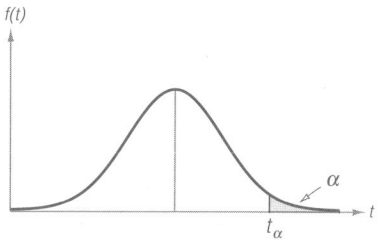

ν	$t_{.100}$	$t_{.050}$	$t_{.025}$	$t_{.010}$	$t_{.005}$	$t_{.001}$	$t_{.0005}$
1	3.078	6.314	12.706	31.821	63.657	318.31	636.62
2	1.886	2.920	4.303	6.965	9.925	22.326	31.598
3	1.638	2.353	3.182	4.541	5.841	10.213	12.924
4	1.533	2.132	2.776	3.747	4.604	7.173	8.610
5	1.476	2.015	2.571	3.365	4.032	5.893	6.869
6	1.440	1.943	2.447	3.143	3.707	5.208	5.959
7	1.415	1.895	2.365	2.998	3.499	4.785	5.408
8	1.397	1.860	2.306	2.896	3.355	4.501	5.041
9	1.383	1.833	2.262	2.821	3.250	4.297	4.781
10	1.372	1.812	2.228	2.764	3.169	4.144	4.587
11	1.363	1.796	2.201	2.718	3.106	4.025	4.437
12	1.356	1.782	2.179	2.681	3.055	3.930	4.318
13	1.350	1.771	2.160	2.650	3.012	3.852	4.221
14	1.345	1.761	2.145	2.624	2.977	3.787	4.140
15	1.341	1.753	2.131	2.602	2.947	3.733	4.073
16	1.337	1.746	2.120	2.583	2.921	3.686	4.015
17	1.333	1.740	2.110	2.567	2.898	3.646	3.965
18	1.330	1.734	2.101	2.552	2.878	3.610	3.922
19	1.328	1.729	2.093	2.539	2.861	3.579	3.883
20	1.325	1.725	2.086	2.528	2.845	3.552	3.850
21	1.323	1.721	2.080	2.518	2.831	3.527	3.819
22	1.321	1.717	2.074	2.508	2.819	3.505	3.792
23	1.319	1.714	2.069	2.500	2.807	3.485	3.767
24	1.318	1.711	2.064	2.492	2.797	3.467	3.745
25	1.316	1.708	2.060	2.485	2.787	3.450	3.725
26	1.315	1.706	2.056	2.479	2.779	3.435	3.707
27	1.314	1.703	2.052	2.473	2.771	3.421	3.690
28	1.313	1.701	2.048	2.467	2.763	3.408	3.674
29	1.311	1.699	2.045	2.462	2.756	3.396	3.659
30	1.310	1.697	2.042	2.457	2.750	3.385	3.646
40	1.303	1.684	2.021	2.423	2.704	3.307	3.551
60	1.296	1.671	2.000	2.390	2.660	3.232	3.460
120	1.289	1.658	1.980	2.358	2.617	3.160	3.373
∞	1.282	1.645	1.960	2.326	2.576	3.090	3.291

Source: This table is reproduced with the kind permission of the Trustees of Biometrika from E. S. Pearson and H. O. Hartley (eds.), *The Biometrika Tables for Statisticians*, Vol. 1, 3d ed., *Biometrika*, 1966.

A First Course in
BUSINESS
STATISTICS

Contents

CHAPTER SEVEN

Inferences Based on a Single Sample: Tests of Hypotheses   327

CHAPTER EIGHT

Comparing Two Population Means   385

CHAPTER NINE

Comparing Population Proportions   447

APPENDIX C

APPENDIX D

Case Studies

List of Exercise Data Sets

Most of the exercise data sets that contain 30 or more measurements are listed below and are available on a computer disk (ASCII format). Instructors who adopt this text may obtain a copy of the disk by writing to the publisher.

Preface

The sixth edition of *A First Course in Business Statistics* has three primary objectives: (1) increased emphasis on methods for quality improvement, (2) greater use of statistical computer output, and (3) many new business applications.

Accomplishing the first objective includes adding cause-and-effect diagrams to Chapter 11, Methods for Quality Improvement. The second and third objectives were achieved by adding many modern business applications, with emphasis on computer output, and the interpretation of observed significance levels (p-values) that are typically produced by statistical software. A list of major revisions follows:

Revisions

1. **Single Chapter on Describing Data (Chapter 2).** Chapter 2 (Graphical Descriptions of Data) and Chapter 3 (Numerical Descriptive Measures) from the previous edition have been combined, with coverage of some of the graphical methods relating to categorical (nominal and ordinal) data through examples, case studies, and exercises rather than separate sections.

2. **Probability (Chapter 3).** The concepts of mutually exclusive and independent events are now in separate sections to improve readability of the chapter.

3. **Methods for Quality Improvement (Chapter 11).** A new section on "Diagnosing Causes of Variation" with cause-and-effect diagrams has been added. To make the chapter more traditional and teachable in a first course, we have also condensed the material on quality, systems, and process management into a single section. Despite this reduction, we believe this chapter represents the most authoritative treatment of quality improvement in any introductory statistics text.

4. **Updated Exercises.** The exercises have been updated, with many new business applications added.

5. **A Complete Set of Answers.** At the request of reviewers, we now include short answers to both odd- and even-numbered exercises in the appendix.

6. **ASP Statistical Software Disk** included with the text. (A description of the software is given later in this preface.)

We continue to make statistical inference the primary theme of the text, but we think that our treatment blends well with contemporary thinking about teaching statistics. Our text is intended for use in the traditional one-quarter or one-semester business statistics course that is offered at many universities and community colleges.

It may also be used in a single introductory business statistics course that stresses the understanding and application of concepts along with the ability to apply some of the basic statistical methods for analyzing data.

We have maintained the features of this text that we believe make it unique among introductory statistics texts for business courses. These features, which assist the student in achieving an overview of statistics and an understanding of its relevance in the solution of business problems, are as follows:

Features:

1. Case Studies.   (See the list of case studies on page x.) Many important concepts are emphasized by the inclusion of case studies, which consist of brief summaries of actual business applications of the concepts and are often drawn directly from the business literature. These case studies allow the student to see business applications of important statistical concepts immediately after introduction of the concepts. The case studies also help to answer by example the often asked questions, "Why should I study statistics? Of what relevance is statistics to business?" Finally, the case studies constantly remind the student that each concept is related to the dominant theme—statistical inference.

2. Where We've Been . . . Where We're Going .   The first page of each chapter is a "unification" page. Our purpose is to allow the student to see how the chapter fits into the scheme of statistical inference. First, we briefly show how the material presented in previous chapters helps us to achieve our goal (Where We've Been). Then, we indicate what the next chapter (or chapters) contributes to the overall objective (Where We're Going). This feature allows us to point out that we are constructing the foundation block by block, with each chapter an important component in the structure of statistical inference. Furthermore, this feature provides a series of brief résumés of the material covered as well as glimpses of future topics.

3. Many Examples and Exercises.   We believe that most students learn by doing. The text contains many worked examples to demonstrate how to solve various types of problems. We then provide the student with a large number of exercises. The answers for all the exercises are included at the end of the text. The exercises are of two types:

    a. Learning the Mechanics.   These exercises are intended to be straightforward applications of the new concepts. They are introduced in a few words and are unhampered by a barrage of background information designed to make them "practical," but which often detracts from instructional objectives. Thus, with a minimum of labor, the student can recheck his or her ability to comprehend a concept or a definition.

    b. Applying the Concepts.   The mechanical exercises described above are followed by realistic exercises that allow the student to see applications of statistics to the solution of problems encountered in business and economics. Once the mechanics are mastered, these exercises develop the student's skills at comprehending realistic problems that describe situations to which the techniques may be applied.

4. **On Your Own . . .**   The chapters end with an exercise entitled **On Your Own . . . .** The intent of this exercise is to give the student some hands-on experience with a business application of the statistical concepts introduced in the chapter. In most cases, the student is required to collect, analyze, and interpret data relating to some business phenomenon.

5. **Using the Computer.**   Another feature at the end of most chapters encourages the use of computers in the analysis of real data. A demographic data base, consisting of 1,000 observations on 15 variables, has been described in Appendix C and is available on diskette from the publisher. Each **Using the Computer** section provides one or more computer exercises that utilize the data in Appendix C and enhance the new material covered in the chapter.

6. **A Simple, Clear Style.**   We have tried to achieve a simple and clear writing style. Subjects that are tangential to our objective have been avoided, even though some may be of academic interest to those well versed in statistics. We have not taken an encyclopedic approach in the presentation of material.

7. **Footnotes and Appendix A.**   Although the text is designed for students with a noncalculus background, footnotes explain the role of calculus in various derivations. Footnotes are also used to inform the student about some of the theory underlying certain results. Appendix A presents some useful counting rules for the instructor who wishes to place greater emphasis on probability. Consequently, we think the footnotes and Appendix A provide an opportunity for flexibility in the mathematical and theoretical level at which the material is presented.

8. **Supplementary Material.**   Solutions manuals, a study guide, a Minitab supplement, an integrated software system, a computer-generated test system, a test bank, and a 1,000-observation demographic data base, and data on disk are available.

   a. **Student Solutions Manual** (by Nancy S. Boudreau).   The student solutions manual presents detailed solutions to most odd-numbered exercises in the text. Many points are clarified and expanded to provide maximum insight into and benefits from each exercise. ISBN 0-02-312715-5.

   b. **Instructor's Solutions Manual** (by Nancy S. Boudreau).   The instructor's solutions manual presents the full solutions to the even-numbered exercises contained in the text. For adopters, the manual is complimentary from the publisher. ISBN 0-02-379176-4.

   c. **Minitab Supplement** (by Ruth K. Meyer and David D. Krueger).   The Minitab computer supplement was developed to be used with Minitab Release 8.0, a general-purpose statistical computing system. The supplement, which was written especially for the student with no previous experience with computers, provides step-by-step descriptions of how to use Minitab effectively as an aid in data analysis. Each chapter begins with a list of new commands introduced in the chapter. Brief examples are then given to explain new commands, followed by examples from the text illustrating the new and previously learned commands. Where appropriate, simulation examples are included. Exercises, many of which are drawn from the text, conclude each chapter.

A special feature of the supplement is a chapter describing a survey sampling project. The objectives of the project are to illustrate the evaluation of a questionnaire, provide a review of statistical techniques, and illustrate the use of Minitab for questionnaire evaluation. ISBN 0-02-381000-9.

d. ASP Statistical Software Diskette. The text includes a 3½" diskette containing the ASP program, *A Statistical Package for Business, Economics, and the Social Sciences*. ASP, from DMC Software, Inc., is a user-friendly, totally menu-driven program that contains all of the major statistical applications covered in the text, plus many more. ASP runs on any IBM-compatible PC with at least 516K of memory. With ASP, students with no knowledge of computer programming can create and analyze data sets easily and quickly. Appendix D contains start-up procedures and a short tutorial on the use of ASP. Full documentation is provided complimentary to adopters of the text.

e. ASP Tutorial and Student Guide (by George Blackford). Most students have little trouble learning to use ASP without documentation. Some, however, may want to purchase the *ASP Tutorial and Student Guide*. Bookstores can order the tutorial from DMC Software, Inc., 6169 Pebbleshire Drive, Grand Blanc, MI 48439.

f. Test Bank (by Mark Dummeldinger). This manual provides a large number of test items utilizing real data. ISBN 0-02-379177-2.

g. PH Test Manager IBM 3.5". This program allows users to generate tests and quizzes by chapter or section number, choosing from numerous questions. Full editing and graphing capabilities are included; instructors may modify existing questions or create their own questions as well as original graphics. ISBN 0-13-359704-0.

h. Data Base. A demographic data set was assembled based on a systematic random sample of 1,000 U.S. zip codes. Demographic data for each zip code area selected were supplied by CACI, an international demographic and market information firm. Fifteen demographic measurements (including population, number of households, median age, median household income, variables related to the cost of housing, educational levels, the work force, and purchasing potential indexes based on the Bureau of the Census Consumer Expenditure Surveys) are presented for each zip code area.

Some of the data are referenced in the **Using the Computer** sections. The objectives are to enable the student to analyze real data in a relatively large sample using the computer, and to gain experience using the statistical techniques and concepts on real data.

i. Data Sets on Disk. All of the large exercise data sets, as well as the demographic data set, are available on a computer disk. A list of the exercise data sets, with the exercise number, the page number, and the file name for each data set, is given on pages xi–xii. ISBN 0-02-379178-0.

Full Version Available

A full-sized one- or two-term business statistics text is also available: *Statistics for Business and Economics* by James T. McClave (University of Florida) and P. George Benson (Rutgers University); © 1994, 985 pp. cloth, ISBN 0-02-379201-9 (U4602-1).

Contents.   1: What Is Statistics?   2: Methods for Describing Sets of Data.   3: Probability.   4: Discrete Random Variables.   5: Continuous Random Variables.   6: Sampling Distributions.   7: Inferences Based on a Single Sample: Estimation.   8: Inferences Based on a Single Sample: Tests of Hypotheses.   9: Inferences Based on Two Samples: Estimation and Tests of Hypotheses.   10: Simple Linear Regression.   11: Multiple Regression.   12: Introduction to Model Building.   13. Methods for Quality Improvement.   14: Time Series: Index Numbers and Descriptive Analyses.   15: Time Series: Models and Forecasting.   16: Design of Experiments and Analysis of Variance.   17: Nonparametric Statistics.   18: The Chi-Square Test and Analysis of Contingency Tables.   19: Decision Analysis.   20: Survey Sampling. Appendix A: Basic Counting Rules.   Appendix B: Tables.   Appendix C: Demographic Data Set.   Appendix D: Calculation Formulas for Analysis of Variance. Appendix E: ASP Tutorial.   Answers to Selected Exercises.   Index.   Call Prentice-Hall Faculty Services at 1-800-526-0485, or your local representative.

Acknowledgments

We owe thanks to the many people who assisted in reviewing and preparing this textbook. Their names appear in the following list. We particularly acknowledge the editorial assistance of Susan L. Reiland, the typing and assistance of Brenda Dobson, and the administrative support of Jane Oas Benson. Without these three, we never could have completed this work.

Gordon J. Alexander
University of Minnesota

Richard W. Andrews
University of Michigan

Larry M. Austin
Texas Tech University

Golam Azam
North Carolina Agricultural
& Technical University

Donald W. Bartlett
University of Minnesota

Clarence Bayne
Concordia University

Carl Bedell
Philadelphia College of Textiles and
Science

David M. Bergman
University of Minnesota

William H. Beyer
University of Akron

Atul Bhatia
University of Minnesota

Jim Branscome
University of Texas at Arlington

Francis J. Brewerton
Middle Tennessee State University

Daniel G. Brick
University of St. Thomas

Robert W. Brobst
University of Texas at Arlington

Michael Broida
Miami University of Ohio

Glenn J. Browne
University of Maryland,
Baltimore

Edward Carlstein
University of North Carolina at
Chapel Hill

John M. Charnes
University of Miami

Chih-Hsu Cheng
Ohio State University

Larry Claypool
Oklahoma State University

Edward R. Clayton
Virginia Polytechnic Institute and
State University

Ronald L. Coccari
Cleveland State University

Ken Constantine
University of New Hampshire

Robert Curley
University of Central Oklahoma

Joyce Curry-Daly
California Polytechnic State
University

Jim Daly
California Polytechnic State
University

Jim Davis
Golden Gate University

Dileep Dhavale
University of Northern Iowa

Mark Eakin
University of Texas at Arlington

Rick L. Edgeman
Colorado State University

Carol Eger
Stanford University

Robert Elrod
Georgia State University

Douglas A. Elvers
University of North Carolina at
Chapel Hill

Iris Fetta
Clemson University

Susan Flach
General Mills, Inc.

Alan E. Gelfand
University of Connecticut

Joseph Glaz
University of Connecticut

Edit Gombay
University of Alberta

Paul W. Guy
California State University, Chico

Michael E. Hanna
University of Texas at Arlington

Don Holbert
East Carolina University

James Holstein
University of Missouri, Columbia

Warren M. Holt
Southeastern Massachusetts
University

Steve Hora
University of Hawaii, Hilo

Iris B. Ibrahim
Clemson University

Petros Ioannatos
GMI Engineering & Management
Institute

Chipei Tseng
Northern Illinois University

Edna White
Florida Atlantic University

Pankaj Vaish
Arthur Andersen & Company

Steve Wickstrom
University of Minnesota

Robert W. Van Cleave
University of Minnesota

James Willis
Louisiana State University

Ken Wallenius
Clemson University

Douglas A. Wolfe
Ohio State University

Charles F. Warnock
Colorado State University

Oilek Yeldan
Bilkent University, Turkey

William J. Weida
United States Air Force Academy

Gary Yoshimoto
St. Cloud State University

T. J. Wharton
Oakland University

Fike Zahroon
Moorhead State University

Kathleen M. Whitcomb
University of South Carolina

Christopher J. Zappe
Bucknell University

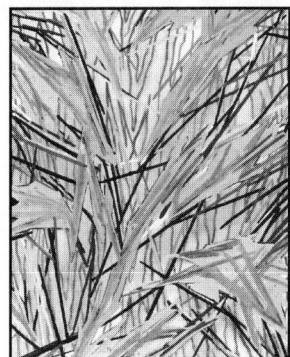

CHAPTER ONE

What Is Statistics?

Contents

Case Studies

Where We're Going

What is statistics? Is it a field of study, a group of numbers that summarize a business operation, or—as the title of a popular book (Tanur et al., 1989) suggests—"a guide to the unknown"? We will begin to see in Chapter 1 that each of these descriptions has some applicability in understanding statistics. We will see that *descriptive statistics* focuses on developing numerical summaries that describe some business phenomenon, whereas *inferential statistics* uses numerical summaries to assist in making business decisions. Our main objective is to show how statistics can be useful to you in business decision-making, so the primary theme of this text is inferential statistics.

1.1   Statistics: What Is It?

What does statistics mean to you? Does it bring to mind batting averages, the Dow Jones Industrial Average, unemployment figures, numerical distortions of facts (lying with statistics!), or simply a college requirement you have to complete? We hope to convince you that statistics is a meaningful, useful science with a broad, almost limitless scope of application to business and economic problems. We also want to show that statistics lie only when they are misapplied. Finally, our objective is to paint a unified picture of statistics to leave you with the impression that your time was well spent studying a subject that will prove useful to you in many ways.

Statistics means "numerical descriptions" to most people. The Dow Jones Industrial Average, monthly unemployment figures, and the fraction of women executives in a particular industry are all statistical descriptions of large sets of data. Often, the purpose of calculating these numbers goes beyond the description of the particular set of data. Frequently, the data are regarded as a sample selected from some larger set of data whose characteristics we wish to estimate. For example, a sampling of unpaid accounts for a large merchandiser would allow you to calculate an estimate of the average value of unpaid accounts. This estimate could be used as an audit check on the total value of all unpaid accounts held by the merchandiser. So, the applications of statistics can be divided into two broad areas: **descriptive** and **inferential** statistics.

> **Descriptive statistics** utilizes numerical and graphical methods to look for patterns, summarize, and present the information in a set of data.
>
> **Inferential statistics** utilizes sample data to make estimates, predictions, or other generalizations about a larger set of data, frequently as an aid to decision making.

Although both descriptive and inferential statistics are discussed in the following chapters, the primary theme of the text is **inference**. Let us examine some case studies that illustrate applications of descriptive and inferential statistics in business and government.

CASE STUDY 1.1 / The Consumer Price Index

A data set of interest to virtually all Americans is the set of prices charged for goods and services in the U.S. economy. The general upward movement in this set of prices is referred to as *inflation*; the general downward movement is referred to as *deflation*. In order to *estimate* the change in prices over time, the Bureau of Labor Statistics (BLS) of the U.S. Department of Labor developed the Consumer Price Index (CPI). Each month, the BLS collects price data about a specific collection of goods and services (called a *market basket*) from 85 urban areas around the country. Statistical procedures are used to compute the CPI (a descriptive statistic) from this sample price data and other information about consumers' spending habits. By comparing the level of the CPI at different points in time, it is possible to *estimate* (make an inference about) the rate of inflation over particular time intervals and to compare the purchasing power of a dollar at different points in time.

One major use of the CPI as an index of inflation is as an indicator of the success or failure of government economic policies. A second use of the CPI is to escalate income payments. Millions of workers have *escalator clauses* in their collective bargaining contracts; these clauses call for increases in wage rates based on increases in the CPI. In addition, the incomes of Social Security beneficiaries and retired military and federal civil service employees are tied to the CPI. It has been estimated that a 1% increase in the CPI can trigger an increase of over $1 billion in income payments. Thus, it can be said that the very livelihoods of millions of Americans depend on the behavior of a statistical estimator, the CPI (U.S. Department of Labor, 1978).

CASE STUDY 1.2 / Taste-Preference Scores for Beer

Two sets of data of interest to the marketing department of a food-products firm are (1) the set of taste-preference scores given by consumers to its product and to competitors' products when all brands are clearly labeled and (2) the taste-preference scores given by the same set of consumers when all brand labels have been removed and the consumer's only means of product identification is taste. With such information, the marketing department should be able to determine whether taste preference arose because of perceived physical differences in the products or as a result of the consumer's image of the brand. (Brand image is, of course, largely a result of a firm's marketing efforts.) Such a determination should help the firm develop marketing strategies for its product.

A study using these two types of data was conducted by Ralph Allison and Kenneth Uhl (1965) to determine whether beer drinkers could distinguish among major brands of unlabeled beer. A sample of 326 beer drinkers was randomly selected from the set of beer drinkers identified as males who drank beer at least three times a week. During the first week of the study, each of the 326 participants was given a six-pack of unlabeled beer containing three major brands and was asked to taste-rate each beer on a scale from 1 (poor) to 10 (excellent). During the second week, the same set of drinkers was given a six-pack containing six major brands. This time, however, each bottle carried its usual label. Again, the drinkers were asked to taste-rate each beer from 1 to 10. From a statistical analysis of the two sets of data yielded by the study, Allison and Uhl concluded that the 326 beer drinkers studied could not distinguish among brands by taste on an overall basis. This result enabled them to *infer* statistically that such was also the case for beer drinkers in general. Their results also indicated that brand labels and their associations did significantly influence the tasters' evaluations. These findings suggest that physical differences in the products have less to do with their success or failure in the marketplace than the image of the brand in the consumers' minds. As to the benefits of such a study, Allison and Uhl note, "to the extent that product images, and their changes, are believed to be a result of advertising . . . the ability of firms' advertising programs to influence product images can be more thoroughly examined."

The employment status (employed or unemployed) of each individual in the U.S. work force is a set of data that is of interest to economists, businesspeople, and sociologists. These data provide information on the social and economic health of our society. To obtain information about the employment status of the work force, the U.S. Bureau of the Census conducts what is known as the *Current Population Survey*. Each month approximately 1,500 interviewers visit about 59,000 of the 91.9 million households in the United States and question the occupants over 14 years of age about their employment status. Their responses enable the Bureau of the Census to *estimate* the percentage of people in the labor force who are unemployed (the *unemployment rate*). Thus, a *statistical estimator* serves as a monthly indicator of the nation's economic welfare.

Perhaps you are wondering how a reliable estimate of this percentage can be obtained from a sample that includes only about .1% of the households in the United States. The answer lies in the method used to select the sample of households. The method was designed to enable the Bureau of the Census to control the precision of its estimate while obtaining a sample that is representative of the set of all households in the country. That reliable estimates of nationwide characteristics can be obtained from relatively small sample sizes is an illustration of the power of statistics (U.S. Department of Commerce, 1978).

The United Airlines Maintenance Base in San Francisco is responsible for the maintenance and overhaul of all United Airlines aircraft. Its storeroom receives, stores, and distributes all the parts needed for maintenance of the aircraft. To control the stock of spare parts and to determine the value of parts on hand, *inventory counts* (a descriptive statistic) of the number of each item in stock are taken. It is the responsibility of the Auditing Division of United Airlines to verify the accuracy of the inventory counts. Rather than verifying the accuracy of the counts by recounting all of the inventory item groups, the accountants sample a small number of these groups and recount them. If they find a large number of discrepancies between the original counts and their sample counts, they *infer* that many of the rest of the item counts (those not sampled and recounted) are also in error. They conclude that the original inventory counts are unacceptable and must be recounted. On the other hand, if they find only a small number of discrepancies, they *infer* that most of the item counts not rechecked are accurate, and conclude that the original inventory counts are satisfactory.

Before this inferential statistical procedure was implemented, the Auditing Division verified inventory counts by recounting all the items in stock. The inferential procedure enables the accountants to maintain the quality of their verifications with a substantial reduction in work-hours (Hunz, 1956).

CASE STUDY 1.5 / The Decennial Census of the United States

The following description is quoted from the U.S. Bureau of the Census, *Statistical Abstract of the United States: 1992:*

The U.S. Constitution provides for a census of the population every 10 years, primarily to establish a basis for apportionment of members of the House of Representatives among the States. For over a century after the first census in 1790, the census organization was a temporary one, created only for each decennial census. In 1902, the Bureau of the Census was established as a permanent Federal agency, responsible for enumerating the population and also for compiling statistics on other subjects.

The census of the population is a complete count. That is, an attempt is made to account for every person, for each person's residence, and for other characteristics (sex, age, family relationships, etc.). Since the 1940 census, in addition to the complete count information, some data have been obtained from representative samples of the population. In the 1990 census, variable sampling rates were employed. For most of the country, one in every six households (about 17%) received the long form or sample questionnaire; in governmental units estimated to have fewer than 2500 inhabitants, every other household (50%) received the sample questionnaire to enhance the reliability of sample data for small areas. Exact agreement is not to be expected between sample data and the complete census count.

Census statistics regarding total numbers of people in various age groups are examples of numerical *descriptions* that require no statistical inference, since they are (purportedly) complete counts. However, income data collected by the Bureau of the Census from "representative samples" might be used to make *inferences* about the incomes of *all* persons. You will learn that the reliability of statistical inferences is dependent on the sampling procedure, characteristics of the data, and the methodology employed to make the inferences.

Why study statistics in a business program? The quantification of business research and business operations (quality control, statistical auditing, forecasting, etc.) has been truly astounding over the past several decades. Econometric modeling, market surveys, and the creation of indexes such as the Consumer Price Index all represent relatively recent attempts to quantify economic behavior. It is extremely important that today's business graduate understand the methods and language of statistics, since the alternative is to be swamped by a flood of numbers that are more confusing than enlightening to the untutored mind. The business student should develop a discerning sense of rational thought that will distill the information contained in these numbers so it can be used to make intelligent decisions, inferences, and generalizations. We believe that the study of statistics is essential to the ability to operate effectively in the modern business environment.

1.2   The Elements of Statistics

Statistical methods are particularly useful for studying, analyzing, and learning about **populations**.

> ### Definition 1.1
>
> A **population** is a set of existing units (usually people, objects, transactions, or events).

Examples of populations include (1) all employed workers in the United States, (2) all registered voters in California, (3) everyone who has purchased a particular brand of cellular telephone, (4) all the cars produced last year by a particular assembly line, (5) the current stock of spare parts at United Airlines' maintenance facility, (6) all sales made at the drive-in window of a fast-food restaurant during a given year, and (7) the set of all accidents occurring on a particular stretch of interstate highway during a holiday period. Notice that the first three population examples (1–3) are sets (groups) of people; the next two (4–5) are sets of objects; the next (6) is a set of transactions; and the last (7) is a set of events.

In studying a population, we focus on one or more characteristics or properties of the units in the population. For example, we may be interested in the age, income, or the number of years of education of the people currently unemployed in the United States. We call such characteristics **variables**.

> ### Definition 1.2
>
> A **variable** is a characteristic or property of an individual population unit. The name *variable* is derived from the fact that any particular characteristic may *vary* among the units in a population.

In studying a particular variable, it is helpful—as we will see in forthcoming chapters—to be able to obtain a numerical representation for the variable. Thus, when numerical representations are not readily available, the process of measurement plays an important supporting role in statistical studies. **Measurement** is the process by which numbers are assigned to variables of individual population units. Measurement may entail asking a consumer to rate the taste of a product on a scale from 1 to 10 or simply asking a worker how old she is. Frequently, however, it involves the use of instruments such as stopwatches, scales, calipers, etc. We discuss measurement in more detail in the next chapter.

If the population you wish to study is small in size, then it is feasible to measure a variable for every unit in the population. For example, if you are measuring the starting salary for all University of Michigan MBA graduates in 1993, it is at least feasible to obtain every salary. When we measure a variable for every unit of a population, it is called a **census** of the population. However, the populations of interest in business problems are typically much larger, involving perhaps many thousands of units. Some examples of large populations were given after Definition 1.1; others are all invoices produced in the last year by a Fortune 500 company, all potential buyers of a new facsimile machine, and all stockholders of a firm listed on the New York Stock Exchange. In studying such populations it would typically be too time-consuming or too costly to conduct a census. A more reasonable alternative would be to select and study a subset (a portion) of the units in the population.

Thus, for example, instead of examining all 15,472 invoices produced by a company during a given year, an auditor may select and examine a **sample** of only 100 invoices. If he is interested in the variable *dollar value*, then he would record (measure) the dollar value of each invoice.

Definition 1.3
. . . .

A **sample** is a subset of the units of a population.

The method of selecting the sample is called the sampling procedure, or sampling plan. One very important sampling procedure is **random sampling**, one that assures that every subset of units in the population has the same chance of being included in the sample. Thus, if an auditor samples 100 of the 15,472 invoices in the population so that every invoice (and subset of invoices) has an equal chance of being included in the sample, he has devised a random sample. Random sampling is discussed in Chapter 3.

After selecting the sample and measuring the variable(s) of interest for every sampled unit, the information contained in the sample is used to make *inferences* about the population.

Definition 1.4
. . . .

A **statistical inference** is an estimate, prediction, or other generalization about a population based on information contained in a sample.

That is, *we use the information contained in the smaller sample to learn about the larger population.* * Thus, from an examination of the sample of 100 invoices, the auditor may estimate the total number of invoices containing errors in the population

---

*The terms *population* and *sample* are often used to refer to the sets of measurements themselves, in addition to the units on which the measurements are made. For applications in which a single variable of interest is being measured, this will cause little confusion. When the terminology is potentially ambiguous, the measurements will be referred to as *population data sets* and *sample data sets*, respectively.

of 15,472 invoices or predict the total number of invoices with errors in next year's population of invoices.

Managers use statistical inferences to guide and support their decisions. For example, the auditor's inference about the quality of the firm's invoices can be used in deciding whether to modify the firm's billing operations. The decision to market a new product may hinge on an inference about the willingness of a population of consumers to buy the product—an inference based on the results of testing the product on a sample of consumers.

The preceding definitions identify four of the five elements of an inferential statistical problem: a population, one or more variables of interest, a sample, and an inference. The fifth—and perhaps most important—is a measure of reliability for the inference. This is the topic of Section 1.3.

EXAMPLE 1.1

A large paint retailer has had numerous complaints from customers about underfilled paint cans. As a result, the retailer has begun inspecting incoming shipments of paint from suppliers. Shipments with underfill problems will be returned to the supplier. A recent shipment contained 2,440 gallon-size cans. The retailer randomly selected 100 cans and weighed each on a scale capable of measuring weight to four decimal places. Properly filled cans weigh 10 pounds.

a. Describe the population.

b. Describe the variable of interest.

c. Describe the sample.

d. Describe the inference.

Solution

a. The population is the set of units of interest to the retailer, which is the shipment of 2,440 cans of paint.

b. The weight of the paint cans is the variable the retailer wishes to evaluate.

c. The sample must be a subset of the population. In this case, it is the 100 cans of paint selected by the retailer. If the 100 cans represent a random sample, then the sampling procedure used must be such that each of the 2,440 cans had an equal chance of being included in the sample.

d. The inference of interest involves the *generalization* of the information contained in the weights of the sample of paint cans to the population of paint cans. In particular, the retailer wants to learn about the extent of the underfill problem (if any) in the population. This might be accomplished by finding the average* weight of the cans in the sample and using it to estimate the average weight of the cans in the population.

---

*Although we will not formally define the term *average* until Chapter 2, *typical* or *middle* can be substituted here without confusion.

EXAMPLE 1.2

Cola wars is the popular media term for the intense competition between the marketing campaigns of Coca-Cola and Pepsi. The campaigns have featured movie and television stars, rock videos, athletic endorsements, and claims of consumer preference based on taste tests. Suppose a particular Pepsi bottler gives 1,000 cola consumers in the bottler's marketing region a "blind" taste test (i.e., a taste test in which the two brand names are disguised). Each consumer is asked to state a preference for brand A or brand B.

a. Describe the population.
b. Describe the variable of interest.
c. Describe the sample.
d. Describe the inference.

Solution

a. The population of interest to the Pepsi bottler is the collection or set of all cola consumers in the marketing region.
b. The characteristic of each cola consumer that the bottler wishes to study is the consumer's cola preference as revealed under the conditions of a blind taste test. Thus, cola preference is the variable of interest.
c. The sample is the group of 1,000 cola consumers from the bottler's marketing region.
d. The inference of interest is the *generalization* of the cola preferences of the 1,000 sampled consumers to the population of all cola consumers in the bottler's marketing region. In particular, the preferences of the consumers in the sample can be used to *estimate* the percentage of all cola consumers in the region who prefer each brand.

1.3 Statistics: Witchcraft or Science?

The primary objective of statistics is inference. In the previous section, we described inference as making generalizations about populations based on information contained in a sample. But making the inference is only part of the story. We also need to know how good the inference is. The only way we could be reasonably certain that an inference about a population is correct would be to include the entire population in our sample. But, due to resource constraints (i.e., insufficient time or money), this is generally not an option. In basing inferences on only a portion of the population (a sample), we introduce an element of uncertainty into our inferences. In general, the smaller the sample size, the less certain we are about the inference. Thus, an inference based on a sample of size 5 is (usually) less reliable than an inference based on a sample of size 100. Consequently, whenever possible, it is important to determine and report the **reliability** of each inference made; this is the fifth element of a statistical problem.

The measure of reliability that accompanies an inference separates the science of statistics from the art of fortune-telling. A palm reader, like a statistician, may examine a sample (your hand) and make inferences about the population (your life). However, unlike statistical inferences, no measure of reliability can be attached to the palm reader's inferences.

Suppose, as in Example 1.1, we are interested in estimating the average weight of a population of paint cans from the average weight of a sample of cans. Using statistical methods, we can determine a *bound on the estimation error*. This bound is simply a number that our estimation error (the difference between the average weight of the sample and the average weight of the population of cans) is not likely to exceed. We will see in later chapters that this bound is a measure of the uncertainty of our inference. The reliability of statistical inferences is discussed throughout this text. For now, we simply want you to realize that an inference is incomplete without a measure of its reliability.

We conclude this section with a summary of the elements of inferential statistical problems and an example to illustrate a measure of reliability.

Five Elements of Inferential Statistical Problems

1. The population of interest
2. One or more variables (characteristics of the population units) that are to be investigated
3. The sample of population units
4. The inference about the population based on information contained in the sample
5. A measure of reliability for the inference

EXAMPLE 1.3

Refer to Example 1.2, in which 1,000 consumers indicated their cola preferences in a taste test. Describe how the reliability of an inference concerning the preferences of all cola consumers in the Pepsi bottler's marketing region could be measured.

Solution

When the preferences of 1,000 consumers are used to estimate the preferences of all consumers in the region, the estimate will not exactly mirror the preferences of the population. For example, if the taste test shows that 56% of the 1,000 consumers preferred Pepsi, it does not follow (nor is it likely) that exactly 56% of all cola drinkers in the region prefer Pepsi. Nevertheless, we may be able to use sound statistical reasoning (which is presented later in the text) to ensure that the sampling procedure used will generate estimates that are almost certainly within a specified limit of the true percentage of all consumers who prefer Pepsi. For example, such reasoning might assure us that the estimate of the preference for Pepsi is almost certainly within 5% of the actual population preference. The implication is that the actual preference for

Pepsi is between 51% [i.e., (56 − 5)%] and 61% [i.e., (56 + 5)%]. This interval represents a measure of reliability for the inference.

1.4   Processes (Optional)

Sections 1.2 and 1.3 focused on the use of statistical methods to analyze and learn about populations, which are sets of *existing* units. Statistical methods are equally useful for analyzing and making inferences about **processes**.

Definition 1.5

A **process** is a series of actions or operations that transforms inputs to outputs. A process produces or generates output over time.

The most obvious processes that are of interest to businesses are production or manufacturing processes. A manufacturing process uses a series of operations performed by people and machines to convert inputs, such as raw materials and parts, to finished products (the outputs). Examples include the process used to produce the paper on which these words are printed, automobile assembly lines, and oil refineries.

Figure 1.1 presents a general description of a process and its inputs and outputs. In the context of manufacturing, the process in the figure (i.e., the transformation process) could be a depiction of the overall production process or it could be a depiction of one of the many processes (sometimes called subprocesses) that exist within an overall production process. Thus, the output shown could be finished goods that will be shipped to an external customer or merely the output of one of the steps or subprocesses of the overall process. In the latter case, the output becomes input for the next subprocess. For example, Figure 1.1 could represent the overall automobile assembly process, with its output being fully assembled cars ready for shipment to dealers. Or, it could depict the windshield-assembly subprocess, with its output of partially assembled cars with windshields ready for "shipment" to the next subprocess in the assembly line.

FIGURE 1.1 ▶
Graphical depiction of a manufacturing process

Besides physical products and services, businesses and other organizations generate streams of numerical data over time that are used to evaluate the performance of the organization. Examples include weekly sales figures, quarterly earnings, and yearly profits. The U.S. economy (a complex organization) can be thought of as generating streams of data that include the Gross National Product (GNP), stock prices, and the Consumer Price Index. Statisticians and other analysts conceptualize these data streams as being generated by processes. Typically, however, the series of operations or actions that cause particular data to be realized are either unknown or so complex (or both) that the processes are treated as **black boxes**.

Definition 1.6

A process whose operations or actions are unknown or unspecified is called a **black box**.

Frequently, when a process is treated as a black box, its inputs are not specified either. The entire focus is on the output of the process. A black box process is illustrated in Figure 1.2.

FIGURE 1.2 ▶
A black box process with numerical output

In studying a process, we generally focus on one or more characteristics, or properties, of the output. For example, we may be interested in the weight or the length of the units produced or even the time it takes to produce each unit. As with characteristics of population units, we call these characteristics **variables**. In studying processes whose output is already in numerical form (i.e., a stream of numbers), the characteristic, or property, represented by the numbers (e.g., sales, GNP, or stock prices) is typically the variable of interest. If the output is not numeric, we use **measurement processes** to assign numerical values to variables. * For example, if in the automobile assembly process the weight of the fully assembled automobile is the variable of interest, a measurement process involving a large scale will be used to assign a numerical value to each automobile.

---

*A process whose output is already in numerical form necessarily includes a measurement process as one of its subprocesses.

As with populations, we use sample data to analyze and make inferences (estimates, predictions, or other generalizations) about processes. But the concept of a sample is defined differently when dealing with processes. Recall that a population is a set of existing units and that a sample is a subset of those units. In the case of processes, however, the concept of a set of existing units is not relevant or appropriate. Processes generate or create their output *over time*—one unit after another. For example, a particular automobile assembly line produces a completed vehicle every 4 minutes. We define a sample from a process in the box.

Definition 1.7

Any set of output (objects or numbers) produced by a process is called a **sample**.

Thus, the next 10 cars turned out by the assembly line constitute a sample from the process, as do the next 100 cars or every fifth car produced today.

EXAMPLE 1.4

A particular fast-food restaurant chain has 6,289 outlets with drive-through windows. To attract more customers to its drive-through services, the company is considering offering a 50% discount on the price of an order that a customer must wait more than a specified number of minutes to receive. To help determine what the time limit should be, the company decided to estimate the average waiting time at a particular drive-through window in Dallas, Texas. For 7 consecutive days, the worker taking customers' orders recorded the time that every order was placed. The worker who handed the order to the customer recorded the time of delivery. In both cases, workers used synchronized digital clocks that reported the time to the nearest second. At the end of the 7-day period, 2,109 orders had been timed.

a. Describe the process of interest at the Dallas restaurant.
b. Describe the variable of interest.
c. Describe the sample.
d. Describe the inference of interest.
e. Describe how the reliability of the inference could be measured.

Solution

a. The process of interest is the drive-through window at a particular fast-food restaurant in Dallas, Texas. It is a process because it "produces," or "generates," meals over time. That is, it services customers over time.

b. The variable the company monitored is customer waiting time, the length of time a customer waits to receive a meal after placing an order. Since the study is focusing only on the output of the process (the time to produce the output) and not the internal operations of the process (the tasks required to produce a meal for a customer), the process is being treated as a black box.

c. The sampling plan was to monitor every order over a particular 7-day period. The sample is the 2,109 orders that were processed during the 7-day period.

d. The company's immediate interest is in learning about the drive-through window in Dallas. They plan to do this by using the waiting times from the sample to make a statistical inference about the drive-through process. In particular, they might use the average waiting time for the sample to estimate the average waiting time at the Dallas facility.

e. As for inferences about populations, measures of reliability can be developed for inferences about processes. The reliability of the estimate of the average waiting time for the Dallas restaurant could be measured by a bound on the error of estimation. That is, we might find that the average waiting time is 4.2 minutes, with a bound on the error of estimation of .5 minute. The implication would be that we could be reasonably certain that the true average waiting time for the Dallas process is between 3.7 and 4.7 minutes.

Notice that there is also a population described in this example: the company's 6,289 existing outlets with drive-through facilities. In the final analysis, the company will use what it learns about the process in Dallas and, perhaps, similar studies at other locations to make an inference about the waiting times in its populations of outlets.

Note that output already generated by a process can be viewed as a population. Suppose a soft-drink canning process produced 2,000 twelve-packs yesterday, all of which were stored in a warehouse. If we were interested in learning something about those 2,000 packages—such as the percentage with defective cardboard packaging—we could treat the 2,000 packages as a population. We might draw a sample from the population in the warehouse, measure the variable of interest, and use the sample data to make a statistical inference about the 2,000 packages, as described in Sections 1.2 and 1.3.

CASE STUDY 1.6 / Quality Improvement: U.S. Firms Respond to the Challenge from Japan

Over the last 2 decades, U.S. firms have been seriously challenged by products of superior quality from overseas, particularly from Japan. Japan currently produces 26% of the cars sold in the United States, and some predict this figure will climb to 40% within a decade. Only one U.S. firm still manufactures televisions; the rest are made in Japan.

To meet this competitive challenge, more and more U.S. firms—both manufacturing and service firms—have begun quality-improvement initiatives of their own. Many of these firms now stress the management of quality in all phases and aspects of their business, from the design of their products to production, distribution, sales, and service.

Broadly speaking, quality-improvement programs are concerned with (1) finding out what the customer wants, (2) translating those wants into a product design, and (3) producing and delivering a product or service that meets or exceeds the specifications of the product design. In all these areas, but particularly in the third, *improvement of quality requires improvement of processes*—including production processes, distribution processes, and service processes.

But what does it mean to say that a process has been improved? Generally speaking, it means that the customer of the process (i.e., the user of the output) indicates a greater satisfaction with the output. Frequently, such increases in satisfaction require a reduction in the variation of one or more process variables. That is, a reduction in the variation of the output stream of the process is needed.

But how can process variation be monitored and reduced? In the mid-1920s, Walter Shewhart of the Bell Telephone Laboratories made perhaps the most significant breakthrough of this century for the improvement of processes. He recognized that variation in process output was inevitable. No two parts produced by a given machine are the same; no two transactions performed by a given bank teller are the same. He also recognized that variation could be understood, monitored, and controlled using statistical methods. He developed a simple graphical technique—called a **control chart**—for determining whether product variation is within acceptable limits. This method provides guidance for when to adjust or change a production process and when to leave it alone. It can be used at the end of the production process or, most significantly, at different points within the process. We discuss control charts and other tools for improving processes in Chapter 11.

In recent years, largely as a result of the Japanese challenge to the supremacy of U.S. products, control charts and other statistical tools have gained widespread use in the United States. As evidence for the claim that U.S. firms are responding well to Japan's competitive challenge, consider this: The most prestigious quality improvement prize in the world that a firm can win is the Deming Prize. It is awarded by the Japanese. In 1989 it was won for the first time by an American company—Florida Power and light Company.

In this section we have presented a brief introduction to processes and the use of statistical methods to analyze and learn about processes. In Chapter 11 we present an in-depth treatment of these subjects. If you would like further amplification now of the ideas presented in this section, we suggest that you read Section 11.1 "Quality, Processes, and Systems."

1.5   The Role of Statistics in Managerial Decision-Making

Managers frequently rely on input from statistical analyses to help them make decisions. The role statistics can play in managerial decision-making is indicated in the flow diagram in Figure 1.3. Every managerial decision-making problem begins with a real-world problem. This problem is then formulated in managerial terms and framed as a managerial question. The next sequence of steps (proceeding counterclockwise around the flow diagram) identifies the role that statistics can play in this process. The managerial question is translated into a statistical question, the sample data are collected and analyzed, and the statistical question is answered. The next step in the process is using the answer to the statistical question to reach an answer to the managerial question. The answer to the managerial question may suggest a reformulation of the original managerial problem, suggest a new managerial question, or lead to the solution of the managerial problem.

FIGURE 1.3 ▶

Flow diagram showing the role of statistics in managerial decision-making

Source: Chervany, Benson, and Iyer (1980)

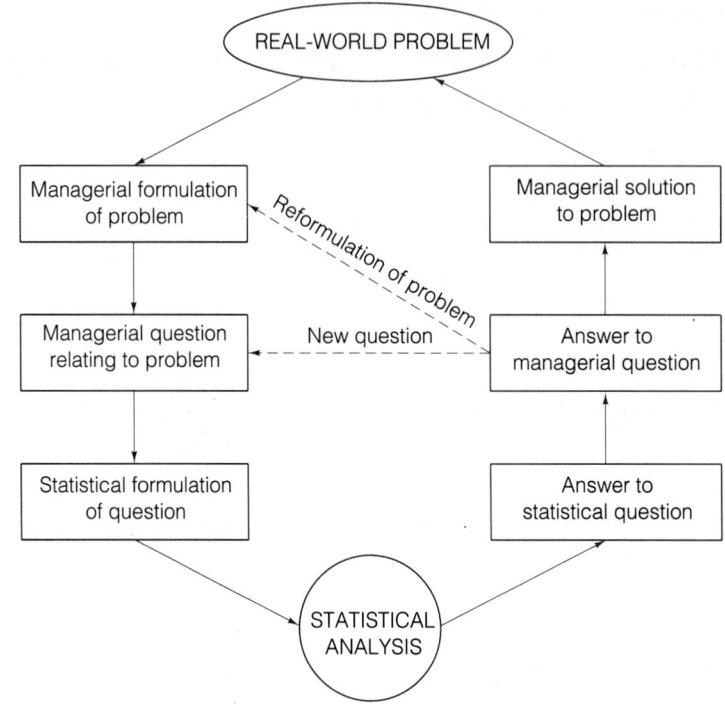

One of the most difficult steps in the decision-making process—one that requires a cooperative effort among managers and statisticians—is the translation of the managerial question into statistical terms (for example, into a question about a population). This statistical question must be formulated so that, when answered, it will provide the key to the answer to the managerial question. Thus, as in the game of chess, you must formulate the statistical question with the end result, the solution to the managerial question, in mind.

Exercises 1.1 – 1.18

Note: *Starred (*) exercises refer to the optional section.*

Learning the Mechanics

1.1   Explain the difference between descriptive and inferential statistics.

1.2   List and define the five elements of an inferential statistical problem.

1.3   Explain how populations and variables differ.

1.4   Explain how populations and samples differ.

1.5   Why would a statistician consider an inference incomplete without an accompanying measure of its reliability?

*1.6   Explain the difference between a population and a process.

1.7   Consider the set of all students enrolled in your statistics course this term. Suppose you are interested in learning about the current grade point averages (GPAs) of this group.
  a. Define the population and variable of interest.
  b. Suppose you determine the GPA of every member of the class. What would this represent, a census or a sample?
  c. Suppose you determine the GPA of 10 members of the class. Would this represent a census or a sample?
  d. If you determine the GPA of every member of the class and then calculate the average, how much reliability does this have as an "estimate" of the class average GPA?
  e. If you determine the GPA of ten members of the class and then calculate the average, will the number you get necessarily be the same as the average GPA for the whole class? On what factors would you expect the reliability of the estimate to depend?

1.8   Refer to Exercise 1.7. What must be true in order for the sample of 10 students you select from your class to be considered a random sample?

Applying the Concepts

1.9   Pollsters regularly conduct opinion polls to determine the popularity rating of the current president. Suppose a poll is to be conducted tomorrow in which 2,000 individuals will be asked whether the president is doing a good or poor job.
  a. What is the relevant population?
  b. What is the variable of interest? Is it numerical or nonnumerical?
  c. What is the sample?
  d. What is the inference of interest to the pollster?

1.10   Refer to Exercise 1.9. Suppose the poll is conducted as described therein, except that each of the 2,000 individuals polled is asked to rate the job performance of the president on a scale from 0 to 100. How do your answers to parts **a–d** change, if at all?

1.11   *Fortune* publishes a list of the 500 industrial corporations in the United States with the largest annual sales volume ("The Fortune 500," 1992). Throughout the year, each of these companies is then referred to as a *Fortune 500 company*. Assume a researcher with limited time and money wants to predict the number of new employees these 500 companies anticipate hiring next year. She selects 50 of the 500 companies, and asks a representative of each company how many new employees the company is likely to hire in the coming year.
  a. Identify the population from which the sample was drawn.
  b. What is the variable of interest?
  c. Identify the sample.
  d. What could we infer about the population from the sample data?
  e. When answering part **d**, are we employing descriptive or inferential statistics? Explain.
  f. *Fortune* lists the net profit of each of the 500 companies. If we compute the average of these 500 net profits to learn more about the Fortune 500 companies, are we employing descriptive or inferential statistics? Explain.

*1.12 Coca-Cola and Schweppes Beverages Limited (CCSB), which was formed in 1987, is 49% owned by the Coca-Cola Company. David Nellist (1992) reports that CCSB's new Wakefield plant can produce 4,000 cans of soft drink per minute. The automated process consists of measuring and dispensing the raw ingredients into storage vessels to create the syrup, and then injecting the syrup, along with carbon dioxide, into the beverage cans. Suppose that to monitor the subprocess that adds carbon dioxide to the cans, five filled cans are pulled off the line every 15 minutes and the amount of carbon dioxide in each of these five is measured to determine whether the amounts are within prescribed limits.

a. Describe the process studied.
b. Describe the variable of interest.
c. Describe the sample.
d. Describe the inference of interest.
e. *Brix* is a unit for measuring sugar concentration. If a technician is assigned the task of estimating the average brix level of all 240,000 cans of beverage stored in a warehouse near Wakefield, will the technician be examining a process or a population? Explain.

1.13 An insurance company would like to determine the proportion of all medical doctors who have been involved in one or more malpractice suits. The company selects 500 doctors at random from a professional directory and determines the number in the sample who have ever been involved in a malpractice suit.

a. Identify the population and variable of interest to the insurance company.
b. Describe the sample and identify the type of inference the insurance company wishes to make.
c. What is meant by the phrase *at random* in the context of this exercise?

1.14 *Corporate merger* is a means through which one firm (the bidder) acquires control of the assets of another firm (the target). Carol E. Eger (1982) identified a total of 497 mergers between firms listed on the New York Stock Exchange that resulted in delisting of the acquired (target) firm's stock during the period 1958–1980. She sampled 38 of these mergers and evaluated the effects of the merger on the value of the holdings of the bidder firm's bondholders. In particular, she wanted to learn whether the value of the holdings increased or decreased as a result of the merger.

a. Identify the population studied.
b. Identify the variable of interest.
c. Describe the sample.
d. Discuss types of inferences we might wish to make about the population.

1.15 *Job-sharing* is an innovative employment alternative that originated in Sweden and is becoming very popular in the United States. Firms that offer job-sharing plans allow two or more persons to work part-time, sharing one full-time job. For example, two job-sharers might alternate work weeks, with one working while the other is off. Job-sharers never work at the same time and may not even know each other. Job-sharing is particularly attractive to working mothers and to people who frequently lose their jobs due to fluctuations in the economy ("Your Job in the 1980's," 1980). To evaluate employers' satisfaction with job-sharing plans, a government agency contacted 100 firms that offer job-sharing. Each firm's director of personnel was asked whether the firm was satisfied with the productivity of workers with shared jobs.

a. Identify the population from which the sample was selected.
b. Identify the variable measured.
c. Identify the sample selected.
d. What type of inference is of interest to the government agency?

1.16   Myron Gable and Martin T. Topol (1988) sampled 218 department-store executives to study the relationship between job satisfaction and the degree of Machiavellian orientation. Briefly, the Machiavellian orientation is one in which the executive exerts very strong control—even to the point of deception and cruelty—over the employees supervised. The authors administered a questionnaire to each of the sampled executives and obtained both a job satisfaction score and a Machiavellian rating. They concluded that those with higher satisfaction scores are likely to have a lower "Mach" rating.

    a. What is the population from which the sample was selected?

    b. What variables were measured by the authors?

    c. Identify the sample.

    d. What inference was made by the authors?

1.17   Manufacturers of consumer goods rely on the information provided by consumer preference surveys to guide both the design and the marketing of new products. In the winter of 1986, Onan Corporation, a manufacturer of built-in generators for recreational vehicles (RVs), was considering developing and marketing a portable generator. Such a product could potentially be marketed both to RV owners and RV manufacturers. To determine RV owners' preferences with respect to the features of a portable generator (e.g., size and manual or electric start), 3,000 questionnaires were mailed to RV owners in the continental United States. One thousand fifty-two (1,052) responses were received by Onan.*

    a. Identify the population, the variables, the sample, and the inferences of interest to Onan.

    b. Chapters 5–8 indicate that the reliability of an inference is related to the size of the sample used. In addition to sample size, what other factors might affect the reliability of inferences based on the responses to a mailed questionnaire?

1.18   The Wallace Company of Houston is a distributor of pipes, valves, and fittings to the refining, chemical, and petrochemical industries. The company was one of four winners of the Malcolm Baldrige National Quality Award in 1990. Don Nichols (1991) explains that one of the steps the company takes to monitor the quality of its distribution process is to send out a survey twice a year to a subset of its current customers, asking the customers to rate the speed of deliveries, the accuracy of invoices, and the quality of the packaging of the products they have received from Wallace.

    a. Describe the process studied.

    b. Describe the variables of interest.

    c. Describe the sample.

    d. Describe the inferences of interest.

    e. What are some of the factors that are likely to affect the reliability of the inferences?

On Your Own

If you could start your own business right now, what kind would it be? Identify a large population and a characteristic of the units in the population (i.e., a variable) that would be of interest to you and your firm. How would you measure the variable of interest for a sample of units drawn from the population? Is the data set you identified a sample data set or a population data set? How could you use this data set in the operation of your business?

---

*Information by personal communication with Thomas J. Roess, Manager, Market Analysis, Onan Corporation, Fridley, Minnesota.

References

Allison, R. I. and Uhl, K. P. "Influence of beer brand identification on taste perception." *Journal of Marketing Research*, Aug. 1965, pp. 36–39.

Careers in Statistics. Washington, D.C.: American Statistical Association and the Institute of Mathematical Statistics, 1974.

Chervany, N. L., Benson, P. G., and Iyer, R. K. "The planning stage in statistical reasoning." *The American Statistician*, Nov. 1980, pp. 222–226.

Eger, C. E. "Corporate mergers: An analytical analysis of the role of risky debt." Unpublished Ph.D. dissertation. University of Minnesota, 1982.

"The Fortune 500." *Fortune*, Apr. 20, 1992, pp. 220–239.

Gable, M. and Topol, M. T. "Machiavellianism and the department-store executive." *Journal of Retailing*, Spring 1988, pp. 68–84.

Hunz, E. "Application of statistical sampling to inventory audits." *The Internal Auditor*, 1956, *13*, p. 38.

Nellist, David. "Quality teamwork at Wakefield." *Industrial Management and Data Systems*, 1992, Vol. 92, No. 2, pp. 21–23.

Nichols, Don. "Quality wins." *Small Business Reports*, May 1991, pp. 26–35.

Tanur, J. M., Mosteller, F., Kruskal, W. H., Link, R. F., Pieters, R. S., and Rising, G. R. *Statistics: A Guide to the Unknown.* San Francisco: Holden-Day, 1989.

U.S. Bureau of the Census. *Statistical Abstract of the United States: 1989.* Washington, D.C.: U.S. Government Printing Office, 1989.

U.S. Department of Commerce. *An Error Profile: Employment as Measured by the Current Population Survey.* Statistical Policy Working Paper 3. Washington, D.C.: U.S. Government Printing Office, 1978.

U.S. Department of Labor. *The Consumer Price Index: Concepts and Content over the Years.* Bureau of Labor Statistics, Report 517. Washington, D.C.: U.S. Government Printing Office, May 1978.

Willis, R. E. and Chervany, N. L. *Statistical Analysis and Modeling for Management Decision-making.* Belmont, Calif.: Wadsworth, 1974, Chapter 1.

"Your job in the 1980's." *Consumer's Digest*, Nov.–Dec. 1980, pp. 32–36.

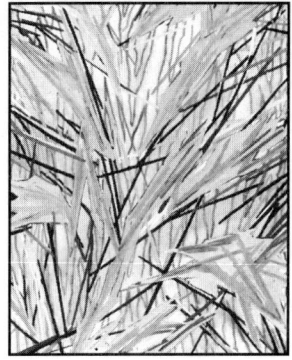

CHAPTER TWO

Methods for Describing Sets of Data

Contents

Case Studies

Where We've Been

In Chapter 1, we examined some examples of the use of statistics in business. We discussed the role that statistics plays in supporting managerial decision-making. We introduced you to descriptive and inferential statistics and to the five elements of inferential statistics: a population, one or more variables, a sample, an inference, and a measure of reliability for the inference. We described the primary goal of inferential statistics as using sample data to make inferences (estimates, predictions, or other generalizations) about the population from which the sample was drawn.

Where We're Going

Before we make an inference, we must be able to describe and extract information from the sample data. This can be accomplished through both graphical and numerical methods.

Before we can use the information in a sample to make inferences about a population, we must be able to extract the relevant information from the sample. That is, we need methods to summarize and describe the sample measurements. For example, if we look at last year's sales for 100 randomly selected companies, we are unlikely to extract much information by looking at the set of 100 sales figures. We would get a clearer picture of the data by calculating the average sales for all 100 companies, by determining the highest and lowest company sales, by drawing a graph that shows the spread of the 100 sales figures, or, in general, by using some technique that will extract and summarize relevant information from the data and, at the same time, allow us to obtain a clearer understanding of the sample.

In this chapter, we first define four different types of data and then present some graphical and numerical methods for describing data of each type. You will see that graphical methods for describing data are intuitively appealing and can be used to describe either a sample or a population. However, numerical methods for describing data are the keys that unlock the door to population inference-making.

2.1   Types of Data

In Chapter 1, you learned that statistics, both descriptive and inferential, is concerned with measurements of one or more variables of a sample of units drawn from a population. These measurements are referred to as **data**. We will generally classify data as one of four types: **nominal**, **ordinal**, **interval**, or **ratio**.

> ### Definition 2.1
>
> **Nominal data** are measurements that simply classify the units of the sample (or population) into categories.

Nominal data (also referred to as **categorical data**) are labels or names that identify the category to which each unit belongs. The following are examples of nominal data:

1. The political party affiliation of each individual in a sample of 50 business executives
2. The gender of each individual in a sample of seven applicants for a computer programming job
3. The state in which each of a sample of 100 U.S. firms had its highest sales revenue in 1993.

Note that in each case—political party, gender, and state—the measurement is no more than a categorization of each sample unit. Nominal data are often reported as nonnumerical labels, such as Democrat, woman, and Ohio. Even if the labels are converted to numbers, as they often are for ease of computer entry and analysis, the numerical values are simply codes. They cannot be meaningfully added, subtracted, multiplied, or divided. For example, we might code Democrat = 1, Republican = 2, and Other = 3. These are simply numerical codes for each of the categories into which units may fall and have no further significance.

Definition 2.2

....

Ordinal data are measurements that enable the units of the sample (or population) to be ordered with respect to the variable of interest.

Ordinal data are measurements that indicate the *relative* amount of a property possessed by the units. The following are examples of ordinal data:

1. The size of car rented by each individual in a sample of 30 business travelers: compact, subcompact, midsize, or full-size
2. A taste-tester's ranking of four brands of barbecue sauce
3. A supervisor's annual ranking of the performance of her 10 employees using a scale of 1 (worst performance) to 10 (best performance)

Note that in each case—size, flavor preference, and performance ranking—more than a categorization of units is involved. In addition to providing a categorization, the measurements actually rank the units. For example, we know that a midsize car is larger than a subcompact and that an employee with a performance ranking of 9 performed better, in the opinion of the supervisor, than one with a ranking of 7. We also know that a taster preferred brand C barbecue sauce to brand A if he gives brand C a higher flavor-preference ranking than brand A.

Ordinal data are said to represent a "higher" level of measurement than nominal data because ordinal data contain all the information of nominal data (i.e., category labels that differentiate units) *plus* an ordering of the units. As with nominal measurements, the distance between ordinal measurements is not meaningful. For example, we do not know whether the difference in size between a full-size and a midsize car is the same as the difference between the midsize and the subcompact. Nor do we know whether the extent of flavor preference between barbecue sauce brands C and A is the same as that between brands A and B if a taster reports her flavor preference as $C > A > B > D$, where > means "more flavorful than."

As with nominal data, ordinal data can be reported with or without numbers. For example, the automobile sizes are nonnumerically labeled, whereas the supervisor's performance rankings are numerical. Even if numbers are used, we must again be careful: They simply provide an ordering or ranking of the units in the sample or population. The arithmetic operations of addition, subtraction, multiplication, and division are not meaningful for ordinal data.

> ## Definition 2.3
>
> **Interval data** are measurements that enable the determination of how much more or less of the measured characteristic is possessed by one unit of the sample (or population) than another.

Interval data are always numerical, and the numbers assigned to two units can be subtracted to determine the *difference* between the units with respect to the variable measured. The following are examples of interval data:

1. The temperature (in degrees Fahrenheit) at which each of a sample of 20 pieces of heat-resistant plastic begins to melt

2. The scores of a sample of 150 MBA applicants on the GMAT, a standardized business graduate school entrance exam administered nationwide

3. The time at which the 5 P.M. Washington–to–New York air shuttle arrives at LaGuardia on each of a sample of 30 weekdays

Note that in each case—temperature, score, and arrival time—more than a ranking is involved. The difference between the numerical values assigned to the units is meaningful. For example, the difference between scores of 600 and 580 on the GMAT is the same as that between scores of 520 and 500. Also, the morning shuttle due at 9 A.M. but arriving at 9:20 A.M. is just as late as the afternoon shuttle due at 5:30 P.M. and arriving at 5:50 P.M. Note in each case that the difference is the key, not the numerical measurement itself.

Interval data represent a higher level of measurement than ordinal data, because in addition to ranking the units, interval data reflect the difference between the units with respect to the variable measured. Although adding or subtracting interval data is valid, multiplying or dividing them is not. This is because the zero point (the origin, or 0) does not indicate an absence of the characteristic of interest. For example, the origin on the temperature scale differs for the Fahrenheit and Celsius scales and does not indicate an absence of heat on either scale. Temperatures lower than $0°$ (e.g., $-10°C$ and $-10°F$) indicate that less heat is present, so $0°$ does not mean "no heat." The result is that we cannot say that a temperature of $100°F$ indicates twice the heat of $50°F$. Similarly, since GMAT scores range from 200 to 800, a zero score is not even possible, and thus has no meaning. The result is that a score of 600 cannot be interpreted as being 50% higher than a score of 400.

Most numerical business data are measured on scales for which the origin is meaningful. Thus, most numerical measurements encountered in business are *ratio data*.

Definition 2.4

Ratio data are measurements that enable the determination of how many times as much of the measured characteristic is possessed by one unit of the sample (or population) than another.

Ratio data are always numerical, and the ratio between the numbers assigned to two units can be interpreted as the multiple by which the units differ. The following are examples of ratio data:

1. The sales revenue for each firm in a sample of 100 U.S. firms
2. The unemployment rate (reported as a percentage) in the United States for each of the past 60 months
3. The number of female executives employed in each of a sample of 50 manufacturing companies

Note that in each case—dollars of revenue, percentage unemployed, and count of female executives—the scale measures the absolute amount of the characteristic possessed by the unit. The result is that the ratio of measurements between units is meaningful. That is, a company with revenue of $100 million has twice the revenue of a company with $50 million in revenue. Similarly, an unemployment rate of 8% means twice as many unemployed as with a rate of 4%. And a company with 30 female executives has 1.5 times as many as one with 20 female executives.

Ratio data represent the highest level of measurement. The numbers can be used to categorize, rank, differentiate, and measure multiples of one unit with respect to another. All arithmetic operations performed on ratio data are meaningful.

The key to differentiating interval and ratio data is that for ratio data the zero point, or origin, denotes an absence of the characteristic being measured. For example, zero revenue, zero unemployment, and zero female executives mean *absence* of income, unemployment, and female executives, respectively. Most measurement scales utilized in business yield ratio data: measures of monetary value, distance, weight, height, percentages, and numerical counts all usually generate ratio data.

The four types of data are often combined into two classes that are sufficient for most statistical applications. Nominal and ordinal data are often referred to as **qualitative** data, whereas interval and ratio data are called **quantitative** data.

The properties of the four types of data are summarized in the box. As you would expect, the methods for describing and reporting data depend on the type of data analyzed. We devote the remainder of this chapter to graphical methods for describing qualitative and quantitative data.

Types of Data

Nominal	Classification of sample (or population) units into categories
	Often uses labels rather than numbers
Ordinal	Rank-orders the sample (or population) units
	May be verbal labels or numbers
Interval	Enables comparison of sample (or population) units according to differences between values
	Always numerical, but the zero point on the scale does not indicate an absence of the measured characteristic
Ratio	Enables comparison of sample (or population) units according to multiples of the values
	Always numerical, and the zero point on the scale denotes an absence of the measured characteristic

Qualitative	Includes nominal and ordinal data types
Quantitative	Includes interval and ratio data types

Exercises 2.1 – 2.8

Learning the Mechanics

2.1
 a. Explain the difference between nominal and ordinal data.
 b. Explain the difference between interval and ratio data.
 c. Explain the difference between qualitative and quantitative data.

2.2 Each of the following descriptions of data defines one of the following types: nominal, ordinal, interval, ratio. Match the correct type to each description.
 a. Data that enable the units of the sample to be compared by the differences between their numerical values
 b. Data that enable the units of the sample to be classified into categories
 c. Data that enable the units of the sample to be rank-ordered
 d. Data that enable the units of the sample to be compared by computing the ratios of the numerical values

2.3 Suppose you are provided a data set that classifies each sample unit into one of four categories: A, B, C, or D. You plan to create a computer database consisting of these data, and you decide to code the data as A = 1, B = 2, C = 3, and D = 4 for entering them into the computer. Are the data consisting of the classifications A, B, C, and D qualitative or quantitative? After the data are entered as 1, 2, 3, or 4, are they qualitative or quantitative? Explain your answers.

Applying the Concepts

2.4 A food-products company is considering marketing a new snack food. To see how consumers react to the product, the company conducted a taste-test using a sample of 100 shoppers at a suburban shopping mall. The shoppers were asked to taste the snack food and then fill out a short questionnaire that requested the following information:
  a. What is your age?
  b. Are you the person who typically does the food shopping for your household?
  c. How many people are in your family?
  d. How would you rate the taste of the snack food on a scale of 1 to 10, where 1 is least tasty?
  e. Would you purchase this snack food if it were available on the market?
  f. If you answered yes to question **e**, how often would you purchase it?

Each of these questions defines a variable of interest to the company. Classify the data generated for each variable as nominal, ordinal, interval, or ratio. Justify your classification.

2.5 Classify the following examples of data as nominal, ordinal, interval, or ratio. Justify your classification.
  a. Ten college freshmen were asked to indicate the brand of jeans they prefer.
  b. Fifteen television cable companies were asked how many hours of sports programming they carry in a typical week.
  c. Fifty executives were asked what percentage of their workday is spent in meetings.
  d. The number of long-distance phone calls made from each of 100 public telephone booths on a particular day was recorded.
  e. The Scholastic Aptitude Test (SAT) scores of 250 incoming freshmen to a small college were compiled.

2.6 Classify the following examples of data as either qualitative or quantitative:
  a. The brand of calculator purchased by each of 20 business statistics students
  b. The list price of calculators purchased by each of 20 business statistics students
  c. The number of automobiles purchased during the past 5 years by each household in a sample of 50 randomly selected households
  d. The month indicated by each of 41 randomly selected business firms as the month during which it had the highest sales
  e. The depth of tread remaining on each of 137 randomly selected automobile tires after 20,000 miles of wear

2.7 Windows is a computer software product made by Microsoft Corporation. In designing Windows Version 3.1, Microsoft telephoned 60,000 users of Windows 3.0 (an older version) and asked them how the product could be improved (Roberts, 1992). Assume customers were asked the following questions:

  I. Are you the most frequent user of Windows 3.0 in your household?
  II. What is your age?
  III. How would you rate the helpfulness of the Tutorial instructions that accompany Windows 3.0, on a scale of 1 to 10, where 1 is not helpful?
  IV. When using a printer with Windows 3.0, do you most frequently use a dot-matrix printer or another type of printer?
  V. If the speed of Windows 3.0 could be changed, which one of the following would you prefer: slower, unchanged, faster?

VI. How many people in your household have used Windows 3.0 at least once?

Each of these questions defines a variable of interest to the company. Classify the data generated for each variable as nominal, ordinal, interval, or ratio. Justify your classification.

2.8 Classify the examples of data in parts **a–d** as either qualitative or quantitative:
    a. The number of corporate mergers during each of the last 15 years
    b. The change in the Consumer Price Index during each of the last 6 months
    c. The length of time before each of 30 dry-cell batteries goes dead
    d. The American automobile manufacturer that each of 25 service station mechanics indicated as producing the most reliable cars
    e. Classify each of the preceding as nominal, ordinal, interval or ratio data.

2.2 Graphical Methods for Describing Quantitative Data: Histograms and Stem-and-Leaf Displays

Recall from Section 2.1 that quantitative data sets consist of either interval or ratio data. Most business data are quantitative, so that methods for summarizing quantitative data are especially important.

For example, suppose a financial analyst is interested in the amount of resources spent by computer hardware and software companies on research and development (R&D). She samples 50 of these high-technology firms and calculates the amount each spent last year on R&D as a percentage of their total revenues. The results are given in Table 2.1. As numerical measurements made on the sample of 50 units (the firms),

TABLE 2.1 Percentage of Revenues Spent on Research and Development

Company	Percentage	Company	Percentage	Company	Percentage	Company	Percentage
1	13.5	14	9.5	27	8.2	39	6.5
2	8.4	15	8.1	28	6.9	40	7.5
3	10.5	16	13.5	29	7.2	41	7.1
4	9.0	17	9.9	30	8.2	42	13 2
5	9.2	18	6.9	31	9.6	43	7.7
6	9.7	19	7.5	32	7.2	44	5.9
7	6.6	20	11.1	33	8.8	45	5.2
8	10.6	21	8.2	34	11.3	46	5.6
9	10.1	22	8.0	35	8.5	47	11.7
10	7.1	23	7.7	36	9.4	48	6.0
11	8.0	24	7.4	37	10.5	49	7.8
12	7.9	25	6.5	38	6.9	50	6.5
13	6.8	26	9.5				

these percentages represent quantitative data. The analyst's initial objective is to describe these data in order to extract relevant information.

A **relative frequency histogram** for these 50 R&D percentages is shown in Figure 2.1. The horizontal axis of Figure 2.1, which gives the percentage spent on R&D for each company, is divided into intervals commencing with the interval from 5.15 to 6.25 and proceeding in intervals of equal size to 12.85 to 13.95 percent. The vertical axis gives the proportion (or **relative frequency**) of the 50 percentages that fall in each interval. Thus, you can see that the bulk of the companies spend between 6.25% and 10.65% of their revenues on research and development, while only .06 of the companies spend more than 12%. Many other summary statements can be made by further study of the histogram.

FIGURE 2.1 ►
Relative frequency histogram for the 50 computer companies' R&D percentages

Another graphic representation of these same data, a **stem-and-leaf** display, is shown below. In these displays the **stem** is the portion of the observation to the left of the decimal point, whereas the remaining portion to the right of the decimal point is the **leaf**.

The stems and leaves for the R&D percentages 7.4, 10.5, and 13.2 are shown here:

Stem	Leaf		Stem	Leaf		Stem	Leaf
7	4		10	5		13	2

The stem-and-leaf display for all 50 R&D percentages is shown in Figure 2.2 (page 30). Note that the leaves corresponding to each stem are arranged in ascending order, and a key is included with the display to specify the units of the leaf (and, by implication, the units of the stem).

FIGURE 2.2 ▶

Stem-and-leaf display for 50
computer companies' research and
development percentages

Stem	Leaf
5	2 6 9
6	0 5 5 5 6 8 9 9 9
7	1 1 2 2 4 5 5 7 7 8 9
8	0 0 1 2 2 2 4 5 8
9	0 2 4 5 5 6 7 9
10	1 5 5 6
11	1 3 7
12	
13	2 5 5

Key: Leaf units are tenths.

Note that although the stem 12 has no leaves (meaning that none of the 50 observations fell in the range from 12.0 to 12.9), we include the 12 stem in the display so that this fact is visually obvious. Note also that the decimal point is not included in the display. When there is no confusion caused by its omission, we can usually obtain a less cluttered graphical description without it.

Several descriptive facts about these data are easily seen in the stem-and-leaf display. Most of the sampled computer companies (37 of 50) spent between 6.0% and 9.9% of their revenues on R&D, and 11 of them spent between 7.0% and 7.9%. Relative to the rest of the sampled companies, three spent a high percentage of revenues on R&D—in excess of 13%.

Both the histogram and stem-and-leaf displays provide useful graphic descriptions of quantitative data. Since most statistical software packages can be used to construct these displays, we will focus on their interpretation rather than their construction.

Histograms can be used to display either the **frequency** or **relative frequency** of the measurements falling into specified intervals (called **measurement classes**). The frequency is just a count of the number of measurements in a class, while the relative frequency is the proportion, or fraction, of measurements in the class. The measurement classes, frequencies, and relative frequencies for the R&D data are shown in Table 2.2.

By looking at a histogram (say, the relative frequency histogram in Figure 2.1), you can see two important facts. First, note the total area under the histogram, and then note the proportion of the total area that falls over a particular interval of the horizontal axis. You will see that the proportion of the total area that falls above an interval is equal to the relative frequency of the measurements that fall in the interval. *

---

*Some histograms are constructed with all class intervals of equal width except the first and last, which are open-ended. The proportionality between area and relative frequency will not hold for such histograms. We will restrict our attention to histograms that have equal-sized class intervals, because later we will want to establish a correspondence between relative frequency histograms and probability distributions. ·

TABLE 2.2   Measurement Classes, Frequencies, and Relative Frequencies for the R&D Percentage Data

Class	Measurement Class	Class Frequency	Class Relative Frequency
1	5.15– 6.25	4	$4/50 = .08$
2	6.25– 7.35	12	$12/50 = .24$
3	7.35– 8.45	14	$14/50 = .28$
4	8.45– 9.55	7	$7/50 = .14$
5	9.55–10.65	7	$7/50 = .14$
6	10.65–11.75	3	$3/50 = .06$
7	11.75–12.85	0	$0/50 = .00$
8	12.85–13.95	3	$3/50 = \underline{.06}$
			1.00

For example, the relative frequency for the class interval 5.15–6.25 is .08. Consequently, the rectangle above that interval contains 8% of the total area under the histogram.

Second, you can imagine the appearance of the relative frequency histogram for a very large set of data (say, a population). As the number of measurements in a data set is increased, you can obtain a better description of the data by decreasing the width of the class intervals. When the class intervals become small enough, a relative frequency histogram will (for all practical purposes) appear as a smooth curve (see Figure 2.3).

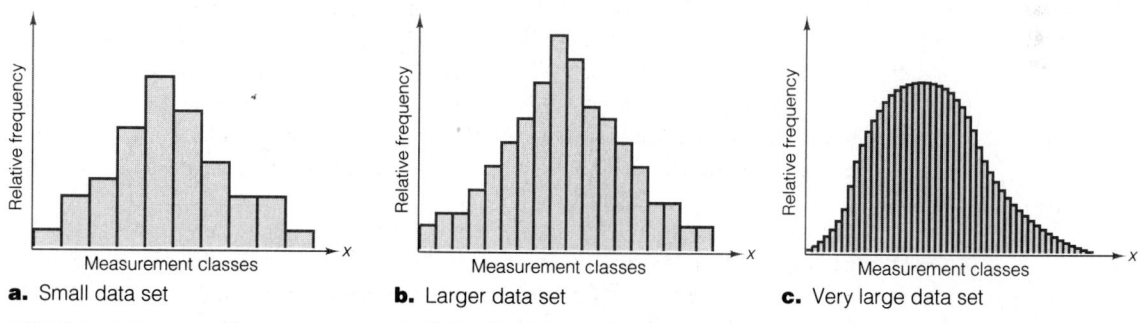

a. Small data set   **b.** Larger data set   **c.** Very large data set

FIGURE 2.3 ▲ The effect of the size of a data set on the outline of a histogram

While histograms provide good visual descriptions, particularly of very large data sets, individual measurements cannot be identified by looking at a histogram. In contrast, each of the original measurements is "visible" in a stem-and-leaf display. The stem-and-leaf display arranges the data in ascending order, which enables easy location of the individual measurements. For example, in Figure 2.2 we can easily see that three of the R&D measurements are equal to 8.2%, whereas that fact is not evident by inspection of the histogram in Figure 2.1. However, stem-and-leaf displays can become unwieldy for very large data sets. A very large number of stems and leaves causes the vertical and horizontal dimensions of the display to become cumbersome, so that the usefulness of the visual display is diminished.

EXAMPLE 2.1

A manufacturer of industrial wheels suspects that profitable orders are being lost because of the long time the firm takes to develop price quotes for potential customers. To investigate this possibility, 50 requests for price quotes were randomly selected from the set of all quotes made last year, and the processing time was determined for each quote. The processing times are displayed in Table 2.3, and each quote was classified according to whether the order was "lost" or not (i.e., whether or not the customer placed an order after receiving a price quote).

TABLE 2.3   Price Quote Processing Times (Days)

Request Number	Processing Time	Lost?	Request Number	Processing Time	Lost?
1	2.36	No	26	3.34	No
2	5.73	No	27	6.00	No
3	6.60	No	28	5.92	No
4	10.05	Yes	29	7.28	Yes
5	5.13	No	30	1.25	No
6	1.88	No	31	4.01	No
7	2.52	No	32	7.59	No
8	2.00	No	33	13.42	Yes
9	4.69	No	34	3.24	No
10	1.91	No	35	3.37	No
11	6.75	Yes	36	14.06	Yes
12	3.92	No	37	5.10	No
13	3.46	No	38	6.44	No
14	2.64	No	39	7.76	No
15	3.63	No	40	4.40	No
16	3.44	No	41	5.48	No
17	9.49	Yes	42	7.51	No
18	4.90	No	43	6.18	No
19	7.45	No	44	8.22	Yes
20	20.23	Yes	45	4.37	No
21	3.91	No	46	2.93	No
22	1.70	No	47	9.95	Yes
23	16.29	Yes	48	4.46	No
24	5.52	No	49	14.32	Yes
25	1.44	No	50	9.01	No

a. Use a statistical software package to create a frequency histogram for these data. Then shade the area under the histogram that corresponds to lost orders.

b. Use a statistical software package to create a stem-and-leaf display for these data. Then shade each leaf of the display that corresponds to a lost order.

c. Compare and interpret the two graphic displays of these data.

Solution

a. We used SAS to generate the relative frequency histogram in Figure 2.4.

FIGURE 2.4 ▶

Frequency histogram for the quote processing time data

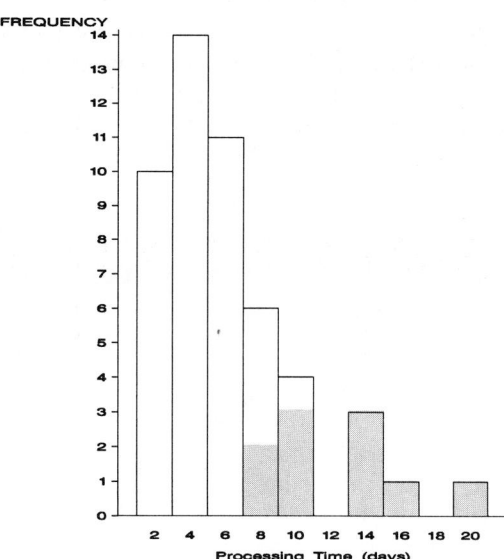

SAS, like most statistical software, offers the user the choice of accepting default class intervals and interval widths, or the user can make his or her own selections. After some experimenting with various numbers of class intervals and interval widths, we used 10 intervals. SAS then created intervals of width 2 days, beginning at 1 day, just below the smallest measurement of 1.25 days, and ending with 21 days, just above the largest measurement of 20.2 days. Note that SAS labels the midpoint of each bar, rather than its endpoints. Thus, the bar labeled "2" represents measurements from 1.00 to 2.99, the bar labeled "4" represents measurements from 3.00 to 4.99, etc. This histogram clearly shows the clustering of the measurements in the lower end of the distribution (between approximately 1 and 7 days), and the relatively few measurements in the upper end of the distribution (greater than 12 days). The shading of the area of the frequency histogram corresponding to lost orders clearly indicates that they lie in the upper tail of the distribution.

b. We used the statistical package SPSS[R] to generate the stem-and-leaf display in Figure 2.5 (page 34).

FIGURE 2.5 ▶

Stem-and-leaf display for the quote processing time data

```
Frequency      Stem &  Leaf

   5.00          1 .   24789
   5.00          2 .   03569
   8.00          3 .   23344699
   6.00          4 .   034469
   6.00          5 .   114579
   5.00          6 .   01467
   5.00          7 .   24557
   1.00          8 .   2
   3.00          9 .   049
   1.00         10 .   0
    .00         11 .
    .00         12 .
   1.00         13 .   4
   4.00 Extremes       (14.1), (14.3), (16.3), (20.2)

Stem width:      1.00
Each leaf:           1 case(s)
```

Note that the stem consists of the number of whole days (units and ten digits), and the leaf is the tenths digit (first digit after the decimal) of each measurement.* The hundredths digit has been dropped to make the display more visually effective. Thus, the first processing time in Table 2.3, 2.36 days, is partitioned as follows:

Stem	Leaf
2	3

Note that SPSS also includes a column titled "Frequency" showing the number of measurements corresponding to each stem. Also, note that instead of extending the stems all the way to 20 days to show the largest measurement, SPSS truncates the display after the stem corresponding to 13 days, labels the largest four measurements as "Extremes," and simply lists them horizontally in the last row of the display. Extreme observations that are detached from the remainder of the data are called **outliers**, and they usually receive special attention in statistical analyses. Although outliers may represent legitimate measurements, they are frequently mistakes: incorrectly recorded, miscoded during data entry, or taken from a population different from the one from which the rest of the sample was selected. Stem-and-leaf displays are useful for identifying outliers.

c. As is usually the case for data sets that are not too large (say, fewer than 100 measurements), the stem-and-leaf display provides more detail than the histogram without being unwieldy. For the processing time data, note that the stem-and-leaf display in Figure 2.5 clearly indicates not only that the lost orders are associated with high processing times (as does the histogram in Figure 2.4), but also exactly which of the times correspond to lost orders. Histograms are most useful for displaying very large data sets, when the overall shape of the distribution of measure-

---

*In the examples in this section, the stem was formed from the digits to the left of the decimal. This is not always the case. For example, in the following data set the stems could be the tenths digit and the leaves the hundredths digit: .12, .15, .22, .25, .28, .33.

ments is more important than the identification of individual measurements. Nevertheless, the message of both graphical displays is clear: establishing processing time limits may well result in fewer lost orders.

While stem-and-leaf displays may generally provide more information than histograms for quantitative (interval or ratio) data, they are not useful for qualitative (nominal or ordinal) data. However, histograms can be used to graph the **frequency** or **relative frequency** corresponding to each classification of the qualitative variable. Histograms for qualitative data are often called **bar charts**, and their usefulness is demonstrated in the Case Study 2.1.

CASE STUDY 2.1 / Pareto Analysis

Vilfredo Pareto (1843–1923), an Italian economist, discovered that approximately 80% of the wealth of a country lies with approximately 20% of the people. Others have noted similar findings in other areas: 80% of sales are attributable to 20% of the customers; 80% of customer complaints result from 20% of the components of a product; 80% of defective items produced by a process result from 20% of the types of errors that are made in production (Kane, 1989). These examples illustrate the idea of "the vital few and the trivial many," the **Pareto principle**. As applied to the last example, a "vital few" errors account for most of the defectives produced. The remaining defectives are due to many different errors, the "trivial many."

In general, **Pareto analysis** involves the categorization of items and the determination of which categories contain the most observations. These are the "vital few" categories. Pareto analysis is used in industry today as a problem-identification tool. Managers and workers use it to identify the most important problems or causes of problems that plague them. Knowledge of the "vital few" problems permits management to set priorities and focus their problem-solving efforts.

The primary tool of Pareto analysis is the **Pareto diagram**. The Pareto diagram is simply a frequency or relative frequency histogram, or bar chart, with the bars arranged in descending order of height from left to right across the horizontal axis. That is, the tallest bar is

positioned at the left and the shortest is at the far right. This arrangement locates the most important categories—those with the largest frequencies—at the left of the chart. Since the data are qualitative, there is no inherent numerical order: They can be rearranged to make the display more useful.

Consider the following example from the automobile industry (adapted from Kane, 1989). All cars produced on a particular day were inspected for defects. The defects were categorized by type as follows: body, accessories, electrical, transmission, and engine. The resulting Pareto diagram for these qualitative data is shown in Figure 2.6(a) on page 36. The diagram reveals that most of the defects were found on the bodies of the cars or in their accessories (radio, wipers, etc.).

Sufficient data were collected when the cars were inspected to take the Pareto analysis one step farther. All 70 body defects were further classified as to whether they were paint defects, dents, upholstery defects, windshield defects, or chrome defects. All 50 accessory defects were further classified as to whether they were defects in the air conditioning (A/C) system, the radio, the power steering, the cruise control, or the windshield (W/S) wipers. Two more Pareto diagrams were constructed from these data. They are shown in panels (b) and (c) of Figure 2.6. This decomposition of the original Pareto diagram is called **exploding the Pareto diagram**.

It can be seen that paint defects and dents were the predominant types of body defects and that the accessory with the most problems is the air conditioning system. These are the "vital few" types of defects. Their identification permitted management to target them for special attention by managers, engineers, and assembly-line workers.

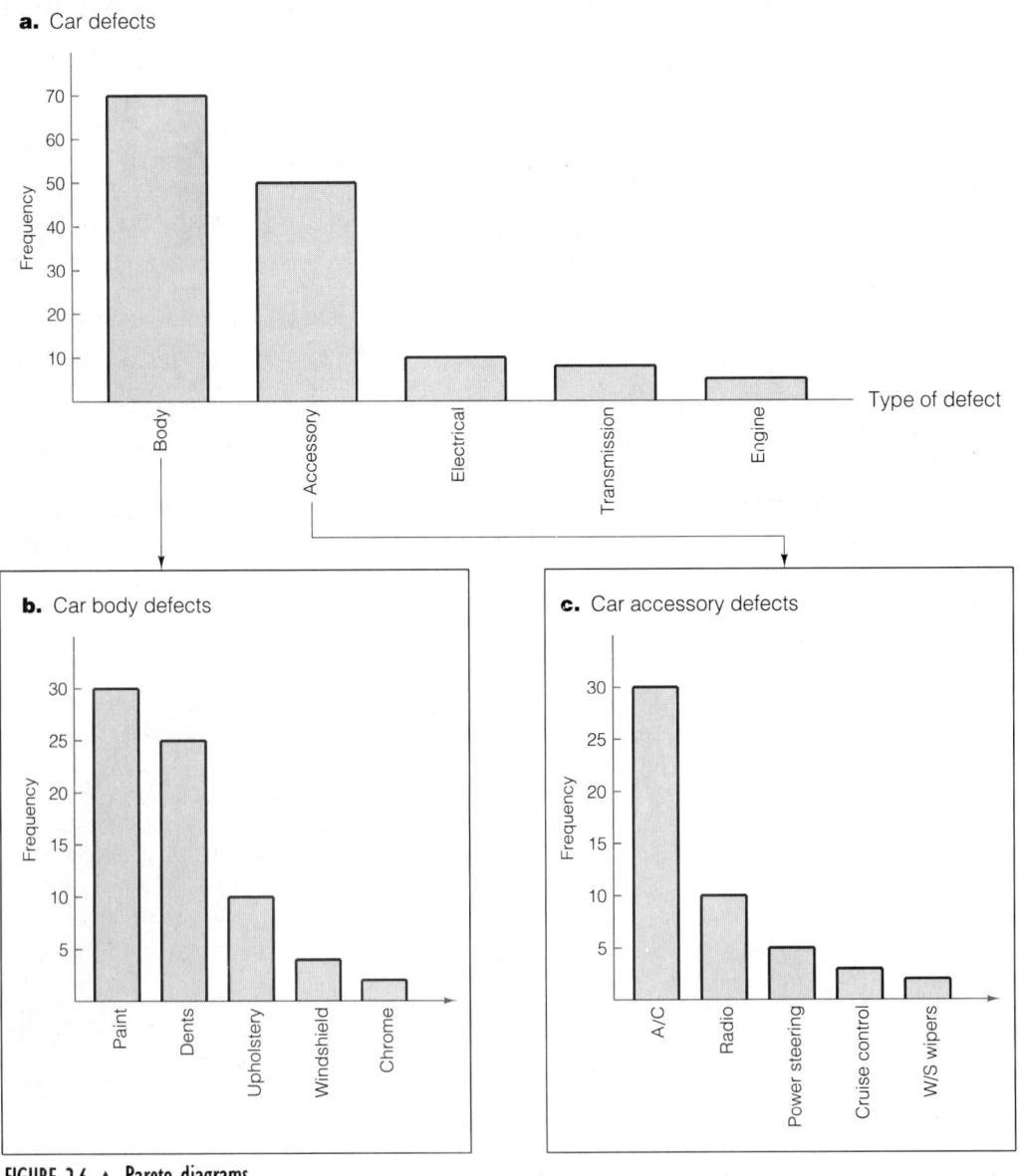

FIGURE 2.6 ▲ Pareto diagrams

Most statistical software packages can be used to generate histograms and stem-and-leaf displays. Both are useful tools for graphically describing data sets. We recommend generating and comparing both displays when feasible. The histogram will generally be more useful for very large data sets or for qualitative data, whereas the stem-and-leaf display provides useful detail for smaller quantitative data sets.

CASE STUDY 2.2 / Appraising the Market Value of an Asset

The *market value* of an asset is the price negotiated by a willing buyer and a willing seller of the asset, each acting rationally in his or her own self-interest. The *book value* of an asset is the value of the asset as shown in its owner's accounting records. Generally speaking, it is the amount the owner paid for the asset, less any depreciation expense (Davidson, Stickney, and Weil, 1979).

Robert R. Sterling and Raymond Radosevich (1969) examined the hypothesis that accountants generally agree on the book value of a depreciable asset but do not agree on its current market value. A questionnaire was prepared in which the installment purchase of a depreciable asset was described and the respondent was asked to determine the market value of the asset. The questionnaire also contained a series of questions relating to the book value of the asset. These questions

enabled Sterling and Radosevich to calculate a book value for the asset for each of the respondents. The questionnaire was mailed to 500 randomly selected certified public accountants (CPAs) in the United States; 114 and 99 usable book value and market value responses, respectively, were returned.

The frequency distributions of book values and market values obtained from the returned questionnaires appear in Figure 2.7. In both histograms, the intervals from $150 to $200 and $600 to $650 include all responses less than $200 and greater than $600, respectively. The histograms suggest disagreement among the CPAs as to both the book value and the market value of the asset. Thus, Sterling and Radosevich rejected the hypothesis that accountants tend to agree on book values and to disagree on market values.

a. Book values

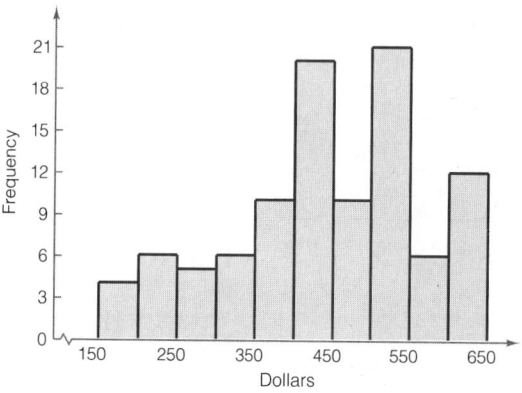

b. Market values

FIGURE 2.7 ▲ Frequency histograms for book and market values as assessed by CPAs

Note that decisions based on a visual comparison of histograms (or other graphical descriptions) are risky because they are subject to an unknown probability of error. For example, we might wonder whether dis-

agreement among the CPAs really exists or whether the difference we see in the histogram is due to random variation that would be present from sample to sample. We begin to answer questions of this type in Chapter 5.

Exercises 2.9–2.22

Note: Starred exercises (*) require the use of a computer.

Learning the Mechanics

2.9   Graph the relative frequency histogram for the 500 measurements summarized in the accompanying relative frequency table.

Measurement Class	Relative Frequency
.5– 2.5	.10
2.5– 4.5	.15
4.5– 6.5	.25
6.5– 8.5	.20
8.5–10.5	.05
10.5–12.5	.10
12.5–14.5	.10
14.6–16.5	.05

2.10   Refer to Exercise 2.9. Calculate the number of the 500 measurements falling into each of the measurement classes. Then graph a frequency histogram for these data.

2.11   The statistical package Minitab was used to generate the following histogram:

```
MIDDLE OF       NUMBER OF
INTERVAL        OBSERVATIONS
   20              1        *
   22              3        ***
   24              2        **
   26              3        ***
   28              4        ****
   30              7        *******
   32             11        ***********
   34              6        ******
   36              2        **
   38              3        ***
   40              3        ***
   42              2        **
   44              1        *
   46              1        *
```

a. Is this a frequency histogram or relative frequency histogram? Explain.

b. How many measurement classes were used in the construction of this histogram?

c. How many measurements are there in the data set described by this histogram?

2.12 SAS was used to generate the stem-and-leaf display below. Note that SAS arranges the stems in descending order. Also, the instruction to "Multiply Stem.Leaf by $10^{**}+0.1$" indicates that each number should be multiplied by 10. For example, the top number in the display, 5.1, represents an observation of $10(5.1) = 51$.

```
Stem Leaf                          #
   5  1                            1
   4  457                          3
   3  00036                        5
   2  1134599                      7
   1  2248                         4
   0  012                          3
      ----+----+----+----+
Multiply Stem.Leaf by 10**+01
```

a. How many observations were in the original data set?

b. In the bottom row of the stem-and-leaf display, identify the stem, the leaves, and the numbers in the original data set represented by this stem and its leaves.

2.13 Bonds can be issued by the federal government, state and local governments, and U.S. corporations. A *mortgage bond* is a promissory note in which the issuing company pledges certain real assets as security in exchange for a specified amount of money. A *debenture* is an unsecured promissory note, backed only by the general credit of the issuer. The bond price of either a mortgage bond or debenture is negotiated between the asked price (the lowest price anyone will accept) and the bid price (the highest price anyone wants to pay). (See *How the Bond Market Works*, 1988.) The accompanying table contains the bid prices on December 31, 1991, for a sample of 30 publicly traded debenture bonds issued by utility companies.

Utility Company	Bid Price	Utility Company	Bid Price
Gulf States Utilities	108⅜	Indiana & Michigan Electric	98¼
Northern Natural Gas	101⅛	Toledo Edison Co.	105⅛
Indiana Gas	101	Dayton Power and Light	102¼
Appalachian Power	99⅞	Atlantic City Electric	94¼
Empire Gas Corp.	57½	Long Island Lighting	105⅛
Wisconsin Electric Power	100⅜	Portland General Electric	108
Pennsylvania Electric	99⅞	Boston Gas	105⅛
Commonwealth Edison	88	Duquesne Light Co.	69¾
El Paso Natural Gas	106⅜	General Electric Co.	99⅜
Montana Power Co.	100¼	Ohio Power Co.	94⅜
Elizabethtown Water	99⅞	Texas Power and Light	100½
Cascade Natural Gas	109¾	Columbia Gas System	78
Tennessee Gas Pipeline	102⅝	Central Power and Light	108⅛
Western Electric	99¾	Boston Edison	113⅛
Dallas Power and Light	108⅛	Philadelphia Electric	102⅝

Source: *Bond Guide* (a publication of the Standard & Poor Corporation), January 1992.

a. A frequency histogram was generated using a statistical software package. (See the accompanying figure.) Note that the software labels the midpoint of each measurement class rather than the two endpoints, and plots the bars horizontally rather than vertically. Interpret the histogram.

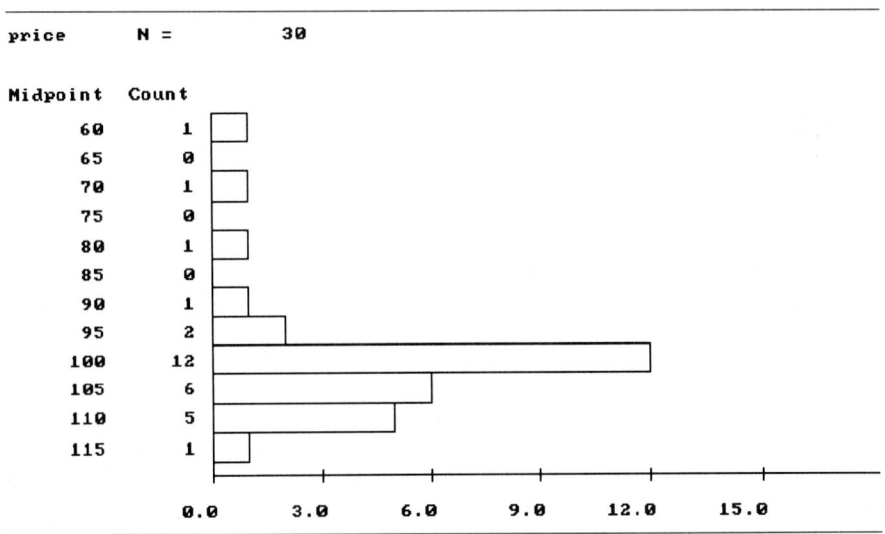

```
price        N =         30

Midpoint   Count
    60        1
    65        0
    70        1
    75        0
    80        1
    85        0
    90        1
    95        2
   100       12
   105        6
   110        5
   115        1

            0.0    3.0    6.0    9.0   12.0   15.0
```

b. Use the histogram to determine the number of bonds in the sample that had a bid price greater than $97.50. What proportion of the total number of bonds is this group?

c. Identify the area under the histogram of part **a** that corresponds to this proportion.

Applying the Concepts

2.14 Production processes may be classified as *make-to-stock processes* or *make-to-order* processes. Make-to-stock processes are designed to produce a standardized product that can be sold to customers from the firm's inventory. Make-to-order processes are designed to produce products according to customer specifications. The McDonald's and Burger King fast-food chains are classic examples of these two types of processes. McDonald's produces and stocks standardized hamburgers; Burger King—whose slogan is "Your way, right away"—makes hamburgers according to the ingredients specified by the customer (Schroeder, 1993). In general, performance of make-to-order processes is measured by delivery time—the time from receipt of an order until the product is delivered to the customer. The following data set is a sample of delivery times (in days) for a particular make-to-order firm last year. The delivery times marked by an asterisk are associated with customers who subsequently placed additional orders with the firm.

50*	64*	56*	43*	64*
82*	65*	49*	32*	63*
44*	71	54*	51*	102
49*	73*	50*	39*	86
33*	95	59*	51*	68

The Minitab stem-and-leaf display of these data is shown here.

```
Stem-and-leaf of Time      N  = 25
Leaf Unit = 1.0
        3      3 239
        7      4 3499
       (7)     5 0011469
       11      6 34458
        6      7 13
        4      8 26
        2      9 5
        1     10 2
```

a. Circle the individual leaves that are associated with customers who did not place a subsequent order.
b. Concerned that they are losing potential repeat customers because of long delivery times, the management would like to establish a guideline for the maximum tolerable delivery time. Using the stem-and-leaf display, suggest a guideline. Explain your reasoning.

2.15   In order to better understand the interactions that take place between salespeople and customers, Ronald P. Willett and Allan L. Pennington (1966) monitored the interactions of appliance salespeople and customers on the floor of a large department store. Part of their research involved observing the length of time customers and salespeople interacted prior to the close of the sale or the departure of the customer. The data below, adapted from the article, are the lengths of time (in minutes) from the first customer–salesperson contact to the close of the sale or the customer's departure for 132 customers who completed their appliance purchase either at the time they were observed or within the following 2 weeks. Instances where a purchase was made by the customer at the time he or she was observed are denoted with an asterisk.

1.0*	3.2	49.1*	3.3	5.4*	6.0*	7.9*	39.9	1.1	25.4*	14.9
7.4*	12.4	10.9*	20.1*	30.5	27.2*	.9	50.1	48.6	10.0*	40.0
41.3*	26.2	118.4	12.0*	30.5	7.0*	66.1*	105.2*	47.6*	10.1*	12.2*
15.1*	33.3	8.8	30.0*	26.4*	8.4	1.7	12.5	23.0	11.1	21.9
6.1	.7	1.5	13.0	9.0*	7.6	10.9	13.5	8.0*	35.1	41.6
22.3	44.4*	18.4	8.9*	16.9*	34.6*	16.2	98.2	11.0	43.1	31.8
.4*	32.2	37.0	18.0*	14.2	39.2*	8.1*	4.5*	69.1	24.8	15.0*
17.4*	28.7	15.0*	14.2*	20.6*	27.7	7.9	18.7*	8.4	15.9	38.2
11.0*	7.8*	15.0	6.0	77.1	26.0	7.0*	7.4*	3.0	11.1	35.0*
35.4	25.6*	1.9*	40.1	.8	19.2*	42.3	15.5	13.3*	81.0	20.1*
12.8*	14.9	38.1	9.7	17.7*	7.7	42.1	4.1*	17.6*	5.1*	30.0
8.1*	25.1*	29.2	12.3	15.9	60.2*	27.7	10.3	14.0*	30.0*	10.5

SAS was used to construct a relative frequency histogram for each of the following data sets (see page 42):
(1) The complete set of 132 times
(2) The set of times associated with customers who made appliance purchases at the time they were being observed
(3) The set of times associated with customers who made the appliance purchases at a later date

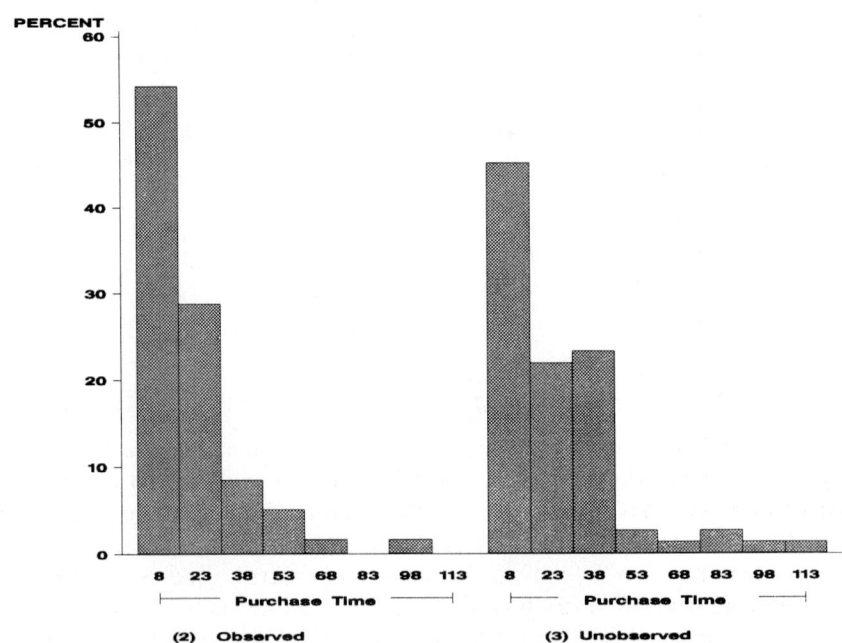

a. Interpret the three histograms. Describe any differences you detect between the histograms of parts (2) and (3).

b. Suggest possible explanations for the differences you noted in part a.

2.16 In a manufacturing plant a *work center* is a specific production facility that consists of one or more people and/or machines and is treated as one unit for the purposes of capacity requirements planning and job scheduling. If jobs arrive at a particular work center at a faster rate than they depart, the work center impedes the overall production process and is referred to as a *bottleneck* (Fogarty, Blackstone, and Hoffmann, 1991). The data in the table were collected by an operations manager for use in investigating a potential bottleneck work center.

Number of Items Arriving at Work Center per Hour

155	115	156	156	109	127
150	159	163	148	135	119
172	143	159	140	127	115
166	148	175	122	99	106
151	161	138	171	123	135
148	129	135	125	107	152
140	152	139	111	137	161

The stem-and-leaf displays for the two sets of data are shown below:

Arrivals			*Departures*	
Stem	**Leaf**		**Stem**	**Leaf**
			9	9
			10	6 7 9
11	5		11	1 5 9
12	9		12	2 3 5 7 7
13	5 8 9		13	5 5 7
14	0 3 8 8		14	0 8
15	0 1 2 5 6 9 9		15	2 6
16	1 3 6		16	1
17	2 5		17	1

Do the stem-and-leaf displays suggest that the work center may be a bottleneck? Explain.

*2.17 The ability to fill a customer's order on time depends to a great extent on being able to estimate how long it will take to produce the product in question. In most production processes, the time required to complete a particular task will be shorter each time the task is undertaken. Furthermore, it has been observed that in most cases the task time will decrease at a decreasing rate the more times the task is undertaken. Thus, in order to estimate how long it will take to produce a particular product, a manufacturer may want to study the relationship between production time per unit and the number of units that have been produced. The line or curve characterizing this relationship is called a *learning curve* (Adler and Clark, 1991). Twenty-five employees, all of whom were performing the same production task for the tenth time, were observed. Each person's task-completion time (in minutes) was recorded. The same 25 employees were observed again the 30th time they performed the same task and the 50th time they performed the task. The resulting completion times are shown in the table at the top of page 44.

Tenth Performance		Thirtieth Performance		Fiftieth Performance	
15	19	16	11	10	8
21	20	10	10	5	10
30	22	12	13	7	8
17	20	9	12	9	7
18	19	7	8	8	8
22	18	11	20	11	6
33	17	8	7	12	5
41	16	9	6	9	6
10	20	5	9	7	4
14	22	15	10	6	15
18	19	10	10	8	7
25	24	11	11	14	20
23		9		9	

a. Use a statistical software package to construct a frequency histogram for each of the three data sets.

b. Compare the histograms. Does it appear that the relationship between task completion time and the number of times the task is performed is in agreement with the observations noted above about production processes in general? Explain.

*2.18 When two firms announce plans to merge, it frequently happens that within a few weeks one firm or the other becomes dissatisfied with the consequences of merging and the merger is canceled. Dodd (1980) reported that of 151 merger announcements that he identified, 80 were canceled. Thus, at the time a proposed merger is announced, there exists a great amount of uncertainty concerning whether the merger will take place. This uncertainty may persist for a considerable period of time and it may be many months after the announcement that the merger actually occurs. In her study of 38 mergers that were consummated, Eger (1982) reported the number of *trading days* (days the New York Stock Exchange is open for business) between the merger announcement (defined as the first mention of the potential merger in the *Wall Street Journal*) and the effective date of the merger. These data are listed next:

74	45	55	74	64	97	65	82	92	116
140	62	92	78	45	93	94	57	123	128
92	73	173	116	35	124	64	84	255	277
123	80	143	112	76	214	64	86		

a. Use a statistical software package to construct a stem-and-leaf display for these data.

b. Summarize the information reflected in your stem-and-leaf display concerning the number of trading days between announcement and the effective merger date for this sample of mergers.

2.19 Typically, the more attractive a corporate common stock is to an investor, the higher the stock's price–earnings (P/E) ratio. For example, if investors expect the stock's future earnings per share to increase, the price of the stock will be bid up and a high P/E ratio will result. Thus, the level of a stock's P/E ratio is a function of both the current financial performance of the firm and an investor's expectation of future performance (Spiro, 1982). The table contains the 1986 P/E ratios for samples of firms from the electronics industry and the auto parts industry.

	Auto Parts			Electronics	
Firm	P/E Ratio		Firm	P/E Ratio	
Lear Siegler	9		AMP Inc.	22	
Genuine Parts	15		Raytheon	12	
Federal–Mogul	12		Intel	85	
PPG Industries	13		Avnet	24	
Borg–Warner	13		Perkin Elmer	14	
Hoover Universal	12		TRW Inc.	15	
Libbey–Owens–Ford	8		Motorola	39	
Dana	8		Hewlett–Packard	20	
Champion Spark Plug	15		Honeywell	12	
Dayco	10		American District	27	
Sheller–Globe	7		Corning Glass Works	27	
Arvin Industries	10		EG&G	19	
Allen Group	13		Varian Associates	14	
Eaton	9		M/A-Com, Inc.	14	
Cummins Engine	10		Harris Corp.	19	
Barnes Group	11		Texas Instruments	10	
Echlin	14		IT&T	12	
Johnson Controls	9		North American Philips	11	
Rockwell Int.	9		GTE	8	
Snap-on-Tools	14		Tektronix	16	

Source: Stock reports (OTC, NYSE, American), Standard & Poor's 1986.

a. Construct a stem-and-leaf display for each of these data sets.

b. What do your stem-and-leaf displays suggest about the level of the P/E ratios of firms in the electronics industry as compared to firms in the auto parts industry? Explain.

2.20   Consider the accompanying **bar chart** (a histogram for qualitative data), which shows 1985 cigarette sales (in billions of cigarettes) by company.

a. In general, what is described by the bar chart?
b. Which company sold the most cigarettes in 1985? Approximately how many cigarettes did the company sell?
c. Convert the bar chart to a relative frequency bar chart. Describe any problems you encounter in making the conversion.

2.21 A large midwestern city conducted a study of commuter traffic patterns and modes of transportation in 1990 and compared the results with those of a similar 1970 study ("In Twin Cities, Free(way)'s a Crowd," 1992). The comparisons will be used by the Metropolitan Council when making decisions about road improvements and mass transit. Some of the general findings were: Due to suburban job growth, most work trips are from suburb to suburb; the average commuting time has increased only 1 minute over the average in 1970. The accompanying table shows additional study findings.

	1970	1990
Drive alone	3,720	8,500
Carpool	1,680	1,000
Use mass transit	360	400
Other	240	100

Data: Metropolitan Council, Minneapolis, MN.

a. Construct two relative frequency bar charts for these data, one for 1970 and one for 1990.
b. Combine the bar charts you constructed in part **a** by plotting the eight relative frequencies on the same bar chart. You can do this by drawing two bars side by side for each category listed on the horizontal axis of your chart. Such a chart facilitates comparison of the two data sets.
c. *Stacking* is the combining of all the bar charts for any one time period into a single bar, by drawing one on top of the other and distinguishing one from another by the use of colors or patterns. Stack the relative frequencies of the four categories for 1970. Do the same for 1990.
d. Describe the changes in commuter behavior revealed by these data.

2.22 A research company conducted a written customer survey for a computer manufacturer to evaluate the services provided by its dealerships. Customers who had purchased personal computers were asked which one of the following four items they were least satisfied with: service, technical assistance, training, or the salesperson. Within the indicated category, each customer was asked to select the one aspect with which they were least satisfied. The accompanying table describes their responses.

	No. of Customers
Service	10,002
Timely completion of maintenance/service	6,040
Availability of service, repairs, and maintenance support	1,518
Responsiveness of dealer to your service needs	1,426
Quality of maintenance/service work completed	1,018
Technical Assistance	8,555
Ability of staff to answer technical questions about installation, operations, and applications of the product	6,001
Availability of staff to assist with set-up or operation of the product	2,099
Courtesy of staff providing technical support	455

	No. of Customers
Training	1,202
Quality of training provided by the dealer	820
Ability of dealer to provide training to meet your specific needs and level of expertise	212
Availability of individualized training or classroom sessions to assist you in the use of your product	90
Courtesy of the person who provided training	80
Salesperson	4,100
Salesperson's ability to clearly explain the features and benefits of the product	1,515
Salesperson's understanding of your needs	765
Salesperson's ability to provide solutions to your needs	556
Ease of contacting sales staff	451
Convenience of delivery schedule	410
Condition of product on delivery	300
Courtesy of your salesperson	103

a. How many customers responded to the survey?

b. Construct a Pareto diagram for the four categories. According to your diagram, which category represents the greatest opportunity for increasing customer satisfaction? Explain.

c. For the category you identified in part **b**, explode the Pareto diagram and identify more specifically (than in part **b**) how customer satisfaction can be increased.

2.3 Graphical Methods for Describing Quantitative Data Produced Over Time: The Time Series Plot (Optional)

Each of the previous sections has been concerned with describing the information contained in a sample or population of data. Often these data are viewed as having been produced at essentially the same point in time. Thus, time has not been a factor in any of the graphical methods described so far.

Data of interest to managers are often produced and monitored over time. Examples include the daily closing price of their company's common stock, the company's weekly sales volume and quarterly profits, and characteristics—such as weight and length—of products produced by the company.

> **Definition 2.5**
>
> Data that are produced and monitored over time are called **time series** data.

Recall from Section 1.4 that a process is a series of actions or operations that generates output over time. Accordingly, measurements taken of a sequence of units produced by a process—such as a production process—are time series data. In general, any sequence of numbers produced over time can be thought of as being generated by a process.

When measurements are made over time, it is important to record both the numerical value and the time or the time period associated with each measurement. With this information a **time series plot**—sometimes called a **run chart**—can be constructed to describe the time series data and to learn about the process that generated the data. A time series plot is a graph of the measurements (on the vertical axis) plotted against time or against the order in which the measurements were made (on the horizontal axis). The plotted points are usually connected by straight lines to make it easier to see the changes and movement in the measurements over time. For example, Figure 2.8 is a time series plot of a particular company's monthly sales (number of units sold per month). And Figure 2.9 is a time series plot of the weights of 30 one-gallon paint cans that were consecutively filled by the same filling head. Notice that the weights are plotted against the order in which the cans were filled rather than some unit of time. When monitoring production processes, it is often more convenient to record the order rather than the exact time at which each measurement was made.

Time series plots reveal the movement (trend) and changes (variation) in the variable being monitored. Notice how sales trend upward in the summer and how the variation in the weights of the paint cans increases over time. This kind of information would not be revealed by stem-and-leaf displays or histograms, as the following case study illustrates.

FIGURE 2.8 ▶

Time series plot of company sales

FIGURE 2.9 ▲ Time series plot of paint can weights

CASE STUDY 2.3 / Deming Warns Against Knee-Jerk Use of Histograms

W. Edwards Deming is one of America's most famous statisticians. He is best known for the role he played after World War II in teaching the Japanese how to improve the quality of their products by monitoring and continually improving their production processes. In his book *Out of the Crisis* (1986), Deming warns against the knee-jerk (i.e., automatic) use of histograms to display and extract information from data. As evidence he offers the following example.

Fifty camera springs were tested in the order in which they were produced. The elongation of each

spring was measured under the pull of 20 grams. Both a time series plot and a histogram were constructed from the measurements. They are shown in Figure 2.10, which has been reproduced from Deming's book. If you had to predict the elongation measurement of the next spring to be produced (i.e., spring 51) and could use only one of the two plots to guide your prediction, which would you use? Why?

Only the time series plot describes the behavior *over time* of the process that produces the springs. The fact that the elongation measurements are decreasing

FIGURE 2.10 ►
Deming's time series plot
and histogram

over time can only be gleaned from the time series plot. Because the histogram does not reflect the order in which the springs were produced, it in effect represents all observations as having been produced simultaneously. Using the histogram to predict the elongation of the 51st spring would very likely lead to an overestimate.

The lesson from Deming's example is this: For displaying and analyzing data that have been generated over time by a process, the primary graphical tool is the time series plot, not the histogram.

2.4   Numerical Methods for Measuring Central Tendency

Now that we have presented some graphic techniques for summarizing and describing data sets, we turn to numerical methods for accomplishing this objective. When we speak of a data set, we refer to either a sample or a population. If statistical inference is our goal, we will wish ultimately to use sample numerical descriptive measures to make inferences about the corresponding measures for a population.

As you will see, there are a large number of numerical methods available to describe data sets. Most of these methods measure one of two data characteristics:

1. The **central tendency** of the set of measurements; i.e., the tendency of the data to cluster or to center about certain numerical values.

2. The **variability** of the set of measurements; i.e., the spread of the data.

In this section, we concentrate on measures of central tendency. In the next section, we discuss measures of variability.

The most popular and best understood measure of central tendency for a quantitative data set is the **arithmetic mean** (or simply the **mean**) of a data set.

> ### Definition 2.6
>
> The **mean** of a set of quantitative data is equal to the sum of the measurements divided by the number of measurements contained in the data set.

In everyday terms, the mean is the average value of the data set.

We will denote the measurements of a data set as follows:

$$x_1, x_2, x_3, \ldots, x_n$$

where x_1 is the first measurement in the data set, x_2 is the second measurement in the data set, x_3 is the third measurement in the data set, . . . , and x_n is the nth (and last) measurement in the data set. Thus, if we have five measurements in a set of data, we will write x_1, x_2, x_3, x_4, x_5 to represent the measurements. If the actual numbers are 5, 3, 8, 5, and 4, we have $x_1 = 5$, $x_2 = 3$, $x_3 = 8$, $x_4 = 5$, and $x_5 = 4$.

To calculate the mean of a set of measurements, we must sum them and divide by n, the number of measurements in the set. The sum of measurements x_1, x_2, . . . , x_n is

$$x_1 + x_2 + \cdot \cdot \cdot + x_n$$

To shorten the notation, we will write this sum as

$$x_1 + x_2 + \cdot \cdot \cdot + x_n = \sum_{i=1}^{n} x_i$$

where $\sum$ is the symbol for the summation. Verbally translate $\sum_{i=1}^{n} x_i$ as follows: "The sum of the measurements, whose typical member is x_i, beginning with the member x_1 and ending with the member x_n."

Finally, we will denote the mean of a sample of measurements by $\bar{x}$ (read "x-bar"), and represent the formula for its calculation as follows:

$$\bar{x} = \frac{\sum_{i=1}^{n} x_i}{n}$$

EXAMPLE 2.2

Calculate the mean of the following five sample measurements:　5, 3, 8, 5, 6.

Solution

Using the definition of sample mean and the shorthand notation, we find

$$\bar{x} = \frac{\sum_{i=1}^{5} x_i}{5} = \frac{5 + 3 + 8 + 5 + 6}{5} = \frac{27}{5} = 5.4$$

Thus, the mean of this sample is 5.4.[*]

---

[*]In the examples given here, $\bar{x}$ is sometimes rounded to the nearest tenth, sometimes the nearest hundredth, sometimes the nearest thousandth. There is no specific rule for rounding when calculating $\bar{x}$ because $\bar{x}$ is specifically defined to be the sum of all measurements divided by n; i.e., it is a specific fraction. When $\bar{x}$ is used for descriptive purposes, it is often convenient to round the calculated value of $\bar{x}$ to the number of significant figures used for the original measurements. When $\bar{x}$ is to be used in other calculations, however, it may be necessary to retain more significant figures.

EXAMPLE 2.3

Refer to Table 2.4. Calculate the mean of the percentages of revenues spent by the 50 companies on research and development.

TABLE 2.4	Percentages of Revenues Spent on Research and Development						
Company	Percentage	Company	Percentage	Company	Percentage	Company	Percentage
1	13.5	14	9.5	27	8.2	39	6.5
2	8.4	15	8.1	28	6.9	40	7.5
3	10.5	16	13.5	29	7.2	41	7.1
4	9.0	17	9.9	30	8.2	42	13.2
5	9.2	18	6.9	31	9.6	43	7.7
6	9.7	19	7.5	32	7.2	44	5.9
7	6.6	20	11.1	33	8.8	45	5.2
8	10.6	21	8.2	34	11.3	46	5.6
9	10.1	22	8.0	35	8.5	47	11.7
10	7.1	23	7.7	36	9.4	48	6.0
11	8.0	24	7.4	37	10.5	49	7.8
12	7.9	25	6.5	38	6.9	50	6.5
13	6.8	26	9.5				

Solution

Using the data in Table 2.4, we have

$$\bar{x} = \frac{\sum_{i=1}^{50} x_i}{50} = \frac{13.5 + 8.4 + \cdots + 6.5}{50} = \frac{424.6}{50} = 8.49$$

The average expenditure on research and development for the 50 companies is 8.49% of revenues. Glancing at the relative frequency histogram for these data (Figure 2.11), we note that the mean falls in the middle of this data set.

FIGURE 2.11 ▶
Relative frequency histogram for the 50 computer companies' R&D percentages: The mean

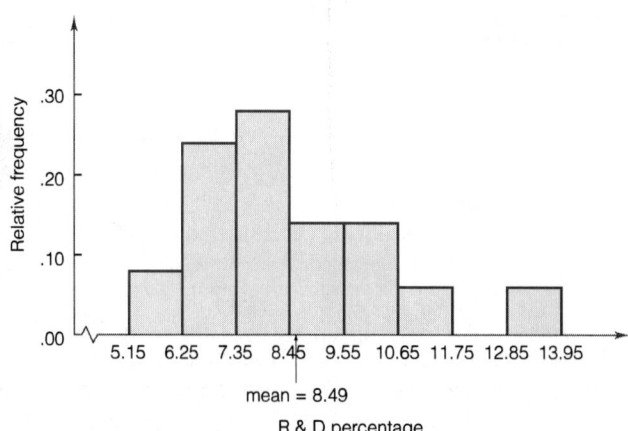

The sample mean will play an important role in accomplishing our objective of making inferences about populations based on sample information. For this reason, it is important to use a different symbol when we want to discuss the **mean of a population**—i.e., the mean of the set of measurements on every unit in the population. We use the Greek letter μ (mu) for the population mean. We will adopt a general policy of using Greek letters to represent population numerical descriptive measures and Roman letters to represent corresponding descriptive measures for the sample.

$$\bar{x} = \text{Sample mean} \qquad \mu = \text{Population mean}$$

The sample mean, $\bar{x}$, will often be used to estimate (make an inference about) the population mean, μ. For example, the percentages of revenues spent on research and development by the population consisting of *all* U.S. companies has a mean equal to some value, μ. Our sample of 50 companies yielded percentages with a mean of $\bar{x} = 8.49$. If, as is usually the case, we did not have access to the measurements for the entire population, we could use $\bar{x}$ as an estimator or approximator for μ. Then we would need to know something about the reliability of our inference. That is, we would need to know how accurately we might expect $\bar{x}$ to estimate μ. In Chapter 6, we will find that this accuracy depends on two factors:

1. *The size of the sample.* The larger the sample, the more accurate the estimate will tend to be.
2. *The variability, or spread, of the data.* All other factors remaining constant, the more variable the data, the less accurate the estimate.

In summary, the mean provides a valuable measure of the central tendency for a set of measurements. It is a very common tool in business and economic research, and therefore the mean will be the focus of much of our discussion of inferential statistics.

CASE STUDY 2.4 / Hotels: A Rational Method for Overbooking

The most outstanding characteristic of the general hotel reservation system is the option of the prospective guest, without penalty, to change or cancel his reservation or even to "no-show" (fail to arrive without notice). Overbooking (taking reservations in excess of the hotel capacity) is practiced widely throughout the industry as a compensating economic measure. This has motivated our research into the problem of determining policies for overbooking which are based on some set of rational criteria.

So said Marvin Rothstein (1974) in an article that appeared in *Decision Sciences*, a journal published by the Decision Sciences Institute. In this paper Rothstein introduces a method for scientifically determining hotel booking policies and applies it to the booking problems of the 133-room Sheraton Pocono Inn at Stroudsburg, Pennsylvania.

From the Sheraton Pocono Inn's records, the number of reservations, walk-ins (people without reservations who expect to be accommodated), cancellations, and no-shows were tabulated for each day during the period August 1–28, 1971. The inn's records for this period included approximately 3,100 guest histories. From the tabulated data, the mean or average number of room reservations per day for each of the seven days of the week was computed, as shown in Table 2.5. In applying his booking policy decision

TABLE 2.5 Mean Number of Room Reservations, August 1–28, 1971, 133 Rooms						
Sunday	Monday	Tuesday	Wednesday	Thursday	Friday	Saturday
138	126	149	160	150	150	169

method to the Sheraton's data, Rothstein used the means listed in Table 2.5 to help portray the inn's demand for rooms.

The mean number of Saturday reservations during the period August 1–28, 1971, is 169. This may be interpreted as an estimate of μ, the mean number of rooms demanded via reservations (walk-ins also contribute to the demand for rooms) on a Saturday during 1971. If the reservation data for all Saturdays during 1971 had been tabulated, μ could have been computed. But, since only the August data are available, they were used to estimate μ. Can you think of some problems associated with using August's data to estimate the mean for the entire year?

Another very important measure of central tendency is the **median** of a set of measurements:

Definition 2.7

The **median** of a data set is the middle number when the measurements are arranged in ascending (or descending) order.

The median is of most value in describing large data sets. If the data set is characterized by a relative frequency histogram (see Figure 2.12), the median is the point on the x-axis such that half the area under the histogram lies above the median and half lies below. [*Note:* In Section 2.2, we observed that the relative frequency associated with a particular interval on the x-axis is proportional to the area under the histogram that lies above the interval.]

FIGURE 2.12 ▶
Location of the median

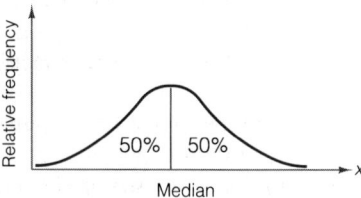

For a small—or even a large but finite—number of measurements, there may be many numbers that satisfy the property indicated in Figure 2.12. For this reason, we will arbitrarily calculate the median of a data set as follows:

Calculating the Median

Arrange the n measurements from the smallest to the largest.

1. If n is odd, the median is the middle number.
2. If n is even, the median is the mean (average) of the middle two numbers.

EXAMPLE 2.4

Consider the following sample of $n = 7$ measurements: 5, 7, 4, 5, 20, 6, 2.

a. Calculate the median of this sample.
b. Eliminate the last measurement (the 2), and calculate the median of the remaining $n = 6$ measurements.

Solution

a. The seven measurements in the sample are first ranked in ascending order:

   2, 4, 5, 5, 6, 7, 20

   Since the number of measurements is odd, the median is the middle measurement. Thus, the median of this sample is 5.

b. After removing the 2 from the set of measurements, we rank the sample measurements in ascending order as follows:

   4, 5, 5, 6, 7, 20

   Now the number of measurements is even, so we average the middle two measurements. The median is $(5 + 6)/2 = 5.5$.

In certain situations, the median may be a better measure of central tendency than the mean. In particular, the median is less sensitive than the mean to extremely large or small measurements. To illustrate, note that all but one of the measurements in Example 2.4 center about $x = 5$. The single large measurement, $x = 20$, does not affect the value of the median, 5, but it causes the mean, $\bar{x} = 7$, to lie to the right of most of the measurements.

As another example, if you were interested in computing a measure of central tendency of the incomes of a company's employees, the mean might be misleading. If all blue- and white-collar employees' incomes are included in the data set, the high incomes of a few executives will influence the mean more than the median. Thus, the median will often provide a more accurate picture of the typical income for an employee. Similarly, the median yearly sales for a set of companies would locate the middle of the sales data. However, the very large yearly sales of a few companies would

TABLE 2.6 Percentages of Revenues Spent on Research and Development, in Ascending Order			
5.2	7.1	8.2	9.9
5.6	7.2	8.2	10.1
5.9	7.2	8.2	10.5
6.0	7.4	8.4	10.5
6.5	7.5	8.5	10.6
6.5	7.5	8.8	11.1
6.5	7.7	9.0	11.3
6.6	7.7	9.2	11.7
6.8	7.8	9.4	13.2
6.9	7.9	9.5	13.5
6.9	8.0	9.5	13.5
6.9	8.0	9.6	
7.1	8.1	9.7	

greatly influence the mean, making it deceptively large. That is, the mean could exceed a vast majority of the sample measurements, making it a misleading measure of central tendency.

For an example using more measurements, we have arranged the 50 R&D percentages in ascending order in Table 2.6. Since the number of measurements is even, the median equals the mean of the middle two numbers (shaded)—that is, the mean of the 25th and 26th numbers in the ordered list:

$$\frac{8.0 + 8.1}{2} = 8.05$$

Note that the median is smaller than the mean (8.49) for these data. This fact indicates that the data are **skewed** to the right—i.e., there are more extreme measurements in the right tail of the distribution than in the left tail. This affects the mean more than the median, because the extreme values (large or small) are used explicitly in the calculation of the mean. On the other hand, the median is not affected directly by extreme measurements, since the middle measurement(s) is (are) the only one(s) explicitly used to calculate the median. Consequently, if measurements are pulled toward one end of the distribution, the mean will shift toward that tail more than the median. The skewness of the R&D data set is evident in Figure 2.13, where we show the median and mean of the R&D percentages.

FIGURE 2.13 ▶
Relative frequency histogram for the R&D percentages: Mean and median

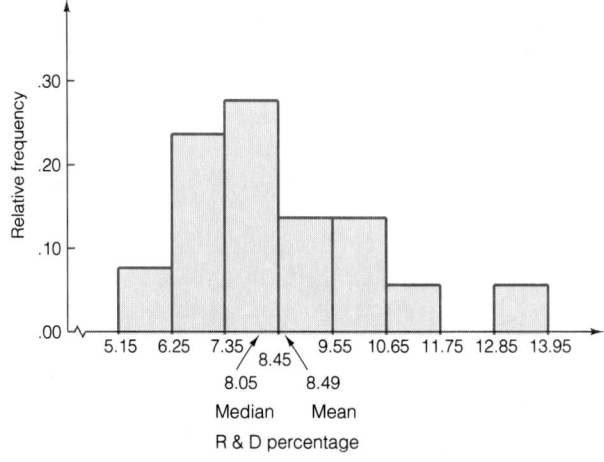

A comparison of the mean and median gives us a general method for detecting skewness in data sets, as shown in the box.

Comparing the Mean and the Median

1. If the median is less than the mean, the data set is skewed to the right:

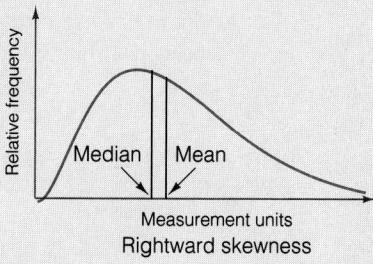

2. The median will equal the mean when the data set is symmetric:

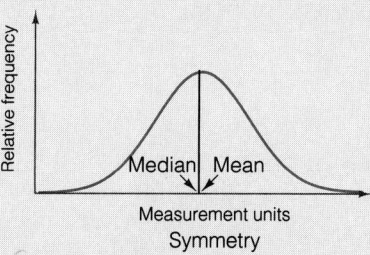

3. If the median is greater than the mean, the data set is skewed to the left:

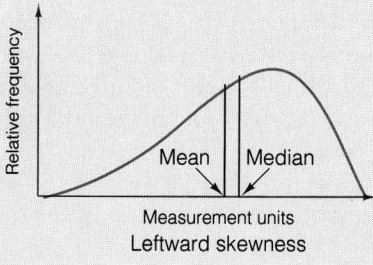

CASE STUDY 2.5 / The Delphi Technique for Obtaining a Consensus of Opinion

George T. Milkovich, Anthony J. Annoni, and Thomas A. Mahoney (1972) explain the delphi technique as follows:

The delphi technique, a set of procedures originally developed by the Rand Corporation in the late 1940's, is designed to obtain the most reliable consensus of opinion of a group of experts. Essentially, the delphi is a series of intensive interrogations of each individual expert (by a series of questionnaires) concerning some primary question interspersed with controlled feedback. The procedures are designed to avoid direct confrontation of the experts with one another.

The interaction among the experts is accomplished through an intermediary who gathers the data requests of the experts and summarizes them along with the experts' answers to the primary question. This mode of controlled interaction among the experts is a deliberate attempt to avoid the disadvantages associated with more conventional use of experts such as in round table discussions or direct confrontation of opposing views. The developers of the delphi argue the procedures are more conducive to independent thought and allow more gradual formulation to a considered opinion.

This article presents a study of the usefulness of the delphi procedure in projecting labor requirements in a low profit margin national retail firm. Seven company executives formed the panel of experts. Five questionnaires submitted at approximately 8-day intervals were used to interrogate the seven experts. On questionnaires 2–5, they were each asked the primary question, "How many buyers will the firm need 1 year from now?" Their individual responses along with the median response of the group for each questionnaire appear in Table 2.7.

TABLE 2.7   Projected Demand for Buyers

Questionnaire	Experts							Median
	A	B	C	D	E	F	G	
2	55	35	33	35	55	33	32	35
3	45	35	41	35	41	34	32	35
4	45	38	41	35	41	34	34	38
5	45	38	41	35	45	34	34	38

Note that the median response increased from 35 on questionnaire 2 to 38 on questionnaires 4 and 5. This increase indicates an upward shift in the distribution of the experts' forecasts as to the number of buyers the firm would need a year from now. If a single number is needed to represent the group's forecast, the median of the last questionnaire—in this case 38—is frequently used.

One conclusion of the study was that the delphi technique provided a better forecast of the actual number of buyers (37) needed by the firm 1 year later than did other more conventional forecasting techniques.

A third measure of central tendency is the **mode** of a set of measurements.

> ### Definition 2.8
>
> The **mode** is the measurement that occurs with greatest frequency in the data set.

Because it emphasizes data concentration, the mode is often used with large data sets to locate the region in which much of the data is concentrated. A retailer of men's clothing would be interested in the modal neck size and sleeve length of potential customers. The modal income class of the laborers in the United States is of interest to the Labor Department. Thus, the mode provides a useful measure of central tendency for many business applications.

Unless a quantitative data set is very large, its mode may not be very meaningful. For example, consider the percentage of revenues spent on research and development (R&D) by 50 companies. These data, first presented in Table 2.1, were analyzed in Section 2.2. A reexamination of the data reveals that three of the measurements are repeated three times: 6.5%, 6.9%, and 8.2%. Thus, there are three modes in the sample, and none is particularly useful as a measure of central tendency.

We can calculate a more meaningful measure by first constructing a relative frequency histogram for the data. The measurement class containing the most measurements is called the **modal class**, and the mode is taken to be the midpoint of this interval. For the R&D data, the modal class is the one corresponding to the interval 7.35 to 8.45, as shown by the shaded rectangle in Figure 2.14. The mode is taken to be the midpoint of this interval, that is, $(7.35 + 8.45)/2 = 7.90$. This modal class (and the mode itself) identifies the area in which the data are most concentrated, and in that sense is a measure of central tendency. However, for most applications involving quantitative data, the mean and median provide more descriptive information than the mode.

FIGURE 2.14 ▶
Relative frequency histogram for the computer companies' R&D percentages: The modal class

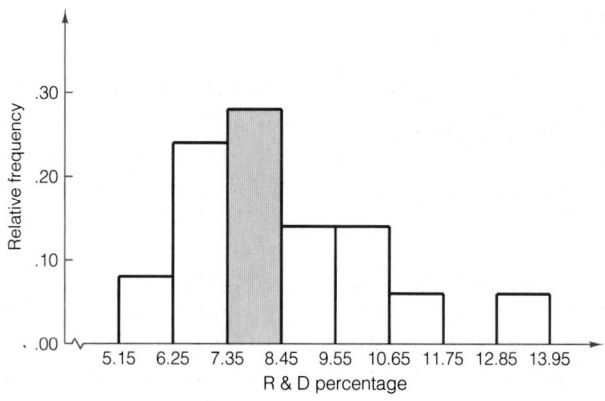

Exercises 2.23–2.34

Learning the Mechanics

2.23 Calculate the mean, median, and mode of the following data: 18, 10, 15, 13, 17, 15, 12, 15, 18, 16, 11.

2.24 Calculate the mean and median of the following grade-point averages: 3.2, 2.5, 2.1, 3.7, 2.8, 2.0.

2.25 Explain the difference between the calculation of the median for an odd and an even number of measurements. Construct one data set consisting of 5 measurements and another consisting of 6 measurements for which the medians are equal.

2.26 Explain how the relationship between the mean and median provides information about the symmetry or skewness of the data's distribution.

2.27 Refer to Case Study 2.5. Practitioners of the delphi technique frequently use the median of the set of responses given by the panel of experts on the last questionnaire to describe "the opinion of the experts." Why do you suppose the median response is used rather than the mean response?

Applying the Concepts

2.28 According to *Consumers' Digest* (Nov.–Dec. 1980), in 1980 sugar was the leading food additive in the U.S. food supply. Sugar may be listed more than once on a product's ingredient list since it goes by different names depending on its source (e.g., sucrose, corn sweetener, fructose, and dextrose). Thus, when you read a product's label you may have to total up the sugar in the product to see how much sweetener it contains. The accompanying table gives a list of candy bars and the percentage of sugar they contain relative to their weight.

Brand	Percentage of Sugar by Weight	Brand	Percentage of Sugar by Weight
Baby Ruth	23.7	Power House	30.6
Butterfinger	29.5	Bit-O-Honey	23.5
Mr. Goodbar	34.2	Chunky	38.4
Milk Duds	36.0	Milk Chocolate Covered Raisinettes	24.7
Mello Mint	79.6	Oh Henry!	31.2
M & M Plain Chocolate Candies	52.2	Borden Cracker Jack	14.7
Mars Chocolate Almond	36.4	Good & Plenty Licorice	28.2
Milky Way	26.8	Nestle's Crunch	43.5
Marathon	36.7	Planter Jumbo Block Peanut Candy	21.5
Snickers	28.0	Switzer Licorice	8.4
3 Musketeers	36.1	Switzer Red Licorice	2.8
Junior Mints	45.3	Tootsie Pop Drops	54.1
Pom Poms	29.5	Tootsie Roll	21.1
Sugar Babies	41.0	Fancy Fruit Lifesavers	77.6
Sugar Daddy	22.0	Spear-O-Mint Lifesavers	67.6
Almond Joy	20.0		

Source: *National Confectioners Association Brand Name Guide to Sugar* (Nelson Hall Paperback).
Secondary Source: *Consumers' Digest*, Nov.–Dec. 1980, p. 11.

a. Calculate the mean percentage of sugar per bar for the candy bars listed.
b. Find the median for the data set.
c. What do the mean and median indicate about the skewness of the data set?
d. Construct a relative frequency histogram for the data set. Indicate the location of the mean, median, and modal class of the data set on your histogram.

2.29   During the 1980s the pharmaceutical industry placed an increased emphasis on producing revolutionary new products. As a result, R&D costs increased and companies took a greater interest in R&D management. The table lists the 1984 R&D expenditures (in millions of dollars) of the world's largest pharmaceutical manufacturers.

Company	R&D Expenditures	Company	R&D Expenditures
Abbott	$110	Pfizer	159
American Home	90	Rhone–Poulenc	110
Bayer	200	Sandoz	181
Boehringer Ingelheim	176	Schering–Plough	129
Bristol–Myers	162	Smith Kline–Beckman	158
Ciba–Geigy	230	Squibb	114
Hoechst	274	Takeda	125
Hoffmann–LaRoche	363	Upjohn	200
Johnson & Johnson	187	Warner–Lambert	162
Merck	290		

Source: *Business Quarterly*, Fall 1985, p. 81.

a. Calculate the mean and median for this data set.

b. What do the mean and median indicate about the skewness of this data set?

c. Will the median of a data set always be equal to an actual value in the data set, as was the case in part **a**?

2.30   The table lists the mean age for each team in the National Basketball Association (NBA), along with the number of players on each team at the start of the 1982–1983 season. What was the population mean age at the start of the 1982–1983 season? [*Hint:* $\sum_{i=1}^{n} x_i = n\bar{x}$]

Team	Number of Players	Mean Age	Team	Number of Players	Mean Age
1. Indiana	12	24.720	13. San Antonio	12	26.25
2. Portland	12	24.724	14. Los Angeles	13	26.42
3. Golden State	15	24.96	15. New York	14	26.45
4. Dallas	13	25.17	16. Cleveland	14	26.48
5. New Jersey	13	25.26	17. San Diego	13	26.71
6. Kansas City	12	25.27	18. Boston	12	26.94
7. Chicago	12	25.32	19. Seattle	11	27.09
8. Detroit	13	25.65	20. Atlanta	12	27.12
9. Philadelphia	12	25.96	21. Denver	11	27.59
10. Phoenix	13	26.10	22. Houston	12	29.21
11. Washington	13	26.10	23. Milwaukee	13	29.72
12. Utah	11	26.13			

Source: *Basketball Weekly*, Jan. 3, 1983, Vol. 16, No. 5, pp. 10–11.

2.31 According to the U.S. Energy Information Association, the average price of regular unleaded gasoline in the United States as of March 1989 was 14.4 cents per gallon cheaper than the average price of premium gas. The table lists the average price excluding excise tax (in cents per gallon) of regular unleaded gas in each of a sample of 20 states.

State	Price	State	Price
Alaska	92.5	Nevada	64.9
Arkansas	63.3	New Hampshire	74.7
Connecticut	76.8	New York	70.6
Delaware	68.5	North Dakota	72.4
Louisiana	67.6	Oklahoma	64.6
Maine	76.8	Oregon	70.8
Massachusetts	74.9	Pennsylvania	65.5
Michigan	63.9	Texas	64.6
Missouri	63.4	Wisconsin	65.7
Montana	69.0	Wyoming	69.7

Data: U.S. Energy Information Association, *Petroleum Marketing Monthly*, March 1989.
Source: *Statistical Abstract of the United States*, 1989.

a. Calculate the mean, median, and mode of this data set.
b. Eliminate the highest price from the data set and repeat part **a**. What effect does dropping this measurement have on the measures of central tendency calculated in part **a**?
c. Arrange the 20 prices in order from lowest to highest. Next, eliminate the lowest two prices and the highest two prices from the data set and calculate the mean of the remaining prices. The result is called an **80% trimmed mean**, since it is calculated using the central 80% of the values in the data set. An advantage of the trimmed mean is that it is not as sensitive as the arithmetic mean to extreme observations in the data set.

2.32 At the end of 1982, McDonald's had 7,300 restaurants and total sales for the year of $7.8 billion. Burger King had 3,400 restaurants and total sales of $2.4 billion. McDonald's opens new restaurants at the rate of 500 per year and Burger King at the rate of 200 per year (*Minneapolis Tribune*, July 3, 1983).
a. Calculate the average sales per restaurant for McDonald's in 1982 and compare it with the average sales per restaurant for Burger King in 1982.
b. On average, how many restaurants did McDonald's open per month? Per week? Per day?

2.33 In 1985, U.S. consumers redeemed 6.49 billion manufacturers' coupons worth a total of $2.24 billion (McCullough, 1986). Find the mean value per coupon.

2.34 In 1972, Kroger Corporation, one of the largest supermarket chains in the United States, made a major strategic decision. Instead of continuing to hold prices high and trying to attract customers with weekend specials and heavy advertising, Kroger decided to emphasize price competition all week long. Its new strategy involved selling "brand-name groceries for less, on average, than its competitors were doing, and to advertise this fact strenuously" ("Keeping Up," 1979). For the situation described, explain what is meant by "on average" in the preceding quote.

2.5   Numerical Methods for Measuring Variability

Measures of central tendency provide only a partial description of a quantitative data set. Our information is incomplete without a measure of the **variability**, or **spread**, of the data set. Note that in describing a data set, we refer to either the sample or the population. Ultimately (in Chapter 6) we will use the sample numerical descriptive measures to make inferences about the corresponding descriptive measures for the population from which the sample was selected.

If you examine the two histograms in Figure 2.15, you will notice that both hypothetical data sets are symmetric, with equal modes, medians, and means. However, in data set 1 in Figure 2.15(a), the measurements occur with almost equal frequency in the measurement classes, whereas in data set 2 in Figure 2.15(b), most of the measurements are clustered about the center. For this reason, a measure of variability is needed, along with a measure of central tendency, to describe a data set.

FIGURE 2.15 ▶
Two hypothetical data sets

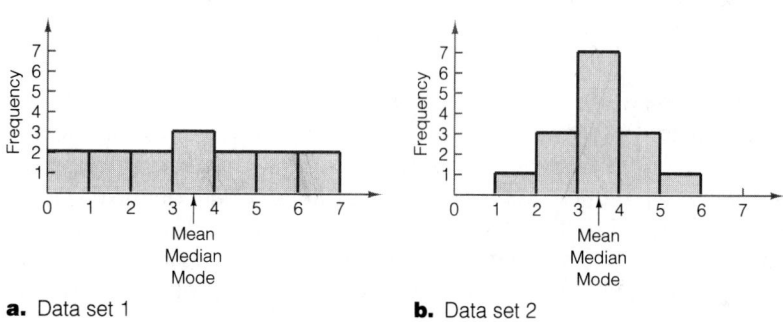

a. Data set 1   **b.** Data set 2

Perhaps the simplest measure of the variability of a quantitative data set is its **range**.

Definition 2.9

The **range** of a data set is equal to the largest measurement minus the smallest measurement.

The range measures the spread of the data by measuring the distance between the smallest and largest measurements. For example, stock A may vary in price during a given year from $32 to $36, whereas stock B may vary from $10 to $58, as shown in

Figure 2.16. The range in price of stock A is $36 − $32 = $4, while that for stock B is $58 − $10 = $48. A comparison of ranges tells us that the price of stock B was much more variable than the price of stock A.

FIGURE 2.16 ▶
Ranges of stock prices for two companies

Because it is easy to calculate, the range is a popular tool for measuring process variation in quality control (see Section 11.5). However, the range is not always a satisfactory measure of variability. For example, suppose we are comparing the profit margin (as a percentage of the total bid price) per construction job for 100 construction jobs for each of two cost estimators working for a large construction company. We find that the profit margins range from −10% (loss) to +40% (profit) for both cost estimators and therefore that the ranges for the two data sets, $40\% - (-10\%) = 50\%$, are equal. Because of this, we might be inclined to conclude that there is little or no difference in the performance of the two estimators.

But, suppose the histograms for the two sets of 100 profit margin measurements appear as shown in Figure 2.17. Although the ranges are equal and all central tendency measures are the same for these two symmetric data sets, there is an obvious difference between the two sets of measurements. The difference is that estimator B's profit margins tend to be more stable—i.e., to pile up or to cluster about the center of the data set. In contrast, estimator A's profit margins are more spread out over the range, indicating a higher incidence of some high profit margins, but also a greater risk of losses. Thus, even though the ranges are equal, the profit margin record of estimator A is more variable than that of estimator B, indicating a distinct difference in their cost estimating characteristics. We therefore need to develop more informative numerical measures of variability than the range. In particular, we need a measure that takes into consideration the magnitude of all measurements, not just the largest and smallest.

FIGURE 2.17 ▶
Profit margin histograms for two cost estimators

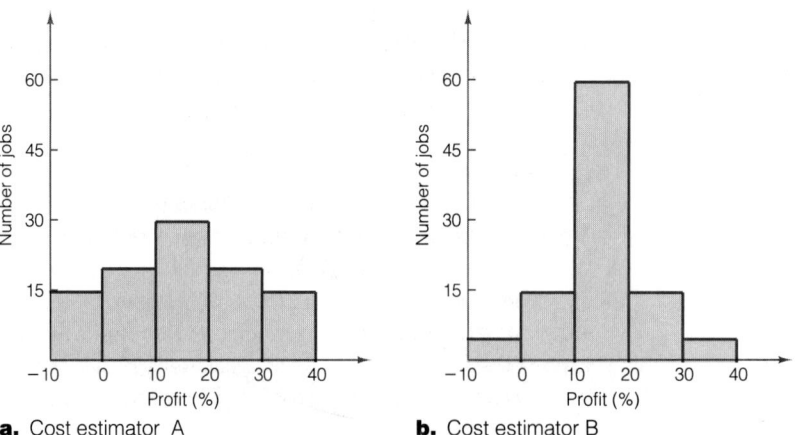

CASE STUDY 2.6 / More on the Delphi Technique

You will recall from Case Study 2.5 that the delphi technique is a set of procedures that may be used to obtain a consensus opinion from a group of experts through a series of questionnaires. Case Study 2.5 illustrated the use of the median as a measure of central tendency for the distribution of expert opinions elicited by the questionnaires. As a measure of variability of the data (i.e., the opinions), Milkovich et al. (1972) used the range. Table 2.7, showing the experts' opinions, is repeated here as Table 2.8, with the addition of the range of the distribution

of opinions of each questionnaire in the right-hand column.

The range of 23 on questionnaire 2 indicates that at that time the experts' opinions were widely dispersed. The decrease in the range to 11 following questionnaire 4 indicates that as the experts received more information about the firm's needs and learned about one another's opinions, the variability in the distribution of their opinions decreased. Milkovich et al. noted that the decrease in the range was an indication that experts' opinions were converging.

TABLE 2.8   Projected Demand for Buyers

Questionnaire	Experts							Median	Range
	A	B	C	D	E	F	G		
2	55	35	33	35	55	33	32	35	23
3	45	35	41	35	41	34	32	35	13
4	45	38	41	35	41	34	34	38	11
5	45	38	41	35	45	34	34	38	11

Let us see if we can find a measure of data variability that is more sensitive than the range. Recall that we represent the n measurements in a sample by the symbols x_1, $x_2, \ldots, x_n$, and we represent their mean by $\bar{x}$. What would be the interpretation of $x_1 - \bar{x}$? It is the distance, or **deviation**, between the first sample measurement, x_1, and the sample mean, $\bar{x}$. If we were to calculate this distance for *every* measurement in the sample, we would create a set of distances from the mean:

$$x_1 - \bar{x}, \quad x_2 - \bar{x}, \quad x_3 - \bar{x}, \quad \ldots, \quad x_n - \bar{x}$$

What information do these distances contain? If they tend to be large, the interpretation is that the data are spread out or highly variable. If the distances are mostly small, the data are clustered around the mean $\bar{x}$ and therefore do not exhibit much variability. As a simple example, consider the two samples in Table 2.9 (page 66), which have five measurements (we have ordered the numbers for convenience). You will note that both samples have a mean of 3. However, a glance at the distances shows that sample 1 has greater variability —i.e., more large distances from $\bar{x}$—than sample

2, which is clustered around $\bar{x}$. You can see this clearly by looking at these distances in Figure 2.18. Thus, the distances provide information about the variability of the sample measurements.

TABLE 2.9

	Sample 1	Sample 2
Measurements	1, 2, 3, 4, 5	2, 3, 3, 3, 4
Mean	$\bar{x} = \dfrac{1 + 2 + 3 + 4 + 5}{5} = \dfrac{15}{5} = 3$	$\bar{x} = \dfrac{2 + 3 + 3 + 3 + 4}{5} = \dfrac{15}{5} = 3$
Distances from $\bar{x}$	$1 - 3,\ 2 - 3,\ 3 - 3,\ 4 - 3,\ 5 - 3$ or $-2,\quad -1,\quad 0,\quad 1,\quad 2$	$2 - 3,\ 3 - 3,\ 3 - 3,\ 3 - 3,\ 4 - 3$ or $-1,\quad 0,\quad 0,\quad 0,\quad 1$

FIGURE 2.18 ▶

Distances from the mean for two data sets

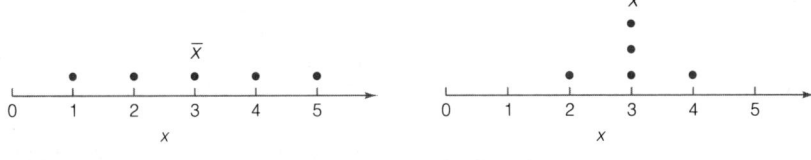

a. Sample 1   **b.** Sample 2

The next step is to condense the information on distances from $\bar{x}$ into a single numerical measure of variability. Simply averaging the distances from $\bar{x}$ will not help. For example, in samples 1 and 2 the negative and positive distances cancel, so that the average distance is 0. Since this is true for any data set—i.e., the sum of the deviations, $\sum_{i=1}^{n} (x_i - \bar{x})$, is always 0—we gain no information by averaging the distances from $\bar{x}$.

There are two methods for dealing with the fact that positive and negative distances from the mean cancel. The first is to treat all the distances as though they were positive, ignoring the sign of the negative distances. We will not pursue this line of thought because the resulting measure of variability (the mean of the absolute values of the distances) presents analytical difficulties beyond the scope of this text. A second method of eliminating the minus signs associated with the distances is to square them. The quantity we can calculate from the squared distances will provide a meaningful description of the variability of a data set.

To use the squared distances calculated from a data set, we first calculate the **sample variance**.

Definition 2.10

The **sample variance** for a sample of n measurements is equal to the sum of the squared distances from the mean divided by $(n - 1)$. In symbols, using s^2 to represent the sample variance,

$$s^2 = \frac{\sum_{i=1}^{n} (x_i - \bar{x})^2}{n - 1}$$

Referring to the two samples in Table 2.9, you can calculate the variance for sample 1 as follows:

$$s^2 = \frac{(1 - 3)^2 + (2 - 3)^2 + (3 - 3)^2 + (4 - 3)^2 + (5 - 3)^2}{5 - 1}$$

$$= \frac{4 + 1 + 0 + 1 + 4}{4} = 2.5$$

The second step in finding a meaningful measure of data variability is to calculate the **standard deviation** of the data set.

Definition 2.11

The **sample standard deviation**, s, is defined as the positive square root of the sample variance, s^2. Thus,

$$s = \sqrt{s^2} = \sqrt{\frac{\sum_{i=1}^{n} (x_i - \bar{x})^2}{n - 1}}$$

The **population variance**, denoted by the symbol σ^2 (sigma squared), is the average of the squared distances of the measurements of *all* units in the population from the mean, μ. σ (sigma) is the square root of this quantity. Since we never really compute σ^2 or σ from the population (the object of sampling is to avoid this costly procedure), we simply denote these two quantities by their respective symbols.

$s^2 = $ Sample variance	$s = $ Sample standard deviation
$\sigma^2 = $ Population variance	$\sigma = $ Population standard deviation

In contrast to the variance, the standard deviation is expressed in the original units of measurement. For example, if the original measurements are in dollars, the variance is expressed in the peculiar units "dollars squared," but the standard deviation is expressed in dollars.

You may wonder why we use the divisor $(n - 1)$ instead of n when calculating the sample variance. Although the use of n may seem logical, since then the sample variance would be the average squared distance from the mean, the use of n tends to underestimate the population variance, σ^2. The use of $(n - 1)$ in the denominator provides the appropriate correction for this tendency.[*] Since the primary use of sample statistics like s^2 is to estimate population parameters like σ^2, $(n - 1)$ is preferred to n when defining the sample variance.

EXAMPLE 2.5

Calculate the standard deviation of the following sample: 2, 3, 3, 3, 4.

Solution

For this set of data, $\bar{x} = 3$. Then,

$$s = \sqrt{\frac{(2 - 3)^2 + (3 - 3)^2 + (3 - 3)^2 + (3 - 3)^2 + (4 - 3)^2}{5 - 1}}$$

$$= \sqrt{\frac{2}{4}} = \sqrt{.5} = .71$$

As the number of measurements in the sample becomes larger, the sample variance becomes more difficult to calculate. We must calculate the distance between each measurement and the mean, square it, sum the squared distances, and finally divide by $(n - 1)$. Fortunately, as we show in Example 2.8, we can get around this difficulty by using a statistical software package (or most handheld calculators) to compute s^2 and s. However, if you must calculate it by hand, there is a shortcut formula for computing the sample variance.

---

[*]*Appropriate* here means that s^2 with a divisor of $(n - 1)$ is an **unbiased** estimator of σ^2. We define and discuss unbiasedness of estimators in Chapter 5.

Shortcut Formula for Sample Variance

$$s^2 = \frac{\left(\begin{array}{c}\text{Sum of squares of}\\ \text{sample measurements}\end{array}\right) - \dfrac{\left(\begin{array}{c}\text{Sum of sample}\\ \text{measurements}\end{array}\right)^2}{n}}{n-1} = \frac{\sum\limits_{i=1}^{n} x_i^2 - \dfrac{\left(\sum\limits_{i=1}^{n} x_i\right)^2}{n}}{n-1}$$

Note that the formula requires only the sum of the sample measurements, $\sum\limits_{i=1}^{n} x_i$, and the sum of the squares of the sample measurements, $\sum\limits_{i=1}^{n} x_i^2$. Be careful when you calculate these two sums. Rounding the values of x^2 that appear in $\sum\limits_{i=1}^{n} x_i^2$ or rounding the quantity $\left(\sum\limits_{i=1}^{n} x_i\right)^2 \!\!\Big/ n$ can lead to substantial errors in the calculation of s^2.

EXAMPLE 2.6

Use the shortcut formula to compute the variances of these two samples of five measurements each:

    Sample 1:   1, 2, 3, 4, 5   *Sample 2:*   2, 3, 3, 3, 4

Solution

We first work with sample 1. The two quantities needed are

$$\sum_{i=1}^{5} x_i = 1 + 2 + 3 + 4 + 5 = 15$$

and

$$\sum_{i=1}^{5} x_i^2 = 1^2 + 2^2 + 3^2 + 4^2 + 5^2 = 1 + 4 + 9 + 16 + 25 = 55$$

Then the sample variance for sample 1 is

$$s^2 = \frac{\sum\limits_{i=1}^{5} x_i^2 - \dfrac{\left(\sum\limits_{i=1}^{5} x_i\right)^2}{5}}{5-1} = \frac{55 - \dfrac{(15)^2}{5}}{4} = \frac{55 - 45}{4} = \frac{10}{4} = 2.5$$

Similarly, for sample 2 we get

$$\sum_{i=1}^{5} x_i = 2 + 3 + 3 + 3 + 4 = 15$$

and

$$\sum_{i=1}^{5} x_i^2 = 2^2 + 3^2 + 3^2 + 3^2 + 4^2 = 4 + 9 + 9 + 9 + 16 = 47$$

Then the variance for sample 2 is

$$s^2 = \frac{\sum_{i=1}^{5} x_i^2 - \dfrac{\left(\sum_{i=1}^{5} x_i\right)^2}{5}}{5 - 1} = \frac{47 - \dfrac{(15)^2}{5}}{4} = \frac{47 - 45}{4} = \frac{2}{4} = .5$$

EXAMPLE 2.7

The 50 companies' percentages of revenues spent on R&D are repeated here. Calculate the sample variance, s^2, and the standard deviation, s, for these measurements.

13.5	9.5	8.2	6.5	8.4	8.1	6.9	7.5	10.5	13.5
7.2	7.1	9.0	9.9	8.2	13.2	9.2	6.9	9.6	7.7
9.7	7.5	7.2	5.9	6.6	11.1	8.8	5.2	10.6	8.2
11.3	5.6	10.1	8.0	8.5	11.7	7.1	7.7	9.4	6.0
8.0	7.4	10.5	7.8	7.9	6.5	6.9	6.5	6.8	9.5

Solution

The calculation of the sample variance, s^2, would be very tedious for this sample if we tried to use the formula

$$s^2 = \frac{\sum_{i=1}^{50} (x_i - \bar{x})^2}{50 - 1}$$

because it would be necessary to compute all 50 squared distances from the mean. However, for the shortcut formula we need compute only

$$\sum_{i=1}^{50} x_i = 13.5 + 8.4 + \cdots + 6.5 = 424.6$$

and

$$\sum_{i=1}^{50} x_i^2 = (13.5)^2 + (8.4)^2 + \cdots + (6.5)^2 = 3,797.92$$

Then

$$s^2 = \frac{\sum_{i=1}^{50} x_i^2 - \dfrac{\left(\sum_{i=1}^{50} x_i\right)^2}{50}}{50 - 1} = \frac{3{,}797.92 - \dfrac{(424.6)^2}{50}}{49} = 3.9228$$

The standard deviation is

$$s = \sqrt{s^2} = \sqrt{3.9228} = 1.98$$

Notice that we retained all the decimal places in the calculation of the sum of squares of the measurements. This was done to reduce the rounding error in the calculations, even though the original data were accurate to only one decimal place.*

EXAMPLE 2.8

Use a statistical software package to compute the median, mean, variance, and standard deviation of the R&D data given in Example 2.7.

Solution

The SAS/PC printout is shown in Figure 2.19. The median, mean, variance, and standard deviation are shaded on the printout. Although the SAS procedure (PROC

FIGURE 2.19 ▶
SAS/PC printout for mean, median, variance, and standard deviation

	Moments		
N	50	Sum Wgts	50
Mean	8.492	Sum	424.6
Std Dev	1.980604	Variance	3.922792
Skewness	.8546013	Kurtosis	.4192877
USS	3797.92	CSS	192.2168
CV	23.32317	Std Mean	.2800997
T:Mean=0	30.31778	Prob>¦T¦	0.0001
Sgn Rank	637.5	Prob>¦S¦	0.0001
Num ^= 0	50		
W:Normal	.9328984	Prob<W	0.009

	Quantiles(Def=5)		
100% Max	13.5	99%	13.5
75% Q3	9.6	95%	13.2
50% Med	8.05	90%	11.2
25% Q1	7.1	10%	6.5
0% Min	5.2	5%	5.9
		1%	5.2

*The accuracy of the original data has nothing to do with the degree of accuracy used in computing s^2 and s. You should retain twice as many decimal places in s^2 as you want in s. For example, if you want to calculate s to the nearest hundredth, you should calculate s^2 to the nearest ten-thousandth.

UNIVARIATE) generates many other descriptive statistics, some of which we discuss later, we can easily pick out those of interest to us. Note that many decimal places are carried by the program, but when we round to the same number of decimal places used in the previous examples, we find

$$\text{Median} = 8.05 \qquad s^2 = 3.9228$$
$$\bar{x} = 8.49 \qquad s = 1.98$$

The answers are identical to those obtained by hand calculation.

You know that the standard deviation measures the variability of a set of data and you know how to calculate it. But how can we interpret and use the standard deviation? This is the topic of Section 2.6.

Exercises 2.35–2.46

Learning the Mechanics

2.35   The range, variance, and standard deviation provide information about the variation in a data set.
  a. Describe the information each conveys.
  b. Discuss the advantages and disadvantages of using each to measure the variability of a data set.

2.36   Describe the sample variance using words rather than a formula. Do the same with the population variance.

2.37   Given the following information about two data sets, compute $\bar{x}$, the sample variance, and the standard deviation for each:

  a. $n = 25,\quad \sum_{i=1}^{n} x_i^2 = 1{,}000,\quad \sum_{i=1}^{n} x_i = 50$ **b.** $n = 80,\quad \sum_{i=1}^{n} x_i^2 = 270,\quad \sum_{i=1}^{n} x_i = 100$

2.38   For each of the following data sets, compute $\sum_{i=1}^{n} x_i$, $\sum_{i=1}^{n} x_i^2$, and $\left(\sum_{i=1}^{n} x_i \right)^2$:

  a. 5, 9, 6, 3, 7   **b.** 3, 1, 4, 3, 0, −2   **c.** 90, 12, 40, 15
  d. −1, 4, 1, 0, 5   **e.** 1, 0, 0, 1, 0, 10

2.39   Compute $\bar{x}$, s^2, and s for each of the following data sets:
  a. 10, 1, 0, 0, 20   **b.** 5, 9, −1, 100

2.40   Compute $\bar{x}$, s^2, and s for each of the following data sets. If appropriate, specify the units in which your answer is expressed.
  a. 3, 1, 10, 10, 4   **b.** 8 feet, 10 feet, 32 feet, 5 feet   **c.** −1, −4, −3, 1, −4, −4
  d. ⅕ ounce, ⅕ ounce, ⅕ ounce, ⅖ ounce, ⅕ ounce, ⅘ ounce

2.41   Using only integers between 0 and 10, construct two data sets with at least ten observations each that have the same mean but different variances. Construct dot diagrams for each of your data sets (see Figure 2.18), and mark the mean of each data set on its dot diagram.

2.42   Using only integers between 0 and 10, construct two data sets with at least ten observations each that have the same range but different means. Construct a dot diagram for each of your data sets (see Figure 2.18), and mark the mean of each data set on its dot diagram.

2.43   Can the variance of a data set ever be negative? Explain. Can the variance ever be smaller than the standard deviation? Explain.

Applying the Concepts

2.44   The Consumer Price Index (CPI) measures the price change of a constant market basket of goods and services. The Bureau of Labor Statistics publishes a national CPI (called the U.S. City Average Index) as well as separate indexes for each of 28 different cities in the United States. The national index and some of the city indexes are published monthly; the remainder of the city indexes are published semiannually. The CPI is used in cost-of-living escalator clauses of many labor contracts to adjust wages for inflation (U.S. Department of Labor, 1978). For example, in the printing industry of Minneapolis and St. Paul, hourly wages are adjusted every 6 months (based on October and April values of the CPI) by 4¢ for every point change in the Minneapolis/St. Paul CPI.

   The table lists the published values of the U.S. City Average Index and the Chicago Index during 1991 and 1992. The sums and sums of squares for the U.S. City Average Index are $\Sigma x = 3{,}318.1$ and $\Sigma x^2 = 458{,}877.49$, respectively. For the Chicago Index, these quantities are $\Sigma x = 3{,}337.2$ and $\Sigma x^2 = 464{,}169.38$.

Month	U.S. City Average Index	Chicago	Month	U.S. City Average Index	Chicago
January 1991	134.6	135.1	January 1992	138.1	138.9
February	134.8	135.5	February	138.6	139.2
March	135.0	136.2	March	139.3	139.7
April	135.2	136.1	April	139.5	139.8
May	135.6	136.8	May	139.7	140.5
June	136.0	137.3	June	140.2	141.2
July	136.2	137.3	July	140.5	141.4
August	136.6	137.6	August	140.9	141.9
September	137.2	138.3	September	141.3	142.7
October	137.4	138.0	October	141.8	142.1
November	137.8	138.0	November	142.0	142.4
December	137.9	138.3	December	141.9	142.9

Source: U.S. Department of Labor: Labor Statistics, 1991–1993.
Secondary Source: CPI Chicago, pp. 91–93.

   a.   Calculate the mean values for the U.S. City Average Index and the Chicago Index.
   b.   Find the ranges of the U.S. City Average Index and the Chicago Index.
   c.   The standard deviation of the U.S. City Average Index over the 24 months described in the table is 2.43. Calculate the standard deviation for the Chicago Index over the time period described in the table.

   d. Which index displays greater variation about its mean over the time period in question? Justify your response.

2.45 To set an appropriate price for a product, it is necessary to be able to estimate its cost of production. One element of the cost is based on the length of time it takes workers to produce the product. The most widely used technique for making such measurements is the **time study**. In a time study, the task to be studied is divided into measurable parts and each is timed with a stopwatch or filmed for later analysis. For each worker, this process is repeated many times for each subtask. Then the average and standard deviation of the time required to complete each subtask are computed for each worker. A worker's overall time to complete the task under study is then determined by adding his or her subtask-time averages (Chase and Aquilano, 1977). The data (in minutes) given in the table are the result of a time study of a production operation involving two subtasks.

Repetition	Worker A		Worker B	
	Subtask 1	Subtask 2	Subtask 1	Subtask 2
1	30	2	31	7
2	28	4	30	2
3	31	3	32	6
4	38	3	30	5
5	25	2	29	4
6	29	4	30	1
7	30	3	31	4

   a. Find the overall time it took each worker to complete the manufacturing operation under study.
   b. For each worker, find the standard deviation of the seven times for subtask 1.
   c. In the context of this problem, what are the standard deviations you computed in part **b** measuring?
   d. Repeat part **b** for subtask 2.
   e. If you could choose workers similar to A or workers similar to B to perform subtasks 1 and 2, which type would you assign to each subtask? Explain your decisions on the basis of your answers to parts **a–d**.

2.46 The table lists the 1989 profits (in millions of dollars) for a sample of seven airlines.

Airline	Profit
Continental	3.06
Eastern	−852.32
Northwest	355.25
Pan Am	−414.73
Delta	473.17
TWA	−298.55
United	358.09

Source: *Air Transport* (Washington, D.C.: Air Transport Association of America, 1990).

   a. Calculate the range, variance, and standard deviation of the data set.
   b. Specify the units in which each of your answers to part **a** is expressed.
   c. Suppose Eastern Airlines had a profit of $0 instead of a loss of $852.32 million. Would the range of the data set increase or decrease? Why? Would the standard deviation of the data set increase or decrease? Why?

2.6   Interpreting the Standard Deviation

As we have seen, if we are comparing the variability of two samples selected from a population, the sample with the larger standard deviation is the more variable of the two. Thus, we know how to interpret the standard deviation on a relative or comparative basis, but we have not explained how it provides a measure of variability for a single sample.

One way to interpret the standard deviation as a measure of variability of a data set would be to answer questions such as the following: How many measurements are within 1 standard deviation of the mean? How many measurements are within 2 standard deviations? For a specific data set, we can answer the questions by counting the number of measurements in each of the intervals. However, if we are interested in obtaining a general answer to these questions, the problem is more difficult.

In Table 2.10, we present two sets of guidelines to help answer the questions of how many measurements fall within 1, 2, and 3 standard deviations of the mean. The first set, which applies to any sample, is derived from a theorem proved by the Russian mathematician, Chebyshev. The second set, the Empirical Rule, is based on empirical evidence that has accumulated over time and applies to samples that possess mound-shaped frequency distributions—those that are approximately symmetric, with a clustering of measurements about the midpoint of the distribution (the mean, median, and mode should all be about the same) and that tail off as we move away from the center of the histogram. Thus, the histogram will have the appearance of a mound or bell, as shown in Figure 2.20 on page 76. The percentages given for the various intervals (particularly the interval $\bar{x} - 2s$ to $\bar{x} + 2s$) in Table 2.10 provide remarkably good approximations even when the distribution of the data is slightly skewed or asymmetric.*

TABLE 2.10   Aids to the Interpretation and Use of a Standard Deviation

1. A rule (from Chebyshev's theorem) that applies to any sample of measurements, regardless of the shape of the frequency distribution:
   a. It is possible that none of the measurements will fall within the interval $\bar{x} \pm s$ or ($\bar{x} - s$, $\bar{x} + s$)—i.e., within 1 standard deviation of the mean.
   b. At least $\frac{3}{4}$ of the measurements will fall within ($\bar{x} - 2s$, $\bar{x} + 2s$)—i.e., within 2 standard deviations of the mean.
   c. At least $\frac{8}{9}$ of the measurements will fall within ($\bar{x} - 3s$, $\bar{x} + 3s$)—i.e., within 3 standard deviations of the mean.
   d. Generally, at least $(1 - 1/k^2)$ of the measurements will fall within ($\bar{x} - ks$, $\bar{x} + ks$)—i.e., within k standard deviations of the mean, where k is any number greater than 1.

Note to the instructor: It is our intention to imply that the Empirical Rule of Table 2.10 not only applies to normal distributions of data, but also applies very well to mound-shaped distributions of large data sets and to distributions that are moderately skewed.

2. A rule of thumb called the Empirical Rule applies to samples with frequency distributions that are mound-shaped:
   a. Approximately 68% of the measurements will fall within the interval $\bar{x} \pm s$ or $(\bar{x} - s, \bar{x} + s)$—i.e., within 1 standard deviation of the mean.
   b. Approximately 95% of the measurements will fall within $(\bar{x} - 2s, \bar{x} + 2s)$—i.e., within 2 standard deviations of the mean.
   c. Essentially all the measurements will fall within $(\bar{x} - 3s, \bar{x} + 3s)$—i.e., within 3 standard deviations of the mean.

FIGURE 2.20 ▶
Histogram of a mound-shaped sample

EXAMPLE 2.9

The 50 companies' percentages of revenues spent on R&D are repeated here:

13.5	9.5	8.2	6.5	8.4	8.1	6.9	7.5	10.5	13.5
7.2	7.1	9.0	9.9	8.2	13.2	9.2	6.9	9.6	7.7
9.7	7.5	7.2	5.9	6.6	11.1	8.8	5.2	10.6	8.2
11.3	5.6	10.1	8.0	8.5	11.7	7.1	7.7	9.4	6.0
8.0	7.4	10.5	7.8	7.9	6.5	6.9	6.5	6.8	9.5

We have previously shown that the mean and standard deviation of these data are 8.49 and 1.98, respectively. Calculate the fraction of these measurements that lie within the intervals $\bar{x} \pm s$, $\bar{x} \pm 2s$, and $\bar{x} \pm 3s$, and compare the results with those in Table 2.10.

Solution

We first form the interval

$$(\bar{x} - s, \bar{x} + s) = (8.49 - 1.98, 8.49 + 1.98) = (6.51, 10.47)$$

A check of the measurements reveals that 34 of the 50 measurements, or 68%, are within 1 standard deviation of the mean.

The interval

$$(\bar{x} - 2s, \bar{x} + 2s) = (8.49 - 3.96, 8.49 + 3.96) = (4.53, 12.45)$$

contains 47 of the 50 measurements, or 94%.

The 3 standard deviation interval around $\bar{x}$,

$$(\bar{x} - 3s, \bar{x} + 3s) = (8.49 - 5.94, 8.49 + 5.94) = (2.55, 14.43)$$

contains all the measurements.

In spite of the fact that the distribution of these data is skewed to the right (see Figure 2.13), the percentages within 1, 2, and 3 standard deviations (68%, 94%, and 100%) agree very well with the approximations of 68%, 95%, and 100% given by the Empirical Rule. You will find that unless the distribution is extremely skewed, the mound-shaped approximations will be reasonably accurate. Of course, no matter what the shape of the distribution, Chebyshev's theorem from Table 2.10 assures that at least 75% and at least 89% ($\frac{8}{9}$) of the measurements will lie within 2 and 3 standard deviations of the mean, respectively.

EXAMPLE 2.10

Chebyshev's theorem and the Empirical Rule (Table 2.10) are useful as a check on the calculation of the standard deviation. For example, suppose we calculated the standard deviation of the R&D percentages to be 3.92. Are there any clues in the data that enable us to judge whether this number is reasonable?

Solution

The range of the R&D percentages is $13.5 - 5.2 = 8.3$. From the Empirical Rule we know that most of the measurements (approximately 95% if the distribution is not extremely skewed) will be within 2 standard deviations of the mean. And from Chebyshev's theorem, regardless of the shape of the distribution, almost all of the measurements (at least $\frac{8}{9}$) will fall within 3 standard deviations of the mean. Consequently, we would expect the range of measurements to be between 4 (± 2) and 6 (± 3) standard deviations in length (see Figure 2.21). For the R&D data, this means that the standard deviation s should fall between

$$\frac{\text{Range}}{6} = \frac{8.3}{6} = 1.38 \quad \text{and} \quad \frac{\text{Range}}{4} = \frac{8.3}{4} = 2.08$$

FIGURE 2.21 ▶
The relation between the range and the standard deviation

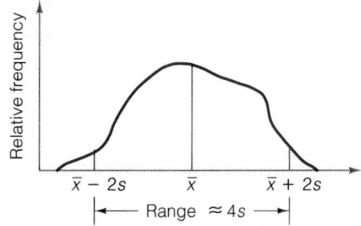

Thus, we would have reason to believe that a calculated standard deviation of 3.92 for these data is too large, since it far exceeds one-fourth the range, 2.08. A check of our work reveals that 3.92 is the variance s^2, not the standard deviation s (see Example 2.7). We "forgot" to take the square root, a common error. The correct value of 1.98 is between one-sixth and one-fourth the range.

In examples and exercises we will sometimes use $s \approx$ range/4 to obtain a crude, and usually conservatively large, approximation for s. However, we stress that this is no substitute for calculating the exact value of s when possible.

Beginning with the following example, we will use the concepts in Chebyshev's theorem and the Empirical Rule to build the foundation for statistical inference-making.

EXAMPLE 2.11

A manufacturer of automobile batteries claims that the average length of useful life for its grade A battery is 60 months. However, the guarantee on this brand is for only 36 months. Assume that the standard deviation of the lifelengths is known to be 10 months and that the frequency distribution of the lifelengths is known to be mound-shaped.

a. Approximately what percentage of the manufacturer's grade A batteries will last more than 50 months, assuming the manufacturer's claim about the mean lifelength is true?

b. Approximately what percentage of the manufacturer's batteries will last less than 40 months, assuming that the manufacturer's claim about the mean lifelength is true?

c. Suppose that your grade A battery lasts 37 months. What would you infer about the manufacturer's claim that the mean lifelength is 60 months?

Solution

Assuming that the distribution of lifelengths is approximately mound-shaped, with a mean of 60 months and a standard deviation of 10 months, it would appear as shown in Figure 2.22. Note that we can take advantage of the fact that mound-shaped distributions are (approximately) symmetric about the mean, so that the percentages given by the Empirical Rule can be split equally between the halves of the distribution on each side of the mean. The approximations given in Figure 2.22 are more dependent on the assumption of a mound-shaped distribution than those given by the Empirical Rule because the approximations in the figure depend on the (approximate) symmetry of the mound-shaped distribution. We saw in Example 2.9 that the Empirical Rule can yield good approximations even for skewed distributions. This will *not* be true of the approximations in Figure 2.22; the distribution must be mound-shaped and (approximately) symmetric.

FIGURE 2.22 ▶
Grade A battery lifelength distribution; manufacturer's claim assumed true

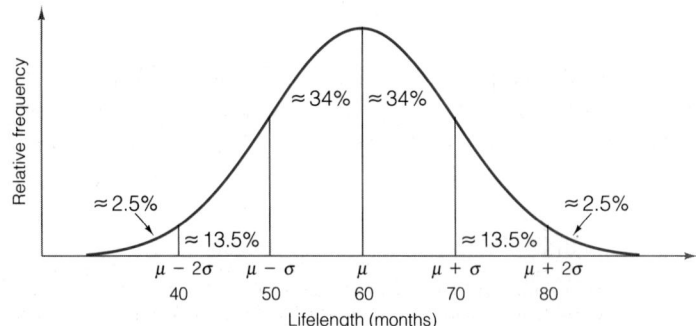

For example, since approximately 68% of the measurements will fall within 1 standard deviation on both sides of the mean, the distribution's symmetry implies that approximately ½ (68%) = 34% of the measurements will fall between the mean and 1 standard deviation on each side. This concept is demonstrated in Figure 2.22. Note that the 2.5% of the measurements beyond 2 standard deviations in each direction from the mean follows from the fact that, if approximately 95% of the measurements fall within 2 standard deviations, then about 5% fall outside 2 standard deviations. If the distribution is approximately symmetric, then about 2.5% fall beyond 2 standard deviations on each side of the mean.

a. Using Figure 2.22, it is easy to see that the percentage of batteries lasting more than 50 months is, approximately, 34% (between 50 and 60 months) plus 50% (greater than 60 months). Thus, approximately (50 + 34)% = 84% of the batteries should last longer than 50 months.

b. The percentage of batteries that last less than 40 months can also be determined from Figure 2.22. Since 40 is 2 standard deviations below the claimed mean of 60 months, approximately 2.5% of the batteries should fail prior to 40 months, assuming the manufacturer's claim is true.

c. If you are so unfortunate that your grade A battery fails at 37 months, one or two inferences can be made: Either your battery was one of the approximately 2.5% that fail prior to 40 months, or the manufacturer's claim is not true. Because the chances are so small that a battery fails before 40 months if the claim is true, you would have good reason to have serious doubts about the manufacturer's claim. A mean smaller than 60 months and/or a standard deviation greater than 10 months would increase the likelihood of a battery's failure prior to 40 months.*

Example 2.11 is our initial demonstration of the statistical inference-making process. At this point you should realize that we will use sample information (in Example 2.11 your battery's failure at 37 months) to make inferences about the population (in Example 2.11, the manufacturer's claim about the mean lifelength for the population of all batteries). We will build on this foundation as we proceed.

CASE STUDY 2.7 / Becoming More Sensitive to Customer Needs

The degree of sensitization on the part of a firm to the needs and wants of its consumers is frequently an important factor in determining the firm's overall success.

Namias (1964) presents a procedure for achieving such sensitivity. The procedure uses the rate of consumer complaints about a product to determine when and

---

*The assumption that the distribution is mound-shaped and symmetric may also be incorrect. However, if the distribution were skewed to the right, as lifelength distributions often tend to be, the percentage of measurements more than 2 standard deviations *below* the mean would be even less than 2.5%.

when not to conduct a search for specific causes of consumer complaints. For simplification, we will discuss Namias's paper as if the procedure described used the number of complaints per 10,000 units of a product sold to determine when and when not to conduct a search for specific causes of consumer complaints. The details of the procedure are discussed in Case Study 2.8.

Namias's procedure, given our simplification, makes use of the **distribution** of the number of consumer complaints received about a product per 10,000 units of the product sold. To visualize such a distribution, imagine that a company produces its product in lots of 10,000 units and keeps track of the number of complaints received about items in each lot. The company's complaint records will show a series of numbers, perhaps 100, 96, 145, 201, etc., each of which is the number of complaints received about a particular lot of 10,000 units. This series of numbers is a quantitative data set from which a relative frequency histogram can be drawn. The histogram constructed from this data set is a representation of the distribution of interest—i.e.,

the distribution of the number of consumer complaints received about a product per 10,000 units of the product sold. It is assumed that this distribution remains stable over time. The variance and standard deviation of this distribution are measures of the variation in the number of consumer complaints received. Namias determined that this distribution was mound-shaped. Accordingly, it can be said that approximately 95% of the time the number of complaints about a product will be within 2 standard deviations of the mean number of complaints. It is upon this fact, as we shall see in Case Study 2.8, that Namias's procedure for determining when it would be worthwhile to conduct a search for specific causes of consumer complaints is founded.

If it could not have been determined that the distribution of the number of complaints was mound-shaped, it would have been necessary for Namias to use Chebyshev's theorem (Table 2.10). In that case, it could have been said only that at least 75% of the time the number of complaints about a product will be within 2 standard deviations of the mean number of complaints.

Exercises 2.47–2.61

Learning the Mechanics

2.47 To what kind of data sets can Chebyshev's theorem be applied? The Empirical Rule?

2.48 The output from a statistical computer program indicates that the mean and standard deviation of a data set consisting of 200 measurements are $1,500 and $300, respectively.
  a. What are the units of measurement of the variable of interest? Based on the units, are these data nominal, ordinal, interval, or ratio?
  b. What can be said about the number of measurements between $900 and $2,100? Between $600 and $2,400? Between $1,200 and $1,800? Between $1,500 and $2,100?

2.49 For any set of data, what can be said about the percentage of the measurements contained in each of the following intervals?
  a. $\bar{x} - s$ to $\bar{x} + s$ **b.** $\bar{x} - 2s$ to $\bar{x} + 2s$ **c.** $\bar{x} - 3s$ to $\bar{x} + 3s$

2.50 As a result of government and consumer pressure, automobile manufacturers in the United States are deeply involved in research to improve their products' gasoline mileage. One manufacturer, hoping to achieve 40 miles per gallon on one of its compact models, measured the mileage obtained by 36 test versions of the model with the following results (rounded to the nearest mile for convenience):

43	35	41	42	42	38	40	41	41
40	40	41	42	36	43	40	38	40
38	45	39	41	42	37	40	40	44
39	40	37	39	41	39	41	37	40

The mean and standard deviation of these data are 40.1 and 2.2, respectively.

a. What are the units in which the mean and standard deviation are expressed?

b. If the manufacturer would be satisfied with a (population) mean of 40 miles per gallon, how would it react to the above test data?

c. Use the information in Table 2.10 to check the reasonableness of the calculated standard deviation, $s = 2.2$.

d. Construct a relative frequency histogram of the data set. Is the data set mound-shaped?

e. What percentage of the measurements would you expect to find within the intervals $\bar{x} \pm s$, $\bar{x} \pm 2s$, and $\bar{x} \pm 3s$?

f. Count the number of measurements that actually fall within the intervals of part e. Express each interval count as a percentage of the total number of measurements. Compare these results with your answers to part e.

2.51 Given a data set with a largest value of 760 and a smallest value of 135, what would you estimate the standard deviation to be? Explain the logic behind the procedure you used to estimate the standard deviation. Suppose the standard deviation is reported to be 25. Is this feasible? Explain.

Applying the Concepts

2.52 A manufacturer of video cassette recorders is disturbed because retailers were complaining that they were not receiving shipments of recorders as fast as they had been promised. The manufacturer decided to run a check on the distribution network. Each of the 50 warehouses owned by the manufacturer throughout the country had been instructed to maintain at least 200 recorders in stock at all times so that a supply would always be readily available for retailers. The manufacturer checked the inventories of 20 of these warehouses and obtained the following numbers of video cassette recorders in stock:

40	10	44	142	14	301	175	0	38	202
220	32	400	78	16	99	0	176	5	86

The mean and standard deviation are 103.9 and 111.3, respectively.

a. Calculate the median. Is the distribution of measurements skewed or symmetric? Explain.

b. Using your answer to part **a**, would you advise using the Empirical Rule to describe these data? Why?

c. According to Chebyshev's theorem, what percentage of the measurements would you expect to find outside the intervals $\bar{x} \pm s$, $\bar{x} \pm 2s$, and $\bar{x} \pm 3s$?

d. Check the numbers of measurements that actually fall outside the intervals specified in part **c**. Express each count as a percentage of the total number of measurements. Compare these results with your answers to part **c**.

2.53 Twenty-five mergers were sampled from the population of mergers that occurred between firms (excluding railroads) listed on the New York Stock Exchange during the period 1958–1980. For each merger, the ratio of the target firm's sales for the preceding year to the bidder firm's sales was calculated. (See Exercise 1.14 for definitions of target and bidder firms.) The 25 sales ratios are listed below (Eger, 1982, p. 133):

.16	.07	.32	.05	.79
.30	.18	.04	.04	.05
.14	.08	.14	.29	.02
.14	.10	.34	.10	.02
.03	.15	.09	.06	.02

For these data, $\Sigma x = 3.72$ and $\Sigma x^2 = 1.2088$.

a. What is the mean sales ratio, $\bar{x}$, for this sample of mergers? Also, find s^2 and s.
b. According to Chebyshev's theorem, what percentage of the measurements would you expect to find in the intervals $\bar{x} \pm .75s$, $\bar{x} \pm 2.5s$, and $\bar{x} \pm 4s$?
c. What percentage of measurements actually fall in the intervals of part b? Compare these results with the results of part b.
d. What percentage of the mergers involved a target firm with larger sales than the bidder firm?

2.54 Tests have demonstrated that the shelf life of cake mix A has a mound-shaped distribution with a mean of 275 days and a standard deviation of 55 days. Mix B has a shelf life whose distribution is also mound-shaped, but with a mean of 286 days and a standard deviation of 22 days.

a. What percentage of boxes of cake mix A remain fresh for 330 days or more?
b. What percentage of boxes of mix B remain fresh for 330 days or more?
c. Which cake mix is more likely to remain fresh for more than 330 days? Explain.
d. Now assume the shapes of the two shelf-life distributions are unknown. Answer parts a–c by applying Chebyshev's theorem.

2.55 A company that bottles sparkling water has determined that it lost an average of 30.4 cases per week last year due to breakage in transit. The standard deviation of the number of cases lost per week was 3.8 cases. With only this information, what can you say about the number of weeks last year that the company lost more than 38 cases due to breakage in transit? Justify your answer.

2.56 A chemical company produces a substance composed of 98% cracked corn particles and 2% zinc phosphide for use in controlling rat populations in sugarcane fields. Production must be carefully controlled to maintain the zinc phosphide at 2% because too much zinc phosphide will damage the sugarcane and too little will be ineffective in controlling the rat population. Records from past production indicate that the distribution of the actual percentage of zinc phosphide present in the substance is approximately mound-shaped, with a mean of 2.0% and a standard deviation of .08%. If the production line is operating correctly and a batch is chosen at random from a day's production, what is the approximate probability that it will contain less than 1.84% zinc phosphide?

2.57 For 50 randomly selected days, the number of vehicles that used a certain road was ascertained by a city engineer. The mean was 385; the standard deviation was 15. Suppose you are interested in the proportion of days that there were between 340 and 430 vehicles using the road. What does Chebyshev's theorem tell you about this proportion?

2.58 A boat dealer has determined that the frequency distribution of the number of outboard motor sales per month over the last five years is mound-shaped, with a sample mean of 30 and a sample variance of 4. Approximately what percentage of the recorded monthly sales figures of the past five years would be expected to be greater than 34? Less than 26? Greater than 36?

2.59 Solar energy is considered by many to be the energy of the future. A recent survey was taken to compare the cost of solar energy with the cost of gas or electric energy. Results of the survey revealed that the average monthly utility bill of a three-bedroom house using gas or electric energy was $125 and the standard deviation was $15.

    a. If nothing is known about the distribution of utility bills, what can you say about the fraction of all three-bedroom homes with gas or electric energy that have bills between $80 and $170?

    b. If it is reasonable to assume that the distribution of utility bills is mound-shaped, approximately what proportion of three-bedroom homes would have monthly bills less than $110?

    c. Suppose that three houses with solar energy units had the following utility bills: $78, $92, $87. Does this suggest that solar energy units might result in lower utility bills? Explain. [*Note:* We present a statistical method for testing this conjecture in Chapter 6.]

2.60 When it is working properly, a machine that fills 25-pound bags of flour dispenses an average of 25 pounds per fill; the standard deviation of the amount of fill is .1 pound. To monitor the performance of the machine, an inspector weighs the contents of a bag coming off the machine's conveyor belt every half-hour during the day. If the contents of two consecutive bags fall more than 2 standard deviations from the mean (using the mean and standard deviation given above), the filling process is said to be out of control and the machine is shut down briefly for adjustments. The data given in the table are the weights measured by the inspector yesterday. Assume the machine is never shut down for more than 15 minutes at a time. At what times yesterday was the process shut down for adjustment? Justify your answer.

Time	Weight (pounds)	Time	Weight (pounds)
8:00 A.M.	25.10	12:30 P.M.	25.06
8:30	25.15	1:00	24.95
9:00	24.81	1:30	24.80
9:30	24.75	2:00	24.95
10:00	25.00	2:30	25.21
10:30	25.05	3:00	24.90
11:00	25.23	3:30	24.71
11:30	25.25	4:00	25.31
12:00	25.01	4:30	25.15
		5:00	25.20

2.61 A buyer for a lumber company must determine whether to buy a piece of land containing 5,000 pine trees. If 1,000 of the trees are at least 40 feet tall, he will purchase the land; otherwise, he will not. The owner of the land reports that the distribution of the heights of the trees has a mean of 30 feet, and a standard deviation of 3 feet. Based on this information, what should the buyer decide?

2.7 Measures of Relative Standing

As we have seen, numerical measures of central tendency and variability describe the general nature of a data set (either a sample or a population). We may also be interested in describing the relative location of a particular measurement within a data set.

Descriptive measures of the relationship of a measurement to the rest of the data are called **measures of relative standing**.

One measure of the relative standing of a particular measurement is its **percentile ranking**:

Definition 2.12

Let $x_1, x_2, \ldots, x_n$ be a set of n measurements (n large) arranged in increasing (or decreasing) order. The **pth percentile** is a number x such that $p\%$ of the measurements fall below the pth percentile and $(100 - p)\%$ fall above it.

For example, if oil company A reports that its yearly sales are in the 90th percentile of all companies in the industry, the implication is that 90% of all oil companies have yearly sales less than company A's, and only 10% have yearly sales exceeding company A's. This is demonstrated in Figure 2.23.

FIGURE 2.23 ▶
Relative frequency distribution for yearly sales of oil companies

Another measure of relative standing in popular use is the **z-score**. As you can see in Definition 2.13, the z-score makes use of the mean and standard deviation of the data set in order to specify the location of a measurement:

Definition 2.13

The **sample z-score** for a measurement x is

$$z = \frac{x - \bar{x}}{s}$$

The **population z-score** for a measurement x is

$$z = \frac{x - \mu}{\sigma}$$

Note that the z-score is calculated by subtracting $\bar{x}$ (or μ) from the measurement x and then dividing the result by s (or σ). The result, the z-score, represents the distance between a given measurement, x, and the mean, expressed in standard deviations.

EXAMPLE 2.12

Suppose 200 steelworkers are selected, and the annual income of each is determined. The mean and standard deviation are $\bar{x} = \$24,000$ and $s = \$2,000$. Suppose Joe Smith's annual income is $22,000. What is his sample z-score?

FIGURE 2.24 ▶
Annual income of steelworkers

$18,000	$22,000	$24,000	$30,000
$\bar{x} - 3s$	Joe Smith's income	$\bar{x}$	$\bar{x} + 3s$

Solution

Joe Smith's annual income lies below the mean income of the 200 steelworkers (see Figure 2.24). We compute

$$z = \frac{x - \bar{x}}{s} = \frac{\$22,000 - \$24,000}{\$2,000} = -1.0$$

which tells us that Joe Smith's annual income is 1.0 standard deviation *below* the sample mean, or, in short, his sample z-score is -1.0.

The numerical value of the z-score reflects the relative standing of the measurement. A large positive z-score implies that the measurement is larger than almost all other measurements, whereas a large negative z-score indicates that the measurement is smaller than almost every other measurement. If a z-score is 0 or near 0, the measurement is located at or near the mean of the sample or population.

We can be more specific if we know that the frequency distribution of the measurements is mound-shaped. In this case, the following interpretation of the z-scores can be given:

Interpretation of z-Scores for Mound-Shaped Distributions of Data

1. Approximately 68% of the measurements will have a z-score between -1 and 1.

2. Approximately 95% of the measurements will have a z-score between -2 and 2.

3. All or almost all the measurements will have a z-score between -3 and 3.

Note that this interpretation of z-scores is identical to that given in Table 2.10 for samples that exhibit mound-shaped frequency distributions. The statement that a measurement falls in the interval $(\mu - \sigma, \mu + \sigma)$ is identical to the statement that a measurement has a population z-score between -1 and 1, since all measurements between $(\mu - \sigma)$ and $(\mu + \sigma)$ are within 1 standard deviation of μ (see Figure 2.25 on page 86).

FIGURE 2.25 ▶
Population z-scores for a mound-shaped distribution

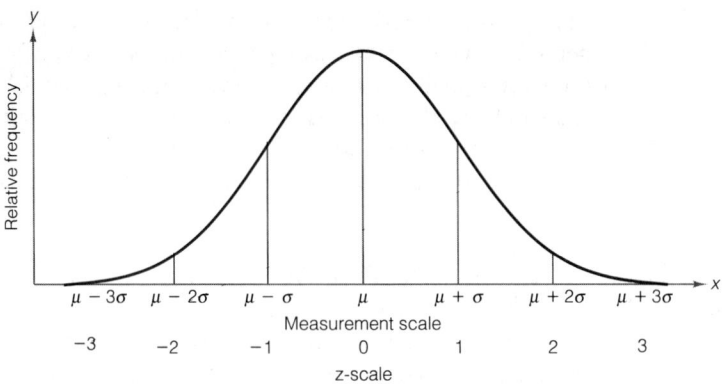

EXAMPLE 2.13

Suppose a female bank employee believes her salary is low as a result of sex discrimination. To substantiate her belief, she collects information on the salaries of her male counterparts in the banking business. She finds that their salaries have a mean of $34,000 and a standard deviation of $2,000. Her salary is $27,000. Does this information support her claim of sex discrimination?

Solution

The analysis might proceed as follows. First, we calculate the z-score for the woman's salary with respect to those of her male counterparts. Thus,

$$z = \frac{\$27,000 - \$34,000}{\$2,000} = -3.5$$

The implication is that the woman's salary is 3.5 standard deviations *below* the mean of the male salary distribution. Furthermore, if a check of the male salary data shows that the frequency distribution is mound-shaped, we can infer that very few salaries in this distribution should have a z-score less than −3, as shown in Figure 2.26. Therefore, a z-score of −3.5 represents either a measurement from a distribution different from the male salary distribution or a very unusual (highly improbable) measurement for the male salary distribution.

FIGURE 2.26 ▶
Male salary distribution

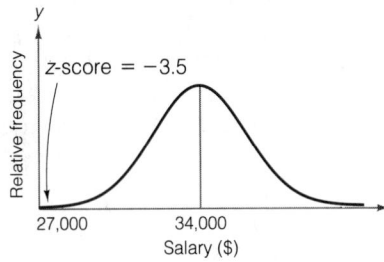

Which of the two situations do you think prevails? Do you think the woman's salary is simply an unusually low one in the distribution of salaries, or do you think her claim of salary discrimination is justified? Most people would probably conclude that her salary does not come from the male salary distribution. However, the careful investigator should require more information before inferring sex discrimination as the cause. We would want to know more about the data collection technique the woman used, and more about her competence at her job. Also, perhaps other factors such as the length of employment should be considered in the analysis.

The method of Example 2.13 exemplifies an approach to statistical inference that might be called the **rare event approach**. An experimenter hypothesizes a specific frequency distribution to describe a population of measurements. Then a sample of measurements is drawn from the population. If the experimenter finds it unlikely that the sample came from the hypothesized distribution, the hypothesis is concluded to be false. Thus, in Example 2.13 the woman believes her salary reflects sex discrimination. She hypothesizes that her salary should be just another measurement in the distribution of her male counterparts' salaries if no discrimination exists. However, it is so unlikely that the sample (in this case, her salary) came from the male frequency distribution that she rejects that hypothesis, concluding that the distribution from which her salary was drawn is different from the distribution for the men.

This rare event approach to inference-making is discussed further in later chapters. Proper application of the approach requires a knowledge of probability, the subject of our next chapter.

CASE STUDY 2.8 / Deciding When to Respond to Consumer Complaints

Now we will finish the discussion begun in Case Study 2.7 of a method proposed by Namias (1964) to determine when and when not to conduct a search for specific causes of consumer complaints.

The rate of consumer complaints about a product may change or vary merely as a result of chance or fate, or perhaps because of some specific cause, such as a decline in the quality of the product. Concerning the former, Namias says:

In any operation or production process, variability in the output or product will occur, and no two operational results may be expected to be exactly alike. Complete constancy of consumer rates of complaint is not possible, for the vagaries of fate and chance operate even within the most rigid framework of quality or operation control.

Namias provides a decision rule with which to determine when the observed variation in the rate of consumer complaints is due to chance and when it is due to specific causes. If the observed rate is 2 standard deviations or less away from the mean rate of complaint, it is attributed to chance. If the observed rate is farther than 2 standard deviations above the mean rate, it is attributed to a specific problem in the production or distribution of the product. The reasoning is that if there are no problems with the production and distribution of the product, 95% of the time the rate of complaints should be within 2 standard deviations of the mean rate. If the production and distribution processes were operating normally, it would be very unlikely for a rate higher than 2 standard deviations above the mean to occur. Instead, it is more likely that the high complaint rate is caused by abnormal operation of the production and/or distribution process; that is, something specific is wrong with the process.

Namias recommends searching for the cause (or causes) only if the observed variation in the rate of complaints is determined by the rule to be the result of a specific cause (or causes). The degree of variability due to chance must be tolerated. Namias says,

As long as the results exhibit chance variability, the causes are common, and there is no need to attempt to improve the product by making specific changes. Indeed this may only create more variability, not less, and it may inject trouble where none existed, with waste of time and money. . . . On the other hand, time and money are again wasted through failure to recognize specific conditions when they arise. It is therefore economical to look for a specific cause when there is more variability than is expected on the basis of chance alone.

Namias collected data from the records of a beverage company for a two-week period to demonstrate the effectiveness of the rule. Consumer complaints concerned chipped bottles that looked dangerous. For one of the firm's brands the mean complaint rate was determined to be 26.01 and the rate 2 standard deviations above the mean was determined to be 48.78 complaints per 10,000 bottles sold. The complaint rate observed during the two weeks under study was 93.12 complaints per 10,000 bottles sold. Since 93.12 is many more than 2 standard deviations above the mean rate, it was concluded that the high rate of complaints must have been caused by some specific problem in the production or distribution of the particular brand of beverage and that a search for the problem would probably be worthwhile. The problem was traced to rough handling of the bottled beverage in the warehouse by newly hired workers. As a result, a training program for new workers was instituted.

In Chapter 11, "Methods for Quality Improvement," we discuss in detail methods for monitoring the variation of a production process and deciding when to take action to improve the process.

Exercises 2.62–2.74

Learning the Mechanics

2.62 What is the 50th percentile of a quantitative data set? What is another name for the 50th percentile?

2.63 In each of the following compute the z-score for the x value, and note whether your result is a sample z-score or a population z-score:
   a. $x = 31$, $s = 7$, $\bar{x} = 24$ **b.** $x = 95$, $s = 4$, $\bar{x} = 101$
   c. $x = 5$, $\mu = 2$, $\sigma = 1.7$ **d.** $\mu = 17$, $\sigma = 5$, $x = 14$

2.64 Compare the z-scores to determine which of the following x values lie the greatest distance above the mean and the greatest distance below the mean.
   a. $x = 100$, $\mu = 50$, $\sigma = 25$ **b.** $x = 1$, $\mu = 4$, $\sigma = 1$
   c. $x = 0$, $\mu = 200$, $\sigma = 100$ **d.** $x = 10$, $\mu = 5$, $\sigma = 3$

2.65 At the University of Statistics (US), the students are given z-scores at the end of each semester rather than the traditional GPAs. The mean and standard deviation of all students' cumulative GPAs at US, on which the z-scores are based, are 2.7 and .5, respectively.
   a. Translate each of the following z-scores to a corresponding GPA: $z = 2.0$, $z = -1.0$, $z = .5$, $z = -2.5$.
   b. Students with z-scores below -1.6 are put on probation at US. What is the corresponding probationary GPA?

c. The president of US wishes to graduate the top 16% of the students with cum laude honors and the top 2.5% with summa cum laude honors. Where should the limits be set in terms of z-scores? In terms of GPAs? What assumption, if any, did you make about the distribution of the GPAs at US?

2.66 Suppose that 40 and 90 are two elements of a population data set and that their z-scores are -2 and 3, respectively. Using only this information, is it possible to determine the population's mean and standard deviation? If so, find them. If not, explain why it is not possible.

Applying the Concepts

2.67 In 1987 the United States imported merchandise valued at $406 billion and exported merchandise worth $253 billion. The difference between these two quantities (exports minus imports) is referred to as the *merchandise trade balance*. Since more goods were imported than exported in 1987, the merchandise trade balance was a *negative* $153 billion. The accompanying table lists the United States exports to and imports from a sample of ten countries in 1987 (in millions of dollars).

Country	Exports	Imports
Brazil	4,040	7,865
Egypt	2,210	465
France	7,943	10,730
Italy	5,530	11,040
Japan	28,249	84,575
Mexico	14,582	20,271
Panama	743	356
Soviet Union	1,480	425
Sweden	1,894	4,758
Turkey	1,483	821

Source: *Statistical Abstract of the United States: 1989,* pp. 788–791.

a. Calculate the U.S. merchandise trade balance with each of the ten countries. Express your answers in billions of dollars.

b. Use a z-score to identify the relative position of the U.S. trade balance with Japan within the data set you developed in part **a**. Do the same for the trade balance with the Soviet Union. Write a sentence or two that describes the relative positions of these two trade balances.

2.68 The accompanying table lists the unemployment rate in 1987 for a sample of nine countries.

Country	Percent Unemployed	Country	Percent Unemployed
Australia	8.1	Italy	7.9
Canada	8.9	Japan	2.9
France	11.1	Sweden	1.9
Germany	6.9	United States	6.2
Great Britain	10.3		

Source: *Statistical Abstract of the United States: 1989,* p. 829.

The mean and standard deviation of the nine countries' unemployment rates are 7.1 and 3.1, respectively.

a. Calculate the z-scores of the unemployment rates of the United States, Australia, and Japan.

b. Describe the information conveyed by the sign (positive or negative) of the z-scores you calculated in part a.

2.69 In *Fortune*'s 1990 ranking of the 500 largest industrial corporations in the United States, Control Data Corporation ranked 153rd in terms of 1989 sales. In 1985, it ranked 71st. Use percentiles to describe Control Data Corporation's position in each year's sales distribution.

2.70 A parking lot owner's accountant determined the owner's receipts for each of 100 randomly chosen days from the past year. The mean and standard deviation for the 100 days were $360 and $25, respectively. Yesterday's receipts amounted to $370.

a. Find the sample z-score for yesterday's receipts.

b. How many standard deviations away from the mean is the value of yesterday's receipts?

c. Would you consider yesterday's receipts to be unusually high? Why or why not?

2.71 It is known that the frequency distribution of the number of videocassette recorders (VCRs) sold each week by a large department store in Atlanta is mound-shaped, with a mean of 35 and a variance of 9.

a. Approximately what percentage of the measurements in the frequency distribution should fall between 32 and 38? Between 26 and 44?

b. If the z-score for last week's sales was -1.33, how many VCRs did the store sell last week?

c. If it is known that the number of VCRs sold each week by a rival department store has a mound-shaped frequency distribution with a mean of 35 and a standard deviation of 2, for which store is it more likely that more than 41 VCRs will be sold in a week? Why?

2.72 One of the ways the federal government raises money is through the sale of securities such as **Treasury bonds**, **Treasury bills (T-bills)**, and **U.S. savings bonds**. Treasury bonds and bills are marketable (i.e., they can be traded in the securities market) long-term and short-term notes, respectively. U.S. savings bonds are non-marketable notes; they can be purchased and redeemed only from the U.S. Treasury. On June 30, 1983, the interest rate on 3-month T-bills was 8.75%. Within the next week, the *Wall Street Journal* sampled 17 economists and asked them to forecast the interest rate of 3-month T-bills on September 30, 1983. (T-bills are offered for sale weekly by the government, and their interest rates typically vary with each offering.) The forecasts obtained are listed in the table.

Economist	Interest Rate Forecast (%)	Economist	Interest Rate Forecast (%)
Alan Greenspan	8.70	Robert Parry	8.50
Timothy Howard	8.75	John Paulus	9.50
Lacy H. Hunt	9.35	Norman Robertson	8.50
Edward Hyman	7.80	Francis Schott	8.50
David Jones	9.25	Stuart Schweitzer	9.00
Irwin Kellner	8.25	Allen Sinai	9.15
Alan Lerner	9.25	Thomas Thompson	9.25
Donald Maude	7.70	John Wilson	10.00
Anne Parker Mills	8.50		

Source: *Wall Street Journal*, July 5, 1983, p. 2. Reprinted by permission. © Dow Jones & Company, Inc. 1983. All rights reserved.

The mean and standard deviation of the 17 forecasts are 8.82% and .61%, respectively.
   a. Calculate the z-scores of Alan Greenspan's forecast and John Wilson's forecast. What do the z-scores tell you about their forecasts relative to the forecasts of the other economists?
   b. Write a sentence or two that summarizes the 17 forecasts. In your summary, use a measure of central tendency and a measure of variability.

2.73   The mean and standard deviation of the gross weekly income distribution of a local firm's 120 employees were determined to be $170 and $10, respectively.
   a. Approximately what percentage of the employees would be expected to have incomes over $190 per week? Under $160 per week? Over $200 per week?
   b. If you were employed by this firm and your weekly income was $185, what would your z-score be, and how many standard deviations would your salary be away from the mean salary?

2.74   Refer to Exercise 2.73. Suppose it is known that the weekly gross income distribution is mound-shaped.
   a. Approximately what percentage of the employees would be expected to have incomes over $190 per week? Under $160 per week? Over $200 per week?
   b. If you and a friend both worked at the firm and your income was $160 per week and hers was $195 per week, how many standard deviations apart are your incomes?
   c. If you randomly chose an employee of this firm, is it more likely that his or her gross income is over $190 per week or under $145 per week? Why?

2.8   Box Plots: Graphical Descriptions Based on Quartiles (Optional)

The **box plot**, a relatively recent introduction to the methodology of descriptive measures, is based on the **quartiles** of a data set. Quartiles are values that partition the data set into four groups, each containing 25% of the measurements. The lower quartile Q_L is the 25th percentile, the middle quartile is the median m (the 50th percentile), and the upper quartile Q_U is the 75th percentile (see Figure 2.27).

FIGURE 2.27 ▶
The quartiles for a data set

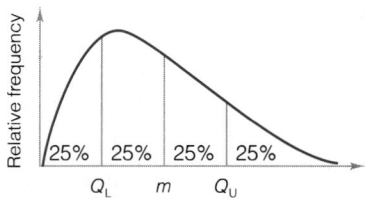

Definition 2.14

The **lower quartile** is the 25th percentile of a data set, the **middle quartile** is the median, and the **upper quartile** is the 75th percentile.

A box plot is based on the **interquartile range (IQR)**, the distance between the lower and upper quartiles:

$$IQR = Q_U - Q_L$$

Definition 2.15

The **interquartile range** is the distance between the lower and upper quartiles:

$$IQR = Q_U - Q_L$$

The box plot for the 50 companies' percentages of revenues spent on R&D (Table 2.6) is given in Figure 2.28. The box plot shown there was generated by the Minitab statistical software package for personal computers.* Note that a rectangle (the *box*) is drawn, with the ends of the rectangle (the *hinges*, represented by the "I's" at the ends of the box drawn by the Minitab program) drawn at the quartiles Q_L and Q_U. By definition, then, the "middle" 50% of the observations—those between Q_L and Q_U—fall inside the box. For the R&D data, these quartiles appear to be at (approximately) 7.0 and 9.5 Thus,

$$IQR = 9.5 - 7.0 = 2.5 \quad \text{(approximately)}$$

The median is shown at about 8.0 by a + sign within the box.

FIGURE 2.28 ▶
Minitab box plot for R&D percentages

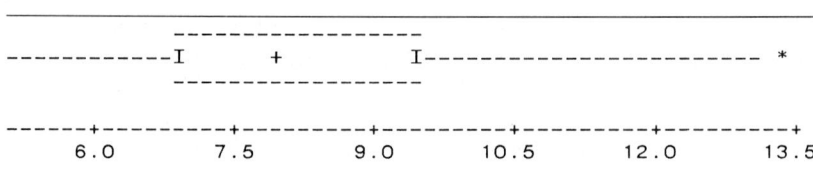

To guide the construction of the "tails" of the box plot, two sets of limits, called *inner fences* and *outer fences*, are used. Neither set of fences actually appears on the box plot. Inner fences are located at a distance of $1.5(IQR)$ from the hinges. Emanating from each hinge of the box are dashed lines called the *whiskers*. The two whiskers will

---

*Although box plots can be generated by hand, the amount of detail required makes them particularly well-suited for computer generation. We will use computer software to generate the box plots in this section.

extend to the most extreme observation inside the inner fences. For example, the inner fence on the lower side of the R&D percentage plot is (approximately):

$$\text{Lower inner fence} = \text{Lower hinge} - 1.5(\text{IQR})$$
$$\approx 7.0 - 1.5(2.5)$$
$$= 7.0 - 3.75 = 3.25$$

The smallest measurement in the data set is 5.2, which is well inside this inner fence. Thus, the lower whisker extends to 5.2. On the upper end, the inner fence is at about $(9.5 + 3.75) = 13.25$. The largest measurement inside this fence is the third largest measurement, 13.2. Note that the longer upper whisker reveals the rightward skewness of the R&D distribution.

Values that are beyond the inner fences receive special attention, because they are extreme values that represent relatively rare occurrences. In fact, for mound-shaped distributions, fewer than 1% of the observations are expected to fall outside the inner fences. As discussed above, none of the R&D measurements fall outside the lower inner fence. However, the two measurements at 13.5 fall outside the upper inner fence which is located at 13.25. These measurements are represented by asterisks (*), and they further emphasize the rightward skewness of the distribution. Note that the box plot does not reveal that there are *two* measurements at 13.5, since only a single symbol is used to represent both observations at that point.

The other pair of imaginary fences, the outer fences, are defined at a distance 3(IQR) from each end of the box. Measurements that fall beyond the outer fences are represented by zeros (0) and are very extreme measurements that require special attention and analysis. Less than one-hundredth of 1% (.01%, or .0001) of the measurements from mound-shaped distributions are expected to fall beyond the outer fences. Since no measurement in the R&D box plot (Figure 2.28) is represented by a 0, we know that none of the measurements fall outside the outer fences.

Generally, any measurements that fall beyond the inner fences, and certainly any that fall beyond the outer fences, are considered potential **outliers**. Outliers are extreme measurements that stand out from the rest of the sample and may be faulty— incorrectly recorded observations or members of a different population from the rest of the sample. At the least, they are very unusual measurements from the same population. For example, the two R&D measurements at 13.5 may be considered outliers, because they exceed the inner fence ("*" representation in Figure 2.28). When we analyze these measurements, we find they are correctly recorded. However, it turns out that both represent R&D expenditures of relatively young and fast-growing companies. Thus, the outlier analysis may have revealed important factors that relate to the R&D expenditures of high-tech companies: their age and rate of growth. Outlier analysis often reveals useful information of this kind, and therefore plays an important role in the statistical inference-making process.

The elements (and nomenclature) of box plots are summarized in the next box. Some aids to the interpretation of box plots are also given.

Elements of a Box Plot

1. A rectangle (the **box**) is drawn with the ends (the **hinges**) drawn at the lower and upper quartiles (Q_L and Q_U). The median of the data is shown in the box, usually by a "+".

2. The points at distances 1.5(IQR) from each hinge mark the **inner fences** of the data set. Horizontal lines (the **whiskers**) are drawn from each hinge to the most extreme measurement inside the inner fence.

3. A second pair of fences, the **outer fences**, exist at a distance of 3 interquartile ranges, 3(IQR), from the hinges. One symbol (usually "*") is used to represent measurements falling between the inner and outer fences, and another (usually "0") is used to represent measurements beyond the outer fences.

4. The symbols used to represent the median and the extreme data points (those beyond the fences) will vary depending on the software you use to construct the box plot. (You may use your own symbols if you are constructing a box plot by hand.) You should consult the program's documentation to determine exactly which symbols are used.

Aids to the Interpretation of Box Plots

1. Examine the length of the box. The IQR is a measure of the sample's variability, and is especially useful for the comparison of two samples (see Example 2.15).

2. Visually compare the lengths of the whiskers. If one is clearly longer, the distribution of the data is probably skewed in the direction of the longer whisker.

3. Analyze any measurements that lie beyond the fences. Fewer than 5% should fall beyond the inner fences, even for very skewed distributions. Measurements beyond the outer fences are probably **outliers**, with one of the following explanations:

   a. The measurement is incorrect. It may have been observed, recorded, or entered into the computer incorrectly.

   b. The measurement belongs to a population different from that from which the rest of the sample was drawn (see Example 2.15).

   c. The measurement may be correct and from the same population as the rest, but represents a rare event. Generally, we accept this explanation only after carefully ruling out all others.

EXAMPLE 2.14

In Example 2.1 we analyzed 50 processing times for the development of price quotes by the manufacturer of industrial wheels. The intent was to determine whether the success or failure in obtaining the order was related to the amount of time to process the price quotes. Each quote that corresponds to "lost" business was so classified. The data are repeated in Table 2.11. Use a statistical software package to draw a box plot for these data.

TABLE 2.11   Price Quote Processing Times (Days)

Request Number	Processing Time	Lost?	Request Number	Processing Time	Lost?
1	2.36	No	26	3.34	No
2	5.73	No	27	6.00	No
3	6.60	No	28	5.92	No
4	10.05	Yes	29	7.28	Yes
5	5.13	No	30	1.25	No
6	1.88	No	31	4.01	No
7	2.52	No	32	7.59	No
8	2.00	No	33	13.42	Yes
9	4.69	No	34	3.24	No
10	1.91	No	35	3.37	No
11	6.75	Yes	36	14.06	Yes
12	3.92	No	37	5.10	No
13	3.46	No	38	6.44	No
14	2.64	No	39	7.76	No
15	3.63	No	40	4.40	No
16	3.44	No	41	5.48	No
17	9.49	Yes	42	7.51	No
18	4.90	No	43	6.18	No
19	7.45	No	44	8.22	Yes
20	20.23	Yes	45	4.37	No
21	3.91	No	46	2.93	No
22	1.70	No	47	9.95	Yes
23	16.29	Yes	48	4.46	No
24	5.52	No	49	14.32	Yes
25	1.44	No	50	9.01	No

Solution

The SAS/PC box plot printout for these data is shown in Figure 2.29 (page 96). Note that the SAS program draws the box plot vertically, and shows a scale for the processing times on the left. SAS uses a horizontal dashed line in the box to represent the median, and a plus (+) sign to represent the mean. (SAS shows the mean in box plots, unlike many other statistical programs.) Also, note that SAS uses the symbol "0" to represent measurements between the inner and outer fences and "*" to represent observations beyond the outer fences.

FIGURE 2.29 ▶
SAS box plot for processing time
data

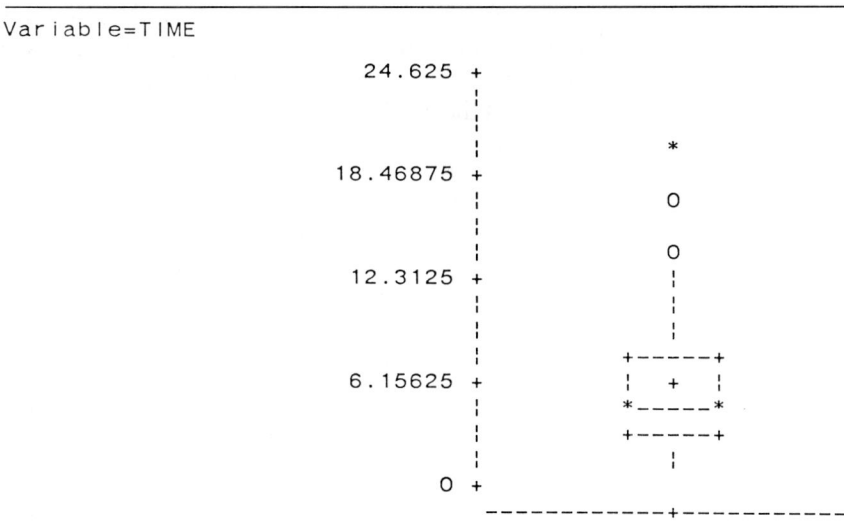

Note that the upper whisker is longer than the lower whisker and that the mean lies above the median; these characteristics reveal the rightward skewness of the data. However, the most important feature of the data is made very obvious by the box plot: There are at least two measurements between the inner and outer fences (in fact, there are three, but two are almost equal and are represented by the same "0") and at least one beyond the outer fence, all on the upper end of the distribution. Thus, the distribution is extremely skewed to the right, and several measurements need special attention in our analysis. We offer an explanation for the outliers in the following example.

EXAMPLE 2.15

The box plot for the 50 processing times (Figure 2.29) does not explicitly reveal the differences, if any, between the set of times corresponding to the success and the set of times corresponding to the failure to obtain the business. Box plots corresponding to the 39 "won" and 11 "lost" bids were generated using the SAS/PC program, and are shown in Figure 2.30. Interpret them.

Solution

The division of the data set into two parts, corresponding to won and lost bids, eliminates any observations that are beyond inner or outer fences. Furthermore, the skewness in the distributions has been reduced, as evidenced by the facts that the upper whiskers are only slightly longer than the lower, and that the means are closer to the medians than for the combined sample. The box plots also reveal that the processing times corresponding to the lost bids tend to exceed those of the won bids. A plausible explanation for the outliers in the combined box plot (Figure 2.29) is that they are from a different population than the bulk of the times. In other words, there are two populations represented by the sample of processing times—one corresponding to lost bids, and the other to won bids.

FIGURE 2.30 ▶
Box plots of processing time data:
Won and lost bids

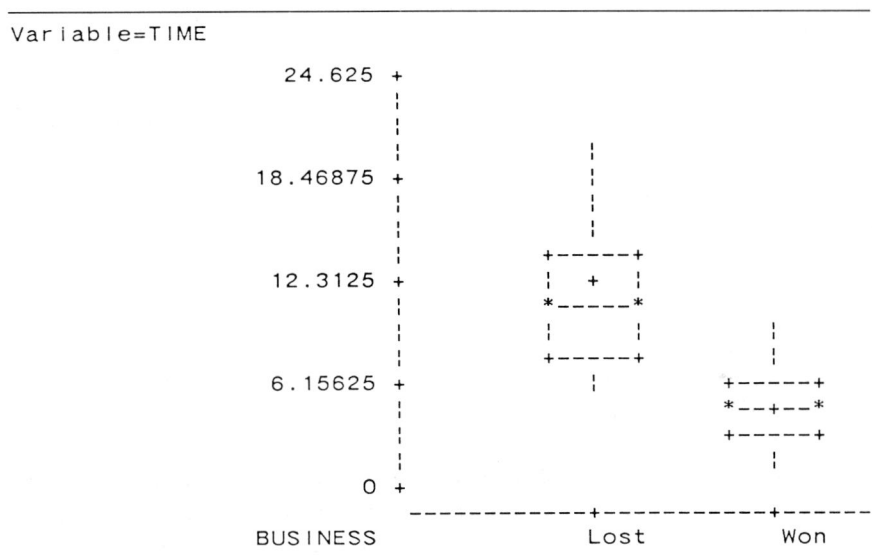

```
Variable=TIME

    24.625 +
           I
           I
           I
 18.46875 +
           I
           I
           I
   12.3125 +
           I
           I
           I
   6.15625 +
           I
           I
           I
         0 +

             BUSINESS           Lost           Won
```

The box plots lend support to the conclusion that the price quote processing time and the success of acquiring the business are related. However, whether the visual differences between the box plots generalize to inferences about the populations corresponding to these two samples is a matter for inferential statistics, not graphical descriptions. We will discuss how to use samples to compare two quantitative populations using inferential statistics in Chapter 8.

Exercises 2.75–2.84

Note: Starred (*) exercises require the use of a computer.

Learning the Mechanics

2.75   Define the 25th, 50th, and 75th percentiles of a data set. Explain how they provide a description of the data.

2.76   Suppose a data set consisting of exam scores has a lower quartile $Q_L = 60$, a median $m = 75$, and an upper quartile $Q_U = 85$. The scores on the exam ranged from 18 to 100. Without having the actual scores available to you, construct as much of the box plot as possible.

2.77   Minitab was used to generate the following box plot:

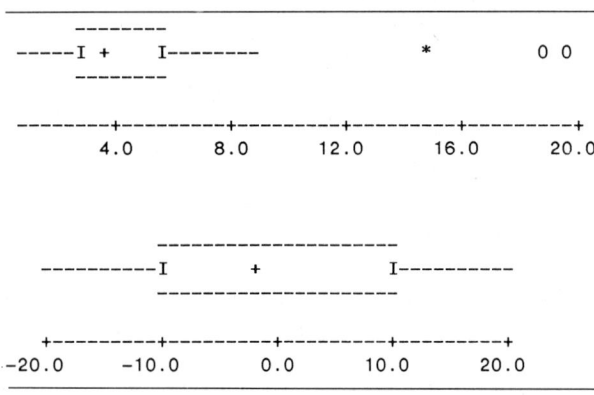

```
         -------- ----
* *    --------------I    +    I--------
         ----------

+---------+---------+---------+---------+
0.0      15.0      30.0      45.0      60.0
```

a. What is the median of the data set (approximately)?
b. What are the upper and lower quartiles of the data set (approximately)?
c. What is the interquartile range of the data set (approximately)?
d. Is the data set skewed to the left, skewed to the right, or symmetric?
e. What percentage of the measurements in the data set lie to the right of the median? To the left of the upper quartile?

2.78   Minitab was used to generate the accompanying box plots. Compare and contrast the frequency distributions of the two data sets. Your answer should include comparisons of the following characteristics: central tendency, variation, skewness, and outliers.

```
         --------
-----I +    I--------            *         0 0
         --------

--------+---------+---------+---------+---------+
       4.0       8.0       12.0      16.0      20.0
```

```
         --------------------
----------I      +            I----------
         --------------------

+---------+---------+---------+---------+
-20.0    -10.0     0.0       10.0      20.0
```

*2.79   Use a statistical software package to construct a box plot for the following set of sample measurements:

1.11	1.39	1.66	1.33	1.30
1.72	1.36	1.26	1.35	1.46
1.55	1.24	1.65	1.40	1.50
1.31	1.41	1.24	1.38	1.28
2.00	1.12	1.25	1.49	2.10
1.86	1.55	1.31	1.14	1.82

*2.80 Consider the following two sample data sets:

Sample A			Sample B		
121	171	158	171	152	170
173	184	163	168	169	171
157	85	145	190	183	185
165	172	196	140	173	206
170	159	172	172	174	169
161	187	100	199	151	180
142	166	171	167	170	188

a. Use a statistical software package to construct a box plot for each data set.
b. Using the information reflected in your box plots, describe the similarities and differences between the two data sets.
c. Identify any outliers that may exist in the two data sets.

Applying the Concepts

2.81 The table contains the top salary offer (in thousands of dollars) received by each member of a sample of 50 undergraduate business majors (excluding accounting majors) who graduated from the Carlson School of Management at the University of Minnesota in 1991–1992.

Salary Offers to 1991–1992 Graduates

23.7	26.1	26.6	27.9	40.0	22.8	26.0	26.5	27.5	37.2
22.0	25.9	26.5	27.5	36.1	21.6	25.7	24.7	27.3	34.8
20.9	25.6	24.6	27.2	32.8	20.7	25.4	25.6	26.9	29.1
19.8	25.3	26.4	26.9	28.9	18.7	24.8	26.4	26.8	28.3
17.5	24.2	26.3	26.7	28.2	14.0	23.9	26.1	26.7	28.1

Source: Placement Office, Carlson School of Management, University of Minnesota.

a. The mean and standard deviation are 26.2 and 4.56, respectively. Find and interpret the z-score associated with the highest salary offer, the lowest salary offer, and the mean salary offer. Would you consider the highest offer to be unusually high? Why or why not?
*b. Use a statistical software package to construct a box plot for this data set. Which salary offers (if any) are potentially faulty observations? Explain.

*2.82 A firm's earnings per share (E/S) of common stock is a measure used by investors to monitor the financial performance of a firm. Thirty firms were sampled from *Fortune's* 1990 listing of the 500 largest corporations in the United States, and their earnings per share for 1989 are recorded in the table at the top of page 100.

a. Use a statistical software package to construct a box plot for this data set. Identify any outliers that may exist in this data set.
b. For each outlier identified in part a, determine how many standard deviations it lies from the mean of the E/S data set.

Firm	E/S	Firm	E/S
Illinois Tool Works	$3.06	Dow Jones	$ 3.15
Sara Lee	3.50	United Brands	1.70
Reynolds Metals	9.20	Washington Post	15.50
Scott Paper	5.11	Avon Products	.34
Phelps Dodge	7.59	Valhi	.91
Westmoreland Coal	1.39	American Cyanamid	3.12
Avery International	1.96	EG&G	2.40
Warner–Lambert	6.10	Asarco	5.50
Borden	−.41	Snap-on Tools	2.55
General Electric	4.36	McCormick	3.09
Cooper Industries	2.51	Exxon	2.74
Lockheed	.03	Georgia–Pacific	7.42
Kellogg	3.85	Crown Cork & Seal	3.58
FMC	3.79	DuPont (E.I.) de Nemours	3.53
Oxford Industries	.99	Molex	2.28

Source: *Fortune*, Apr. 23, 1990, pp. 337–396.

*2.83   A manufacturer of minicomputer systems is interested in improving its customer support services. As a first step, its marketing department has been charged with the responsibility of summarizing the extent of customer problems in terms of system down time. The 40 most recent customers were surveyed to determine the amount of down time (in hours) they had experienced during the previous month. These data are listed in the table.

Customer Number	Down Time	Customer Number	Down Time	Customer Number	Down Time	Customer Number	Down Time
230	12	240	24	250	4	260	34
231	16	241	15	251	10	261	26
232	5	242	13	252	15	262	17
233	16	243	8	253	7	263	11
234	21	244	2	254	20	264	64
235	29	245	11	255	9	265	19
236	38	246	22	256	22	266	18
237	14	247	17	257	18	267	24
238	47	248	31	258	28	268	49
239	0	249	10	259	19	269	50

a. Use a statistical software package to construct a box plot for these data. Use the information reflected in the box plot to describe the frequency distribution of the data set. Your description should address central tendency, variation, and skewness.

b. Use your box plot to determine which customers are having unusually lengthy down times.

c. Find and interpret the z-scores associated with the customers you identified in part b.

2.84   The accompanying Minitab-generated box plots describe the U.S. Environmental Protection Agency's 1986 automobile mileage estimates for all models manufactured by Ford and Honda.

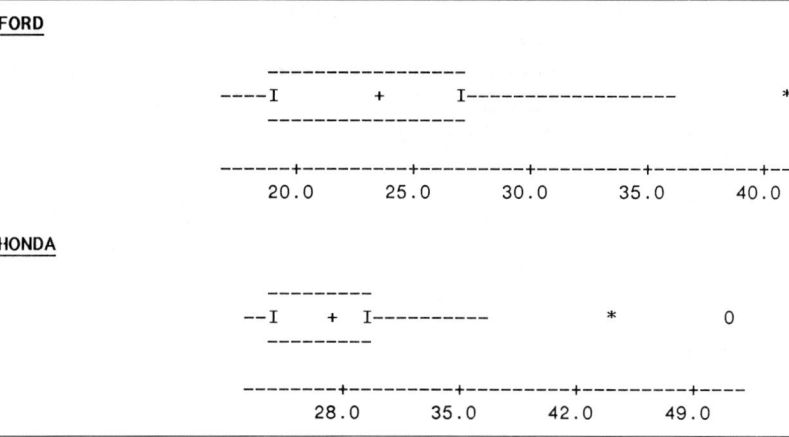

a. Which manufacturer has the higher median mileage estimate?
b. Which manufacturer's mileage estimates have the greater range?
c. Which manufacturer's mileage estimates have the greater interquartile range?
d. Which manufacturer has the model with the highest mileage estimate? Approximately what is that mileage?

2.9   Distorting the Truth with Descriptive Techniques

While it may be true in telling a story that a picture is worth a thousand words, it is also true that pictures can be used to convey a colored and distorted message to the viewer. So the old adage "Let the buyer (reader) beware" applies. Examine relative frequency histograms, time series plots, and, in general, all graphical descriptions with care. In this section, we mention a few of the pitfalls to watch for when analyzing a chart or graph.

One common way to change the impression conveyed by a graph is to change the scale on the vertical axis, the horizontal axis, or both. For example, if you want to show that the change in firm A's market share over time is moderate, you could pack in a large number of units per inch on the vertical axis. That is, make the distance between successive units on the vertical scale small, as shown in Figure 2.31. You can see that the change in the firm's market share over time appears to be minimal.

FIGURE 2.31 ▶
Firm A's market share, 1980–1990: Packed vertical axis

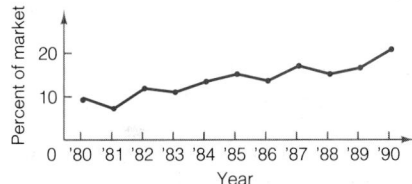

To make the changes in firm A's market share appear large, you could increase the distance between successive units on the vertical axis. That is, you stretch the vertical axis by graphing only a few units per inch, as shown in Figure 2.32. The telltale sign of stretching is a long vertical axis, but this is often hidden by starting the vertical axis at some point above 0, as shown in Figure 2.33(a). Or, the same effect can be achieved by using a broken line called a *scale break* for the vertical axis, as shown in Figure 2.33(b).

FIGURE 2.32 ▶
Firm A's market share, 1980–1990: Stretched vertical axis

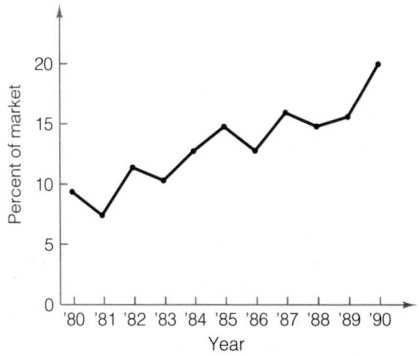

FIGURE 2.33 ▶
Daily stock sales on the New York Stock Exchange from May to July 1979

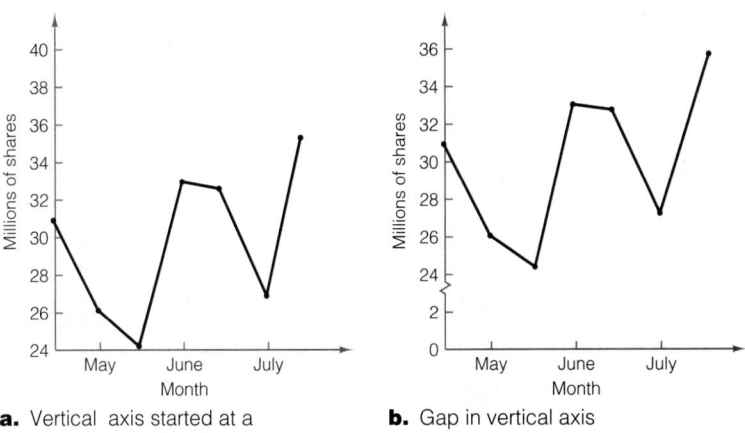

a. Vertical axis started at a point greater than 0

b. Gap in vertical axis

Stretching the horizontal axis (increasing the distance between successive units) may also lead you to incorrect conclusions. For example, Figure 2.34(a) depicts rental income in the United States from the first quarter of 1978 to the first quarter of 1980. If you increase the length of the horizontal axis, as in Figure 2.34(b), the change in the rental income over time seems to be less pronounced.

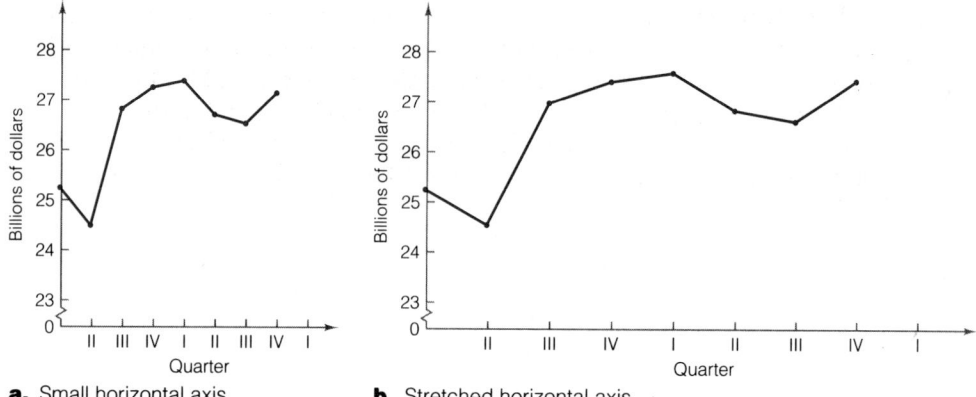

a. Small horizontal axis   **b.** Stretched horizontal axis

FIGURE 2.34 ▲ Rental income from the first quarter of 1978 to the first quarter of 1980

The changes in categories indicated by a bar chart can also be emphasized or deemphasized by stretching or shrinking the vertical axis. Another method of achieving visual distortion with bar charts is by making the width of the bars proportional to their height. For example, look at the bar chart in Figure 2.35(a), which depicts the percentage of a year's total automobile sales attributable to each of the four major manufacturers. Now suppose we make the width as well as the height grow as the market share grows. This is shown in Figure 2.35(b). The reader may tend to equate the *area* of the bars with the relative market share of each manufacturer. In fact, the true relative market share is proportional only to the height of the bars.

FIGURE 2.35 ►

Relative share of the automobile market for each of four major manufacturers

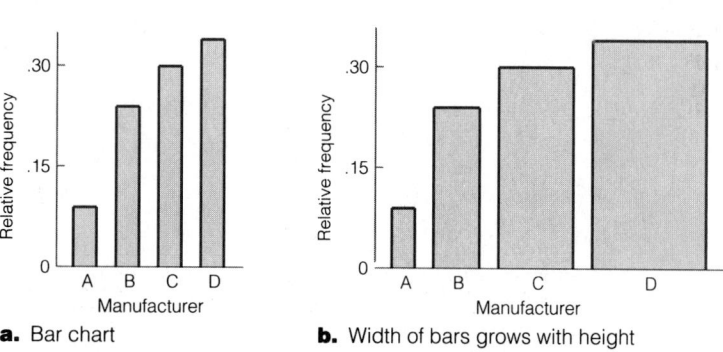

a. Bar chart   **b.** Width of bars grows with height

Sometimes, as noted by Selazny (1975), we do not need to manipulate the graph to distort the impression it creates. Modifying the verbal description that accompanies the graph can change the interpretation that will be made by the viewer. Figure 2.36 (page 104) provides a good illustration of this ploy.

We have presented only a few of the ways that graphs can be used to convey misleading pictures of business phenomena. However, the lesson is clear. Examine all graphical descriptions of data with care. In particular, check the axes and the size of the units on each axis. Ignore visual changes and concentrate on the actual numerical changes indicated by the graph or chart.

FIGURE 2.36 ▶

Changing the verbal description to change a viewer's interpretation. Source: Reprinted by permission of the publisher, from "Grappling with Graphics," by Gene Selazny, *Management Review*, Oct. 1975, p. 7. © 1975 American Management Association, New York. All rights reserved.

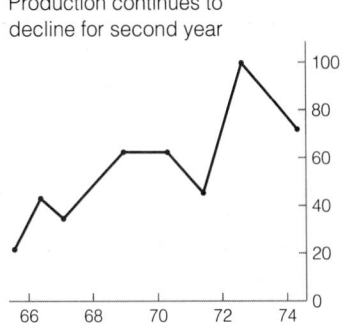

Production continues to decline for second year

For our production, we need not even change the chart, so we can't be accused of fudging the data. Here we'll simply change the title so that for the Senate subcommittee, we'll indicate that we're not doing as well as in the past...

1974: 3rd best year for production

whereas for the general public, we'll tell them that we're still in the prime years.

The information in a data set can also be distorted by using numerical descriptive measures, as Example 2.16 indicates.

EXAMPLE 2.16

Suppose you are considering working for a small firm that presently has a senior member and three junior members. You inquire about the salary you could expect to earn if you join the firm. Unfortunately, you receive two answers:

Answer A: The senior member tells you that an "average employee" earns $57,500.

Answer B: One of the junior members later tells you that an "average employee" earns $45,000.

Which answer can you believe? The confusion exists because the phrase "average employee" has not been clearly defined. Suppose the four salaries paid are $45,000 for each of the three junior members and $95,000 for the senior member. Thus,

$$\bar{x} = \frac{3(\$45,000) + \$95,000}{4} = \frac{\$230,000}{4} = \$57,500$$

Median = $45,000

You can now see how the two answers were obtained. The senior member reported the mean of the four salaries, and the junior member reported the median. The information you received was distorted because neither person stated which measure of central tendency was being used.

Another distortion of information in a sample occurs when *only* a measure of central tendency is reported. Both a measure of central tendency and a measure of variability are needed to obtain an accurate mental image of a data set.

Suppose you want to buy a new car and are trying to decide which of two models to purchase. Since energy and economy are both important issues, you decide to purchase model A because its EPA mileage rating is 32 miles per gallon in the city, whereas the mileage rating for model B is only 30 miles per gallon in the city.

However, you may have acted too quickly. How much variability is associated with the ratings? As an extreme example, suppose that further investigation reveals that the standard deviation for model A mileages is 5 miles per gallon, whereas that for model B is only 1 mile per gallon. If the mileages form a mound-shaped distribution, they might appear as shown in Figure 2.37. Note that the larger amount of variability associated with model A implies that more risk is involved in purchasing model A. That is, the particular car you purchase is more likely to have a mileage rating that will greatly differ from the EPA rating of 32 miles per gallon if you purchase model A, while a model B car is not likely to vary from the 30 miles per gallon rating by more than 2 miles per gallon.

FIGURE 2.37 ▶
Mileage distributions for two car models

Summary

Data may be classified as one of four types: **nominal, ordinal, interval**, and **ratio**. Nominal data simply classify the sample or population units, whereas ordinal data enable the units to be ranked. Nominal and ordinal data are often referred to collectively as **qualitative**. Interval data are numbers that enable the comparison of sample or population units by calculation of their numerical differences, whereas ratio data enable the comparison using multiples, or ratios, of the numerical values. Interval and ratio data are often referred to collectively as **quantitative**. Since we want to use sample data to make inferences about the population from which it is drawn, it is important for us to be able to describe the data. **Graphic methods** are important and useful tools for describing data sets. Our ultimate goal, however, is to use the sample to make inferences about the population. We are wary of using graphic techniques to accomplish this goal, since they do not lend themselves to a measure of the reliability for an inference. We therefore developed **numerical measures** to describe a data set.

These numerical methods for describing **quantitative** data sets can be grouped as follows:

1. Measures of central tendency
2. Measures of variability

The measures of central tendency we presented were the **mean, median**, and **mode**. The relationship between the mean and median provides information about the **skewness** of the frequency distribution. For making inferences about the population, the sample mean will usually be preferred to the other measures of central tendency. The **range, variance**, and **standard deviation** all represent numerical measures of variability. Of these, the variance and standard deviation are in most common use, especially when the ultimate objective is to make inferences about a population.

The mean and standard deviation may be used to make statements about the fraction of measurements in a given interval. For example, we know that at least 75% of the measurements in a data set lie within 2 standard deviations of the mean. If the frequency distribution of the data set is mound-shaped, approximately 95% of the measurements will lie within 2 standard deviations of the mean.

Measures of relative standing provide still another dimension on which to describe a data set. The objective of these measures is to describe the location of a specific measurement relative to the rest of the data set. By doing so, you can construct a mental image of the relative frequency distribution. **Percentiles** and **z-scores** are important examples of measures of relative standing.

The **rare event** concept of statistical inference means that if the chance that a particular sample came from a hypothesized population is very small, we can conclude either that the sample is extremely rare or that the hypothesized population is not the one from which the sample was drawn. The more unlikely it is that the sample came from the hypothesized population, the more strongly we favor the conclusion that the hypothesized population is not the true one. We need to be able to assess accurately the rarity of a sample, and this requires knowledge of probability, the subject of our next chapter.

Finally, we gave some examples that demonstrated how descriptive statistics may be used to distort the truth. You should be very critical when interpreting graphic or numerical descriptions of data sets.

Supplementary Exercises 2.85–2.122

Note: Starred (*) exercises require the use of a computer. Double-starred exercises (**) refer to optional sections in this chapter.

2.85   Classify the following data as one of four types: nominal, ordinal, interval, or ratio.
   a. The length of time it takes each of 15 telephone installers to hook up a wall phone
   b. The style of music preferred by each of 30 randomly selected radio listeners
   c. The arrival time of the 5 P.M. train from New York to Newark
   d. A sample of 100 customers in a fast-food restaurant asked to rate their hamburger on the following scale: poor, fair, good, excellent
   e. Classify each of the data sets in parts **a–d** as qualitative or quantitative.

2.86   Discuss the conditions under which the median is preferred to the mean as a measure of central tendency.

2.87   Compute $\sum_{i=1}^{n} x_i^2$, $\sum_{i=1}^{n} x_i$, and $\left(\sum_{i=1}^{n} x_i \right)^2$ for each of the following data sets:
   a. 11, 1, 2, 8, 7   **b.** 15, 15, 2, 6, 12   **c.** -1, 2, 0, -4, -8, 13   **d.** 100, 0, 0, 2

2.88   Compute s^2 and s for each of the data sets in Exercise 2.87.

**2.89   A time series plot similar to the one shown here appeared in a recent advertisement for a well-known golf magazine. One person might interpret the plot's message as the longer you subscribe to the magazine, the better golfer you should become. Another person might interpret it as indicating that if you subscribe for 3 years, your game should improve dramatically.

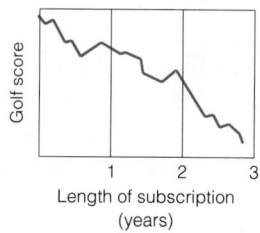

   a. Explain why the plot can be interpreted in more than one way.
   b. How could the plot be altered to rectify the current distortion?

2.90   Explain why we generally prefer the standard deviation to the range as a measure of variability for quantitative data.

2.91   Construct a relative frequency histogram for the data summarized in the accompanying table.

Measurement Class	Relative Frequency	Measurement Class	Relative Frequency
.00–.75	.02	5.25–6.00	.15
.75–1.50	.01	6.00–6.75	.12
1.50–2.25	.03	6.75–7.50	.09
2.25–3.00	.05	7.50–8.25	.05
3.00–3.75	.10	8.25–9.00	.04
3.75–4.50	.14	9.00–9.75	.01
4.50–5.25	.19		

2.92   Compute s^2 for data sets with the following characteristics:

a. $\sum_{i=1}^{n} x_i^2 = 246$, $\sum_{i=1}^{n} x_i = 63$, $n = 22$ b. $\sum_{i=1}^{n} x_i^2 = 666$, $\sum_{i=1}^{n} x_i = 106$, $n = 25$

c. $\sum_{i=1}^{n} x_i^2 = 76$, $\sum_{i=1}^{n} x_i = 11$, $n = 7$

2.93   Climatologists around the world use a 30-year mean as a standard of "normal" temperature or precipitation for a region. These data are regularly used by the tourist, transportation, and construction industries, as well as by farmers. Normals are computed every 10 years. The normals used from 1990–1999 are based on 1961–1990 National Weather Service data ("A Plain Old '30-Year Mean' Is Forecaster's Yardstick," 1990). The table contains 1961–1990 temperature data in degrees Fahrenheit for Minnesota.

Year	Mean Daily January Temperature	Year	Mean Daily January Temperature
1961	12.0	1976	11.6
1962	7.1	1977	.3
1963	2.9	1978	5.5
1964	20.0	1979	3.2
1965	10.0	1980	15.3
1966	3.3	1981	18.0
1967	14.6	1982	2.3
1968	14.3	1983	19.6
1969	9.4	1984	12.0
1970	5.6	1985	10.1
1971	6.5	1986	17.5
1972	5.5	1987	21.2
1973	17.4	1988	10.4
1974	11.9	1989	21.2
1975	14.5	1990	26.3

a. What is the "normal" Minnesota temperature for January?
b. What is the standard deviation of the 30 temperatures? What information about the temperatures is conveyed by the standard deviation?
c. According to Chebyshev's theorem, what percentage of the 30 temperatures would be expected to fall within 2 standard deviations of the normal temperature? How many actually fell in that interval?

*2.94   If it is not examined carefully, the graphical description of U.S. peanut production shown here can be misleading.

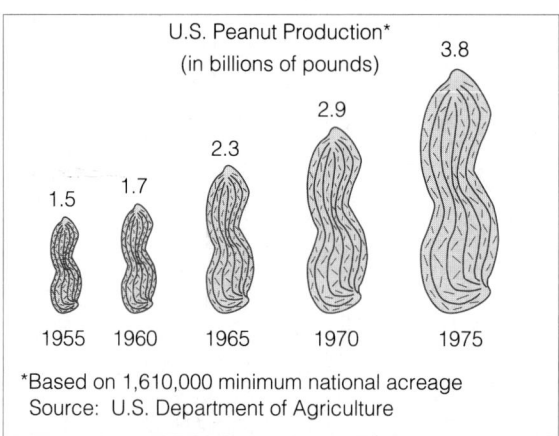

U.S. Peanut Production*
(in billions of pounds)

1.5   1.7   2.3   2.9   3.8

1955   1960   1965   1970   1975

*Based on 1,610,000 minimum national acreage
Source: U.S. Department of Agriculture

a. Explain why the graph may mislead some readers.
b. Construct an undistorted graph of U.S. peanut production for the given years.

2.95   In some locations, radiation levels in homes are measured at well above normal background levels in the environment. As a result many architects and builders are making design changes to assure adequate air exchange so that radioactive radon gas will not be trapped in homes. In one such location, 50 homes' radon levels were measured, and the mean level was 10 ppb (parts per billion), the median was 8 ppb, and the standard deviation was 3 ppb. Background levels in this location are at about 4 ppb.
a. Based on these results, is the distribution of the 50 homes' radon levels symmetric, skewed to the left, or skewed to the right? Why?
b. Use both Chebyshev's theorem and the Empirical Rule to describe the distribution of radon levels. Which do you think is most appropriate in this case? Why?
c. Use the results from part **b** to approximate the number of homes in this sample with radioactive radon gas levels above the background level.
d. Suppose another home is measured at a location 10 miles from the one sampled, and has a level of 20 ppb. What is the z-score for this measurement relative to the 50 homes sampled in the other location? Is it likely that this new measurement comes from the same distribution of levels as the other 50? Why? How would you confirm your conclusion?

2.96   As part of a study of property values in Minneapolis, the Robinson Appraisal Company sampled 79 apartment buildings and determined, among other things, each building's size, age, and condition as of January 1982. The following data are the ages (in years) of the buildings:

82	67	18	82	21	65	79	13	70	74	65	82	22	21	57	36
62	72	50	69	58	66	82	18	55	23	82	70	82	24	82	10
59	56	19	32	82	13	71	63	19	70	67	15	67	64	23	56
51	70	50	21	18	22	66	69	82	13	73	57	55	14	69	82
18	53	64	82	19	71	72	75	21	79	76	54	70	3	71	

Consider the following computer-generated stem-and-leaf display for these data:

```
Stem Leaf                            #
   8 22222222222                    11
   7 5699                            4
   7 000001112234                   12
   6 5566777999                     10
   6 2344                            4
   5 55667789                       8
   5 00134                          5
   4
   4
   3 6                              1
   3 2                              1
   2
   2 111122334                      9
   1 58888999                       8
   1 03334                          5
   0
   0 3                              1
      ----+----+----+----+
   Multiply Stem.Leaf by 10**+1
```

a. Use the display to determine the age that approximately 50% of the buildings exceed.
b. How many buildings are more than 75 years old? Less than 10 years old?

2.97 In experimenting with a new technique for imprinting paper napkins with designs, names, etc., a paper products company discovered that four different results were possible:

(A) Imprint successful

(B) Imprint smeared

(C) Imprint off-center to the left

(D) Imprint off-center to the right

To test the reliability of the technique, the company imprinted 1,000 napkins and obtained the results shown in the accompanying graph.

a. What type of graphical tool is the figure?
b. What information does the graph convey to you?
c. From the information provided by the graph, how might you numerically describe the reliability of the imprinting technique?

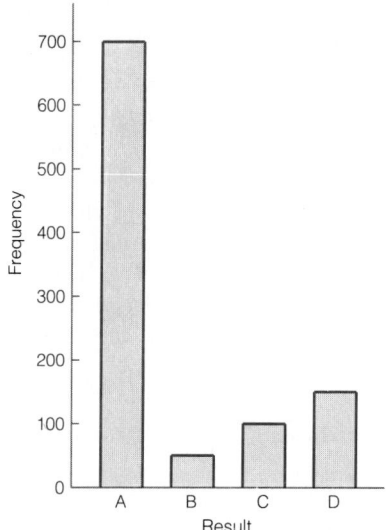

2.98 The data in the table describe the distribution of rent amounts paid by U.S. apartment dwellers in 1987. Use a relative frequency histogram to describe the data.

Rent (in Dollars)	Percentage of Renters in Rent Class
Less than 350	7%
350–399	12%
400–449	12%
450–499	15%
500–549	11%
550 or more	43%

Source: U.S. Bureau of the Census, *Statistical Abstract of the United States: 1988.*

2.99 Under what circumstances might the standard deviation be preferred to the variance as a measure of the variation in a data set?

2.100 In reference to a particular measurement, what is a measure of relative standing?

2.101 How does a z-score locate a measurement within a set of measurements? Explain.

2.102 In 1985, consumers spent an estimated average of $11,883 for a new car, compared with $5,414 in 1976 (*Minneapolis Star and Tribune*, Mar. 15, 1985). To be able to determine the 1985 average *exactly*, what information is needed?

2.103 Explain why the mode is often an unacceptable measure of central tendency for quantitative data sets.

2.104 A quality control inspector is interested in determining whether a metal lathe used to produce machine bearings is properly adjusted. He plans to do so by using 30 bearings selected randomly from the last 2,000 bearings produced by the machine to estimate the average diameter of bearings being produced. Define and explain the meanings of the following symbols *in the context of this problem*:

a. μ b. $\bar{x}$ c. σ d. s e. $\mu + 2\sigma$

2.105 A manufacturer of industrial wheels is losing many profitable orders because of the long time it takes the firm's marketing, engineering, and accounting departments to develop price quotes for potential customers. To remedy this problem the firm's management would like to set guidelines for the length of time each department should spend developing price quotes. To help develop these guidelines, 50 requests for price quotes were randomly selected from the set of all price quotes made last year; the processing time was determined for each price quote for each department. These times are displayed in the table. The price quotes are also classified by whether they were "lost" (i.e., whether or not the customer placed an order after receiving the price quote).

Price Quote Processing Times (in Days)

Request Number	Marketing	Engineering	Accounting	Lost?	Request Number	Marketing	Engineering	Accounting	Lost?
1	7.0	6.2	.1	No	26	.6	2.2	.5	No
2	.4	5.2	.1	No	27	6.0	1.8	.2	No
3	2.4	4.6	.6	No	28	5.8	.6	.5	No
4	6.2	13.0	.8	Yes	29	7.8	7.2	2.2	Yes
5	4.7	.9	.5	No	30	3.2	6.9	.1	No
6	1.3	.4	.1	No	31	11.0	1.7	3.3	No
7	7.3	6.1	.1	No	32	6.2	1.3	2.0	No
8	5.6	3.6	3.8	No	33	6.9	6.0	10.5	Yes
9	5.5	9.6	.5	No	34	5.4	.4	8.4	No
10	5.3	4.8	.8	No	35	6.0	7.9	.4	No
11	6.0	2.6	.1	No	36	4.0	1.8	18.2	Yes
12	2.6	11.3	1.0	No	37	4.5	1.3	.3	No
13	2.0	.6	.8	No	38	2.2	4.8	.4	No
14	.4	12.2	1.0	No	39	3.5	7.2	7.0	Yes
15	8.7	2.2	3.7	No	40	.1	.9	14.4	No
16	4.7	9.6	.1	No	41	2.9	7.7	5.8	No
17	6.9	12.3	.2	Yes	42	5.4	3.8	.3	No
18	.2	4.2	.3	No	43	6.7	1.3	.1	No
19	5.5	3.5	.4	No	44	2.0	6.3	9.9	Yes
20	2.9	5.3	22.0	No	45	.1	12.0	3.2	No
21	5.9	7.3	1.7	No	46	6.4	1.3	6.2	No
22	6.2	4.4	.1	No	47	4.0	2.4	13.5	Yes
23	4.1	2.1	30.0	Yes	48	10.0	5.3	.1	No
24	5.8	.6	.1	No	49	8.0	14.4	1.9	Yes
25	5.0	3.1	2.3	No	50	7.0	10.0	2.0	No

a. Stem-and-leaf displays for each of the departments and for the total processing time were produced using Minitab. Note that very high processing times that are "disconnected" from the other times are shown in a list under the heading of "HI" at the bottom of the display. Also, note that the units of the leaves for the total processing time are units (1.0), while the leaf units for each of the three components are tenths (.1). Shade the leaves that correspond to "lost" orders in each of the displays, and interpret each of the displays.

```
Stem-and-leaf of Mkt          Stem-and-leaf of Engr
Leaf Unit = 0.10             Leaf Unit = 0.10

    6      0  112446              7      0  4466699
    7      1  3                  14      1  3333788
   14      2  0024699            19      2  12246
   16      3  25                 23      3  1568
   22      4  001577            (5)      4  24688
  (10)     5  0344556889         22      5  233
   18      6  0002224799         19      6  01239
    8      7  0038               14      7  22379
    4      8  07                  9      8
    2      9                      9      9  66
    2     10  0                   7     10  0
    1     11  0                   6     11  3
                                  5     12  023
                                  2     13  0
                                  1     14  4
```

```
Stem-and-leaf of Accnt                Stem-and-leaf of Total
Leaf Unit = 0.10                     Leaf Unit = 1.0

   19      0  1111111111122333444      1      0  1
   (8)     0  55556888                 3      0  33
   23      1  00                        5      0  45
   21      1  79                       11      0  666677
   19      2  0023                      17      0  888999
   15      2                            21      1  0000
   15      3  23                       (5)      1  33333
   13      3  78                        24      1  4444445555
   11      4                            14      1  6677
   11      4                            10      1  8999
   11      5                             6      2  0
   11      5  8                          5      2  3
   10      6  2                          4      2  44
    9      6
    9      7  0                               HI   30, 36
    8      7
    8      8  4

   HI     99, 105, 135, 144,
          182, 220, 300
```

b. Using your results from part **a**, develop "maximum processing time" guidelines for each department that, if followed, will help the firm reduce the number of lost orders.

2.106 Refer to Exercise 2.105. The means and standard deviations for the processing times are given here.

	Marketing	Engineering	Accounting	Total
$\bar{x}$	4.77	5.04	3.65	13.46
s	2.58	3.84	6.26	6.82

a. Calculate the z-score corresponding to the maximum processing time guideline you developed in Exercise 2.105 for each department, and for the total processing time.

    b. Calculate the maximum processing time corresponding to a z-score of 3 for each of the departments. What percentage of the orders exceed these guidelines? How does this agree with Chebyshev's theorem and the Empirical Rule?

    c. Repeat part **b** using a z-score of 2.

    d. Compare the percentage of "lost" quotes with corresponding times that exceed at least one of the guidelines in part **b** to the same percentage using the guidelines in part **c**. Which set of guidelines would you recommend be adopted? Why?

2.107   What is Pareto analysis?

2.108   A company has roughly the same number of people in each of five departments: Production, Sales, R&D, Maintenance, and Administration. The following table lists the number and type of major injuries that occurred in each department last year.

Type of Injury	Department	Number of Injuries	Type of Injury	Department	Number of Injuries
Burn	Production	3	Cuts	Production	4
	Maintenance	6		Sales	1
Back strain	Production	2		R&D	1
	Sales	1		Maintenance	10
	R&D	1	Broken arm	Production	2
	Maintenance	5		Maintenance	2
	Administration	2	Broken leg	Sales	1
Eye damage	Production	1		Maintenance	1
	Maintenance	2	Broken finger	Administration	1
	Administration	1	Concussion	Maintenance	3
Deafness	Production	1		Administration	1
			Hearing loss	Maintenance	2

    a. Construct a Pareto diagram to identify which department or departments have the worst safety record.

    b. Explode the Pareto diagram of part **a** to identify the most prevalent type of injury in the department with the worst safety record.

2.109   One hundred management trainees were given an examination in basic accounting. Their test scores were found to have a mean and variance of 75 and 36, respectively.

    a. Make a statement about the percentage of the test scores that would be expected to fall between 69 and 81.

    b. If a grade of 63 was required to pass the test, make a statement about the percentage of the trainees who would be expected to fail.

2.110   Redo Exercise 2.109 assuming that the distribution of test scores was determined to be mound-shaped.

2.111   A national chain of automobile oil-change franchises claims that "your hood will be open for less than 12 minutes when we service your car." To check their claim, an undercover consumer reporter from a local television station monitored the "hood time" of 25 consecutive customers at one of the chain's franchises. The resulting data follow. Construct a time series plot for these data and describe in words what it reveals.

Customer Number	Hood Open (Minutes)	Customer Number	Hood Open (Minutes)
1	11.50	14	12.50
2	13.50	15	13.75
3	12.25	16	12.00
4	15.00	17	11.50
5	14.50	18	14.25
6	13.75	19	15.50
7	14.00	20	13.00
8	11.00	21	18.25
9	12.75	22	11.75
10	11.50	23	12.50
11	11.00	24	11.25
12	13.00	25	14.75
13	16.25		

2.112 The vice president in charge of sales for the conglomerate you work for has asked you to evaluate the sales records of two of the firm's divisions. You note that the range of monthly sales for division A over the last 2 years is $50,000 and the range for division B is only $30,000. You compute each division's mean monthly sales for the same time period and discover that both divisions have a mean of $110,000. Assume that is all the information you have about the division's sales records. Would you be willing to say which of the divisions has a more consistent sales record? Why or why not?

2.113 Refer to Exercise 2.112.
   a. Estimate the standard deviation of the monthly sales distribution of division B.
   b. Based on your estimate in part **a**, would you say it is more likely that division B's sales next month will be over $120,000 or under $90,000?
   c. Is it possible for division B's sales next month to be over $160,000? Explain.

2.114 The Age Discrimination in Employment Act mandates that workers 40 years of age or older be treated without regard to age in all phases of employment (hiring, promotions, firing, etc.). Age discrimination cases are of two types: *disparate treatment* and *disparate impact*. In the former, the issue is whether workers have been intentionally discriminated against. In the latter, the issue is whether employment practices adversely affect the protected class (i.e., workers 40 and over) even though no such effect was intended by the employer (Zabell, 1989). During the recession of the early 1990s, a small computer manufacturer laid off 10 of its 20 software engineers. The ages of all the engineers at the time of the lay-off are shown in the table.

Not Laid off:	34	55	42	38	42	32	40	40	46	29
Laid off:	52	35	40	41	40	39	40	64	47	44

   a. Find the standard deviation of the 20 ages. Describe how the standard deviation can be used to characterize the set of ages.
   b. If a software engineer were selected at random from these 20 to be laid off, what is the probability that the engineer would be 40 or older? [*Note:* We will formally define "probability" in the next chapter.]
   c. Find the median age of all 20 engineers and the median age of the 10 who were not laid off.
   d. Given your answers to parts **b** and **c** (and any other evidence you care to use), does it appear that the company may be vulnerable to a disparate impact claim? Explain.

2.115 Suppose you used the following formula as a measure of the variability (V) of a data set:

$$V = \frac{\sum_{i=1}^{n} (x_i - \bar{x})}{n}$$

What information can be learned about the variability of a data set using this formula? Using the data in part **a** of Exercise 2.87, find V.

2.116 Many firms use on-the-job training to teach their employees computer programming. Suppose you work in the personnel department of a firm that just finished training a group of its employees to program, and you have been requested to review the performance of one of the trainees on the final test that was given to all trainees. The mean and standard deviation of the test scores are 80 and 5, respectively, and the distribution of scores is mound-shaped.

a. The employee in question scored 65 on the final test. Compute the employee's z-score.

b. Approximately what percentage of the trainees will have z-scores equal to or less than the employee of part **a**?

c. If a trainee were randomly selected from those who had taken the final test, is it more likely that he or she would score 90 or above, or 65 or below?

*2.117 A company that bags and sells wild rice has received numerous complaints from its customers about underfilled bags. Most complaints concern their 5-pound bag. The operations manager suspects that the problem may be due to differences between fill-machine operators. To investigate her suspicion, the manager weighed the last 10 bags filled by machine operator 1 before operator 2 took over at 3:00 P.M. She also weighed the first 10 bags produced by operator 2. The data follow.

Bag Number	Operator Number	Bag Weight (Pounds)	Bag Number	Operator Number	Bag Weight (Pounds)
1	1	5.00	11	2	5.35
2	1	5.10	12	2	4.70
3	1	4.90	13	2	5.05
4	1	5.05	14	2	5.30
5	1	5.05	15	2	4.50
6	1	4.95	16	2	5.40
7	1	5.00	17	2	5.20
8	1	4.90	18	2	5.00
9	1	5.10	19	2	5.20
10	1	5.00	20	2	4.60

a. Construct a time series plot for these data.

b. What do these data reveal about differences in the performances of the two operators?

c. Could such differences account for the customer complaints? Explain.

d. Describe any other filling problems revealed by the plot.

e. Suggest a better plan for selecting the bags to be weighed.

2.118 The advertising expenditures (in thousands of dollars) by media for a recent year are described for the 16 top-selling brandies and cordials by the following Minitab-generated box plots.

MAGAZINES

BILLBOARDS

NEWSPAPERS

a. For which medium are median expenditures the highest?
b. For which medium is the range of expenditures the largest? The smallest?
c. For which medium is the interquartile range the largest? The smallest?
d. Describe the shape of each data set's frequency distribution.
e. Do any of the media receive advertising expenditures from all 16 brands of brandies and cordials? Explain.

2.119   Economic theory suggests that the vigor of competition in an industry is related to the number of firms in the industry. As a measure of competitiveness, however, the number of firms in an industry does not take into consideration the extent to which a few firms may dominate that industry. For example, in an industry with 100 firms, each may produce 1% of industry output, or three firms may dominate, producing 75% compared to the other 97 firms' 25%. The *market concentration ratio* is a measure of competitiveness that reflects such inequalities among firms in an industry. The market concentration ratio is usually defined as the percentage of total industry sales contributed by the largest few firms (usually three or four). A high concentration ratio indicates an industry dominated by a few firms. A low concentration ratio indicates an industry with much competition among many firms. The table on page 118 contains 1970 three-firm market concentration ratios for 12 industries in each of six different countries. Answer the following questions using the methods from this chapter that you deem appropriate.

Industry	United States	Canada	United Kingdom	Sweden	France	West Germany
Brewing	39	89	47	70	63	17
Cigarettes	68	90	94	100	100	94
Fabric weaving	30	67	28	50	23	16
Paints	26	40	40	92	14	32
Petroleum refining	25	64	79	100	60	47
Shoes (except rubber)	17	18	17	37	13	20
Glass bottles	65	100	73	100	84	93
Cement	20	65	86	100	81	54
Ordinary steel	42	80	39	63	84	56
Antifriction bearings	43	89	82	100	80	90
Refrigerators	64	75	65	89	100	72
Storage batteries	54	73	75	100	94	82

Source: F. M. Scherer, Alan Beckenstein, Erich Kaufer, and R. D. Murphy. *The Economics of Multiplant Operation: An International Comparisons Study* (Cambridge, Mass.: Harvard University Press, 1975). Reprinted by permission.

a. For each of the six countries, characterize the magnitude and variability of the sample of 12 market concentration ratios.

b. For each of the 12 industries, characterize the magnitude and variability of the sample of six market concentration ratios.

c. Which nation has on average the most competition within its industries? The least competition?

d. Which are the three most competitive industries? The three least competitive industries?

2.120 The **pie chart** is an alternative graphic technique for describing qualitative data sets. Each category of the data set is assigned one slice of the pie, the size of which is proportional to the relative frequency of the category. The sequence of pie charts on page 119 portrays the evolution of the structure of the top 500 firms in the United States and the top 200 firms in the United Kingdom over the period 1950–1980. Describe the trends that are revealed by these pie charts.

*2.121 *Consumer Reports* is a magazine that contains ratings and reports for consumers on goods, services, health, and personal finances. It is published by Consumers Union, a nonprofit organization established in 1936. Consumers Union reported on the testing of 46 brands of toothpaste ("A Guide to Good Dental Care," 1992). Each was rated on: package design, flavor, cleaning ability, fluoride content, and cost per month (a cost estimate based on brushing with ½ inch of toothpaste twice daily). The accompanying data are the costs per month for the 46 brands. Costs marked by an asterisk represent those brands that carry the American Dental Association (ADA) seal verifying effective decay prevention.

.58	.66	1.02	1.11	1.77	1.40	.73*	.53*	.57*	1.34
1.29	.89*	.49	.53*	.52	3.90	4.73	1.26	.71*	.55*
.59*	.97	.44*	.74*	.51*	.68*	.67	1.22	.39	.55
.62	.66*	1.07	.64	1.32*	1.77*	.80*	.79	.89*	.64
.81*	.79*	.44*	1.09	1.04	1.12				

a. Use a statistical software package to construct a stem-and-leaf display for the data.

b. Circle the individual leaves that represent those brands that carry the ADA seal.

c. What does the pattern of circles suggest about the costs of those brands approved by the ADA?

Growth of Diversification of Large Companies

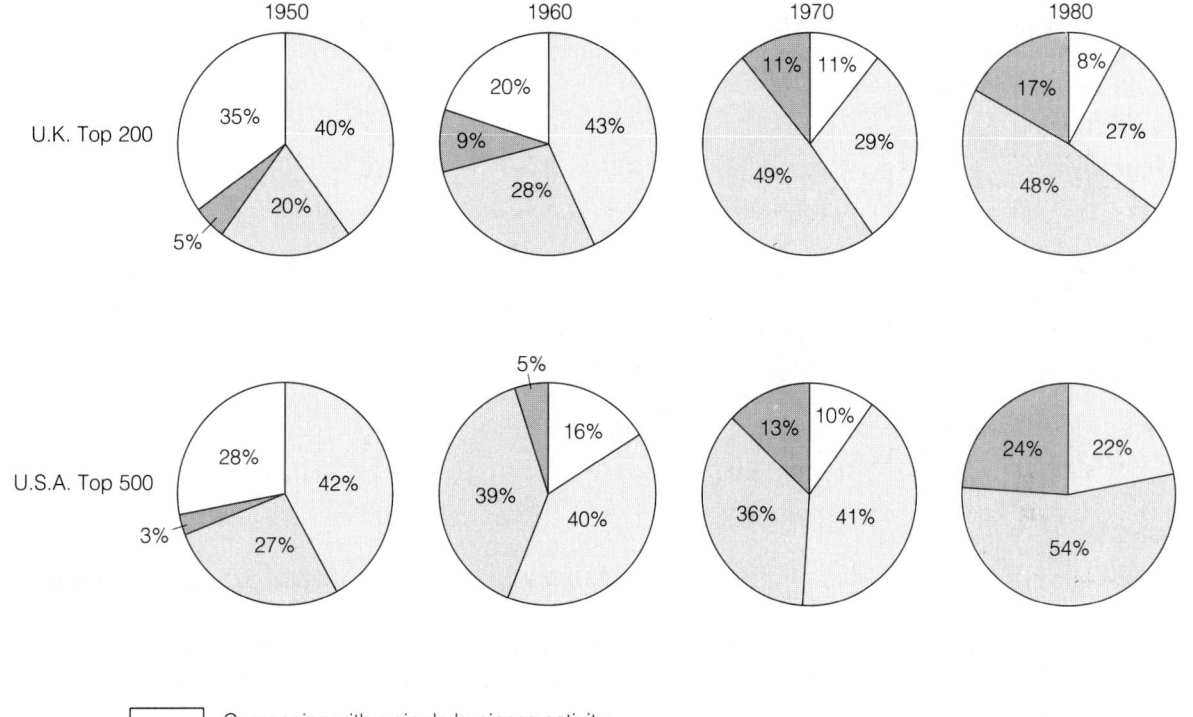

Source: Adapted from *Long Range Planning*. Vol 19, No 1, 1986, pp. 52-60. Reprinted with permission. Copyright 1986, Pergamon Press, Ltd.

▲ **Pie charts for Exercise 2.120**

*2.122   Newly manufactured tires are rated for traction, heat, and tread wear according to the Uniform Tire Quality Grading System. Traction is rated using an A-B-C system to indicate the tire's braking performance on wet pavement. The tire's ability to dissipate heat is also measured using an A-B-C scale (with A representing the highest rating for both traction and heat). "Tread wear is graded on a number system with the rating for any particular tire expressed as a comparison of that tire with a tire rated at 100. Thus, if the tire tested wore twice as long as the baseline tire, it would carry a rating of 200" (Brand, 1991). Forty new tires, all of the same type and manufactured by the same company, were tested and each tire's tread-wear life in months was recorded. The data are listed below.

48	46	45	48	51	53	49	46	48	47
50	49	43	52	52	50	43	44	43	52
44	47	51	52	45	49	48	43	53	50
53	51	44	43	45	47	53	44	46	53

    a. If a tire with a tread-wear rating of 100 lasts 48 months, compute the tread-wear ratings of each of the 40 tires tested. Round the ratings to the nearest whole number.

    b. Use a statistical software package to construct a histogram for these 40 ratings.

    c. Based on the shape of the histogram, is there reason for concern about the quality of the manufacturing process that is producing these particular tires? Explain.

On Your Own

A number of sources of business data are listed on the following page. Use these and any others you or your instructor can find to select two real business-oriented data sets, one qualitative and one quantitative. Describe both data sets using the graphic and numerical descriptive tools introduced in this chapter. Count the number of observations in your quantitative data set within 1, 2, and 3 standard deviations of the mean of the data and compare the counts with those you would expect using either Chebyshev's theorem or the Empirical Rule.

    Be sure to select data of interest to you, since we will be referring to these data sets in **On Your Own** sections of later chapters.

Suggested Secondary Data Sources*

Annual Reports to Shareholders.

Board of Governors of the Federal Reserve System. *Federal Reserve Bulletin* (monthly).

Business Week (magazine).

Dun & Bradstreet's *Million Dollar Directory* (yearly).

Economic Indicators. Council of Economic Advisors.

Forbes (magazine).

Fortune (magazine).

Handbook of Basic Economic Statistics. Economic Statistics Bureau of Washington, D.C.

Moody's Manuals (set of 8).

Simmons Study of Media and Markets. Simmons Market Research Bureau, Inc.

Sourcebook of Zip Code Demographics.

State Demographics: Population Profiles of the 50 States. Dow Jones-Irwin.

Survey of Buying Power Demographics USA.

Thomas Register of America Manufacturers.

U.S. Bureau of the Census. *Census of Manufacturers* (every 5 years).

U.S. Bureau of the Census. *County Census Patterns* (yearly).

U.S. Bureau of the Census. *Statistical Abstract of the United States* (yearly).

U.S. Department of Commerce, Office of Business Economics, *Business Statistics.*

U.S. Bureau of Commerce, Office of Business Economics. *Survey of Current Business* (monthly).

U.S. Department of Health and Human Services. *Vital Statistics of the United States.*

U.S. Department of Labor. *Monthly Labor Review.*

U.S. Department of Labor, Bureau of Labor Statistics. *Employment and Earnings.*

U.S. Department of Labor, Bureau of Labor Statistics. *National Survey of Professional Administrative, Technical, and Clerical Pay.*

Value Line Investment Survey, Value Line, Inc.

Wall Street Journal (daily).

Your state's statistical abstract.

---

*Primary data are data you (or someone in your organization) collect for the study at hand. *Secondary data* are data collected by someone outside the organization for purposes other than the study at hand.

    Many of these sources and guides are now available on computer media, including CD-ROMs and online data services.

Guides to Finding Secondary Data*

American Statistical Index: A Comprehensive Guide to the Statistical Publications of the United States Government.

Business Periodical Index.

Business Rankings and Salaries Index. Detroit: Gale Research Co.

Encyclopedia of Business Information Sources. Detroit: Gale Research Co.

Federal Statistical Directory: The Guide to Personnel and Data Sources.

Guide to Bureau of Economic Analysis.

Guide to Special Issues and Indexes of Periodicals.

Houser and Leonard. *Government Statistics for Business Use.*

New York Times Index.

Predicasts F&S Indexes.

Sourcebook of Global Statistics.

Statistical Reference Index: A Selective Guide to American Statistical Publications from Sources Other Than the U.S. Government. Congressional Information Services, Inc.

Statistics Sources, edited by Paul Wasserman. Detroit: Gale Research Co.

U.S. Bureau of the Census. *Directory of Non-federal Statistics for States and Local Areas.*

Wall Street Journal Index.

Your local Chamber of Commerce.

Using the Computer

We have supplied a set of data in Appendix C (also available on diskette from the publisher) that will be used as a source for the **Using the Computer** exercises at the end of most chapters. A complete description of the data can be found in Appendix C. Briefly, the data set includes such variables as population size, number of households, average household size, average income, percentage of college graduates, percentage of women in the work force, and purchasing-potential indexes for groceries, sporting goods, and home improvements for each of 1,000 U.S. zip codes.

a. Consider the percentage of women in the work force. Use a statistical software package to generate a stem-and-leaf display and a relative frequency histogram for these 1,000 percentages. Compare the graphical descriptions you obtain, and discuss what each reveals about the distribution of the percentage of women in the work force in the sample of 1,000 zip codes.

b. Repeat part **a** for one of the census regions, perhaps the one in which you currently reside. Compare the regional distribution to the national distribution you obtained in part **a**.

c. Finally, repeat part **a** for the zip codes corresponding to one state, perhaps the one in which you currently reside. Compare the state distribution to the national and regional distributions of parts **a** and **b**.

d. Now compute the mean and standard deviation of the same data set over the 1,000 zip codes and over the zip codes in the region you selected. Use the computer to count the number of zip codes' percentages within the intervals $\bar{x} \pm s$, $\bar{x} \pm 2s$, and $\bar{x} \pm 3s$. Compare the results with those given by Chebyshev's theorem and the Empirical Rule (Table 2.10).

---

*Primary data are data you (or someone in your organization) collect for the study at hand. *Secondary data* are data collected by someone outside the organization for purposes other than the study at hand.

Many of these sources and guides are now available on computer media, including CD-ROMs and online data services.

References

Adler, Paul S. and Clark, Kim B. "Behind the learning curve: A sketch of the learning process." *Management Science*, Mar. 1991, p. 267.

"A guide to good dental care." *Consumer Reports*, Consumers Union, Sept. 1992, p. 601.

"A plain old '30-year mean' is forecaster's yardstick." *Star Tribune* (Minneapolis). Sept. 2, 1990.

Brand, Paul. "Tire's initial grade loses importance as tread depth starts to wear down." *Star Tribune* (Minneapolis). Sept. 22, 1991.

Chase, R. B. and Aquilano, N. J. *Production and Operations Management*, rev. ed. Homewood, Ill.: Richard D. Irwin, 1977.

Davidson, S., Stickney, C. P., and Weil, R. L. *Financial Accounting*, 2d ed. Chicago: Dryden Press, 1979.

Deming, W. E. *Out of the Crisis*. Cambridge, Mass. M.I.T. Center for Advanced Engineering Study, 1986.

Dixon, W. J., Brown, M. B., Engelman, L., Frane, J. W., Hill, M. A., Jennrich, R. I., and Toporek, J. D. *BMDP Statistical Software*. Berkeley: University of California Press, 1983.

Dodd, P. "Merger proposals, management discretion, and stockholder wealth." *Journal of Financial Economics*, 1980, 8, pp. 105–137.

Eger, C. E. "Corporate mergers: An empirical analysis of the role of risky debt." Unpublished Ph.D. dissertation. School of Management, University of Minnesota, 1982.

Fogarty, D. W., Blackstone, J. H., Jr., and Hoffmann, T. R. *Production and Inventory Management*. Cincinnati, Ohio: South-Western, 1991.

"The *Fortune* 500." *Fortune*, Apr. 23, 1990, pp. 337–396.

Gitlow, H., Gitlow, S., Oppenheim, A., and Oppenheim, R. *Tools and Methods for the Improvement of Quality*. Homewood, Ill.: Irwin, 1989.

How the Bond Market Works. The New York Institute of Finance. New York: 1988.

Huff, D. *How to Lie with Statistics*. New York: Norton, 1954.

Ishikawa, K. *Guide to Quality Control*, 2d ed. White Plains, N.Y.: Kraus International Publications, 1982.

Juran, J. M. *Juran on Planning for Quality*. New York: The Free Press, 1988.

Kane, V. E. *Defect Prevention*. New York: Marcel Dekker, Inc., 1989.

"Keeping up." *Fortune*, Aug. 13, 1979, p. 100.

McCullough, B. "Should you be a coupon clipper?" *Minneapolis Star and Tribune*, Mar. 17, 1986.

Mendenhall, W. *Introduction to Probability and Statistics*, 8th ed. Boston: Duxbury, 1991. Chapter 3.

Milkovich, G. T., Annoni, A. J., and Mahoney, T. A. "The use of the delphi procedures in manpower forecasting." *Management Science*, Dec. 1972, 19, part 1, pp. 381–388.

Minitab Reference Manual, Release 8. Minitab, Inc., State College, Penn., 1991.

Namias, J. "A method to detect specific causes of consumer complaints." *Journal of Marketing Research*, Aug. 1964, pp. 63–68.

Neter, J., Wasserman, W., and Whitmore, G. A. *Applied Statistics*, 2d ed. Boston: Allyn & Bacon, 1982. Chapter 3.

Nie, N., Hull, C. H., Jenkins, J. G., Steinbrenner, K., and Bent, D. H. *Statistical Package for the Social Sciences*, 2nd ed. New York: McGraw-Hill, 1975.

Postlewaite, S. "Salad bars sprout as fast-food battle turns from the burger." *Minneapolis Tribune*, July 3, 1983.

Roberts, Jonathan. "Microsoft speaks: Windows Version 3.1 succeeds by listening to users." *Cue News*. Egghead Software, June 1992, p. 3.

Rothstein, M. "Hotel overbooking as a Markovian sequential decision process." *Decision Sciences*, July 1974, 5, pp. 389–405.

SAS User's Guide: Statistics, Version 5 ed. SAS Institute, Inc., Cary, N.C., 1985.

Schroeder, R. G. *Operations Management*, 4th ed. New York: McGraw-Hill, 1993.

Selazny, G. "Grappling with graphics." *Management Review*, Oct. 1975, p. 7.

Spiro, H. T. *Finance for the Nonfinancial Manager*. New York: Wiley, 1982. Chapter 17.

Sterling, R. R. and Radosevich, R. "A valuation experiment." *Journal of Accounting Research*, Spring 1969, pp. 90–95.

Willett, R. P. and Pennington, A. L. "Customer and salesman: The anatomy of choice and influence in a retail setting." *Science, Technology and Marketing*, Proceedings of the 1966 Fall Conference of the American Marketing Association, Raymond M. Haas (ed.), 1966, pp. 598–616.

U.S. Department of Labor. *The Consumer Price Index: Concepts and Content over the Years*. Bureau of Labor Statistics, Report 517, May 1978.

Zabell, S. L. "Statistical proof of employment discrimination." *Statistics: A Guide to the Unknown*, 3d ed. Pacific Grove, Calif.: Wadsworth, 1989.

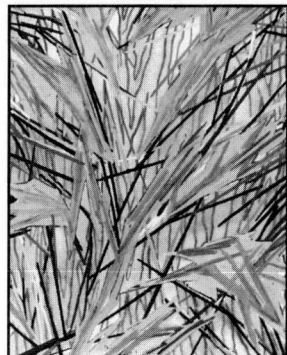

CHAPTER THREE
Probability

Contents

Case Studies

Where We've Been

In Chapter 1, we identified inference from a sample to a population as one of the major goals of statistics. In Chapter 2, we learned how to describe a set of measurements using graphical and numerical descriptive methods.

Where We're Going

We now begin to consider the problem of making an inference. What permits us to make the inferential jump from sample to population and then to give a measure of reliability for the inference? As you will see, the answer is *probability*. This chapter is devoted to probability—what it is and some of the basic concepts of the theory that surrounds it.

You will recall that statistics is concerned with inferences about a population based on sample information. Understanding how this will be accomplished is easier if you understand the relationship between population and sample. This understanding is enhanced by reversing the statistical procedure of making inferences from sample to population. In this chapter we assume the population *known* and calculate the chances of obtaining various samples from the population. Thus, probability is the "reverse" of statistics: In probability we use the population information to infer the probable nature of the sample.

Probability plays an important role in inference-making. To illustrate, suppose you have an opportunity to invest in an oil exploration company. Past records show that for ten out of ten previous oil drillings (a sample of the company's experiences), all ten resulted in dry wells. What do you conclude? Do you think the chances are better than 50–50 that the company will hit a producing well? Should you invest in this company? We think your answer to these questions will be an emphatic no. If the company's exploratory prowess is sufficient to hit a producing well 50% of the time, a record of ten dry wells out of ten drilled is an event that is just too *improbable*. Do you agree?

As another illustration, suppose you are playing poker with what your opponents assure you is a well-shuffled deck of cards. In three consecutive five-card hands, the person on your right is dealt four aces. Based on this sample of three deals, do you think the cards are being adequately shuffled? Again, we think your answer will be no and that you will reach this conclusion because dealing three hands of four aces is just too improbable, assuming that the cards were properly shuffled.

Note that the conclusion concerning the potential success of the oil drilling company and the conclusion concerning the card shuffling were both based on probabilities—namely, the probabilities of certain sample results. Both situations were contrived so you could easily conclude that the probabilities of the sample results were small. Unfortunately, the probabilities of many observed sample results are not so easy to evaluate. For these cases, we will need the assistance of a theory of probability.

3.1 Events, Sample Spaces, and Probability

Most sets of data that are of interest to the business community are generated by some **experiment**.

> ### Definition 3.1
> An **experiment** is an act or process that leads to a single outcome that cannot be predicted with certainty.

Our definition of *experiment* is broader than that used in the physical sciences, where we might picture test tubes, microscopes, and other equipment. Examples of statistical experiments in business are recording whether a customer prefers one of two brands of coffee (say, brand A or brand B), measuring the change in the Dow Jones Industrial Average from one day to the next, recording the weekly sales of a business firm, and counting the number of errors on a page of an accountant's ledger.

A "single outcome" of an experiment is called a **simple event**.

Definition 3.2

A **simple event** is an outcome of an experiment that cannot be decomposed into a simpler outcome.

In Table 3.1 we present three examples of experiments and their simple events. We begin with simple coin and dice examples because they are most likely to be familiar to you. Experiment **a** in Table 3.1 is to toss a coin and observe the up face. You will undoubtedly agree that the most basic possible outcomes of this experiment are Observe a head and Observe a tail. Experiment **b** in Table 3.1 is to toss a die and observe the up face. Notice that the simple events Observe a 1, Observe a 2, etc., cannot be decomposed into simpler outcomes. However, the outcome Observe an even number can be decomposed into Observe a 2, Observe a 4, and Observe a 6. Thus, Observe an even number is not a simple event. The reasoning is similar for experiment **c** in Table 3.1.

TABLE 3.1   Experiments and Their Simple Events

a. Experiment: Toss a coin and observe the up face.
Simple events: 1. Observe a head
2. Observe a tail

b. Experiment: Toss a die and observe the up face.
Simple events: 1. Observe a 1
2. Observe a 2
3. Observe a 3
4. Observe a 4
5. Observe a 5
6. Observe a 6

c. Experiment: Toss two coins and observe the up faces.
Simple events: 1. Observe H_1, H_2
2. Observe H_1, T_2
3. Observe T_1, H_2
4. Observe T_1, T_2
(where H_1 means head on coin 1, H_2 means head on coin 2, etc.)

Outcomes such as Observe an even number, which can be decomposed into simpler outcomes (Observe a 2, Observe a 4, Observe a 6), are called **events**.

> ### Definition 3.3
>
> An **event** is a collection of one or more simple events.

Thus, in experiment **b** of Table 3.1, three examples of events are Observe an even number, Observe a number less than 4, and Observe a 6. Note that the last event, Observe a 6, cannot be decomposed into a simpler outcome and so is also a simple event. If the experiment is counting the number of errors on a page of an accountant's ledger, three examples of events are Observe no errors, Observe fewer than five errors, and Observe more than ten errors. Only the first, Observe no errors, is also a simple event. Our goal is to be able to calculate the probability that a particular event will occur when an experiment is performed.

The first step in achieving this goal is to note that simple events have an important property. If the experiment is conducted once, you will observe one and only one simple event. For example, if the experiment is to toss a coin and observe the up face, you cannot Observe a tail and Observe a head on the same toss. Or, if you toss a die and Observe a 2, you cannot Observe a 6 on the same toss. That is, for a single performance of an experiment, one and only one of the simple events will occur. To see that this property does not hold for all events, consider the event Observe an even number. It is possible to Observe an even number and Observe a 2 on the same toss of a die.

The collection of all the simple events of an experiment is called the **sample space**.

> ### Definition 3.4
>
> The **sample space** of an experiment is the collection of all its simple events.

For example, there are six simple events associated with experiment **b** in Table 3.1. These six simple events comprise the sample space for the experiment. Similarly, for experiment **c** in Table 3.1, there are four simple events in the sample space.

A graphical method called a **Venn diagram** is useful for presenting a sample space and its simple events. The sample space is shown as a closed figure, labeled S. This figure contains a set of points, called **sample points**, with each point representing a simple event. Figure 3.1 shows the Venn diagram for each of the three experiments in Table 3.1. Note that the number of sample points in a sample space S is equal to the number of simple events associated with the respective experiment: two for experiment **a**, six for experiment **b**, and four for experiment **c**.

Now that we have defined the terms *simple event* and *sample space*, we are prepared to define the **probabilities of simple events**. The probability of a simple event is a number that indicates the likelihood that the event will occur when the experiment is performed. This number is usually taken to be the relative frequency of the occur-

a. Experiment: Observe the up face on a coin

b. Experiment: Observe the up face on a die

c. Experiment: Observe the up faces on two coins

FIGURE 3.1 ▲

Venn diagrams for the three experiments from Table 3.1

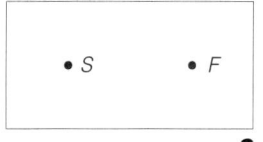

FIGURE 3.2 ▲
Experiment: Invest in a business venture and observe whether it succeeds (*S*) or fails (*F*)

rence of a simple event in a very long series of repetitions of the experiment. Or, when this information is not available, we select the number based on experience. For example, if we are assigning probabilities to the two simple events in the coin-toss experiment (Observe a head and Observe a tail), we might reason that if we toss a balanced coin a very large number of times, the simple events Observe a head and Observe a tail will occur with the same relative frequency of .5. Thus, the probability of each simple event is .5.

For some experiments we may assign probabilities to the simple events based on general information about the experiment. For example, if the experiment is to invest in a business venture and to observe whether it succeeds or fails, the sample space would appear as in Figure 3.2.

We are unlikely to be able to assign probabilities to the simple events of this experiment based on a long series of repetitions, since unique factors govern each performance of this kind of experiment. Instead, we may consider factors such as the personnel managing the venture, the general state of the economy at the time, the rate of success of similar ventures, and any other information deemed pertinent. If we finally decide that the venture has an 80% chance of succeeding, we assign a probability of .8 to the simple event Success. This probability can be interpreted as a measure of our degree of belief in the outcome of the business venture.

Such subjective probabilities should be based on expert information and must be carefully assessed. Otherwise, we run the risk of being misled by uninformed and/or biased probability statements. That is, we may be misled on any decisions based on these probabilities or based on any calculations in which they appear.*

No matter how you assign the probabilities to simple events, the probabilities assigned must obey two rules:

1. All simple event probabilities must lie between 0 and 1, inclusive.
2. The probabilities of all the simple events in the sample space must sum to 1.

Recall that an event is a collection of one or more simple events. Let us examine this statement in greater detail. Consider the die-tossing experiment and the event Observe an even number. This event will occur if and only if one of the three simple events, Observe a 2, Observe a 4, or Observe a 6, occurs. Consequently, you can think of the event Observe an even number as the collection of the three simple events, Observe a 2, Observe a 4, and Observe a 6. This event, which we will denote by the symbol A, can be represented in a Venn diagram by a closed figure inside the sample space S. The closed figure A will contain the simple events that constitute event A, as shown in Figure 3.3.

How do you decide which simple events belong to the set associated with an event A? Test each simple event in the sample space S. If event A occurs when a particular simple event occurs, then that simple event is in the event A. For example, in the die-toss experiment, the event Observe an even number (event A) will occur if the

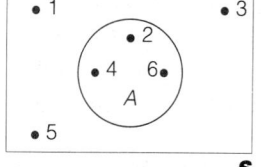

FIGURE 3.3 ▲
Die-toss experiment with event *A*: Observe an even number

*For a text that deals in detail with subjective probabilities, see Winkler (1972) or Lindley (1985).

Bloom County Probabilities

The issue of whether probability should be defined as the relative frequency in a long series of repetitions of an experiment or as a subjective measure of belief is one that has been debated for many years by probabilists, statisticians, and even philosophers. A considerably lighter side of this debate is illustrated in the accompanying Bloom County comic strip.

© 1986, Washington Post Writers Group, reprinted with permission.

simple event Observe a 2 occurs. By the same reasoning, the simple events Observe a 4 and Observe a 6 are in event A.

Now return to our original objective—finding the probability of an event. Consider the problem of finding the probability of observing an even number (event A) in the single toss of a die. You will recall that A will occur if one of the three simple events, toss a 2, 4, or 6, occurs. Since two or more simple events cannot occur at the same time, we can easily calculate the probability of event A by summing the probabilities of the three simple events. If we assume the die is fair (i.e., balanced), then each simple event is equally likely to occur. Accordingly, we would attach a probability equal to ⅙ to each of the simple events, so the probability of observing an even number (event A), denoted by the symbol $P(A)$, would be

$$P(A) = P(\text{Observe a 2}) + P(\text{Observe a 4}) + P(\text{Observe a 6})$$
$$= \tfrac{1}{6} + \tfrac{1}{6} + \tfrac{1}{6} = \tfrac{1}{2}$$

The previous example leads us to a general procedure for finding the probability of an event A.

> The probability of an event A is calculated by summing the probabilities of the simple events in A.

Thus, we can summarize the steps for calculating the probability of any event.

> **Steps for Calculating Probabilities of Events**
>
> 1. Define the experiment.
> 2. List the simple events.
> 3. Assign probabilities to the simple events.
> 4. Determine the collection of simple events contained in the event of interest.
> 5. Sum the simple event probabilities to obtain the event probability.

EXAMPLE 3.1

Consider the experiment of tossing two coins and observing the up faces. Assume both coins are fair.

a. List the simple events and assign them reasonable probabilities.

b. Consider the events

$$A: \{\text{Observe exactly one head}\} \qquad B: \{\text{Observe at least one head}\}$$

and calculate $P(A)$ and $P(B)$.

Solution

a. The simple events are

$$H_1, H_2 \qquad H_1, T_2 \qquad T_1, H_2 \qquad T_1, T_2$$

where H_1 denotes Observe a head on coin 1, H_2 denotes Observe a head on coin 2, etc. If both coins are fair, we can again use the concept of relative frequency in a long series of experimental repetitions to conclude that each simple event should be assigned a probability of $\frac{1}{4}$.

b. We use a Venn diagram to show the events A: {Observe exactly one head} and B: {Observe at least one head} (Figure 3.4). Using the collection of simple events in A and B, we may calculate the probabilities by adding the appropriate simple event probabilities:

$$P(A) = P(H_1, T_2) + P(T_1, H_2) = \frac{1}{4} + \frac{1}{4} = \frac{1}{2}$$
$$P(B) = P(H_1, H_2) + P(H_1, T_2) + P(T_1, H_2) = \frac{1}{4} + \frac{1}{4} + \frac{1}{4} = \frac{3}{4}$$

FIGURE 3.4 ▲
Venn diagram of the two-coin toss

EXAMPLE 3.2

A retail computer store owner sells two basic types of microcomputers: IBM personal computers (IBM PCs) and IBM compatibles (PCs that run all or most of the same software as an IBM PC, but that are not manufactured by IBM). One problem facing the owner is deciding how many of each type of PC to stock. One important factor affecting the solution is the proportion of customers who purchase each type of PC. Show how this problem might be formulated in the framework of an experiment, with simple events and a sample space. Indicate how probabilities might be assigned to the simple events.

Solution

Using the term *customer* to refer to a person who purchases one of the two types of PCs, we can define the experiment as the entrance of a customer and the observation of which type of PC is purchased. There are two simple events in the sample space corresponding to this experiment:

Experiment: Observe the type of PC purchased by a customer.

Simple events: 1. *I*: {The customer purchases an IBM PC}
2. *C*: {The customer purchases an IBM compatible}

The difference between this experiment and the coin-toss experiment becomes apparent when we attempt to assign probabilities to the two simple events. What probability should we assign to the simple event *I*? If you answer .5, you are assuming that the events *I* and *C* should occur with equal likelihood, just as the simple events Heads and Tails in the coin-toss experiment. The assignment of simple event probabilities for the PC purchase experiment is not so easy. Suppose a check of the store's records indicates that 80% of its customers purchase IBM PCs. Then it might be reasonable to assign the probability of the simple event *I* as .8 and that of the simple event *C* as .2. The important points are that simple events are not always equally likely, and that the probabilities of simple events are not always easy to assign, particularly for experiments that represent real applications (as opposed to coin- and die-toss experiments).

EXAMPLE 3.3

A poll of "computer-familiar" adults who do not own a home computer was conducted by *USA Today* (Sept. 25, 1985). Each adult was asked to identify which of 10 electronic appliances was his or her highest-priority purchase, if any. The results are summarized in Table 3.2.

TABLE 3.2   Electronic Appliances of Highest Priority to Purchase by Computer-Familiar Adults

Electronic Appliance	Percent Response[a]	Electronic Appliance	Percent Response[a]
Home computer (HC)	24	Video cassette recorder (VCR)	17
Microwave oven (MO)	13	Video camera (VC)	9
Compact disc player (CDP)	4	Big-screen TV (BSTV)	7
Phone-answering machine (PAM)	6	Movie camera (MC)	3
Car telephone (CT)	5	None (N)	9
Programmable phone (PP)	3		

[a]Response percentages in the *USA Today* article did not add to 100% due to rounding. We have added 1% to the two smallest responses to facilitate the solution to this example.

Source: "Buying a computer is in our budget," *USA Today*, Sept. 25, 1985. Copyright 1985, USA Today. Excerpted with permission.

a. Define the experiment that generated the data in Table 3.2 and list the simple events.

b. Assign probabilities to the simple events.

c. What is the probability that a telephonic appliance is of highest priority?

d. What is the probability that a video appliance is of highest priority?

Solution

a. The experiment is the act of polling a computer-familiar adult. The simple events, the simplest outcomes of the experiment, are the 11 response categories listed in Table 3.2. They are shown in the Venn diagram in Figure 3.5.

FIGURE 3.5 ▶
Venn diagram for electronic appliance poll

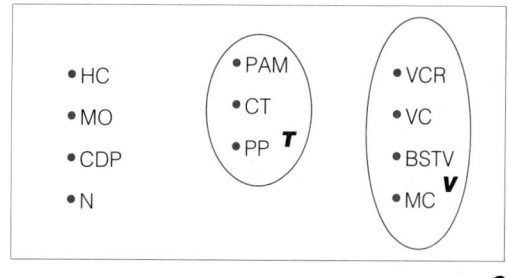

b. In Example 3.1, the simple events were assigned equal probabilities. If we were to assign equal probabilities in this case, each of the response categories would be assigned a probability of ¹⁄₁₁, or .09. However, you can see by examining Table 3.2 that equal probabilities are not reasonable in this case, because the response percentages were not the same in the 11 classifications. Instead, we assign a probability equal to the actual response percentage in each class, as shown in Table 3.3.

TABLE 3.3   Simple Event Probabilities for Electronic Appliance Poll

Simple Event	Probability
HC	.24
MO	.13
CDP	.04
PAM	.06
CT	.05
PP	.03
VCR	.17
VC	.09
BSTV	.07
MC	.03
N	.09

c. The event T that a telephonic appliance is the highest priority is not a simple event, because it consists of more than one of the response classifications (the simple events). In fact, as shown in Figure 3.5, T consists of three simple events. The probability of T is defined to be the sum of the probabilities of the simple events in T:

$$P(T) = P(PAM) + P(CT) + P(PP) = .06 + .05 + .03 = .14$$

d. The event V that a video appliance is identified as the highest priority purchase consists of four simple events, and the probability of V is the sum of the corresponding simple event probabilities:

$$P(V) = P(VCR) + P(VC) + P(BSTV) + P(MC)$$
$$= .17 + .09 + .07 + .03 = .36$$

EXAMPLE 3.4

You have the capital to invest in two of four ventures, each of which requires approximately the same amount of investment capital. Unknown to you, two of the investments will eventually fail and two will be successful. You research the four ventures because you think that your research will increase your probability of a successful choice over a purely random selection, and you eventually decide on two. What is the lower limit of your probability of selecting the two best out of four? That is, if you used none of the information generated by your research, and selected two ventures at random, what is the probability that you would select the two successful ventures? At least one?

Solution

Denote the two successful enterprises as S_1 and S_2 and the two failing enterprises as F_1 and F_2. The experiment involves a random selection of two out of the four ventures, and each possible pair of ventures represents a simple event. The six simple events that make up the sample space are

1. S_1, S_2 2. S_1, F_1
3. S_1, F_2 4. S_2, F_1
5. S_2, F_2 6. F_1, F_2

The next step is to assign probabilities to the simple events. If we assume that the choice of any one pair is as likely as any other, then the probability of each simple event is $\frac{1}{6}$. Now check to see which simple events result in the choice of two successful ventures. Only one such simple event exists—namely, S_1, S_2. Therefore, the probability of choosing two successful ventures out of the four is

$$P(S_1, S_2) = \frac{1}{6}$$

The event of selecting at least one of the two successful ventures includes all the simple events except F_1, F_2.

P(Select at least one success)

$$= P(S_1, S_2) + P(S_1, F_1) + P(S_1, F_2) + P(S_2, F_1) + P(S_2, F_2)$$
$$= \frac{1}{6} + \frac{1}{6} + \frac{1}{6} + \frac{1}{6} + \frac{1}{6} = \frac{5}{6}$$

Therefore, the worst that you could do in selecting two ventures out of four may not be too bad. With a random selection, the probability of selecting two successful ventures will be at least $\frac{1}{6}$ and the probability of selecting at least one successful venture out of two is at least $\frac{5}{6}$.

The preceding examples have one thing in common: The number of simple events in each of the sample spaces was small; hence, the simple events were easy to identify and list. How can we manage this when the simple events run into the thousands or millions? For example, suppose you wish to select five business ventures from a group of 1,000. Then each different group of five ventures would represent a simple event. How can you determine the number of simple events associated with this experiment?

One method of determining the number of simple events for a complex experiment is to develop a counting system. Start by examining a simple version of the experiment. For example, see if you can develop a system for counting the number of ways to select two people from a total of four (this is exactly what was done in Example 3.4). If the ventures are represented by the symbols V_1, V_2, V_3, and V_4, the simple events could be listed in the following pattern:

$$V_1, V_2 \qquad V_2, V_3 \qquad V_3, V_4$$
$$V_1, V_3 \qquad V_2, V_4$$
$$V_1, V_4$$

Note the pattern and now try a more complex situation—say, sampling three ventures out of five. List the simple events and observe the pattern. Finally, see if you can deduce the pattern for the general case. Perhaps you can program a computer to produce the matching and counting for the number of samples of 5 selected from a total of 1,000.

A second method of determining the number of simple events for an experiment is to use **combinatorial mathematics**. This branch of mathematics is concerned with developing counting rules for given situations. For example, there is a simple rule for finding the number of different samples of five ventures selected from 1,000. This rule is given by the formula

$$\binom{N}{n} = \frac{N!}{n!(N - n)!}$$

where N is the number of elements in the population; n is the number of elements in the sample; and the factorial symbol (!) means that, say,

$$n! = n(n - 1)(n - 2) \cdots \cdots 3 \cdot 2 \cdot 1$$

Thus, $5! = 5 \cdot 4 \cdot 3 \cdot 2 \cdot 1$. (The quantity 0! is defined to be equal to 1.)

EXAMPLE 3.5

Refer to Example 3.4, in which we selected two ventures from four in which to invest. Use the combinatorial counting rule to determine how many different selections can be made.

Solution

For this example, $N = 4$, $n = 2$, and

$$\binom{4}{2} = \frac{4!}{2!2!} = \frac{4 \cdot 3 \cdot 2 \cdot 1}{(2 \cdot 1)(2 \cdot 1)} = 6$$

You can see that this agrees with the number of simple events obtained in Example 3.4.

EXAMPLE 3.6

Suppose you plan to invest equal amounts of money in each of five business ventures. If you have 20 ventures from which to make the selection, how many different samples of five ventures can be selected from the 20?

Solution

For this example, $N = 20$ and $n = 5$. Then the number of different samples of 5 that can be selected from the 20 ventures is

$$\binom{20}{5} = \frac{20!}{5!(20 - 5)!} = \frac{20!}{5!15!}$$

$$= \frac{20 \cdot 19 \cdot 18 \cdot \cdots \cdot 3 \cdot 2 \cdot 1}{(5 \cdot 4 \cdot 3 \cdot 2 \cdot 1)(15 \cdot 14 \cdot 13 \cdot \cdots \cdot 3 \cdot 2 \cdot 1)} = 15,504$$

The symbol $\binom{N}{n}$, meaning the **number of combinations of N elements taken n at a time**, is just one of a large number of counting rules that have been developed by combinatorial mathematicians. This counting rule applies to situations in which the experiment calls for selecting n elements from a total of N elements, without replacing each element before the next is selected. If you are interested in learning other methods for counting simple events for various types of experiments, you will find a few of the basic counting rules in Appendix A. Others can be found in the references listed at the end of this chapter.

Exercises 3.1 – 3.15

Learning the Mechanics

3.1 What is the difference between a *simple event* and an *event*?

3.2 The diagram describes the sample space of a particular experiment and events A and B.

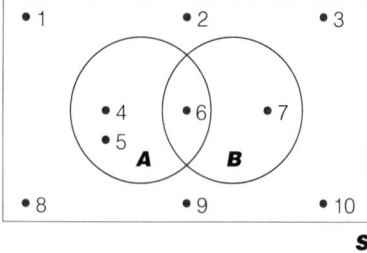

a. What is this type of diagram called?
b. Suppose the simple events are equally likely. Find $P(A)$ and $P(B)$.

c. Suppose $P(1) = P(2) = P(3) = P(4) = P(5) = \frac{1}{20}$ and $P(6) = P(7) = P(8) = P(9) = P(10) = \frac{3}{20}$. Find $P(A)$ and $P(B)$.

3.3 An experiment results in one of the following simple events: E_1, E_2, E_3, E_4, and E_5.
    a. Find $P(E_3)$ if $P(E_1) = .1$, $P(E_2) = .2$, $P(E_4) = .3$, and $P(E_5) = .1$.
    b. Find $P(E_3)$ if $P(E_1) = P(E_3)$, $P(E_2) = .1$, $P(E_4) = .2$, and $P(E_5) = .2$.
    c. Find $P(E_3)$ if $P(E_1) = P(E_2) = P(E_4) = P(E_5) = .1$.

3.4 Compute each of the following:

    a. $\begin{pmatrix} 9 \\ 4 \end{pmatrix}$ **b.** $\begin{pmatrix} 7 \\ 2 \end{pmatrix}$ **c.** $\begin{pmatrix} 4 \\ 4 \end{pmatrix}$ **d.** $\begin{pmatrix} 5 \\ 0 \end{pmatrix}$ **e.** $\begin{pmatrix} 6 \\ 5 \end{pmatrix}$

Applying the Concepts

3.5 The population of the amounts of 500 automobile loans made by a bank last year can be described as shown in the table. For the purpose of checking the accuracy of the bank's records, an auditor will randomly select one of these loans for inspection (i.e., each loan has an equal probability of being selected).

Amount of Loan ($)			
Under 2,000	2,000–4,999	5,000–7,999	8,000 or more
35	73	300	92

    a. List the simple events in this experiment.
    b. What is the probability that the loan selected will be for $8,000 or more?
    c. What is the probability that the loan will be for less than $5,000?

3.6 Communications products (telephones, fax machines, etc.) can be designed to operate on either an analog or a digital system. Because of improved accuracy, it is likely that a digital signal will soon replace the current analog signal used in telephone lines. The result will be a flood of new digital products for consumers to choose from (Kozlov, 1992). Suppose a particular firm plans to produce a new fax machine in both analog and digital forms. Concerned with whether the products will succeed or fail in the marketplace, a market analysis is conducted that results in the simple events and associated probabilities of occurrence listed in the table (S_a: analog succeeds, F_a: analog fails, etc.). Find the probability of each of the following events:

    A: {Both new products are successful}
    B: {The analog design is successful}
    C: {The digital design is successful}
    D: {At least one of the two products is successful}

Simple Events	Probabilities
$S_a S_d$	.31
$S_a F_d$	.10
$F_a S_d$	.50
$F_a F_d$	.09

3.7 Of six cars produced at a particular factory between 8 and 10 A.M. last Monday morning, three are known to be "lemons." Three of the six cars were shipped to dealer A and the other three to dealer B. Just by chance, dealer A received all three lemons. What is the probability of this event occurring if, in fact, the three cars shipped to dealer A were selected at random from the six produced?

3.8 A buyer for a large metropolitan department store must choose two firms from the four available to supply the store's fall line of men's pants. The buyer has not dealt with any of the four firms before and considers their products equally suitable. Unknown to the buyer, two of the four firms are having serious financial problems that may result in their not being able to deliver the pants as soon as promised. The firms are identified as G_1 and G_2 (firms in good financial condition) and P_1 and P_2 (firms in poor financial condition).

a. List each simple event (i.e., list each possible pair of firms that could be selected by the buyer).

b. Assume the probability of selecting a particular pair from among the four firms is the same for each pair. What is that probability?

c. Find the probability of each of the following events:

  A: {Buyer selects two firms in poor financial condition}

  B: {Buyer selects at least one firm in poor financial condition}

3.9 Simulate the experiment in Exercise 3.8 by marking four poker chips (or cards), one corresponding to each of the four firms. Mix the chips, randomly draw two, and record the results. Replace the chips. Now repeat the experiment a large number of times (at least 100).

a. Calculate the proportion of times event A occurs. How does this proportion compare with $P(A)$? Should the proportion equal $P(A)$? Explain.

b. Calculate the proportion of times event B occurs and compare it with $P(B)$.

3.10 The Value Line Survey, a service for common stock investors, provides its subscribers with up-to-date evaluations of the prospects and risks associated with the purchase of a large number of common stocks. Each stock is ranked 1 (highest) to 5 (lowest) according to Value Line's estimate of the stock's potential for price appreciation during the next 12 months.

  Suppose you plan to purchase stock in three electrical utility companies from among seven that possess rankings of 2 for price appreciation. Unknown to you, two of the companies will experience serious difficulties with their nuclear facilities during the coming year. If you randomly select the three companies from among the seven, what is the probability that you select:

a. None of the companies with prospective nuclear difficulties?

b. One of the companies with prospective nuclear difficulties?

c. Both of the companies with prospective nuclear difficulties?

3.11 Approximately 77 million Visa and 60 million Mastercard credit cards had been issued in the United States by the end of 1984. Both were issued by thousands of banks, including Citicorp. Citicorp also issued competing cards of its own: Diners Club, Carte Blanche, and Choice are wholly owned by Citicorp. The accompanying table describes the population of credit cards issued by Citicorp. One Citicorp credit card customer is to be selected at random and the type of credit card will be recorded. (Assume that each customer has only one Citicorp-issued card.)

Credit Card	Number Issued (in millions)	Credit Card	Number Issued (in millions)
Visa and Mastercard	6.0	Carte Blanche	.3
Diners Club	2.2	Choice	1.0

Source: *Fortune*, Feb. 4, 1985, p. 21.

a. List the simple events in this experiment.
b. Find the probability of each simple event.
c. What is the probability that the customer selected uses one of Citicorp's wholly owned credit cards?

3.12 You are a lawyer for a client who has committed a felony, and there are seven judges who could hear your motion to set bail. Four judges are strict, and the other three are lenient. As you walk into the courtroom, judge A (a strict judge) is leaving to go home.
a. What is the probability of drawing a lenient judge for your client?
b. What is the probability of drawing a lenient judge for your client if the probability of getting judge B (a strict judge) is .3, the probability of getting judge C (a strict judge) is .4, and the probabilities of getting any of the other four judges are equally likely?
c. Suppose you know that judge D (a lenient judge) never follows judge A. What is the probability of drawing a lenient judge for your client if the probabilities in part **b** are valid?

3.13 *Sustainable development* or *sustainable farming* means "finding ways to live and work the Earth without jeopardizing the future" (Schmickle, 1992). Studies were concluded in five midwestern states to develop a profile of a sustainable farmer. Study results revealed that farmers can be classified along a sustainability scale, depending on whether they are likely or unlikely to engage in the following practices: (1) Raise a broad mix of crops; (2) Raise livestock; (3) Use chemicals sparingly; (4) Use techniques for regenerating the soil, such as crop rotation.
a. List the different sets of classifications that are possible.
b. Suppose you are planning to interview farmers across the country to determine the frequency with which they fall into the classification sets you listed for part **a**. Since no information is yet available, assume initially that there is an equal chance of a farmer falling into any single classification set. Using that assumption, what is the probability that a farmer will be classified as unlikely on all four criteria (i.e., classified as a non-sustainable farmer)?
c. Using the same assumption as in part **b**, what is the probability that a farmer will be classified as likely on at least three of the criteria (i.e., classified as a near-sustainable farmer)?

3.14 J. D. Power, a market-research firm in Agoura Hills, California, annually surveys thousands of U.S. motor vehicle owners to determine which automobiles and trucks the consumers believe to be the best based on such criteria as repair frequency, mileage, and dealer etiquette. The top three automobiles for 1991 were (in no particular order): Infiniti, Saturn sedan, and Lexus ("GM's Saturn Takes 3rd in New-Car Owner Poll," 1992).
a. List all possible sets of rankings for these three automobiles.
b. Assuming that each set of rankings in part **a** is equally likely, what is the probability that consumers ranked Saturn first? That consumers ranked Saturn last? That consumers ranked Lexus first and Infiniti second (which is, in fact, what they did)?

3.15 Probabilities are often expressed in terms of **odds**, especially in gambling settings. For example, handicappers for horse races express their belief about the probability of each horse winning a race in terms of odds. If the probability of event E is $P(E)$, then the **odds in favor of** E are $P(E)$ to $[1 - P(E)]$. Thus, if a handicapper assesses a probability of .25 that Snow Chief will win the Belmont Stakes, the odds in favor of Snow Chief are $25/100$ to $75/100$, or 1 to 3. It follows that the **odds against** E are $[1 - P(E)]$ to $P(E)$, or 3 to 1 against a win by Snow Chief. In general, if the odds in favor of event E are a to b, then $P(E) = a/(a + b)$.
a. A second handicapper assesses the probability of a win by Snow Chief to be $1/3$. According to the second handicapper, what are the odds in favor of a Snow Chief win?
b. A third handicapper assesses the odds in favor of Snow Chief to be 1 to 1. According to the third handicapper, what is the probability of a Snow Chief win?

c. A fourth handicapper assesses the odds against Snow Chief winning to be 3 to 2. Find this handicapper's assessment of the probability that Snow Chief will win.

3.2   Unions and Intersections

An event can often be viewed as a composition of two or more other events. Such an event, called a **compound event**, can be formed (composed) in two ways:

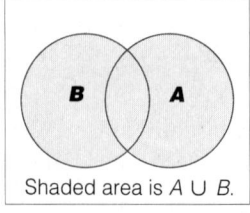

Shaded area is $A \cup B$.

Definition 3.5

The **union** of two events A and B is the event that occurs if either A or B or both occur on a single performance of the experiment. We will denote the union of events A and B by the symbol $A \cup B$.

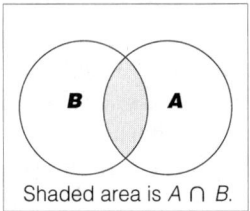

Shaded area is $A \cap B$.

Definition 3.6

The **intersection** of two events A and B is the event that occurs if both A and B occur on a single performance of the experiment. We will write $A \cap B$ for the intersection of events A and B.

EXAMPLE 3.7

Consider the die-toss experiment. Define the following events:

   A: {Toss an even number}
   B: {Toss a number less than or equal to 3}

a. Describe $A \cup B$ for this experiment.

b. Describe $A \cap B$ for this experiment.

c. Calculate $P(A \cup B)$ and $P(A \cap B)$ assuming the die is fair.

Solution

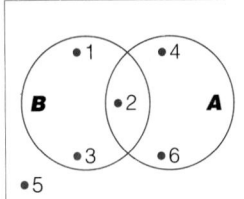

a. The **union** of A and B is the event that occurs if we observe an even number, a number less than or equal to 3, or both on a single throw of the die. Consequently, the simple events in the event $A \cup B$ are those for which A occurs, B occurs, or both A and B occur. Testing the simple events in the entire sample space, we find that the collection of simple events in the union of A and B is

$$A \cup B = \{1, 2, 3, 4, 6\}$$

b. The **intersection** of A and B is the event that occurs if we observe *both* an even number and a number less than or equal to 3 on a single throw of the die. Testing the simple events to see which imply the occurrence of *both* events A and B, we see that the intersection contains only one simple event:

$$A \cap B = \{2\}$$

In other words, the intersection of A and B is the simple event Observe a 2.

c. Recalling that the probability of an event is the sum of the probabilities of the simple events of which the event is composed, we have

$$P(A \cup B) = P(1) + P(2) + P(3) + P(4) + P(6)$$
$$= \frac{1}{6} + \frac{1}{6} + \frac{1}{6} + \frac{1}{6} + \frac{1}{6} = \frac{5}{6}$$

and

$$P(A \cap B) = P(2) = \frac{1}{6}$$

EXAMPLE 3.8

Many firms undertake direct marketing campaigns to promote their products. The campaigns typically involve mailing information to millions of households; the responses to the mailings are carefully monitored to determine the demographic characteristics of respondents. By studying tendencies to respond, the firm can better target future mailings to those segments of the population most likely to purchase the products.

Suppose a distributor of mail-order tools is analyzing the results of a recent mailing. The probability of response is believed to be related to income and age of the head of the household. The percentages of the total number of respondents to the mailing are given by income and age classification in Table 3.4.

TABLE 3.4   Percentage of Respondents in Age–Income Classes

		Income		
		<$25,000	$25,000–$50,000	>$50,000
	<30 yrs.	5%	12%	10%
Age	30–50 yrs.	14%	22%	16%
	>50 yrs.	8%	10%	3%

Define the following events:

A: {A respondent's income is more than $50,000}
B: {A respondent's age is 30 years or more}

a. Find $P(A)$ and $P(B)$.   b. Find $P(A \cup B)$.   c. Find $P(A \cap B)$.

Solution

Following the steps for calculating probabilities of events (given in the box on page 131), we first note that the objective is to characterize the income and age distribution of respondents to the mailing. To accomplish this, we define the experiment as selecting a respondent from the collection of all respondents, and observing which income and age class he or she occupies. The simple events are the nine different age–income classes:

E_1: {<30 yrs., <$25,000}
E_2: {30–50 yrs., <$25,000}
    ⋮   ⋮
E_9: {>50 yrs., >$50,000}

Next, we assign probabilities to the simple events. If we blindly select one of the respondents, the probability that he or she will occupy a particular age–income class is just the proportion, or relative frequency, of respondents in that class. These proportions are given (as percentages) in Table 3.4. Thus,

$P(E_1)$ = Relative frequency of respondents in
        age–income class (<30 yrs., <$25,000)
    = .05
$P(E_2)$ = .14

and so forth. You may verify that the simple event probabilities add to 1.

a. To find $P(A)$ we first determine the collection of simple events contained in event A. Since A is defined as {>$50,000}, we see from Table 3.4 that A contains the three simple events represented by the last column of the table. In words, the event A consists of the income class (>$50,000) and all three age classes within that income class. The probability of A is the sum of the probabilities of the simple events in A:

$P(A) = .10 + .16 + .03 = .29$

Similarly, B consists of the six simple events in the second and third rows of Table 3.4:

$P(B) = .14 + .22 + .16 + .08 + .10 + .03 = .73$

b. The union of events A and B, $A \cup B$, consists of all simple events in *either* A *or* B *or both* A *and* B. That is, the union of A and B consists of all respondents whose income exceeds $50,000 *or* whose age is 30 or more. In Table 3.4 this is any simple event found in the third column *or* the last two rows. Thus,

$P(A \cup B) = .10 + .14 + .22 + .16 + .08 + .10 + .03 = .83$

c. The intersection of events A and B, $A \cap B$, consists of all simple events in *both* A *and* B. That is, the intersection of A and B consists of all respondents whose income exceeds $50,000 *and* whose age is 30 or more. In Table 3.4 this is any simple event found in the third column *and* the last two rows (i.e., in the last two rows of the third column). Thus,

$$P(A \cap B) = .16 + .03 = .19$$

3.3   The Additive Rule and Mutually Exclusive Events

In the previous section, we showed how to determine which simple events are contained in a union. Then we showed that the probability of the union can be calculated by adding the probabilities of the simple events in the union. It is also possible to obtain the probability of a union of two events by using the additive rule.

The union of two events will often contain many simple events, since the union occurs if either one or both of the events occur. By studying the Venn diagram in Figure 3.6, you can see that the probability of the union of two events A and B can be obtained by summing $P(A)$ and $P(B)$ and subtracting the probability corresponding to $A \cap B$. Therefore, the formula for calculating the probability of the union of two events is as given in the box.

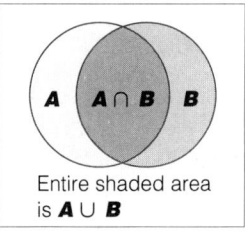

Entire shaded area
is **A** ∪ **B**

FIGURE 3.6 ▲
Venn diagram of union

Additive Rule of Probability

The probability of the union of events A and B is the sum of the probabilities of events A and B minus the probability of the intersection of events A and B:

$$P(A \cup B) = P(A) + P(B) - P(A \cap B)$$

Note that we must subtract the probability of the intersection because, when we add the probabilities of A and B, the intersection probability is counted twice.

EXAMPLE 3.9

Consider the die-toss experiment. Define the events

    A: {Observe an even number}
    B: {Observe a number less than or equal to 3}

Assuming the die is fair, calculate the probability of the union of A and B by using the additive rule of probability.

Solution

The formula for the probability of a union requires that we calculate the following:

$$P(A) = P(2) + P(4) + P(6) = \frac{1}{6} + \frac{1}{6} + \frac{1}{6} = \frac{3}{6}$$
$$P(B) = P(1) + P(2) + P(3) = \frac{1}{6} + \frac{1}{6} + \frac{1}{6} = \frac{3}{6}$$
$$P(A \cap B) = P(2) = \frac{1}{6}$$

Now we can calculate the probability of $A \cup B$:

$$P(A \cup B) = P(A) + P(B) - P(A \cap B) = \tfrac{3}{6} + \tfrac{3}{6} - \tfrac{1}{6} = \tfrac{5}{6}$$

If two events A and B do not intersect—i.e., when $A \cap B$ contains no simple events—we call the events A and B **mutually exclusive** events:

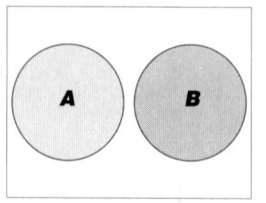

FIGURE 3.7 ▲
Venn diagram of mutually exclusive events

Definition 3.7

Events A and B are **mutually exclusive** if $A \cap B$ contains no simple events.

Figure 3.7 shows a Venn diagram of two mutually exclusive events. The events A and B have no simple events in common; i.e., A and B cannot occur simultaneously, and $P(A \cap B) = 0$. Thus, we have the following important relationship:

If two events A and B are mutually exclusive, the probability of the union of A and B equals the sum of the probabilities of A and B:

$$P(A \cup B) = P(A) + P(B)$$

EXAMPLE 3.10

Consider the experiment of tossing two balanced coins. Find the probability of observing *at least* one head.

Solution

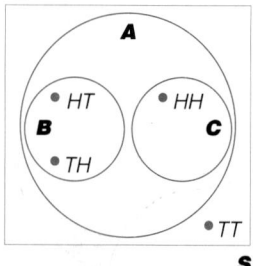

FIGURE 3.8 ▲
Venn diagram for coin toss experiment

Define the events

> A: {Observe at least one head}
> B: {Observe exactly one head}
> C: {Observe exactly two heads}

Note that

$$A = B \cup C$$

and that $B \cap C$ contains no simple events (see Figure 3.8). Thus, B and C are mutually exclusive, so that

$$P(A) = P(B \cup C) = P(B) + P(C) = \tfrac{1}{2} + \tfrac{1}{4} = \tfrac{3}{4}$$

Although Example 3.10 is very simple, the concept of writing events with verbal descriptions that include the phrases "at least" or "at most" as unions of mutually exclusive events is a very useful one. This enables us to find the probability of the event by adding the probabilities of the mutually exclusive events.

3.4   Complementary Events

A very useful concept in the calculation of event probabilities is the notion of **complementary events**:

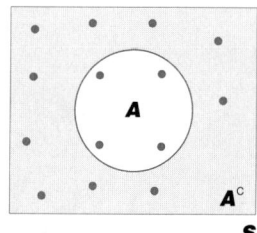

FIGURE 3.9 ▲
Venn diagram of complementary events

> ### Definition 3.8
>
> The **complement** of any event A is the event that A does not occur. We will denote the complement of A by A^c.

Since an event A is a collection of simple events, the simple events included in A^c are just those that are not in A. Figure 3.9 demonstrates this. You will note from the figure that all simple events in S are included in either A or A^c, and that *no* simple event is in both A and A^c. This leads us to conclude that the probabilities of an event and its complement *must sum to* 1:

> The sum of the probabilities of complementary events equals 1; i.e.,
>
> $$P(A) + P(A^c) = 1$$

In many probability problems, it will be easier to calculate the probability of the complement of the event of interest than the event itself. Then, since

$$P(A) + P(A^c) = 1$$

we can calculate $P(A)$ by using the relationship

$$P(A) = 1 - P(A^c)$$

EXAMPLE 3.11

Consider the experiment of tossing two fair coins. Calculate the probability of event A: {Observe at least one head} by using the complementary relationship.

Solution

We know that the event A: {Observe at least one head} consists of the simple events

$$A = \{H_1, H_2;\ \ H_1, T_2;\ \ T_1, H_2\}$$

The complement of A is defined as the event that occurs when A does not occur. Therefore,

$$A^c = \{T_1, T_2\}$$

FIGURE 3.10 ▶
Complementary events in the toss
of two coins

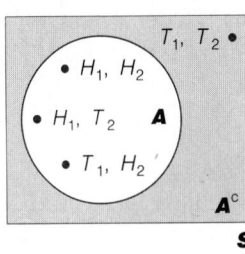

This complementary relationship is shown in Figure 3.10. Assuming the coins are balanced,

$$P(A^c) = P(T_1, T_2) = \tfrac{1}{4} \quad \text{and} \quad P(A) = 1 - P(A^c) = 1 - \tfrac{1}{4} = \tfrac{3}{4}$$

Exercises 3.16–3.31

Learning the Mechanics

3.16 Consider the Venn diagram shown, where $P(E_1) = .13$, $P(E_2) = .05$, $P(E_3) = P(E_4) = .2$, $P(E_5) = .06$, $P(E_6) = .3$, and $P(E_7) = .06$. Find each of the following probabilities.

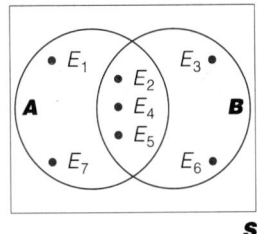

a. $P(A^c)$ b. $P(B^c)$ c. $P(A^c \cap B)$
d. $P(A \cup B)$ e. $P(A \cap B)$ f. $P(A^c \cup B^c)$

3.17 What are mutually exclusive events? Give a verbal description, and then draw a Venn diagram.

3.18 Two dice are tossed and the following events are defined:

  A: {The total number of dots on the upper faces of the two dice is equal to 5}
  B: {At least one of the two dice has three dots on the upper face}

a. Identify the simple events in each of the following events: A, B, A ∩ B, and A ∪ B.
b. Find P(A) and P(B) by summing the probabilities of the appropriate simple events.
c. Find P(A ∩ B) and P(A ∪ B) by summing the probabilities of the appropriate simple events.
d. Find P(A ∪ B) using the additive rule. Compare your answer to that for the same event in part **c**.
e. Are A and B mutually exclusive events? Why?

3.19 Three coins are tossed and the following events are defined:

> A: {Observe at least one head}
> B: {Observe exactly two heads}
> C: {Observe exactly two tails}

Assume that the coins are balanced. Calculate the following probabilities by summing the probabilities of the appropriate simple events:

a. $P(A \cup B)$ **b.** $P(A \cap B)$ **c.** $P(A \cap C)$ **d.** $P(B \cap C)$
e. Are events B and C mutually exclusive?
f. Find $P(B \cup C)$.

3.20 The accompanying table describes the adult population of a small suburb of a large southern city.

		Income		
		Under $20,000	$20,000–$50,000	Over $50,000
	Under 25	950	1,000	50
Age	25–45	450	2,050	1,500
	Over 45	50	950	1,000

A marketing research firm plans to randomly select one adult from this suburb to evaluate a new food product. For this experiment the nine age–income categories are the simple events. Consider the following events:

> A: {Person is under 25}
> B: {Person is between 25 and 45}
> C: {Person is over 45}
> D: {Person has income under $20,000}
> E: {Person has income of $20,000–$50,000}
> F: {Person has income over $50,000}

Convert the frequencies in the table to relative frequencies and use them to calculate the following probabilities:

a. $P(B)$ **b.** $P(F)$ **c.** $P(C \cap F)$ **d.** $P(B \cup C)$ **e.** $P(A^c)$ **f.** $P(A^c \cap F)$
g. Consider each pair of events (A and B, A and C, etc.) and list the pairs of events that are mutually exclusive. Justify your choices.

3.21 Refer to Exercise 3.20 and use the same event definitions to solve the following.

a. Write the event that the person selected is under 25 with an income over $50,000 as an intersection of two of the events defined in Exercise 3.20.
b. Write the event that a person of age 25 or over is selected as the union of two mutually exclusive events.
c. Write the event that a person of age 25 or over is selected as the complement of an event.

3.22 Three fair coins are tossed, and we wish to find the probability of the event A: {Observe at least one head}.
  a. Express A as the union of three mutually exclusive events. Find the probability of A using this expression.
  b. Express A as the complement of an event. Find the probability of A using this expression.

Applying the Concepts

3.23 A state energy agency mailed questionnaires on energy conservation to 1,000 homeowners in the state capital. Five hundred questionnaires were returned. Suppose an experiment consists of randomly selecting and reviewing one of the returned questionnaires. Consider the events:

  A: {The home is constructed of brick}

  B: {The home is more than 30 years old}

  C: {The home is heated with oil}

Describe each of the following events in terms of unions, intersections, and complements (i.e., A ∪ B, A ∩ B, A^c, etc.):
  a. The home is more than 30 years old and is heated with oil.
  b. The home is not constructed of brick.
  c. The home is heated with oil or is more than 30 years old.
  d. The home is constructed of brick and is not heated with oil.

3.24 Identifying managerial prospects who are both talented and motivated is difficult. A personnel manager constructed the table shown here to define nine combinations of talent–motivation levels. The numbers in the table are the manager's assessments of the probabilities that a managerial prospect will be classified in the respective categories.

		Talent		
		High	Medium	Low
	High	.05	.16	.05
Motivation	**Medium**	.19	.32	.05
	Low	.11	.05	.02

Suppose the personnel manager has decided to hire a new manager. Define the following events:

  A: {Prospect places in the high motivation category}

  B: {Prospect places in the high talent category}

  C: {Prospect rates medium or better in both categories}

  D: {Prospect rates low in at least one of the categories}

  E: {Prospect places high in both categories}

  a. Does the sum of the probabilities in the table equal 1?
  b. Find the probability of each event defined above.
  c. Find $P(A \cup B)$, $P(A \cap B)$, and $P(A \cup C)$.
  d. Find $P(A^c)$ and explain what this means from a practical point of view.

e. Consider each pair of events (A and B, A and C, etc.) and list the pairs of events that are mutually exclusive. Justify your choices.

3.25 After completing an inventory of three warehouses, a manufacturer of golf club shafts described its stock of 20,125 shafts with the percentages given in the table. Suppose a shaft is selected at random from the 20,125 currently in stock and the warehouse number and type of shaft are observed.

		Regular	Stiff	Extra Stiff
	1	41%	6%	0%
Warehouse	2	10%	15%	4%
	3	11%	7%	6%

Type of Shaft

a. List all the simple events for this experiment.
b. What is the set of all simple events called?
c. Let C be the event that the shaft selected is from warehouse 3. Find P(C) by summing the probabilities of the simple events in C.
d. Let F be the event that the shaft chosen is an extra stiff type. Find P(F).
e. Let A be the event that the shaft selected is from warehouse 1. Find P(A).
f. Let D be the event that the shaft selected is a regular type. Find P(D).
g. Let E be the event that the shaft selected is a stiff type. Find P(E).

3.26 Refer to Exercise 3.25. Define the characteristics of a golf club shaft portrayed by the following events, and then find the probability of each. For each union, use the additive rule to find the probability. Also, determine whether the events are mutually exclusive.
a. $A \cap F$ b. $C \cup E$ c. $C \cap D$ d. $A \cup F$ e. $A \cup D$

3.27 Refer to Exercise 3.5, in which a bank's loan records were being audited. Suppose each of the 500 automobile loans made by the bank last year is now classified according to two characteristics: amount of loan and length of loan. As before, an auditor is planning to choose one loan at random for inspection.

		Under 2,000	2,000–4,999	5,000–7,999	8,000 or more
	12	30	4	0	0
	24	5	18	2	0
Length of Loan (Months)	36	0	20	89	4
	42	0	31	95	37
	48	0	0	114	51

Amount of Loan ($)

a. List the simple events in this experiment.
b. What is the probability that the loan selected will be for $8,000 or more? Does your answer agree with your answer to part **b** in Exercise 3.5?
c. What is the probability that the loan selected is a 3-year loan for more than $7,999?

   d. What is the probability that the loan selected is a 3- or 4-year loan?

   e. What is the probability that the loan selected is a 42-month loan for $2,000 or more?

3.28 The long-run success of a business depends on its ability to market products with superior characteristics that maximize consumer satisfaction and that give the firm a competitive advantage (Bagozzi, 1986). Ten new products have been developed by a food products firm. Market research has indicated that the 10 products have the characteristics described by the Venn diagram shown here.

   a. Write the event that a product possesses all the desired characteristics as an intersection of the events defined in the Venn diagram. Which products are contained in this intersection?

   b. If one of the 10 products were selected at random to be marketed, what is the probability that it would possess all the desired characteristics?

   c. Write the event that the randomly selected product would give the firm a competitive advantage or would satisfy consumers as a union of the events defined in the Venn diagram. Find the probability of this union.

   d. Write the event that the randomly selected product would possess superior product characteristics and satisfy consumers. Find the probability of this intersection.

3.29 Whether purchases are made by cash or credit card is of concern to merchandisers because they must pay a certain percentage of the sale value to the credit agency. To better understand the relationship between type of purchase (credit or cash) and type of merchandise, a department store analyzed 10,000 sales and placed them in the categories shown in the table. Suppose a single sale is selected at random from the 10,000 and the following events are defined:

   A: {Sale was paid by credit card}

   B: {Merchandise purchased was women's wear}

   C: {Merchandise purchased was men's wear}

   D: {Merchandise purchased was sportswear}

		Type of Merchandise			
		Women's Wear	Men's Wear	Sportswear	Household
Type of Purchase	Cash	6%	9%	3%	7%
	Credit Card	41%	9%	22%	3%

Describe the characteristics of a sale implied by the following events, and find the probability of each.
a. $A \cup B$ b. $B \cup C$ c. $B \cap A$ d. $D \cap A$
e. Which pairs of events are mutually exclusive? Why?

3.30 Refer to Exercise 3.29. The following events are defined:

A: {Sale was paid by credit card}

B: {Merchandise purchased was women's wear}

a. Describe the events A^c and B^c.   b. Find $P(A^c)$.   c. Find $P(B^c)$.
d. Find the probability that the sale was in neither men's wear nor women's wear.
e. Find the probability that the sale was *not* a credit card purchase in the sportswear department.

3.31 The types of occupations of the 117,342,000 employed workers (age 16 years and older) in the United States in 1989 are described in the table, and their relative frequencies are listed. A worker is to be selected at random from this population and his or her occupation is to be determined. (Assume that each worker in the population has only one occupation.)

Occupation	Relative Frequency	
Male worker	.548	
Managerial/professional		.142
Technical/sales/administrative		.108
Service		.052
Precision production, craft, and repair		.108
Operators/fabricators		.114
Farming, forestry, and fishing		.024
Female workers	.452	
Managerial/professional		.117
Technical/sales/administrative		.200
Service		.080
Precision production, craft, and repair		.010
Operators/fabricators		.040
Farming, forestry, and fishing		.005

Source: *Statistical Abstract of the United States: 1991*, p. 395.

a. What is the probability that the worker will be a male service worker?
b. What is the probability that the worker will be a manager or a professional?
c. What is the probability that the worker will be a female professional or a female operator/fabricator?
d. What is the probability that the worker will not be in a technical/sales/administrative occupation?

3.5 Conditional Probability

FIGURE 3.11 ▲
Reduced sample space for the die-toss experiment — given that event *B* has occurred

The probabilities we assign to the simple events of an experiment are measures of our belief that they will occur when the experiment is performed. When we assign these probabilities, we should make no assumptions other than those contained in or implied by the definition of the experiment. However, at times we will want to make assumptions other than those implied by the experimental description, and these extra assumptions may alter the probabilities we assign to the simple events of an experiment.

For example, we have shown that the probability of observing an even number (event A) on a toss of a fair die is ½. However, suppose you are given the information that on a particular throw of the die the result was a number less than or equal to 3 (event B). Would you still believe that the probability of observing an even number on that throw of the die is equal to ½? If you reason that making the assumption that B has occurred reduces the sample space from six simple events to three simple events (namely, those contained in event B), the reduced sample space is as shown in Figure 3.11.

Since the reduced sample space contains only three simple events (Observe a 1, Observe a 2, Observe a 3), each is assigned a new probability, called a **conditional probability**. Because the simple events for the die-toss experiment are equally likely, each of the three simple events in the reduced sample space is assigned a conditional probability of ⅓. Since the only even number of the three numbers in the reduced sample space B is the number 2 and since the die is fair, we conclude that the probability that A occurs *given that B occurs* is one in three, or ⅓. We will use the symbol $P(A \mid B)$ to represent the probability of event A given that event B occurs. For the die-toss example,

$$P(A \mid B) = \tfrac{1}{3}$$

To get the probability of event A given that event B occurs, we proceed as follows: We divide the probability of the part of A that falls within the reduced sample space B—namely, $P(A \cap B)$—by the total probability of the reduced sample space—namely, $P(B)$. Thus, for the die-toss example with event A: {Observe an even number} and event B: {Observe a number less than or equal to 3}, we find

$$P(A \mid B) = \frac{P(A \cap B)}{P(B)} = \frac{P(2)}{P(1) + P(2) + P(3)} = \frac{\tfrac{1}{6}}{\tfrac{3}{6}} = \tfrac{1}{3}$$

This formula for $P(A \mid B)$ is true in general:

To find the **conditional probability that event A occurs given that event B occurs**, divide the probability that *both* A and B occur by the probability that B occurs; that is,

$$P(A \mid B) = \frac{P(A \cap B)}{P(B)}$$

This formula adjusts the probability of $A \cap B$ from its original value in the complete sample space S to a conditional probability in the reduced sample space B. If the simple events in the complete sample space are equally likely, then the formula will assign equal probabilities to the simple events in the reduced sample space, as in the die-toss experiment. If, on the other hand, the simple events have unequal probabilities, the formula will assign conditional probabilities proportional to the probabilities in the complete sample space.

EXAMPLE 3.12

Suppose you are interested in the probability of the sale of a large piece of earth-moving equipment. A single prospect is contacted. Let F be the event that the buyer has sufficient money (or credit) to buy the product and let F^c denote the complement of F (the event that the prospect does not have the financial capability to buy the product). Similarly, let B be the event that the buyer wishes to buy the product and let B^c be the complement of that event. Then the four simple events associated with the experiment are shown in Figure 3.12, and their probabilities are given in Table 3.5.

FIGURE 3.12 ▲
Sample space for contacting a sales prospect

TABLE 3.5   Probabilities of Customer Desire to Buy and Ability to Finance

		Desire	
		To Buy, B	Not to Buy, B^c
Able to Finance	Yes, F	.2	.1
	No, F^c	.4	.3

Find the probability that a single prospect will buy, given that the prospect is able to finance the purchase.

Solution

Suppose you consider the large collection of prospects for the sale of your product and randomly select one person from this collection. What is the probability that the person selected will buy the product? In order to buy the product, the customer must be financially able and have the desire to buy, so this probability would correspond to

FIGURE 3.13 ▲
Subspace (shaded) containing sample points implying a financially able prospect

the entry in Table 3.5 below B and next to F, or $P(B \cap F) = .2$. This is called the **unconditional probability** of the event $B \cap F$.

In contrast, suppose you know that the prospect selected has the financial capability for purchasing the product. Now you are seeking the probability that the customer will buy given (the condition) that the customer has the financial ability to pay. This probability, the **conditional probability** of B given that F has occurred and denoted by the symbol $P(B \mid F)$, would be determined by considering only the simple events in the reduced sample space containing the simple events $B \cap F$ and $B^c \cap F$—i.e., simple events that imply the prospect is financially able to buy. (This subspace is shaded in Figure 3.13.) From our definition of conditional probability,

$$P(B \mid F) = \frac{P(B \cap F)}{P(F)}$$

where $P(F)$ is the sum of the probabilities of the two simple events corresponding to $B \cap F$ and $B^c \cap F$ (given in Table 3.5). Then

$$P(F) = P(B \cap F) + P(B^c \cap F) = .2 + .1 = .3$$

and the conditional probability that a prospect buys, given that the prospect is financially able, is

$$P(B \mid F) = \frac{P(B \cap F)}{P(F)} = \frac{.2}{.3} = .667$$

As we would expect, the probability that the prospect will buy, given that he or she is financially able, is higher than the unconditional probability of selecting a prospect who will buy.

. . . .

Note in Example 3.12, that the conditional probability formula assigns a probability to the event $(B \cap F)$ in the reduced sample space that is proportional to the probability of the event in the complete sample space. To see this, note that the two simple events in the reduced sample space, $(B \cap F)$ and $(B^c \cap F)$, have probabilities of .2 and .1, respectively, in the complete sample space S. The formula assigns conditional probabilities ⅔ and ⅓ (use the formula to check the second one) to these events in the reduced sample space F, so that the conditional probabilities retain the 2 to 1 proportionality of the original simple event probabilities.

. . . .

EXAMPLE 3.13

The investigation of consumer product complaints by the Federal Trade Commission has generated much interest by manufacturers in the quality of their products. A manufacturer of an electromechanical kitchen aid conducted an analysis of a large number of consumer complaints and found that they fell into the six categories shown in Table 3.6. If a consumer complaint is received, what is the probability that the cause of the complaint was product appearance, given that the complaint originated prior to the end of the guarantee period?

TABLE 3.6   Distribution of Product Complaints

	Reason for Complaint		
	Electrical	Mechanical	Appearance
During Guarantee Period	18%	13%	32%
After Guarantee Period	12%	22%	3%

Solution

Let A represent the event that the cause of a particular complaint was product appearance and let B represent the event that the complaint occurred during the guarantee period. Checking Table 3.6, you can see that (18 + 13 + 32)% = 63% of the complaints occurred during the guarantee time. Hence, $P(B) = .63$. The percentage of complaints that were caused by appearance, A, *and* occurred during the guarantee period, B, is 32%. Therefore, $P(A \cap B) = .32$. Using these probability values, we can calculate the conditional probability $P(A \mid B)$ that the cause of a complaint is appearance given that the complaint occurred prior to the termination of the guarantee time:

$$P(A \mid B) = \frac{P(A \cap B)}{P(B)} = \frac{.32}{.63} = .51$$

Consequently, you can see that slightly more than half of the complaints that occurred during the guarantee period were due to scratches, dents, or other imperfections in the surface of the kitchen devices.

You will see in later chapters that conditional probability plays a key role in many applications of statistics. For example, we may be interested in the probability that a particular stock gains 10% during the next year. We may assess this probability using information such as the past performance of the stock or the general state of the economy at present. However, our probability may change drastically if we assume that the Gross Domestic Product (GDP) will increase by 10% in the next year. We would then be assessing the *conditional probability* that our stock gains 10% in the next year given that the GDP gains 10% in the same year. Thus, the probability of any event that is calculated or assessed based on an assumption that some other event occurs concurrently is a conditional probability.

CASE STUDY 3.1 / Purchase Patterns and the Conditional Probability of Purchasing

In his doctoral dissertation, Alfred A. Kuehn (1958) examined sequential purchase data to gain some insight into consumer brand switching. He analyzed the frozen orange juice purchases of approximately 600 Chicago families during 1950–1952. The data were collected by the *Chicago Tribune* Consumer Panel. Kuehn was interested in determining the influence of a consumer's last four orange juice purchases on the next purchase. Thus, sequences of five purchases were analyzed.

Table 3.7 contains a summary of the data collected for Snow Crop brand orange juice and part of Kuehn's analysis of the data. In the column labeled "Previous Purchase Pattern" an S stands for the purchase of Snow Crop by a consumer and an O stands for the purchase of a brand other than Snow Crop. Thus, for example, SSSO is used to represent the purchase of Snow Crop three times in a row followed by the purchase of some other brand of frozen orange juice. The column labeled "Sample Size" lists the number of occurrences of the purchase sequences in the first column. The column labeled "Frequency" lists the number of times the associated purchase sequence in the first column led to the next purchase (i.e., the fifth purchase in the sequence) being Snow Crop.

The column labeled "Observed Approximate Probability of Purchase" contains the relative frequency with which each sequence of the first column led to the next purchase being Snow Crop. These relative frequencies, which give approximate probabilities, are computed for each sequence of the first column by dividing the frequency of the sequence by the sample size of the sequence. Notice that these approximate probabilities are really conditional probabilities. For the sequences of five purchases analyzed, each of the entries in the fourth column is the approximate probability that the next purchase is Snow Crop, given that the previous four purchases were as noted in the first column. For example, .806 is the approximate probability that the next purchase will be Snow Crop given that the previous four purchases were also Snow Crop.

An examination of the approximate probabilities in the fourth column indicates that both the most recent brand purchased and the number of times a brand is purchased have an effect on the next brand purchased. It appears that the influence on the next brand of orange juice purchased by the second most recent

TABLE 3.7   Observed Approximate Probability of Purchasing Snow Crop, Given the Four Previous Brand Purchases

Previous Purchase Pattern S = Snow Crop, O = Other Brand	Sample Size	Frequency	Observed Approximate Probability of Purchase
SSSS	1,047	844	.806
OSSS	277	191	.690
SOSS	206	137	.665
SSOS	222	132	.595
SSSO	296	144	.486
OOSS	248	137	.552
SOOS	138	78	.565
OSOS	149	74	.497
SOSO	163	66	.405
OSSO	181	75	.414
SSOO	256	78	.305
OOOS	500	165	.330
OOSO	404	77	.191
OSOO	433	56	.129
SOOO	557	86	.154
OOOO	8,442	405	.048

purchase is not so strong as the most recent purchase but is stronger than the third most recent purchase. In general, it appears that the probability of a particular consumer purchasing Snow Crop the next time he or she buys orange juice is inversely related to the number of consecutive purchases of another brand he or she made since last purchasing Snow Crop and is directly proportional to the number of Snow Crop purchases among the four purchases.

Kuehn, of course, goes on to conduct a more formal statistical analysis of these data, which we will not pursue here. We simply want you to see that probability is a basic tool for making inferences about populations using sample data.

3.6   The Multiplicative Rule and Independent Events

The probability of an intersection of two events can be calculated using the multiplicative rule, which employs the conditional probabilities we defined in the previous section. Actually, we have already developed the formula in another context. You will recall that the formula for calculating the conditional probability of B given A is

$$P(B \mid A) = \frac{P(A \cap B)}{P(A)}$$

If we multiply both sides of this equation by $P(A)$, we get a formula for the probability of the intersection of events A and B:

Multiplicative Rule of Probability

$P(A \cap B) = P(A)P(B \mid A)$ or, equivalently, $P(A \cap B) = P(B)P(A \mid B)$

The second expression in the box is obtained by multiplying both sides of the equation $P(A \mid B) = P(A \cap B)/P(B)$ by $P(B)$.

Before working an example, we emphasize that the intersection often contains only a few simple events, in which case the probability is easy to calculate by summing the appropriate simple event probabilities.

The formula for calculating intersection probabilities plays a very important role in an area of statistics known as **Bayesian statistics**. (For a complete discussion of Bayesian statistics, consult the references at the end of this chapter.)

EXAMPLE 3.14

Suppose an investment firm is interested in the following events:

A: {Gross Domestic Product gains 10% next year}

B: {Common stock in XYZ Corporation gains 10% next year}

The firm has assigned the following probabilities on the basis of available information:

$P(B \mid A) = .8$ $P(A) = .3$

That is, the investment company believes the probability is .8 that XYZ common stock will gain 10% in the next year *assuming that* the GDP gains 10% in the same time period. In addition, the company believes the probability is only .3 that the GDP will gain 10% in the next year. Use the formula for calculating the probability of an intersection to determine the probability that XYZ common stock *and* the GDP gain 10% in the next year.

Solution

We want to calculate $P(A \cap B)$. The formula is

$$P(A \cap B) = P(A)P(B \mid A) = (.3)(.8) = .24$$

Thus, according to this investment firm, the probability is .24 that both XYZ common stock and the GDP will gain 10% in the next year.

In the previous section, we showed that the probability of an event A may be substantially altered by the knowledge that the event B has occurred. However, this will not always be the case. In some instances the assumption that event B has occurred will not alter the probability of event A at all. When this is true, we call events A and B **independent**.

Definition 3.9

Events A and B are **independent** if the assumption that B has occurred does not alter the probability that A occurs; i.e., events A and B are independent if

$$P(A \mid B) = P(A)$$

Equivalently, events A and B are **independent** if

$$P(B \mid A) = P(B)$$

Events that are not independent are said to be **dependent**.

EXAMPLE 3.15

Suppose that we decide to change the definition of event B in the die-toss experiment to {Observe a number less than or equal to 4} but we let event A remain {Observe an even number}. Are events A and B independent (assuming a fair die)?

Solution

The Venn diagram for this experiment is shown in Figure 3.14. We first calculate

$$P(A) = \tfrac{1}{2}$$

$$P(B) = P(1) + P(2) + P(3) + P(4) = \tfrac{4}{6} = \tfrac{2}{3}$$

$$P(A \cap B) = P(2) + P(4) = \tfrac{2}{6} = \tfrac{1}{3}$$

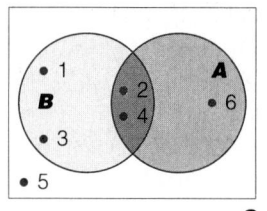

FIGURE 3.14
Die-toss experiment, Example 3.15

Now assuming B has occurred, the conditional probability of A is

$$P(A \mid B) = \frac{P(A \cap B)}{P(B)} = \frac{\frac{1}{3}}{\frac{2}{3}} = \frac{1}{2} = P(A)$$

Thus, the assumption of the occurrence of event B does not alter the probability of observing an even number—it remains $\frac{1}{2}$. Therefore, the events A and B are independent. Note that if we calculate the conditional probability of B given A, our conclusion is the same:

$$P(B \mid A) = \frac{P(A \cap B)}{P(A)} = \frac{\frac{1}{3}}{\frac{1}{2}} = \frac{2}{3} = P(B)$$

EXAMPLE 3.16

Refer to the consumer product complaint study in Example 3.13. The percentages of complaints of various types in the pre- and post-guarantee periods are shown in Table 3.6. Define the following events:

A: {Cause of complaint is product appearance}

B: {Complaint occurred during the guarantee term}

Are A and B independent events?

Solution

Events A and B are independent if $P(A \mid B) = P(A)$. We calculated $P(A \mid B)$ in Example 3.13 to be .51, and from Table 3.6 (page 155) we can see that

$$P(A) = .32 + .03 = .35$$

Therefore, $P(A \mid B) \neq P(A)$, and A and B are not independent events.

To gain an intuitive understanding of independence, think of situations in which the occurrence of one event does not alter the probability that a second event will occur. For example, suppose two small companies are being monitored by a financier for possible investment. If the businesses are in different industries and they are otherwise unrelated, then the success or failure of one company may be *independent* of the success or failure of the other. That is, the event that company A fails may not alter the probability that company B will fail.

As a second example, consider an election poll in which 1,000 registered voters are asked to state their preference between two candidates. One objective of the pollsters is to select a sample of voters so that the responses will be independent. That is, the sample is selected so that the event that one polled voter prefers candidate A does not alter the probability that a second polled voter prefers candidate A.

We will make three final points about independence. The first is that the property of independence, unlike the mutually exclusive property, cannot be shown on or gleaned from a Venn diagram. In general, the only way to check for independence is by performing the calculations of the probabilities in the definition.

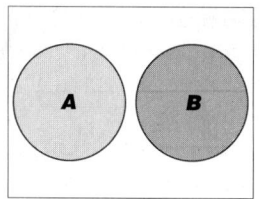

S

FIGURE 3.15 ▲
Mutually exclusive events are
dependent.

The second point concerns the relationship between the mutually exclusive and independence properties. Suppose that events A and B are mutually exclusive, as shown in Figure 3.15. Are these events independent or dependent? That is, does the assumption that B occurs alter the probability of the occurrence of A? It certainly does, because if we assume that B has occurred, it is impossible for A to have occurred simultaneously. Thus, mutually exclusive events are dependent events.

The third point is that the probability of the intersection of independent events is very easy to calculate. Referring to the formula for calculating the probability of an intersection, we find

$$P(A \cap B) = P(B)P(A \mid B)$$

Thus, since $P(A \mid B) = P(A)$ when A and B are independent, we have the following useful rule:

If events A and B are independent, the probability of the intersection of A and B equals the product of the probabilities of A and B:

$$P(A \cap B) = P(A)P(B)$$

The converse is also true: If $P(A \cap B) = P(A)P(B)$, then events A and B are independent.

In the die-toss experiment, we showed in Example 3.15 that the events A: {Observe an even number} and B: {Observe a number less than or equal to 4} are independent if the die is fair. Thus,

$$P(A \cap B) = P(A)P(B) = (\tfrac{1}{2})(\tfrac{2}{3}) = \tfrac{1}{3}$$

This agrees with the result

$$P(A \cap B) = P(2) + P(4) = \tfrac{2}{6} = \tfrac{1}{3}$$

that we obtained in the example.

. . . .

EXAMPLE 3.17

Almost every retail business has the problem of determining how much inventory to purchase. Insufficient inventory may result in lost business, and excess inventory will have a detrimental effect on profits. Suppose a retail computer store owner is planning to place an order for personal computers (PCs). She is trying to decide how many IBM PCs and how many IBM compatibles (personal computers that run all or most of the same software as the IBM PC but that are not manufactured by IBM) to order. The owner's records indicate that 80% of the previous PC customers purchased IBM PCs, and 20% purchased compatibles.

a. What is the probability that the next two customers will purchase compatibles?

b. What is the probability that the next 10 customers will purchase compatibles?

Solution

a. Let C_1 represent the event that customer 1 will purchase a compatible, and C_2 the event that customer 2 will purchase a compatible. The event that *both* customers purchase compatibles is the intersection of these events, $C_1 \cap C_2$. From past records, the store owner could reasonably conclude that the probability of C_1 is equal to .2 (based on the fact that 20% of past customers have purchased compatibles), and the same reasoning would apply to C_2. However, in order to compute the probability of the intersection $C_1 \cap C_2$, more information is needed. Either the records must be examined for the occurrence of consecutive purchases of compatibles, or some assumption must be made to enable the calculation of $P(C_1 \cap C_2)$ from the multiplicative rule. It seems reasonable to make the assumption that the two events are independent, since the decision of the first customer is not likely to affect that of the second customer. Assuming independence, we have

$$P(C_1 \cap C_2) = P(C_1)P(C_2) = (.2)(.2) = .04$$

b. To see how to compute the probability that 10 consecutive purchases will be of compatibles, first consider the event that three consecutive customers purchase compatibles. If C_3 represents the event that the third customer purchases a compatible, then we want to compute the probability of the intersection of $C_1 \cap C_2$ with C_3. Again assuming independence of the purchasing decisions, we have

$$P(C_1 \cap C_2 \cap C_3) = P(C_1 \cap C_2)P(C_3) = (.2)^2(.2) = .008$$

Similar reasoning leads to the conclusion that the intersection of 10 such events can be calculated as follows:

$$P(C_1 \cap C_2 \cap \cdots \cap C_{10}) = P(C_1)P(C_2) \cdots P(C_{10})$$
$$= (.2)^{10}$$
$$= .0000001024$$

Thus, the probability that 10 consecutive customers purchase IBM compatibles is about 1 in 10 million, assuming that the probability of each customer's purchase of a compatible is .2, and that the purchase decisions are independent.

Exercises 3.32–3.47

Learning the Mechanics

3.32 An experiment results in one of three mutually exclusive events, A, B, or C. It is known that $P(A) = .30$, $P(B) = .55$, and $P(C) = .15$. Find each of the following probabilities:
a. $P(A \cup B)$ **b.** $P(A \cap C)$ **c.** $P(A \mid B)$ **d.** $P(B \cup C)$
e. Are B and C independent events? Explain.

3.33 Consider the experiment depicted by the Venn diagram on page 162, with the sample space S containing five simple events. The simple events are assigned the following probabilities: $P(E_1) = .20$, $P(E_2) = .30$, $P(E_3) = .30$, $P(E_4) = .10$, $P(E_5) = .10$.

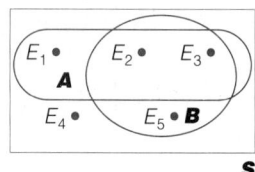

a. Calculate $P(A)$, $P(B)$, and $P(A \cap B)$.
b. Suppose we know that event A has occurred, so that the reduced sample space consists of the three simple events in A—namely, E_1, E_2, and E_3. Use the formula for conditional probability to adjust the probabilities of these three simple events for the knowledge that A has occurred [i.e., $P(E_i \mid A)$]. Verify that the conditional probabilities are in the same proportion to one another as the original simple event probabilities.
c. Calculate the conditional probability $P(B \mid A)$ in two ways: (1) Add the adjusted (conditional) probabilities of the simple events in the intersection $A \cap B$, since these represent the event that B occurs given that A has occurred; (2) Use the formula for conditional probability:

$$P(B \mid A) = \frac{P(A \cap B)}{P(A)}$$

Verify that the two methods yield the same result.
d. Are events A and B independent? Why or why not?

3.34 An experiment results in one of five simple events, with the following probabilities: $P(E_1) = .22$, $P(E_2) = .31$, $P(E_3) = .15$, $P(E_4) = .22$, and $P(E_5) = .10$. The following events have been defined:

$$A = \{E_1, E_3\} \qquad B = \{E_2, E_3, E_4\} \qquad C = \{E_1, E_5\}$$

Find each of the following probabilities:
a. $P(A)$ b. $P(B)$ c. $P(A \cap B)$ d. $P(A \mid B)$ e. $P(B \cap C)$ f. $P(C \mid B)$

3.35 Refer to Exercise 3.34. Which of the following pairs of events are independent? Explain.
a. A and B b. A and C c. B and C

3.36 Three coins are tossed and the following events are defined:

A: {Observe exactly two heads}
B: {Observe at least one head}
C: {Observe at most one head}
D: {Observe at least two tails}

Use the formulas of this section to calculate the following:
a. $P(B \cap C)$ b. $P(B \cup C)$
c. $P(A \cap D)$ d. $P(A \cup D)$
e. $P(B^c \cap C)$ f. $P(A \cap C)$
g. Determine which pairs of events, if any, are independent.

3.37 Defend or refute each of the following statements:
a. Dependent events are always mutually exclusive.
b. Mutually exclusive events are always dependent.

c. Independent events are always mutually exclusive.

d. Mutually exclusive events are always independent.

3.38 If $P(R) = \frac{1}{3}$, $P(S) = \frac{1}{3}$, and events R and S are mutually exclusive, find $P(R \mid S)$ and $P(S \mid R)$.

3.39 Two dice are tossed and the following events are defined:

> A: {Sum of the numbers showing is an odd number}
>
> B: {Sum of the numbers showing is 8, 9, 10, or 11}

Are A and B independent?

3.40 Two hundred shoppers at a large suburban mall were asked two questions: (1) Did you see a television ad for the sale at department store X during the past 2 weeks? (2) Did you shop at department store X during the past 2 weeks? The responses to these questions are summarized in the table. One of the 200 shoppers questioned is to be chosen at random.

	Shopped at X	Did Not Shop at X
Saw ad	100	25
Did not see ad	25	50

a. What is the probability that the person selected saw the ad?

b. What is the probability that the person selected saw the ad and shopped at store X?

c. Find the conditional probability that the person shopped at store X given that the person saw the ad.

d. What is the probability that the person selected shopped at store X?

e. Use your answers to parts **a**, **b**, and **d** to check the independence of the events Saw ad and Shopped at X.

f. Are the two events {Did not see ad} and {Did not shop at X} mutually exclusive? Explain.

Applying the Concepts

3.41 Businesses that offer credit to their customers are inevitably faced with the task of collecting unpaid bills. Richard L. Peterson (1986) conducted a study of collection remedies used by creditors. As part of the study he asked samples of creditors in four states about how they deal with past-due bills. Their responses are tallied in the table. "Tough actions" included filing a legal action, turning the debt over to a third party such as an attorney or collection agency, garnishing wages, and repossessing secured property. Suppose one of the creditors questioned is selected at random.

	Wisconsin	Illinois	Arkansas	Louisiana
Take tough action early	0	1	5	1
Take tough action late	37	23	22	21
Never take tough action	9	11	6	15

a. What is the probability that the creditor is from Wisconsin or Louisiana?

b. What is the probability that the creditor is not from Wisconsin or Louisiana?

c. What is the probability that the creditor never takes tough action?

d. What is the probability that the creditor is from Arkansas and never takes tough action?

e. What is the probability that the creditor never takes tough action, given that the creditor is from Arkansas?

f. If the creditor takes tough action early, what is the probability that the creditor is from Arkansas or Louisiana?

g. What is the probability that a creditor from Arkansas never takes tough action?

3.42 A particular automatic sprinkler system for high-rise apartment buildings, office buildings, and hotels has two different types of activation devices for each sprinkler head. One type has a reliability of .91 (i.e., the probability that it will activate the sprinkler when it should is .91). The other type, which operates independently of the first type, has a reliability of .87. Suppose a serious fire starts near a particular sprinkler head.
   a. What is the probability that the sprinkler head will be activated?
   b. What is the probability that the sprinkler head will not be activated?
   c. What is the probability that both activation devices will work properly?
   d. What is the probability that only the device with reliability .91 will work properly?

3.43 A soft-drink bottler has two quality control inspectors independently check each case of soft drinks for chipped or cracked bottles before the cases leave the bottling plant. Having observed the work of the two trusted inspectors over several years, the bottler has determined that the probability of a defective case getting by the first inspector is .05 and the probability of a defective case getting by the second inspector is .10. What is the probability that a defective case gets by both inspectors?

3.44 The table describes the 67.1 million U.S. long-form federal tax returns filed with the Internal Revenue Service (IRS) in 1989 and the percentage of those returns that were audited by the IRS.

Income	Number of Tax Filers (Millions)	Percentage Audited
Under $25,000	29.1	.5
$25,000–$49,999	25.8	1.0
$50,000–$99,999	10.0	1.0
$100,000 or more	2.2	5.5

Source: *Statistical Abstract of the United States: 1991*, p. 324.

   a. If a tax filer is randomly selected from this population of tax filers (i.e., each tax filer has an equal probability of being selected), what is the probability that the tax filer was audited?
   b. If a tax filer is randomly selected from this population of tax filers, what is the probability that the tax filer had an income of $25,000–$49,999 in 1989 *and* was audited? What is the probability that the tax filer had an income of $50,000 or more in 1989 *or* was not audited?

3.45 Even with strong advertising programs, new products are often unsuccessful. A company that produces a variety of household items found that only 18% of the new products it introduced over the last 10 years have become profitable. When two new products were introduced during the same year, only 5% of the time did both products become profitable. Suppose the company plans to introduce two new products, A and B, next year. If the percentages just cited define the probabilities of success, what is the probability that:
   a. Product A will become profitable?
   b. Product B will not become profitable?
   c. At least one of the two products will become profitable?
   d. Neither of the two products will become profitable?
   e. Either product A or product B (but not both) will become profitable?

3.46 Refer to Exercise 3.45.
   a. If product B is profitable, what is the probability that product A becomes profitable?
   b. If at least one of the products will be profitable, what is the probability that the profitable product is A?

3.47 **Total quality management (TQM)** is a management philosophy and system of management techniques to improve product and service quality and worker productivity. TQM involves such techniques as teamwork, empowerment of workers, improved communication with customers, evaluation of work processes, and statistical analysis of processes and their output (Benson, 1992). One hundred U.S. companies were surveyed and it was found that 30 had implemented TQM. Among the 100 companies surveyed, 60 reported an increase in sales last year. Of those 60, 20 had implemented TQM. Suppose one of the 100 surveyed companies is to be selected at random for additional analysis.

a. What is the probability that a firm that implemented TQM is selected? That a firm whose sales increased is selected?

b. Are the two events {TQM implemented} and {Sales increased} independent or dependent? Explain.

c. Suppose that instead of 20 TQM-implementers among the 60 firms reporting sales increases, there were 18. Now are the events {TQM implemented} and {Sales increased} independent or dependent? Explain.

3.7   Random Sampling

How a sample is selected from a population is of vital importance in statistical inference because the probability of an observed sample will be used to infer the characteristics of the sampled population. To illustrate, suppose you deal yourself four cards from a deck of 52 cards, and all four cards are aces. Do you conclude that your deck is an ordinary bridge deck, containing only four aces, or do you conclude that the deck is stacked with more than four aces? It depends on how the cards were drawn. If the four aces were always placed on the top of a standard bridge deck, drawing four aces would not be unusual—it would be certain. On the other hand, if the cards were thoroughly mixed, drawing four aces in a sample of four cards would be highly improbable. The point, of course, is that, in order to use the observed sample of four cards to make inferences about the population (the deck of 52 cards), you need to know how the sample was selected from the deck.

One of the simplest and most frequently used sampling procedures (implied in the previous examples and exercises) produces what is known as a **random sample**.

Definition 3.10

If n elements are selected from a population in such a way that every possible combination of n elements in the population has an equal probability of being selected, the n elements are said to be a **random sample**.[*]

---

[*]Strictly speaking, this is a **simple random sample**. There are many different types of random samples. The simple random sample is the most frequently employed. Consult the references for a discussion of other types of sampling procedures.

If a population is not too large and the elements can be marked on slips of paper or poker chips, you can physically mix the slips of paper or chips and remove *n* elements from the total. Then the elements that appear on the slips or chips selected would indicate the population elements to be included in the sample. Such a procedure would not guarantee a random sample because it is often difficult to achieve a thorough mix, but it provides a reasonably good approximation to random sampling.

Many samplers use a table of random numbers (see Table I in Appendix B) or a statistical software package to generate a random sample. Random-number tables are constructed in such a way that every digit occurs with (approximately) equal probability. To use a table of random numbers, we number the N elements in the population from 1 to N. Then we turn to Table I and haphazardly select a number in the table. Proceeding from this number across the row or down the column (either will do), remove and record *n* numbers from the table. Use only the necessary number of digits in each random number to identify the element to be included in the sample. If, in the course of recording the *n* numbers from the table, you obtain a number that has already been selected, simply discard the duplicate, and select a replacement at the end of the sequence. Thus, you may have to select more than *n* numbers to obtain a random sample of *n* unique numbers.

We illustrate this procedure with an example.

EXAMPLE 3.18

Suppose you wish to randomly sample five households (we will keep the number in the sample small to simplify our example) from a population of 100,000 households. Use Table I in Appendix B to select a random sample.

TABLE 3.8   Reproduction of Part of Table I of Appendix B: Random Numbers

Row \ Column	1	2	3	4	5	6
1	10480	15011	01536	02011	81647	91646
2	22368	46573	25595	85393	30995	89198
3	24130	48360	22527	97265	76393	64809
4	42167	93093	06243	61680	07856	16376
5	37570	39975	81837	16656	06121	91782
6	77921	06907	11008	42751	27756	53498
7	99562	72905	56420	69994	98872	31016
8	96301	91977	05463	07972	18876	20922
9	89579	14342	63661	10281	17453	18103
10	85475	36857	53342	53988	53060	59533
11	28918	69578	88231	33276	70997	79936
12	63553	40961	48235	03427	49626	69445
13	09429	93969	52636	92737	88974	33488
14	10365	61129	87529	85689	48237	52267
15	07119	97336	71048	08178	77233	13916

Solution

First, number the households in the population from 1 to 100,000. Then, turn to a page of Table I, say, the first page. A reproduction of part of the first page of Table I is shown in Table 3.8. Now, commence with the random number that appears in the third row, second column. This number is 48360. Proceed down the second column to obtain the remaining four random numbers. The five selected random numbers are shaded in Table 3.8. Using the first five digits to represent the households from 1 to 99,999 and the number 00000 to represent household 100,000, you can see that the households numbered

$$48,360 \qquad 93,093 \qquad 39,975 \qquad 6,907 \qquad 72,905$$

should be included in your sample.

CASE STUDY 3.2 / The 1970 Draft Lottery

From 1948 through the early years of the Vietnam War, the Selective Service System drafted men into the military service by age—oldest first, starting with 25-year-olds. A network of local draft boards was used to implement the selection process. Then, on the evening of December 1, 1969, the Selective Service System conducted a lottery to determine the order of selection for 1970 in an attempt to overcome what many believed were inequities in the system. (Such lotteries had been used during World Wars I and II, but it had been 27 years since the last one.)

The objective of the lottery was to randomly order the induction sequence of men between the ages of 19 and 26. To do this, the 366 possible days in a year were written on slips of paper and placed in egg-shaped capsules that were stored in monthly lots. The monthly lots were placed one by one into a wooden box that was ". . . turned end over end several times to mix the numbers" ("Random or not? Judge studies lottery protest," 1970). The capsules were then dumped into a large glass bowl and drawn one by one to obtain the order of induction. All men born on the first day drawn would be inducted first; those born on the second day drawn would be drafted next, etc. Thus, the lottery assigned a rank to each of the 366 birthdays. The results of the lottery are shown in Table 3.9 on page 168.

For a random sequence of numbers to be generated with this procedure, it is necessary for each (re-

maining) capsule in the bowl to have an equal probability of being selected on each draw. That is, by means of thorough mixing, each capsule must have an equal opportunity to come to rest precisely where the sampler's hand closes within the bowl. Although a mixing procedure with this property is almost impossible to achieve, the ideal can be closely approximated. Unfortunately, this was apparently not the case in the 1970 lottery. Even though the sequence of dates in Table 3.9 may appear to be random, there is ample statistical evidence to indicate a nonrandom selection of induction dates.[*]

To obtain an understanding of the problem with the 1970 lottery, we calculated the median rank for each month and plotted the medians in Figure 3.16(a) on page 169. If the sequence of ranks were randomly generated, there should be no relationship between the size of the median ranks and the months of the year. The medians should vary randomly above and below a horizontal line with intercept 183.5 (the median of the integers 1 through 366). However, Figure 3.16(a) reveals a general downward trend in the medians. Men born later in the year were more likely to be drafted before men born early in the year. Furthermore, since not all men between the ages of 19 and 25 would be

---

[*]We discuss procedures for detecting nonrandomness in Chapter 11.

TABLE 3.9 1970 Draft Lottery Results

No.	Date		No.	Date		No.	Date		No.	Date		No.	Date		No.	Date
1	Sept.	14	62	April	21	123	Dec.	28	184	Sept.	8	245	Aug.	26	306	Jan.	7
2	April	24	63	Sept.	20	124	April	13	185	Nov.	20	246	Sept.	18	307	Aug.	13
3	Dec.	30	64	June	27	125	Oct.	2	186	Jan.	21	247	June	22	308	May	28
4	Feb.	14	65	May	10	126	Nov.	13	187	July	20	248	July	11	309	Nov.	26
5	Oct.	18	66	Nov.	12	127	Nov.	14	188	July	5	249	June	1	310	Nov.	5
6	Sept.	6	67	July	25	128	Dec.	18	189	Feb.	17	250	May	21	311	Aug.	19
7	Oct.	26	68	Feb.	12	129	Dec.	1	190	July	18	251	Jan.	3	312	April	8
8	Sept.	7	69	June	13	130	May	15	191	April	29	252	April	23	313	May	31
9	Nov.	22	70	Dec.	21	131	Nov.	15	192	Oct.	20	253	April	6	314	Dec.	12
10	Dec.	6	71	Sept.	10	132	Nov.	25	193	July	31	254	Oct.	16	315	Sept.	30
11	Aug.	31	72	Oct.	12	133	May	12	194	Jan.	9	255	Sept.	17	316	April	22
12	Dec.	7	73	June	17	134	June	11	195	Sept.	24	256	Mar.	23	317	Mar.	9
13	July	8	74	April	27	135	Dec.	20	196	Oct.	24	257	Sept.	28	318	Jan.	13
14	April	11	75	May	19	136	Mar.	11	197	May	9	258	Mar.	24	319	May	23
15	July	12	76	Nov.	6	137	June	25	198	Aug.	14	259	Mar.	13	320	Dec.	15
16	Dec.	29	77	Jan.	28	138	Oct.	13	199	Jan.	8	260	April	17	321	May	8
17	Jan.	15	78	Dec.	27	139	Mar.	6	200	Mar.	19	261	Aug.	3	322	July	15
18	Sept.	26	79	Oct.	31	140	Jan.	18	201	Oct.	23	262	April	28	323	Mar.	10
19	Nov.	1	80	Nov.	9	141	Aug.	18	202	Oct.	4	263	Sept.	9	324	Aug.	11
20	June	4	81	April	4	142	Aug.	12	203	Nov.	19	264	Oct.	27	325	Jan.	10
21	Aug.	10	82	Sept.	5	143	Nov.	17	204	Sept.	21	265	Mar.	22	326	May	22
22	June	26	83	April	3	144	Feb.	2	205	Feb.	27	266	Nov.	4	327	July	6
23	July	24	84	Dec.	25	145	Aug.	4	206	June	10	267	Mar.	3	328	Dec.	2
24	Oct.	5	85	June	7	146	Nov.	18	207	Sept.	16	268	Mar.	27	329	Jan.	11
25	Feb.	19	86	Feb.	1	147	April	7	208	April	30	269	April	5	330	May	1
26	Dec.	14	87	Oct.	6	148	April	16	209	June	30	270	July	29	331	July	14
27	July	21	88	July	28	149	Sept.	25	210	Feb.	4	271	April	2	332	Mar.	18
28	June	5	89	Feb.	15	150	Feb.	11	211	Jan.	31	272	June	12	333	Aug.	30
29	Mar.	2	90	April	18	151	Sept.	29	212	Feb.	16	273	April	15	334	Mar.	21
30	Mar.	31	91	Feb.	7	152	Feb.	13	213	Mar.	8	274	June	16	335	June	9
31	May	24	92	Jan.	26	153	July	22	214	Feb.	5	275	Mar.	4	336	April	19
32	April	1	93	July	1	154	Aug.	17	215	Jan.	4	276	May	4	337	Jan.	22
33	Mar.	17	94	Oct.	28	155	May	6	216	Feb.	10	277	July	9	338	Feb.	9
34	Nov.	2	95	Dec.	24	156	Nov.	21	217	Mar.	30	278	May	18	339	Aug.	22
35	May	7	96	Dec.	16	157	Dec.	3	218	April	10	279	July	4	340	April	26
36	Aug.	24	97	Nov.	8	158	Sept.	11	219	April	9	280	Jan.	20	341	June	18
37	May	11	98	July	17	159	Jan.	2	220	Oct.	10	281	Nov.	28	342	Oct.	9
38	Oct.	30	99	Nov.	29	160	Sept.	22	221	Jan.	12	282	Nov.	10	343	Mar.	25
39	Dec.	11	100	Dec.	31	161	Sept.	2	222	Jan.	28	283	Oct.	8	334	Aug.	20
40	May	3	101	Jan.	5	162	Dec.	23	223	Mar.	28	284	July	10	345	April	20
41	Dec.	10	102	Aug.	15	163	Dec.	13	224	Jan.	6	285	Feb.	29	346	April	12
42	July	13	103	May	30	164	Jan.	30	225	Sept.	1	286	Aug.	25	347	Feb.	6
43	Dec.	9	104	June	19	165	Dec.	4	226	May	29	287	July	30	348	Nov.	3
44	Aug.	16	105	Dec.	8	166	Mar.	16	227	July	19	288	Oct.	17	349	Jan.	29
45	Aug.	2	106	Aug.	9	167	Aug.	28	228	June	2	289	July	27	350	July	2
46	Nov.	11	107	Nov.	16	168	Aug.	7	229	Oct.	29	290	Feb.	22	351	April	25
47	Nov.	27	108	Mar.	1	169	Mar.	15	230	Nov.	24	291	Aug.	21	352	Aug.	27
48	Aug.	8	109	June	23	170	Mar.	26	231	April	14	292	Feb.	18	353	June	29
49	Sept.	3	110	June	6	171	Oct.	15	232	Sept.	4	293	Mar.	5	354	Mar.	14
50	July	7	111	Aug.	1	172	July	23	233	Sept.	27	294	Oct.	14	355	Jan.	27
51	Nov.	7	112	May	17	173	Dec.	26	234	Oct.	7	295	May	13	356	June	14
52	Jan.	25	113	Sept.	15	174	Nov.	30	235	Jan.	17	296	May	27	357	May	26
53	Dec.	22	114	Aug.	6	175	Sept.	13	236	Feb.	24	297	Feb.	3	358	June	24
54	Aug.	5	115	July	3	176	Oct.	25	237	Oct.	11	298	May	2	359	Oct.	1
55	May	16	116	Aug.	23	177	Sept.	19	238	Jan.	14	299	Feb.	28	360	June	20
56	Dec.	5	117	Oct.	22	178	May	14	239	Mar.	20	300	Mar.	12	361	May	25
57	Feb.	23	118	Jan.	23	179	Feb.	25	240	Dec.	19	301	June	3	362	Mar.	29
58	Jan.	19	119	Sept.	23	180	June	15	241	Oct.	19	302	Feb.	20	363	Feb.	21
59	Jan.	24	120	July	16	181	Feb.	8	242	Sept.	12	303	July	26	364	May	5
60	June	21	121	Jan.	16	182	Nov.	23	243	Oct.	21	304	Dec.	17	365	Feb.	26
61	Aug.	29	122	Mar.	7	183	May	20	244	Oct.	3	305	Jan.	1	366	June	8

FIGURE 3.16 ▶
Median plots for lottery results:
1970 and 1971

a. 1970 lottery

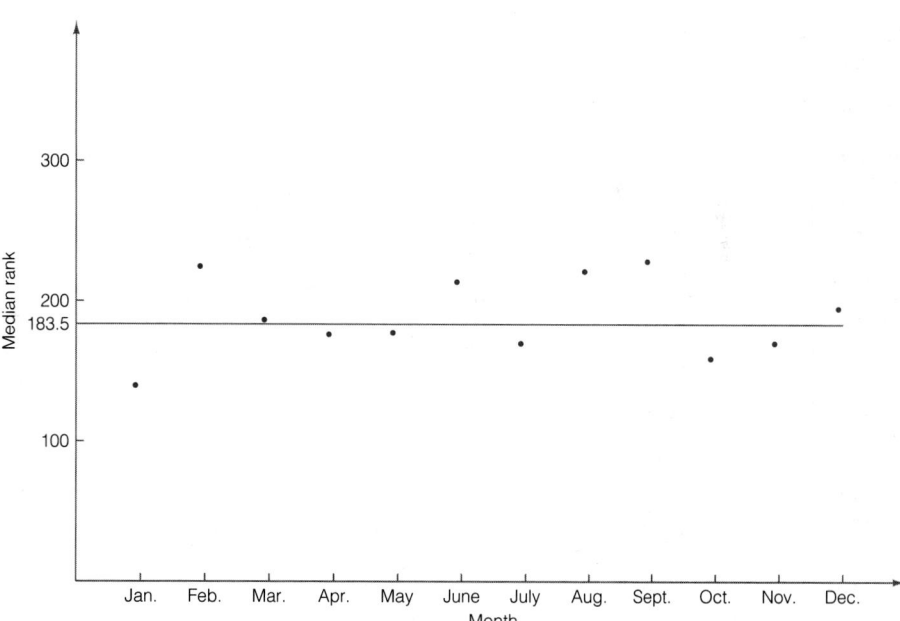

b. 1971 lottery

drafted in 1970, men born earlier in the year were more likely not to be drafted at all. Although it is possible to observe such a sequence of medians when random sampling is employed, it is highly unlikely. It is more likely that the capsules were not mixed thoroughly enough to give every capsule an equal chance of selection on each draw. The graph indicates that capsules tended to be drawn in monthly groups, and thus suggests that monthly lots of capsules in the wooden boxes were not mixed thoroughly enough after they were dumped into the large glass bowl (Williams, 1978).

The following year, the Selective Service System used more sophisticated mixing techniques to guard against the monthly clustering of selections. The me-

dian plot for the 1971 lottery is shown in Figure 3.16(b). [*Note:* The 1971 lottery involved only men born in 1951. Thus, only 365 birthdays were ranked and the sequence of monthly ranked medians should be compared to 183 instead of 183.5.] Note that no apparent trend remains; the new mixing technique appears to have been successful.

This case study emphasizes the value of using a random-number table or a random number generator of a statistical software package in the selection of a random sample. Most important, it points out the problems that may be encountered when attempting to acquire a random sample by a mechanical selection process.

Exercises 3.48 – 3.54

Learning the Mechanics

3.48 Suppose you wish to draw a sample of $n = 2$ elements from a population that contains $N = 10$ elements.
  a. List all possible different samples of $n = 2$ elements, and also use combinatorial mathematics (see Section 3.1) to count the number of different samples that can be selected. How many different samples of $n = 2$ elements can be selected?
  b. If random sampling is employed, what is the probability of drawing a particular pair of elements in your sample?

3.49 Use Table I of Appendix B to select a random sample of size $n = 20$ from among the digits 0, 1, 2, . . . , 9. (Digits may repeat themselves.) Explain your procedure.

3.50 Suppose that a population contains $N = 200,000$ elements. Use Table I of Appendix B to select a random sample of $n = 10$ elements from the population. Explain how you selected your sample.

3.51 Consider the population of new savings accounts opened in one business day at a bank, as shown in the table. Suppose you wish to draw a random sample of two accounts from this population.

Account Number	0001	0002	0003	0004	0005
Account Balance	$1,000	$12,500	$850	$1,000	$3,450

  a. List all possible different pairs of accounts that could be obtained.
  b. What is the probability of selecting accounts 0001 and 0004?
  c. What is the probability of selecting two accounts that each have a balance of $1,000? That each have a balance other than $1,000?

Applying the Concepts

3.52 To ascertain the effectiveness of their advertising campaigns, firms frequently conduct telephone interviews with consumers. Samples of telephone numbers may be randomly or systematically selected from telephone directories, or a more recent innovation called **random-digit dialing** may be employed. This approach involves using a random-number generator to create the sample of phone numbers to be called. Use the random-number table (Table I of Appendix B) to generate a sample of 10 seven-digit telephone numbers from area code 215. Describe the procedure you used.

3.53 When a company sells shares of stock to investors, the transaction is said to take place in the *primary market*. To enable investors to resell the stock when they wish, *secondary markets* called *stock exchanges* were created. Stock exchange transactions involve buyers and sellers exchanging cash for shares of stock, with none of the proceeds going to the companies that issued the shares (Greenleaf, Foster, and Prinsky, 1982). The results of the previous business day's transactions for stocks traded on the New York Stock Exchange (NYSE) and five regional exchanges—the Midwest, Pacific, Philadelphia, Boston, and Cincinnati stock exchanges—are summarized each business day in the NYSE–Composite Transactions table in the *Wall Street Journal*.
  a. Examine the NYSE–Composite Transactions table in a recent issue of the *Wall Street Journal* and explain how to draw a random sample of stocks from the table.
  b. Use the procedure you described in part **a** to draw a random sample of 20 stocks from a recent NYSE–Composite Transactions table. For each stock in the sample, list its name (i.e., the abbreviation given in the table), its sales volume, and its closing price.

3.54 The total labor force has increased annually, from 69.6 million in 1960 to 106.9 million in 1980 to 124.8 million in 1990. From 1960 to 1980, the percentage of the labor force age 16–34 steadily increased, and the percentage of the labor force age 35–64 decreased. However, beginning around 1980, with the aging of the baby-boom generation, these percentages began moving in the opposite directions.

Age	*Percent in the Labor Force*		
	1960	*1980*	*1990*
16–34	37.3	51.0	45.7
35–64	58.1	46.1	51.4
65+	4.6	2.9	2.8

Source: *Statistical Abstract of the United States: 1991*, p. 388.

  a. If the year were 1990 and one laborer were randomly selected from the labor force, what is the probability that a particular laborer would be selected? What is the probability that the laborer would be between 16 and 34 years of age?
  b. Repeat part **a** for the year 1960, and compare the answers.
  c. If two laborers were randomly selected from the 1990 labor force, what is the probability of selecting a particular pair of laborers?

Summary

We have developed some of the basic tools of probability that enable us to determine the probabilities of various sample outcomes, given a specific population structure. Although many of the examples we presented were of no practical importance, they accomplished their purpose if you now understand the basic concepts and definitions of probability.

The basic understanding of probability presented in this chapter includes the following concepts: **Experiments** are the basis for the generation of data. The most basic outcomes of experiments, called **simple events**, cannot be predicted with certainty. Therefore, we assign **probabilities** to the simple events, such that they obey two rules: (1) all probabilities must be between 0 and 1, and (2) the simple event probabilities must sum to 1. The collection of all the simple events is called the **sample space** of the experiment.

Unions and **intersections** are useful combinations of events. **Unions** are inclusive: either or both events occur. **Intersections** are limiting: both events occur. **Complements** are exclusive: the event does not occur. The **additive rule** is useful for calculating the probability of unions, and is particularly simple when the events have no intersection, in which case they are said to be **mutually exclusive**.

Conditional probability applies when we have some knowledge about what has occurred, reducing the size of the sample space. The **multiplicative rule** is useful for relating the probability of an intersection to conditional probability. When an intersection probability is equal to the product of the two (unconditional) event probabilities, we say the events are **independent**.

Our primary reason for studying the basics of probability is to enable the quantitative evaluation of alternative explanations (or models) of real data. To be able to rule out some explanations as "unlikely" and to accept others as "probable," we must first be able to quantify "unlikely" and "probable," and the theory of probability will provide the foundation for this endeavor.

In the next several chapters, we will present probability models that can be used to solve practical business problems. You will see that for most applications, we will need to make inferences about unknown aspects of these probability models; i.e., we will need to apply inferential statistics to the problem.

Supplementary Exercises 3.55–3.79

3.55 What are the two rules that probabilities assigned to simple events must obey?

3.56 Are mutually exclusive events also dependent events? Explain.

3.57 Given that $P(A \cap B) = .4$ and $P(A \mid B) = .8$, find $P(B)$.

3.58 Which of the following pairs of events are mutually exclusive? Justify your response.
  a. The Dow Jones Industrial Average increases on Monday.
    A large New York bank decreases its prime interest rate on Monday.
  b. The next sale by a PC retailer is an IBM microcomputer.
    The next sale by a PC retailer is an Apple microcomputer.
  c. You reinvest all your dividend income for 1990 in a limited partnership.
    You reinvest all your dividend income for 1990 in a money market fund.

3.59 A manufacturer of electronic digital watches claims that the probability of its watch running more than 1 minute slow or 1 minute fast after 1 year of use is .05. A consumer protection agency has purchased four of the manufacturer's watches with the intention of testing the claim.

   a. Assuming that the manufacturer's claim is correct, what is the probability that all four of the watches are as accurate as claimed?

   b. Assuming that the manufacturer's claim is correct, what is the probability that exactly two of the four watches fail to meet the claim?

   c. Suppose that three of the four tested watches failed to meet the claim. What inference can be made about the manufacturer's claim? Explain.

   d. Suppose that all four tested watches failed to meet the claim. Is it necessarily true that the manufacturer's claim is false? Explain.

3.60 The state legislature has appropriated $1 million to be distributed in the form of grants to individuals and organizations engaged in the research and development of alternative energy sources. You have been hired by the state's energy agency to assemble a panel of five energy experts whose task it will be to determine which individuals and organizations should receive the grant money. You have identified 11 equally qualified individuals who are willing to serve on the panel. How many different panels of five experts could be formed from these 11 individuals?

3.61 A research and development company surveyed all 200 of its employees over the age of 60 and obtained the information given in the table. One of these 200 employees is selected at random.

	Under 20 Years with Company		Over 20 Years with Company	
	Technical Staff	Nontechnical Staff	Technical Staff	Nontechnical Staff
Plan to Retire at Age 65	31	5	45	12
Plan to Retire at Age 68	59	25	15	8

   a. What is the probability that the person selected is on the technical staff?

   b. If the person selected has over 20 years of service with the company, what is the probability that the person plans to retire at age 68?

   c. If the person selected is on the technical staff, what is the probability that the person has been with the company less than 20 years?

   d. What is the probability that the person selected has over 20 years with the company, is on the nontechnical staff, and plans to retire at age 65?

3.62 Refer to Exercise 3.61.

   a. Consider the events A: {Plan to retire at age 68} and B: {On the technical staff}. Are events A and B independent? Explain.

   b. Consider the event D: {Plan to retire at age 68 *and* on the technical staff}. Describe the complement of event D.

   c. Consider the event E: {On the nontechnical staff}. Are events B and E mutually exclusive? Explain.

3.63 Two marketing research companies, Richard Saunders International and Marketing Intelligence Service, joined forces to create a consumer preference poll called Acupoll. Acupoll is used to predict whether newly developed products will succeed if they are brought to market. The reliability of the Acupoll has been described as follows: The probability that Acupoll predicts the success of a particular product, given that later the product actually is successful, is .89 (Hall, 1992). A company is considering the introduction of a new product and assesses the product's probability of success to be .90. If this company were to have its product evaluated through Acupoll, what is the probability that Acupoll predicts success for the product and the product actually turns out to be successful?

3.64 The performance of quality inspectors affects both the quality and the cost of outgoing products. A product that passes inspection is assumed to meet quality standards; a product that fails inspection may be reworked, scrapped, or reinspected. Quality engineers at Westinghouse Electric Corporation evaluated inspectors' performances in judging the quality of solder joints by comparing each inspector's classifications of a set of 153 joints with the consensus evaluation of a panel of experts (Meagher and Scazzero, 1985). Suppose the results for a particular inspector are as shown in the table, and that one of the 153 solder joints is to be selected at random.

		Inspector's Judgment	
		Joint Acceptable	Joint Rejectable
Committee's Judgment	Joint Acceptable	101	10
	Joint Rejectable	23	19

a. What is the probability that the inspector judges the joint to be acceptable? That the committee judges the joint to be acceptable?
b. What is the probability that both the inspector and the committee judge the joint to be acceptable? That neither judges the joint to be acceptable?
c. What is the probability that the inspector and the committee disagree? Agree?

3.65 A local country club has a membership of 600 and operates facilities that include an 18-hole championship golf course and 12 tennis courts. Before deciding whether to accept new members, the club president would like to know how many members regularly use each facility. A survey of the membership indicates that 70% regularly use the golf course, 50% regularly use the tennis courts, and 5% use neither of these facilities regularly.
a. Construct a Venn diagram to describe the results of the survey.
b. If one club member is chosen at random, what is the probability that the member uses either the golf course or the tennis courts or both?
c. If one member is chosen at random, what is the probability that the member uses both the golf and the tennis facilities?
d. A member is chosen at random from among those known to use the tennis courts regularly. What is the probability that the member also uses the golf course regularly?

3.66 Insurance companies use *mortality tables* to help them determine how large a premium to charge a particular individual for a particular life insurance policy. The accompanying table shows the probability of survival to age 65 for persons of the specified ages.

Age	Probability of Survival to Age 65	Age	Probability of Survival to Age 65
0	.72	40	.77
10	.74	45	.79
20	.74	50	.81
30	.75	55	.85
35	.76	60	.90

a. For a person 20 years old, what is the probability that he or she will die before age 65?

b. Describe in words the trend indicated by the increasing probabilities in the second and fourth columns.

3.67 Explain why the following statement is or is not valid: If an individual is chosen at random from all U.S. citizens living in the 50 states, the probability that this individual lives in New Hampshire is $\frac{1}{50}$.

3.68 A manufacturer of 35-mm cameras knows that a shipment of 30 cameras sent to a large discount store contains six defective cameras. The manufacturer also knows that the store will choose two of the cameras at random, test them, and accept the shipment if neither is defective.

a. What is the probability that the first camera chosen by the store will be defective?

b. Given that the first camera chosen passed inspection, what is the probability that the second camera chosen will fail inspection?

c. What is the probability that the shipment will be accepted?

3.69 The accompanying figure is a schematic representation of a system comprised of three components connected *in series*. The system functions properly only if all three components operate properly. The components could be mechanical or electrical; they could be work stations in an assembly process; or could represent the functions of three different departments in an organization. The probability of failure for each of the components follows: #1 = .12, #2 = .09, #3 = .11.

A System Comprised of Three
Components in Series

a. Find the probability that the system operates properly.

b. What is the probability that at least one of the components will fail and, therefore, that the system will fail?

3.70 To accompanying figure is a representation of a system comprised of two subsystems that are said to operate *in parallel*. Each subsystem has two components that operate in series (refer to Exercise 3.69). The system will operate properly as long as at least one of the subsystems functions properly. The probability of failure for each component in the system is .1. Assume that the components operate independently of each other.

A System Comprised of Two Parallel Subsystems
Subsystem A

a. Find the probability that the system operates properly.

b. Find the probability that exactly one subsystem fails.

c. Find the probability that the system fails to operate properly.

d. How many parallel subsystems like the two shown here would be required to guarantee that the system would operate properly more than 99% of the time?

3.71 Your firm has decided to market two new products. The manager of the Marketing Department believes the probability of product A being accepted by the public and product B not being accepted is .3, of product B being accepted and product A not being accepted is .4, and of both products A and B being accepted is .2. Given these probabilities the manager has concluded that the probability of both products failing is .01. Do you agree with this conclusion? Explain.

3.72 Suppose only two daily newspapers are available in your town—a local paper and one from a nearby city—and that 1,000 people in town subscribe to a daily paper. Assume that 65% of the people in town who subscribe to a daily newspaper subscribe to the local paper and 40% of those who subscribe to a daily paper subscribe to the city paper.

a. Use a Venn diagram to describe the population of newspaper subscribers.

b. If one of the 1,000 subscribers is chosen at random, what is the probability that he or she subscribes to both newspapers?

3.73 Six people apply for two identical positions in a company. Four are minority applicants and the remainder are nonminority. Define the following events:

A: {Both persons selected for the positions are nonminority candidates}

B: {Both persons selected for the positions are minority candidates}

C: {At least one of the persons selected is a minority candidate}

If all the applicants are equally qualified and the choice is therefore a random selection of two applicants from the six available, find the following:

a. $P(A)$ b. $P(B)$ c. $P(C)$ d. $P(B \mid C)$

e. For the purpose of identification, assume that the minority candidates are numbered 1, 2, 3, and 4. Define the event D: {Minority candidate 1 is selected}. Find $P(D \mid C)$.

3.74 Suppose there are 500 applicants for five equivalent positions at a factory and the company is able to narrow the field to 30 equally qualified applicants. Seven of the finalists are minority candidates. Assume that the five who are chosen are selected at random from this final group of 30.

a. What is the probability that none of the minority candidates is hired?

b. What is the probability that no more than one minority candidate is hired?

3.75 The probability that a microcomputer salesperson sells a computer to a prospective customer on the first visit to the customer is .4. If the salesperson fails to make the sale on the first visit, the probability that the sale will be made on the second visit is .65. The salesperson never visits a prospective customer more than twice. What is the probability that the salesperson will make a sale to a particular customer?

3.76 A credit counselor claims that the probability that at least two local firms go bankrupt next year is .15, and the probability that exactly two local firms go bankrupt is .20. Can this statement be true? Explain.

3.77 Use a Venn diagram to show that

$$P(A \cap B^c) = P(A) - P(A \cap B)$$

3.78 Use your intuitive understanding of independence to form an opinion about whether each of the following scenarios represents independent events.

    a. The results of consecutive tosses of a coin

    b. The opinions of randomly selected individuals in a pre-election poll

    c. A major-league baseball player's results in two consecutive at-bats

    d. The amount of gain or loss associated with investments in different stocks that are bought on the same day, and sold on the same day 1 month later

    e. The amount of gain or loss associated with investments in different stocks that are bought and sold in different time periods, 5 years apart

    f. The prices bid by two different development firms in response to a building construction proposal issued by a university.

3.79 A fair coin is flipped 20 times and 20 heads are observed. In such cases it is often said that a tail is due on the next flip. Is this statement true or false? Explain.

On Your Own

Obtain a standard bridge deck of 52 cards and think of the cards as the 52 items your firm produces each day. Let the four aces and four kings in the deck represent defective items.

a. If one item is randomly sampled from a day's production, what is the probability of its being defective?

b. Shuffle the cards, draw one, and record whether it is a defective item. Then replace the card and repeat the process. After each draw, recalculate the proportion of the draws that have resulted in a defective item. Construct a graph with the proportion of defectives on the y-axis and the number of draws on the x-axis. Notice how the proportion defective stabilizes as the number of draws increases.

c. Draw a horizontal line on the graph in part **b** at a height equal to the probability you calculated in part **a**. Compare the calculated proportion of defectives to this probability. As the number of draws is increased, does the calculated proportion of defectives more closely approach the actual probability of drawing a defective?

Using the Computer

Suppose a large bank is planning a national mailing to market a major credit card. However, the bank will first test its marketing materials by mailing to a single zip code.

a. If one of the 1,000 zip codes in Appendix C were to be selected randomly for a test mailing, what is the probability that the selected zone is one for which the average income exceeds $35,000?

b. Suppose the zip code were to be selected from the Northeast census region (among those in Appendix C). What is the probability that the selected zone is one for which the average income exceeds $35,000?

c. Are the events described in parts **a** and **b** independent? Why or why not? What are the practical implications of the independence, or dependence, of the events?

References

Bagozzi, R. P. *Principles of Marketing Management*. Chicago: SRA, 1986, p. 215.

Benson, P. George. "Process thinking: The quality catalyst." *Minnesota Management Review*, Carlson School of Management, University of Minnesota, Minneapolis, Fall 1992.

Feller, W. *An Introduction to Probability Theory and Its Applications*, 3d ed. Vol. 1. New York: Wiley, 1968. Chapters 1, 4, and 5.

"GM's Saturn takes 3rd in new-car owner poll." *Star Tribune* (Minneapolis). June 30, 1992.

Greenleaf, J., Foster, R., and Prinsky, R. "Understanding financial data in the *Wall Street Journal*." *Wall Street Journal*, Special Education Edition, 1982, p. 19.

Hall, Trish. "Pollsters think they have trick for product picks." *Star Tribune* (Minneapolis). Dec. 16, 1992.

Kozlov, Alex. "Business products for the technophobic and parsimonious." *Newsweek*, Nov. 16, 1992, p. 7.

Kuehn, A. A. "An analysis of the dynamics of consumer behavior and its implications for marketing management." Unpublished doctoral dissertation, Graduate School of Industrial Administration, Carnegie Institute of Technology, 1958.

Lindley, D. V. *Making Decisions*, 2d ed. London: Wiley, 1985.

Meagher, J. J. and Scazzero, J. A. "Measuring inspector variability." *39th Annual Quality Congress Transactions*, American Society for Quality Control, May 1985, pp. 75–81.

Parzen, E. *Modern Probability Theory and Its Applications*. New York: Wiley, 1960. Chapters 1 and 2.

Peterson, R. L. "Creditors' use of collection remedies." *Journal of Financial Research*, Vol. 9 , No. 1, Spring 1986, pp. 71–86.

Press, S. J. *Bayesian Statistics*. New York: Wiley, 1989.

"Random or not? Judge studies lottery protest." *The National Observer*, Jan. 12, 1970, p. 2.

Schmickle, Sharon. " 'Sustainable' farming viable, study suggests." *Star Tribune* (Minneapolis). June 20, 1992.

Williams, B. *A Sampler on Sampling*. New York: Wiley, 1978. pp. 5–8.

Winkler, R. L. *An Introduction to Bayesian Inference and Decision*. New York: Holt, Rinehart and Winston, 1972. Chapter 2.

Winkler, R. L. and Hays, W. L. *Statistics: Probability, Inference, and Decision*, 2d ed. New York: Holt, Rinehart and Winston, 1975. Chapters 1 and 2.

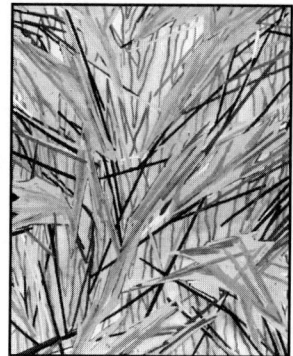

CHAPTER FOUR

Random Variables and Probability Distributions

Contents

Case Studies

Where We've Been

By illustration, we indicated in Chapter 3 how probability would be used to make an inference about a population from information contained in a sample. We also noted that probability would be used to measure the reliability of the inference.

Where We're Going

Most events in Chapter 3 were described in words or were denoted by capital letters. In real life, most sample observations are numerical—in other words, they are quantitative data. In this chapter, we will learn that data can be characterized as observed values of random variables. We will study several important random variables and will learn how to find the probabilities of specific numerical outcomes.

You may have noticed that most of the examples of experiments given in Chapter 3 generated quantitative (numerical) data. This is frequently true; observations on many types of phenomena are numerical measurements. The Consumer Price Index, unemployment rate, number of sales made in a week, and yearly profit of a company are all examples of numerical measurements of some business phenomenon. Thus, most experiments have simple events that correspond to values of some numerical variable.

Definition 4.1

A **random variable** is a rule that assigns one (and only one) numerical value to each simple event of an experiment.*

The term **random variable** is more meaningful than the simpler term *variable* because the adjective *random* indicates that the experiment may result in one of the several possible values of the variable, according to the *random* outcome of the experiment. For example, if the experiment is to count the number of customers who use the drive-up window of a bank each day, the random variable (the number of customers) will vary from day to day, partly because of the random phenomena that influence whether customers use the drive-up window. Thus, the possible values of this random variable range from zero to the maximum number of customers the window could possibly serve in a day.

We define two different types of random variables, *discrete* and *continuous*, in Section 4.1. Then we spend the remainder of the chapter discussing specific types of random variables and the aspects that make them important in business applications.

4.1   Two Types of Random Variables

Recall that the simple event probabilities corresponding to an experiment must sum to 1. Assigning one unit of probability to the simple events in a sample space, and consequently to the values of a random variable, is not always as easy as the examples in Chapter 3 may lead you to believe. If the number of simple events is finite, the job is easy. If the number of simple events is infinite but you can list them in order (we call this **countable**), the task is still not too difficult. But if the simple events are numerical and correspond to the infinitely large number of points contained in an interval, the task is impossible. Why? Because you cannot assign a small portion of probability to each of the simple events in this infinitely large set—the sum of the probabilities will exceed 1 (in fact, the sum will be infinitely large). The consequences of this mathe-

---

*By *experiment*, we mean an experiment that yields random outcomes (as defined in Chapter 3).

matical fact are important. We will have to use two different probability models, depending on whether the number of simple events in a sample space (or equivalently, the values that a random variable can assume) are countable or they correspond to the infinitely large number of points contained in one or more intervals.

Definition 4.2

Random variables that can assume a *countable* number of values are called **discrete**.

Definition 4.3

Random variables that can assume values corresponding to any of the points contained in one or more intervals are called **continuous**.

Examples of **discrete** random variables are:

1. The number of sales made by a salesperson in a given week: $x = 0, 1, 2, \ldots$
2. The number of people in a sample of 500 who favor a particular product over all competitors: $x = 0, 1, 2, \ldots, 499, 500$.
3. The number of bids received in a bond offering: $x = 0, 1, 2, \ldots$
4. The number of errors on a page of an accountant's ledger: $x = 0, 1, 2, \ldots$
5. The number of customers waiting to be served in a restaurant at a particular time: $x = 0, 1, 2, \ldots$

Note that each of the examples of discrete random variables begins with the words "the number of." This is very common because the discrete random variables most frequently observed are counts.

Examples of **continuous** random variables are:

1. The length of time between arrivals at a hospital clinic: $0 \leq x < \infty$ (infinity).
2. For a new apartment complex, the length of time from completion until a specified number of apartments are rented: $0 \leq x < \infty$.
3. The amount of carbonated beverage loaded into a 12-ounce can in a can filling operation: $0 \leq x \leq 12$.
4. The depth at which a successful oil drilling venture first strikes oil.
5. The weight of a food item bought in a supermarket.

In Sections 4.2–4.4 we discuss the probability distributions for discrete random variables. Probability distributions for continuous random variables are covered in Sections 4.5–4.9. Along the way we will discover two random variables that play important roles in business decisions—the binomial (a discrete) random variable and the normal (a continuous) random variable.

Exercises 4.1 – 4.10

Applying the Concepts

4.1   What is a random variable?

4.2   How do discrete and continuous random variables differ?

4.3   Which of the following describe continuous random variables, and which describe discrete random variables? Justify your answers.
   a. The amount of water flowing through the Hoover Dam in a year
   b. The number of people who fly American Airlines each day
   c. The length of time it takes to assemble one Ford Thunderbird
   d. The number of patients that are admitted per week in a particular hospital

4.4   Which of the following describe continuous random variables, and which describe discrete random variables?
   a. The number of newspapers sold by the *New York Times* each month
   b. The amount of ink used in printing a Sunday edition of the *New York Times*
   c. The actual number of ounces in a 1-gallon bottle of laundry detergent
   d. The number of defective parts in a shipment of nuts and bolts
   e. The number of people collecting unemployment insurance each month

4.5   Give two examples of a business-oriented discrete random variable. Do the same for a continuous random variable.

4.6   Give an example of a discrete random variable that would be of interest to a banker.

4.7   Give an example of a continuous random variable that would be of interest to an economist.

4.8   Give an example of a discrete random variable that would be of interest to the manager of a hotel.

4.9   Give two examples of discrete random variables that would be of interest to the manager of a clothing store.

4.10 Give an example of a continuous random variable that would be of interest to a stockbroker.

4.2   Probability Distributions for Discrete Random Variables

Since a random variable assigns a numerical value to each of the simple events associated with an experiment, a complete description of a random variable requires that we specify its **probability distribution**. Note that each simple event is assigned one and only one value of the random variable, and hence, the values of the random variable represent mutually exclusive events.

> ### Definition 4.4
>
> The **probability distribution** of a discrete random variable is a graph, table, or formula that specifies the probability associated with each possible value the random variable can assume.

To illustrate, consider Example 4.1.

EXAMPLE 4.1

Recall the experiment of tossing two coins (Chapter 3), and let x be the number of heads observed. Find the probability distribution for the random variable x, assuming the two coins are fair.

Solution

Recall from Chapter 3 that the sample space and simple events for this experiment are as shown in Figure 4.1, and the probability associated with each of the four simple events is $\frac{1}{4}$. The random variable x can assume values 0, 1, 2. Then, identifying the probabilities of the simple events associated with each of these values of x, we have

$$P(x = 0) = P(T_1, T_2) = \frac{1}{4}$$
$$P(x = 1) = P(T_1, H_2) + P(H_1, T_2) = \frac{1}{4} + \frac{1}{4} = \frac{1}{2}$$
$$P(x = 2) = P(H_1, H_2) = \frac{1}{4}$$

We denote the probability of the discrete random variable x by the symbol $p(x)$. Then, for this example, $p(0) = \frac{1}{4}$, $p(1) = \frac{1}{2}$, and $p(2) = \frac{1}{4}$. Table 4.1 shows the probability distribution of x in tabular form, and Figure 4.2 on page 184 shows it in two alternative graphical forms. Figure 4.2(a) shows the probabilities concentrated at the points, $x = 0$, 1, and 2. The heights of the vertical line segments give the probabilities that correspond to each of these values of x. The probability distribution in Figure 4.2(b) is shown as a histogram with one class corresponding to each of the three values of x. Although the probabilities for discrete random variables are, in fact, concentrated at specific points, the probability histogram will be a convenient way of viewing the probability distribution for a discrete random variable when we attempt to approximate certain probabilities in Section 4.9.

FIGURE 4.1 ▶
Venn diagram for the two-coin-toss experiment

H_1, H_2	T_1, H_2
•	•
$x = 2$	$x = 1$
H_1, T_2	T_1, T_2
•	•
$x = 1$	$x = 0$

S

TABLE 4.1 Probability Distribution: Tabular Form

x	0	1	2
$p(x)$	$\frac{1}{4}$	$\frac{1}{2}$	$\frac{1}{4}$

FIGURE 4.2 ▶
Probability distribution: Graphical forms

 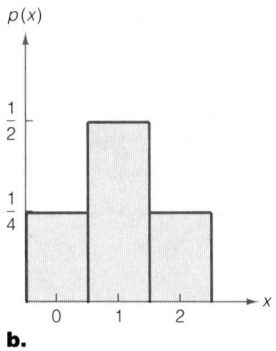

We could also present the probability distribution for x as a formula, but this would unnecessarily complicate a very simple example. We will give the formulas for the probability distributions of some discrete random variables later in this chapter.

Two requirements must be satisfied by all probability distributions for discrete random variables:

Requirements for the Probability Distribution of a Discrete Random Variable x

1. $p(x) \geq 0$ for all values of x
2. $\sum_{\text{All } x} p(x) = 1$

CASE STUDY 4.1 / Assessing the Effects of the Deadly Dutch Elm Disease

Since 1930 when the Dutch elm disease fungus was first discovered in the U.S. on the east coast, it has spread westward destroying elm trees all across the continent. It has been called ". . . the most destructive and widespread plague of trees of our time" (Webster, 1978). The fungus is spread primarily by English bark beetles which breed in diseased elm trees. Because of a lack of an effective chemical treatment, the major tactic in combating Dutch elm disease is a sanitation program which involves the removal of the diseased elm trees before they become a breeding ground for the fungus-carrying beetle (Chervany et al., 1980).

At the start of 1977, the city of Minneapolis had approximately 200,000 elms and had not lost more than 7,200 elms in any single year to Dutch elm disease. Since a major reforestation program had recently been inaugurated, this loss rate was not overly alarming. In 1977, however, Minneapolis lost 31,475 elms, approximately 16% of the existing elm population.

Prior to the 1978 growing season the Minneapolis Park and Recreation Board (Park Board), the organization responsible for managing the city's Dutch Elm Disease Sanitation Program, hired a team of management scientists to help in the design and operation of a sanitation program capable of dealing with the increased disease incidence. An integral part of the program proposed by the team involved forecasting the number of elms to be lost in the coming growing season. This information would enable the Park Board to plan staffing, evaluate potential bottlenecks in the elm removal operation, and inform the citizenry of the extent of the damage to the urban forest expected during the next year.

Because of the scarcity of historical data, the forecast was developed from the opinions of four disease experts. Each expert developed a discrete probability distribution to represent his beliefs regarding the num-

ber of elms that would be infected by the disease during the 1978 growing season. These four probability distributions were combined (by averaging using equal weights) to obtain a single discrete probability distribution reflecting the beliefs of all the experts regarding the number of elms to be infected. A slightly modified version of this probability distribution appears in the table.

This distribution was used to make probabilistic forecasts of the number of trees that would be infected in 1978. It indicated that, according to the combined opinions of the disease experts, it was most likely that the number of trees to be infected would be between 20,000 and 24,999. Furthermore, probability statements like the following were made about the number of trees to be infected, x:

Number of Elms that Would be Infected in 1978

x	$p(x)$
5,000– 9,999	.02
10,000–14,999	.07
15,000–19,999	.16
20,000–24,999	.17
25,000–29,999	.12
30,000–34,999	.13
35,000–39,999	.11
40,000–44,999	.08
45,000–49,999	.07
50,000 or more	.07

$$P(15,000 \leq x \leq 29,999) = .45$$
$$P(15,000 \leq x \leq 39,999) = .69$$
$$P(10,000 \leq x \leq 49,999) = .91$$
$$P(x < 15,000) = .09$$
$$P(x \geq 40,000) = .22$$

It is interesting to note that the actual number of losses to Dutch elm disease in 1978 was 20,817 trees, which is within the modal interval of the forecast distribution (Chervany et al., 1980).

Example 4.1 and Case Study 4.1 illustrate how the probability distribution for a discrete random variable can be derived, but for many practical examples, the task is much more difficult. Fortunately, experiments and associated discrete random variables with identical characteristics are found in many different areas of business. That is, although the data may be collected in an area of accounting, marketing, economics, or management, for all practical purposes the data may represent observed values of the same type of random variable. This fact simplifies the problem for the business analyst. All that must be done is to define the nature of the experiment, define the type of random variable, and specify the probability distribution of the random variable.

In Sections 4.3 and 4.4 we describe two important types of discrete random variables, give their probability distributions, and explain where and how they can be applied in business. (Mathematical derivations of the probability distributions will be omitted, but these details can be found in the references at the end of the chapter.)

But first, we discuss some descriptive measures of these sometimes complex probability distributions. Since probability distributions are analogous to the relative fre-

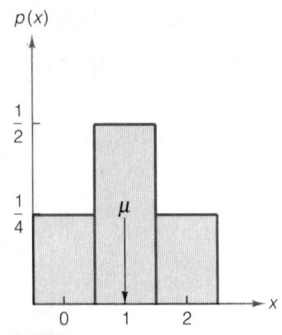

$p(x)$

FIGURE 4.3 ▲

Probability distribution for a
two-coin toss

quency distributions of Chapter 2, it should be no surprise that the mean and standard deviation are useful descriptive measures.

If a discrete random variable, x, were observed a very large number of times and if the data generated were arranged in a relative frequency distribution, the relative frequency distribution would be indistinguishable from the probability distribution for the random variable. Thus, the probability distribution for a random variable can be viewed as a theoretical model for the relative frequency distribution of a population. To the extent that the two distributions are equivalent (and we will assume they are), the probability distribution for x possesses a mean μ and a variance σ^2 that are identical to the corresponding descriptive measures for the population. The purpose of this section is to explain how you can find the mean value—or *expected value*, as it is called—for a random variable. We will illustrate the procedure with an example.

Examine the probability distribution for x (the number of heads observed in the toss of two fair coins) in Figure 4.3. Try to locate the mean of the distribution intuitively. We may reason as follows that the mean μ of this distribution is equal to 1: In a large number of experiments, ¼ should result in $x = 0$, ½ in $x = 1$, and ¼ in $x = 2$ heads. For example, if you were to perform the experiment 1,000 times, approximately 250 should result in $x = 0$, approximately 500 in $x = 1$, and approximately 250 in $x = 2$. Therefore, the average number of heads is

$$\mu = \frac{250(0) + 500(1) + 250(2)}{1,000} = 0(\tfrac{1}{4}) + 1(\tfrac{1}{2}) + 2(\tfrac{1}{4}) = 0 + \tfrac{1}{2} + \tfrac{1}{2} = 1$$

Note that to obtain the mean of the random variable x, we multiply each possible value of x by its probability $p(x)$, and then we sum this product over all possible values of x. The **mean of x** is also referred to as the **expected value of x**, denoted by $E(x)$.

Definition 4.5

The **mean**, or **expected value**, of a discrete random variable x is

$$\mu = E(x) = \sum_{\text{All } x} xp(x)$$

The term *expected* is a mathematical term and should not be interpreted as it is typically used. Specifically, it is possible that a random variable might never equal its *expected* value. Rather, the expected value is the mean of the probability distribution, a measure of its central tendency. You can think of μ as the mean value of x in a *very large* (actually, infinite) number of repetitions of the experiment.

EXAMPLE 4.2

Suppose you work for an insurance company and you sell a $10,000 whole-life insurance policy at an annual premium of $290. Actuarial tables show that the probability of death during the next year for a person of your customer's age, sex, health, etc., is .001. What is the expected gain (amount of money made by the company) for a policy of this type?

Solution

The experiment is to observe whether the customer survives the upcoming year. The probabilities associated with the two simple events, Live and Die, are .999 and .001, respectively. The random variable you are interested in is the gain, x, which can assume the following values:

Gain x	Simple Event	Probability
\$290	Customer lives	.999
\$290–\$10,000	Customer dies	.001

If the customer lives, the company gains the \$290 premium as profit. If the customer dies, the gain is negative because the company must pay \$10,000, for a net "gain" of $(290 - 10,000)$. The expected gain is therefore

$$\mu = E(x) = \sum_{\text{All } x} xp(x) = (290)(.999) + (290 - 10,000)(.001) = \$280$$

In other words, if the company were to sell a very large number of 1-year \$10,000 policies to customers possessing the characteristics just described, it would (on the average) net \$280 per sale in the next year.

This example illustrates that the expected value of a random variable x need not be a possible value of x. That is, the expected value is \$280, but x will equal either \$290 or $-\$9,710$ each time the experiment is performed (a policy is sold and a year elapses). The expected value is the mean, a measure of central tendency—but not necessarily a possible value of x.

We found in Chapter 2 that the mean and other measures of central tendency tell only part of the story about a set of data. The same is true about probability distributions. We need to measure variability as well. Since a probability distribution can be viewed as a representation of a population, we will use the population variance to measure its variability.

The **population variance**, σ^2, is defined as the average squared distance of x from the population mean, μ. Since x is a random variable, the squared distance, $(x - \mu)^2$, is also a random variable. Applying the same logic used to find the mean value of x, we find the mean value of $(x - \mu)^2$ by multiplying all possible values of $(x - \mu)^2$ by $p(x)$ and then summing over all possible x values. This quantity,

$$E[(x - \mu)^2] = \sum_{\text{All } x} (x - \mu)^2 p(x)$$

is also called the **expected value of the squared distance from the mean**; i.e., $\sigma^2 = E[(x - \mu)^2]$.[*] The **standard deviation of** x is defined as the square root of the variance.

Definition 4.6

The **variance** of a discrete random variable x is

$$\sigma^2 = E[(x - \mu)^2] = \sum_{\text{All } x} (x - \mu)^2 p(x)$$

EXAMPLE 4.3

Suppose you invest a fixed sum of money in each of five business ventures. Assume you know that 70% of such ventures are successful, the outcomes of the ventures are independent of one another, and the probability distribution for the number, x, of successful ventures out of five is:

x	0	1	2	3	4	5
$p(x)$	.002	.029	.132	.309	.360	.168

a. Find $\mu = E(x)$.

b. Find $\sigma = \sqrt{E[(x - \mu)^2]}$.

c. Graph $p(x)$. Locate μ and the interval $\mu \pm 2\sigma$ on the graph. Explain how μ and σ can be used to describe $p(x)$.

Solution

a. Applying the formula, we obtain

$$\mu = E(x) = \sum_{\text{All } x} xp(x)$$

$$= 0(.002) + 1(.029) + 2(.132) + 3(.309) + 4(.360) + 5(.168)$$

$$= 3.50$$

---

[*]It can be shown that $E[(x - \mu)^2] = E(x^2) - \mu^2$, where $E(x^2) = \sum_{\text{All } x} x^2 p(x)$. Note the similarity between this expression and the shortcut formula $\sum_{i=1}^{n} (x_i - \bar{x})^2 = \sum_{i=1}^{n} x_i^2 - \frac{(\sum x_i)^2}{n}$ given in Chapter 2.

b. Now we calculate the variance of x:

$$\sigma^2 = E[(x - \mu)^2] = \sum_{\text{All } x} (x - \mu)^2 p(x)$$

$$= (0 - 3.5)^2(.002) + (1 - 3.5)^2(.029) + (2 - 3.5)^2(.132)$$
$$+ (3 - 3.5)^2(.309) + (4 - 3.5)^2(.360) + (5 - 3.5)^2(.168)$$
$$= 1.05$$

Thus, the standard deviation is

$$\sigma = \sqrt{\sigma^2} = \sqrt{1.05} = 1.02$$

c. The graph of $p(x)$ is shown in Figure 4.4. Note that the mean μ and the interval $\mu \pm 2\sigma$ are shown on the graph. We can use μ and σ to describe the probability distribution in the same way that we used $\bar{x}$ and s to describe a relative frequency distribution in Chapter 2. Note in particular that $\mu = 3.5$ locates the probability distribution along the x-axis. If the investment is made in the five ventures, we expect to obtain a number x of successes near 3.5. Similarly, $\sigma = 1.02$ measures the spread of the probability distribution. Since this distribution can be interpreted as a relative frequency distribution that is moderately mound-shaped (see Figure 4.4), we expect (see Table 2.10 on page 75) at least 75% and, more likely, near 95% of observed x values to fall in the interval $\mu \pm 2\sigma$—i.e., between 1.46 and 5.54. Compare this with the actual probability that x falls in the interval $\mu \pm 2\sigma$. From Figure 4.4 you can see that this probability includes the sum of $p(x)$ for all values of x except $p(0) = .002$ and $p(1) = .029$. Therefore, 96.9% of the probability distribution lies within 2 standard deviations of the mean. This percentage is consistent with Table 2.10.

FIGURE 4.4 ▶
Graph of $p(x)$ for
Example 4.3

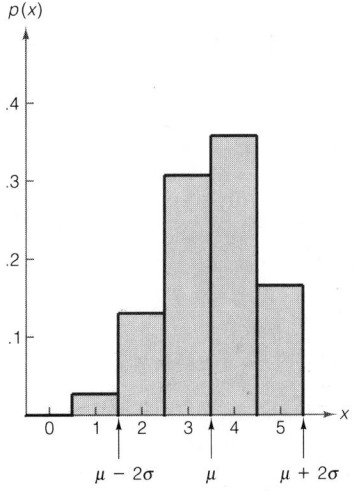

Exercises 4.11 – 4.25

Learning the Mechanics

4.11   Three coins are tossed. Let x equal the number of heads observed.
  a. Identify the simple events associated with this experiment and assign a value of x to each simple event, assuming the coins are fair.
  b. Calculate $p(x)$ for each value of x.
  c. Display the probability distribution of x in graphical form.

4.12   A die is tossed. Let x be the number of spots observed on the upturned face of the die.
  a. Find the probability distribution of x and display it in tabular form.
  b. Display the probability distribution of x in graphical form.

4.13   Explain why each of the following is or is not a valid probability distribution for a random variable x.

a.

x	0	1	2	3
$p(x)$	.1	.3	.3	.2

b.

x	-2	-1	0
$p(x)$	.25	.50	.25

c.

x	4	9	20
$p(x)$	$-.3$	.4	.3

d.

x	2	3	5	6
$p(x)$	.15	.15	.45	.35

4.14   The random variable x has the following discrete probability distribution:

x	1	3	5	7	9
$p(x)$	.1	.2	.4	.2	.1

  a. Find $P(x \le 3)$.   **b.** Find $P(x < 3)$.   **c.** Find $P(x = 7)$.
  d. Find $P(x \ge 5)$.   **e.** Find $P(x > 2)$.   **f.** Find $P(3 \le x \le 9)$.

4.15   Consider the following probability distribution for the random variable x:

x	0	1	2	5	10
$p(x)$	.05	.25	.30	.20	.20

  a. Find $E(x)$.   **b.** Graph $p(x)$ and locate $E(x)$ on the graph.
  c. Interpret the value you obtained for $E(x)$.

4.16   Consider the following probability distribution for the random variable x:

x	-3	-1	0	1	5
$p(x)$	.05	.25	.45	.15	.10

a. Find μ, σ^2, and σ.   b. Graph $p(x)$.
c. Locate μ and the interval $\mu \pm \sigma$ on your graph. What is the probability that x will fall within the interval $\mu \pm \sigma$?
d. Locate the interval $\mu \pm 3\sigma$ on your graph. What is the probability that x falls within this interval?

Applying the Concepts

4.17 The following probability distribution characterizes a marketing analyst's beliefs concerning the probabilities associated with the number, x, of sales that a company might expect per month for a new super-computer:

x	0	1	2	3	4	5	6	7	8
$p(x)$	.02	.08	.15	.19	.24	.17	.10	.04	.01

a. Display the probability distribution for x in graphical form.
b. Based on the probability distribution for x, what is the probability that the company will sell more than three computers per month? More than four?

4.18 Experience has shown that a builder of custom houses makes a profit on 95% of his contracts. Assume the event that the builder makes a profit on any one job is independent of whether he makes a profit on any other. The builder typically contracts to build three houses per month. Let x equal the number of houses per month that result in a profit.
a. Find $p(x)$.   b. Graph $p(x)$.   c. Find the probablity that $x \geq 2$.

4.19 **Economic risk** is sometimes measured by computing the variance or standard deviation of the probability distribution that describes the potential gains or losses of the firm. This follows from the fact that the greater the variation in potential outcomes, the greater the uncertainty faced by the firm; the smaller the variation, the more predictable the firm's gains or losses (Williams and Heins, 1986). The two discrete probability distributions given in the table were developed from historical data. They describe the potential total physical damage losses next year to the fleets of delivery trucks of two different firms.

Firm A		Firm B	
Loss next year	Probability	Loss next year	Probability
$ 0	.01	$ 0	.00
500	.01	200	.01
1,000	.01	700	.02
1,500	.02	1,200	.02
2,000	.35	1,700	.15
2,500	.30	2,200	.30
3,000	.25	2,700	.30
3,500	.02	3,200	.15
4,000	.01	3,700	.02
4,500	.01	4,200	.02
5,000	.01	4,700	.01

a. Verify that both firms have the same expected total physical damage loss.

b. Compute the standard deviation of each probability distribution, and determine which firm faces the greater risk of physical damage to its fleet next year.

4.20 In 1965 the U.S. Weather Bureau (now called the National Weather Service) initiated a nationwide program in which precipitation probabilities were included in all public weather forecasts. This was the first time in any field of application that probabilities were issued on such a large scale. The program continues today. Precipitation forecasts indicate the likelihood of measurable precipitation ($\geq .01$ inch) at a specific point (the official rain gauge) during a given time period (Murphy and Winkler, 1984). Suppose that if a measurable amount of rain falls during the next 24 hours, a river will reach flood stage and a business will incur damages of \$300,000. The National Weather Service has indicated that there is a 30% chance of a measurable amount of rain during the next 24 hours.
a. Construct the probability distribution that describes the potential flood damages.
b. Find the firm's expected loss due to flood damage.

4.21 The state of Minnesota has a "Pick Three" lottery game. The object of the game is to pick three numbers between 0 and 9, inclusive, that match three numbers selected in an official daily drawing. In the drawing, one ball is randomly selected from each of three bins containing the numbers 0–9. To win, the order of the numbers drawn must match the order in which you selected the numbers.
a. Suppose you picked the numbers 1, 3, and 7. What is the probability that none of your numbers will match those of the official drawing? That all three of your numbers will match?
b. What is the probability that you will match one number? Two numbers?
c. Will your answers to parts **a** and **b** change if it is not required that the order of the numbers drawn match the order in which you selected the numbers? Explain.

4.22 Banks and finance companies compete for personal loan customers. For purposes of product design and marketing, it is important for these financial institutions to understand the similarities and differences of the customers they attract. To further such an understanding, Robert W. Johnson and A. Charlene Sullivan (1981) sampled and questioned 488 bank borrowers and 87 finance company borrowers. One of the characteristics they investigated was the credit-worthiness of borrowers. They evaluated each borrower using a credit-scoring system of a large commercial bank. (Credit score is inversely related to credit risk.) The table summarizes the scores they obtained. The relative frequencies can be thought of as the approximate probabilities of a randomly selected borrower having the associated credit score.

Credit Score	Relative Frequency		Credit Score	Relative Frequency	
	Bank Customers	Finance Company Customers		Bank Customers	Finance Company Customers
210	.109	.000	160	.102	.069
200	.117	.023	150	.102	.161
190	.109	.034	140	.074	.172
180	.113	.034	130	.035	.105
170	.219	.184	120	.020	.218

a. Find the expected credit score for bank borrowers. Find the expected credit score for finance company borrowers. Interpret both these values in the context of the problem.
b. Find the standard deviation for the credit scores of bank borrowers. For finance company borrowers.
c. Using the probability distributions in the table and your results from parts **a** and **b**, compare the credit-worthiness of bank borrowers and finance company borrowers.

4.23 A patient complaining of severe stomach pains checked into a local hospital. After a series of tests, the doctors narrowed their diagnosis to four possible ailments. They believe there is a 40% chance that the patient has hepatitis; a 10% chance that she has cirrhosis; a 45% chance of gallstones; and a 5% chance of cancer of the pancreas. The doctors feel certain that the patient has only one of the diseases, but will not know which disease until further tests are performed. The cost associated with treating each disease is given in the table:

Disease	Hepatitis	Cirrhosis	Gallstones	Pancreatic Cancer
Cost	$700	$1,110	$3,320	$16,450

    a. Construct the probability distribution for the cost of treating the patient.
    b. Calculate the mean of the probability distribution you constructed in part **a.** What does this number represent?
    c. Further testing reveals that the patient has either hepatitis or cirrhosis. Given this information, construct the new probability distribution for the cost of treating the patient.
    d. Calculate the mean of the probability distribution you constructed in part **c.** What does this number represent?

4.24 Suppose you own a company that bonds financial managers. Based on past experience, you assess the probability that you will have to forfeit any particular bond to be .001. How much should you charge for a $1 million bond in order to break even on all such bonds?

4.25 One of the primary responsibilities of the personnel department of a firm is to maintain accurate and up-to-date professional and personal profiles of current employees and potential employees. Such information is utilized to match people to project assignments within the firm (Misshauk, 1979). A company is interested in hiring a person with an MBA degree and at least 2 years experience in a marketing department of a computer products firm. The company's personnel department has determined that it will cost the company $1,000 per job candidate to collect the required background information and to interview the candidate. As a result, the company will hire the first qualified person it finds and will interview no more than three candidates. The company has received job applications from four persons who appear to be qualified but, unknown to the company, only one actually possesses the required background. Candidates to be interviewed will be randomly selected from the pool of four applicants.
    a. Construct the probability distribution for the total cost to the firm of the interviewing strategy.
    b. What is the probability that the firm's interviewing strategy will result in none of the four applicants being hired?
    c. Calculate the mean of the probability distribution you constructed in part **a.**
    d. What is the expected total cost of the interviewing strategy?

4.3   The Binomial Distribution

A common source of business data is an opinion or preference survey. Many of these surveys result in dichotomous responses—i.e., responses that admit one of two possible alternatives, such as Yes–No. The number of Yes responses (or No responses) will usually have a **binomial probability distribution**. For example, suppose a random sample of current customers is selected from a firm's data base to evaluate a new product. The number of customers in the sample who prefer the product to its competition is a random variable that has a binomial probability distribution.

All experiments that have the characteristics of the coin-tossing experiments of Chapter 3 and the preceding sections of this chapter yield **binomial random variables**. Imagine an experiment that is equivalent to tossing a coin n times. You are interested in observing the number of heads, x, in the n tosses. For such an experiment, x is a binomial random variable. In general, to decide whether a discrete random variable has a binomial probability distribution, check it against the characteristics listed in the box.

Characteristics of a Binomial Random Variable

1. The experiment consists of n identical trials.
2. There are only two possible outcomes on each trial. We denote one outcome by S (for Success) and the other by F (for Failure).
3. The probability of S remains the same from trial to trial. This probability is denoted by p, and the probability of F is denoted by q. Note that $p + q = 1$.
4. The trials are independent.
5. The binomial random variable x is the number of S's in n trials.

EXAMPLE 4.4

For each of the following examples, decide whether x is a binomial random variable:

a. You randomly select three bonds out of a possible ten for an investment portfolio. Unknown to you, eight of the ten will maintain their present value, and the other two will lose value due to a change in their ratings. Let x be the number of the three bonds you select that lose value.

b. Before marketing a new product on a large scale, many companies conduct a consumer preference survey to determine whether the product is likely to be successful. Suppose a company develops a new diet soda and then conducts a taste-preference survey with 100 randomly chosen consumers stating their preference among the new soda and the two leading sellers. Let x be the number of the 100 who choose the new brand over the two others.

c. Some surveys are conducted using a method of sampling other than simple random sampling (defined in Chapter 3). For example, suppose a television cable company is trying to decide whether to establish a branch in a particular city. The company plans to conduct a survey to determine the fraction of households in the city that would use the cable television service. The sampling method is to choose a city block at random and then to survey every household on that block. This sampling technique is called **cluster sampling**. Suppose 10 blocks are sampled in this manner, producing a total of 124 household responses. Let x be the number of the 124 households that would use the cable television service.

Solution

a. In checking the binomial characteristics, a problem arises with independence (characteristic 4 in the box). Suppose the first bond you picked was one of the two that will lose value. This reduces the chance that the second bond you pick will lose value, since now only one of the nine remaining bonds are in that category. Thus, the choices you make are dependent, and therefore x, the number of the three bonds you select that lose value, is *not* a binomial random variable.

b. Surveys that produce dichotomous responses and use random sampling techniques are classic examples of binomial experiments. In our example, each randomly selected consumer either states a preference for the new diet soda or does not. The sample of 100 consumers is a very small proportion of the totality of potential consumers, so the response of one would be, for all practical purposes, independent of another. Thus, x is a binomial random variable.

c. This example is a survey with dichotomous responses (Yes or No to the cable service), but the sampling method is not simple random sampling. Again, the binomial characteristic of independent trials would probably not be satisfied. The responses of households within a particular block would almost surely be dependent, since households within a block tend to be similar with respect to income, level of education, and general interests. Thus, the binomial model would not be satisfactory for x if the cluster sampling technique were used.

To see how to compute probabilities for binomial random variables, consider the following example.

EXAMPLE 4.5

A retail computer store sells IBM personal computers (PCs) and compatibles. Assume that 80% of the PCs that the store sells are IBM PCs, and 20% are compatibles.

a. Use the steps given in Chapter 3 (box on page 131) to find the probability that all of the next four PC purchases are compatibles.

b. Find the probability that three of the next four PC purchases are compatibles.

c. Let x represent the number of the next four PC purchases that are compatibles. Explain why x is a binomial random variable.

d. Use the answers to parts **a** and **b** to derive a formula for $p(x)$, the probability distribution of the binomial random variable, x.

Solution

a. 1. The first step is to define the experiment. Here we are interested in observing the type of PC purchased by each of the next four (buying) customers: IBM (I) or compatible (C).

2. Next, we list the simple events associated with the experiment. Each simple event consists of the purchase decisions made by the four customers. For ex-

ample, *IIII* represents the simple event that all four purchase IBM PCs, and *CIII* represents the simple event that customer 1 purchases a compatible, while customers 2, 3, and 4 purchase IBM PCs. The 16 simple events are listed in Table 4.2.

TABLE 4.2 Simple Events for PC Experiment of Example 4.5				
IIII	*CIII*	*CCII*	*ICCC*	*CCCC*
	ICII	*CICI*	*CICC*	
	IICI	*CIIC*	*CCIC*	
	IIIC	*ICCI*	*CCCI*	
		ICIC		
		IICC		

3. We now assign probabilities to the simple events. Note that each simple event can be viewed as the intersection of four customers' decisions and, assuming the decisions are made independently, the probability of each simple event can be obtained using the multiplicative rule, as follows:

$$P(IIII) = P[(\text{customer 1 chooses IBM}) \cap (\text{customer 2 chooses IBM})$$
$$\cap (\text{customer 3 chooses IBM}) \cap (\text{customer 4 chooses IBM})]$$
$$= P(\text{customer 1 chooses IBM}) \times P(\text{customer 2 chooses IBM})$$
$$\times P(\text{customer 3 chooses IBM}) \times P(\text{customer 4 chooses IBM})$$
$$= (.8)(.8)(.8)(.8) = (.8)^4$$
$$= .4096$$

All other simple event probabilities are calculated using similar reasoning. For example,

$$P(CIII) = (.2)(.8)(.8)(.8) = (.2)(.8)^3 = .1024$$

You can check that this reasoning results in simple event probabilities that add to 1 over the 16 simple events in the sample space.

4. Finally, we add the appropriate simple event probabilities to obtain the desired event probability. The event of interest is that all four customers purchase compatibles. In Table 4.2 we find only one simple event, *CCCC*, contained in this event. All other simple events imply that at least one IBM is purchased. Thus,

$$P(\text{All four purchase compatibles}) = P(CCCC) = (.2)^4 = .0016$$

That is, the probability is only 16 in 10,000 that all four customers purchase compatibles.

b. The event that three of the next four buyers purchase compatibles consists of the four simple events in the fourth column of Table 4.2: *ICCC*, *CICC*, *CCIC*, and *CCCI*. To obtain the event probability we add the simple event probabilities:

$P(3$ of next 4 customers purchase compatibles)
$$= P(ICCC) + P(CICC) + P(CCIC) + P(CCCI)$$
$$= (.2)^3(.8) + (.2)^3(.8) + (.2)^3(.8) + (.2)^3(.8)$$
$$= 4(.2)^3(.8) = .0256$$

Note that each of the four simple event probabilities is the same, because each simple event consists of three Cs and one I; the order does not affect the probability because the customers' decisions are (assumed) independent.

c. We can characterize the experiment as consisting of four identical trials—the four customers' purchase decisions. There are two possible outcomes to each trial, I or C, and the probability of C, $p = .2$, is the same for each trial. Finally, we are assuming that each customer's purchase decision is independent of all others, so that the four trials are independent. Then it follows that x, the number of the next four purchases that are compatibles, is a binomial random variable.

d. The event probabilities in parts **a** and **b** provide insight into the formula for the probability distribution $p(x)$. First, consider the event that three purchases are compatibles (part **b**). We found that

$$P(x = 3) = 4(.2)^3(.8)$$

Recall that this probability is the sum of four simple event probabilities, each equal to $(.2)^3(.8)$. This line of reasoning leads to the following formula:

$$P(x = 3) = (\text{Number of simple events for which } x = 3)$$
$$\times (.2)^{\text{Number of compatibles purchased}}$$
$$\times (.8)^{\text{Number of IBMs purchased}}$$
$$= 4(.2)^3(.8)^1$$

In general, we can use combinatorial mathematics to count the number of simple events. For example,

Number of simple events for which $x = 3$

$= $ Number of different ways of selecting 3 of the 4 trials for C purchases

$$= \binom{4}{3} = \frac{4!}{3!(4-3)!} = \frac{4 \cdot 3 \cdot 2 \cdot 1}{(3 \cdot 2 \cdot 1) \cdot 1} = 4$$

The formula that works for any value of x can be deduced as follows:

$$P(x = 3) = \binom{4}{3}(.2)^3(.8)^1 = \binom{4}{x}(.2)^x(.8)^{4-x}$$

The component $\binom{4}{x}$ counts the number of simple events with x compatibles, and the component $(.2)^x(.8)^{4-x}$ is the probability associated with each simple event having x compatibles.

For the general binomial experiment, with n trials and probability of Success p on each trial, the probability of x Successes is

$$p(x) = \binom{n}{x} \qquad p^x(1-p)^{n-x}$$

$\uparrow$ $\uparrow$

No. of simple events   Probability of x S's
with x S's   and $(n - x)$ F's in
                         any simple event

In theory, you could always resort to first principles to calculate binomial probabilities: list the simple events and sum their probabilities. However, as the number of trials (n) increases, the number of simple events grows very rapidly (the number of simple events is 2^n). Thus, we prefer the formula for calculating binomial probabilities, since its use avoids listing simple events.

The binomial probability distribution is summarized in the box.

The Binomial Probability Distribution

$$p(x) = \binom{n}{x} p^x q^{n-x} \qquad (x = 0, 1, 2, \ldots, n)$$

where p = Probability of a success on a single trial

        $q = 1 - p$

        n = Number of trials

        x = Number of successes in n trials

$$\binom{n}{x} = \frac{n!}{x!(n-x)!}$$

As noted in Chapter 3, the symbol 5! means $5 \cdot 4 \cdot 3 \cdot 2 \cdot 1 = 120$. Similarly, $n! = n(n-1)(n-2) \cdots \cdot 3 \cdot 2 \cdot 1$; remember, $0! = 1$.

The mean, variance, and standard deviation for the binomial random variable x are shown in the box.

Mean, Variance, and Standard Deviation for a Binomial Random Variable

Mean: $\mu = np$

Variance: $\sigma^2 = npq$

Standard deviation: $\sigma = \sqrt{npq}$

As we demonstrated in Chapter 2, the mean and standard deviation provide measures of the central tendency and variability, respectively, of a distribution. Thus, we can use μ and σ to obtain a rough visualization of the probability distribution for

x when the calculation of the probabilities is too tedious. To illustrate the use of the binomial probability distribution, consider Example 4.6.

EXAMPLE 4.6

A machine that produces stampings for automobile engines is malfunctioning and producing 10% defectives. The defective and nondefective stampings proceed from the machine in a random manner. If the next five stampings are tested, find the probability that three of them are defective.

Solution

Let x equal the number of defectives in $n = 5$ trials. Then x is a binomial random variable with p, the probability that a single stamping will be defective, equal to $.1$, and $q = 1 - p = 1 - .1 = .9$. The probability distribution for x is given by the expression

$$p(x) = \binom{n}{x} p^x q^{n-x} = \binom{5}{x}(.1)^x(.9)^{5-x}$$

$$= \frac{5!}{x!(5 - x)!}(.1)^x(.9)^{5-x} \qquad (x = 0, 1, 2, 3, 4, 5)$$

To find the probability of observing $x = 3$ defectives in a sample of $n = 5$, substitute $x = 3$ into the formula for $p(x)$ to obtain

$$p(3) = \frac{5!}{3!(5 - 3)!}(.1)^3(.9)^{5-3} = \frac{5!}{3!2!}(.1)^3(.9)^2$$

$$= \frac{5 \cdot 4 \cdot 3 \cdot 2 \cdot 1}{(3 \cdot 2 \cdot 1)(2 \cdot 1)}(.1)^3(.9)^2 = 10(.1)^3(.9)^2$$

$$= .0081$$

Note that the binomial formula tells us that there are 10 simple events having 3 defectives (check this by listing them), each with probability $(.1)^3(.9)^2$.

EXAMPLE 4.7

Refer to Example 4.6 and find the values of $p(0)$, $p(1)$, $p(2)$, $p(4)$, and $p(5)$. Graph $p(x)$. Calculate the mean μ and standard deviation σ. Locate μ and the interval $\mu - 2\sigma$ to $\mu + 2\sigma$ on the graph. If the experiment were to be repeated many times, what proportion of the x observations would fall within the interval $\mu - 2\sigma$ to $\mu + 2\sigma$?

Solution

Again, $n = 5$, $p = .1$, and $q = .9$. Then, substituting into the formula for $p(x)$:

$$p(0) = \frac{5!}{0!(5 - 0)!}(.1)^0(.9)^{5-0} = \frac{5 \cdot 4 \cdot 3 \cdot 2 \cdot 1}{(1)(5 \cdot 4 \cdot 3 \cdot 2 \cdot 1)}(1)(.9)^5 = .59049$$

$$p(1) = \frac{5!}{1!(5 - 1)!}(.1)^1(.9)^{5-1} = 5(.1)(.9)^4 = .32805$$

$$p(2) = \frac{5!}{2!(5 - 2)!}(.1)^2(.9)^{5-2} = (10)(.1)^2(.9)^3 = .07290$$

$$p(4) = \frac{5!}{4!(5-4)!}(.1)^4(.9)^{5-4} = 5(.1)^4(.9) = .00045$$

$$p(5) = \frac{5!}{5!(5-5)!}(.1)^5(.9)^{5-5} = (.1)^5 = .00001$$

The graph of $p(x)$ is shown as a probability histogram in Figure 4.5. [$p(3)$ is taken from Example 4.6 to be .0081.]

To calculate the values of μ and σ, substitute $n = 5$ and $p = .1$ into the following formulas:

$$\mu = np = (5)(.1) = .5 \qquad \sigma = \sqrt{npq} = \sqrt{(5)(.1)(.9)} = \sqrt{.45} = .67$$

To find the interval $\mu - 2\sigma$ to $\mu + 2\sigma$, we calculate

$$\mu - 2\sigma = .5 - 2(.67) = -.84 \qquad \mu + 2\sigma = .5 + 2(.67) = 1.84$$

If the experiment were to be repeated a large number of times, what proportion of the x observations would fall within the interval $\mu - 2\sigma$ to $\mu + 2\sigma$? You can see from Figure 4.5 that all observations equal to 0 or 1 will fall within the interval. The

FIGURE 4.5 ▶
The binomial distribution: $n = 5$, $p = .1$

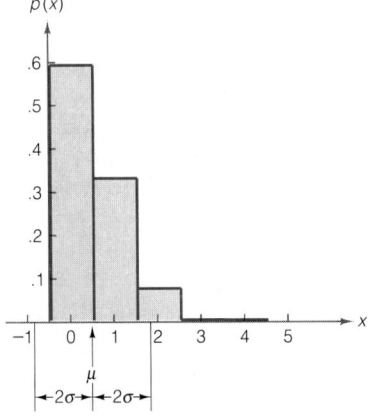

probabilities corresponding to these values are .5905 and .3280, respectively. Consequently, you would expect $.5905 + .3280 = .9185$, or approximately 91.9%, of the observations to fall within the interval $\mu - 2\sigma$ or $\mu + 2\sigma$. This again emphasizes that for most probability distributions, observations rarely fall more than 2 standard deviations from μ.

CASE STUDY 4.2 / The Space Shuttle *Challenger:* Catastrophe in Space

On January 28, 1986, at 11:39.13 A.M., while traveling at Mach 1.92 at an altitude of 46,000 feet, the space shuttle *Challenger* was totally enveloped in an explosive burn that destroyed the shuttle and resulted in the deaths of all seven astronauts aboard. What happened? What was the cause of this catastrophe? This was the 25th shuttle mission. Each of the preceding 24 missions had been successful.

The report of the Presidential Commission assigned to investigate the accident concluded that the explosion was caused by the failure of the O-ring seal in the joint between the two lower segments of the right solid rocket booster. The seal is supposed to prevent superhot gases from leaking through the joint during the propellant burn of the booster rocket. The failure of the seal permitted a jet of white-hot gases to escape and to ignite the liquid fuel of the external fuel tank. The fuel tank fireburst destroyed the *Challenger.*

What were the chances of this event occurring? In a 1985 report, the National Aeronautics and Space Administration (NASA) claimed that the probability of such a failure was about $\frac{1}{60,000}$, or about once in every 60,000 flights. But a 1983 risk-assessment study conducted for the Air Force assessed the probability of a shuttle catastrophe due to booster rocket "burn-through" to be $\frac{1}{35}$, or about once in every 35 missions.

If it is assumed that (1) p, the probability of shuttle catastrophe due to booster failure, remains the same from mission to mission, and (2) the performance of the booster rockets on one mission is independent of the performance of the boosters on other missions, then the number, x, of shuttle catastrophes due to booster failure in n missions can be treated as a binomial random variable. Accordingly, the probability that no disasters would have occurred during 25 missions is

$$P(x = 0) = \binom{25}{0} p^0 (1 - p)^{25-0}$$
$$= \frac{25!}{0!25!} p^0 (1 - p)^{25} = (1 - p)^{25}$$

If we use NASA's probability of shuttle catastrophe ($p = \frac{1}{60,000} = .0000167$), the probability of no catastrophes in 25 missions is approximately .9996. If we use the probability of catastrophe from the study prepared for the Air Force ($p = \frac{1}{35} = .02857$), the probability of no catastrophes in 25 missions is approximately .4845. Or, if we consider the complementary event that at least one catastrophe occurs in 25 missions, the chances are .0004, or about 4 in 10,000, given NASA's assumptions. On the other hand, the probability of at least one catastrophe under the Air Force's assumptions is .5155, or slightly more than 50–50. Given the events of January 28, 1986, which risk assessment—NASA's or the Air Force's—appears to be more appropriate? The probability of one or more disasters in 25 missions is so remote using NASA's assessment that it casts serious doubt on the risk assessment practices used by NASA prior to the *Challenger's* fatal mission (McKean, 1986; Biddle, 1986; Robinson, 1986; "'83 Report Put Booster Accident as Most Likely," 1986).

Using Binomial Tables

Calculating binomial probabilities becomes tedious when n is large. For some values of n and p the binomial probabilities have been tabulated in Table II of Appendix B. Part of Table II is shown in Table 4.3; a graph of the binomial probability distribution for $n = 10$ and $p = .10$ is shown in Figure 4.6. Table II actually contains a total of nine tables, labeled (**a**) through (**i**), one each corresponding to $n = 5, 6, 7, 8, 9, 10,$

15, 20, and 25. In each of these tables the columns correspond to values of p, and the rows correspond to values of the random variable x. The entries in the table represent **cumulative** binomial probabilities. Thus, for example, the entry in the column corresponding to $p = .10$ and the row corresponding to $x = 2$ is .930 (shaded), and its interpretation is

$$P(x \leq 2) = P(x = 0) + P(x = 1) + P(x = 2) = .930$$

TABLE 4.3   Reproduction of Part of Table II of Appendix B: Cumulative Binomial Probabilities for $n = 10$

k \ p	.01	.05	.10	.20	.30	.40	.50	.60	.70	.80	.90	.95	.99
0	.904	.599	.349	.107	.028	.006	.001	.000	.000	.000	.000	.000	.000
1	.996	.914	.736	.376	.149	.046	.011	.002	.000	.000	.000	.000	.000
2	1.000	.988	.930	.678	.383	.167	.055	.012	.002	.000	.000	.000	.000
3	1.000	.999	.987	.879	.650	.382	.172	.055	.011	.001	.000	.000	.000
4	1.000	1.000	.998	.967	.850	.633	.377	.166	.047	.006	.000	.000	.000
5	1.000	1.000	1.000	.994	.953	.834	.623	.367	.150	.033	.002	.000	.000
6	1.000	1.000	1.000	.999	.989	.945	.828	.618	.350	.121	.013	.001	.000
7	1.000	1.000	1.000	1.000	.998	.988	.945	.833	.617	.322	.070	.012	.000
8	1.000	1.000	1.000	1.000	1.000	.998	.989	.954	.851	.624	.264	.086	.004
9	1.000	1.000	1.000	1.000	1.000	1.000	.999	.994	.972	.893	.651	.401	.096

This probability is also shaded in the graphical representation of the binomial distribution with $n = 10$ and $p = .10$ in Figure 4.6.

FIGURE 4.6 ▶
Binomial probability distribution for $n = 10$ and $p = .10$; $P(x \leq 2)$ shaded

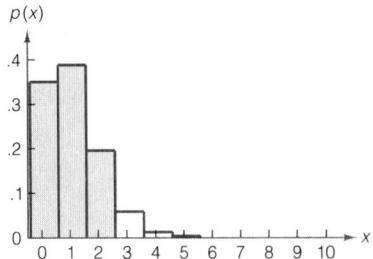

You can also use Table II to find the probability that x equals a specific value. For example, suppose you want to find the probability that $x = 2$ in the binomial distribution with $n = 10$ and $p = .10$. This is found by subtraction as follows:

$$P(x = 2) = [P(x = 0) + P(x = 1) + P(x = 2)] - [P(x = 0) + P(x = 1)]$$
$$= P(x \le 2) - P(x \le 1)$$
$$= .930 - .736 = .194$$

The probability that a binomial random variable exceeds a specified value can be found using Table II and the notion of complementary events. For example, to find the probability that x exceeds 2 when $n = 10$ and $p = .10$, we use

$$P(x > 2) = 1 - P(x \le 2) = 1 - .930 = .070$$

Note that this probability is represented by the unshaded portion of the graph in Figure 4.6.

All probabilities in Table II are rounded to three decimal places. Thus, although none of the binomial probabilities in the table is exactly zero, some are small enough (less than .0005) to round to .000. For example, using the formula to find $P(x = 0)$ when $n = 10$ and $p = .6$, we obtain

$$P(x = 0) = \binom{10}{0}(.6)^0(.4)^{10-0} = .4^{10} = .00010486$$

but this is rounded to .000 in Table II of Appendix B (see Table 4.3).

Similarly, none of the table entries is exactly 1.0, but when the cumulative probabilities exceed .9995, they are rounded to 1.000. The row corresponding to the largest possible value for x, $x = n$, is omitted, because all the cumulative probabilities in that row are equal to 1.0 (exactly). For example, in Table 4.3 with $n = 10$, $P(x \le 10) = 1.0$, no matter what the value of p.

The following example further illustrates the use of Table II.

EXAMPLE 4.8

Suppose a poll of 20 employees is taken in a large company. The purpose is to determine x, the number who favor unionization. Suppose that 60% of all the company's employees favor unionization.

a. Find the mean and standard deviation of x.

b. Use Table II of Appendix B to find the probability that $x < 10$.

c. Use Table II to find the probability that $x > 12$.

d. Use Table II to find the probability that $x = 11$.

Solution

a. The number of employees polled is presumably small compared with the total number of employees in this company. Thus, we may treat x, the number of the 20 who favor unionization, as a binomial random variable. The value of p is the fraction of the total employees who favor unionization; i.e., $p = .6$. Therefore, we calculate the mean and variance:

$$\mu = np = 20(.6) = 12 \qquad \sigma^2 = npq = 20(.6)(.4) = 4.8$$

The standard deviation is then

$$\sigma = \sqrt{4.8} = 2.19$$

b. The tabulated value is

$$P(x \le 9) = .128$$

c. To find the probability

$$P(x > 12) = \sum_{x=13}^{20} p(x)$$

we use the fact that for all probability distributions, $\sum_{\text{All } x} p(x) = 1$. Therefore,

$$P(x > 12) = 1 - P(x \le 12) = 1 - \sum_{x=0}^{12} p(x)$$

Consulting Table II, we find the entry in row $k = 12$, column $p = .6$ to be .584. Thus,

$$P(x > 12) = 1 - .584 = .416$$

d. To find the probability that exactly 11 employees favor unionization, recall that the entries in Table II are cumulative probabilities and use the relationship

$$P(x = 11) = [p(0) + p(1) + \cdots + p(10) + p(11)]$$
$$- [p(0) + p(1) + \cdots + p(9) + p(10)]$$
$$= P(x \le 11) - P(x \le 10)$$

Then

$$P(x = 11) = .404 - .245 = .159$$

The probability distribution for x in this example is shown in Figure 4.7. Note that the interval $\mu \pm 2\sigma$ is $(7.6,\ 16.4)$.

FIGURE 4.7 ▶
The binomial probability distribution for x in Example 4.8: $n = 20$, $p = .6$

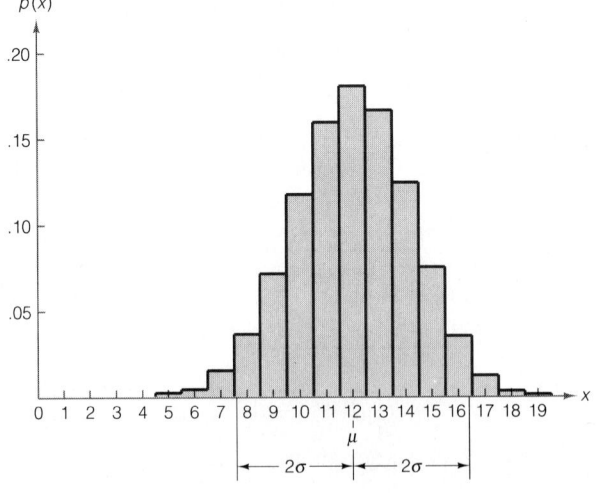

· · · · · · · · · · · · · · · · · · ·

CASE STUDY 4.3 / Evaluating Customer Response to a New Sales Program

Arthur A. Brown, Frank T. Hulswit, and John D. Kettelle (1956) were asked by a large firm to study, and perhaps determine reasons for and solutions to, its lack of growth over the prior 5 years. In their article, Brown et al. refer to the firm as "Penstock Press, a large commercial printing company."

The primary concern of the study was Penstock's sales operations. Accordingly, Brown et al. conducted an experiment to study the sales effectiveness of Penstock's salespeople. The salespeople were instructed to increase their sales efforts toward all of Penstock's customers, but in particular toward 60 of the larger customers, for a 4-month experimental period. At the end of the 4-month period it was determined that the probability of a customer making a genuinely positive response to the increased sales effort merely by chance was .25. Of Penstock's 60 large customers, it was noted that 24 made what appeared to be genuinely positive responses. But before concluding that the increased sales effort toward the 60 large customers had paid off, Brown et al. felt it was important to determine how likely it would be for 24 or more of the 60 customers to make positive responses merely by chance. Assuming that the probability of a positive response occurring by chance (.25) is the same for each of the 60 customers and that the response of one customer does not affect that of another, the number of positive responses observed has a binomial probability distribution. Accordingly, the probability of 24 or more positive responses from the 60 customers can be determined as follows:

$$P(x \geq 24) = \sum_{x=24}^{60} \binom{60}{x} .25^x (.75)^{60-x} = .004$$

(Due to the large value of n, the number of customers in the experiment, it would be unrealistic to try to compute the above probability by hand. If you had access to binomial tables for $n = 60$ and $p = .25$, the probability could be found using the tables. Otherwise, it would be necessary to use a computer or an approximation such as the one we will discuss in Section 4.9.) The fact that the probability of observing 24 or more genuinely positive responses from the 60 customers merely by chance is only .004 indicates that in actually observing 24 such responses either a very rare event has occurred or the responses were in fact genuine and the increased sales effort did influence the increase in sales.

Brown and his colleagues concluded that the number of positive responses could not be explained by chance, but that they in fact "implied deliberate continuing business from the customers," i.e., genuine responses. The authors noted that this conclusion was supported by Penstock's salespeople.

Exercises 4.26–4.39

Learning the Mechanics

4.26 Suppose x is a binomial random variable with $n = 4$ and $p = .7$.
a. Use the formula for the binomial probability distribution to calculate the values of $p(x)$ for $x = 0, 1, 2, 3, 4$.
b. Graph $p(x)$.

4.27 Given that x is a binomial random variable, compute $p(x)$ for each of the following cases:
a. $n = 8$, $x = 5$, $p = .5$ b. $n = 7$, $x = 2$, $q = .3$ c. $n = 4$, $x = 4$, $p = .6$

4.28 Suppose x is a binomial random variable with $n = 13$ and $p = .6$.
a. Display $p(x)$ in tabular form.   b. Compute the mean and variance of x.

    c. Graph $p(x)$ and locate $E(x)$ and the interval $\mu \pm 2\sigma$ on the graph.

    d. What is the probability that x falls within the interval $\mu \pm 2\sigma$?

4.29 Use the results of Exercise 4.28 to find the following probabilities:

    a. $P(x \leq 5)$ b. $P(x \geq 3)$ c. $P(x < 7)$

4.30 Given that x is a binomial random variable with $n = 15$ and $p = .7$, use Table II of Appendix B to find the following probabilities:

    a. $P(x \geq 11)$ b. $P(x < 7)$ c. $P(x > 7)$ d. $P(x = 9)$ e. $P(x \leq 5)$ f. $P(x > 4)$

4.31 The binomial probability distribution is a family of probability distributions, with each individual distribution depending on the values of n and p. Assume that x is a binomial random variable with $n = 6$.

    a. Determine the value of p such that the probability distribution of x is symmetric.

    b. Determine a value of p such that the probability distribution of x is skewed to the right.

    c. Determine a value of p such that the probability distribution of x is skewed to the left.

    d. Graph each of the binomial distributions you obtained in parts **a**, **b**, and **c**. Locate the mean for each distribution on its graph.

    e. In general, for what values of p will a binomial distribution be symmetric? Skewed to the right? Skewed to the left?

Applying the Concepts

4.32 Your firm's accountant believes that 10% of the company's invoices contain arithmetic errors. To check this theory, the accountant randomly samples 25 invoices and finds that seven contain errors. What is the probability that of the 25 invoices written, seven or more would contain errors if the accountant's theory was valid? What assumptions do you have to make to solve this problem using the methodology of this chapter?

4.33 According to the Internal Revenue Service (IRS), the chances of your tax return being audited are about 6 in 1,000 if your income is less than \$25,000; they increase to about 14 in 1,000 if your income is \$25,000 or more; they increase to about 46 in 1,000 if your income is \$100,000 or more (*Statistical Abstract of the United States: 1991*, p. 324).

    a. What is the probability that a taxpayer with income less than \$25,000 will be audited by the IRS? With income \$25,000 or more? With income \$100,000 or more?

    b. If five taxpayers with incomes under \$25,000 are randomly selected, what is the probability that exactly one will be audited? That more than one will be audited?

    c. Repeat part **b** assuming that five taxpayers with incomes of \$25,000 or more are randomly selected.

    d. If two taxpayers with incomes under \$25,000 are randomly selected and two with incomes more than \$100,000 are randomly selected, what is the probability that none of these taxpayers will be audited by the IRS?

    e. What assumptions did you have to make in order to answer these questions using the methodology presented in this section?

4.34 A problem of considerable economic impact on the economy is the burgeoning cost of Medicare and other public-funded medical services. One aspect of this problem concerns the high percentage of people seeking medical treatment who, in fact, have no physical basis for their ailments. One conservative estimate is that the percentage of people who seek medical assistance and who have no real physical ailment is 10%, and some doctors believe that it may be as high as 40%. Suppose we were to randomly sample the records of a doctor and found that five of 15 patients seeking medical assistance were physically healthy.

a. What is the probability of observing five or more physically healthy patients in a sample of 15 if the proportion, p, that the doctor normally sees is 10%?

b. What is the probability of observing five or more physically healthy patients in a sample of 15 if the proportion, p, that the doctor normally sees is 40%?

c. Why might your answer to part **a** make you believe that p is larger than .10?

4.35 According to the U.S. Golf Association (USGA), "The weight of the [golf] ball shall not be greater than 1.620 ounces avoirdupois (45.93 grams). The diameter of the ball shall not be less than 1.680 inches. The velocity of the ball shall be not greater than 250 feet per second" (USGA, 1993). The USGA periodically checks the specifications of golf balls sold in the United States by randomly sampling balls from pro shops around the country. Two dozen of each kind are sampled, and if more than three do not meet size and/or velocity requirements, that kind of ball is removed from the USGA's approved-ball list (*Golf World*, Sept. 10, 1982).

a. What assumptions must be made and what information must be known in order to use the binomial probability distribution to calculate the probability that the USGA will remove a particular kind of golf ball from its approved-ball list?

b. Suppose 10% of all balls produced by a particular manufacturer are less than 1.680 inches in diameter, and assume that the number of such balls, x, in a sample of two dozen balls can be adequately characterized by a binomial probability distribution. Find the mean and standard deviation of the binomial distribution.

c. Refer to part **b**. If x has a binomial distribution, then so does the number, y, of balls in the sample that meet the USGA's minimum diameter. [*Note:* $x + y = 24$.] Describe the distribution of y. In particular, what are p, q, and n? Also, find $E(y)$ and the standard deviation of y.

4.36 Suppose you have purchased 50,000 electrical switches and have been guaranteed by the supplier that the shipment will contain no more than .1% defectives. To check the shipment, you randomly sample 500 switches, test them, and find that four are defective. Assuming the supplier's claim is true, compute μ and σ for the number of defectives in a sample of 500 switches. If the supplier's claim is true, is it likely that you would have found four defective switches in the sample? Based on this sample, what inference would you make concerning the supplier's guarantee?

4.37 Many firms utilize sampling plans to control the quality of manufactured items ready for shipment or the quality of incoming items (parts, raw materials, etc.) that have been purchased. To illustrate the use of a sampling plan, suppose you are shipping electrical fuses in lots, each containing 5,000 fuses. The plan specifies that you will randomly sample 25 fuses from each lot and accept (and ship) the lot if the number of defective fuses, x, in the sample is less than 3. If $x \geq 3$, you will reject the lot. Find the probability of accepting a lot ($x = 0$, 1, or 2) if the actual fraction defective in the lot is:

a. 0   b. .01   c. .10   d. .30   e. .50   f. .80   g. .95   h. 1

Construct a graph showing $P(A)$, the probability of lot acceptance, as a function of the lot fraction defective, p. This graph is called the **operating characteristic curve** for the sampling plan.

4.38 Refer to Exercise 4.37. Suppose the sampling plan called for sampling $n = 25$ fuses and accepting a lot of $x \leq 3$. Calculate the quantities specified in Exercise 4.37, and construct the operating characteristic curve for this sampling plan. Compare this curve with the curve obtained in Exercise 4.37. (Note how the curve characterizes the ability of the plan to screen bad lots from shipment.)

4.39 A local newspaper claims that 65% of the items advertised in its classified advertisement section are sold within 1 week of the first appearance of the ad. To check the validity of its claim, the newspaper randomly selected $n = 800$ advertisements from last year's classified advertisements and contacted the people who placed the ads. They found that $x = 472$ of the 800 items sold within 1 week.

a. Compute μ and σ for the random variable x, the number of items sold within 1 week.

b. Based on a sample of 800, is it likely that you would observe $x \leq 472$ if the newspaper's claim were true? Explain.

c. Do the results of the newspaper's survey support the newspaper's claim? Explain.

4.4   The Poisson Distribution (Optional)

A type of probability distribution useful in describing the number of events that will occur in a specific period of time or in a specific area or volume is the **Poisson distribution** (named after the 18th-century physicist and mathematician, Siméon Poisson). The following are typical examples of random variables for which the Poisson probability distribution provides a good model:

1. The number of industrial accidents in a given manufacturing plant per month

2. The number of noticeable surface defects (scratches, dents, etc.) found by quality inspectors on a new automobile (or any manufactured product)

3. The parts per million of some toxicant found in water or air emission from a manufacturing plant (a random variable of great interest to both the business community and the Environmental Protection Agency)

4. The number of arithmetic errors per 100 invoices (or per 1,000 invoices, etc.) in the accounting records of a company

5. The number of customer arrivals per unit time at a service counter (a service station, a hospital clinic, a supermarket checkout counter, etc.)

6. The number of death claims per day received by an insurance company

7. The number of breakdowns of an electronic computer per month

---

Characteristics of a Poisson Random Variable

1. The experiment consists of counting the number of times a particular event occurs during a given unit of time or in a given area or volume (or weight, distance, or any other unit of measurement).

2. The probability that an event occurs in a given unit of time, area, or volume is the same for all the units.

3. The number of events that occur in one unit of time, area, or volume is independent of the number that occur in other units.

4. The mean (or expected) number of events in each unit will be denoted by the Greek letter lambda, λ.

The characteristics of the Poisson random variable described in the box are usually difficult to verify for practical examples. The previous examples satisfy them well enough that the Poisson distribution provides a good model. As with all probability models, the real test of the adequacy of the Poisson model is whether it provides a reasonable approximation to reality—that is, whether empirical data support it.

The probability distribution, mean, and variance for a Poisson random variable are shown in the next box.

The calculation of Poisson probabilities is made easier by the use of Table III in Appendix B. There the cumulative probabilities $P(x \leq k)$ for various values of λ are given. The use of Table III is illustrated in Example 4.9.

Probability Distribution, Mean, and Variance for a Poisson Random Variable*

$$p(x) = \frac{\lambda^x e^{-\lambda}}{x!} \quad (x = 0, 1, 2, \ldots)$$

$$\mu = \lambda \qquad \sigma^2 = \lambda$$

where λ = Mean number of events during a given time period, or over a specific area or volume

$e = 2.71828.\ .\ .$

EXAMPLE 4.9

Suppose the number, x, of a company's employees who are absent on Mondays has (approximately) a Poisson probability distribution. Furthermore, assume that the average number of Monday absentees is 2.6.

a. Find the mean and standard deviation of x, the number of employees absent on Monday.

b. Use Table III of Appendix B to find the probability that fewer than two employees are absent on a given Monday.

c. Use Table III to find the probability that more than five employees are absent on a given Monday.

d. Use Table III to find the probability that exactly five employees are absent on a given Monday.

Solution

a. The mean and variance of a Poisson random variable are both equal to λ. Thus, for this example,

$$\mu = \lambda = 2.6 \qquad \sigma^2 = \lambda = 2.6$$

---

*The Poisson probability distribution also provides a good approximation to a binomial probability distribution with mean $\lambda = np$ when n is large and p is small (say, $np \leq 7$).

Then the standard deviation of x is

$$\sigma = \sqrt{2.6} = 1.61$$

Remember that the mean measures the central tendency of the distribution, and does not necessarily equal a possible value of x. In this example, the mean is 2.6 absences, and of course there cannot be 2.6 absences on a given Monday. Similarly, the standard deviation of 1.61 measures the variability of the number of Monday absences. Perhaps a more helpful measure is the interval $\mu \pm 2\sigma$, which in this case stretches from $-.62$ to 5.82. We expect the number of absences to fall in this interval most of the time—with at least 75% relative frequency, and probably with more than 90% relative frequency. The mean and the 2-standard-deviation interval around it are shown in Figure 4.8.

FIGURE 4.8 ▶

Probability distribution for number of Monday absences

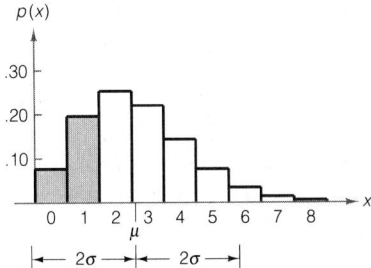

b. A partial reproduction of Table III is shown in Table 4.4. The rows of the table correspond to different values of λ, and the columns correspond to different values of the Poisson random variable x. The entries in the table are cumulative probabilities (much like the binomial probabilities in Table II).

To find the probability that fewer than two employees are absent on a given Monday, we first note that

$$P(x < 2) = P(x \leq 1)$$

This probability is a cumulative probability and is therefore the entry in Table III in the row corresponding to $\lambda = 2.6$ and the column corresponding to $x = 1$. The entry is .267, shown shaded in Table 4.4. This probability corresponds to the shaded area in Figure 4.8, and may be interpreted as meaning that there is a 26.7% chance that fewer than two employees will be absent on a given Monday.

c. To find the probability that more than five employees are absent on a given Monday, we consider the complementary event:

$$P(x > 5) = 1 - P(x \leq 5) = 1 - .951 = .049$$

where .951 is the entry in Table III corresponding to $\lambda = 2.6$ and $x = 5$ (see Table 4.4). Note from Figure 4.8 that this is the area in the interval $\mu \pm 2\sigma$, or $-.62$ to 5.82. Then the number of absences should exceed 5 or, equivalently, should be more than 2 standard deviations from the mean, on only about 4.9% of all Mondays. Note that this percentage agrees remarkably well with that given by the

TABLE 4.4   Reproduction of Part of Table III of Appendix B: Poisson Probabilities

λ \ x	0	1	2	3	4	5	6	7	8	9
2.2	.111	.335	.623	.819	.928	.975	.993	.998	1.000	
2.4	.091	.308	.570	.779	.904	.964	.988	.997	.999	1.000
2.6	.074	.267	.518	.736	.877	.951	.983	.995	.999	1.000
2.8	.061	.231	.469	.692	.848	.935	.976	.992	.998	.999
3.0	.050	.199	.423	.647	.815	.916	.966	.988	.996	.999
3.2	.041	.171	.380	.603	.781	.895	.955	.983	.994	.998
3.4	.033	.147	.340	.558	.744	.871	.942	.977	.992	.997
3.6	.027	.126	.303	.515	.706	.844	.927	.969	.988	.996
3.8	.022	.107	.269	.473	.668	.816	.909	.960	.984	.994
4.0	.018	.092	.238	.433	.629	.785	.889	.949	.979	.992
4.2	.015	.078	.210	.395	.590	.753	.867	.936	.972	.989
4.4	.012	.066	.185	.359	.551	.720	.844	.921	.964	.985
4.6	.010	.056	.163	.326	.513	.686	.818	.905	.955	.980
4.8	.008	.048	.143	.294	.476	.651	.791	.887	.944	.975
5.0	.007	.040	.125	.265	.440	.616	.762	.867	.932	.968
5.2	.006	.034	.109	.238	.406	.581	.732	.845	.918	.960
5.4	.005	.029	.095	.213	.373	.546	.702	.822	.903	.951
5.6	.004	.024	.082	.191	.342	.512	.670	.797	.886	.941
5.8	.003	.021	.072	.170	.313	.478	.638	.771	.867	.929
6.0	.002	.017	.062	.151	.285	.446	.606	.744	.847	.916

Empirical Rule for mound-shaped distributions, which tells us to expect approximately 5% of the measurements (observed values of the random variable) to lie further than 2 standard deviations from the mean.

d. To use Table III to find the probability that *exactly* five employees are absent on a given Monday, we must write the probability as the difference between two cumulative probabilities:

$$P(x = 5) = P(x \le 5) - P(x \le 4) = .951 - .877 = .074$$

Note that probabilities in Table III are all rounded to three decimal places. Thus, although in theory a Poisson random variable can assume infinitely large values, the values of x in Table III are extended only until the cumulative probability is 1.000. This does not mean that x *cannot* assume larger values, but only that the likelihood is less than .001 (in fact, less than .0005) that it will do so.

Finally, you may need to calculate Poisson probabilities for values of λ not found in Table III. You may be able to obtain an adequate approximation by interpolation, but if not, consult more extensive tables for the Poisson distribution.

Exercises 4.40–4.52

Learning the Mechanics

4.40 Consider the following probability distribution:

$$p(x) = \frac{2^x e^{-2}}{x!} \qquad (x = 0, 1, 2, \ldots)$$

  a. Is x a discrete or continuous random variable? Explain.
  b. What is the name of this probability distribution?
  c. Graph the probability distribution.
  d. Find the mean and standard deviation of x.
  e. Find the mean and standard deviation of the probability distribution.

4.41 Given that x is a random variable for which a Poisson probability distribution provides a good approximation, use Table III of Appendix B to compute the following:
  a. $P(x \le 3)$ when $\lambda = 5$
  b. $P(x \le 3)$ when $\lambda = 3$
  c. $P(x \le 3)$ when $\lambda = 1$
  d. What happens to the probability of the event $\{x \le 3\}$ as λ decreases from 5 to 1? Is this intuitively reasonable?

4.42 Assume that x is a random variable having a Poisson probability distribution with a mean of 3.2. Use Table III of Appendix B to find the following probabilities:
  a. $P(x \ge 4)$ b. $P(x > 2)$ c. $P(x = 3)$
  d. $P(x < 7)$ e. $P(x \le 4)$ f. $P(2 \le x \le 6)$

4.43 Given that x is a random variable for which a Poisson probability distribution with $\lambda = 5$ provides a good characterization:
  a. Graph $p(x)$ for $x = 0, 1, 2, \ldots, 13, 14, 15$.
  b. Find μ and σ for x, and locate μ and the interval $\mu \pm 2\sigma$ on the graph.
  c. What is the probability that x will fall within the interval $\mu \pm 2\sigma$?

Applying the Concepts

4.44 The Federal Deposit Insurance Corporation (FDIC), established in 1933, insures deposits of up to $100,000 in banks that are members of the Federal Reserve System (and others that voluntarily join the insurance fund) against losses due to bank failure or theft. From 1981 through 1990 the average number of bank failures per year among insured banks was approximately 124.5 (*Statistical Abstract of the United States: 1991*, p. 502). Assume that x, the number of bank failures per year among insured banks, can be adequately characterized by a Poisson probability distribution with mean 124.5.
  a. Find the expected value and standard deviation of x.
  b. In 1988, 221 insured banks failed. How far (in standard deviations) does $x = 221$ lie above the mean of the Poisson distribution? That is, find the z-score for $x = 221$.
  c. In 1986, 145 insured banks failed. Indicate how to calculate $P(x \le 145)$. Do not actually perform the calculation.
  d. Discuss conditions that would make the Poisson assumption plausible.

4.45 The Environmental Protection Agency (EPA), established in 1970 as part of the executive branch of the federal government, issues pollution standards that vitally affect the safety of consumers and the operations of industry (*The United States Government Manual 1985–1986*). For example, the EPA states that manufacturers of vinyl chloride and similar compounds must limit the amount of these chemicals in plant air emissions to no more than 10 parts per million. Suppose the mean emission of vinyl chloride for a particular plant is 4 parts per million. Assume that the number of parts per million of vinyl chloride in air samples, x, follows a Poisson probability distribution.

    a. What is the standard deviation of x for the plant?

    b. Is it likely that a sample of air from the plant would yield a value of x that would exceed the EPA limit? Explain.

    c. Discuss conditions that would make the Poisson assumption plausible.

4.46 U.S. airlines fly aproximately 26 billion passenger-miles per month and average about 11.8 fatalities per month (*Statistical Abstract of the United States: 1991*, pp. 627, 629). Assume the probability distribution for x, the number of fatalities per month, can be approximated by a Poisson probability distribution.

    a. What is the probability that no fatalities will occur during any given month? [*Hint:* Either use Table III of Appendix B and interpolate to approximate the probability, or use a calculator or computer to calculate the probability exactly.]

    b. Find $E(x)$ and the standard deviation of x.

    c. Use your answers to part **b** to describe the probability that as many as 20 fatalities will occur in any given month.

    d. Discuss conditions that would make the Poisson assumption plausible.

4.47 The safety supervisor at a large manufacturing plant believes the expected number of industrial accidents per month to be 3.4. What is the probability of exactly two accidents occurring next month? Three or more? What assumptions do you need to make to solve this problem using the methodology of this chapter?

4.48 As a check on the quality of the wooden doors produced by a company, its owner requested that each door undergo inspection for defects before leaving the plant. The plant's quality control inspector found that 1 square foot of door surface contains, on the average, .5 minor flaw. Subsequently, 1 square foot of each door's surface was examined for flaws. The owner decided to have all doors reworked that were found to have two or more minor flaws in the square foot of surface that was inspected. What is the probability that a door will fail inspection and be sent back for reworking? What is the probability that a door will pass inspection?

4.49 A large manufacturing plant has 3,200 incandescent light bulbs illuminating the manufacturing floor. If the rate at which the bulbs fail follows a Poisson distribution with a mean of three bulbs per hour, what is the probability that exactly three light bulbs fail in an hour? What is the probability that no bulbs fail in an hour? That no bulbs fail in an 8-hour shift? What assumption is required to calculate the last probability?

4.50 The random variable x, the number of people who arrive at a cashier's counter in a bank during a specified period of time, often possesses (approximately) a Poisson probability distribution. If the mean arrival rate, λ, is known, the Poisson probability distribution can be used to aid in the design of the customer service facility. Suppose you estimate that the mean number of arrivals per minute for cashier service at a bank is one person per minute. What is the probability that in a given minute, the number of arrivals will equal three or more? Can you tell the bank manager that the number of arrivals will rarely exceed three per minute?

4.51 The probability that a health insurance company must pay a major medical claim for a policy is .001. If a group of 1,000 policyholders represents a random sample of all possible policyholders, what is the probability that the insurance company will have to pay at least one major medical claim in this sample?

4.52 The Department of Commerce in a particular state has determined that the number of small businesses that declare bankruptcy per month has approximately a Poisson distribution with a mean equal to 6.4.
  a. Find the probability of at least five bankruptcies occurring next month.
  b. Find the probability of exactly four bankruptcies occurring next month.

4.5   Probability Distributions for Continuous Random Variables

Recall that a continuous random variable is one that can assume any value within some interval or intervals. For example, the length of time between a consumer's purchase of new automobiles, the thickness of sheets of steel produced in a rolling mill, and the actual weight of the contents of 1-gallon cans of paint are all continuous random variables.

The graphical form of the probability distribution for a continuous random variable, x, will be a smooth curve that might appear as shown in Figure 4.9. This curve, a function of x, is denoted by the symbol $f(x)$ and is variously called a **probability density function**, a **frequency function**, or a **probability distribution**.

The areas under a probability distribution correspond to probabilities for x. For example, the area A between the two points a and b, as shown in Figure 4.9, is the probability that x assumes a value between a and b ($a < x < b$). Because areas over intervals represent probabilities, it follows that the total area under a probability distribution, the probability assigned to all values of x, should equal 1. Note that probability distributions for continuous random variables will have different shapes depending on the relative frequency distributions of the real data that the probability distribution is supposed to model. Note too that the events $\{a < x < b\}$ and $\{a \leq x \leq b\}$ are equivalent for continuous random variables, because no probability is assigned to individual points. In terms of the probability distribution $f(x)$, no area is added by the addition of a single point (or two points) to the interval.

FIGURE 4.9 ▶
A probability distribution $f(x)$ for a continuous random variable x

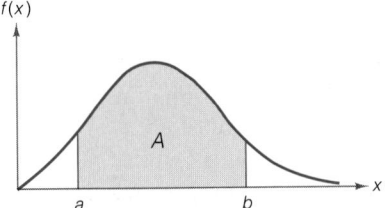

The areas under most probability distributions are obtained by the use of calculus* or numerical methods. Because this is often a difficult procedure, we give the areas for

---

*Students with knowledge of calculus should note that the probability that x assumes a value in the interval $a < x < b$ is $P(a < x < b) = \int_a^b f(x)\, dx$, assuming the integral exists. Similar to the requirements for a discrete probability distribution, we require $f(x) \geq 0$ and $\int_{-\infty}^{\infty} f(x)\, dx = 1$.

some of the most common probability distributions in tabular form in Appendix B. Then, to find the area between two values of x, say $x = a$ and $x = b$, you can simply consult the appropriate table.

For each of the continuous random variables presented in the remainder of this chapter, we will give the formula for the probability distribution along with its mean and standard deviation. These two numbers, μ and σ, will enable you to make some approximate probability statements about a random variable even when you do not have access to a table of areas under the probability distribution.

4.6   The Uniform Distribution (Optional)

Perhaps the simplest of all the continuous probability distributions is the **uniform distribution**. The frequency function has a rectangular shape, as shown in Figure 4.10. The possible values of x consist of all points on the real line between point c and point d. The height of $f(x)$ is constant in that interval and equals $1/(d - c)$. Therefore, the total area under $f(x)$ is given by

$$\text{Total area of rectangle} = (\text{Base})(\text{Height}) = (d - c)\left(\frac{1}{d - c}\right) = 1$$

The uniform probability distribution provides a model for continuous random variables that are *evenly distributed* over a certain interval. That is, a uniform random variable is one that is just as likely to assume a value in one interval as it is to assume a value in any other interval of equal size. There is no clustering of values around any value; instead, there is an even spread over the entire region of possible values.

FIGURE 4.10 ▶
The uniform probability distribution

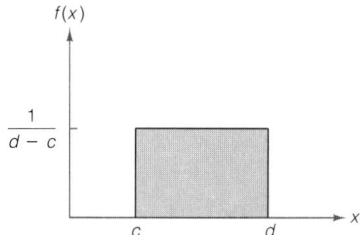

The uniform distribution is sometimes referred to as the **randomness distribution**, since one way of generating a uniform random variable is to perform an experiment in which a point is *randomly* selected on the horizontal axis between the points c and d. If we were to repeat this experiment infinitely often and construct a relative frequency histogram for the outcomes, we would create a uniform probability distribution like that shown in Figure 4.10. The random selection of points on a line can also be used to generate random numbers such as those in a random number table (e.g., Table I of Appendix B). Recall that random numbers are selected in such a way that every digit has an equal probability of selection. Therefore, random numbers are realizations of a uniform random variable. (Random numbers were used to draw random samples in Section 3.7.)

The formulas for the uniform probability distribution and its mean and standard deviation are shown in the box.

Probability Distribution, Mean, and Standard Deviation of a Uniform Random Variable x

$$f(x) = \frac{1}{d - c} \quad (c < x < d)$$

$$\mu = \frac{c + d}{2} \qquad \sigma = \frac{d - c}{\sqrt{12}}$$

Suppose the interval $a < x < b$ lies within the domain of x—i.e., it falls within the larger interval $c < x < d$. Then the probability that x assumes a value within the interval $a < x < b$ is the area of the rectangle over the interval—namely,[*]

$$\frac{b - a}{d - c}$$

. . . .

EXAMPLE 4.10

Suppose the research department of a steel manufacturer believes that one of the company's rolling machines is producing sheets of steel of varying thickness. The thickness is a uniform random variable with values between 150 and 200 millimeters. Any sheets less than 160 millimeters thick must be scrapped because they are unacceptable to buyers.

a. Calculate the mean and standard deviation of x, the thickness of the sheets produced by this machine. Then graph the probability distribution and show the mean on the horizontal axis. Also show 1- and 2-standard-deviation intervals around the mean.

b. Calculate the fraction of steel sheets produced by this machine that have to be scrapped.

Solution

a. To calculate the mean and standard deviation for x, we substitute 150 and 200 millimeters for c and d, respectively, in the formulas. Thus,

---

[*]The student who has knowledge of calculus should note that
$$P(a < x < b) = \int_a^b f(x)\, dx = \int_a^b 1/(d - c)\, dx = (b - a)/(d - c)$$

$$\mu = \frac{c + d}{2} = \frac{150 + 200}{2} = 175 \text{ millimeters}$$

and

$$\sigma = \frac{d - c}{\sqrt{12}} = \frac{200 - 150}{\sqrt{12}} = \frac{50}{3.464} = 14.43$$

The uniform probability distribution is

$$f(x) = \frac{1}{d - c} = \frac{1}{200 - 150} = \frac{1}{50}$$

The graph of this function is shown in Figure 4.11. The mean and the 1- and 2-standard-deviation intervals around the mean are shown on the horizontal axis.

FIGURE 4.11 ▶

Distribution for x in Example 4.10

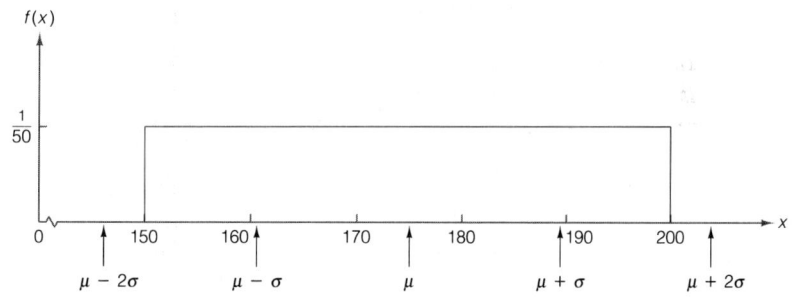

b. To find the fraction of steel sheets produced by the machine that have to be scrapped, we must find the probability that x, the thickness, is less than 160 millimeters. As indicated in Figure 4.12, we need to calculate the area under the frequency function $f(x)$ between the points $x = 150$ and $x = 160$. This is the area of a rectangle with base $160 - 150 = 10$ and height $\frac{1}{50}$. The fraction that has to be scrapped is then

$$P(x < 160) = (\text{Base})(\text{Height}) = (10)\left(\frac{1}{50}\right) = \frac{1}{5}$$

That is, 20% of all the sheets made by this machine must be scrapped.

FIGURE 4.12 ▶

Probability that sheet thickness, x, is between 150 and 160 millimeters

Exercises 4.53 – 4.63

Learning the Mechanics

4.53 Suppose x is a random variable best described by a uniform probability distribution with $c = 20$ and $d = 45$.
  a. Find $f(x)$.   **b.** Find the mean and variance of x.
  c. Graph $f(x)$ and locate μ and the interval $\mu \pm 2\sigma$ on the graph. Find the probability that x assumes a value within the interval $\mu \pm 2\sigma$.

4.54 Refer to Exercise 4.53. Find the following probabilities:
  a. $P(20 \le x \le 30)$ **b.** $P(20 < x < 30)$ **c.** $P(x \ge 30)$ **d.** $P(x \ge 45)$
  e. $P(x \le 40)$ **f.** $P(x < 40)$ **g.** $P(15 \le x \le 35)$ **h.** $P(21.5 \le x \le 31.5)$

4.55 Suppose x is a random variable best described by a uniform probability distribution with $c = 3$ and $d = 7$.
  a. Find $f(x)$.   **b.** Find the mean and variance of x.
  c. Graph $f(x)$ and locate μ and the interval $\mu \pm \sigma$. Find the probability that x assumes a value within the interval $\mu \pm \sigma$.

4.56 Use the probability distribution of Exercise 4.55 to find the value of a that makes each of the following probability statements true:
  a. $P(x \ge a) = .6$ **b.** $P(x \le a) = .25$ **c.** $P(x \le a) = 1$ **d.** $P(4 \le x \le a) = .5$
  e. $P(x > a) = .2$

4.57 The random variable x is best described by a uniform probability distribution with $c = 100$ and $d = 200$. Find the probability that x assumes a value:
  a. More than 2 standard deviations from μ.   **b.** Less than 3 standard deviations from μ.
  c. Within 2 standard deviations of μ.

4.58 The random variable x is best described by a uniform probability distribution with mean 10 and standard deviation 1. Find c, d, and $f(x)$. Graph the probability distribution.

Applying the Concepts

4.59 As we noted in this section, random numbers are values of a uniform random variable. Construct a relative frequency histogram for the data set listed below. (It was created by the random-number generator of the Minitab computer package.) Except for the expected variation in relative frequencies among the class intervals, does your histogram suggest that the data are observations on a uniform random variable with $c = 0$ and $d = 100$? Explain.

38.8759	98.0716	64.5788	60.8422	.8413
88.3734	31.8792	32.9847	.7434	93.3017
12.4337	11.7828	87.4506	94.1727	23.0892
47.0121	43.3629	50.7119	88.2612	69.2875
62.6626	55.6267	78.3936	28.6777	71.6829
44.0466	57.8870	71.8318	28.9622	23.0278
35.6438	38.6584	46.7404	11.2159	96.1009
95.3660	21.5478	87.7819	12.0605	75.1015

4.60   A bus is scheduled to stop at a certain bus stop every half hour on the hour and half hour. At end of the day, buses still stop about every 30 minutes, but due to delays earlier in the day, they are equally likely to stop at any time during any given half hour. If you arrive at a bus stop at the end of the day, what is the probability that you will have to wait more than 20 minutes for the bus (no matter when you show up)? How long do you expect to wait for the bus?

4.61   Probability distributions and event probabilities can be used to express uncertainty about future events. For example, security analysts use probability distributions to forecast stock prices and quarterly earnings; weather forecasters use event probabilities to forecast precipitation, temperature ranges, and the location of a hurricane's landfall. Such forecasts are known as **probability forecasts** (Murphy and Winkler, 1984). Probability forecasts can be derived from sample data, expert judgment, or a combination of both. When a forecaster possesses relatively little information about the future value of a random variable, the uniform distribution is frequently used to make a probability forecast. Suppose a security analyst believes that the closing price of a particular stock 3 months from today will be between $30 and $40, but has no idea where within the interval the price will be.
a. Graph the uniform distribution the security analyst should use as a probability forecast.
b. According to the analyst's forecast, what is the probability that the stock will close higher than $35? Higher than $38? Between $34 and $36, inclusive? Higher than $50?

4.62   The **reliability** of a piece of equipment is frequently defined to be the probability, p, that the equipment performs its intended function successfully for a given period of time under specific conditions (Martz and Waller, 1982). Because p varies from one point in time to another, some reliability analysts treat p as if it were a random variable. Suppose an analyst characterizes the uncertainty about the reliability of a particular robotic device used in an automobile assembly line using the following distribution:

$$f(p) = \begin{cases} 1 & 0 \leq p \leq 1 \\ 0 & \text{otherwise} \end{cases}$$

a. Graph the analyst's probability distribution for p.   **b.** Find the mean and variance of p.
c. According to the analyst's probability distribution for p, what is the probability that p is greater than .95? Less than .95?
d. Suppose the analyst receives the additional information that p is definitely between .90 and .95, but that there is complete uncertainty about where it lies between these values. Describe the probability distribution the analyst should now use to describe p.

4.63   A tool and die machine shop produces extremely high-tolerance spindles. The spindles are 18-inch slender rods used in a variety of military equipment. A piece of equipment used in the manufacture of the spindles malfunctions on occasion and places a single gouge somewhere on the spindle. However, if the spindle can be cut so that it has 14 consecutive inches without a gouge, then the spindle can be salvaged for other purposes. Assuming that the location of the gouge along the spindle is best described by a uniform distribution, what is the probability that a defective spindle can be salvaged?

4.7   The Normal Distribution

One of the most useful and frequently encountered continuous random variables has a **bell-shaped** probability distribution, as shown in Figure 4.13. It is known as a **normal random variable**, and its probability distribution is called a **normal distribution**.

FIGURE 4.13 ▶
A normal probability distribution

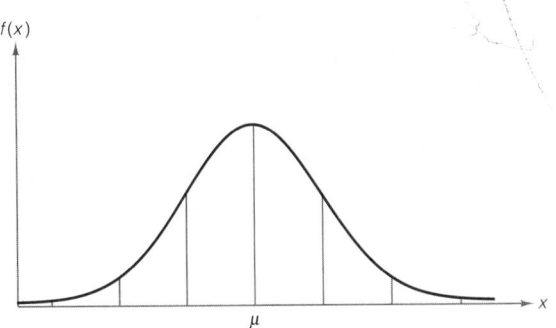

You will see during the remainder of this text that the normal distribution plays a very important role in the science of statistical inference. Many business phenomena generate random variables with probability distributions that are very well approximated by a normal distribution. For example, it has been demonstrated that the monthly rate of return for a particular stock is approximately a normal random variable, and the probability distribution for the weekly sales of a corporation might be approximated by a normal probability distribution. The normal distribution might also provide an accurate model for the distribution of the scores on an unemployment aptitude test. You can determine the adequacy of the normal approximation to an existing population of data by comparing the relative frequency distribution of a large sample of the data to the normal probability distribution.

The normal distribution is perfectly symmetric about its mean, μ, as can be seen in the examples in Figure 4.14. Its spread is determined by the value of its standard deviation, σ.

FIGURE 4.14 ▶
Several normal distributions, with different means and standard deviations

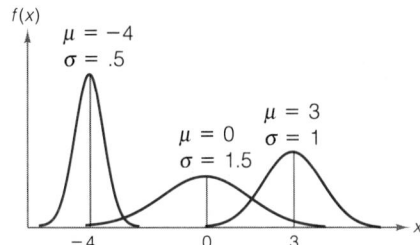

The formula for the normal probability distribution is shown in the next box. When plotted, this formula yields a curve like that shown in Figure 4.13. Note that the mean μ and the variance σ^2 appear in this formula, so that no separate formulas for μ and σ^2 are necessary. To graph the normal curve we will have to know the numerical values of μ and σ.

Probability Distribution for a Normal Variable x

$$f(x) = \frac{1}{\sigma\sqrt{2\pi}}\, e^{-(1/2)[(x-\mu)/\sigma]^2}$$

where μ = Mean of the normal random variable, x
   σ^2 = Variance of the normal random variable, x
   π = 3.1416. . .
   e = 2.71828. . .

Computing the area over intervals under the normal probability distribution is a difficult task.* Consequently, we will use the computed areas listed in Table IV of Appendix B (and inside the front cover). Although there is an infinitely large number of normal curves—one for each pair of values for μ and σ—we have formed a single table that will apply to any normal curve. This was done by constructing the table of areas as a function of the z-score (presented in Section 2.7). The population z-score for a measurement was defined as the *distance* between the measurement and the population mean, divided by the population standard deviation. Thus, the z-score gives the distance between a measurement and the mean in units equal to the standard deviation. In symbolic form, the z-score for the measurement x is

$$z = \frac{x - \mu}{\sigma}$$

To illustrate the use of Table IV, suppose we know that the length of time between charges of a pocket calculator has a normal distribution, with a mean of 50 hours and a standard deviation of 15 hours. If we were to observe the length of time that elapses before the need for the next charge, what is the probability that this measurement would assume a value between 50 hours and 70 hours? This probability is the area under the normal probability distribution between 50 and 70, as shown in the shaded area, A, of Figure 4.15.

FIGURE 4.15 ▶
Normal distribution: $\mu = 50$, $\sigma = 15$

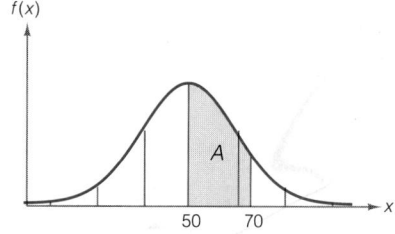

---

*The student with knowledge of calculus should note that there is not a closed-form expression for $P(a < x < b) = \int_a^b f(x)\, dx$ for the normal probability distribution. However, the value of this definite integral can be obtained to any desired degree of accuracy by numerical approximation procedures. The areas in Table IV of Appendix B were obtained by using such a procedure.

The first step in finding the area A is to calculate the z-score corresponding to the measurement 70. We calculate

$$z = \frac{x - \mu}{\sigma}$$

$$= \frac{70 - 50}{15}$$

$$= \frac{20}{15} = 1.33$$

Thus, the measurement 70 is 1.33 standard deviations above the mean, 50. The second step is to refer to Table IV (a partial reproduction of this table is shown in Table 4.5). Note that z-scores are listed in the left-hand column of the table. To find the area corresponding to a z-score of 1.33, we first locate the value 1.3 in the left-hand column. Since this column lists z values to one decimal place only, we refer to the top

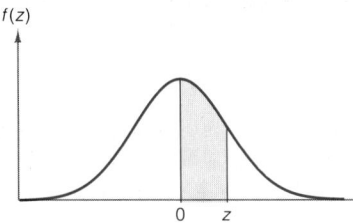

TABLE 4.5   Reproduction of Part of Table IV of Appendix B (and inside front cover): Normal Curve Areas

z	.00	.01	.02	.03	.04	.05	.06	.07	.08	.09
.0	.0000	.0040	.0080	.0120	.0160	.0199	.0239	.0279	.0319	.0359
.1	.0398	.0438	.0478	.0517	.0557	.0596	.0636	.0675	.0714	.0753
.2	.0793	.0832	.0871	.0910	.0948	.0987	.1026	.1064	.1103	.1141
.3	.1179	.1217	.1255	.1293	.1331	.1368	.1406	.1443	.1480	.1517
.4	.1554	.1591	.1628	.1664	.1700	.1736	.1772	.1808	.1844	.1879
.5	.1915	.1950	.1985	.2019	.2054	.2088	.2123	.2157	.2190	.2224
.6	.2257	.2291	.2324	.2357	.2389	.2422	.2454	.2486	.2517	.2549
.7	.2580	.2611	.2642	.2673	.2704	.2734	.2764	.2794	.2823	.2852
.8	.2881	.2910	.2939	.2967	.2995	.3023	.3051	.3078	.3106	.3133
.9	.3159	.3186	.3212	.3238	.3264	.3289	.3315	.3340	.3365	.3389
1.0	.3413	.3438	.3461	.3485	.3508	.3531	.3554	.3577	.3599	.3621
1.1	.3643	.3665	.3686	.3708	.3729	.3749	.3770	.3790	.3810	.3830
1.2	.3849	.3869	.3888	.3907	.3925	.3944	.3962	.3980	.3997	.4015
1.3	.4032	.4049	.4066	.4082	.4099	.4115	.4131	.4147	.4162	.4177
1.4	.4192	.4207	.4222	.4236	.4251	.4265	.4279	.4292	.4306	.4319
1.5	.4332	.4345	.4357	.4370	.4382	.4394	.4406	.4418	.4429	.4441

row of the table to get the second decimal place, .03. Finally, we locate the number where the row labeled $z = 1.3$ and the column labeled .03 meet. This number represents the area between the mean, μ, and the measurement that has a z-score of 1.33:

$$A = .4082$$

Thus, the probability that the calculator operates between 50 and 70 hours before needing a charge is .4082.

The use of the z-score simplifies the calculation of normal probabilities because if x is normally distributed with any mean and standard deviation, z is *always* a normal random variable with a mean of 0 and a standard deviation of 1. For this reason z is often referred to as the **standard normal random variable**.

Definition 4.7

The **standard normal random variable** z is defined by the formula

$$z = \frac{x - \mu}{\sigma}$$

where x is a normal random variable with mean μ and standard deviation σ. The standard normal random variable z is normally distributed with mean 0 and standard deviation 1, and can be described as the number of standard deviations between x and μ.

Since we will convert all normal random variables to standard normal in order to find probabilities based on Table IV of Appendix B, it is important that you learn to use Table IV well. The following examples illustrate its use.

EXAMPLE 4.11

Find the probability that the standard normal random variable z falls between -1.33 and $+1.33$.

Solution

The standard normal distribution is shown in Figure 4.16. Since all probabilities associated with standard normal random variables can be depicted as areas under the standard normal curve, you should always draw the curve and then equate the desired probability to an area.

FIGURE 4.16 ▶
A distribution of z-scores (a standard normal distribution)

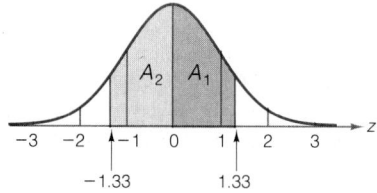

In this example we want to find the probability that z falls between -1.33 and $+1.33$, which is equivalent to the area between -1.33 and $+1.33$, shown shaded in Figure 4.16. Table IV of Appendix B provides the area between $z = 0$ and any value of z looked up, so that if we look up $z = 1.33$ we find that the area between $z = 0$ and $z = 1.33$ is .4082. This is the area labeled A_1 in Figure 4.16. To find the area A_2 between $z = 0$ and $z = -1.33$, we note that the symmetry of the normal distribution implies that the area between $z = 0$ and any point to the left is equal to the area between $z = 0$ and the point equidistant to the right. Thus, in this example the area between $z = 0$ and $z = -1.33$ is equal to the area between $z = 0$ and $z = +1.33$. That is,

$$A_1 = A_2 = .4082$$

The probability that z falls between -1.33 and $+1.33$ is the sum of the areas A_1 and A_2. Using probabilistic notation, we summarize as follows:

$$P(-1.33 < z < +1.33) = P(-1.33 < z < 0) + P(0 \leq z < 1.33)$$
$$= A_1 + A_2 = .4082 + .4082$$
$$= .8164$$

Remember that $<$ and $\leq$ are equivalent in events involving z because the inclusion (or exclusion) of a single point does not alter the probability of an event involving a continuous random variable.

. . . .

EXAMPLE 4.12

Find the probability that a standard normal random variable exceeds 1.64, i.e., find $P(z > 1.64)$.

Solution

The area under the standard normal distribution to the right of 1.64 is the shaded area labeled A_1 in Figure 4.17. This area represents the desired probability that z exceeds 1.64. However, when we look up $z = 1.64$ in Table IV of Appendix B, we must remember that the probability given in the table corresponds to the area between $z = 0$ and $z = 1.64$ (the area labeled A_2 in Figure 4.17). From Table IV we find that $A_2 = .4495$. To find the area A_1 to the right of 1.64, we make use of two facts:

1. The standard normal distribution is symmetric about its mean, $z = 0$.
2. The total area under the standard normal probability distribution equals 1.

FIGURE 4.17 ▶
Standard normal distribution:
$\mu = 0, \sigma = 1$

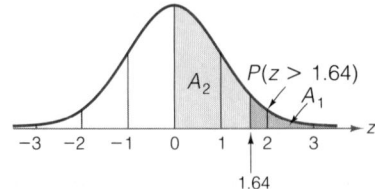

Taken together, these two facts imply that the areas on either side of the mean $z = 0$ equal .5; thus, the area to the right of $z = 0$ in Figure 4.17 is $A_1 + A_2 = .5$. Then

$$P(z > 1.64) = A_1 = .5 - A_2 = .5 - .4495 = .0505$$

To attach some practical significance to this probability, note that the implication is that the chance of a standard normal random variable exceeding 1.64 is approximately .05. Or, since z represents the number of standard deviations between *any* normal random variable and its mean, a normal random variable will exceed its mean by more than 1.64 standard deviations only about 5% of the time.

EXAMPLE 4.13

Find the probability that a normal random variable lies to the right of a point $-.74$ standard deviation from its mean.

Solution

We must first interpret the event in terms of a standard normal random variable, so that we can use Table IV of Appendix B to find the event's probability. Since the standard normal random variable z is simply the number of standard deviations between a normal random variable and its mean, the event that a normal random variable lies to the right of a point $-.74$ standard deviation from the mean is equivalent to the event that the standard normal random variable z exceeds $-.74$. The event is shown as the shaded area in Figure 4.18, and we want to find $P(z > -.74)$.

FIGURE 4.18 ▶
Standard normal distribution:
$\mu = 0, \sigma = 1$

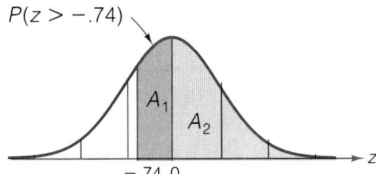

We divide the shaded area into two parts: the area A_1 between $z = -.74$ and $z = 0$, and the area A_2 to the right of $z = 0$. We must always make such a division when the desired area lies on both sides of the mean ($z = 0$), because Table IV contains areas between $z = 0$ and the point you look up. To find A_1, we remember that the sign of z is unimportant when determining the area, because the standard normal distribution is symmetric about its mean. We look up $z = .74$ in Table IV to find that $A_1 = .2704$. The symmetry also implies that half the distribution lies on each side of the mean, so the area A_2 to the right of $z = 0$ is .5. Then

$$P(z > -.74) = A_1 + A_2 = .2704 + .5 = .7704$$

EXAMPLE 4.14

Find the probability that a normal random variable lies more than 1.96 standard deviations from its mean *in either direction*.

Solution

The event that a normal random variable lies beyond 1.96 standard deviations in either direction from its mean is equivalent to the event that the standard normal random variable z exceeds 1.96 in absolute value. That is, we want to find

$$P(z > |1.96|) = P(z < -1.96 \text{ or } z > 1.96)$$

This probability is the shaded area in Figure 4.19. Note that the total shaded area is the sum of two areas, A_1 and A_2—areas that are equal because of the symmetry of the normal distribution.

FIGURE 4.19 ▶
Standard normal distribution:
$\mu = 0,\ \sigma = 1$

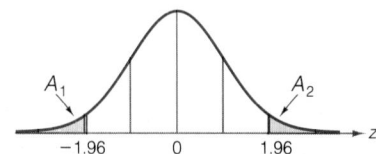

We look up $z = 1.96$ and find the area between $z = 0$ and $z = 1.96$ to be .4750. Then the area to the right of 1.96 is $.5 - .4750 = .0250$, so that

$$P(z > |1.96|) = .0250 + .0250 = .05$$

The implication is that any normal random variable lies more than 1.96 standard deviations from its mean 5% of the time. Recall (Chapter 2) that the Empirical Rule tells us that about 5% of the measurements in mound-shaped distributions will lie beyond 2 standard deviations from the mean; the normal distribution, which is certainly mound-shaped, has 5% of its area beyond 1.96 standard deviations. In fact, the normal distribution provides the model on which the Empirical Rule is based, along with much "empirical" experience with real data that often approximately obey the rule, whether they are drawn from a normal distribution or not.

EXAMPLE 4.15

Assume that the length of time, x, between charges of a pocket calculator is normally distributed with a mean of 50 hours and a standard deviation of 15 hours. Find the probability that the calculator will last between 30 and 70 hours between charges.

Solution

The normal distribution with mean $\mu = 50$ and $\sigma = 15$ is shown in Figure 4.20; the desired probability that the calculator lasts between 30 and 70 hours is shaded. In order to find the probability, we must first convert the distribution to standard normal, which we do by calculating the z-score:

$$z = \frac{x - \mu}{\sigma}$$

The z-scores corresponding to the important values of x are shown just under the x values on the horizontal axis in Figure 4.20. Note that $z = 0$ corresponds to the mean

FIGURE 4.20 ▶
Normal probability distribution:
$\mu = 50, \sigma = 15$

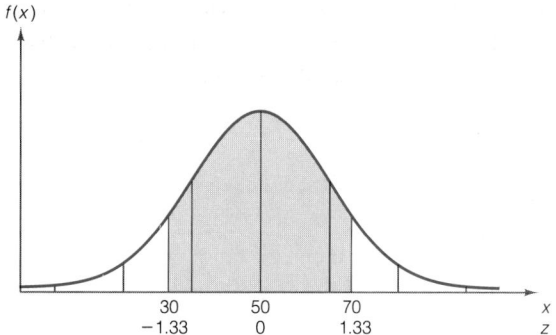

$f(x)$

30	50	70	x
−1.33	0	1.33	z

of $\mu = 50$ hours, while the x values 30 and 70 yield z-scores of -1.33 and $+1.33$, respectively. Thus, the event that the calculator lasts between 30 and 70 hours is equivalent to the event that a standard normal random variable lies between -1.33 and $+1.33$. We found this probability in Example 4.11 (see Figure 4.16) by doubling the area corresponding to $z = 1.33$ in Table IV. That is,

$$P(30 \le x \le 70) = P(-1.33 \le z \le 1.33) = 2(.4082) = .8164$$

The steps to follow when calculating a probability corresponding to a normal random variable are summarized in the box.

Steps for Finding a Probability Corresponding to a Normal Random Variable

1. Sketch the normal distribution and indicate the mean of the random variable x. Then shade the area corresponding to the probability you want to find.

2. Convert the boundaries of the shaded area from x values to standard normal random variable z values using the formula

$$z = \frac{x - \mu}{\sigma}$$

Show the z values under the corresponding x values on your sketch.

3. Use Table IV of Appendix B (and inside the front cover) to find the areas corresponding to the z values. If necessary, use the symmetry of the normal distribution to find areas corresponding to negative z values and the fact that the total area on each side of the mean equals .5 to convert the areas from Table IV to the probabilities of the event you have shaded.

EXAMPLE 4.16

Suppose an automobile manufacturer introduces a new model that has an advertised mean in-city mileage of 27 miles per gallon. Although such advertisements seldom report any measure of variability, suppose you write the manufacturer for the details of the tests, and you find that the standard deviation is 3 miles per gallon. This information leads you to formulate a probability model for the random variable x, the in-city mileage for this car model. You believe that the probability distribution of x can be approximated by a normal distribution with a mean of 27 and a standard deviation of .3.

a. If you were to buy this model of automobile, what is the probability you would purchase one that averages less than 20 miles per gallon for in-city driving?

b. Suppose you purchase one of these new models, and it does get less than 20 miles per gallon for in-city driving. Should you conclude that your probability model is incorrect?

Solution

a. The probability model proposed for x, the in-city mileage, is shown in Figure 4.21. We are interested in finding the area, A, to the left of 20, since this area corresponds to the probability that a measurement chosen from this distribution falls below 20. Or in other words, if this model is correct, the area A represents the fraction of cars that can be expected to get less than 20 miles per gallon for in-city driving. To find A, we first calculate the z value corresponding to $x = 20$. That is,

$$z = \frac{x - \mu}{\sigma} = \frac{20 - 27}{3} = -\frac{7}{3} = -2.33$$

This z value is shown in Figure 4.21 under the corresponding x value.

FIGURE 4.21 ▶

Normal probability distribution for x in Example 4.16: $\mu = 27$ miles per gallon, $\sigma = 3$ miles per gallon

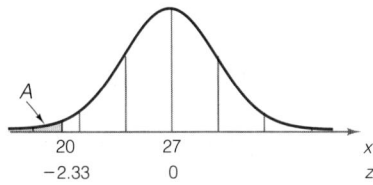

Because of the symmetry of the normal distribution about its mean and because Table IV provides only areas to the right of the mean, we look up 2.33 in Table IV and find that the corresponding area is .4901. This is the area between $z = 0$ and $z = -2.33$, so we find

$$A = .5 - .4901 = .0099 \approx .01$$

According to this probability model, you should have only about a 1% chance of purchasing a car of this make with an in-city mileage under 20 miles per gallon.

b. Now you are asked to make an inference based on a sample—the car you purchased. You are getting less than 20 miles per gallon for in-city driving. What do you infer? We think you will agree that one of two possibilities is true:

The probability model is correct, and you simply were unfortunate to have purchased one of the cars in the 1% that get less than 20 miles per gallon in the city.

The probability model is incorrect. Perhaps the assumption of a normal distribution is unwarranted, or the mean of 27 is an overestimate, or the standard deviation of 3 is an underestimate, or some combination of these errors was made. At any rate, the form of the actual probability model certainly merits further investigation.

You have no way of knowing with certainty which possibility is the correct one, but the evidence points to the second one. We are again relying on the rare event approach to statistical inference that we introduced earlier. The basic idea is that the sample (one measurement in this case) was so unlikely to have been drawn from the proposed probability model that it casts serious doubt on the model. We would be inclined to believe that the model is somehow in error.

Occasionally you will be given a probability and want to find the values of the normal random variable that correspond to the probability. For example, suppose the average daily production of a manufacturer is known to be normally distributed, and management wants to pay an incentive bonus to the crew when their level of production exceeds the 90th percentile of the daily production distribution. To determine the production level at which bonuses will be paid, you will need to be able to use the normal distribution probability table in reverse, as demonstrated in the following example.

EXAMPLE 4.17

Find the value of z, call it z_0, in the standard normal distribution that will be exceeded only 10% of the time. That is, find z_0 such that $P(z \geq z_0) = .10$.

Solution

In this case we are given a probability, or an area, and asked to find the value of the standard normal random variable that corresponds to the area. Specifically, we want to find the value z_0 such that only 10% of the standard normal distribution exceeds z_0 (see Figure 4.22).

FIGURE 4.22 ▶
Standard normal distribution for Example 4.17

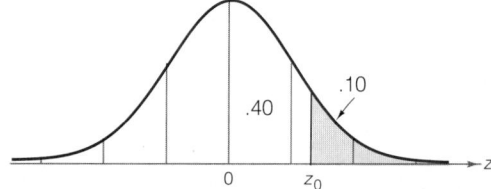

We know that the total area to the right of the mean $z = 0$ is .5, which implies that z_0 must lie to the right of (above) 0. To pinpoint the value, we use the fact that the area to the right of z_0 is .10, which implies that the area between $z = 0$ and z_0 is $.5 - .1 = .4$. But areas between $z = 0$ and some other z value are exactly the types given in Table IV of Appendix B. Therefore, we look up the *area* .4000 in the body of Table IV, and find that the corresponding z value is (to the closest approximation) $z_0 = 1.28$. Thus, the point 1.28 standard deviations above the mean is the 90th percentile of a normal distribution.

EXAMPLE 4.18

Find the value of z_0 such that 95% of the standard normal z values lie between $-z_0$ and $+z_0$, i.e.,

$$P(-z_0 \leq z \leq z_0) = .95$$

Solution

Here we wish to move an equal distance z_0 in the positive and negative direction from the mean $z = 0$ until 95% of the standard normal distribution is enclosed. This means that the area on each side of the mean will be equal to $\frac{1}{2}(.95) = .475$, as shown in Figure 4.23. Since the area between $z = 0$ and z_0 is .475, we look up .475 in the body of Table IV and find the corresponding z value $z_0 = 1.96$. Thus, as we found in the reverse order in Example 4.14, 95% of a normal distribution lies between plus and minus 1.96 standard deviations of the mean.

FIGURE 4.23 ▶
Standard normal distribution:
$\mu = 0, \sigma = 1$

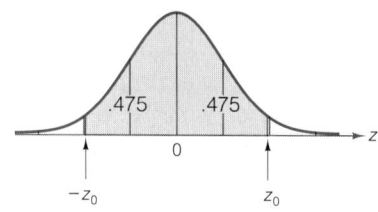

Now that you have learned to use Table IV to find a standard normal z value that corresponds to a specified probability, we will demonstrate a practical application in Example 4.19.

EXAMPLE 4.19

Suppose a paint manufacturer has a daily production, x, that is normally distributed with a mean of 100,000 gallons and a standard deviation of 10,000 gallons. Management wants to create an incentive bonus for the production crew when the daily production exceeds the 90th percentile of the distribution, in hopes that the crew will, in turn, become more productive. At what level of production should management pay the incentive bonus?

Solution

First, we need to find the 90th percentile in the standard normal distribution. We did this in Example 4.17 (see Figure 4.22) and found that $z = 1.28$ is the standard normal value that will be exceeded only 10% of the time.

Next, we want to convert the standard normal value to an x value, a production level in this example. We know that the production level at which the incentive bonus will be paid is $z = 1.28$ standard deviations above the mean level. To determine the production level, remember that

$$z = \frac{x - \mu}{\sigma}$$

If we solve this equation for x, we find

$$x = \mu + z\sigma$$

In this example, $\mu = 100{,}000$, $z = 1.28$, and $\sigma = 10{,}000$ so

$$x = 100{,}000 + 1.28(10{,}000) = 100{,}000 + 12{,}800$$
$$= 112{,}800$$

Thus, the 90th percentile of the production distribution is 112,800 gallons. Management should pay an incentive bonus when a day's production exceeds this level if its objective is to pay only when the production is in the top 10% of the current production distribution.

CASE STUDY 4.4 / Evaluating an Investment's Risk

Frederick S. Hillier (1963) described several ways a business firm can easily, but effectively, evaluate risky investment projects. He noted that, up to the time of his writing,

Such procedures as have been suggested for dealing with risk have tended to be either quite simplified or somewhat theoretical. Thus, these procedures have tended to provide management with only a portion of the information required for a sound decision, or they have assumed the availability of information which is almost impossible to obtain.

In one of his approaches to handling risk, Hillier assumes that the cash flow from an investment to the firm in the ith future year after the investment is made is normally distributed, and shows that the present worth, P, of the proposed investment is therefore normally distributed with mean μ_P and variance σ_P^2. He points out that by describing P with a probability distribution as he has done, management is provided with information about P and, as a result, with some basis upon which to evaluate the risk of the investment decision.

Hillier provides an example of how management can evaluate the risk of an investment by assuming its present worth is normally distributed:

Suppose that, on the basis of the forecasts regarding prospective cash flow from a proposed invest-

ment of $10,000, it is determined that $\mu_P =$ $1,000 and $\sigma_P =$ $2,000. Ordinarily, the current procedure would be to approve the investment since $\mu_P > 0$. However, with additional information available ($\sigma_P =$ $2,000) regarding the considerable risk of the investment, the executive can analyze the situation further. Using widely available tables for the normal distribution, he could note that the probability that $P < 0$, so that the investment won't pay, is 0.31. Furthermore, the probability is 0.16, 0.023, and 0.0013, respectively, that the investment will lose the present worth equivalent of at least $1,000, $3,000, and $5,000, respectively. Considering the financial status of the firm, the executive can use this and similar information to make his decision. Suppose, instead, that the executive is attempting to choose between this investment and a second investment with $\mu_P =$ $500 and $\sigma_P =$ $500. By conducting a similar analysis for the second investment, the executive can decide whether the greater expected earnings of the first investment justifies the greater risk. A useful technique for making this comparison is to superimpose the drawing of the probability distribution of P for the second investment upon the corresponding drawing for the first investment. This same approach generalizes to the comparison of more than two investments.

Exercises 4.64 – 4.83

Learning the Mechanics

4.64 Use Table IV in Appendix B (and inside front cover) to calculate the area under the standard normal distribution between the following pairs of z-scores:

a. $z = 0$ and $z = 2$ b. $z = 0$ and $z = 3.0$ c. $z = 0$ and $z = 1.5$ d. $z = 0$ and $z = .80$

4.65 Repeat Exercise 4.64 for each of the following pairs of standard normal z values:

a. $z = -1.33$ and $z = -.33$ b. $z = -2$ and $z = 2$ c. $z = -2.33$ and $z = -1.33$
d. $z = -3$ and $z = 3$ e. $z = -2.25$ and $z = 0$ f. $z = 0.0$ and $z = 2.25$

4.66 Find each of the following probabilities for the standard normal random variable z:

a. $P(z \leq -1)$ b. $P(z \geq 2.32)$ c. $P(z \leq -2.58)$
d. $P(z \geq 2)$ e. $P(z = 0)$ f. $P(z \leq -1.645)$

4.67 Find each of the following probabilities for the standard normal random variable z:

a. $P(-1 \leq z \leq 1)$ b. $P(-1.96 \leq z \leq 1.96)$
c. $P(-1.645 \leq z \leq 1.645)$ d. $P(-2 \leq z \leq 2)$

4.68 Find a value of the standard normal random variable z, call it z_0, such that:

a. $P(z \geq z_0) = .05$ b. $P(z \geq z_0) = .025$ c. $P(z \leq z_0) = .025$
d. $P(z \geq z_0) = .10$ e. $P(z > z_0) = .10$

4.69 Find a value of the standard normal random variable z, call it z_0, such that:

a. $P(z \leq z_0) = .2090$ b. $P(z \leq z_0) = .7090$ c. $P(-z_0 \leq z < z_0) = .8472$
d. $P(-z_0 \leq z \leq z_0) = .1664$ e. $P(z_0 \leq z \leq 0) = .4798$ f. $P(-1 < z < z_0) = .5328$

4.70 Suppose the random variable x is best described by a normal distribution with $\mu = 30$ and $\sigma = 4$. Find the value of the standard normal random variable z that corresponds to each of the following x values:

a. $x = 20$ b. $x = 30$ c. $x = 27.5$ d. $x = 15$ e. $x = 35$ f. $x = 25$

4.71 Refer to Exercise 4.70. How many standard deviations away from the mean of x are each of the following x values?

a. $x = 25$ b. $x = 37.5$ c. $x = 30$ d. $x = 36$

4.72 Suppose the continuous random variable x has a normal probability distribution with mean 120 and variance 36. Draw a rough sketch (i.e., a graph) of the frequency function of x. Locate μ and the interval $\mu \pm 2\sigma$ on the graph. Find the following probabilities:

a. $P(\mu - 2\sigma \leq x \leq \mu + 2\sigma)$ b. $P(x \geq 128)$ c. $P(x \leq 108)$
d. $P(112 \leq x \leq 130)$ e. $P(114 \leq x \leq 116)$ f. $P(115 \leq x \leq 128)$

4.73 The random variable x has a normal distribution with $\mu = 1,000$ and $\sigma = 10$.

a. Find the probability that x assumes a value more than 2 standard deviations from its mean. More than 3 standard deviations from μ.

b. Find the probability that x assumes a value within 1 standard deviation of its mean. Within 2 standard deviations of μ.

c. Find the value of x that represents the 80th percentile of this distribution. The 10th percentile.

4.74 The random variable x has a normal distribution with mean 50 and variance 9. Find the value of x, call it x_0, such that:
    a. $P(x \leq x_0) = .8413$ **b.** $P(x > x_0) = .025$
    c. $P(x > x_0) = .95$ **d.** $P(41 \leq x < x_0) = .8630$

4.75 The random variable x has a normal distribution with standard deviation 25. It is known that the probability that x exceeds 150 is .90. Find the mean μ of the probability distribution.

Applying the Concepts

4.76 The tread life of a particular brand of tire is a random variable best described by a normal distribution with a mean of 60,000 miles and a standard deviation of 8,300 miles. If the manufacturer warrants the tires for the first 45,000 miles, what proportion of the tires will need to be replaced under warranty? What if the warranty is for the first 40,000 miles?

4.77 A company that sells annuities must base the annual payout on the probability distribution of the length of life of the participants in the plan. Suppose the probability distribution of the lifetimes of the participants in the plan is approximately a normal distribution with $\mu = 68$ years and $\sigma = 3.5$ years.
    a. What proportion of the plan participants would receive payments beyond age 70?
    b. Beyond age 75?
    c. Complete the following statement: Only 15% of plan participants will receive payment beyond age
    _____.

4.78 **Personnel tests** are designed to test a job applicant's cognitive and/or physical abilities. An IQ test is an example of the former; a speed test involving the arrangement of pegs on a peg board is an example of the latter. (Dessler, 1986). A particular dexterity test is administered nationwide by a private testing service. It is known that for all tests administered last year the distribution of scores was approximately normal with mean 75 and standard deviation 7.5
    a. A particular employer requires job candidates to score at least 80 on the dexterity test. Approximately what percentage of the test scores during the past year exceeded 80?
    b. The testing service reported to a particular employer that the score of one of its job candidates fell at the 98th percentile of the distribution (i.e., approximately 98% of the scores were lower than the candidate's, and only 2% were higher). What was the candidate's score?

4.79 Ideally, a worker seeking a new job in a particular industry should acquire information about wage rates offered by all firms in the industry. However, workers may not find it worthwhile to search until they find the highest available wage rate. The result is that managers may not have to pay top dollar to attract workers. These factors help explain the existing disparity in wage rates among firms (Blair and Kenny, 1982). Suppose the distribution of wage rates nationwide that would be offered to a particular skilled worker can be approximated by a normal distribution with $\mu = \$10.50$ per hour and $\sigma = \$1.25$ per hour. In addition, assume that the worker is offered $12.00 per hour by the first firm contacted.
    a. Suppose the worker were to undertake a nationwide job search. What proportion of the wage rates that would be offered to the worker would be greater than $12.00 per hour?
    b. If the worker were to complete a nationwide job search and then randomly select one of the many job offers received, what is the probability that the wage rate would be more than $10.00 per hour?
    c. The **median**, call it m, of a continuous random variable x is the value such that $P(x \geq m) = P(x \leq m) = .5$. That is, the median is the value m such that half the area under the probability distribution lies above

m and half lies below it. Find the median of the random variable corresponding to the wage rate and compare it to the mean wage rate.

4.80   An important quality characteristic for soft-drink bottlers is the amount of soft drink injected into each bottle. This volume is determined (approximately) by measuring the height of the soft drink in the neck of the bottle and comparing it to a scale that converts the height measurement to a volume measurement (Montgomery, 1991). In a particular filling process, the number of ounces injected into 8-ounce bottles is approximately normally distributed with mean 8.00 ounces and standard deviation .05 ounce. Bottles that contain less than 7.9 ounces do not meet the bottler's quality standard and are sold at a substantial discount.
   a. If 20,000 bottles are filled, approximately how many will fail to meet the quality standard?
   b. Suppose that, due to the failure of one of the filling system's components, the mean of the filling process shifts to 7.95 ounces. (Assume that the standard deviation remains .05 ounce.) If 20,000 bottles are filled, approximately how many will fail to meet the quality standard?
   c. Suppose that a different component fails and, although the mean of the filling process remains 8.00 ounces, the standard deviation increases to .1 ounce. If 20,000 bottles are filled, approximately how many will fail to meet the quality standard?

4.81   The **monthly rate of return** of a stock is a measure investors frequently use for evaluating the behavior of a stock over time. A stock's monthly rate of return generally reflects the amount of money an investor makes (or loses if the return is negative) for every dollar invested in the stock in a given month. Thus, stocks with high average monthly rates of return typically offer more lucrative investment opportunities than stocks with low average monthly rates of return. Eugene Fama (1976) has demonstrated that the probability distribution for the monthly rate of return of a stock can be approximated by a normal probability distribution. Suppose the monthly rates of return to stock ABC are normally distributed with mean .05 and standard deviation .03, and the monthly rates of return to stock XYZ are normally distributed with mean .07 and standard deviation .05. Assume that you have $100 invested in each stock.
   a. Over the long run, which stock will yield the higher average monthly rate of return? Why?
   b. Suppose you plan to hold each stock for only 1 month. What is the expected value of each investment at the end of 1 month?
   c. Which stock offers greater protection against incurring a loss on your investment next month? Why?

4.82   Do security analysts do a good job of forecasting corporate earnings growth and advising their clientele? David Dreman, a *Forbes* columnist, addresses this question in an article titled "Astrology Might Be Better" (*Forbes*, Mar. 26, 1984). The basis of Dreman's article is a study by Professors Michael Sandretto of Harvard and Sudhir Milkrishnamurthi of the Massachusetts Institute of Technology. The study surveys security analysts' forecasts of annual earnings for the (then) current year for more than 769 companies with five or more forecasts per company per year. The average forecast error for this large number of forecasts was 31.3%. To apply this information to a practical situation, suppose the population of analysts' forecast errors is normally distributed with a mean of 31.3% and a standard deviation of 10%.
   a. If you obtain a security analyst's forecast for a particular company, what is the probability that it will be in error by more than 50%?
   b. If three analysts make the forecast, what is the probability that at least one of the analysts will err by more than 50%?

4.83   A machine used to regulate the amount of dye dispensed for mixing shades of paint can be set so that it discharges an average of μ milliliters of dye per can of paint. The amount of dye discharged is known to have a normal distribution with variance equal to .160. If more than 6 milliliters of dye are discharged when making a particular shade of blue paint, the shade is unacceptable. Determine the setting for μ so that no more than 1% of the cans of paint will be unacceptable.

4.8   The Exponential Distribution (Optional)

Another important probability distribution that is useful for describing business data is the **exponential probability distribution**. Two business phenomena with frequency functions that might be well approximated by the exponential distribution are the length of time between arrivals at a fast-food drive-through restaurant and the length of time between the filing of claims in a small insurance office. Note that in each of these examples, the measurements are the lengths of time between certain events. For this reason, the exponential distribution is sometimes called the **waiting time distribution**.

The formula for the exponential probability distribution is shown in the box, along with its mean and standard deviation.

Probability Distribution, Mean, and Standard Deviation for an Exponential Random Variable x

$$f(x) = \lambda e^{-\lambda x} \quad (x > 0)$$

$$\mu = \frac{1}{\lambda} \qquad \sigma = \frac{1}{\lambda}$$

Unlike the normal distribution, which has a shape and location determined by the values of the two quantities μ and σ, the shape of the exponential distribution is governed by a single quantity, λ. Further, it is a probability distribution with the property that its mean equals its standard deviation. Exponential distributions corresponding to $\lambda = .5$, 1, and 2 are shown in Figure 4.24.

FIGURE 4.24 ▶
Exponential distributions

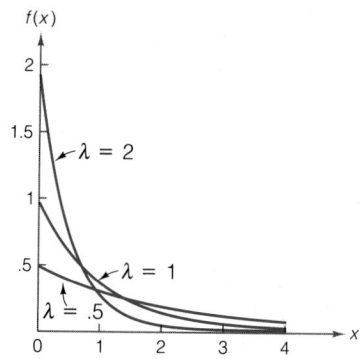

To calculate probabilities for exponential random variables, we need to be able to find areas under the exponential probability distribution. Suppose we want to find the area, A, to the right of some number, a, as shown in Figure 4.25. This area can be calculated by using the formula given in the box.

FIGURE 4.25 ▶
The area, **A**, to the right of a number, **a**, for an exponential distribution

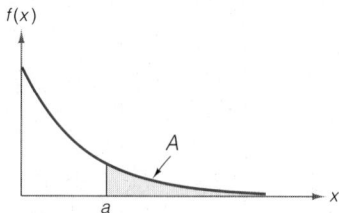

Finding the Area, **A**, to the Right of a Number, **a**, for an Exponential Distribution*

$$A = P(x \geq a) = e^{-\lambda a}$$

Use Table V in Appendix B to find the value of $e^{-\lambda a}$ after substituting the appropriate numerical values for λ and a.

EXAMPLE 4.20

Suppose the length of time (in days) between sales for an automobile salesperson is modeled as an exponential random variable with $\lambda = .5$. What is the probability that the salesperson goes more than 5 days without a sale?

Solution

The probability we want is the area, A, to the right of $a = 5$ in Figure 4.26.

FIGURE 4.26 ▶
Exponential distribution for Example 4.20: $\lambda = .5$

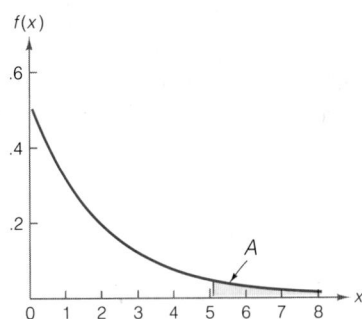

---

*This area is calculated by integration:

$$\int_a^\infty \lambda e^{-\lambda x} \, dx = -e^{-\lambda x} \Big|_a^\infty = e^{-\lambda a}$$

To find this probability, use the formula given for area:

$$A = e^{-\lambda a} = e^{-(.5)(5)} = e^{-2.5}$$

Referring to Table V, we find

$$A = e^{-2.5} = .082085$$

That is, our model indicates that the automobile salesperson has a probability of about .08 of going more than 5 days without a sale.

EXAMPLE 4.21

A microwave oven manufacturer is trying to determine the length of warranty period it should attach to its magnetron tube, the most critical component in the oven. Preliminary testing has shown that the length of life (in years), x, of a magnetron tube has an exponential probability distribution with $\lambda = .16$.

a. Find the mean and standard deviation of x.

b. If a warranty period of 5 years is attached to the magnetron tube, what fraction of tubes must the manufacturer plan to replace (assuming the exponential model with $\lambda = .16$ is correct)?

c. Find the probability that the length of life of a magnetron tube will fall within the interval $\mu \pm 2\sigma$.

Solution

a. Using the formulas for the mean and standard deviation for an exponential random variable, we find

$$\mu = \frac{1}{\lambda} = \frac{1}{.16} = 6.25 \text{ years}$$

Also, since $\mu = \sigma$, $\sigma = 6.25$ years.

b. To find the fraction of tubes that will have to be replaced before the 5-year warranty period expires, we need to find the area between 0 and 5 under the distribution. This area, A, is shown in Figure 4.27. To find the required probability, we recall the formula

$$P(x > a) = e^{-\lambda a}$$

FIGURE 4.27 ▶
Exponential distribution for
Example 4.21: $\lambda = .16$

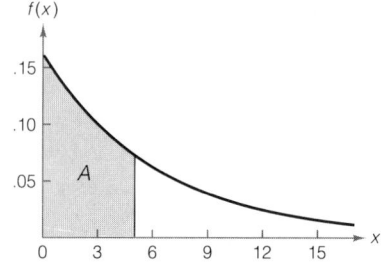

Using this formula and Table V of Appendix B, we find

$$P(x > 5) = e^{-\lambda(5)} = e^{-(.16)(5)} = e^{-.80} = .449329$$

To find the area A, we use the complementary relationship:

$$P(x \le 5) = 1 - P(x > 5) = 1 - .449329 = .550671$$

So, approximately 55% of the magnetron tubes will have to be replaced during the 5-year warranty period.

c. We would expect the probability that the life of a magnetron tube, x, falls within the interval $\mu \pm 2\sigma$ to be quite large (near .95 if we think the Empirical Rule in Table 2.10 might apply). A graph of the exponential distribution showing the interval from $\mu - 2\sigma$ to $\mu + 2\sigma$ is shown in Figure 4.28. Since the point $\mu - 2\sigma$ lies below $x = 0$, we need to find only the area between $x = 0$ and $a = \mu + 2\sigma = 6.25 + 2(6.25) = 18.75$. This area, A, which is shaded in Figure 4.28, is

$$A = 1 - P(x > 18.75)$$
$$= 1 - e^{-\lambda(18.75)} = 1 - e^{-(.16)(18.75)} = 1 - e^{-3}$$

FIGURE 4.28 ▶

Exponential distribution for
Example 4.21: $\lambda = .16$

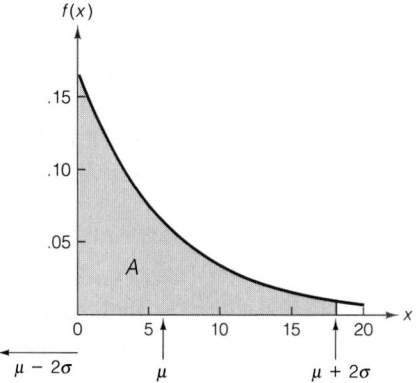

Checking Table V of Appendix B for the value of e^{-3}, we find $e^{-3} = .049787$. Therefore, the probability that the life, x, of a magnetron tube falls within the interval $\mu \pm 2\sigma$ is

$$A = 1 - e^{-3} = 1 - .049787 = .950213$$

You can see that this probability agrees very well with the Empirical Rule even though this probability distribution is not mound-shaped (it is strongly skewed to the right).

CASE STUDY 4.5 / Assessing the Reliability of Computer Software

In a discussion about the reliability of computer software, G. J. Schick (1974) says the following:

Custom software . . . is expensive to develop and requires extensive testing—the goal being to certify that the software is in error-free condition, ready to support the mission for which it was designed. Similar economies should also be expected from an integrated statistical software test program. Traditionally, there are never enough time or resources to test all possible branches and data combinations in a computer program of reasonable size.

Current practice is to design and develop a software system and then to test it to detect errors, until the amount of time and expense required to discover remaining errors is too great to justify further testing. . . . In principle, few large real-time computer programs ever have been tested completely and unequivocally in the sense that every logical data path has been successfully executed under every logical combination for the data at hand for all possible options. One management objective would be to test every logical path in the computer program at least once with some kind of numerical check. At the present state of the art, such a degree of testing is neither feasible nor realistic. In practice, the contractor must be willing to release and the customer willing to accept a level of risk associated with a program that has been less than completely checked.

In finding and correcting errors in a computer program (*debugging*) and determining the program's reliability, Schick and others have noted the importance of the distribution of the time until the next program error is found. If this distribution is assumed to be exponential, with

$$f(x) = \lambda e^{-\lambda x} \quad (x > 0, \quad \lambda > 0)$$

then, as Schick points out, its mean, $1/\lambda$, would be the average time required to find the next error.

In his article, Schick describes a method relevant to software reliability for estimating the parameter, λ, of the exponential distribution. Using computer debugging data supplied by the U.S. Navy, Schick demonstrates how this estimation procedure and the exponential distribution can be used to estimate the reliability of a computer program. [*Note:* The model used by Schick to represent the distribution for the time until the next error is based on the exponential distribution, but it is slightly more complicated because he assumes that λ varies. For our purposes, however, nothing is lost by assuming the distribution to be exponential.

After 26 program errors were found, Schick estimated λ to be .042. Accordingly, $1/\lambda = 23.8$ days. This means that the average time it would take to find the next (27th) error would be about 24 days. Thus, the probability of it taking, say, 60 or more days to find the next error is

$$P(x \geq 60) = e^{-(.042)(60)} = .08046$$

Over the next 290 days, five more errors were detected. Since this is a rate of about one error every 60 days and since $P(x \geq 60) \approx .08$, it seems unlikely that an exponential distribution with $\lambda = .042$ is an appropriate representation of the distribution for the time until the next error. Based on the number of new errors found and the length of time it took to find them, Schick reestimated λ. He found $\lambda = .0036$. Thus, $1/\lambda = 278$ days, meaning that on average the next error (32nd) would not occur for 278 days. At this point, the length of time and, therefore, the cost required to find any remaining program errors may be prohibitive. Debugging should probably be discontinued.

Exercises 4.84 – 4.95

Learning the Mechanics

4.84   The random variables x and y have exponential distributions with $\lambda = 3$ and $\lambda = .75$, respectively. Using Table V in Appendix B, carefully plot both distributions on the same set of axes.

4.85   Use Table V in Appendix B to determine the value of $e^{-\lambda a}$ for each of the following cases:
   a. $\lambda = 1$, $a = 1$ **b.** $\lambda = 1$, $a = 2.5$ **c.** $\lambda = 2.5$, $a = 3$ **d.** $\lambda = 5$, $a = .3$

4.86   Suppose x has an exponential distribution with $\lambda = 3$. Find the following probabilities:
   a. $P(x > 2)$ **b.** $P(x > 1.5)$ **c.** $P(x > 3)$ **d.** $P(x > .45)$

4.87   Suppose x has an exponential distribution with $\lambda = 2.5$. Find the following probabilities:
   a. $P(x \leq 3)$ **b.** $P(x \leq 4)$ **c.** $P(x \leq 1.6)$ **d.** $P(x \leq .4)$

4.88   Suppose the random variable x is best approximated by an exponential probability distribution with $\lambda = 2$. Find the mean and variance of x. Find the probability that x will assume a value within the interval $\mu \pm 2\sigma$.

4.89   The random variable x can be adequately approximated by an exponential probability distribution with $\lambda = 1$. Find the probability that x assumes a value:
   a. More than 3 standard deviations from μ.   **b.** Less than 2 standard deviations from μ.
   c. Within .5 standard deviation of μ.

Applying the Concepts

4.90   A taxi service based at an airport can be characterized as a transportation system with one source terminal and a fleet of vehicles that take passengers from the terminal to different destinations. Each vehicle returns to the terminal after some random trip time and makes another trip. To improve the vehicle-dispatching decisions involved in such a system (e.g., how many passengers should be allocated to a waiting taxi?), Sims and Templeton (1985) used queueing theory to model and to evaluate the system. In their model, they assumed travel times of successive trips are independent exponential random variables. Assume $\lambda = .05$.
   a. What is the mean trip time for the taxi service?
   b. What is the probability that a particular trip will take more than 30 minutes?
   c. Two taxis have just been dispatched. What is the probability that both will be gone for more than 30 minutes? That at least one of the taxis will return within 30 minutes?

4.91   The shelf-life of a product is a random variable that is related to consumer acceptance and, ultimately, to sales and profit. Suppose the shelf-life of bread is best approximated by an exponential distribution with mean equal to 2 days. What fraction of the loaves stocked today would you expect to still be saleable (i.e., not stale) 3 days from now?

4.92   A catalog company that receives the majority of its orders by telephone conducted a study to determine how long customers were willing to wait on hold before ordering a product. The length of time was found to be a random variable best approximated by an exponential distribution with a mean equal to 2.8 minutes. What proportion of customers having to hold more than 3 minutes will hang up before placing an order? More than 2 minutes? More than 1 minute?

4.93 Bolling (1972) used an exponential distribution with mean 58 minutes to model the service-time distribution of each of eight treatment tables in the emergency room of Richmond Memorial Hospital.

    a. Using this distribution, find the probability that it will take more than 58 minutes to treat a patient in the emergency room. More than 1.5 hours.

    b. What is the probability that each of the next three patients will require more than 58 minutes for treatment?

    c. Recall from part c of Exercise 4.79 that the median, m, of a continuous random variable x is the value such that $P(x \geq m) = P(x \leq m) = .5$. Is the median time required to treat a patient more or less than 58 minutes?

    d. Using Table V in Appendix B, approximate the median of the service-time distribution.

4.94 In Case Study 4.5, the exponential distribution was used to help evaluate the reliability of a computer program. After 26 program errors were found, the time (in days) required to find the next error was determined to have an exponential distribution with $\lambda = .042$.

    a. Graph this exponential distribution, and locate its mean and the interval $\mu \pm \sigma$ on your graph.

    b. What is the mean time required to find the 27th program error?

    c. What is the probability that it will take less than 30 days to find the 27th error?

    d. Find the probability that the time required to find the 27th error is within the interval $\mu \pm \sigma$.

    e. Find the probability that the time required to find the 27th error is within the interval $\mu \pm 2\sigma$. How does your answer compare with the approximate probability provided by the Empirical Rule of Chapter 2?

4.95 **Product reliability** has been defined as the probability that a product will perform its intended function satisfactorily for its intended life when operating under specified conditions (Lamberson, 1985). The **reliability function**, $R(x)$, for a product indicates the probability of the product's life exceeding x time periods. When the time until failure of a product can be adequately modeled by an exponential distribution, the product's reliability function is $R(x) = e^{-\lambda x}$. Suppose that the time to failure (in years) of a particular product is modeled by an exponential distribution with $\lambda = .5$.

    a. What is the product's reliability function?

    b. What is the probability that the product will perform satisfactorily for at least 4 years?

    c. What is the probability that a particular product will survive longer than the mean life of the product?

    d. If λ changes, will the probability that you calculated in part c change? Explain.

    e. If 10,000 units of the product are sold, approximately how many will perform satisfactorily for more than 5 years? About how many will fail within 1 year?

    f. How long should the length of the warranty period be for the product if the manufacturer wants to replace no more than 5% of the units sold while under warranty?

4.9 Approximating a Binomial Distribution with a Normal Distribution

When a binomial random variable can assume a large number of values, the calculation of its probabilities may become very tedious. To contend with this problem, we provide tables in Appendix B to give the probabilities for some values of n and p, but these tables are by necessity incomplete. For example, the binomial table (Table II) can be used only for $n = 5, 6, 7, 8, 9, 10, 15, 20,$ or 25. To get around this limitation, we seek approximation procedures for calculating the probabilities associated with binomial random variables.

When n is large, a normal probability distribution can provide a good approximation to the probability distribution of a binomial random variable. To show how the approximation works, we refer to Example 4.8, in which we used the binomial distribution to model the number x of 20 employees who favor unionization. We assumed that 60% of all the company's employees favored unionization. The mean and standard deviation of x were found to be $\mu = 12$ and $\sigma = 2.19$. The binomial distribution for $n = 20$ and $p = .6$ is shown in Figure 4.29 and the approximating normal distribution with mean $\mu = 12$ and standard deviation $\sigma = 2.19$ is superimposed.

FIGURE 4.29 ▶
Binomial distribution for $n = 20$, $p = .6$ and normal distribution with $\mu = 12$, $\sigma = 2.19$

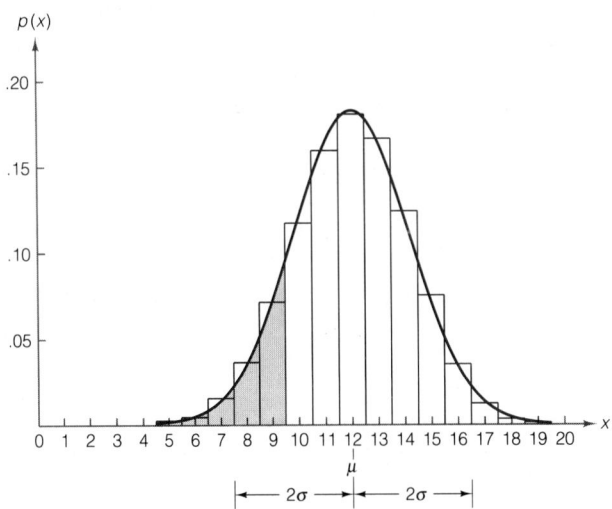

As part of Example 4.8, we used Table II to find the probability that $x < 10$. This probability, which is shaded in Figure 4.29, was found to equal .128. To find the normal approximation, we first note that $P(0 \le x < 10)$ corresponds to the area to the left of $x = 9.5$ on the normal curve in the figure. We use $x = 9.5$ rather than $x = 9$ or $x = 10$ so that all the binomial probability corresponding to $x = 9$ is included in the approximating normal curve area, but none of that corresponding to $x = 10$ is included. Because we are approximating a discrete distribution (the binomial) with a continuous distribution (the normal), we call the use of 9.5 (instead of 9 or 10) a **correction for continuity**. That is, we are correcting the discrete distribution so that it can be approximated by the continuous one. The use of the correction for continuity leads to the calculation of the following standard normal z value:

$$z = \frac{x - \mu}{\sigma} = \frac{9.5 - 12}{2.19} = -1.14$$

Using Table IV of Appendix B, we find the area between $z = 0$ and $z = -1.14$ to be .3729. Then the probability that x is less than 10 is approximated by the area under the normal distribution to the left of 9.5, shown shaded in Figure 4.29. That is,

$$P(x \le 9) \approx P(z \le -1.14)$$
$$= .5 - P(-1.14 < z \le 0)$$
$$= .5 - .3729 = .1271$$

The approximation differs only slightly from the exact binomial probability, .128. Of course, when tables of exact binomial probabilities are available, we will use the exact value rather than a normal approximation.

Use of the normal distribution will not always provide a good approximation for binomial probabilities. The following is a useful rule of thumb to determine when n is large enough for the approximation to be effective: the interval $\mu \pm 3\sigma$ should lie within the range of the binomial random variable x (i.e., 0 to n) in order for the normal approximation to be adequate. The rule works well because almost all of the normal distribution falls within 3 standard deviations of the mean, so if this interval is contained within the range of x values, there is "room" for the normal approximation to work.

As shown in Figure 4.30(a) for the example above with $n = 20$ and $p = .6$, the interval

$$\mu \pm 3\sigma = 12 \pm 3(2.19) = (5.43, \ 18.57)$$

lies within the range 0 to 20. However, if we were to try to use the normal approximation with $n = 10$ and $p = .1$, the interval $\mu \pm 3\sigma$ is

$$1 \pm 3(.95) \quad \text{or} \quad (-1.85, \ 3.85)$$

As shown in Figure 4.30(b) (page 244), this interval is not contained within the range of x, since $x = 0$ is a lower bound for the binomial distribution. Note in Figure 4.30(b)

FIGURE 4.30a ▶

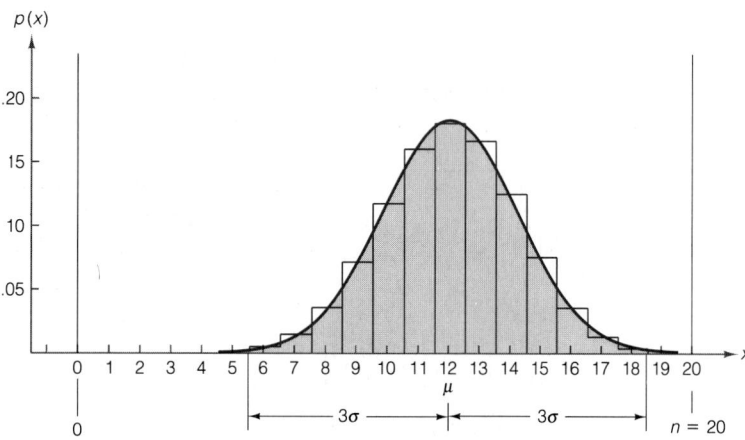

a. $n = 20$, $p = .6$: Normal approximation is good

FIGURE 4.30b ▶

Rule of thumb for normal approximation to binomial probabilities

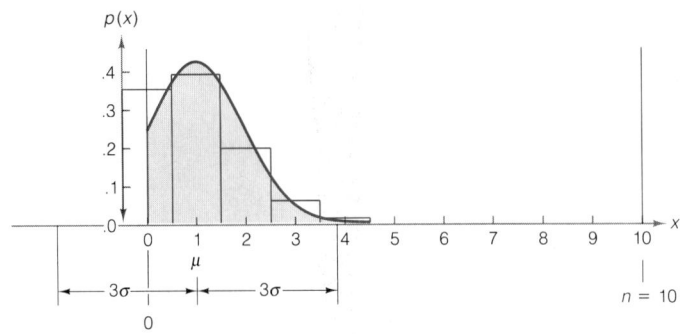

b. $n = 10$, $p = .1$:   Normal approximation is poor

that the normal distribution will not "fit" in the range of x, and therefore will not provide a good approximation to the binomial probabilities.

Using a Normal Distribution to Approximate Binomial Probabilities

1. After you have determined n and p for the binomial distribution, calculate the interval $\mu \pm 3\sigma = np \pm 3\sqrt{npq}$. If the interval lies in the range 0 to n, the normal distribution will provide a reasonable approximation to the probabilities of most binomial events.

2. Write the binomial probability of interest in the form $P(x \leq a)$ or $P(x \geq a)$ or $P(a \leq x \leq b)$.

3. If the binomial probability to be approximated is of the form $P(x \leq a)$, the correction for continuity is $(a + .5)$, and the approximating standard normal z value is $z = \dfrac{(a + .5) - \mu}{\sigma}$ See Figure 4.31(a).

4. If the binomial probability to be approximated is of the form $P(x \geq a)$, the correction for continuity is $(a - .5)$, and the approximating standard normal z value is $z = \dfrac{(a - .5) - \mu}{\sigma}$ See Figure 4.31(b).

5. If the binomial probability to be approximated is of the form $P(a \leq x \leq b)$, treat the ends of the interval separately, calculating two distinct z values according to step 3. [*Note:* $P(a \leq x \leq b) = P(x \leq b) - P(x \leq a - 1)$]

6. Sketch the approximating normal distribution and shade the area corresponding to the probability of the event of interest, as in Figure 4.31. Using Table IV of Appendix B and the z value(s) you calculated in steps 3–5, find the shaded area. This is the approximate probability of the binomial event.

FIGURE 4.31 ▶
Approximating binomial
probabilities by normal
probabilities

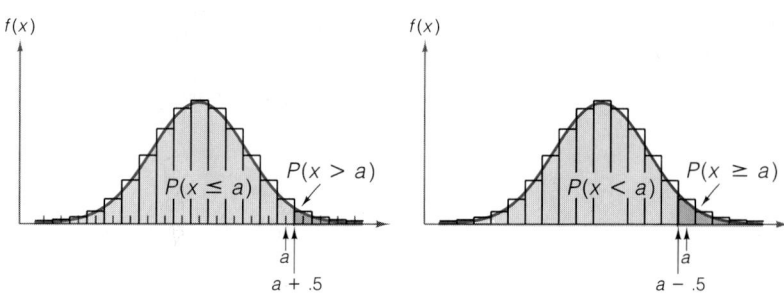

a. $P(x \le a)$ or $P(x > a)$ **b.** $P(x < a)$ or $P(x \ge a)$

The steps for approximating a binomial probability by a normal probability are given in the preceding box.

EXAMPLE 4.22

The pocket calculator has become relatively inexpensive because its solid-state circuitry is stamped by machine, thus making mass production feasible. One problem with anything that is mass-produced is quality. The production process must be monitored or audited to be sure the output of the process conforms to requirements.

One method of dealing with this problem is **lot acceptance sampling**, in which items being produced are sampled at various stages of the production process and are carefully inspected. The lot of items from which the sample is drawn is then accepted or rejected, based on the number of defectives in the sample. Lots that are accepted may be sent forward for further processing or may be shipped to customers; lots that are rejected may be reworked or scrapped. For example, suppose a manufacturer of calculators chooses 200 stamped circuits from the day's production and determines x, the number of defective circuits in the sample. Suppose that up to a 6% rate of defectives is considered acceptable for the process.

a. Find the mean and standard deviation of x, assuming the defective rate is 6%.

b. Use the normal approximation to determine the probability that 20 or more defectives are observed in the sample of 200 circuits—i.e., find the approximate probability that $x \ge 20$.

Solution

a. The random variable x is binomial, with $n = 200$ and the fraction defective $p = .06$. Thus,

$$\mu = np = 200(.06) = 12$$
$$\sigma = \sqrt{npq} = \sqrt{200(.06)(.94)} = \sqrt{11.28} = 3.36$$

b. We first note that

$$\mu \pm 3\sigma = 12 \pm 3(3.36) = 12 \pm 10.08 = (1.92, 22.08)$$

lies completely within the range from 0 to 200, so a normal probability distribution should provide an adequate approximation to this binomial distribution.

To find the approximating area corresponding to $x \geq 20$, refer to Figure 4.32. Note that we want to include all of the binomial probability histogram from 20 to 200, inclusive. But in order to include the entire rectangle corresponding to $x = 20$,

FIGURE 4.32 ▶
Normal approximation to the binomial distribution with $n = 200$, $p = .06$

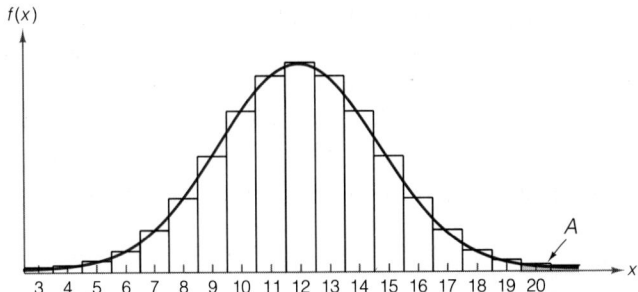

we must begin the approximating area at $20 - .5 = 19.5$. In other words, since the event is of the form $x \geq a$ with $a = 20$, the correction for continuity is $a - .5 = 20 - .5 = 19.5$. Thus, the z value is

$$z = \frac{(a - .5) - \mu}{\sigma} = \frac{19.5 - 12}{3.36} = \frac{7.5}{3.36} = 2.23$$

Referring to Table IV of Appendix B, we observe that the area to the right of the mean corresponding to $z = 2.23$ (see Figure 4.33) is .4871. So, the area A is

$$A = .5 - .4871 = .0129$$

FIGURE 4.33 ▶
Standard normal distribution

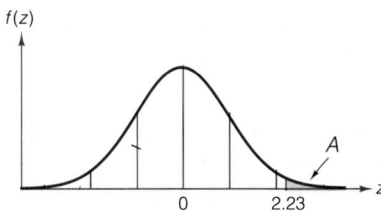

Thus, the normal approximation to the binomial probability is

$$P(x \geq 20) \approx .0129$$

In other words, the probability is extremely small that 20 or more defectives would be observed in a sample of 200 circuits, *if in fact the true defective rate is 6%*. If the manufacturer were to observe $x \geq 20$, the likely reason is that the process is producing more than the acceptable 6% defectives.

Exercises 4.96–4.104

Learning the Mechanics

4.96 Assume that x is a binomial random variable with n and p as specified in parts **a–f**. For which cases would it be appropriate to use a normal distribution to approximate the binomial distribution?

    a. $n = 100$, $p = .05$ **b.** $n = 100$, $p = .2$ **c.** $n = 25$, $p = .5$
    d. $n = 1,000$, $p = .01$ **e.** $n = 60$, $p = .95$ **f.** $n = 1,000$, $p = .95$

4.97 Suppose that x is a binomial random variable with $p = .7$ and $n = 25$.

    a. Would it be appropriate to approximate the probability distribution of x with a normal distribution? Explain.
    b. Assuming that a normal distribution provides an adequate approximation to the distribution of x, what are the mean and variance of the approximating normal distribution?
    c. Use Table II of Appendix B to find the exact value of $P(x \geq 15)$.
    d. Use the normal approximation to find $P(x \geq 15)$.

4.98 Assume that x is a binomial random variable with $n = 100$ and $p = .45$. Use a normal approximation to find the following:

    a. $P(x \leq 45)$ **b.** $P(40 \leq x \leq 50)$ **c.** $P(x \geq 38)$

4.99 Assume that x is a binomial random variable with $n = 1,000$ and $p = .50$. Find each of the following probabilities:

    a. $P(x > 500)$ **b.** $P(490 \leq x < 500)$ **c.** $P(x > 1,000)$

Applying the Concepts

4.100 The *Statistical Abstract of the United States: 1992* (p. 46) reports that 25% of the country's 94,312,000 households are inhabited by one person. If 1,000 randomly selected homes are to participate in a survey to determine television ratings, find the approximate probability that no more than 250 of these homes are inhabited by one person.

4.101 In 1982, General Motors Corporation's auto assembly plant in Fremont, California, was shut down and turned over to Toyota Motor Corporation as part of a joint venture with the Japanese firm. Before the shutdown, 5,000 workers produced 240,000 cars a year and had an absentee rate of 20%. After the Japanese took over and introduced their distinctive management style, the same number of cars were produced by only 2,500 workers and the absentee rate dropped to 2% ("The Difference Japanese Management Makes," *Business Week*, July 14, 1986, p. 47).

    a. With an absentee rate of 20%, what is the probability that at least 90% of a random sample of 50 workers will be on the job on a particular day?
    b. What assumption must we make in order to use the normal distribution to approximate the probability required in part **a**?
    c. If the absentee rate were 2%, should the probability of the event in part **b** be approximated using a normal distribution? Explain.

4.102 In Case Study 4.2, the number of shuttle catastrophes due to booster failure in n missions was treated as a binomial random variable. Using the binomial distribution and the probability of catastrophe determined by the Air Force's risk assessment study ($\frac{1}{35}$), we determined the probability of at least 1 shuttle catastrophe in 25 missions to be .5155.

a. Based on the guidelines presented in this section, would it have been advisable to approximate this probability using the normal approximation to the binomial distribution? Explain.

b. Regardless of your answer to part **a**, use the normal distribution to approximate the binomial probability. Comment on the difference between the exact and approximate probabilities.

c. Refer to part **a**. Would the normal approximation be advisable if $n = 100$? $n = 500$? $n = 1,000$?

d. Approximate the probability that more than 25 catastrophes occur in 1,000 flights, assuming that the probability of a catastrophe in any given flight remains $\frac{1}{35}$.

4.103 In May 1983, after an extensive investigation by the Consumer Product Safety Commission, Honeywell agreed to recall 770,000 potentially defective smoke detectors. The commission suggested that about 40% of the Honeywell detectors were defective. However, Honeywell found only four defectives in a random sample of 2,000 detectors and claimed the recall was not justified (Gross, 1983). Let x be the number of defective smoke detectors found in a random sample of 2,000 detectors.

a. What assumptions must be made in order to characterize x as a binomial random variable? Do these assumptions appear to be satisfied?

b. Assume that the conditions of part **a** hold. Determine the approximate probability of finding four or fewer defective smoke detectors in a random sample of 2,000 if, in fact, 40% of all detectors are defective.

c. Assume that Honeywell's sample data have been reported accurately. Is it *likely* that 40% of their detectors are defective? Explain.

d. Refer to part **c**. Is it *possible* that 40% of Honeywell's detectors are defective? Explain.

4.104 A computer disk manufacturer claims that 99.4% of its disks are defect-free. A large software company that buys and uses large numbers of the disks wants to verify this claim, and selects 1,600 disks to be tested. The tests reveal 12 defective disks. Assuming that the disk manufacturer's claim is correct, what is the probability of finding 12 or more defective disks in a sample of 1,600? Does your answer cast doubt on the manufacturer's claim? Explain.

Summary

Random variables are rules that assign numerical values to the outcomes of an experiment. **Discrete random variables** have countable numbers of possible values, and **continuous random variables** can assume an uncountable number of values corresponding to the points in one or more intervals. For purposes of distinguishing the two, the values of a discrete random variable can be listed, whereas those of a continuous random variable cannot.

The **probability distribution** of a discrete random variable specifies the probability associated with each possible value the random variable can assume. The mean and standard deviation of the probability distribution provide numerical descriptive measures of the distribution. Many applications of statistics involve the estimation of the mean and standard deviation of a probability distribution based on sample data.

The **binomial** and **Poisson** probability distributions describe two specific types of discrete random variables that have many applications in business. Many **continuous** random variables in business applications have probability distributions that are well approximated by the **normal, uniform,** or **exponential probability distributions**. In this chapter we described each probability distribution with a table, formula, or graph, gave its mean and variance, and pointed out some practical applications of each probability model. In addition, we showed that the normal probability distribution provides a good approximation for the binomial distribution when n is sufficiently large.

In the following chapters we will learn that the normal distribution plays a primary role in statistical inference.

Supplementary Exercises 4.105 – 4.131

Note: *Starred (*) exercises refer to optional sections in this chapter.*

Learning the Meachanics

4.105   Given that x is a binomial random variable, compute $p(x)$ for each of the following cases:
   a. $n = 7$, $x = 3$, $p = .5$
   b. $n = 4$, $x = 3$, $p = .8$
   c. $n = 15$, $x = 1$, $p = .1$

4.106   For each of the following examples, decide whether x is a binomial random variable, and explain your decision:
   a. Of five applicants for a job in the accounting department, two will be selected. Although all applicants appear to be equally qualified, only three have the ability to fulfill the expectations of the company. Suppose that the two selections are made at random from the five applicants, and let x be the number of qualified applicants selected.
   b. A software developer establishes a support hotline for customers to call in with questions regarding use of the software. Let x represent the number of calls received on the support hotline during a specified workday.
   c. Florida is one of a minority of states with no state income tax. A poll of 1,000 registered voters is conducted to determine how many would favor a state income tax in light of the state's current fiscal condition. Let x be the number in the sample who would favor the tax.

*4.107   Assume that x is a random variable best described by a uniform distribution with $c = 10$ and $d = 90$.
   a. Find $f(x)$.   **b.** Find the mean and standard deviation of x.
   c. Graph the probability distribution for x, and locate its mean and the interval $\mu \pm 2\sigma$ on the graph.
   d. Find $P(x \leq 60)$.   **e.** Find $P(x \geq 90)$.   **f.** Find $P(x \leq 80)$.
   g. Find $P(\mu - \sigma \leq x \leq \mu + \sigma)$.   **h.** Find $P(x > 75)$.

4.108   The random variable x has a normal distribution with $\mu = 75$ and $\sigma = 10$. Find the following probabilities:
   a. $P(x \leq 80)$ **b.** $P(x \geq 85)$ **c.** $P(70 \leq x \leq 75)$
   d. $P(x > 80)$ **e.** $P(x = 78)$ **f.** $P(x \leq 110)$

*4.109   Given that x is a Poisson random variable, compute $p(x)$ for each of the following cases:
   a. $\lambda = 14$, $x = 11$ **b.** $\lambda = 11$, $x = 14$ **c.** $\lambda = 13$, $x = 7$

4.110 Suppose x is a normal random variable with mean 40 and standard deviation 6. Find the value of x, call it x_0, such that:

    a. $P(\mu \leq x < x_0) = .40$ **b.** $P(x \geq x_0) = .10$ **c.** $P(x_0 \leq x < \mu) = .45$

    d. $P(x < x_0) = .05$ **e.** $P(x > x_0) = .40$ **f.** $P(x \leq x_0) = .40$

*4.111 Suppose x has an exponential distribution with $\lambda = .3$. Find the following probabilities:

    a. $P(x \leq 2)$ **b.** $P(x > 3)$ **c.** $P(x = 1)$ **d.** $P(x \leq 7)$ **e.** $P(4 \leq x \leq 12)$ **f.** $P(x = 2.5)$

4.112 Assume that x is a binomial random variable with $n = 50$ and $p = .6$. Find approximate values for the following probabilities:

    a. $P(x \leq 35)$ **b.** $P(25 \leq x \leq 40)$ **c.** $P(x \geq 20)$ **d.** $P(40 \leq x \leq 50)$

4.113 Which of the following describe discrete random variables, and which describe continuous random variables?

    a. The number of damaged inventory items

    b. The average monthly sales revenue generated by a salesperson over the past year

    c. The number of square feet of warehouse space a company rents

    d. The length of time a firm must wait before its copying machine is fixed

Applying the Concepts

4.114 The Environmental Protection Agency (EPA) tested 842 in-use automobiles to determine whether there were differences between the cars' actual gas mileage and the mileage projected in the EPA's mileage guide. For highway driving, they found that only 68% of the cars tested had fuel economies within 2 miles per gallon of the mileage guide's projection (*Environmental News*, 1978). Assume this figure holds for the population of cars currently in use for which the EPA has determined projected gas mileages. Suppose the EPA is planning to select 20 cars at random from this population and test their fuel economies to determine how many are within 2 miles per gallon of their EPA projections.

    a. Decide whether the following statement is true or false and explain: The number of cars in the sample of 20 that have mileages within 2 miles per gallon of their EPA projections is not a binomial random variable but, for convenience, could be treated as a binomial random variable.

    b. What is the probability (approximately) that fewer than 10 of the 20 cars selected will be within 2 miles per gallon of their EPA projections? (For convenience, use 70% as an approximation to 68%.)

4.115 As part of a study of how pricing decisions are made by fabricare firms (the dry cleaning and laundry industry), Joe F. Goetz, Jr. (1985) contacted and questioned 103 fabricare firms. The accompanying table describes the sales volumes of these firms. Assume that the sales volume, x, for each of the six intervals can be adequately approximated by the midpoint of the interval. These midpoints are shown in the second column of the table. One of the 103 firms is to be randomly selected for more intensive questioning. In this situation the relative frequencies in the table can be interpreted as probabilities that describe the approximate likelihood of the sampled firm having sales volume x.

Sales Volume	x	Relative Frequency
Over $0 to $75,000	$ 37,500	.14
Over $75,000 to $150,000	112,500	.30
Over $150,000 to $300,000	225,000	.20
Over $300,000 to $500,000	400,000	.17
Over $500,000 to $1,000,000	750,000	.10
Over $1,000,000 to $5,000,000	3,000,000	.09

a. Find $E(x)$.   **b.** Find $E[(x - \mu)^2]$.

c. Interpret the values you obtained in parts **a** and **b** in the context of the problem.

4.116 E. Brewer and P. Kaeser (1963) conducted a study of the factors that affect the level of production of workers paid on a piecework basis (i.e., paid according to the number of items they produce or process). Their study involved observing the performance of 36 quality control inspectors at a paper mill in England over an 8-week period. The inspectors were responsible for detecting and sorting out paper with defects such as holes, spots, creases, and rust marks. Part of the study entailed computing and analyzing the average hourly earnings for each inspector for each week of the 8-week observation period. Brewer and Kaeser constructed a frequency histogram of the average earnings data and noted that the histogram could be approximated by a normal distribution.

a. How many observations are there in the average earnings data set?

b. Suppose the average-earnings histogram can be approximated by a normal distribution with $\mu = \$7.65$ and $\sigma = \$1.25$. Approximately what proportion of the weekly average earnings are over $8.50 per hour?

c. Using the normal distribution of part **b**, is it possible to determine approximately how many inspectors averaged over $8.50 per hour for the 8-week period? If so, how many? If not, why not?

4.117 The **tolerance limits** for a particular quality characteristic (e.g., length, weight, or strength) of a product are the minimum and/or maximum values at which the product will operate properly. Tolerance limits are set by the engineering design function of the manufacturing operation (Juran and Gryna, 1980). The tensile strength of a particular metal part can be characterized as being normally distributed with a mean of 25 pounds and a standard deviation of 2 pounds. The upper and lower tolerance limits for the part are 30 pounds and 21 pounds, respectively. A part that falls within the tolerance limits results in a profit of $10. A part that falls below the lower tolerance limit costs the company $2; a part that falls above the upper tolerance limit costs the company $1. Find the company's expected profit per metal part produced.

4.118 An experiment is to be conducted to determine whether an acclaimed stock market analyst has extrasensory perception (ESP). Five different cards are shuffled and one is chosen at random. The analyst will try to identify which card was drawn without seeing it. The experiment is repeated 20 times and x, the number of correct decisions, is recorded. (Assume that the 20 trials are independent.)

a. If the stock market analyst is guessing (i.e., if the analyst does not possess ESP), what is the value of p, the probability of a correct decision on each trial?

b. If the analyst is guessing, what is the probability of a correct decision on at least half the trials?

c. Suppose the analyst makes the correct decision on 10 of the 20 trials. Do you think this performance is good enough to suggest that the analyst possesses ESP? Support or refute the proposition that the analyst possesses ESP using your results from part **b**.

4.119 The metropolitan airport commission is considering the establishment of limitations on noise pollution around a local airport. At the present time, the noise level per jet takeoff in one neighborhood near the airport is approximately normally distributed with a mean of 100 decibels and a standard deviation of 6 decibels.

a. What is the probability that a randomly selected jet will generate a noise level greater than 108 decibels in this neighborhood?

b. What is the probability that a randomly selected jet will generate a noise level of exactly 100 decibels?

c. Suppose a regulation is passed that requires jet noise in this neighborhood to be lower than 105 decibels 95% of the time. Assuming the standard deviation of the noise distribution remains the same, how much will the mean level of noise have to be lowered to comply with the regulation?

4.120 When the price of grain is low, many farmers participate in government-financed, on-farm storage programs rather than selling their grain. But storage invites insect infestations, and grain elevators penalize farmers who sell them insect-infested grain. In 1982, the U.S. Grain Marketing Research Laboratory estimated that 80% of the storage bins of corn in the country were infested with insects, and it has been estimated that the economic loss to farmers in the state of Minnesota alone is $12.6 million annually (*Minneapolis Tribune*, Aug. 8, 1982). Suppose 20 storage bins of corn are randomly selected and examined for insect infestation.
   a. What is the probability (approximately) that less than one-half of the bins are infested?
   b. What assumptions did you make in answering part **a**?
   c. Why is your answer to part **a** an approximation?
   d. Would you be surprised if all 20 of the bins were infested? Explain.

*4.121 A wholesale office equipment outlet claims that on an average it sells 2.4 typewriters per day. If it has only five typewriters in stock at the close of business today and does not expect to receive a shipment of new typewriters until some time after the close of business tomorrow, what is the probability that the outlet's current supply of typewriters will not be sufficient to meet tomorrow's demand?

*4.122 Assume that the length of the active life of baking yeast has an exponential distribution with a mean equal to 6 months. If the expiration date marked on a package of yeast is based on a life of 6 months, what is the probability that a package of the yeast will lose its potency before its expiration date?

4.123 A company has a lump-sum incentive plan for salespeople that is dependent on their level of sales. If they sell less than $100,000 per year, they receive a $1,000 bonus; from $100,000 to $200,000, they receive $5,000; and above $200,000, they receive $10,000. If the annual sales per salesperson has approximately a normal distribution with $\mu = \$180,000$ and $\sigma = \$50,000$:
   a. Find p_1, the proportion of salespeople who receive a $1,000 bonus.
   b. Find p_2, the proportion of salespeople who receive a $5,000 bonus.
   c. Find p_3, the proportion of salespeople who receive a $10,000 bonus.
   d. What is the mean value of the bonus payout for the company? [*Hint:* Review the definition for the expected value of a random variable.]

4.124 If the probability of a customer responding to one of your marketing department's mail questionnaires is .6, what is the probability that, of 20 questionnaires mailed, more than 15 will be returned?

*4.125 Based on sample data collected in the Denver area, Nicholas Kiefer (1985) found that in some cases the exponential distribution is an adequate approximation for the distribution of the time (in weeks) an individual is unemployed. In particular, he found the exponential distribution to be appropriate for white and black workers, but not for Hispanics. Use $\lambda = .075$ to answer the following questions.
   a. What is the mean time workers are unemployed according to the exponential distribution?
   b. What is the probability that a white worker who just lost her job will be unemployed for at least 2 weeks? More than 6 weeks?
   c. What is the probability that an unemployed worker will find a new job within 12 weeks?

4.126 Contrary to our intuition, very reliable decisions concerning the proportion of a large group of consumers who favor a particular product or a particular social issue can be based on relatively small samples. For example, suppose the target population of consumers contains 50,000,000 people and we want to decide whether the proportion of consumers, p, in the population who favor some product (or issue) is as large as some value, say .2. Suppose you randomly select a sample as small as 1,600 from the 50,000,000 and you observe the number, x, of consumers in the sample who favor the new product. Assuming that $p = .2$, find the mean and standard deviation of x. Suppose that 400 (or 25%) of the sample of 1,600 consumers favor the new product. Why might this sample result lead you to conclude that p (the proportion of consumers who favor the product in the population of 50,000,000) is larger than .2? [*Hint:* Compare the observed value of x with the values of μ and σ calculated on the assumption that $p = .2$.]

4.127 In recent years, the use of the telephone as a data collection instrument for public opinion polls has been steadily increasing. However, one of the major factors bearing on the extent to which the telephone will become an acceptable data collection tool in the future is the *refusal rate*—i.e., the percentage of the eligible people actually contacted who refuse to take part in the poll. Suppose that past records indicate a refusal rate of 20% in a large city. A poll of 25 city residents is to be taken, and x is the number of residents contacted by telephone who refuse to take part in the poll.
  a. Find the mean and variance of x.   **b.** Find $P(x \leq 5)$.   **c.** Find $P(x > 10)$.

*4.128 A small life insurance company has determined that on the average it receives five death claims per day. What is the probability that the company will receive three claims or less on a particular day? Exactly five claims? What assumptions must you make to find these probabilities?

4.129 To help highway planners anticipate the need for road repairs and design future construction projects, data are collected on the volume and weight of truck traffic on specific roadways. Recently, equipment has been developed that can be built into road surfaces to measure traffic volumes and to weigh trucks without requiring them to stop at roadside weigh stations. As with any measuring device, however, the "weigh-in-motion" equipment does not always record truck weights accurately. In an experiment performed by the Minnesota Department of Transportation involving repeated weighing of a 27,907-pound truck, it was found that the weights recorded by the weigh-in-motion equipment were approximately normally distributed with mean 27,315 and a standard deviation of 628 pounds (Dahlin, 1982; Wright, Owen, and Pena, 1983). It follows that the difference between the actual weight and recorded weight, the error of measurement, is normally distributed with mean 592 pounds and standard deviation 628 pounds.
  a. What is the probability that the weigh-in-motion equipment understates the actual weight of the truck?
  b. If a 27,907-pound truck were driven over the weigh-in-motion equipment 100 times, approximately how many times would the equipment overstate the truck's weight?
  c. What is the probability that the error in the weight recorded by the weigh-in-motion equipment for a 27,907-pound truck exceeds 400 pounds?
  d. It is possible to adjust (or *calibrate*) the weigh-in-motion equipment to control the mean error of measurement. At what level should the mean error be set so the equipment will understate the weight of a 27,907-pound truck 50% of the time? Only 40% of the time?

4.130 The owner of construction company A makes bids on jobs so that, if it is awarded the job, company A will make a $10,000 profit. The owner of construction company B makes bids on jobs so that, if it is awarded the job, company B will make a $15,000 profit. Each company describes the probability distribution of the number of jobs the company is awarded per year as shown in the table.

Company A		Company B	
x	$p(x)$	x	$p(x)$
2	.05	2	.15
3	.15	3	.30
4	.20	4	.30
5	.35	5	.20
6	.25	6	.05

    a. Find the expected number of jobs each will be awarded in a year.
    b. What is the expected profit for each company?
    c. Find the variance and standard deviation of the distribution of the number of jobs awarded per year for each company.
    d. Graph $p(x)$ for both companies A and B. For each company, what proportion of the time will x fall in the interval $\mu \pm 2\sigma$?

4.131 A manufacturer considers a production lot unacceptable if 10% or more of the units in the lot are defective. In such cases the company wants to scrap (not ship) the entire lot. A company quality control inspector has proposed the following criterion for determining whether to reject a lot: In a sample of 10 units from a lot, if two or more are defective, reject the entire lot. If the lot currently under examination is 11% defective, what is the probability that this decision rule will lead the quality control inspector to the correct decision?

On Your Own

To control the quality of incoming or outgoing large lots of manufactured items, manufacturers use lot acceptance sampling plans. For example, if each lot consists of 1,000 items, the plan will call for the selection of a random sample of n items (n is usually small) from each lot. The items in each sample are carefully inspected, the number of defectives recorded, and the lot considered to be of acceptable quality if the number of defectives is less than or equal to some specified number, a. The number a is called the **acceptance number** for the plan.

    To illustrate, simulate sampling from a large lot of items that contains 10% defectives. Place 10 poker chips (or marbles, etc.) in a bowl and mark one of the 10 as defective. Randomly select a sample of five items from a lot by selecting a chip from the 10, replacing it, and repeating the process four more times. Count the number of times, x, that you observe the defective chip. This process is equivalent to selecting a random sample of $n = 5$ items from a large lot containing 10% defectives.

    If you choose $a = 1$ as the acceptance number for the plan, then you will accept only lots for which $x \leq 1$.

    By choosing n and a, you change the ability of a sampling plan to screen out bad lots. To investigate the properties of a sampling plan with $n = 5$ and $a = 1$, simulate the process of sampling from 100 lots.

a. Collect the 100 values of x obtained from the simulation, and construct a relative frequency histogram for x. Note that this histogram is an approximation to $p(x)$. Estimate the proportion of lots that will be accepted by the plan by dividing the number of lots accepted by 100.
b. Calculate the exact values of $p(x)$ for $n = 5$ and $p = .1$, and compare these with the results of part **a**.

Using the Computer

Calculate the mean percentage of college graduates over all the zip codes for one of the census regions listed in Appendix C. Round the mean to the nearest integer, and use the result as an estimate of the percentage of college graduates among all people at least 25 years old in the region.

a. Suppose that 20 individuals from the region respond to an advertisement by an employment agency. If these people represent a random sample of all individuals at least 25 years of age in the region, what is the probability that more than half of them have college degrees?

b. If 2,000 individuals respond, find the mean μ and standard deviation σ of the number of them who have college degrees. Calculate $\mu \pm 2\sigma$ and $\mu \pm 3\sigma$, and use Chebyshev's theorem and the Empirical Rule to estimate the probability that the number of respondents with college degrees falls in each of the intervals. Based on your answers, assess the likelihood that more than half the applicants will have college degrees.

c. What are the potential problems with using the mean percentage of college graduates as an estimate of the percentage for the region? How could the estimate be improved?

d. Use the normal approximation to the binomial to estimate the probability that fewer than 10% of 20 applicants (still assuming they represent a random sample) have a college education. Compare your answer with the exact binomial probability of the same event.

e. Use the normal approximation to the binomial to estimate the probability that fewer than 10% of 200 applicants have a college education. If your statistical software package has a function that calculates exact binomial probabilities, use it to calculate the same probability you approximated, and compare the results.

References

Biddle, W. "What destroyed *Challenger?*" *Discover*, Apr. 1986, pp. 40–47.

Blair, R. D. and Kenny, L. W. *Microeconomics for Managerial Decision Making*. New York: McGraw-Hill, 1982. Chapter 10.

Brewer, E. and Kaeser, P. "A comparative analysis of incentive plans." *Journal of Industrial Relations*, July 1963, *11*, pp. 183–198.

Brown, A. A., Hulswit, F. T., and Kettelle, J. D. "A study of sales operations." *Operations Research*, June 1956, *4*, pp. 296–308.

Chervany, N. L., Anderson, J. C., Benson, P. G., and Hill, A. V. "A management science approach to a Dutch elm disease sanitation program." *Interfaces*, Apr. 1980, *10*, p. 108.

Dahlin, C. *Minnesota's Experience with Weighing Trucks in Motion*. St. Paul: Minnesota Department of Transportation, 1982.

Dessler, G. "Personnel tests gain in popularity." *St. Paul Pioneer Press and Dispatch*, Mar. 17, 1986.

"'83 report put booster accident as most likely." *Minneapolis Star and Tribune*, Feb. 11, 1986.

Environmental News. Environmental Protection Agency. New England Regional Office, Boston, Jan. 1978, pp. 11–12.

Fama, E. F. *Foundations of Finance*. New York: Basic Books, 1976. Chapter 1.

Goetz, J. F., Jr. "The pricing decision: A service industry's experience." *Journal of Small Business Management*, Apr. 1985, *23*, pp. 61–67.

Gross, S. "Honeywell smoke detectors recalled after 18-month probe." *Minneapolis Star and Tribune*, May 25, 1983.

Hillier, F. S. "The derivation of probabilistic information for the evaluation of risky investments." *Management Science*, Apr. 1963, *9*, pp. 443–457.

Hogg, R. V. and Craig, A. T. *Introduction to Mathematical Statistics*, 4th ed. New York: Macmillan, 1978.

Johnson, R. W. and Sullivan, A. C. "Segmentation of the consumer loan market." *Journal of Retail Banking*, Sept. 1981, *3*, pp. 1–7.

Juran, J. M. and Gryna, F. M., Jr. *Quality Planning and Analysis*, 2d ed. New York: McGraw-Hill, 1980.

Kiefer, N. M. "Specification diagnostics based on Laguerre alternatives for econometric models of duration." *Journal of Econometrics*, 1985, *28*, pp. 135–154.

Lamberson, L. R. "Reliability tutorial." *American Society for Quality Control Quality Congress Transaction*, Baltimore, 1985, pp. 88–99.

Lindgren, B. W. *Statistical Theory*, 3d ed. New York: Macmillan, 1976. Chapters 2 and 3.

Martz, H. F. and Waller, R. A. *Bayesian Reliability Analysis*. New York: Wiley, 1982, pp. 1, 256.

McKean, K. "They fly in the face of danger." *Discover*, Apr. 1986, pp. 48–58.

Mendenhall, W. *Introduction to Probability and Statistics*, 8th ed. Boston: Duxbury, 1991. Chapters 5 and 6.

Misshauk, M. J. *Management Theory and Practice*. Boston: Little, Brown, 1979. Chapter 13.

Montgomery, D. C. *Introduction to Statistical Quality Control*, 2d ed. New York: Wiley, 1991.

Mood, A. M., Graybill, F. A., and Boes, D. C. *Introduction to the Theory of Statistics*, 3d ed. New York: McGraw-Hill, 1974. Chapter 3.

Murphy, A. H. and Winkler, R. L. "Probability forecasting in meteorology." *Journal of the American Statistical Association*, Sept. 1984, 79, pp. 489–500.

Neter, J., Wasserman, W., and Whitmore, G. A. *Applied Statistics*, 4th ed. Boston: Allyn & Bacon, 1993.

Parzen, E. *Modern Probability Theory and Its Applications*. New York: Wiley, 1960. Chapters 3, 4, 6, and 7.

Robinson, W. V. "NASA blamed for shuttle disaster." *Boston Globe*, June 10, 1986.

Schick, G. J. "The search for a software reliability model." *Decision Sciences*, Oct. 1974, 5, p. 529.

Sims, S. H. and Templeton, J. G. C. "Steady state results for the M/M (a, b)/c batch-service system." *European Journal of Operational Research*, 1985, 21, pp. 260–267.

U.S. Golf Association. *The Rules of Golf*. 1993, p. 110.

The United States Government Manual 1985–1986. Office of the Federal Register, revised July 1, 1985, pp. 485–487.

Webster, A. H. "Straight answers about Dutch elm disease." *Flower and Garden*, May 1978, pp. 28–33, 46–47.

Williams, C. A., Jr., and Heins, R. M. *Risk Management and Insurance*, 6th ed. New York: McGraw-Hill, 1986.

Willis, R. E. and Chervany, N. L. *Statistical Analysis and Modeling for Management Decision-Making*. Belmont, Calif.: Wadsworth, 1974. Chapter 5.

Winkler, R. L. and Hays, W. *Statistics: Probability, Inference, and Decision*, 2d ed. New York: Holt, Rinehart and Winston, 1975. Chapter 3.

Wright, J. L., Owen, F., and Pena, D. *Status of Mn/DOT's Weigh-in-Motion Program*. St. Paul: Minnesota Department of Transportation, Jan. 1983.

CHAPTER FIVE

Sampling Distributions

Contents

Case Studies

Where We've Been

We have learned in earlier chapters that the objective of most statistical investigations is inference—that is, estimating some numerical descriptive measure (a parameter) of a population based on sample data. To estimate a population parameter, we use sample data to compute numerical descriptive measures (sample statistics) such as the sample mean or variance.

Where We're Going

Because sample measurements are observed values of random variables, the value of a sample statistic will vary in a random manner from sample to sample. In other words, since sample statistics are computed from random variables, they themselves are random variables, and they have probability distributions that are either discrete or continuous. The probability distribution of a sample statistic is called a *sampling distribution* because it characterizes the distribution of values of the statistic over a very large number of samples. Sampling distributions are the topic of this chapter. We will discuss why many sampling distributions tend to be approximately normal, and you will see how sampling distributions can be used to evaluate the accuracy of parameter estimates. Then in subsequent chapters we will show how to use sampling distributions to make inferences in a variety of business and industrial applications.

In Chapter 4 we assumed that we knew the probability distribution of a random variable, and based on this knowledge, we were able to compute the mean, variance, and probability that the random variable assumed specific values. However, in most practical applications, this information will not be available. To illustrate, in Example 4.8, we calculated the probability that the binomial random variable x—the number of 20 polled employees who favor unionization—assumed specific values. To do this, it was necessary to assume some value for p, the proportion of the employees in the population who favor unionization. Thus, for the purpose of illustration we assumed $p = .6$. Typically, however, the exact value of p would be unknown. In fact, the probable purpose of taking the poll was to estimate p. Similarly, when we modeled the in-city gas mileage of a certain type of automobile in Example 4.16, we used the normal probability distribution with an *assumed* mean and standard deviation of 27 and 3 miles per gallon, respectively. In reality, the true mean and standard deviation are unknown quantities that would have to be estimated.

Numerical quantities that describe probability distributions are called **parameters**. Thus, p, the probability of a success in a binomial experiment, and μ and σ, the mean and standard deviation of a normal distribution, are examples of parameters. Since probability distributions are used to characterize populations, it follows that parameters are also numerical descriptive measures of populations.

Definition 5.1

A **parameter** is a numerical descriptive measure of a population. It is calculated from the observations in the population.

Since it is almost always too costly and/or time-consuming to conduct a census of a population and compute its parameters, we use the information contained in a sample to make inferences about the parameters of a population. In order to make such inferences, we must compute **sample statistics** that will aid in making these inferences.

Definition 5.2

A **sample statistic** is a numerical descriptive measure of a sample. It is calculated from the observations in the sample.

Some examples of useful sample statistics we have already discussed are the sample mean, $\bar{x}$; sample median; sample variance, s^2; and the sample standard deviation, s. Before we can use these and other sample statistics to make inferences about population parameters, we have to be able to evaluate their properties. How can we decide which sample statistic contains the most information about a population parameter? One purpose of this chapter is to answer this question.

5.1   Introduction to Sampling Distributions

If we want to estimate a parameter of a population—say, the population mean, μ—there are a number of sample statistics that we could use for the estimate. Two possibilities are the sample mean, $\bar{x}$, and the sample median, m. Which of these do you think will provide a better estimate of μ?

Before answering this question, consider the following example: Toss a fair die and let x equal the number of dots showing on the up face. Suppose the die is tossed three times, producing the sample measurements 2, 2, 6. The sample mean is $\bar{x} = 3.33$ and the sample median is $m = 2$. Since the mean of x is $\mu = 3.5$, you can see that for this sample of three measurements, the sample mean $\bar{x}$ provides an estimate that falls closer to μ than does the sample median [see Figure 5.1(a)].

FIGURE 5.1 ▶
Comparing the sample mean ($\bar{x}$) and sample median (m) as estimators of the population mean (μ)

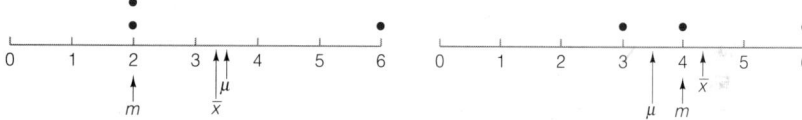

a. Sample 1: $\bar{x}$ is closer than m to μ **b.** Sample 2: m is closer than $\bar{x}$ to μ

Now suppose we toss the die three more times and obtain the sample measurements, 3, 4, 6. The mean and median of this sample are $\bar{x} = 4.33$ and $m = 4$, respectively. This time m is closer to μ [see Figure 5.1(b)].

This simple example illustrates an important point: Neither the sample mean nor the sample median will *always* fall closer to the population mean. Consequently, we cannot compare these two sample statistics or, in general, any two sample statistics on the basis of their performance for a single sample. Instead, we need to recognize that sample statistics are themselves random variables because different samples can lead to different values for the sample statistics. As random variables, sample statistics must be judged and compared on the basis of their probability distributions—i.e., the collection of values and associated probabilities of each statistic that would be obtained if the sampling experiment were repeated a *very large number of times*. We will illustrate this concept with an example.

Suppose it is known that in a certain part of Canada the daily high temperature recorded for all past months of January has a mean of $\mu = 10°F$ and a standard deviation of $\sigma = 5°F$. Consider an experiment consisting of randomly selecting 25 daily high temperatures from the records of past months of January and calculating the sample mean, $\bar{x}$. If this experiment were repeated a very large number of times, the value of $\bar{x}$ would vary from sample to sample. For example, the first sample of 25 temperature measurements might have a mean of $\bar{x} = 9.8$; the second sample, a mean of $\bar{x} = 11.4$; the third sample, a mean of $\bar{x} = 10.5$; etc. If the sampling experiment were repeated a very large number of times and the resulting values of $\bar{x}$ were displayed in a histogram, the histogram would be the approximate probability distribution of $\bar{x}$. If $\bar{x}$ is a good estimator of μ, we would expect the values of $\bar{x}$ to cluster around μ as shown in Figure 5.2. This probability distribution is called a **sampling distribution** because it describes the potential outcomes of $\bar{x}$ in repeated sampling.

FIGURE 5.2 ►
Sampling distribution for $\bar{x}$ based on a sample of $n = 25$ measurements: $\mu = 10$, $\sigma = 5$

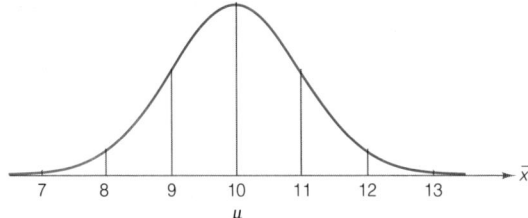

In actual practice, the sampling distribution of a statistic is obtained mathematically or (approximately) by simulating the sampling on a computer using the procedure just described.

Definition 5.3

. . . .

The **sampling distribution** for a sample statistic (calculated from a sample of n measurements) is the probability distribution of the statistic.

If $\bar{x}$ has been calculated from a sample of $n = 25$ measurements selected from a population with mean $\mu = 10$ and standard deviation $\sigma = 5$, the sampling distribution (Figure 5.2) provides information about the behavior of $\bar{x}$ in repeated sampling. For example, the probability that you will draw a sample of 25 measurements and obtain a value of $\bar{x}$ in the interval $9 \leq \bar{x} \leq 10$ will be the area under the sampling distribution over that interval.

Since the properties of a statistic are typified by its sampling distribution, it follows that, to compare two statistics, you compare their sampling distributions. For example, if you have two statistics, A and B, for estimating the same parameter (for purposes of illustration, suppose the parameter is the population variance σ^2) and if their sampling distributions are as shown in Figure 5.3, you would choose statistic A in preference to statistic B. You would make this choice because the sampling distribution for statistic

FIGURE 5.3 ►
Two sampling distributions for estimating the population variance, σ^2

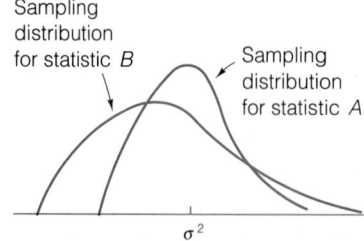

A centers over σ^2 and has less spread (variation) than the sampling distribution for statistic B. When you draw a single sample in a practical sampling situation, the probability is higher that statistic A will fall closer to σ^2.

Remember that in practice we will not know the numerical value of the unknown parameter, σ^2, so we will not know whether statistic A or statistic B is closer to σ^2 for particular samples. We have to rely on our theoretical knowledge of the sampling distributions to choose the better sample statistic and then use it sample after sample.

EXAMPLE 5.1

Consider a large population consisting only of the measurements 0, 3, and 12 and described by the probability distribution shown in the table. A random sample of $n = 3$ measurements is selected from the population.

x	0	3	12
$p(x)$	$\frac{1}{3}$	$\frac{1}{3}$	$\frac{1}{3}$

a. Find the sampling distribution of the sample mean $\bar{x}$.
b. Find the sampling distribution of the sample median m.

Solution

Every possible sample of $n = 3$ measurements is listed in Table 5.1, along with the sample mean and median. Because any one sample is as likely to be selected as any other (random sampling), the probability of observing any particular sample is $\frac{1}{27}$. This probability is also listed in Table 5.1.

TABLE 5.1   Possible Samples of $n = 3$ Measurements

Possible Samples	$\bar{x}$	m	Probability	Possible Samples	$\bar{x}$	m	Probability
0, 0, 0	0	0	$\frac{1}{27}$	3, 3, 12	6	3	$\frac{1}{27}$
0, 0, 3	1	0	$\frac{1}{27}$	3, 12, 0	5	3	$\frac{1}{27}$
0, 0, 12	4	0	$\frac{1}{27}$	3, 12, 3	6	3	$\frac{1}{27}$
0, 3, 0	1	0	$\frac{1}{27}$	3, 12, 12	9	12	$\frac{1}{27}$
0, 3, 3	2	3	$\frac{1}{27}$	12, 0, 0	4	0	$\frac{1}{27}$
0, 3, 12	5	3	$\frac{1}{27}$	12, 0, 3	5	3	$\frac{1}{27}$
0, 12, 0	4	0	$\frac{1}{27}$	12, 0, 12	8	12	$\frac{1}{27}$
0, 12, 3	5	3	$\frac{1}{27}$	12, 3, 0	5	3	$\frac{1}{27}$
0, 12, 12	8	12	$\frac{1}{27}$	12, 3, 3	6	3	$\frac{1}{27}$
3, 0, 0	1	0	$\frac{1}{27}$	12, 3, 12	9	12	$\frac{1}{27}$
3, 0, 3	2	3	$\frac{1}{27}$	12, 12, 0	8	12	$\frac{1}{27}$
3, 0, 12	5	3	$\frac{1}{27}$	12, 12, 3	9	12	$\frac{1}{27}$
3, 3, 0	2	3	$\frac{1}{27}$	12, 12, 12	12	12	$\frac{1}{27}$
3, 3, 3	3	3	$\frac{1}{27}$				

a. From Table 5.1 you can see that $\bar{x}$ can assume the values 0, 1, 2, 3, 4, 5, 6, 8, 9, and 12. Because $\bar{x} = 0$ occurs in only one sample, $P(\bar{x} = 0) = \frac{1}{27}$. Similarly, $\bar{x} =$

1 occurs in three samples: (0, 0, 3), (0, 3, 0), and (3, 0, 0). Therefore, $P(\bar{x} = 1) =$ $3/27 = 1/9$. Calculating the probabilities of the remaining values of $\bar{x}$ and arranging them in a table, we obtain the following probability distribution:

$\bar{x}$	0	1	2	3	4	5	6	8	9	12
$p(x)$	$1/27$	$3/27$	$3/27$	$1/27$	$3/27$	$6/27$	$3/27$	$3/27$	$3/27$	$1/27$

This is the sampling distribution for $\bar{x}$, because it specifies the probability associated with each possible value of $\bar{x}$.

b. In Table 5.1 you can see that the median m can assume one of the three values 0, 3, or 12. The value $m = 0$ occurs in seven different samples. Therefore, $P(m = 0) = 7/27$. Similarly, $m = 3$ occurs in thirteen samples and $m = 12$ occurs in seven samples. Therefore, the probability distribution (i.e., the sampling distribution) for the median m is as follows:

m	0	3	12
$p(m)$	$7/27$	$13/27$	$7/27$

Example 5.1 demonstrates the procedure for finding the exact sampling distribution of a statistic when the number of different samples that could be selected from the population is relatively small. In the real world, populations often consist of a large number of different values, making samples difficult (or impossible) to enumerate. When such a situation occurs, we may choose to obtain the approximate sampling distribution for a statistic by simulating the sampling over and over again and recording the proportion of times different values of the statistic occur. Example 5.2 illustrates this procedure.

EXAMPLE 5.2

Suppose we perform the following experiment: Take a sample of 11 measurements from the uniform distribution shown in Figure 5.4. Calculate the two sample statistics

$$\bar{x} = \text{Sample mean} = \frac{\sum_{i=1}^{11} x_i}{11}$$

$m = \text{Median} = \text{Sixth sample measurement when the 11 measurements}$ are arranged in ascending order

In this particular example we *know* that the population mean is $\mu = .5$. The objective will be to find out which sample statistic contains more information about μ. We use a computer to generate 1,000 samples, each with $n = 11$ observations. Then, we compute $\bar{x}$ and m for each sample. Our goal is to find the resulting approximate sampling distributions for $\bar{x}$ and m.

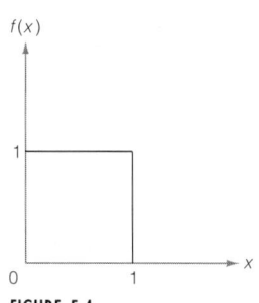

FIGURE 5.4 ▲
Uniform distribution from 0 to 1

Solution   The first 10 of the 1,000 samples generated are presented in Table 5.2. For each of the 1,000 samples we compute the sample mean, $\bar{x}$, and the sample median, m. For example, the first computer-generated sample from the uniform distribution (arranged in ascending order) contained the following measurements: .125, .138, .139, .217, .419, .506, .516, .757, .771, .786, .919. The sample mean, $\bar{x}$, and median, m, computed for this sample are

$$\bar{x} = \frac{.125 + .138 + \cdots + .919}{11} = .481$$

$$m = \text{Sixth ordered measurement} = .506$$

TABLE 5.2   First 10 Samples of $n = 11$ Measurements from a Uniform Distribution

Sample	Measurements										
1	.217	.786	.757	.125	.139	.919	.506	.771	.138	.516	.419
2	.303	.703	.812	.650	.848	.392	.988	.469	.632	.012	.065
3	.383	.547	.383	.584	.098	.676	.091	.535	.256	.163	.390
4	.218	.376	.248	.606	.610	.055	.095	.311	.086	.165	.665
5	.144	.069	.485	.739	.491	.054	.953	.179	.865	.429	.648
6	.426	.563	.186	.896	.628	.075	.283	.549	.295	.522	.674
7	.643	.828	.465	.672	.074	.300	.319	.254	.708	.384	.534
8	.616	.049	.324	.700	.803	.399	.557	.975	.569	.023	.072
9	.093	.835	.534	.212	.201	.041	.889	.728	.466	.142	.574
10	.957	.253	.983	.904	.696	.766	.880	.485	.035	.881	.732

The relative frequency histograms for $\bar{x}$ and m for the 1,000 samples of size $n = 11$ are shown in Figure 5.5.

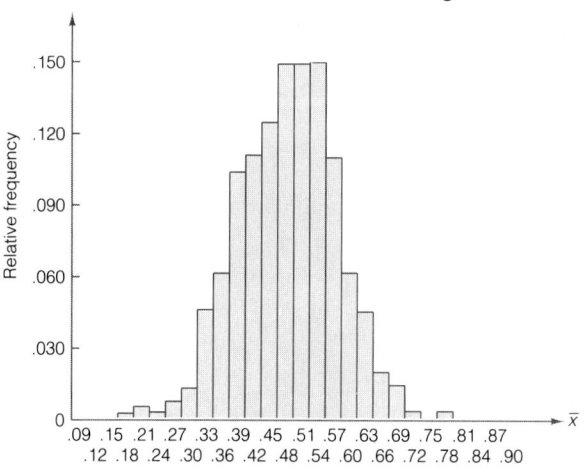

a. Sampling distribution for $\bar{x}$ (based on 1,000 samples of $n = 11$ measurements)

b. Sampling distribution for m (based on 1,000 samples of $n = 11$ measurements)

FIGURE 5.5 ▲ Approximate sampling distributions for $\bar{x}$ and m, Example 5.2

You can see that the values of $\bar{x}$ tend to cluster around μ to a greater extent than do the values of m. Thus, on the basis of the observed sampling distributions, we conclude that $\bar{x}$ contains more information about μ than m does—at least for samples of $n = 11$ measurements from the uniform distribution.

We will not always have to simulate repeated sampling on a computer to find sampling distributions. Many sampling distributions can be derived mathematically, but the theory necessary to do this is beyond the scope of this text. Consequently, when we need to know the properties of a statistic, we will present its sampling distribution and simply describe its properties. Several of the important properties of sampling distributions are discussed in the next section.

5.2 Properties of Sampling Distributions: Unbiasedness and Minimum Variance

A sample statistic that is used to make inferences about a population parameter is called a **point estimator**. A point estimator is a rule or formula that tells us how to use the sample data to calculate a single number that can be used as an **estimate** of the value of some population parameter. For example, the sample mean, $\bar{x}$, is a point estimator of the population mean, μ. Similarly, the sample variance, s^2, is a point estimator of the population variance, σ^2.

Definition 5.4

A **point estimator** of a population parameter is a rule or formula that tells us how to use the sample data to calculate a single number that can be used as an **estimate** of the population parameter.

Often, many different point estimators can be found to estimate the same parameter. Each will have a sampling distribution that provides information about the point estimator. By examining the sampling distribution, we can determine how large the difference between an estimate and the true value of the parameter—called the **error of estimation**—is likely to be. We can also determine whether an estimator is likely to overestimate or to underestimate a parameter.

Since the sampling distribution of a point estimator (or of any statistic) describes its behavior in repeated sampling, we look to the sampling distribution to identify characteristics or properties that we would want an estimator to have. As a first consideration, we would like the sampling distribution to center over the value of the parameter we want to estimate. One way to express centrality is in terms of the mean of the sampling distribution. Consequently, we say that a statistic is **unbiased** if its sampling distribution has a mean equal to the parameter it is intended to estimate.

When this occurs, the sampling distribution of the statistic will be centered over the parameter as shown in Figure 5.6(a). If the mean of a sampling distribution is not equal to the parameter it is intended to estimate, the statistic is said to be **biased**. The amount of bias is the difference between the mean of the sampling distribution and the value of the parameter you wish to estimate. The sampling distribution for a biased statistic is shown in Figure 5.6(b).

FIGURE 5.6 ▶
Sampling distributions for unbiased and biased estimators

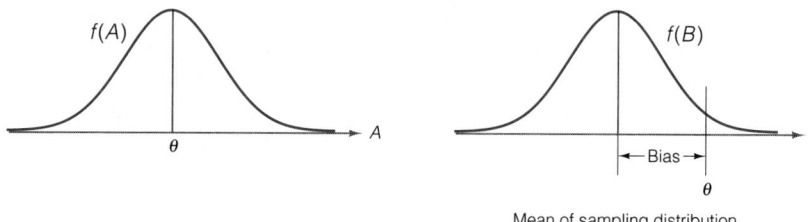

a. Unbiased sample statistic for the parameter θ

b. Biased sample statistic for the parameter θ

Definition 5.5

If a sample statistic has a sampling distribution with a mean equal to the population parameter the statistic is intended to estimate, the statistic is said to be an **unbiased** estimator of the parameter.

If the mean of the sampling distribution is not equal to the parameter, the statistic is said to be a **biased** estimator of the parameter.

The standard deviation of a sampling distribution measures another important property of a statistic—the spread of the estimates generated by repeated sampling. Suppose two statistics, A and B, are both unbiased estimators of the population parameter called θ (theta). Note that θ could by any parameter, such as μ, σ^2, or σ. Since the means of the two sampling distributions are the same, we turn to their standard deviations to decide which will provide estimates that fall closer to the unknown population parameter we are estimating. Naturally, we will choose the sample statistic that has the smaller standard deviation. Figure 5.7 depicts sampling distribu-

FIGURE 5.7 ▶
Sampling distributions for two unbiased estimators

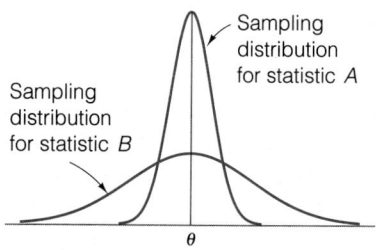

tions for A and B. Note that the standard deviation of the distribution of A is smaller than the standard deviation for B, indicating that over a large number of samples, the values of A cluster more closely around the unknown population parameter than do the values of B. Stated differently, the probability is high that A is closer to the parameter value than B is. Therefore, we would choose statistic A instead of statistic B as an estimator of θ.

In summary, to make an inference about a population parameter, use the sample statistic with a sampling distribution that is unbiased and has a small standard deviation (usually smaller than the standard deviation of other unbiased sample statistics). How to find this sample statistic will not concern us, because the "best" statistic for estimating a particular parameter is a matter of record. We will simply present an unbiased estimator with its standard deviation for each population parameter we consider. [*Note:* The standard deviation of the sampling distribution for a statistic is often called the **standard error** of the statistic.]

EXAMPLE 5.3

In Example 5.1, we found the sampling distributions of the sample mean $\bar{x}$ and the sample median m for random samples of $n = 3$ measurements from a population defined by the following probability distribution:

x	0	3	12
$p(x)$	$1/3$	$1/3$	$1/3$

The sampling distributions of $\bar{x}$ and m were found to be the following:

$\bar{x}$	0	1	2	3	4	5	6	8	9	12
$p(x)$	$1/27$	$3/27$	$3/27$	$1/27$	$3/27$	$6/27$	$3/27$	$3/27$	$3/27$	$1/27$

m	0	3	12
$p(m)$	$7/27$	$13/27$	$7/27$

a. Show that $\bar{x}$ is an unbiased estimator of μ in this situation.

b. Show that m is a biased estimator of μ in this situation.

Solution

a. The expected value of a discrete random variable x (see Section 4.2) is defined to be $E(x) = \sum xp(x)$, where the summation is over all values of x. Then

$$E(x) = \mu = \sum xp(x) = (0)(1/3) + (3)(1/3) + (12)(1/3) = 5$$

The expected value of the discrete random variable $\bar{x}$ is

$$E(\bar{x}) = \sum (\bar{x})p(\bar{x})$$

summed over all values of $\bar{x}$. Or

$$E(\bar{x}) = (0)(\tfrac{1}{27}) + (1)(\tfrac{3}{27}) + 2(\tfrac{3}{27}) + \cdots + (12)(\tfrac{1}{27}) = 5$$

Since $E(\bar{x}) = \mu$, we see that $\bar{x}$ is an unbiased estimator of μ.

b. The expected value of the sample median m is

$$E(m) = \sum mp(m) = (0)(\tfrac{7}{27}) + (3)(\tfrac{13}{27}) + (12)(\tfrac{7}{27}) = 4.56$$

Since the expected value of m is not equal to μ ($\mu = 5$), the sample median m is a biased estimator of μ.

EXAMPLE 5.4

Refer to Example 5.3 and find the standard deviations of the sampling distributions of $\bar{x}$ and m. Which statistic would appear to be a better estimator for μ?

Solution

The variance of the sampling distribution of $\bar{x}$ (we will denote it by the symbol $\sigma_{\bar{x}}^2$) is found to be

$$\sigma_{\bar{x}}^2 = E\{[\bar{x} - E(\bar{x})]^2\} = \sum (\bar{x} - \mu)^2 p(\bar{x})$$

where, from Example 5.3,

$$E(\bar{x}) = \mu = 5$$

Then

$$\sigma_{\bar{x}}^2 = (0 - 5)^2(\tfrac{1}{27}) + (1 - 5)^2(\tfrac{3}{27}) + (2 - 5)^2(\tfrac{3}{27}) + \cdots + (12 - 5)^2(\tfrac{1}{27})$$
$$= 8.6667$$

and

$$\sigma_{\bar{x}} = \sqrt{8.6667} = 2.94$$

Similarly, the variance of the sampling distribution of m (we will denote it by σ_m^2) is

$$\sigma_m^2 = E\{[m - E(m)]^2\}$$

where, from Example 5.3, the expected value of m is $E(m) = 4.56$. Then

$$\sigma_m^2 = E\{[m - E(m)]^2\} = \sum [m - E(m)]^2 p(m)$$
$$= (0 - 4.56)^2(\tfrac{7}{27}) + (3 - 4.56)^2(\tfrac{13}{27}) + (12 - 4.56)^2(\tfrac{7}{27}) = 20.9136$$

and

$$\sigma_m = \sqrt{20.9136} = 4.57$$

Which statistic appears to be the better estimator for the population mean μ: the sample mean $\bar{x}$ or the median m? To answer this question, we compare the sampling distributions of the two statistics. The sampling distribution of the sample median m is biased (i.e., it is located to the left of the mean μ) and its standard deviation $\sigma_m = 4.57$ is much larger than the standard deviation of the sampling distribution of $\bar{x}$, $\sigma_{\bar{x}} = 2.94$. Consequently, the sample mean $\bar{x}$ would be a better estimator of the population mean μ, for the population in question, than would the sample median m.

5.3 The Sampling Distribution of the Sample Mean

Estimating the mean useful life of automobiles, the mean monthly sales for all automobile dealers in a large city, and the mean breaking strength of a new plastic are practical problems with something in common. In each, we are interested in making an inference about the mean, μ, of some population. Because many practical business problems involve estimating μ, it is particularly important to have a sample statistic that is a good estimator of μ. As we mentioned in Chapter 2, the sample mean, $\bar{x}$, is generally a good choice as an estimator of μ. The mean and standard deviation of the sampling distribution of this useful statistic are related to the mean, μ, and standard deviation, σ, of the sampled population as described in the box.

The Mean and Standard Deviation of the Sampling Distribution of $\bar{x}$

Regardless of the shape of the population relative frequency distribution,

1. The mean of the sampling distribution of $\bar{x}$ will equal μ, the mean of the sampled population; i.e., $\mu_{\bar{x}} = \mu$.[*]
2. The standard deviation of the sampling distribution of $\bar{x}$ will equal σ, the standard deviation of the sampled population, divided by the square root of the sample size, n; i.e.,

$$\sigma_{\bar{x}} = \frac{\sigma^{\dagger}}{\sqrt{n}}$$

The standard deviation $\sigma_{\bar{x}}$ is often referred to as the **standard error of the mean**.

---

[*] $\mu_{\bar{x}}$ is an alternative (but equivalent) symbol for $E(\bar{x})$.

[†] If the sample size, n, is large relative to the number, N, of elements in the population, (e.g., 5% or more), $\sigma/\sqrt{n}$ must be multiplied by a finite population correction factor, $\sqrt{(N - n)/(N - 1)}$. For most sampling situations, this correction factor will be close to 1 and can be ignored.

Thus, $\bar{x}$ is an unbiased estimator of the population mean μ [i.e., $E(\bar{x}) = \mu$], and the standard deviation of $\bar{x}$ is inversely related to the (square root of the) sample size (i.e., $\sigma_{\bar{x}} = \sigma/\sqrt{n}$).

For example, suppose the sampled population has the uniform probability distribution shown in Figure 5.8(a). The mean and standard deviation of this probability distribution are $\mu = .5$ and $\sigma = .29$ (refer to optional Section 4.6 for the formulas for μ and σ). Now suppose a sample of 11 measurements is selected from this population. The sampling distribution of the sample mean for samples of size 11 will also have a mean of .5, with a standard deviation

$$\sigma_{\bar{x}} = \frac{\sigma}{\sqrt{n}} = \frac{.29}{\sqrt{11}} = .09$$

(That is, the standard error of $\bar{x}$ is $\sigma/\sqrt{n} = .09$.)

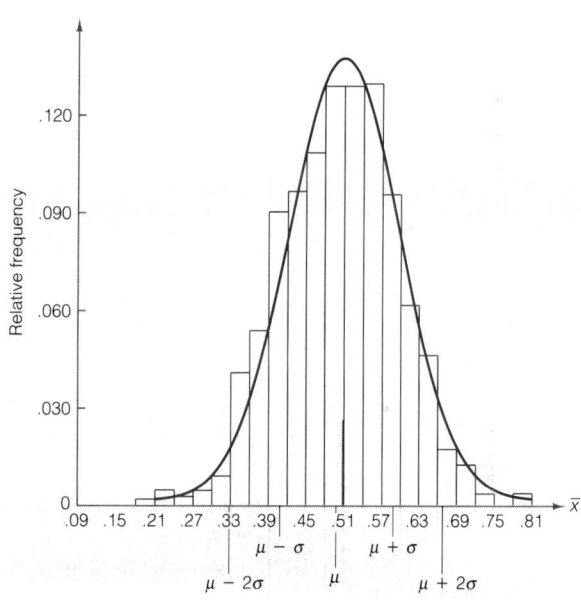

a. Relative frequency distribution of the sampled population

b. Relative frequency histogram for $\bar{x}$ in 1,000 samples of $n = 11$ measurements from a uniform distribution

FIGURE 5.8 ▲

What can be said about the shape of the sampling distribution of $\bar{x}$? Two important theorems provide this information.

Theorem 5.1

If a random sample of n observations is selected from a population with a normal distribution, the sampling distribution of $\bar{x}$ will be a normal distribution.

Theorem 5.2: The Central Limit Theorem

If a random sample of n observations is selected from a population (any population), then, when n is sufficiently large, the sampling distribution of $\bar{x}$ will be approximately a normal distribution. The larger the sample size, n, the better will be the normal approximation to the sampling distribution of $\bar{x}$.[*]

Thus, for sufficiently large samples, the sampling distribution of $\bar{x}$ will be approximately normal. How large must the sample size, n, be so that $\bar{x}$ has a normal sampling distribution? The answer depends on the shape of the relative frequency distribution of the sampled population, as shown in Figure 5.9.

Generally speaking, the greater the skewness of the distribution of the sampled population, the larger the sample size must be to obtain an adequate normal approximation to the sampling distribution of $\bar{x}$. But for some populations, particularly those with symmetric distributions, n may be fairly small and the sampling distribution of $\bar{x}$ will be approximately normal.

To demonstrate how small n can be and still achieve approximate normality for the sampling distribution of $\bar{x}$, recall Example 5.2, in which we generated 1,000 samples of $n = 11$ measurements from a uniform distribution. The relative frequency histogram for the 1,000 sample means is shown in Figure 5.8(b), and the normal probability distribution with a mean of .5 and a standard deviation of .09 is superimposed. You can see that this normal probability distribution approximates the computer-generated sampling distribution very well, even though the sample size is only $n = 11$.

The implications of the Central Limit Theorem are apparent by comparing the sampling distribution of $\bar{x}$ in Figure 5.8(b) with the distribution of the sampled population in Figure 5.8(a). In this situation, the population relative frequency distribution is not skewed and, as a result, a very small sample size proved large enough to apply the Central Limit Theorem. The sampling distribution of $\bar{x}$ is approximately normal, even though the distribution of the sampled population is decidedly nonnormal. You will also note that the mean of the sampling distribution is equal to the mean of the distribution of the sampled population, but that the variability of the sampling distribution is substantially less than the variability of the sampled population.

In most real-life applications, the shape of the population distribution will *not* be known. In such cases, we typically require $n \geq 30$ in order to invoke the Central Limit Theorem.

---

[*]Also, because of the Central Limit Theorem, the sum of a random sample of n observations, $\sum_{i=1}^{n} x_i$, will have a sampling distribution that will be approximately normal for large samples. This distribution will have a mean equal to $n\mu$ and a variance equal to $n\sigma^2$.

FIGURE 5.9 ▶

Sampling distribution of $\bar{x}$ for different populations and different sample sizes

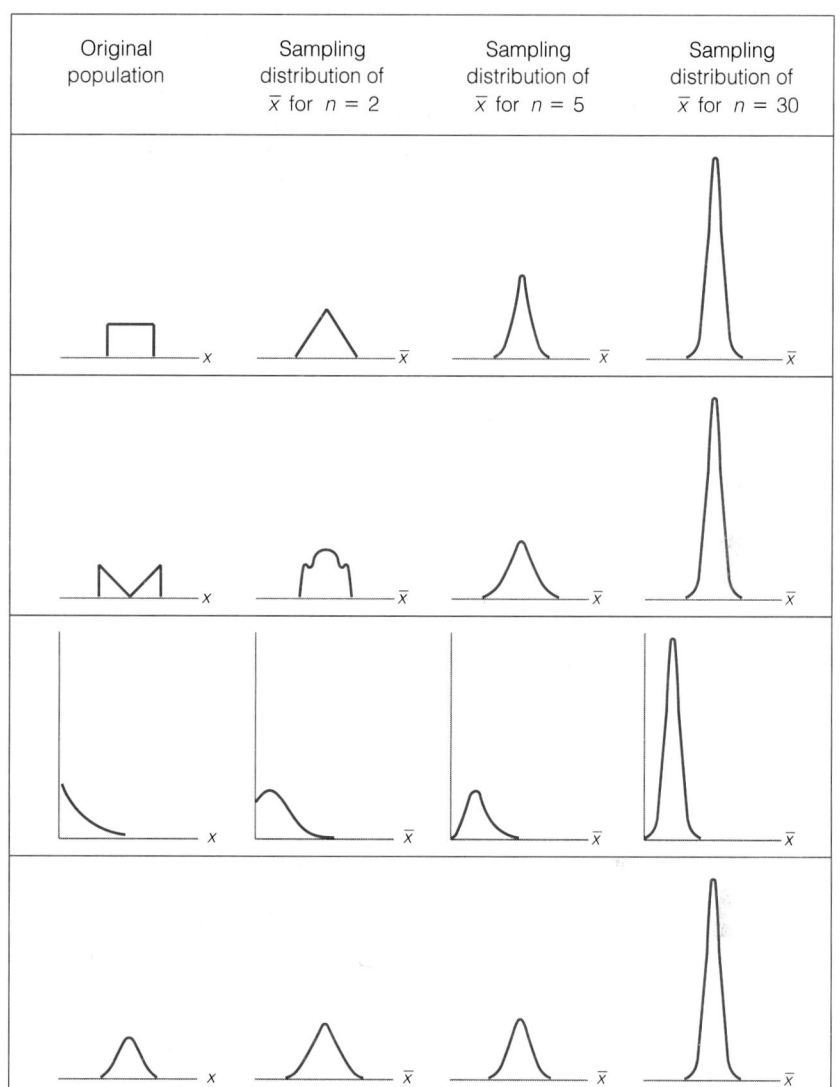

. . . . ▶

EXAMPLE 5.5

Suppose we have selected a random sample of $n = 25$ observations from a population with mean equal to 80 and standard deviation equal to 5. It is known that the population is not extremely skewed.

a. Sketch the relative frequency distributions for the population and for the sampling distribution of the sample mean, $\bar{x}$.

b. Find the probability that $\bar{x}$ will be larger than 82.

Solution

a. We do not know the exact shape of the population relative frequency distribution, but we do know that it should be centered about $\mu = 80$, its spread should be measured by $\sigma = 5$, and it is not highly skewed. One possibility is shown in Figure 5.10(a). From the Central Limit Theorem, we know that the sampling distribution of $\bar{x}$ will be approximately normal since the sampled population distribution is not extremely skewed. We also know that the sampling distribution will have mean and standard deviation

$$\mu_{\bar{x}} = \mu = 80 \quad \text{and} \quad \sigma_{\bar{x}} = \frac{\sigma}{\sqrt{n}} = \frac{5}{\sqrt{25}} = 1$$

The sampling distribution of $\bar{x}$ is shown in Figure 5.10(b).

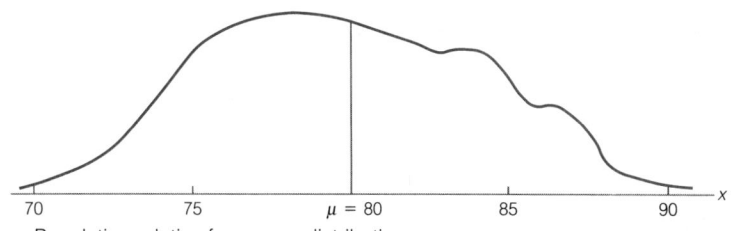

a. Population relative frequency distribution

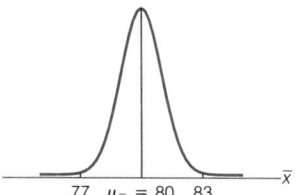

b. Sampling distribution of $\bar{x}$

FIGURE 5.10 ▲ A population relative frequency distribution and the sampling distribution for $\bar{x}$

b. The probability that $\bar{x}$ will exceed 82 is equal to the darker shaded area in Figure 5.11. To find this area, we need to find the z value corresponding to $\bar{x} = 82$. Recall

FIGURE 5.11 ▶

The sampling distribution of $\bar{x}$

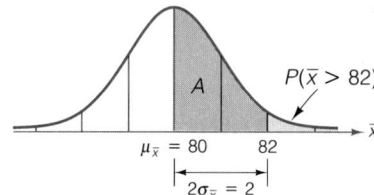

that the standard normal random variable z is the difference between any normally distributed random variable and its mean, expressed in units of its standard deviation. Since $\bar{x}$ is a normally distributed random variable with mean $\mu_{\bar{x}} = \mu$ and standard deviation $\sigma_{\bar{x}} = \sigma/\sqrt{n}$, it follows that the standard normal z value corresponding to the sample mean, $\bar{x}$, is

$$z = \frac{(\text{Normal random variable}) - (\text{Mean})}{\text{Standard deviation}} = \frac{\bar{x} - \mu_{\bar{x}}}{\sigma_{\bar{x}}}$$

Therefore, for $\bar{x} = 82$, we have

$$z = \frac{\bar{x} - \mu_{\bar{x}}}{\sigma_{\bar{x}}} = \frac{82 - 80}{1} = 2$$

The area A in Figure 5.11 corresponding to $z = 2$ is given in the table of areas under the normal curve (see Table IV of Appendix B) as .4772. Therefore, the tail area corresponding to the probability that $\bar{x}$ exceeds 82 is

$$P(\bar{x} > 82) = P(z > 2) = .5 - .4772 = .0228$$

EXAMPLE 5.6

A manufacturer of automobile batteries claims that the distribution of the lifetimes of its best battery has a mean of 54 months and a standard deviation of 6 months. Suppose a consumer group decides to check the claim by purchasing a sample of 50 of these batteries and subjecting them to tests that determine their lifetimes.

a. Assuming the manufacturer's claim is true, describe the sampling distribution of the mean lifetime of a sample of 50 batteries.

b. Assuming the manufacturer's claim is true, what is the probability that the consumer group's sample has a mean lifetime of 52 months or less?

Solution

a. Even though we have no information about the shape of the probability distribution of the lifetimes of the batteries, we can use the Central Limit Theorem to deduce that the sampling distribution for a sample mean lifetime of 50 batteries is approximately normally distributed. Furthermore, the mean of this sampling distribution is the same as the mean of the sampled population, which is $\mu = 54$ months, according to the manufacturer's claim. Finally, the standard deviation of the sampling distribution is given by

$$\sigma_{\bar{x}} = \frac{\sigma}{\sqrt{n}} = \frac{6}{\sqrt{50}} = .85 \text{ month}$$

Thus, if we assume the claim is true, the sampling distribution of the mean lifetime of the 50 batteries is approximately normal with mean 54 months and standard deviation .85 month. The sampling distribution is shown in Figure 5.12.

FIGURE 5.12 ▶
Sampling distribution of $\bar{x}$ in Example 5.6

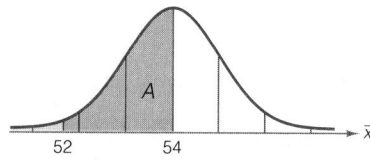

b. If the manufacturer's claim is true, the probability that the consumer group observes a mean battery lifetime of 52 months or less for their sample of 50 batteries, $P(\bar{x} \leq 52)$, is equivalent to the darker shaded area in Figure 5.12. Since the sampling distribution is approximately normal, we can find this area by computing the standard normal z value:

$$z = \frac{\bar{x} - \mu_{\bar{x}}}{\sigma_{\bar{x}}} = \frac{\bar{x} - \mu}{\sigma_{\bar{x}}} = \frac{52 - 54}{.85} = -2.35$$

where $\mu_{\bar{x}}$, the mean of the sampling distribution of $\bar{x}$, is equal to μ, the mean of the sampled population.

The area A shown in Figure 5.12 between $\bar{x} = 52$ and 54 is found in Table IV of Appendix B to be .4906, so the area to the left of 52 is

$$P(\bar{x} \leq 52) = .5 - A = .5 - .4906 = .0094$$

Thus, the probability that the consumer group will observe a sample mean of 52 or less is only .0094 if the manufacturer's claim is true. If the 50 tested batteries do result in a mean of 52 months or less, the consumer group will have strong evidence that the manufacturer's claim is untrue, because such an event is very unlikely to occur if the claim is true. (This is still another application of the rare event approach to statistical inference.)

In addition to providing a very useful approximation for the sampling distribution of a sample mean, the Central Limit Theorem offers an explanation for the fact that many relative frequency distributions of data are mound-shaped. Many of the macroscopic measurements we take in business research are really means or sums of many microscopic phenomena. For example, a company's sales for one year is the total of the many individual sales the company made during the year. Thus, the year's sales for a sample of similar companies may have a mound-shaped relative frequency distribution. Similarly, the length of time a construction company takes to complete a house might be viewed as the total of the time each of the large number of distinct jobs necessary to build the house takes to complete. The monthly profit of a firm can be viewed as the sum of the profits of all the transactions of the firm for that month. If we adopt viewpoints like these, the Central Limit Theorem offers some explanation for the frequent occurrence of mound-shaped distributions in nature.

CASE STUDY 5.1 / Evaluating the Condition of Rental Cars

In the summer of 1986, National Car Rental Systems, Inc., commissioned USAC Properties, Inc. [the performance testing/endorsement arm of the United States Automobile Club (USAC)] to conduct a survey of the general condition of the cars rented to the public by Hertz, Avis, National, and Budget Rent-a-Car.* National was interested in comparing the conditions of the cars it rented with those of the other leading car-rental companies.

Teams of USAC officials would evaluate each company's cars on appearance and cleanliness, accessory performance, mechanical functions, and vehicle safety using a demerit point system designed specifically for this survey. Each car would start with a perfect score of 0 points and would incur demerit points for each discrepancy noted by the inspectors. The number of demerits associated with a discrepancy would be based on the seriousness of the discrepancy.

---

*Information by personal communication with Rajiv Tandon, Corporate Vice President and General Manager of the Car Rental Division, National Car Rental Systems, Inc., Minneapolis, Minn.

If all cars in each company's fleet could be inspected and graded, one measure of the overall condition of a company's cars would be the mean of all scores received by the company, i.e., the company's *fleet mean score*. Such a census, however, besides being virtually impossible to conduct logistically, would be prohibitively expensive. It was therefore decided that the fleet mean score would have to be estimated. Accordingly, 10 major airports were randomly selected, and 10 cars from each company were randomly rented for inspection from each airport by USAC officials; i.e., a sample of size $n = 100$ cars from each company's fleet was drawn and inspected. In the analysis of USAC's inspection results, each company's mean score was used to estimate the company's unknown fleet mean score. (The use of a sample mean to estimate a

population mean will be discussed in detail in Chapter 6). As we have seen in this chapter, $\bar{x}$ is a random variable with a sampling distribution that has a mean equal to the mean of the population from which the sample was drawn. Thus, in the context of this case study, the mean of the sampling distribution of $\bar{x}$ is the unknown fleet mean score. Since the sample size used by USAC was 100, the statisticians who evaluated USAC's inspection results were able to invoke the Central Limit Theorem and assume the sampling distribution of $\bar{x}$ to be approximately normally distributed. This assumption enabled comparisons of fleet mean scores for Hertz, Avis, National, and Budget Rent-a-Car to be made using the conventional large-sample testing procedures that are presented in Chapters 7 and 8.

CASE STUDY 5.2 / Reducing Investment Risk Through Diversification

A number of studies by financial analysts have shown that the total risk (total variation) of a stock, as measured by the variance of the stock's rates of return over time, is comprised of two components: **systematic risk** and **unsystematic risk**. Systematic risk (systematic variability) is the portion of total risk caused by factors that simultaneously influence the prices of all stocks. Examples of such factors are changes in federal economic policies and changes in the national political climate. These factors explain why the prices of all stocks tend to move together over time (i.e., generally upward or generally downward). Unsystematic risk (unsystematic variability) is the portion of the total risk of a particular stock due to factors that influence the firm in question but generally do not influence other firms. Examples of such factors are labor strikes, management errors, and lawsuits (Francis, 1986). Although the proportions of systematic and unsystematic risk vary from firm to firm, it has been determined that, for many of the stocks listed on the New York Stock Exchange, systematic risk comprises about 25% and unsystematic risk comprises about 75% of the stock's total risk (Blume, 1971). As is demonstrated in this case study, an investor can use diversification to reduce the unsystematic portion of the total investment risk.

Suppose an investor is considering investing a total of $5,000 in one or more of five different stocks. We denote the monthly rates of return of these stocks by r_1, r_2, r_3, r_4, and r_5. For simplicity, we assume these monthly returns are independent and identically distributed random variables with mean $\mu = 10\%$ and standard deviation $\sigma = 4\%$. Suppose the investor has narrowed the choice to two options: (1) invest $5,000 in stock 1 or (2) invest $1,000 in each of the five stocks.

Under the first option, the investor's monthly rate of return is r_1. Under the second option, since equal amounts of money were invested in each stock, the investor's monthly rate of return is $\bar{r} = \sum_{i=1}^{5} r_i/5$. If the first option is chosen, the investor's expected monthly rate of return, $E(r_i)$, is $\mu = 10\%$ and the risk, as measured by the variance of the stock's rate of return, is $\sigma^2 = 16$. If the second option is chosen, the investor's expected monthly rate of return, $E(\bar{r})$, can be shown to be the same as in the first option. However, since the numerator of $\bar{r}$ is the sum of $n = 5$ independent and identically distributed random variables, each with mean μ and variance σ^2, the variance of $\bar{r}$ is $\sigma_{\bar{r}}^2 = \sigma^2/n$. Accordingly, the risk faced by the investor is

$^{16}/_5 = 3.2$ and is lower than under the first option. Thus, the uncertainty faced by the investor is lower if the investor diversifies, rather than putting "all the eggs in one basket." For a more detailed discussion of risk reduction through diversification, see Sharpe and Alexander (1990) and Elton and Gruber (1987), or Alexander and Francis (1986).

5.4   The Relationship Between Sample Size and a Sampling Distribution

Suppose you draw two random samples from a population—one sample containing $n = 5$ observations and the second containing $n = 10$—and you want to compute $\bar{x}$ for each sample and use these statistics to estimate the population mean, μ. Intuitively, it would seem that the $\bar{x}$ based on the sample of 10 measurements would contain more information about μ than the $\bar{x}$ based on five measurements. But how is this larger sample size reflected in the sampling distribution of a statistic?

For the statistics you will encounter in this text, the variance of a statistic's sampling distribution will be inversely proportional to the sample size.* Or, since the standard deviation of $\bar{x}$ is equal to $\sigma/\sqrt{n}$, you can say that the standard deviation of the sampling distribution is proportional to $1/\sqrt{n}$. So, to reduce the standard deviation of the sampling distribution of a statistic to $\frac{1}{2}$ its original value you will need 4 times as many observations in your sample $(1/\sqrt{n} = 1/\sqrt{4} = \frac{1}{2})$. Or to reduce the standard deviation to $\frac{1}{3}$ its original value, you will need 9 times as many observations.

The sampling distributions for the sample mean, $\bar{x}$, based on random samples from a normally distributed population, are shown in Figure 5.13 for $n = 1$, 4, and

FIGURE 5.13 ▶

Three sampling distributions of $\bar{x}$

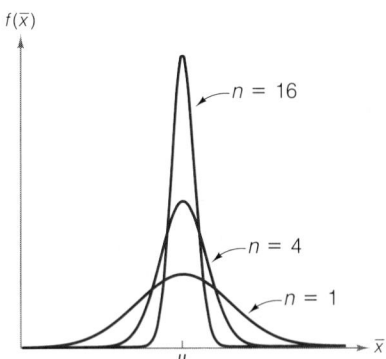

---

*Note that this is not true of all statistics, but it is true for most.

16 observations. The curve for $n = 1$ represents the probability distribution of the population. Those for $n = 4$ and $n = 16$ are sampling distributions of $\bar{x}$. Note how the distributions contract (variation decreases) as n increases from 1 to 4 to 16. The standard deviation of $\bar{x}$ based on $n = 16$ measurements is half the corresponding standard deviation of the distribution based on $n = 4$ measurements.

EXAMPLE 5.7

Consider the **Bernoulli** random variable x that can assume the values 0 and 1 with probabilities p and $q = (1 - p)$, respectively. The distribution is summarized in Table 5.3, where we have associated the term *Success* with the outcome $x = 1$, and *Failure* with the outcome $x = 0$. The Bernoulli random variable is just a binomial random variable with $n = 1$ trial.

Suppose a random sample of n measurements is drawn from this Bernoulli distribution, and the sample mean $\bar{x}$ is calculated. Note that

TABLE 5.3 Bernoulli Distribution

Outcome	x	$p(x)$
Failure	0	q
Success	1	p

$$\bar{x} = \frac{\sum_{i=1}^{n} x_i}{n}$$

and that $\sum_{i=1}^{n} x_i$ is the total number of successes (the number of 1's in the sample) in the random sample of n measurements (or *trials*). This sum is therefore a binomial random variable, with n trials and probability of success p. For example, the Bernoulli random variable might be the status of a single computer microchip (nondefective or defective), x the number of n such chips that are good, and $\bar{x}$ the fraction of nondefective (good) chips in a set of n.

a. Find the mean and standard deviation of the sampling distribution of $\bar{x}$.

b. Simulate the distribution of $\bar{x}$ using $p = .8$, and $n = 1, 10, 25,$ and 100 by generating 1,000 samples for each sample size and creating a histogram of the 1,000 sample means.

Solution

a. The mean and variance of the Bernoulli random variable are

$$\mu = E(x) = 0(q) + 1(p) = p$$
$$\sigma^2 = E[(x - \mu)^2] = (0 - p)^2(q) + (1 - p)^2(p)$$
$$= p^2q + q^2p = pq(p + q) = pq$$

Note that these are the mean and standard deviation of a binomial random variable with $n = 1$, which is another description of a Bernoulli random variable.

We know that the mean $\bar{x}$ of a random sample is unbiased, so that

$$E(\bar{x}) = \mu = p$$

and the standard error is

$$\sigma_{\bar{x}} = \frac{\sigma}{\sqrt{n}} = \frac{\sqrt{pq}}{\sqrt{n}} = \sqrt{\frac{pq}{n}}$$

Because $\bar{x}$ provides an unbiased estimate of the probability of success p and has a standard error that decreases as the sample size increases, we use it to estimate p in subsequent chapters, where we refer to it as the sample fraction of successes, $\hat{p}$ (read "p hat"). We refer to its standard error as $\sigma_{\hat{p}}$.

b. The mean and standard error of $\bar{x}$ when $p = .8$ are

$$\mu_{\bar{x}} = p = .8$$

$$\sigma_{\bar{x}} = \sqrt{\frac{pq}{n}} = \sqrt{\frac{(.8)(.2)}{n}} = \frac{.4}{\sqrt{n}}$$

TABLE 5.4   Mean and Standard Error of $\bar{x}$ for Bernoulli Random Variable with $p = .8$

n	$\mu_{\bar{x}}$	$\sigma_{\bar{x}}$
1	.8	$\frac{.4}{\sqrt{1}} = .400$
10	.8	$\frac{.4}{\sqrt{10}} = .1265$
25	.8	$\frac{.4}{\sqrt{25}} = .0800$
100	.8	$\frac{.4}{\sqrt{100}} = .0400$

You can see in Table 5.4 how the standard error of $\bar{x}$ decreases as n increases.

The simulation of 1,000 sample means with each of the sample sizes given in Table 5.4 resulted in the sampling distributions shown in Figure 5.14. A relative frequency histogram is used to display each sampling distribution. Note that each sampling distribution more closely resembles a normal distribution than the previous one. As the Central Limit Theorem promises, the distribution of $\bar{x}$ becomes approximately normal for large n, and the approximation improves as n increases. Note too that the values of $\bar{x}$ cluster more closely around their mean (.8) as n is increased. We will make use of these properties to estimate p for binomial random variables in Chapter 6.

a. $n = 1$

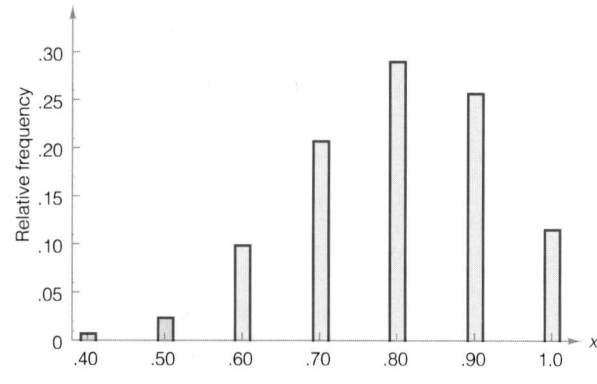

b. $n = 10$

FIGURE 5.14 ▲ Sampling distributions for Bernoulli sample means

c. $n = 25$

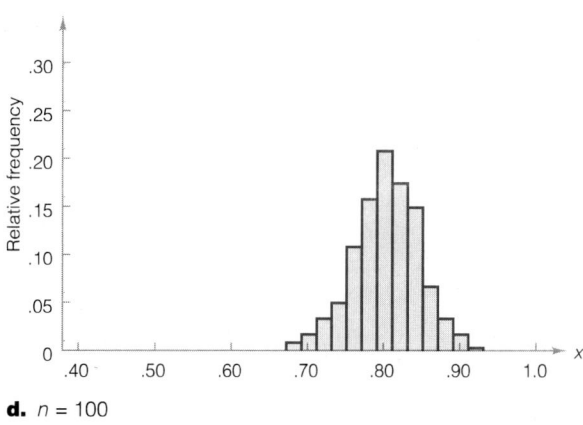

d. $n = 100$

EXAMPLE 5.8

Refer to Example 5.7. Suppose $n = 400$ microchips are to be sampled from a very large batch, of which a proportion p are good. The proportion of good chips in the sample will be determined by assigning a 1 to each good chip, a 0 to each defective chip, and calculating the sample mean of the 400 Bernoulli observations. Assuming that the approximate value of p is .8, what is the probability that $\bar{x}$ will fall within .03 of the exact value of p?

Solution

We first note (see Example 5.7) that the mean and standard deviation of $\bar{x}$ are

$$E(\bar{x}) = p \qquad \text{and} \qquad \sigma_{\bar{x}} = \sqrt{\frac{pq}{n}} = \sqrt{\frac{pq}{400}}$$

Using the approximate value of p to obtain an approximation for the standard deviation of the sampling distribution of $\bar{x}$, we find

$$\sigma_{\bar{x}} \approx \sqrt{\frac{(.8)(.2)}{400}} = .02$$

Next, the Central Limit Theorem implies that the distribution of $\bar{x}$ based on a sample of size 400 is approximately normal. The properties are summarized in Figure 5.15 on page 280. Note that the mean of the sampling distribution is p, so that the standard normal z value is given by the formula

$$z = \frac{\bar{x} - \mu_{\bar{x}}}{\sigma_{\bar{x}}} = \frac{\bar{x} - p}{.02}$$

Even though the value of p is unknown, we can find the probability that $\bar{x}$ is within .03 of p by first calculating the z value corresponding to the $\bar{x}$ value that is .03 greater than p:

$$z = \frac{(p + .03) - p}{.02} = \frac{.03}{.02} = 1.5$$

Similarly, the value .03 less than p is 1.5 standard deviations *below* the mean and has a z value of -1.5. Thus, the event that $\bar{x}$ falls within .03 of p is equivalent to the event that the standard normal random variable z is between -1.5 and 1.5. Using Table IV of Appendix B, we find the probability that $\bar{x}$ falls within 1.5 standard deviations of p is $2(.4332) = .8664$, the area shown shaded in Figure 5.15. The interpretation of this

FIGURE 5.15 ▶
Sampling distribution of $\bar{x}$

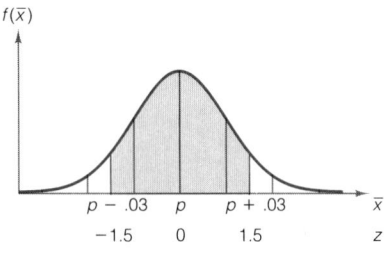

probability is that there is about an 87% chance that the proportion of good chips in the sample of 400 will fall within .03 of the exact proportion of good chips in the entire batch.

. . . .

For most sampling distributions, the standard deviation of the distribution decreases as the sample size increases. We use this result in Chapters 6, 7, and 8 to help us determine the sample size needed to obtain a specified accuracy of estimation.

Summary

. . . .

Many practical business problems require that an inference be made about some population **parameter** (for example, a mean, standard deviation, etc.). If we want to make this inference on the basis of sample information, we need to compute a **sample statistic** that contains information about the population parameter. The amount of such information is reflected in the sample statistic's **sampling distribution**—that is, the probability distribution of the sample statistic. The sampling distribution describes the behavior of the statistic in repeated sampling. We want a sample statistic that is an **unbiased** estimator of the population parameter and has a smaller variance than any other unbiased sample statistic.

When the population parameter of interest is the mean, μ, the sample mean, $\bar{x}$, provides an unbiased estimator with a standard deviation of $\sigma/\sqrt{n}$. In addition, the **Central Limit Theorem** assures us that the sampling distribution of the mean of a large sample will be approximately normally distributed, no matter what the shape of the relative frequency distribution of the sampled population.

The amount of information in a sample that is relevant to some population parameter is related to the sample size. Another way of saying this is that as n gets larger, the standard deviations of most sample statistics get smaller.

The sampling distributions for all the many statistics that can be computed from sample data could be discussed in detail, but this would delay discussion of the practical objective of this course—the role of statistical inference in business decision-making. Consequently, we will comment further on the sampling distributions of particular statistics when we use them as estimators in the following chapters.

Exercises 5.1 – 5.32

Note: *Starred (*) exercises require the use of a computer.*

Learning the Mechanics

5.1 Consider a sample statistic, A. As with all sample statistics, A is computed by utilizing a specified function (formula) of the sample measurements. (For example, if A were the sample mean, the specified formula would be to sum the measurements and divide by the number of measurements.)
   a. Describe what we mean by the phrase "the sampling distribution of the sample statistic A."
   b. Suppose A is to be used to estimate a population parameter α. Explain what is meant by the assertion: A is an unbiased estimator of α.
   c. Consider another sample statistic, B. Assume that B is also an unbiased estimator of the population parameter α. How can we use the sampling distributions of A and B to decide which is the better estimator of α?

5.2 The standard deviation (or, as it is frequently called, the standard error) of the sampling distribution for the sample mean, $\bar{x}$, is equal to the standard deviation of the population from which the sample was selected, divided by the square root of the sample size. That is,

$$\sigma_{\bar{x}} = \frac{\sigma}{\sqrt{n}}$$

   a. As the sample size is increased, what happens to the standard error of $\bar{x}$? Why is this property important?
   b. Suppose that a sample statistic has a standard error that is not a function of the sample size. In other words, the standard error remains constant as n changes. What would this imply about the statistic as an estimator of a population parameter?
   c. Suppose another unbiased estimator (call it A) of the population mean is a sample statistic with a standard error equal to

$$\sigma_A = \frac{\sigma}{\sqrt[3]{n}}$$

   Which of the sample statistics, $\bar{x}$ or A, is preferable as an estimator of the population mean? Why?
   d. Suppose that the population standard deviation σ is equal to 10 and that the sample size is 64. Calculate the standard errors of $\bar{x}$ and A. Assuming that the sampling distribution A is approximately normal, interpret the standard errors. Why is the assumption of (approximate) normality unnecessary for the sampling distribution of $\bar{x}$?

5.3 In each of the following cases, find the mean and standard deviation of the sampling distribution of the sample mean, $\bar{x}$, for a random sample of size n drawn from a population with mean μ and standard deviation σ:
   a. $n = 16$, $\mu = 8$, $\sigma = 3$ b. $n = 15$, $\mu = 200$, $\sigma = 15$
   c. $n = 100$, $\mu = 50$, $\sigma = 4$ d. $n = 110$, $\mu = -10$, $\sigma = 17$

5.4 A random sample of $n = 36$ observations is drawn from a normal population with mean equal to 10 and standard deviation equal to 12.
   a. Give the mean and standard deviation of the (repeated) sampling distribution of $\bar{x}$.
   b. Describe the shape of the sampling distribution of $\bar{x}$. Does your answer depend on the sample size?
   c. Calculate the z-score corresponding to a value of $\bar{x} = 13.4$.
   d. Calculate the z-score corresponding to $\bar{x} = 8.3$.

5.5 Refer to Exercise 5.4. Find the probability that:
   a. $\bar{x}$ is larger than 11   b. $\bar{x}$ is less than 11   c. $\bar{x}$ is larger than 13.1
   d. $\bar{x}$ falls between 9 and 11   e. $\bar{x}$ is less than 6.7

5.6 A random sample of 64 observations is to be drawn from a large population with mean 500 and standard deviation 80. Find the probability that:
   a. $\bar{x} \le 500$ b. $\bar{x} < 500$ c. $\bar{x} < 510$
   d. $\bar{x} > 480$ e. $\bar{x} < 491.9$ f. $487 \le \bar{x} \le 525.3$
   g. $488 \le \bar{x} \le 495.2$ h. $501.7 \le \bar{x} \le 511.7$

5.7 A random sample of 40 observations is to be drawn from a large population of measurements. It is known that 30% of the measurements in the population are 1's, 20% of the measurements are 2's, 20% are 3's, and 30% are 4's.
   a. Give the mean and standard deviation of the sampling distribution of $\bar{x}$, the sample mean of the 40 observations.
   b. Describe the sampling distribution of $\bar{x}$. Does your answer depend on the sample size?

*5.8 Use a statistical software package to generate 100 random samples of size $n = 2$ from a population characterized by a uniform probability distribution (Section 4.6) with $c = 0$ and $d = 10$. Compute $\bar{x}$ for each sample and plot a frequency distribution for the 100 values of $\bar{x}$. Repeat this process for $n = 5, 10, 30$, and 50. Explain how your plots illustrate the Central Limit Theorem.

*5.9 Use a statistical software package to generate 100 random samples of size $n = 2$ from a population characterized by a normal probability distribution with mean 100 and standard deviation 10. Compute $\bar{x}$ for each sample and plot a frequency distribution for the 100 values of $\bar{x}$. Repeat this process for $n = 5, 10, 30$, and 50. Explain how your plots illustrate the Central Limit Theorem.

5.10 Suppose a sample of $n = 50$ items is drawn from a population of manufactured products and the weight, x, of each item is recorded. Prior experience has shown that the weight has a probability distribution with $\mu = 6$ ounces and $\sigma = 2.5$ ounces. Then $\bar{x}$, the sample mean, will be approximately normally distributed (because of the Central Limit Theorem).
   a. Calculate $\mu_{\bar{x}}$ and $\sigma_{\bar{x}}$.
   b. What is the probability that the manufacturer's sample has a mean weight of between 5.75 and 6.25 ounces?
   c. What is the probability that the manufacturer's sample has a mean weight of less than 5.5 ounces?
   d. How would the sampling distribution of $\bar{x}$ change if the sample size, n, were increased from 50 to 100?

5.11 A population consists of four numbers, 1, 2, 2, and 3, marked on poker chips.

    a. How many different samples of $n = 2$ chips could be selected (without replacement) from the population? List the possible samples.

    b. Give the probability of selecting any one of these samples (assume that the sampling is random).

    c. Calculate $\bar{x}$ for each of the samples in part **b**.

    d. Calculate the probability associated with each of the possible values of $\bar{x}$.

    e. Graph the population probability distribution and the sampling distribution of $\bar{x}$ (obtained in part **d**).

5.12 Suppose x equals the number of heads observed when a single coin is tossed (i.e., $x = 0$ or $x = 1$). The population corresponding to x is the set of 0's and 1's generated when the coin is tossed repeatedly a large number of times. Suppose we select $n = 3$ observations from this population (i.e., we toss the coin three times and observe the three values of x).

    a. List the four different samples (combinations of 0's and 1's) that could be obtained.

    b. Calculate the value of $\bar{x}$ for each of the samples.

    c. List the values that $\bar{x}$ can assume, and find the probabilities of observing these values.

    d. Construct a graph of the sampling distribution of $\bar{x}$.

5.13 A random sample of size n is to be drawn from a large population with mean 100 and standard deviation 10, and the sample mean, $\bar{x}$, is to be calculated. To see the effect of different sample sizes on the standard deviation of the sampling distribution of $\bar{x}$, plot $\sigma/\sqrt{n}$ against n for $n = 1, 5, 10, 20, 30, 40$, and 50.

5.14 Refer to Exercise 5.13. If you increase the sample size from $n = 5$ to $n = 25$, does the information in the sample mean, $\bar{x}$, pertinent to μ increase by the same amount as it does for an increase in sample size from $n = 30$ to $n = 50$? How is this answer shown in the graph you constructed for Exercise 5.13?

5.15 A random sample of size $n = 30$ is to be drawn from a large population with $\mu = 500$ and $\sigma = 200$.

    a. What is the standard deviation of the sampling distribution of $\bar{x}$?

    b. In order to reduce the standard deviation of $\bar{x}$ to 50% of the value in part **a**, how much larger would n need to be?

    c. In order to reduce $\sigma_{\bar{x}}$ to 75% of the value in part **a**, how much larger would n need to be?

Applying the Concepts

5.16 A soft-drink bottler requires bottles with an internal pressure strength of at least 150 pounds per square inch (psi). A prospective bottle vendor claims that its production process yields bottles with a mean internal strength of 157 psi and a standard deviation of 3 psi. As part of its vendor surveillance, the bottler strikes an agreement with the vendor that permits the bottler to sample from the vendor's production process to verify the vendor's claim. The bottler randomly selected 40 bottles from the last 10,000 produced, measured the internal pressure strength of each, and found the mean strength for the sample to be 1.3 psi below the process mean cited by the vendor.

    a. Assuming the vendor's claim to be true, what is the probability of obtaining a sample mean 1.3 psi or more below the process mean? What does your answer suggest about the validity of the vendor's claim?

    b. If the process standard deviation were 3 psi (as claimed by the vendor), but the mean were 156 psi, would the observed sample result be more or less likely than in part **a**? What if the mean were 158 psi?

    c. If the process mean were 157 psi as claimed, but the process standard deviation were 2 psi, would the observed sample result be more or less likely than in part **a**? What if the standard deviation were 6 psi?

5.17 Steven Hartley (1983) conducted an experiment to evaluate the forecasting skills of 140 retail buyers of two large midwestern retail organizations. In one part of the experiment, 61 of the buyers were given historical sales data for the previous 30 months and asked to forecast sales 6 months from now. For each buyer, Hartley calculated the difference between the actual number of units sold 6 months later and the buyer's forecast. This difference is sometimes called **forecast error** and is denoted here as x. In order to characterize the accuracy of this group of 61 buyers, Hartley calculated $\bar{x}$, the mean forecast error for the sample.

    a. Assume the sample of 61 buyers was randomly selected from a large population of buyers whose forecast errors have a distribution with mean 10 and standard deviation 16. Describe the sampling distribution of $\bar{x}$.

    b. Hartley found $\bar{x} = 13.49$. Given the information in part **a** about the population of buyers, is this a likely result? Explain.

    c. Suppose $\bar{x} = 0$ and $s^2 = 1$. What do these statistics tell you about the accuracy of the forecasts of the 61 buyers?

5.18 In Case Study 5.2, an individual was considering investing $1,000 in each of $n = 5$ different stocks. The monthly rate of return on each stock had mean $\mu = 10\%$ and standard deviation $\sigma = 4\%$. The investor's monthly rate of return for the portfolio of five stocks was $\bar{r} = \sum r_i/5$. It was shown that the variance of the investor's monthly rate of return was $\sigma_{\bar{r}}^2 = \sigma^2/n = 3.2$ and that this number is a measure of the risk faced by the investor.

    a. If instead the individual were to invest $1,000 in only three of the five stocks, would the risk faced by the investor increase or decrease? Explain.

    b. Suppose $1,000 was invested in each of 10 stocks with rate-of-return characteristics identical to those described above. Measure the risk faced by the investor and compare it to the risk associated with investing in just five of the stocks.

5.19 It was not until the 1950s that manufacturing companies began to measure and account for the costs of their quality functions. In general, quality costs are those associated with producing, identifying, avoiding, or repairing products that do not meet requirements. They are often divided into four categories: prevention costs, appraisal costs, internal failure costs, and external failure costs (Montgomery, 1991). This exercise is concerned with an inspection and evaluation activity that would generate appraisal costs.

    A particular manufacturing process requires steel rods that are at least 3 meters in length. The rods are purchased in lots of 50,000. To determine whether the lot meets the required quality standards, 100 rods are randomly sampled from each incoming lot and the mean length of rods in the sample is calculated. The quality manager has decided to accept lots whose sample mean is 3.005 meters or more. Assume that the standard deviation of the rod lengths in a lot is .03 meter.

    a. If in fact each lot has a mean length of 3 meters, what percentage of the lots received by the manufacturer will be returned to the vendor (i.e., the supplier)?

    b. If in fact all of the rods in all of the lots received by the manufacturer are between 2.999 and 3.004 meters in length, what percentage of the lots will be returned to the vendor?

5.20 A local bank reported to the federal government that its 5,246 savings accounts have a mean balance of $1,000 and a standard deviation of $240. Government auditors have asked to randomly sample 64 of the bank's accounts in order to assess the reliability of the mean balance reported by the bank. The auditors say they will certify the bank's report only if the sample mean balance is within $60 of the reported mean balance. What is the probability that the auditors will *not* certify the bank's report, even if the mean balance really is $1,000? (Assume the standard deviation reported by the bank is accurate.)

5.21 A manufacturer produces safety jackets for competitive fencers. These jackets are rated by the minimum force, in newtons, that will allow a weapon to pierce the jacket. When this process is operating correctly, it produces jackets that have ratings with an average of 840 newtons and a standard deviation of 15 newtons. FIE, the international governing body for fencing, requires jackets to be rated at a minimum of 800 newtons. To check whether the process is operating correctly, a manager takes a sample of 50 jackets from the process, rates them, and calculates $\bar{x}$, the mean rating for jackets in the sample. She assumes that the standard deviation of the process is fixed, but is worried that the mean rating of the process may have changed.
   a. What is the sampling distribution of $\bar{x}$ if the process is still operating correctly?
   b. Suppose the manager's sample has a mean rating of 830 newtons. What is the probability of getting an $\bar{x}$ of 830 newtons or lower if the process is operating correctly?
   c. Given the manager's assumption that the standard deviation of the process is fixed, what does your answer to part **b** suggest about the current state of the process (i.e., does it appear that the mean jacket rating is still 840 newtons)?
   d. Now suppose that the mean of the process has not changed, but the standard deviation of the process has increased from 15 newtons to 45 newtons. What is the sampling distribution of $\bar{x}$ in this case? What is the probability of getting an $\bar{x}$ of 830 newtons or lower when $\bar{x}$ has this distribution?

5.22 A machine for filling cereal boxes can be set to dispense a mean weight of between 12 and 20 ounces. The standard deviation of the weight of boxes filled with the machine is 1 ounce and is independent of the mean. The product is shipped in cases of 36 boxes. Assume each case represents a random sample from the population of boxes filled by this machine at a fixed setting of the mean weight dispensed.
   a. At what level should the mean be set so that 95% of all cases produced will have a mean weight of at least 16 ounces?
   b. Repeat part **a**, this time assuming that the standard deviation of the weight of boxes filled by the machine is 2 ounces.
   c. Repeat part **b**, but for cases of 64 boxes.
   d. Do any of these answers depend on the distribution of weights for individual boxes filled by the machine? Why or why not?

5.23 To determine whether a metal lathe that produces machine bearings is properly adjusted, a sample of 36 bearings is collected and the diameter of each is measured. Assume the standard deviation of the diameter of the machine bearings is stable and equal to .001 inch. What is the probability that the mean diameter $\bar{x}$ of the sample will lie within .0001 inch of the process mean?

5.24 Refer to Exercise 5.23. Suppose the mean diameter of the bearings produced by the machine is supposed to be .5 inch. The company decides to use the sample mean (from Exercise 5.23) to decide whether the process is in control—i.e., whether it is producing bearings with a mean diameter of .5 inch. The machine will be considered out of control if the mean of the sample of $n = 36$ diameters is less than .4994 inch or larger than .5006 inch. If the true mean diameter of the bearings produced by the machine is .501 inch, what is the probability that the test will fail to imply that the process is out of control?

5.25 In 1981, Northern States Power (NSP), a private utility in Minnesota, mailed many of its customers an offer for an in-home energy audit designed to encourage households to conserve energy, but the response rate fell far short of expectations. To improve the response rate, Richard Weijo (1983) evaluated alternative means of making NSP customers aware of the audit program and of motivating them to make inexpensive energy-saving changes to their homes. As part of the study, two independent samples were selected from among the 9,900 customers scheduled to receive energy-audit offers by April 1982. The 280 households in the first sample received an inexpensive water-flow controller with their energy-audit offer, while the 348 households in the second sample received only the energy-audit offer. All of the households in both samples were surveyed by telephone and assigned a score from 0 to 5 based on how much they remembered about the energy-audit offers. To compare the effectiveness of the two types of mailings with respect to information recall, Weijo calculated $\bar{x}$ and $\bar{y}$ (the sample means of the scores for households receiving and not receiving the water-flow controller, respectively).

a. The scores received by the 280 households that were mailed the water-flow controller can be viewed as a sample from the population of scores that would exist if all 9,900 households had been sent the water-flow controller and then been interviewed. Suppose this hypothetical population of scores has standard deviation 1.2. Describe the sampling distribution of $\bar{x}$.

b. Suppose all 9,900 households had received only the energy-audit offer and were later scored with respect to their recall of information about the mailing. Assume that the standard deviation of this population of scores is 1.0, and describe the sampling distribution of $\bar{y}$.

c. How large would the sample of households receiving the water-flow controller have to be in order to have $\sigma_{\bar{x}} = \sigma_{\bar{y}}$?

5.26 The primary responsibility of government tax assessors is to estimate the market values of all properties in their respective jurisdictions. These estimates form the basis upon which property tax bills are determined. To estimate the mean market value for single-family homes in a particular county in 1994, a county tax assessor uses the mean sale price for all single-family homes that sold during 1994. Such a sample is typically treated by tax assessors as if it were a random sample from the population of properties in question (*Standard on Assessment-Ratio Studies,* 1980). Suppose 400 properties sold during 1994 and assume that the standard deviation of the market value for the population of properties is about $50,000.

a. What is the population in question?

b. What is the probability that the assessor's sample mean will overestimate the actual mean market value of the population?

c. What is the probability that the assessor's sample mean will fall within $4,000 of the actual mean market value for the population?

5.27 In any production process, some variation in the quality of the product is unavoidable. Variation in product can be divided into two categories: **variation due to special causes** and **variation due to common causes**. The former includes variation due to a specific worker or group of workers, a specific machine, or a specific local condition. The latter includes variation due to faults of the overall production system, such as poor working conditions for workers, use of raw materials of inferior quality, poor design of the product, etc. The discovery and removal of special causes is generally the responsibility of a person directly involved with the production operation in question. In contrast, common causes are the responsibility of management.

A production process in which all special causes of variation have been eliminated is said to be **stable** or **in statistical control**. The variation that remains is simply random variation. If the magnitude of the random variation is unacceptable to management, it can be reduced through the elimination of common causes (Deming, 1982, 1986).

It is common practice to monitor the variation in the quality characteristic of a product over time by plotting the quality characteristic on a **control chart**. For example, the amount of alkali in soap might be monitored each hour by randomly selecting from the production process and measuring the quantity of alkali in $n = 5$ test specimens of soap. The mean, $\bar{x}$, of the sample alkaline measurements would be plotted against time, as shown in the accompanying figure. If the process is in statistical control, $\bar{x}$ should assume a distribution with a mean equal to the process mean, μ, with standard deviation equal to the process standard deviation divided by the square root of the sample size, $\sigma_{\bar{x}} = \sigma/\sqrt{n}$. The control chart shown here includes a horizontal line to locate the process mean and two lines, called **control limits**, located $3\sigma_{\bar{x}}$ above and below μ. If $\bar{x}$ falls within the control limits, the process is deemed to be in control. If $\bar{x}$ is outside the limits, there is strong evidence that special causes of variation are present, and the process is deemed to be out of control. We discuss control charts in detail in Chapter 11.

When the production process is in statistical control, the percentage of alkali in a test specimen of soap follows approximately a normal distribution with $\mu = 2\%$ and $\sigma = 1\%$.

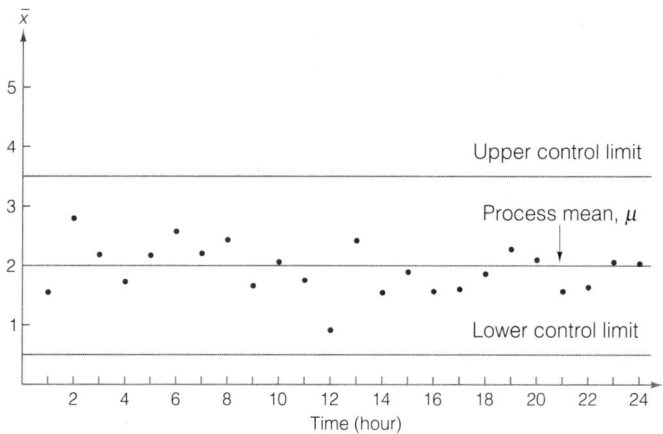

a. If $n = 4$, how far from μ should the upper and lower control limits be located?
b. If the process is in control, what is the probability that $\bar{x}$ will fall outside the control limits?
c. If the process mean shifts to $\mu = 3\%$ before the sample is drawn, what is the probability that the sample will lead to the (correct) conclusion that the process is out of control?

5.28 Refer to Exercise 5.27. The soap company has decided to set tighter control limits than the $3\sigma_{\bar{x}}$ limits described in Exercise 5.27. In particular, when the process is in control, the company is willing to risk a .10 probability that $\bar{x}$ falls outside the control limits.

a. The company still wants the control limits to be located at equal distances above and below the process mean and is still planning to use $n = 4$ measurements in each hourly sample. Where should the control limits be located?
b. Suppose the control limits developed in part **a** are implemented, but unknown to the company, μ is currently 3% (not 2%). What is the probability that $\bar{x}$ will fall outside the control limits if $n = 4$? If $n = 9$?

5.29 Refer to Exercise 5.28. To improve the sensitivity of control charts, **warning limits** are sometimes included on the chart along with the control limits. These limits are typically set at $\mu \pm 1.96\sigma_{\bar{x}}$. If two successive data points fall outside the warning limits, the process is deemed to be out of control (Wetherhill, 1977).

a. If the soap process is in control (i.e., it follows a normal distribution with $\mu = 2\%$ and $\sigma = 1\%$), what is the probability that the next value of $\bar{x}$ will fall outside the warning limits?
b. If the soap process is in control, how many of the next 40 values of $\bar{x}$ plotted on the control chart would be expected to fall above the upper warning limit?
c. If the soap process is in control, what is the probability that the next two values of $\bar{x}$ will fall below the lower warning limit?

5.30 A manufacturer of aluminum foil claims that its 75-foot roll has a mean length of 75.11 feet per roll and a standard deviation of .15 foot. To check this claim, a consumer group plans to purchase 36 of the company's 75-foot rolls, measure the length of each, and compute the sample mean length. Treat the sample as if it were a random sample from the population of rolls currently stocked by grocery stores.
  a. Assuming the manufacturer's claim is true, describe the sampling distribution of the sample mean.
  b. Assuming the manufacturer's claim is true, what is the probability that the sample mean will be less than 75 feet?
  c. Suppose the sample mean actually equals 74.95 feet. Can this evidence be used to refute the manufacturer's claim? Explain.

5.31 A building contractor has decided to purchase a load of factory-reject aluminum siding if the average number of flaws per piece of siding in a sample of size 35 from the factory's reject pile is 2.1 or less. Suppose the number of flaws per piece of siding in the factory's reject pile has a Poisson probability distribution with a mean of 2.5. Find the probability that the contractor will not purchase a load of siding. [*Hint:* If x is a Poisson random variable with mean λ, then the variance of the random variable x is also equal to λ.]

5.32 The distribution of the number of loaves of bread sold per day by a large bakery over the past 5 years has a mean of 250 and a standard deviation of 45 loaves.
  a. Describe the sampling distribution of the total number of loaves of bread sold in 30 randomly selected days. [*Hint:* See the footnote on page 270 that gives the application of the Central Limit Theorem to the sum of the measurements in a sample.]
  b. What is the approximate probability that the total number of loaves sold in 30 randomly selected days is between 7,000 and 8,000?
  c. What is the approximate probability that the total number of loaves sold in 30 randomly selected days is greater than 8,100 loaves?

Using the Computer

Calculate the mean and standard deviation for the 1,000 zip codes' median household incomes (Appendix C). We will treat these quantities as the population mean μ and standard deviation σ for this exercise.

  a. Draw 100 random samples of $n = 20$ observations from the 1,000 zip codes' median household incomes. Select the samples with replacement, i.e., replace each measurement before selecting the next.* Calculate the 100 sample means. Generate a stem-and-leaf display or a relative frequency histogram for the 100 means. Then count the number of the 100 sample means that fall in the intervals $\mu \pm \sigma/\sqrt{n}$, $\mu \pm 2\sigma/\sqrt{n}$, and $\mu \pm 3\sigma/\sqrt{n}$. How do the graphical description and the percentage of means falling in the intervals agree with a normal distribution having mean μ and standard deviation $\sigma/\sqrt{n}$?
  b. Repeat part **a** using a sample size of $n = 50$. Is the sampling distribution of the sample means closer to normal for the larger sample size? Why?

---

*In this and some future exercises we specify "sampling with replacement" to simulate the sampling from very large populations. Consult the references at the end of this chapter for the use of finite population correction factors.

References

Alexander, G. J. and Francis, J. C. *Portfolio Analysis*. Englewood Cliffs, N.J.: Prentice-Hall, Inc., 1986. Chapters 4 and 5.

Blume, M. "On the assessment of risk." *Journal of Finance*, Mar. 1971, 26, pp. 1–10.

Deming, W. E. *Out of the Crisis*. Cambridge, Mass.: MIT Center for Advanced Engineering Study, 1986.

Deming, W. E. *Quality, Productivity, and Competitive Position*. Cambridge, Mass.: MIT Center for Advanced Engineering Study, 1982. Chapter 7.

Elton, E. J. and Gruber, M. J. *Modern Portfolio Theory and Investment Analysis*, 3rd ed. New York: Wiley, 1987.

Francis, J. C. *Investments: Analysis and Management*, 4th ed. New York: McGraw-Hill, 1986.

Hartley, S. W. *Judgmental Sales Forecasting: An Experimental Investigation of Task Structure and Environmental Complexity*. Unpublished Ph.D. dissertation, University of Minnesota, 1983.

Hogg, R. V. and Craig, A. T. *Introduction to Mathematical Statistics*, 4th ed. New York: Macmillan, 1978. Chapter 4.

Lindgren, B. W. *Statistical Theory*, 3rd ed. New York: Macmillan, 1976. Chapter 2.

Montgomery, D. C. *Introduction to Statistical Quality Control*, 2d ed. New York: Wiley, 1991.

Neter, J., Wasserman, W., and Whitmore, G. A. *Applied Statistics*, 2d ed. Boston: Allyn & Bacon, 1983. Chapters 8 and 9.

Sharpe, W. F. and Alexander, G. J. *Investments*, 4th ed. Englewood Cliffs, N.J.: Prentice-Hall, 1990. Chapter 7.

Standard on Assessment-Ratio Studies. Chicago: International Association of Assessing Officers, 1980.

Weijo, R. O. *Evaluating Information, Incentive, and Door-to-door Interventions for the MECS Energy Audit Program: A Theoretical Application of the Petty and Cacippo Elaboration Likelihood Model*. Unpublished Ph.D. dissertation, University of Minnesota, 1983.

Wetherill, G. B. *Sampling Inspection and Quality Control*, 2d ed. New York: Chapman and Hall, 1977. Chapter 3.

Winkler, R. L. and Hays, W. *Statistics: Probability, Inference, and Decision*, 2d ed. New York: Holt, Rinehart and Winston, 1975. Chapter 5.

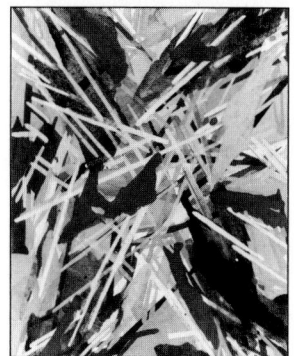

CHAPTER SIX

Inferences Based on a Single Sample: Estimation

Contents

Case Study

Where We've Been

In the preceding chapters we learned that populations are characterized by numerical descriptive measures (called *parameters*), and that decisions about their values are based on sample statistics computed from sample data. Since statistics vary in a random manner from sample to sample, inferences based on them will be subject to uncertainty. This property is reflected in the sampling (probability) distribution of a statistic.

Where We're Going

This chapter puts all the preceding material into practice; that is, we estimate population means and proportions based on a single sample selected from the population of interest. Most important, we use the sampling distribution of a sample statistic to assess the reliability of the estimate.

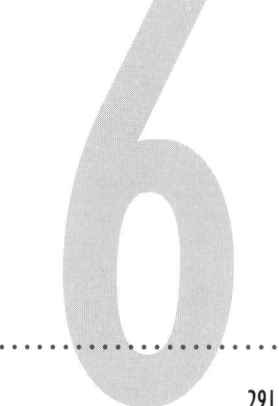

The estimation of the mean gas mileage for a new car model, the estimation of the expected life of a computer monitor, and the estimation of the mean yearly sales for companies in the steel industry are problems with a common element: In each case, we are interested in estimating the mean of a population of measurements. This important problem constitutes the primary topic of this chapter.

You will see that different techniques are used for estimating a mean, depending on whether a sample contains a large or small number of measurements. Regardless, our objectives remain the same. We want to use the sample information to estimate the mean and to assess the reliability of the estimate.

In Sections 6.1 and 6.2, we consider a method of estimating a population mean using a large sample and develop a formula to determine just how large the sample must be to achieve a specified degree of reliability. In Section 6.3, we show how a mean can be estimated when only a small sample is available. Finally, estimation of binomial probabilities (e.g., population proportions) and the determination of sample sizes necessary to make reliable estimates are covered in Sections 6.4 and 6.5, respectively.

6.1   Large-Sample Estimation of a Population Mean

Suppose a large credit corporation wants to estimate the average amount of money owed by its delinquent debtors—i.e., debtors who are more than 2 months behind in payment. To accomplish this objective, the company plans to sample 100 of its delinquent accounts and to use the sample mean, $\bar{x}$, of the amounts overdue to estimate μ, the mean for *all* delinquent accounts. The sample mean $\bar{x}$ represents a **point estimator** of the population mean μ (Definition 5.4). How can we assess the accuracy of this point estimator?

Recall that for sufficiently large samples the sampling distribution of the sample mean is approximately normal, as shown in Figure 6.1. Now, suppose you plan to take a sample of $n = 100$ measurements and calculate the following interval:

$$\bar{x} \pm 2\sigma_{\bar{x}} = \bar{x} \pm \frac{2\sigma}{\sqrt{n}}$$

FIGURE 6.1 ▶
Sampling distribution of $\bar{x}$

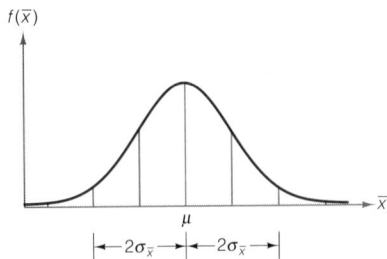

That is, you will form an interval 4 standard deviations wide: from 2 standard deviations below the sample mean to 2 standard deviations above the sample mean. What is the chance, *before we have drawn the sample*, that this interval will enclose μ, the population mean?

To answer this question, refer to Figure 6.1. If the 100 measurements yield a value of $\bar{x}$ that falls between the two lines on either side of μ—i.e., within 2 standard deviations of μ—then the interval $\bar{x} \pm 2\sigma_{\bar{x}}$ will contain μ. If $\bar{x}$ falls outside either of these boundaries, then the interval $\bar{x} \pm 2\sigma_{\bar{x}}$ will not contain μ. Since the area under the normal curve (the sampling distribution of $\bar{x}$) between these boundaries is approximately .95 (more precisely, from Table IV of Appendix B, the area is .9544), we know that the interval $\bar{x} \pm 2\sigma_{\bar{x}}$ will contain μ with a probability approximately equal to .95.

To illustrate, suppose that the sum and the sum of squared deviations for the sample of debts of 100 delinquent accounts are

$$\sum_{i=1}^{n} x_i = \$23,300 \qquad \sum_{i=1}^{n} (x_i - \bar{x})^2 = 801,900$$

We first calculate the sample mean and standard deviation:

$$\bar{x} = \frac{\sum_{i=1}^{100} x_i}{n} = \frac{23,300}{100} = \$233 \qquad s = \sqrt{\frac{\sum_{i=1}^{100} (x_i - \bar{x})^2}{n-1}} = \sqrt{\frac{801,900}{99}} = \$90$$

We next substitute for $\bar{x}$ in

$$\bar{x} \pm 2\sigma_{\bar{x}} = 233 \pm 2\left(\frac{\sigma}{\sqrt{100}}\right)$$

But now we face a problem. You can see that without knowing the standard deviation, σ, of the original population—i.e., the standard deviation of the amounts of *all* delinquent accounts—we cannot calculate this interval. However, since we have a large sample ($n = 100$ measurements), we can approximate the interval by using the sample standard deviation, s, to approximate σ. Thus,

$$\bar{x} \pm 2\left(\frac{\sigma}{\sqrt{100}}\right) \approx \bar{x} \pm 2\left(\frac{s}{\sqrt{100}}\right) = 233 \pm 2\left(\frac{90}{10}\right) = 233 \pm 18$$

That is, we estimate the mean amount of delinquency for all accounts to fall within the interval ($215, $251).

Can we be sure that μ, the true mean amount due, is within the interval ($215, $251)? We cannot be certain, but we can be reasonably confident that it is. This confidence is derived from the knowledge that if we were to repeatedly draw samples of 100 accounts from this group of delinquent accounts and form the interval $\bar{x} \pm 2\sigma_{\bar{x}}$ each time, approximately 95% of the intervals would contain μ. We have no way of knowing (without looking at *all* the delinquent accounts) whether our sample interval is one of the 95% that contain μ or one of the 5% that do not, so we simply state that we are 95% confident our interval ($215, $251) contains μ. Thus, we have given an interval estimate of the mean delinquency per account and a measure of the reliability of the estimate.

The formula that tells us how to calculate an interval estimate based on sample data is called an **interval estimator**. The probability .95, that measures the confidence that we can place in the interval estimate is called a **confidence coefficient**. The percentage, 95%, is called the **confidence level** for the interval estimate.

Definition 6.1

An **interval estimator** is a formula that tells us how to use sample data to calculate an interval that estimates a population parameter.

Definition 6.2

The **confidence coefficient** is the probability that an interval estimator encloses the population parameter—that is, the relative frequency with which the interval estimator encloses the population parameter when the estimator is used repeatedly a very large number of times. The **confidence level** is the confidence coefficient expressed as a percentage.

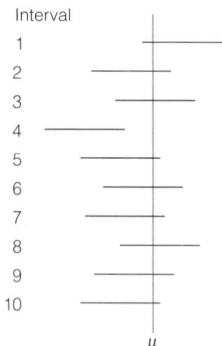

FIGURE 6.2 ▲
Interval estimators for μ:
10 samples

The foregoing describes how an interval can be used to estimate a population mean. When we use an interval estimator, we can usually calculate the probability that the interval estimation *process* will result in an interval that contains the true value of the population mean. That is, the probability that the interval contains the parameter in repeated usage is usually known. Figure 6.2 shows what happens when a number of samples are drawn from a population and a confidence interval for μ is calculated from each. The location of μ is indicated by the vertical line in the figure. Ten confidence intervals, each based on one of 10 samples, are shown as horizontal line segments. Note that the confidence intervals move from sample to sample—sometimes containing μ and other times missing μ. If our confidence level is 95%, then in the long run, 95% of our sample confidence intervals will contain μ.

Suppose you wish to choose a **confidence coefficient** other than .95. Notice that in Figure 6.1 the confidence coefficient .95 is equal to the total area under the sampling distribution, less .05 of the area; this .05 is divided equally between the two tails. Using this idea, we can construct a confidence interval with any desired confidence coefficient by increasing or decreasing the area (call it α) assigned to the tails of the sampling distribution (see Figure 6.3). For example, if we place $\alpha/2$ in each tail and if $z_{\alpha/2}$ is the z value such that the area $\alpha/2$ will lie to its right, then the confidence interval with confidence coefficient $(1 - \alpha)$ is

$$\bar{x} \pm z_{\alpha/2}\sigma_{\bar{x}}$$

FIGURE 6.3 ▶

Locating $z_{\alpha/2}$ on the standard normal curve

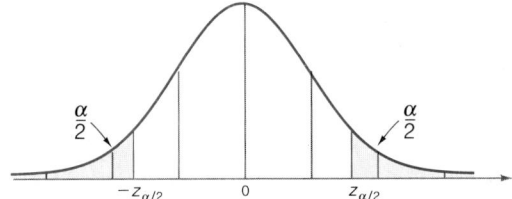

Large-Sample $100(1 - \alpha)\%$ Confidence Interval for μ

$$\bar{x} \pm z_{\alpha/2}\sigma_{\bar{x}}$$

where $z_{\alpha/2}$ is the z value with an area $\alpha/2$ to its right (see Figure 6.3) and $\sigma_{\bar{x}} = \sigma/\sqrt{n}$. The parameter σ is the standard deviation of the sampled population and n is the sample size. When σ is unknown (as is almost always the case) and n is large (say, $n \geq 30$), the value of σ can be approximated by the sample standard deviation, s.

To illustrate, for a confidence coefficient of .90, $(1 - \alpha) = .90$, $\alpha = .10$, $\alpha/2 = .05$, and $z_{.05}$ is the z value that locates .05 in one tail of the sampling distribution. Recall that Table IV of Appendix B (and inside front cover) gives the areas between the mean and a specified z value. Since the total area to the right of the mean is .50, $z_{.05}$ will be the z value corresponding to the tabulated area to the right of the mean equal to .4500. This z value is $z_{.05} = 1.645$. Confidence coefficients used in practice (in reports and published articles) usually range from .90 to .99. The most commonly used confidence coefficients with corresponding values of α and $z_{\alpha/2}$ are shown in Table 6.1.

TABLE 6.1   Commonly Used Values of $z_{\alpha/2}$

Confidence Level $100(1 - \alpha)$	α	$\alpha/2$	$z_{\alpha/2}$
90%	.10	.05	1.645
95%	.05	.025	1.96
99%	.01	.005	2.575

EXAMPLE 6.1

Unoccupied seats on flights cause the airlines to lose revenue. Suppose a large airline wants to estimate its average number of unoccupied seats per flight over the past year. To accomplish this, the records of 225 flights are randomly selected and the number of unoccupied seats is noted for each of the sampled flights. The sample mean and standard deviation are

$$\bar{x} = 11.6 \text{ seats} \qquad s = 4.1 \text{ seats}$$

Estimate μ, the mean number of unoccupied seats per flight during the past year, using a 90% confidence interval.

Solution

The general form of the large-sample 90% confidence interval for a population mean is

$$\bar{x} \pm z_{\alpha/2}\sigma_{\bar{x}} = \bar{x} \pm z_{.05}\sigma_{\bar{x}} = \bar{x} \pm 1.645\left(\frac{\sigma}{\sqrt{n}}\right)$$

For the 225 records sampled, we have

$$11.6 \pm 1.645\left(\frac{\sigma}{\sqrt{225}}\right)$$

Since we do not know the value of σ (the standard deviation of the number of unoccupied seats per flight for all flights of the year), we use our best approximation, the sample standard deviation s. Then the 90% confidence interval is, approximately,

$$11.6 \pm 1.645\left(\frac{4.1}{\sqrt{225}}\right) = 11.6 \pm .45$$

or from 11.15 to 12.05. That is, the airline can be 90% confident that the mean number of unoccupied seats per flight was between 11.15 and 12.05 during the sampled year.

Remember that the 90% confidence comes from the knowledge that the interval estimation process will result in an interval that contains μ 90% of the time in repeated sampling. We do not know whether this particular interval (11.15, 12.05) is one of the 90% that contain μ, or one of the 10% that do not.

The interpretation of confidence intervals for a population mean is summarized in the box.

Interpretation of a Confidence Interval for a Population Mean

When we form a $100(1 - \alpha)\%$ confidence interval for μ, we usually express our confidence in the interval with a statement such as, "We can be $100(1 - \alpha)\%$ confident that μ lies between the lower and upper bounds of the confidence interval," where for a particular application we substitute the appropriate numerical values for the confidence, and the lower and upper bounds. **The statement reflects our confidence in the estimation process rather than in the particular interval that is calculated from sample data.** We know that repeated application of the same procedure will result in different lower and upper bounds on the interval. Furthermore, we know that $100(1 - \alpha)\%$ of the resulting intervals will contain μ. There is (usually) no way to determine whether a particular interval is one of those that contain μ, or one that does not. However, unlike point estimators, confidence intervals have some measure of reliability, the confidence coefficient, associated with them, and for that reason are generally preferred to point estimators.

CASE STUDY 6.1 / Dancing to the Customer's Tune: The Need to Assess Customer Preferences

We sometimes lose sight of the fact that many firms were customer-oriented long before the quality movement swept through the U.S. in the 1980s and early 1990s. The following quotations were extracted from the Dec. 13, 1976, issue of *Business Week*:

"We're dancing to the tune of the customer as never before," says J. Janvier Wetzel, vice-president for sales promotion at Los Angeles–based Broadway Department Stores. "With population growth down to a trickle compared with its previous level, we're no longer spoiled with instant success every time we open a new store. Traditional department stores are locked in the biggest competitive battle in their history."

The nation's retailers are becoming uncomfortably aware that today's operating environment is vastly different from that of the 1960s. Population growth is slowing, a growing singles market is emerging, family formations are coming at later ages, and more women are embarking on careers. Of the 71 million households in the U.S. today, the dominant consumer buying segment is families headed by persons over 45. But by 1980 this group will have lost its majority status to the 25 to 40 year-old group. Merchants must now reposition their stores to attract these new customers.

To do so retailers are using market research

to ferret out new purchasing attitudes and lifestyles and then translating this into customer buying segments. Data on demographics, psychographics (measurement of attitudes), and lifestyles are being fed into retailers' computers so they can make marketing decisions based on actual spending patterns and estimate their inventory needs with less risk.

To stock its various departments with the type and style of goods that appeal to its potential group of customers, a downtown department store should be interested in estimating the average age of downtown shoppers, not shoppers in general. Suppose a downtown department store questions 49 downtown shoppers concerning their age (the offer of a small gift certificate may help convince shoppers to respond to such questions). The sample mean and standard deviation are found to be 40.1 and 8.6, respectively. The store could then estimate μ, the mean age of all downtown shoppers, with a 95% confidence interval as follows:

$$\bar{x} \pm 1.96\left(\frac{s}{\sqrt{n}}\right) = 40.1 \pm 1.96\left(\frac{8.6}{\sqrt{49}}\right)$$

$$= 40.1 \pm 2.4$$

Thus, the department store should gear its sales to the segment of consumers with average age between 37.7 and 42.5.

Exercises 6.1 – 6.15

Learning the Mechanics

6.1 Find $z_{\alpha/2}$ for each of the following:
   a. $\alpha = .10$ b. $\alpha = .01$ c. $\alpha = .05$ d. $\alpha = .20$

6.2 What is the confidence level of each of the following confidence intervals for μ?
   a. $\bar{x} \pm 1.96\sigma/\sqrt{n}$ b. $\bar{x} \pm 1.645\sigma/\sqrt{n}$ c. $\bar{x} \pm 2.575\sigma/\sqrt{n}$
   d. $\bar{x} \pm 1.282\sigma/\sqrt{n}$ e. $\bar{x} \pm .99\sigma/\sqrt{n}$

6.3 A random sample of 50 observations from a population produced the following summary statistics:

$$\sum x = 850 \qquad \sum (x_i - \bar{x})^2 = 4{,}720$$

   a. Find a 95% confidence interval for μ.   b. Interpret the confidence interval you found in part **a**.

6.4 A random sample of 70 observations from a normally distributed population produced a sample mean of 26.2 and a standard deviation of 4.1.
   a. Find a 95% confidence interval for μ.   b. Find a 99% confidence interval for μ.
   c. What happens to the width of a confidence interval as the sample size is held fixed and the value of the confidence coefficient is increased?
   d. Would your confidence intervals of parts **a** and **b** be valid if the distribution of the original population were not normal? Explain.

6.5 Refer to Exercise 6.4. Suppose the sample contained only 40 observations.
   a. Recompute the 95% confidence interval for μ.
   b. What is the effect on the width of a confidence interval of reducing the sample size as the confidence coefficient remains fixed? Of increasing the sample size as the confidence coefficient remains fixed?

6.6 Explain what is meant by the statement "We are 95% confident that our interval estimate contains μ."

6.7 Explain the difference between an interval estimator and a point estimator for μ.

6.8 Describe the relationship between the size of the confidence coefficient and the width of the confidence interval.

6.9 Describe the relationship between the sample size and the width of the confidence interval.

Applying the Concepts

6.10 To assess the magnitude of recent rent increases in metropolitan Minneapolis, an apartment referral service randomly sampled and interviewed 32 apartment building owners. They obtained the following data concerning the change in rent for two-bedroom apartments between May 1989 and May 1990:

1.13%	2.03%	1.79%	1.00%	−.45%	2.03%	1.41%	.34%
2.61	2.42	2.06	−1.07	1.25	2.27	.61	.68
−1.22	1.00	5.20	.62	.00	.05	1.82	1.39
7.33	3.32	.68	3.59	.90	1.42	1.80	.00

a. Carefully describe the population from which the sample was drawn.

b. Use a 95% confidence interval to estimate the mean percentage change in rent for two-bedroom apartments.

c. In constructing the confidence interval of part **b**, was it necessary to assume that the population was normally distributed? Explain.

6.11 A major department store chain is interested in estimating the average amount its credit card customers spent on their first visit to the chain's new store in the mall. Fifty credit card accounts were randomly sampled and analyzed with the following results: $\bar{x} = \$62.56$ and $s^2 = 400$.

a. Identify the population the department store chain is interested in learning about.

b. Which population parameter does the chain wish to estimate?

c. Construct a 90% confidence interval for the parameter identified in part **b**.

6.12 At the end of 1989, 1990, and 1991, the average prices of a share of stock on the New York Stock Exchange (NYSE) were $36.51, $31.08, and $37.27, respectively (*Statistical Abstract of the United States: 1992*, p. 512). To investigate the average share price at the end of 1992, a random sample of 30 NYSE stocks was drawn. Their closing prices on December 31, 1992, are listed (by their NYSE abbreviations) in the table.

Stock	Price	Stock	Price	Stock	Price
RowanCos	7⅞	LaZ Boy	25⅞	Supervalu	31⅛
Huntway	2	Tektronix	20⅛	Tambrands	64⅛
ChemBank	38⅝	GiantInd	5⅜	Crane	23⅝
Advest	5⅞	CalMat	22½	Ameritech	71¼
Caterpillar	53⅝	Omnicom	41¼	Goodyear	68⅜
Sears	45½	HewlettPk	69⅞	WellsF	76⅜
UnElec	37⅜	StrtGlob	12⅛	Boeing	40⅛
Travelers	27¼	VanDorn	20⅜	BankAmer	46½
Rockwell	29	MinnMngMfg	100⅝	ZurnInd	39⅜
HomeShop	8¼	HondaMotor	20¾	Equimark	8⅛

Source: *Wall Street Journal*, January 4, 1993.

a. Using a 90% confidence interval, estimate the average price of a share of stock at the end of 1992.

b. Use the latest edition of the *Statistical Abstract of the United States* to find the actual average price of a stock on the NYSE at the end of 1992. Is this figure in agreement with your confidence interval? Explain. If not, provide a possible explanation for the disagreement.

6.13 An auditor was hired to verify the accuracy of a company's new billing system. The auditor randomly sampled 35 invoices produced since the system was installed. Each invoice was compared against the relevant internal records to determine by how much the invoice was in error. The amount of the error, x, was defined as $(A - I)$, where A is the actual amount owed the company and I is the amount indicated on the invoice. The auditor found that $\bar{x} = \$1$ and $s = \$124$.

a. Identify the population the auditor studied.

b. Describe the variable that the auditor measured.

c. Construct a 98% confidence interval for the mean error per invoice.

d. Interpret the confidence interval.

e. Comment on the accuracy of the billing system.

6.14 A process has been developed that can transform ordinary iron into a kind of super-iron called *metallic glass* ("One Answer to Imports," 1981). Metallic glass is 3 to 4 times as strong as the toughest steel alloys, but it becomes brittle at very high temperatures. To estimate the mean temperature, μ, at which a particular type of metallic glass becomes brittle, 36 pieces of the metallic glass were randomly sampled from a recent production run. Each piece was independently subjected to higher and higher temperatures until it became brittle. The temperature at which brittleness was first noticed was recorded for each piece in the sample. The following results were obtained: $\bar{x} = 480°F$, $s = 11°F$. Use a 90% confidence interval to estimate μ. Interpret your confidence interval.

6.15 Nasser Arshadi and Edward Lawrence (1984) investigated the profiles (i.e., career patterns, social backgrounds, and so forth) of the top executives in the U.S. banking industry. They sampled 96 executives and found that 80% studied business or economics and that 45% had a graduate degree. With respect to the number of years of service, x, at the same bank, the group had a mean of 23.43 years and a standard deviation of 10.82 years.
   a. Construct a 90% confidence interval for $E(x) = \mu$.
   b. Interpret your interval in the context of the problem.
   c. What assumption(s) was it necessary to make in order to construct the confidence interval of part **a**?
   d. Is your interval estimate for $E(x)$ also an interval estimate for $E(\bar{x})$? Explain. [*Hint:*   See Chapter 5.]

6.2   Determining the Sample Size Necessary to Estimate a Population Mean

Typically, an analyst must plan the sampling study that produces the data used to estimate a population mean. Perhaps the most important design decision faced by the analyst is to determine the size of the sample. We will show in this section that the appropriate sample size for estimating a population mean depends on the desired reliability.

To see this, consider the example from Section 6.1, in which we estimated the mean overdue amount for all delinquent accounts in a large credit corporation. A sample of 100 delinquent accounts produced an estimate $\bar{x}$ that was within \$18 of the true mean amount due, μ, for all delinquent accounts at the 95% confidence level. That is, the 95% confidence interval for μ was \$36 wide when 100 accounts were sampled. This is illustrated in Figure 6.4(a).

Now suppose that we want to estimate μ to within \$5 with 95% confidence. That is, we want to narrow the width of the confidence interval from \$36 to \$10, as shown in Figure 6.4(b). How much will the sample size have to be increased to accomplish this? If we want the estimator $\bar{x}$ to be within \$5 of μ, we must have

$$1.96\sigma_{\bar{x}} = 5 \quad \text{or, equivalently,} \quad 1.96\left(\frac{\sigma}{\sqrt{n}}\right) = 5$$

The necessary sample size is obtained by solving this equation for n. To do this we need an approximation for σ. We have an approximation from the initial sample of 100 accounts—namely, the sample standard deviation, $s = 90$. Thus,

a. $n = 100$

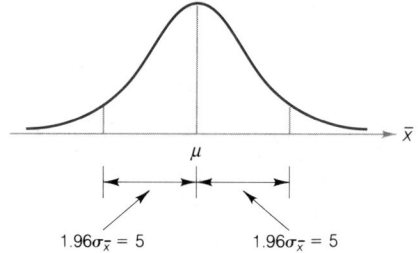

b. $n = 1,300$

FIGURE 6.4 ▲

Relationship between sample size and width of confidence interval for delinquent creditors example

$$1.96\left(\frac{\sigma}{\sqrt{n}}\right) \approx 1.96\left(\frac{s}{\sqrt{n}}\right) = 1.96\left(\frac{90}{\sqrt{n}}\right) = 5$$

$$\sqrt{n} = \frac{1.96(90)}{5} = 35.28$$

$$n = (35.28)^2 = 1,244.68$$

Approximately 1,245 accounts will have to be sampled to estimate the mean overdue amount μ to within \$5 with (approximately) 95% confidence. The confidence interval resulting from a sample of this size will be approximately \$10 wide [see Figure 6.4(b)].

In general, we can express the reliability associated with a confidence interval for the population mean μ in one of two equivalent ways: We can specify the bound, B, within which we want to estimate μ with $100(1 - \alpha)\%$ confidence. This bound B then is equal to the half-width of the confidence interval, as shown in Figure 6.5. Equivalently, we can specify the total width, W, of the $100(1 - \alpha)\%$ confidence interval for μ, also shown in Figure 6.5. Note that $W = 2B$.

FIGURE 6.5 ▶

Specifying the bound B or total width W for a confidence interval

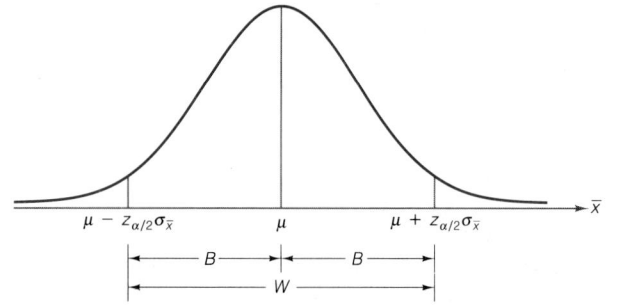

The procedure for finding the sample size necessary to estimate μ to within a given bound B or with a total interval width W is given in the box.

Sample Size Determination for $100(1 - \alpha)\%$ Confidence Intervals for μ

To estimate μ to within a bound B or, equivalently, with a confidence interval of total width W, with $100(1 - \alpha)\%$ confidence, the required sample size is found by solving one of the following equations for n:

$$z_{\alpha/2}\left(\frac{\sigma}{\sqrt{n}}\right) = B \qquad z_{\alpha/2}\left(\frac{\sigma}{\sqrt{n}}\right) = \frac{W}{2}$$

The solution can be written in terms of either B or W:

$$n = \frac{(z_{\alpha/2})^2\sigma^2}{B^2} \qquad n = \frac{4(z_{\alpha/2})^2\sigma^2}{W^2}$$

The value of σ is almost always unknown. It can be estimated by the standard deviation, s, from a prior sample. Alternatively, we may approximate the range R of observations in the population, and (conservatively) estimate $\sigma \approx R/4$. In any case, you should round the value of n you obtain *upward* to ensure that the sample size will be sufficient to achieve the specified reliability.

EXAMPLE 6.2

Suppose the manufacturer of official NFL footballs uses a machine to inflate the new balls to a pressure of 13.5 pounds. When the machine is properly calibrated, the mean inflation pressure is 13.5, but uncontrollable factors cause the pressures of individual footballs to vary randomly from about 13.3 to 13.7 pounds. For quality control purposes, the manufacturer wishes to estimate the true mean inflation pressure for a particular shipment of balls with a 99% confidence interval that is only .05 pound wide. What sample size should be used?

Solution

For a 99% confidence interval we have $z_{\alpha/2} = z_{.005} = 2.575$, and to estimate σ we note that the range of observations is $R = 13.7 - 13.3 = .4$ and use $\sigma \approx R/4 = .1$. Thus, in order to have a confidence interval of width $W = .05$, we use the formula derived in the box to find the sample size n:

$$n = \frac{4(z_{\alpha/2})^2\sigma^2}{W^2} \approx \frac{4(2.575)^2(.1)^2}{(.05)^2} = 106.09$$

We round this up to $n = 107$ and, realizing that σ was approximated by $R/4$, we might even advise that the sample size be specified as $n = 110$ to be more certain of attaining the objective of a 99% confidence interval with width $W = .05$ pound or less.

Sometimes the formulas will lead to a solution that indicates a small sample size is sufficient to achieve the confidence interval goal. As we will see in Section 6.3, the procedures and assumptions for making inferences from small samples differ from those for large samples. Therefore, if the formulas yield a small sample size ($n < 30$), one simple strategy is to select a sample size $n \geq 30$.

The cost of sampling must also be considered when the sample size is being determined. Although more complex formulas can be derived to take sampling costs into account, these are beyond the scope of this text. For our purposes, it is sufficient to realize that a sampling budget may prove to be a restriction on the sample size, and therefore on the reliability of the confidence interval.

Exercises 6.16–6.25

Learning the Mechanics

6.16 If you wish to estimate a population mean correct to within a bound $B = .3$ with probability .95 and you know from prior sampling that σ^2 is approximately equal to 7.2, how many observations would have to be included in your sample?

6.17 If you wish to estimate a population mean with a 95% confidence interval of width $W = .3$ and you know from prior sampling that σ^2 is approximately equal to 7.2, how many observations would have to be included in your sample? Compare your answer to that for Exercise 6.16. Explain the difference.

6.18 Suppose you wish to estimate the mean of a normal population using a 99% confidence interval and you know from prior information that $\sigma^2 \approx 1$.
  a. To see the effect of the sample size on the width of the confidence interval, calculate the width W of the confidence interval for $n = 9, 36, 81, 400$.
  b. Plot the width as a function of sample size n on graph paper. Connect the points by a smooth curve and note how the width decreases as n increases.

6.19 Suppose you wish to estimate a population mean correct to within a bound $B = .20$ with probability equal to .90. You do not know σ^2, but you know that the observations will range in value between 30 and 34.
  a. Find the approximate sample size that will produce the desired accuracy of the estimate. You wish to be conservative to ensure that the sample size will be ample to achieve the desired accuracy of the estimate. [*Hint:* Using your knowledge of data variation from Section 2.6, assume that the range of the observations will equal 4σ.]
  b. Calculate the approximate sample size making the less conservative assumption that the range of the observations is equal to 6σ.

6.20 It costs you $10 to draw a sample of size $n = 1$ and measure the attribute of interest. You have a budget of $1,500.
  a. Do you have sufficient funds to estimate the population mean for the attribute of interest with a 95% confidence interval 5 units in width? Assume $\sigma = 14$.
  b. If a 90% confidence level were used, would your answer to part **a** change? Explain.

Applying the Concepts

6.21 It costs more to produce defective items—since they must be scrapped or reworked—than it does to produce nondefective items. This simple fact suggests that manufacturers should ensure the quality of their products by perfecting their production processes rather than through inspection of finished products (Deming, 1986). To better understand a particular metal-stamping process, a manufacturer wishes to estimate the mean length of items produced by the process during the past 24 hours.

   a. How many parts should be sampled in order to estimate the population mean to within .1 mm with 80% confidence? Previous studies of this machine have indicated that the standard deviation of lengths produced by the stamping operation is about 2 mm.

   b. Time permits the use of a sample size no larger than 100. If an 80% confidence interval for μ is constructed using $n = 100$, will it be wider or narrower than the interval that would have been obtained using the sample size determined in part **a**? Explain.

   c. If management requires that μ be estimated to within .1 mm and that a sample of size no more than 100 be used, what is (approximately) the maximum confidence level that could be attained for a confidence interval that meets management's specifications?

6.22 A large food-products company receives about 100,000 phone calls a year from consumers on its toll-free number. A computer monitors and records how many rings it takes for an operator to answer, how much time each caller spends "on hold," and other data. However, the reliability of the monitoring system has been called into question by the operators and their labor union. As a check on the computer system, approximately how many calls should be manually monitored during the next year to estimate the true mean time that callers spend on hold to within 3 seconds with 95% confidence? Answer this question for the following values of the standard deviation of waiting times (in seconds):   10, 20, and 30.

6.23 Suppose a department store wants to estimate μ, the average age of the customers of its contemporary apparel department, correct to within 2 years with probability equal to .95. Approximately how large a sample would be required? [*Note:*   Management does not know the standard deviation σ but estimates that the ages of its customers range from 15 to 45. Use a conservative approximation for σ to calculate n.]

6.24 Mortgage companies and banks use professional appraisers to determine the value of properties (e.g., single-family homes) that their customers offer as security when applying for a loan. In a year's time, a real estate appraiser may appraise 500 properties. Norwest Mortgage requires its appraisers to keep track of their turnaround time for each property—the time it takes an appraiser from receipt of the appraisal request to the submission of the completed appraisal to a loan officer. How large a sample of properties would be needed to estimate the mean turnaround time for a particular appraiser during the previous 12 months with an 80% confidence interval of width no more than 2 days? The turnaround times range from 2 days to 18 days.

6.25 The United States Golf Association (USGA) tests all new brands of golf balls to assure that they meet USGA specifications. One test is intended to measure the average distance travelled when the ball is hit by a machine called "Iron Byron," a name inspired by the swing of the famous golfer Byron Nelson. Suppose the USGA wants to estimate the mean distance for a new brand with a 90% confidence interval of width 2 yards. Assume that past tests have indicated that the standard deviation of the distances "Iron Byron" hits golf balls is approximately 10 yards. How many golf balls should be hit by "Iron Byron" to achieve the desired accuracy in estimating the mean?

6.3   Small-Sample Estimation of a Population Mean

One of the items of interest to an investor in a company is a forecast of the company's annual earnings per share for the next year. Recall that earnings per share is computed by dividing the total annual earnings of the company by the total number of shares of stock outstanding. One way of trying to project the earnings per share is to ask the opinion of several experts, thus obtaining a sample of projections for the particular company. Then, this sample of opinions can be used to make an inference about the mean projected earnings per share, μ, of all stock analysts. However, time and cost restrictions would probably limit the sample of opinions to a small number, and thus the large-sample estimation technique of Section 6.1 may not be applicable.

Many inferences in business must be made on the basis of very limited information—i.e., **small samples**. When an inference is to be made about a population mean, μ, small samples have two immediate problematic effects:

PROBLEM 1

The shape of the sampling distribution of the sample mean $\bar{x}$ now depends on the shape of the population that is sampled. Because the Central Limit Theorem applies only to large samples, we can no longer assume that the sampling distribution of $\bar{x}$ is approximately normal.

PROBLEM 2

Although it is still true that $\sigma_{\bar{x}} = \sigma/\sqrt{n}$, the sample standard deviation s may provide a poor approximation of the population standard deviation σ when the sample size is small.

Solution to Problem 1

According to Theorem 5.1, the sampling distribution of $\bar{x}$ will be normal (approximately normal) even for small samples *if the population being sampled is normal* (*approximately normal*).

Solution to Problem 2

Instead of using the standard normal statistic

$$z = \frac{\bar{x} - \mu}{\sigma_{\bar{x}}} = \frac{\bar{x} - \mu}{\sigma/\sqrt{n}}$$

which requires knowledge of, or a good approximation to, σ, we define and use the statistic

$$t = \frac{\bar{x} - \mu}{s/\sqrt{n}}$$

in which the sample standard deviation, s, replaces the population standard deviation, σ.

The distribution of the **t statistic** in repeated sampling was discovered by W. S. Gosset, a scientist in the Guinness brewery in Ireland, who published his discovery in 1908 under the pen name of Student. The main result of Gosset's work is that if we are sampling from a normal distribution, the t statistic will have a sampling distribution very much like that of the z statistic: mound-shaped, symmetric, and with mean 0. The primary difference between the sampling distributions of t and z is that the t statistic is more variable than the z, which follows intuitively when you realize that t contains two random quantities ($\bar{x}$ and s), while z contains only one ($\bar{x}$).

The actual increase in variability in the sampling distribution of t depends on the sample size, n. In particular, the smaller the value of n, the more variable will be the sampling distribution of t. A convenient way of expressing this dependence is to say that the t statistic has $(n - 1)$ **degrees of freedom (df)**. Recall that the quantity $(n - 1)$ is the divisor that appears in the formula for s^2. This number plays a key role in the sampling distribution of s^2 and appears in discussions of other statistics in later chapters.

In Figure 6.6, we show both the sampling distribution of z and the sampling distribution of a t statistic with 4 df. You can see that the increased variability of the t statistic means that the t value, t_α, that locates an area α in the upper tail of the t distribution will be larger than the corresponding value z_α. Values of t that will be used in forming small-sample confidence intervals for μ are given in Table VI of Appendix B (and inside front cover). A partial reproduction of this table is shown in Table 6.2. Note that t_α values are listed for degrees of freedom from 1 to 29, where α refers to the tail area to the right of t_α. For example, if we want the t value with an area of .025 to its right and 4 df, we look in the table under the column $t_{.025}$ for the entry in the row corresponding to 4 df. This entry is $t_{.025} = 2.776$, as shown in Figure 6.7. The corresponding standard normal z-score is $z_{.025} = 1.96$.

FIGURE 6.6 ▶
Standard normal (z) distribution
and t distribution with 4 df

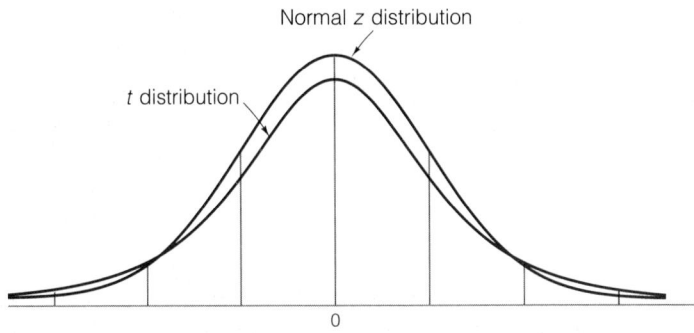

Note that the last row of Table VI, where df = infinity, contains the standard normal z values. This follows from the fact that as the sample size n grows very large, s becomes closer to σ, and thus t becomes closer in distribution to z. In fact, when df = 29, there is little difference between corresponding tabulated values of z and t. Thus, we choose the arbitrary cutoff of $n = 30$ (df = 29) to distinguish between the large- and small-sample inferential techniques.

TABLE 6.2   Reproduction of Part of Table VI of Appendix B: Critical Values of the t Statistic

Degrees of Freedom	$t_{.100}$	$t_{.050}$	$t_{.025}$	$t_{.010}$	$t_{.005}$	$t_{.001}$	$t_{.0005}$
1	3.078	6.314	12.706	31.821	63.657	318.31	636.62
2	1.886	2.920	4.303	6.965	9.925	22.326	31.598
3	1.638	2.353	3.182	4.541	5.841	10.213	12.924
4	1.533	2.132	2.776	3.747	4.604	7.173	8.610
5	1.476	2.015	2.571	3.365	4.032	5.893	6.869
6	1.440	1.943	2.447	3.143	3.707	5.208	5.959
7	1.415	1.895	2.365	2.998	3.499	4.785	5.408
8	1.397	1.860	2.306	2.896	3.355	4.501	5.041
9	1.383	1.833	2.262	2.821	3.250	4.297	4.781
10	1.372	1.812	2.228	2.764	3.169	4.144	4.587
11	1.363	1.796	2.201	2.718	3.106	4.025	4.437
12	1.356	1.782	2.179	2.681	3.055	3.930	4.318
13	1.350	1.771	2.160	2.650	3.012	3.852	4.221
14	1.345	1.761	2.145	2.624	2.977	3.787	4.140
15	1.341	1.753	2.131	2.602	2.947	3.733	4.073
⋮	⋮	⋮	⋮	⋮	⋮	⋮	⋮
∞	1.282	1.645	1.960	2.326	2.576	3.090	3.291

FIGURE 6.7 ▶

The $t_{.025}$ value in a t distribution with 4 df and the corresponding $z_{.025}$ value

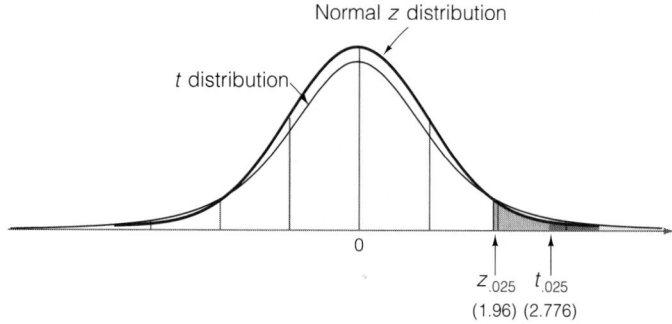

Returning to the projected earnings per share example, suppose we can get a sample of five expert opinions about next year's earnings per share for a stock. We calculate the mean and standard deviation of these five projections to be

$$\bar{x} = \$2.63 \qquad s = \$.72$$

How can we use this information to construct a 95% confidence interval for μ, the mean projected earnings per share for all stock analysts in the population?

First, we know that we are dealing with a sample too small to assume that the sample mean $\bar{x}$ is approximately normally distributed by the Central Limit Theorem.

That is, we cannot "automatically" conclude that $\bar{x}$ is normally distributed from the Central Limit Theorem when the sample size is small. Instead, we must assume the measured variable, in this case the earnings per share projection, is normally distributed in order for the distribution of $\bar{x}$ to be normal.

Second, unless we are fortunate enough to know the population standard deviation σ, which in this case represents the standard deviation of *all* the analysts' projections of the stock's earnings per share, we cannot use the standard normal z statistic to form our confidence interval for μ. Instead, we must use the t distribution, with $(n - 1)$ degrees of freedom.

In this case, $n - 1 = 4$ df, and the t value is found in the table (Table 6.2 or inside front cover) to be

$$t_{.025} = 2.766 \quad \text{with 4 df}$$

Recall that the large-sample confidence interval would have been of the form

$$\bar{x} \pm z_{\alpha/2}\sigma_{\bar{x}} = \bar{x} \pm z_{\alpha/2}\frac{\sigma}{\sqrt{n}} = \bar{x} \pm z_{.025}\frac{\sigma}{\sqrt{n}}$$

where 95% is the desired confidence level. To form the interval for a small sample *from a normal distribution, we simply substitute t for z and s for σ in the preceding formula*:

$$\bar{x} \pm t_{\alpha/2}\frac{s}{\sqrt{n}}$$

Substituting the numerical values, we get

$$2.63 \pm (2.776)\frac{(.72)}{\sqrt{5}} = 2.63 \pm .89$$

or \$1.77 to \$3.52 per share. That is, we can be 95% confident that the mean of *all* analysts' earnings per share projections for this stock is between \$1.77 and \$3.52. As with our large-sample interval estimates, our confidence is in the process, not in this particular interval. We know that the procedure we used will produce an interval that contains the true mean, μ, 95% of the time we utilize it, *assuming that the population of earnings-per-share projections from which our sample was selected is normally distributed*. The latter assumption is necessary for the small-sample interval to be valid.

What price did we pay for having to utilize a small sample to make the inference? First, we had to assume the underlying population is normally distributed; if the assumption is invalid, our interval might also be invalid.* Second, we had to form the interval using a t value of 2.776 rather than a z value of 1.96, resulting in a wider interval to achieve the same 95% level of confidence. If the interval from \$1.77 to \$3.52 is too wide to be of use, then we know how to remedy the situation: increase the number of analysts sampled in order to decrease the interval width (on average).

---

*By *invalid* we mean that the probability that the procedure will yield an interval that contains μ is not equal to $(1 - \alpha)$. Generally, if the underlying population is approximately normal, then the confidence coefficient will approximate the probability that the interval contains μ.

The procedure for forming a small-sample confidence interval is summarized in the accompanying box.

Small-Sample Confidence Interval for μ^*

$$\bar{x} \pm t_{\alpha/2}\left(\frac{s}{\sqrt{n}}\right)$$

where $t_{\alpha/2}$ is based on $(n - 1)$ degrees of freedom.

Assumption: The relative frequency distribution of the sampled population is approximately normal.

EXAMPLE 6.3

Some quality control experiments require **destructive sampling** in order to measure some particular characteristic of the product. For example, suppose a manufacturer of printers for personal computers wishes to estimate the mean number of characters printed before the printhead fails. The cost of destructive sampling often dictates small samples. Suppose the printer manufacturer tests $n = 15$ printheads and calculates the following statistics:

$$\bar{x} = 1.23 \text{ million characters} \qquad s = .27 \text{ million characters}$$

Form a 99% confidence interval for the mean number of characters printed before the head fails.

Solution

If we assume that the number of characters printed before printhead failure is normally distributed, we can use the t statistic to form the confidence interval. We use a confidence coefficient of .99 and degrees of freedom $n - 1 = 14$ to find in Table VI of Appendix B:

$$t_{\alpha/2} = t_{.005} = 2.977$$

Thus, the small sample forces us to assume normality and extend the interval almost 3 standard deviations (of $\bar{x}$) on each side of the sample mean in order to form the 99% confidence interval. For these data, the interval is

$$\bar{x} \pm t_{.005}\left(\frac{s}{\sqrt{n}}\right) = 1.23 \pm 2.977\left(\frac{.27}{\sqrt{15}}\right) = 1.23 \pm .21 \quad \text{or} \quad (1.02, 1.44)$$

---

*The procedure given in the box assumes that the population standard deviation σ is unknown, which is almost always the case. If σ is known, we can form the small-sample confidence interval just as we would a large-sample confidence interval using a standard normal z value instead of t. However, we must still assume that the underlying population is approximately normal.

Thus, the manufacturer can be 99% confident that the printhead has a mean life between 1.02 and 1.44 million characters. If the manufacturer were to advertise that the mean life of its printheads is (at least) 1 million characters, the interval would support such a claim. Our confidence is derived from the knowledge that 99% of the intervals formed in repeated applications of this procedure will contain μ.

We have emphasized throughout this section that the assumption of a normally distributed population is necessary for making small-sample inferences about μ when using the t statistic. While many business phenomena do have approximately normal distributions, it is also true that many have distributions that are not normal or even mound-shaped. Empirical evidence acquired over the years has shown that the t distribution is rather insensitive to moderate departures from normality. That is, the use of the t statistic when sampling from mound-shaped populations generally produces credible results; however, for cases in which the distribution is distinctly non-normal, *nonparametric methods* should be used. A simple nonparametric procedure for making inferences about a population mean is described in Chapter 7.

Exercises 6.26 – 6.37

Learning the Mechanics

6.26 Explain the differences in the sampling distributions of $\bar{x}$ for large and small samples under the following assumptions:
a. The variable of interest, x, is normally distributed.
b. Nothing is known about the distribution of the variable x.

6.27 Suppose you have selected a random sample of $n = 5$ measurements from a normal distribution. Compare the standard normal z values with the corresponding t values if you were forming the following confidence intervals:
a. 80% confidence interval   b. 90% confidence interval   c. 95% confidence interval
d. 98% confidence interval   e. 99% confidence interval
f. Use the table values you obtained in parts a–e to sketch the z and t distributions. What are the similarities and differences?

6.28 Let t_0 be a particular value of t. Use Table VI of Appendix B to find t_0 values such that the following statements are true:
a. $P(t \geq t_0) = .025$ where df $= 11$ b. $P(t \geq t_0) = .01$ where df $= 9$
c. $P(t \leq t_0) = .005$ where df $= 6$ d. $P(t \leq t_0) = .05$ where df $= 18$

6.29 Let t_0 be a particular value of t. Use Table VI of Appendix B to find t_0 values such that the following statements are true:
a. $P(-t_0 < t < t_0) = .95$ where df $= 10$ b. $P(t \leq -t_0$ or $t \geq t_0) = .05$ where df $= 10$
c. $P(t \leq t_0) = .05$ where df $= 10$ d. $P(t \leq -t_0$ or $t \geq t_0) = .05$ where df $= 20$
e. $P(t \leq -t_0$ or $t \geq t_0) = .01$ where df $= 5$

6.30 The following random sample was selected from a normal distribution: 5, 6, 2, 8, 4
   a. Construct a 90% confidence interval for the population mean μ.
   b. Construct a 95% confidence interval for the population mean μ.
   c. Construct a 99% confidence interval for the population mean μ.
   d. Assume that the sample mean $\bar{x}$ and sample standard deviation s remain exactly the same as those you just calculated, but that they are based on a sample of $n = 20$ observations rather than $n = 6$ observations. Repeat parts **a–c**. What is the effect of increasing the sample size on the width of the confidence intervals?

6.31 The following sample of 24 measurements was selected from a population that is approximately normally distributed:

91	80	99	110	95	106	78	121
106	100	97	82	100	83	115	104
114	118	96	101	79	130	94	101

   a. Construct an 80% confidence interval for the population mean.
   b. Construct a 95% confidence interval for the population mean and compare the width of this interval with that of part **a**.
   c. Carefully interpret each of the confidence intervals, and explain why the 80% confidence interval is narrower.

Applying the Concepts

6.32 Health insurers and the federal government are both putting pressure on hospitals to shorten the average length of stay (LOS) of their patients. A random sample of 20 hospitals in one state had a mean LOS in 1990 of 3.8 days, and a standard deviation of 1.2 days.
   a. Use a 90% confidence interval to estimate the population mean LOS for the state's hospitals in 1990.
   b. Interpret the interval in terms of this application.
   c. What is meant by the phrase "90% confidence interval"?

6.33 Named for the section of the 1978 Internal Revenue Code that authorized it, a 401(k) plan permits employees to shift part of their before-tax salaries into investments such as mutual funds. Employers typically match 50% of the employee's contribution up to about 6% of salary (Paré, 1992). Concerned with what it believed was a low employee-participation rate in its 401(k) plan, a particular Fortune 500 company sampled 11 other Fortune 500 companies and asked for their 401(k) participation rates. The following answers were obtained (in percentages):

80	76	81	77	82	80	85	60	80	79	82

   a. Use a 95% confidence interval to estimate the mean participation rate for Fortune 500 companies.
   b. Interpret the interval in the context of this problem.
   c. What assumption is necessary to ensure the validity of this confidence interval?
   d. If the value 60% in the above data set were instead 80%, how would the center and width of confidence interval you constructed in part **a** be affected?

6.34 A **mortgage** is a type of loan that is secured by a designated piece of property. If the borrower defaults on the loan, the lender can sell the property to recover the outstanding debt. The home mortgage is the most important type of personal loan in the United States. In a home mortgage, the borrower pledges the home in question as security for the loan (Sharpe and Alexander, 1990). A federal bank examiner is interested in estimating the mean outstanding principal balance of all home mortgages foreclosed by the bank due to default by the borrower during the last 3 years. A random sample of 12 foreclosed mortgages yielded the following data (in dollars):

95,982	81,422	39,888	46,836	66,899	69,110
59,200	62,331	105,812	55,545	56,635	72,123

a. Describe the population from which the bank examiner collected the sample data. What characteristic must this population possess to enable us to construct a confidence interval for the mean outstanding principal balance using the method described in this section?
b. Construct a 90% confidence interval for the mean of interest.
c. Carefully interpret your confidence interval in the context of the problem.

6.35 A study indicated that the cost of hiring an employee (excluding salary) ranges from about $1,500 for a secretary to more than $40,000 for a manager (Dessler, 1986). In order to estimate its mean cost of hiring an entry-level secretary, a large corporation randomly selected eight of the entry-level secretaries it hired during the last 2 years and determined the costs (in dollars) involved in hiring each. The following data were obtained:

2,100	1,650	1,315	2,035	2,245	1,980	1,700	2,190

Assume that the population from which these data were sampled is approximately normally distributed.
a. Describe the population from which the corporation collected the sample data.
b. Use a 90% confidence interval to estimate the mean of interest to the corporation.
c. How wide is the confidence interval you constructed in part **b**? Would a 95% confidence interval be wider or narrower? Explain.

6.36 Private colleges and universities rely on money contributed by individuals and corporations for their operating expenses. Much of this money is put into a fund called an **endowment**, and the college spends only the interest earned by the fund. A recent survey of eight private colleges in the United States revealed the following endowments (in millions of dollars):   60.2, 47.0, 235.1, 490.0, 122.6, 177.5, 95.4, and 220.0. Estimate the mean endowment for private colleges, using a 95% confidence interval. List any assumptions you make.

6.37 One of the concerns of U.S. industry as we enter the mid-1990s is the increasing cost of health insurance for its workers. A random sample of 23 small companies (companies with less than $10 million in annual revenues) that offer paid health insurance as a benefit was selected. The mean health insurance cost per worker per month was $135, and the standard deviation was $32.
a. Use a 95% confidence interval to estimate the mean cost per worker per month for all small companies.
b. What assumption is necessary to ensure the validity of the confidence interval?
c. What is meant by the phrase "95% confidence interval"?

6.4   Large-Sample Estimation of a Binomial Probability

Many market studies are conducted by companies with the objective of determining the fraction of buyers of a particular product who prefer the company's brand. For example, a tobacco company may conduct a market study by sampling and interviewing 1,000 smokers to determine their brand preference. The objective of the survey is to estimate the proportion of all smokers who smoke the company's brand. The number, x, of the 1,000 sampled who smoke the company's brand is a binomial random variable. (See Section 4.3 for a description of the binomial experiment.) The probability, p, that a smoker prefers the company's brand is the parameter to be estimated. That is, we want to estimate the proportion p of all smokers who prefer the company's brand.

How would you estimate the probability, p, of success in a binomial experiment? One logical answer is to use the proportion of successes in the sample. That is, we can estimate p by calculating

$$\hat{p} = \frac{\text{Number of successes in the sample}}{\text{Number of trials}} = \frac{x}{n}$$

Thus, if 313 of the 1,000 smokers were found to smoke the company's brand, we would estimate the proportion p of all smokers who prefer the brand to be

$$\hat{p} = \frac{x}{n} = \frac{313}{1,000} = .313$$

To determine the reliability of the estimator $\hat{p}$, we need to know its sampling distribution. That is, if we were to draw samples of 1,000 smokers over and over again, each time calculating a new estimate $\hat{p}$, what would be the frequency distribution of all the $\hat{p}$ values? The answer lies in viewing $\hat{p}$ as the average or mean number of successes per trial over the n trials. Thus, if each success in the sample is assigned a value equal to 1 and each failure is assigned a 0, then the sum of all n sample observations is x, the total number of successes; and $\hat{p} = x/n$ is the average or mean number of successes per trial in the n trials. The Central Limit Theorem tells us that for any population the relative frequency distribution of the sample mean is approximately normal for sufficiently large samples. We demonstrated the properties of $\hat{p}$ in Example 5.7. The sampling distribution of $\hat{p}$ has the characteristics indicated in Figure 6.8 and listed in the next box.

FIGURE 6.8 ▶
Sampling distribution of $\hat{p}$

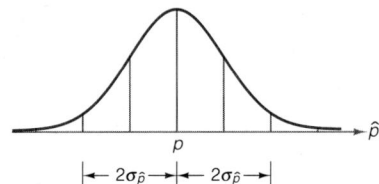

Sampling Distribution of $\hat{p}$

1. The mean of the sampling distribution of $\hat{p}$ is p; i.e., $\hat{p}$ is an unbiased estimator of p.

Continued

2. The standard deviation of the sampling distribution of $\hat{p}$ is $\sqrt{pq/n}$; i.e., $\sigma_{\hat{p}} = \sqrt{pq/n}$, where $q = 1 - p$.

3. For large samples, the sampling distribution of $\hat{p}$ is approximately normal. A sample size will be considered large if the interval $\hat{p} \pm 3\sigma_{\hat{p}}$ does not include 0 or 1. [*Note:* This requirement is almost equivalent to that given in Section 4.9 for approximating a binomial distribution with a normal one. The main difference is that we assumed p to be known in Section 4.9; now we are trying to make inferences about an unknown p, so we use $\hat{p}$ to estimate p in checking the adequacy of the normal approximation.]

The fact that $\hat{p}$ is a mean number of successes per trial allows us to form confidence intervals in a manner that is completely analogous to that used for large-sample inferences about μ:

Large-Sample Confidence Interval for p

$$\hat{p} \pm z_{\alpha/2}\sigma_{\hat{p}} = \hat{p} \pm z_{\alpha/2}\sqrt{\frac{pq}{n}} \approx \hat{p} \pm z_{\alpha/2}\sqrt{\frac{\hat{p}\hat{q}}{n}}$$

where $\hat{p} = \dfrac{x}{n}$ and $\hat{q} = 1 - \hat{p}$

[*Note:* When n is large, we can use $\hat{p}$ to approximate the value of p in the formula for $\sigma_{\hat{p}}$.]

Thus, if 313 of 1,000 smokers smoke the company's brand, a 95% confidence interval for the proportion of all smokers who prefer the company's brand is

$$\hat{p} \pm z_{\alpha/2}\sigma_{\hat{p}} = .313 \pm 1.96\sqrt{\frac{pq}{1,000}}$$

where $q = 1 - p$. Just as we needed an approximator for σ in calculating a large-sample confidence interval for μ, we now need an approximation for p. As Table 6.3 shows, the approximation for p need not be especially accurate, because the value of pq needed for the confidence interval is relatively insensitive to changes in p. Therefore, we can use $\hat{p}$ to approximate p. Keeping in mind that $\hat{q} = 1 - \hat{p}$, we substitute these values into the formula for the confidence interval:

$$\hat{p} \pm 1.96\sqrt{\frac{pq}{1,000}} \approx \hat{p} \pm 1.96\sqrt{\frac{\hat{p}\hat{q}}{1,000}}$$

$$= .313 \pm 1.96\sqrt{\frac{(.313)(.687)}{1,000}} = .313 \pm .029$$

$$= (.284, .342)$$

TABLE 6.3   Values of pq for Several Different p Values

p	pq
.5	.25
.6 or .4	.24
.7 or .3	.21
.8 or .2	.16
.9 or .1	.09

The company can be 95% confident that the interval from 28.4% to 34.2% contains the true percentage of all smokers who prefer its brand. That is, in repeated construction of confidence intervals, approximately 95% of all samples would produce confidence intervals that enclose p. Note that confidence intervals for p are interpreted in the same manner as confidence intervals for μ.

EXAMPLE 6.4

Many public polling agencies conduct surveys to determine the current consumer sentiment concerning the state of the economy. For example, the Bureau of Economic and Business Research (BEBR) at the University of Florida conducts quarterly surveys to gauge consumer sentiment in the Sunshine State. Suppose that BEBR randomly samples 484 consumers and finds that 257 are optimistic about the state of the economy. Use a 90% confidence interval to estimate the proportion of all consumers in Florida who are optimistic about the state of the economy. Based on the confidence interval, can BEBR infer that the majority of Florida consumers are optimistic about the economy?

Solution

The number, x, of the 484 sampled consumers who are optimistic about the Florida economy is a binomial random variable if we can assume that the sample was randomly selected from the population of Florida consumers and that the poll was conducted identically for each sampled consumer.

The point estimate of the proportion of Florida consumers who are optimistic about the economy is

$$\hat{p} = \frac{x}{n} = \frac{257}{484} = .531$$

We first check to be sure that the sample size is sufficiently large that the normal distribution provides a reasonable approximation for the sampling distribution of $\hat{p}$. We check the 3-standard-deviation interval around $\hat{p}$:

$$\hat{p} \pm 3\sigma_{\hat{p}} \approx \hat{p} \pm 3\sqrt{\frac{\hat{p}\hat{q}}{n}}$$

$$= .531 \pm 3\sqrt{\frac{(.531)(.469)}{484}} = .531 \pm .068 = (.463, .599)$$

Since this interval is wholly contained in the interval $(0, 1)$, we may conclude that the normal approximation is reasonable.

We now proceed to form the 90% confidence interval for p, the true proportion of Florida consumers who are optimistic about the state of the economy:

$$\hat{p} \pm z_{\alpha/2}\sigma_{\hat{p}} = \hat{p} \pm z_{\alpha/2}\sqrt{\frac{pq}{n}} \approx \hat{p} \pm z_{\alpha/2}\sqrt{\frac{\hat{p}\hat{q}}{n}}$$

$$= .531 \pm 1.645\sqrt{\frac{(.531)(.469)}{484}} = .531 \pm .037 = (.494, .568)$$

Thus, we can be 90% confident that the proportion of all Florida consumers who are confident about the economy is between .494 and .568. As always, our confidence stems from the fact that 90% of all similarly formed intervals will contain the true proportion p and not from any knowledge about whether this particular interval does.

Can we conclude that the majority of Florida consumers are optimistic about the economy based on this interval? If we wished to use this interval to infer that a majority is optimistic, the interval would have to support the inference that p exceeds .5 — that is, that more than 50% of the Florida consumers are optimistic about the economy. Note that the interval contains some values below .5 (as low as .494) as well as some above .5 (as high as .568). Therefore, we cannot conclude that the true value of p exceeds .5 based on this 90% confidence interval.

In Example 6.4, we used a confidence interval to make an inference about whether the true value of p exceeds .5. That is, we used the sample to *test* whether p exceeds .5. When we want to use sample information to test the value of a population parameter, we usually use a *test of hypothesis*, the subject of the next chapter.

We conclude Chapter 6 by showing how to determine the sample size necessary to make inferences about a binomial probability with a specified reliability.

Exercises 6.38–6.48

Learning the Mechanics

6.38 Describe the sampling distribution of $\hat{p}$ based on the large samples of size n. That is, give the mean, the standard deviation, and the (approximate) shape of the distribution of $\hat{p}$ when large samples of size n are (repeatedly) selected from a binomial distribution with probability of success p.

6.39 Explain the meaning of the phrase "$\hat{p}$ is an unbiased estimator of p."

6.40 A random sample of size $n = 225$ yielded $\hat{p} = .46$.
a. Is the sample size large enough to use the methods of this section to construct a confidence interval for p? Explain.
b. Construct a 95% confidence interval for p.
c. Interpret the 95% confidence interval.
d. Explain what is meant by the phrase "95% confidence interval."

6.41 A random sample of size $n = 121$ yielded $\hat{p} = .88$.
a. Is the sample size large enough to use the methods of this section to construct a confidence interval for p? Explain.
b. Construct a 90% confidence interval for p.
c. What assumption is necessary to assure the validity of this confidence interval?

6.42 For the binomial sample information summarized in each part, indicate whether the sample size is large enough to use the methods of this chapter to construct a confidence interval for p.
a. $n = 400$, $\hat{p} = .10$ b. $n = 50$, $\hat{p} = .10$ c. $n = 20$, $\hat{p} = .5$ d. $n = 20$, $\hat{p} = .3$

6.43 A random sample of 50 consumers taste-tested a new snack food. Their responses were coded (0: do not like; 1: like; 2: indifferent) and listed:

```
1  0  0  1  2  0  1  1  0  0  0  1  0  2  0  2  2  0  0  1  1  0  0  0  0
1  0  2  0  0  0  1  0  0  1  0  0  1  0  1  0  2  0  0  1  1  0  0  0  1
```

a. Use an 80% confidence interval to estimate the proportion of consumers who like the snack food.

b. Provide a statistical interpretation for the confidence interval constructed in part **a**.

Applying the Concepts

6.44 A random sample of 122 Illinois law firms was selected to determine their degree of computer usage (Wentling, 1988). This survey showed that 76 of the firms used microcomputers (PCs).

a. Use a 95% confidence interval to estimate the proportion of all Illinois law firms who used microcomputers at the time of the survey.

b. Interpret the interval in the terms of this application.

c. What is meant by the phrase "95% confidence interval"?

d. Do you think this interval provides an estimate for the proportion of all U.S. law firms who were using microcomputers at the time of the survey? Why or why not?

6.45 For decades, U.S. companies have tied a portion of the compensation of many upper-management employees to the performance of the firm. In the last few years, however, a growing number of companies have begun offering similar performance incentives to all of their employees. What instigated this change in pay structures? Of 46 companies (surveyed by the American Compensation Association) that had modified their traditional pay structures, 26 reported making the modification in response to profound market changes in the last decade: global competition, consumer demand for high-quality goods and services, etc. They needed new ways to improve performance and cut costs (Alters, 1992). For the population of U.S. firms that have switched to nontraditional pay structures, estimate the proportion that have done so in response to market forces (rather than to growth, downsizing, or some other reason). Use a 90% confidence interval and specify whatever assumptions are necessary to assure the validity of the estimate.

6.46 Following a year-long investigation begun in 1985, a congressional subcommittee concluded that inflated home appraisals are responsible, in part, for many defaulted home mortgages. One insurer sampled 300 defaulted home mortgages and found that 120 of them involved defective appraisals.

a. Assume that the 300 defaulted mortgages were randomly sampled from all defaulted mortgages during 1985. Use a 90% confidence interval to estimate the proportion of all defaulted home mortgages in 1985 that involved a defective home appraisal.

b. How wide is the confidence interval you constructed in part **a**? Would an 80% confidence interval be wider or narrower than your interval of part **a**? Explain.

6.47 In February and March 1985, the Gallup Organization conducted telephone interviews with a random sample of 258 owners and managers of small U.S. businesses (i.e., firms with 20 or more employees but with less than $50 million in sales). Forty percent of those interviewed were under 45 years of age and 30% have worked at four or more companies (Graham, 1985).

a. Describe the population of interest to the Gallup Organization.

b. Is the sample size large enough to construct a confidence interval for the proportion of owners and managers who are under 45 years of age? Explain.

c. Construct a 95% confidence interval for the proportion of interest in part **b**.

    d. If a 95% confidence interval were used to estimate the proportion of owners and managers who have worked at four or more companies, would the interval be wider, narrower, or the same width as the interval estimate of part **c**? Explain.

6.48 Shoplifting is an escalating problem for retailers. Recently, one New York City store randomly selected 500 shoppers and observed them while they were in the store. Two in 25 were seen stealing. How accurate is this estimate? To help you answer this question, construct a 95% confidence interval for p, the proportion of all the store's customers who are shoplifters.

6.5 Determining the Sample Size Necessary to Estimate a Binomial Probability

We showed in Section 6.2 that samples can be designed to estimate a population mean μ with a specified degree of reliability. An analogous situation exists for estimating a binomial probability p. For example, in Section 6.4 a tobacco company used a sample of 1,000 smokers to calculate a 95% confidence interval for the proportion of smokers who preferred its brand, obtaining the interval .284 to .342. Note that the total width of the interval is about .06 $(.342 - .284 \approx .06)$. Suppose the company wants to estimate its market share more precisely, say with a 95% confidence interval having a width of .03.

    The company wants a confidence interval width W of .03. This corresponds to a half-width, or bound B on the estimate of p, of $B = W/2 = .015$. The sample size n to generate such an interval is found by solving the following equation for n:

$$z_{\alpha/2}\sigma_{\hat{p}} = B \quad \text{or} \quad z_{\alpha/2}\sqrt{\frac{pq}{n}} = .015 \quad \text{(see Figure 6.9)}$$

FIGURE 6.9 ▶
Specifying the total width **W** (or bound **B**) of a confidence interval for a binomial probability **p**

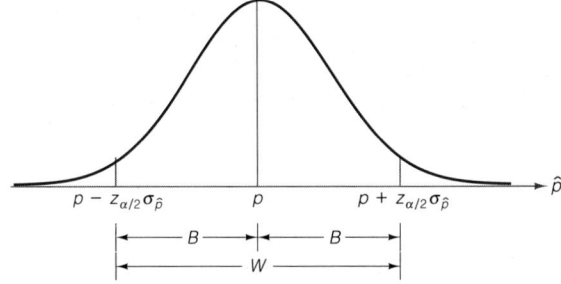

Since a 95% confidence interval is desired, the appropriate z value is $z_{\alpha/2} = z_{.025} = 1.96$. We must approximate the value of the product pq before we can solve the equation for n. As shown in Table 6.3, the closer the values of p and q to .5, the larger the product pq. Thus, to find a conservatively large sample size that will generate a confidence interval with the specified reliability, we generally choose an approximation of p close to .5. In the case of the tobacco company, however, we have an initial sample estimate of $\hat{p} = .313$. A conservatively large estimate of pq can therefore be obtained by using, say, $p = .35$. We now substitute into the equation and solve for n:

$$1.96\sqrt{\frac{(.35)(.65)}{n}} = .015$$

$$n = \frac{(1.96)^2(.35)(.65)}{(.015)^2} = 3,884.28 \approx 3,885$$

The company must sample about 3,885 smokers to estimate the percentage who prefer its brand with a 95% confidence interval of width .03.

The procedure for finding the sample size necessary to estimate a binomial probability p to within a given bound B or with a total interval width W is given in the box.

Sample Size Determination for $100(1 - \alpha)$% Confidence Interval for p

In order to estimate a binomial probability p to within a bound B or, equivalently, with a confidence interval of total width W with $100(1 - \alpha)$% confidence, the required sample size is found by solving one of the following equations for n:

$$z_{\alpha/2}\sqrt{\frac{pq}{n}} = B \qquad z_{\alpha/2}\sqrt{\frac{pq}{n}} = \frac{W}{2}$$

The solution can be written in terms of either B or W:

$$n = \frac{(z_{\alpha/2})^2(pq)}{B^2} \qquad n = \frac{4(z_{\alpha/2})^2(pq)}{W^2}$$

The value of the product pq is usually unknown. It can be estimated by using the sample fraction of successes, $\hat{p}$, from a prior sample. Alternatively, remember from Table 6.3 that the value of pq is at its maximum when p equals .5, so that you can obtain conservatively large values of n by approximating p by .5, or values close to .5. In any case, you should round the value of n you obtain *upward* to ensure that the sample size will be sufficient to achieve the specified reliability.

EXAMPLE 6.5

Since the deregulation of the telephonic communications industry, many firms have begun manufacturing telephones. Suppose one large manufacturer that entered the market quickly has an initial problem with excessive customer complaints and consequent returns of the phones for repair or replacement. The manufacturer wants to estimate the magnitude of the problem in order to estimate potential warranty costs. How many telephones should be sampled from the warehouse and checked in order to estimate the fraction defective p to within .01 with 90% confidence?

Solution

In order to estimate p to within a bound of .01, we set the half-width of the confidence interval equal to $B = .01$, as shown in Figure 6.10.

FIGURE 6.10 ▶
Specified reliability for estimate of fraction defective in Example 6.5

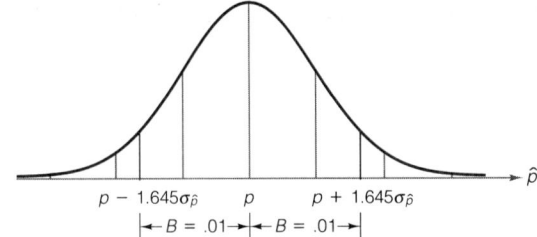

The equation for the sample size n requires an estimate of the product pq. We could most conservatively estimate $pq = .25$ (i.e., use $p = .5$), but this may be overly conservative when estimating a fraction defective (as consumers, we hope so!). A value of .1, corresponding to 10% defective, will probably be conservatively large for this application. The solution is, therefore,

$$n = \frac{(z_{\alpha/2})^2(pq)}{B^2} \approx \frac{(1.645)^2(.1)(.9)}{(.01)^2} = 2,435.4 \approx 2,436$$

Thus, the manufacturer should sample 2,436 telephones in order to estimate the fraction defective p to within .01 with 90% confidence. Remember that this answer depends on our approximation for pq, where we used .09. If the fraction defective is closer to .05 than .10, we can use a sample of 1,286 telephones (check this) to estimate p to within .01 with 90% confidence.

. . . .

The cost of sampling will play an important role in the final determination of the sample size to be selected to estimate a binomial probability p. Although more complex formulas can be derived to balance the reliability and cost considerations, we will solve for the necessary sample size and note that the sampling budget may be a limiting factor. Consult the references for a more complete treatment of this problem.

Exercises 6.49–6.56

. . . .

Learning the Mechanics

6.49   In each case, find the approximate sample size necessary to estimate a binomial proportion p correct to within .03 with probability equal to .90.
   a. Assume you know p is near .8.

b. Assume you have no knowledge of the value of p, but you want to be certain that your sample is large enough to achieve the specified accuracy for the estimate.

6.50 In each case, find the approximate sample size required to construct a 95% confidence interval for p that has width .08.

   a. Assume p is near .2.   **b.** Assume you have no prior knowledge about p.

6.51 The following is a 90% confidence interval for p: (.26, .54). How large was the sample used to construct this interval?

Applying the Concepts

6.52 According to estimates made by the General Accounting Office, the Internal Revenue Service (IRS) answered 18.3 million telephone inquiries during the 1986 tax season and 17% of the IRS offices provided answers that were wrong. These estimates were based on data collected from sample calls to numerous IRS offices (Roper, 1986). How many IRS offices should be randomly selected and contacted in order to estimate the proportion of IRS offices that fail to correctly answer questions about gift taxes with a 90% confidence interval of width .06?

6.53 While corporate executives are probably not as highly stressed as air traffic controllers or inner-city police, research has indicated that they are among the more highly pressured work groups. In order to estimate p, the proportion of managers who perceive themselves to be frequently under stress, Hall and Savery (1986) sampled 532 managers in Western Australian corporations. One hundred ninety of these managers fell into the "high-stress" group. Assume that random sampling was used in this study. Was the sample size large enough to estimate p to within .03 with 95% confidence? Explain.

6.54 The quality director of a firm that manufactures videotapes has recommended that the percentage of defective tapes produced each hour be monitored using 90% confidence intervals. Based on previous testing and consumer complaints, it is believed that about 3% of the tapes produced each hour are defective. How many tapes should be sampled and tested each hour for the sample proportion to be within .01 of the true hourly percentage defective with 90% confidence?

6.55 Suppose you are a retailer and you want to estimate the proportion of your customers who are shoplifters. You decide to select a sample of shoppers and check closely to determine whether they steal any merchandise while in the store. Suppose experience suggests that the percentage of customers who are shoplifters is near 5%. How many customers should you include in your sample if you want to estimate the proportion of shoplifters in your store correct to within .02 with 90% confidence?

6.56 Some quality control testing involves destructive sampling, i.e., the test to determine whether the item is defective destroys the product. This type of sampling is generally expensive, and high costs often prohibit large sample sizes. For example, suppose the National Highway Safety Administration (NHSA) wishes to determine the proportion of new tires that will fail when subjected to hard braking at a speed of 60 miles per hour. NHSA can obtain the tires for $25 (wholesale price) each. Suppose the budget for the experiment is $10,000, and NHSA wishes to estimate the percentage that will fail to within .02 with 95% confidence. If the entire $10,000 can be spent on tires (i.e., ignoring other costs), and assuming that the true fraction that will fail is approximately .05, can NHSA attain its goal while staying within the budget? Explain.

Summary

From the beginning we have stressed that the theme of this text is the use of sample information to make inferences about the parameters of a population. For the first seven chapters, we developed the tools necessary to perform inference-making procedures. In Chapter 6 we discussed the inferential procedure called **estimation**.

Estimation involves both **point estimates** and **interval estimates**. Point estimates are single points calculated from a sample to estimate a population parameter. Interval estimates utilize **confidence coefficients** to express the reliability of the estimate. The confidence coefficient is the probability that the estimation procedure will generate an interval that contains the parameter being estimated. Thus, confidence is expressed in terms of the long-run performance of the estimation procedure.

We used the standard normal z distribution to develop large-sample interval estimates for the population mean μ and the binomial probability p. The t distribution was used to form confidence intervals for the mean of normal distributions when n is small.

Supplementary Exercises 6.57–6.71

6.57 In each of the following instances, determine whether you would use a z statistic, a t statistic, or neither to form a 95% confidence interval; then look up the appropriate z or t value in the tables.
  a. Random sample of size $n = 23$ from a normal distribution with unknown mean μ and standard deviation σ
  b. Random sample of size $n = 135$ from a normal distribution with unknown mean μ and standard deviation σ
  c. Random sample of size $n = 10$ from a normal distribution with unknown mean μ and known standard deviation $\sigma = 5$
  d. Random sample of size $n = 73$ from a distribution about which nothing is known
  e. Random sample of size $n = 12$ from a distribution about which nothing is known

6.58 Let t_0 represent a particular value of t from Table VI of Appendix B. Find the table values such that the following statements are true:
  a. $P(t \leq t_0) = .05$ where df $= 20$
  b. $P(t \geq t_0) = .005$ where df $= 9$
  c. $P(t \leq -t_0$ or $t \geq t_0) = .10$ where df $= 8$
  d. $P(t \leq -t_0$ or $t \geq t_0) = .01$ where df $= 17$

6.59 A large New York City bank is interested in estimating (1) the proportion of weeks in which it processes more than 100,000 checks and (2) the average number of checks it processes per week. The bank maintains records of x, the number of checks processed each week. Suppose the bank records the number of checks, x, processed per week for 50 weeks randomly sampled from among the past 6 years. Define each of the following *in the context of the problem*:

a. $\bar{x}$ b. $\hat{p}$ c. σ_x d. μ_x e. n f. $\sigma_{\bar{x}}$ g. p h. s_x

6.60 A company is interested in estimating μ, the mean number of days of sick leave taken by all its employees. The firm's statistician selects at random 100 personnel files and notes the number of sick days taken by each employee. The following sample statistics are computed:

$$\bar{x} = 12.2 \text{ days} \qquad s = 10 \text{ days}$$

a. Estimate μ using a 90% confidence interval.
b. How many personnel files would the statistician have to select in order to estimate μ to within 2 days with 99% confidence?

6.61 A firm's president, vice presidents, department managers, and others use financial data generated by the firm's accounting system to help them make decisions regarding such things as pricing, budgeting, and plant expansion. To provide reasonable certainty that the system provides reliable data, internal auditors periodically perform various checks of the system (Taylor and Glezen, 1979). Suppose an internal auditor is interested in determining the proportion of sales invoices in a population of 5,000 sales invoices for which the "total sales" figure is in error. She plans to estimate the true proportion of invoices in error based on a random sample of size 100.

a. Assume that the population of invoices is numbered from 1 to 5,000 and that every invoice ending with a 0 is in error (i.e., 10% are in error). Use the random number table (Table I in Appendix B) to draw a random sample of 100 invoices from the population of 5,000 invoices. For example, random number 456 stands for invoice number 456. List the invoice numbers in your sample and indicate which of your sampled invoices are in error (i.e., those ending in a 0).
b. Use the results of your sample of part **a** to construct a 90% confidence interval for the true proportion of invoices in error.
c. Recall that the true population proportion of invoices in error is equal to .1. Compare the true proportion with the estimate of the true proportion you developed in part **b**. Does your confidence interval include the true proportion?

6.62 When companies employ control charts to monitor the quality of their products, a series of small samples is typically used to determine if the process is "in control" during the period of time in which each sample is selected. (We cover quality control charts in Chapter 11.) Suppose a concrete-block manufacturer samples nine blocks per hour and tests the breaking strength of each. During one hour's test the mean and standard deviation are 985.6 pounds per square inch (psi) and 22.9 psi, respectively.

a. Construct a 99% confidence interval for the mean breaking strength of blocks produced during the hour in which the sample was selected.
b. The process is to be considered "out of control" if the mean strength differs from 1,000 psi. What would you conclude based on the confidence interval constructed in part **a**?
c. Repeat parts **a** and **b** using a 90% confidence interval.
d. The manufacturer wants to be reasonably certain that the process is really out of control before shutting down the process and trying to determine the problem. Which interval, the 99% or 90% confidence interval, is more appropriate for making the decision? Explain.
e. Which assumptions are necessary to assure the validity of the confidence intervals?

6.63 The Internal Revenue Service is conducting an audit of the 10,000 outlets of a large fast-food chain. It is interested in determining the average error in reported income last year for all outlets in the chain. The size of the chain precludes a census (an audit of all 10,000 outlets), so 100 outlets are randomly selected and audited. Let x = error in reported income = (actual income − reported income) for a given firm. The audits yielded the following statistics:

$$\bar{x} = \$12,522 \qquad s = \$4,000$$

    a. Construct a 95% confidence interval for the mean error in reported income per outlet.
    b. What does the confidence interval from part **a** reflect regarding the chain's income-reporting behavior last year?

6.64 A market researcher wants to select one sample to estimate both μ, the average age of people living within 5 miles of a proposed shopping mall site, and p, the proportion of people within that 5-mile radius who are between 20 and 40 years of age. He wants to estimate μ with a 95% confidence interval that is no more than 6 years wide and p with a 90% confidence interval of width no greater than .1. It is known from previous studies of this population that the standard deviation of the ages in the population is 10 years, and it is believed that p is near .4. How large a sample does the researcher need to draw to construct confidence intervals for both μ and p that satisfy the above specifications?

6.65 Recycling has received increasing emphasis among environmental concerns as a means of dealing with the significant growth in the trash and garbage of our "throw-away" society. To estimate the degrees of awareness about recycling in one major city, a random sample of 346 households was selected, and 212 were found to use available recycling facilities. Use a 95% confidence interval to estimate the proportion of households in the city who are using available recycling facilities.

6.66 In 1988, tire sales in the United States reached a historic high ("Bounce for Synthetic Rubber: Tires Are Back in the Fast Lane," 1989). Tires made of synthetic rubber are accounting for much of this growth. Suppose one manufacturer is testing a new synthetic rubber design. Twenty tires of the new design are produced and subjected to wear tests. The results indicate that the mean wear for the test tires is 42,250 miles, and the standard deviation is 4,355 miles.
    a. What is the point estimate of the true mean wear for the new design?
    b. Construct a 90% confidence interval estimate for the mean wear associated with the new design.
    c. Which method of estimation is better, point estimation or interval estimation? Why?

6.67 Refer to Exercise 6.66. Suppose that 200 tires rather than 20 were tested, and assume that the sample mean and standard deviation for the 200 tires remain the same: $\bar{x} = 42,250$ miles, $s = 4,355$ miles. Repeat parts **a–c** of Exercise 6.66 and comment on the similarities and differences in your answers.

6.68 In 1987, a case of salmonella (bacterial) poisoning was traced to a particular brand of ice cream bar, and the manufacturer removed its bars from the market. Despite this response, many consumers refused to purchase any brand of ice cream bars for some period of time after the event (McClave, personal communication). One manufacturer conducted a survey of consumers 6 months after the poisoning. A sample of 244 ice cream bar consumers was contacted, and 23 consumers indicated that they would not purchase ice cream bars because of the potential for food poisoning.
    a. What is the point estimate of the true fraction of the entire market who refuse to purchase bars 6 months after the poisoning?
    b. Is the sample size large enough to use the normal approximation for the sampling distribution of the estimator of the binomial probability? Justify your response.

c. Construct a 95% confidence interval for the true proportion of the market who still refuse to purchase ice cream bars 6 months after the event. What assumptions are necessary to assure the validity of the interval?

d. Interpret both the point estimate and confidence interval in terms of this application.

6.69 Refer to Exercise 6.68. Suppose it is now 1 year after the poisoning was traced to ice cream bars. The manufacturer wishes to estimate the proportion who will still not purchase bars using a 95% confidence interval of width .04. How many consumers should be sampled?

6.70 Medicaid health assistance programs are administered by the individual states, even though part of the funding is federal. The federal government requires that the states perform regular audits in order to assure that payments are accurate. One Florida hospital was audited by the Florida Department of Health and Rehabilitative Services (HRS) in 1989, and a random sample of 25 Medicaid claims was selected. The sample mean of the claims was $34.76, and the standard deviation was $11.34.

a. Use a 99% confidence interval to estimate the mean of all claims submitted by this hospital.

b. What assumptions are necessary to assure the validity of this confidence interval?

6.71 Refer to Exercise 6.70.

a. How many claims must be sampled if the HRS wants to estimate the mean size of the hospital's claims to within $1.00 using a 99% confidence interval?

b. If a sample of this size were to be selected and a 99% confidence interval constructed, what assumptions would be necessary to assure the validity of the interval?

On Your Own

Choose a population pertinent to your major area of interest that has an unknown mean (or, if the population is binomial, that has an unknown proportion of success). For example, a marketing major may be interested in the proportion of consumers who prefer a particular product. An advertising major might want to estimate the proportion of the television viewing audience who regularly watch a particular program. An economics major may want to estimate the mean monthly expenditure of college students on food.

Define the parameter you want to estimate and conduct a **pilot study** to obtain an initial estimate of the parameter of interest and, more important, an estimate of the variability associated with the estimator. A pilot study employs a small sample (perhaps 20 to 30 observations) to gain some information about the population of interest. The purpose is to help plan more elaborate future studies. Based on the results of your pilot study, determine the sample size necessary to estimate the parameter to within a reasonable bound (of your choice) with a 95% confidence interval.

Using the Computer

Refer to **Using the Computer** in Chapter 5. Recall the values of the "population" mean μ and standard deviation σ for the 1,000 zip code income measurements. Suppose our objective is to sample from this population and to estimate the mean μ using a 95% confidence interval.

a. Determine the sample size n_1 necessary to estimate μ to within $2,000 with 95% confidence. Then generate 100 95% confidence intervals by repeatedly drawing samples of size n_1 (with replacement) from the 1,000 measurements, and using the sample statistics to form a confidence interval. Treat σ as unknown when forming the confidence intervals. What percentage of the confidence intervals contain μ?

b. Determine the sample size n_2 necessary to estimate μ to within $500 with 95% confidence. Then generate 100 95% confidence intervals by repeatedly drawing samples of size n_2 (with replacement) from the 1,000 measurements, and using the sample statistics to form a confidence interval. Treat σ as unknown when forming the confidence intervals. What percentage of the confidence intervals contain μ?

c. Repeat parts **a** and **b** using an 80% confidence interval. Compare the results.

References

Alters, D. "Teamwork means a share of the gain." *Star Tribune* (Minneapolis), June 29, 1992.

Arshadi, N. and Lawrence, E. C. "A characteristic appraisal of top bank executives." *Journal of Retail Banking*, Winter 1983–1984, Vol. 5, No. 4, pp. 19–25.

"Bounce for synthetic rubber: Tires are back in the fast lane." *Chemical Week*, Apr. 19, 1989, pp. 40–44.

Deming, W. E. *Out of the Crisis*. Cambridge, Mass.: M.I.T. Center for Advanced Study of Engineering, 1986.

Dessler, G. "Personnel tests gain in popularity." *St. Paul Pioneer Press and Dispatch*, Mar. 17, 1986.

Graham, E. "The entrepreneurial mystique." *Wall Street Journal*, May 20, 1985.

Hall, K. and Savery, L. K. "Tight rein, more stress." *Harvard Business Review*, Jan.–Feb. 1986, pp. 160–164.

"One answer to imports: Wonder-iron." *Fortune*, Feb. 9, 1981, p. 71.

Paré, T. P. "Is your 401(k) plan good enough?" *Fortune*, Dec. 28, 1992, pp. 78–83.

Roper, J. E. "Survey: 17% of IRS phone answers wrong." *Minneapolis Star and Tribune*, July 26, 1986.

Sharpe, W. F. and Alexander, G. J. *Investments*, 4th ed. Englewood Cliffs, N.J.: Prentice-Hall, Inc., 1990.

Taylor, D. H. and Glezen, G. W. *Auditing, Integrated Concepts and Procedures*. New York: Wiley, 1979, p. 3.

U.S. Bureau of the Census. *Statistical Abstract of the United States: 1992*. Washington, D.C.: U.S. Government Printing Office, 1992.

Wentling, R. M. "Master the software explosion." *Legal Assistant Today*, Mar./Apr. 1988, Vol. 5, No. 4, pp. 44–51.

CHAPTER SEVEN

Inferences Based on a Single Sample: Tests of Hypotheses

Contents

Case Studies

Where We've Been

We showed how to use sample information to estimate population parameters in Chapter 6. The sampling distribution of a statistic was used to assess the reliability of an estimate, which was expressed in terms of a confidence interval.

Where We're Going

We now show how to utilize sample information to test whether a population parameter is less than, equal to, or greater than a specified value. This type of inference is called a *test of hypothesis*. We show how to conduct a test of hypothesis about a population mean μ and a binomial probability p. But just as with estimation, we stress the measurement of the reliability of the inference. An inference without a measure of reliability is little more than a guess.

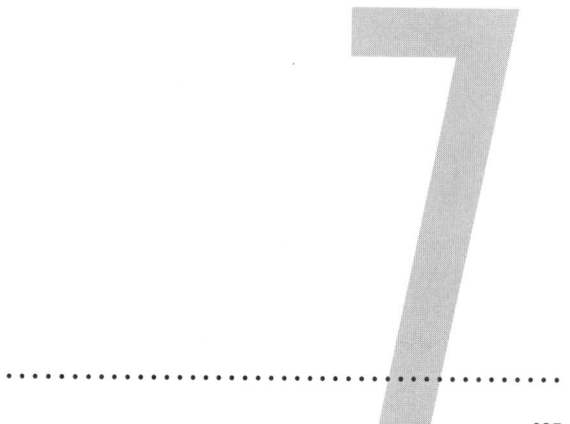

Suppose you want to determine whether the mean waiting time in the drive-through line of a fast-food restaurant exceeds 5 minutes, whether the mean breaking strength of sewer pipe exceeds 2,400 pounds per foot, or whether the majority of consumers are optimistic about the economy. In each case you are interested in making an inference about how the value of a parameter relates to a specific numerical value: Is it less than, equal to, or greater than the specified number? This type of inference is called a **test of hypothesis**, and testing hypotheses is the subject of this chapter.

We introduce the elements of a test of hypothesis in Section 7.1. We then show how to conduct a large-sample test of hypothesis about a population mean in Sections 7.2 and 7.3. In Section 7.4 we utilize small samples to conduct tests about means, while in optional Section 7.5 we consider an alternative nonparametric test. Large-sample tests about binomial probabilities (e.g., population proportions) are the subject of Section 7.6, and some advanced methods for determining the reliability of a test are covered in the optional Section 7.7.

7.1   The Elements of a Test of Hypothesis

Suppose building specifications in a certain city require that the average breaking strength of residential sewer pipe be more than 2,400 pounds per foot of length (that is, per lineal foot). Each manufacturer who wants to sell pipe in this city must demonstrate that its product meets the specification. Note that we are again interested in making an inference about the mean, μ, of a population. However, in this example, we are less interested in estimating the value of μ than we are in **testing a hypothesis** about its value. That is, we want to decide whether the mean breaking strength of the pipe exceeds 2,400 pounds per lineal foot.

The method used to reach a decision is based on the rare event concept explained in earlier chapters. We define two hypotheses: (1) The **null hypothesis** is that which represents the status quo to the party performing the sampling experiment—the hypothesis that will not be rejected unless the data provide convincing evidence that it is false. (2) The **alternative**, or **research, hypothesis** is that which will be accepted only if the data provide convincing evidence of its truth. From the point of view of the city conducting the tests, the null hypothesis is that the manufacturer's pipe does *not* meet specifications unless the tests provide convincing evidence otherwise. The null and alternative hypotheses are therefore:

> *Null hypothesis* (H_0): $\mu \leq 2{,}400$ (i.e., the manufacturer's pipe does not meet specifications)
>
> *Alternative (research) hypothesis* (H_a): $\mu > 2{,}400$ (i.e., the manufacturer's pipe meets specifications)

How can the city decide when enough evidence exists to conclude that the manufacturer's pipe meets specifications? Since the hypotheses concern the value of the population mean μ, it is reasonable to use the sample mean $\bar{x}$ to make the inference, just as we did when forming confidence intervals for μ in Sections 6.1 and 6.2. The city will conclude that the pipe meets specifications only when the sample mean $\bar{x}$ convincingly indicates that the population mean exceeds 2,400 pounds per lineal foot.

"Convincing" evidence in favor of the alternative hypothesis will exist when the value of $\bar{x}$ exceeds 2,400 by an amount that cannot be readily attributed to sampling variability. To decide, we compute a **test statistic**, which will be the z value that measures the distance between the value of $\bar{x}$ and the value of μ specified in the null hypothesis. When the null hypothesis contains more than one value of μ, as in this case (H_0: $\mu \leq 2,400$), we use the value of μ closest to the values specified in the alternative hypothesis. The idea is that if the hypothesis that μ *equals* 2,400 can be rejected in favor of $\mu > 2,400$, then μ *less than or equal to* 2,400 can certainly be rejected. Thus, the test statistic is

$$z = \frac{\bar{x} - 2,400}{\sigma_{\bar{x}}} = \frac{\bar{x} - 2,400}{\sigma/\sqrt{n}}$$

Note that a value of $z = 1$ means that $\bar{x}$ is 1 standard deviation above $\mu = 2,400$; a value of $z = 1.5$ means that $\bar{x}$ is 1.5 standard deviations above $\mu = 2,400$, etc. How large must z be before the city can be convinced that the null hypothesis can be rejected in favor of the alternative, and conclude that the pipe meets specifications?

If you examine Figure 7.1, you will note that the chance of observing a value of $\bar{x}$ more than 1.645 standard deviations above 2,400 is only .05, *if in fact the true mean μ is 2,400.* Thus, if the sample mean is more than 1.645 standard deviations above 2,400, either H_0 is true and a relatively rare event has occurred (probability .05 or less) or H_a is true and the population mean exceeds 2,400. Since we would most likely reject the notion that a rare event has occurred, we would reject the null hypothesis ($\mu \leq 2,400$) and conclude that the alternative hypothesis ($\mu > 2,400$) is true. What is the probability that this procedure will lead us to a wrong decision?

FIGURE 7.1 ▶
The sampling distribution of $\bar{x}$, assuming $\mu = 2,400$

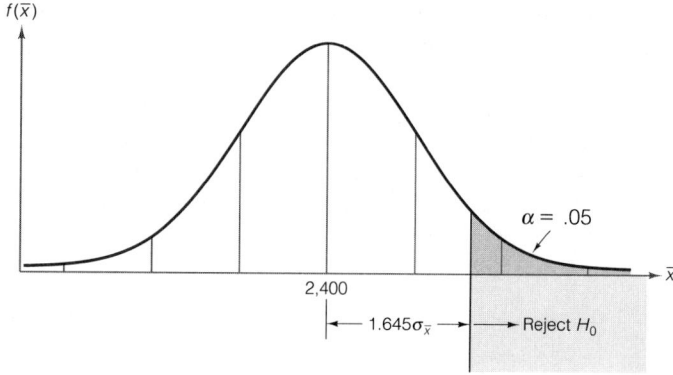

Deciding that the null hypothesis is false when in fact it is true is called a **Type I error**. As indicated in Figure 7.1, the probability of making a Type I error—that is, deciding in favor of the alternative hypothesis when in fact the null hypothesis is true—is only $\alpha = .05$. That is,

$$\alpha = P(\text{Type I error})$$
$$= P(\text{Rejecting the null hypothesis when in fact the null hypothesis is true})$$

In our example,

$$\alpha = P(z > 1.645 \text{ when in fact } \mu = 2,400) = .05$$

Therefore, the test can be summarized as follows:

Null and alternative hypotheses: H_0: $\mu = 2,400$ H_a: $\mu > 2,400$

Test statistic: $z = \dfrac{\bar{x} - 2,400}{\sigma_{\bar{x}}}$

Rejection region: $z > 1.645$ for $\alpha = .05$

To illustrate the use of the test, suppose we tested 50 sections of sewer pipe and found the mean and standard deviation for these 50 measurements of breaking strength to be

$$\bar{x} = 2,460 \text{ pounds per lineal foot} \qquad s = 200 \text{ pounds per lineal foot}$$

As in the case of estimation, we can use s to approximate σ when s is calculated from a large set of sample measurements.

The test statistic is

$$z = \frac{\bar{x} - 2,400}{\sigma_{\bar{x}}} = \frac{\bar{x} - 2,400}{\sigma/\sqrt{n}} \approx \frac{\bar{x} - 2,400}{s/\sqrt{n}}$$

Substituting $\bar{x} = 2,460$, $n = 50$, and $s = 200$, we have

$$z \approx \frac{2,460 - 2,400}{200/\sqrt{50}} = \frac{60}{28.28} = 2.12$$

Therefore, the sample mean lies $2.12\sigma_{\bar{x}}$ above the hypothesized value of μ, 2,400, as shown in Figure 7.2. Since this value of z exceeds 1.645, it falls in the rejection

FIGURE 7.2 ▶
Location of test statistic when $\bar{x} = 2,460$

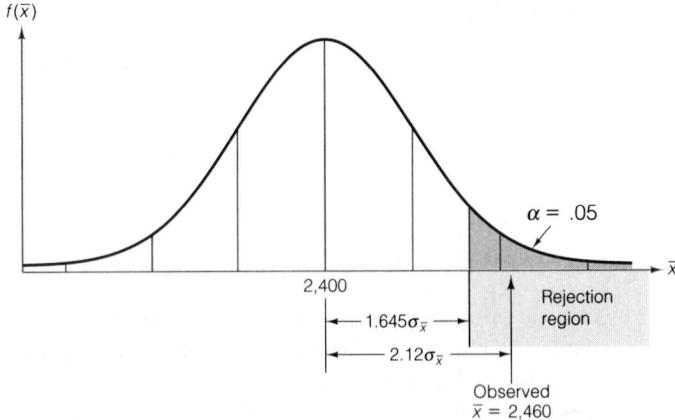

region. That is, we reject the null hypothesis that $\mu = 2,400$ and conclude that $\mu > 2,400$. Thus, it appears that the company's pipe has a mean strength that exceeds 2,400 pounds per lineal foot.

How much faith can be placed in this conclusion? What is the probability that our statistical test would lead us to reject the null hypothesis (and conclude that the company's pipe met the city's specifications) when in fact the null hypothesis was true? The answer is "$\alpha = .05$." That is, we selected the level of risk, α, of making a Type I error when we constructed the test. Thus, the chance is only 1 in 20 that our test would lead us to conclude the manufacturer's pipe satisfied the city's specifications when in fact the pipe does *not* meet specifications.

Now, suppose the sample mean breaking strength for the 50 sections of sewer pipe turned out to be $\bar{x} = 2,430$ pounds per lineal foot. Assuming the sample standard deviation is still $s = 200$, the test statistic is

$$z = \frac{2,430 - 2,400}{200/\sqrt{50}} = \frac{30}{28.28} = 1.06$$

Therefore, the sample mean $\bar{x} = 2,430$ is only 1.06 standard deviations above the null hypothesized value of $\mu = 2,400$. As shown in Figure 7.3, this value does not fall in the rejection region ($z > 1.645$). Therefore, we cannot reject H_0 using $\alpha = .05$. Even though the sample mean exceeds the city's specification of 2,400 by 30 pounds per lineal foot, it does not exceed the specification by enough to provide *convincing* evidence that the *population mean* exceeds 2,400.

FIGURE 7.3 ▶
Location of test statistic when $\bar{x} = 2,430$

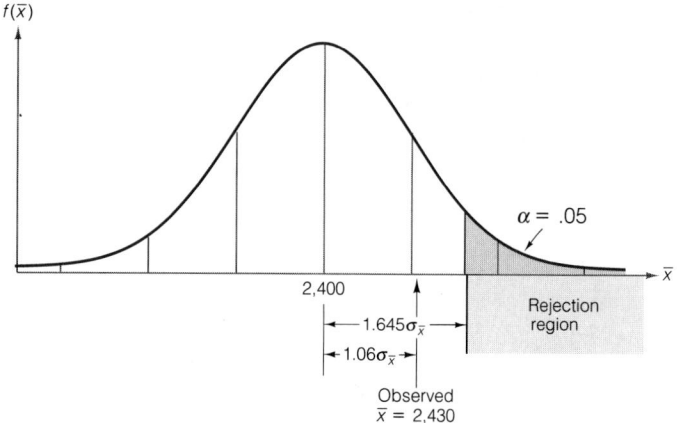

Should we accept the null hypothesis H_0: $\mu \leq 2,400$, and conclude that the manufacturer's pipe does not meet specifications? To do so would be to risk a **Type II error**—that of concluding that the null hypothesis is true (the pipe does not meet specifications) when in fact it is false (the pipe does meet specifications). We will denote the probability of committing a Type II error by β, and we will show in optional Section 7.7 that β is often difficult to determine precisely. Rather than make a decision (accept H_0) for which the probability of error (β) is unknown, we avoid the potential

Type II error by avoiding the conclusion that the null hypothesis is true. Instead, we will simply state that *the sample evidence is insufficient to reject H_0 at α = .05*. Since the null hypothesis is the "status-quo" hypothesis, the effect of not rejecting H_0 is to maintain the status quo. In our pipe-testing example, the effect of having insufficient evidence to reject the null hypothesis that the pipe does not meet specifications is probably to prohibit the utilization of the manufacturer's pipe unless and until there is sufficient evidence that the pipe does meet specifications. That is, until the data indicate convincingly that the null hypothesis is false, we usually maintain the status quo implied by its truth.

Table 7.1 summarizes the four possible outcomes of a test of hypothesis. The "true state of nature" columns in Table 7.1 refer to the fact that either the null hypothesis H_0 is true, or the alternative hypothesis H_a is true. Note that the true state of nature is unknown to the researcher conducting the test. The "decision" rows in Table 7.1 refer to the action of the researcher, assuming that he or she will either conclude that H_0 is true or that H_a is true based on the results of the sampling experiment. Note that a Type I error can be made *only* when the alternative hypothesis is accepted (equivalently, when the null hypothesis is rejected) and a Type II error can be made *only* when the null hypothesis is accepted. Our policy will be to make a decision only when we know the probability of making the error that corresponds to that decision. Since α is usually specified by the analyst, we will generally be able to reject H_0 (accept H_a) when the sample evidence supports that decision. However, since β is usually not specified, we will generally avoid the decision to accept H_0, preferring instead to state that the sample evidence is insufficient to reject H_0 when the test statistic is not in the rejection region.

TABLE 7.1   Decisions and Consequences for a Test of Hypothesis

		True State of Nature	
		H_0 True	H_a True
Decision	H_0 True	Correct decision	Type II error (probability β)
	H_a True	Type I error (probability α)	Correct decision

Elements of a Test of Hypothesis

1. *Null hypothesis* (H_0):   A theory about the values of one or more population parameters. The theory generally represents the status quo, which we do not reject unless we have strong contradictory evidence.

2. *Alternative (research) hypothesis* (H_a):   A theory that contradicts the null hypothesis. The theory generally represents that which we will accept only when sufficient supporting evidence exists.

3. *Test statistic*:   A sample statistic used to decide whether to reject the null hypothesis.

4. *Rejection region*:   The numerical values of the test statistic for which the null hypothesis will be rejected. The rejected region is chosen so that the probability is α that it will contain the test statistic when the null hypothesis is true, thereby leading to a Type I error. The value of α is usually chosen to be small (e.g., .01, .05, or .10), and is referred to as the **level of significance** of the test.

5. *Assumptions*:   Any assumptions made about the population(s) being sampled should be clearly stated.

6. *Sample and calculate test statistic*:   The sample is drawn and the numerical value of the test statistic is determined.

7. *Conclusion*:
   a. If the numerical value of the test statistic falls in the rejection region, we reject the null hypothesis and conclude that the alternative hypothesis is true. We know that the hypothesis-testing process will lead to this conclusion incorrectly (Type I error) only $100\alpha\%$ of the time when H_0 is true.
   b. If the test statistic does not fall in the rejection region, we do not reject H_0. Thus, we reserve judgment about which hypothesis is true. We do not conclude that the null hypothesis is true, because we do not (in general) know the probability β that our test procedure will lead to an incorrect acceptance of H_0 (Type II error).*

The elements of a test of hypothesis are summarized in the preceding box. Note that the first four elements are all specified *before* the sample is drawn. In no case will the results of the sample be used to determine the hypotheses: the data are collected to test the (predetermined) hypotheses, not to formulate them.

CASE STUDY 7.1 / Statistics Is Murder!

The jury trial of an accused murderer is analogous to the statistical hypothesis-testing process. Each of the elements of a test of hypothesis applies to the jury system of deciding the guilt or innocence of the accused:

1. H_0:   The null hypothesis in a jury trial is that the accused is not guilty. The status-quo hypothesis in the American system of justice is innocence, which is assumed to be true until proven otherwise.

---

*In many practical business applications of hypothesis testing, nonrejection leads management to behave as if the null hypothesis were accepted. Accordingly, the distinction between acceptance and nonrejection is frequently blurred in practice. We discuss the issues connected with the acceptance of the null hypothesis and the calculation of β in more detail in (optional) Section 7.7.

2. H_a: The alternative hypothesis is guilt, which is accepted only when sufficient evidence exists to establish its truth.

3. *Test statistic*: The test statistic in a trial is the final vote of the jury, i.e., the number of the jury members who vote "guilty."

4. *Rejection region*: In a murder trial the jury vote must be unanimous in favor of guilt before the null hypothesis of innocence is rejected in favor of the alternative hypothesis of guilt. Thus, for a 12-member jury trial, the rejection region is $x = 12$, where x is the number of "guilty" votes.

5. *Assumption*: The primary assumption made in jury trials concerns the method of selecting the jury. The jury is assumed to represent a random sample of citizens who have no prejudice concerning the case.

6. *Sample and calculate the test statistic*: Sample data are generated through the trial jury's deliberations. The final vote of the jury is analogous to the calculation of the test statistic.

7. *Conclusion*:
   a. If the vote of the jury is unanimous in favor of guilt, the null hypothesis of innocence is rejected and the court concludes that the accused murderer is guilty. Although the court does not, in general, know the probability α that the conclusion is in error, the system relies on the belief that the value is made very small by requiring a unanimous vote before guilt is concluded.

   b. Any vote other than a unanimous one for guilt results in the court reserving judgment about the hypotheses, either by declaring the accused "not guilty," or by declaring a mistrial and repeating the "test" with a new jury. (The latter is analogous to collecting more data and repeating a statistical test of hypothesis.) The court never accepts the null hypothesis by declaring the accused "innocent," perhaps recognizing both that innocence is the "status-quo" hypothesis and does not need to be proved, and that the probability β of incorrectly concluding innocence may be large.

As in the case of tests of statistical hypotheses, we may never know whether the verdict in a murder trial is correct. Instead, we rely on the knowledge that the trial procedure will lead to incorrect conclusions (especially, guilt when the accused is in fact innocent) in only a very small percentage of trials.

Exercises 7.1 – 7.10

Learning the Mechanics

7.1 Which hypothesis, the null or the alternative, is the status-quo hypothesis? Which is the research hypothesis?

7.2 Which elements of a test of hypothesis are used to decide whether to reject the null hypothesis?

7.3 What is the level of significance of a test of a hypothesis?

7.4 What is the difference between Type I and Type II errors in hypothesis testing? How do α and β relate to Type I and Type II errors?

7.5 List the four possible combinations of decisions and true states of nature for a test of hypothesis.

7.6 Why do we (generally) reject the null hypothesis when the test statistic falls in the rejection region, but do not accept the null hypothesis when the test statistic does not fall in the rejection region?

7.7 If you test a hypothesis and reject the null hypothesis in favor of the alternative hypothesis, does your test prove that the alternative hypothesis is correct? Explain.

Applying the Concepts

7.8   In 1895 an Italian criminologist, Cesare Lombroso, proposed that blood pressure be used to test for truthfulness. In the 1930s, William Marston added the measurements of respiration and perspiration to the process and called his machine the **polygraph**—or lie detector. Today, its use in screening job applicants is on the rise in both industry and government (Dujack, 1986). But how well does it work? Physicians Michael Phillips, Allan Brett, and John Beary subjected the polygraph to the same careful testing given to medical diagnostic tests. They found that if 1,000 people were subjected to the polygraph and 500 told the truth and 500 lied, the polygraph would indicate that approximately 185 of the truth-tellers were liars and that approximately 120 of the liars were truth-tellers ("Lie Detectors Can Make a Liar of You," *Discover*, June 1986, p. 7).

   a. In the application of a polygraph test, an individual is presumed to be a truth-teller (H_0) until "proven" a liar (H_a). In this context, what is a Type I error? A Type II error?

   b. According to Phillips, Brett, and Beary, what is the probability (approximately) that a polygraph test will result in a Type I error? A Type II error?

7.9   Pharmaceutical companies spend millions of dollars annually on research and development of new drugs to benefit society. After a new drug is formulated, the pharmaceutical company must subject it to lengthy and involved testing before receiving the necessary permission from the Food and Drug Administration (FDA) to market the drug. The pharmaceutical company must provide substantial evidence that a new drug is safe prior to receiving FDA approval, so that the FDA can confidently certify the safety of the drug.

   a. If the new drug testing were to be placed in a test-of-hypothesis framework, would the null hypothesis be that the drug is safe or unsafe? The alternative hypothesis?

   b. Given the choice of null and alternative hypotheses in part **a**, describe Type I and Type II errors in terms of this application. Define α and β in terms of this application.

   c. If the FDA wants to be very confident that the drug is safe before permitting it to be marketed, is it more important that α or β be small? Explain.

7.10   Sometimes monetary costs can be assigned to the commission of Type I and Type II errors. A comparison of these costs helps to decide how large or small to set α—the probability over which the tester usually has control. Suppose you are the owner of a small company that produces a single product and that has averaged sales of $1,000,000 per year for the past 3 years. One of your employees has conducted a survey and recommends you switch to a different product immediately. If you change your product and he is correct, sales will be $1,010,000 per year. If you change and he is wrong, your company's yearly sales will drop to $400,000. Assume your sales will remain at $1,000,000 per year if you stay with the current product. You are testing with the following hypotheses: H_0: The current product is better; H_a: The new product is better.

   a. Define Type I and Type II errors in terms of this example.

   b. What is the cost over the next three years of a Type I error? Of a Type II error?

   c. Based on your answer to part **b**, at which of the following levels would you set α: .01, .05, .10? Explain.

7.2   Large-Sample Test of Hypothesis About a Population Mean

In Section 7.1 we learned that the null and alternative hypotheses form the basis for a test of hypothesis inference. The null and alternative hypotheses may take one of several forms. In the sewer pipe example, we tested the null hypothesis that the population mean strength of the pipe is less than or equal to 2,400 pounds per lineal foot, against the alternative hypothesis that the mean strength exceeds 2,400. That is, we tested

$$H_0: \quad \mu \leq 2{,}400$$

$$H_a: \quad \mu > 2{,}400$$

This is a **one-tailed** (or **one-sided**) statistical test because the alternative hypothesis specifies that the population parameter (the population mean μ, in this example) is strictly greater than a specified value (2,400, in this example). If the null hypothesis had been $H_0: \mu \geq 2{,}400$ and the alternative hypothesis had been $H_a: \mu < 2{,}400$, the test would still be one-sided, because the parameter is still specified to be on "one side" of the null hypothesis value.

Some statistical investigations seek to show that the population parameter is *either larger or smaller* than some specified value. Such an alternative hypothesis is called a **two-tailed** (or **two-sided**) hypothesis.

While alternative hypotheses are always specified as strict inequalities, such as $\mu < 2{,}400$, $\mu > 2{,}400$, or $\mu \neq 2{,}400$, null hypotheses are usually specified as equalities, such as $\mu = 2{,}400$. Even when the null hypothesis is an inequality, such as $\mu \leq 2{,}400$, we specify $H_0: \mu = 2{,}400$, reasoning that if sufficient evidence exists to show that $H_a: \mu > 2{,}400$ is true when tested against $H_0: \mu = 2{,}400$, then surely sufficient evidence exists to reject $\mu < 2{,}400$ as well. Therefore, the null hypothesis is specified as the value of μ closest to a one-sided alternative hypothesis, and as the only value *not* specified in a two-tailed alternative hypothesis. The steps for selecting the null and alternative hypotheses are summarized in the box.

Steps for Selecting the Null and Alternative Hypotheses

1. Select the **alternative hypothesis** as that which the sampling experiment is intended to establish. The alternative hypothesis will assume one of three forms:

Form	*Example*
One-tailed, upper-tailed	$H_a: \quad \mu > 2{,}400$
One-tailed, lower-tailed	$H_a: \quad \mu < 2{,}400$
Two-tailed	$H_a: \quad \mu \neq 2{,}400$

2. Select the **null hypothesis** as the status quo, that which will be presumed true unless the sample evidence conclusively establishes the alternative hypothesis. The null hypothesis will be specified as the parameter value closest to the alternative in one-tailed tests, and as the complementary (or only unspecified) value to the alternative in two-tailed tests.

   Example: $H_0: \quad \mu = 2{,}400$

The rejection region for a two-tailed test differs from that for a one-tailed test. When we are trying to detect departure from the null hypothesis value in *either* direction, we must establish a rejection region in both tails of the sampling distribution of the test statistic. Figure 7.4(a) and (b) show the one-tailed rejection regions for lower- and upper-tailed tests, respectively. The two-tailed rejection region is illustrated in Figure 7.4(c). Note that a rejection region is established in each tail of the sampling distribution for a two-tailed test.

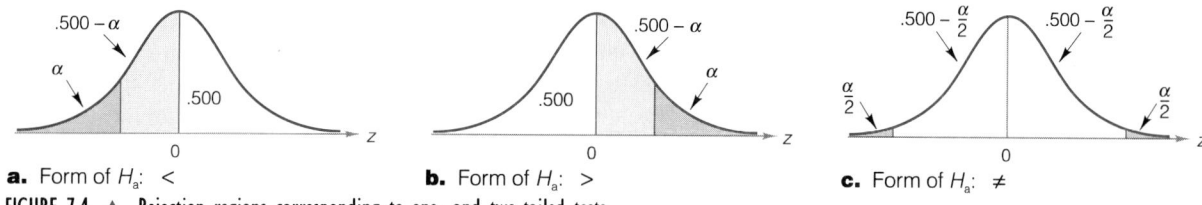

a. Form of H_a: $<$ **b.** Form of H_a: $>$ **c.** Form of H_a: $\neq$

FIGURE 7.4 ▲ Rejection regions corresponding to one- and two-tailed tests

The rejection regions corresponding to typical values selected for α are shown in Table 7.2 for one- and two-tailed tests. Note that the smaller α you select, the more evidence (the larger z) is required before you can reject H_0.

TABLE 7.2   Rejection Regions for Common Values of α

	Alternative Hypothesis		
	Lower-Tailed	Upper-Tailed	Two-tailed
$\alpha = .10$	$z < -1.28$	$z > 1.28$	$z < -1.645$ or $z > 1.645$
$\alpha = .05$	$z < -1.645$	$z > 1.645$	$z < -1.96$ or $z > 1.96$
$\alpha = .01$	$z < -2.33$	$z > 2.33$	$z < -2.576$ or $z > 2.576$

EXAMPLE 7.1

A manufacturer of cereal wants to test the performance of one of its filling machines. The machine is designed to discharge a mean amount of $\mu = 12$ ounces per box, and the manufacturer wants to detect any departure from this setting. This quality control study calls for sampling 100 boxes to determine whether the machine is performing to specifications. Set up a test of hypothesis for this study, using $\alpha = .01$.

Solution

Since the manufacturer wishes to detect a departure from the setting of $\mu = 12$ in either direction, $\mu < 12$ or $\mu > 12$, we conduct a two-tailed statistical test. Following the procedure for selecting the null and alternative hypotheses, we specify as the alternative hypothesis that the mean differs from 12 ounces, since detecting the machine's departure from specifications is the purpose of the quality control study. The null hypothesis is the presumption that the fill machine is operating properly unless the sample data indicate otherwise.

Thus,

$$H_0: \quad \mu = 12$$
$$H_a: \quad \mu \neq 12 \quad \text{(i.e., } \mu < 12 \quad \text{or} \quad \mu > 12)$$

The test statistic measures the number of standard deviations between the observed value of $\bar{x}$ and the null hypothesized value $\mu = 12$:

$$\text{Test statistic:} \quad z = \frac{\bar{x} - 12}{\sigma_{\bar{x}}}$$

The rejection region must be designated to detect a departure from $\mu = 12$ in *either* direction, so we will reject H_0 for values of z that are either too small (negative) or too large (positive). To determine the precise values of z that comprise the rejection region, we first select α, the probability that the test will lead to incorrect rejection of the null hypothesis. Then we divide α equally between the lower and upper tails of the distribution of z, as shown in Figure 7.5. In this example, $\alpha = .01$, so $\alpha/2 = .005$ is placed in each tail. These tail areas correspond to $z = -2.576$ and $z =. 2.576$, respectively (from Table 7.2):

Rejection region: $\quad z < -2.576 \quad$ or $\quad z > 2.576 \quad$ (Figure 7.5)

Assumptions: Since the sample size is large enough ($n > 30$), the Central Limit Theorem will apply, and no assumptions need to be made about the population of fill measurements. The sampling distribution of the sample mean fill of 100 boxes will be approximately normal regardless of the distribution of the individual boxes' fills.

FIGURE 7.5 ►
Two-tailed rejection region:
$\alpha = .01$

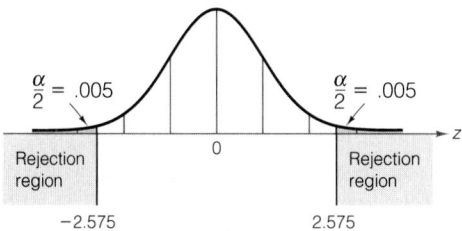

Note that the test in Example 7.1 is set up *before* the sample is drawn; the data are not used to develop the test. Evidently, the manufacturer does not want to disrupt the filling process to adjust the machine unless the sample data provide very convincing evidence that it is not meeting specifications, because the value of α has been set quite low at .01. If the sample evidence results in the rejection of H_0, the manufacturer can be 99% confident that the machine needs adjustment.

Once the test is set up, we are ready to perform the sampling experiment and conduct the test. The test is performed in Example 7.2.

EXAMPLE 7.2

Refer to the quality control test set up in Example 7.1. Suppose the sample yields the following results:

$$n = 100 \text{ observations} \qquad \bar{x} = 11.85 \text{ ounces} \qquad s = .5 \text{ ounce}$$

Use these data to conduct the test of hypothesis.

Solution

Since the test is completely specified in Example 7.1, we simply substitute the sample statistics into the test statistic:

$$z = \frac{\bar{x} - 12}{\sigma_{\bar{x}}} = \frac{\bar{x} - 12}{\sigma/\sqrt{n}} = \frac{11.85 - 12}{\sigma/\sqrt{100}}$$

$$\approx \frac{11.85 - 12}{s/10} = \frac{-.15}{.5/10} = -3.0$$

The implication is that the sample mean, 11.85, is (approximately) 3 standard deviations below the null hypothesized value of 12.0 in the sampling distribution of $\bar{x}$. You can see in Figure 7.5 that this value of z is in the lower-tail rejection region, which consists of all values of $z < -2.575$. These sample data provide sufficient evidence to reject H_0 and conclude, at the $\alpha = .01$ level of significance, that the mean fill differs from the specification of $\mu = 12$ ounces. It appears that the machine is, on average, underfilling the boxes.

Two final points about the test of hypothesis in Example 7.2 apply to all statistical tests:

1. Since z is less than -2.576, it is tempting to state our conclusion at a significance level lower than $\alpha = .01$. We resist the temptation because the level of α is determined *before* the sampling experiment is performed. If we decide that we are willing to tolerate a 1% Type I error rate, the result of the sampling experiment should have no effect on that decision. *In general, the same data should not be used both to determine the significance level and to conduct the test.*

2. When we state our conclusion at the .01 level of significance, we are referring to the failure rate of the *procedure*, not the result of this particular test. We know that the test procedure will lead to the rejection of the null hypothesis only 1% of the time when in fact $\mu = 12$. *Therefore, when the test statistic falls in the rejection region, we infer that the alternative $\mu \neq 12$ is true and express our confidence in the procedure by quoting the α level of significance—that is, the probability that the test leads to a rejection of the null hypothesis when it is true.*

The set-up of a large-sample test of hypothesis about a population mean is summarized in the next box. Both the one- and two-tailed tests are shown.

Large-Sample Test of Hypothesis About μ

One-Tailed Test

H_0: $\mu = \mu_0{}^*$

H_a: $\mu < \mu_0$
     (or H_a: $\mu > \mu_0$)

Test statistic: $z = \dfrac{\bar{x} - \mu_0}{\sigma_{\bar{x}}}$

Rejection region: $z < -z_\alpha$
   (or $z > z_\alpha$ when H_a: $\mu > \mu_0$)

where z_α is chosen so that

$$P(z > z_\alpha) = \alpha$$

Two-Tailed Test

H_0: $\mu = \mu_0{}^*$

H_a: $\mu \neq \mu_0$

Test statistic: $z = \dfrac{\bar{x} - \mu_0}{\sigma_{\bar{x}}}$

Rejection region: $z < -z_{\alpha/2}$
   or $z > z_{\alpha/2}$

where $z_{\alpha/2}$ is chosen so that

$$P(z > z_{\alpha/2}) = \alpha/2$$

Assumptions: No assumptions need to be made about the probability distribution of the population, because the Central Limit Theorem assures us that, for large samples, the test statistic will be approximately normally distributed regardless of the shape of the underlying probability distribution of the population.

Note: μ_0 is the symbol for the numerical value assigned to μ under the null hypothesis.

Once the test has been set up, the sample is drawn and the test statistic is calculated. The next box contains possible conclusions for a test of hypothesis, depending on the result of the sampling experiment.

Possible Conclusions for a Test of Hypothesis

1. If the calculated test statistic falls in the rejection region, reject H_0 and conclude that the alternative hypothesis H_a is true. State that you are rejecting H_0 at the α level of significance. Remember that the significance level refers to the Type I error rate for the testing process, not the particular result of a single test.

2. If the test statistic does not fall in the rejection region, conclude that the sample data do not provide sufficient evidence to reject H_0 at the α level of significance. [Generally, we will not "accept" the null hypothesis unless the probability β of a Type II error has been calculated (see optional Section 7.7).]

CASE STUDY 7.2 / Statistical Quality Control, Part I

In Exercise 5.27 we described a graphical device, known as a control chart, that can be used in business operations to monitor the variation over time in the quality of products and services being produced. The control chart was developed by Walter A. Shewhart of Bell Telephone Laboratories in 1924 and has become a basic tool of quality control engineers and operations managers the world over. Japan's emergence as an industrial superpower is due in part to their early adoption and refinement of quality control techniques, such as the control chart (Duncan, 1986). In this case study and Case Study 7.3, we expand the discussion of control charts and demonstrate that they are simply vehicles for conducting hypothesis tests. We discuss control charts in detail in Chapter 11.

Suppose it is desired to monitor the pitch diameter of the threads on a particular aircraft fitting. When the process is in control, the pitch diameters follow a normal distribution with mean μ_0 and standard deviation σ_0. Recall from Exercise 5.27 that such monitoring can be accomplished by (1) sampling n items from the production process at regular time intervals, (2) measuring the pitch diameter of each item sampled, and (3) plotting the mean diameter of each sample, $\bar{x}$, on a control chart like that in Figure 7.6. Such a control

chart is called an $\bar{x}$-**chart**. If a value of $\bar{x}$ falls above the upper control limit or below the lower control limit, there is strong evidence that the process is out of control—i.e., that the quality of the product being produced does not meet established standards. Otherwise, the process is deemed to be in control.

In the language of hypothesis testing, this decision process can be described as follows:

1. There are two hypotheses of interest:

H_0: Process is in control, $\mu = \mu_0$
H_a: Process is out of control, $\mu \neq \mu_0$

2. The test statistic used to investigate these hypotheses is $\bar{x}$.

3. The upper and lower control limits define the rejection region for the test.

4. Since the control limits are located at $\mu_0 \pm 3\sigma_{\bar{x}}$, the probability of committing a Type I error is $\alpha = .0026$. (Why?)

Thus, each time an analyst plots a sample mean on an $\bar{x}$-chart and observes where it falls in relation to the control limits, the analyst is conducting a two-tailed hypothesis test.

FIGURE 7.6 ▶
$\bar{x}$-chart

Exercises 7.11–7.19

Learning the Mechanics

7.11 For each of the following rejection regions, sketch the sampling distribution of z and indicate the location of the rejection region:

a. $z > 1.96$ b. $z > 1.645$ c. $z > 2.575$

d. $z < -1.29$ e. $z < -1.645$ or $z > 1.645$ f. $z < -2.575$ or $z > 2.575$

g. For each of the rejection regions specified in parts **a–f**, what is the probability that a Type I error will be made?

7.12 A random sample of 64 observations produced the following sums:

$$\sum_{i=1}^{64} x_i = 59.65 \qquad \sum_{i=1}^{64} (x_i - \bar{x})^2 = 8.63$$

a. Test the null hypothesis that $\mu = 1.00$ against the alternative hypothesis that $\mu < 1.00$ using $\alpha = .10$. Interpret the results of the test.

b. Test the null hypothesis that $\mu = 1.00$ against the alternative hypothesis that $\mu \neq 1.00$ using $\alpha = .10$. Interpret the results of the test.

7.13 Suppose you are interested in conducting the following statistical test:

$$H_0: \ \mu = 255 \qquad H_a: \ \mu > 255$$

and you have decided to use the following decision rule: "Reject H_0 if the sample mean of a random sample of 81 items is more than 270." Assume the standard deviation of the population is 63.

a. Express the decision rule in terms of z.

b. Find α, the probability of making a Type I error, for this decision rule.

7.14 A random sample of 70 observations produced the following sums:

$$\sum x_i = 47.46 \qquad \sum x_i^2 = 40.81$$

a. Test the null hypothesis that $\mu = .60$ against the alternative hypothesis that $\mu > .60$. Test using $\alpha = .05$. Interpret the results.

b. Test the null hypothesis that $\mu = .60$ against the alternative hypothesis that $\mu \neq .60$. Test using $\alpha = .05$. Interpret the results.

Applying the Concepts

7.15 A telephone company's records indicate that private customers pay an average of $23.14 per month for long-distance telephone calls; the standard deviation of the amounts paid for long-distance calls is $10.48.

a. If a random sample of 50 bills is taken, what is the probability that the sample mean is greater than $25?

b. If a random sample of 100 bills is taken, what is the probability that the sample mean is greater than $25?

c. The telephone company suspects that the mean amount paid per month per customer for long-distance service has increased. A random sample of 100 customers' bills during a given month produced a sample mean of $27.21 expended for long-distance calls. Do the data indicate that the mean level of the amounts billed per month for long-distance telephone calls has increased from $23.14? Test using $\alpha = .05$.

7.16   In quality control applications of hypothesis testing, the null and alternative hypotheses are frequently specified as

H_0:   The production process is performing satisfactorily.

H_a: The process is performing in an unsatisfactory manner.

Accordingly, α is sometimes referred to as the **producer's risk**, while β is called the **consumer's risk** (Montgomery, 1991). An injection molder produces plastic golf tees. The process is designed to produce tees with a mean weight of .250 ounce. To investigate whether the injection molder is operating satisfactorily, 40 tees were randomly sampled from the last hour's production. Their weights (in ounces) are listed below:

```
.247  .251  .254  .253  .253  .248  .253  .255  .256  .252
.253  .252  .253  .256  .254  .256  .252  .251  .253  .251
.253  .253  .248  .251  .253  .256  .254  .250  .254  .255
.249  .250  .254  .251  .251  .255  .251  .253  .252  .253
```

a. Do the data provide sufficient evidence to conclude that the process is not operating satisfactorily? Test using $\alpha = .05$.
b. In the context of this problem, explain why it makes sense to call α the producer's risk and β the consumer's risk.

7.17   The Environmental Protection Agency (EPA) estimated that the 1994 Polaris automobile obtains a mean of 35 miles per gallon (mpg) on the highway. However, the company that manufactures the car claims that the EPA has underestimated the Polaris' mileage. To support its assertion, the company selects 36 1994 Polaris cars and records the mileage obtained for each car over a driving course similar to the one used by the EPA. The following data resulted:

$$\bar{x} = 37.3 \text{ mpg} \qquad s = 6.4 \text{ mpg}$$

a. If the auto manufacturer wishes to show that the mean mpg for 1994 Polaris autos is greater than 35 mpg, what should the alternative hypothesis be? The null hypothesis?
b. Do the data provide sufficient evidence to support the auto manufacturer's claim? Test using $\alpha = .05$. List any assumptions you make in conducting the test.

7.18   The introduction of printed circuit boards (PCBs) in the 1950s revolutionized the electronics industry. However, solder-joint defects on PCBs have always been a problem. A single PCB may contain thousands of solder joints. Until the 1980s the only way of checking the quality of solder joints was by visual inspection. Because of the low reliability of visual inspection, some manufacturers required each of their joints to be inspected four times by four different people. Now both X-ray and laser technologies are available for use in inspection (Streeter, 1986). A particular manufacturer of laser-based inspection equipment claims that its product can inspect on average at least 10 solder joints per second when the joints are spaced .1 inch apart. The equipment was tested by a potential buyer on 48 different PCBs. In each case, the equipment was operated for exactly 1 second. The numbers of solder joints inspected on each run are as follows:

```
10   9  10  10  11   9  12   8   8   9   6  10   7  10  11   9
 9  13   9  10  11  10  12   8   9   9   9   7  12   6   9  10
10   8   7   9  11  12  10   0  10  11  12   9   7   9   9  10
```

a. The potential buyer wants to know whether the sample data refute the manufacturer's claim. Specify the null and alternative hypotheses that the buyer should test.
b. In the context of this exercise, what is a Type I error? A Type II error?
c. Conduct the hypothesis test described in part **a** and interpret the results in the context of this exercise. Use $\alpha = .05$.

7.19 A company has devised a new ink-jet cartridge for its plain-paper fax machine that it believes has a longer lifetime (on average) than the one currently being produced. To investigate its length of life, 225 of the new cartridges were tested by counting the number of high-quality printed pages each was able to produce. The sample mean and standard deviation were determined to be 1,511.4 pages and 35.7 pages, respectively. The historical average lifetime for cartridges produced by the current process is 1,502.5 pages; the historical standard deviation is 97.3 pages.

a. What are the appropriate null and alternative hypotheses to test whether the mean lifetime of the new cartridges exceeds that of the old cartridges?
b. Use $\alpha = .005$ to conduct the test in part **a**. Do the new cartridges have an average lifetime that is statistically significantly longer than the cartridges currently in production?
c. Does the difference in average lifetimes appear to be of practical significance from the perspective of the consumer? Explain.
d. Should the apparent decrease in the standard deviation in lifetimes associated with the new cartridges be viewed as an improvement over the old cartridges? Explain.

7.3 Observed Significance Levels: *p*-Values

According to the statistical test procedure described in Section 7.2, the value of α and, correspondingly, the rejection region are selected prior to conducting the test, and the conclusion is stated in terms of rejecting or not rejecting the null hypothesis. A second method of presenting the results of a statistical test reports the extent to which the test statistic disagrees with the null hypothesis and leaves to the reader the task of deciding whether to reject the null hypothesis. This measure of disagreement is called the **observed significance level** (or ***p*-value**) for the test.

> ### Definition 7.1
>
> The **observed significance level**, or ***p*-value**, for a specific statistical test is the probability, assuming H_0 is true, of observing a value of the test statistic that is at least as contradictory to the null hypothesis (and as supportive of the alternative hypothesis) as the actual one computed from the sample data.

For example, the value of the test statistic computed for the sample of $n = 50$ sections of sewer pipe was $z = 2.12$. Since the test was one-tailed—i.e., $H_a: \mu > 2,400$—values of the test statistic even more contradictory to H_0 than the one observed would be values larger than $z = 2.12$. Therefore, the observed significance level (*p*-value) for this test is

$$p\text{-value} = P(z \geq 2.12)$$

or, equivalently, the area under the standard normal curve to the right of $z = 2.12$ (see Figure 7.7).

FIGURE 7.7 ▶
Finding the *p*-value for an upper-tail test when $z = 2.12$

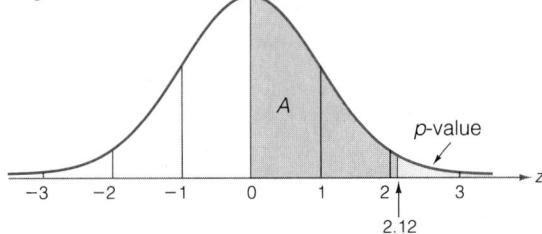

The area A in Figure 7.7 is given in Table IV of Appendix B as .4830. Therefore, the upper-tail area corresponding to $z = 2.12$ is

$$p\text{-value} = .5 - .4830 = .0170$$

Consequently, we say these test results are highly significant; that is, they disagree rather strongly with the null hypothesis, $H_0: \mu = 2{,}400$, and favor $H_a: \mu > 2{,}400$. The probability of observing a z value at least as large as 2.12 is only .0170, if in fact H_0 is true.

If you are inclined to select $\alpha = .05$ for this test, then you would reject the null hypothesis because the *p*-value for the test, .0170, is less than .05. In contrast, if you choose $\alpha = .01$, you would not reject the null hypothesis because the *p*-value for the test is larger than .01. Thus, the use of the observed significance level is identical to the test procedure described in the preceding sections except that the choice of α is left to the reader.

The steps for calculating the *p*-value corresponding to a test statistic for a population mean are given in the box.

Steps for Calculating the *p*-Value for a Test of Hypothesis

1. Determine the value of the test statistic z from the sample data.
2. a. If the test is one-tailed, the *p*-value is equal to the tail area beyond z in the same direction as the alternative hypothesis. Thus, if the alternative hypothesis is of the form ">," the *p*-value is the area to the right of, or above, the observed z value. Conversely, if the alternative is of the form "<," the *p*-value is the area to the left of, or below, the observed z value.
   b. If the test is two-tailed, the *p*-value is equal to twice the tail area beyond the observed z value in the direction of the sign of z. That is, if z is positive, the *p*-value is twice the area to the right of, or above, the observed z value. Conversely, if z is negative, the *p*-value is twice the area to the left of, or below, the observed z value.

EXAMPLE 7.3

Find the observed significance level for the test of the mean filling weight in Examples 7.1 and 7.2.

Solution

Example 7.1 presented a two-tailed test of the hypothesis

$$H_0: \quad \mu = 12 \text{ ounces}$$

against the alternative hypothesis

$$H_a: \quad \mu \neq 12 \text{ ounces}$$

The observed value of the test statistic in Example 7.2 was $z = -3.0$, and any value of z less than -3.0 or greater than $+3.0$ (because this is a two-tailed test) would be even more contradictory to H_0. Therefore, the observed significance level for the test is

$$p\text{-value} = P(z < -3.0 \quad \text{or} \quad z > +3.0)$$

Thus, we calculate the area below the observed z value, $z = -3.0$, and double it. From Table IV of Appendix B, we find that $P(z < -3.0) = .5 - .4987 = .0013$. Therefore, the p-value for this two-tailed test is

$$2P(z < -3.0) = 2(.0013)$$
$$= .0026$$

We can interpret this p-value as a strong indication that the machine is not filling the boxes according to specifications since we would observe a test statistic this extreme or more extreme only 26 in 10,000 times if the machine were meeting specifications ($\mu = 12$). The extent to which the mean differs from 12 could be better determined by calculating a confidence interval for μ.

When publishing the results of a statistical test of hypothesis in journals, case studies, reports, etc., many researchers make use of p-values. Instead of selecting α and then conducting a test as outlined in this chapter, the researcher will compute and report the value of the approximate test statistic and its associated p-value. It is left to the reader of the report to judge the significance of the result—i.e., the reader must determine whether to reject the null hypothesis in favor of the alternative hypothesis, based on the reported p-value. This p-value is often referred to as the **observed significance level** of the test. Usually, the null hypothesis will be rejected if the observed significance level is *less* than the fixed significance level, α, chosen by the reader. The inherent advantages of reporting test results in this manner are twofold: (1) readers are able to draw their own conclusions about the reported hypothesis test by choosing α themselves and comparing it to the reported p-value and (2) a measure of the degree of significance of the test result (i.e., the p-value) is provided.

> ### How to Decide Whether to Reject H_0 Using Reported p-Values
>
> 1. Choose the maximum value of α you are willing to tolerate.
> 2. If the observed significance level (p-value) of the test is less than the chosen value of α, then reject the null hypothesis. Otherwise, do not reject the null hypothesis.

Exercises 7.20–7.33

Learning the Mechanics

7.20 If a hypothesis test were conducted using $\alpha = .05$, for which of the following p-values would the null hypothesis be rejected?
a. .06   b. .10   c. .01   d. .001   e. .251   f. .042

7.21 For each α and observed significance level (p-value) pair, indicate whether the null hypothesis would be rejected.
a. $\alpha = .05$, p-value $= .10$ b. $\alpha = .10$, p-value $= .05$ c. $\alpha = .01$, p-value $= .001$
d. $\alpha = .025$, p-value $= .05$ e. $\alpha = .10$, p-value $= .45$

7.22 Explain the difference between statistical significance and practical significance.

7.23 An analyst tested the null hypothesis $\mu \geq 34$ against the alternative hypothesis that $\mu < 34$. The analyst reported a p-value of .083. What is the smallest value of α for which the null hypothesis would be rejected?

7.24 In a test of H_0: $\mu \leq 178$ against H_a: $\mu > 178$, the sample data yielded the test statistic $z = 1.83$. Find the p-value for the test.

7.25 In a test of H_0: $\mu = 178$ against H_a: $\mu \neq 178$, the sample data yielded the test statistic $z = 1.77$. Find the p-value for the test.

7.26 In a test of H_0: $\mu \geq 178$ against H_a: $\mu < 178$, the sample data yielded the test statistic $z = -2.13$. Find the observed significance level of the test.

7.27 In a test of the hypothesis H_0: $\mu = 35$ versus H_a: $\mu > 35$, a sample of $n = 100$ observations possessed mean $\bar{x} = 35.7$ and standard deviation $s = 3.1$. Find and interpret the p-value for this test.

7.28 In a test of the hypothesis H_0: $\mu = 70$ versus H_a: $\mu \neq 70$, a sample of $n = 50$ observations possessed mean $\bar{x} = 69.4$ and standard deviation $s = 2.9$. Find and interpret the p-value for this test.

Applying the Concepts

7.29 The manufacturer of an over-the-counter pain reliever claims that its product brings pain relief to headache sufferers in less than 3.5 minutes, on average. To be able to make this claim in its television advertisements, the manufacturer was required by a particular television network to present statistical evidence in support of the claim. The manufacturer reported that for a random sample of 50 headache sufferers, the mean time to relief was 3.3 minutes and the standard deviation was 66 seconds.

a. Do these data support the manufacturer's claim? Test using $\alpha = .05$.

b. Report the p-value of the test.

c. In general, do large p-values or small p-values support the manufacturer's claim? Explain.

7.30 Refer to Exercise 7.16, in which the performance of an injection molder that produces plastic golf tees was investigated. Find the p-value for the test and interpret its value.

7.31 The *Chronicle of Higher Education Almanac* (Aug. 1992) reported that for the 1990–1991 academic year, 4-year private colleges charged students an average of $9,083 for tuition and fees, whereas at 4-year public colleges the average was $1,888. Suppose that for 1992–1993 a random sample of 30 private colleges yielded the following data on tuition and fees: $\bar{x} = \$9,667$ and $s = \$1,721$. Assume that $9,083 is the population mean for 1990–1991.

a. Specify the null and alternative hypotheses you would use to investigate whether the mean amount for tuition and fees in 1992–1993 was significantly larger (in the statistical sense) than it was in 1990–1991.

b. The data are submitted to a statistical software package, and the following results are obtained:

```
Z = 1.86        P-VALUE = .0314
```

Check these calculations, and interpret the result.

c. Explain the difference between statistical significance and practical significance in the context of this exercise.

7.32 Florida's housing market remains strong due to the steady stream of new residents fleeing harsh northern winters. The state association of realtors claims that during the last 6 months the mean sale price of a new home in Florida was $101,335. A realtor who believes this figure is too low obtains a random sample of 40 sale prices from a list of all homes sold in Florida during the last 6 months. The sample mean and standard deviation were: $\bar{x} = \$104,754$, $s = \$10,254$.

a. The realtor wishes to conduct a hypothesis test to substantiate her belief. Identify the null and alternative hypotheses of interest to the realtor.

b. Find the observed significance level for this test and interpret its value.

7.33 Recall Exercise 7.19, in which we tested the null hypothesis $H_0: \mu \leq 1,502.5$ versus the alternative $H_a: \mu > 1,502.5$, where μ is the mean lifetime of new cartridges for fax machines. The sample data were analyzed using a statistical software package, with the following results:

```
Z = 1.37        P-VALUE = .0853
```

a. Interpret the results.

b. If the test were two-tailed, how would the p-value change? Interpret the two-tailed p-value.

7.4   Small-Sample Test of Hypothesis About a Population Mean

A manufacturer of computer disk drives monitors the retail prices of its drives in order to gauge the market. For one type of drive the list price is $750, and the manufacturer wishes to know whether the current mean retail price differs from the list price. Seventeen retail establishments are sampled, and their current prices for the drive are determined. The mean and standard deviation for the 17 retail prices are calculated:

$$\bar{x} = \$732 \qquad s = \$38$$

Does this sample provide sufficient evidence to conclude that the mean retail price differs from the list price of $750?

This inference can be placed in a test of hypothesis framework. We establish the null hypothesized value as the list price and then utilize a two-tailed alternative to test whether the true mean retail price differs from the list price:

$$H_0: \quad \mu = \$750$$
$$H_a: \quad \mu \neq \$750$$

Recall from Section 6.3 that when we are faced with making inferences about a population mean using the information in a small sample, two problems emerge:

1. The normality of the sampling distribution for $\bar{x}$ does not follow from the Central Limit Theorem when the sample size is small. We must assume that the distribution of measurements from which the sample was selected is approximately normally distributed in order to assure the approximate normality of the sampling distribution of $\bar{x}$.

2. If the population standard deviation σ is unknown, as is usually the case, then we cannot assume that s will provide a good approximation for σ when the sample size is small. Instead, we must use the t distribution rather than the standard normal z distribution to make inferences about the population mean μ.

Therefore, for the test statistic of a small-sample test of a population mean, we use the t statistic:

$$\textit{Test statistic:} \quad t = \frac{\bar{x} - \mu_0}{s/\sqrt{n}} = \frac{\bar{x} - 750}{s/\sqrt{n}}$$

where μ_0 is the null hypothesized value of the population mean, μ. In our example, $\mu_0 = \$750$.

To find the rejection region we must specify the value of α, the probability that the test will lead to rejection of the null hypothesis when it is true, and then consult the t table (Table VI of Appendix B or inside front cover). Using $\alpha = .05$, the two-tailed rejection region is:

$$\textit{Rejection region:} \quad t_{\alpha/2} = t_{.025} = 2.120 \text{ with } n - 1 = 16 \text{ degrees of freedom.}$$
$$\text{Reject } H_0 \text{ if } t < -2.120 \text{ or } t > 2.120.$$

The rejection region is shown in Figure 7.8.

FIGURE 7.8 ▶
Two-tailed rejection region for
small-sample *t*-test

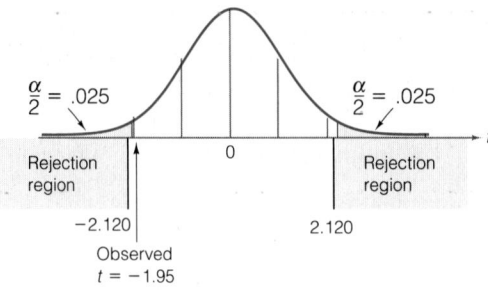

We are now prepared to calculate the test statistic and reach a conclusion:

$$t = \frac{\bar{x} - \mu_0}{s/\sqrt{n}} = \frac{732 - 750}{38/\sqrt{17}} = \frac{-18}{9.22} = -1.95$$

Since the calculated value of t does not fall in the rejection region (Figure 7.8), we cannot reject H_0 at the $\alpha = .05$ level of significance. Thus, based on the sample evidence, the manufacturer should not conclude that the mean retail price differs from the \$750 list price based on the sample evidence.

We summarize the technique for conducting a small-sample test of hypothesis about a population mean in the box.

Small-Sample Test of Hypothesis About μ

One-Tailed Test

H_0: $\mu = \mu_0$

H_a: $\mu < \mu_0$
   (or H_a: $\mu > \mu_0$)

Test statistic: $t = \dfrac{\bar{x} - \mu_0}{s/\sqrt{n}}$

Rejection region: $t < -t_\alpha$
   (or $t > t_\alpha$ when H_a: $\mu > \mu_0$)

Two-Tailed Test

H_0: $\mu = \mu_0$

H_a: $\mu \neq \mu_0$

Test statistic: $t = \dfrac{\bar{x} - \mu_0}{s/\sqrt{n}}$

Rejection region: $t < -t_{\alpha/2}$
   or $t > t_{\alpha/2}$

where t_α and $t_{\alpha/2}$ are based on $(n - 1)$ degrees of freedom.

Assumption: A random sample is selected from a population with a relative frequency distribution that is approximately normal.

Remember, the basic assumption necessary for the use of the t statistic is that the sampled population has a relative frequency distribution that is approximately normal.

What can be done if you know that the population relative frequency distribution is decidedly nonnormal, say highly skewed?

> ### What Can Be Done If the Population Relative Frequency Distribution Departs Greatly From Normal?
>
> *Answer:*   Use the nonparametric sign test described in optional Section 7.5.

EXAMPLE 7.4

A major car manufacturer wants to test a new engine to determine whether it meets new air pollution standards. The mean emission, μ, of all engines of this type must be less than 20 parts per million of carbon. Ten engines are manufactured for testing purposes, and the mean and standard deviation of the emissions for this sample of engines are determined to be

$$\bar{x} = 17.1 \text{ parts per million} \qquad s = 3.0 \text{ parts per million}$$

Do the data supply sufficient evidence to allow the manufacturer to conclude that this type of engine meets the pollution standard? Assume that the manufacturer is willing to risk a Type I error with probability equal to $\alpha = .01$.

Solution

The manufacturer wants to establish the alternative hypothesis that the mean emission level, μ, for all engines of this type is less than 20 ppm. The elements of this small-sample one-tailed test are

H_0: $\mu = 20$

H_a: $\mu < 20$

Test statistic: $t = \dfrac{\bar{x} - 20}{s/\sqrt{n}}$

Assumption: The relative frequency distribution of the population of emission levels for all engines of this type is approximately normal.

Rejection region: For $\alpha = .01$ and df $= n - 1 = 9$, the one-tailed rejection region (see Figure 7.9) is $t < -t_{.01} = -2.821$.

FIGURE 7.9 ▶

Rejection region for Example 7.4

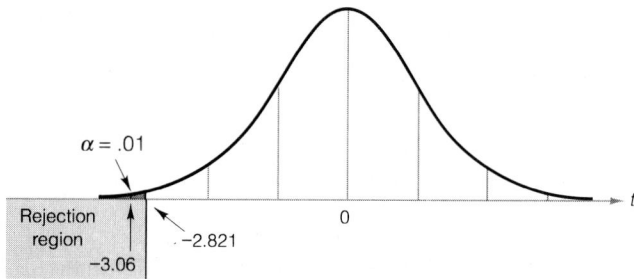

Rejection region

$\alpha = .01$

-3.06 -2.821 0 t

We now calculate the test statistic:

$$t = \frac{\bar{x} - 20}{s/\sqrt{n}} = \frac{17.1 - 20}{3.0/\sqrt{10}} = -3.06$$

Since the calculated t falls in the rejection region (see Figure 7.9), the manufacturer concludes that $\mu < 20$ parts per million and the new engine type meets the pollution standard. Are you satisfied with the reliability associated with this inference? The probability is only $\alpha = .01$ that the test would support the alternative hypothesis if in fact it was false.

EXAMPLE 7.5

Find the observed significance level for the test in Example 7.4.

Solution

The test performed in Example 7.4 was a one-tailed test, in which $H_0: \mu = 20$ would be rejected in favor of $H_a: \mu < 20$ for values of t in the lower tail of the t distribution. Since the value of t computed from the sample data was $t = -3.06$, the observed significance level (or p-value) for the test is equal to the probability that t would assume a value less than or equal to -3.06, if in fact H_0 were true. This is equal to the area in the lower tail of the t distribution (shaded in Figure 7.10). To find this area—i.e., the p-value for the test—we consult the t table in Table VI of Appendix B. Unlike the table of areas under the normal curve, Table VI gives only the t values corresponding to the areas .100, .050, .025, .010, .005, .001, and .0005. Therefore, we can only approximate the p-value for the test. Since the observed t value was based on 9 degrees of freedom, we use the df = 9 row in Table VI and move across the row until we reach the t value that is closest to the observed $t = -3.06$. [Note: We ignore the minus sign.] The t values corresponding to p-values of .010 and .005 are 2.821 and 3.250, respectively. Since the observed t value falls between $t_{.010}$ and $t_{.005}$, the p-value for the test lies between .010 and .005.

FIGURE 7.10 ▶
The observed significance level for the test in Example 7.4

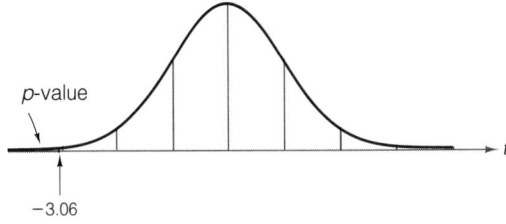

p-value

-3.06

t

Small-sample inferences typically require more assumptions and provide less information about the population parameter than do large-sample inferences. Nevertheless, the t test is a viable method of testing a hypothesis about a population mean of a normal distribution when only a small number of observations is available.

Exercises 7.34–7.46

Learning the Mechanics

7.34 In what ways are the distributions of the z-test statistic and t-test statistic alike? How do they differ?

7.35 Under what circumstances should you use the t distribution in testing a hypothesis about a population mean?

7.36 For each of the following rejection regions, sketch the sampling distribution of t and indicate the location of the rejection region on your sketch:
a. $t > 1.440$ where df $= 6$ **b.** $t < -1.782$ where df $= 12$
c. $t < -2.060$ or $t > 2.060$ where df $= 25$

7.37 For each of the rejection regions defined in Exercise 7.36, what is the probability that a Type I error will be made?

7.38 The following sample of five measurements was randomly selected from a normally distributed population: 11.78, 11.14, 9.81, 9.25, 8.75, 10.34.
a. Test the null hypothesis that the mean of the population is 11 against the alternative hypothesis, $\mu < 11$. Use $\alpha = .05$.
b. Test the null hypothesis that the mean of the population is 11 against the alternative hypothesis, $\mu \neq 11$. Use $\alpha = .05$.

7.39 Find the observed significance level for each test in Exercise 7.38.

7.40 Refer to Exercise 7.38.
a. Find a 95% confidence interval for μ.
b. Give the value of t that would be used to form a 90% confidence interval for μ.
c. Describe a practical situation that would motivate you to form a confidence interval for μ rather than testing a hypothesis about μ.

7.41 A statistical software package is used to conduct a t-test for the null hypothesis $H_0: \mu = 1,000$ versus the alternative hypothesis $H_a: \mu > 1,000$ based on a sample of 17 observations. The software's output is:

$$\overline{\text{T = 1.894} \qquad \text{P-VALUE = .0382}}$$

a. Most software does not indicate what assumptions are necessary for the validity of a statistical procedure. What assumptions are necessary for the validity of this procedure?
b. Interpret the results of the test.
c. Suppose the alternative hypothesis had been the two-tailed $H_a: \mu \neq 1,000$. If the t statistic were unchanged, then what would the p-value be for this test? Interpret the p-value for the two-tailed test.

Applying the Concepts

7.42 In any bottling process, a manufacturer will lose money if the bottles contain either more or less than is claimed on the label. Suppose a quality manager for a catsup company is interested in testing whether the mean number of ounces of catsup per family-size bottle differs from the labeled amount of 20 ounces. The manager samples nine bottles, measures the weight of their contents, and finds that $\bar{x} = 19.7$ ounces and $s = .3$ ounce.

a. Does the sample evidence indicate that the catsup dispensing machine needs adjustment? Test at $\alpha = .05$.
b. What is the p-value for the hypothesis test you conducted in part **a**?
c. What assumptions are necessary so that the procedure used in part **a** is valid?
d. Find a 90% confidence interval for the mean number of ounces of catsup being dispensed.

7.43 A company purchases large quantities of naphtha in 50-gallon drums. Because the purchases are ongoing, small shortages in the drums can represent a sizable loss to the company. The weights of the drums vary slightly from drum to drum, so the weight of the naphtha is measured after removing it from the drums. Suppose the company samples the contents of 20 drums, measures the naphtha in each, and calculates $\bar{x} = 49.70$ gallons and $s = .32$ gallon. Do the sample statistics provide sufficient evidence to indicate that the mean fill per 50-gallon drum is less than 50 gallons? Use $\alpha = .10$. List your assumptions.

7.44 To instill customer loyalty, airlines, hotels, rental car companies, and credit card companies (among others) have initiated **frequency marketing programs** that reward their regular customers. In the United States alone, 30 million people are members of the frequent flier programs of the airline industry (Rice, 1993). A large fast-food restaurant chain wished to explore the profitability of such a program. They randomly selected 12 of their 1,200 restaurants nationwide and instituted a frequency program that rewarded customers with a $5.00 gift certificate after every 10 meals purchased at full price. They ran the trial program for 3 months. The restaurants not in the sample had an average increase in profits of $1,047.34 over the previous 3 months, whereas the restaurants in the sample had the following changes in profit:

$2,232.90　$ 545.47　$3,440.70　$1,809.10　$6,552.70　　$4,798.70
$2,965.00　$2,610.70　$3,381.30　$1,591.40　$2,376.20　−$2,191.00

Note that the last number is negative, representing a decrease in profits.
a. Specify the appropriate null and alternative hypotheses for determining whether the mean profit change for restaurants with frequency programs is significantly greater (in a statistical sense) than $1,047.34.
b. Conduct the test of part **b** using $\alpha = .05$. Does it appear that the frequency program would be profitable for the company if adopted nationwide?

7.45 In a nationwide survey of 1,000 men and women conducted by Caldwell Davis Partners (an advertising agency), it was found that two-thirds of the people surveyed perceived themselves as younger than their actual chronological age. This may explain the recent failures of a line of food advertised for senior citizens and a shampoo directed at "hair over 40." However, men and women under 30 generally perceived themselves as older than their actual age (Nemy, 1982). A researcher randomly sampled 10 college students under the age of 30 and asked them how old they were and how old they perceived themselves to be. The results are shown in the table:

Chronological Age:　20 19 25 22 26 19 18 20 20 21
Perceived Age:　　　22 21 30 25 22 19 20 18 21 21

a. Do the sample data support the survey's findings with respect to the perceptions of men and women under age 30? Test using $\alpha = .10$.
b. What assumption must hold for the procedure you used in part **a** to be valid?

7.46 The Occupational Safety and Health Act of 1970 (OSHA) allows issuance of engineering standards to assure safe workplaces for all Americans. In 1975, the standards for exposure to arsenic in smelters, herbicide production facilities, and other places where arsenic is used were reviewed, and the previous maximum allowable level of .5 milligram per cubic meter of air was reduced to .004. Suppose smelters at two plants are being investigated to determine whether they are meeting OSHA standards. Two analyses of the air are made at each plant, and the results (in milligrams per cubic meter of air) are shown in the table.

Plant 1		Plant 2	
Observation	Arsenic Level	Observation	Arsenic Level
1	.01	1	.05
2	.005	2	.09

a. What are the appropriate null and alternative hypotheses if we wish to test whether the plants meet the current OSHA standard?

b. These data are analyzed by statistical software, with the following results:

```
PLANT 1      T = 1.40      P-VALUE = .200
PLANT 2      T = 3.30      P-VALUE = .094
```

Check the calculations of the t statistics and p-values.

c. Interpret the results of the two tests.

7.5 A Nonparametric Test About a Population Median (Optional)

In Sections 7.2–7.4 we utilized the z and t statistics for testing hypotheses about a population mean. The z statistic is appropriate for large random samples selected from "general" populations—i.e., with few limitations on the probability distribution of the underlying population. The t statistic was developed for small-sample tests when the sample is selected at random from a *normal* distribution. The question is: How can we conduct a test of hypothesis when we have a small sample from a **nonnormal** distribution?

The **sign test** is a relatively simple nonparametric procedure to test hypotheses about the central tendency of a nonnormal probability distribution. Note that we used the phrase *central tendency* rather than *population mean*. This is because the sign test, like many nonparametric procedures, provides inferences about the population **median**, M, rather than the population mean, μ. Remember (Chapter 2) that the median is the 50th percentile of the distribution (Figure 7.11 on page 356) and as such is less affected by the skewness of the distribution and the presence of outliers (extreme observations) than the mean. Since the nonparametric test must be suitable for all distributions, not just the normal, it is reasonable for nonparametric tests to focus on the more robust (less sensitive to extreme values) measure of central tendency, the median.

FIGURE 7.11 ▶
Location of the population median, M

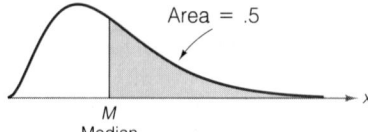

For example, suppose that a large metropolitan bank regularly samples several of its commercial loan accounts in order to audit their current financial stability. One of the important financial statistics calculated is the debt-to-equity ratio, and the bank's board of directors wants to be sure that at least 50% of its commercial loan accounts have debt-to-equity ratios of less than 1.25 (that is, corporate debt is less than 1.25 times the company's equity). An audit of a random sample of eight commercial accounts produced the following debt-to-equity ratios:

1.18	.51	4.79	1.20	.77	1.23	1.06	1.04

If the objective is to determine whether the median is less than 1.25, we establish that as our alternative hypothesis and test

$$H_0: \quad M = 1.25 \qquad H_a: \quad M < 1.25$$

The one-tailed sign test is conducted by counting the number of sample measurements that "favor" the alternative hypothesis—in this case, the number that are less than 1.25. If the null hypothesis is true, we expect approximately half of the measurements to fall on each side of the hypothesized median; and if the alternative is true, we expect significantly more than half to favor the alternative—i.e., to be less than 1.25. Thus:

Test statistic: $\ S = $ Number of measurements less than 1.25, the null hypothesized median

If we wish to conduct the test at the $\alpha = .05$ level of significance, then the rejection region can be expressed in terms of the observed significance level, or p-value, of the test:

Rejection region: $\ p$-value $\leq .05$

In this example, $S = 7$ of the 8 companies have debt-to-equity ratios less than 1.25. To determine the observed significance level associated with this outcome, we note that the number of measurements less than 1.25 is a binomial random variable (check the binomial characteristics presented in Chapter 4), and *if H_0 is true,* the binomial probability p that a measurement lies below (or above) the median 1.25 is equal to .5 (Figure 7.11. What is the probability of obtaining a result *as contrary or more contrary* to H_0 than the one observed? That is, what is the probability that 7 *or more* of 8 binomial measurements will result in success (be less than 1.25) if the probability of success is .5? Table II in Appendix B indicates that

$$P(x \geq 7) = 1 - P(x \leq 6)$$
$$= 1 - .965$$
$$= .035$$

using $n = 8$ and $p = .5$. Thus, the probability that at least 7 of 8 companies would have ratios less than 1.25 *if the true median were* 1.25 is only .035. The p-value of the test is therefore .035, which is less than $\alpha = .05$. We therefore conclude that this sample provides sufficient evidence to reject the null hypothesis. The implication of this rejection is that the bank can conclude at the $\alpha = .05$ level of significance that the true median debt-to-equity ratio of its commercial loans is less than 1.25. However, we note that one of the loans greatly exceeds the others, with a ratio of 4.79, and deserves special attention. Note that this large ratio is an outlier that would make the use of a t test and its commensurate assumption of normality dubious.

The use of the sign test for testing hypotheses about population medians is summarized in the box.

Sign Test for a Population Median *M*

One-Tailed Test	*Two-Tailed Test*
H_0: $M = M_0$	H_0: $M = M_0$
H_a: $M > M_0$	H_a: $M \neq M_0$
[or H_a: $M < M_0$]	

Test statistic:

S = Number of sample measurements greater than M_0
[or S = Number of sample measurements less than M_0]

Test statistic:

S = Larger of S_1 and S_2 where S_1 = Number of measurements less than M_0 and S_2 = Number of measurements greater than M_0

Observed significance level:

p-value = $P(x \geq S)$

Observed significance level:

p-value = $2P(x \geq S)$

where x has a binomial distribution with parameters n and $p = .5$. (Use Table II, Appendix B.)

Rejection region: Reject H_0 if p-value $\leq .05$.

Assumption: The sample is selected randomly from a continuous probability distribution. [*Note:* No assumptions need to be made about the shape of the probability distribution.]

Recall that the normal probability distribution provides a good approximation for the binomial distribution when the sample size is large. For tests about the median of a distribution, the null hypothesis implies that $p = .5$, and the normal distribution will provide a good approximation if $n \geq 10$. (Samples with $n \geq 10$ satisfy the condition that $np \pm 3\sqrt{npq}$ be contained in the interval 0 to n.) Thus, we can use the standard normal z distribution to conduct the sign test for large samples. The large-sample sign test is summarized in the box.

Large-Sample Sign Test for a Population Median M

One-Tailed Test	Two-Tailed Test
H_0: $M = M_0$	H_0: $M = M_0$
H_a: $M > M_0$	H_a: $M \neq M_0$
[or H_a: $M < M_0$]	

Test statistic: $z = \dfrac{(S - .5) - .5n}{.5\sqrt{n}}$

[Note: S is calculated as shown in the previous box. We subtract .5 from S as the "correction for continuity." The null hypothesized mean value is $np = .5n$, and the standard deviation is

$$\sqrt{npq} = \sqrt{n(.5)(.5)} = .5\sqrt{n}$$

See Chapter 4 for details on the normal approximation to the binomial distribution.]

Rejection region: $z > z_\alpha$	Rejection region: $z > z_{\alpha/2}$

where tabulated z values can be found inside the front cover.

EXAMPLE 7.6

A manufacturer of compact disk (CD) players has established that the median time to failure for its players is 5,250 hours of utilization. A sample of 20 CD players from a competitor is obtained, and they are continuously tested until each fails. The 20 failure times range from 5 hours (a "defective" player) to 6,575 hours, and 14 of the 20 exceed 5,250 hours. Is there evidence that the median failure time of the competitor differs from 5,250 hours? Use $\alpha = .10$.

Solution

The null and alternative hypotheses of interest are

H_0: $M = 5{,}250$ hours H_a: $M \neq 5{,}250$ hours

Test statistic: Since $n \geq 10$, we use the standard normal z statistic:

$$z = \frac{(S - .5) - .5n}{.5\sqrt{n}}$$

where S is the maximum of S_1, the number of measurements greater than 5,250, and S_2, the number of measurements less than 5,250.

Rejection region: $z > 1.645$, where $z_{\alpha/2} = z_{.05} = 1.645$

Assumptions: The distribution of the failure times is continuous (time is a continous variable), but nothing is assumed about the shape of its probability distribution.

Since the number of measurements exceeding $5{,}250$ is $S_1 = 14$, and thus the number of measurements less than $5{,}250$ is $S_2 = 6$, then S is 14, the greater of S_1 and S_2. The calculated z statistic is, therefore,

$$z = \frac{(S - .5) - .5n}{.5\sqrt{n}} = \frac{13.5 - 10}{.5\sqrt{20}} = \frac{3.5}{2.236} = 1.565$$

The value of z is not in the rejection region, so we cannot reject the null hypothesis at the $\alpha = .10$ level of significance. Thus, the CD manufacturer should not conclude, on the basis of this sample, that its competitor's CD players have a failure time median that differs from $5{,}250$ hours.

The one-sample nonparametric sign test for a median provides an alternative to the t test for small samples from nonnormal distributions. However, if the distribution is approximately normal, the t test provides a more powerful test about the central tendency of the distribution.

Exercises 7.47–7.54

Learning the Mechanics

7.47   Under what circumstances is the sign test preferred to the t test for making inferences about the central tendency of a population?

7.48   What is the probability that a randomly selected observation exceeds each of the following?
   a. Mean of a normal distribution   **b.** Median of a normal distribution
   c. Mean of a nonnormal distribution   **d.** Median of a nonnormal distribution

7.49   Use Table II of Appendix B to calculate the following binomial probabilities:
   a. $P(x \geq 7)$ when $n = 8$ and $p = .5$
   b. $P(x \geq 5)$ when $n = 8$ and $p = .5$
   c. $P(x \geq 8)$ when $n = 8$ and $p = .5$
   d. $P(x \geq 10)$ when $n = 15$ and $p = .5$. Also use the normal approximation to calculate this probability, and compare the approximation with the exact value.
   e. $P(x \geq 15)$ when $n = 25$ and $p = .5$. Also use the normal approximation to calculate this probability, and compare the approximation with the exact value.

7.50   Consider the following sample of ten measurements:

   12.1   8.5   15.8   17.7   9.6   4.0   25.2   10.3   6.2   13.9

Use these data to conduct each of the following sign tests using the binomial tables (Table II, Appendix B) and $\alpha = .05$:

a. $H_0: M = 10$ versus $H_a: M > 10$ **b.** $H_0: M = 10$ versus $H_a: M \neq 10$
c. $H_0: M = 18$ versus $H_a: M < 18$ **d.** $H_0: M = 18$ versus $H_a: M \neq 18$
e. Repeat each of the preceding tests using the normal approximation to the binomial probabilities. Compare the results.
f. What assumptions are necessary to assure the validity of each test?

7.51 Suppose you wish to conduct a test of the research hypothesis that the median of a population is greater than 75. You randomly sample 25 measurements from the population and determine that 17 of them exceed 75. Set up and conduct the appropriate test of hypothesis at the .10 level of significance. Be sure to specify all necessary assumptions.

Applying the Concepts

7.52 In the early 1990s many firms found it necessary to reduce the size of their workforces in order to reduce costs. These reductions were referred to as *corporate downsizing* and *reductions in force* (RIF) by the business community and media. Subsequently, many companies were sued by former employees who alleged that the RIFs were discriminatory with regard to age. Federal law protects employees over 40 years of age against such discrimination.

Suppose one large company's employees have a median age of 37. Its RIF plan is to fire 15 employees aged 43, 32, 39, 28, 54, 41, 50, 62, 22, 45, 47, 54, 43, 33, and 59 years.

a. Calculate the median age of the employees who are being terminated.
b. What are the appropriate null and alternative hypotheses to test whether the population from which the terminated employees were selected has a median age that exceeds the entire company's median age?
c. Conduct the test of part **b**, and report the significance level of the test.
d. Assuming that courts generally require statistical evidence at the .10 level of significance before ruling that age discrimination laws were violated, what do you advise the company about its planned RIF? Explain.

7.53 Airline industry analysts expect that the Federal Aviation Administration (FAA) will increase the frequency and thoroughness of its review of aircraft maintenance procedures in response to the admission by Eastern Airlines in the summer of 1990 that it had not met some maintenance requirements. Suppose that the FAA samples the records of six aircraft currently utilized by one airline and determines the number of flights between the last two complete engine maintenances for each, with the following results: 24, 27, 25, 94, 29, 28.

The FAA requires that this maintenance be performed at least every 30 flights. Although it is obvious that not all aircraft are meeting the requirement, the FAA wishes to test whether the airline is meeting this particular maintenance requirement "on average."

a. Would you suggest the t test or sign test to conduct the test? Why?
b. Set up the null and alternative hypotheses such that the burden of proof is on the airline to show it is meeting the "on-average" requirement.
c. What are the test statistic and rejection region for this test if the level of significance is $\alpha = .01$? Why would the level of significance be set at such a low value?
d. Conduct the test, and state the conclusion in terms of this application.

7.54 A paper company requires that the median height of pine trees exceed 40 feet before they are harvested. A sample of 24 trees in one large plot is selected, and 17 of them are over 40 feet.

   a. Test whether the company can conclude at the .05 level of significance that the median height of trees in the plot exceeds 40 feet.

   b. Calculate and interpret the *p*-value of this test.

   c. What assumptions must be made about the probability distribution of the tree heights in the plot in order to assure the validity of the test?

7.6 Large-Sample Test of Hypothesis About a Binomial Probability

Inferences about proportions (or percentages) are often made in the context of the probability, *p*, of "success" for a binomial distribution. We showed how to use large samples from binomial distributions to form confidence intervals for *p* in Section 6.5. We now consider tests of hypotheses about a binomial probability *p*.

For example, consider the problem of *insider trading* in the stock market. Insider trading is the buying and selling of stock by an individual privy to inside information in a company, usually a high-level executive in the firm. The Securities and Exchange Commission (SEC) imposes strict guidelines about insider trading so that all investors can have equal access to information that may affect the stock's price. An investor wishing to test the effectiveness of the SEC guidelines monitors the market for a period of a year and records the number of times a stock price increases the day following a significant purchase of stock by an insider. For a total of 576 such transactions, the stock increased the following day 327 times. Does this sample provide evidence that the stock price may be affected by insider trading?

We first view this as a binomial experiment, with the 576 transactions as the trials, and success representing an increase in the stock's price the following day. Let *p* represent the probability that the stock price will increase following a large insider purchase. If the insider purchase has no effect on the stock price (that is, if the information available to the insider is identical to that available to the general market), then the investor expects the probability of a stock increase to be the same as that of a decrease, or $p = .5$. On the other hand, if insider trading affects the stock price (indicating that the market has not fully accounted for the information known to the insiders), then the investor expects the stock either to decrease or to increase more than half the time following significant insider transactions; that is, $p \neq .5$.

We can now place the problem in the context of a test of hypothesis:

$$H_0: \quad p = .5$$
$$H_a: \quad p \neq .5$$

Recall that the sample proportion, $\hat{p}$, is really just the sample mean of the outcomes of the individual binomial trials, and as such is approximately normally distributed (for large samples) according to the Central Limit Theorem. Thus, for large samples we can use the standard normal *z* as the test statistic:

$$\text{Test statistic:} \quad z = \frac{(\text{Sample proportion} - \text{Null hypothesized proportion})}{\text{Standard deviation of sample proportion}}$$

$$= \frac{\hat{p} - p_0}{\sigma_{\hat{p}}}$$

where we use the symbol p_0 to represent the null hypothesized value of p.

Rejection region: We use the standard normal distribution to find the appropriate rejection region for the specified value of α. Using $\alpha = .05$, the two-tailed rejection region is

$$z < -z_{\alpha/2} = -z_{.025} = -1.96 \quad \text{or} \quad z > z_{\alpha/2} = z_{.025} = 1.96$$

See Figure 7.12.

FIGURE 7.12 ▶
Rejection region for insider trading example

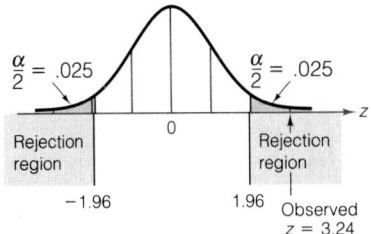

We are now prepared to calculate the value of the test statistic. Before doing so, we want to be sure that the sample size is large enough to assure that the normal approximation for the sampling distribution of $\hat{p}$ is reasonable. To check this, we calculate a 3-standard-deviation interval around the null hypothesized value, p_0, which is assumed to be the true value of p until our test procedure might prove otherwise. Recall that $\sigma_{\hat{p}} = \sqrt{(pq)/n}$ and that we will need an estimate of the product (pq) in order to calculate a numerical value of the test statistic z. Since the null hypothesized value is generally the "accepted until proven otherwise" value, we use the value of $p_0 q_0$ (where $q_0 = 1 - p_0$) to estimate pq in the calculation of z. Thus,

$$\sigma_{\hat{p}} = \sqrt{\frac{pq}{n}} \approx \sqrt{\frac{p_0 q_0}{n}} = \sqrt{\frac{(.5)(.5)}{576}} = .021$$

and the 3-standard-deviation interval around p_0 is

$$p_0 \pm 3\sigma_{\hat{p}} \approx .5 \pm 3(.021) = (.437, .563)$$

As long as this interval does not contain 0 or 1 (i.e., is completely contained in the interval 0 to 1), as is the case here, then the normal distribution will provide a reasonable approximation for the sampling distribution of $\hat{p}$.

Returning to the hypothesis test at hand, the proportion of the sampled transactions that resulted in a stock increase is

$$\hat{p} = \frac{327}{576} = .568$$

Finally, we calculate the number of standard deviations (the z value) between the sampled and hypothesized value of the binomial probability:

$$z = \frac{\hat{p} - p_0}{\sigma_{\hat{p}}} \approx \frac{\hat{p} - p_0}{\sqrt{(p_0 q_0)/n}} = \frac{.568 - .5}{.021} = \frac{.068}{.021} = 3.24$$

The implication is that the observed sample proportion is (approximately) 3.24 standard deviations above the null hypothesized probability, .5 (Figure 7.12). Therefore, we reject the null hypothesis, concluding at the .05 level of significance that the true probability of an increase or decrease in a stock's price differs from .5 the day following significant insider purchase of the stock. It appears that an insider purchase significantly *increases* the probability that the stock price will increase the following day.

The test of hypothesis about a binomial probability p is summarized in the box. Note that the procedure is entirely analogous to that used for conducting large-sample tests about a population mean.

Large-Sample Test of Hypothesis About p

One-Tailed Test	Two-Tailed Test
H_0: $p = p_0$	H_0: $p = p_0$
H_a: $p < p_0$	H_a: $p \neq p_0$
(or H_a: $p > p_0$)	

where p_0 = the hypothesized value of p

Test statistic: $z = \dfrac{\hat{p} - p_0}{\sigma_{\hat{p}}}$ Test statistic: $z = \dfrac{\hat{p} - p_0}{\sigma_{\hat{p}}}$

where $\sigma_{\hat{p}} = \sqrt{[p_0(q_0)]/n}$, and, as usual, we assume H_0 is true until convinced otherwise.

Rejection region: $z < -z_\alpha$ Rejection region: $z < -z_{\alpha/2}$
   (or $z > z_\alpha$ when H_a: $p > p_0$)   or $z > z_{\alpha/2}$

Assumption: The experiment is binomial, and the sample size is large enough that the interval $p_0 \pm 3\sigma_{\hat{p}}$ does not include 0 or 1.

EXAMPLE 7.7

The reputations (and hence, sales) of many businesses can be severely damaged by shipments of manufactured items that contain a large percentage of defectives. For example, a manufacturer of alkaline batteries may want to be reasonably certain that less than 5% of the batteries are defective. Suppose 300 batteries are randomly selected from a very large shipment, each is tested, and 10 defective batteries are found. Does this provide sufficient evidence for the manufacturer to conclude that the fraction defective in the entire shipment is less than .05? Use $\alpha = .01$.

Solution

Before conducting the test of hypothesis, we check to determine whether the sample size is large enough to use the normal approximation for the sampling distribution of $\hat{p}$. To do this, the following interval is constructed:

$$p_0 \pm 3\sigma_{\hat{p}} = p_0 \pm 3\sqrt{\frac{p_0 q_0}{n}} = .05 \pm 3\sqrt{\frac{(.05)(.95)}{300}}$$

$$= .05 \pm .04 \quad \text{or} \quad (.01, .09)$$

Since the interval lies within the interval $(0, 1)$, the normal approximation will be adequate.

The objective of our analysis is to determine whether there is sufficient evidence to indicate that p is less than .05. Consequently, we will test the null hypothesis that $p = .05$ against the alternative hypothesis that $p < .05$. The elements of the test are

$$H_0: \quad p = .05$$
$$H_a: \quad p < .05$$

Test statistic: $\quad z = \dfrac{\hat{p} - p_0}{\sigma_{\hat{p}}}$

Rejection region: $\quad z < -z_{.01} = -2.33 \qquad$ (see Figure 7.13)

FIGURE 7.13 ▶
Rejection region for Example 7.7

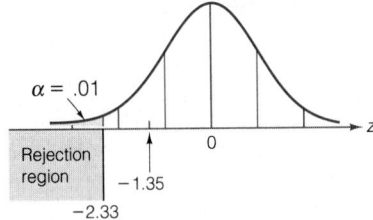

We now calculate the test statistic:

$$z = \frac{\hat{p} - .05}{\sigma_{\hat{p}}} \approx \frac{(10/300) - .05}{\sqrt{p_0 q_0/n}} = \frac{.033 - .05}{\sqrt{p_0 q_0/300}}$$

Substituting the values for p_0 and q_0 into the z statistic, we obtain

$$z \approx \frac{-.017}{\sqrt{(.05)(.95)/300}} = \frac{-.017}{.0126} = -1.35$$

As shown in Figure 7.13, the calculated z value does not fall in the rejection region. Therefore, there is insufficient evidence at the .01 level of significance to indicate that the shipment contains fewer than 5% defective batteries.

EXAMPLE 7.8

In Example 7.7 we found that we did not have sufficient evidence, at the $\alpha = .01$ level of significance, to indicate that the fraction defective, p, of alkaline batteries was less than $p = .05$. How strong was the weight of evidence favoring the alternative hypothesis ($H_a: p < .05$)? Find the observed significance level for the test.

Solution

The computed value of the test statistic was $z = -1.35$. Therefore, for this one-tailed test,

$$\text{Observed significance level} = P(z \leq -1.35)$$

This lower-tail area is shown in Figure 7.14. The area A between $z = 0$ and $z = 1.35$ is given in Table IV of Appendix B as .4115. Therefore, the observed significance level is $.5 - .4115 = .0885$. Note that this probability is quite small. That is, the probability of observing a z value as small as or smaller than -1.35 is only .0885. Therefore, we would reject H_0 if we choose $\alpha = .10$ (since the observed significance level is less than .10), but we would not reject H_0 (the conclusion of Example 7.7) if we choose $\alpha = .05$ or $\alpha = .01$.

FIGURE 7.14 ▶
The observed significance level for Example 7.8

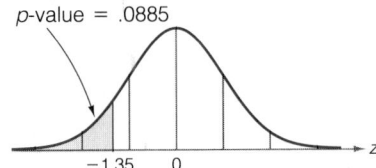

p-value = .0885

$-1.35 \quad 0$

Small-sample test procedures are also available for p. These are omitted from our discussion because most surveys conducted in business use samples that are large enough to employ the large-sample tests presented in this section.

CASE STUDY 7.3 / Statistical Quality Control, Part 2

In complicated assembly operations (such as railway-car assembly), many quality variables could be measured (e.g., strength of welds, degree of corrosion, and number of paint flaws), and in principle, each could be monitored over time using control charts, as described in Case Study 7.2. In some situations, however, an alternative, simpler procedure may be more appropriate. For example, n finished products could be randomly sampled at regular time intervals, inspected for defects, and simply classified as being defective or nondefective products. Then $\hat{p}$, the proportion of defectives in each sample, could be determined and plotted on a control chart called a **p-chart**, as illustrated in Figure 7.15. In this way, the proportion of defective products

produced and, therefore, product quality and the current capability of the production process could be monitored over time (Wetherill, 1977; Montgomery, 1991).

In order to construct the control chart shown in Figure 7.15 on page 366, it is necessary to know (i.e., have a good estimate for) p_0, the proportion of defectives produced when the process is operating properly (i.e., in control). Then, assuming n is large enough to use the normal distribution to approximate the sampling distribution of $\hat{p}$, the control limits are located $3\sigma_{\hat{p}}$ above and below p_0. If a value of $\hat{p}$ falls above the upper limit, it is a signal that the process is turning out more defectives than usual and may be out of control. But what is the significance of the lower control limit?

FIGURE 7.15 ▶

p-chart for proportion defective

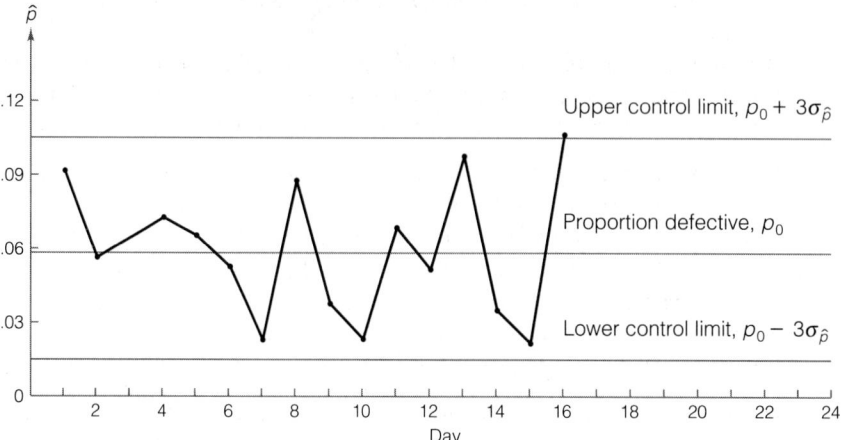

Why should the manufacturer be concerned if fewer defectives than usual are being produced? Two important reasons follow (Caplen, 1970):

1. It may be an indication that the inspector is not performing his or her job carefully and may be missing defectives that normally would be identified. As a result, defective products may be sold to customers.

2. If the inspector is performing adequately, it may be an indication that the production process is temporarily better. If so, the low $\hat{p}$ value signals management to begin a search for the causes for the improvement. If found, it may be possible to improve the production process permanently.

As in Case Study 7.2, this control chart procedure for monitoring the proportion of defective products is nothing more than a two-tailed hypothesis test with the following elements:

1. H_0: Process is in control, $p = p_0$
   H_a: Process is out of control, $p \neq p_0$

2. The test statistic is $\hat{p}$.

3. The rejection region is defined by the upper and lower control limits.

4. Since the control limits are located at $p_0 \pm 3\sigma_{\hat{p}}$, the probability of committing a Type I error is approximately $\alpha = .0026$. (Why?)

We discuss *p*-charts in more detail in Chapter 11.

Exercises 7.55 – 7.65

Learning the Mechanics

7.55 For the binomial sample sizes and null hypothesized values of p in each part, determine whether the sample size is large enough to use the normal approximation methodology presented in this section to conduct a test of the null hypothesis $H_0: p = p_0$.
a. $n = 900$, $p_0 = .975$ b. $n = 125$, $p_0 = .01$ c. $n = 40$, $p_0 = .75$
d. $n = 15$, $p_0 = .75$ e. $n = 12$, $p_0 = .62$

7.56 Suppose a random sample of 100 observations from a binomial population gave a value of $\hat{p} = .63$ and you wish to test the null hypothesis that the population parameter p is equal to .70 against the alternative hypothesis that $p < .70$.

a. Noting that $\hat{p} = .63$, what does your intuition tell you? Does the value of $\hat{p}$ appear to contradict the null hypothesis?

b. Use the large-sample z test to test H_0: $p = .70$ against the alternative hypothesis H_a: $p < .70$ at the $\alpha = .05$ significance level. How do the test results compare with your intuitive decision from part a?

c. Find and interpret the p-value for the hypothesis test you conducted in part b.

7.57 Suppose the sample in Exercise 7.56 has produced $\hat{p} = .83$ and we wish to test H_0: $p = .9$ against the alternative hypothesis H_a: $p < .9$.

a. Calculate the value of the z statistic for this test.

b. Notice that $\hat{p} - p_0 = .83 - .9 = -.07$ is the same as for Exercise 7.56. Considering this, why is the absolute value of z for this exercise larger than that calculated in Exercise 7.56?

c. Complete the test using $\alpha = .05$ and interpret the results.

d. Find the observed significance level for your hypothesis test, and interpret its value.

7.58 A statistics student used a computer program to test the null hypothesis H_0: $p = .5$ against the one-tailed alternative H_a: $p > .5$. A sample of 500 observations are input into the computer, which returns the following result:

```
Z = 0.44          P-VALUE = 0.3300
```

a. The student concludes, based on the p-value, that there is a 33% chance that the alternative hypothesis is true. Do you agree? If not, correct the interpretation.

b. How would the p-value change if the alternative hypothesis were two-tailed, H_a: $p \neq .5$? Interpret this p-value.

Applying the Concepts

7.59 A random sample of 50 consumers taste-tested a new snack food. Their responses were coded (0: do not like; 1: like; 2: indifferent) and listed as follows:

```
1 0 0 1 2 0 1 1 0 0 0 1 0 2 0 2 2 0 0 1
1 0 0 0 0 1 0 2 0 0 0 1 0 0 1 0 0 1 0 1
0 2 0 0 1 1 0 0 0 1
```

a. Test H_0: $p = .5$ against H_a: $p > .5$, where p is the proportion of customers who do not like the snack food. Use $\alpha = .10$.

b. Report the observed significance level of your test.

7.60 According to a spokesperson for General Mills, the company's cents-off coupon offers are designed to get people to buy its products and its refund offers (money returned with proof of repeated purchases) are designed to encourage people to continue buying its products. In a national survey conducted by the Nielsen Clearing House in 1975, 65% of the respondents indicated that they used cents-off coupons when grocery shopping. In a 1980 survey, the Nielsen organization found that 76% of those surveyed used cents-off coupons (*Minneapolis Star*, Nov. 29, 1981). Suppose the 1980 survey consisted of a random sample of 100 shoppers, of whom 76 indicated that they used cents-off coupons.

    a. Does the 1980 sample provide sufficient evidence that the percentage of shoppers using cents-off coupons exceeds 65%? Test using $\alpha = .05$.

    b. Is the sample size large enough to use the inferential procedures presented in this section? Explain.

    c. Find the observed significance level for the test you conducted in part **a**, and interpret its value.

7.61 In gambling, a *system* is a strategy for playing a game that is thought to improve one's chances of winning. A small gambling school teaches customers how to play casino blackjack. Their published advertisements claim that they ". . . teach a system that guarantees winning results on average." A customer who lost thousands of dollars while using the system decided to sue the school for false advertising. To test the school's claim, the customer's lawyer commissioned a computer simulation study. The computer "played" 1,000,000 independent games of blackjack with the "player" following the school's system and the "dealer" obeying the standard house rules. The "player" won 497,584 of the simulated games.

    a. Letting p represent the long-run proportion of games won by players using the system, test $H_0: p \geq .50$ versus $H_a: p < .50$ using $\alpha = .01$.

    b. Do the results of this test contradict the advertised claim? Explain.

    c. Suppose the simulation had been run only 10,000 times. Would the results of the test be the same if the "player" won the same proportion of the simulated games (i.e., 4,976)?

    d. List any assumptions that you made in answering parts **a** and **c**.

7.62 Refer to Exercise 7.61. Find the observed significance levels for the tests you conducted in parts **a** and **c** and interpret their values.

7.63 Marketing research has been defined by the American Marketing Association as the "systematic gathering, recording, and analyzing of data about problems relating to the marketing of goods and services" (*Report of Definitions Committee of the American Marketing Association*, 1961). Companies may have their own marketing research departments, or they may use the services of a marketing research firm. The marketing research department of a large West Coast manufacturer of facial tissue paper was charged with the responsibility of determining customer preferences regarding the softness of its newly developed product (brand A) relative to the industry leader (brand B). A random sample of 250 customers was selected. Each customer was asked to rank the softness of brands A and B: 146 ranked brand A softer and 104 ranked brand B softer.

    a. Do the data indicate that brand A is perceived as softer than brand B? Test using $\alpha = .05$.

    b. Find the p-value for the test and interpret its value.

7.64 A producer of frozen orange juice claims that 52% of all orange-juice drinkers prefer its product. To test the validity of this claim, a competitor samples 200 orange-juice drinkers and finds that only 95 prefer the producer's brand.

    a. What are the appropriate null and alternative hypotheses to test the producer's claim?

    b. When these data are analyzed by a statistical software program, the following results are obtained:

```
Z = -1.27          P-VALUE = .1020
```

    Check the computer calculations.

    c. Interpret the results.

    d. How would the p-value change if the test were two-tailed rather than one-tailed?

7.65   A major videocassette rental chain is considering opening a new store in an area that currently does not have any such stores. The chain will open a store if there is evidence that at least 5,000 of the 20,000 households in the area are equipped with videocassette recorders (VCRs). It conducts a telephone poll of 300 randomly selected households in the area and finds that 96 have VCRs. Is this enough evidence to conclude that more than 5,000 of the homes in the area are equipped with VCRs? Test at $\alpha = .01$.

7.7   Calculating Type II Error Probabilities: More About β (Optional)

In our introduction to hypothesis testing in Section 7.1, we showed that the probability of committing a Type I error, α, can be controlled by the selection of the rejection region for the test. Thus, when the test statistic falls in the rejection region and we make the decision to reject the null hypothesis, we do so knowing the error rate for incorrect rejections of H_0. The situation corresponding to accepting the null hypothesis, and thereby risking a Type II error, is not generally as controllable. For that reason, we adopted a policy of nonrejection of H_0 when the test statistic does not fall in the rejection region, rather than risking an error of unknown magnitude.

To see how β, the probability of a Type II error, can be calculated for a test of hypothesis, recall the example in Section 7.2 in which a city tests a manufacturer's pipe to see whether it meets the requirement that the mean strength exceeds 2,400 pounds per lineal foot. The setup for the test is as follows:

$$H_0: \quad \mu = 2,400$$
$$H_a: \quad \mu > 2,400$$

Test statistic: $z = \dfrac{\bar{x} - 2,400}{\sigma/\sqrt{n}}$

Rejection region: $z > 1.645$ for $\alpha = .05$

Figure 7.16(a) on page 370 shows the rejection region for the **null distribution**—that is, the distribution of the test statistic assuming the null hypothesis is true. The area in the rejection region is .05, and this area represents α, the probability that the test statistic leads to rejection of H_0 when, in fact, H_0 is true.

The Type II error probability β is calculated assuming that the null hypothesis is false, because it is defined as the *probability of accepting H_0 when it is false*. Since H_0 is false for any value of μ exceeding 2,400, one value of β exists for each possible value of μ greater than 2,400 (an infinite number of possibilities). Figure 7.16(b), (c), and (d) show three of the possibilities, corresponding to alternative hypothesis values of μ equal to 2,425, 2,450, and 2,475, respectively. Note that β is the area in the *nonrejection (or acceptance) region* in each of these distributions, and that β decreases as the true value of μ moves farther from the null-hypothesized value of $\mu = 2,400$. This is sensible, because the probability of incorrectly accepting the null hypothesis should decrease as the distance between the null and alternative values of μ increases.

FIGURE 7.16 ▶
Values of α and β for various
values of μ

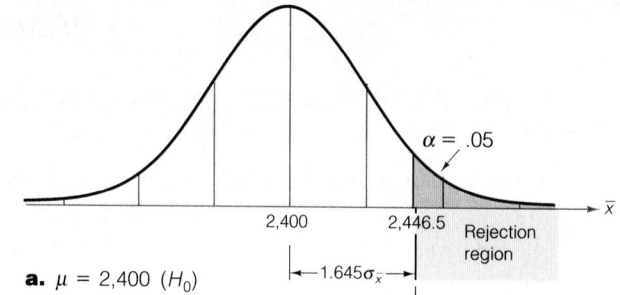

a. $\mu = 2,400$ (H_0)

b. $\mu = 2,425$ (H_a)

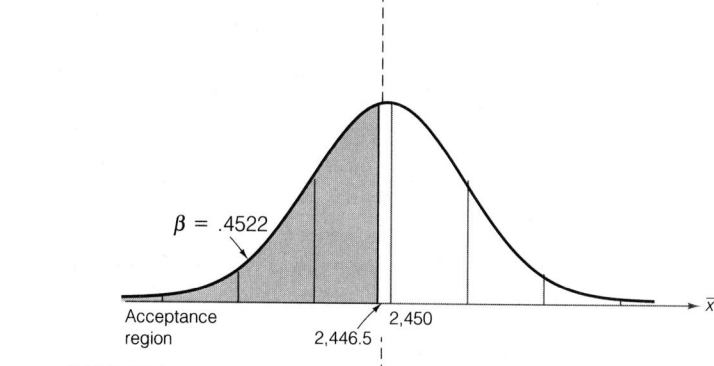

c. $\mu = 2,450$ (H_a)

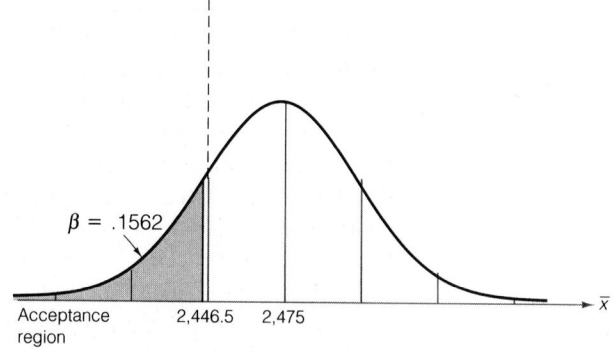

d. $\mu = 2,475$ (H_a)

In order to calculate the value of β for a specific value of μ in H_a, we proceed as follows:

1. First, calculate the value of $\bar{x}$ that corresponds to the border between the acceptance and rejection regions. For the sewer pipe example, that is the value of $\bar{x}$ that lies 1.645 standard deviations above $\mu = 2{,}400$ in the sampling distribution of $\bar{x}$. Denoting this value by $\bar{x}_0$, corresponding to the largest value of $\bar{x}$ that supports the null hypothesis, we find (recalling that $s = 200$ and $n = 50$):

$$\bar{x}_0 = \mu_0 + 1.645\sigma_{\bar{x}} = 2{,}400 + 1.645\left(\frac{\sigma}{\sqrt{n}}\right)$$

$$\approx 2{,}400 + 1.645\left(\frac{s}{\sqrt{n}}\right) = 2{,}400 + 1.645\left(\frac{200}{\sqrt{50}}\right)$$

$$= 2{,}400 + 1.645(28.28) = 2{,}446.5$$

2. Next, for a particular alternative distribution corresponding to a value of μ, denoted by μ_a, we calculate the z value corresponding to $\bar{x}_0$, the border between the rejection and acceptance regions. We then use this z value and Table IV of Appendix B to determine the area in the *acceptance* region under the alternative distribution. This area is the value of β corresponding to the particular alternative μ_a. For example, for the alternative $\mu_a = 2{,}425$, we calculate

$$z = \frac{\bar{x}_0 - 2{,}425}{\sigma_{\bar{x}}} = \frac{\bar{x}_0 - 2{,}425}{\sigma/\sqrt{n}}$$

$$\approx \frac{\bar{x}_0 - 2{,}425}{s/\sqrt{n}} = \frac{2{,}446.5 - 2{,}425}{28.28} = .76$$

Note in Figure 7.16(b) that the area in the acceptance region is the area to the left of $z = .76$. This area is

$$\beta = .5 + .2764 = .7764$$

Thus, the probability that the test procedure will lead to an incorrect acceptance of the null hypothesis $\mu = 2{,}400$ when in fact $\mu = 2{,}425$ is about .78. As the average strength of the pipe increases to 2,450, the value of β decreases to .4522 [Figure 7.16(c)]. If the mean strength is further increased to 2,475, the value of β is further decreased to .1562 [Figure 7.16(d)]. Thus, even if the true mean strength of the pipe exceeds the minimum specification by 75 pounds per lineal foot, the test procedure will lead to an incorrect acceptance of the null hypothesis (rejection of the pipe) approximately 16% of the time. The upshot is that the pipe must be manufactured so that the mean strength well exceeds the minimum requirement if the manufacturer wants the probability of its acceptance by the city to be large (i.e., β to be small).

The steps for calculating β for a large-sample test about a population mean are summarized in the following box.

Steps for Calculating β for a Large-Sample Test About μ

1. Calculate the value(s) of $\bar{x}$ corresponding to the border(s) of the rejection region. There will be one border value for a one-tailed test and two for a two-tailed test. The formula is one of the following, corresponding to a test with level of significance α:

$$\textit{Upper-tailed test:} \quad \bar{x}_0 = \mu_0 + z_\alpha \sigma_{\bar{x}} \approx \mu_0 + z_\alpha \left(\frac{s}{\sqrt{n}} \right)$$

$$\textit{Lower-tailed test:} \quad \bar{x}_0 = \mu_0 - z_\alpha \sigma_{\bar{x}} \approx \mu_0 - z_\alpha \left(\frac{s}{\sqrt{n}} \right)$$

$$\textit{Two-tailed test:} \quad \bar{x}_{0,L} = \mu_0 - z_{\alpha/2} \sigma_{\bar{x}} \approx \mu_0 - z_{\alpha/2} \left(\frac{s}{\sqrt{n}} \right)$$

$$\bar{x}_{0,U} = \mu_0 + z_{\alpha/2} \sigma_{\bar{x}} \approx \mu_0 + z_{\alpha/2} \left(\frac{s}{\sqrt{n}} \right)$$

2. Specify the value of μ_a in the alternative hypothesis for which the value of β is to be calculated. Then convert the border value(s) of $\bar{x}_0$ to z value(s) using the alternative distribution with mean μ_a. The general formula for the z value is

$$z = \frac{\bar{x}_0 - \mu_a}{\sigma_{\bar{x}}}$$

Sketch the alternative distribution (centered at μ_a), and shade the area above the acceptance (nonrejection) region. Use the z statistic(s) and Table IV of Appendix B to find the shaded area, which is β.

Following the calculation of β for a particular value of μ_a, you should interpret the value in the context of the hypothesis-testing application. It is often useful to interpret the value of $1 - \beta$, which is known as the **power of the test**, corresponding to a particular alternative, μ_a. Since β is the probability of accepting the null hypothesis when the alternative hypothesis is true with $\mu = \mu_a$, $1 - \beta$ is the probability of the complementary event, or the probability of rejecting the null hypothesis when the alternative $\mu = \mu_a$ is true. That is, the power $1 - \beta$ measures the likelihood that the test procedure will lead to the *correct* decision (reject H_0) for a particular value of the mean in the alternative hypothesis.

For example, in the sewer pipe example we found that $\beta = .7764$ when $\mu = 2,425$. This is the probability that the test leads to the (incorrect) acceptance of the null hypothesis when $\mu = 2,425$. Or, equivalently, the power of the test is $1 - .7764 = .2236$, which means that the test will lead to the (correct) rejection of the null hypothesis only 22% of the time when the pipe exceeds specifications by 25 pounds per lineal foot. When the manufacturer's pipe has a mean strength of 2,475 (that is, 75

> **Definition 7.2**
>
> The **power** of a test is the probability that the test will correctly lead to the rejection of the null hypothesis for a particular value of μ in the alternative hypothesis. The power is equal to $1 - \beta$ for the particular alternative considered.

pounds per lineal foot in excess of specifications), the power of the test increases to $1 - .1562 = .8438$. That is, the test will lead to the acceptance of the manufacturer's pipe 84% of the time if $\mu = 2,475$.

. . . .

EXAMPLE 7.9

Recall the quality control study in Examples 7.1 and 7.2, in which we tested to determine whether a cereal box filling machine was deviating from the specified mean fill of $\mu = 12$ ounces. The test setup is repeated here:

$$H_0: \quad \mu = 12$$
$$H_a: \quad \mu \neq 12 \quad (\text{i.e., } \mu < 12 \quad \text{or} \quad \mu > 12)$$

Test statistic: $\quad z = \dfrac{\bar{x} - 12}{\sigma_{\bar{x}}}$

Rejection region: $\quad z < -1.96 \quad \text{or} \quad z > 1.96 \qquad \text{for } \alpha = .05$
$$\qquad\qquad\qquad z < -2.575 \quad \text{or} \quad z > 2.575 \qquad \text{for } \alpha = .01$$

Note that two rejection regions have been specified corresponding to values of $\alpha = .05$ and $\alpha = .01$, respectively. Assume that $n = 100$ and $s = .5$.

a. Suppose the machine is underfilling the boxes by an average of .1 ounce, i.e., $\mu = 11.9$. Calculate the values of β corresponding to the two rejection regions. Discuss the relationship between the values of α and β.

b. Calculate the power of the test for each of the rejection regions when $\mu = 11.9$.

Solution

a. We first consider the rejection region corresponding to $\alpha = .05$. The first step is to calculate the border values of $\bar{x}$ corresponding to the two-tailed rejection region, $z < -1.96$ or $z > 1.96$:

$$\bar{x}_{0,L} = \mu_0 - 1.96\sigma_{\bar{x}} \approx \mu_0 - 1.96\left(\frac{s}{\sqrt{n}}\right) = 12.0 - 1.96\left(\frac{.5}{10}\right) = 11.902$$

$$\bar{x}_{0,U} = \mu_0 + 1.96\sigma_{\bar{x}} \approx \mu_0 + 1.96\left(\frac{s}{\sqrt{n}}\right) = 12.0 + 1.96\left(\frac{.5}{10}\right) = 12.098$$

These border values are shown in Figure 7.17(a) on page 374.

FIGURE 7.17 ▶
Calculation for β for Example 7.9

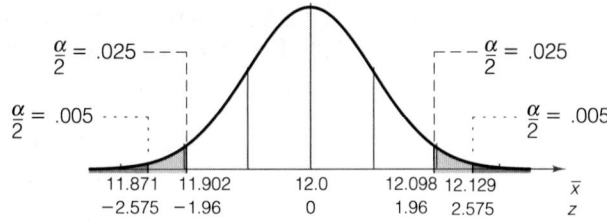

a. $\mu = 12\ (H_0)$
Two rejection regions
$\alpha = .05$ and $\alpha = .01$

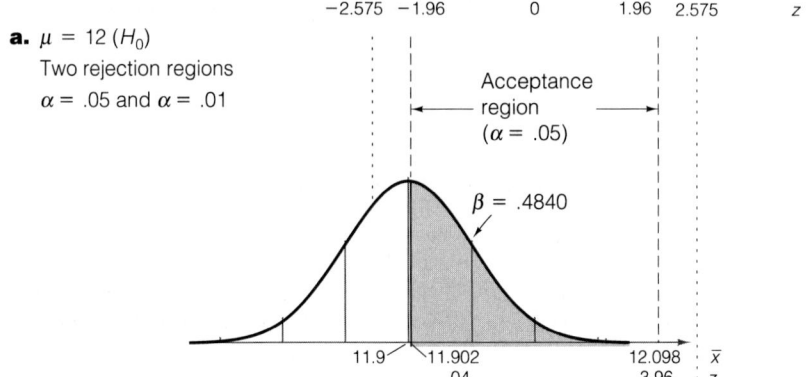

b. $\mu = 11.9\ (H_a)$
β for $\alpha = .05$ rejection region

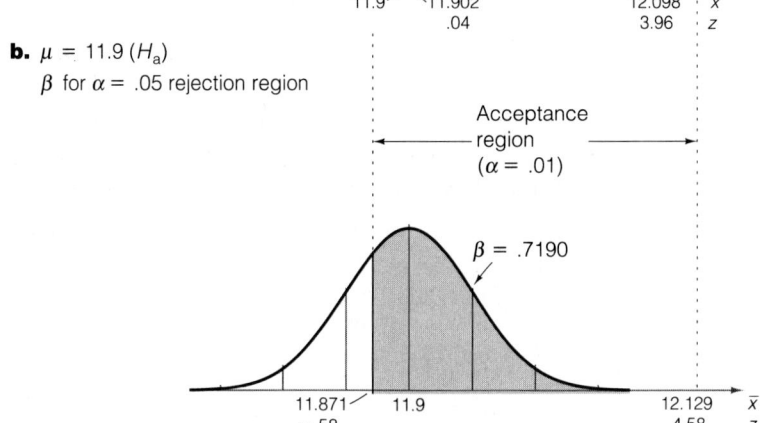

c. $\mu = 11.9\ (H_a)$
β for $\alpha = .01$ rejection region

Next, we convert these values to z values in the alternative distribution with $\mu_a = 11.9$:

$$z_{\mathrm{L}} = \frac{\bar{x}_{0,\mathrm{L}} - \mu_a}{\sigma_{\bar{x}}} \approx \frac{11.902 - 11.9}{.05} = .04$$

$$z_{\mathrm{U}} = \frac{\bar{x}_{0,\mathrm{U}} - \mu_a}{\sigma_{\bar{x}}} \approx \frac{12.098 - 11.9}{.05} = 3.96$$

These z values are shown in Figure 7.17(b), and you can see that the acceptance (or nonrejection) region is the area between them. Using Table IV of Appendix B, we find that the area between $z = 0$ and $z = .04$ is .0160, and the area between

$z = 0$ and $z = 3.96$ is (approximately) .5 (since $z = 3.96$ is off the scale of Table IV). Then the area between $z = .04$ and $z = 3.96$ is approximately

$$\beta = .5 - .0160 = .4840$$

Thus, the test with $\alpha = .05$ will lead to a Type II error about 48% of the time when the machine is underfilling by .1 ounce.

For the rejection region corresponding to $\alpha = .01$, $z < -2.575$ or $z > 2.575$, we find

$$\bar{x}_{0,L} = 12.0 - 2.575\left(\frac{.5}{10}\right) = 11.871$$

$$\bar{x}_{0,U} = 12.0 + 2.575\left(\frac{.5}{10}\right) = 12.129$$

These border values of the rejection region are shown in Figure 7.17(c).

Converting these to z values in the alternative distribution with $\mu_a = 11.9$, we find $z_L = -.58$ and $z_U = 4.58$. The area between these values is approximately

$$\beta = .2190 + .5 = .7190$$

Thus, the chance that the test procedure with $\alpha = .01$ will lead to an incorrect acceptance of H_0 is about 72%.

Note that the value of β increases from .4840 to .7190 when we decrease the value of α from .05 to .01. This is a general property of the relationship between α and β: *as α is decreased (increased), β is increased (decreased).*

b. The power is defined to be the probability of (correctly) rejecting the null hypothesis when the alternative is true. When $\mu = 11.9$ and $\alpha = .05$, we find

$$\text{Power} = 1 - \beta = 1 - .4840 = .5160$$

When $\mu = 11.9$ and $\alpha = .01$,

$$\text{Power} = 1 - \beta = 1 - .7190 = .2810$$

You can see that the power of the test is decreased as the level of α is decreased. This means that as the probability of incorrectly rejecting the null hypothesis is decreased, the probability of correctly accepting the null hypothesis for a given alternative is also decreased. Thus, the value of α must be selected carefully, with the realization that a test is made less powerful to detect departures from the null hypothesis when the value of α is decreased.

We have shown that the probability of committing a Type II error, β, is inversely related to α (Example 7.9), and that the value of β decreases as the value of μ moves farther from the null hypothesis value (sewer pipe example). The sample size n also affects β. Remember that the standard deviation of the sampling distribution of $\bar{x}$ is inversely proportional to the (square root of the) sample size: $\sigma_{\bar{x}} = \sigma/\sqrt{n}$. Thus, as illustrated in Figure 7.18 (page 376), the variability of both the null and alternative sampling distributions is decreased as n is increased. If the value of α is specified and remains fixed, the value of β decreases as n increases, as illustrated in Figure 7.18(b). Conversely, the power of the test for a given alternative hypothesis is increased as the sample size is increased.

FIGURE 7.18 ▶
Relationship between α, β, and n

a. Small n

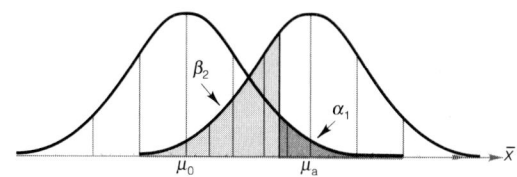

b. Large n, fixed α $(\beta_2 < \beta_1)$

The properties of β and power are summarized in the box.

Properties of β and Power

1. The value of β decreases and the power increases as the distance between the null and alternative values of μ increases (see Figure 7.16).
2. The value of β increases and the power decreases as the value of α is decreased (see Figure 7.17).
3. The value of β decreases and the power increases as the sample size is increased, assuming α remains fixed (see Figure 7.18).

Exercises 7.66–7.77

Learning the Mechanics

7.66   What is the relationship between β, the probability of committing a Type II error, and the power of a test?

7.67   List three factors that increase the power of a test.

7.68   Suppose you want to test H_0: $\mu = 500$ against H_a: $\mu > 500$ using $\alpha = .05$. The population in question is normally distributed with standard deviation 100. A random sample of size $n = 25$ will be used.
   a. Sketch the sampling distribution of $\bar{x}$ assuming that H_0 is true.
   b. Find the value of $\bar{x}_0$, that value of $\bar{x}$ above which the null hypothesis will be rejected. Indicate the rejection region on your graph of part **a**. Shade the area above the rejection region and label it α.

c. On your graph of part **a**, sketch the sampling distribution of $\bar{x}$ if $\mu = 550$. Shade the area under this distribution that corresponds to the probability that $\bar{x}$ falls in the nonrejection region when $\mu = 550$. Label this area β.

d. Find β.

e. Compute the power of this test for detecting the alternative $H_a: \mu = 550$.

7.69 Refer to Exercise 7.68.

a. If $\mu = 575$ instead of 550, what is the probability that the hypothesis test will incorrectly fail to reject H_0? That is, what is β?

b. If $\mu = 575$, what is the probability that the test will correctly reject the null hypothesis? That is, what is the power of the test?

c. Compare β and the power of the test when $\mu = 575$ to the values you obtained in Exercise 7.68 for $\mu = 550$. Explain the differences.

7.70 It is desired to test $H_0: \mu = 75$ against $H_a: \mu < 75$ using $\alpha = .10$. The population in question is uniformly distributed with standard deviation 15. A random sample of size 49 will be drawn from the population.

a. Describe the (approximate) sampling distribution of $\bar{x}$ under the assumption that H_0 is true.

b. Describe the (approximate) sampling distribution of $\bar{x}$ under the assumption that the population mean is 70.

c. If μ were really equal to 70, what is the probability that the hypothesis test would lead the investigator to commit a type II error?

d. What is the power of this test for detecting the alternative $H_a: \mu = 70$?

7.71 Refer to Exercise 7.70. If the true value of the population mean is $\mu = 73$, what is the power of the test? How does it compare with the power when $\mu = 70$?

7.72 Refer to Exercises 7.70 and 7.71.

a. Find β for each of the following values of the population mean: 74, 72, 70, 68, 66.

b. Plot each value of β you obtained in part **a** against its associated population mean. Show β on the vertical axis and μ on the horizontal axis. Draw a curve through the five points on your graph.

c. Use your graph of part **b** to find the approximate probability that the hypothesis test will lead to a type II error when $\mu = 73$. Compare your answer to the result you obtained in Exercise 7.71.

d. Convert each of the β values you calculated in part **a** to the power of the test at the specified value of μ. Plot the power on the vertical axis against μ on the horizontal axis. Compare the β graph of part **b** to the **power curve** of this part.

e. Examine the graphs of parts **b** and **d**. Explain what they reveal about the relationships among the distance between the true mean μ and the null hypothesized mean μ_0, the value of β, and the power.

7.73 Suppose you want to conduct the two-tailed test of $H_0: \mu = 30$ against $H_a: \mu \neq 30$ using $\alpha = .05$. A random sample of size 121 will be drawn from the population in question. Assume the population has a standard deviation equal to 1.2.

a. Describe the sampling distribution of $\bar{x}$ under the assumption that H_0 is true.

b. Describe the sampling distribution of $\bar{x}$ under the assumption that $\mu = 29.8$.

c. If μ were really equal to 29.8, find the value of β associated with the test.

d. Find the value of β for the alternative $H_a: \mu = 30.4$.

Applying the Concepts

7.74 If a manufacturer (the vendee) buys all items of a particular type from a particular vendor, the manufacturer is practicing *sole sourcing*. Sole sourcing is a purchasing policy that is generally recognized as an important component of a firm's quality system. One of the major benefits of sole sourcing for the vendee is the improved communication that results from the closer vendee/vendor relationship (Treleven, 1986). As part of a sole sourcing arrangement, a vendor agreed to periodically supply its vendee with sample data from its production process. The vendee uses the data to investigate whether the mean length of rods produced by the vendor's production process is truly 5.0 millimeters or more, as claimed by the vendor and desired by the vendee.

    a. If the production process has a standard deviation of .01 millimeter, the vendor supplies $n = 100$ items to the vendee, and the vendee uses $\alpha = .05$ in testing H_0: $\mu = 5.0$ millimeters against H_a: $\mu < 5.0$ millimeters, what is the probability that the vendee's test will fail to reject the null hypothesis when in fact $\mu = 4.9975$ millimeters? What is the name given to this type of error?

    b. Refer to part **a**. What is the probability that the vendee's test will reject the null hypothesis when in fact $\mu = 5.0$? What is the name given to this type of error?

    c. What is the power of the test to detect a departure of .0025 millimeter below the specified mean rod length of 5.0 millimeters?

7.75 Refer to Exercise 7.18 in which the performance of a particular type of laser-based inspection equipment was investigated. Assume that the standard deviation of the number of solder joints inspected on each run is 1.2. If $\alpha = .05$ is used in conducting the hypothesis test of interest using a sample of 48 circuit boards, and if the true mean number of solder joints that can be inspected is really equal to 9.5, what is the probability that the test will result in a Type II error?

7.76 Refer to Exercise 7.17, in which the alternative hypothesis that the mean miles per gallon achieved by 1994 Polaris automobiles exceeds 35 is tested against the null hypothesis that the mean is 35 (or less). A sample of 36 automobiles were tested; assume that the resulting standard deviation of $s = 6$ is a good estimate of the true standard deviation.

    a. Calculate the power of the test for the mean values of 35.5, 36.0, 36.5, 37.0, and 37.5.

    b. Plot the power of the test on the vertical axis against the mean on the horizontal axis. Draw a curve through the points.

    c. Use the power curve of part **b** to estimate the power for the mean value $\mu = 36.75$. Calculate the power for this value of μ, and compare it to your approximation.

    d. Use the power curve to approximate the power of the test when $\mu = 40$. If the true value of the mean mpg for this model is really 40, what (approximately) are the chances that the test will fail to reject the null hypothesis that the mean is 35?

7.77 Refer to Exercise 7.76. Show what happens to the power curve when the sample size is increased from $n = 36$ to $n = 100$. Assume that the standard deviation is $\sigma = 6$.

Summary

We have extended the concept of making inferences from using samples to estimate parameters of a distribution to performing tests of hypotheses about these parameters. The essential elements of a test of hypothesis are the **null** and **alternative hypotheses**, the **test statistic**, the **rejection region**, the **calculation of the test statistic**, and the **conclusion**.

The null hypothesis is the *status-quo* hypothesis, the hypothesis not rejected until contradicted by sufficient sample evidence. The alternative is the *research hypothesis*, the hypothesis that will not be accepted until convincingly established by sample information. The test statistic is a value calculated from the sample information and utilized to decide whether to reject the null hypothesis. The rejection region is the collection of values of the test statistic that will cause us to reject the null hypothesis.

We design the test to have a specified **Type I error probability**, α, so that we know the probability of rejecting H_0 when H_0 is true. When the test statistic falls in the rejection region, we infer that the null hypothesis is false (that is, the alternative is true) at the α level of significance. If the test statistic does not fall in the rejection region, then we fail to reject the null hypothesis. We do not accept the null hypothesis in this case unless we know the **Type II error probability**, β.

We have covered large-sample tests involving the population mean μ and the binomial probability p, both using the standard normal z as a test statistic. We have also discussed the small-sample test involving the mean of a normal distribution using the t statistic. A **nonparametric** procedure is required when a small sample is drawn from a nonnormal population.

Supplementary Exercises 7.78 – 7.101

Note: Starred (*) exercises refer to the optional sections.

Learning the Mechanics

7.78   Which of the elements of a test of hypothesis can and should be specified *prior* to analyzing the data that are to be utilized to conduct the test?

7.79   Complete the following statement: The smaller the *p*-value associated with a test of hypothesis, the stronger the support for the _____ hypothesis. Explain your answer.

7.80   Specify the differences between a large-sample and small-sample test of hypothesis about a population mean μ. Focus on the assumptions and test statistics.

7.81   Medical tests have been developed to detect most serious diseases. A medical test is designed to minimize the probability that it will produce a "false positive" or a "false negative." A false positive refers to a positive test result when, in fact, the individual does not have the disease, whereas a false negative is a negative test result for an individual who does have the disease.
   a. If we treat a medical test for a disease as a statistical test of hypothesis, what are the null and alternative hypotheses for the medical test?
   b. What are the Type I and Type II errors for the test? Relate each to false positives and false negatives.
   c. Considering which of the errors has more serious consequences, is it more important to minimize α or β? Explain.

7.82   If the rejection of the null hypothesis of a particular test would cause your firm to go out of business, would you want α to be small or large? Explain.

7.83 In conducting a hypothesis test, if you select a very small value for α, will β tend to be large or small? Explain.

Applying the Concepts

7.84 The EPA sets a limit of 5 parts per million (ppm) on PCB (a dangerous substance) in water. A major manufacturing firm producing PCB for electrical insulation discharges small amounts from the plant. The company management, attempting to control the amount of PCB in its discharge, has given instructions to halt production if the mean amount of PCB in the effluent exceeds 3 ppm. A random sample of 50 water specimens produced the following statistics: $\bar{x} = 3.1$ ppm, $s = .5$ ppm.

   a. Do these statistics provide sufficient evidence to halt the production process? Use $\alpha = .01$.

   b. If you were the plant manager, would you want to use a large or a small value for α for the test in part **a**? Explain.

   c. Find the p-value for the test and interpret its value.

*7.85 Refer to Exercise 7.84.

   a. In the context of the problem, define a Type II error.

   b. Calculate β for the test described in part **a** of Exercise 7.84 assuming that the true mean is $\mu = 3.1$ ppm.

   c. What is the power of the test to detect the effluent's departure from the standard of 3.0 ppm when the mean is 3.1 ppm?

   d. Repeat parts **b** and **c** assuming that the true mean is 3.2 ppm. What happens to the power of the test as the plant's mean PCB departs further from the standard?

*7.86 Refer to Exercises 7.84 and 7.85.

   a. Suppose an α value of .05 is used to conduct the test. Does this change favor the manufacturer? Explain.

   b. Determine the value of β and the power for the test when $\alpha = .05$ and $\mu = 3.1$.

   c. What happens to the power of the test when α is increased?

7.87 According to the Internal Revenue Service (IRS), in 1980, 4,414 taxpayers reported earning more than $1 million in adjusted gross income. By 1990 that number had grown to 63,642. Interestingly, as the number of millionaires rose dramatically, their charitable contributions nose-dived from an average of $207,089 in 1980 to $83,929 in 1989 (Farhi, 1992). Will this trend continue into the mid 1990s? The IRS sampled six 1993 tax returns of millionaires and found the following charitable contributions (in thousands of dollars):

      91.1   103.2   62.9   150.4   209.5   31.7

   a. Do the sample data indicate that annual charitable contributions by millionaires have increased since 1989? Conduct the test using $\alpha = .05$.

   b. What assumptions are necessary to assure the validity of the test conducted in part **a**? Comment on the validity of the assumptions.

   *c. Conduct a nonparametric test on the data. Compare the results to the results obtained in part **a**.

7.88 During the 1980s, testing products for quality during production became a way of life for most successful businesses. Although first applications of quality testing were primarily in the manufacturing sector, companies in the service sector have increasingly turned to quality improvement techniques to compete effectively. For example, suppose a drive-in bank wants to assure that the mean waiting time for its customers will be less than 2 minutes. A random sample of 20 drive-in customers is selected daily, and the waiting times are recorded and analyzed. On one busy day the sample results were: $\bar{x} = 112$ seconds, $s = 28$ seconds. Can the bank safely conclude that the mean waiting time was less than 2 minutes on this day? Use $\alpha = .05$.

7.89   Refer to Exercise 7.88. What is the approximate observed significance level associated with this test?

7.90   In the past, a chemical company produced 880 pounds of a certain type of plastic per day. Now, using a newly developed and less expensive process, the mean daily yield of plastic for the first 50 days of production was 871 pounds, and the standard deviation was 21 pounds.

   a. Do the data provide sufficient evidence to indicate that the mean daily yield for the new process is less than for the old procedure? (Test using $\alpha = .01$.)

   b. What assumptions must you make in order to use the statistical test you employed?

7.91   Refer to Exercise 7.90. Find and interpret the p-value for the test conducted.

7.92   Refer to Exercise 7.90. Calculate the probability β that the test fails to reject the null hypothesis that the new process has a mean daily yield of $\mu = 880$ when in fact the true mean is $\mu = 875$. What is the power of the test to determine that $\mu < 880$ when $\mu = 875$?

7.93   A discount store chain claims that its steel-belted radial tires are more resistant to wear than those of a major tire company. The following experiment was performed to test this claim. On each of 40 cars, one discount tire and one rubber company tire were mounted on the rear axle. After each car was driven 8,000 miles, the tires were inspected for wear. Suppose the tires of the discount chain show less wear on 32 of the cars. What would you conclude about the discount chain's claim? Why?

7.94   The *beta coefficients* of stocks are a measure of their volatility (or risk) relative to the market as a whole. Stocks with beta coefficients greater than 1 generally bear greater risk (more volatile) than the market, whereas stocks with beta coefficients less than 1 are less risky (less volatile) than the overall market (Sharpe and Alexander, 1990). A random sample of 15 high-technology stocks was selected at the end of 1990, and the mean and standard deviation of the beta coefficients were calculated: $\bar{x} = 1.23$, $s = .37$.

   a. Set up the appropriate null and alternative hypotheses to test that the average high-technology stock is riskier than the market as a whole.

   b. Establish the appropriate test statistic and rejection region for the test. Use $\alpha = .10$.

   c. What assumptions are necessary to assure the validity of the test?

   d. Calculate the test statistic and state your conclusion.

   e. What is the approximate p-value associated with this test? Interpret it.

7.95   Refer to Exercise 7.94. When the data were analyzed with a statistical software package, the output was:

$$T = 2.408 \qquad P\text{-}VALUE = 0.0304$$

The p-value corresponds to a two-tailed test of the null hypothesis $\mu = 1$.

   a. Interpret the p-value of the computer output.

   b. If the alternative hypothesis of interest is $\mu > 1$, what is the appropriate p-value of the test?

7.96   One study of gambling newsletters that purport to improve a bettor's odds of winning bets on NFL football games indicates that the newsletters' betting schemes were not profitable (Sauer et al., 1988). Suppose a random sample of 50 games is selected to test one gambling newsletter. Following the newsletter's recommendations, 30 of the 50 games produced winning wagers. Test to see whether the newsletter can be said to increase the odds of winning significantly over what one could expect by selecting winners at random. Use $\alpha = .05$.

7.97   Refer to Exercise 7.96. Calculate and interpret the p-value for the test.

*7.98   Refer to Exercise 7.96.
    a. Describe a Type II error in terms of this application.
    b. Calculate the probability β of a Type II error for this test assuming that the newsletter really does increase the probability of winning a wager on an NFL game to $p = .55$
    c. Suppose the number of games sampled is increased from 50 to 100. How does this affect the probability of the Type II error in part **b**?

7.99   A random sample of 200 residents in one large city is selected, and each is asked whether a new increase in the property tax would be favored if the income were used for public education. A total of 113 indicate support for the tax.
    a. What are the appropriate null and alternative hypotheses to test whether a majority of residents in the city favor the tax?
    b. The data are analyzed using a statistical software package, with the following output:

Z = 1.84   P-VALUE = .0329

    Interpret the results.
    c. What assumptions, if any, are necessary to assure the validity of this test?

*7.100   Increasing numbers of private and public agencies require employee testing for substance abuse. One laboratory has developed a system with a normalized measurement scale, in which values less than 1.00 indicate normal ranges while values of or greater than 1.00 indicate potential substance abuse. The lab reports a normal result as long as the median level for an individual is less than 1.00. Nine independent measurements of each individual's sample are made; suppose that one individual's results were as follows:

    .78   .51   4.32   .23   .77   .98   .96   .89   1.11

    a. Set up the appropriate null and alternative hypotheses if the employer wants "proof" beyond a reasonable doubt that the individual is in the normal range.
    b. Test to determine whether the laboratory can conclude that the individual's median level is in the normal range using a .05 level of significance.
    c. What assumptions are necessary to assure the validity of this test?

*7.101   Many water treatment facilities add hydrofluorosilicic acid to the water to supplement the natural fluoride concentration in order to reach a target concentration of fluoride in the drinking water. Certain levels are thought to enhance dental health, but very high concentrations can be dangerous. Suppose that one such treatment plant targets .75 milligram per liter (mg/L) for its water. The plant tests 25 samples each day to determine whether the median level differs from the target.
    a. Set up the null and alternative hypotheses.
    b. Set up the test statistic and rejection region using $\alpha = .10$.
    c. Explain the implication of a Type I error in the context of this application. A Type II error.
    d. Suppose that one day's samples result in 18 values that exceed .75 mg/L. Conduct the test and state the appropriate conclusion in the context of this application.
    e. When it was suggested to the plant's supervisor that a t test should be used to conduct the daily test, she replied that the probability distribution of the fluoride concentrations was "heavily skewed to the right."

Show graphically what she meant by this, and explain why this is a reason to prefer the sign test to the t test.

On Your Own

The **efficient market** theory postulates that the best predictor of a stock's price at some point in the future is the current price of the stock (with some adjustments for inflation and transaction costs, which we shall assume to be negligible for the purpose of this exercise). To test this theory, select a random sample of 25 stocks on the New York Stock Exchange and record the closing prices on the last day of each of two recent consecutive months. Calculate the increase or decrease in the stock price over the 1 month period.

a. Define μ as the mean change in price of all stocks over a 1-month period. Set up the appropriate null and alternative hypothesis in terms of μ.

b. Use the sample of the 25 stock price differences to conduct the test of hypothesis established in part **a**. Use $\alpha = .05$.

c. Tabulate the number of rejections and nonrejections of the null hypothesis obtained by all the students in your class. If the null hypothesis were true, how many rejections of the null hypothesis would you expect among those in your class? How does this expectation compare with the actual number of nonrejections? What does the result of this exercise indicate about the efficient market theory?

Using the Computer

Refer to **Using the Computer** in Chapters 5 and 6. Let μ_0 be the mean of the population of 1,000 zip codes you selected (that is, μ_0 is the "true" value of the population mean). In each of the following scenarios you will be testing the null hypothesis $H_0: \mu = \mu_0$ against the two-tailed alternative hypothesis $H_a: \mu \neq \mu_0$. Thus, in this exercise you know that the null hypothesis is true.

a. Select 100 samples of size 50 (with replacement) from the 1,000 zip codes, and conduct the test for each sample using $\alpha = .05$. In how many of the tests did the sample lead to an incorrect rejection of the null hypothesis? How does this compare with what you expected to occur? Repeat the exercise using $\alpha = .10$.

b. Select 100 samples of size 20 (with replacement) from the 1,000 zip codes, and conduct the test for each sample using $\alpha = .05$. In how many of the tests did the sample lead to an incorrect rejection of the null hypothesis? How does this compare with what you expected to occur? Repeat the exercise using $\alpha = .10$.

References

Caplen, R. *A Practical Approach to Quality Control*. London: Business Books, 1970. Chapter 15.

Conover, W. J. *Practical Nonparametric Statistics*, 2d ed. New York: Wiley, 1980.

Dujack, S. R. "Science leaves no doubt: The polygraph lies." *Minneapolis Star and Tribune*, July 31, 1986.

Duncan, A. J. *Quality Control and Industrial Statistics*, 5th ed. Homewood, Ill.: Richard D. Irwin, 1986. Chapter 1.

Farhi, P. "Multiplying millionaires." *Star Tribune* (Minneapolis), July 14, 1992.

Hollander, M. and Wolfe, D. A. *Nonparametric Statistical Methods*, New York: Wiley, 1973.

Montgomery, D. C. *Introduction to Statistical Quality Control*, 2d ed. New York: Wiley, 1991.

Nemy, E. "Survey says two-thirds of Americans see themselves as younger than they are." *Minneapolis Tribune*, Dec. 19, 1982.

Report of Definitions Committee of the American Marketing Association. Chicago: American Marketing Association, 1961.

Rice, F. "Be a smarter frequent flier." *Fortune*, Feb. 22, 1993, pp. 108–112.

Sauer, R. D., Brajer, V., Ferris, S. P., and Marr, M. W. "Hold your bets: Another look at the efficiency of the gambling market for National Football League games." *Journal of Political Economy*, Feb. 1988, Vol. 96, No. 1, pp. 260–273.

Sharpe, W. F. and Alexander, G. J. *Investments*, 4th ed. Englewood Cliffs, N.J.: Prentice-Hall, 1990.

Streeter, J. P. "Solder joint inspection using a laser inspector." *Quality Congress Transactions*. Milwaukee: American Society for Quality Control, 1986. pp. 507–515.

Treleven, M. "Sole sourcing from the vendor side."*Quality Congress Transactions*. Milwaukee: American Society for Quality Control, 1986. pp. 584–590.

Wetherill, G. B. *Sampling, Inspection, and Quality Control*, 2d ed. London: Chapman and Hall, 1977. Chapter 3.

Willis, R. E. and Chervany, N. L. *Statistical Analysis and Modeling for Management Decision-making*. Belmont, Calif.: Wadsworth, 1974. Chapters 8 and 11.

CHAPTER EIGHT

Comparing Two Population Means

Where We've Been

The two methods for making statistical inferences, estimation and tests of hypotheses, were presented in Chapters 6 and 7. Confidence intervals and tests of hypotheses based on single samples were used to make inferences about sampled populations. We gave confidence intervals and tests of hypotheses concerning a population mean, μ, and a binomial proportion, p, and learned how to select the sample size necessary to obtain a specified amount of information concerning a parameter.

Where We're Going

Now that we have learned to make inferences about a single population, it is natural that we would want to compare two populations. We may want to compare the mean costs per pound in the manufacture of two drugs or the mean shelf lives of two industrial products. How to decide whether differences exist in population means and how to estimate these differences is the subject of this chapter. We will learn how to compare population proportions in Chapter 9.

8.1 Large-Sample Inferences About the Difference Between Two Population Means: Independent Sampling

Suppose a chain of department stores is considering two suburbs of a large city as alternatives for locating a new store. The final decision about which location to choose will be based on a comparison of the mean incomes of families living in the two suburbs.* The store is to be located in the suburb that has the higher mean income per household.

Let μ_1 represent the mean income of families in suburb 1 and μ_2 represent the mean income of families in suburb 2. Then our objective is to make an inference about $(\mu_1 - \mu_2)$, the difference between the mean incomes for the two suburbs.

Suppose independent samples of 100 households are randomly selected from each suburb, and the mean incomes, $\bar{x}_1$ and $\bar{x}_2$, are calculated for the two samples. An intuitively appealing estimator for $(\mu_1 - \mu_2)$ is the difference between the sample means, $(\bar{x}_1 - \bar{x}_2)$. The performance of this estimator in repeated sampling is summarized by the properties of its sampling distribution (see Figure 8.1).

FIGURE 8.1 ▶
Sampling distribution of $(\bar{x}_1 - \bar{x}_2)$

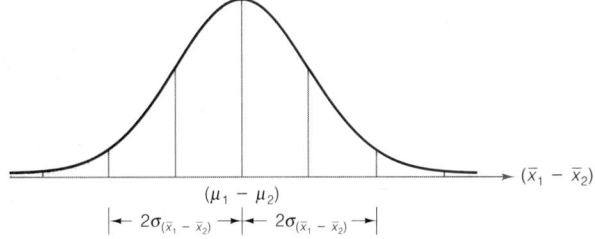

$(\mu_1 - \mu_2)$

$\leftarrow 2\sigma_{(\bar{x}_1 - \bar{x}_2)} \rightarrow \leftarrow 2\sigma_{(\bar{x}_1 - \bar{x}_2)} \rightarrow$

$(\bar{x}_1 - \bar{x}_2)$

Properties of the Sampling Distribution $(\bar{x}_1 - \bar{x}_2)$

1. The mean of the sampling distribution of $(\bar{x}_1 - \bar{x}_2)$ is $(\mu_1 - \mu_2)$.

2. If the two samples are independent, the standard deviation of the sampling distribution is

$$\sigma_{(\bar{x}_1 - \bar{x}_2)} = \sqrt{\frac{\sigma_1^2}{n_1} + \frac{\sigma_2^2}{n_2}}$$

where σ_1^2 and σ_2^2 are the variances of the two populations being sampled, and n_1 and n_2 are the respective sample sizes. We also refer to $\sigma_{(\bar{x}_1 - \bar{x}_2)}$ as the **standard error** of the statistic $(\bar{x}_1 - \bar{x}_2)$.

3. The sampling distribution of $(\bar{x}_1 - \bar{x}_2)$ is approximately normal for *large* samples by the Central Limit Theorem.

---

*Assume that the incomes within a suburb are moderately homogeneous, hence the distributions are not heavily skewed, so the mean would be a satisfactory measure of central tendency for the data.

Since the shape of the sampling distribution is approximately normal for large samples, we can use the z statistic to make inferences about $(\mu_1 - \mu_2)$, just as we did for a single mean. The procedures for forming confidence intervals and testing hypotheses are summarized in the boxes. Note the similarity of these procedures to their counterparts for a single mean (Sections 6.1 and 7.2).

Large-Sample Confidence Interval for $(\mu_1 - \mu_2)$

$$(\bar{x}_1 - \bar{x}_2) \pm z_{\alpha/2}\sigma_{(\bar{x}_1 - \bar{x}_2)} = (\bar{x}_1 - \bar{x}_2) \pm z_{\alpha/2}\sqrt{\frac{\sigma_1^2}{n_1} + \frac{\sigma_2^2}{n_2}}$$

Assumptions: The two samples are randomly selected in an independent manner from the two populations. The sample sizes, n_1 and n_2, are large enough so that $\bar{x}_1$ and $\bar{x}_2$ each have approximately normal sampling distributions and so that s_1^2 and s_2^2 provide good approximations to σ_1^2 and σ_2^2. This will generally be true if $n_1 \geq 30$ and $n_2 \geq 30$.

Large-Sample Test of Hypothesis for $(\mu_1 - \mu_2)$

One-Tailed Test

H_0: $(\mu_1 - \mu_2) = D_0$
H_a: $(\mu_1 - \mu_2) < D_0$
   [or H_a: $(\mu_1 - \mu_2) > D_0$]

Two-Tailed Test

H_0: $(\mu_1 - \mu_2) = D_0$
H_a: $(\mu_1 - \mu_2) \neq D_0$

where D_0 = Hypothesized difference between the means (this is often 0)

Test statistic: $z = \dfrac{(\bar{x}_1 - \bar{x}_2) - D_0}{\sigma_{(\bar{x}_1 - \bar{x}_2)}}$

Test statistic: $z = \dfrac{(\bar{x}_1 - \bar{x}_2) - D_0}{\sigma_{(\bar{x}_1 - \bar{x}_2)}}$

where $\sigma_{(\bar{x}_1 - \bar{x}_2)} = \sqrt{\dfrac{\sigma_1^2}{n_1} + \dfrac{\sigma_2^2}{n_2}}$

Rejection region: $z < -z_\alpha$
[or $z > z_\alpha$ when H_a: $(\mu_1 - \mu_2) > D_0$]

Rejection region: $z < -z_{\alpha/2}$
   or $z > z_{\alpha/2}$

Assumptions: Same as for the large-sample confidence interval.

Suburb 1	Suburb 2
$\bar{x}_1 = \$38,750$	$\bar{x}_2 = \$35,150$
$s_1 = \$3,200$	$s_2 = \$2,700$
$n_1 = 100$	$n_2 = 100$

For example, suppose the means and standard deviations of the incomes of sampled households from the two suburbs are as shown. Then to form a 95% confidence interval for the difference $(\mu_1 - \mu_2)$ between the true mean suburban incomes, we calculate

$$(\bar{x}_1 - \bar{x}_2) \pm 1.96 \sqrt{\frac{\sigma_1^2}{n_1} + \frac{\sigma_2^2}{n_2}} = (38{,}750 - 35{,}150) \pm 1.96 \sqrt{\frac{\sigma_1^2}{100} + \frac{\sigma_2^2}{100}}$$

To complete the calculations for this confidence interval, we must estimate σ_1^2 and σ_2^2. Since the samples are both relatively large, the sample variances s_1^2 and s_2^2 will provide reasonable approximations. Thus, our interval is approximately

$$3{,}600 \pm 1.96 \sqrt{\frac{(3{,}200)^2}{100} + \frac{(2{,}700)^2}{100}} = 3{,}600 \pm 821 = (2{,}779,\ 4{,}421)$$

When this estimation procedure is used, confidence intervals of this type will enclose the difference in population means, $(\mu_1 - \mu_2)$, 95% of the time. Therefore, we are reasonably confident that the mean income of households in suburb 1 is between \$2,779 and \$4,421 higher than the mean income of households in suburb 2. Based on this information, the department store chain should build the new store in suburb 1.

EXAMPLE 8.1

In the late 1980s and early 1990s the United States and Japan engaged in intense negotiations regarding restrictions on trade between the two countries. One of the claims made repeatedly by U.S. officials was that many Japanese manufacturers price their goods higher in Japan than in the United States, in effect subsidizing low prices in the United States by extremely high prices in Japan. The basis of the U.S. argument was that Japan was able to do that only by keeping competitive U.S. goods from reaching the Japanese marketplace.

An economist decided to test the hypothesis that higher retail prices were being charged for Japanese automobiles in Japan than in the United States. She obtained random samples of 50 retail sales in the United States and 30 retail sales in Japan over the same time period and for the same model of automobile, converted the Japanese sales prices from yen to dollars using current conversion rates, and obtained the summary shown in the table. Do these data provide sufficient evidence for the economist to conclude that the mean sales price for this model is higher in Japan than in the United States?

U.S. Sales	Japanese Sales
$n_1 = 50$	$n_2 = 30$
$\bar{x}_1 = \$11{,}545$	$\bar{x}_2 = \$12{,}243$
$s_1 = \$1{,}989$	$s_2 = \$1{,}843$

Solution

We can best answer this question by performing a test of hypothesis. Defining μ_1 as the mean sales price in the United States and μ_2 as the mean sales price in Japan during this period and for this model of automobile, we want to test whether the data support the alternative (research) hypothesis that $\mu_2 > \mu_1$ [i.e., that $(\mu_1 - \mu_2) < 0$]. Thus, we test the null hypothesis, $(\mu_1 - \mu_2) = 0$. The evidence necessary to reject this hypothesis in favor of the alternative is a sufficiently large negative value of the difference between the sample means, $(\bar{x}_1 - \bar{x}_2)$.

The elements of the test are as follows:

$$H_0: \quad (\mu_1 - \mu_2) = 0 \quad \text{(i.e., } \mu_1 = \mu_2; \text{ note that } D_0 = 0 \text{ for this hypothesis test)}$$

$$H_a: \quad (\mu_1 - \mu_2) < 0 \quad \text{(i.e., } \mu_1 < \mu_2)$$

$$\textit{Test statistic:} \quad z = \frac{(\bar{x}_1 - \bar{x}_2) - D_0}{\sigma_{(\bar{x}_1 - \bar{x}_2)}} = \frac{(\bar{x}_1 - \bar{x}_2) - 0}{\sigma_{(\bar{x}_1 - \bar{x}_2)}}$$

$$\textit{Rejection region:} \quad z < -z_\alpha = -1.645 \quad \text{(see Figure 8.2)}$$

FIGURE 8.2 ▶
Rejection region for Example 8.1

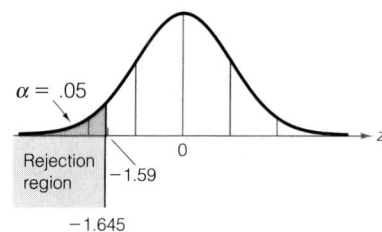

$\alpha = .05$

Rejection region

-1.59

0

z

-1.645

Assuming the samples from the United States and Japan are independent, we now calculate

$$z = \frac{(\bar{x}_1 - \bar{x}_2) - 0}{\sigma_{(\bar{x}_1 - \bar{x}_2)}} = \frac{(11,545 - 12,243)}{\sqrt{\dfrac{\sigma_1^2}{n_1} + \dfrac{\sigma_2^2}{n_2}}}$$

$$\approx \frac{-698}{\sqrt{\dfrac{s_1^2}{n_1} + \dfrac{s_2^2}{n_2}}} = \frac{-698}{\sqrt{\dfrac{(1,989)^2}{50} + \dfrac{(1,843)^2}{30}}} = \frac{-698}{438.57} = -1.59$$

As you can see in Figure 8.2, the calculated z value does not fall in the rejection region. The samples do not provide sufficient evidence, at $\alpha = .05$, for the economist to conclude that the mean retail price in Japan exceeds that in the United States.

EXAMPLE 8.2

Find the observed significance level for the test from Example 8.1.

Solution

The alternative hypothesis in Example 8.1, $H_a: (\mu_1 - \mu_2) < 0$, required a lower one-tailed test using

$$z = \frac{\bar{x}_1 - \bar{x}_2}{\sigma_{(\bar{x}_1 - \bar{x}_2)}}$$

as a test statistic. Since the value of z calculated from the sample data was -1.59, the observed significance level (p-value) for the test is the probability of observing a value of z at least as contradictory to the null hypothesis as $z = -1.59$; i.e.,

$$p\text{-value} = P(z \le -1.59)$$

This probability is computed assuming H_0 is true and is equal to the shaded area shown in Figure 8.3.

FIGURE 8.3 ▶
The observed significance level
for Example 8.1

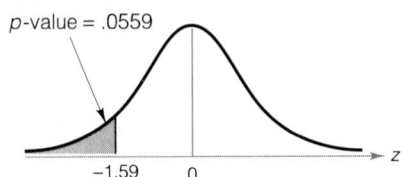

p-value = .0559

$-1.59 \quad 0$

z

The tabulated area corresponding to $z = 1.59$ in Table IV of Appendix B is .4441. Therefore, the observed significance level for the test is

$$p\text{-value} = .5 - .4441$$
$$= .0559$$

You will recall that in Example 8.1, we chose $\alpha = .05$ as the probability of a Type I error and consequently did not reject H_0; that is, we did not find sufficient evidence to indicate that $(\mu_1 - \mu_2) < 0$. If the results of the test had been presented in terms of an observed significance level and left for us to interpret, we might not have reached such an inflexible conclusion. Observing a value of z as small as $z = -1.59$ is an improbable event (rare event) if, in fact, $\mu_1 = \mu_2$. Since the probability is fairly small (.0559)—in fact, quite close to .05—we would conclude that there is some evidence to suggest that $\mu_1 < \mu_2$. Naturally, we would be more certain of this conclusion if the observed significance level were smaller, say, .05, .01, or, better yet, .001. However, the practical question to be answered is not whether the test results are statistically significant but whether the difference between μ_1 and μ_2 is large enough to be significant from a practical business perspective. To shed light on this question, we will wish to estimate the difference, $(\mu_1 - \mu_2)$.

EXAMPLE 8.3

Find a 95% confidence interval for the difference in mean retail prices in the United States and Japan of Example 8.1 and discuss the implications of the confidence interval.

Solution

The 95% confidence interval for $(\mu_1 - \mu_2)$ is

$$(\bar{x}_1 - \bar{x}_2) \pm z_{\alpha/2} \sqrt{\frac{\sigma_1^2}{n_1} + \frac{\sigma_2^2}{n_2}}$$

Once again, we will substitute s_1^2 and s_2^2 for σ_1^2 and σ_2^2 because these quantities will provide good approximations to σ_1^2 and σ_2^2 for samples as large as $n_1 = 50$ and $n_2 = 30$. Then, the 95% confidence interval for $(\mu_1 - \mu_2)$ is

$$(11{,}545 - 12{,}243) \pm 1.96\sqrt{\frac{(1{,}989)^2}{50} + \frac{(1{,}843)^2}{30}} = -698 \pm 859.60$$

Thus, we estimate the difference in mean retail prices to fall in the interval $-\$1{,}557.60$ to $\$161.60$. In other words, we estimate that μ_2, the mean retail price in Japan, could be larger than μ_1, the mean retail price in the United States, by as much as $\$1{,}557.60$, or it could be less than μ_1 by as much as $\$161.60$.

What is the practical interpretation of all this? By all appearances, the Japanese retail price for this model car was indeed higher than the U.S. retail price during the same time period. However, the data collected were insufficient to provide statistical support for this conclusion at the specified level of significance.

What can be done further to refine and sharpen the analysis? The first and most obvious improvement would be to increase the sample sizes: Sample sizes of 50 and 30 yield a rather wide confidence interval (total width of $\$1{,}719.20$) for estimating the difference between the means. Increasing the sample sizes will decrease the standard error $\sigma_{(\bar{x}_1 - \bar{x}_2)}$; hence, the width of the confidence interval will also decrease.

A second, less obvious, refinement to the analysis would be somehow to decrease the rather large standard deviations associated with the samples, s_1 and s_2. Both exceed $\$1{,}800$, indicating that the retail prices contained within each sample vary widely. Perhaps the options available on this model result in significant price discrepancies, or perhaps the dealerships in urban settings have significantly different pricing strategies from those in rural settings. *Regression analysis* is a useful statistical methodology for comparing population means while controlling for other factors affecting the variability of the measurements, such as options and geographic location in this example. Regression analysis is the subject of Chapter 10.

Exercises 8.1 – 8.13

Learning the Mechanics

8.1 The purpose of this exercise is to compare the variation of $\bar{x}_1$ and $\bar{x}_2$ with the variation of $(\bar{x}_1 - \bar{x}_2)$.

 a. Suppose the first sample is selected from a population with mean $\mu_1 = 150$ and variance $\sigma_1^2 = 900$. Within what range should the sample mean vary about 95% of the time in repeated samples of 100 measurements from this distribution? That is, construct an interval extending 2 standard deviations of $\bar{x}_1$ on each side of μ_1.

 b. Suppose the second sample is selected independently of the first from a second population with mean $\mu_2 = 150$ and variance $\sigma_2^2 = 1{,}600$. Within what range should the sample mean vary about 95% of the time in repeated samples of 100 measurements from this distribution? That is, construct an interval extending 2 standard deviations of $\bar{x}_2$ on each side of μ_2.

   c. Now consider the difference between the two sample means, $(\bar{x}_1 - \bar{x}_2)$. What are the mean and standard deviation of the sampling distribution of $(\bar{x}_1 - \bar{x}_2)$?

   d. Within what range should the difference in sample means vary about 95% of the time in repeated independent samples of 100 measurements each from the two populations? That is, construct an interval extending 2 standard deviations of $(\bar{x}_1 - \bar{x}_2)$ on each side of $(\mu_1 - \mu_2)$.

   e. What, in general, can be said about the variability of the difference between independent sample means relative to the variability of the individual sample means?

8.2 Independent random samples of 64 observations each are chosen from two normal populations with $\mu_1 = 12$, $\mu_2 = 10$, $\sigma_1 = 4$, and $\sigma_2 = 3$. Let $\bar{x}_1$ and $\bar{x}_2$ denote the two sample means.
   a. Give the mean and standard deviation of the sampling distribution of $\bar{x}_1$.
   b. Give the mean and standard deviation of the sampling distribution of $\bar{x}_2$.
   c. Find the mean and standard deviation of the sampling distribution of $(\bar{x}_1 - \bar{x}_2)$.
   d. Will the statistic $(\bar{x}_1 - \bar{x}_2)$ be normally distributed? Explain.

8.3 Refer to Exercise 8.2.
   a. Give the z-score corresponding to $(\bar{x}_1 - \bar{x}_2) = 2.25$.
   b. Find the probability that $(\bar{x}_1 - \bar{x}_2)$ is larger than 2.25.
   c. Find the probability that $(\bar{x}_1 - \bar{x}_2)$ is less than 2.25.
   d. Find the probability that $(\bar{x}_1 - \bar{x}_2)$ is less than $-.8$ or larger than $.8$.

8.4 Two independent random samples have been selected, 100 observations from population 1 and 100 from population 2. Sample means $\bar{x}_1 = 15.5$ and $\bar{x}_2 = 26.6$ were obtained. From previous experience with these populations, it is known that the variances are $\sigma_1^2 = 9$ and $\sigma_2^2 = 16$.
   a. Find $\sigma_{(\bar{x}_1 - \bar{x}_2)}$.
   b. Sketch the approximate sampling distribution for $(\bar{x}_1 - \bar{x}_2)$ assuming $(\mu_1 - \mu_2) = 10$.
   c. Locate the observed value of $(\bar{x}_1 - \bar{x}_2)$ on the graph you drew in part **b**. Does it appear that this value contradicts the null hypothesis H_0: $(\mu_1 - \mu_2) = 10$?
   d. Use the z table on the inside front cover to determine the rejection region for the test of the hypothesis H_0: $(\mu_1 - \mu_2) = 10$ against H_a: $(\mu_1 - \mu_2) \neq 10$. Use $\alpha = .05$.
   e. Conduct the hypothesis test of part **d** and interpret your results.
   f. Construct a 95% confidence interval for $(\mu_1 - \mu_2)$. Interpret the interval.
   g. Which inference provides more information about the value of $(\mu_1 - \mu_2)$—the test of hypothesis in part **e** or the confidence interval in part **f**?

8.5 Independent random samples are selected from two populations and are used to test the hypothesis H_0: $(\mu_1 - \mu_2) = 0$ against the alternative H_a: $(\mu_1 - \mu_2) \neq 0$. A total of 233 observations from population 1 and 312 from population 2 are analyzed with a statistical software package, with the results shown.

$\overline{X}_1 = 473$	$\overline{X}_2 = 485$
$S_1 = 84$	$S_2 = 93$
$Z = -1.576$	P-VALUE $= .1150$

   a. Interpret the results of the computer analysis.
   b. If the alternative hypothesis had been H_a: $(\mu_1 - \mu_2) < 0$, how would the p-value change? Interpret the p-value for this one-tailed test.

Applying the Concepts

8.6 Wansley, Roenfeldt, and Cooley (1983) compared the profiles of a sample of 44 firms that merged during 1975–1976 with those of a sample of 44 firms that did not merge. The table displays information obtained on the firms' price–earnings ratios.

	Merged Firms	Nonmerged Firms
Sample mean	7.295	14.666
Sample standard deviation	7.374	16.089

a. The analysis indicated that merged firms generally have smaller price–earnings ratios. Do you agree? Test using $\alpha = .05$.

b. Report and interpret the p-value of the test you conducted in part **a**.

c. What assumption(s) was it necessary to make in order to perform the test in part **a**?

d. Do you think that the distributions of the price–earnings ratios for the populations from which these samples were drawn are normally distributed? Why or why not? [*Hint:* Note the relative values of the sample means and standard deviations.]

8.7 A paper company conducted an experiment to compare the mean time to unload shipments of logs for two different unloading procedures. Two samples of 50 trucks each were unloaded using a new method and the company's current method. The objective of the experiment is to determine whether the new method will reduce the mean unloading time. The sample means and standard deviations are shown in the table.

New Method	Current Method
$n_1 = 50$	$n_2 = 50$
$\bar{x}_1 = 25.4$ minutes	$\bar{x}_2 = 27.3$ minutes
$s_1 = 3.1$ minutes	$s_2 = 3.7$ minutes

a. Do the data provide sufficient evidence to indicate that the mean unloading time for the new method is less than the mean unloading time for the method currently in use? Test using $\alpha = .05$.

b. Give the observed significance level for the test.

8.8 Refer to Exercise 8.7. Find a 90% confidence interval for the difference in mean unloading times between the two methods.

8.9 For over a decade, Tennant Co., a Minnesota manufacturer of industrial floor-cleaning machines, has been using quality circles to help improve its product. The term *quality circles* describes a process in which groups comprising both white-collar and blue-collar employees attempt to solve quality, productivity, or work environment problems.

When Tennant began its quality circles program in 1979, a sample of finished machines was found to have an average of 4.2 defects per machine. Because of such defects, the company had to pay its employees $16.6 million for the 39,600 hours of labor required to rework the defective machines. In 1982, a sample of machines revealed a substantial improvement in quality. The mean number of defectives was reduced to 1.3 defects per machine, and rework was down to 3,500 hours of labor (Marcotty, 1983a, 1983b). Assume that each sample of machines was randomly selected and was of size 100. Further, assume that the sample standard deviations for 1979 and 1983 were 2.0 and 1.1, respectively.

a. Although the decline in the average number of defects per machine between 1979 and 1982 appears to be significant from a managerial perspective, is it statistically significant? To answer the question, conduct the appropriate hypothesis test and report and interpret the observed significance level of the test.

b. In the context of the problem, describe the Type I and Type II errors associated with your hypothesis test of part **a**.

8.10 As part of a study of participative management, George H. Hines (1974) sampled workers from two types of New Zealand sociocultural backgrounds: those who believe in the existence of a class system and those who believe that they live and work in a classless society. Each worker in the sampling was selected from a work environment with a high degree of participatory management. Do workers who consider themselves to be social equals with their management superiors possess other levels of job satisfaction than those workers who see themselves as socially different from management? Each worker in the independent random samples answered this question by rating his or her job satisfaction on a scale of 1 (poor) to 7 (excellent). Based on the results shown in the table, what can you say about differences in job satisfaction for the two different sociocultural types of workers? Use $\alpha = .10$.

	Believe Class System Exists	Believe No Class System Exists
Sample size	175	277
Mean	5.42	5.19
Standard deviation	1.24	1.17

8.11 An experiment has been conducted to compare the productivity of two machines. Machine 1 produced an average of 51.4 items per hour and a standard deviation of $s_1 = 2.1$ for 35 randomly selected hours during the past 2 weeks. Machine 2 produced an average of 49.5 items per hour and a standard deviation of $s_2 = 1.8$ for 45 randomly selected hours during the past 2 weeks.
a. Describe the populations being compared.
b. Do the samples provide sufficient evidence at $\alpha = .10$ to conclude that machine 1 produces more items per hour, on the average, than machine 2?
c. Report the p-value for the test you conducted in part b.

8.12 Refer to Exercise 8.11. Construct a 95% confidence interval for $(\mu_1 - \mu_2)$. Would a 99% confidence interval be narrower or wider than the one you constructed? Why?

8.13 The mean or median value of a community's single-family homes is sometimes used as an indicator of local wealth or "buying power." Such information may be useful to retail merchants looking for communities in which to locate their businesses or deciding where to concentrate their advertising. A retailer believes that the mean price of a single-family home in Edina, Minnesota, is substantially more than in St. Louis Park, Minnesota. If this is confirmed by a statistical hypothesis test, the retailer will increase her advertising budget for the Edina area. The table contains the asking prices of a random sample of 30 homes up for sale in Edina in late February 1993 and a random sample of 30 homes also on the market then in St. Louis Park.

Edina			St. Louis Park		
$215,000	179,900	134,600	$134,900	89,900	180,000
205,000	225,000	179,750	84,900	153,500	94,900
214,900	145,000	165,900	90,000	34,900	87,900
178,500	329,500	164,900	110,000	109,000	89,900
349,900	142,900	119,000	78,700	103,900	69,500
145,900	140,900	159,900	74,900	104,900	66,900
82,000	189,500	179,000	69,900	87,900	54,900
402,500	203,900	160,000	149,900	120,000	69,900
217,500	672,900	116,700	116,900	86,500	73,900
138,000	205,900	129,900	84,900	89,900	65,800

Source: Minneapolis Area Association of Realtors, 1993.

a. Describe the populations from which the sample data were selected.
b. What are the parameters of interest to the retailer?
c. For Edina, $\bar{x}_1 = \$203,142$ and $s_1 = \$112,285$. For St. Louis Park, $\bar{x}_2 = \$94,300$ and $s_2 = \$30,687$. Do the data indicate that the mean price of a home in Edina is more than $\$60,000$ greater than the mean price in St. Louis Park? Test using $\alpha = .05$.
d. Use a 95% confidence interval to estimate the true difference in the mean prices for Edina and St. Louis Park.

8.2 Small-Sample Inferences About the Difference Between Two Population Means: Independent Sampling

Suppose a television network wanted to determine whether major sports events or first-run movies attract more viewers in the prime-time hours. It selected 28 prime-time evenings; of these, 13 had programs devoted to major sports events and the remaining 15 had first-run movies. The number of viewers (estimated by a television viewer rating firm) was recorded for each program. If μ_1 is the mean number of sports viewers per evening of sports programming and μ_2 is the mean number of movie viewers per evening of movie programming, we want to detect a difference between μ_1 and μ_2—if such a difference exists. Therefore, we want to test the null hypothesis

$$H_0: \quad (\mu_1 - \mu_2) = 0$$

against the alternative hypothesis

$$H_a: \quad (\mu_1 - \mu_2) \neq 0 \qquad \text{(i.e., either } \mu_1 > \mu_2 \text{ or } \mu_2 > \mu_1)$$

Since the sample sizes are small, s_1^2 and s_2^2 will be unreliable estimates of σ_1^2 and σ_2^2 and the z test statistic will be inappropriate for the test. But, as in the case of a single mean (Section 7.4), we can construct a Student's t statistic. This statistic (formula to be given subsequently) has the familiar t distribution described in Chapter 6. **To use the t statistic, both sampled populations must be approximately normally distributed with equal population variances, and the random samples must be selected independently of each other.** The normality and equal variances assumptions would imply relative frequency distributions for the populations that would appear as shown in Figure 8.4. We will assume that the distributions of the two populations of numbers of television viewers will approximately satisfy these assumptions.

FIGURE 8.4 ▶
Assumptions for the two-sample t:
(1) normal populations
(2) equal variances

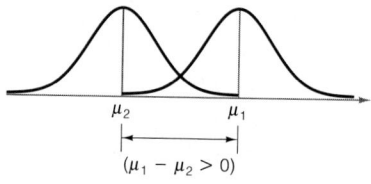

Since we assume the two populations have equal variances ($\sigma_1^2 = \sigma_2^2 = \sigma^2$), it is reasonable to combine the sum of squares of deviations from the two samples to construct a pooled sample estimator of σ^2 for use in the t statistic. Thus, if s_1^2 and s_2^2 are the two sample variances (each estimating the variance σ^2 common to both populations), the pooled estimator of σ^2, denoted as s_p^2, is

$$s_p^2 = \frac{\overbrace{\sum_{i=1}^{n_1} (x_i - \bar{x}_1)^2}^{\substack{\text{From} \\ \text{sample 1}}} + \overbrace{\sum_{i=1}^{n_2} (x_i - \bar{x}_2)^2}^{\substack{\text{From} \\ \text{sample 2}}}}{n_1 + n_2 - 2}$$

or

$$s_p^2 = \frac{(n_1 - 1)s_1^2 + (n_2 - 1)s_2^2}{(n_1 - 1) + (n_2 - 1)} = \frac{(n_1 - 1)s_1^2 + (n_2 - 1)s_2^2}{n_1 + n_2 - 2}$$

where x_1 represents a measurement from sample 1 and x_2 represents a measurement from sample 2. Recall that the term **degrees of freedom** was defined in Section 6.3 as 1 less than the sample size. Thus, in this case we have $(n_1 - 1)$ degrees of freedom for sample 1 and $(n_2 - 1)$ degrees of freedom for sample 2. Since we are pooling the information on σ^2 obtained from both samples, the degrees of freedom associated with the pooled variance s_p^2 is equal to the sum of the degrees of freedom for the two samples, namely, the denominator of s_p^2—i.e., $(n_1 - 1) + (n_2 - 1) = n_1 + n_2 - 2$.

Note that the second formula given for s_p^2 shows that the pooled variance is simply a *weighted average* of the two sample variances, s_1^2 and s_2^2. The weight given each variance is proportional to its degrees of freedom. If the two variances have the same number of degrees of freedom (i.e., if the sample sizes are equal), then the pooled variance is a simple average of the two sample variances. The result is an average or pooled variance that is a better estimate of σ_2 than either s_1^2 or s_2^2 alone.

To obtain the small-sample test statistic for testing $H_0: (\mu_1 - \mu_2) = D_0$, substitute the pooled estimate of σ^2 into the formula for the two-sample z statistic (Section 8.1) to obtain

$$t = \frac{(\bar{x}_1 - \bar{x}_2) - D_0}{\sqrt{s_p^2 \left(\frac{1}{n_1} + \frac{1}{n_2} \right)}}$$

It can be shown that this statistic, like the t statistic of Chapter 6, has a t distribution, but with $(n_1 + n_2 - 2)$ degrees of freedom.

We will use the television viewer example to outline the final steps for this t test. The hypothesized difference in mean number of viewers is $D_0 = 0$. The rejection region will be two-tailed and will be based on a t distribution with $(n_1 + n_2 - 2)$ or $(13 + 15 - 2) = 26$ df. Letting $\alpha = .05$, the rejection region for the test would be

$$t < -t_{\alpha/2} \quad \text{or} \quad t > t_{\alpha/2}$$

The value for $t_{.025}$ with df $= 26$ given in Table VI of Appendix B is 2.056. Thus, the rejection region for the television example is

$$t < -2.056 \quad \text{or} \quad t > 2.056$$

This rejection region is shown in Figure 8.5.

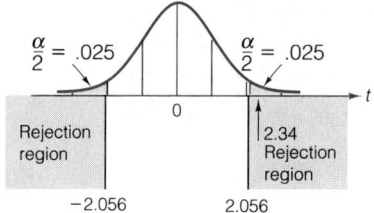

Now, suppose the television network's samples produce the results shown in the table:

Sports	Movie
$n_1 = 13$	$n_2 = 15$
$\bar{x}_1 = 6.8$ million	$\bar{x}_2 = 5.3$ million
$s_1 = 1.8$ million	$s_2 = 1.6$ million

We must assume that these independent samples were selected from normal distributions (i.e., the number of viewers per evening is normally distributed for each type of program) with equal variances. [*Note:*   Although the sample estimates of variance are not equal, the assumption that the population variances are equal may still be valid. Consult the references at the end of this chapter for methods for checking this assumption statistically.] We now calculate

$$s_p^2 = \frac{(n_1 - 1)s_1^2 + (n_2 - 1)s_2^2}{n_1 + n_2 - 2}$$

$$= \frac{(13 - 1)(1.8)^2 + (15 - 1)(1.6)^2}{13 + 15 - 2} = \frac{74.72}{26} = 2.87$$

Then,

$$t = \frac{(\bar{x}_1 - \bar{x}_2) - D_0}{\sqrt{s_p^2\left(\dfrac{1}{n_1} + \dfrac{1}{n_2}\right)}} = \frac{(6.8 - 5.3) - 0}{\sqrt{2.87\left(\dfrac{1}{13} + \dfrac{1}{15}\right)}} = \frac{1.5}{.64} = 2.34$$

Since the observed value of t, $t = 2.34$, falls in the rejection region (see Figure 8.5), the samples provide sufficient evidence to indicate that the mean numbers of viewers differ for major sports events and first-run movies shown in prime time. Or, we say that the test results are statistically significant at the $\alpha = .05$ level of significance. Because the rejection was in the positive or upper tail of the t distribution, the indication is that the mean number of viewers for sports events exceeds that for movies.

The t statistic can also be used to construct a confidence interval for the difference between population means. Both the confidence interval and the test of hypothesis procedures are summarized in the boxes.

Small-Sample Confidence Interval for $(\mu_1 - \mu_2)$

$$(\bar{x}_1 - \bar{x}_2) \pm t_{\alpha/2} \sqrt{s_p^2 \left(\frac{1}{n_1} + \frac{1}{n_2} \right)}$$

where $\quad s_p^2 = \dfrac{(n_1 - 1)s_1^2 + (n_2 - 1)s_2^2}{n_1 + n_2 - 2}$

and $t_{\alpha/2}$ is based on $(n_1 + n_2 - 2)$ df.

Assumptions: 1. Both sampled populations have relative frequency distributions that are approximately normal.
2. The population variances are equal.
3. The samples are randomly and independently selected from the populations.

Small-Sample Test of Hypothesis for $(\mu_1 - \mu_2)$ (Independent Samples)

One-Tailed Test

H_0: $(\mu_1 - \mu_2) = D_0$
H_a: $(\mu_1 - \mu_2) < D_0$
 [or H_a: $(\mu_1 - \mu_2) > D_0$]

Test statistic:

$$t = \frac{(\bar{x}_1 - \bar{x}_2) - D_0}{\sqrt{s_p^2 \left(\dfrac{1}{n_1} + \dfrac{1}{n_2} \right)}}$$

Rejection region: $\quad t < -t_\alpha$
 [or $t > t_\alpha$ when
 H_a: $(\mu_1 - \mu_2) > D_0$]
where $t_{\alpha/2}$ is based on
$(n_1 + n_2 - 2)$ df.

Two-Tailed Test

H_0: $(\mu_1 - \mu_2) = D_0$
H_a: $(\mu_1 - \mu_2) \neq D_0$

Test statistic:

$$t = \frac{(\bar{x}_1 - \bar{x}_2) - D_0}{\sqrt{s_p^2 \left(\dfrac{1}{n_1} + \dfrac{1}{n_2} \right)}}$$

Rejection region: $\quad t < -t_{\alpha/2}$
 or $t > t_{\alpha/2}$
where t_α is based on
$(n_1 + n_2 - 2)$ df.

Assumptions: Same as for the small-sample confidence interval for $(\mu_1 - \mu_2)$.

EXAMPLE 8.4

Suppose you want to estimate the difference in annual operating costs for automobiles with automatic transmissions and those with standard transmissions. Using the records of a local automobile club, you randomly select 8 owners of cars with automatic transmissions and 12 owners of cars with standard transmissions who have purchased their cars within the last 2 years. Each of the 20 owners keeps accurate records of the amount spent on operating his or her car (including gasoline, oil, repairs, etc.) for a 12-month period. All costs are recorded on a per-thousand-mile basis to adjust for differences in mileage driven during the 12-month period. The results are summarized in the table. Estimate the true difference $(\mu_1 - \mu_2)$ in the mean operating costs per thousand miles between cars with automatic and cars with standard transmissions. Use a 90% confidence interval.

Automatic	*Standard*
$n_1 = 8$	$n_2 = 12$
$\bar{x}_1 = 156.96$	$\bar{x}_2 = 152.73$
$s_1 = \$4.85$	$s_2 = \$6.35$

Solution

The objective of this experiment is to obtain a 90% confidence interval for $(\mu_1 - \mu_2)$. To use the small-sample confidence interval for $(\mu_1 - \mu_2)$, the following assumptions must be satisfied:

1. The operating cost per thousand miles is normally distributed for cars with both automatic and standard transmissions. Since these costs are averages (because we observe them on a per-thousand-mile basis), the Central Limit Theorem lends credence to this assumption.

2. The variance in cost is the same for the two types of cars. Under these circumstances, we might expect the variation in costs from automobile to automobile to be about the same for both types of transmissions.

3. The samples are randomly and independently selected from the two populations. We have randomly chosen 20 different owners for the two samples in such a way that the cost measurement for one owner is not dependent on the cost measurement for any other owner. Therefore, this assumption would be valid.

The first step in performing the test is to calculate the pooled estimate of variance:

$$s_p^2 = \frac{(n_1 - 1)s_1^2 + (n_2 - 1)s_2^2}{n_1 + n_2 - 2}$$

$$= \frac{(8 - 1)(4.85)^2 + (12 - 1)(6.35)^2}{8 + 12 - 2} = 33.7892$$

where s_p^2 possesses $(n_1 + n_2 - 2) = (8 + 12 - 2) = 18$ df. Then, the 90% confidence interval for $(\mu_1 - \mu_2)$, the difference in mean operating costs for the two types of automobiles, is

$$(\bar{x}_1 - \bar{x}_2) \pm t_{\alpha/2} \sqrt{s_p^2 \left(\frac{1}{n_1} + \frac{1}{n_2} \right)} = (156.96 - 152.73) \pm t_{.05} \sqrt{33.7892 \left(\frac{1}{8} + \frac{1}{12} \right)}$$

$$= 4.23 \pm 1.734(2.653) = 4.23 \pm 4.60$$

$$= (-.37, \ 8.83)$$

This means that, with 90% confidence, we estimate the difference in mean operating costs per thousand miles between cars with automatic transmissions and those with standard transmissions to fall in the interval from $-\$.37$ to $\$8.83$. In other words, we estimate the mean operating costs for cars with automatic transmissions to be anywhere from $\$.37$ less than to $\$8.83$ more than the operating costs per thousand miles for cars with standard transmissions. Although the sample means seem to suggest that cars with automatic transmissions cost more to operate, there is insufficient evidence to indicate that $(\mu_1 - \mu_2)$ differs from 0 because the interval includes 0 as a possible value for $(\mu_1 - \mu_2)$. To show a difference in mean operating costs (if it exists), it would be necessary to increase the sample sizes and thereby narrow the width of the confidence interval for $(\mu_1 - \mu_2)$.

The two-sample t statistic is a powerful tool for comparing population means when the assumptions are satisfied. It has also been shown to retain its usefulness when the sampled populations are only approximately normally distributed. Furthermore, when the sample sizes are equal, the assumption of equal population variances can be relaxed. That is, when $n_1 = n_2$, σ_1^2 and σ_2^2 can be quite different and the test statistic will still have (approximately) a Student's t distribution. When the assumptions are not satisfied, other statistical tests are available. For example, the nonparametric statistical tests discussed in optional Section 8.5 may be appropriate.

What Can Be Done If the Assumptions Are Not Satisfied?

Answer: If you are concerned that your assumptions are not satisfied, use the Wilcoxon rank sum test for independent samples to test for a shift in population distributions. (See optional Section 8.5.)

Exercises 8.14–8.26

Learning the Mechanics

8.14 To use the t statistic to test for differences in the means of two populations, what assumptions must be made about the two populations? About the two samples?

8.15 Two populations are described in each of the following cases. In which cases would it be appropriate to apply the small-sample t test to investigate the difference between the population means?

a. Population 1:   Normal distribution with variance σ_1^2
   Population 2:   Skewed to the right with variance $\sigma_2^2 = \sigma_1^2$

b. Population 1:   Normal distribution with variance σ_1^2
   Population 2:   Normal distribution with variance $\sigma_2^2 \neq \sigma_1^2$

c. Population 1:   Skewed to the left with variance σ_1^2
   Population 2:   Skewed to the left with variance $\sigma_2^2 = \sigma_1^2$

d. Population 1:   Normal distribution with variance σ_1^2
   Population 2:   Normal distribution with variance $\sigma_2^2 = \sigma_1^2$

e. Population 1:   Uniform distribution with variance σ_1^2
   Population 2:   Uniform distribution with variance $\sigma_2^2 = \sigma_1^2$

8.16 In the t tests of this section, σ_1^2 and σ_2^2 are assumed to be equal. Thus, we say $\sigma_1^2 = \sigma_2^2 = \sigma^2$. Why is a pooled estimator of σ^2 used instead of either s_1^2 or s_2^2?

8.17 Assume that $\sigma_1^2 = \sigma_2^2 = \sigma^2$. Calculate the pooled estimator of σ^2 for each of the following cases:
a. $s_1^2 = 120$, $s_2^2 = 100$, $n_1 = n_2 = 25$ b. $s_1^2 = 12$, $s_2^2 = 20$, $n_1 = 20$, $n_2 = 10$
c. $s_1^2 = .15$, $s_2^2 = .20$, $n_1 = 6$, $n_2 = 10$ d. $s_1^2 = 3,000$, $s_2^2 = 2,500$, $n_1 = 16$, $n_2 = 17$
e. Note that the pooled estimate is a weighted average of the sample variances. Which of the variances does the pooled estimate fall nearer in each of the above cases?

8.18 Independent random samples from normal populations produced the results shown in the table.

Sample 1	2.1	3.4	1.4	3.0	2.9	3.3
Sample 2	3.4	3.0	4.2	3.8	3.5	

a. Calculate the pooled estimate of σ^2.
b. Do the data provide sufficient evidence to indicate that $\mu_2 > \mu_1$? Test using $\alpha = .10$.
c. Find the approximate observed significance level for the test, part **b**, and interpret its value.
d. Find a 90% confidence interval for $(\mu_1 - \mu_2)$. Interpret the confidence interval.
e. Which of the two inferential procedures, the test of hypothesis in part **b** or the confidence interval in part **d**, provides more information about $(\mu_1 - \mu_2)$? Justify your answer.

8.19 Independent random samples from two normal populations produced the results shown in the table.

Sample 1	Sample 2
$n_1 = 12$	$n_2 = 16$
$\bar{x}_1 = 35$	$\bar{x}_2 = 43$
$s_1 = 4.2$	$s_2 = 3.7$

a. Calculate the pooled estimate of σ^2.
b. Do these data provide sufficient evidence to indicate that $\mu_1 \neq \mu_2$? Test using $\alpha = .05$.
c. Find the approximate p-value for the test, part **b**, and interpret its value.
d. Find a 95% confidence interval for $(\mu_1 - \mu_2)$. Interpret the confidence interval.

8.20 Independent random samples from approximately normal populations produced the results shown in the table at the top of page 402.

	Sample 1						
52	33	42	44	41	50	44	51
45	38	37	40	44	50	43	

	Sample 2						
52	43	47	56	62	53	61	50
56	52	53	60	50	48	60	55

a. Do the data provide sufficient evidence to conclude that $(\mu_2 - \mu_1) > 10$? Test using $\alpha = .01$.
b. Construct a 98% confidence interval for $(\mu_2 - \mu_1)$. Interpret your result.

Applying the Concepts

8.21 While cable television companies in Minnesota are prohibited from holding exclusive rights to an area, the laws do not demand that a company face competition (Gross, 1993). Many subscribers feel that these *de facto* monopolies exploit consumers by charging excessive monthly cable fees. Suppose a congressional subcommittee considering regulation of the cable industry investigates whether cable rates are higher in areas with no competition than in areas with competition. They randomly sample basic rates for six cable companies that have no competition and for six companies that face competition (but not from each other). The observed rates are shown in the table.

No competition $18.44 $26.88 $22.87 $25.78 $23.34 $27.52

Competition $18.95 $23.74 $17.25 $20.14 $18.98 $20.14

a. What are the appropriate null and alternative hypotheses to test the research hypothesis of the subcommittee?
b. Conduct the test of part **a** using $\alpha = .05$. Report and interpret the approximate significance level of the test.
c. What assumptions are necessary to assure the validity of the test? Why does it matter that none of the companies in the sample compete against each other?

8.22 An industrial plant wants to determine which of two types of fuel—gas or electric—will produce more useful energy at a lower cost. One measure of economical energy production, the *plant investment per delivered quad*, is calculated by taking the amount of money (in dollars) invested in the particular utility by the plant and dividing by the delivered amount of energy (in quadrillion British thermal units). The smaller this ratio, the less an industrial plant pays for its delivered energy.

Random samples of 11 plants using electrical utilities and 16 plants using gas utilities were taken, and plant investment per quad was calculated for each. The data produced the results shown in the table.

	Electric	*Gas*
Sample size	11	16
Mean investment/quad (billions)	$22.5	$17.5
Variance	17.5	15

a. Do these data provide sufficient evidence at $\alpha = .05$ to indicate a difference in the average investment per quad between the plants using gas and those using electrical utilities?
b. Find a 90% confidence interval for $(\mu_1 - \mu_2)$. Give a practical interpretation of this interval.

8.23 Marketing strategists would like to be able to predict consumer response to new products and their accompanying promotional schemes. To this end, studies that examine the differences between buyers and nonbuyers of a product are of interest. One such study conducted by Shuchman and Riesz (1975) was aimed at characterizing the purchasers and nonpurchasers of Crest toothpaste. Purchasers were defined as households that converted to Crest following its endorsement by the Council on Dental Therapeutics of the American Dental Association on August 1, 1960, and remained "loyal" to Crest until at least April 1963. Nonpurchasers were defined as households that did not convert to Crest during the same time period. Using demographic data collected from a sample of 499 purchasers and 499 nonpurchasers, Shuchman and Riesz demonstrated that both the mean household size (number of persons) and mean household income were significantly larger for purchasers than for nonpurchasers. A similar study utilized random samples of size 20 and yielded the data shown in the table on the age of the householder primarily responsible for buying toothpaste.

	Purchasers											*Nonpurchasers*								
34	35	23	44	52	46	28	48	28	34		28	22	44	33	55	63	45	31	60	54
33	52	41	32	34	49	50	45	29	59		53	58	52	52	66	35	25	48	59	61

a. Do the data present sufficient evidence to conclude there is a difference in the mean age of purchasers and nonpurchasers? Use $\alpha = .10$.
b. What assumptions are necessary in order to answer part **a**?
c. Give the observed significance level for the test, and interpret its value.
d. Find a 90% confidence interval for the difference between the mean ages of purchasers and nonpurchasers.

8.24 One way corporations raise money for expansion is to issue *bonds*, loan agreements to repay the purchaser a specified amount with a fixed rate of interest paid periodically over the life of the bond. The sale of bonds is usually handled by an underwriting firm. In a study described in the *Harvard Business Review* (July–Aug. 1979), D. Logue and R. Rogalski asked, "Does It Pay to Shop for Your Bond Underwriter?" The reason for the question is that the price of a bond may rise or fall after its issuance. Therefore, whether a corporation receives the market price for a bond depends on the skill of its underwriter. The mean change in the prices of 27 bonds handled over a 12-month period by one underwriter and in the prices of 23 bonds handled by another are shown.

	Underwriter 1	*Underwriter 2*
Sample size	27	23
Sample mean	−.0491	−.0307
Sample variance	.009800	.002465

a. Do the data provide sufficient evidence to indicate a difference in the mean change in bond prices handled by the two underwriters? Test using $\alpha = .05$.
b. Find a 95% confidence interval for the mean difference for the two underwriters, and interpret it.

8.25 With the emergence of Japan as an industrial superpower, U.S. businesses are looking closely at Japanese management styles and philosophies. Some of the credit for the high quality of Japanese products is attributed to the Japanese system of permanent employment for their workers. In the United States, high job turnover rates are common in many industries and are associated with high product defect rates. High turnover rates mean U.S. plants have more inexperienced workers who are unfamiliar with the company's product lines than Japan has. In a study of the air conditioner industry in Japan and the United States, David Garvin (1983) reported that the difference in the average annual turnover rate of workers between U.S. plants and Japanese plants was 3.1%. In another study, five Japanese and five U.S. plants that manufacture air conditioners were randomly sampled; their turnover rates are listed in the table.

U.S. Plants	Japanese Plants
7.11%	3.52%
6.06	2.02
8.00	4.91
6.87	3.22
4.77	1.92

a. Do the data provide sufficient evidence to indicate that the mean annual percentage turnover for U.S. plants exceeds the corresponding mean percentage for Japanese plants? Test using $\alpha = .05$.

b. Report and interpret the observed significance level of the test you conducted in part a.

c. List any assumptions you made in conducting the hypothesis test of part a. Comment on their validity for this application.

8.26 *Sales quotas* are volume objectives assigned to specific sales units, such as regions, districts, or salespersons' territories. Sometimes to achieve manufacturing efficiency or long-term goals, sales managers set quotas for specific products at challenging levels. The underlying idea is that setting challenging quotas and attaching significant rewards will direct salespersons' efforts along desired paths (Winer, 1973). The Universal Products Company (real company, fictitious name) manufactures and markets electronic and electromechanical industrial equipment. It has a sales force of over 1,000, organized in ten districts and 135 branch offices. Salespersons have sales quotas on two specific products, Dataprinters and Micromagnetics, as well as an overall sales volume quota. Many salespersons have complained that having to make the quota on Dataprinters takes so much time that it keeps them from generating a higher overall sales volume. To determine how reducing the Dataprinter quota would affect total sales volume, Winer compared the sales volumes of a sample of branch offices whose salespersons all worked under the standard quota with the sales volumes of a sample of branch offices whose salespersons all were given a lower Dataprinter quota. Data were collected for a 7-month period and are reported in the table in terms of total sales per worker-month (in thousands of dollars).

Branch	Lower Quota	Standard Quota
1		17.7
2	15.6	
3		15.1
4	14.0	
5		12.3
6		12.0
7	11.2	
8	11.0	
9		10.5
10	10.3	
11		10.0
12	9.4	

a. What are the appropriate null and alternative hypotheses for testing whether salespersons on the two types of quotas differ in their mean sales per worker-month? Define any symbols you use.

b. The data in the table are submitted to a statistical software program, with results as shown. Interpret this output. What do you conclude about the test set up in part a?

```
MEAN DIFFERENCE = -1.02
T-VALUE = -0.66    DF = 10    TWO-TAILED P-VALUE = .525
```

c. The same software package yielded the output shown. Interpret the interval. Does its width imply that little or much information about the difference in mean sales is contained in these data? How could the amount of information be increased?

```
90% CONFIDENCE INTERVAL: (-3.814, 1.781)
```

8.3 Inferences About the Difference Between Two Population Means: Paired Difference Experiments

Suppose you want to compare the mean daily sales of two restaurants located in the same city. If you were to record the restaurants' total sales for each of 12 days (2 work weeks), the results might appear as shown in Table 8.1.

TABLE 8.1   Daily Sales for Two Restaurants

Day	Restaurant 1	Restaurant 2
1 (Monday)	$ 759	$ 678
2 (Tuesday)	981	933
3 (Wednesday)	1,005	918
4 (Thursday)	1,449	1,302
5 (Friday)	1,905	1,782
6 (Saturday)	2,073	1,971
7 (Monday)	693	639
8 (Tuesday)	873	825
9 (Wednesday)	1,074	999
10 (Thursday)	1,338	1,281
11 (Friday)	1,932	1,827
12 (Saturday)	2,106	2,049
	$\bar{x}_1 = \$1,349.00$	$\bar{x}_2 = \$1,267.00$
	$s_1 = \$530.07$	$s_2 = \$516.03$

Test the null hypothesis that the mean daily sales, μ_1 and μ_2, for the two restaurants are equal against the alternative hypothesis that they differ; i.e.,

$$H_0: (\mu_1 - \mu_2) = 0 \qquad H_a: (\mu_1 - \mu_2) \neq 0$$

Using the two-sample t statistic (Section 8.2) we would calculate

$$s_p^2 = \frac{(n_1 - 1)s_1^2 + (n_2 - 1)s_2^2}{n_1 + n_2 - 2}$$

$$= \frac{(12 - 1)(530.07)^2 + (12 - 1)(516.03)^2}{12 + 2 - 2} = 273{,}630.6$$

and

$$t = \frac{(\bar{x}_1 - \bar{x}_2) - 0}{\sqrt{s_p^2\left(\dfrac{1}{n_1} + \dfrac{1}{n_2}\right)}} = \frac{(1{,}349.00 - 1{,}267.00)}{\sqrt{273{,}630.6\left(\dfrac{1}{12} + \dfrac{1}{12}\right)}} = \frac{82.0}{213.54} = .38$$

This small t value will not lead to rejection of H_0 when compared to the t distribution with $n_1 + n_2 - 2 = 22$ df, even if α were chosen as large as $.20$ ($t_{\alpha/2} = t_{.10} = 1.321$). Thus, we might conclude that insufficient evidence exists to infer that there is a difference in mean daily sales for the two restaurants.

However, if you examine the data in Table 8.1 more closely, you will find this conclusion difficult to accept. The sales of restaurant 1 exceed those of restaurant 2 *for every one of the 12 days*. This, in itself, is strong evidence to indicate that μ_1 differs from μ_2, and we will subsequently confirm this fact. Why, then, was the t test unable to detect this difference?

The cause of this apparent inconsistency is that the two-sample t is inappropriate, because the assumption of independent samples is invalid. If you examine the pairs of daily sales, you will note that the sales of the two restaurants tend to rise and fall together over the days of the week. This pattern suggests a very strong daily dependence between the two samples and a violation of the assumption of independence required for the two-sample t test of Section 8.2. In this particular situation, note the *large variation within samples* (reflected by the large value of s_p^2) in comparison to the *small difference between the sample means*. Because s_p^2 was so large, the t test was unable to detect a possible difference between μ_1 and μ_2.

Now, consider a valid method to analyze the data of Table 8.1. We add to this table a column of differences between the daily sales of the restaurants, and thus form Table 8.2. We can regard these daily differences in sales as a sample of all daily differences, past and present. Then we can use this sample to make inferences about the mean, μ_D, of the population of differences, *which is equal to the difference* $(\mu_1 - \mu_2)$: i.e., the mean of the population (sample) of differences equals the difference between the population (sample) means. Thus, our test becomes

H_0: $\mu_D = 0$ (i.e., $\mu_1 - \mu_2 = 0$)

H_a: $\mu_D \neq 0$ (i.e., $\mu_1 - \mu_2 \neq 0$)

TABLE 8.2   Daily Sales and Differences for Two Restaurants

Day	Restaurant 1	Restaurant 2	(Restaurant 1 − Restaurant 2)
1 (Monday)	$ 759	$ 678	$ 81
2 (Tuesday)	981	933	48
3 (Wednesday)	1,005	918	87
4 (Thursday)	1,449	1,302	147
5 (Friday)	1,905	1,782	123
6 (Saturday)	2,073	1,971	102
7 (Monday)	693	639	54
8 (Tuesday)	873	825	48
9 (Wednesday)	1,074	999	75
10 (Thursday)	1,338	1,281	57
11 (Friday)	1,932	1,827	105
12 (Saturday)	2,106	2,049	57

$$\bar{x}_D = \$82.00$$
$$s_D = \$32.00$$

The test statistic is a one-sample t (Section 7.4), since we are now analyzing a single sample of differences:

$$\text{Test statistic:} \quad t = \frac{\bar{x}_D - 0}{s_D/\sqrt{n_D}}$$

where

$\bar{x}_D =$ Sample mean of differences

$s_D =$ Sample standard deviation of differences

$n_D =$ Number of differences

Assumptions: 1. The population of differences in daily sales is approximately normally distributed.

2. The sample differences are randomly selected from a population of differences.

To find the rejection region, we first choose $\alpha = .05$. Then we will reject H_0 if

$$t < -t_{.025} \quad \text{or} \quad t > t_{.025}$$

where $t_{.025}$ is based on $(n_D - 1)$ degrees of freedom.

Referring to Table VI of Appendix B, we find the t value corresponding to $\alpha/2 = .025$ and $n_D - 1 = 12 - 1 = 11$ df to be $t_{.025} = 2.201$. Thus, the null hypothesis will be rejected if $t < -2.201$ or $t > 2.201$. Note that the number of degrees of freedom has decreased from $n_1 + n_2 - 2 = 22$ to 11 by using the *paired difference experiment* rather than the two independent random samples design.

Now calculate

$$t = \frac{\bar{x}_D - 0}{s_D/\sqrt{n_D}} = \frac{82.00}{32.00/\sqrt{12}} = 8.88$$

Because this computed value of t falls in the rejection region, we conclude that the difference in mean daily sales for the two restaurants differs from 0. The fact that $\bar{x}_1 - \bar{x}_2 = \bar{x}_D = \$82.00$ strongly suggests that the mean daily sales for restaurant 1 exceed the mean daily sales for restaurant 2.

This kind of experiment, in which observations are paired and the differences analyzed, is called a **paired difference experiment**. In many cases a paired difference experiment can provide more information about the difference between population means than an independent samples experiment. The differencing removes the variability due to the dimension on which the observations are paired. For instance, in the restaurant example, the day-to-day variability in daily sales is removed by analyzing the differences between the restaurants' daily sales. The removal of the variability due to this extra dimension is called **blocking**, and the paired difference experiment is a simple example of a **randomized block experiment**. In our example, the days represent the blocks.

Some other examples for which the paired difference experiment might be appropriate are the following:

1. To compare the performance of two automobile salespeople, we might test a hypothesis about the difference $(\mu_1 - \mu_2)$ in their respective mean monthly sales. If we randomly choose n_1 months of salesperson 1's sales and independently choose n_2 months of salesperson 2's sales, the month-to-month variability caused by the seasonal nature of new car sales might inflate s_p^2 and prevent the two-sample t statistic from detecting a difference between μ_1 and μ_2, if such a difference actually exists. However, by taking the difference in monthly sales for the two salespeople for each of n months, we eliminate the month-to-month variability (seasonal variation) in sales, and the probability of detecting a difference between μ_1 and μ_2, if a difference exists, is increased.

2. Suppose you want to estimate the difference $(\mu_1 - \mu_2)$ in mean price between two major brands of premium gasoline. If you were to choose two independent random samples of stations for each brand, the variability in price due to geographic location may be large. To eliminate this source of variability, you could choose pairs of stations, one station for each brand, in close geographic proximity and use the sample of differences between the prices of the brands to make an inference about $(\mu_1 - \mu_2)$.

3. Suppose a college placement center wants to estimate the difference $(\mu_1 - \mu_2)$ in mean starting salaries for men and women graduates who seek jobs through the center. If it independently samples men and women, the starting salaries may vary due to their different college majors and differences in grade-point averages. To eliminate these sources of variability, the placement center could match male and female job-seekers according to their majors and grade-point averages. Then the difference between the starting salaries of each pair in the sample could be used to make an inference about $(\mu_1 - \mu_2)$.

The hypothesis-testing and confidence interval procedures based on a paired difference experiment are summarized in the next two boxes.

Paired Difference Test of Hypothesis

One-Tailed Test

H_0: $(\mu_1 - \mu_2) = D_0$,
 i.e., $\mu_D = D_0$

H_a: $(\mu_1 - \mu_2) < D_0$,
 i.e., $\mu_D < D_0$
 [or H_a: $(\mu_1 - \mu_2) > D_0$,
 i.e., $\mu_D > D_0$]

Test statistic: $\quad t = \dfrac{\bar{x}_D - D_0}{s_D/\sqrt{n_D}}$

Rejection region: $\quad t < -t_\alpha$
 [or $t > t_\alpha$ when
 H_a: $(\mu_1 - \mu_2) > D_0$]

where t_α has $(n_D - 1)$ df.

Two-Tailed Test

H_0: $(\mu_1 - \mu_2) = D_0$,
 i.e., $\mu_D = D_0$

H_a: $(\mu_1 - \mu_2) \neq D_0$,
 i.e., $\mu_D \neq D_0$

Test statistic: $\quad t = \dfrac{\bar{x}_D - D_0}{s_D/\sqrt{n_D}}$

Rejection region: $\quad t < -t_{\alpha/2}$
 $\quad$ or $t > t_{\alpha/2}$

where $t_{\alpha/2}$ has $(n_D - 1)$ df.

Assumptions: 1. The relative frequency distribution of the population of differences is normal.
  2. The differences are randomly selected from the population of differences.

Paired Difference Confidence Interval

$$\bar{x}_D \pm t_{\alpha/2}\, \frac{s_D}{\sqrt{n_D}}$$

where $t_{\alpha/2}$ has $(n_D - 1)$ df.

Assumption: Same as for the paired difference test (previous box).

EXAMPLE 8.5

A paired difference experiment is conducted to compare the starting salaries of male and female college graduates who find jobs. Pairs are formed by choosing a male and a female with the same major and similar grade-point averages. Suppose a random sample of 10 pairs is formed in this manner, and the starting annual salary of each person is recorded. The results are shown in Table 8.3 on page 410. Test to see whether there is evidence that the mean starting salary, μ_1, for males exceeds the mean starting salary, μ_2, for females. Use $\alpha = .05$.

TABLE 8.3	Starting Salaries		
Pair	Male	Female	Difference
			(Male − Female)
1	$24,300	$23,800	$ 500
2	26,500	26,600	−100
3	25,400	24,800	600
4	23,500	23,500	0
5	28,500	27,600	900
6	22,800	23,000	−200
7	24,500	24,200	300
8	26,200	25,100	1,100
9	23,400	23,200	200
10	24,200	23,500	700

Solution

Since we are interested in determining whether the data indicate that μ_1 exceeds μ_2—i.e., whether the mean starting salary for men exceeds the mean starting salary for women—we will choose a one-sided alternative (research) hypothesis. Then the elements of the paired difference test are

$$H_0: \quad \mu_D = 0 \quad (\mu_1 - \mu_2 = 0)$$
$$H_a: \quad \mu_D > 0 \quad (\mu_1 - \mu_2 > 0)$$

Test statistic: $\quad t = \dfrac{\bar{x}_D - 0}{s_D/\sqrt{n_D}}$

Assumption: The relative frequency distribution for the population of differences is normal.

Since the test is upper-tailed, we will reject H_0 if $t > t_\alpha = t_{.05} = 1.833$, where t_α is based on $n_D - 1 = 9$ df. The rejection region is shown in Figure 8.6.

FIGURE 8.6 ▶
Rejection region for Example 8.5

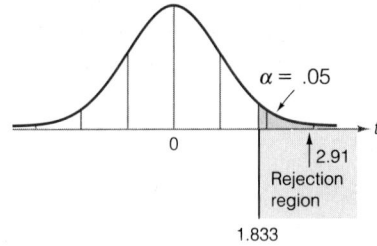

$\alpha = .05$

2.91
Rejection region

1.833

Using x_{Di} to represent the ith difference measurement, we now calculate

$$\sum_{i=1}^{10} x_{Di} = 500 + (-100) + \cdots + 700 = 4,000$$

and

$$\sum_{i=1}^{10} x_{Di}^2 = 3,300,000$$

Then,

$$\bar{x}_D = \frac{\sum_{i=1}^{10} x_{Di}}{10} = \frac{4,000}{10} = 400$$

$$s_D^2 = \frac{\sum_{i=1}^{n_D} (x_{Di} - \bar{x}_D)^2}{n_D - 1} = \frac{\sum_{i=1}^{10} x_{Di}^2 - \left(\sum_{i=1}^{10} x_{Di}\right)^2 / 10}{9}$$

$$= \frac{3,300,000 - (4,000)^2 / 10}{9} = 188,888.89$$

$$s_D = \sqrt{s_D^2} = 434.61$$

Substituting these values into the formula for the test statistic, we find that

$$t = \frac{\bar{x}_D - 0}{s_D / \sqrt{n_D}} = \frac{400}{434.61/\sqrt{10}} = \frac{400}{137.44} = 2.91$$

As you can see in Figure 8.6, the calculated t falls in the rejection region. Thus, we conclude at $\alpha = .05$ that the mean starting salary for males exceeds the mean starting salary for females.

. . . .

One measure of the amount of information about $(\mu_1 - \mu_2)$ gained by using a paired difference experiment rather than an independent samples experiment in Example 8.5 is the relative widths of the confidence intervals obtained by the two methods. A 95% confidence interval for $(\mu_1 - \mu_2)$ using the paired difference experiment is

$$\bar{x}_D \pm t_{\alpha/2} \frac{s_D}{\sqrt{n_D}}$$

where t_α has $n_D - 1 = 9$ df. Substituting into this formula, we obtain

$$400 \pm t_{.025} \frac{434.61}{\sqrt{10}} = 400 \pm 2.262 \frac{434.61}{\sqrt{10}} = 400 \pm 310.88$$

$$\approx 400 \pm 311 = (\$89, \$711)$$

If we analyzed the same data as though they were from an independent samples experiment,* we would first calculate the following quantities:

$$\begin{array}{ll} \textit{Males} & \textit{Females} \\ \bar{x}_1 = \$24{,}930 & \bar{x}_2 = \$24{,}530 \\ s_1^2 = 3{,}009{,}000 & s_2^2 = 2{,}331{,}222.22 \end{array}$$

Then

$$s_p^2 = \frac{(n_1 - 1)s_1^2 + (n_2 - 1)s_2^2}{n_1 + n_2 - 2} = \frac{9(3{,}009{,}000) + 9(2{,}331{,}222.22)}{18}$$

$$= 2{,}670{,}111.11$$

where s_p^2 is based on $(n_1 + n_2 - 2) = (10 + 10 - 2) = 18$ df.

The 95% confidence interval is

$$(\bar{x}_1 - \bar{x}_2) \pm t_{\alpha/2} \sqrt{s_p^2\left(\frac{1}{n_1} + \frac{1}{n_2}\right)} = 400 \pm t_{.025} \sqrt{2{,}670{,}111.11\left(\frac{1}{10} + \frac{1}{10}\right)}$$

$$= 400 \pm 2.101 \sqrt{2{,}670{,}111.11\left(\frac{1}{10} + \frac{1}{10}\right)}$$

$$= 400 \pm 1{,}535.35$$

$$\approx 400 \pm 1{,}535 = (-\$1{,}135, \$1{,}935)$$

The confidence interval for the independent sampling experiment is about five times wider than the corresponding paired difference confidence interval. Blocking out the variability due to differences in majors and grade-point averages significantly increases the information about the difference in mean male and female starting salaries by providing a much more accurate (smaller confidence interval for the same confidence coefficient) estimate of $(\mu_1 - \mu_2)$.

You may wonder whether a paired difference experiment is always superior to an independent samples experiment. The answer is: most of the time, but not always. We sacrifice half the degrees of freedom in the t statistic when a paired difference design is used instead of an independent samples design. This is a *loss* of information, and unless this loss is more than compensated for by the reduction in variability obtained by blocking (pairing), the paired difference experiment will result in a net loss of information about $(\mu_1 - \mu_2)$. Thus, we should be convinced that the pairing will significantly reduce variability before performing the paired difference experiment. Most of the time this will happen.

One final note: The pairing of the observations is determined *before* the experiment is performed (that is, by the *design* of the experiment). **A paired difference**

---

*This is done only to indicate how much more information is obtained by a paired design versus an unpaired design. Actually, for an experiment designed using pairing, an unpaired analysis is invalid because the assumption of independent samples is not satisfied.

experiment is never obtained by pairing the sample observations after the measurements have been acquired. Such is the stuff of which statistical lies are made!

What Do You Do When the Assumption of a Normal Distribution for the Population of Differences Is Not Satisfied?

Answer: Use the Wilcoxon signed rank test for the paired difference design. (See optional Section 8.6.)

CASE STUDY 8.1 / Comparing Salaries for Equivalent Work

Procedures to maintain comparable salaries between federal white-collar workers and those in the private sector are mandated by federal law. William M. Smith (1976) discussed one statistical mechanism used in complying with this law. An annual survey, the *National Survey for Professional, Administrative, Technical, and Clerical Pay*, is conducted by the Bureau of Labor Statistics. Salary information is collected for approximately 85 work-level categories ranging from clerical to administrative positions in 20 occupations.

The design of the survey resembles a paired difference design because the occupation and experience of employees in the private and government sectors are matched as closely as possible before a comparison is made. Test statistics like the paired difference t can be used to compare the mean salaries for the two sectors. Then, if the data indicate that the mean salaries differ for certain levels, the need for an adjustment is indicated.

Smith points out that presidential or legislative intervention often prevents the adjustments indicated by the data from being enacted. Regardless, the results of the survey are valuable as a salary guide for the private sector and to those performing general economic analyses.

Exercises 8.27–8.38

Learning the Mechanics

8.27 A paired difference experiment yielded n_D pairs of observations. In each case, what is the rejection region for testing H_0: $\mu_D = 2$ against H_a: $\mu_D > 2$?
  a. $n_D = 12$, $\alpha = .05$ **b.** $n_D = 24$, $\alpha = .10$
  c. $n_D = 4$, $\alpha = .025$ **d.** $n_D = 8$, $\alpha = .01$

8.28 A paired difference experiment yielded the data shown in the table at the top of page 414.

Person	Before, x_1	After, x_2
1	82	92
2	60	72
3	55	57
4	97	104
5	79	89

a. Compute $\bar{x}_D$ and s_D.   b. Demonstrate that $\bar{x}_D = \bar{x}_1 - \bar{x}_2$.
c. Is there sufficient evidence to conclude that $\mu_1 \neq \mu_2$? Test using $\alpha = .05$.
d. Find and interpret the approximate p-value for the paired difference test.
e. What assumptions are necessary so the paired difference test will be valid?

8.29 Refer to Exercise 8.28. Construct a 95% confidence interval for μ_D.

8.30 A paired difference experiment produced the following data:

$$n_D = 18 \qquad \bar{x}_1 = 92 \qquad \bar{x}_2 = 95.5 \qquad \bar{x}_D = -3.5 \qquad s_D^2 = 21$$

a. Determine the values of t for which the null hypothesis $(\mu_1 - \mu_2) = 0$ would be rejected in favor of the alternative hypothesis $(\mu_1 - \mu_2) < 0$. Use $\alpha = .10$.
b. Conduct the paired difference test described in part **a**. Draw the appropriate conclusions.
c. What assumptions are necessary so that the paired difference test will be valid?
d. Construct a 90% confidence interval for the mean difference μ_D.
e. Which of the two inferential procedures, the confidence interval of part **d** or the test of hypothesis of part **b**, provides more information about the difference between the population means?

8.31 Frequently, a paired difference experiment provides more information about the difference between two population means than an independent random samples experiment. Explain. When may it not?

8.32 A paired difference experiment yielded the data shown in the table.

Pair	1	2	3	4	5	6	7
x	24.4	86.3	43.2	69.5	93.0	29.9	67.3
y	12.3	74.3	34.4	61.6	84.3	23.4	59.9

a. Test H_0: $\mu_D = 10$ against H_a: $\mu_D \neq 10$, where $\mu_D = (\mu_x - \mu_y)$. Use $\alpha = .05$.
b. Report and interpret the p-value for the test you conducted in part **a**.

Applying the Concepts

8.33 Do people generally receive the asking price when they sell their home? The accompanying table lists the asking price and sale price for a random sample of 10 1993 single-family home sales in Eden Prairie, Minnesota.

House	Asked	Received	House	Asked	Received
1	$312,900	$305,600	6	122,855	121,000
2	142,900	142,900	7	164,900	159,900
3	136,700	135,000	8	74,900	74,900
4	134,900	125,700	9	129,900	132,000
5	196,900	200,000	10	150,000	146,500

Source: Minneapolis Area Association of Realtors, 1993.

a. Explain why the samples are not independent.

b. What is the dimension on which the samples are paired or matched?

c. Defining D as (Price asked − Price received), $\sum x_{D_i} = \$23,355$ and $\sum x_{D_i}^2 = 195,531,025$. Conduct a test of hypothesis that will help answer the question of interest for people in Eden Prairie who sold their homes in 1993. Use $\alpha = .05$.

8.34 *Time* (Dec. 7, 1981) reported that many corporations now encourage their employees to "get things off their chests" by communicating directly to management on hot-line phones, through the mail, or in face-to-face meetings. For example, American Express Corp. instituted a mail program that guaranteed its employees anonymity (if desired) and an answer from the responsible person (including the company chairperson) within 10 days. A similar program at IBM generated an average of 13,000 letters a year from IBM's 195,000 U.S. employees. Such programs reflect the constant search by American business for ways to improve worker productivity.

Before instituting an employee complaint/suggestion program in its manufacturing plant, a company randomly sampled eight workers and measured their productivity in terms of the number of items produced per day. A year after the start of the complaint program the productivity of seven of these workers was reevaluated. (The eighth had been promoted in the interim.) The productivity data are shown in the table.

Employee ID Number	August 1992	August 1993
1011	10	9
0033	9	11
0998	12	14
0006	8	9
1802	10	9
0246	11	14
0777	14	–
1112	11	13

a. Do the data provide evidence that the complaint/suggestion program has helped to increase worker productivity? Test using $\alpha = .10$, and clearly state any assumptions you make in conducting the test.

b. Discuss how the 1-year gap between productivity evaluations could weaken the results of the study.

8.35 Among the better known and most frequently enforced antitrust laws are those against price fixing (Sherman Act, Section One) and monopoly or attempt to monopolize (Sherman Act, Section Two). Other antitrust violations include price discrimination, retail price maintenance, and tying the sale of a product to the purchase of another product. Alan R. Beckenstein, H. Landis Gabel, and Karlene Roberts (1983) surveyed 188 Fortune 500 industrial companies and found that, on average (without adjusting for inflation), these companies "spent 3½ times the amount on antitrust investigations, legal fees, fines, damages, court costs, and out-of-court settlements in the 1970s as they did in the 1960s." Further, on average, these companies faced 3.22 more antitrust litigations in the 1970s than in the 1960s. Beckenstein, Gabel, and Roberts observed that companies must now consider the possible legal consequences of their actions more than they used to. They concluded that with today's legal risks managers at all levels should be helping to design and implement strategies to comply with the antitrust laws. Another survey of 10 Fortune 500 companies yielded the data in the table about the number of litigations faced by the firms in the 1960s and 1970s.

Firm	1960s	1970s	Firm	1960s	1970s
1	10	10	6	7	6
2	8	12	7	6	11
3	9	8	8	9	12
4	7	16	9	8	11
5	8	14	10	7	12

a. Do the data provide sufficient evidence to reject the researchers' claim? Conduct a test of hypothesis and use the p-value of your test to help you answer this question.
b. Use a 90% confidence interval to estimate the difference in the mean number of antitrust litigations per firm in the 1970s and the 1960s. Compare your results to the reported survey finding.

8.36 A manufacturer of automobile shock absorbers was interested in comparing the durability of its shocks with that of the shocks produced by its biggest competitor. To make the comparison, one of the manufacturer's and one of the competitor's shocks were randomly selected and installed on the rear wheels of each of six cars. After the cars had been driven 20,000 miles, the strength of each test shock was measured, coded, and recorded. Results of the examination are shown in the table.

Car Number	Manufacturer's Shock	Competitor's Shock
1	8.8	8.4
2	10.5	10.1
3	12.5	12.0
4	9.7	9.3
5	9.6	9.0
6	13.2	13.0

a. Do the data present sufficient evidence to conclude that there is a difference in the mean strength of the two types of shocks after 20,000 miles of use? Use $\alpha = .05$.
b. Find the approximate observed significance level for the test, and interpret its value.
c. What assumptions are necessary to apply a paired difference analysis to the data?
d. Construct a 95% confidence interval for $(\mu_1 - \mu_2)$. Interpret the confidence interval.

8.37 Suppose the data in Exercise 8.36 are based on independent random samples.
a. Do the data provide sufficient evidence to indicate a difference between the mean strengths for the two types of shocks? Use $\alpha = .05$.
b. Construct a 95% confidence interval for $(\mu_1 - \mu_2)$. Interpret your result.
c. Compare the confidence intervals you obtained in Exercise 8.36 and in part b of this exercise. Which is wider? To what do you attribute the difference in width? Assuming in each case that the appropriate assumptions are satisfied, which interval provides you with more information about $(\mu_1 - \mu_2)$? Explain.
d. Are the results of an unpaired analysis valid if the data come from a paired experiment?

8.38 A *pupillometer* is a device used to observe changes in pupil dilations as the eye is exposed to different visual stimuli. Since there is a direct correlation between the amount an individual's pupil dilates and his or her interest in the stimuli, marketing organizations sometimes use pupillometers to help them evaluate potential consumer interest in new products, alternative package designs, and other factors. The Design and Market Research Laboratories of the Container Corporation of America used a pupillometer to evaluate consumer reaction to different silverware patterns for a client (McGuire, 1973). Suppose 15 consumers were chosen at random, and each was shown two silverware patterns. Their pupillometer readings are shown in the table (in millimeters).

Consumer	Pattern 1	Pattern 2	Consumer	Pattern 1	Pattern 2
1	1.00	.80	9	.98	.91
2	.97	.66	10	1.46	1.10
3	1.45	1.22	11	1.85	1.60
4	1.21	1.00	12	.33	.21
5	.77	.81	13	1.77	1.50
6	1.32	1.11	14	.85	.65
7	1.81	1.30	15	.15	.05
8	.91	.32			

a. What are the appropriate null and alternative hypotheses to test whether the mean amount of pupil dilation differs for the two patterns? Define any symbols you use.

b. The data were analyzed using a statistical software package, with the results shown. Interpret these results. Do you think that the *p*-value is exactly equal to zero? Explain.

```
MEAN DIFFERENCE (1 - 2) = .239
T = 5.76     DF = 14     TWO-TAILED P-VALUE = .000
```

c. Another part of the computer output was the confidence interval. Interpret the interval.

```
95% CONFIDENCE INTERVAL: (.150, .328)
```

d. Is the paired difference design used for this study preferable to an independent samples design? For independent samples we could select 30 consumers, divide them into two groups of 15, and show each group a different pattern. Explain your preference.

8.4 Determining the Sample Size

You can find the appropriate sample size to estimate the difference between two population parameters with a specified degree of reliability by using the method described in Section 6.2. That is, to estimate the difference between two parameters correct to within B units with probability $(1 - \alpha)$, set $z_{\alpha/2}$ standard deviations of the sampling distribution of the estimator equal to B. Then solve for the sample size. To do this, you have to specify a particular ratio between n_1 and n_2. Most often, you will want to have equal sample sizes—i.e., $n_1 = n_2 = n$. We will illustrate the procedure with two examples.

EXAMPLE 8.6

The sales manager for a chain of supermarkets wants to determine whether store location, management, and other factors produce a difference in the mean meat purchase per customer (zero purchases to be excluded) at two different stores. The manager would like the estimate of the difference in mean meat purchase per customer to be correct to within $2.00 with probability equal to .95. If the two sample sizes are to be equal, find $n_1 = n_2 = n$, the number of customer meat sales to be randomly selected from each store.

Solution

To solve the problem, you have to know something about the variation in the dollar amount of meat sales per customer. Suppose you know that the sales have a range of approximately $30 at each store. Then you could approximate $\sigma_1 = \sigma_2 = \sigma$ by letting the range equal 4σ, and

$$4\sigma \approx \$30 \quad \text{so} \quad \sigma \approx \$7.50$$

The next step is to solve the equation

$$z_{\alpha/2} \sqrt{\frac{\sigma_1^2}{n_1} + \frac{\sigma_2^2}{n_2}} = B$$

for n, where $n = n_1 = n_2$. Since we want the estimate to lie within $B = \$2.00$ of $(\mu_1 - \mu_2)$ with probability equal to .95, $z_{\alpha/2} = z_{.025} = 1.96$. Then, letting $\sigma_1 = \sigma_2 = 7.5$ and solving for n, we have

$$1.96 \sqrt{\frac{(7.5)^2}{n} + \frac{(7.5)^2}{n}} = 2.00$$

$$1.96 \sqrt{\frac{2(7.5)^2}{n}} = 2.00$$

$$n = 108.05 \approx 109 \quad \text{(rounding upward)}$$

Consequently, you will have to randomly sample 109 meat sales per store to estimate the difference in mean meat sales per customer correct to within $2.00 with probability approximately equal to .95.

EXAMPLE 8.7

A laboratory manager wishes to compare the difference in the mean readings of two instruments, A and B, designed to measure the potency (in parts per million) of an antibiotic. To conduct the experiment, the manager plans to select n_D specimens of the antibiotic from a vat and to measure each specimen with both instruments. The difference $(\mu_A - \mu_B)$ will be estimated based on the n_D paired differences $(x_A - x_B)$ obtained in the experiment. If preliminary measurements suggest that the differences will range between plus or minus 10 parts per million, how many differences will be needed to estimate $(\mu_A - \mu_B)$ correct to within 1 part per million with confidence coefficient equal to .99?

Solution

The estimator for $(\mu_A - \mu_B)$, based on a paired difference experiment, is $\bar{x}_D = (\bar{x}_A - \bar{x}_B)$ and

$$\sigma_{\bar{x}_D} = \frac{\sigma_D}{\sqrt{n_D}}$$

Thus, the number n_D of pairs of measurements needed to estimate $(\mu_A - \mu_B)$ to within 1 part per million can be obtained by solving for n_D in the equation

$$z_{\alpha/2} \frac{\sigma_D}{\sqrt{n_D}} = B$$

where $z_{.005} = 2.58$ and $B = 1$. To solve this equation for n_D, we need to have an approximate value for σ_D.

We are given the information that the differences are expected to range from -10 to 10 parts per million. Letting the range equal $4\sigma_D$, we find

$$\text{Range} = 20 \approx 4\sigma_D$$
$$\sigma_D \approx 5$$

Substituting $\sigma_D = 5$, $B = 1$, and $z_{.005} = 2.58$ into the equation and solving for n_D, we obtain

$$2.58 \frac{5}{\sqrt{n_D}} = 1$$
$$n_D = [(2.58)(5)]^2 = 166.41$$

Therefore, it will require approximately $n_D = 166$ pairs of measurements to estimate $(\mu_A - \mu_B)$ correct to within 1 part per million using the paired difference experiment.

The next box summarizes the procedures for determining the sample sizes necessary for estimating $(\mu_1 - \mu_2)$ for the case $n_1 = n_2 = n$ and for estimating μ_D.

Determination of Sample Size for Comparing Two Means

Independent Random Samples

To estimate $(\mu_1 - \mu_2)$ to within a given bound B with probability $(1 - \alpha)$ or, equivalently, with a $100(1 - \alpha)\%$ confidence interval of width $W = 2B$, use the following formula to solve for equal sample sizes that will achieve the desired reliability:

$$n_1 = n_2 = \frac{(z_{\alpha/2})^2(\sigma_1^2 + \sigma_2^2)}{B^2} = \frac{4(z_{\alpha/2})^2(\sigma_1^2 + \sigma_2^2)}{W^2}$$

You will need to substitute estimates for the values of σ_1^2 and σ_2^2 before solving for the sample size. These estimates might be sample variances s_1^2 *and* s_2^2 from prior sampling (e.g., a pilot sample), or from an educated (and conservatively large) guess based on the range, i.e., $s \approx R/4$.

Paired Difference Experiment

To estimate μ_D to within a given bound B with probability $(1 - \alpha)$ or, equivalently, with a $100(1 - \alpha)\%$ confidence interval of width $W = 2B$, use the following formula to solve for n_D that will achieve the desired reliability

$$n_D = \frac{(z_{\alpha/2})^2\sigma_D^2}{B^2} = \frac{4(z_{\alpha/2})^2\sigma_D^2}{W^2}$$

You will need to substitute an estimate for the value of σ_D^2 before solving for the sample size. This estimate might be a sample variance s_D^2 from prior sampling (e.g., a pilot study), or from an educated (and conservatively large) guess based on the range, i.e., $s_D \approx R/4$.

Exercises 8.39–8.46

Learning the Mechanics

8.39 Suppose you want to estimate the difference between two population means correct to within 1.8 with probability $.95$. If prior information suggests that the population variances are approximately equal to $\sigma_1^2 = \sigma_2^2 = 14$ and you want to select independent random samples of equal size from the populations, how large should the sample sizes, n_1 and n_2, be?

8.40 Suppose you want to estimate the difference $(\mu_1 - \mu_2)$ between a pair of population means correct to within 1.8 with probability equal to $.90$. If the estimate is to be based on a paired difference experiment and you know from prior experiments that the approximate range of the paired differences is 28, approximately how many paired differences would you need?

8.41 Suppose you want to estimate the difference $(\mu_1 - \mu_2)$ between a pair of population means correct to within 4.7 with probability equal to $.95$. If the estimate is to be based on a paired difference experiment and you know from prior experiments that the approximate range of the paired differences is 60, approximately how many paired differences would you need?

Applying the Concepts

8.42 Is housework hazardous to your health? A recent study (Rogot, Sorlie, and Johnson, 1992) compares the life expectancies for 25-year-old white women who are in the labor force to those who are housewives. How large a sample must be taken from each group to be 95% confident that the estimate of difference in life expectancies for the two groups is within 1 year of the true difference in life expectancies? Assume that equal sample sizes will be selected from the two groups, and that the standard deviation for both groups is approximately 15 years.

8.43 Even though Japan is an economic superpower, Japanese workers are in many ways worse off than their U.S. and European counterparts. For example, in 1991 the estimated average housing space per person (in square feet) was 665.2 in the United States, 400.4 in Germany, and only 269 in Japan (Berg, 1993). Next year a team of economists and sociologists from the United Nations plans to reestimate the difference in the mean housing space per person for U.S. and Japanese workers. Assume that equal sample sizes will be used for each country and that the standard deviation is 35 square feet for Japan and 80 for the United States. How many people should be sampled in each country to estimate the difference to within 10 square feet with 95% confidence?

8.44 An investment analyst wishes to estimate the difference in mean rates of return between short- and long-term corporate bonds. The estimate is to be based on matched pairs of the annual rates of return, one representing the rate of return on a short-term bond of a particular corporation, and the other representing the rate of return of a long-term bond of the same corporation. A brief examination of the current prices of a few of these pairs suggests a range of differences equal to approximately 2%. If the analyst wishes to estimate the difference in mean rates of return correct to within .2% with probability equal to .99, approximately how many pairs of bonds must be included in the sample?

8.45 In Exercise 8.34, a company compared the productivity of workers (number of items produced per day) before and after the institution of an employee complaint/suggestion program. Suppose the company now wants to estimate the difference in mean numbers of items produced per day before and after institution of the program correct to within .5 item with probability equal to .95. How many employees should be included in the sample? [*Hint:* Use the value of s_D calculated in Exercise 8.34 to approximate σ_D.]

8.46 Refer to Exercise 8.22. Suppose you want to estimate the difference in mean investment per delivered quad between electric and gas utilities correct to within \$1.50 with probability equal to .95. If the estimate is to be based on independent random samples of equal size, approximately how many plants must be included in each sample? [*Hint:* Use the pooled estimate, s_p^2, obtained in Exercise 8.22 as an approximation to σ^2.]

8.5 A Nonparametric Test for Comparing Two Populations: Independent Sampling (Optional)

The independent-samples t test for comparing two populations (Section 8.2) is unsuitable for some types of business data. These data fall into two categories: (1) data sets that do not satisfy the assumptions upon which the t test is based—namely, that the random variables being measured have normal probability distributions with equal variances; and (2) data that are not susceptible to measurement but that can be *ranked in order of magnitude*. An example of the second type of data occurs during new product testing. For a food product this may entail taste tests in which consumers rank the new product in order of preference with respect to one or more currently popular brands. A consumer probably has a preference for each product, but the strength of the preference is difficult, if not impossible, to measure. Consequently, the best we can do is have each consumer examine the new product along with a few established products, and rank them according to preference: 1 for the most preferred, 2 for second, etc.

Suppose two independent random samples are to be used to compare two population means, and the *t* test of Section 8.2 is inappropriate for making the comparison. Either we are unwilling to make assumptions about the form of the underlying probability distributions, or we are unable to obtain exact values of the sample measurements but can rank them in order of magnitude. For either of these situations, if the data can be ordered, the **Wilcoxon rank sum test** (developed by Frank Wilcoxon) can be applied. The Wilcoxon rank sum procedure compares the probability distributions associated with the two sampled populations, rather than the specific parameters of these populations (such as the means). Consequently, it is a **nonparametric test.**

For example, suppose six economists who work for the federal government and seven university economists are randomly selected, and each is asked to predict next year's percentage change in cost of living as compared with this year's figure. The objective of the study is to compare the government economists' predictions to those of the university economists. The data are shown in Table 8.4.

TABLE 8.4 Percentage Cost of Living Change, as Predicted by Government and University Economists

Government Economist		University Economist	
Prediction	Rank	Prediction	Rank
3.1	4	4.4	6
4.8	7	5.8	9
2.3	2	3.9	5
5.6	8	8.7	11
0.0	1	6.3	10
2.9	3	10.5	12
		10.8	13

The two populations of predictions are those that would be obtained from *all* government and *all* university economists if they could all be questioned. If it can be inferred that, say, the distribution of predictions for university economists lies above (to the right of) the distribution of predictions for government economists (see Figure 8.7),

FIGURE 8.7
Probability distributions of economists' predictions of percentage change in cost of living

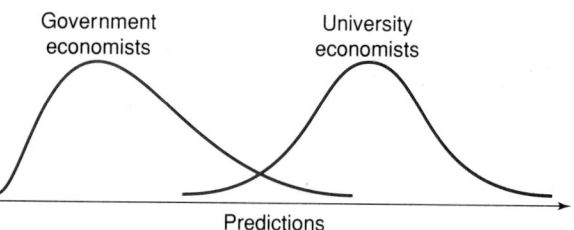

the implication is that university economists' predictions of next year's percentage change in cost of living tend to be higher than government economists' predictions.

To compare their probability distributions using Wilcoxon's procedure, we first *rank the sample observations as though they were all drawn from the same population.* That is, we pool the measurements from both samples and then rank the measurements from the smallest (a rank of 1) to the largest (a rank of 13). The ranks of the economists' predictions are indicated in Table 8.4.

The test statistic for the Wilcoxon test is based on the totals of the ranks for each of the two samples—that is, on the **rank sums.** If the two rank sums are nearly equal, the implication is that there is no evidence that the probability distributions from which the samples were drawn are different. On the other hand, if the two rank sums are very different, the implication is that the two samples may have come from different populations.

For the economists' predictions, we arbitrarily denote the rank sum for government economists by T_A and that for university economists by T_B. Then

$$T_A = 4 + 7 + 2 + 8 + 1 + 3 = 25$$
$$T_B = 6 + 9 + 5 + 11 + 10 + 12 + 13 = 66$$

The sum of T_A and T_B will always equal $n(n + 1)/2$, where $n = n_1 + n_2$. So, for this example, $n_1 = 6$, $n_2 = 7$, and

$$T_A + T_B = \frac{13(13 + 1)}{2} = 91$$

Since $T_A + T_B$ is fixed, a small value for T_A implies a large value for T_B (and vice versa) and a large difference between T_A and T_B. Therefore, the smaller the value of one of the rank sums, the greater is the evidence to indicate that the samples were selected from different populations.

Values that locate the rejection region for the rank sum associated with the smaller sample are given in Table XI of Appendix B. A partial reproduction of this table is shown in Table 8.5 (page 425). The columns of the table represent n_1, the first sample size, and the rows represent n_2, the second sample size. *The T_L and T_U entries in the table are the boundaries of the lower and upper regions, respectively, for the rank sum associated with the sample that has fewer measurements.* If the sample sizes n_1 and n_2 are the same, either rank sum may be used as the test statistic. To illustrate, suppose $n_1 = 8$ and $n_2 = 10$. For a two-tailed test with $\alpha = .05$, we consult part **a** of the table and find that the null hypothesis will be rejected if the rank sum of sample 1 (the sample with fewer measurements), T, is less than or equal to $T_L = 54$ *or* greater than or equal to $T_U = 98$. The Wilcoxon rank sum test is summarized in the box.

Wilcoxon Rank Sum Test: Independent Samples[*]

<table>
<tr><td align="center">One-Tailed Test</td><td align="center">Two-Tailed Test</td></tr>
<tr>
<td>H_0: Two sampled populations have identical probability distributions

H_a: The probability distribution for population A is shifted to the right of that for B</td>
<td>H_0: Two sampled populations have identical probability distributions

H_a: The probability distribution for population A is shifted to the left or to the right of that for B</td>
</tr>
<tr>
<td>Test statistic: The rank sum T associated with the sample with fewer measurements (for equal sample sizes, use either rank sum)</td>
<td>Test statistic: The rank sum T associated with the sample with fewer measurements (for equal sample sizes, use either rank sum)</td>
</tr>
<tr>
<td>Rejection region: Assuming the smaller sample size is associated with distribution A (or, for equal sample sizes, use the rank sum T_A), we reject H_0 if $T_A \geq T_U$, where T_U is the upper value given by Table XI in Appendix B for the chosen one-tailed α value.</td>
<td>Rejection region: $T \leq T_L$ or $T \geq T_U$, where T_L is the lower value given by Table XI in Appendix B for the chosen two-tailed α value, and T_U is the upper value from Table XI.</td>
</tr>
</table>

[*Note*: If the one-sided alternative is that the probability distribution for A is shifted to the *left* of B (and T_A is the test statistic), we reject H_0 if $T_A \leq T_L$.]

Assumptions: 1. The two samples are random and independent.
  2. The two probability distributions from which the samples are drawn are continuous.

Ties: Assign tied measurements the average of the ranks they would receive if they were unequal but occurred in successive order. For example, if the third-ranked and fourth-ranked measurements are tied, assign each a rank of $(3 + 4)/2 = 3.5$.

Note that the assumptions necessary for the validity of the Wilcoxon rank sum test do not specify the shape or type of probability distribution. However, the distributions are assumed to be continuous so that the probability of tied measurements is 0 (see Chapter 4), and each measurement can be assigned a unique rank. In practice, however, rounding of continuous measurements will sometimes produce ties. As long as the number of ties is small relative to the sample sizes, the Wilcoxon test procedure will still have approximate significance level α. The test is not recommended to compare discrete distributions for which many ties are expected.

---

[*]Another statistic used for comparing two populations based on independent random samples is the **Mann-Whitney U statistic**. The U statistic is a simple function of the rank sums. It can be shown that the Wilcoxon rank sum test and the Mann-Whitney U test are equivalent.

TABLE 8.5   Reproduction of Part of Table XI of Appendix B: Critical Values of T_L and T_U for the Wilcoxon Rank Sum Test: Independent Samples

a. $\alpha = .025$ one-tailed; $\alpha = .05$ two tailed

n_2 \\ n_1	3		4		5		6		7		8		9		10	
	T_L	T_U	T_L	T_U	T_L	T_U	T_L	T_U	T_L	T_U	T_L	T_U	T_L	T_U	T_L	T_U
3	5	16	6	18	6	21	7	23	7	26	8	28	8	31	9	33
4	6	18	11	25	12	28	12	32	13	35	14	38	15	41	16	44
5	6	21	12	28	18	37	19	41	20	45	21	49	22	53	24	56
6	7	23	12	32	19	41	26	52	28	56	29	61	31	65	32	70
7	7	26	13	35	20	45	28	56	37	68	39	73	41	78	43	83
8	8	28	14	38	21	49	29	61	39	73	49	87	51	93	54	98
9	8	31	15	41	22	53	31	65	41	78	51	93	63	108	66	114
10	9	33	16	44	24	56	32	70	43	83	54	98	66	114	79	131

EXAMPLE 8.8

Test the hypothesis that the university economists' predictions of next year's percentage change in cost of living tend to be higher than the government economists'. Conduct the test using the data in Table 8.4 and $\alpha = .05$.

Solution

H_0:   The probability distributions corresponding to the government and university economists' predictions of inflation rate are identical

H_a: The probability distribution for the university economists' predictions lies above (to the right of) the probability distribution for the government economists' predictions*

Test statistic: Since fewer government economists ($n_1 = 6$) than university economists ($n_2 = 7$) were sampled, the test statistic is T_A, the rank sum of the government economists' predictions.

Rejection region: Since the test is one-sided, we consult part **b** of Table XI for the rejection region corresponding to $\alpha = .05$. We reject H_0 only for $T_A \leq T_L$, the lower value from Table XI, since we are specifically testing that the distribution of the government economists' predictions lies *below* the distribution of university economists' predictions, as shown in Figure 8.8. Thus, we reject H_0 if $T_A \leq 30$.

Since T_A, the rank sum of the government economists' predictions in Table 8.4, is 25, it is in the rejection region (see Figure 8.8 on page 426). Therefore, we can conclude that the university economists' predictions tend, in general, to exceed the government economists' predictions.

---

*The alternative hypotheses in this chapter will be stated in terms of a difference in the *location* of the distributions. However, since the shapes of the distributions may also differ under H_a, some figures (e.g., Figure 8.8) depicting H_a will show probability distributions with different shapes.

FIGURE 8.8 ▶
Alternative hypothesis and rejection region for Example 8.8

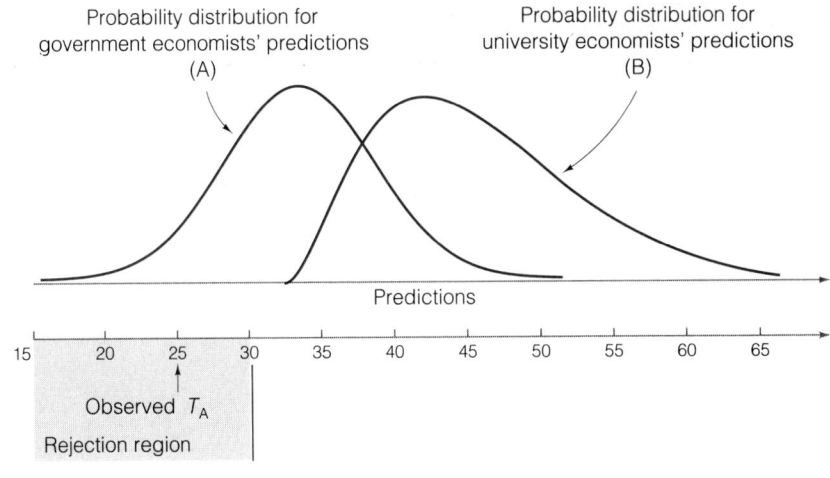

Probability distribution for government economists' predictions (A)

Probability distribution for university economists' predictions (B)

Predictions

Observed T_A

Rejection region

Table XI of Appendix B gives values of T_L and T_U for sample sizes n_1 and n_2 less than or equal to 10. When both sample sizes are 10 or larger, the sampling distribution of T_A can be approximated by a normal distribution with mean and variance

$$E(T_A) = \frac{n_1(n_1 + n_2 + 1)}{2} \quad \text{and} \quad \sigma^2_{T_A} = \frac{n_1 n_2(n_1 + n_2 + 1)}{12}$$

Therefore, for $n_1 \geq 10$ and $n_2 \geq 10$, we can conduct the Wilcoxon rank sum test using the familiar z test of Chapters 7 and 8. The large-sample test is summarized in the next box.

Wilcoxon Rank Sum Test: Large Independent Samples

One-Tailed Test

H_0: Two sampled populations have identical probability distributions

H_a: The probability distribution for population A is shifted to the right of that for B

Test statistic: $z = \dfrac{T_A - \dfrac{n_1(n_1 + n_2 + 1)}{2}}{\sqrt{\dfrac{n_1 n_2(n_1 + n_2 + 1)}{12}}}$

Rejection region: $z > z_\alpha$

Assumptions: $n_1 \geq 10$ and $n_2 \geq 10$

Two-Tailed Test

H_0: Two sampled populations have identical probability distributions

H_a: The probability distribution for population A is shifted left *or* right of that for B

Test statistic: $z = \dfrac{T_A - \dfrac{n_1(n_1 + n_2 + 1)}{2}}{\sqrt{\dfrac{n_1 n_2(n_1 + n_2 + 1)}{12}}}$

Rejection region: $z < -z_{\alpha/2}$ or $z > z_{\alpha/2}$

Exercises 8.47–8.56

Learning the Mechanics

8.47 Specify the test statistic and the rejection region for the Wilcoxon rank sum test for independent samples in each of the following situations.

 a. H_0: Two probability distributions, A and B, are identical
   H_a: Probability distribution for population A is shifted to the right or left of the probability distribution for population B
   $n_A = 10$, $n_B = 6$, $\alpha = .10$

 b. H_0: Two probability distributions, A and B, are identical
   H_a: Probability distribution for population A is shifted to the right of the probability distribution for population B
   $n_A = 5$, $n_B = 7$, $\alpha = .05$

 c. H_0: Two probability distributions, A and B, are identical
   H_a: Probability distribution for population A is shifted to the left of the probability distribution for population B
   $n_A = 9$, $n_B = 8$, $\alpha = .025$

 d. H_0: Two probability distributions, A and B, are identical
   H_a: Probability distribution for population A is shifted to the right or left of the probability distribution for population B
   $n_A = 15$, $n_B = 15$, $\alpha = .05$

8.48 Suppose you want to compare two treatments, A and B. In particular, you wish to determine whether the distribution for population B is shifted to the right of the distribution for population A. You plan to use the Wilcoxon rank sum test.

 a. Specify the null and alternative hypotheses you would test.

 b. Suppose you obtained the following independent random samples of observations on experimental units subjected to the two treatments:

 A: 36, 39, 33, 29, 42, 33, 35, 28, 34

 B: 35, 48, 52, 66

 Conduct a test of the hypotheses described in part **a**. Test using $\alpha = .05$.

8.49 Explain the difference between the one- and two-tailed versions of the Wilcoxon rank sum test for independent random samples.

8.50 Random samples of sizes $n_1 = 20$ and $n_2 = 15$ were drawn from populations 1 and 2, respectively. The measurements obtained are listed in the table.

Population 1				Population 2		
9.0	17.9	25.6	31.1	10.1	11.1	13.5
21.1	26.9	24.6	23.1	12.0	18.2	10.3
24.8	16.5	26.0	25.1	9.2	7.0	14.2
17.2	30.1	14.3	26.1	12.2	13.6	13.2
18.9	25.4	22.0	23.3	8.8	12.5	21.5

a. Conduct a hypothesis test to determine whether the probability distribution for population 2 is shifted to the left of the probability distribution for population 1. Use $\alpha = .05$.

b. What is the approximate p-value of the test of part **a**?

Applying the Concepts

8.51 A property's *assessment ratio* is calculated by dividing the property's assessed value (for tax purposes) by its market value (or a proxy for market value, such as a recent sale price; Freedman, 1985). Tax assessors' valuations are often evaluated by private real estate appraisers and government agencies using procedures such as the Wilcoxon rank sum test to compare the distributions of the assessment ratios for different groups of properties. The table lists the assessment ratios for random samples of 10 properties in neighborhood A and eight properties in neighborhood B.

Neighborhood A		Neighborhood B	
.850	.880	.911	.835
1.060	.895	.770	.800
.910	.844	.815	.793
.813	.965	.748	.796
.737	.875		

a. Use the Wilcoxon rank sum test to investigate the fairness of the assessments between the two neighborhoods. Use $\alpha = .05$ and interpret your findings in the context of the problem.

b. Under what circumstances could the two-sample t test be used to investigate the fairness issue of part **a**?

c. What assumptions are necessary to assure the validity of the test you conducted in part **a**?

8.52 Recall that the variance of a binomial sample proportion, $\hat{p}$, depends on the value of the population parameter, p. As a consequence, the variance of a sample percentage, $(100\hat{p})\%$, also depends on p. Thus if you conduct an unpaired t test (Section 8.2) to compare the means of two populations of percentages, you may be violating the assumption that $\sigma_1^2 = \sigma_2^2$, upon which the t test is based. If the disparity in the variances is large, you will obtain more reliable test results using the Wilcoxon rank sum test for independent samples. In Exercises 8.25, we used a Student's t test to compare the mean annual percentages of labor turnover between U.S. and Japanese manufacturers of air conditioners. The annual percentage turnover rates for five U.S. and five Japanese plants are shown in the table. Do the data provide sufficient evidence to indicate that the mean annual percentage turnover for American plants exceeds the corresponding mean for Japanese plants? Test using the Wilcoxon rank sum test with $\alpha = .05$. Do your test conclusions agree with those of the t test in Exercise 8.25?

U.S. Plants	Japanese Plants
7.11%	3.52%
6.06	2.02
8.00	4.91
6.87	3.22
4.77	1.92

8.53 A state highway department has decided to investigate the increased severity of automobile accidents occurring at an urban intersection since the adoption of the right-turn-on-red law. From police records, it chooses a random sample of eight accidents that occurred at the intersection before the law was enacted and a random sample of eight accidents that occurred after the law was enacted. The total damage estimate for each accident was the measure of severity. The damage estimates are recorded in the table. Use the Wilcoxon rank sum test to determine whether the damages tended to increase after the enactment of the law. Test using $\alpha = .05$. Draw appropriate conclusions.

Damage per Accident

Before Right-Turn Law		After Right-Turn Law	
$150	$242	$145	$ 899
500	435	390	1,250
250	100	680	290
301	402	560	963

8.54 A major razor blade manufacturer advertises that its twin-blade disposable razor "gets you lots more shaves" than any single-blade disposable razor on the market. A rival company that has been very successful in selling single-blade razors plans to test this claim. Independent random samples of eight single-blade users and eight twin-blade users are taken, and the number of shaves that each gets before indicating a preference to change blades is recorded. The results are shown in the table.

Twin Blades		Single Blades	
8	15	10	13
17	10	6	14
9	6	3	5
11	12	7	7

a. Do the data support the twin-blade manufacturer's claim? Use $\alpha = .05$.
b. Do you think this experiment was designed in the best possible way? If not, what design might have been better?
c. What assumptions are necessary for the validity of the test you performed in part **a**? Do the assumptions seem reasonable for this application?

8.55 A realtor wants to determine whether a difference exists between home prices in two subdivisions. Six homes from subdivision A and eight homes from subdivision B are sampled, and the prices (in thousands of dollars) are recorded in the table.

Subdivision A		Subdivision B	
43	39	57	88
48	47	39	46
42		55	41
60		52	64

a. Use the two-sample t test to compare the population mean prices per house in the two subdivisions. What assumptions are necessary for the validity of this procedure? Do you think they are reasonable in this case?
b. Use the Wilcoxon rank sum test to determine whether there is a shift in the locations of the probability distributions of house prices in the two subdivisions.

8.56 A *management information system* (MIS) is a computer-based information-processing system designed to support the operations, management, and decision functions of an organization. The development of an MIS involves three stages: definition, physical design, and implementation of the system (Davis and Olson, 1985).

The successful implementation of an MIS is related to the quality of the entire development process. It could fail due to inadequate planning by and negotiating between the designers and the future users of the system prior to construction, or simply because the users were improperly trained (Alter and Ginzberg, 1978).

Thirty firms that recently implemented an MIS were surveyed: 16 were satisfied with the implementation results, 14 were not. Each firm was asked to rate the quality of the planning and negotiation stages of the development process, using a scale of 0 to 100, with higher numbers indicating better quality. (A score of 100 indicates that all the problems that occurred in the planning and negotiation stages were successfully resolved, while 0 indicates that none were resolved.) The results obtained are shown in the table.

Firms with Good MIS			Firms with Poor MIS		
52	59	95	60	40	90
70	60	90	50	55	85
40	90	86	55	65	80
80	75	95	70	55	90
82	80	93	41	70	
65					

a. Alter and Ginzberg used the Mann-Whitney U test (a procedure equivalent to the Wilcoxon rank sum test) on similar data to compare the quality of the development processes of successfully and unsuccessfully implemented MISs. Use the large-sample Wilcoxon rank sum test to determine whether the distribution of quality scores for successfully implemented systems lies above the distribution of scores for unsuccessfully implemented systems. Test using $\alpha = .05$.

b. Under what circumstances could you use the two-sample t test to conduct the same test?

8.6   A Nonparametric Test for Comparing Two Populations: Paired Difference Experiment (Optional)

Nonparametric techniques can also be used to compare two probability distributions when a paired difference design is used. For example, for some paper products, softness is an important consideration in determining consumer acceptance. One method of determining softness is to have judges give a sample of the products a softness rating. Suppose each of 10 judges is given a sample of two products that a company wants to compare. Each judge rates the softness of each product on a scale from 1 to 10, with higher ratings implying a softer product. The results are shown in Table 8.6.

Since this is a paired difference experiment, we analyze the differences between the measurements (see Section 8.3). However, the nonparametric approach requires that we calculate the ranks of the *absolute values* of the differences between the measurements—i.e., the ranks of the differences after removing any minus signs. Note that tied absolute differences are assigned the average of the ranks they would receive if they were unequal but successive measurements. After the absolute differences are ranked, the sum of the ranks of the positive differences, T_+, and the sum of

TABLE 8.6   Paper Softness Ratings

Judge	Product		Difference	Absolute Value of Difference	Rank of Absolute Value
	A	B	(A − B)		
1	6	4	2	2	5
2	8	5	3	3	7.5
3	4	5	−1	1	2
4	9	8	1	1	2
5	4	1	3	3	7.5
6	7	9	−2	2	5
7	6	2	4	4	9
8	5	3	2	2	5
9	6	7	−1	1	2
10	8	2	6	6	10

$$T_+ = \text{Sum of positive ranks} = 46$$
$$T_- = \text{Sum of negative ranks} = 9$$

the ranks of the negative differences, T_-, are computed.

We are now prepared to test the nonparametric hypotheses:

H_0:   The probability distributions of the ratings for products A and B are identical

H_a: The probability distribution for product A is shifted to the right or left of the probability distribution of the ratings for product B

Test statistic: $T = $ Smaller of the positive and negative rank sums T_+ and T_-

The smaller the value of T, the greater will be the evidence to indicate that the two probability distributions differ in location. The rejection region for T can be determined by consulting Table XII of Appendix B. A portion of that table is shown in Table 8.7 (page 432). This table gives a value, T_0, for each value of n, the number of matched pairs.

The values of T_0 are tabulated for both a one- and two-tailed test. For a two-tailed test with $\alpha = .05$, we will reject H_0 if $T \leq T_0$. The T_0 value that locates the rejection region for the judges' ratings in Table 8.6 is the value indicated for $n = 10$ pairs of observations. This value of T_0 is 8. Therefore, the rejection region for the test (see Figure 8.9 on page 432) is

Rejection region: $T \leq 8$ for $\alpha = .05$

Since the smaller rank sum for the paper data, $T = T_- = 9$, does not fall within the rejection region, the experiment has not provided sufficient evidence to indicate that the two paper products differ with respect to their softness ratings at $\alpha = .05$.

TABLE 8.7 Reproduction of Part of Table XII of Appendix B: Critical Values of T_0 in the Wilcoxon Paired Difference Signed Rank Test

One-tailed	Two-tailed	$n = 5$	$n = 6$	$n = 7$	$n = 8$	$n = 9$	$n = 10$
$\alpha = .05$	$\alpha = .10$	1	2	4	6	8	11
$\alpha = .025$	$\alpha = .05$		1	2	4	6	8
$\alpha = .01$	$\alpha = .02$			0	2	3	5
$\alpha = .005$	$\alpha = .01$				0	2	3
		$n = 11$	$n = 12$	$n = 13$	$n = 14$	$n = 15$	$n = 16$
$\alpha = .05$	$\alpha = .10$	14	17	21	26	30	36
$\alpha = .025$	$\alpha = .05$	11	14	17	21	25	30
$\alpha = .01$	$\alpha = .02$	7	10	13	16	20	24
$\alpha = .005$	$\alpha = .01$	5	7	10	13	16	19
		$n = 17$	$n = 18$	$n = 19$	$n = 20$	$n = 21$	$n = 22$
$\alpha = .05$	$\alpha = .10$	41	47	54	60	68	75
$\alpha = .025$	$\alpha = .05$	35	40	46	52	59	66
$\alpha = .01$	$\alpha = .02$	28	33	38	43	49	56
$\alpha = .005$	$\alpha = .01$	23	28	32	37	43	49
		$n = 23$	$n = 24$	$n = 25$	$n = 26$	$n = 27$	$n = 28$
$\alpha = .05$	$\alpha = .10$	83	92	101	110	120	130
$\alpha = .025$	$\alpha = .05$	73	81	90	98	107	117
$\alpha = .01$	$\alpha = .02$	62	69	77	85	93	102
$\alpha = .005$	$\alpha = .01$	55	61	68	76	84	92

FIGURE 8.9 ►
Rejection region for paired difference experiment

Note that, if a significance level of $\alpha = .10$ had been used, the rejection region would have been $T \leq 11$, and we would have rejected H_0. In other words, the samples do provide evidence that the probability distributions of the softness ratings differ at $\alpha = .10$.

The **Wilcoxon signed rank test** is summarized in the next box. Note that the difference measurements are assumed to have a continuous probability distribution so that the absolute differences will have unique ranks. Although tied (absolute) differences can be assigned ranks by averaging, the number of ties should be small relative to the number of observations to assure the validity of the test.

Wilcoxon Signed Rank Test for a Paired Difference Experiment

One-Tailed Test

H_0: Two sampled populations have identical probability distributions

H_a: The probability distribution for population A is shifted to the right of that for population B

Test statistic: T_-, the negative rank sum (we assume the differences are computed by subtracting each paired B measurement from the corresponding A measurement)

Rejection region: $T_- \leq T_0$, where T_0 is found in Table XII in Appendix B for the one-tailed significance level α and the number of untied pairs, n.

Two-Tailed Test

H_0: Two sampled populations have identical probability distributions

H_a: The probability distribution for population A is shifted to the right *or* to the left of that for population B

Test statistic: T, the smaller of the positive and negative rank sums, T_+ and T_-

Rejection region: $T \leq T_0$, where T_0 is found in Table XII in Appendix B for the two-tailed significance level α and the number of untied pairs, n.

[Note: If the alternative hypothesis is that the probability distribution for A is shifted to the left of B, we use T_+ as the test statistic and reject H_0 if $T_+ \leq T_0$.]

Assumptions: 1. The sample of differences is randomly selected from the population of differences.
2. The probability distribution from which the sample of paired differences is drawn is continuous.

Ties: Assign tied absolute differences the average of the ranks they would receive if they were unequal but occurred in successive order. For example, if the third-ranked and fourth-ranked differences are tied, assign both a rank of $(3 + 4)/2 = 3.5$.

EXAMPLE 8.9

Suppose the U.S. Consumer Product Safety Commission (CPSC) wants to test the hypothesis that New York City electrical contractors are more likely to install unsafe electrical outlets in urban homes than in suburban homes. A pair of homes, one urban and one suburban and both serviced by the same electrical contractor, is chosen for each of ten randomly selected electrical contractors. A CPSC inspector assigns each of the 20 homes a safety rating between 1 and 10, with higher numbers implying safer electrical conditions. The results are shown in Table 8.8. Use the Wilcoxon signed rank test to determine whether the CPSC hypothesis is supported at the $\alpha = .05$ level.

TABLE 8.8 Electrical Safety Ratings for 10 Pairs of New York City Homes

Contractor	Urban	Suburban	Contractor	Urban	Suburban
1	7	9	6	6	10
2	4	5	7	8	9
3	8	8	8	10	8
4	9	8	9	9	4
5	3	6	10	5	9

Solution

The null and alternative hypotheses are

H_0: The probability distributions of home electrical ratings are identical for urban and suburban homes

H_a: The electrical ratings for suburban homes tend to exceed the electrical ratings for urban homes

These hypotheses can be tested for the data in Table 8.8 using the Wilcoxon signed rank test. Since a paired difference design was used (the homes were selected in urban–suburban pairs so that the electrical contractor was the same for both), we first calculate the difference between the ratings for each pair of homes, and then rank the absolute values of the differences (see Table 8.9). Note that one pair of ratings was the same (both 8), and the resulting 0 difference contributes to neither the positive nor the negative rank sum. Thus, we eliminate this pair from the calculation of the test statistic.

Test statistic: T_+, the positive rank sum

In Table 8.9, we compute the urban minus suburban rating differences, and if the alternative hypothesis is true, we would expect most of these differences to be negative. Or, in other words, we would expect the *positive* rank sum T_+ to be small if the alternative hypothesis is true (see Figure 8.10).

TABLE 8.9 Differences in Ratings and the Ranks of Their Absolute Values

Rating		Difference	Rank of Absolute Difference
Urban	Suburban	(Urban — Suburban)	
7	9	-2	4.5
4	5	-1	2
8	8	0	(Eliminated)
9	8	1	2
3	6	-3	6
6	10	-4	7.5
8	9	-1	2
10	8	2	4.5
9	4	5	9
5	9	-4	7.5
			Positive rank sum $= T_+ = 15.5$

Rejection region: For $\alpha = .05$, from Table XII of Appendix B, we use $n = 9$ (remember, one pair of observations was eliminated) to find the rejection region for this one-tailed test: $T_+ \le 8$.

FIGURE 8.10 ▶
The alternative hypothesis for
Example 8.9. We expect T_+ to
be small.

Since the computed value $T_+ = 15.5$ exceeds the critical value of 8, we conclude that this sample provides insufficient evidence at $\alpha = .05$ to support the alternative hypothesis. We *cannot* conclude on the basis of this sample information that suburban homes have safer electrical outlets than urban homes.

As in the case for the rank sum test for independent samples, the sampling distribution of the signed rank statistic can be approximated by a normal distribution when the number n of paired observations is large (say, $n \geq 25$). The large-sample z test is summarized in the box.

Wilcoxon Signed Rank Test for a Paired Difference Experiment: Large Sample

One-Tailed Test	*Two-Tailed Test*

H_0: Two sampled populations have identical probability distributions

H_a: The probability distribution for population A is shifted to the right of that for population B

Test statistic: $z = \dfrac{T_+ - \dfrac{n(n+1)}{4}}{\sqrt{\dfrac{n(n+1)(2n+1)}{24}}}$

Rejection region: $z > z_\alpha$

Assumptions: $n \geq 25$

H_0: Two sampled populations have identical probability distributions

H_a: The probability distribution for population A is shifted to the right *or* to the left of that for population B

Test statistic: $z = \dfrac{T_+ - \dfrac{n(n+1)}{4}}{\sqrt{\dfrac{n(n+1)(2n+1)}{24}}}$

Rejection region: $z < -z_{\alpha/2}$ or $z > z_{\alpha/2}$

Exercises 8.57 – 8.67

Learning the Mechanics

8.57 Specify the test statistic and the rejection region for the Wilcoxon signed rank test for the paired difference design in each of the following situations.

a. H_0: Two probability distributions, A and B, are identical
H_a: Probability distribution for population A is shifted to the right or left of the probability distribution for population B
$n = 30$, $\alpha = .10$

b. H_0: Two probability distributions, A and B, are identical.
H_a: Probability distribution for population A is shifted to the right of the probability distribution for population B
$n = 20$, $\alpha = .05$

c. H_0: Two probability distributions, A and B, are identical
H_a: Probability distribution for population A is shifted to the left of the probability distribution for population B
$n = 8$, $\alpha = .005$

8.58 Suppose you want to test a hypothesis that two treatments, A and B, are equivalent against the alternative hypothesis that the responses for A tend to be larger than those for B. You plan to use a paired difference experiment and to analyze the resulting data using the Wilcoxon signed rank test.

a. Specify the null and alternative hypotheses you would test.

b. Suppose the paired difference experiment yielded the data in the table. Conduct the test of part **a** using $\alpha = .025$.

Pair of Experimental Units	Treatment A	Treatment B	Pair of Experimental Units	Treatment A	Treatment B
1	56	42	6	76	75
2	54	45	7	74	63
3	98	87	8	29	35
4	45	25	9	63	59
5	82	71	10	80	81

8.59 Explain the difference between the one- and two-tailed versions of the Wilcoxon signed rank test for the paired difference experiment.

8.60 In order to conduct the Wilcoxon signed rank test, why do we need to assume that the probability distribution of differences is continuous?

8.61 A paired difference experiment with $n = 30$ pairs yielded $T_+ = 354$.

a. Specify the null and alternative hypotheses that should be used in conducting a hypothesis test to determine whether the probability distribution for population A is located to the right of that for population B.

b. Conduct the test of part **a** using $\alpha = .05$.

c. What is the approximate p-value of the test of part **b**?

d. What assumptions are necessary to assure the validity of the test you performed in part **b**?

Applying the Concepts

8.62 Which is the more effective means of dealing with complex group problem-solving tasks: face-to-face meetings or video teleconferencing? A report of an experiment (Rosetti and Surynt, 1985) concluded that video teleconferencing may be the more effective method. Ten groups of four people each were randomly assigned both to a specific communication setting (face-to-face or video teleconference) and to one of two specific complex problems. Upon completion of the problem-solving task, the same groups were placed in the alternative communication setting and asked to complete the second problem-solving task. The percentage of each problem task correctly completed was recorded for each group. Suppose the results were as given in the table.

Group	Face-to-Face	Video Teleconferencing	Group	Face-to-Face	Video Teleconferencing
1	65%	75%	6	85%	90%
2	82	80	7	98	98
3	54	60	8	35	40
4	69	65	9	85	89
5	40	55	10	70	80

a. What type of experimental design was used in this study?

b. Specify the null and alternative hypotheses that should be used in determining whether the data provide sufficient evidence to conclude that the problem-solving performance of video teleconferencing groups is superior to that of groups that interact face-to-face.

c. Conduct the hypothesis test of part **b**. Use $\alpha = .05$. Interpret the results of your test in the context of the problem.

d. What is the p-value of the test in part **c**?

8.63 Traditionally, workers in the United States have had a fixed 8-hour workday. A recent job-scheduling innovation that is helping managers to overcome the motivation and absenteeism problems associated with the fixed workday is a concept called *flextime*. This flexible working hours program permits employees to design their own 40-hour work week (Certo, 1980). The management of a large manufacturing firm may adopt a flextime program for its hourly employees, depending on the success or failure of a pilot program. Ten employees were randomly selected and given a questionnaire designed to measure their attitude toward their job. Each was then permitted to design and follow a flextime workday. After 6 months, attitudes toward their jobs were again measured. The resulting attitude scores are displayed in the table. The higher the score, the more favorable is the employee's attitude toward his or her work. Use a nonparametric test procedure to evaluate the success of the pilot flextime program. Test using $\alpha = .05$.

Employee	Before	After	Employee	Before	After
1	54	68	6	82	88
2	25	42	7	94	90
3	80	80	8	72	81
4	76	91	9	33	39
5	63	70	10	90	93

8.64 In Exercise 8.35, a paired difference test was used to compare the mean number of antitrust litigations per firm in the 1960s with the mean number per firm in the 1970s. The data are repeated in the table at the top of page 438. Beckenstein, Gabel, and Roberts (1983) claimed that, on average, companies faced more antitrust litigations in the 1970s than in the 1960s. Do the data support their claim? Test using the Wilcoxon signed rank test with $\alpha = .05$. Be sure to specify your null and alternative hypotheses.

Firm	1960s	1970s	Firm	1960s	1970s
1	10	10	6	7	6
2	8	12	7	6	11
3	9	8	8	9	12
4	7	16	9	8	11
5	8	14	10	7	12

8.65 A manufacturer of household appliances is considering one of two chains of department stores to be the sales merchandiser for its product in a particular region of the United States. Before choosing one chain, the manufacturer wants to compare the product exposure that might be expected for the two chains. Eight locations are selected where both chains have stores, and on a specific day, the number of shoppers entering each store is recorded. The data are shown in the table. Is there sufficient evidence to indicate that one chain tends to have more customers per day than the other? Test using $\alpha = .05$.

Location	A	B	Location	A	B
1	879	1,085	5	2,326	2,778
2	445	325	6	857	992
3	692	848	7	1,250	1,303
4	1,565	1,421	8	773	1,215

8.66 A food vending company currently uses vending machines made by two different manufacturers. Before purchasing new machines, the company wants to compare the two types in terms of reliability. Records for 7 weeks are given in the table; the data indicate the number of breakdowns per week for each type of machine. The company has the same number of machines of each type. Is the probability distribution of the number of breakdowns for machine A shifted to the left or to the right of the probability distribution of the number of breakdowns for machine B? Use $\alpha = .05$.

Week	Machine A	Machine B
1	14	12
2	17	13
3	10	14
4	15	12
5	14	9
6	9	11
7	12	11

8.67 Economic indexes provide measures of economic change. The table lists the producer commodity price indexes for January 1985 and January 1986, for six product categories. By comparing these two sets of indexes, you can obtain information regarding changes in the economy that occurred during 1985.

Product Category	January 1985	January 1986
Processed poultry	198.8	192.4
Concrete ingredients	331.0	339.0
Lumber	343.0	329.6
Gas fuels	1,073.0	1,034.3
Drugs and pharmaceuticals	247.4	265.9
Synthetic fibers	157.6	151.1

Source: *Standard & Poor's Statistical Service, Current Statistics*, Jan. 1987, pp. 12–13.

a. Conduct a paired difference t test to compare the mean values of these indexes for January 1985 and January 1986. Use $\alpha = .05$. What assumptions are necessary for the validity of this procedure? Why might these assumptions be in doubt?

b. Use the Wilcoxon signed rank test to determine whether the data provide evidence that the probability distribution of the economic indexes has changed. Use $\alpha = .05$. What assumptions are necessary to assure the validity of this test?

Summary

We have presented various techniques for using the information in two samples to make inferences about the difference between population means. As you would expect, we can make reliable inferences with fewer assumptions about the sampled populations when the sample sizes are large. When we cannot take large samples from the populations, the **two-sample t statistic** permits us to use the limited sample information to make inferences about the **difference between means** when the assumptions of normality and equal population variances are at least approximately true. The **paired difference experiment** offers the possibility of increasing the information about $(\mu_1 - \mu_2)$ by pairing similar observational units to control variability. In designing a paired difference experiment, we expect that the reduction in variability will more than compensate for the loss in degrees of freedom.

For situations when the assumptions required to conduct a t test are invalid (e.g., nonnormal populations or unequal variances), **nonparametric** procedures are available. The **Wilcoxon rank sum test** can be used to compare two populations based on independent samples and the **Wilcoxon signed rank test** can be used for a paired difference experiment.

Supplementary Exercises 8.68–8.82

Note: Starred (*) exercises refer to optional sections.

8.68   Was the average amount spent by firms in the electronics industry on company-sponsored research and development (R&D) higher in 1989 than in 1988? The table below lists R&D expenditures (in millions of dollars) for a sample of firms in the electronics industry.

Firm	1988	1989
Adams-Russell	6.3	5.1
Harris	116.9	104.0
Aydin	8.5	6.6
Andrew	14.1	17.0
Compudyn	2.3	1.8
Raytheon	271.0	274.7
Varian Associates	80.2	83.1
General Instr.	37.5	46.9

Source: *Business Week*, Special Issue on Innovation in America, 1989, 1990.

    a. A securities analyst who follows the electronics industry believes R&D expenditures have increased. Do the data support the analyst's belief? Test using $\alpha = .10$.

    b. What are the Type I and Type II errors associated with your hypothesis test of part **a**?

    c. What assumptions must hold in order for your test of part **a** to be valid?

8.69 Refer to Exercise 8.68. Use a 95% confidence interval to estimate the mean difference between 1989 and 1988 R&D expenditures. Interpret the interval.

8.70 List the assumptions necessary for each of the following inferential techniques:

    a. Large-sample inferences about the difference $(\mu_1 - \mu_2)$ between population means using a two-sample z statistic

    b. Small-sample inferences about $(\mu_1 - \mu_2)$ using an independent samples design and a two-sample t statistic

    c. Small-sample inferences about $(\mu_1 - \mu_2)$ using a paired difference design and a single-sample t statistic to analyze the differences

    d. Large-sample inferences about the difference $(p_1 - p_2)$ between binomial proportions using a two-sample z statistic

8.71 How does gender affect what type of advertising proves most effective? Because numerous studies have shown that males tend to be more competitive with others than with themselves, an advertising researcher created two versions of a soft drink ad (Prokash, 1990):

    Ad 1:   Four men compete in racquetball.

    Ad 2:   One man competes against himself in racquetball.

The author hypothesized that men would find the first ad more effective. To test this hypothesis, 43 males were shown both ads and asked to measure their attitude toward the advertisement (*Aad*), their attitude toward the brand of soft drink (*Ab*), and their intention to purchase the soft drink (*Intention*). Each variable was measured on a 7-point scale, with higher scores indicating a more favorable attitude. The results are in the table.

	Aad	*Ab*	*Intention*
Ad 1 sample mean	4.465	3.311	4.366
Ad 2 sample mean	4.150	2.902	3.813
Level of significance	$p = .091$	$p = .032$	$p = .050$

    a. What are the appropriate null and alternative hypotheses to test the author's research hypothesis? Define any symbols you use.

    b. Do you think this is an independent samples experiment or a paired difference experiment? Explain.

    c. Interpret the p-value for each test.

    d. What assumptions are necessary for the validity of the tests?

*8.72 A study was conducted to determine whether the installation of a traffic light was effective in reducing the number of accidents at a busy intersection. Samples of 6 months prior to installation and 5 months after installation of the light yielded the numbers of accidents per month listed in the table.

Before	After
12	4
5	2
10	7
9	3
14	8
6	

a. Is there sufficient evidence to conclude that the traffic light aided in reducing the number of accidents? Test using $\alpha = .025$.

b. Explain why this type of data might or might not be suitable for analysis using the t test.

*8.73 The Wilcoxon signed rank test was used to compare the performance of organizations using an innovative decentralized organization structure, the M-form, and their principal competitors. Teece (1981) identified the first firm in each of 20 industries that adopted the M-form structure. The principal competitor of each of these firms was identified, and if it also had adopted the M-form structure, but at a later date, it qualified for the sample. The difference in performance within the 14 qualifying pairs of firms was measured over two 3-year time periods: "before," when only the M-form originator in each pair used the M-form, and "after," when both had M-form structures. Differential performance in each time period was measured as the average difference in yearly return on stockholders' equity, where the differences were formed by subtracting the competitor's return on equity from the M-form originator's. The performance data appear in the accompanying table.

Industry	Average Difference in Yearly Return on Equity		Industry	Average Difference in Yearly Return on Equity	
	Before	After		Before	After
Grocery	25.70%	10.78%	Grain milling	3.86	4.81
Chemicals	6.26	−.39	Petroleum	3.29	2.38
Textiles	5.84	1.94	Tires	−3.36	−2.46
Aluminum	4.16	.56	Autos	13.48	14.38
Meat packing	−2.43	−5.80	Electrical equipment	−10.85	−10.40
Packaged foods	.77	−1.18	Tobacco	1.50	1.90
Can manufacturing	3.79	2.49	Retail department stores	12.32	12.37

a. Teece concluded that "the M-form innovation has been shown to display a statistically significant impact on firm performance." Do you agree? Test using $\alpha = .05$.

b. What is the approximate p-value of the test of part a?

c. What assumptions are necessary to assure the validity of the test procedure you used in part a?

8.74 Management training programs are often instituted to teach supervisory skills and thereby increase productivity. Suppose a company psychologist administers a set of examinations to each of ten supervisors before such a training program begins and then administers similar examinations at the end of the program. The examinations are designed to measure supervisory skills, with higher scores indicating increased skill. The results of the tests are shown in the table at the top of page 442.

Supervisor	Pre-Test	Post-Test	Supervisor	Pre-Test	Post-Test
1	63	78	6	72	85
2	93	92	7	91	99
3	84	91	8	84	82
4	72	80	9	71	81
5	65	69	10	80	87

a. Do the data provide evidence that the training program is effective in increasing supervisory skills, as measured by the examination scores? Use $\alpha = .10$.

b. Find and interpret the approximate p-value for the test.

8.75 A recent study (Jackson, Jackson, and Newmiller, 1992) investigated how much Americans worry about product tampering. Random samples of male and female consumers were asked to rate their concern about product tampering on a scale of 1 (little or no concern) to 9 (very concerned).

a. What are the appropriate null and alternative hypotheses to determine whether a difference exists in the mean level of concern about product tampering between men and women? Define any symbols you use.

b. Some of the statistics reported are shown here. Interpret these results.

```
MEAN SCORES:  MEN = 3.209     WOMEN = 3.923
       Z = -2.69     TWO-TAILED P-VALUE = .0072
```

c. What assumptions are necessary to assure the validity of this test?

8.76 You have been offered similar jobs in two different locales. To help decide which job to accept, you want to compare the cost of living in both cities. One of your primary concerns is the cost of housing, so you obtain a newspaper from each locale and study the housing prices in the classified ads. One convenient way to get a general idea of prices is to compute the prices per square foot. This is done by dividing the price of the house by its heated area (in square feet). Random samples of 63 ads in locale 1 and 78 in locale 2 produce the results shown in the table. Is there evidence that the mean housing price per square foot differs in the two locales? Use $\alpha = .01$.

Locale 1	Locale 2
$\bar{x}_1 = \$50.40$ per square foot	$\bar{x}_2 = \$53.70$ per square foot
$s_1 = \$4.50$ per square foot	$s_2 = \$5.30$ per square foot

8.77 Many computer programs are available to conduct two-sample tests of hypotheses to compare the means of two populations, for both independent and paired samples. Most of these report both the test statistic and the observed significance level for the test, but some report only the observed significance level of the test. Suppose you use one of these programs to test the null hypothesis $H_0: (\mu_1 - \mu_2) = 0$ versus the alternative $H_a: (\mu_1 - \mu_2) \neq 0$ with independent samples of size 12 and 10, respectively. Using $\alpha = .05$, what conclusions would you reach for the following observed significance levels reported by the program?

a. P-VALUE = .0429   b. P-VALUE = .1984   c. P-VALUE = .0001
d. P-VALUE = .0344   e. P-VALUE = .0545   f. P-VALUE = .9633

g. Always make sure that the program is performing the calculations correctly, especially with an unfamiliar program. Even programs that perform the calculations correctly usually do not remind you of the assumptions necessary for the validity of the procedure. What assumptions are necessary for this test?

8.78 Does the time of day during which one works affect job satisfaction? A recent study examined differences in job satisfaction between day-shift and night-shift nurses. Satisfaction with the hours of work, free time away from work, and breaks during work was measured. The table shows the mean scores for each measure of job satisfaction (higher scores indicate increased satisfaction), along with the observed significance level comparing the means for the day-shift and night-shift samples:

	Mean Satisfaction		
	Day Shift	Night Shift	p-Value
Hours of work	3.91	3.56	.813
Free time	2.55	1.72	.047
Breaks	2.53	3.75	.0073

Source: Barton, J., and Folkard, S. "The response of day and night nurses to their work schedules." *Occupational Psychology*, Sept. 1991, Vol. 64, pp. 207–218.

a. Specify the null and alternative hypotheses if we wish to test whether a difference in job satisfaction exists between day-shift and night-shift nurses on each of the three measures. Define any symbols you use.
b. Interpret the p-value for each test (each p-value in the table is two-tailed).
c. Assume that each test is based on a small sample of nurses from each group. What assumptions are necessary in order for the tests to be valid?

8.79 Japanese laborers worked 2,120 hours on average in 1991, while their American counterparts worked only 1,940 hours. The Japanese government, hoping to avoid a trade war and recognizing the lower quality of life for Japanese workers, has set a goal of 1,800 hours per year on average for its workers (Berg, 1993). A large Japanese company wants to test whether the gap in average hours worked in 1993 differed from 1991. A sample of 50 American workers had a sample mean of 1,933 hours worked and a sample standard deviation of 38 hours. A sample of 60 Japanese workers had a mean of 2,097 hours worked and a standard deviation of 43 hours.
a. What are the null and alternative hypotheses of interest?
b. Test the null hypothesis and report the p-value. Is there evidence that the difference in average hours between U.S. and Japanese workers has changed?
c. What assumptions must be made for the methodology you employed in part **b** to be valid?
d. Construct a 95% confidence interval to estimate the true difference in average hours between American and Japanese workers in 1993. Does this confidence interval cover the hypothesized value of D_0 in part **a**?

8.80 A state highway patrol was interested in knowing whether frequent patrolling of highways substantially reduced the number of speeders. Two similar interstate highways were selected for the study—one heavily patrolled and the other only occasionally patrolled. After 1 month, random samples of 100 cars were chosen on each highway and the number of cars exceeding the speed limit was recorded. This process was repeated on 5 randomly selected days. The data are shown in the table.

Day	Well Patrolled Road	Seldom Patrolled Road
1	35	60
2	40	36
3	25	48
4	38	54
5	47	63

a. Use the paired t test with $\alpha = .10$ to compare the population mean number of speeders per 100 cars for the two highways. What assumptions are necessary for the validity of this procedure? Do you think the assumptions are reasonable in this situation?

*__b.__ Use a nonparametric procedure to determine whether the data provide evidence to indicate that heavy patrolling tends to reduce the number of speeders. Test using $\alpha = .10$.

8.81 A hotel had a problem with people reserving rooms for a weekend and then not honoring their reservations (no-shows). As a result, the hotel developed a new reservation and deposit plan that it hoped would reduce the number of no-shows. One year after the policy was initiated, management evaluated its effect in comparison with the old policy. Compare the records given in the table on the number of no-shows for the ten nonholiday weekends preceding the institution of the new policy and the ten nonholiday weekends preceding the evaluation time. Has the situation improved under the new policy? Test at $\alpha = .05$.

Before		After	
10	11	4	4
5	8	3	2
3	9	8	5
6	6	5	7
7	5	6	1

*__8.82__ The personnel director of a company interviewed six potential job applicants without knowing anything about their backgrounds and then rated them on a scale from 1 to 10. Independently, the director's supervisor made an evaluation of the background qualifications of each candidate on the same scale. The results are shown in the table. Is there evidence that candidates' qualification scores are related to their interview performance? Use $\alpha = .10$.

Candidate	Qualifications	Interview Performance
1	10	8
2	8	9
3	9	10
4	4	5
5	5	3
6	6	6

On Your Own

Many stock market indexes, such as the Dow Jones Industrial Average, act both as indicators of stock market trends and as economic indicators. One way of comparing economic conditions at the end of two consecutive years is to estimate the difference in the mean closing prices of all stocks on the New York Stock Exchange. We outline two methods of sampling to estimate the difference in mean closing prices on the last day of market operations for two consecutive years, 1993 and 1994.

Method 1: Two Independent Samples

Step 1   Obtain lists of the closing prices of all stocks on the New York Stock Exchange for the last operating days of 1993 and 1994. (Any library will have these available.)

Step 2   Using a table of random numbers, randomly choose 15 stocks from the 1993 list and record the closing price of each.

Step 3   Again refer to a table of random numbers and choose a second (independent) sample of 15 closing prices from the 1994 list.

Step 4   Using the two samples of closing prices, form a 95% confidence interval for the true difference in mean closing prices for the two years.

Method 2: Paired Samples

Step 1   Same as for method 1.

Step 2   Same as for method 1.

Step 3   Obtain the 1994 closing prices for the *same stocks as those used in 1993.*

Step 4   Using this set of paired observations, form a 95% confidence interval for the true mean difference in closing prices for the two years.

Before actually collecting any data, state which method you think will provide more information (and why). Then, to compare the two methods, first perform the entire experiment outlined in method 1. After you have completed this, obtain the 1994 closing prices for the *same* stocks as the 1993 stocks analyzed and complete step 4 of method 2.

Which method provided a narrower confidence interval and thus more information on this performance of the experiment? Does this agree with your preliminary answer?

Using the Computer

Select two census regions from Appendix C, and consider the sports purchasing index. A marketing firm wants to target one of the two regions for a sports magazine marketing campaign.

a. Treat the sports index measurements for the zip codes in the regions as a random sample of sports index measurements from all the zip codes for the regions. Test the null hypothesis that the populations' mean sports purchasing indexes are equal using $\alpha = .01$, and place a 99% confidence interval on the true difference between the mean purchasing index for the two regions.

b. Repeat part **a** using the following pairs of α and confidence levels for the tests and confidence intervals: (.05, 95%), (.10, 90%), and (.20, 80%). Describe what happens to the tests and confidence intervals as α is increased and the confidence level is decreased. Which do you think is more informative, the tests or the confidence intervals? Explain.

References

Alter, S., and Ginzberg, M. "Managing uncertainty in MIS implementation." *Sloan Management Review*, Fall 1978, Vol. 20, pp. 23–31.

Beckenstein, A. R., Gabel, H. L., and Roberts, K. "An executive's guide to antitrust compliance." *Harvard Business Review*, Sept.–Oct. 1983, pp. 94–102.

Berg, S. "Land of rising fun?" *Minneapolis Star Tribune*, Jan. 31, 1993.

Certo, S. C. *Principles of Modern Management*. Dubuque, IA: Wm. C. Brown 1980. Chapter 14.

Davis, G. B., and Olson, M. H. *Management Information Systems*, 2nd ed. New York: McGraw-Hill, 1985.

Freedman, D. A. "The mean versus the median: A case study in 4-R Act litigation." *Journal of Business and Economic Statistics*, Jan. 1985, Vol. 3, pp. 1–13.

Garvin, D. A. "Quality on the line." *Harvard Business Review*, Sept.–Oct. 1983, pp. 65–75.

Gibbons, J. D. *Nonparametric Statistical Inference*, 2d ed. New York: McGraw-Hill, 1985.

Gross, S. "Cable TV—An industry in flux." *Minneapolis Star Tribune*, Jan. 10, 1993.

Hines, G. H. "Sociocultural influences on employee expectancy and participative management." *Academy of Management Journal*, 1974, Vol. 17, No. 2.

Hollander, M., and Wolfe, D. A. *Nonparametric Statistical Methods*. New York: Wiley, 1973.

Jackson, G. B., Jackson, R. W., and Newmiller, C. E., Jr. "Consumer demographics and reaction to product tampering." *Journal of Psychology and Marketing*, Jan. 1992, Vol. 9, No. 1, pp. 45–57.

Lehmann, E. L. *Nonparametrics: Statistical Methods Based on Ranks*. San Francisco: Holden-Day, 1975.

Logue, D., and Rogalski, R. *Harvard Business Review*, July–Aug. 1979.

Marcotty, J. "Quantity of quality circles proves they're no fad." *Minneapolis Tribune*, Nov. 20, 1983a.

Marcotty, J. "Tennant tightens up loose screws." *Minneapolis Tribune*, Nov. 20, 1983b.

McGuire, E. P. *Evaluating New Product Proposals*. New York: National Industrial Conference Board, 1973. Pp. 54–55.

Neter, J., Wasserman, W., and Whitmore, G. A. *Applied Statistics*, 2d ed. Boston: Allyn & Bacon, 1982. Chapter 13.

Prokash, V. "Sex roles and advertising preferences." *Advertising Research*, May/June 1990, pp. 43–50.

Rogot, E., Sorlie, P. D., and Johnson, N. T. "Life expectancy by employment status, income, and education in the national longitudinal mortality study." *Public Health Reports*, July–Aug. 1992, Vol. 107, No. 4, p. 457.

Rosetti, D. K., and Surynt, T. J. "Video teleconferencing and performance." *Journal of Business Communication*, Fall 1985, Vol. 22, pp. 25–31.

Shuchman, A., and Riesz, P. C. "Correlates of persuasibility: The Crest case." *Journal of Marketing Research*, Feb. 1975, Vol. 12, pp. 7–11.

Siegel, S. *Nonparametric Statistics for the Behavioral Sciences*. New York: McGraw-Hill, 1956.

Smith, W. M. "Federal pay procedures and the comparability survey." *Monthly Labor Review*, Aug. 1976, pp. 27–31.

Teece, D. J. "Internal organization and economic performance: An empirical analysis of the profitability of principal firms." *The Journal of Industrial Economics*, Dec. 1981, Vol. 30, pp. 173–199.

Wansley, J. W., Roenfeldt, R. L., and Cooley, P. L. "Abnormal returns from merger profiles." *Journal of Financial and Quantitative Analysis*, June 1983, Vol. 18, No. 2, pp. 149–162.

Winer, L. "The effect of product sales quotas on sales force productivity." *Journal of Marketing Research*, May 1973, Vol. 10, p. 180.

Winkler, R. L., and Hays, W. L. *Statistics: Probability, Inference, and Decision*, 2d ed. New York: Holt, Rinehart and Winston, 1975. Chapter 6.

CHAPTER NINE

Comparing Population Proportions

Contents

Case Studies

Where We've Been

Chapter 8 presented methods for comparing two population means using z and t statistics and for comparing two populations using nonparametric methods.

Where We're Going

In this chapter, we will consider a problem of comparable importance—comparing two or more population proportions. The need to compare population proportions arises because many business and social experiments involve questioning people and classifying their responses. We will learn how to determine whether the proportion of consumers favoring product A differs from the proportion favoring product B, and we will learn how to estimate the difference with a confidence interval.

Many experiments are conducted in business and the biological, physical, and social sciences to compare two or more population proportions. Those conducted in business and the social sciences to sample the opinions of people are called **sample surveys.** For example, a breakfast cereal producer might wish to estimate the difference in the proportions of consumers in two sales regions who prefer their product over the competition's. Or, after an innovative process change, an engineer might wish to determine whether the proportion of defective items produced by a manufacturing process was less than the proportion of defectives produced before the change. This chapter will show you how to test hypotheses about the difference between two population proportions based on independent random sampling. We will also show how to find a confidence interval for the difference. Then, in optional Section 9.3 we will compare more than two population proportions, and in optional section 9.4 we will present a related problem.

9.1   Inferences About the Difference Between Two Population Proportions: Independent Binomial Experiments

Suppose a manufacturer of camper vans wants to compare the potential market for its products in the northeastern United States to the market in the southeastern United States. Such a comparison would help the manufacturer decide where to concentrate sales efforts. Using telephone directories, the company randomly chooses 1,000 households in the northeast (NE) and 1,000 households in the southeast (SE) and determines whether each household plans to buy a camper within the next 5 years. The objective is to use this sample information to make an inference about the difference $(p_1 - p_2)$ between the proportion p_1 of *all* households in the NE and the proportion p_2 of *all* households in the SE that plan to purchase a camper within 5 years.

The two samples represent independent binomial experiments (see Section 4.3 for the characteristics of binomial experiments), with the binomial random variables x_1 and x_2 being the numbers of the 1,000 sampled households in each area that indicate they will purchase a camper within 5 years. The results of the sampling can be summarized as shown in the table. We can now calculate the *sample* proportions $\hat{p}_1$ and $\hat{p}_2$ of the households in the NE and SE, respectively, that are prospective buyers:

NE	SE
$n_1 = 1{,}000$	$n_2 = 1{,}000$
$x_1 = 42$	$x_2 = 24$

$$\hat{p}_1 = \frac{x_1}{n_1} = \frac{42}{1{,}000} = .042 \qquad \hat{p}_2 = \frac{x_2}{n_2} = \frac{24}{1{,}000} = .024$$

The difference between the sample proportions, $(\hat{p}_1 - \hat{p}_2)$, is an intuitively appealing point estimator of the difference between the population parameters, $(p_1 - p_2)$. For our example, the estimate is

$$(\hat{p}_1 - \hat{p}_2) = .042 - .024 = .018$$

To judge the reliability of the estimator $(\hat{p}_1 - \hat{p}_2)$, we must know something about its behavior in repeated sampling from the two populations. That is, we need to know the sampling distribution of $(\hat{p}_1 - \hat{p}_2)$. Properties of the sampling distribution are given in the box. Remember that $\hat{p}_1$ and $\hat{p}_2$ can be viewed as means of the number of successes in the respective samples so that the Central Limit Theorem will apply when the sample sizes are large.

Properties of the Sampling Distribution of $(\hat{p}_1 - \hat{p}_2)$

1. If the sample sizes n_1 and n_2 are large (see Section 6.4 for a guideline), the sampling distribution of $(\hat{p}_1 - \hat{p}_2)$ is approximately normal.

2. The mean of the sampling distribution if $(\hat{p}_1 - \hat{p}_2)$ is $(p_1 - p_2)$; i.e.,

$$E(\hat{p}_1 - \hat{p}_2) = p_1 - p_2$$

Thus, $(\hat{p}_1 - \hat{p}_2)$ is an unbiased estimator of $(p_1 - p_2)$.

3. The standard deviation of the sampling distribution of $(\hat{p}_1 - \hat{p}_2)$ is

$$\sigma_{(\hat{p}_1-\hat{p}_2)} = \sqrt{\frac{p_1 q_1}{n_1} + \frac{p_2 q_2}{n_2}}$$

Since the distribution of $(\hat{p}_1 - \hat{p}_2)$ in repeated sampling is approximately normal, we can use the z statistic to derive confidence intervals for $(p_1 - p_2)$ or to test a hypothesis about $(p_1 - p_2)$. For the camper example, a 95% confidence interval for the difference $(p_1 - p_2)$ is

$$(\hat{p}_1 - \hat{p}_2) \pm 1.96 \sigma_{(\hat{p}_1-\hat{p}_2)} = (\hat{p}_1 - \hat{p}_2) \pm 1.96 \sqrt{\frac{p_1 q_1}{n_1} + \frac{p_2 q_2}{n_2}}$$

The quantities $p_1 q_1$ and $p_2 q_2$ must be estimated in order to complete the calculation of the standard deviation, $\sigma_{(\hat{p}_1-\hat{p}_2)}$, and hence of the confidence interval. In Section 6.4, we showed that the value of pq is relatively insensitive to the value chosen to approximate p. Therefore, $\hat{p}_1 \hat{q}_1$ and $\hat{p}_2 \hat{q}_2$ will provide satisfactory estimates of $p_1 q_1$ and $p_2 q_2$, respectively. Then

$$(\hat{p}_1 - \hat{p}_2) \pm 1.96 \sqrt{\frac{p_1 q_1}{n_1} + \frac{p_2 q_2}{n_2}} \approx (\hat{p}_1 - \hat{p}_2) \pm 1.96 \sqrt{\frac{\hat{p}_1 \hat{q}_1}{n_1} + \frac{\hat{p}_2 \hat{q}_2}{n_2}}$$

$$= (.042 - .024) \pm 1.96 \sqrt{\frac{(.042)(.958)}{1,000} + \frac{(.024)(.976)}{1,000}}$$

$$= .018 \pm .016 = (.002, .034)$$

Thus, we are 95% confident that the interval (.002, .034) contains $(p_1 - p_2)$. It appears that there are between .2% and 3.4% more households in the NE than in the SE that plan to purchase campers in the next 5 years.

Large-Sample $100(1 - \alpha)\%$ Confidence Interval for $(p_1 - p_2)$

$$(\hat{p}_1 - \hat{p}_2) \pm z_{\alpha/2}\, \sigma_{(\hat{p}_1 - \hat{p}_2)} = (\hat{p}_1 - \hat{p}_2) \pm z_{\alpha/2} \sqrt{\frac{p_1 q_1}{n_1} + \frac{p_2 q_2}{n_2}}$$

$$\approx (\hat{p}_1 - \hat{p}_2) \pm z_{\alpha/2} \sqrt{\frac{\hat{p}_1 \hat{q}_1}{n_1} + \frac{\hat{p}_2 \hat{q}_2}{n_2}}$$

Assumptions: The two samples are independent random samples from binomial distributions. Both samples should be large enough that the normal distribution provides an adequate approximation to the sampling distribution of $\hat{p}_1$ and $\hat{p}_2$ (see Section 6.4).

The z statistic,

$$z = \frac{(\hat{p}_1 - \hat{p}_2) - (p_1 - p_2)}{\sigma_{(\hat{p}_1 - \hat{p}_2)}}$$

is used to test the null hypothesis that $(p_1 - p_2)$ equals some specified difference— say, D_0. For the special case where $D_0 = 0$—i.e., where we want to test the null hypothesis that $(p_1 - p_2) = 0$ (or, equivalently, that $p_1 = p_2$)—the best estimate of $p_1 = p_2 = p$ is obtained by dividing the total number of successes $(x_1 + x_2)$ for the two samples by the total number of observations $(n_1 + n_2)$; i.e.,

$$\hat{p} = \frac{x_1 + x_2}{n_1 + n_2} \qquad \text{or} \qquad \hat{p} = \frac{n_1 \hat{p}_1 + n_2 \hat{p}_2}{n_1 + n_2}$$

The second equation shows that $\hat{p}$ is a weighted average of $\hat{p}_1$ and $\hat{p}_2$, with the larger sample receiving more weight. If the sample sizes are equal, then $\hat{p}$ is a simple average of the two sample proportions of successes.

We now substitute the weighted average $\hat{p}$ for both p_1 and p_2 in the formula for the standard deviation of $(\hat{p}_1 - \hat{p}_2)$:

$$\sigma_{(\hat{p}_1 - \hat{p}_2)} = \sqrt{\frac{p_1 q_1}{n_1} + \frac{p_2 q_2}{n_2}} \approx \sqrt{\frac{\hat{p}\hat{q}}{n_1} + \frac{\hat{p}\hat{q}}{n_2}} = \sqrt{\hat{p}\hat{q}\left(\frac{1}{n_1} + \frac{1}{n_2}\right)}$$

The test is summarized in the box.

Large-Sample Test of Hypothesis About $(p_1 - p_2)$

One-Tailed Test

H_0: $(p_1 - p_2) = 0$*
H_a: $(p_1 - p_2) < 0$
[or H_a: $(p_1 - p_2) > 0$]

Test statistic: $z = \dfrac{(\hat{p}_1 - \hat{p}_2)}{\sigma_{(\hat{p}_1 - \hat{p}_2)}}$

Rejection region: $z < -z_\alpha$
[or $z > z_\alpha$ when
H_a: $(p_1 - p_2) > 0$]

Two-Tailed Test

H_0: $(p_1 - p_2) = 0$
H_a: $(p_1 - p_2) \neq 0$

Test statistic: $z = \dfrac{(\hat{p}_1 - \hat{p}_2)}{\sigma_{(\hat{p}_1 - \hat{p}_2)}}$

Rejection region: $z < -z_{\alpha/2}$
or $z > z_{\alpha/2}$

Note: $\sigma_{(\hat{p}_1 - \hat{p}_2)} = \sqrt{\dfrac{p_1 q_1}{n_1} + \dfrac{p_2 q_2}{n_2}} \approx \sqrt{\hat{p}\hat{q}\left(\dfrac{1}{n_1} + \dfrac{1}{n_2}\right)}$

where $\hat{p} = \dfrac{x_1 + x_2}{n_1 + n_2} = \dfrac{n_1\hat{p}_1 + n_2\hat{p}_2}{n_1 + n_2}$

Assumption: Same as for large-sample confidence interval for $(p_1 - p_2)$. (See previous box.)

EXAMPLE 9.1

A consumer agency wants to determine whether there is a difference between the proportions of the two leading automobile models that need major repairs (more than $500) within 2 years of their purchase. A sample of 400 2-year owners of model 1 are contacted, and a sample of 500 2-year owners of model 2 are contacted. The numbers x_1 and x_2 of owners who report that their cars needed major repairs within the first 2 years are 53 and 78, respectively. Test the null hypothesis that no difference exists between the proportions in populations 1 and 2 needing major repairs against the alternative that a difference does exist. Use $\alpha = .10$.

Solution

If we define p_1 and p_2 as the true proportions of model 1 and model 2 owners, respectively, whose cars need major repairs within 2 years, the elements of the test are

---

*The test can be adapted to test for a difference $D_0 \neq 0$. Because most applications call for a comparison of p_1 and p_2, implying $D_0 = 0$, we will confine our attention to this case.

$$H_0: (p_1 - p_2) = 0 \qquad H_a: (p_1 - p_2) \neq 0$$

Test statistic: $\quad z = \dfrac{(\hat{p}_1 - \hat{p}_2)}{\sigma_{(\hat{p}_1 - \hat{p}_2)}}$

Rejection region: $(\alpha = .10)$: $\quad z > z_{\alpha/2} = z_{.05} = 1.645$
$\qquad\qquad\qquad\qquad$ or $z < -z_{\alpha/2} = -z_{.05} = -1.645$
$\qquad\qquad\qquad\qquad$ (see Figure 9.1)

FIGURE 9.1 ▶
Rejection region for Example 9.1

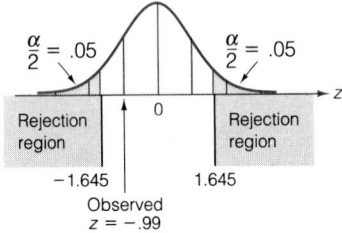

$\dfrac{\alpha}{2} = .05$ $\dfrac{\alpha}{2} = .05$

Rejection region   0   Rejection region

−1.645   1.645

Observed
$z = -.99$

We now calculate

$$z = \frac{(\hat{p}_1 - \hat{p}_2)}{\sigma_{(\hat{p}_1 - \hat{p}_2)}} = \frac{(\hat{p}_1 - \hat{p}_2)}{\sqrt{\dfrac{p_1 q_1}{n_1} + \dfrac{p_2 q_2}{n_2}}} \approx \frac{(\hat{p}_1 - \hat{p}_2)}{\sqrt{\hat{p}\hat{q}\left(\dfrac{1}{n_1} + \dfrac{1}{n_2}\right)}}$$

where

$$\hat{p}_1 = \frac{x_1}{n_1} = \frac{53}{400} = .1325$$

$$\hat{p}_2 = \frac{x_2}{n_2} = \frac{78}{500} = .1560$$

and

$$\hat{p} = \frac{n_1 \hat{p}_1 + n_2 \hat{p}_2}{n_1 + n_2} = \frac{400(.1325) + 500(.1560)}{400 + 500} = .1456$$

Thus, $\hat{p}$ is a weighted average of $\hat{p}_1$ and $\hat{p}_2$, with more weight given the larger sample of model 2 owners. We substitute to obtain the (approximate) z test statistic:

$$z \approx \frac{.1325 - .1560}{\sqrt{(.1456)(.8544)\left(\dfrac{1}{400} + \dfrac{1}{500}\right)}} = \frac{-.0235}{.0237} = -.99$$

The samples provide insufficient evidence at $\alpha = .10$ to detect a difference between the proportions of the two models that need repairs within 2 years. Even though 2.35% more sampled owners of model 2 found major repairs, this difference is only .99 standard deviation ($z = -.99$) from the hypothesized zero difference between the true proportions.

EXAMPLE 9.2

Find the observed significance level for the test in Example 9.1.

Solution

The observed value of z for this two-tailed test was $z = -.99$. Therefore, the observed significance level is

$$p\text{-value} = P(z < -.99 \text{ or } z > .99)$$

This probability is equal to the shaded area shown in Figure 9.2. The area corresponding to $z = .99$ is given in Table IV of Appendix B as .3389. Therefore, the

FIGURE 9.2 ▶
The observed significance level for the test of Example 9.2

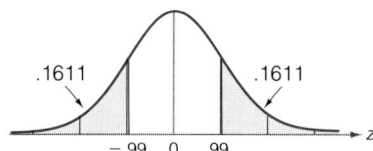

observed significance level for the test, the sum of the two shaded tail areas under the standard normal curve, is

$$p\text{-value} = 2(.5 - .3389) = .3222$$

The probability of observing a z as large as .99 or less than $-.99$ if in fact $p_1 = p_2$ is .3222. This large p-value indicates that there is little or no evidence of a difference between p_1 and p_2.

CASE STUDY 9.1 / Hotel Room Interviewing—Anxiety and Suspicion

Writing in the *Sloan Management Review*, Lois Kaufman and John Wolf (1982) describe the typical approach used by sales managers for attracting and interviewing prospective sales representatives:

To maintain product distribution and enhance customer service, corporate sales personnel are typically assigned to a district sales office that is tied to a regional office by telephone or telex. The managers who are responsible for staffing sales territories usually operate with considerable autonomy. When hiring sales representatives, they usually advertise for these positions in local newspapers, and traditionally invite applicants to interviews which are held in hotel rooms.

The purpose of the article was to examine the effects of the hotel interview site on prospective sales representatives, and on women in particular.

As part of their study, Kaufman and Wolf asked a sample of 74* female college students from Rutgers University, Montclair State College, and Union College whether they would agree to a job interview in a room at a local hotel; 62% said they would. Another sample of 74 college women was asked whether they would agree to a job interview in a room of a local office building, and 98% said yes. The authors used a one-tailed hypothesis test to examine the following hypotheses:

$$H_0: \quad p_1 - p_2 = 0 \qquad H_a: \quad p_1 - p_2 > 0$$

where

p_1 = Proportion of female college students who, if offered a job interview in a room of a local office building, would say they would attend the interview

p_2 = Proportion of female college students who, if offered a job interview in a room of a local hotel, would say they would attend the interview

They obtained an observed significance level of less than .05 for their z statistic and concluded that the proportion of women who would agree to an interview in an office building is significantly greater than the proportion willing to interview in a hotel room.

A similar but less extreme result was obtained when college men were asked the same questions. For the women $\hat{p}_1 - \hat{p}_2 = .36$, whereas for the men $\hat{p}_1 - \hat{p}_2 = .09$. Based on these results and other information supplied by the men and women who participated in their study, Kaufman and Wolf explained the study's findings as follows:

Both men and women find hotel rooms more stressful than offices, but women are even more anxious than men about the prospect of interviewing in hotels. Most respondents said they would take precautions if they interviewed in hotels. Hotel room hiring was described with such words as "shady," "suspicious," "secretive," and "fishy."

Kaufman and Wolf summarized the implications of their findings by saying:

We believe that companies should reexamine their hiring practices and recognize that hotel room interviewing may not be the best approach to recruiting and hiring talented employees. Companies should consider using college campuses, local placement agencies, civic centers, libraries, or government buildings as possible interview sites. Although companies may not intend to discourage applicants when they interview in hotels, our survey showed that many women as well as some men will not attend an interview held in a hotel.

Exercises 9.1 – 9.16

Learning the Mechanics

9.1 What are the characteristics of a binomial experiment?

9.2 The quantities $\hat{p}_1$ and $\hat{p}_2$ have been defined as x_1/n_1 and x_2/n_2, respectively. What assumptions do we make about x_1 and x_2? Describe the sampling distributions of $\hat{p}_1$ and $\hat{p}_2$, assuming n_1 and n_2 are large.

9.3 In each case, determine whether the sample sizes are large enough to conclude that the sampling distribution of $(\hat{p}_1 - \hat{p}_2)$ is approximately normal.

---

*Sample sizes were obtained via personal communication from Professor Kaufman.

a. $n_1 = 12,$ $n_2 = 14,$ $\hat{p}_1 = .42,$ $\hat{p}_2 = .57$
b. $n_1 = 12,$ $n_2 = 14,$ $\hat{p}_1 = .92,$ $\hat{p}_2 = .86$
c. $n_1 = 30,$ $n_2 = 30,$ $\hat{p}_1 = .70,$ $\hat{p}_2 = .73$
d. $n_1 = 100,$ $n_2 = 250,$ $\hat{p}_1 = .93,$ $\hat{p}_2 = .97$
e. $n_1 = 125,$ $n_2 = 200,$ $\hat{p}_1 = .08,$ $\hat{p}_2 = .12$

9.4 In each case, find the values of z for which H_0: $(p_1 - p_2) = 0$ would be rejected in favor of H_a: $(p_1 - p_2) < 0$.
a. $\alpha = .01$ b. $\alpha = .025$ c. $\alpha = .05$ d. $\alpha = .10$

9.5 Random samples of $n_1 = 200$ and $n_2 = 220$ from two binomial populations produced $x_1 = 47$ and $x_2 = 72$ successes, respectively.
a. Compute the sample proportions, $\hat{p}_1$ and $\hat{p}_2$.
b. Find the values of z for which the null hypothesis H_0: $(p_1 - p_2) = 0$ would be rejected in favor of the alternative hypothesis H_a: $(p_1 - p_2) \neq 0$. Use $\alpha = .10$.
c. Test the hypotheses described in part b. Interpret your results.
d. Find and interpret the p-value for the test.
e. What assumptions must be satisfied so the test will be valid?
f. Construct a 98% confidence interval for $(p_1 - p_2)$. Interpret your confidence interval.

9.6 A random sample of size $n_1 = 1,000$ from population 1 and a random sample of size $n_2 = 1,000$ from population 2 yielded $x_1 = 290$ and $x_2 = 343$ successes, respectively.
a. Given H_0: $(p_1 - p_2) = 0$ and H_a: $(p_1 - p_2) < 0$, find the values of z for which the null hypothesis would be rejected in favor of the alternative hypothesis. Use $\alpha = .025$.
b. Conduct the test described above. Interpret the results.
c. Find the observed significance level of the hypothesis test, and interpret its value.
d. What assumptions must be satisfied so the test will be valid?
e. Construct and interpret an 80% confidence interval for $(p_1 - p_2)$.

9.7 Random samples of size $n_1 = 55$ and $n_2 = 65$ were drawn from populations 1 and 2, respectively. The samples yielded $\hat{p}_1 = .7$ and $\hat{p}_2 = .6$. Test H_0: $(p_1 - p_2) = 0$ against H_a: $(p_1 - p_2) > 0$ using $\alpha = .05$.

Applying the Concepts

9.8 Despite company policies allowing unpaid family leave for new fathers, many men fear that exercising this option would be held against them by their superiors (*Minneapolis Star Tribune*, February 14, 1993). In a random sample of 100 male workers planning to become fathers, 35 agreed with the statement, "If I knew there would be no repercussions, I would choose to participate in the family leave program after the birth of a son or daughter." However, of 96 men who became fathers in the previous 16 months, only nine participated in the program.
a. Specify the appropriate null and alternative hypotheses to test whether the sample data provide sufficient evidence to reject the hypothesis that the proportion of new fathers participating in the program is the same as the proportion that would like to participate. Define any symbols you use.
b. Are the sample sizes large enough to conclude that the sampling distribution of $(\hat{p}_1 - \hat{p}_2)$ is approximately normal?
c. Conduct the hypothesis test using $\alpha = .05$. Report the observed significance level of the test.
d. What assumptions must be satisfied for the test to be valid?

9.9 Women are filling managerial positions in increasing numbers, although whether they progress fast enough it still debated. Does marriage hinder a woman's career progression more than a man's? A recent article (Stroh, Brett, and Reilly, 1992) investigated this and other questions relating to managerial careers of men and women in today's work force. In a random sample of 795 male managers and 223 female managers from 20 Fortune 500 corporations, 86% of the male managers and 45% of the female managers were married.

    a. Use a 95% confidence interval to estimate the difference between the proportions of men and women managers who are married.

    b. Interpret the interval. State your conclusion in terms of the population from which the sample was drawn.

9.10 What makes entrepreneurs different from chief executive officers (CEOs) of Fortune 500 companies? The *Wall Street Journal* hired the Gallup Organization to investigate this question. For the study, entrepreneurs were defined as chief executive officers of companies listed by *Inc.* magazine as among the 500 fastest-growing smaller companies in the United States. The Gallup Organization sampled 207 CEOs of Fortune 500 companies and 153 entrepreneurs. They obtained the results shown in the table.

	Fortune 500 CEOs	*Entrepreneurs*
Age: Under 45 years old	19	96
Education: Completed 4 years of college	195	116
Employment record: Have been fired or dismissed from a job	19	47

Source: Graham, E. "The entrepreneurial mystique." *Wall Street Journal*, May 20, 1985.

    a. In each of the three areas—age, education, and employment record—are the sample sizes large enough to use the inferential methods of this section to investigate the differences between Fortune 500 CEOs and entrepreneurs? Justify your answer.

    b. Do the data indicate that Fortune 500 CEOs and entrepreneurs differ in terms of education? Test using $\alpha = .05$.

    c. What assumption(s) must be satisfied in order for your test of part **b** to be valid?

9.11 Refer to Exercise 9.10. Use a 95% confidence interval to estimate the difference in the proportions of Fortune 500 CEOs and entrepreneurs who are under 45 years of age.

9.12 Refer to Exercise 9.10.

    a. Test to determine whether the data indicate that the fractions of CEOs and entrepreneurs who have been fired or dismissed from a job differ at the $\alpha = .01$ level of significance.

    b. Construct a 99% confidence interval for the difference between the fractions of CEOs and entrepreneurs who have been fired or dismissed from a job.

    c. Which inferential procedure provides more information about the difference between employment records, the test of hypothesis of part **a** or the confidence interval of part **b**? Explain.

9.13 To aid in the development of new products and to guide their marketing programs, food producers attempt to identify the taste preferences of various segments of the population. A study by Professor Susan Schiffman of the Duke University Center for the Study of Aging and Human Development showed that a person's ability to identify food by smell and taste decreases with increasing age. As a result, she recommends adding simulated odors to the food of older people to improve its flavor. Part of Professor Schiffman's experiment involved asking a random sample of older persons and a random sample of college students to smell, taste, and identify a variety of foods that had been blended to prevent identification by "feel." Subjects were blindfolded during the experiment (Meier, 1980). Suppose that blended apple was correctly identified by 81 of 100 students and by 51 of 100 older people.

a. Would these data support the conclusion that the ability to identify food decreases with age? Test using $\alpha = .05$.

b. Report the p-value of the hypothesis test, and interpret its value.

c. What assumption must be satisfied so the hypothesis test of part **a** will be valid? Why was this assumption necessary?

9.14 Moving companies (home movers, etc.) are required by the government to publish a Carrier Performance Report each year. One of the descriptive statistics they must include is the annual percentage of shipments on which a $50 or greater claim for loss or damage was filed. Suppose company A and company B each decide to estimate this figure by sampling their records, and they obtain the data shown in the table.

	Company A	Company B
Total shipments delivered	9,542	6,631
Number of shipments with a claim $\geq$ $50	1,653	501

a. Estimate the true proportion of shipments on which a claim of $50 or more was made against company A. Use an estimate that reflects its reliability.

b. Repeat part **a** for company B.

c. Use a 95% confidence interval to estimate the true difference in the proportions of shipments that result in claims being made against company A and company B.

9.15 Refer to Exercise 9.14. Test the null hypothesis that no difference exists between the true percentage of shipments resulting in claims made against company A and company B against the alternative hypothesis that a difference does exist. Use $\alpha = .05$. Do your test results indicate that one carrier is superior to the other? If so, which one? Explain how you arrived at your conclusion.

9.16 If α were set at .01 in Exercise 9.15, would you be more or less likely to reject the null hypothesis if in fact it is true? Explain.

9.2 Determining the Sample Size

The sample sizes n_1 and n_2 required to compare two population proportions can be found in a manner similar to the method described in Section 8.4 for comparing two population means. We will assume equal sample sizes, i.e., $n_1 = n_2 = n$, and then choose n so that ($\hat{p}_1 - \hat{p}_2$) will differ from ($p_1 - p_2$) by no more than a bound B with a specified probability. We will illustrate the procedure with an example.

EXAMPLE 9.3

A production supervisor suspects a difference exists between the proportions of defective items produced by two different machines. Experience has shown that the proportion defective for the two machines is in the neighborhood of .03. If the supervisor wants to estimate the difference in the proportions using a 95% confidence interval of width .01, how many items must be randomly sampled from the production of each machine? (Assume that you want $n_1 = n_2 = n$.)

Solution

For the specified level of reliability, $z_{\alpha/2} = z_{.025} = 1.96$. Then, letting $p_1 = p_2 = .03$ and $n_1 = n_2 = n$, we find the required sample size per machine by solving the following equation for n:

$$z_{\alpha/2} \sqrt{\frac{p_1 q_1}{n_1} + \frac{p_2 q_2}{n_2}} = \frac{W}{2}$$

where W is the desired width of the confidence interval, i.e., $W = .01$. Substituting and solving for n, we obtain

$$1.96 \sqrt{\frac{(.03)(.97)}{n} + \frac{(.03)(.97)}{n}} = .005$$

$$1.96 \sqrt{\frac{2(.03)(.97)}{n}} = .005$$

$$n = 8,943.2$$

You can see that this may be a tedious sampling procedure. If the supervisor insists on estimating $(p_1 - p_2)$ correct to within .005 with probability equal to .95, approximately 9,000 items will have to be inspected for each machine.

. . . .

You can see from the calculations in Example 9.3 that $\sigma_{\hat{p}_1 - \hat{p}_2}$ (and hence the solution, $n_1 = n_2 = n$) depends on the actual (but unknown) values of p_1 and p_2.

In fact, the solution for $n_1 = n_2 = n$ is largest when $p_1 = p_2 = .5$. Therefore, if we have no prior information on the approximate values of p_1 and p_2, we use $p_1 = p_2 = .5$ in the formula for $\sigma_{\hat{p}_1 - \hat{p}_2}$. If p_1 and p_2 really are close to .5, then the values of n_1 and n_2 that you have calculated will be appropriate. If p_1 and p_2 differ substantially from .5, then your solutions for n_1 and n_2 will be larger than needed. Consequently, using $p_1 = p_2 = .5$ when solving for n_1 and n_2 is a conservative procedure because the sample sizes n_1 and n_2 will be at least as large as (and probably larger than) needed.

The procedure for determining sample sizes necessary for estimating $(p_1 - p_2)$ for the case $n_1 = n_2$ is given in the box.

Determination of Sample Size for Comparing Two Proportions

To estimate $(p_1 - p_2)$ to within a given bound B with probability $(1 - \alpha)$ or, equivalently, with a $100(1 - \alpha)\%$ confidence interval of width $W = 2B$, use the following formula to solve for equal sample sizes that will achieve the desired reliability:

$$n_1 = n_2 = \frac{(z_{\alpha/2})^2 (p_1 q_1 + p_2 q_2)}{B^2} = \frac{4(z_{\alpha/2})^2 (p_1 q_1 + p_2 q_2)}{W^2}$$

You will need to substitute estimates for the values of p_1 and p_2 before solving for the sample size. These estimates might be based on prior samples, obtained from educateed guesses, or, most conservatively, specified as $p_1 = p_2 = .5$.

Exercises 9.17–9.24

Learning the Mechanics

9.17 Assuming that $n_1 = n_2$, find the appropriate sample sizes needed to estimate $(p_1 - p_2)$ for each of the following situations:

a. $W = .2$ with 99% confidence. Assume that $p_1 \approx .3$ and $p_2 \approx .6$.

b. $B = .05$ with 90% confidence. Assume there is no prior information available to obtain approximate values of p_1 and p_2.

c. $B = .05$ with 90% confidence. Assume that $p_1 \approx .1$ and $p_2 \approx .2$.

9.18 A pollster wants to estimate the difference between the proportions of men and women who favor a particular national political candidate using a 90% confidence interval of width .04. Suppose the pollster has no prior information about the proportions. If equal numbers of men and women are to be polled, how large should the samples be?

9.19 You want to estimate the difference between two population proportions correct to within .04 with confidence coefficient equal to .90. You think both p_1 and p_2 are near .4, and you want to select samples of equal size from the two populations. Find the required sample sizes, n_1 and n_2.

9.20 Enough money has been budgeted to collect independent random samples of size $n_1 = n_2 = 100$ from populations 1 and 2 in order to estimate $(\mu_1 - \mu_2)$. Prior information indicates that $\sigma_1 = \sigma_2 = 10$. Have sufficient funds been allocated to construct a 90% confidence interval for $(\mu_1 - \mu_2)$ of width 4 or less? Justify your answer.

Applying the Concepts

9.21 Nationally televised home shopping was introduced in 1985. Overnight it became the hottest craze in television programming. By December 1986 there were 34 home shopping cable services (Covert, 1986), and now nearly every cable service carries at least one such channel. Who uses these home shopping services? Are the shoppers primarily men or women? Suppose you want to estimate the difference in the proportions of men and women who say they have used or expect to use televised home shopping using an 80% confidence interval of width .06 or less.

a. Approximately how many people should be included in your samples?

b. Suppose you want to obtain individual estimates for the two proportions of interest. Will the sample size found in part **a** be large enough to provide estimates of each proportion correct to within .02 with probability equal to .90? Justify your response.

9.22 Refer to Exercise 9.13 and the study of whether a person's ability to identify food by smell and taste decreases with increasing age. How large should the samples be to estimate the difference in the proportion of students and the proportion of older people who are able to identify blended apple to within .05 with probability .90?

9.23 Rat damage is a costly nuisance in the production of sugarcane. One aspect of the problem that has been investigated by the U.S. Department of Agriculture concerns the optimal place to locate rat poison. To be most effective, should the poison be in the middle of the field or on the outer perimeter? One way to answer this question is to determine where more damage occurs. If damage is measured by the proportion of cane stalks that have been damaged by rats, how many stalks from each section of the field should be sampled in order to estimate the true difference between the proportions of stalks damaged in the two sections to within .02 with probability .95?

9.24 A television manufacturer wants to compare the proportions of its sets that need repair within 1 year with the proportion of a competitor's sets that need repair within 1 year. If it is desired to estimate the difference in proportions to within .05 with 90% confidence, how many buyers of each brand must be sampled? Assume the proportion of sets that need repair will be about .2 for both brands.

9.3   Comparing Population Proportions for a Multinomial Experiment (Optional)

TABLE 9.1   Consumer Preference Survey

A	B	Store Brand
61	53	36

Consumer preference surveys can be valuable aids in making marketing decisions. Suppose a large supermarket chain conducts a consumer preference survey by recording the brand of bread purchased by customers in its stores. Assume the chain carries three brands of bread—two major brands (A and B) and its own store brand. The brand preferences of a random sample of 150 buyers are observed, and the resulting count data appear in Table 9.1. Do these data indicate that a preference exists for any of the brands?

To answer this question, we have to know the underlying probability distribution of these count data. This distribution, called the **multinomial probability distribution**, is an extension of the binomial distribution (Section 4.3). The properties of the multinomial distribution are shown in the box.

Properties of the Multinomial Probability Distribution

1. The experiment consists of n identical trials.
2. There are k possible outcomes to each trial.
3. The probabilities of the k outcomes, denoted by $p_1, p_2, \ldots, p_k$, remain the same from trial to trial, where $p_1 + p_2 + \cdots + p_k = 1$.
4. The trials are independent.
5. The random variables of interest are the counts $n_1, n_2, \ldots, n_k$ in each of the k cells.

You can see that the properties of the multinomial experiment closely resemble those of the binomial experiment and that, in fact, a binomial experiment is a multinomial experiment for the special case where $k = 2$.

In most practical applications involving a multinomial experiment, the true values of the k outcome probabilities, $p_1, p_2, \ldots, p_k$, will be unknown. The objective is therefore to make inferences about these probabilities.

Note that the consumer preference survey given in Table 9.1 satisfies the multinomial conditions. Suppose we want to test the null hypothesis that there is no preference for any of the three brands versus the alternative hypothesis that a preference exists for one or more of the brands. Then, letting

p_1 = Proportion of all customers who prefer brand A

p_2 = Proportion of all customers who prefer brand B

p_3 = Proportion of all customers who prefer the store brand

we want to test

H_0: $p_1 = p_2 = p_3 = \frac{1}{3}$ (No preference)

H_a: At least one of the proportions exceeds $\frac{1}{3}$ (A preference exists)

If the null hypothesis is true (i.e., if $p_1 = p_2 = p_3 = \frac{1}{3}$), then we would expect to see approximately $\frac{1}{3}$ of the customers in the sample purchase each brand. Or, more formally, the expected value (mean value) of the number of customers purchasing brand A is given by

$$E(n_1) = np_1 = n(\tfrac{1}{3}) = 150(\tfrac{1}{3}) = 50$$

Similarly, $E(n_2) = E(n_3) = 50$ if no preference exists.

The following test statistic measures the degree of disagreement between the data and the null hypothesis:

$$X^2 = \frac{[n_1 - E(n_1)]^2}{E(n_1)} + \frac{[n_2 - E(n_2)]^2}{E(n_2)} + \frac{[n_3 - E(n_3)]^2}{E(n_3)}$$
$$= \frac{(n_1 - 50)^2}{50} + \frac{(n_2 - 50)^2}{50} + \frac{(n_3 - 50)^2}{50}$$

Note that the farther the observed numbers n_1, n_2, and n_3 are from their expected value (50), the larger X^2 will become. That is, large values of X^2 cast doubt on the null hypothesis and suggest that it is false.

We have to know the distribution of X^2 in repeated sampling before we can decide whether the data indicate that a preference exists. If in fact H_0 is true, X^2 can be shown to have approximately a **chi-square distribution.** The shape of the chi-square distribution will depend on the degrees of freedom (df) associated with Table 9.1. For this application, the number of degrees of freedom will always be $(k - 1)$.[*]

Critical values of χ^2 are given in Table XIII of Appendix B, a portion of which is shown in Table 9.2. For the consumer preference survey in Table 9.1, with $\alpha = .05$ and $k - 1 = 3 - 1 = 2$ df, we will reject H_0 if

$$X^2 > \chi^2_{.05}$$

---

[*]Deriving the df involves the number of linear restrictions imposed on the count data, so we will simply give the df for each X^2. See the references at the end of the chapter for more detail.

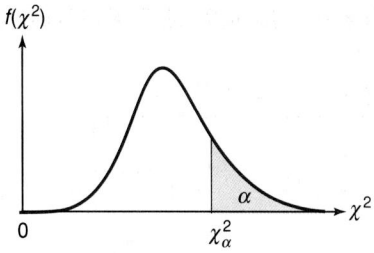

TABLE 9.2   Reproduction of Part of Table XIII in Appendix B

Degrees of Freedom	$\chi^2_{.100}$	$\chi^2_{.050}$	$\chi^2_{.025}$	$\chi^2_{.010}$	$\chi^2_{.005}$
1	2.70554	3.84146	5.02389	6.63490	7.87944
2	4.60517	5.99147	7.37776	9.21034	10.5966
3	6.25139	7.81473	9.34840	11.3449	12.8381
4	7.77944	9.48773	11.1433	13.2767	14.8602
5	9.23635	11.0705	12.8325	15.0863	16.7496
6	10.6446	12.5916	14.4494	16.8119	18.5476
7	12.0170	14.0671	16.0128	18.4753	20.2777
8	13.3616	15.5073	17.5346	20.0902	21.9550
9	14.6837	16.9190	19.0228	21.6660	23.5893
10	15.9871	18.3070	20.4831	23.2093	25.1882
11	17.2750	19.6751	21.9200	24.7250	26.7569

FIGURE 9.3 ▶
Rejection region for consumer preference survey

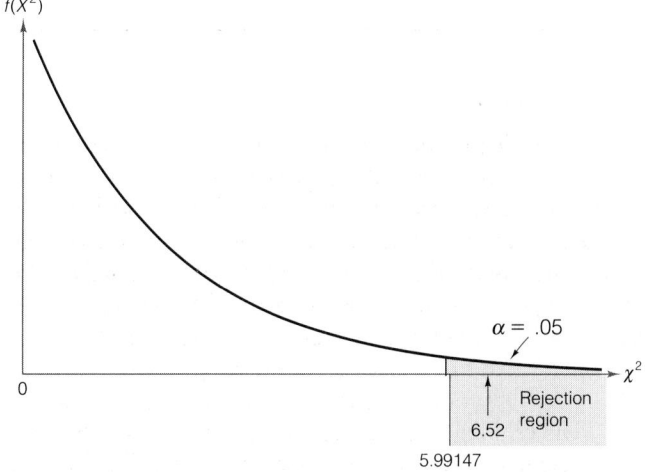

This value of χ^2 (shaded in Table 9.2) is 5.99147 (see Figure 9.3). The computed value of the test statistic is

$$X^2 = \frac{(n_1 - 50)^2}{50} + \frac{(n_2 - 50)^2}{50} + \frac{(n_3 - 50)^2}{50}$$

$$= \frac{(61 - 50)^2}{50} + \frac{(53 - 50)^2}{50} + \frac{(36 - 50)^2}{50} = 6.52$$

Since the computed $X^2 = 6.52$ exceeds the critical value of 5.99147, we conclude at $\alpha = .05$ that there is a customer preference for one or more of the brands of bread.

The general form for a test of hypothesis concerning multinomial probabilities is shown in the next box.

A Test of Hypothesis About Multinomial Probabilities

H_0: $p_1 = p_{1,0}, p_2 = p_{2,0}, \ldots, p_k = p_{k,0}$, where $p_{1,0}, p_{2,0}, \ldots, p_{k,0}$ represent the hypothesized values of the multinomial probabilities

H_a: At least one of the multinomial probabilities does not equal its hypothesized value

Test statistic: $X^2 = \sum_{i=1}^{k} \frac{[n_i - E(n_i)]^2}{E(n_i)}$

where $E(n_i) = np_{i,0}$, the expected number of outcomes of type i assuming H_0 is true. The total sample size is n.

Rejection region: $X^2 > \chi_\alpha^2$ where df $= k - 1$

Assumptions: The sample size n will be large enough so that, for every cell, the expected cell count, $E(n_i)$, will be equal to 5 or more.

EXAMPLE 9.4

TABLE 9.3   Distribution of Pay Increases

None	Standard	Merit
42	365	193

A large firm has established what it hopes is an objective system of deciding on annual pay increases for its employees. The system is based on a series of evaluation scores determined by the supervisors of each employee. Employees with scores above 80 receive a merit pay increase, those with scores between 50 and 80 receive the standard increase, and those below 50 receive no increase. The firm designed the plan with the objective that, on the average, 25% of its employees would receive merit increases, 65% would receive standard increases, and 10% would receive no increase.

After 1 year of operation using the new plan, the distribution of pay increases for the 600 company employees was as shown in Table 9.3. Test at the $\alpha = .01$ level to determine whether these data indicate that the distribution of pay increases differs significantly from the proportions established by the firm.

Solution   Define

p_1 = Proportion of employees who receive no pay increase

p_2 = Proportion of emloyees who receive a standard increase

p_3 = Proportion of employees who receive a merit increase

Then the null and alternative hypotheses representing the intent are

H_0: $p_1 = .10$, $p_2 = .65$, $p_3 = .25$

H_a: At least two of the proportions differ from the firm's proposed plan

Test statistic: $X^2 = \sum \dfrac{[n_i - E(n_i)]^2}{E(n_i)}$

where

$E(n_1) = np_{1,0} = 600(.10) = 60$

$E(n_2) = np_{2,0} = 600(.65) = 390$

$E(n_3) = np_{3,0} = 600(.25) = 150$

Rejection region: For $\alpha = .01$ and df $= k - 1 = 2$, reject H_0 if $X^2 > \chi^2_{.01}$, where (from Table XIII of Appendix B) $\chi^2_{.01} = 9.21034$.

We now calculate the test statistic:

$$X^2 = \frac{(42 - 60)^2}{60} + \frac{(365 - 390)^2}{390} + \frac{(193 - 150)^2}{150} = 19.33$$

Since this value exceeds the table value of χ^2 (9.21034), the data provide strong evidence ($\alpha = .01$) that the company's pay plan is not working as planned.

. . . .

By focusing on one particular outcome of a multinomial experiment, we can use the methods developed in Section 6.4 for a binomial proportion to establish a confidence interval for any one of the multinomial probabilities. * For example, if we want a 95% confidence interval for the proportion of the company's employees who will receive merit increases under the new system, we calculate

$$\hat{p}_3 \pm 1.96\sigma_{\hat{p}_3} \approx \hat{p}_3 \pm 1.96\sqrt{\frac{\hat{p}_3(1 - \hat{p}_3)}{n}} \quad \text{where } \hat{p}_3 = \frac{n_3}{n} = \frac{193}{600} = .32$$

$$= .32 \pm 1.96\sqrt{\frac{(.32)(1 - .32)}{600}} = .32 \pm .04$$

---

*Note that focusing on one outcome has the effect of combining the other $(k - 1)$ outcomes into a single group. Thus, we obtain, in effect, two outcomes—or a binomial experiment.

Thus, we estimate that between 28% and 36% of the firm's employees will qualify for merit increases under the new plan. It appears that the firm will have to raise the requirements for merit increases in order to achieve the stated goal of a 25% employee qualification rate.

CASE STUDY 9.2 / Investigating Response Bias in a Diary Survey

Marketing researchers sometimes collect data from consumers by asking them to keep diaries of their purchases or product usage. Such *diary methods* generally provide more accurate data than collection methods (such as the telephone interview) that require the consumer to recall from memory the details of purchases and activities. However, diary methods are not problem-free. Frequently, response rates by consumers to requests for diary data are lower than for other types of market research surveys such as mailed questionnaires. In addition, recording biases (such as not recording some events or recording inappropriate events) may be present in diary data.

John McKenzie (1983) studied the accuracy of telephone-call data collected by diary methods in Great Britain. This required comparing the demographic profile of a sample of 1,802 telephone users who responded to a request for diary data to the demographic profile of the population from which the sample of all those who were asked to keep diaries was selected. The population data were available from telephone company records for the study population of 29,507 households.

Table 9.4 shows the education profiles of the population and the sample. These data can be used to determine if the distribution of the age at which schooling ended for the sample differs significantly from the distribution for the population. If a significant difference exists, then it can be inferred that the sample is not representative of the population and that the survey results have been affected by **response bias**.

The sample data should lead to rejection of the following null hypothesis if the population and sample profiles differ:

TABLE 9.4   Terminal Education Age of Head of Household

	Population		Sample	
	Frequency	Relative Frequency	Frequency	Relative Frequency
Up to 15	13,137	$p_1 = .445$	791	.439
16–18	7,021	$p_2 = .238$	531	.295
19+	3,074	$p_3 = .104$	202	.112
Not Known	6,275	$p_4 = .213$	278	.154

H_0: $p_1 = .445$, $p_2 = .238$, $p_3 = .104$, $p_4 = .213$

H_a: At least one of the relative frequencies differs from its hypothesized value

The sample data yield

$$X^2 = \frac{(791 - 801.89)^2}{801.89} + \frac{(531 - 428.88)^2}{428.88}$$
$$+ \frac{(202 - 187.41)^2}{187.41} + \frac{(278 - 383.83)^2}{383.83}$$
$$= 54.78$$

Since $X^2 = 54.78 > \chi^2_{.005} = 12.8381$ (df = 3), the null hypothesis is rejected and the existence of response bias is confirmed. McKenzie found similar discrepancies between the population and sample with respect to the age, sex, and social class of the head of household.

When response biases such as these can be identified or are suspected, they can generally be overcome by increasing the response rates of the survey. For a discussion of ways to increase response rates, see Sudman and Ferber (1971, 1974).

Exercises 9.25 – 9.38

Learning the Mechanics

9.25 Use Table XIII of Appendix B to find each of the following χ^2 values.
a. $\chi^2_{.05}$ for df = 17
b. $\chi^2_{.990}$ for df = 100
c. $\chi^2_{.10}$ for df = 15
d. $\chi^2_{.005}$ for df = 3

9.26 Find the following probabilities.
a. $P(\chi^2 \leq .872085)$ for df = 6
b. $P(\chi^2 > 30.5779)$ for df = 15
c. $P(\chi^2 \geq 82.3581)$ for df = 100
d. $P(\chi^2 < 13.7867)$ for df = 30

9.27 Find the rejection region for a one-dimensional χ^2 test of a null hypothesis concerning $p_1, p_2, \ldots, p_k$ if:
a. $k = 4$ and $\alpha = .10$
b. $k = 6$ and $\alpha = .01$
c. $k = 8$ and $\alpha = .05$

9.28 What are the characteristics of a multinomial experiment? Compare the characteristics to those of a binomial experiment.

9.29 What conditions must n satisfy to make the χ^2 test valid?

9.30 A multinomial experiment with $k = 5$ cells and $n = 300$ produced the data shown in the table.

Cell	n_i
1	48
2	69
3	83
4	61
5	39

a. Do these data provide sufficient evidence to contradict the null hypothesis that $p_1 = .15$, $p_2 = .25$, $p_3 = .30$, $p_4 = .20$, and $p_5 = .10$? Test using $\alpha = .05$.
b. Find the approximate observed significance level for the test in part **a**.

9.31 A multinomial experiment with $k = 4$ cells and $n = 200$ produced the data shown in the table.

Cell	1	2	3	4
n_i	48	56	63	53

a. Do these data provide sufficient evidence to conclude that the multinomial probabilities differ? Test using $\alpha = .05$.
b. What are the Type I and Type II errors associated with the test of part **a**?

9.32 Refer to Exercise 9.31. Construct a 95% confidence interval for the multinomial probability associated with cell 3.

Applying the Concepts

9.33 A 1985 Gallup survey portrayed U.S. entrepreneurs as "the mavericks, dreamers, and loners whose rough edges and uncompromising need to do it their own way set them in sharp contrast to senior executives in major

American corporations" (Graham, 1985). One of the many questions put to a sample of $n = 100$ entrepreneurs about their job characteristics, work habits, social activities, etc. concerned the origin of the car they usually drive. The responses are given in the table.

United States	Europe	Japan
45	46	9

a. Do these data provide evidence of a difference in the preference of entrepreneurs for the cars of the United States, Europe, and Japan? Test using $\alpha = .05$.
b. Do these data provide evidence of a difference in the preference of entrepreneurs for domestic versus foreign cars? Test using $\alpha = .05$.
c. What assumptions must be made in order for your inferences of parts **a** and **b** to be valid?

9.34 Refer to Exercise 9.33. Use a 90% confidence interval to estimate the proportion of U.S. entrepreneurs who drive foreign cars.

9.35 Overweight trucks are responsible for much of the damage sustained by our local, state, and federal highway systems. Although illegal, overloading is common. Truckers may avoid weigh stations run by enforcement officers by taking back roads or by traveling when weigh stations are likely to be closed. A state highway planning agency monitored the movements of overweight trucks on an interstate highway using an unmanned, computerized scale that is built into the highway (Dahlin and Owen, 1984). Unknown to the truckers, the scale weighed their vehicles as they passed over it. Each day's proportion of one week's total truck traffic (5-axle tractor truck semitrailers) is shown in the table.

Monday	Tuesday	Wednesday	Thursday	Friday	Saturday	Sunday
.191	.198	.187	.180	.155	.043	.046

During the same week, the number of overweight trucks per day was as follows:

Monday	Tuesday	Wednesday	Thursday	Friday	Saturday	Sunday
90	82	72	70	51	18	31

a. The planning agency would like to know whether the number of overweight trucks per week is distributed over the 7 days of the week in direct proportion to the volume of truck traffic. Test using $\alpha = .05$.
b. Find the approximate p-value for the test of part **a**.

9.36 The manager of a firm's data processing division believes that the distribution of the number of errors per invoice has changed dramatically since the physical layout of the fields (areas of information) on the invoices was changed 6 months ago. The table describes the distribution of the number of errors per invoice using the previous format.

Errors per Invoice	0	1	2	3	4	4+
Proportion of Finished Invoices	.90	.04	.03	.02	.005	.005

A random sample of 300 printed invoices was selected from those that printed last week. Each invoice was examined for errors. The following data resulted:

Errors per Invoice	0	1	2	3	4	4+
Number of Invoices	150	120	15	7	4	4

a. Do the data provide sufficient evidence to indicate that the proportions of printed invoices in the six error categories differ from the proportions using the previous format?

b. Find the approximate observed significance level for the test in part **a**.

9.37 A company that manufactures dice for gambling casinos in Nevada and New Jersey regularly inspects its product to be sure that only "fair" (balanced) dice are supplied to the casinos. One die was randomly chosen from a production lot and rolled 120 times. Counts of the numbers showing face up are recorded in the table. Do the data provide sufficient evidence to indicate that the die is unbalanced? Test using $\alpha = .10$.

Numbers Face Up	1	2	3	4	5	6
Frequency	28	27	20	18	15	12

9.38 The threat of earthquakes is a part of life in California, where scientists have warned about "the big one" for decades. A recent article (Palm and Hodgson, 1992) investigated what influences homeowners in purchasing earthquake insurance. One factor investigated was the proximity to a major fault. The researchers hypothesized that the nearer a county is to a major fault, the more likely residents are to own earthquake insurance. Suppose that a random sample of 700 earthquake-insured residents from four California counties is selected, and the number in each county is counted and recorded in the table:

	Contra Costa	Santa Clara	Los Angeles	San Bernardino
Number insured:	103	213	241	143

a. What are the appropriate null and alternative hypotheses to test whether the proportions of all earthquake-insured residents in the four counties differ?

b. Do the data provide sufficient evidence that the proportions of all earthquake-insured residents differ among the four counties? Test using $\alpha = .05$.

c. Los Angeles County is closest to a major earthquake fault. Construct a 95% confidence interval for the proportion of all earthquake-insured residents in the four counties that reside in Los Angeles County.

d. Does the confidence interval you formed in part **c** support the conclusion of the test conducted in part **b**? Explain.

9.4 Contingency Table Analysis (Optional)

Rising fuel prices have made consumers more aware of what size cars they purchase. An automobile manufacturer who is interested in determining the relationship between the size and make of newly purchased automobiles randomly samples 1,000 recent buyers of American-made cars. The manufacturer classifies each purchase with respect to the size and manufacturer of the purchased automobile. The data are shown in Table 9.5, which is an example of a **contingency table**. Contingency tables consist of **multinomial count data classified on two scales**, or **dimensions**.

Let the probabilities for the multinomial experiment in Table 9.5 be those shown in Table 9.6. Thus, p_{11} is the probability that a new-car buyer purchases a small car of manufacturer A. Note the probability totals, called **marginal probabilities**, for each row and column. The marginal probability p_1 is the probability that a small car is

TABLE 9.5 Contingency Table for Automobile Size Example

		Manufacturer				Totals
		A	B	C	D	
Size	Small	157	65	181	10	413
	Intermediate	126	82	142	46	396
	Large	58	45	60	28	191
	Totals	341	192	383	84	1,000

TABLE 9.6 Probabilities for Contingency Table 9.5

		Manufacturer				Totals
		A	B	C	D	
Size	Small	p_{11}	p_{12}	p_{13}	p_{14}	p_1
	Intermediate	p_{21}	p_{22}	p_{23}	p_{24}	p_2
	Large	p_{31}	p_{32}	p_{33}	p_{34}	p_3
	Totals	p_A	p_B	p_C	p_D	1

purchased, and the marginal probability p_A is the probability that a car of manufacturer A is purchased.

Suppose we want to know whether the two classifications, manufacturer and size, are dependent. That is, if we know which size car a buyer will choose, does that information give us a clue about which manufacturer the buyer will choose? In a probabilistic sense we know (Chapter 3) that independence of events A and B implies that $P(A \cap B) = P(A)P(B)$. Similarly, in the contingency table analysis, if the classifications are independent, the probability that an item is classified in any particular cell of the table is the product of the corresponding marginal probabilities. Thus, under the hypothesis of independence, in Table 9.6 we must have

$$p_{11} = p_1 p_A \qquad p_{12} = p_1 p_B$$

and so forth.

To test the hypothesis of independence, we use the same reasoning employed in the one-dimensional tests of optional Section 9.3. First, we calculate the expected (or mean) count in each cell assuming the null hypothesis of independence is true. We do this by noting that the expected count in the upper left-hand corner of the table, for example, is just the total number of multinomial trials, n, times the probability, p_{11}. Then $E(n_{11}) = np_{11}$ and, if the classifications are independent, $E(n_{11}) = np_1 p_A$.

We can estimate p_1 and p_A by the sample proportions $\hat{p}_1 = n_1/n$ and $\hat{p}_A = n_A/n$. Thus, the estimate of the expected value $E(n_{11})$ is

$$\hat{E}(n_{11}) = n\left(\frac{n_1}{n}\right)\left(\frac{n_A}{n}\right) = \frac{n_1 n_A}{n}$$

Similarly,

$$\hat{E}(n_{12}) = \frac{n_1 n_B}{n}$$

$$\vdots$$

$$\hat{E}(n_{34}) = \frac{n_3 n_D}{n}$$

Using the data in Table 9.5, we find

$$\hat{E}(n_{11}) = \frac{n_1 n_A}{n} = \frac{(413)(341)}{1,000} = 140.833$$

$$\hat{E}(n_{12}) = \frac{n_1 n_B}{n} = \frac{(413)(192)}{1,000} = 79.296$$

$$\vdots$$

$$\hat{E}(n_{34}) = \frac{n_3 n_D}{n} = \frac{(191)(84)}{1,000} = 16.044$$

The observed data and the estimated expected values are shown in Table 9.7.

TABLE 9.7   Observed and Estimated Expected (in Parentheses) Counts

		Manufacturer				Totals
		A	B	C	D	
	Small	157 (140.833)	65 (79.296)	181 (158.179)	10 (34.692)	413
Size	Intermediate	126 (135.036)	82 (76.032)	142 (151.668)	46 (33.264)	396
	Large	58 (65.131)	45 (36.672)	60 (73.153)	28 (16.044)	191
	Totals	341	192	383	84	1,000

We now use the X^2 statistic to compare the observed and expected (estimated) counts in each cell of the contingency table:

$$X^2 = \frac{[n_{11} - \hat{E}(n_{11})]^2}{\hat{E}(n_{11})} + \frac{[n_{12} - \hat{E}(n_{12})]^2}{\hat{E}(n_{12})} + \cdots + \frac{[n_{34} - \hat{E}(n_{34})]^2}{\hat{E}(n_{34})}$$

$$= \sum_{i=1}^{3} \sum_{j=1}^{4} \frac{[n_{ij} - \hat{E}(n_{ij})]^2}{\hat{E}(n_{ij})}$$

Substituting the data of Table 9.7 into this expression yields

$$X^2 = \frac{(157 - 140.833)^2}{140.833} + \frac{(65 - 79.296)^2}{79.296} + \cdots + \frac{(28 - 16.044)^2}{16.044} = 45.81$$

Large values of X^2 imply that the observed and expected counts do not closely agree and therefore that the hypothesis of independence is false. To determine how large X^2 must be before it is too large to be attributed to chance, we make use of the fact that the sampling distribution of X^2 is approximately a χ^2 probability distribution when the classifications are independent. The number of degrees of freedom for the approximating χ^2 distribution will be $(r - 1)(c - 1)$, where r is the number of rows and c is the number of columns in the table.

For the size and manufacturer of automobiles example, the number of degrees of freedom for χ^2 is $(r - 1)(c - 1) = (3 - 1)(4 - 1) = 6$. Then, for $\alpha = .05$, we reject the hypothesis of independence if

$$X^2 > \chi^2_{.05} = 12.5916$$

Since the computed $X^2 = 45.81$ exceeds the value 12.5916, we conclude that the size and manufacturer of a car selected by a purchaser are dependent events.

What is the observed significance level of X^2 for this test? While we cannot use Table XIII to find the exact significance level, we can use it to place bounds on the p-value. Note that the value of X^2 exceeds even the χ^2 value corresponding to a significance level of .005 with 6 degrees of freedom, 18.5476. Thus, we know that the observed significance level corresponding to the test statistic, 45.81, is smaller than .005, i.e., p-value $< .005$. The evidence in favor of the alternative hypothesis that the manufacturer and size of car are dependent is therefore quite strong.

The pattern of dependence can be seen more clearly by expressing the data as percentages. We first select one of the two classifications to be used as the base variable. In the automobile size preference example, suppose we select manufacturer as the classificatory variable to be the base. Next, we represent the responses for each level of the second categorical variable (car size) as a percentage of the subtotal for the base variable. For example, from Table 9.7 we convert the response for small car sales for manufacturer A (157) to a percentage of the total sales for manufacturer A (341).

That is,

$$\left(\frac{157}{341}\right)100\% = 46\%$$

The conversion of all Table 9.7 entries is accomplished in the same way, and the values are shown in Table 9.8. The value shown at the right of each row is the row's total expressed as a percentage of the total number of responses in the entire table. Thus, the small car percentage is $^{413}\!/_{1,000}(100)\% = 41\%$ (rounded to the nearest percent).

TABLE 9.8   Percentages of Car Sizes by Manufacturer

		Manufacturer				All
		A	B	C	D	
	Small	46	34	47	12	41
Size	Intermediate	37	43	37	55	40
	Large	17	23	16	33	19
	Totals	100	100	100	100	100

If the size and manufacturer variables are independent, then the percentages in the cells of the table are expected to be approximately equal to the row percentages. Thus, we would expect the small car percentages for each of the four manufacturers to be approximately 41% if size and manufacturer were independent. The extent to which each manufacturer's percentage departs from this value determines the dependence of the two classifications, with greater variability of the row percentages meaning a greater degree of dependence. A plot of the percentages helps summarize the observed pattern. In Figure 9.4 we show the manufacturer (the base variable) on the horizontal axis and the size percentages on the vertical axis. The "expected" percentages under the assumption of independence are shown as horizontal lines, and each observed value is represented by a symbol indicating the size category.

Figure 9.4 clearly indicates why the test resulted in the conclusion that the two classifications in the contingency table are dependent. Note that the sales of manufacturers A, B, and C fall relatively close to the expected percentages under the assumption of independence. However, the sales of manufacturer D deviate significantly from the expected values, with much higher percentages for large and intermediate cars and a much smaller percentage for small cars than expected under independence. Also, manufacturer B deviates slightly from the expected pattern, with a greater percentage of intermediate than small car sales. Statistical measures of the

FIGURE 9.4 ▶

Size as a percentage of manufacturer subtotals

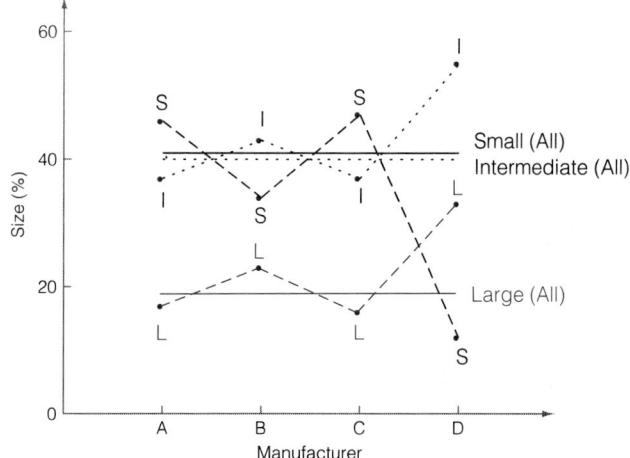

degree of dependence and procedures for making comparisons of pairs of levels for classifications are available. They are beyond the scope of this text but can be found in the references at the end of the chapter. We do, however, utilize descriptive summaries such as Figure 9.4 to examine the degree of dependence exhibited by the sample data.

The general form of a contingency table is shown in Table 9.9. Note that the observed count in the cell located in the ith row and the jth column is denoted by n_{ij}, the ith row total is r_i, the jth column total is c_j, and the total sample size is n. Using

TABLE 9.9   General $r \times c$ Contingency Table

		Column				Row Totals
		1	2	$\cdots$	c	
	1	n_{11}	n_{12}	$\cdots$	n_{1c}	r_1
	2	n_{21}	n_{22}	$\cdots$	n_{2c}	r_2
Row	$\vdots$	$\vdots$	$\vdots$		$\vdots$	$\vdots$
	r	n_{r1}	n_{r2}	$\cdots$	n_{rc}	r_r
Column Totals		c_1	c_2	$\cdots$	c_c	n

this notation, we give the general form of the contingency table test for independent classifications in the box.

General Form of a Contingency Table Analysis: A Test for Independence

H_0: The two classifications are independent

H_a: The two classifications are dependent

Test statistic: $X^2 = \sum\limits_{i=1}^{r} \sum\limits_{j=1}^{c} \dfrac{[n_{ij} - \hat{E}(n_{ij})]^2}{\hat{E}(n_{ij})}$

where $\hat{E}(n_{ij}) = \dfrac{r_i c_j}{n}$

Rejection region: $X^2 > \chi_\alpha^2$, where χ_α^2 is based on $(r - 1)(c - 1)$ df

Assumption: The sample size, n, is large enough so that, for every cell, the expected cell count, $E(n_{ij})$, is equal to 5 or more.

EXAMPLE 9.5

A large brokerage firm wants to determine whether the service it provides to affluent customers differs from the service it provides to lower-income customers. A sample of 500 customers is selected, and each customer is asked to rate his or her broker. The results are shown in Table 9.10.

TABLE 9.10   Observed and Estimated Expected (in Parentheses) Counts for Example 9.5

		Customer's Income			Totals
		Under $20,000	$20,000–$50,000	Over $50,000	
Broker Rating	Outstanding	48 (53.856)	64 (66.402)	41 (32.742)	153
	Average	98 (94.336)	120 (116.312)	50 (57.352)	268
	Poor	30 (27.808)	33 (34.286)	16 (16.906)	79
Totals		176	217	107	500

a. Test to determine whether there is evidence that broker rating and customer income are independent. Use $\alpha = .10$.

b. Plot the data and describe the patterns revealed. Is the result of the test supported by the plot?

Solution

a. The first step is to calculate estimated expected cell frequencies under the assumption that the classifications are independent. Thus,

$$\hat{E}(n_{11}) = \frac{r_1 c_1}{n} = \frac{(153)(176)}{500} = 53.856$$

$$\hat{E}(n_{12}) = \frac{r_1 c_2}{n} = \frac{(153)(217)}{500} = 66.402$$

and so forth. All the estimated expected counts are shown in Table 9.10. We are now ready to conduct the test for independence:

H_0: The rating a customer gives his or her broker is independent of the customer's income

H_a: Broker rating and customer income are dependent

Test statistic: $\quad X^2 = \sum\limits_{i=1}^{3} \sum\limits_{j=1}^{3} \dfrac{[n_{ij} - \hat{E}(n_{ij})]^2}{\hat{E}(n_{ij})}$

Rejection region: For $\alpha = .10$ and $(r - 1)(c - 1) = (2)(2) = 4$ df, reject H_0 if $X^2 > \chi^2_{.10}$, where $\chi^2_{.10} = 7.77944$.

The calculated value of X^2 is

$$X^2 = \frac{(48 - 53.856)^2}{53.856} + \frac{(64 - 66.402)^2}{66.402} + \cdots + \frac{(16 - 16.906)^2}{16.906}$$

$$= 4.28$$

Since $X^2 = 4.28$ does not exceed the critical value, 7.77944, there is insufficient evidence at $\alpha = .10$ to conclude that broker rating and customer income are dependent. This survey does not support the firm's alternative hypothesis that affluent customers get broker service different from lower-income customers.

b. The broker rating frequencies are expressed as percentages of income category frequencies in Table 9.11. The expected percentages under the assumption of independence are shown at the right of each row. The plot of the percentage data

TABLE 9.11   Broker Ratings as Percentages of Income Class

		Customer's Income			All
		Under $20,000	$20,000–$50,000	Over $50,000	
	Outstanding	27	29	38	31
Broker Rating	Average	56	55	47	54
	Poor	17	15	15	16
Totals		100	99[a]	100	101[a]

[a]Percentages do not add to 100 because of rounding.

is shown in Figure 9.5, where horizontal lines represent the expected percentages assuming independence. Note that the response percentages deviate only slightly from those expected under the assumption of independence, supporting the result of the test in part **a**. That is, neither the descriptive plot nor the statistical test provides evidence that the rating given the broker services depends on (varies with) the customer's income.

FIGURE 9.5 ▶

Plot of broker rating – customer income contingency table

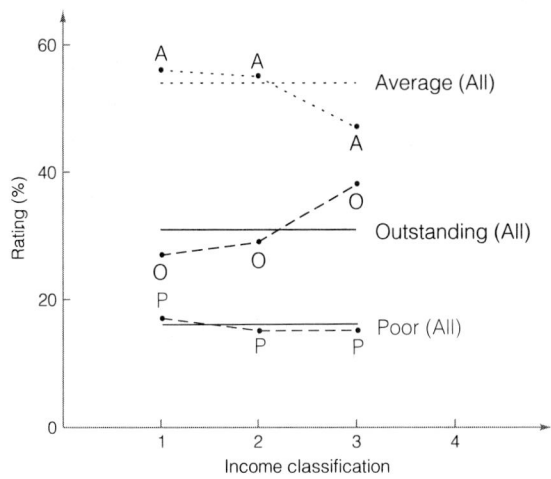

CASE STUDY 9.3 / Deceived Survey Respondents: Once Bitten, Twice Shy

An article by Sheets et al. (1974) explores a situation sometimes encountered by marketing research personnel:

For some time, people engaged in marketing and other field-based research have had to contend with the consequences of a fairly widely used ploy in the direct selling field: gaining a potential customer's attention and interest by requesting cooperation in some sort of false survey. Despite the efforts of the American Association for Public Opinion Research, the American Marketing Association, and other groups, and regardless of Federal Trade Commission orders, this gambit is still in use, although perhaps somewhat modified.

The authors hypothesized that a previous exposure to a false survey increases the probability that a person will refuse to respond to a legitimate survey. They conducted an experiment in which 104 individuals were asked to cooperate in a marketing research study. The 54 people who agreed to participate were then given a low-key sales presentation for a fictitious encyclopedia. Two to 4 days later, 49 of the original 54 participants (five were not available) and 70 completely new individuals (the control group) were interviewed. Each group was asked the same opening question. The results of this survey are presented in Table 9.12.

TABLE 9.12   Experimental and Control Group Willingness to Participate in True Market Research

	Experimental	Control	Totals
Consented	12	36	48
Refused	37	34	71
Totals	49	70	119

A χ^2 test was used to analyze these count data. The χ^2 test statistic is 8.691, significant at $\alpha = .005$. This indicates dependence of the refusal rate on previous exposure to false surveys. The interpretation given to these data by Sheets et al. (1974) is:

The findings indicate support for the hypothesis: false market surveys have a deleterious effect upon respondent willingness to cooperate in subsequent market research studies. By inference, households that have been previously exposed to false research are half again as likely to refuse to cooperate in legitimate field research as those who have not. The implication for field researchers is either to stay away from areas that have had recent, heavy, direct, sales efforts or to plan for higher refusal rates in such areas.

Exercises 9.39–9.52

Learning the Mechanics

9.39   Find the rejection region for a test of independence of two classifications where the contingency table contains r rows and c columns and
a. $r = 5, \quad c = 4, \quad \alpha = .05$ **b.** $r = 4, \quad c = 6, \quad \alpha = .10$ **c.** $r = 3, \quad c = 3, \quad \alpha = .01$

9.40   Consider the accompanying 2×3 (i.e., $r = 2$ and $c = 3$) contingency table:

		Column 1	Column 2	Column 3
Row	1	12	32	45
	2	16	29	25

a. Specify the null and alternative hypotheses that should be used in testing the independence of the row and column classifications.
b. Specify the test statistic and the rejection region that should be used in conducting the hypothesis test of part **a**. Use $\alpha = .01$.
c. Assuming the row classification and the column classification are independent, find estimates for the expected cell counts.
d. Conduct the hypothesis test of part **a**. Interpret your result.

9.41 Refer to Exercise 9.40.

    a. Convert the frequency responses to percentages by calculating the percentage of each column total falling in each row. Also convert the row totals to percentages of the total number of responses. Display the percentages in a table.

    b. Create a graph with percentage on the vertical axis and the column number on the horizontal axis. Show the row total percentages as horizontal lines on the plot, and plot the cell percentages from part **a** using the row number as a plotting symbol.

    c. What pattern do you expect to see if the rows and columns are independent? Does the plot support the results of the test of independence in Exercise 9.40?

9.42 Test the null hypothesis of independence of the two classifications, A and B, of the 3 × 3 contingency table shown. Test using $\alpha = .05$.

		B		
		B_1	B_2	B_3
	A_1	39	70	42
A	A_2	67	51	70
	A_3	30	38	26

9.43 Refer to Exercise 9.42. Convert the responses to percentages by calculating the percentage of each B class total falling into each A classification. Also, calculate the percentage of the total number of responses that constitute each of the A classification totals. Create a graph with percentage on the vertical axis and the B classification on the horizontal axis. Show the A classification total percentages as horizontal lines on the graph, and plot the individual cell percentages using the A class number as a plotting symbol. Does the graph support the result of the test of hypothesis in Exercise 9.42? Explain.

9.44 Test the null hypothesis of independence of the two classifications, A and B, of the 3 × 4 contingency table shown below. Test using $\alpha = .05$.

		B			
		B_1	B_2	B_3	B_4
	A_1	22	38	29	47
A	A_2	42	24	68	53
	A_3	29	85	105	68

9.45 A chi-square test was applied to each of the following contingency tables and the null hypothesis of independence was rejected. Construct a graph for each table that enables you to interpret the pattern of dependence in each case.

a.

A		B_1	B_2
	A_1	50	10
	A_2	10	40

b.

C		D_1	D_2
	C_1	15	70
	C_2	80	15

c.

E		F_1	F_2	F_3
	E_1	10	30	15
	E_2	30	10	15

9.46 In a contingency table test for independence, explain why the null hypothesis is independence and the alternative hypothesis is dependence (instead of vice versa).

Applying the Concepts

9.47 Are all employees equally likely to have accidents? Are certain employee groups—say, younger employees—more prone to particular kinds of accidents? The effective implementation of hiring policies, training programs, and safety programs requires such knowledge. A study was recently conducted to address these questions for a particular manufacturing company. A portion of the research results is summarized in the accompanying contingency table.

		Kind of Accident		
		Sprain	Burn	Cut
Age	Under 25	9	17	5
	25 and Over	61	13	12

Source: Parry, A. E. "Changing assumptions about loss frequency." *Professional Safety*, Oct. 1985, pp. 39–43.

a. From the contingency table, the researcher concluded that there is a relationship between an employee's age and the kind of accident that the employee may have. Do you agree? Test using $\alpha = .05$.

b. According to the frequencies of the contingency table, which is the most frequent type of accident? Are younger or older employees more likely to have sprains? Burns? Justify your answers.

c. What assumptions must hold in order for your test of part **a** to be valid?

d. Plot the percentage of employees under 25 who are injured based on the total injuries for each kind of accident. Compare this to the percentage of the total number of employees under 25 who are injured based on the total of all kinds of accidents. What does the plot indicate about the pattern of dependence in the data?

9.48 Over the years, pollsters have found that the public's confidence in big business is closely tied to the economic climate. When businesses are growing and employment is increasing, public confidence is high. When the opposite occurs, public confidence is low. Harvey Kahalas (1981) hypothesized that there is a relationship between the level of confidence in business and job satisfaction, and that this is true for both union and nonunion workers. He analyzed sample data collected by the National Opinion Research Center and shown in the tables at the top of page 480.

		Job Satisfaction			
		Very Satisfied	Moderately Satisfied	A Little Dissatisfied	Very Dissatisfied
Union Member Confidence in Major Corporations	A Great Deal	26	15	2	1
	Only Some	95	73	16	5
	Hardly Any	34	28	10	9

		Job Satisfaction			
		Very Satisfied	Moderately Satisfied	A Little Dissatisfied	Very Dissatisfied
Nonunion Confidence in Major Corporations	A Great Deal	111	52	12	4
	Only Some	246	142	37	18
	Hardly Any	73	51	19	9

a. Kahalas concluded that his hypothesis was not supported by the data. Do you agree? Conduct the appropriate tests using $\alpha = .05$. Be sure to specify your null and alternative hypotheses.

b. Find and interpret the approximate p-values of the tests you conducted in part **a**.

9.49 A study was conducted to determine the effects of television viewing on the purchase of products advertised on television. A sample of 2,452 women from the Davenport, Iowa, metropolitan area was interviewed, first in February and then again in May. Each time, the women were asked whether they watch a specific program and whether they purchase the product advertised during the program. Their responses are categorized in the table.

		Buying, Feb./May				Totals
		Yes/Yes	Yes/No	No/Yes	No/No	
	Yes/Yes	460	173	191	351	1,175
Viewing Feb./May	Yes/No	76	59	44	113	292
	No/Yes	86	27	53	80	246
	No/No	175	104	113	347	739
Totals		797	363	401	891	2,452

Source: *Journal of Marketing Research*, Feb. 1966, pp. 13–24.

a. If a χ^2 test of independence were conducted for the table, what would be the null and alternative hypotheses?

b. Conduct the test referred to in part **a**. Test using $\alpha = .05$.

c. What assumptions must you make so that the χ^2 test in part **b** will be valid?

9.50 In recent years, corporate boards of directors have been pressed to improve their monitoring of corporate economic performance and to become more careful overseers of the activities of management. In addition, boards are being asked to guide the long-term responsiveness of their respective organizations to the economic and social climate. These pressures have forced many boards of directors to better articulate the mission and strategies of their firms. To study the extent and nature of strategic planning being undertaken by boards of directors, Ahmed Tashakori and William Boulton (1983) questioned a sample of 119 chief executive officers of major U.S. corporations. One objective was to determine if a relationship exists between the composition of a board—i.e., a majority of outside directors versus a majority of in-house directors—and its level of participation in the strategic planning process. To this end, the questionnaire data were used to classify the responding corporations according to the level of their board's participation in the strategic planning process:

Level 1: Board participates in formulation or implementation or evaluation of strategy

Level 2: Board participates in formulation and implementation, formulation and evaluation, or implementation and evaluation of strategy

Level 3: Board participates in formulation, implementation, and evaluation of strategy

The results obtained are shown in the left-hand table. Of these 119 firms, 100 had boards where outside directors constituted a majority. Their levels of participation in strategic planning are shown at the right.

All Firms				*Outside Directed*			
Level	1	2	3	*Level*	1	2	3
Number of Firms	22	37	60	*Number of Firms*	20	27	53

a. Tashakori and Boulton concluded that a relationship exists between a board's level of participation in the strategic planning process and the composition of the board. Do you agree? Construct the appropriate contingency table, and test using $\alpha = .10$.

b. In the context of the problem, specify the Type I and Type II errors associated with the test of part **a**.

c. Find the approximate p-value for the test in part **a**. Based on the p-value, would the null hypothesis have been rejected at $\alpha = .05$? Explain.

d. Construct a graph that helps to interpret the result of the test in part **a**.

9.51 An insurance company that sells hospitalization policies wants to know whether there is a relationship between the amount of hospitalization coverage a person has and the length of stay in the hospital. Records are selected at random at a large hospital by hospital personnel, and the information on length of stay and hospitalization coverage is given to the insurance company. The results are summarized in the table. Can you conclude that there is a relationship between length of stay and hospitalization coverage? Use $\alpha = .01$.

		Length of Stay (days)			
		5 or Under	6–10	11–15	Over 15
	Under 25%	26	30	6	5
Coverage of Costs	25–50%	21	30	11	7
	51–75%	25	25	45	9
	Over 75%	11	32	17	11

9.52 One criterion used to evaluate employees in the assembly section of a large factory is the number of defective pieces per 1,000 parts produced. The quality control department wants to find out whether there is a relationship between years of experience and defect rate. Since the job is repetitious, after the initial training period any improvement due to a learning effect might be offset by a loss of motivation. A defect rate is calculated for each worker in a yearly evaluation. The results for 100 workers are given in the table.

		Years Since Training Period		
		<1	1–4	5–9
	High	6	9	9
Defect Rate	Average	9	19	23
	Low	7	8	10

a. Is there evidence of a relationship between defect rate and years of experience? Use $\alpha = .05$.

b. Find the approximate observed significance level for the test in part **a**.

Summary

This chapter showed you how to compare two population proportions using methodology that is very similar to the methodology used to compare two population means (Chapter 8). When the samples have been randomly and independently selected from two binomial populations and when the sample sizes are large, the difference $(\hat{p}_1 - \hat{p}_2)$ between the sample proportions will be approximately normally distributed (the Central Limit Theorem, Section 5.3). This enables us to form a large-sample standard normal z statistic similar to the one used to compare two population means. This statistic is then used as a test statistic for testing hypotheses about the difference between two population proportions and to construct a confidence interval for $(p_1 - p_2)$. The width of this confidence interval can be controlled by adjusting the sample sizes n_1 and n_2.

Optional Section 9.3 discussed how to compare two population proportions from a **multinomial experiment** using a **chi-square test**. This methodology was applied in optional Section 9.4 to test for dependence between two methods of classification in a **contingency table**.

Supplementary Exercises 9.53–9.72

Note: *Exercises marked with an asterisk* (*) *are from the optional sections.*

9.53 The threat of earthquakes is a part of life for homeowners in California. Scientists have been warning about the "big one" for decades. A recent article considered some factors involved when California homeowners purchase earthquake insurance, including the proximity to a major earthquake fault. Surveys were mailed to residents in four California counties. The data collected are shown in the table.

	Contra Costa	Santa Clara	Los Angeles	San Bernardino
Sample Size	521	556	337	372
Number with Earthquake Insurance	117	222	133	109

Source: Palm, R., and Hodgson, M. "Earthquake insurance: Mandated disclosure and homeowner response in California." *Annals of the Association of American Geographers*, June 1992, Vol. 82, No. 2, pp. 207–221.

a. Los Angeles County is the closest of the four to a major earthquake fault. Calculate 95% confidence intervals for the difference in the proportion of earthquake-insured residents in Los Angeles County and each of the other counties.
b. Do these results support the contention that closer proximities to major earthquake faults result in higher proportions of earthquake-insured residents?

9.54 Refer to Exercise 9.53. How large must the samples from Los Angeles and San Bernardino counties be to estimate the difference between earthquake-insured proportions to within .03 with 95% confidence?

9.55 The relationships among physical fitness, stress, and worker productivity have been the subject of much research during the past decade. One sports psychology researcher focused on the relationship between level of fitness and stress among employees of companies offering health and fitness programs. Random samples of employees were selected from each of three fitness-level categories, and each person was evaluated for signs of stress. The resulting data are shown.

Fitness Level	Sample Size	Proportion with Signs of Stress
Poor	242	.155
Average	212	.133
Good	95	.108

Source: Tucker, L. A. "Physical fitness and psychological distress." *International Journal of Sports Psychology*, July–Sept. 1990, Vol. 21, pp. 185–201.

a. What are the appropriate null and alternative hypotheses to test whether a greater proportion of employees in the poor fitness category show signs of stress than those in the average fitness category? Define any symbols you use.
b. Conduct the test constructed in part **a** using $\alpha = .10$. Interpret the result.
c. How would your null and alternative hypotheses change if you wanted to compare the proportions showing signs of stress in the poor and good fitness categories?
d. To conduct the test in part **c**, the data were analyzed by a statistical software package with the results shown. Based on these results, would you agree that fitness level has no bearing on whether an individual shows signs of stress? Explain.

```
Z = 1.11        P-VALUE = .1335
```

9.56 Refer to Exercise 9.55. Even though the sample proportions differed by nearly .05 (that is, almost 5% more of those in poor condition exhibited signs of stress than those in good condition), the p-value was not small enough to reject the null hypothesis that the corresponding population proportions are equal.

    a. How large would the samples have to be to estimate the difference in the proportions showing signs of stress to within .04 with 95% confidence? Assume equal sample sizes for the two groups, and remember that the first sample selected resulted in proportions of .155 and .108 for the poor and good fitness levels, respectively.

    b. Suppose samples of the size you calculated in part **a** were selected from each group, and the sample proportions again turned out to be .155 and .108. Test the null hypothesis $H_0: (p_1 - p_2) = 0$ against the alternative $H_a: (p_1 - p_2) > 0$, where p_1 is the proportion of all employees in the poor fitness category who show signs of stress and p_2 is the proportion of all employees having good fitness who show signs of stress. Calculate and interpret the observed significance level.

*9.57 In Case Study 9.1, we described part of a statistical analysis (Kaufman and Wolf, 1982) examining the preferences and anxieties of men and women with respect to attending job interviews in hotel rooms. The table gives additional data from this study. A random sample of 302 students (95 men and 207 women) was asked whether they would be uncomfortable about interviewing in a hotel room. The responses are shown in the table. Do these data provide sufficient evidence to conclude that anxiety over hotel room interviewing is related to the interviewee's sex? Test using $\alpha = .05$.

	Yes	No
Men	63.16%	36.84%
Women	77.29%	22.71%

9.58 A procedure developed by Tele-Research, Inc., evaluates the effectiveness of newly developed television commercials prior to their release. A study using this procedure (Jenssen, 1966) randomly selected 392 shoppers as they entered a large Los Angeles supermarket and asked their preferences for several product brands. One was brand XYZ, whose new television commercial was the object of the study. Ostensibly in exchange for their time, the shoppers were given a packet of ten cents-off coupons for various products sold in the supermarket, including XYZ. The coupons could be used only in that store and only on that day. A second sample of 387 shoppers was given the same interview, but was also asked to watch four television commercials in a trailer parked outside the supermarket. One commercial was the newly developed ad for XYZ. Following the viewing, the shoppers were asked for their reactions to the commercials, then were given the same packet of coupons. Of the 392 shoppers not exposed to the television commercials, 57 redeemed the coupon for XYZ. Of the 387 shoppers who saw XYZ's commercial, 84 redeemed the XYZ coupon.

    a. Do the sample data provide sufficient evidence to conclude that the new XYZ commercial motivates shoppers to purchase the XYZ brand? Use $\alpha = .05$.

    b. Find and interpret the observed significance level for the test.

*9.59 Many investors believe that the stock market's directional change in January signals the market's direction for the remainder of the year. This so-called January indicator is frequently cited in the popular press. But is this indicator valid? If so, the well-known *random walk and efficient markets* theories (basically postulating that market movements are unpredictable) of stock-price behavior would be called into question. The accompanying table summarizes the relevant changes in the Dow Jones Industrial Average for the period December 31,

1927, through January 31, 1981. Joseph S. Martinich (1984) applied the chi-square test of independence to these data to investigate the January indicator.

		Next 11-Month Change	
		Up	Down
January Change	Up	25	10
	Down	9	9

a. Examine the contingency table. Based solely on your visual inspection, do the data appear to confirm the validity of the January indicator? Explain.

b. Construct a plot of the percentage of years for which the 11-month movement is up based on the January change. Compare these two percentages to the percentage of times the market moved up during the last 11 months over all years in the sample. What do you think of the January indicator now?

c. If a chi-square test of independence is to be used to investigate the January indicator, what are the appropriate null and alternative hypotheses?

d. Conduct the test of part **c**. Use $\alpha = .05$. Interpret your results in the context of the problem.

e. Would you get the same result in part **d** if $\alpha = .10$ were used? Explain.

9.60 Advertising companies often try to characterize the average user of a client's product so ads can be targeted at particular segments of the buying community. A new movie is about to be released, and the advertising company wants to determine whether to aim the ad campaign at people under or over 25 years of age. It plans to arrange an advance showing of the movie to an audience from each group, then obtain an opinion about the movie from each individual. How many individuals should be included in each sample if the advertising company wants to estimate the difference in the proportions of viewers in each age group who will like the movie to within .05 with 90% confidence? Assume the sample size for each group will be the same and about half of each group will like the movie.

***9.61** The classification of solder joints as acceptable or not is a difficult inspection task due to its subjective nature. Westinghouse Electric Company has experimented with different means of evaluating the performance of solder inspectors. One approach involves comparing an individual inspector's classifications with those of the group of experts that comprise Westinghouse's Work Standards Committee. In an experiment 153 solder connections were evaluated by the committee and 111 were classified as acceptable. An inspector evaluated the same 153 connections and classified 124 as acceptable. Of the items rejected by the inspector, the committee agreed with 19 (Meagher and Scazzero, 1985).

a. Construct a contingency table that summarizes the classifications of the committee and the inspectors.

b. Based on a visual examination of the table you constructed in part **a**, does it appear that there is a relationship between the inspector's classifications and the committee's? Explain. (A plot of the percentage rejected by committee and inspector will aid your examination.)

c. Conduct a chi-square test of independence for these data. Use $\alpha = .05$. Carefully interpret the results of your test in the context of the problem.

9.62 An important interaction occurs when a consumer dissatisfied with a purchase returns to the retailer to obtain satisfaction. The action taken by the retailer, however, may not conform to the consumer's expectations, and the resulting frustration and ill will benefit neither party. Ronald Dornoff and Clint Tankersley (1975) conducted a study to test the hypothesis that differences exist between retailers' and consumers' perceptions regarding actions taken by retailers in market transactions. A random sample of 300 consumers selected from the Cincinnati Metropolitan Area Telephone Directory was asked via mail questionnaire to react to scenarios like the following:

> A customer calls the retailer to report that her refrigerator purchased 2 weeks ago is not cooling properly and that all the food has spoiled.
>
> Action that should be taken by the retailer: The customer should be reimbursed for the value of the spoiled food.

One hundred usable questionnaires were returned. The same questionnaire was presented in person to 100 managers and assistant managers of a random sample of 40 retail establishments drawn from the yellow pages of the Cincinnati Telephone Directory. For the preceding scenario, 89 consumers agreed with the action prescribed for the retailer, 3 disagreed, and 8 had no opinion. Thirty-seven retailers (managers or assistant managers) agreed with the prescribed action, 54 disagreed, and 9 had no opinion.

a. Use a 95% confidence interval to estimate the difference in the proportions of consumers and retailers who agree with the action prescribed. Draw appropriate conclusions regarding the hypothesis of interest to Dornoff and Tankersley.

b. What assumption(s), if any, must be made in constructing the confidence interval?

c. Discuss the implications of the composition of the sample of retailers for the validity of the conclusions you made in part **a**. How would you improve the sampling procedure?

9.63 In 1986, the American Society for Quality Control commissioned the Gallup Organization to explore the attitudes, beliefs, and experiences of upper-level executives in U.S. businesses with respect to the quality and quality practices related to their companies' products and services. One of the questions was: "Poor quality—as measured by repair, rework and scrap costs, lost sales, and so on—is said to cost American business billions of dollars annually. How much does poor quality cost your company, as a percent of gross sales?" The table describes the responses (rounded to the nearest percent) of 387 service company executives and 311 industrial company executives.

	Service Companies	Industrial Companies
Less than 5%	45%	47%
5%–10%	24	23
11%–19%	5	12
20%–29%	3	6
30%–49%	2	2
50% or more	1	0
Don't know	20	10

Source: "Gallup survey: Top executives talk quality." *Quality Progress*, Dec. 1986, pp. 49–54.

a. Use a 90% confidence interval to estimate the proportion of all executives in U.S. service companies who believe poor quality costs their firm 10% or less of gross sales.

b. Use a 90% confidence interval to estimate the difference between the proportion of all executives in service companies and the proportion of all executives in industrial companies who believe poor quality costs their companies 10% or less of gross sales.

c. What assumptions must hold in order for your confidence intervals of parts **a** and **b** to be valid?

*9.64 Consumers have traditionally viewed products with warranties more favorably than products without warranties. In fact, when given the choice between two similar products, one of which is warranted, consumers prefer the warranted product, even at a higher price. Thus, consumers generally perceive warranties as a kind of value added to the product. However, a substantial number of firms perceive their warranties primarily as legal disclaimers of responsibility and nothing more. As a result of the differences in perceptions by consumers and businesses, Congress passed the Magnuson-Moss Warranty Act, which took effect in 1977. According to this act, all warranties must be designated as "full" or "limited," must be clearly written in readily understood language, and must contain specific information.

McDaniel and Rao (1982) investigated consumer satisfaction with warranty practices since the advent of the Magnuson-Moss Warranty Act. Using a mailed questionnaire, they sampled 237 midwestern consumers who had purchased a major appliance within the past 6 to 18 months. One question was, "Do most retailers and dealers make a conscientious effort to satisfy their customers' warranty claims?" One hundred fifty-six answered yes, 61 were uncertain, and 20 said no.

The population of consumers from which this sample was drawn had also been investigated 2 years prior to the Magnuson-Moss Warranty Act. At that time, 37.0% of the population answered yes to the same question, 53.3% were uncertain, and 9.7% said no.

a. As reflected in the answers to the preceding question, have consumer attitudes toward warranties changed since the earlier study? Test using $\alpha = .05$.

b. Compare the pre- and post-Magnuson-Moss Warranty Act responses, and describe any changes.

*9.65 Organizations that loan money to businesses are in effect gambling that the business will become (or remain) successful long enough so that the loan will not be defaulted. Loan applicants are carefully screened to weed out those firms with a high probability of defaulting. Characteristics of an applicant firm that might be examined by a loan officer include such things as the firm's age and legal structure. The loan officer's evaluation will also consider the amount of the requested loan, its duration, and its type (e.g., for an existing business, to buy an existing business, or to start a new business).

Albert L. Page et al. (1977) conducted an empirical investigation of the past loan performance of the Greater Cleveland Growth Corporation, an affiliate of the Office of Minority Business Enterprise. Part of the study involved identifying demographic and firm characteristic variables that relate to the status of the loans made. Loans were classified as paid off, current, or defaulted. Paid off and current loans are regarded as good loans.

In a sample of 64 loan histories, the frequencies for six loan status and legal structure categories were as shown in the table.

Loan Status	Firm's Legal Structure	Frequency
Defaulted	Sole proprietorship	14
Paid off or current	Sole proprietorship	13
Defaulted	Partnership	10
Paid off or current	Partnership	1
Defaulted	Corporation	12
Paid off or current	Corporation	14

a. From a contingency table analysis of the data, Page et al. reported a relationship between the legal structure of an applicant firm and the success or failure of the loan. Test their conclusion using $\alpha = .05$.

b. Find the approximate observed significance level for the test in part **a.**

c. What assumptions must you make so that the test conclusions in part **a** will be valid?

   d. Use a 95% confidence interval to estimate the proportion of loans made by the Growth Corporation that will be defaulted.

*9.66   The U.S. Postal Service is investigating the effect of alternative mail-sorting procedures on the percentage of sorting errors. A sorting error occurs when a piece of mail is placed into an incorrect zip code category. The three alternatives to be evaluated are:

   1. All manual (i.e., mail clerks sort all mail)
   2. Mixed manual–automated (i.e., mail clerks sort handwritten addresses and optical scanning machines sort typewritten addresses)
   3. All automated (i.e., optical scanning machines sort all mail)

   To evaluate these three alternatives, the Postal Service randomly selects 1,500 pieces of mail from the main post office in Washington, D.C. Five hundred pieces of mail are randomly assigned to each of the three sorting procedures. The experiment produced these error rates for the three sorting procedures:

All manual:	19%
Mixed manual–automated:	17%
All automated:	24%

   a. Based on these sample data, would you conclude that the error rates differ among the mail sorting procedures? Test using $\alpha = .05$.
   b. Find the approximate observed significance level for the test.

*9.67   It is commonly assumed that the more experience a job applicant has, the better that person will perform the necessary duties. Other factors, such as whether the person has a college degree or is male or female, may also be indicative of future performance. H. M. Greenberg and J. Greenberg (1980) argue that for sales jobs, the most important factor is matching the job requirement with an applicant's personal characteristics. This, they claim, will result in better retention rates and higher levels of job performance. To validate this claim they studied two groups of recently hired sales personnel. In the first group, which numbered 1,980, all were job-matched; the 3,961 members of the second group were not. After 6 months they were evaluated, and the aggregate data are shown in the table (1, highest performance; 4, lowest). The tabulated values are the percentages of total sales personnel contained in the respective samples.

	Performance					Totals
	1	2	3	4	Quit or Fired	
Job-Matched	9%	40%	32%	14%	5%	100%
Not Job-Matched	2%	17%	25%	31%	25%	100%

   a. Use both the percentages given in the table and the sample sizes to construct a contingency table that shows the numbers of sales personnel falling in each category of the table.
   b. Do the data provide sufficient evidence to indicate that the proportions of sales personnel falling in the performance categories depend on whether the people are job-matched? Test using $\alpha = .05$.

c. Do the data provide sufficient evidence to indicate the proportion of sales personnel receiving the highest rating (1) is larger if job-matched than if not? Test using $\alpha = .05$. [*Note:* This will require a one-sided test.]

9.68 An economist wants to investigate the difference in unemployment rates between an urban industrial community and a university community in the same state. She interviews 525 potential members of the work force in the industrial community and 375 in the university community. Of these, 47 and 22, respectively, are unemployed. Use a 95% confidence interval to estimate the difference in unemployment rates in the two communities.

****9.69** Smoke detectors are highly recommended safety devices for early fire detection in homes and businesses. It is vital that the devices be nondefective. Suppose 100 brand A smoke detectors are tested and 12 fail to emit a warning signal. Subjected to the same test, 15 out of 90 brand B detectors fail to operate. Form a 90% confidence interval to estimate the difference in the fractions of defective smoke detectors produced by the two companies. Interpret this confidence interval.

****9.70** A corporation owns several convenience stores that are open 24 hours a day. It is interested in knowing whether there is a relationship between time of day and size of purchase. One of its stores is selected at random to be involved in a study. Store records are collected over a period of several weeks and then 300 purchases are randomly selected. Since the register also prints the time of the purchase, this random selection procedure yields both amount and time of purchase. The information is summarized in the table. Is there a relationship between time and size of purchase? Use $\alpha = .05$.

		Size of Purchase		
		$2 or Less	$2.01–$7	Over $7
	8 A.M.–3.59 P.M.	65	38	14
Time of Purchase	4 P.M.–11:59 P.M.	61	49	10
	12 Midnight–7:59 A.M.	29	27	7

****9.71** Product or service quality is often defined as *fitness for use*. This means the product or service meets the customer's needs. Generally speaking, fitness for use is based on five quality characteristics: technological (e.g., strength, hardness), psychological (taste, beauty), time-oriented (reliability), contractual (guarantee provisions), and ethical (courtesy, honesty). The quality of a service may involve all these characteristics, while the quality of a manufactured product generally depends on technological and time-oriented characteristics (Schroeder, 1993). After a barrage of customer complaints about poor quality, a manufacturer of gasoline filters for cars had its quality inspectors sample 600 filters—200 per work shift—and check for defects. The data in the table resulted.

Shift	Defectives Produced
First	25
Second	35
Third	80

    a. Do the data indicate that the quality of the filters being produced may be related to the shift producing the filter? Test using $\alpha = .05$.

    b. Estimate the proportion of defective filters produced by the first shift. Use a 95% confidence interval.

*9.72 Several life insurance firms have policies geared to college students. To get more information about this group, a major insurance firm interviewed college students to find out the type of life insurance they preferred, if any. The accompanying table was produced after surveying 1,600 students.

	Term Policy	Whole-Life Policy	No Preference
Females	116	27	676
Males	215	33	533

    a. Is there evidence that the life insurance preference of students depends on their sex?

    b. Find the approximate observed significance level for the test in part **a**.

    c. Construct a plot of percentage responses that will help to interpret the result of the test in part **a**.

On Your Own

Market researchers rely on surveys to estimate the proportions of the consumer market that prefer various brands of a product. Choose a product with which you are familiar, and guess the proportion of consumers you think favor the major brands of the product. (Choose a product for which there are at least three major brands sold in the same store.)

    Now go to a store that carries these brands, and observe how many consumers purchase each brand. Be sure to observe long enough so that at least five (and preferably at least ten) purchases of each brand have been made. Stop sampling after a predetermined length of time or after a predetermined number of total purchases, rather than at some arbitrary time, which could bias your results.

    Use the count data to test the null hypothesis that the true proportions of consumers who favor each brand equal your presampling guesses of the proportions. Would failure to reject this null hypothesis imply that your guesses are correct?

Using the Computer

Are monthly homeowner costs related to the region of the country in which a homeowner lives? Use the zip code data of Appendix C to investigate this question.

    a. Conduct a χ^2 test of independence to answer the question. Treat the variable median monthly homeowner cost as if it had four classes: \$0–\$200, \$200.01–\$400, \$400.01–\$600, and \$601.01–\$800.

    b. Construct a table similar to Table 9.11 and a graph similar to Figure 9.5 to help explain the results of the test you conducted in part **a**. Interpret your results.

References

Cochran, W. G. "The χ^2 test of goodness of fit." *Annals of Mathematical Statistics*, 1952, Vol. 23, 315–345.

Conover, W. J. *Practical Nonparametric Statistics*, 2nd ed. New York: Wiley, 1980.

Covert, C. "Television viewers snapping up Home Shopping Network." *Minneapolis Star and Tribune*, Dec. 16, 1986.

Dahlin, C., and Owen, F. *An Analysis of Data Collected at the I-494 Weighing-in-Motion Site*. St. Paul: Minnesota Department of Transportation, 1984.

Dornoff, R. J., and Tankersley, C. B. "Perceptual differences in market transactions: A source of customer frustration," *Journal of Consumer Affairs*, Summer 1975, Vol. 9, pp. 97–103.

Graham, E. "The entrepreneurial mystique." *Wall Street Journal*, May 20, 1985.

Greenberg, H. M., and Greenberg, J. "Job-matching for better sales performance." *Harvard Business Review*, Sept.–Oct. 1980.

Hollander, M., and Wolfe, D. A. *Nonparametric Statistical Methods*. New York: Wiley, 1973.

Jenssen, W. J. "Sales effects of TV, radio, and print advertising." *Journal of Advertising Research*, June 1966, Vol. 6, pp. 2–7.

Kahalas, H. "The relationship between confidence in business and job satisfaction for union and nonunion members." *Baylor Business Studies*, Feb.–Apr. 1981, Vol. 127, pp. 45–53.

Kaufman, L., and Wolf, J. "Hotel room interviewing—Anxiety and suspicion." *Sloan Management Review*, Spring 1982, Vol. 23, pp. 57–64.

"Many fathers are reluctant to take time for family leave." *Minneapolis Star Tribune*, Feb. 14, 1993.

Martinich, J. S. "The January indicator: A nonrandom but unprofitable walk." *Mid-South Business Journal*, 1984, Vol. 4, No. 4.

McDaniel, S. W., and Rao, C. P. "Consumer attitudes toward and satisfaction with warranties and warranty performance—Before and after Magnuson-Moss." *Baylor Business Studies*. Nov.–Dec. 1982, Vol. 130, pp. 47–61.

McKenzie, J. "The accuracy of telephone call data collected by diary methods." *Journal of Marketing Research*, Nov. 1983, Vol. 20, pp. 417–427.

Meagher, J. J., and Scazzero, J. A. "Measuring inspector variability." *1985 ASQC Quality Congress Transaction*, Baltimore, May 1985, pp. 75–81.

Meier, P. "Taste: It's in the buds—and they don't improve with age." *Minneapolis Tribune*, June 8, 1980.

Neter, J., Wasserman, W., and Whitmore, G. A. *Applied Statistics*, 2nd ed. Boston: Allyn & Bacon, 1982. Chapter 17.

Page, A. L., Trombetta, W. L., Werner, C., and Kulifay, M. "Identifying successful versus unsuccessful loans held by the minority small business clients of an OMBE affiliate." *Journal of Business Research*, June 1977, Vol. 5, pp. 139–153.

Palm, R., and Hodgson, M. "Earthquake insurance: Mandated disclosure and homeowner response in California." *Annals of the Association of American Geographers*, June 1992, Vol. 82, No. 2.

Schroeder, R. G. *Operations Management*, 4th ed. New York: McGraw-Hill, 1993.

Sheets, T., Radlinski, A., Kohne, J., and Brunner, G. A. "Deceived respondents: Once bitten, twice shy." *Public Opinion Quarterly*, 1974, Vol. 18, pp. 261–263.

Siegel, S. *Nonparametric Statistics for the Behavioral Sciences*. New York: McGraw-Hill, 1956. Chapter 9.

Sudman, S., and Ferber, R. "A comparison of alternative procedures for collecting consumer expenditure data for frequently purchased products." *Journal of Marketing Research*, May 1974, Vol. 11, pp. 129–135.

Sudman, S., and Ferber, R. "Experiments in obtaining consumer expenditures by diary methods." *Journal of the American Statistical Association*, Dec. 1971, Vol. 66, pp. 725–735.

Tashakori, A., and Boulton, W. "A look at the board's role in planning." *Journal of Business Strategy*, Winter 1983, Vol. 3, pp. 64–70.

Winkler, R. L., and Hays, W. L. *Statistics: Probability, Inference and Decision*, 2nd ed. New York: Holt, Rinehart and Winston, 1975. Chapter 12.

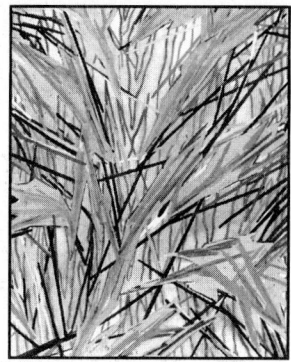

CHAPTER TEN

Regression Analysis

Contents

Case Studies

Where We've Been

The answers to many questions that arise in business require knowledge about the mean of a population or about the difference between two population means. Estimating and testing hypotheses about means, or the difference between two means, were the subjects of Chapters 6, 7, and 8.

Where We're Going

Suppose you want to predict the assessed value of a house in a particular community. Using the methods of Chapter 6, you could select a random sample of houses from the community and use the mean of their assessed values to predict the assessed value of the house of interest to you. But using this procedure would ignore the information contained in easily observed variables that are related to assessed house value—namely, the square feet of floor space, number of bathrooms, age of the house, etc. In this chapter we consider the problem of modeling the mean value of a single dependent variable y (for example, assessed house value) as a function of one or more independent variables (e.g., square feet of floor space, number of bathrooms, etc.).

In Chapters 6–8 we described methods for making inferences about population means. The mean of a population was treated as a **constant**, and we showed how to use sample data to estimate or to test hypotheses about this constant mean. In many business applications, the mean of a population is not viewed as a constant but instead as a variable. For example, the mean sales price of residences in a large city during 1990 can be treated as a constant and might be equal to $150,000. But we might also treat the mean sales price as a variable that depends on the square feet of living space in the residence. For example, the relationship might be

$$\text{Mean sales price} = \$30,000 + \$60 \cdot (\text{Square feet})$$

The formula implies that the mean sales price of 1,000-square-foot homes is $90,000, the mean sales price of 2,000-square-foot homes is $150,000, and the mean sales price of 3,000-square-foot homes is $210,000.

What do we gain by treating the mean as a variable rather than a constant? In many practical applications we are dealing with highly variable data, data for which the standard deviation is so large that a constant mean is almost "lost" in a sea of variability. For example, if the mean residential sales price is $150,000 but the standard deviation is $75,000, then the actual sales prices will vary considerably, and the mean price is not a very meaningful or useful characterization of the price distribution. On the other hand, if the mean sales price is treated as a variable that depends on the square feet of living space, the standard deviation of sales prices for any given size of home might be only $10,000. In this case, the mean price provides a much better characterization of sales prices when it is treated as a variable rather than a constant.

In this chapter we discuss situations in which the mean of the population is treated as a variable, dependent on the value of another variable. The preceding example of residential sales price depending on the square feet of living space is one illustration. Other examples are the mean sales revenue of a firm depending on the advertising expenditure, the mean price of a specific stock depending on the Dow Jones Industrial Stock Average, and the mean monthly production of automobiles depending on the total number of sales in the previous month.

We begin by discussing the simplest of all models relating a population mean to another variable, using the **straight-line model**. We show how to use sample data to estimate the straight-line relationship between the mean value of one variable, y, as it relates to a second variable, x. The methodology of estimating and using a straight-line relationship we call **simple linear regression analysis**. Then, in the optional sections, we consider the more general **multiple regression model** that relates y to several variables, $x_1, x_2, \ldots$.

10.1 Probabilistic Models

An important consideration in merchandising a product is the amount of money spent on advertising. Suppose you want to model the monthly sales revenue of an appliance store as a function of the monthly advertising expenditure. The first question to be answered is this: Do you think an exact relationship exists between these two variables? That is, can the exact value of sales revenue be predicted if the advertising expenditure is specified? We think you will agree this is not possible for several reasons. Sales depend on many variables other than advertising expenditure—for example, time of year, state of general economy, inventory, and price structure. However, even if many variables are included in the model (the topic of optional Section 10.9), it is still unlikely that we can predict the monthly sales *exactly*. There will almost certainly be some variation in sales due strictly to **random phenomena** that cannot be anticipated or explained. We will refer to all unexplained variation in sales—caused by important but unincluded variables or by unexplainable random phenomena—as **random error**.

If we construct a model that hypothesizes an exact relationship between variables, it is called a **deterministic model**. For example, if we believe that monthly sales revenue y will be exactly 10 times the monthly advertising expenditure x, we write

$$y = 10x$$

to represent a **deterministic** relationship between the variables y and x.

On the other hand, if we believe that the model should be constructed to allow for random error, then we hypothesize a **probabilistic model**. This includes both a deterministic component and a random error component. For example, if we hypothesize that the sales y is related to advertising x by

$$y = 10x + \text{Random error}$$

we are hypothesizing a **probabilistic** relationship between y and x. Note that the deterministic component of this probabilistic model is $10x$.

General Form of a Probabilistic Model

$$y = \text{Deterministic component} + \text{Random error}$$

where y is the variable of interest.

As you will see, the random error plays an important role in testing hypotheses and finding confidence intervals for the deterministic portion of the model and enables us to estimate the magnitude of the error of prediction when the model is used to predict some value of y to be observed in the future.

We begin with the simplest of probabilistic models—**a first-order linear model**, which graphs as a straight line. The elements of the straight-line model are summarized in the next box.

A First-Order (Straight-Line) Model

$$y = \beta_0 + \beta_1 x + \epsilon$$

where

> $y = $ **Dependent** or **response variable** (variable to be modeled)
>
> $x = $ **Independent*** or **predictor variable** (variable used as a predictor of y)
>
> ϵ (epsilon) $= $ Random error component
>
> β_0 (beta zero) $= $ y-intercept of the line—i.e., point at which the line intercepts or cuts through the y-axis (see Figure 10.1)
>
> β_1 (beta one) $= $ Slope of the line—i.e., amount of increase (or decrease) in the deterministic component of y for every 1-unit increase in x (see Figure 10.1)

FIGURE 10.1 ▶

The straight-line model

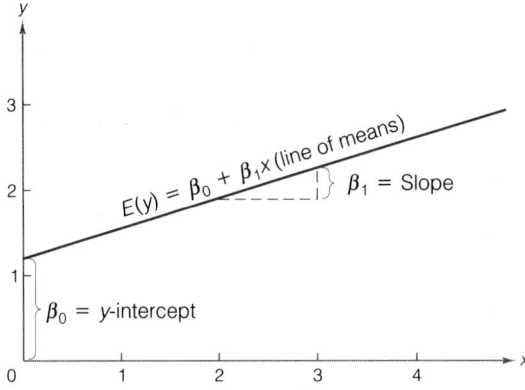

In the probabilistic model the deterministic component is referred to as the **line of means** because the mean of y, $E(y)$, is equal to the straight-line component of the model. That is,

$$E(y) = \beta_0 + \beta_1 x$$

Note that the Greek symbols β_0 and β_1 represent the y-intercept and slope of the model. They are population parameters that would be known only if we had access to the entire population of (x, y) measurements. Together with a specific value of the

---

*The word *independent* should not be interpreted in a probabilistic sense. The phrase *independent variable* is used in regression analysis to refer to a predictor variable for the response y.

independent variable x, they determine the mean value of y, which is just a specific point on the line of means (Figure 10.1).

The values of β_0 and β_1 are unknown in almost all practical applications of regression analysis. The process of developing a model, estimating the unknown parameters, and using the model can be viewed as the five-step procedure shown in the box.

Step 1 Hypothesize the deterministic component of the model that relates the mean, $E(y)$, to the independent variable x (Section 10.1).

Step 2 Use the sample data to estimate unknown parameters in the model (Section 10.2).

Step 3 Specify the probability distribution of the random error term, and estimate the standard deviation of this distribution (Section 10.3).

Step 4 Statistically evaluate the usefulness of the model (Sections 10.4, 10.5, and 10.6).

Step 5 When satisfied that the model is useful, use it for prediction, estimation, and other purposes (Section 10.7).

The focus of this chapter is on the straight-line model; more complex models are addressed in optional Section 10.9.

Exercises 10.1 – 10.8

Learning the Mechanics

10.1 In each case, graph the line that passes through the given points.
    a. (2, 0) and (5, 5)   **b.** (0, 0) and (4, 3)   **c.** (0, −2) and (7, 6)   **d.** (−1, −3) and (4, 4)

10.2 The equation for a straight line (deterministic) is

$$y = \beta_0 + \beta_1 x$$

If the line passes through the point (−2, 1), then $x = -2$, $y = 1$ must satisfy the equation; i.e.,

$$1 = \beta_0 + \beta_1(-2)$$

Similarly, if the line passes through the point (6, 6), then $x = 6$, $y = 6$ must satisfy the equation; i.e.,

$$6 = \beta_0 + \beta_1(6)$$

Use these two equations to solve for β_0 and β_1, and find the equation of the line that passes through the points $(-2, 1)$ and $(6, 6)$.

10.3 Refer to Exercise 10.2. Find the equations of the lines that pass through the points listed in Exercise 10.1.

10.4 Plot the following lines:
a. $y = 4 + x$ b. $y = -4 + x$ c. $y = 4 + 2x$
d. $y = -2x$ e. $y = x$ f. $y = .50 + .75x$

10.5 Give the slope and y-intercept for each of the lines defined in Exercise 10.4.

10.6 Why do we generally prefer a probabilistic model to a deterministic model? Give examples for which the two types of models might be appropriate.

10.7 What is the line of means?

10.8 If a straight-line probabilistic relationship relates the mean $E(y)$ to an independent variable x, does it imply that every value of the variable y will always fall exactly on the line of means? Why or why not?

10.2 Fitting the Straight-Line Model: The Method of Least Squares

After the straight-line model has been hypothesized as being appropriate for relating the mean $E(y)$ to the independent variable x, the next step is to collect data and to estimate the (unknown) population parameters—the y-intercept β_0 and the slope β_1.

To begin with a simple example, suppose an appliance store conducts a 5-month experiment to determine the effect of advertising on sales revenue. The results are shown in Table 10.1. (The number of measurements is small, and the measurements themselves are unrealistically simple to avoid arithmetic confusion in this initial example.) The relationship between sales revenue y and advertising expenditure x is hypothesized to follow a first-order linear model, that is,

$$y = \beta_0 + \beta_1 x + \epsilon$$

The question is this: How can we best use the information in the sample of five observations in Table 10.1 to estimate the unknown y-intercept β_0 and slope β_1?

TABLE 10.1   Advertising–Sales Data

Month	Advertising Expenditure x ($\$100$s)	Sales Revenue y ($\$1,000$s)
1	1	1
2	2	1
3	3	2
4	4	2
5	5	4

To gain information on the approximate values of these parameters, it is helpful to construct a **scattergram** for the sample data. Such a plot, also called a **scatter plot** or **scatter diagram**, locates each of the five data points on a graph, as in Figure 10.2. Note that the scattergram suggests a general tendency for y to increase as x increases. If you place a ruler on the scattergram, you will see that a line may be drawn through three of the five points, as shown in Figure 10.3. To obtain the equation of this visually fitted line, note that the line intersects the y-axis at $y = -1$, so the y-intercept is -1. Also, y increases exactly 1 unit for every 1-unit increase in x, indicating that the slope is $+1$. Therefore, the equation is

$$\tilde{y} = -1 + 1(x) = -1 + x$$

where $\tilde{y}$ is used to denote the value of y predicted from the visually fitted model.

FIGURE 10.2 ▶

Scattergram for data in Table 10.1

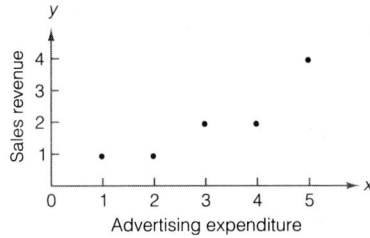

FIGURE 10.3 ▶

Visual straight-line fit to the data

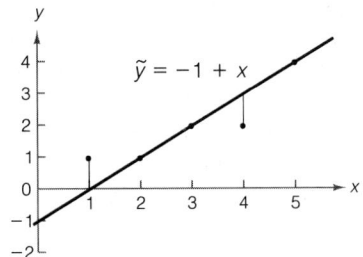

One way to decide quantitatively how well a straight line fits a set of data is to note the extent to which the data points deviate from the line. For example, to evaluate the visual model in Figure 10.3 we calculate the **deviations**—i.e., the differences between the observed and the predicted values of y. These deviations, or **errors**, are the vertical distances between observed and predicted values (see Figure 10.3). The observed and predicted values of y, their differences, and their squared differences are shown in Table 10.2 on page 500. Note that the **sum of errors** equals 0 and the **sum of squares of the errors (SSE)** is equal to 2.

You can see by shifting the ruler around the graph that it is possible to find many lines for which the sum of the errors is equal to 0, but it can be shown that there is one (and only one) line for which the *SSE is a minimum*. This line is called by various names, including the **least squares line**, the **regression line**, the **least squares prediction equation**, or the **fitted line**. We will typically refer to it as the least squares line.

TABLE 10.2 Comparing Observed and Predicted Values for the Visual Model

x	y	$\hat{y} = -1 + x$	$(y - \hat{y})$	$(y - \hat{y})^2$
1	1	0	$(1 - 0) = \quad 1$	1
2	1	1	$(1 - 1) = \quad 0$	0
3	2	2	$(2 - 2) = \quad 0$	0
4	2	3	$(2 - 3) = -1$	1
5	4	4	$(4 - 4) = \quad 0$	0
			Sum of errors $= \quad 0$	Sum of squared errors (SSE) $= 2$

To find the least squares line for a set of data, assume that we have a sample of n data points consisting of values of x and y, say $(x_1, y_1), (x_2, y_2), \ldots, (x_n, y_n)$. For example, the $n = 5$ data points shown in Table 10.2 are $(1, 1), (2, 1), (3, 2), (4, 2)$, and $(5, 4)$. The fitted line, which we calculate using the five data points, is represented as

$$\hat{y} = \hat{\beta}_0 + \hat{\beta}_1 x$$

The "hats" can be read as "estimator of." Thus, $\hat{y}$ is an estimator of the mean value of y, $E(y)$, and $\hat{\beta}_0$ and $\hat{\beta}_1$ are estimators of β_0 and β_1, respectively.

For a given data point, say the point (x_i, y_i), the observed value of y is y_i and the predicted value of y would be obtained by substituting x_i into the prediction equation:

$$\hat{y}_i = \hat{\beta}_0 + \hat{\beta}_1 x_i$$

And the deviation of the ith value of y from its predicted value is

$$y_i - \hat{y}_i = y_i - (\hat{\beta}_0 + \hat{\beta}_1 x_i)$$

Then the sum of squares of the deviations of the y values about their predicted values for all the n data points is

$$\text{SSE} = \sum_{i=1}^{n} [y_i - (\hat{\beta}_0 + \hat{\beta}_1 x_i)]^2$$

The quantities $\hat{\beta}_0$ and $\hat{\beta}_1$ that make the SSE a minimum are called the **least squares estimates** of the population parameters β_0 and β_1, and the prediction equation $\hat{y} = \hat{\beta}_0 + \hat{\beta}_1 x$, as noted above, is called the *least squares line*.

Definition 10.1

The **least squares line** is one that has a smaller sum of squared errors than any other straight-line model.

The values of $\hat{\beta}_0$ and $\hat{\beta}_1$ that minimize the SSE (proof omitted) are given by the formulas in the accompanying box.*

Formulas for the Least Squares Estimates

Slope: $\hat{\beta}_1 = \dfrac{SS_{xy}}{SS_{xx}}$ y-intercept: $\hat{\beta}_0 = \bar{y} - \hat{\beta}_1 \bar{x}$

where

$$SS_{xy} = \sum_{i=1}^{n} x_i y_i - \frac{\left(\sum_{i=1}^{n} x_i\right)\left(\sum_{i=1}^{n} y_i\right)}{n}$$

$$SS_{xx} = \sum_{i=1}^{n} x_i^2 - \frac{\left(\sum_{i=1}^{n} x_i\right)^2}{n}$$

n = Sample size

Preliminary computations for finding the least squares line for the advertising–sales example are contained in Table 10.3.

TABLE 10.3   Preliminary Computations for the Advertising–Sales Example

	x_i	y_i	x_i^2	$x_i y_i$
	1	1	1	1
	2	1	4	2
	3	2	9	6
	4	2	16	8
	5	4	25	20
Totals	$\Sigma x_i = 15$	$\Sigma y_i = 10$	$\Sigma x_i^2 = 55$	$\Sigma x_i y_i = 37$

---

*Students who are familiar with calculus should note that the values of $\hat{\beta}_0$ and $\hat{\beta}_1$ that minimize SSE = $\sum_{i=1}^{n} (y_i - \hat{y}_i)^2$ are obtained by setting the two partial derivatives $\partial SSE/\partial\beta_0$ and $\partial SSE/\partial\beta_1$ equal to 0. The *sample* solutions to these equations are denoted by $\hat{\beta}_0$ and $\hat{\beta}_1$, where the ˆ (hat) denotes that these are sample estimates of the true population intercept β_0 and slope β_1. The solutions to these two equations yield the formulas shown in the box.

We can now calculate*

$$SS_{xy} = \sum x_i y_i - \frac{\left(\sum x_i\right)\left(\sum y_i\right)}{5} = 37 - \frac{(15)(10)}{5} = 37 - 30 = 7$$

$$SS_{xx} = \sum x_i^2 - \frac{\left(\sum x_i\right)^2}{5} = 55 - \frac{(15)^2}{5} = 55 - 45 = 10$$

Then, the slope of the least squares line is

$$\hat{\beta}_1 = \frac{SS_{xy}}{SS_{xx}} = \frac{7}{10} = .7$$

and the y-intercept is

$$\hat{\beta}_0 = \bar{y} - \hat{\beta}_1 \bar{x} = \frac{\sum y_i}{5} - \hat{\beta}_1 \frac{\left(\sum x_i\right)}{5}$$

$$= \frac{10}{5} - (.7)\frac{15}{5} = 2 - (.7)(3) = 2 - 2.1 = -.1$$

The least squares line is thus

$$\hat{y} = \hat{\beta}_0 + \hat{\beta}_1 x = -.1 + .7x$$

The graph of this line is shown in Figure 10.4.

FIGURE 10.4 ▶
The line $\hat{y} = -.1 + .7x$ fit to the data

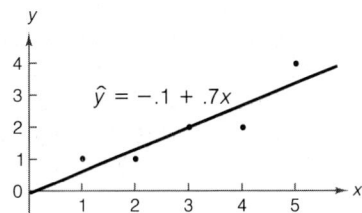

The observed and predicted values of y, the deviations of the y values about their predicted values, and the squares of these deviations are shown in Table 10.4. Note that the sum of squares of the deviations (SSE) is 1.10, and (as we would expect) this is less than the SSE = 2.0 obtained in Table 10.2 for the visually fitted line.

It is important that you be able to interpret the intercept and slope in terms of the data being utilized to fit the model. In the sales–advertising example, the estimated y-intercept, $\hat{\beta}_0$, is $-.1$. This value would seem to imply that the estimated mean sales are equal to $-.1$, or $-\$100$, when the advertising expenditure, x, is equal to $\$0$. Since negative sales are not possible, this seems to make the model nonsensical. However, *the model parameters should be interpreted only within the sampled range of the*

---

*Since summations are used extensively from this point on, we omit the limits on Σ when the summation includes all the measurements in the sample; i.e., when the symbol is $\sum_{i=1}^{n}$, we write Σ.

TABLE 10.4   Comparing Observed and Predicted Values for the Least Squares Model

x	y	$\hat{y} = -.1 + .7x$	$(y - \hat{y})$	$(y - \hat{y})^2$
1	1	.6	$(1 - .6) = .4$	.16
2	1	1.3	$(1 - 1.3) = -.3$	.09
3	2	2.0	$(2 - 2.0) = 0$	.00
4	2	2.7	$(2 - 2.7) = -.7$	.49
5	4	3.4	$(4 - 3.4) = .6$	.36
			Sum of errors = 0	SSE = 1.10

independent variable—in this case, for advertising expenditures between 1 ($100) and 5 ($500). Thus, the y-intercept—which is defined at $x = 0$ ($0 advertising expenditure)—is not within the range of the sampled values of x and is not subject to meaningful interpretation.

The slope, $\hat{\beta}_1$, of the least squares line was calculated to be .7. The implication is that for every unit increase of x, the mean value of y is estimated to increase by .7 unit. In terms of this example, for every $100 increase in advertising, the mean sales are estimated to increase by $700 *over the sampled range of advertising from $100 to $500*. Thus, the model does not imply that increasing the advertising expenditure from $500 to $1,000 will result in an increase in mean sales of $3,500 because the range of x in the sample does not extend to $1,000 ($x = 10$). Be careful to interpret the estimated parameters only within the sampled range of x.

Even when the interpretations of the estimated parameters are meaningful, it should be remembered that they are only estimates based on the sample. As such, their values will typically change in repeated sampling. How much confidence do we have that the estimated slope $\hat{\beta}_1$ accurately estimates the true slope β_1? This requires statistical inference, in the form of confidence intervals and tests of hypotheses, which we address in Section 10.4.

To summarize, we define the best-fitting straight line to be the one that minimizes the sum of squared errors around the line, and we call it the least squares line. We should interpret the least squares line only within the sampled range of the independent variable. In subsequent sections we show how to make statistical inferences about the model.

Exercises 10.9–10.18

Learning the Mechanics

10.9 The table on page 504 is similar to Tables 10.3 and 10.4. Columns 3 and 4 are for the preliminary computations to find the least squares line for the given pairs of x and y values. After the least squares line has been obtained, columns 5, 6, and 7 are used to compare the observed and predicted values of y and to calculate the SSE.

x_i	y_i	x_i^2	$x_i y_i$	$\hat{y} =$	$(y - \hat{y})$	$(y - \hat{y})^2$
7	2					
4	4					
6	2					
2	5					
1	7					
1	6					
3	5					
Totals $\Sigma x_i =$	$\Sigma y_i =$	$\Sigma x_i^2 =$	$\Sigma x_i y_i =$		$\Sigma(y - \hat{y}) =$	SSE $= \Sigma(y - \hat{y})^2 =$

a. Complete columns 3 and 4 of the table and calculate the totals for columns 1–4.
b. Find SS_{xy}.
c. Find SS_{xx}.
d. Find $\hat{\beta}_1$.
e. Find $\bar{x}$ and $\bar{y}$.
f. Find $\hat{\beta}_0$.
g. Find the least squares line and write it at the top of column 5.
h. Complete columns 5, 6 and 7 of the table.

10.10 Refer to Exercise 10.9.
a. Plot the least squares line on a scattergram of the data.
b. Plot this line on the same graph: $\hat{y} = 14 - 2.5x$.
c. Show that SSE is larger for the line of part **b** than it is for the least squares line.

10.11 Construct a scattergram for the data in the table.

x	.5	1	1.5
y	2	1	3

a. Plot these two lines on your scattergram:

$$y = 3 - x \quad \text{and} \quad y = 1 + x$$

b. Which of these lines would you choose to characterize the relationship between x and y? Explain.
c. Show that the sum of errors for both of these lines equals 0.
d. Which of these lines has the smaller SSE?
e. Find the least squares line for the data, and compare it to the two lines described in part **a**.

10.12 Consider the following pairs of measurements:

x	8	5	4	6	2	5	3
y	1	3	6	3	7	2	5

a. Construct a scattergram for the data.
b. What does the scattergram suggest about the relationship between x and y?
c. Given that $SS_{xx} = 23.4286$, $SS_{xy} = -23.2857$, $\bar{y} = 3.8571$, and $\bar{x} = 4.7143$, calculate the least squares estimates of β_0 and β_1.

d. Plot the least squares line on your scattergram. Does the line appear to fit the data well? Explain.
e. Interpret the y-intercept and slope of the least squares line. Over what range of x are these interpretations meaningful?

10.13 Suppose that $n = 100$ recent residential home sales in a city are used to fit a least squares straight-line model relating the sales price, y, to the square feet of living space, x. Homes in the sample range from $1,500$ square feet to $4,000$ square feet of living space, and the resulting least squares equation is

$$\hat{y} = -30,000 + 70x$$

a. What is the underlying hypothesized probabilistic model for this application? What does it imply about the relationship between the mean sales price and living space?
b. Identify the least squares estimates of the y-intercept and slope of the model.
c. Interpret the least squares estimate of the y-intercept. Is it meaningful for this application? Explain.
d. Interpret the least squares estimate of the slope of the model. Over what range of x is the interpretation meaningful?
e. Use the least squares model to estimate the mean sales price of a 3,000-square-foot home. Is the estimate meaningful? Explain.
f. Use the least squares model to estimate the mean sales price of a 5,000-square-foot home. Is the estimate meaningful? Explain. [*Note:* We show how to measure the statistical reliability of these least squares estimates in subsequent sections.]

Applying the Concepts

10.14 Individuals who report perceived wrongdoing of a corporation or public agency are known as *whistle blowers*. Two researchers developed an index to measure the extent of retaliation against a whistle blower. The index was based on the number of forms of reprisal actually experienced, the number of forms of reprisal threatened, and the number of people within the organization (e.g., coworkers or immediate supervisor) who retaliated against them. The table lists the retaliation index (higher numbers indicate more extensive retaliation) and salary for a sample of 15 whistle blowers from federal agencies.

Retaliation Index	Salary	Retaliation Index	Salary
301	$62,000	535	$15,800
550	36,500	455	44,000
755	17,600	615	46,600
327	20,000	700	12,100
500	30,100	650	62,000
377	35,000	630	21,000
290	47,500	360	11,900
452	54,000		

Source: Data adapted from Near, J. P., and Miceli, M. P. "Retaliation against whistle blowers: Predictors and effects." *Journal of Applied Psychology*, 1986, Vol. 71, No. 1, pp. 137–145.

a. Construct a scattergram for the data. Does it appear that the extent of retaliation increases, decreases, or stays the same with an increase in salary? Explain.
b. Use the method of least squares to fit a straight line to the data.

c. Graph the least squares line on your scattergram. Does the least squares line support your answer to the question in part **a**? Explain.

d. Interpret the y-intercept, $\hat{\beta}_0$, of the least squares line in terms of this application. Is the interpretation meaningful?

e. Interpret the slope, $\hat{\beta}_1$, of the least squares line in terms of this application. Over what range of x is this interpretation meaningful?

10.15 Due primarily to the price controls of the Organization of Petroleum Exporting Countries (OPEC), a cartel of crude oil suppliers, the price of crude oil rose dramatically from the mid-1970s to the mid-1980s. As a result, motorists saw an upward spiral in gasoline prices. The data in the table are typical prices for a gallon of regular leaded gasoline and a barrel of crude oil (refiner acquisition cost) for the indicated years, and $\Sigma y = 1,521$, $\Sigma x = 330.28$, $\Sigma y^2 = 153,735$, $\Sigma x^2 = 7,824.1822$, and $\Sigma xy = 34,259.58$.

Year	Gasoline	Crude Oil	Year	Gasoline	Crude Oil
	y (¢/gal.)	x ($/bbl.)		y (ct/gal.)	x ($/bbl.)
1975	57	10.38	1983	116	28.99
1976	59	10.89	1984	113	28.63
1977	62	11.96	1985	112	26.75
1978	63	12.46	1986	86	14.55
1979	86	17.72	1987	90	17.90
1980	119	28.07	1988	90	14.67
1981	131	35.24	1989	100	17.97
1982	122	31.87	1990	115	22.23

Source: U.S. Bureau of the Census. *Statistical Abstract of the United States: 1982–1992.*

a. Use the data to calculate the least squares line that describes the relationship between the price of a gallon of gasoline and the price of a barrel of crude oil.

b. Plot your least squares line on a scattergram of the data. Does your least squares line appear to be an appropriate characterization of the relationship between y and x? Explain.

c. If the price of crude oil fell to $15 per barrel, to what level (approximately) would the price of regular gasoline fall? Justify your response.

10.16 A car dealer is interested in modeling the relationship between the number of cars sold by the firm each week and the average number of salespeople who work on the showroom floor per day during the week. The dealer believes the relationship between the two variables can best be described by a straight line. The sample data shown in the table were supplied by the car dealer.

Week of	Cars Sold, y	Average Salespeople on Duty, x
January 30	20	6
June 29	18	6
March 2	10	4
October 26	6	2
February 7	11	3

a. Construct a scattergram for the data.

b. Assuming the relationship between the variables is best described by a straight line, use the method of least squares to estimate the y-intercept and the slope of the line.

c. Plot the least squares line on your scattergram.

d. Interpret the least squares estimates of the y-intercept and slope of the line of means. Are the interpretations meaningful?

e. According to your least squares line, approximately how many cars should the dealer expect to sell in a week if an average of five salespeople is on the showroom floor each day? [*Note:* A measure of the reliability of these predictions is discussed in Section 10.7.]

10.17 Baseball wisdom says if you can't hit, you can't win. But is the number of games won by a major league baseball team in a season related to the team's batting average? The accompanying table shows the number of games won and the batting averages for the 14 teams in the American League for the 1991 season.

Team	Games Won, y	Team Batting Average, x	Team	Games Won, y	Team Batting Average, x
Cleveland	57	.254	Baltimore	67	.254
New York	71	.256	California	81	.255
Boston	84	.269	Milwaukee	83	.271
Toronto	91	.257	Seattle	83	.255
Texas	85	.270	Kansas City	82	.264
Detroit	84	.247	Oakland	84	.248
Minnesota	95	.280	Chicago	87	.262

Source: *Official Major League Baseball 1992 Stat Book.* Major League Baseball Properties, Inc., and the editors of *The Baseball Encyclopedia*, New York.

a. If you were to model the relationship between the mean (or expected) number of games won by a major league team and the team's batting average x, using a straight line, would you expect the slope of the line to be positive or negative? Explain.

b. Construct a scattergram for the data. Does the pattern revealed by the scattergram agree with your answer to part **a**?

c. Given that $\Sigma y = 1,134$, $\Sigma x = 3.642$, $\Sigma y^2 = 93,110$, $\Sigma x^2 = .948622$, and $\Sigma xy = 295.54$, fit a simple linear regression model to the data.

d. Graph the least squares line on your scattergram. Does your least squares line seem to fit the points on your scattergram?

e. Why might the mean (or expected) number of games won not appear to be strongly related to a team's batting average?

10.18 The 1990 winner of Britain's Best Factory Award, NCR Ltd., manufactures automated teller machines. NCR management attributes its success to Total Quality Management (TQM) strategies, including reducing inventory levels through just-in-time (JIT) inventory ordering policies, instructing operators to stop the assembly line when quality problems are detected, and using only high-quality suppliers. This last strategy helped NCR cut the number of suppliers from 430 to 180 between 1980 and 1989. It saw a corresponding increase in the percentage of products that passed final inspection, from 40% to 98%.

	1980	1982	1985	1987	1989
Number of Suppliers, x	430	395	360	270	180
Products Passing Inspection, y (%)	40	60	80	88	98

Source: Lee-Mortimer, A. "Best of the best." *Total Quality Management*, Dec. 1990, p. 317.

a. Given that $SS_{xx} = 41,180.0$, $SS_{xy} = -8,582.0$, $\bar{y} = 73.2$, and $\bar{x} = 327.0$, find the least squares line relating y to x.

b. Plot the data and graph the least squares line as a check on your calculations.

c. Interpret the least squares estimates $\hat{\beta}_0$ and $\hat{\beta}_1$ in the context of this problem.

10.3   Model Assumptions

In Section 10.2, we assumed that the probabilistic model relating the firm's sales revenue y to advertising dollars x is

$$y = \beta_0 + \beta_1 x + \epsilon$$

We also recall that the least squares estimate of the deterministic component of the model $\beta_0 + \beta_1 x$ is

$$\hat{y} = \hat{\beta}_0 + \hat{\beta}_1 x = -.1 + .7x$$

Now we turn our attention to the random component ϵ of the probabilistic model and its relation to the errors in estimating β_0 and β_1. We use a probability distribution to characterize the behavior of ϵ. We will see how the probability distribution of ϵ determines how well the regression model describes the relationship between the dependent variable y and the independent variable x.

We make four basic assumptions about the general form of the probability distribution of ϵ:

Assumption 1   The mean of the probability distribution of ϵ is 0. That is, the average of the values of ϵ over an infinitely long series of experiments is 0 for each setting of the independent variable x. This assumption implies that the mean value of y, $E(y)$, for a given value of x is $E(y) = \beta_0 + \beta_1 x$.

Assumption 2   The variance of the probability distribution of ϵ is constant for all values of the independent variable, x. For our straight-line model, this assumption means that the variance of ϵ is equal to a constant, say σ^2, for all values of x.

Assumption 3   The probability distribution of ϵ is normal.

Assumption 4   The values of ϵ associated with any two observed values of y are independent. That is, the value of ϵ associated with one value of y has no effect on the values of ϵ associated with other y values.

The implications of the first three assumptions can be seen in Figure 10.5, which shows distributions of errors for three particular values of x—namely, x_1, x_2, and x_3. Note that the relative frequency distributions of the errors are normal, with a mean of 0 and a constant variance σ^2 (all the distributions shown have the same amount of spread or variability). The straight line shown in Figure 10.5 is the line of means. It indicates the mean value $E(y)$ for a given value of x and is given by the equation

$$E(y) = \beta_0 + \beta_1 x$$

FIGURE 10.5 ►

The probability distribution of ϵ

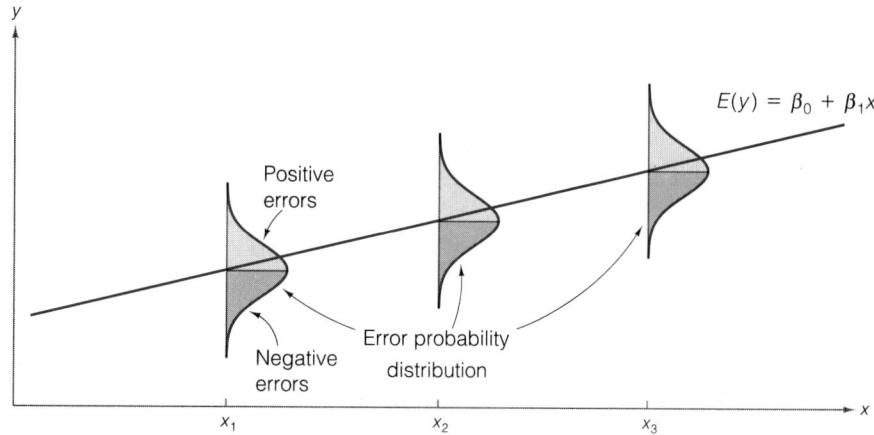

In most practical situations, the constant σ^2 in Assumption 3 will be unknown, and we must use our data to estimate its value. The best estimate of σ^2, denoted by s^2, is obtained by dividing the sum of squares of deviations,

$$\text{SSE} = \sum (y_i - \hat{y}_i)^2$$

by the number of degrees of freedom (df) associated with this quantity. We use 2 df to estimate the y-intercept and slope in the straight-line model, leaving $(n - 2)$ df for the error variance estimation (see the formulas in the box). In general, the number of degrees of freedom for estimating σ^2 will be $n - (k + 1)$, where k is the total number of independent variables in the model.

Estimation of σ^2, Straight-Line Model

$$s^2 = \frac{\text{SSE}}{\text{Degrees of freedom for error}} = \frac{\text{SSE}}{n - 2}$$

where

$$\text{SSE} = \sum (y_i - \hat{y}_i)^2 = \text{SS}_{yy} - \hat{\beta}_1 \text{SS}_{xy}$$

$$\text{SS}_{yy} = \sum (y_i - \bar{y})^2 = \sum y_i^2 - \frac{\left(\sum y_i \right)^2}{n}$$

Warning: When performing these calculations, you may be tempted to round the calculated values of SS_{yy}, $\hat{\beta}_1$, and SS_{xy}. Be certain to carry at least six significant figures for each of these quantities to avoid substantial errors in the calculation of SSE.

In the advertising–sales example, we previously calculated SSE $= 1.10$ for the least squares line $\hat{y} = -.1 + .7x$. Recalling that there were $n = 5$ data points, we have $n - 2 = 5 - 2 = 3$ df for estimating σ^2. Thus,

$$s^2 = \frac{SSE}{n - 2}$$

$$= \frac{1.10}{3} = .367$$

is the estimated variance, and

$$s = \sqrt{.367} = .61$$

is the estimated standard deviation of ϵ.

You may be able to obtain an intuitive feeling for s by recalling the interpretation given to a standard deviation in Chapter 2 and remembering that the least squares line estimates the mean value of y for a given value of x. Since s measures the spread of the distribution of y values about the least squares line, we should not be surprised to find that most of the observations lie within $2s$ or $2(.61) = 1.22$ of the least squares line. For this simple example (only five data points), all five data points fall within $2s$ of the least squares line. In Section 10.7, we use s to evaluate the error of prediction when the least squares line is used to predict a value of y to be observed for a given value of x.

The four assumptions listed previously make it possible for us to develop measures of reliability for the least squares estimators and to develop hypothesis tests for examining the usefulness of the least squares line. Various techniques exist for checking the validity of these assumptions, and there are remedies to be applied when they appear to be invalid. We discuss some of these techniques and remedies in optional Section 10.10.

In actual practice, the assumptions need not hold exactly in order for least squares estimators to be useful. The assumptions will be satisfied adequately for many applications encountered in business.

Exercises 10.19 – 10.26

Learning the Mechanics

10.19   Suppose you fit a least squares line to 26 data points and calculate SSE $= 8.34$. Find s^2, the estimator of σ^2, the variance of the random error term ϵ.

10.20   Calculate SSE and s^2 for each of the following cases:
    a. $n = 15$, $SS_{yy} = 7{,}492.91$, $SS_{xy} = 261.43$, $\hat{\beta}_1 = 26.97$
    b. $n = 87$, $\Sigma y^2 = 10{,}235.76$, $\Sigma y = 672.60$, $SS_{xy} = 340.85$, $\hat{\beta}_1 = .04$
    c. $n = 9$, $\Sigma(y_i - \bar{y})^2 = 38{,}377.81$, $SS_{xy} = -12{,}824.93$, $SS_{xx} = 8{,}221.11$

10.21 Refer to Exercises 10.9 and 10.12. Calculate s^2 and s for the least squares lines obtained in those exercises.

10.22 Visually compare the given scattergrams. If a least squares line were determined for each data set, which do you think would have the smallest variance, s^2? Explain.

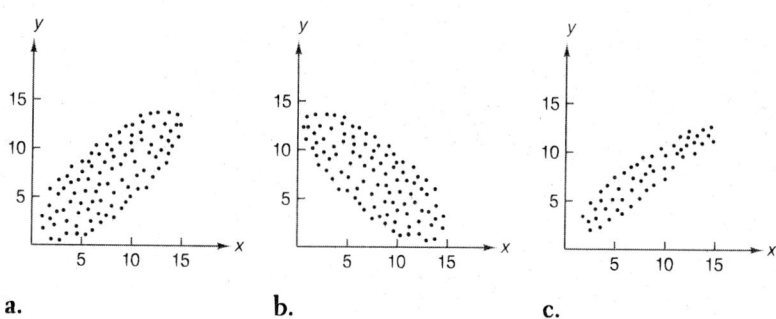

a.   b.   c.

Applying the Concepts

10.23 Prior to the 1970s the developing countries played a small role in world trade because their own economic policies hindered integration with the world economy. However, many of these countries have since changed their policies and vastly improved their importance to the global economy (Krueger, 1992). The table provides data for investigating the relationship between developing countries and industrial countries in annual import levels (given in billions of U.S. dollars).

	1950	1960	1970	1980	1989
Industrial Countries' Imports, x	39.8	85.4	226.9	1,370.2	2,237.9
Developing Countries' Imports, y	21.1	40.1	75.6	556.4	819.4

a. Given that $SS_{xx} = 3,809,368.452$, $SS_{xy} = 1,419,492.796$, $SS_{yy} = 531,174.148$, $\bar{x} = 792.04$, and $\bar{y} = 302.52$, fit a least squares line to the data. Plot the data points and graph the least squares line as a check on your calculations.

b. According to your least squares line, approximately what would you expect annual imports for developing countries to be if annual imports for industrial countries were $1,600 billion?

c. Calculate SSE and s^2.

d. Interpret the standard deviation s in the context of this problem.

10.24 To improve the quality of the output of any production process, we must first understand the capabilities of the process (Deming, 1986). In a particular manufacturing process, the useful life of a cutting tool is related to the speed at which the tool is operated. If we understand this relationship we can predict when the tool should be replaced and how many spare tools should be available. The data in the table at the top of page 512 were derived from life tests for the two brands of cutting tools currently in use.

Cutting Speed	Useful Life (hrs.)	
(meters/min.)	Brand A	Brand B
30	4.5	6.0
30	3.5	6.5
30	5.2	5.0
40	5.2	6.0
40	4.0	4.5
40	2.5	5.0
50	4.4	4.5
50	2.8	4.0
50	1.0	3.7
60	4.0	3.8
60	2.0	3.0
60	1.1	2.4
70	1.1	1.5
70	.5	2.0
70	3.0	1.0

a. Construct a scattergram for each brand of cutting tool.
b. For each brand, use the method of least squares to model the relationship between useful life and cutting speed.
c. Find SSE, s^2, and s for each least squares line.
d. For a cutting speed of 70 meters per minute, find $\hat{y} \pm 2s$ for each least squares line.
e. For which brand would you feel more confident in using the least squares line to predict useful life for a given cutting speed? Explain.

10.25   Although the cable television industry could provide viewers with 100 or more channels, a study by the A. C. Nielsen Co. suggests that viewers may not want so many. The Nielsen survey indicates that as television channels increase, the *percentage* of channels viewed for 10 minutes a week or more declines (Landro and Mayer, 1982). In a similar study, 20 households were sampled, and the number of channels available to each household was recorded. In addition, each household was asked to monitor its television viewing for 1 week and report the number of channels watched for 10 minutes or more. The results appear in the accompanying table.

Household	Number of Channels Available	Number of Channels Watched $\geq$ 10 Minutes	Household	Number of Channels Available	Number of Channels Watched $\geq$ 10 Minutes
1	12	6	11	25	10
2	29	10	12	8	6
3	4	3	13	5	4
4	20	8	14	10	4
5	40	12	15	16	9
6	5	3	16	4	4
7	6	5	17	5	1
8	4	4	18	45	13
9	14	8	19	35	5
10	20	6	20	50	10

a. Do these data tend to support the Nielsen findings? Find the appropriate least squares line and use it to justify your answer.

b. Plot your least squares line on a scattergram of the data.

c. Calculate SSE, s^2, and s. For the given number of channels available to a particular household, within what approximate bounds would you expect this least squares line to be able to predict the percentage of channels watched for 10 minutes or more?

10.26 A much larger proportion of U.S. teenagers work while attending high school than was the case a decade ago, and this proportion exceeds that in Japan, Germany, and Sweden. The change was fueled by the growth of the service sector after World War II, the rise of the fast-food industry in the 1960s and 1970s, and the larger number of teenage girls entering the work force. Because heavy workloads often result in poor classroom performance and lower grades, many states are tightening the child labor laws. A 1991 study of high school students in California and Wisconsin showed that those who worked only a few hours per week had the highest grade-point averages. The table shows GPAs and work hours per week for a sample of five students.

Grade-Point Average, y	2.93	3.00	2.86	3.04	2.66
Hours Worked per Week, x	12	0	17	5	21

Source: Adapted from Waldman, S., and Springen, K. "Too old, too fast." *Newsweek*, Nov. 16, 1992, p. 80.

a. Given that $SS_{xx} = 294.00000$, $SS_{xy} = -4.55000$, $SS_{yy} = .08968$, $\bar{x} = 11.00000$, and $\bar{y} = 2.89800$, fit a least squares line to the data.

b. Plot the data and graph the least squares line.

c. Predict the GPA of a high school student who works 10 hours per week. Repeat this for one who works 16 hours per week.

d. Calculate SSE, s^2, and s.

e. Within what approximate distance do you expect your predictions in part **c** to fall from the true GPA earned by the high school student? [*Note:* A more precise measure of reliability for these predictions is discussed in Section 10.7.]

10.4   Inferences About the Slope β_1 of the Straight-Line Model

Refer again to the data of Table 10.1 and suppose that the appliance store's sales revenue is *completely unrelated* to the advertising expenditure. What could be said about the values of β_0 and β_1 in the hypothesized probabilistic model

$$y = \beta_0 + \beta_1 x + \epsilon$$

if x contributes no information for the prediction of y? The implication is that the mean of y—i.e., the deterministic part of the model $E(y) = \beta_0 + \beta_1 x$—does not change as x changes. Regardless of the value of x, you always predict the same value of y. In the straight-line model, this means that the true slope, β_1, is equal to 0. Therefore, to test the null hypothesis that the linear model contributes no information for the prediction of y against the alternative hypothesis that the linear model is useful for predicting y, we test

$$H_0: \quad \beta_1 = 0 \qquad H_a: \quad \beta_1 \neq 0$$

If the data support the alternative hypothesis, we conclude that x does contribute information for the prediction of y using the straight-line model [although the true relationship between $E(y)$ and x could be more complex than a straight line]. Thus, in effect, this is a test of the usefulness of the hypothesized model.

The appropriate test statistic is found by considering the sampling distribution of $\hat{\beta}_1$, the least squares estimator of the slope β_1.

Sampling Distribution of $\hat{\beta}_1$

If the four assumptions about ϵ (see Section 10.3) are satisfied, then the sampling distribution of $\hat{\beta}_1$, the least squares estimator of slope, will be normal with mean β_1 (the true slope) and standard deviation

$$\sigma_{\hat{\beta}_1} = \frac{\sigma}{\sqrt{SS_{xx}}} \qquad \text{(see Figure 10.6)}$$

FIGURE 10.6 ▶
Sampling distribution of $\hat{\beta}_1$

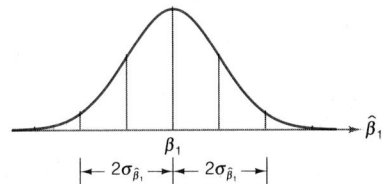

Since σ will usually be unknown, the appropriate test statistic is generally a Student's t statistic, formed as follows:

$$t = \frac{\hat{\beta}_1 - \text{Hypothesized value of } \beta_1}{s_{\hat{\beta}_1}} = \frac{\hat{\beta}_1 - 0}{s/\sqrt{SS_{xx}}}$$

$$\text{where} \quad s_{\hat{\beta}_1} = \frac{s}{\sqrt{SS_{xx}}}$$

Note that we have substituted the estimator s for σ, and then formed $s_{\hat{\beta}_1}$, the estimator of the standard deviation of $\hat{\beta}_1$, by dividing s by $\sqrt{SS_{xx}}$. The number of degrees of freedom associated with this t statistic is the same as the number of degrees of freedom associated with s. Recall that this is $(n - 2)$ when the hypothesized model is a straight line (see Section 10.3).

The setup of our test of the usefulness of the straight-line model is summarized in the box.

A Test of Usefulness of the Straight-Line Model

One-Tailed Test

H_0: $\beta_1 = 0$

H_a: $\beta_1 < 0$
  (or H_a: $\beta_1 > 0$)

Test statistic: $t = \dfrac{\hat{\beta}_1}{s_{\hat{\beta}_1}} = \dfrac{\hat{\beta}_1}{s/\sqrt{SS_{xx}}}$

Rejection region: $t < -t_\alpha$
  (or $t > t_\alpha$)

where t_α is based on $(n - 2)$ df.

Two-Tailed Test

H_0: $\beta_1 = 0$

H_a: $\beta_1 \neq 0$

Test statistic: $t = \dfrac{\hat{\beta}_1}{s_{\hat{\beta}_1}} = \dfrac{\hat{\beta}_1}{s/\sqrt{SS_{xx}}}$

Rejection region: $t < -t_{\alpha/2}$
  or $t > t_{\alpha/2}$

where $t_{\alpha/2}$ is based on $(n - 2)$ df.

Assumptions: The four assumptions about ϵ listed in Section 10.3

For the advertising–sales example, we will choose $\alpha = .05$ and, since $n = 5$, df $= (n - 2) = 5 - 2 = 3$. Then the rejection region for the two-tailed test is

$$t < -t_{.025} = -3.182 \quad \text{or} \quad t > t_{.025} = 3.182$$

We previously calculated $\hat{\beta}_1 = .7$, $s = .61$, and $SS_{xx} = 10$. Thus,

$$t = \frac{\hat{\beta}_1}{s/\sqrt{SS_{xx}}} = \frac{.7}{.61/\sqrt{10}} = \frac{.7}{.19} = 3.7$$

Since this calculated t value falls in the upper-tail rejection region (see Figure 10.7), we reject the null hypothesis and conclude that the slope β_1 is not 0. The sample evidence indicates that x contributes information for the prediction of y when a linear model is used to characterize the relationship between sales revenue and advertising.

FIGURE 10.7 ▶
Rejection region and calculated t value for testing whether the slope $\beta_1 = 0$

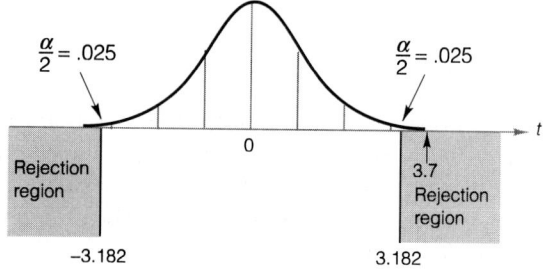

What conclusion can be drawn if the calculated t value does not fall in the rejection region? We know from previous discussions of the philosophy of hypothesis testing that such a t value does *not* lead us to accept the null hypothesis. That is, we do not conclude that $\beta_1 = 0$. Additional data might indicate that β_1 differs from 0, or a more complex relationship may exist between y and x, requiring the fitting of a model other than the straight-line model. We discuss several such models in optional Section 10.9.

Another way to make inferences about the slope β_1 is to estimate it using a confidence interval. This interval is formed as shown in the box.

A $100(1 - \alpha)\%$ Confidence Interval for the Slope β_1

$$\hat{\beta}_1 \pm t_{\alpha/2}\, s_{\hat{\beta}_1} \qquad \text{where} \quad s_{\hat{\beta}_1} = \frac{s}{\sqrt{SS_{xx}}}$$

and $t_{\alpha/2}$ is based on $(n - 2)$ df.

For the advertising–sales example, a 95% confidence interval for the slope β_1 is

$$\hat{\beta}_1 \pm t_{.025}\, s_{\hat{\beta}_1} = .7 \pm 3.182\left(\frac{s}{\sqrt{SS_{xx}}}\right) = .7 \pm 3.182\left(\frac{.61}{\sqrt{10}}\right) = .7 \pm .61$$

Thus, we estimate with 95% confidence that the interval from .09 to 1.31 includes the slope parameter β_1. In terms of this example, the implication is that we can be 95% confident that the *true* mean increase in sales per additional \$100 advertising expenditure is between \$90 and \$1,310. This inference is meaningful only over the sampled range of x—that is, from \$100 to \$500 advertising expenditure.

Since all the values in this interval are positive, it appears that β_1 is positive and that the mean of y, $E(y)$, increases as x increases. However, the rather large width of the confidence interval reflects the small number of data points (and, consequently, a lack of information) in the experiment. Particularly bothersome is the fact that the lower end of the confidence interval implies that we are not even recovering our additional expenditure, since a \$100 increase in advertising may produce as little as a \$90 increase in mean sales. If we wish to tighten this interval, we need to increase the sample size.

Exercises 10.27–10.38

Learning the Mechanics

10.27 Construct both a 95% and a 90% confidence interval for β_1 for each of the following cases:
  a. $\hat{\beta}_1 = 31$, $\quad s = 3$, $\quad SS_{xx} = 35$, $\quad n = 10$
  b. $\hat{\beta}_1 = 64$, $\quad SSE = 1,960$, $\quad SS_{xx} = 30$, $\quad n = 14$
  c. $\hat{\beta}_1 = -8.4$, $\quad SSE = 146$, $\quad SS_{xx} = 64$, $\quad n = 20$

10.28 Consider the following pairs of observations:

x	1	4	3	2	5	6	0
y	1	3	3	1	4	7	2

    a. Construct a scattergram for the data.
    b. Use the method of least squares to fit a straight line to the seven data points in the table.
    c. Plot the least squares line on your scattergram of part **a**.
    d. Specify the null and alternative hypotheses you would use to test whether the data provide sufficient evidence to indicate that x contributes information for the (linear) prediction of y.
    e. What is the test statistic that should be used in conducting the hypothesis test of part **d**? Specify the degrees of freedom associated with the test statistic.
    f. Conduct the hypothesis test of part **d** using $\alpha = .05$.

10.29 Refer to Exercise 10.28. Construct an 80% and a 98% confidence interval for β_1.

10.30 Do the accompanying data provide sufficient evidence to conclude that a straight line is useful for characterizing the relationship between x and y?

y	4	2	4	3	2	4
x	1	6	5	3	2	4

10.31 Suppose that $n = 100$ recent residential home sales in a city are used to fit a least squares straight-line model relating the sales price y to the square feet of living space x. The 100 homes range from 1,500 to 4,000 square feet of living space, and the resulting least squares equation is $\hat{y} = -30,000 + 70x$.
    a. When the null hypothesis that the true slope is zero is tested, the resulting test statistic is $t = 6.572$. Give the approximate p-value of this test, and interpret the result in the context of this application.
    b. The 95% confidence interval for the slope is calculated to be 49.1 to 90.9. Interpret this interval in the context of this application. What can be done to obtain a narrower confidence interval?

Applying the Concepts

10.32 From an observational study of five chief executives, Mintzberg (1973) identified 10 roles found in all managerial jobs: figurehead, leader, liaison, monitor, disseminator, spokesperson, entrepreneur, disturbance handler, resource allocator, and negotiator. An observational study of 19 managers from a medium-sized manufacturing plant (Luthans, Rosenkrantz, and Hennessey, 1985) extended Mintzberg's work by investigating which activities *successful* managers actually perform. A success index considered the manager's length of time in the organization and his or her rank within the firm; the higher the index, the more successful the manager. The table presents similar data that can be used to determine whether managerial success can be partly explained by the extent of network-building interactions with people outside the manager's work unit. Such interactions include phone and face-to-face meetings with customers and suppliers, attending external meetings, and doing public relations work.

Manager	Success Index, y	Interactions With Outsiders, x	Manager	Success Index, y	Interactions With Outsiders, x
1	40	12	11	70	20
2	73	71	12	47	81
3	95	70	13	80	40
4	60	81	14	51	33
5	81	43	15	32	45
6	27	50	16	50	10
7	53	42	17	52	65
8	66	18	18	30	20
9	25	35	19	42	21
10	63	82			

a. Construct a scattergram for the data.

b. Given $SS_{yy} = 7,006.6316$, $SS_{xx} = 10,824.5263$, $SS_{xy} = 2,561.2632$, $\bar{y} = 54.5789$, and $\bar{x} = 44.1579$, use the method of least squares to find a prediction equation for managerial success.

c. Find SSE, s^2, and s for your prediction equation. Interpret the standard deviation s in the context of this problem.

d. Plot the least squares line on your scattergram of part **a**. Does the number of interactions with outsiders seem to help predict managerial success? Explain.

e. Conduct a formal statistical hypothesis test to answer the question posed in part **d**. Use $\alpha = .05$.

f. Construct a 95% confidence interval for β_1. Interpret the interval in the context of the problem.

10.33 The expenses involved in a manufacturing operation may be categorized as being for *raw material, direct labor,* and *overhead.* Direct labor refers to the persons employed to transform the raw materials into the finished product. Overhead refers to all expenses other than those for raw materials and direct labor that are involved with running the factory (e.g., supervisory labor, maintenance of equipment, and office supplies) (Gray and Johnston, 1977). A manufacturer of 10-speed racing bicycles is interested in estimating the relationship between its monthly factory overhead and the total number of bicycles produced per month. The estimate will be used to help develop the manufacturing budget for next year. The data in the table have been collected for the previous 12 months.

Month	Production Level (1,000s of units)	Overhead ($1,000s)	Month	Production Level (1,000 of units)	Overhead ($1,000s)
1	16.9	41.4	7	16.3	37.5
2	15.6	35.0	8	15.5	37.0
3	17.4	38.3	9	23.4	47.9
4	11.6	29.5	10	28.4	55.6
5	17.7	39.6	11	27.1	53.1
6	17.6	37.4	12	19.2	40.6

a. Find the least squares prediction equation relating monthly overhead y to monthly production level x.

b. Does the straight-line model contribute information for predicting overhead costs? Test at $\alpha = .05$.

c. Which of the four assumptions we make about the random error ϵ may be inappropriate in this problem? Explain.

10.34 During June, July, and early August of 1981, 10 bids were made by DuPont, Seagram, and Mobil to take over Conoco. Finally, on August 5, DuPont announced success. The total value of the offer accepted by Conoco was $7.54 billion, making it the largest takeover in the history of American business at that time. A study of the Conoco takeover used regression analysis to examine whether movements in the rate of return of the contending companies' common stock could be explained by movements in the return rate of the stock market as a whole. The model was $y = \beta_0 + \beta_1 x + \epsilon$, where y is the daily rate of return of a stock, x is the daily rate of return of the stock market as a whole (based on Standard & Poor's 500 Composite Index), and ϵ is believed to satisfy the assumptions of Section 10.3. (This model is known in the finance literature as the *market model*. Note that the parameter β_1 reflects the sensitivity of the stock's return rate to movements in the stock market as a whole.) Daily data from early 1979 through 1980 ($n = 504$), yielded the least squares lines shown in the table for the four firms in question. The t statistics and p-values associated with the values of β_1 are also shown.

Firm	Estimated Market Model	t Statistics	p-Values
Conoco	$\hat{y} = .0010 + 1.40x$	$t = 21.93$	.000
DuPont	$\hat{y} = -.0005 + 1.21x$	$t = 18.76$	.000
Mobil	$\hat{y} = .0010 + 1.62x$	$t = 16.21$	.000
Seagram	$\hat{y} = .0013 + .76x$	$t = 6.05$	.000

Source: Ruback, R. S. *Sloan Management Review*, "The Conoco takeover and stockholder returns." Winter 1982, Vol. 23, pp. 13–33.

a. For each of the models, test $H_0: \beta_1 = 0$ versus $H_a: \beta_1 \neq 0$. Use $\alpha = .01$. Draw the appropriate conclusion regarding the usefulness of the market model in each case.

b. If the rate of return of Standard & Poor's 500 Composite Index increased by .10, how much change would occur in the mean rate of return for Conoco's common stock? For Seagram's?

c. Which of the two stocks, Conoco or Seagram, appears to be more responsive to changes in the market as a whole? Explain.

10.35 Refer to Exercise 10.14, in which the extent of retaliation against whistle blowers was investigated. Since salary is a reasonably good indicator of a person's power within an organization, the data of Exercise 10.14 can be used to investigate whether the extent of retaliation is related to the power of the whistle blower in the organization. The researchers were unable to reject the hypothesis that the extent of retaliation is unrelated to power. Do you agree? Test using $\alpha = .05$.

10.36 Buyers are often influenced by bulk advertising of a particular product. For example, if a product that sells for 25¢ is advertised at 2/50¢, 3/75¢, or 4/$1, some people think they are getting a bargain. To test this theory, a store manager advertised an item for equal periods of time at five different bulk rates and achieved the sales volumes listed in the table. Do the data provide sufficient evidence to indicate that mean sales increase as the bulk number increases? Test at $\alpha = .05$.

Advertised Number in Bulk Sale, x	Volume Sold, y
1	27
2	36
3	34
4	63
5	52

10.37 Do the data in Exercise 10.25 support the theory that the expected percentage of channels watched for 10 or more minutes decreases as the number of channels available increases? Test using $\alpha = .10$. Comment on the assumptions necessary for the validity of the test.

10.38 The precision of $\hat{\beta}_1$ as an estimator of β_1 is generally measured by its standard deviation $\sigma_{\hat{\beta}_1}$. In general, the larger the value of $\sigma_{\hat{\beta}_1}$, the wider (less precise) are confidence intervals for β_1; the smaller the value of $\sigma_{\hat{\beta}_1}$, the narrower (more precise) are confidence intervals for β_1.
a. Examine the formula for $\sigma_{\hat{\beta}_1}$ and explain how the observed values of the independent variable influence the size of $\sigma_{\hat{\beta}_1}$.
b. Sometimes it is possible to obtain data for a regression study by setting the independent variable x at different levels and observing the resulting values of the dependent variable y. For example, suppose a supermarket chain is studying the relationship between the sales of a product and how many square feet of display space it is given. Data for such a study will be generated by utilizing display areas of different sizes in different stores and observing the resulting sales. If you were designing such a study, how would your answer to part **a** influence the choice of display area sizes?

10.5   The Coefficient of Correlation

The claim is often made that the crime rate and the unemployment rate are "highly correlated." Another popular belief is that the Gross Domestic Product (GDP) and the rate of inflation are "correlated." Some people even believe that the Dow Jones Industrial Average and the lengths of fashionable skirts are "correlated." Thus, the term **correlation** implies a relationship between two variables.

The **Pearson product moment correlation coefficient** r, defined in the box, provides a quantitative measure of the strength of the linear relationship between x and y, just as does the least squares slope $\hat{\beta}_1$. However, unlike the slope, the correlation coefficient r is *scaleless*. **The value of r is always between -1 and $+1$, no matter what the units of x and y are.**

Definition 10.2

The **Pearson product moment coefficient of correlation** r is a measure of the strength of the linear relationship between two variables x and y. It is computed (for a sample of n measurements on x and y) as follows:

$$r = \frac{SS_{xy}}{\sqrt{SS_{xx}SS_{yy}}}$$

Note that r is computed from the same quantities used in fitting the least squares line. Since both r and $\hat{\beta}_1$ provide information about the utility of the model, it is not surprising that there is a similarity in their computational formulas. In particular, note that SS_{xy} appears in the numerators of both expressions and, since both denominators are always positive, r and $\hat{\beta}_1$ will always be of the same sign (either both positive or both negative). A value of r near or equal to 0 implies little or no linear relationship between the values of y and x that were observed in the sample. In contrast, the closer r is to 1 or -1, the stronger the linear relationship between y and x. And if $r = 1$ or $r = -1$, all the points fall exactly on the least squares line. Positive values of r imply that y increases as x increases; negative values imply that y decreases as x increases. Each of these situations is portrayed in Figure 10.8.

FIGURE 10.8 ▶
Values of r and their implications

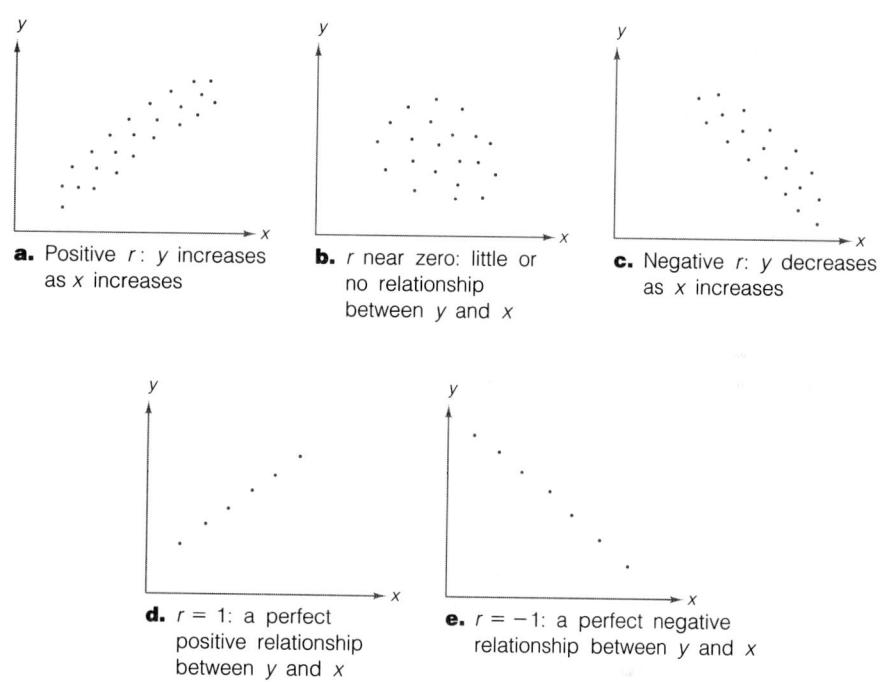

a. Positive r: y increases as x increases

b. r near zero: little or no relationship between y and x

c. Negative r: y decreases as x increases

d. $r = 1$: a perfect positive relationship between y and x

e. $r = -1$: a perfect negative relationship between y and x

EXAMPLE 10.1

A firm wants to know the correlation between the size of its sales force and its yearly sales revenue. The records for the past 10 years are examined, and the results listed in Table 10.5 are obtained. Calculate the coefficient of correlation r for the data.

TABLE 10.5 Sales Force–Revenue Data, Example 10.1

Year	Salespeople	Sales	Year	Salespeople	Sales
	x	y ($100,000s)		x	y ($100,000s)
1981	15	1.35	1986	29	2.93
1982	18	1.63	1987	30	3.41
1983	24	2.33	1988	32	3.26
1984	22	2.41	1989	35	3.63
1985	25	2.63	1990	38	4.15

Solution

We need to calculate SS_{xy}, SS_{xx}, and SS_{yy}:

$$SS_{xy} = \sum x_i y_i - \frac{\left(\sum x_i\right)\left(\sum y_i\right)}{10} = 800.62 - \frac{(268)(27.73)}{10} = 57.456$$

$$SS_{xx} = \sum x_i^2 - \frac{\left(\sum x_i\right)^2}{10} = 7{,}668 - \frac{(268)^2}{10} = 485.6$$

$$SS_{yy} = \sum y_i^2 - \frac{\left(\sum y_i\right)^2}{10} = 83.8733 - \frac{(27.73)^2}{10} = 6.97801$$

Then the coefficient of correlation is

$$r = \frac{SS_{xy}}{\sqrt{SS_{xx}SS_{yy}}} = \frac{57.456}{\sqrt{(485.6)(6.97801)}} = \frac{57.456}{58.211} = .99$$

Thus, the size of the sales force and sales revenue are very highly correlated—at least over the past 10 years. The implication is that a strong positive linear relationship exists between these variables (see Figure 10.9). We must be careful, however, not to jump to unwarranted conclusions. For instance, the firm may be tempted to conclude that the best thing it can do to increase sales is to hire lots of new salespeople. The implication of such a conclusion is that there is a *causal* relationship between the two variables. However, **high correlation does not imply causality**. The fact is that many things have probably contributed both to the increase in the size of the sales force and to the increase in sales revenue. The firm's expertise has undoubtedly grown, the rate of inflation has increased (so that 1990 dollars are not worth as much as 1981 dollars), and perhaps the scope of products and services sold by the firm has widened. We must be careful not to infer a causal relationship on the basis of high sample correlation. The only safe conclusion when a high correlation is observed in the sample data is that a linear trend may exist between x and y.

FIGURE 10.9 ▶
Scattergram for Example 10.1

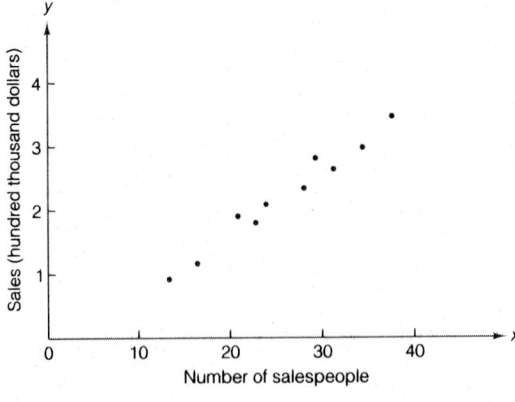

The correlation coefficient r measures the correlation between x values and y values in the sample, and a similar coefficient of correlation exists for the population from which the data points were selected. The **population correlation coefficient** is denoted by the symbol ρ (rho). As you might expect, ρ is estimated by the corresponding sample statistic, r. Or, rather than estimating ρ, we might want to test the hypothesis $H_0\colon \rho = 0$ against $H_a\colon \rho \neq 0$—i.e., test the hypothesis that x contributes no information for the prediction of y using the straight-line model against the alternative that the two variables are at least linearly related. We performed the identical test in Section 10.4 when we tested $H_0\colon \beta_1 = 0$ against $H_a\colon \beta_1 \neq 0$. That is, the null hypothesis $H_0\colon \rho = 0$ is equivalent to the hypothesis $H_0\colon \beta_1 = 0$.* When we tested the null hypothesis $H_0\colon \beta_1 = 0$ in connection with the advertising–sales example, the data led to a rejection of the hypothesis for $\alpha = .05$. This implies that the null hypothesis of a zero linear correlation between the two variables (advertising and sales) can also be rejected at $\alpha = .05$. The only real difference between the least squares slope $\hat{\beta}_1$ and the coefficient of correlation r is the measurement scale. Therefore, the information they provide about the usefulness of the least squares model is to some extent redundant. For this reason, we will use the slope to make inferences about the existence of a positive or negative linear relationship between the two variables.

10.6 The Coefficient of Determination

Another way to measure the usefulness of the model is to measure the contribution of x in predicting y. To accomplish this, we calculate how much the errors of prediction of y were reduced by using the information provided by x. To illustrate, consider the sample shown in the scattergram of Figure 10.10(a) on page 524. If we assume that x contributes no information for the prediction of y, the best prediction for a value of y is the sample mean $\bar{y}$, which is shown as the horizontal line in Figure 10.10(b). The vertical line segments in Figure 10.10(b) are the deviations of the points about the mean $\bar{y}$. Note that the sum of squares of deviations for the prediction equation $\hat{y} = \bar{y}$ is

$$SS_{yy} = \Sigma\,(y_i - \bar{y})^2$$

Now suppose you fit a least squares line to the same set of data and locate the deviations of the points about the line as shown in Figure 10.10(c). Compare the deviations about the prediction lines in parts (b) and (c) of Figure 10.10. You can see that

---

*The correlation test statistic that is equivalent to $t = \hat{\beta}_1/s_{\hat{\beta}_1}$ is

$$t = \frac{r}{\sqrt{(1 - r^2)/(n - 2)}}$$

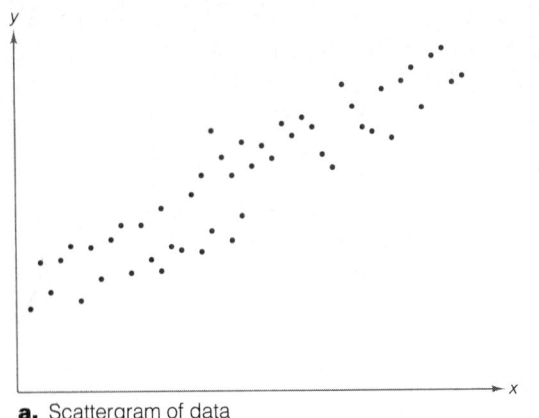

a. Scattergram of data

b. Assumption: x contributes no information for predicting y, $\hat{y} = \bar{y}$

c. Assumption: x contributes information for predicting y, $\hat{y} = \hat{\beta}_0 + \hat{\beta}_1 x$

FIGURE 10.10 ▲
A comparison of the sum of squares of deviations for two models

1. If x contributes little or no information for the prediction of y, the sums of squares of deviations for the two lines,

$$SS_{yy} = \sum (y_i - \bar{y})^2 \quad \text{and} \quad SSE = \sum (y_i - \hat{y}_i)^2$$

will be nearly equal.

2. If x does contribute information for the prediction of y, the SSE will be smaller than SS_{yy}. In fact, if all the points fall on the least squares line, then SSE $= 0$.

Then, the reduction in the sum of squares of deviations that can be attributed to x, expressed as a proportion of SS_{yy}, is

$$\frac{SS_{yy} - SSE}{SS_{yy}}$$

Note that SS_{yy} is the "total sample variation" of the observations around the sample mean $\bar{y}$, and that SSE is the remaining "unexplained sample variability" after fitting the line $\hat{y}$. Thus, the difference $(SS_{yy} - SSE)$ is the "explained sample variability" attributable to the linear relationship with x. Then a verbal description of the proportion is

$$\frac{SS_{yy} - SSE}{SS_{yy}} = \frac{\text{Explained sample variability}}{\text{Total sample variability}} = \frac{\text{Proportion of total sample variability}}{\text{explained by the linear relationship}}$$

It can be shown that this proportion is equal to the square of the simple linear coefficient of correlation r (the Pearson product moment coefficient of correlation).

Definition 10.3

The **coefficient of determination** is the square of the coefficient of correlation. It represents the proportion of the total sample variability around $\bar{y}$ that is explained by the linear relationship between y and x. We compute it as

$$r^2 = \frac{SS_{yy} - SSE}{SS_{yy}} = 1 - \frac{SSE}{SS_{yy}}$$

Note that r^2 is always between 0 and 1, because r is between -1 and $+1$. Thus, an r^2 of .60 means that the sum of squares of deviations of the y values about their predicted values has been reduced 60% by the use of the least squares equation $\hat{y}$, instead of $\bar{y}$, to predict y.

EXAMPLE 10.2

Calculate the coefficient of determination for the advertising–sales example. The data are repeated in Table 10.6.

TABLE 10.6

Advertising Expenditure	Sales Revenue
x ($100s)	y ($1,000s)
1	1
2	1
3	2
4	2
5	4

Solution We first calculate

$$SS_{yy} = \sum y_i^2 - \frac{\left(\sum y_i\right)^2}{5} = 26 - \frac{(10)^2}{5} = 26 - 20 = 6$$

From previous calculations, we know $SSE = \sum (y_i - \hat{y}_i)^2 = 1.10$. Then, the coefficient of determination is given by

$$r^2 = \frac{SS_{yy} - SSE}{SS_{yy}} = \frac{6.0 - 1.1}{6.0} = \frac{4.9}{6.0} = .82$$

So we know that in using the advertising expenditure x to predict y with the least squares line

$$\hat{y} = -.1 + .7x$$

the total sum of squares of deviations of the five sample y values about their predicted values has been reduced 82% by the use of $\hat{y}$, instead of $\bar{y}$, to predict y.

CASE STUDY 10.1 / Estimating the Cost of a Construction Project

As evidenced by the cost overruns of public building projects, the initial estimate of the ultimate cost of a structure is often rather poor. These estimates usually rely on a precise definition of the proposed building in terms of working drawings and specifications. Thus, cost estimators generally use deterministic models that do not take random error into account, so no measure of reliability is possible for their deterministic estimates. Crandall and Cedercreutz (1976) favor a probabilistic model to make cost estimates. They use regression models to relate cost to independent variables like volume, amount of glass, and floor area, explaining that "one of the principal merits of the least squares regression model, for the purpose of preliminary cost estimating, is the method of dealing with anticipated error." Specifically, when random error is anticipated, "statistical methods, such as regression analysis, attack the problem head on."

Crandall and Cedercreutz initially focused on the cost of mechanical work (heating, ventilating, and plumbing), since this part of the total cost is generally difficult to predict. Conventional cost estimates rely

heavily on the amount of ductwork and piping used in construction, but this information is not precisely known until too late to be of use to the cost estimator.

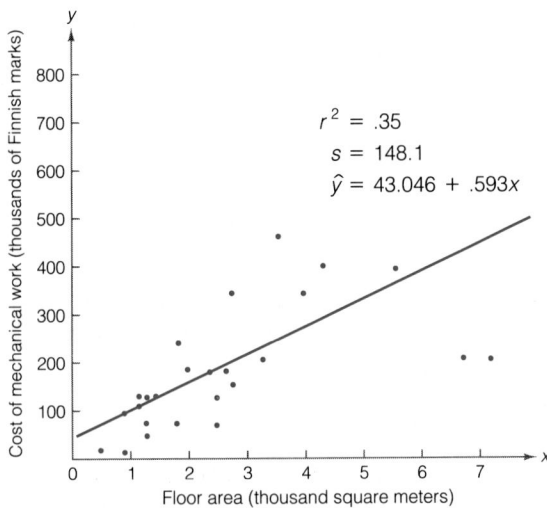

FIGURE 10.11 ▲ Simple linear model relating cost to floor area

One of several models discussed was a simple linear model relating mechanical cost to floor area. Based on the data associated with 26 factory and warehouse buildings, the least squares prediction equation given in Figure 10.11 was found. It was concluded that floor area and mechanical cost are linearly related, since the t statistic (for testing $H_0: \beta_1 = 0$) equalled 3.61, which is significant with an α as small as .002. Thus, floor area should help predict the mechanical cost of a factory or warehouse. In addition, the regression model enables the reliability of the predicted cost to be assessed.

The value of the coefficient of determination r^2 was .35. This tells us that only 35% of the variation among mechanical costs is accounted for by the differences in floor areas. Since there is only one independent variable in the model, this relatively small value of r^2 should not be too surprising. If other variables related to mechanical cost were included in the model, they would probably account for a significant portion of the remaining 65% of the variation in mechanical cost not explained by floor area. In optional Section 10.9, we describe how to build regression models using multiple independent variables.

Exercises 10.39 – 10.48

Learning the Mechanics

10.39 Explain what each of the following sample correlation coefficients tells you about the relationship between the x and y values in the sample:

a. $r = 1$ b. $r = -1$ c. $r = 0$ d. $r = .90$ e. $r = .10$ f. $r = -.88$

10.40 Describe the slope of the least squares line if:

a. $r = .7$ b. $r = -.7$ c. $r = 0$ d. $r^2 = .64$

10.41 Construct a scattergram for each data set. Then calculate r and r^2 for each data set. Interpret their values.

a.

x	−2	−1	0	1	2
y	−2	1	2	5	6

b.

x	−2	−1	0	1	2
y	6	5	3	2	0

c.

x	1	2	2	3	3	3	4
y	2	1	3	1	2	3	2

d.

x	0	1	3	5	6
y	0	1	2	1	0

10.42 Calculate r^2 for the least squares line in each of the following exercises. Interpret their values.

a. Exercise 10.9   b. Exercise 10.12   c. Exercise 10.28

Applying the Concepts

10.43 Find the correlation coefficient and the coefficient of determination for the data listed in the table and interpret your results. Can a causal relationship be inferred? Explain.

Year	Hunting Licenses Sold, x (millions)	Divorces and Annulments, y (millions)
1970	22.2	.71
1975	25.9	1.04
1980	27.0	1.19
1983	28.9	1.16
1984	28.5	1.17
1985	27.7	1.19
1986	27.9	1.18
1987	28.8	1.17
1988	30.0	1.17

Source: U.S. Bureau of the Census. *Statistical Abstract of the United States:*
1992, pp. 90, 238.

10.44 Find the correlation coefficient and the coefficient of determination for the sample data on Gross Domestic Product (GDP) and new housing starts listed in the table and interpret your results. For these data, $SS_{xx} = 27,144,855.71$, $SS_{yy} = 1,132,806.4$, $SS_{xy} = -91,861.52$, $\bar{x} = 3,688.91$, and $\bar{y} = 1,431.2$.

Year	GDP, x ($ billions)	Housing Starts, y (1,000s)	Year	GDP, x ($ billions)	Housing Starts, y (1,000s)
1970	1,010.7	1,434	1985	4,038.7	1,742
1975	1,585.9	1,160	1986	4,268.6	1,805
1979	2,488.6	1,745	1987	4,539.9	1,620
1980	2,708.0	1,292	1988	4,900.4	1,488
1981	3,030.6	1,084	1989	5,244.0	1,376
1982	3,149.6	1,062	1990	5,513.8	1,193
1983	3,405.0	1,703	1991	5,672.6	1,014
1984	3,777.2	1,750			

Source: U.S. Bureau of the Census. *Statistical Abstract of the United States: 1992,* pp. 428, 710.

10.45 Data on monthly sales, y, price per unit during the month, x_1, and amount spent on advertising, x_2, for a product are shown for a 5-month period in the table. Based on this sample, which variable—price or advertising expenditure—appears to provide more information about sales? Explain.

Month	Monthly Sales y (1,000s)	Unit Price x_1	Advertising Costs x_2 (100s)
June	$40	$ .85	$6.0
July	50	.76	5.0
August	55	.75	8.0
September	30	1.00	7.5
October	45	.80	5.5

10.46 A *negotiable certificate of deposit* is a marketable receipt for funds deposited in a bank for a specified period of time at a specified rate of interest (Cook, 1977). The accompanying table lists the end-of-quarter interest rate for 3-month certificates of deposit from January 1980 through December 1991 with the concurrent end-of-quarter values of Standard & Poor's 500 Stock Composite Average (an indicator of stock market activity). For these data, $\Sigma x = 452.96$, $\Sigma y = 10,937.82$, $\Sigma x^2 = 4,780.03$, $\Sigma y^2 = 2,889,220.05$, and $\Sigma xy = 93,654.35$. Find the coefficient of determination and the correlation coefficient for the data, and interpret your results.

Year	Quarter	Interest Rate, x	S&P 500, y	Year	Quarter	Interest Rate, x	S&P 500, y
1980	I	17.57	104.69	1986	I	7.24	238.90
	II	8.49	114.24		II	6.73	250.84
	III	11.29	125.46		III	5.71	231.32
	IV	18.65	135.76		IV	6.04	242.17
1981	I	14.43	136.00	1987	I	6.17	291.70
	II	16.90	131.21		II	6.94	304.00
	III	16.84	116.18		III	7.37	321.83
	IV	12.49	122.55		IV	7.66	247.08
1982	I	14.21	111.96	1988	I	6.63	258.89
	II	14.46	109.61		II	7.51	273.50
	III	10.66	120.42		III	8.23	271.91
	IV	8.66	135.28		IV	9.25	277.72
1983	I	8.69	152.96	1989	I	10.09	294.87
	II	9.20	168.11		II	9.20	317.98
	III	9.39	166.07		III	8.78	349.15
	IV	9.69	164.93		IV	8.32	353.40
1984	I	10.08	159.18	1990	I	8.27	339.94
	II	11.34	153.18		II	8.33	358.02
	III	11.29	166.10		III	8.08	306.05
	IV	8.60	167.24		IV	7.96	330.22
1985	I	9.02	180.66	1991	I	6.71	375.22
	II	7.44	191.85		II	6.01	371.16
	III	7.93	182.08		III	5.70	387.86
	IV	7.80	211.28		IV	4.91	417.09

Source: *Standard & Poor's Statistical Service, Current Statistics.* Standard & Poor's Corporation, 1992.

10.47 The Minnesota Department of Transportation installed a computerized weigh-in-motion scale in the concrete surface of eastbound Interstate 494 in Bloomington, Minnesota. The system monitors traffic continuously and can distinguish among 13 types of vehicles (car, five-axle semi, five-axle twin trailer, etc.). The purpose of the system is to provide traffic counts and weights for use in the planning and design of roadways. A *calibration study* was undertaken to determine whether the scale's readings correspond with the static weights of the vehicles being monitored. After some preliminary comparisons using a two-axle six-tire truck carrying different loads, calibration adjustments were made in the software of the weigh-in-motion system and the scales were reevaluated. The table at the top of page 530 shows the trial data in thousands of pounds.

Trial	Static Weight, x	Initial Motion Reading, y_1	Adjusted Reading, y_2
1	27.9	26.0	27.8
2	29.1	29.9	29.1
3	38.0	39.5	37.8
4	27.0	25.1	27.1
5	30.3	31.6	30.6
6	34.5	36.2	34.3
7	27.8	25.1	26.9
8	29.6	31.0	29.6
9	33.1	35.6	33.0
10	35.5	40.2	35.0

Source: Adapted from data in Wright, J. L., Owen, F., and Pena, D. "Status of MN/DOT's weigh-in-motion program." St. Paul: Minnesota Department of Transportation, Jan. 1983.

a. Construct two scattergrams, one of y_1 versus x and the other of y_2 versus x.
b. Use the scattergram of part **a** to evaluate the performance of the weigh-in-motion scale both before and after the calibration adjustment.
c. Calculate the correlation coefficient for both sets of data, and interpret their values. Explain how these correlation coefficients can be used to evaluate the weigh-in-motion scale.
d. Suppose the sample correlation coefficient for y_2 and x were 1. Could this happen if the static weights and the weigh-in-motion readings disagreed? Explain.

10.48 A firm's *demand curve* describes the quantity of its product that can be sold at various prices, other things being equal (McConnell and Brue, 1990). Over the period of a year, a tire company varied the price of a radial tire to estimate its demand curve. When the price was set very low or very high, few tires sold. The latter result the firm understood; the former it attributed to consumer misperception that low price implies poor quality. The data in the table describe the tire's sales over the experimental period.

Price x (\$)	Sales y (100s)
20	13
35	57
45	85
60	43
70	17

a. Calculate a least squares line to approximate the firm's demand curve.
b. Construct a scattergram and plot your least squares line as a check on your calculations.
c. Test H_0: $\beta_1 = 0$ using a two-tailed test and $\alpha = .05$. Draw the appropriate conclusion in the context of the problem.
d. Does the nonrejection of H_0 in part **c** imply that no relationship exists between tire price and sales volume? Explain.
e. Calculate the coefficient of determination for the least squares line of part **a** and interpret its value in the context of the problem.

10.7   Using the Straight-Line Model for Estimation and Prediction

If we are satisfied that a useful model has been found to describe the relationship between sales revenue and advertising, we are ready to accomplish the original objectives for building the model: using it to estimate or to predict sales on the basis of advertising dollars spent.

The most common uses of a probabilistic model can be divided into two categories. The first is the use of the model for estimating the mean value of y, $E(y)$ for a specific value of x.

For our example, we may want to estimate the mean sales revenue for *all* months during which $400 ($x = 4$) is expended on advertising.

The second use of the model entails predicting a particular y value for a given value of x.

That is, if we decide to expend $400 next month, we want to predict the firm's sales revenue for that month.

In the case of estimating a mean value of y, we are attempting to estimate the mean result of a very large number of experiments at the given x value.
In the second case, we are trying to predict the outcome of a single experiment at the given x value.

In which of these model uses do you expect to have more success; i.e., which value—the mean or individual value of y—can we estimate (or predict) with more accuracy?

Before answering this question, we first consider the problem of choosing an estimator (or predictor) of the mean (or individual) y value. We will use the least squares model

$$\hat{y} = \hat{\beta}_0 + \hat{\beta}_1 x$$

both to estimate the mean value of y and to predict a particular value of y for a given value of x. For our example, we found

$$\hat{y} = -.1 + .7x$$

so that the estimated mean value of sales revenue for all months when $x = 4$ (advertising = 400) is

$$\hat{y} = -.1 + .7(4) = 2.7$$

or $2,700 (the units of y are thousands of dollars). The same value is used to predict the y value when $x = 4$. That is, both the estimated mean value and the predicted value of y equal $\hat{y} = 2.7$ when $x = 4$, as shown in Figure 10.12 (page 532).

FIGURE 10.12 ▶
Estimated mean value and
predicted individual value of sales
revenue y for $x = 4$

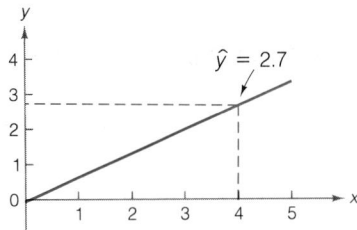

The difference in these two model uses lies in the relative accuracy of the estimate and the prediction. These accuracies are best measured by using the sampling errors of the least squares line when it is used as an estimator and as a predictor, respectively. These errors are reflected in the standard deviations given in the box.

Sampling Errors for the Estimator of the Mean of y and the Predictor of an Individual y

1. The standard deviation of the sampling distribution of the estimator $\hat{y}$ of the mean value of y at a particular value of x, say x_p, is

$$\sigma_{\hat{y}} = \sigma \sqrt{\frac{1}{n} + \frac{(x_p - \bar{x})^2}{SS_{xx}}}$$

where σ is the standard deviation of the random error ϵ.

2. The standard deviation of the prediction error for the predictor $\hat{y}$ of an individual y value for $x = x_p$ is

$$\sigma_{(y-\hat{y})} = \sigma \sqrt{1 + \frac{1}{n} + \frac{(x_p - \bar{x})^2}{SS_{xx}}}$$

where σ is the standard deviation of the random error ϵ.

The true value of σ is rarely known. Thus, we estimate σ by s and calculate the estimation and prediction intervals as shown in the following boxes.

A 100(1 − α)% Confidence Interval for the Mean Value of y for $x = x_p$

$$\hat{y} \pm t_{\alpha/2}(\text{Estimated standard deviation of } \hat{y})$$

or

$$\hat{y} \pm t_{\alpha/2} s \sqrt{\frac{1}{n} + \frac{(x_p - \bar{x})^2}{SS_{xx}}}$$

where $t_{\alpha/2}$ is based on $(n - 2)$ df.

A $100(1 - \alpha)\%$ Prediction Interval for an Individual y for $x = x_p$

$$\hat{y} \pm t_{\alpha/2}[\text{Estimated standard deviation of } (y - \hat{y})]$$

or

$$\hat{y} \pm t_{\alpha/2} s \sqrt{1 + \frac{1}{n} + \frac{(x_p - \bar{x})^2}{SS_{xx}}}$$

where $t_{\alpha/2}$ is based on $(n - 2)$ df.

EXAMPLE 10.3

Find a 95% confidence interval for mean monthly sales when the appliance store spends \$400 on advertising.

Solution

For a \$400 advertising expenditure, $x_p = 4$ and, since $n = 5$, df $= n - 2 = 3$. Then the confidence interval for the mean value of y is

$$\hat{y} \pm t_{\alpha/2} s \sqrt{\frac{1}{n} + \frac{(x_p - \bar{x})^2}{SS_{xx}}} \quad \text{or} \quad \hat{y} \pm t_{.025} s \sqrt{\frac{1}{5} + \frac{(4 - \bar{x})^2}{SS_{xx}}}$$

Recall that $\hat{y} = 2.7$, $s = .61$, $\bar{x} = 3$, and $SS_{xx} = 10$. From Table VI in Appendix B, $t_{.025} = 3.182$. Thus, we have

$$2.7 \pm (3.182)(.61) \sqrt{\frac{1}{5} + \frac{(4 - 3)^2}{10}} = 2.7 \pm (3.182)(.61)(.55)$$

$$= 2.7 \pm 1.1 \quad \text{or} \quad (1.6, 3.8)$$

We are 95% confident that the interval from \$1,600 to \$3,800 encloses the mean sales revenue when the store expends \$400 a month on advertising. Note that we used a small amount of data for purposes of illustration in fitting the least squares line and that the width of the interval could be decreased by using a larger number of data points.

EXAMPLE 10.4

Predict the monthly sales for next month if a \$400 expenditure is to be made on advertising. Use a 95% prediction interval.

Solution

To predict the sales for a particular month for which $x_p = 4$, we calculate the 95% prediction interval as

$$\hat{y} \pm t_{\alpha/2} s \sqrt{1 + \frac{1}{n} + \frac{(x_p - \bar{x})^2}{SS_{xx}}} = 2.7 \pm (3.182)(.61) \sqrt{1 + \frac{1}{5} + \frac{(4 - 3)^2}{10}}$$

$$= 2.7 \pm (3.182)(.61)(1.14)$$

$$= 2.7 \pm 2.2 \quad \text{or} \quad (.5, 4.9)$$

Therefore, we predict with 95% confidence that the sales next month will fall in the interval from $500 to $4,900.

As with the confidence interval for the mean value of y (Example 10.3), the prediction interval for y (Example 10.4) is quite large. This is because we have chosen a small number of data points to fit the least squares line. The width of the prediction interval could be reduced by using more data points.

A comparison of the confidence interval for the mean value of y and the prediction interval for some future value of y for a $400 advertising expenditure ($x = 4$) is illustrated in Figure 10.13. It is important to note that the prediction interval for an individual value of y will always be wider than the confidence interval for a mean value of y. You can see this by examining the formulas for the two intervals, and you can see it in Figure 10.13.

FIGURE 10.13 ▶

A 95% confidence interval for mean sales and a prediction interval for sales when $x = 4$

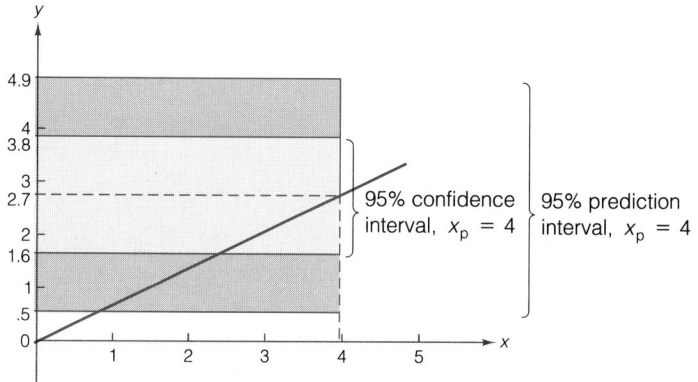

The error in estimating the mean value of y, $E(y)$, for a given value of x, say x_p, is the distance between the least squares line and the true line of means, $E(y) = \beta_0 + \beta_1 x$. This error, $[\hat{y} - E(y)]$, is shown in Figure 10.14. In contrast, the error $(y_p - \hat{y})$ in predicting some future value of y is the sum of two errors—the error of estimating the mean of y, $E(y)$, shown in Figure 10.14, plus the random error that is a component of the value of y to be predicted (see Figure 10.15). Consequently, the error of predicting a particular value of y will be larger than the error of estimating the mean value of y for a particular value of x.

Note from their formulas that both the error of estimation and the error of prediction take their smallest values when $x_p = \bar{x}$. The farther x_p lies from x, the larger will be the errors of estimation and prediction. You can see why this is true by noting the deviations for different values of x_p between the line of means $E(y) = \beta_0 + \beta_1 x$ and the predicted line of means $\hat{y} = \hat{\beta}_0 + \hat{\beta}_1 x$ shown in Figure 10.15. The deviation is larger at the extremities of the interval where the largest and smallest values of x in the data set occur.

FIGURE 10.14 ▶
Error of estimating the mean value of y for a given value of x

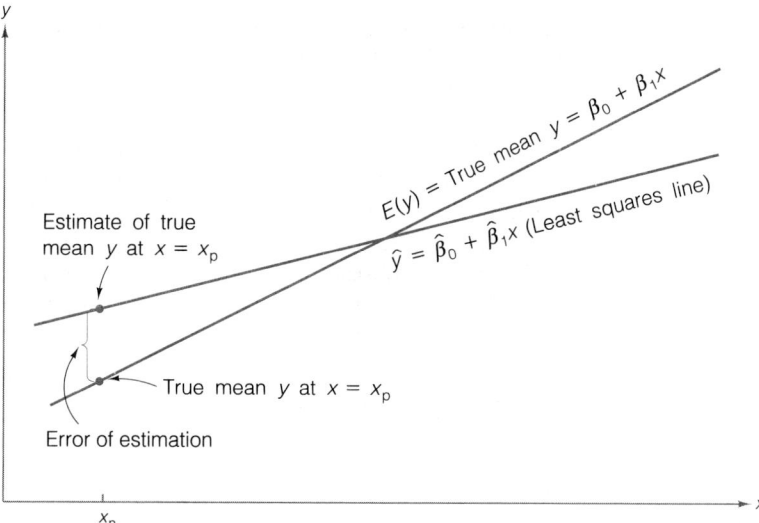

FIGURE 10.15 ▶
Error of predicting a future value of y for a given value of x

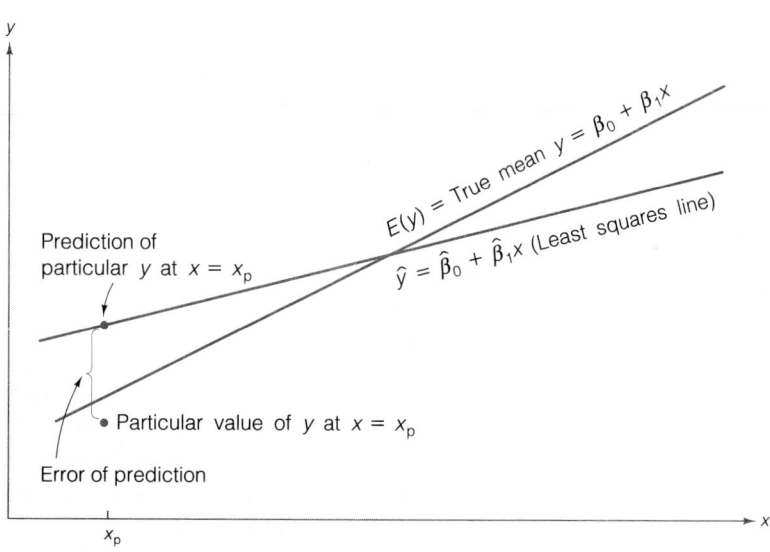

Both the confidence intervals for the mean values and the prediction intervals for individual values are depicted over the entire range of the regression line in Figure 10.16 on page 536. You can see that the confidence interval is always narrower than the prediction interval, and that they are both narrowest at the mean $\bar{x}$, increasing steadily as the distance $|x - \bar{x}|$ increases.

FIGURE 10.16 ▶
Confidence intervals for mean
values and prediction intervals for
individual values

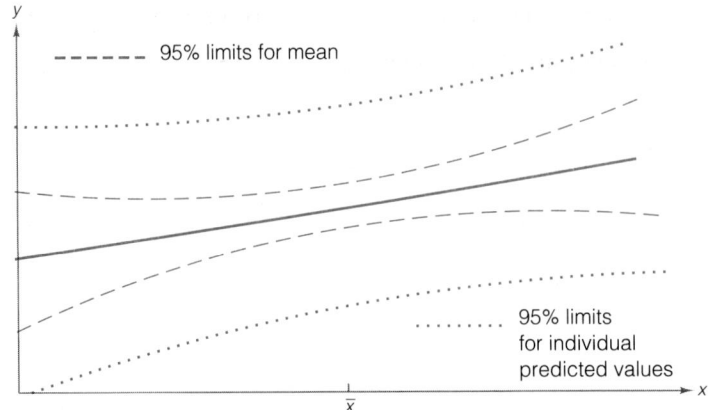

The confidence interval width grows smaller as n is increased; thus, in theory, you can obtain as precise an estimate of the mean value of y as desired (at any given x) by selecting a large enough sample. The prediction interval for a particular value of y also grows smaller as n increases, but there is a lower limit on its width. If you examine the formula for the prediction interval (page 533), you will see that the interval can get no smaller than $\hat{y} \pm z_{\alpha/2}\sigma$.[*] Thus, the only way to obtain more accurate predictions for individual values of y is to reduce the standard deviation of the regression model, σ. This can be accomplished only by improving the model, either by using a curvilinear (rather than linear) relationship with x, or by adding new independent variables to the model, or both. Methods of improving the model are discussed in optional Sections 10.9 and 10.10.

Exercises 10.49–10.58

Learning the Mechanics

10.49 Consider the following pairs of measurements:

x	-2	0	2	4	6	8	10
y	0	3	2	3	8	10	11

  a. Construct a scattergram for these data.
  b. Find the least squares line and plot it on your scattergram.
  c. Find s^2.
  d. Find a 90% confidence interval for the mean value of y when $x_p = 3$. Plot the upper and lower bounds of the confidence interval on your scattergram.
  e. Find a 90% prediction interval for y when $x_p = 3$. Plot the upper and lower bounds of the prediction interval on your scattergram.

---

[*]The result follows from the facts that, for large n, $t_{\alpha/2} \approx z_{\alpha/2}$, $s \approx \sigma$, and the last two terms under the radical in the standard error of the predictor are approximately 0.

f. Compare the widths of the intervals you constructed in parts **d** and **e**. Which is wider and why?

10.50 Consider the following pairs of measurements:

x	4	6	0	5	2	3	2	6	2	1
y	3	5	-1	4	3	2	0	4	1	1

For these data, $SS_{xx} = 38.900$, $SS_{yy} = 33.600$, $SS_{xy} = 32.8$, and $\hat{y} = -.414 + .843x$.
a. Construct a scattergram for the data.
b. Plot the least squares line on your scattergram.
c. Use a 95% confidence interval to estimate the mean value of y when $x_p = 6$. Plot the upper and lower bounds of the interval on your scattergram.
d. Repeat part **c** for $x_p = 3.2$ and $x_p = 0$.
e. Compare the widths of the three confidence intervals you constructed in parts **c** and **d** and explain why they differ.

10.51 Refer to Exercise 10.50.
a. Using no information about x, estimate and calculate a 95% confidence interval for the mean value of y. [*Hint:* Use the one-sample t methodology of Section 6.3.]
b. Plot the estimated mean value and the confidence interval as horizontal lines on your scattergram of Exercise 10.50.
c. Compare the confidence intervals you calculated in parts **c** and **d** of Exercise 10.50 with the one you calculated in part **a** here. Does x seem to contribute information about the mean value of y?
d. Check the answer you gave in part **c** with a statistical test of the null hypothesis $H_0: \beta_1 = 0$ versus $H_a: \beta_1 \neq 0$. Use $\alpha = .05$.

10.52 In fitting a least squares line to $n = 10$ data points, the following quantities were computed: $SS_{xx} = 32$, $\bar{x} = 3$, $SS_{yy} = 26$, $\bar{y} = 4$, and $SS_{xy} = 28$.
a. Find the least squares line.   **b.** Graph the least squares line.
c. Calculate SSE.   **d.** Calculate s^2.
e. Find a 95% confidence interval for the mean value of y when $x_p = 2.5$.
f. Find a 95% prediction interval for y when $x_p = 4$.

Applying the Concepts

10.53 Many variables influence the sales of existing single-family homes. One of these is the interest rate charged for mortgage loans. Shown in the table are the total number of existing single-family homes sold annually, y, and the average annual conventional mortgage interest rate, x, for 1982–1991.

Year	Homes Sold y (1,000s)	Interest Rate x (%)	Year	Homes Sold y (1,000s)	Interest Rate x (%)
1982	1,990	14.8	1987	3,526	8.9
1983	2,719	12.3	1988	3,594	9.0
1984	2,868	12.0	1989	3,346	9.8
1985	3,214	11.2	1990	3,211	9.8
1986	3,565	9.8	1991	3,220	9.2

Source: U.S. Bureau of the Census. *Statistical Abstract of the United States: 1992*, pp. 502, 712.

a. Plot the data points on graph paper.
b. Find the least squares line relating y to x. As a check on your calculations, plot the line on your graph from part **a** to see if the line appears to model the relationship between y and x.
c. Do the data provide sufficient evidence to indicate that mortgage interest rates contribute information for the prediction of annual sales of existing single-family homes? Use $\alpha = .05$.
d. Calculate r and r^2, and interpret their values.
e. Find a 90% confidence interval for the mean annual number of existing single-family homes sold if the average annual mortgage interest rate is 10.0%.
f. Find a 90% prediction interval for the annual number of existing single-family homes sold if the average annual mortgage interest rate is 10.0%.
g. Explain why the widths of the intervals found in parts **e** and **f** differ.

10.54   The reasons given by workers for quitting their jobs generally fall into two categories: (1) seeking or taking a different job; or (2) withdrawing from the labor force. Economic theory suggests that wages and quit rates are related. Evidence regarding this relationship is important for understanding how labor markets operate (Koch and Ragan, 1986). The table lists quit rates (quits per 100 employees) and the average hourly wage in a sample of 15 manufacturing industries during 1986. For these data $\Sigma x_i = 129.050$, $\Sigma x_i^2 = 1,178.960$, $\Sigma y_i = 28.200$, $\Sigma y_i^2 = 64.340$, and $\Sigma x_i y_i = 218.806$.

Industry	Quit Rate	Average Wage	Industry	Quit Rate	Average Wage
1	1.4	$ 8.20	9	2.0	$ 7.99
2	.7	10.35	10	3.8	5.54
3	2.6	6.18	11	2.3	7.50
4	3.4	5.37	12	1.9	6.43
5	1.7	9.94	13	1.4	8.83
6	1.7	9.11	14	1.8	10.93
7	1.0	10.59	15	2.0	8.80
8	.5	13.29			

a. Construct a scattergram for these data.
b. Use the method of least squares to model the quit rate as a function of average hourly wage.
c. Do the data present sufficient evidence to conclude that average hourly wage rate contributes useful information for the prediction of quit rates? What does your model suggest about the relationship between quit rates and wages?
d. Find a 95% prediction interval for the quit rate in an industry with an average hourly wage of $9.00.
e. Estimate the mean quit rate for industries with an average hourly wage of $6.50. Use a 95% confidence interval.

10.55   Refer to Exercise 10.15. Find a 95% confidence interval for the mean price of a gallon of gasoline when crude oil costs $20 per barrel.

10.56   Managers are an important part of any organization's resource base. Accordingly, the organization should be just as concerned about forecasting its future managerial needs as it is with forecasting its needs for, say, the natural resources used in its production processes. According to William F. Glueck (1977), a common forecasting procedure is to model the relationship between sales and the number of managers needed, since "the demand for managers is the result of the increases and decreases in the demand for products and services that an enterprise offers its customers and clients." To develop this relationship, the data shown in the table are collected from a firm's records. For these data $\Sigma x_i = 540$, $\Sigma x_i^2 = 19{,}098$, $\Sigma y_i = 423$, $\Sigma y_i^2 = 10{,}617$, and $\Sigma x_i y_i = 14{,}069$.

Month	Units Sold, x	Managers, y	Month	Units Sold, x	Managers, y
3/88	5	10	9/90	30	22
6/88	4	11	12/90	31	25
9/88	8	10	3/91	36	30
12/88	7	10	6/91	38	30
3/89	9	9	9/91	40	31
6/89	15	10	12/91	41	31
9/89	20	11	3/92	51	32
12/89	21	17	6/92	40	30
3/90	25	19	9/92	48	32
6/90	24	21	12/92	47	32

   a. Use simple linear regression to model the relationship between the number of managers and the number of units sold.

   b. Plot your least squares line on a scattergram of the data. Does it appear that the relationship between y and x is linear? If not, does it appear that your least squares model will provide a useful approximation to the relationship? Explain.

   c. Test the usefulness of your model. Use $\alpha = .05$. State your conclusion in the context of the problem.

   d. The company projects that next May it will sell 39 units. Use your least squares model to construct (1) a 90% confidence interval for the mean number of managers needed when the sales level is 39 and (2) a 90% prediction interval for the number of managers needed next May.

   e. Compare the widths and interpret the two intervals you constructed in part **d**.

10.57 Refer to Exercise 10.24.

   a. Use a 90% confidence interval to estimate the mean useful life of brand A cutting tools when the cutting speed is 45 meters per minute. Repeat for brand B. Compare the width of the two intervals, and comment on the reasons for any difference.

   b. Use a 90% prediction interval to predict the useful life of a brand A cutting tool when the cutting speed is 45 meters per minute. Repeat for brand B. Compare the widths of the two intervals to each other, and to the two intervals you calculated in part **a**. Explain any differences.

   c. Note that the estimation and prediction you performed in parts **a** and **b** were for a value of x that was not included in the original sample; that is, the value $x = 45$ was not part of the sample. However, the value is within the range of x values in the sample, so that the regression model spans the x value for which the estimation and prediction were made. In such situations, estimation and prediction represent *interpolations*.

      Suppose you were asked to predict the useful life for a cutting speed of $x = 100$ meters per minute. Since the given value of x is outside the range of the sample x values, the prediction is an example of *extrapolation*. Predict the useful life of a brand A cutting tool that is operated at 100 meters per minute, and construct a 95% prediction interval for the actual useful life of the tool. What additional assumption do you have to make in order to assure the validity of an extrapolation?

10.58 Explain the implications of using a regression model for estimating the mean value of y for a given value of $x = x_p$ as x_p gets farther from the mean $\bar{x}$. What happens to the width of the confidence interval?

10.8   Using the Computer for Regression

All the examples of simple linear regression that we have presented thus far have required rather tedious calculations involving SS_{yy}, SS_{xx}, SS_{xy}, and so forth. Even with the use of a calculator, the process is laborious and susceptible to error. Fortunately, the use of computers can significantly reduce the labor involved in regression calculations. In this section we introduce the regression output from one statistical software package, the SAS System. Though this is just one of the many statistical packages available that provide regression output, most produce essentially the same quantities, differing only in format and labeling.

To illustrate, suppose a fire insurance company wants to relate the amount of fire damage in major residential fires to the distance between the residence and the nearest fire station. The study is to be conducted in a large suburb of a major city; a sample of 15 recent fires in this suburb is selected. The amount of damage, y, and the distance, x, between the fire and the nearest fire station are recorded for each fire. The results are given in Table 10.7.

TABLE 10.7   Fire Damage Data

Distance from Fire Station	Fire Damage	Distance from Fire Station	Fire Damage
x (miles)	y ($1,000s)	x (miles)	y ($1,000s)
3.4	26.2	2.6	19.6
1.8	17.8	4.3	31.3
4.6	31.3	2.1	24.0
2.3	23.1	1.1	17.3
3.1	27.5	6.1	43.2
5.5	36.0	4.8	36.4
.7	14.1	3.8	26.1
3.0	22.3		

Step 1   First, we hypothesize a model to relate fire damage y to the distance x from the nearest fire station. We will hypothesize a straight-line probabilistic model:

$$y = \beta_0 + \beta_1 x + \epsilon$$

Step 2   Next, we enter the data into the computer and use SAS to estimate the unknown parameters in the deterministic component of the hypothesized model.

The SAS output is presented in Figure 10.17. We have shaded the parts of the printout corresponding to most of the key simple linear regression quantities introduced in this chapter.

FIGURE 10.17 ►

SAS printout for fire damagae regression analysis.

```
                                FIRE DAMAGE EXAMPLE
                     STRAIGHT-LINE MODEL WITH PREDICTION INTERVALS

Model: MODEL1
Dep Variable: Y

                              Analysis of Variance

                         Sum of            Mean
     Source      DF      Squares          Square      F Value     Prob>F

     Model        1     841.76636        841.76636    156.886     0.0001
     Error       13      69.75098          5.36546
     C Total     14     911.51733


           Root MSE       2.31635      R-Square      0.9235
           Dep Mean      26.41333      Adj R-Sq      0.9176
           C.V.           8.76961


                              Parameter Estimates

                       Parameter      Standard     T for H0:
     Variable   DF     Estimate         Error     Parameter=0    Prob > |T|

     INTERCEP    1     10.277929      1.42027781      7.237        0.0001
     X           1      4.919331      0.39274775     12.525        0.0001


                                    Predict              Lower95%   Upper95%
     Obs  X              Y           Value    Residual    Predict    Predict

       1   3.4      26.2000        27.0037    -0.8037     21.8344    32.1729
       2   1.8      17.8000        19.1327    -1.3327     13.8141    24.4514
       3   4.6      31.3000        32.9068    -1.6068     27.6186    38.1951
       4   2.3      23.1000        21.5924     1.5076     16.3577    26.8271
       5   3.1      27.5000        25.5279     1.9721     20.3573    30.6984
       6   5.5      36.0000        37.3342    -1.3342     31.8334    42.8351
       7   0.7      14.1000        13.7215     0.3785      8.1087    19.3342
       8   3        22.3000        25.0359    -2.7359     19.8622    30.2097
       9   2.6      19.6000        23.0682    -3.4682     17.8678    28.2686
      10   4.3      31.3000        31.4311    -0.1311     26.1908    36.6713
      11   2.1      24.0000        20.6085     3.3915     15.3442    25.8729
      12   1.1      17.3000        15.6892     1.6108     10.1999    21.1785
      13   6.1      43.2000        40.2858     2.9142     34.5906    45.9811
      14   4.8      36.4000        33.8907     2.5093     28.5640    39.2175
      15   3.8      26.1000        28.9714    -2.8714     23.7843    34.1585
      16 * 3.5         .           27.4956       .        22.3239    32.6672

Sum of Residuals          -3.73035E-14
Sum of Squared Residuals      69.7510
Predicted Resid SS (Press)    93.2117
```

The estimates of the y-intercept β_0 and the slope β_1 are found about halfway down the printout on the left-hand side, under the column labeled **Parameter Estimate** and in the rows labeled **INTERCEP** and **X,** respectively. The values are $\beta_0 = 10.277929$ and $\hat{\beta}_1 = 4.919331$. Consequently, the least squares equation is

$$\hat{y} = 10.278 + 4.919x$$

This prediction equation is graphed in Figure 10.18, along with a plot of the data points.

FIGURE 10.18 ▶

Least squares model for the fire damage data

The least squares estimate of the slope, $\hat{\beta}_1 = 4.919$, implies that the estimated mean damage increases by \$4,919 per each additional mile from the fire station. This interpretation is valid over the range of x, or from .7 to 6.1 miles from the station. The estimated y-intercept, $\hat{\beta}_0 = 10.278$, has the interpretation that a fire 0 miles from the fire station has an estimated mean damage of \$10,278. Although this would seem to apply to the fire station itself, remember that the y-intercept can be interpreted meaningfully only if $x = 0$ is within the sampled range of the independent variable.

Step 3   Now, we specify the probability distribution of the random error component, ϵ. The assumptions about the distribution will be identical to those listed in Section 10.3. Although we know that these assumptions are not completely satisfied (they rarely are for any practical problem), we are willing to assume they are approximately satisfied for this example.

We also need to estimate σ^2, the variance of ϵ. The estimate of σ^2 is given in the upper portion of the printout under the column heading **Mean Square** and in the row labeled **Error.** The value (shaded) is $s^2 = 5.36546$. The estimate of the standard deviation σ is directly to the right of the heading **Root MSE:** $s = 2.31635$.

Step 4 We can now check the usefulness of the hypothesized model—that is, whether x really contributes information for the prediction of y using the straight-line model. First test the null hypothesis that the slope β_1 is zero—i.e., that there is no linear relationship between fire damage and the distance from the nearest fire station—against the alternative that the slope β_1 differs from zero. We test

$$H_0: \quad \beta_1 = 0$$
$$H_a: \quad \beta_1 \neq 0$$

The t statistic for the test is given (shaded) in the center of the printout under the column heading **T for HO: Parameter = 0** in the row corresponding to **X**. The value shown is $t = 12.525$.

To determine which hypothesis this test statistic supports, we can establish a rejection region using the t table (Table VI of Appendix B). However, the printout makes this unnecessary, because the observed significance level, or p-value, is shown (shaded) immediately to the right of the t statistic, under the column heading **Prob > |T|**. Remember that if the observed significance level is less than the α value you select, then the test statistic supports the alternative hypothesis at that level. For example, if we select $\alpha = .05$ in this example, the observed significance level of .0001 given on the printout indicates that we should reject H_0. We can conclude that there is sufficient evidence at $\alpha = .05$ to infer that a linear relationship between fire damage and distance from the station is useful for predicting damage. Furthermore, it appears (as we might suspect) that fire damage increases as the distance increases.

Note: If you wish to conduct a one-tailed test, the observed significance level is half that given on the printout (assuming the sign of the test statistic agrees with the alternative hypothesis). Thus, if we were testing $H_0: \beta_1 = 0$ versus $H_a: \beta_1 > 0$ in this example, the t statistic is positive, agreeing with H_a, so that the observed significance level would be $\frac{1}{2}(.0001) = .00005$.

We gain additional information about the relationship by forming a confidence interval for the slope β_1. Although a confidence interval for β_1 is not shown on the printout, the estimate of β_1 and the standard error of the estimate, $s_{\hat{\beta}_1}$, are given. Recall that a 95% confidence interval for β_1 is

$$\hat{\beta}_1 \pm t_{.025} s_{\hat{\beta}_1}$$

Substituting $\hat{\beta}_1 = 4.919$ and $s_{\hat{\beta}_1} = .39274775$ (this value is given under the **Standard Error** column in the row corresponding to **X**), we obtain

$$4.919 \pm (2.160)(.393) = 4.919 \pm .849 = (4.070, 5.768)$$

We estimate that the interval from \$4,070 to \$5,768 encloses the mean increase (β_1) in fire damage per additional mile distance from the fire station.

The coefficient of determination for the model is shown (shaded) to the right of **R-square** in the upper portion of the printout. This value

$$r^2 = .9235$$

implies that approximately 92% of the sum of squares of deviations in the sample of y values about $\bar{y}$ is explained by the distance, x, between the fire and the fire station.

For reasons explained in Section 10.5, the coefficient of correlation is not given on the printout. We can compute its value by taking the square root of r^2, but we must remember that r has the same sign (positive or negative) as $\hat{\beta}_1$. Since $\hat{\beta}_1 = 4.919$ is positive, $r = \sqrt{r^2} = \sqrt{.9235} \approx .96$.

The high positive correlation provides further support for our conclusion that β_1 differs from 0; it appears that fire damage and distance from the fire station are highly correlated.

In summary, the inference about β_1 and the values of r^2 and r all point to a strong linear relationship between y and x.

Step 5 We are now prepared to use the least squares model. Suppose the insurance company wants to predict the fire damage if a major residential fire were to occur 3.5 miles from the nearest fire station; i.e., $x_p = 3.5$.

Predicted y values and the corresponding prediction intervals are given in the lower portion of the SAS printout. To find the 95% prediction interval for the fire damage y when the distance from the fire station is $x = 3.5$ miles, first locate the value 3.5 in the column labeled X (the last value in the column). The prediction is given in the center column labeled **Predict Value** in the row corresponding to 3.5:

$$\hat{y} = 27.4956$$

The lower and upper confidence bounds are given in the columns headed **Lower** and **Upper 95% Predict,** respectively:

$$\text{Lower} = 22.3239 \qquad \text{Upper} = 32.6672$$

Thus, the model yields a 95% prediction interval for fire damage in a major residential fire 3.5 miles from the nearest station of \$22,324 to \$32,667.

Caution for Step 5 We would not use this prediction model to make predictions for homes less than .7 mile or more than 6.1 miles from the nearest fire station. A look at the data in Table 10.7 (page 540) reveals that all the x values fall between .7 and 6.1. It is dangerous to use the model to make predictions outside the region in which the sample data fall. A straight line might not provide a good model for the relationship between the mean value of y and x for values of x beyond the range of the sample data.

In this section we showed how the computer can alleviate much of the burden of calculation involved in a regression analysis, and enable us to spend more time on the interpretation of the model. The time spent in learning how to read computer regression output is a good investment. In optional Section 10.9, we rely exclusively on computer printouts to conduct a multiple regression analysis.

Exercises 10.59 – 10.60

Learning the Mechanics

10.59 Refer to Exercise 10.14, in which the extent of retaliation is related to the salary of 15 whistle blowers using a least squares model. A SAS printout for this regression model is given.

```
                    RETALIATION INDEX VS. SALARY

Model: MODEL1
Dep Variable: R_INDEX

                    Analysis of Variance

                     Sum of        Mean
      Source    DF   Squares      Square     F Value     Prob>F

      Model      1  20853.93900  20853.93900   0.925     0.3538
      Error     13 293208.46100  22554.49700
      C Total   14 314062.40000


      Root MSE      150.18155    R-Square    0.0664
      Dep Mean      499.80000    Adj R-Sq   -0.0054
      C.V.           30.04833


                    Parameter Estimates

                  Parameter     Standard    T for H0:
      Variable  DF  Estimate      Error    Parameter=0   Prob > |T|

      INTERCEP   1  575.028672  87.31829499    6.585      0.0001
      SALARY     1   -0.002186   0.00227386   -0.962      0.3538


                             Predict              Lower95%  Upper95%
      Obs  SALARY  R_INDEX    Value   Residual      Mean      Mean

        1   62000   301.0     439.5    -138.5       280.1     598.8
        2   36500   550.0     495.2     54.7770     410.8     579.6
        3   17600   755.0     536.5    218.5        418.9     654.2
        4   20000   327.0     531.3   -204.3        421.6     641.0
        5   30100   500.0     509.2     -9.2163     422.8     595.6
        6   35000   377.0     498.5   -121.5        414.7     582.3
        7   47500   290.0     471.2   -181.2        365.6     576.8
        8   54000   452.0     457.0     -4.9600     329.4     584.6
        9   15800   535.0     540.5     -5.4827     416.5     664.5
       10   44000   455.0     478.8    -23.8246     382.7     574.9
       11   46600   615.0     473.1    141.9        370.2     576.1
       12   12100   700.0     548.6    151.4        410.6     686.5
       13   62000   650.0     439.5    210.5        280.1     598.8
       14   21000   630.0     529.1    100.9        422.6     635.7
       15   11900   360.0     549.0   -189.0        410.3     687.7
```

a. Find the least squares estimates of the intercept β_0 and the slope β_1.

b. Identify the values of SSE, s^2, and s. Based on the standard deviation, how accurately do you expect to be able to predict the retaliation index using the salary of the whistle blower?

c. Find and interpret the coefficient of determination r^2.

d. Find the t statistic and its observed significance level for testing the usefulness of the model. Interpret the values.

e. Find and interpret the 95% confidence interval for the mean retaliation index of whistle blowers with salaries of $35,000.

10.60 Refer to Exercise 10.32, in which an index of managerial success was related to the number of interactions with outsiders. The SAS simple linear regression printout for these data is shown.

Source	DF	Sum of Squares	Mean Square	F Value	Prob>F
Model	1	606.03751	606.03751	1.610	0.2216
Error	17	6400.59407	376.50553		
C Total	18	7006.63158			

Root MSE	19.40375	R-Square	0.0865
Dep Mean	54.57895	Adj R-Sq	0.0328
C.V.	35.55171		

Parameter Estimates

Variable	DF	Parameter Estimate	Standard Error	T for H0: Parameter=0	Prob > |T|
INTERCEP	1	44.130454	9.36159293	4.714	0.0002
INTERACT	1	0.236617	0.18650103	1.269	0.2216

a. Find the least squares equation, and compare it to the one you calculated in Exercise 10.32.

b. Find the standard deviation s, and interpret the value in terms of this exercise.

c. Find and interpret r^2.

d. Is there sufficient evidence to indicate that the model is useful for predicting y? What is the observed significance level of the test?

10.9   Multiple Regression Models (Optional)

Most practical applications of regression use models that are more complex than the first-order (straight-line) model. For example, a realistic probabilistic model for monthly sales revenue would include more than just advertising expenditures in order to provide a good predictive model for sales. Factors such as season, inventory on hand, size of sales force, and price are a few of the many variables that might influence sales. Thus, we would want to incorporate these and other potentially important independent variables into the model if we need to make accurate predictions.

Probabilistic models that include terms involving x^2, x^3 (or higher-order terms), or more than one independent variable are called **multiple regression models**. The general form of these models is

$$\underbrace{y = \beta_0 + \beta_1 x_1 + \beta_2 x_2 + \cdots + \beta_k x_k +}_{\substack{\text{Deterministic}\\\text{portion of model}}} \overbrace{\epsilon}^{\substack{\text{Random}\\\text{error}}}$$

The dependent variable y is now written as a function of k independent variables, $x_1, x_2, \ldots, x_k$. The random error term is added to make the model probabilistic rather than deterministic. The value of the coefficient β_i determines the contribution of the independent variable x_i, given that the other x variables are held constant. β_0 is the y-intercept. The coefficients $\beta_0, \beta_1, \ldots, \beta_k$ will usually be unknown, because they represent population parameters.

At first glance it might appear that the regression model shown above would not allow for anything other than straight-line relationships between y and the independent variables, but this is not true. Actually, $x_1, x_2, \ldots, x_k$ can be functions of variables as long as the functions do not contain unknown parameters. For example, the dollar sales, y, of new housing in a region could be a function of the independent variables

$x_1 = $ Mortgage interest rate

$x_2 = $ (Mortgage interest rate)$^2 = x_1^2$

$x_3 = $ Unemployment rate in the region

$x_4 = x_1 x_3 = $ (Mortgage interest rate) $\times$ (Unemployment rate)

and so on. [*Note:* The variable x_4 representing the cross-product of two other independent variables is called an **interaction term.** You could even insert a cyclical term (if it would be useful) of the form $x_5 = \sin t$, where t is a time variable.] The multiple regression model is quite versatile and can be made to model many different types of response variables. Some typical regression models are shown in the box.

Some Typical Multiple Regression Models

A **first-order model** relating y to $x_1, x_2, \ldots, x_5$:

$$y = \beta_0 + \beta_1 x_1 + \beta_2 x_2 + \beta_3 x_3 + \beta_4 x_4 + \beta_5 x_5 + \epsilon$$

An **interaction model** relating y to x_1, x_2, and x_3:

$$y = \beta_0 + \beta_1 x_1 + \beta_2 x_2 + \beta_3 x_3 + \beta_4 x_1 x_2 + \beta_5 x_1 x_3 + \beta_6 x_2 x_3 + \epsilon$$

A **second-order model** relating y to two quantitative variables, x_1 and x_2:

$$y = \beta_0 + \beta_1 x_1 + \beta_2 x_2 + \beta_3 x_1 x_2 + \beta_4 x_1^2 + \beta_5 x_2^2$$

As shown in the accompanying box, we use the same steps to develop the multiple regression model as we used for the simple regression model.

Step 1   Hypothesize the deterministic component of the model. This component relates the mean, $E(y)$, to the independent variables, $x_1, x_2, \ldots, x_k$. This involves the choice of the independent variables to be included in the model.

Step 2   Use the sample data to estimate the unknown model parameters $\beta_0, \beta_1, \beta_2, \ldots, \beta_k$.

Step 3   Specify the probability distribution of the random error term, ϵ, and estimate the standard deviation of this distribution, σ. The assumptions about the distribution of ϵ are similar to those in Section 10.3:

1. For any given set of values of $x_1, x_2, \ldots, x_k$, the random error ϵ has a normal probability distribution with mean equal to 0 and variance equal to σ^2.

2. The random errors are independent (in a probabilistic sense).

Step 4   Statistically evaluate the usefulness of the model.

Step 5   When satisfied that the model is useful, use it for prediction, estimation, and other purposes.

CASE STUDY 10.2 / Predicting Corporate Executive Compensation

Towers, Perrin, Forster & Crosby (TPF&C), an international management consulting firm, has developed a unique and interesting application of multiple regression analysis. Many firms are interested in evaluating their management salary structure, and TPF&C uses multiple regression models to accomplish this salary evaluation. The Compensation Management Service, as TPF&C calls it, measures both the internal and external consistency of a company's pay policies to determine whether they reflect management's intent.

The dependent variable y used to represent executive compensation is annual salary. The independent variables used to explain salary structure include the executive's age, education, rank, and bonus eligibility; number of employees under the executive's direct supervision; as well as variables that describe the company for which the executive works, such as annual sales, profit, and total assets.

The initial step in developing models for executive compensation is to obtain a sample of executives from various client firms, which TPF&C calls the Compensation Data Bank. The data for these executives are used to estimate the model coefficients (the β parameters), and these estimates are then substituted into the linear model to form a prediction equation. To predict a particular executive's compensation, TPF&C substitutes into the prediction equation the values of the independent variables that pertain to the executive (age, rank, etc.).

The method of fitting multiple regression models is identical to that of fitting the first-order (straight-line) model—namely, the method of least squares. That is, we choose the estimated model

$$\hat{y} = \hat{\beta}_0 + \hat{\beta}_1 x_1 + \cdots + \hat{\beta}_k x_k$$

that minimizes

$$\text{SSE} = \sum (y_i - \hat{y}_i)^2$$

As in the case of the straight-line model, the sample estimates $\hat{\beta}_0, \hat{\beta}_1, \ldots, \hat{\beta}_k$ will be obtained as solutions to a set of simultaneous linear equations.[*]

The primary difference between fitting the simple and multiple regression models is computational difficulty. The $(k + 1)$ simultaneous linear equations that must be solved to find the $(k + 1)$ estimated coefficients $\hat{\beta}_0, \hat{\beta}_1, \ldots, \hat{\beta}_k$ are often difficult (sometimes impossible) to solve with a calculator. Consequently, we resort to the use of computers. Many computer packages have been developed to fit a multiple regression model by the method of least squares. We will present output from several of the more popular computer packages, commencing, in our first example, with the computer output from the SAS System. Since the SAS regression output is similar to that of most other package regression programs, you should have little trouble interpreting regression output from other packages as you encounter them in future examples and exercises, at your computer center, or in using a microcomputer.

EXAMPLE 10.5

A collector of antique grandfather clocks believes that the price received for the clocks at an antique auction increases with the age of the clocks and with the number of bidders. Thus, the following first-order model hypothesized is

$$y = \beta_0 + \beta_1 x_1 + \beta_2 x_2 + \epsilon$$

where

y = Auction price x_1 = Age of clock (years) x_2 = Number of bidders

A sample of 32 auction prices of grandfather clocks, along with their ages and the number of bidders, is given in Table 10.8 on page 550.

---

[*]Students who are familiar with calculus should note that $\hat{\beta}_0, \hat{\beta}_1, \ldots, \hat{\beta}_k$ are the solutions to the set of equations $\partial\text{SSE}/\partial\hat{\beta}_0 = 0$, $\partial\text{SSE}/\partial\hat{\beta}_1 = 0, \ldots, \partial\text{SSE}/\partial\hat{\beta}_k = 0$. The solution, given in matrix notation, is presented in many of the texts listed in the references at the end of the chapter.

TABLE 10.8   Auction Price Data

Age	Bidders	Price	Age	Bidders	Price
x_1	x_2	y	x_1	x_2	y
127	13	$1,235	170	14	$2,131
115	12	1,080	182	8	1,550
127	7	845	162	11	1,884
150	9	1,522	184	10	2,041
156	6	1,047	143	6	854
182	11	1,979	159	9	1,483
156	12	1,822	108	14	1,055
132	10	1,253	175	8	1,545
137	9	1,297	108	6	729
113	9	946	179	9	1,792
137	15	1,713	111	15	1,175
117	11	1,024	187	8	1,593
137	8	1,147	111	7	785
153	6	1,092	115	7	744
117	13	1,152	194	5	1,356
126	10	1,336	168	7	1,262

The model

$$y = \beta_0 + \beta_1 x_1 + \beta_2 x_2 + \epsilon$$

is fit to the data, and a portion of the SAS printout is shown in Figure 10.19.

```
SOURCE              DF    SUM OF SQUARES       MEAN SQUARE     F VALUE          PR > F

MODEL                2    4277159.70340504   2138579.85170252   120.65          0.0001
ERROR               29     514034.51534496     17725.32811534                 ROOT MSE
CORRECTED TOTAL     31    4791194.21875000      R-SQUARE                     133.13650181
                                               0.892713

                                      T FOR H0:        PR > !T!    STD ERROR OF
PARAMETER            ESTIMATE       PARAMETER = 0                   ESTIMATE

INTERCEPT         -1336.72205214        -7.71          0.0001     173.35612607
X1                   12.73619884        14.11          0.0001       0.90238049
X2                   85.81513260         9.86          0.0001       8.70575681
```

FIGURE 10.19 ▲ SAS printout for Example 10.5

a. Give the least squares prediction equation for y.

b. Interpret the β estimates.

c. Test the hypothesis that the auction price increases as the number of bidders increases (and age is held constant), i.e., $\beta_2 > 0$. Use $\alpha = .05$.

d. Find and interpret the coefficient of determination for the model.

e. Test the overall (global) adequacy of the model. Use $\alpha = .05$.

a. The least squares estimates of β_0, β_1, and β_2, shaded on the printout, are

$$\hat{\beta}_0 = -1,336.722 \qquad \hat{\beta}_1 = 12.736 \qquad \hat{\beta}_2 = 85.815$$

Therefore, the least squares prediction equation is

$$\hat{y} = 1,336.722 + 12.736x_1 + 85.815x_2$$

b. For this first-order model, β_1 and β_2 are both slopes and are easily interpreted. For example, β_1 is the change in auction price y for every 1-year increase in age x_1, holding x_2 constant. Since $\hat{\beta}_1 = 12.736$, we estimate that the mean auction price *increases* \$12.74 per year of age of the clock, for a fixed number of bidders. Similarly, since $\hat{\beta}_2 = 85.815$, we estimate that the mean price increases by \$85.82 per additional bidder for a fixed age clock.

We must be careful not to try to interpret the estimated intercept $\hat{\beta}_0 = -1,336.72$ in the same way we interpreted $\hat{\beta}_1$ and $\hat{\beta}_2$. You might think that this implies a negative price for clocks 0 years of age with 0 bidders. However, these zeros are meaningless numbers in this example, since the ages range from 108 to 194 and the number of bidders ranges from 5 to 15. Keep in mind that we are modeling y within the range of values observed for the predictor variables and that the interpretations of the models for values of the independent variables outside their sampled ranges can be very misleading.

c. The hypothesis of interest concerns the parameter β_2. Specifically,

$$H_0: \ \beta_2 = 0$$
$$H_a: \ \beta_2 > 0$$

Testing a hypothesis about a single β parameter that appears in any multiple regression model is accomplished in exactly the same manner as described in Section 10.4. The form of the t test is shown in the preceding box.

The test statistic, shaded on the printout, is $t = 9.86$, and the two-tailed p-value (also shaded) is .0001. For this one-tailed test, the appropriate p-value is $.0001/2 = .00005$. Since $\alpha = .05$ exceeds this p-value, we have sufficient evidence to reject $H_0: \beta_2 = 0$ in favor of $H_a: \beta_2 > 0$. Thus, the collector can conclude that the mean auction price of the clocks increases as the number x_2 of bidders increases, when age (x_1) is held constant.

d. In Section 10.6 we discussed the coefficient of determination r^2 for a straight-line model. The coefficient of determination for a multiple regression model is called the **sample multiple coefficient of determination, R^2**, where

---

*To test the null hypothesis that a parameter, β_i, equals some value other than 0, say $H_0: \beta_i = \beta_{i0}$, use the test statistic $t = (\hat{\beta}_i - \beta_{i0})/s_{\hat{\beta}_i}$. All other aspects of the test are as described in the box.

$$R^2 = 1 - \frac{\Sigma (y_i - \hat{y}_i)^2}{\Sigma (y_i - \bar{y})^2} = 1 - \frac{SSE}{SS_{yy}} = \frac{SS_{yy} - SSE}{SS_{yy}} = \frac{\text{Explained variability}}{\text{Total variability}}$$

and $\hat{y}_i$ is the predicted value of y_i for the model. Just as for the simple linear model, R^2 is a sample statistic that represents the fraction of the sample variation of the y values (measured by SS_{yy}) that is attributable to the regression model. Thus, $R^2 = 0$ implies a complete lack of fit of the model to the data, and $R^2 = 1$ implies a perfect fit, with the model passing through every sample data point. In general, the larger the value of R^2, the better the model fits the data.

The value $R^2 = .8927$ for our model is shaded on the printout. This high value of R^2 implies that about 89% of the sample variation in auction price is attributable to, or explained by, the independent variables, age x_1 and number of bidders x_2. Thus, R^2 is a sample statistic that tells how well the model fits the data, and thereby represents a measure of the usefulness of the model.*

Test of an Individual Parameter Coefficient in the Multiple Regression Model

$$y = \beta_0 + \beta_1 x_1 + \beta_2 x_2 + \cdots + \beta_k x_k + \epsilon$$

One-Tailed Test

H_0: $\beta_i = 0$*
H_a: $\beta_i > 0$
   (or $\beta_i < 0$)

Test statistic: $t = \dfrac{\hat{\beta}_i}{s_{\hat{\beta}_i}}$

Rejection region: $t > t_\alpha$
   (or $t < -t_\alpha$)

Two-Tailed Test

H_0: $\beta_i = 0$*
H_a: $\beta_i \neq 0$

Test statistic: $t = \dfrac{\hat{\beta}_i}{s_{\hat{\beta}_i}}$

Rejection region: $t > t_{\alpha/2}$
   or $t < -t_{\alpha/2}$

where

   n = Number of observations
   k = Number of independent variables in the model

and $t_{\alpha/2}$ is based on $[n - (k + 1)]$ df.

Assumptions: See page 548 for the assumptions about the probability distribution of the random error component ϵ.

---

*The value of R^2 must be examined with care. The value of R^2 will increase as more and more variables are added to the model. Consequently, you could force R^2 to take a value very close to 1 even though the model contributes no information for the prediction of y. In fact, R^2 will equal 1 when the number of terms in the model equals the number of data points. Therefore, you should not rely solely on the value of R^2 to tell you whether the model is useful for predicting y.

e. One method of testing for the overall usefulness of the model is to conduct t tests on each of the slope parameters in the model. In other words, test both null hypotheses $H_0: \beta_1 = 0$ and $H_0: \beta_2 = 0$. Unfortunately, conducting t tests on each β parameter in a model is not a good way to determine whether a model is contributing information for the prediction of y. If we were to conduct a series of t tests to determine whether the independent variables are contributing to the predictive relationship, it is very likely that we would make one or more errors in deciding which terms to retain in the model and which to exclude. For example, suppose that all the β parameters (except β_0) are in fact equal to 0. Although the probability of concluding that any *single* β parameter differs from 0 is only α, the probability of rejecting *at least one* of a set of null hypotheses when each is true is much higher.* Thus, in multiple regression models for which a large number of independent variables are being considered, conducting a series of t tests may include a large number of insignificant variables and exclude some useful ones. If we want to test the usefulness of a multiple regression model, we will need a global test (one that encompasses all the β parameters).

For our model, the test

$$H_0: \quad \beta_1 = \beta_2 = 0$$

$$H_a: \quad \text{At least one of the parameters } \beta_1 \text{ and } \beta_2 \text{ is nonzero}$$

would formally test the global usefulness of the model. The test statistic used to test this hypothesis is called an F statistic. Several equivalent formulas for computing the F statistic are shown in the accompanying box. The computed F statistic is given at the top of the SAS printout, Figure 10.19, under **F VALUE.** This value (shaded) is $F = 120.65$.

The formulas in the box on page 554 indicate that the F statistic is the ratio of the *explained* variability (i.e., R^2) divided by the model degrees of freedom to *unexplained* variability (i.e., $1 - R^2$) divided by the error degrees of freedom. Thus, the larger the proportion of the total variability accounted for by the model, the larger the F statistic. Consequently, "large" values of F will lead us to reject H_0 and conclude that the model is useful for predicting y. The formal rejection region is given by $F > F_\alpha$, where values of F_α are given in Tables VII, VIII, IX, and X of Appendix B. However, since most computer packages provide the observed significance level (p-value) of the F test, we will use the p-value approach to test the hypothesis.

The p-value of the test, given under **PR > F** in Figure 10.19, is .0001. This means that we would reject the null hypothesis $H_0: \beta_1 = \beta_2 = 0$ at any α value greater than .0001. Therefore, the data provide strong evidence that at least one of the model coefficients is nonzero. With a high degree of confidence, the model is statistically useful for predicting auction prices.

---

*You can see why this is true by considering the following analogy. The probability of observing a head on a single toss of a coin is .5, but the probability of observing *at least one* head in five tosses of a coin is .97.

Testing Global Usefulness of the Multiple Regression Model

H_0: $\beta_1 = \beta_2 = \cdots = \beta_k = 0$
   (All model terms are unimportant for predicting y)

H_a: At least one $\beta_i \neq 0$
   (At least one model term is useful for predicting y)

Test statistic: $$F = \frac{(\mathrm{SS}_{yy} - \mathrm{SSE})/k}{\mathrm{SSE}/[n - (k + 1)]}$$

$$= \frac{R^2/k}{(1 - R^2)/[n - (k + 1)]}$$

$$= \frac{\mathrm{MEAN\ SQUARE(MODEL)}}{\mathrm{MEAN\ SQUARE(ERROR)}}$$

where n is the sample size and k is the number of terms in the model.

Rejection region: $F > F_\alpha$, with $\nu_1 = k$ numerator degrees of freedom and $\nu_2 = [n - (k + 1)]$ denominator degrees of freedom. [Values of F_α are given in Tables VII, VIII, IX, and X of Appendix B.]

Assumptions: The standard regression assumptions about the random error component.

Caution: A rejection of the null hypothesis leads to the conclusion (at the α level of significance) that the model is useful. However, "useful" does not necessarily mean "best." Another model may prove even more useful in terms of providing more reliable estimates and predictions. **This global F test is usually regarded as a test that the model *must* pass to merit further consideration.**

Can we be sure that the best prediction model has been found if the global F test indicates that a model is useful? Unfortunately, we cannot. The addition of other independent variables, cross-product (interaction) terms, or second-order (squared) terms may further improve the usefulness of the model as Example 10.6 illustrates.

EXAMPLE 10.6

Refer to Example 10.5. Suppose the collector, having observed many auctions, believes that the *rate of increase* of the auction price with age will be driven upward by a large number of bidders. Thus, instead of a relationship like that shown in Figure 10.20(a), where the rate of increase in price with age is the same for any number of bidders, the collector believes the relationship is like that shown in Figure 10.20(b).

Note that as the number of bidders increases from 5 to 15, the slope of the price versus age line increases. When the slope of the relationship between y and one independent variable (x_1) depends on the value of a second independent variable (x_2), as is the case here, we say that x_1 and x_2 **interact**. A model that accounts for this type of interaction is written

$$y = \beta_0 + \beta_1 x_1 + \beta_2 x_2 + \beta_3 x_1 x_2 + \epsilon$$

FIGURE 10.20 ▶

Examples of no interaction and interaction models

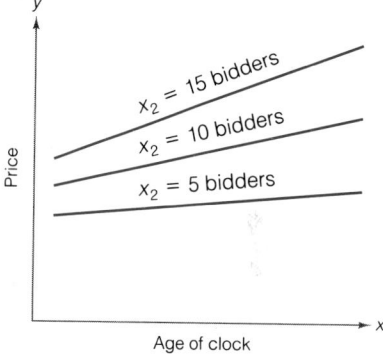

a. No interaction between x_1 and x_2

b. Interaction between x_1 and x_2

Note that the increase in the mean price, $E(y)$, for each 1-year increase in age, x_1, is no longer given by the constant, β_1, but is now $\beta_1 + \beta_3 x_2$. That is, the amount $E(y)$ increases for each 1-unit increase in x_1 is *dependent on the number of bidders*, x_2. Thus, the two variables x_1 and x_2 interact to affect y.

The 32 data points listed in Table 10.8 were used to fit the first-order model with interaction. A portion of the SAS printout is shown in Figure 10.21.

SOURCE	DF	SUM OF SQUARES	MEAN SQUARE	F VALUE	PR > F
MODEL	3	4572547.98717668	1524182.66239223	195.19	0.0001
ERROR	28	218646.23157332	7808.79398476		ROOT MSE
CORRECTED TOTAL	31	4791194.21875000		R-SQUARE	88.36738077
				0.954365	

PARAMETER	ESTIMATE	T FOR H0: PARAMETER = 0	PR > |T|	STD ERROR OF ESTIMATE
INTERCEPT	322.75435309	1.10	0.2806	293.32514660
X1	0.87328775	0.43	0.6688	2.01965115
X2	-93.40991991	-3.14	0.0039	29.70767946
X1*X2	1.29789828	6.15	0.0001	0.21102602

FIGURE 10.21 ▲

Portion of the SAS printout for the model with interaction

Test the hypothesis that the price–age slope increases as the number of bidders increases—i.e., that age x_1 and number of bidders x_2 interact positively.

Solution

The model is

$$y = \beta_0 + \beta_1 x_1 + \beta_2 x_2 + \beta_3 x_1 x_2 + \epsilon$$

and the hypothesis of interest to the collector concerns the parameter β_3. Specifically,

$$H_0: \ \beta_3 = 0 \qquad H_a: \ \beta_3 > 0$$

The test statistic, shaded on the printout, is $t = 6.15$, and the corresponding two-tailed observed significance level (also shaded) is .0001. Thus, the p-value for the test is $.0001/2 = .00005$. At any reasonable α, there is sufficient evidence to reject H_0. Thus, the collector can conclude that the rate of change of the mean price of the clocks with age increases as the number of bidders increases—i.e., x_1 and x_2 interact positively. Thus, it appears that the interaction term should be included in the model.

One Note of Caution   Although the coefficient of x_2 is negative ($\hat{\beta}_2 = -93.41$), this does *not* imply that the auction price decreases as the number of bidders increases. Since interaction is present, the rate of change (slope) of mean auction price with the number of bidders *depends on* x_1, the age of the clock. Thus, for example, the estimated rate of change of y with x_2 for a 150-year-old clock is

$$\text{Estimated } x_2 \text{ slope} = \hat{\beta}_2 + \hat{\beta}_3 x_1 = -93.41 + 1.30(150) = 101.60$$

In other words, we estimate that the auction price of a 150-year-old clock will *increase* by \$101.60 for every additional bidder. Although this rate of increase will vary as x_1 is changed, it will remain positive for the range of values of x_1 included in the sample. Extreme care is needed in interpreting the signs and sizes of coefficients in a multiple regression model.

We conclude this section with a case study summarizing the elements of a multiple regression analysis.

CASE STUDY 10.3 / Predicting the Sales of Crest Toothpaste

Knowing the determinants of demand for its product would help a company focus its marketing efforts on the appropriate market segments (e.g., middle-income families with school-age children). In addition, knowing the relationship between those determinants and product sales would assist the company in predicting sales and, therefore, in its planning throughout the organization. Using a model developed by Roger D. Carlson (1981) as her starting point, Carolyn I. Allmon (1982) employed multiple regression analysis to investigate the determinants of demand for Crest toothpaste and to predict Crest's sales.

Allmon modeled this year's sales of Crest as a function of current advertising expenditures, personal disposable income, and the ratio of Crest's advertising budget to that for Colgate toothpaste, Crest's closest competitor. Specifically, Allmon hypothesized the model

$$y = \beta_0 + \beta_1 x_1 + \beta_2 x_2 + \beta_3 x_3 + \epsilon$$

where

> y = Sales of Crest toothpaste, computed by multiplying Crest's market share by the total market (thousands of dollars)
>
> x_1 = Advertising budget for Crest (thousands of dollars)
>
> x_2 = U.S. personal disposable income (billions of dollars)
>
> x_3 = Ratio of Crest's advertising budget to Colgate's advertising budget (rounded to nearest hundredth)

Allmon hypothesized that the effect of each independent variable on sales is positive—i.e., that β_1, β_2, and β_3 have positive signs. Her belief that β_1 is positive follows from the fact that Procter and Gamble, the firm that manufactures Crest, has advertised Crest heavily for many years. It would be unlikely to do this if advertising did not help sales. That β_2 should be positive follows from a study of toothbrushing frequency which showed that as family income increases, family members brush their teeth more frequently. Allmon argued that since Colgate and Crest are competitors, sales of Colgate should affect sales of Crest and vice versa. Therefore, the larger x_3 is, the higher y should be. Accordingly, β_3 should be positive.

The model was estimated using the method of least squares on data collected for the years 1967–1979. The results were

$$\hat{y} = 30,626 + 3.8932x_1 + 86.519x_2 - 29,607x_3$$
$$\quad\ (19,808)\quad (2.0812)\quad (18.693)\quad (23,822)$$
$$\quad\ \ 1.5461\quad\ \ 1.8706\quad\ \ 4.6283\quad -1.2429$$

$$R^2 = .9575 \qquad F = 67.595$$

where the numbers in parentheses are the standard errors of the coefficient estimates and the numbers below them are the associated t statistics.

Since $F = 67.595 > F_{.01} = 6.99$ (with $\nu_1 = 3$, $\nu_2 = 9$), Allmon concluded that at least one of the model coefficients is nonzero and that the model is

useful for predicting sales. Next, she conducted one-sided, upper-tailed hypothesis tests to determine whether the data supported her expectations about the positive influence of each independent variable on sales. Comparing $t_{.05} = 1.833$ (df = 9) to the t statistics given, we can see that the data support her hypotheses with respect to β_1 and β_2, but that the null hypothesis H_0: $\beta_3 = 0$ cannot be rejected. Thus, she concluded,

. . . my model indicates that income is a significant determinant of sales as is advertising expenditure in the current year. The competition of Colgate dental cream via its advertising expenditure appears not to affect Crest sales significantly. This information could be used by Procter and Gamble in the formulation of their advertising policy, for example, in determining the segment of the market to which most advertising should be directed.

Allmon's primary purpose for developing the model was prediction. As part of her test of the predictive power of the model, Allmon substituted the values for x_1, x_2, and x_3 in 1980 (which were known) into the fitted model and calculated $\hat{y}$. Her model predicted sales of $251,060,340 and actual sales were $245,000,000. Allmon's model did substantially better than Carlson's model, the model she had set out to refine, which predicted sales of $275,447,450.

In concluding her report, Allmon pointed out several limitations of the model. Among them were the following:

1. It was developed from annual data. Accordingly, the results should be viewed cautiously, since the cumulative effect of advertising on sales may last less than a year.

2. The sample is quite small. Even one more data point may substantially change the coefficient estimates and overall model fit.

3. None of the data were obtained from primary sources (such as Procter and Gamble). All data except disposable income were collected from the publication *Advertising Age*, a secondary data source.

Exercises 10.61 – 10.74

Note: *Starred (*) exercises require the use of a computer.*

Learning the Mechanics

10.61 The SAS System was used to fit the model $y = \beta_0 + \beta_1 x_1 + \beta_2 x_2 + \epsilon$ to $n = 20$ data points and the accompanying printout was obtained.

Dep Variable: Y

Analysis of Variance

Source	DF	Sum of Squares	Mean Square	F Value	Prob>F
Model	2	128329.27624	64164.63812	7.223	0.0054
Error	17	151015.72376	8883.27787		
C Total	19	279345.00000			

Root MSE	94.25114	R-Square	0.4594
Dep Mean	360.50000	Adj R-Sq	0.3958
C.V.	26.14456		

Parameter Estimates

Variable	DF	Parameter Estimate	Standard Error	T for H0: Parameter=0	Prob > |T|
INTERCEP	1	506.346067	45.16942487	11.210	0.0001
X1	1	-941.900226	275.08555975	-3.424	0.0032
X2	1	-429.060418	379.82566485	-1.130	0.2743

a. What are the sample estimates of β_0, β_1, and β_2? Interpret each.
b. What is the least squares prediction equation?
c. Find SSE, MSE, and s. Interpret the standard deviation in the context of the problem.
d. Test H_0: $\beta_1 = 0$ against H_a: $\beta_1 \neq 0$. Use $\alpha = .05$.
e. Use a 95% confidence interval to estimate β_2.

10.62 Suppose you fit the multiple regression model

$$y = \beta_0 + \beta_1 x_1 + \beta_2 x_2 + \beta_3 x_3 + \epsilon$$

to $n = 30$ data points and obtained the following result:

$$\hat{y} = 3.4 - 4.6x_1 + 2.7x_2 + .93x_3$$

The estimated standard errors of $\hat{\beta}_2$ and $\hat{\beta}_3$ are 1.86 and .29, respectively.
a. Test the null hypothesis H_0: $\beta_2 = 0$ against the alternative hypothesis H_a: $\beta_2 \neq 0$. Use $\alpha = .05$.
b. Test the null hypothesis H_0: $\beta_3 = 0$ against the alternative hypothesis H_a: $\beta_3 \neq 0$. Use $\alpha = .05$.
c. The null hypothesis H_0: $\beta_2 = 0$ is not rejected. In contrast, the null hypothesis H_0: $\beta_3 = 0$ is rejected. Explain how this can happen even though $\hat{\beta}_2 > \hat{\beta}_3$.

10.63 The model $y = \beta_0 + \beta_1 x + \beta_2 x^2 + \epsilon$ was fit to $n = 19$ data points with the results shown in the accompanying printout.

```
Dep Variable: Y
                         Analysis of Variance

                     Sum of          Mean
   Source     DF     Squares         Square      F Value      Prob>F

   Model       2     24.22335       12.11167      65.478       0.0001
   Error      16      2.95955        0.18497
   C Total    18     27.18289

        Root MSE        0.43008     R-Square       0.8911
        Dep Mean        3.56053     Adj R-Sq       0.8775
        C.V.           12.07921

                       Parameter Estimates

                   Parameter      Standard     T for HO:
   Variable   DF   Estimate       Error        Parameter=0    Prob > |T|

   INTERCEP    1    0.734606      0.29313351      2.506        0.0234
   X           1    0.765179      0.08754136      8.741        0.0001
   XSQ         1   -0.030810      0.00452890     -6.803        0.0001
```

a. Find R^2 and interpret its value.

b. Test the null hypothesis that $\beta_1 = \beta_2 = 0$ against the alternative hypothesis that at least one of β_1 and β_2 are nonzero. Calculate the test statistic using the two formulas given in this section, and compare your results to each other and to that given on the printout. Use $\alpha = .05$ and interpret the result of your test.

c. Find the observed significance level for this test on the printout, and interpret it.

d. Test $H_0: \beta_2 = 0$ against $H_a: \beta_2 \neq 0$. Use $\alpha = .05$ and interpret the result of your test. Report and interpret the observed significance level of the test.

10.64 Suppose you fit the model

$$y = \beta_0 + \beta_1 x_1 + \beta_2 x_2 + \beta_3 x_1 x_2 + \beta_4 x_1^2 + \beta_5 x_2^2 + \epsilon$$

to $n = 30$ data points, and you obtain

$$\text{SSE} = .46 \qquad R^2 = .87$$

a. Do the values of SSE and R^2 suggest that the model provides a good fit to the data? Explain.

b. Is the model of any use in predicting y? Using $\alpha = .05$, test the null hypothesis that $E(y) = \beta_0$, i.e.,

$$H_0: \quad \beta_1 = \beta_2 = \cdots = \beta_5 = 0$$

against the alternative hypothesis

$$H_a: \quad \text{At least one of the parameters } \beta_1, \beta_2, \ldots, \beta_5 \text{ is nonzero}$$

Applying the Concepts

10.65 Economists have two major types of data available to them: *time series data* and *cross-sectional data*. For example, an economist estimating a consumption function, say, household food consumption, as a function of household income and household size, might measure the variables of interest for one sample of households at one point in time. In this case, the economist is using *cross-sectional data*. If instead, the economist is interested in how total consumption in the United States is related to national income, the economist probably would track these variables over time, using *time series data* (Wonnacott and Wonnacott, 1979). The data in the table were collected for a random sample of 25 households in Washington, D.C., during 1990, and therefore are cross-sectional data.

Household	1990 Food Consumption ($1,000s)	1990 Income ($1,000s)	Household Size (Dec. 1990)	Household	1990 Food Consumption ($1,000s)	1990 Income ($1,000s)	Household Size (Dec. 1990)
1	3.2	31.1	4	14	3.1	85.2	2
2	2.4	20.5	2	15	4.5	35.6	9
3	3.8	42.3	4	16	3.5	68.5	3
4	1.9	18.9	1	17	4.0	10.5	5
5	2.5	26.5	2	18	3.5	21.6	4
6	3.0	29.8	4	19	1.8	29.9	1
7	2.6	24.3	3	20	2.9	28.6	3
8	3.2	38.1	4	21	2.6	20.2	2
9	3.9	52.0	5	22	3.6	38.7	5
10	1.7	16.0	1	23	2.8	11.2	3
11	2.9	41.9	3	24	4.5	14.3	7
12	1.7	9.9	1	25	3.5	16.9	5
13	4.5	33.1	7				

a. It has been hypothesized that household food consumption y is related to household income x_1 and to household size x_2 as follows:

$$y = \beta_0 + \beta_1 x_1 + \beta_2 x_2 + \epsilon$$

The SAS computer printout for fitting the model to the data is shown. Give the least squares prediction equation.

```
DEPENDENT VARIABLE: FOOD

SOURCE                       DF  SUM OF SQUARES   MEAN SQUARE  F VALUE

MODEL                         2      15.46228509     7.73114255   100.80
ERROR                        22       1.68731491     0.07669613
CORRECTED TOTAL              24      17.14960000                  PR > F

                                                                 0.0001


R-SQUARE                     C.V.         ROOT MSE      FOOD MEAN

0.901612                     8.9221       0.27694067    3.10400000

                          T FOR H0:    PR > !T!    STD ERROR OF
PARAMETER      ESTIMATE    PARAMETER=0             ESTIMATE

INTERCEPT      1.43260377       9.76      0.0001    0.14673751
INCOME         0.00999062       3.15      0.0046    0.00316806
SIZE           0.37928986      13.68      0.0001    0.02772472
```

b. Do the data provide sufficient evidence to conclude that the mean food consumption increases with household income? Test using $\alpha = .01$.

c. As a check on your conclusion of part **b**, construct a scattergram of household food consumption versus household income. Does the plot support your conclusion in part **b**? Explain.

10.66 Henry and Haynes (1978) report that in the mid-1970s Data Resources, Inc. (DRI), a firm that supplies economic information analyses and advice to government, industry, and financial institutions, used multiple regression to develop a model that characterized a bank's demand for mortgage loans. Working with quarterly time series data on the variables described here, DRI obtained the following least squares model:

$$\hat{y} = 37,350.40 + .61x_1 - 155.74x_2 + 19,934.7x_3 - 5,354.9x_4 + 5,317.61x_5$$
$$\quad\;\; (3.5) \qquad (5.5) \qquad (-2.8) \qquad (4.5) \qquad\quad (-3.9) \qquad\quad (2.7)$$

where

y = Mortgage loan demand (in dollars)

x_1 = Seasonally adjusted mortgage loans outstanding during previous period

x_2 = Deposits at mutual savings banks and savings and loan associations

x_3 = Average number of housing starts per month

x_4 = State's rate of unemployment

x_5 = Conventional mortgage loan interest rate

The numbers in parentheses are the t statistics associated with the estimates of the model coefficients above them. Assume $n = 28$. The preceding model, along with one for the demand for commercial loans and another for the demand for installment loans, became the heart of the bank's loan-demand forecasting system.

a. Find the estimated standard deviation of $\hat{\beta}_2$.

b. Prior to fitting the model, DRI hypothesized that β_2 should be negative because x_2 represents an alternative source of mortgage money available to the consumer. Do the data support this hypothesis? Test using $\alpha = .01$. State your conclusion in the context of the problem.

c. Report the approximate p-value of your test.

d. Provide an economic explanation for why it is reasonable to expect β_4 to be negative.

10.67 Running a manufacturing operation efficiently requires knowledge of the time it takes employees to manufacture the product, otherwise the cost of making the product cannot be determined. Furthermore, management would not be able to establish an effective incentive plan for its employees because it would not know how to set work standards (Chase and Aquilano, 1992). Estimates of production time are frequently obtained using time studies. The data in the table at the top of page 562 came from a recent time study of a sample of 15 employees performing a particular task on an automobile assembly line.

a. The SAS computer printout for fitting the model $y = \beta_0 + \beta_1 x + \beta_2 x^2 + \epsilon$ is shown on page 562. Find the least squares prediction equation. [*Note:* The term $\beta_2 x^2$, called a "quadratic" term, introduces curvature into the hypothesized x–y relationship.]

b. Plot the fitted equation on a scattergram of the data. Is there sufficient evidence to support the inclusion of the quadratic term in the model? Explain.

c. Test the null hypothesis $\beta_2 = 0$ against the alternative that $\beta_2 \neq 0$. Use $\alpha = .01$. Does the quadratic term make an important contribution to the model?

Completion Time, y (mins.)	Experience, x (mos.)	Completion Time, y (mins.)	Experience, x (mos.)
10	24	17	3
20	1	18	1
15	10	16	7
11	15	16	9
11	17	17	7
19	3	18	5
11	20	10	20
13	9		

```
DEPENDENT VARIABLE: Y

SOURCE                        DF    SUM OF SQUARES   MEAN SQUARE   F VALUE

MODEL                          2      156.11947722   78.05973861     65.59
ERROR                         12       14.28052278    1.19004356    PR > F
CORRECTED TOTAL               14      170.40000000                  0.0001

R-SQUARE              C.V.              ROOT MSE        Y MEAN

0.916194            7.3709           1.09089118     14.80000000

                               T FOR H0:      PR > ¦T¦     STD ERROR OF
PARAMETER        ESTIMATE     PARAMETER=0                  ESTIMATE

INTERCEPT       20.09110757        27.72        0.0001      0.72470507
X               -0.67052219        -4.33        0.0010      0.15470634
X*X              0.00953474         1.51        0.1576      0.00632580
```

d. Your conclusion in part **c** should have been to drop the quadratic term from the model. Do so and fit the *reduced model*, $y = \beta_0 + \beta_1 x + \epsilon$, to the data.

e. Define β_1 in the context of this exercise. Find a 90% confidence interval for β_1 in the reduced model of part **d**.

10.68 A researcher wished to investigate the effects of several factors on production line supervisors' attitudes toward handicapped workers. A study was conducted involving 40 randomly selected supervisors. The response y, a supervisor's attitude toward handicapped workers, was measured with a standardized attitude scale. Independent variables used in the study were

$$x_1 = \begin{cases} 1 & \text{if the supervisor is female} \\ 0 & \text{if the supervisor is male} \end{cases} \quad \text{(This is called a dummy variable.)}$$

x_2 = Number of years of experience in a supervisory job

The researcher fit the model

$$y = \beta_0 + \beta_1 x_1 + \beta_2 x_2 + \beta_3 x_2^2 + \epsilon$$

to the data with the following results:

$$\hat{y} = 50 + 5x_1 + 5x_2 - .1x_2^2 \qquad s_{\hat{\beta}_3} = .03$$

a. Is there sufficient evidence to indicate that the quadratic term in years of experience, x_2^2, is useful for predicting attitude score? Use $\alpha = .05$.

b. Sketch the predicted attitude score $\hat{y}$ as a function of the number of years of experience x_2 for male supervisors ($x_1 = 0$). Next, substitute x_1 into the least squares equation and thereby obtain a plot of the prediction equation for female supervisors. [*Note:* For both males and females, plotting $\hat{y}$ for $x_2 = 0, 2, 4, 6, 8,$ and 10 will produce a good picture of the prediction equations. The vertical distance between the males' and females' prediction curves is the same for all values of x_2.]

*10.69 The owner of an apartment building in Minneapolis believed that her 1990 property tax bill was too high due to an overassessment of the property's value by the city tax assessor. The owner hired an independent real estate appraiser to investigate the appropriateness of the city's assessment. The appraiser used regression analysis to explore the relationship between the sale prices of apartment buildings sold in Minneapolis during 1990 and various characteristics of the properties. Twenty-five buildings were randomly sampled from all apartment buildings sold during 1990. The table lists the data collected by the appraiser. The real estate appraiser hypothesized that the sale price (i.e., market value) of an apartment building is related to the other variables in the table according to the model $y = \beta_0 + \beta_1 x_1 + \beta_2 x_2 + \beta_3 x_3 + \beta_4 x_4 + \beta_5 x_5 + \epsilon$.

Code	Sale Price	Apartment Units	Age of Structure	Lot Size	Parking Spaces	Gross Building Area
	y (\$)	x_1	x_2 (yrs.)	x_3 (sq. ft.)	x_4	x_5 (sq. ft.)
0229	90,300	4	82	4,635	0	4,266
0094	384,000	20	13	17,798	0	14,391
0043	157,500	5	66	5,913	0	6,615
0079	676,200	26	64	7,750	6	34,144
0134	165,000	5	55	5,150	0	6,120
0179	300,000	10	65	12,506	0	14,552
0087	108,750	4	82	7,160	0	3,040
0120	276,538	11	23	5,120	0	7,881
0246	420,000	20	18	11,745	20	12,600
0025	950,000	62	71	21,000	3	39,448
0015	560,000	26	74	11,221	0	30,000
0131	268,000	13	56	7,818	13	8,088
0172	290,000	9	76	4,900	0	11,315
0095	173,200	6	21	5,424	6	4,461
0121	323,650	11	24	11,834	8	9,000
0077	162,500	5	19	5,246	5	3,828
0060	353,500	20	62	11,223	2	13,680
0174	134,400	4	70	5,834	0	4,680
0084	187,000	8	19	9,075	0	7,392
0031	155,700	4	57	5,280	0	6,030
0019	93,600	4	82	6,864	0	3,840
0074	110,000	4	50	4,510	0	3,092
0057	573,200	14	10	11,192	0	23,704
0104	79,300	4	82	7,425	0	3,876
0024	272,000	5	82	7,500	0	9,542

a. Fit the real estate appraiser's model to the data in the table. Report the least squares prediction equation.
b. Find the standard deviation of the regression model and interpret its value in the context of this problem.
c. Do the data provide sufficient evidence to conclude that value increases with the number of units in an apartment building? Report the observed significance level, and reach a conclusion using $\alpha = .05$.
d. Interpret the value of $\hat{\beta}_1$ in terms of these data. Remember that your interpretation must recognize the presence of the other variables in the model.
e. Construct a scattergram of sale price versus age. What does your scattergram suggest about the relationship between these variables?
f. Test $H_0: \beta_2 = 0$ against $H_a: \beta_2 < 0$ using $\alpha = .01$. Interpret the result in the context of the problem. Does the result agree with your observation in part e? Why is it reasonable to conduct a one-tailed rather than a two-tailed test of this null hypothesis?
g. What is the observed significance level of the hypothesis test of part f?
h. Find R^2 for the least squares prediction equation found in part a. Interpret its value in the context of the problem.
i. Use an F test to investigate the usefulness of the model hypothesized by the real estate appraiser. Use $\alpha = .01$, and carefully state your conclusion in the context of this application.
j. What is the observed significance level of the F test?

10.70 Much research (and, for that matter, much litigation) has been conducted on the disparity between the salary levels of men and women. Some recent research examined salaries for a sample of 191 Illinois managers using a regression analysis with the following independent variables:

$$x_1 = \text{Gender of manager} = \begin{cases} 1 & \text{if male} \\ 0 & \text{if not} \end{cases} \qquad x_2 = \text{Race of manager} = \begin{cases} 1 & \text{if white} \\ 0 & \text{if not} \end{cases}$$

$x_3 = \text{Education level (in years)}$ $\qquad\qquad$ $x_4 = \text{Tenure with firm (in years)}$
$x_5 = \text{Number of hours worked per week}$

The regression results are shown in the accompanying table for the sample of $n = 191$; $R^2 = .240$.

Variable	$\hat{\beta}$	p-Value
x_1	12.774	<.05
x_2	.713	>.10
x_3	1.519	<.05
x_4	.320	<.05
x_5	.205	<.05
Constant	15.491	–

Source: Reskin, B. F., and Ross, C. E. "Jobs, authority, and earnings among managers: The continuing significance of sex," *Work and Occupations*, Nov. 1992, Vol. 19, No. 4.

a. Write the hypothesized model that was used, and interpret each of its β parameters.
b. Write the least squares equation that estimates the model in part a, and interpret each of the β estimates.
c. Interpret the value of R^2. Is the model useful for predicting annual salary? Test using $\alpha = .05$.

d. Test to determine whether the gender variable indicates that male managers are paid more than female managers, even after adjusting for and holding constant the other four factors in the model. Use $\alpha = .05$. [*Note:* The *p*-values given in the table are two-tailed.]

e. Why would one want to adjust for these other factors prior to conducting a test for salary discrimination?

f. Discuss how the interaction between gender (x_1) and tenure with the firm (x_4) might affect the results of the analysis.

10.71 If producers (providers) of goods (services) are able to reduce the unit cost of their goods by increasing the scale of their operation, they are the beneficiaries of an economic force known as **economies of scale.** Economies of scale cause a firm's long-run average costs to decline (Ferguson and Maurice, 1970). The question of whether economies of scale, diseconomies of scale, or neither (i.e., constant economies of scale) exist in the U.S. motor freight, common carrier industry has been debated for years. In an effort to settle the debate within a specific subsection of the trucking industry, Sugrue, Ledford, and Glaskowsky (1982) used regression analysis to model the relationship between each of a number of cost measures and the size of the operation. In one case, they modeled expense per vehicle-mile, y_1, as a function of the firm's total revenue, x. In another case, they modeled expense per ton-mile, y_2, as a function of x. Data were collected from 264 firms and the least squares results obtained are shown in the table.

Dependent Variable	$\hat{\beta}_0$	$\hat{\beta}_1$	r	F
Expense per vehicle-mile	2.279	$-.00000069$	$-.0783$	1.616
Expense per ton-mile	.1680	$-.000000066$	$-.0902$	2.148

Source: Sugrue, P. K., Ledford, M. H., and Glaskowsky, N. A., Jr. "Operating economies of scale in the U.S. long-haul common carrier, motor freight industry." *Transportation Journal*, Fall 1982, Vol. 22, pp. 27–41.

a. Investigate the usefulness of the two models estimated by Sugrue, Ledford, and Glaskowsky. Use $\alpha = .05$. Draw appropriate conclusions in the context of the problem.

b. Are the observed significance levels of the hypothesis tests you conducted in part **a** greater than .10 or less than .10? Explain.

c. What do your hypothesis tests of part **a** suggest about economies of scale in the subsection of the trucking industry investigated by Sugrue, Ledford, and Glaskowsky—the long-haul, heavy-load, intercity-general-freight common carrier sector? Explain.

10.72 Because the coefficient of determination R^2 always increases when a new independent variable is added to the model, it may be tempting to include many variables in a model to force R^2 to be near 1. However, doing so reduces the degrees of freedom available for estimating σ^2, which adversely affects our ability to make reliable inferences. As an example, suppose you want to use 18 economic indicators to predict next year's GNP. You fit the model

$$y = \beta_0 + \beta_1 x_1 + \beta_2 x_2 + \cdots + \beta_{17} x_{17} + \beta_{18} x_{18} + \epsilon$$

where y = GNP and $x_1, x_2, \ldots, x_{18}$ are indicators. Only 20 years of data ($n = 20$) are used to fit the model, and you obtain $R^2 = .95$. Test to determine whether this impressive-looking R^2 is large enough to infer that the model is useful—i.e., that at least one term in the model is important for predicting GNP. Use $\alpha = .05$.

10.73 A researcher used regression analysis to investigate the determinants of survival size of nonprofit hospitals. For a given sample of hospitals, survival size y is defined as the largest size hospital (in terms of number of beds) exhibiting growth in market share over a specific time interval. Suppose 10 states are randomly selected and the survival size for all nonprofit hospitals in each state is determined for the time periods 1988–1989 and 1991–1992, yielding two observations per state. The 20 survival sizes are listed in the table along with the following data for each state, for the second year in each time interval:

x_1 = Percentage of beds that are in for-profit hospitals
x_2 = Ratio of the number of persons enrolled in health maintenance organizations to the number of persons covered by hospital insurance
x_3 = State populations (in thousands)
x_4 = Percent of state that is urban

It is hypothesized that the model characterizing the relationship between survival size y and the four x variables is

$$y = \beta_0 + \beta_1 x_1 + \beta_2 x_2 + \beta_3 x_3 + \beta_4 x_4 + \epsilon$$

State	Time	y	x_1	x_2	x_3	x_4
1	1	370	.13	.09	5,800	89
1	2	390	.15	.09	5,955	87
2	1	455	.08	.11	17,648	87
2	2	450	.10	.16	17,895	85
3	1	500	.03	.04	7,332	79
3	2	480	.07	.05	7,610	78
4	1	550	.06	.005	11,731	80
4	2	600	.10	.005	11,790	81
5	1	205	.30	.12	2,932	44
5	2	230	.25	.13	3,100	45
6	1	425	.04	.01	4,148	36
6	2	445	.07	.02	4,205	38
7	1	245	.20	.01	1,574	25
7	2	200	.30	.01	1,560	28
8	1	250	.07	.08	2,471	38
8	2	275	.08	.10	2,511	38
9	1	300	.09	.12	4,060	52
9	2	290	.12	.20	4,175	54
10	1	280	.10	.02	2,902	37
10	2	270	.11	.05	2,925	38

Source: Adapted from Bays, C. W. "The determinants of hospital size: A survival analysis." *Applied Economics*, 1986, Vol. 18, pp. 359–377.

The model was fit to the data in the table using the SAS System with the results shown.

```
Dep Variable: Y
                           Analysis of Variance

                        Sum of          Mean
    Source      DF      Squares         Square      F Value      Prob>F

    Model        4  246537.05939  61634.26485      28.180       0.0001
    Error       15   32807.94061   2187.19604
    C Total     19  279345.00000

         Root MSE      46.76747    R-Square       0.8826
         Dep Mean     360.50000    Adj R-Sq       0.8512
         C.V.          12.97295

                        Parameter Estimates

                   Parameter       Standard    T for H0:
    Variable   DF  Estimate        Error       Parameter=0   Prob > |T|

    INTERCEP    1   295.327091    40.17888737      7.350      0.0001
    X1          1  -480.837576   150.39050364     -3.197      0.0060
    X2          1  -829.464955   196.47303539     -4.222      0.0007
    X3          1     0.007934     0.00355335      2.233      0.0412
    X4          1     2.360769     0.76150774      3.100      0.0073
```

a. Report the least squares prediction equation.
b. Find the regression standard deviation s and interpret its value in the context of the problem.
c. Use an F test to investigate the usefulness of the hypothesized model. Report the observed significance level, and use $\alpha = .025$ to reach your conclusion.
d. Prior to collecting the data it was hypothesized that increases in the number of for-profit hospital beds would decrease the survival size of nonprofit hospitals. Do the data support this hypothesis? Testing using $\alpha = .05$.

*10.74 A company that services copy machines is interested in developing a regression model that will assist in personnel planning. It needs a model that describes the relationship between the time spent on a preventive maintenance service call to a customer, y, and two independent variables: the number of copy machines to be serviced, x_1, and the service person's experience in preventive maintenance, x_2. Company records were sampled and the data in the table were obtained.

Hours of Maintenance	Number of Copy Machines	Months of Experience	Hours of Maintenance	Number of Copy Machines	Months of Experience
1.0	1	12	1.8	1	1
3.1	3	8	11.5	10	10
17.0	10	5	9.3	5	2
14.0	8	2	6.0	4	6
6.0	5	10	12.2	10	8

a. Fit the model $y = \beta_0 + \beta_1 x_1 + \beta_2 x_2 + \epsilon$ to the data.
b. Investigate whether the model is useful. Test using $\alpha = .10$.
c. Find R^2 for the fitted model. Interpret your result.
d. Fit the model $y = \beta_0 + \beta_1 x_1 + \beta_2 x_2 + \beta_3 x_1 x_2 + \epsilon$ to the data.
e. Find R^2 for the model of part **d**.
f. Explain why you should not rely solely on a comparison of the two R^2 values for drawing conclusions about which model is more useful for predicting y.
g. Do the data provide sufficient evidence to indicate that the interaction term, $x_1 x_2$, contributes information for the prediction of y? [*Hint:* Test $H_0: \beta_3 = 0$.]
h. Can you be certain that the model you selected in part **f** is the best model to use in predicting maintenance time? Explain.

10.10   Residual Analysis: Checking the Regression Assumptions (Optional)

When we apply regression analysis to a set of data, we never know for certain whether the assumptions of Section 10.3 are satisfied. How far can we deviate from the assumptions and still expect regression analysis to yield results that will have the reliability stated in this chapter? How can we detect departures (if they exist) from the assumptions and what can we do about them? We provide some partial answers to these questions in this section and will direct you to further discussion in succeeding chapters.

Remember from optional Section 10.9 that

$$y = \beta_0 + \beta_1 x_1 + \beta_2 x_2 + \cdots + \beta_k x_k + \epsilon$$

where ϵ is a random error. The first assumption we made was that the mean value of ϵ for *any* given set of values of $x_1, x_2, \ldots, x_k$ is $E(\epsilon) = 0$. One consequence of this assumption is that the mean $E(y)$ for a specific set of values of $x_1, x_2, \ldots, x_k$ is

$$E(y) = \beta_0 + \beta_1 x_1 + \beta_2 x_2 + \cdots + \beta_k x_k$$

That is,

$$\underbrace{y}_{} = \underbrace{E(y)}_{\substack{\text{Mean value of } y \\ \text{for specific values} \\ \text{of } x_1, x_2, \ldots, x_k}} + \underbrace{\epsilon}_{\substack{\text{Random} \\ \text{error}}}$$

The second consequence of the assumption is that the least squares estimators of the model parameters, $\beta_0, \beta_1, \beta_2, \ldots, \beta_k$, will be unbiased regardless of the remaining assumptions that we attribute to the random errors and their probability distributions.

The properties of the sampling distributions of the parameter estimators $\hat{\beta}_0, \hat{\beta}_1, \ldots, \hat{\beta}_k$ will depend on the remaining assumptions that we specify concerning the probability distributions of the random errors. Recall that we assumed that for any given set of values of $x_1, x_2, \ldots, x_k$, ϵ has a normal probability distribution with mean equal to 0 and variance equal to σ^2. Also, we assumed that the random errors are probabilistically independent.

It is unlikely that these assumptions are ever satisfied exactly in a practical application of regression analysis. Fortunately, experience has shown that least squares regression analysis produces reliable statistical tests, confidence intervals, and prediction intervals as long as the departures from the assumptions are not too great. In this section we present some methods for determining whether the data indicate significant departures from the assumptions.

Because the assumptions all concern the random error component ϵ of the model, the first step is to estimate the random error. Since the actual random error associated with a particular value of y is the difference between the actual y value and its unknown mean, we estimate the error by the difference between the actual y value and the *estimated* mean. This estimated error is called a **regression residual**, or simply the **residual**, and is denoted by $\hat{\epsilon}$. The actual error ϵ and residual $\hat{\epsilon}$ are shown in Figure 10.22.

$$\epsilon = \text{Actual random error}$$
$$= (\text{Actual } y \text{ value}) - (\text{Mean of } y)$$
$$= y - E(y) = y - (\beta_0 + \beta_1 x_1 + \beta_2 x_2 + \cdots + \beta_k x_k)$$

$$\hat{\epsilon} = \text{Estimated random error (residual)}$$
$$= (\text{Actual } y \text{ value}) - (\text{Estimated mean of } y)$$
$$= y - \hat{y} = y - (\hat{\beta}_0 + \hat{\beta}_1 x_1 + \hat{\beta}_2 x_2 + \cdots + \hat{\beta}_k x_k)$$

FIGURE 10.22 ▶
Actual random error and regression residual

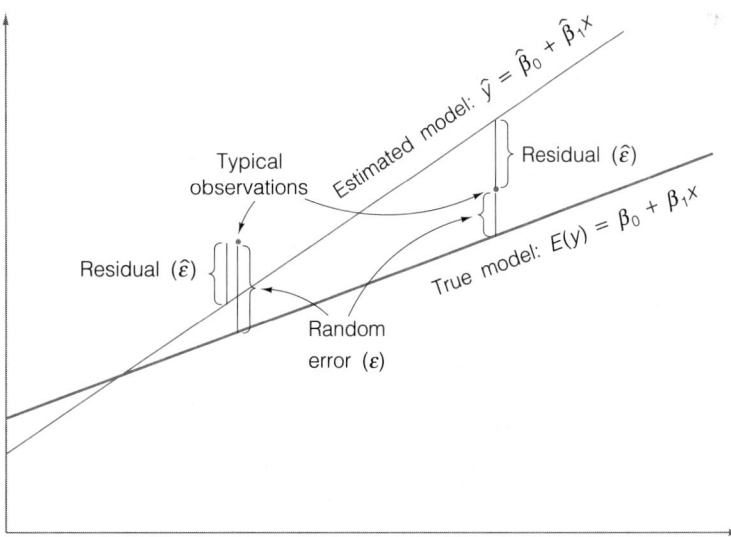

Since the true mean of y (i.e., the true regression model) is not known, the actual random error cannot be calculated. However, because the residual is based on the estimated mean (the least squares regression model), it can be calculated and used to estimate the random error and to check the regression assumptions. Such checks are generally referred to as **residual analyses**. Some useful properties of residuals are given in the box.

Properties of Regression Residuals

1. A residual is equal to the difference between the observed y value and its estimated (regression) mean:

    $$\text{Residual} = y - \hat{y}$$

2. The mean of the residuals is equal to 0. This property follows from the fact that the sum of the differences between the observed y values and the least squares regression model is equal to 0.

    $$\sum (\text{Residuals}) = \sum (y - \hat{y}) = 0$$

3. The standard deviation of the residuals is equal to the standard deviation of the fitted regression model, s. This property follows from the fact that the sum of the squared residuals is equal to SSE, which when divided by the error df is equal to the variance of the fitted regression model, s^2. The square root of the variance is both the standard deviation of the residuals and the standard deviation of the regression model.

    $$\sum (\text{Residuals})^2 = \sum (y - \hat{y})^2 = \text{SSE}$$

    $$s = \sqrt{\frac{\sum (\text{Residuals})^2}{n - (k + 1)}} = \sqrt{\frac{\text{SSE}}{n - (k + 1)}}$$

The following examples show how the analysis of regression residuals can be used to verify the assumptions associated with the model, and to improve the model when the assumptions do not appear to be satisfied. Although the residuals can be calculated and plotted by hand, we rely on the computer for these tasks in the examples and exercises. Most statistical computer packages now include residual analyses as a standard component of their regression modeling programs.

EXAMPLE 10.7

Suppose we theorize that monthly electrical usage, y, in all-electric homes is related to the size, x, of the home. Two competing models are the straight-line model (Model 1) and the second-order (quadratic) model (Model 2), shown below:

Model 1: $E(y) = \beta_0 + \beta_1 x$

Model 2: $E(y) + \beta_0 + \beta_1 x + \beta_2 x^2$

a. $\beta_2 > 0$

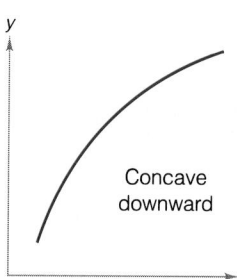

b. $\beta_2 < 0$
FIGURE 10.23 ▲
The interpretation of β_2 for a second-order model

The $\beta_2 x^2$ term in Model 2 allows for a curvilinear relationship between electrical usage and home size to exist, as illustrated in Figure 10.23.

To compare these models, the values of y and x were collected for each of 10 homes during a particular month. The data are shown in Table 10.9. SAS printouts for the straight-line model and the quadratic model fitted to the data are shown in Figures 10.24(a) and 10.24(b) (pages 572–573), respectively. The residuals from these models are shaded in the printouts. The residuals are then plotted on the vertical axis against the variable x, size of home, on the horizontal axis in Figures 10.25(a) and 10.25(b), respectively (page 574).

TABLE 10.9   Home Size–Electrical Usage Data

Size of Home x (square feet)	Monthly Usage y (kilowatt-hours)	Size of Home x (square feet)	Monthly Usage y (kilowatt-hours)
1,290	1,182	1,840	1,711
1,350	1,172	1,980	1,804
1,470	1,264	2,230	1,840
1,600	1,493	2,400	1,956
1,710	1,571	2,930	1,954

a. Verify that each residual is equal to the difference between the observed y value and the estimated mean value, y.

b. Analyze the residual plots.

Solution

a. For the straight-line model the residual is calculated for the first y value as follows:

$$\text{Residual} = (\text{Observed } y \text{ value}) - (\text{Estimated mean})$$
$$= y - \hat{y} = 1{,}182 - 1{,}275.9 = -93.9$$

where the estimated mean is the first number (shaded) in the column labeled **Predict Value** on the SAS printout in Figure 10.24(a). Similarly, the residual for the first y value using the quadratic model is

$$\text{Residual} = 1{,}182 - 1{,}129.6 = 52.4$$

Both residuals agree (after rounding) with the first values given in the column labeled **Residual** in Figures 10.24(a) and 10.24(b), respectively. Although the residuals both correspond to the same observed y value, 1,182, they differ because the estimated mean value changes depending on whether the straight-line model or quadratic model is used. Similar calculations produced the remaining residuals.

FIGURE 10.24 ▶
SAS printouts for electrical usage
example

(a) Straight-line model

Dep Variable: Y

Analysis of Variance

Source	DF	Sum of Squares	Mean Square	F Value	Prob>F
Model	1	703957.18342	703957.18342	39.536	0.0002
Error	8	142444.91658	17805.61457		
C Total	9	846402.10000			

Root MSE	133.43768	R-Square	0.8317
Dep Mean	1594.70000	Adj R-Sq	0.8107
C.V.	8.36757		

Parameter Estimates

Variable	DF	Parameter Estimate	Standard Error	T for HO: Parameter=0	Prob > |T|
INTERCEP	1	578.927752	166.96805715	3.467	0.0085
X	1	0.540304	0.08592981	6.288	0.0002

Obs	Y	Predict Value	Residual
1	1182.0	1275.9	-93.9204
2	1172.0	1308.3	-136.3
3	1264.0	1373.2	-109.2
4	1493.0	1443.4	49.5852
5	1571.0	1502.8	68.1517
6	1711.0	1573.1	137.9
7	1804.0	1648.7	155.3
8	1840.0	1783.8	56.1935
9	1956.0	1875.7	80.3417
10	1954.0	2162.0	-208.0

Sum of Residuals	0
Sum of Squared Residuals	142444.9166

b. The plot of the residuals for the straight-line model, Figure 10.25(a), reveals a nonrandom pattern. The residuals exhibit a mound shape, with the residuals for the small values of x below the horizontal 0 (mean of the residuals) line, the residuals corresponding to the middle values of x above the 0 line, and the residual for the largest value of x again below the 0 line. The indication is that the mean value of the random error ϵ *within* each of these ranges of x (small, medium, large) may not be equal to 0. Such a pattern usually indicates that curvature needs to be added to the model.

FIGURE 10.24 ▶
(b) Quadratic model

Dep Variable: Y

Analysis of Variance

Source	DF	Sum of Squares	Mean Square	F Value	Prob>F
Model	2	831069.54637	415534.77319	189.710	0.0001
Error	7	15332.55363	2190.36480		
C Total	9	846402.10000			

Root MSE	46.80133	R-Square	0.9819	
Dep Mean	1594.70000	Adj R-Sq	0.9767	
C.V.	2.93480			

Parameter Estimates

Variable	DF	Parameter Estimate	Standard Error	T for H0: Parameter=0	Prob > |T|
INTERCEP	1	-1216.143887	242.80636850	-5.009	0.0016
X	1	2.398930	0.24583560	9.758	0.0001
XSQ	1	-0.000450	0.00005908	-7.618	0.0001

Obs	Y	Predict Value	Residual
1	1182.0	1129.6	52.4359
2	1172.0	1202.2	-30.2136
3	1264.0	1337.8	-73.7916
4	1493.0	1470.0	22.9586
5	1571.0	1570.1	0.9359
6	1711.0	1674.2	36.7685
7	1804.0	1769.4	34.5998
8	1840.0	1895.5	-55.4654
9	1956.0	1949.1	6.9431
10	1954.0	1949.2	4.8287

Sum of Residuals   -2.27374E-12
Sum of Squared Residuals   15332.5536

When the second-order term is added to the model, the nonrandom pattern disappears. In Figure 10.25(b), the residuals appear to be randomly distributed around the 0 line, as expected. Note, too, that the ± 2 standard deviation lines are at about ± 95 on the quadratic residual plot, compared to (about) ± 275 on the straight-line plot. The implication is that the quadratic model provides a considerably better model for predicting electrical usage. This conclusion can be verified by noting that the p-value for testing H_0: $\beta_2 = 0$ [shaded in Figure 10.24(b)] is .0001. Consequently, there is strong evidence that curvature is needed in the model.

FIGURE 10.25 ▶

Residual plots for electrical usage example

(a) Straight-line model

(b) Quadratic model

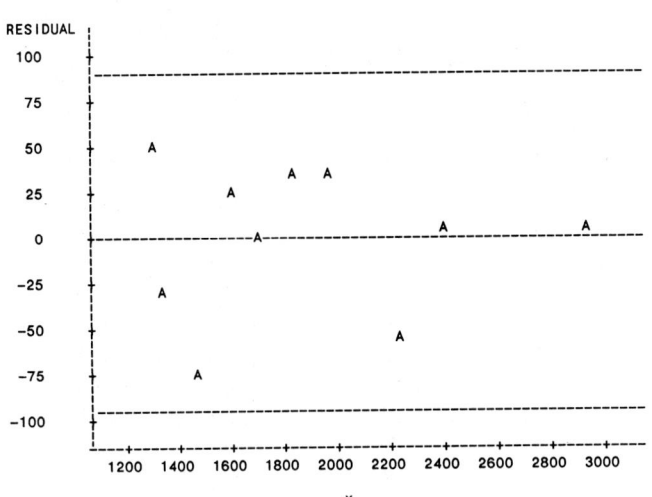

Residual analyses are also useful for detecting one or more observations that deviate significantly from the regression model. We expect approximately 95% of the residuals to fall within 2 standard deviations of the 0 line and all or almost all of them to lie within 3 standard deviations of their mean of 0. Residuals that are extremely far from the 0 line and disconnected from the bulk of the other residuals are called **outliers** and should receive special attention from the regression analyst. You will recall that outliers were first introduced in Chapter 2.

EXAMPLE 10.8

The data for the grandfather clock example are repeated in Table 10.10, with one important difference: The auction price of the clock at the top of the second column has been changed from \$2,131 to \$1,131 (shaded in Table 10.10). The interaction model

$$E(y) = \beta_0 + \beta_1 x_1 + \beta_2 x_2 + \beta_3 x_1 x_2$$

is again fit to these (modified) data, with the printout shown in Figure 10.26 (page 576). The residuals are shown shaded in the printout, and then plotted against the number of bidders, x_2, in Figure 10.27 (page 577). Analyze the residual plot.

TABLE 10.10   Auction Price Data

Age	Bidders	Price	Age	Bidders	Price
x_1	x_2	y	x_1	x_2	y
127	13	\$1,235	170	14	\$1,131
115	12	1,080	182	8	1,550
127	7	845	162	11	1,884
150	9	1,522	184	10	2,041
156	6	1,047	143	6	854
182	11	1,979	159	9	1,483
156	12	1,822	108	14	1,055
132	10	1,253	175	8	1,545
137	9	1,297	108	6	729
113	9	946	179	9	1,792
137	15	1,713	111	15	1,175
117	11	1,024	187	8	1,593
137	8	1,147	111	7	785
153	6	1,092	115	7	744
117	13	1,152	194	5	1,356
126	10	1,336	168	7	1,262

FIGURE 10.26 ▶

Printout for grandfather clock
example with altered data

THE REGRESSION EQUATION IS
PRICE = - 511 + 8.16 AGE + 19.7 BIDDERS + 0.320 AGE-BID

	COEFFICIENT	ST. DEV. OF COEF.	T-RATIO = COEF/S.D.
	-510.5	664.8	-0.77
AGE	8.160	4.577	1.78
BIDDERS	19.74	67.33	0.29
AGE-BID	0.3197	0.4783	0.67

S = 200.3

R-SQUARED = 73.0 PERCENT
R-SQUARED = 70.1 PERCENT, ADJUSTED FOR D.F.

ANALYSIS OF VARIANCE

DUE TO	DF	SS	MS=SS/DF
REGRESSION	3	3029141	1009714
RESIDUAL	28	1123116	40111
TOTAL	31	4152256	

ROW	AGE	Y PRICE	PRED. Y VALUE	ST.DEV. PRED. Y	RESIDUAL
1	127	1235.0	1310.3	59.2	-75.3
2	115	1080.0	1106.0	62.0	-26.0
3	127	845.0	948.2	61.0	-103.2
4	150	1522.0	1322.8	37.1	199.2
5	156	1047.0	1180.2	60.2	-133.2
6	182	1979.0	1831.8	82.8	147.2
7	156	1822.0	1597.9	61.8	224.1
8	132	1253.0	1186.1	39.7	66.9
9	137	1297.0	1179.3	39.0	117.7
10	113	946.0	914.4	58.5	31.6
11	137	1713.0	1560.6	78.3	152.4
12	117	1024.0	1072.8	53.0	-48.8
13	137	1147.0	1115.8	44.2	31.2
14	153	1092.0	1149.9	58.9	-57.9
15	117	1152.0	1187.1	69.6	-35.1
16	126	1336.0	1117.9	43.4	218.1
17	170	1131.0	1914.0	116.5	-783.0
18	182	1550.0	1598.1	62.7	-48.1
19	162	1884.0	1598.3	56.9	285.7
20	184	2041.0	1776.6	70.6	264.4
21	143	854.0	1049.2	58.8	-195.2
22	159	1483.0	1422.1	40.5	60.9
23	108	1055.0	1130.6	97.8	-75.6
24	175	1545.0	1523.0	55.3	22.0
25	108	729.0	696.4	99.5	32.6
26	179	1792.0	1642.9	57.5	149.1
27	111	1175.0	1223.7	107.1	-48.7
28	187	1593.0	1651.7	68.5	-58.7
29	111	785.0	781.9	80.7	3.1
30	115	744.0	823.5	75.4	-79.5
31	194	1356.0	1481.4	133.3	-125.4
32	168	1262.0	1374.6	57.6	-112.6

FIGURE 10.27 ▶

Residual plot vs. number of bidders

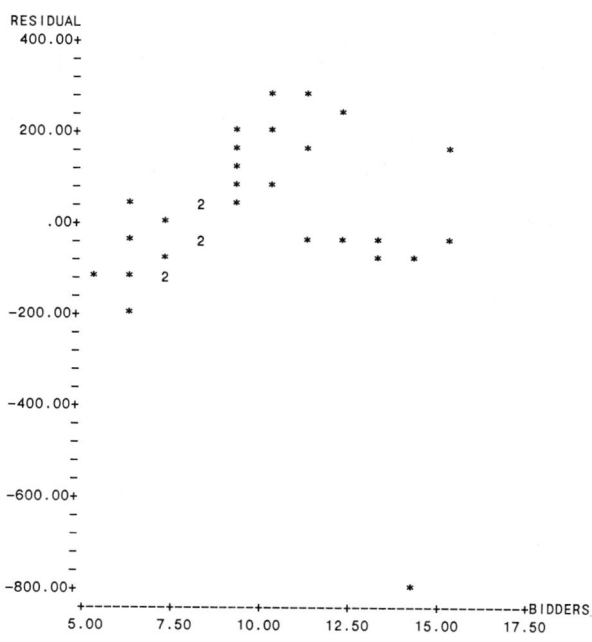

Solution

The residual plot dramatically reveals the one altered measurement. Note that one of the two residuals at $x_2 = 14$ bidders falls more than 3 standard deviations below 0. Note that no other residual lies more than 2 standard deviations from 0.

What do we do with outliers once we identify them? First, we try to determine the cause. Were the data entered into the computer incorrectly? Was the observation recorded incorrectly when the data were collected? If so, correct the observation and rerun the program. Or perhaps the observation is not representative of the conditions you are trying to model. For example, the low price may be attributable to extreme damage or to inferior quality compared to the other clocks. In these cases we probably would exclude the observation from the analysis. Often you may be unable to determine the cause of the outlier. Even so, you may want to rerun the regression analysis excluding the outlier, to assess the effect of that observation on the results of the analysis.

Figure 10.28 shows the printout when the outlier observation is excluded from the grandfather clock analysis, and Figure 10.29 shows the new plot of the residuals versus the number of bidders. Now only one residual lies beyond 2 standard deviations from 0, and none lies beyond 3 standard deviations. Also, the model statistics indicate a much better model without the outlier. Most notably, the standard deviation s has decreased from 200.3 to 85.28, indicating a model that will provide more precise estimates and predictions (narrower confidence and prediction intervals) for clocks like those in the reduced sample. Remember, though, that if you decide to remove the outlier from the analysis, and in fact it belongs to the same population as the rest of the sample, the resulting model may provide misleading estimates and predictions.

FIGURE 10.28 ▶
Minitab printout with outlier
excluded

```
THE REGRESSION EQUATION IS
PRICE-2 = 476 - 0.46 AGE-2 - 114 BIDDERS2 + 1.48 AGE-BID2

                                  ST. DEV.      T-RATIO =
                  COEFFICIENT     OF COEF.      COEF/S.D.
                    475.8           296.2          1.61
AGE-2               -0.465          2.093         -0.22
BIDDERS2           -114.19         31.03          -3.68
AGE-BID2             1.4775         0.2280         6.48


S = 85.28


R-SQUARED = 95.2 PERCENT
R-SQUARED = 94.7 PERCENT, ADJUSTED FOR D.F.


ANALYSIS OF VARIANCE

    DUE TO        DF          SS       MS=SS/DF
    REGRESSION     3       3927844      1309282
    RESIDUAL      27        196341         7272
    TOTAL         30       4124186
```

FIGURE 10.29 ▶
Minitab residual plot

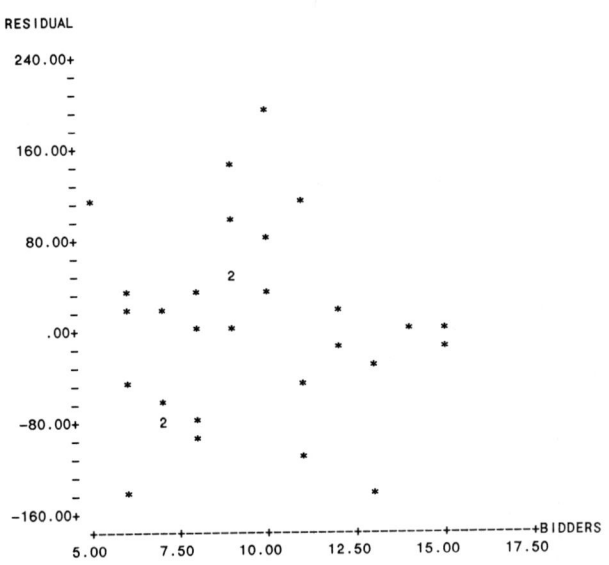

Outlier analysis is another example of testing the assumption that the expected (mean) value of the random error component is 0, since this assumption is in doubt for the error terms corresponding to the outliers. The next example in this section checks the assumption of the normality of the random error component.

EXAMPLE 10.9

Refer to Example 10.8. Use a stem-and-leaf display (Section 2.2) to plot the frequency distribution of the residuals in the grandfather clock example, both before and after the outlier residual is removed. Analyze the plots and determine whether the assumption of normality of the error distribution is reasonable.

Solution

The stem-and-leaf displays for the two sets of residuals are constructed using Minitab as shown in Figure 10.30. Note that the outlier appears to skew the frequency distribution in Figure 10.30(a), whereas the stem-and-leaf display in Figure 10.30(b) appears to be more mound-shaped. Although the displays do not provide formal statistical tests of normality, they do provide a descriptive display. Relative frequency histograms can also be used to check the normality assumption. In this example the normality assumption appears to be more plausible after the outlier is removed. Consult the references for methods to conduct statistical tests of normality using the residuals.

FIGURE 10.30* ▶
Stem-and-leaf displays for grandfather clock example

(a) Outlier included

```
STEM-AND-LEAF DISPLAY OF RESIDUAL
LEAF DIGIT UNIT =   10.0000
1 2 REPRESENTS 120.

        STEM  LEAF

     1    -7   8
     1    -6
     1    -5
     1    -4
     1    -3
     1    -2
     6    -1   93210
    16    -0   7775544432
    16     0   0233366
     9     1   14459
     4     2   1268
```

(b) Outlier excluded

```
STEM-AND-LEAF DISPLAY OF RESIDUAL
LEAF DIGIT UNIT =   10.0000
1 2 REPRESENTS 120.

     3   -1*  331
     9   -0.  987765
    (7)  -0*  4321000
    15   +0*  011223344
     6   +0.  79
     4    1*  004
     1    1.  9
```

*Recall that the left column of the Minitab printout shows the number of measurements at least as extreme as the stem. In Figure 10.30(a) the 6 corresponding to the STEM $= -1$ means that six measurements are less than or equal to -100. If a number in the leftmost column is enclosed in parentheses, it is the number of measurements in that row, and that row contains the median.

In the last example in this section, we show how to use residuals to check the assumption of constant error variance.

EXAMPLE 10.10

The data in Table 10.11 are salaries, y, and years of experience, x, for a sample of 50 managers from a major industry. Fit the second-order model

$$y = \beta_0 + \beta_1 x + \beta_2 x^2 + \epsilon$$

and plot the residuals versus the estimated mean salary, $\hat{y}$. Interpret the plot.

TABLE 10.11   Salary and Experience Data for 50 Managers from a Major Industry

Years of Experience	Salary	Years of Experience	Salary	Years of Experience	Salary
x	y	x	y	x	y
7	$26,075	21	$43,628	28	$99,139
28	79,370	4	16,105	23	52,624
23	65,726	24	65,644	17	50,594
18	41,983	20	63,022	25	53,272
19	62,309	20	47,780	26	65,343
15	41,154	15	38,853	19	46,216
24	53,610	25	66,537	16	54,288
13	33,697	25	67,447	3	20,844
2	22,444	28	64,785	12	32,586
8	32,562	26	61,581	23	71,235
20	43,076	27	70,678	20	36,530
21	56,000	20	51,301	19	52,745
18	58,667	18	39,346	27	67,282
7	22,210	1	24,833	25	80,931
2	20,521	26	65,929	12	32,303
18	49,727	20	41,721	11	38,371
11	33,233	26	82,641		

Solution

We used Minitab to obtain the computer printout for the second-order model shown in Figure 10.31. The least squares prediction equation is

$$\hat{y} = 20{,}242 + 522x + 53x^2$$

The model appears to provide useful information for the prediction of salaries. The F statistic, computed as the ratio of MS(Regression) to MS(Residual), is

$$F = \frac{6{,}861{,}758{,}464}{65{,}984{,}928} = 103.99$$

This provides strong evidence of the model's usefulness. Further confirmation is given by $R^2 = .816$, the significance of the quadratic term ($t = 2.71$), and the estimate of standard deviation, $s = \$8{,}123$. The latter indicates that we would expect to be able to predict a manager's salary based on his or her experience to within (roughly) $\pm 2s \approx \$16{,}000$.

FIGURE 10.31 ▶
Minitab regression printout:
Second-order additive model

```
THE REGRESSION EQUATION IS
Y =   20242, +   522, X1 +   53,0 X2

                                   ST, DEV,     T-RATIO =
              COLUMN   COEFFICIENT   OF COEF,    COEF/S,D,

                --         20242,       4422,       4,58
       X1    C1           522,          617,       0,85
       X2    C3           53,0          19,6       2,71

THE ST, DEV, OF Y ABOUT REGRESSION LINE IS
S =       8123,
WITH (    50- ,3) =   47 DEGREES OF FREEDOM

R-SQUARED = 81,6 PERCENT
R-SQUARED = 80,8 PERCENT, ADJUSTED FOR D,F,

ANALYSIS OF VARIANCE

   DUE TO        DF              SS        MS=SS/DF

REGRESSION      2   13723521024,  6861758464,
RESIDUAL       47    3101292032,    65984928,
TOTAL          49   16824811520,
```

An experienced analyst might regard the increasing rate of increase in salaries and the concept that the prediction intervals are of about the same width ($\approx \$32,000$) for low- and high-salaried managers as tip-offs that an additive model is inappropriate. However, an examination of the residual plot in Figure 10.32 is, perhaps, the first obvious indication of a potential problem. Note that the Minitab program plots **standardized residuals**—residuals divided by the standard deviation, $s = \$8,123$. This makes it easy to determine the deviation of the residuals from their mean of 0, because the vertical axis is simply the number of standard deviations from the mean (much like a z value).

FIGURE 10.32 ▶
Minitab plot of standardized
residuals of second-order additive
model

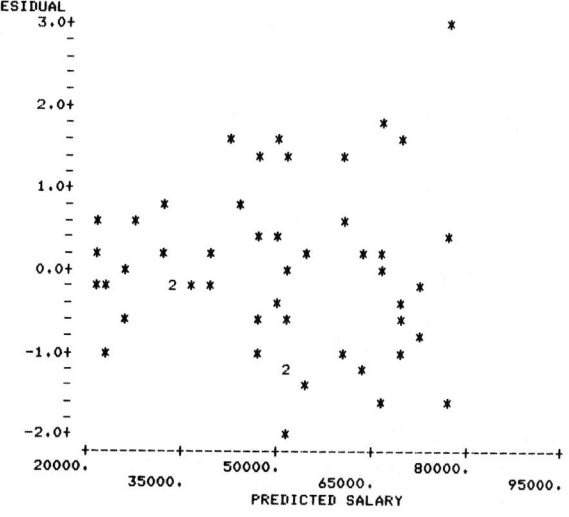

Note the funnel shape of the residuals: the residuals increase in variability as the predicted salary increases. Note that the residuals are all less than 1 standard deviation from the 0 mean when the estimated mean salary, $\hat{y}$, is low, but the range of residual variability stretches to ± 2 standard deviations (or more) for high estimated mean salaries. The residual plot indicates that the assumption of equal variances is likely to be violated, casting doubt on the validity of the inferences made about the model. The problem of nonconstant residual variation can be solved by transforming the dependent variable y and fitting the model to the transformed data. A common transformation in business applications is the logarithmic transformation $y^* = \log(y)$. Consult the references for details on variance-stabilizing transformations in regression.

The box summarizes the residual analyses presented in this section. Residual analysis is a useful tool for the regression analyst, not only to check the assumptions, but also to provide information about how the model can be improved.

Steps in a Residual Analysis

1. Calculate and plot the residuals against each of the independent variables, preferably with the assistance of a computer.

2. Analyze each plot, looking for curvature—either a mound or bowl shape. Both shapes are distinguished by groups of residuals at the low and high values of the x variable on one side of the 0 line, and the residuals for the medium x values on the opposite side of the 0 line. This shape signals the need for a curvature term in the model. Try a second-order term for the variable against which the residuals are plotted.

3. Examine the residual plots for outliers. Draw lines on the residual plots at 3 standard deviations below and above the 0 line. Residuals outside the 3 standard deviation lines are potential outliers. Determine whether each outlier can be explained as an error in data collection or transcription, or belongs to a population different from that of the remainder of the sample, or simply represents an unusual observation. If the observation is an error, fix it or remove it. Even if cause cannot be determined, you may want to rerun the regression analysis without the observation to determine its effect on the analysis.

4. Plot a frequency distribution of the residuals, using a stem-and-leaf display or a histogram. Check to see if obvious departures from normality exist. Extreme skewness of the frequency distribution may indicate the need for a transformation of the dependent variable.

5. Plot the residuals against the predicted response, $\hat{y}$. Check for a pattern that indicates that the variance of the residuals is nonconstant (e.g., increasing as $\hat{y}$ increases). If you detect such a pattern, a transformation of the dependent variable (e.g., $y^* = \log(y)$) may be necessary.

Exercises 10.75 – 10.81

Note: Starred (*) exercises require the use of a computer.

Learning the Mechanics

10.75   Refer to Exercise 10.63, in which a quadratic model was fit to $n = 19$ data points. Two residual plots are shown here—one corresponding to the fitting of a straight-line model to the data, and the other to the quadratic model fit in Exercise 10.63. Analyze the two plots. Is the need for a quadratic term evident from the residual plot for the straight-line model? Does your conclusion agree with your test of the quadratic term in Exercise 10.63?

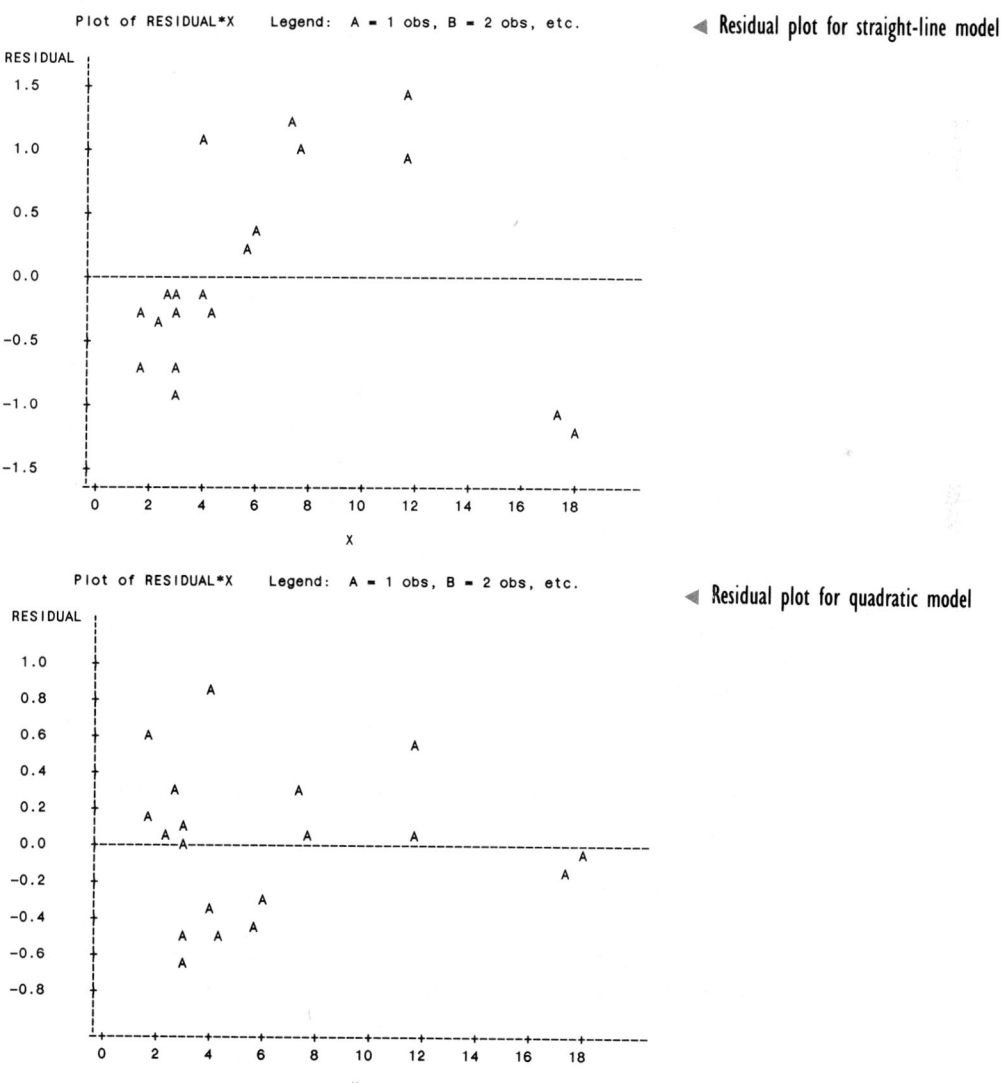

◀ Residual plot for straight-line model

◀ Residual plot for quadratic model

Applying the Concepts

10.76 Refer to Exercise 10.65, in which the 1990 food consumption expenditure y of a sample of 25 households in Washington, D.C., was related to the household income x_1 and size of household x_2 by the model

$$y = \beta_0 + \beta_1 x_1 + \beta_2 x_2 + \epsilon$$

Plots of the residuals from this model are shown—one versus x_1 and one versus x_2. Analyze the plots. Is there visual evidence of a need for a quadratic term in either x_1 or x_2? Explain.

▲ $\hat{\epsilon}$ versus x_1

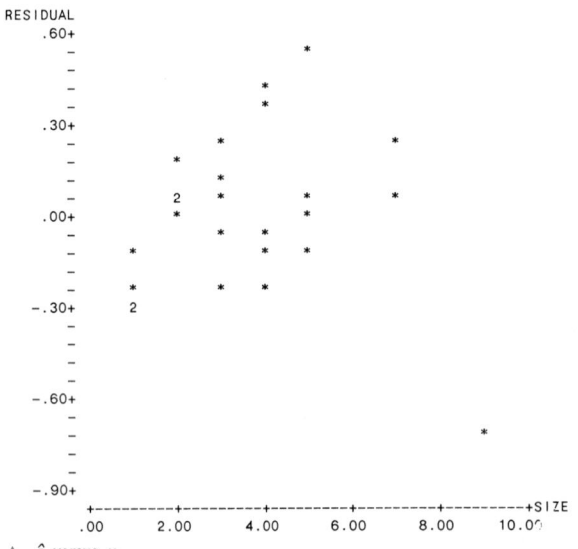

▲ $\hat{\epsilon}$ versus x_2

10.77 Refer to Exercise 10.76. Suppose a 26th household is added to the sample, with the following characteristics:

Food consumption: 6.5   *Income*: 62.3   *Household size*: 5

Two Minitab printouts are shown—one for the same model fit to the first 25 observations, the second fit to all 26 observations.

```
THE REGRESSION EQUATION IS
 FOOD = 1.43 + 0.00999 INCOME + 0.379 SIZE


                                   ST. DEV.      T-RATIO =
                  COEFFICIENT      OF COEF.      COEF/S.D.
                       1.4326        0.1467           9.76
 INCOME            0.009991         0.003168          3.15
 SIZE              0.37929          0.02772          13.68


 S = 0.2769


 R-SQUARED = 90.2 PERCENT
 R-SQUARED = 89.3 PERCENT, ADJUSTED FOR D.F.


 ANALYSIS OF VARIANCE

   DUE TO      DF            SS       MS=SS/DF
 REGRESSION     2       15.4623        7.7311
 RESIDUAL      22        1.6873        0.0767
 TOTAL         24       17.1496
```

▲ Model fit to 25 observations

```
THE REGRESSION EQUATION IS
 FOOD = 1.16 + 0.0187 INCOME + 0.406 SIZE


                                   ST. DEV.      T-RATIO =
 COLUMN       COEFFICIENT         OF COEF.      COEF/S.D.
                    1.1554          0.2882           4.01
 INCOME         0.018735           0.006034         3.11
 SIZE           0.40577            0.05551          7.31


 S = 0.5581

 R-SQUARED = 74.6 PERCENT
 R-SQUARED = 72.4 PERCENT, ADJUSTED FOR D.F.

 ANALYSIS OF VARIANCE

   DUE TO      DF           SS        MS=SS/DF
 REGRESSION     2       21.076        10.538
 RESIDUAL      23        7.163         0.311
 TOTAL         25       28.239
```

▲ Model fit to 26 observations

a. Record the least squares estimates of the model parameters for each model, and note differences in the estimates. Interpret each estimate.

b. Find and interpret the standard deviation for each model.

c. Conduct the analysis of variance F test for each model using $\alpha = .05$.

d. Place a 95% confidence interval on the mean rate of change in food consumption per additional person in the household for each model, assuming household income is constant.

e. According to the results of parts **a–d**, how much influence does the additional observation have on the model?

10.78 Refer to Exercises 10.76 and 10.77. Residual plots against household income and size of household for the models corresponding to 26 observations are shown.

▲ $\hat{e}$ versus x_1

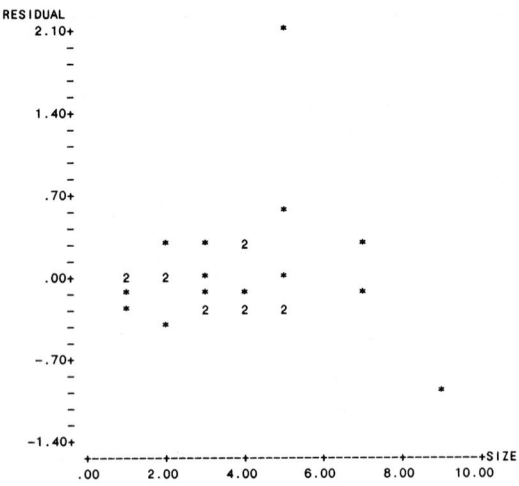

▲ $\hat{e}$ versus x_2

a. Analyze the plots. Are there any outliers? If so, identify them.

b. What are possible explanations for any outliers you identified in part **a**?

10.79 Refer to Exercises 10.76–10.78. The accompanying stem-and-leaf displays represent the frequency distributions of the residuals for the two data sets, one with $n = 25$ and one with $n = 26$. Analyze the displays, especially with regard to the normality assumption.

```
STEM-AND-LEAF DISPLAY OF RESIDUAL
LEAF DIGIT UNIT =    .1000
1 2 REPRESENTS 1.2


    1    -0S   7
    1    -0F
    6    -0T   32222
   11    -0*   11100
   (8)   +0*   00000001
    6    +0T   2223
    2    +0F   45
```

▲ Display for 25 residuals

```
STEM-AND-LEAF DISPLAY OF RESIDUAL
LEAF DIGIT UNIT =    .1000
1 2 REPRESENTS 1.2


    1    -0. 9
  (16)   -0*  4333222211110000
    9    +0*  0022223
    2    +0. 6
    1     1*
    1     1.
    1     2*  1
```

▲ Display for 26 residuals

10.80 State highway agencies regularly invite contractors to submit bids for the construction of new highways. Typical contracts consist of a number of items, and each bidder must quote a cost to the state on an item-by-item basis. One item on most bid specifications is HBP (hot bituminous pavement). The accompanying table contains the winning HBP unit price bids (in dollars/ton) for 30 contracts let over the past 6 months. The total quantity of HBP specified and the number of bidders are also shown for each contract.

Unit Price (per ton)	Quantity (thousands of tons)	Number of Bidders	Unit Price (per ton)	Quantity (thousands of tons)	Number of Bidders
$153.32	1.0	4	$151.13	1.6	7
74.11	7.2	10	79.18	7.3	5
29.72	16.7	5	204.94	.2	9
54.67	11.9	5	81.06	6.8	4
68.39	9.3	4	37.62	11.4	8
119.04	3.7	5	17.13	20.0	3
116.14	1.7	6	37.81	13.4	4
146.49	.1	9	130.72	1.8	2
81.81	7.8	5	26.07	18.5	2
19.58	18.4	9	39.59	14.7	5
141.08	2.9	5	66.20	9.1	4
101.72	4.7	10	160.25	2.4	5
24.88	17.4	10	19.39	17.3	9
19.43	18.4	4	86.60	4.5	9
39.63	11.2	9	47.27	11.6	9

a. Assuming that economies of scale are likely to be present in the supply of HBP for specific contracts, what is the expected relationship between unit price and quantity?

Dep Variable: Y

Analysis of Variance

Source	DF	Sum of Squares	Mean Square	F Value	Prob>F
Model	1	69039.20554	69039.20554	196.615	0.0001
Error	28	9831.89259	351.13902		
C Total	29	78871.09814			

Root MSE	18.73870	R-Square	0.8753
Dep Mean	79.16567	Adj R-Sq	0.8709
C.V.	23.67024		

Parameter Estimates

Variable	DF	Parameter Estimate	Standard Error	T for H0: Parameter=0	Prob > |T|
INTERCEP	1	148.055230	5.98682026	24.730	0.0001
X1	1	−7.570282	0.53988803	−14.022	0.0001

▲ SAS printout for straight-line model in Exercise 10.80

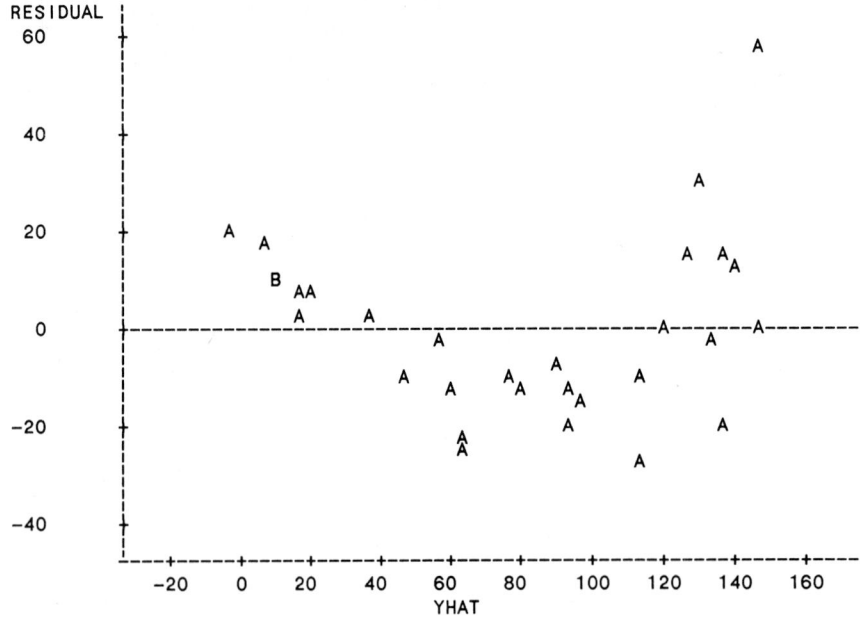

▲ Residual plot for straight-line model in Exercise 10.80

b. Let y represent the unit price, x_1 the quantity, and x_2 the number of bidders. SAS was used to fit the straight-line model

$$y = \beta_0 + \beta_1 x_1 + \epsilon$$

with the results shown in the printout on the previous page. Interpret the least squares estimates, and evaluate the model's usefulness for predicting unit price. Be sure to interpret the estimated standard deviation of the model.

c. The residual plot for this model, with the predicted unit price on the horizontal axis, is also shown on the previous page. What does the pattern of residuals suggest about the assumption that the standard deviation of the error component is constant?

10.81 Refer to Exercise 10.80. We now fit a transformed model by using the logarithmic transformation of unit price in the following model:

$$\log(y) = \beta_0 + \beta_1 x + \epsilon$$

The results are reproduced in the accompanying SAS printout.

Dep Variable: LOG_Y

Analysis of Variance

Source	DF	Sum of Squares	Mean Square	F Value	Prob>F
Model	1	15.59165	15.59165	799.634	0.0001
Error	28	0.54596	0.01950		
C Total	29	16.13761			

Root MSE	0.13964	R-Square	0.9662	
Dep Mean	4.12870	Adj R-Sq	0.9650	
C.V.	3.38210			

Parameter Estimates

Variable	DF	Parameter Estimate	Standard Error	T for H0: Parameter=0	Prob > |T|
INTERCEP	1	5.163967	0.04461255	115.751	0.0001
X1	1	-0.113765	0.00402313	-28.278	0.0001

▲ SAS printout for transformed model in Exercise 10.81

a. Interpret the least squares estimates, and evaluate the usefulness of the model for predicting unit price. Be sure to interpret the estimated standard deviation of the model.

b. The residual plot of the transformed model is shown at the top of page 590, with the predicted value of log(unit price) on the horizontal axis. Evaluate the assumption that the error component of the transformed model has constant standard deviation.

c. Test to determine whether the data support the hypothesis that the mean unit price decreases as the number of bidders increases. Use $\alpha = .05$.

d. With what approximate precision will this model predict the unit price of HBP?

▲ Residual plot for transformed model in Exercise 10.81

Summary

We have introduced an extremely useful tool in this chapter—the **method of least squares** for fitting a prediction equation to a set of data. The application of this methodology, along with the associated inferential procedures, is referred to as **regression analysis**. In Sections 10.1–10.8, we showed how to use sample data to build a model relating a dependent variable y to a single independent variable. The five steps are:

1. Hypothesize a **probabilistic model.** In Sections 10.1–10.8 we confined our attention to the **first-order (straight-line) model,** $y = \beta_0 + \beta_1 x + \epsilon$.

2. Use the method of least squares to estimate the unknown parameters in the **deterministic component,** $\beta_0 + \beta_1 x$. The least squares estimates yield a model $\hat{y} = \hat{\beta}_0 + \hat{\beta}_1 x$ with a **sum of squared errors (SSE)** that is smaller than the SSE for any other straight-line model.

3. Specify the probability distribution of the **random error component, ϵ.**

4. Assess the usefulness of the hypothesized model. Included here are making inferences about the **slope, β_1**; calculating the **coefficient of correlation, r;** and calculating the **coefficient of determination, r^2.**

5. Finally, if we are satisfied with the model, we can use it to **estimate the mean y value,** $E(y)$, for a given x value and/or to **predict an individual y value** for a specific value of x.

In optional Section 10.9, we discussed **multiple regression models,** which relate y to several independent variables, $x_1, x_2, \ldots, x_k$. The steps in a multiple regression analysis are similar to those for the simple straight-line model. Finally, in optional Section 10.10, we showed how **residual analysis** can aid in determining whether the model assumptions (step 3) are satisfied.

Supplementary Exercises 10.82–10.97

Note: *Starred (*) exercises require the use of a computer.*

10.82 Emotional exhaustion, or *burnout*, is a significant problem for people with careers in the field of human services. It seriously affects productivity and feelings of job satisfaction. Leiter and Meechan (1986) used regression analysis to investigate the relationship between burnout and aspects of the human services professional's job and job-related behavior. To measure emotional exhaustion, they used the Maslach Burnout Inventory, a questionnaire. One of the independent variables considered was the proportion of social contacts with individuals who belong to a person's work group. They called this variable *concentration*. The table lists the values of the emotional exhaustion index (higher values indicate greater exhaustion) and concentration for a sample of 25 human services professionals who work in a large public hospital. For this data set, $SS_{yy} = 1,800,417.44$, $SS_{xx} = 14,026.16$, $SS_{xy} = 124,348.520$, $\bar{y} = 578.32$, and $\bar{x} = 68.560$.

Exhaustion Index, y	Concentration, x	Exhaustion Index, y	Concentration, x
100	20%	493	86%
525	60	892	83
300	38	527	79
980	88	600	75
310	79	855	81
900	87	709	75
410	68	791	77
296	12	718	77
120	35	684	77
501	70	141	17
920	80	400	85
810	92	970	96
506	77		

a. Construct a scattergram for the data. Do the variables x and y appear to be related?
b. Calculate the correlation coefficient for the data and interpret its value.
c. Use the method of least squares to estimate the straight-line model relating emotional exhaustion and concentration, and plot it on your scattergram.
d. Calculate the coefficient of determination for your least squares line and interpret it.
e. Test the usefulness of the straight-line relationship with concentration for predicting burnout. Use $\alpha = .05$.

f. Is there evidence that the correlation between emotional exhaustion and concentration differs from 0? Does your conclusion mean that concentration causes emotional exhaustion? Explain.

g. Use a 95% prediction interval to forecast the level of emotional exhaustion for a human services professional for whom 80% of all social contacts are within her work group. Interpret the prediction in the context of the problem.

h. Use a 95% confidence interval to estimate the mean exhaustion level for all professionals who have 80% of their social contacts within their work groups. Interpret the interval, and compare its width with that of the prediction interval in part **g**.

10.83 *Work standards* specify time, cost, and efficiency norms for the performance of work tasks. They are typically used to monitor job performance. In the distribution center of McCormick and Co., Inc., data were collected to develop work standards for the time to assemble or fill customer orders. The table contains data for a random sample of 9 orders.

Time (mins.)	Order Size (cases)
27	36
15	34
71	255
35	103
8	4
60	555
3	6
10	60
10	96

Source: Boyle, D., Ray, B. A., and Kahan, G. "Work standards—the quality way." *Production and Inventory Management Journal,* Second Quarter, 1991, p. 67.

a. Construct a scattergram for these data and interpret it.

b. Fit a least squares line to these data using time as the dependent variable.

c. In general, we would expect the mean time to fill an order to increase with the size of the order. Do the data support this theory? Test using $\alpha = .05$.

d. Find a 95% confidence interval for the mean time to fill an order consisting of 150 cases.

10.84 Refer to Exercise 10.32, in which managerial success y was modeled as a function of the number of contacts x a manager makes with people outside his or her work unit during a specific period of time. Recall that $SS_{yy} = 7,006.6316$, $SS_{xx} = 10,824.5263$, $SS_{xy} = 2,561.2632$, $\bar{y} = 54.5789$, and $\bar{x} = 44.1579$.

a. A manager observed for 2 weeks made 55 contacts with people outside her work unit. Predict the value of the manager's success index. Use a 90% prediction interval.

b. A second manager observed for 2 weeks made 110 contacts outside his work unit. Give two reasons why caution should be exercised in using the least squares model developed from the given data set to construct a prediction interval for this manager's success index.

c. In the context of this problem, determine the value of x whose associated prediction interval for y is the narrowest.

10.85 The preferred mode of long-distance travel has changed dramatically since 1950. The table shows the number of passengers (in millions) carried by scheduled airlines and railroads in the United States over the period from 1950 to 1990. For these data $\Sigma y = 3,917$, $\Sigma x = 5,011$, $\Sigma y^2 = 1,278,301$, $\Sigma x^2 = 1,628,915$, and $\Sigma xy = 1,165,664$.

Year	Air Passengers, y	Rail Passengers, x	Year	Air Passengers, y	Rail Passengers, x
1950	19	488	1977	240	276
1955	42	433	1978	275	262
1960	62	327	1979	317	274
1965	103	306	1980	297	280
1970	169	289	1985	382	275
1974	208	275	1988	455	325
1975	205	270	1989	454	330
1976	223	272	1990	466	329

Source: U.S. Bureau of the Census. *Statistical Abstract of the United States: 1982, 1992.*

a. Find the correlation coefficient and the coefficient of determination for the data in the table and interpret their values.

b. Do the data provide sufficient evidence to indicate that x and y are correlated? Test using $\alpha = .05$.

10.86 *Comparable worth* is a compensation plan designed to eliminate pay inequities among jobs of similar worth. A number of state and municipal governments have adopted such plans, and some unions have sought comparable worth clauses for their contracts. To develop such a plan, a sample of benchmark jobs is evaluated and assigned points (x) based on factors such as responsibility, skill, effort, and working conditions. A market survey is conducted to determine the market rates or salaries (y) of the benchmark jobs. A regression analysis is then used to characterize the relationship between salary and job evaluation points (Scholl and Cooper, 1991). The table gives job evaluation points and salaries for a set of 21 benchmark jobs.

Points, x	Salary, y	Job	Points, x	Salary, y	Job
970	$15,704	Electrician	1865	$17,341	Registered nurse
500	13,984	Semi-skilled laborer	1065	15,194	Licensed practical nurse
370	14,196	Motor equipment operator	880	13,614	Principal clerk typist
220	13,380	Janitor	340	12,594	Clerk typist
250	13,153	Laborer	540	13,126	Senior clerk stenographer
1350	18,472	Senior engineering technician	490	12,958	Senior clerk typist
470	14,193	Senior janitor	940	13,894	Principal clerk stenographer
2040	20,642	Revenue agent	600	13,380	Institutional attendant
370	13,614	Engineering aide	805	15,559	Eligibility technician
1200	16,869	Electrician supervisor	220	13,844	Cook's helper
820	15,184	Senior maintenance technician			

a. Construct a scattergram for these data. What does it suggest about the relationship between salary and job evaluation points?

b. A straight-line model was fit to these data using the SAS system, and the printout is given at the top of page 594. Identify and interpret the least squares equation.

Dependent Variable: Y

Analysis of Variance

Source	DF	Sum of Squares	Mean Square	F Value	Prob>F
Model	1	66801750.334	66801750.334	74.670	0.0001
Error	19	16997968.904	894629.94232		
C Total	20	83799719.238			

Root MSE	945.84879	R-square	0.7972	
Dep Mean	14804.52381	Adj R-sq	0.7865	
C.V.	6.38892			

Parameter Estimates

Variable	DF	Parameter Estimate	Standard Error	T for H0: Parameter=0	Prob > |T|
INTERCEP	1	12024	382.31829064	31.449	0.0001
X	1	3.581616	0.41448305	8.641	0.0001

Obs	X	Dep Var Y	Predict Value	Std Err Predict	Lower95% Predict	Upper95% Predict	Residual
1	970	15704.0	15497.8	221.447	13464.6	17531.0	206.2
2	500	13984.0	13814.5	236.070	11774.1	15854.9	169.5
3	370	14196.0	13348.9	266.420	11292.1	15405.6	847.1
4	220	13380.0	12811.6	309.502	10728.6	14894.6	568.4
5	250	13153.0	12919.1	300.351	10842.0	14996.2	233.9
6	1350	18472.0	16858.8	314.833	14772.4	18945.3	1613.2
7	470	14193.0	13707.0	242.349	11663.4	15750.6	486.0
8	2040	20642.0	19330.2	562.933	17026.4	21633.9	1311.8
9	370	13614.0	13348.9	266.420	11292.1	15405.6	265.1
10	1200	16869.0	16321.6	270.968	14262.3	18380.9	547.4
11	820	15184.0	14960.6	207.190	12934.0	16987.2	223.4
12	1865	17341.0	18703.4	496.163	16467.8	20938.9	-1362.4
13	1065	15194.0	15838.1	238.553	13796.4	17879.8	-644.1
14	880	13614.0	15175.5	210.818	13147.2	17203.7	-1561.5
15	340	12594.0	13241.4	274.451	11180.1	15302.7	-647.4
16	540	13126.0	13957.7	228.483	11921.1	15994.4	-831.7
17	490	12958.0	13778.6	238.109	11737.2	15820.1	-820.6
18	940	13894.0	15390.4	217.251	13359.1	17421.6	-1496.4
19	600	13380.0	14172.6	218.972	12140.6	16204.7	-792.6
20	805	15559.0	14906.9	206.741	12880.4	16933.3	652.1
21	220	13844.0	12811.6	309.502	10728.6	14894.6	1032.4
22	800	.	14888.9	206.632	12862.6	16915.3	.

c. Interpret the value of r^2 for this least squares equation.

d. Is there sufficient evidence to conclude that a straight-line model provides useful information about the relationship in question? Interpret the p-value for this test.

e. A job outside the set of benchmark jobs is evaluated and receives a score of 800 points. Under the comparable worth plan, what is a reasonable range within which a fair salary for this job should be found?

10.87 In the late 1970s and early 1980s, the prices of single-family homes in the United States rose faster than the rate of inflation. As a result, many investors directed their funds to the housing market as a hedge against inflation. One way an investor can assess the value of a specific house is to compare it to recent sale prices for similar houses. Another popular approach, according to Cho and Reichert (1980), uses a regression analysis to model the relationship between price and the variables that influence price. Independent variables that could be utilized are total living area, number of rooms, number of baths, age of property, and so on. Of these factors, Cho and Reichart indicate that total living area provides the most information for determining the worth of a house. The accompanying table lists the final selling price and total living area for a sample of 24 homes in the same geographic area that were sold during the last 3 months of 1990. The regression printout using a straight-line model to relate price to area for these data is given on pages 595–596.

Area (sq. ft.)	Price	Area (sq. ft.)	Price
2,100	$150,000	3,000	205,000
1,455	114,900	1,400	79,400
1,630	106,500	2,750	200,000
2,600	195,000	2,900	215,100
1,210	75,500	2,500	180,800
1,857	126,600	1,535	120,900
2,000	135,400	1,333	70,000
2,400	178,650	2,455	165,200
2,256	145,100	3,010	185,000
1,290	62,600	2,180	160,000
2,332	168,200	1,870	119,900
1,725	138,100	1,582	99,900

a. Construct a scattergram for the data.
b. Find the least squares line and plot it on your scattergram.
c. Find r^2 and interpret its value in the context of the problem.
d. Do the data provide evidence that living area contributes information for predicting the price of a home? Use $\alpha = .05$.
e. Find a 95% confidence interval for β_1. Does your confidence interval support the conclusion you reached in part **d**? Explain. (Note that the standard error of $\hat{\beta}_1$ is given on the printout in the column headed **Standard Error** and in the row corresponding to **AREA**.)
f. Find the observed significance level for the test in part **d**, and interpret its value.
g. Estimate the mean selling price for homes with a total living area of 2,200 square feet. Use a 95% confidence interval.

Source	DF	Sum of Squares	Mean Square	F Value	Prob>F
Model	1	42825909688	42825909688	247.857	0.0001
Error	22	3801265207.6	172784782.16		
C Total	23	46627174896			

Root MSE	13144.76254	R-Square	0.9185	
Dep Mean	141572.91667	Adj R-Sq	0.9148	
C.V.	9.28480			

Parameter Estimates

Variable	DF	Parameter Estimate	Standard Error	T for H0: Parameter=0	Prob > |T|
INTERCEP	1	-15124	10308.485043	-1.467	0.1565
AREA	1	76.174547	4.83848421	15.743	0.0001

Continued

Obs	AREA	PRICE	Predict Value	Residual	Lower 95% Mean	Upper 95% Mean
1	2100	150000	144842	5157.9	139261	150423
2	1455	114900	95709	19190.5	87495.9	103923
3	1630	106500	109040	-2540.0	102017	116064
4	2600	195000	182929	12070.7	175142	190717
5	1210	75500.0	77046.7	-1546.7	66887.4	87206.1
6	1857	126600	126332	268.3	120416	132247
7	2000	135400	137225	-1824.6	131631	142819
8	2400	178650	167694	10955.6	161152	174237
9	2256	145100	156725	-11625.3	150814	162637
10	1290	62600.0	83140.7	-20540.7	73642.8	92638.6
11	2332	168200	162515	5685.4	156304	168725
12	1725	138100	116277	21823.4	109791	122763
13	3000	205000	213399	-8399.2	202423	224376
14	1400	79400.0	91519.9	-12119.9	82892.2	100148
15	2750	200000	194356	5644.5	185450	203261
16	2900	215100	205782	9318.3	195657	215906
17	2500	180800	175312	5488.1	168190	182433
18	1535	120900	101803	19096.5	94160.9	109446
19	1333	70000.0	86416.2	-16416.2	77264.5	95568
20	2455	165200	171884	-6684.0	165035	178733
21	3010	185000	214161	-29160.9	203098	225224
22	2180	160000	150936	9064.0	145236	156636
23	1870	119900	127322	-7421.9	121449	133195
24	1582	99900	105384	-5483.7	98056	112711
25	2200	.	152460	.	146713	158206

10.88 The table lists the 1991 sales y (in millions of dollars) and number of employees x (in thousands) for a random sample of 20 Fortune 500 companies. For this data set, $SS_{yy} = 1,756,002,651.75$, $SS_{xx} = 28,385.22$, $SS_{xy} = 3,881,560.4$, $\bar{y} = 7,740.75$, and $\bar{x} = 39$. Perform a regression analysis that follows the five steps presented in this chapter; be sure to state all assumptions you make. Give a prediction interval for a Fortune 500 company with 50,000 employees.

Company	Sales, y	Employees, x	Company	Sales, y	Employees, x
Procter & Gamble	27,406	94.0	Texaco	37,551	40.2
H. B. Fuller	855	5.6	Westinghouse Electric	12,794	113.7
Johnson & Johnson	12,447	82.7	Tribune	2,035	12.9
Mattel	1,650	12.5	Allied-Signal	11,882	98.3
Intel	4,779	25.1	Polaroid	2,096	12.0
New York Times	1,703	10.1	Leggett & Platt	1,082	10.4
GAF	926	4.1	Gillette	4,706	31.2
Coltec Industries	1,373	11.4	Georgia-Pacific	11,524	57.0
General Mills	7,153	108.1	Compaq Computer	3,271	10.0
ITT Rayonier	979	3.0	Merck	8,603	37.7

Source: "The Fortune 500." *Fortune*, April 20, 1992, pp. 259–284.

*10.89   Since the Great Depression of the 1930s, the link between the suicide rate and the state of the economy has been much researched. Recent work on this link applied regression analysis to data collected from a 45-year-period on the following variables:

y = Suicide rate

x_1 = Unemployment rate

x_2 = Percentage of females in the labor force

x_3 = Divorce rate

x_4 = Log of gross national product (GNP)

x_5 = Annual percent change in GNP

One of the models explored by the authors (Yang, Stack, and Lester, 1992) was a multiple regression model relating y to linear terms in x_1 through x_5. The following least squares model resulted (the observed significance levels of the β estimates are beneath the estimates) and $R^2 = .45$:

$$\hat{y} = .002 + .0204x_1 + (-.0231)x_2 + .0765x_3 + .2760x_4 + .0018x_5$$
$$\quad\quad (.002) \quad\quad (.02) \quad\quad (>.10) \quad\quad (>.10) \quad\quad (>.10)$$

a.   Interpret the value of R^2. Is there sufficient evidence to indicate that the model is useful for predicting the suicide rate? Use $\alpha = .05$.

b.   Interpret each of the coefficients in the model, and each of the corresponding significance levels.

c.   Is there sufficient evidence to indicate that unemployment rate is a useful predictor of the suicide rate? Use $\alpha = .05$.

*10.90   Several states now require all high school seniors to pass an achievement test before they can graduate. On the test, the seniors must demonstrate their familiarity with basic verbal and mathematical skills. Suppose the educational testing company that creates and administers these exams wants to model the score, y, on one of its exams as a function of the student's IQ, x_1, and socioeconomic status (SES), where

$$x_1 = \begin{cases} 1 & \text{if SES is medium} \\ 0 & \text{if SES is low or high} \end{cases} \quad\quad x_3 = \begin{cases} 1 & \text{if SES is high} \\ 0 & \text{if SES is low or medium} \end{cases}$$

Data were collected for a random sample of 60 seniors who took the test, and the model

$$E(y) = \beta_0 + \beta_1 x_1 + \beta_2 x_2 + \beta_3 x_3$$

was fit to the data, with the results shown in the SAS printout.

SOURCE	DF	SUM OF SQUARES	MEAN SQUARE	F VALUE	PR > F
MODEL	3	12268.56439492	4089.52146497	188.33	0.0001
ERROR	56	1216.01893841	21.71462390		
CORRECTED TOTAL	59	13484.58333333		R-SQUARE	ROOT MSE
				0.909822	4.65989527

PARAMETER	ESTIMATE	T FOR H0: PARAMETER=0	PR > !T!	STD ERROR OF ESTIMATE
INTERCEPT	-13.06166081	-3.21	0.0022	4.07101383
X1	0.74193946	17.56	0.0001	0.04224805
X2	18.60320572	12.49	0.0001	1.48895324
X3	13.40965415	8.97	0.0001	1.49417069

a. Identify the least squares equation.
b. Interpret the value of R^2 and test to determine whether the data provide sufficient evidence to indicate that this model is useful for predicting achievement test scores.
c. Sketch the relationship between predicted achievement test score and IQ for the three levels of SES. [Note: Three graphs of $\hat{y}$ versus x_1 must be drawn: the first for the low SES model ($x_2 = x_3 = 0$), the second for the medium SES model ($x_2 = 1$, $x_3 = 0$), and the third for the high SES model ($x_2 = 0$, $x_3 = 1$). The increase in predicted achievement test score per unit increase in IQ is the same for all three levels of SES; i.e., all three lines are parallel.]

*10.91 Refer to Exercise 10.90. We now use the same data to fit the model

$$E(y) = \beta_0 + \beta_1 x_1 + \beta_2 x_2 + \beta_3 x_3 + \beta_4 x_1 x_2 + \beta_5 x_1 x_3$$

Thus, we now add the interaction between IQ and SES to the model. The SAS printout for this model is shown.

SOURCE	DF	SUM OF SQUARES	MEAN SQUARE	F VALUE	PR > F
MODEL	5	12515.10021009	2503.02004202	139.42	0.0001
ERROR	54	969.48312324	17.95339117		
CORRECTED TOTAL	59	13484.58333333		R-SQUARE	ROOT MSE
				0.928104	4.23714422

PARAMETER	ESTIMATE	T FOR H0: PARAMETER = 0	PR > |T|	STD ERROR OF ESTIMATE
INTERCEPT	0.60129643	0.11	0.9096	5.26818519
X1	0.59526252	10.70	0.0001	0.05563379
X2	-3.72536406	-0.37	0.7115	10.01967496
X3	-16.23196444	-1.90	0.0631	8.55429931
X1*X2	0.23492147	2.29	0.0260	0.10263908
X1*X3	0.30807756	3.53	0.0009	0.08739554

a. Identify the least squares prediction equation.
b. Interpret the value of R^2 and test to determine whether the data provide sufficient evidence to indicate that this model is useful for predicting achievement test scores.

*10.92 A metropolitan bus company wants to know whether changes in numbers of bus riders are related to changes in gasoline prices. By using information in the company files and gasoline price information from fuel distributors, the company plans to fit the model

$$y = \beta_0 + \beta_1 x_1 + \beta_2 x_2 + \beta_3 x_1 x_2 + \epsilon$$

where

x_1 = Average wholesale price for regular gasoline in a given month

$x_2 = \begin{cases} 1 & \text{if the bus travels a city route only} \\ 0 & \text{if the bus travels a suburb–city route} \end{cases}$

y = Total number of riders in a bus over the month

a. For the preceding model, how would you test to determine whether the relationship between the mean number of riders and gasoline price is different for the two types of bus routes?

b. Suppose 12 months of data are kept, and the least squares model is

$$\hat{y} = 500 + 50x_1 + 5x_2 - 10x_1x_2$$

Graph the predicted relationship between number of riders and gasoline price for city buses and for suburb–city buses. Compare the slopes.

c. If $s_{\hat{\beta}_3} = 3.0$, do the data indicate that gasoline price affects the number of riders differently for city and suburb–city buses? Use $\alpha = .05$.

*10.93 To increase the motivation and productivity of workers, an electronics manufacturer decides to experiment with a new pay incentive structure at one of two plants. The experimental plan will be tried at plant A for 6 months, whereas workers at plant B will remain on the original pay plan. To evaluate the effectiveness of the new plan, the average assembly time for part of an electronic system was measured for employees at both plants at the beginning and end of the 6-month period. Suppose the model proposed was:

$$y = \beta_0 + \beta_1x_1 + \beta_2x_2 + \epsilon$$

where

  y = Assembly time (hours) at end of 6-month period

  x_1 = Assembly time (hours) at beginning of 6-month period

  $x_2 = \begin{cases} 1 & \text{if plant A} \\ 0 & \text{if plant B} \end{cases}$ (dummy variable)

A sample of $n = 42$ observations yielded

$$\hat{y} = .11 + .98x_1 - .53x_2$$

where

  $s_{\hat{\beta}_1} = .231$ $s_{\hat{\beta}_2} = .48$

Test to see whether, after allowing for the effect of initial assembly time, plant A had a lower mean assembly time than plant B. Use $\alpha = .01$. [*Note:* When the {0, 1} coding is used to define a dummy variable, the coefficient of the variable represents the difference between the mean response at the two levels represented by the variable. Thus, the coefficient β_2 is the difference in mean assembly time between plant A and plant B at the end of the 6-month period, and $\hat{\beta}_2$ is the sample estimator of that difference.]

*10.94 Many colleges and universities develop regression models for predicting the grade-point average (GPA) of incoming freshmen to help make admission decisions. Although most models use many independent variables to predict GPA, we will illustrate by choosing two variables:

  x_1 = Verbal score on college entrance examination (percentile)

  x_2 = Mathematics score on college entrance examination (percentile)

The data in the table on page 600 are obtained for a random sample of 40 freshmen at one college.

Verbal	Math	GPA	Verbal	Math	GPA	Verbal	Math	GPA
x_1	x_2	y	x_1	x_2	y	x_1	x_2	y
81	87	3.49	83	76	3.75	98	67	2.73
68	99	2.89	64	66	2.70	97	80	3.27
57	86	2.73	83	72	3.15	77	90	3.47
100	49	1.54	93	54	2.28	49	54	1.30
54	83	2.56	74	59	2.92	39	81	1.22
82	86	3.43	51	75	2.48	87	69	3.23
75	74	3.59	79	75	3.45	70	95	3.82
58	98	2.86	81	62	2.76	57	89	2.93
55	54	1.46	50	69	1.90	74	67	2.83
49	81	2.11	72	70	3.01	87	93	3.84
64	76	2.69	54	52	1.48	90	65	3.01
66	59	2.16	65	79	2.98	81	76	3.33
80	61	2.60	56	78	2.58	84	69	3.06
100	85	3.30						

The SPSS printout corresponding to the model

$$y = \beta_0 + \beta_1 x_1 + \beta_2 x_2 + \epsilon$$

is shown here.

```
Multiple R            .82527
R Square              .68106
Adjusted R Square     .66382
Standard Error        .40228

Analysis of Variance
                   DF      Sum of Squares      Mean Square
Regression          2          12.78595          6.39297
Residual           37           5.98755           .16183

F =     39.50530        Signif F =  .0000


------------------- 'ariables in the Equation -------------------

Variable            B        SE B        Beta        T    Sig T

X1            .02573 4.02357E-03     .59719     6.395   .0000
X2            .03361 4.92751E-03     .63702     6.822   .0000
(Constant)  -1.57054      .49375                -3.181   .0030
```

a. Interpret the least squares estimates $\hat{\beta}_1$ and $\hat{\beta}_2$ in the context of this application.
b. Interpret the standard deviation and the coefficient of determination of the regression model in the context of this application.
c. Is this model useful for predicting GPA? Conduct a statistical test to justify your answer.
d. Sketch the relationship between predicted GPA, $\hat{y}$, and verbal score, x_1, for the following mathematics scores: $x_2 = 60$, 75, and 90.

*10.95   Refer to Exercise 10.94. The residuals from the first-order model are plotted versus x_1 and versus x_2. Analyze the two plots, and determine whether visual evidence exists that curvature (a quadratic term) for either x_1 or x_2 should be added to the model.

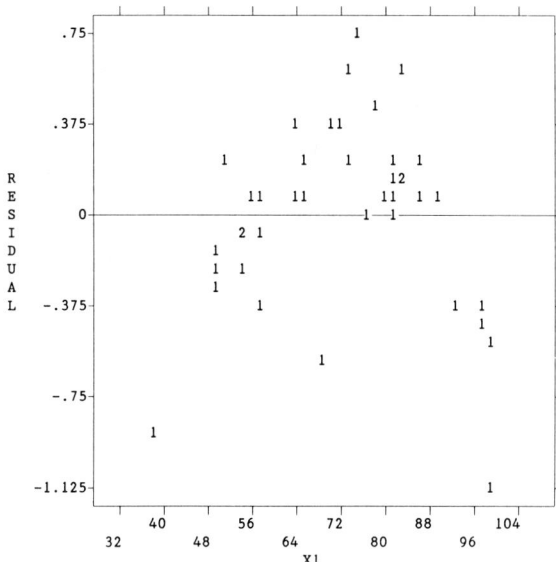

▲ $\hat{e}$ versus x_1 for first-order model

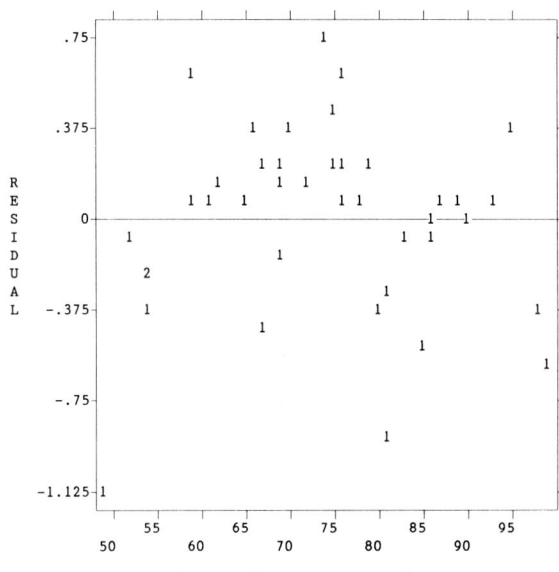

▲ $\hat{e}$ versus x_2 for first-order model

*10.96 Refer to Exercises 10.94 and 10.95. The complete second-order model

$$y = \beta_0 + \beta_1 x_1 + \beta_2 x_2 + \beta_3 x_1^2 + \beta_4 x_2^2 + \beta_5 x_1 x_2 + \epsilon$$

is fit to the data given in Exercise 10.94. The resulting SPSS printout is reproduced here.

```
Multiple R              .96777
R Square                .93657
Adjusted R Square       .92724
Standard Error          .18714

Analysis of Variance
                    DF      Sum of Squares      Mean Square
Regression           5            17.58274          3.51655
Residual            34             1.19076           .03502

F =      100.40901       Signif F =   .0000

------------------ Variables in the Equation -------------------

Variable            B          SE B          Beta         T    Sig T

X1            .16681        .02124       3.87132     7.852    .0000
X2            .13760        .02673       2.60754     5.147    .0000
X1SQ    -1.10825E-03  1.17288E-04      -3.71359    -9.449    .0000
X2SQ    -8.43267E-04  1.59423E-04      -2.37284    -5.290    .0000
X1X2     2.410891E-04  1.43974E-04        .49600     1.675    .1032
(Constant)   -9.91676       1.35441                 -7.322    .0000
```

a. Compare the standard deviations of the first- and second-order regression models. With what relative precision will these two models predict GPA?

b. Test whether this model is useful for predicting GPA. Use $\alpha = .05$.

c. Test whether the interaction term, $\beta_5 x_1 x_2$, is important for the prediction of GPA. Use $\alpha = .10$. Note that this term permits the distance between three mathematics score curves for GPA versus verbal score to change as the verbal score changes.

*10.97 Refer to Exercises 10.94–10.96. The residuals of the second-order model are plotted against both x_1 and x_2. Compare the residual plots to those of the first-order model in Exercise 10.95. Given the analyses you have performed in Exercises 10.94–10.96, which of the two models do you think is preferable as a predictor of GPA: the first- or second-order model?

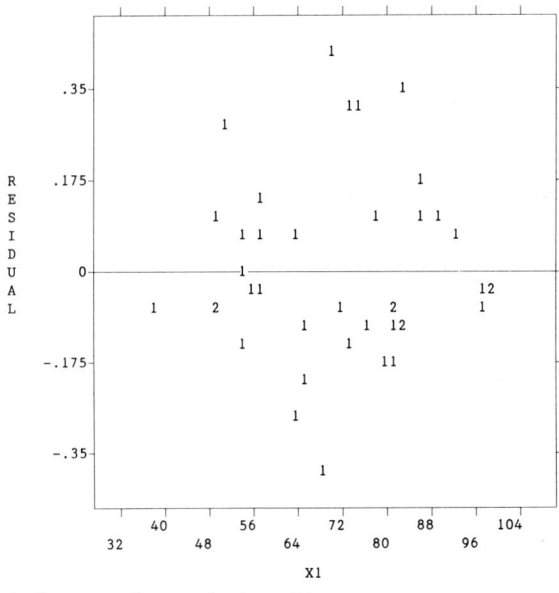

▲ $\hat{e}$ versus x_1 for second-order model

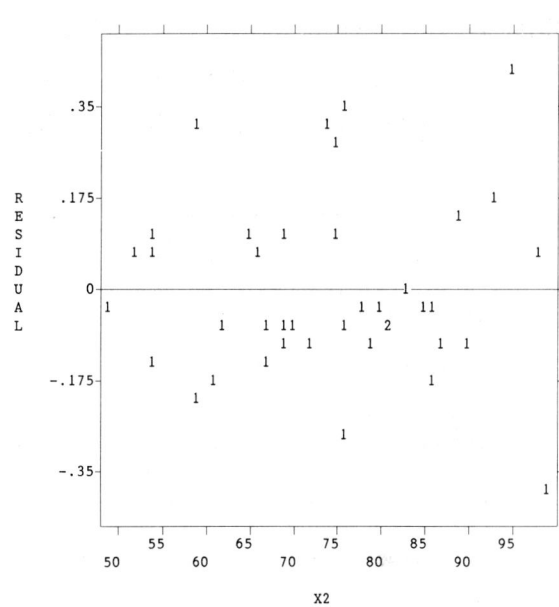

▲ $\hat{e}$ versus x_2 for second-order model

On Your Own

The Gross Domestic Product (GDP) is one of the nation's best-known economic indicators. Many economists have developed models to forecast future values of the GDP. Surely many variables should be included if an accurate prediction is to be made. For the moment, however, consider the simple case of choosing one important variable to include in a simple straight-line model for GDP.

First, list three independent variables (x_1, x_2, and x_3) that you think might be (individually) strongly related to the GDP. Next, obtain 10 yearly values (preferably for the last 10 years) of the three independent variables and the GDP. *

a. Use the least squares formulas given in this chapter to fit three straight-line models—one for each independent variable—for predicting the GDP.
b. Interpret the sign of the estimated slope coefficient, $\hat{\beta}_1$, in each case, and test the utility of each model by testing H_0: $\beta_1 = 0$ against H_a: $\beta_1 \neq 0$.
c. Calculate the coefficient of determination r^2 for each model. Which of the independent variables predicts the GDP best over the 10 sample years when a straight-line model is used? Is this variable necessarily best in general (i.e., for all years)? Explain.

---

*The assumption that the random errors are independent is debatable for time series data. For the purposes of illustration, we assume they are approximately independent. For more on the problem of dependent errors, consult the references at the end of this chapter.

Using the Computer

Suppose we want to model the relationship between the median household income y and the percentage of college graduates x in a zip code using a straight-line model.

a. Draw a random sample of 100 zip codes from the 1,000 described in Appendix C, and extract y and x for each zip code sampled. Use a software package that includes a regression program to obtain the least squares fit for the model of interest.
   1. Graph the fitted model.
   2. Interpret the estimated intercept and slope.
   3. Interpret the estimated standard deviation of the error term.
   4. Evaluate the usefulness of the model.
   5. Estimate the mean median income for all zip codes having 15% college graduates using a 95% confidence interval.
   6. Predict the median income for a particular zip code having 15% college graduates using a 95% prediction interval.

b. Repeat part **a** using the entire set of 1,000 zip codes. Compare the results to those you obtained in part **a**.

References

Allmon, C. I. "Advertising and sales relationships for toothpaste: Another look." *Business Economics*, Sept. 1982, Vol. 17, pp. 55–61.

Blair, R. D., and Kenny, L. W. *Microeconomics for Managerial Decision Making*. New York: McGraw-Hill, 1982. Chapter 3.

Carlson, R. D. "Advertising and sales relationships for toothpaste." *Business Economics*, Sept. 1981, Vol. 16, pp. 36–39.

Chase, R. B., and Aquilano, N. J. *Production and Operations Management*, 6th ed. Homewood, Ill.: Richard D. Irwin, 1992.

Chatterjee S., and Price, B. *Regression Analysis by Example*, 2nd ed. New York: Wiley, 1991.

Cho, C. C., and Reichert, A. "An application of multiple regression analysis for appraising single-family housing values." *Business Economics*, Jan. 1980, Vol. 15, pp. 47–52.

Cook, T. Q. (ed.) *Instruments of the Money Market*, 4th ed. Richmond, Va.: Federal Reserve Bank of Richmond, 1977.

Crandall, J. S., and Cedercreutz, M. "Preliminary cost estimates for mechanical work." *Building Systems Design*, Oct.–Nov. 1976, Vol. 73, pp. 35–51.

Deming, W. E. *Out of the Crisis*. Cambridge, Mass.: MIT Center For Advanced Engineering Study, 1986.

Draper, N. R., and Smith, H. *Applied Regression Analysis*, 2nd ed. New York: Wiley, 1981.

Ferguson, C. E., and Maurice, S. C. *Economics Analysis*. Homewood, Ill.: Richard D. Irwin, 1970. Chapter 6.

Glueck, W. F. *Management*. Hinsdale, Ill.: Dryden Press, 1977. p. 274.

Gray, J., and Johnston, K. S. *Accounting and Management Action*, 2nd ed. New York: McGraw-Hill, 1977. Pp. 267–268.

Henry, W. R., and Haynes, W. W. *Managerial Economics: Analysis and Cases*, 4th ed. Dallas: Business Publications, 1978. Chapter 5.

Koch, P. D., and Ragan, J. F., Jr. "Investigating the causal relationship between quits and wages: An exercise in comparative dynamics." *Economic Inquiry*, Jan. 1986, Vol. 24, pp. 61–83.

Krueger, A. O. "Global trade prospects for the developing countries." *World Economy*, July 1992, Vol. 15, No. 4, p. 457.

Landro, L., and Mayer, J. "Cable-TV viewing study dims prospect of large increase in number of channels." *Wall Street Journal*, Nov. 16, 1982.

Leiter, M. P., and Meechan, K. A. "Role structure and burnout in the field of human services." *Journal of Applied Behavioral Science*, 1986, Vol. 22, No. 1, pp. 47–52.

Luthans, F., Rosenkrantz, S. A., and Hennessey, H. W. "What do successful managers really do? An observational study of managerial activities." *Journal of Applied Behavioral Science*, Aug. 1985, Vol. 21, No. 3, pp. 255–270.

McConnell, C. R., and Brue, S. L. *Economics*. New York: McGraw-Hill, 1990.

Miller, R. B., and Wichern, D. W. *Intermediate Business Statistics: Analysis of Variance, Regression, and Time Series*. New York: Holt, Rinehart and Winston, 1977. Chapter 5–8.

Mintzberg, H. *The Nature of Managerial Work*. New York: Harper and Row, 1973.

Neter, J., Wasserman, W., and Kutner, M. H. *Applied Linear Regression Models*, 2nd ed. Homewood, Ill.: Richard D. Irwin, 1989.

Scholl, R. W., and Cooper, E. "The use of job evaluation to eliminate gender based pay differentials." *Public Personnel Management*, Spring 1991, Vol. 20, No. 1, p. 1.

Weisberg, S. *Applied Linear Regression*, 2nd ed. New York: Wiley, 1985.

Winkler, R. L., and Hays, W. L. *Statistics: Probability, Inference, and Decision*, 2nd ed. New York: Holt, Rinehart and Winston, 1975. Chapter 10.

Wonnacott, R. J., and Wonnacott, T. H. *Econometrics*, 2nd ed. New York: Wiley, 1979. Chapter 6.

Yang, B., Stack, S., and Lester, D. "Suicide and unemployment: Predicting the smoothed trend and yearly fluctuations." *Socio-Economics*, Spring 1992, Vol. 21, No. 1.

Younger, M. S. *First Course in Linear Regression*, 2nd ed. Boston: Duxbury, 1985.

CHAPTER ELEVEN
Methods for Quality Improvement

Contents

Case Study

Where We've Been

In Chapters 6–9, we described methods for making inferences about populations based on sample data. In Chapter 10 we focused on modeling relationships between variables using regression analysis.

Where We're Going

In this chapter, we turn our attention to processes. Recall from Chapter 1 that a process is a series of actions or operations that transform inputs to outputs. This chapter describes methods for improving processes and the quality of the output they produce.

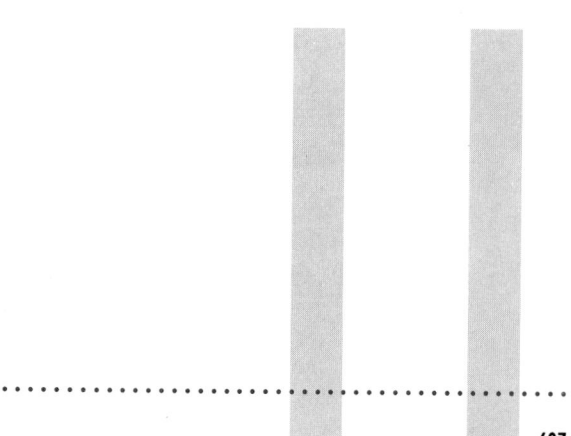

Over the last two decades U.S. firms have been seriously challenged by products of superior quality from overseas, particularly from Japan. Japan currently produces 26% of the cars sold in the United States, and some authorities predict this will climb to 40% within a decade. In 1989, for the first time, the top-selling car in the United States was made in Japan: the Honda Accord. Although it's an American invention, virtually all VCRs are produced in Japan. Only one U.S. firm still manufactures televisions; the rest are made in Japan.

To meet this competitive challenge, more and more U.S. firms—both manufacturing and service firms—have begun quality-improvement initiatives of their own. Many of these firms now stress the management of quality in all phases and aspects of their business, from the design of their products to production, distribution, sales, and service.

Broadly speaking, quality-improvement programs are concerned with (1) finding out what it is that the customer wants, (2) translating those wants into a product or service design, and (3) producing a product or service that meets or exceeds the specifications of the design. In this chapter we focus primarily on the third of these three areas and its major problem—product and service variation.

Variation is inherent in the output of all production and service processes. No two parts produced by a given machine are the same; no two transactions performed by a given bank teller are the same. Why is this a problem? With variation in output comes variation in the quality of the product or service. If this variation is unacceptable to customers, sales are lost, profits suffer, and the firm may not survive.

The existence of this ever-present variation has made statistical methods and statistical training vitally important to industry. In this chapter we present some of the tools and methods currently employed by firms worldwide to monitor and reduce product and service variation.

11.1 Quality, Processes, and Systems

Before describing various tools and methods that can be used to monitor and improve the quality of products and services, we need to consider what is meant by the term **quality**. Quality can be defined from several different perspectives. To the engineers and scientists who design products, quality typically refers to the amount of some ingredient or attribute possessed by the product. For example, high-quality ice cream contains a large amount of butterfat. High-quality rugs have a large number of knots per square inch. A high-quality shirt or blouse has 22 to 26 stitches per inch.

To managers, engineers, and workers involved in the production of a product (or the delivery of a service), quality usually means conformance to requirements, or the degree to which the product or service conforms to its design specifications. For example, in order to fit properly, the cap of a particular molded plastic bottle must be between 1.0000 inch and 1.0015 inches in diameter. Caps that do not conform to this requirement are considered to be of inferior quality.

Although quality can be defined from the perspective of either the designers or the producers of a product, in the final analysis both definitions should be derived from the needs and preferences of the *user* of the product or service. A firm that produces goods that no one wants to purchase cannot stay in business. We define quality accordingly.

Definition 11.1

The **quality** of a good or service is indicated by the extent to which it satisfies the needs and preferences of its users.

Consumers' needs and wants shape their perceptions of quality. Thus, to produce a high-quality product, it is necessary to study the needs and wants of consumers. This is typically one of the major functions of a firm's marketing department. Once the

---

The Eight Dimensions of Quality

1. **Performance**: The primary operating characteristics of the product. For an automobile, these would include acceleration, handling, smoothness of ride, gas mileage, etc.

2. **Features**: The "bells and whistles" that supplement the product's basic functions. Examples include CD players and digital clocks on cars and the frequent-flyer mileage and free drinks offered by airlines.

3. **Reliability**: Reflects the probability that the product will not operate properly within a given period of time.

4. **Conformance**: The extent or degree to which a product meets pre-established standards. This is reflected in, for example, a pharmaceutical manufacturer's concern that the plastic bottles it orders for its drugs have caps that are between 1.0000 and 1.0015 inches in diameter, as specified in their order.

5. **Durability**: The life of the product. If repair is possible, durability relates to the length of time a product can be used before replacement is judged to be preferable to continued repair.

6. **Serviceability**: The ease of repair, speed of repair, and competence and courtesy of the repair staff.

7. **Aesthetics**: How a product looks, feels, sounds, smells, or tastes.

8. **Other perceptions that influence judgments of quality**: Such factors as a firm's reputation and the images of the firm and its products that are created through advertising.

necessary consumer research has been conducted, it is necessary to translate consumers' desires into a product design. This design must then be translated into a production plan and production specifications that, if properly implemented, will turn out a product with characteristics that will satisfy users' needs and wants. In short, consumer perceptions of quality play a role in all phases and aspects of a firm's operations.

But what product characteristics are consumers looking for? What influences users' perceptions of quality? This is the kind of knowledge that firms need to develop and deliver high-quality goods and services. David A. Garvin (1988) summarizes the basic elements of quality in what he calls the **eight dimensions of quality**.

In order to design and produce products of high quality, it is necessary to translate the characteristics described in the box into product attributes that can be built into the product by the manufacturer. That is, user preferences must be interpreted in terms of product variables over which the manufacturer has control. For example, in considering the performance characteristics of a particular brand of wooden pencil, users may indicate a preference for being able to use the pencil for longer periods between sharpenings. The manufacturer may translate this performance characteristic into one or more measurable physical characteristics such as wood hardness, lead hardness, and lead composition. Besides being used to design high-quality products, such variables are used in the process of monitoring and improving quality during production.

In general, a "process" is defined as follows:

Definition 11.2

A **process** is a series of actions or operations that transforms inputs to outputs. A process produces output over time.

Perhaps the best example is a manufacturing process, which consists of a series of operations, performed by people and machines, whereby inputs such as raw materials and parts are converted into finished products (the outputs). Examples of manufacturing processes include automobile assembly lines, oil refineries, and steel mills. Figure 11.1 presents a general description of a process and its inputs.

FIGURE 11.1 ▲ Graphical depiction of a process and its inputs

It is useful to think of processes as *adding value* to the inputs of the process. Manufacturing processes, for example, are designed so that the value of the outputs to potential customers exceeds the value of the inputs—otherwise the firm would have no demand for its products and would not survive.

To understand what causes variation in process output and how processes and their output can be improved, we must understand the role that processes play in *systems*.

Definition 11.3

A **system** is a collection or arrangement of interacting processes that has an ongoing purpose or mission. A system receives inputs from its environment, transforms those inputs to outputs, and delivers them to its environment. In order to survive, a system uses feedback (i.e., information) from its environment to understand and adapt to changes in its environment.

Figure 11.2 presents a model of a basic system. As an example of a system, consider a manufacturing company. It has a collection of interacting processes—marketing research, engineering, purchasing, receiving, production, sales, distribution, billing, etc. Its mission is to make money for its owners, to provide high-quality working conditions for its employees, and to stay in business. The firm receives raw materials and parts (inputs) from outside vendors which, through its production processes, it transforms to finished goods (outputs). The finished goods are distributed to its customers. Through its marketing research, the firm "listens" to (receives feedback from) its customers and potential customers in order to change or adapt its processes and products to meet (or exceed) the needs, preferences, and expectations of the marketplace.

FIGURE 11.2 ▲ Model of a basic system

Since systems are collections of processes, the various types of system inputs are the same as those listed in Figure 11.1 for processes. System outputs are products or services. These outputs may be physical objects made, assembled, repaired, or moved by the system; or they may be symbolical, such as information, ideas, or knowledge.

For example, a brokerage house supplies customers with information about stocks and bonds and the markets where they are traded.

Two important points about systems and the output of their processes are: **(1) No two items produced by a process are the same; (2) Variability is an inherent characteristic of the output of all processes.** This is illustrated in Figure 11.3. No two cars produced by the same assembly line are the same: No two windshields are the same; no two wheels are the same; no two tires are the same; no two lug nuts are the same; no two hubcaps are the same. The same thing can be said for processes that deliver services. Consider the services offered at the teller windows of a bank to two customers waiting in two lines. Will they wait in line the same amount of time? Will they be serviced by tellers with the same degree of expertise and with the same personalities? Assuming the customers' transactions are the same, will they take the same amount of time to execute? The answer to all these questions is no.

FIGURE 11.3 ▶
Output variation

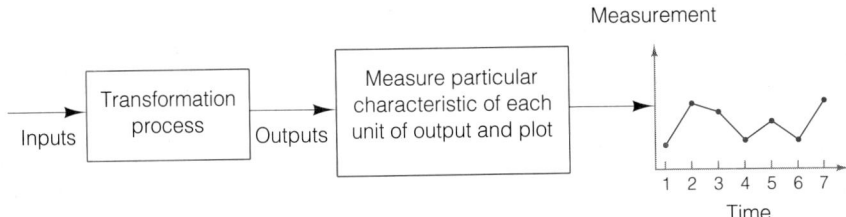

In general, variation in output is caused by the six factors listed in the box.

The Six Major Sources of Process Variation

1. People
2. Machines
3. Materials
4. Methods
5. Measurement
6. Environment

Awareness of this ever-present process variation has made training in statistical thinking and statistical methods highly valued by industry. By **statistical thinking** we mean the knack of recognizing variation, and exploiting it in problem solving and decision-making. The remainder of this chapter is devoted to statistical tools for monitoring process variation.

CASE STUDY 11.1 / Deming's 14 Points

How is it that the Japanese became quality leaders? What inspired their concern for quality? In part, it was the statistical and managerial expertise exported to Japan from the United States following World War II. At the end of the war Japan faced the difficult task of rebuilding its economy. To this end, a group of engineers was assigned by the Allied command to assist the Japanese in improving the quality of their communication systems. These engineers taught the Japanese the statistical quality-control methods that had been developed in the United States under the direction of Walter Shewhart of Bell Laboratories in the 1920s and 1930s. Then, in 1950, the Japanese Union of Scientists and Engineers invited W. Edwards Deming, a statistician who had studied with Shewhart, to present a series of lectures on statistical quality-improvement methods to hundreds of Japanese researchers, plant managers, and engineers. During his stay in Japan he also met with many of the top executives of Japan's largest companies. At the time, Japan was notorious for the inferior quality of its products. Deming told the executives that by listening to what consumers wanted and by applying statistical methods in the production of those goods, they could export high-quality products that would find markets all over the world.

In 1951 the Japanese established the **Deming Prize** to be given annually to companies with significant accomplishments in the area of quality. In 1989, for the first time, the Deming Prize was given to a U.S. company—Florida Power and Light Company

One of W. Edwards Deming's major contributions to the quality movement that is spreading across the major industrialized nations of the world was his recognition that statistical (and other) process improvement methods cannot succeed without the proper organizational climate and culture. Accordingly, he proposed 14 guidelines that, if followed, transform the organizational climate to one in which process-management efforts can flourish. These 14 points are, in essence, Deming's philosophy of management. He ar-

gues convincingly that all 14 should be implemented, not just certain subsets. We list all 14 points here, adding clarifying statements where needed. For a fuller discussion of these points, see Deming (1986), Gitlow et al. (1989), Walton (1986), and Joiner and Goudard (1990).

1. **Create constancy of purpose toward improvement of product and service, with the aim to become competitive and to stay in business, and to provide jobs.** The organization must have a clear goal or purpose. Everyone in the organization must be encouraged to work toward that goal day in and day out, year after year.

2. **Adopt the new philosophy.** Reject detection–rejection management in favor of a customer-oriented, preventative style of management in which never-ending quality improvement is the driving force.

3. **Cease dependence on inspection to achieve quality.** It is because of poorly designed products and excessive process variation that inspection is needed. If quality is designed into products and process management is used in their production, mass inspection of finished products will not be necessary.

4. **End the practice of awarding business on the basis of price tag.** Do not simply buy from the lowest bidder. Consider the quality of the supplier's products along with the supplier's price. Establish long-term relationships with suppliers based on loyalty and trust. Move toward using a single supplier for each item needed.

5. **Improve constantly and forever the system of production and service, to improve quality and productivity, and thus constantly decrease costs.**

6. **Institute training.** Workers are often trained by other workers who were never properly trained themselves. The result is excessive process varia-

tion and inferior products and services. This is not the workers' fault; no one has told them how to do their jobs well.

7. **Institute leadership.** Supervisors should help the workers to do a better job. Their job is to lead, not to order workers around or to punish them.

8. **Drive out fear, so that everyone may work effectively for the company.** Many workers are afraid to ask questions or to bring problems to the attention of management. Such a climate is not conducive to producing high-quality good and services. People work best when they feel secure.

9. **Break down barriers between departments.** Everyone in the organization must work together as a team. Different areas within the firm should have complementary, not conflicting, goals. People across the organization must realize that they are all part of the same system. Pooling their resources to solve problems is better than competing against each other.

10. **Eliminate slogans, exhortations, and arbitrary numerical goals and targets for the work force which urge the workers to achieve new levels of productivity and quality.** Simply asking the workers to improve their work is not enough; they must be shown *how* to improve it. Management must realize that significant improvements can be achieved only if management takes responsibility for quality and makes the necessary changes in the design of the system in which the workers operate.

11. **Eliminate numerical quotas.** Quotas are purely quantitative (e.g., number of pieces to produce per day); they do not take quality into consideration. When faced with quotas, people attempt to meet them at any cost, regardless of the damage to the organization.

12. **Remove barriers that rob employees of their pride of workmanship.** People must be treated as human beings, not commodities. Working conditions must be improved, including the elimination of poor supervision, poor product design, defective materials, and defective machines. These things stand in the way of workers' performing up to their capabilities and producing work they are proud of.

13. **Institute a vigorous program of education and self-improvement.** Continuous improvement requires continuous learning. Everyone in the organization must be trained in the modern methods of quality improvement, including statistical concepts and interdepartmental teamwork. Top management should be the first to be trained.

14. **Take action to accomplish the transformation.** Hire people with the knowledge to implement the 14 points. Build a critical mass of people committed to transforming the organization. Put together a top management team to lead the way. Develop a plan and an organizational structure that will facilitate the transformation.

11.2 Statistical Control

For the rest of this chapter we turn our attention to control charts—graphical devices used for monitoring process variation, for identifying when to take action to improve the process, and for assisting in diagnosing the causes of process variation. Control charts, developed by Walter Shewhart of Bell Laboratories in the mid-1920s, are the tool of choice for continuously monitoring processes. Before we go into the details of control chart construction and use, however, it is important that you have a fuller understanding of process variation. To this end, we discuss patterns of variation in this section.

As was discussed in Chapter 2, the proper graphical method for describing the variation of process output is a **time series plot**, sometimes called a **run chart**. Recall that in a time series plot the measurements of interest are plotted against time or are plotted in the order in which the measurements were made, as in Figure 11.4. Whenever you face the task of analyzing data that were generated over time, your first reaction should be to plot them. The human eye is one of our most sensitive statistical instruments. Take advantage of that sensitivity by plotting the data and allowing your eyes to seek out patterns in the data.

FIGURE 11.4 ▶

Time series plot of fill weights for 50 consecutively produced gallon cans of paint

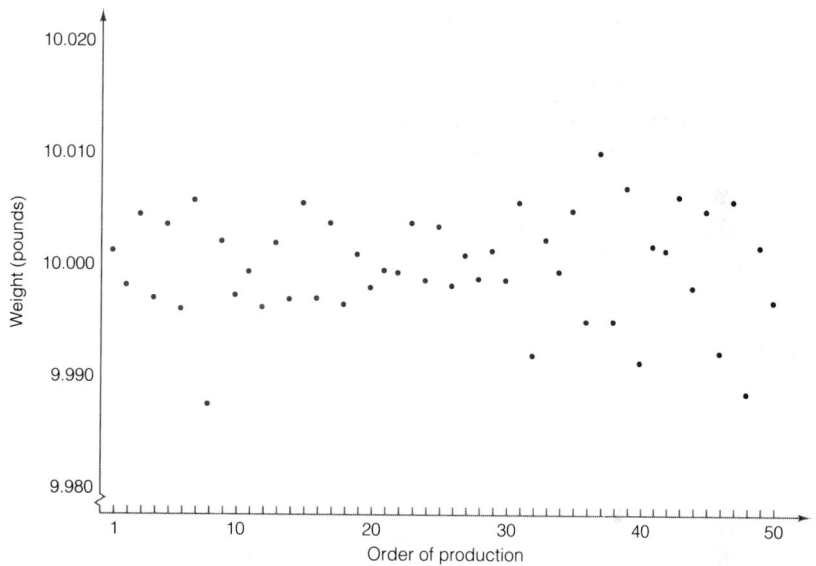

Let's begin thinking about process variation by examining the plot in Figure 11.4 more closely. The measurements, taken from a paint-manufacturing process, are the weights of 50 1-gallon cans of paint that were consecutively filled by the same filling head (nozzle). The weights were plotted in the order of production. Do you detect any systematic, persistent patterns in the sequence of weights? For example, do the weights tend to drift steadily upward or downward over time? Do they oscillate—high, then low, then high, then low, etc.?

To assist your visual examination of this or any other time series plot, Roberts (1991) recommends enhancing the basic plot in two ways. First, compute (or simply estimate) the mean of the set of 50 weights and draw a horizontal line on the graph at the level of the mean. This **centerline** gives you a point of reference in searching for patterns in the data. Second, using straight lines, connect each of the plotted weights in the order in which they were produced. This helps display the sequence of the measurements. Both enhancements are shown in Figure 11.5 on page 616.

FIGURE 11.5 ▶
An enhanced version of the paint
fill time series

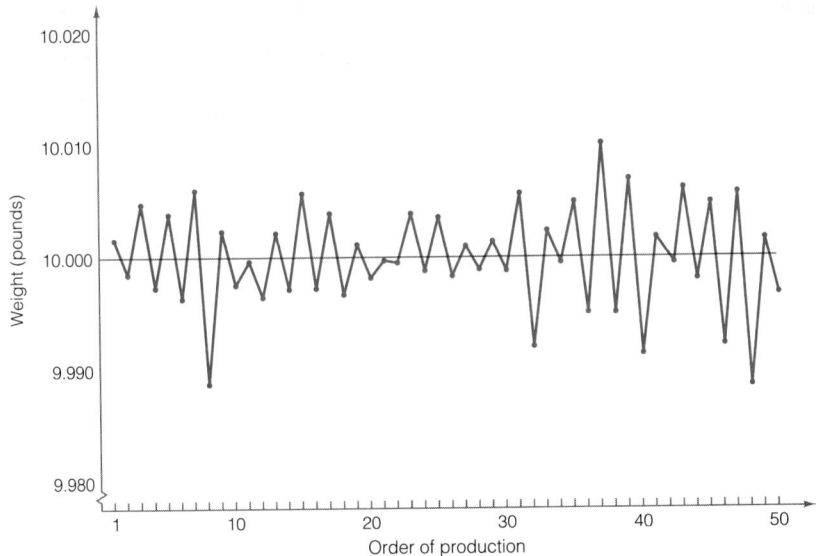

FIGURE 11.6 ▶
Patterns of process variation: Some
examples

a. Uptrend

b. Downtrend

c. Increasing variance

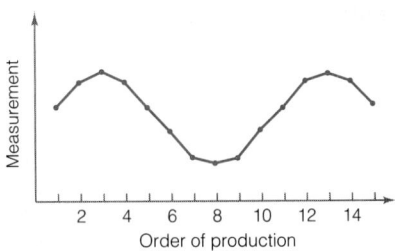

d. Cyclical

(*continued*)

FIGURE 11.6 ▶
Continued

e. Meandering

f. Shock/Freak/Outlier

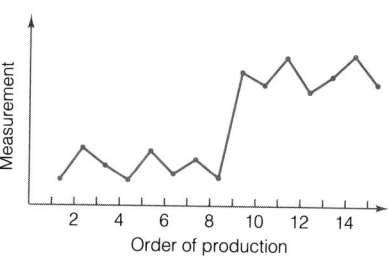

g. Level shift

In trying to describe process variation and diagnose its causes, it helps to think of the sequence of measurements of the output variable (e.g., weight, length, number of defects) as having been generated in the following way:

1. At any point in time, the output variable of interest can be described by a particular probability distribution (or relative frequency distribution). This distribution describes the possible values that the variable can assume and their likelihood of occurrence. Three such distributions are shown in Figure 11.7.

FIGURE 11.7 ▶

Distributions describing one output variable at three points in time

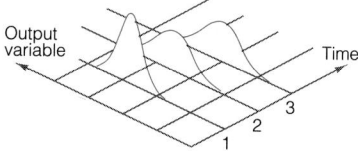

Now do you see a pattern in the data? Successive points alternate up and down, high then low, in an **oscillating sequence**. In this case, the points alternate above and below the centerline. This pattern was caused by a valve in the paint-filling machine that tended to stick in a partially closed position every other time it operated.

Other patterns of process variation are shown in Figure 11.6. We discuss several of them later.

FIGURE 11.8 ▶
Types of changes in output
variables

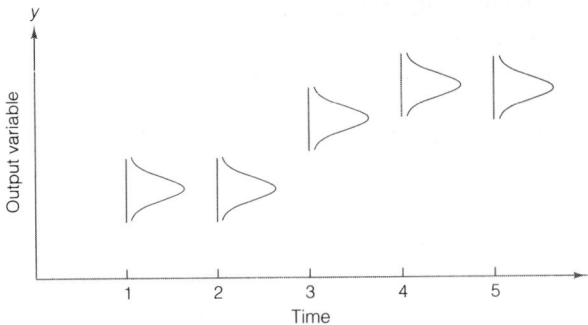

a. Change in mean (i.e., location)

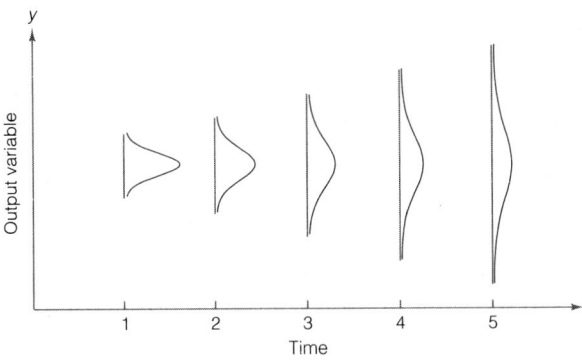

b. Change in variance (i.e., shape)

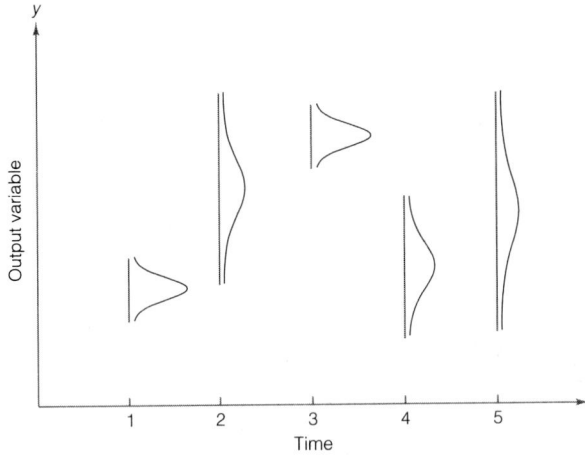

c. Change in mean and variance

2. The particular value of the output variable that is realized at a given time can be thought of as being generated or produced according to the distribution described in point 1. (Alternatively, the realized value can be thought of as being generated by a random sample of size $n = 1$ from a population of values whose relative frequency distribution is that of point 1.)

3. The distribution that describes the output variable may change over time. For simplicity, we characterize the changes as being of three types: the mean (i.e., location) of the distribution may change; the variance (i.e., shape) of the distribution may change; or both. This is illustrated in Figure 11.8.

In general, when the output variable's distribution changes over time, we refer to this as a change in the *process*. Thus, if the mean shifts to a higher level, we say that the process mean has shifted. Accordingly, we sometimes refer to the distribution of the output variable as simply the **distribution of the process**, or the **output distribution of the process**.

Let's reconsider the patterns of variation in Figure 11.6 and model them using this conceptualization. This is done in Figure 11.9. The uptrend of Figure 11.6(a) can be characterized as resulting from a process whose mean is gradually shifting upward over time, as in Figure 11.9(a). Gradual shifts like this are a common phenomenon in manufacturing processes. For example, as a machine wears out (e.g., cutting blades dull), certain characteristics of its output gradually change.

The pattern of increasing dispersion in Figure 11.6(c) can be thought of as resulting from a process whose mean remains constant but whose variance increases over time, as shown in Figure 11.9(c). This type of deterioration in a process may be the

FIGURE 11.9 ▶
Patterns of process variation described by changing distributions

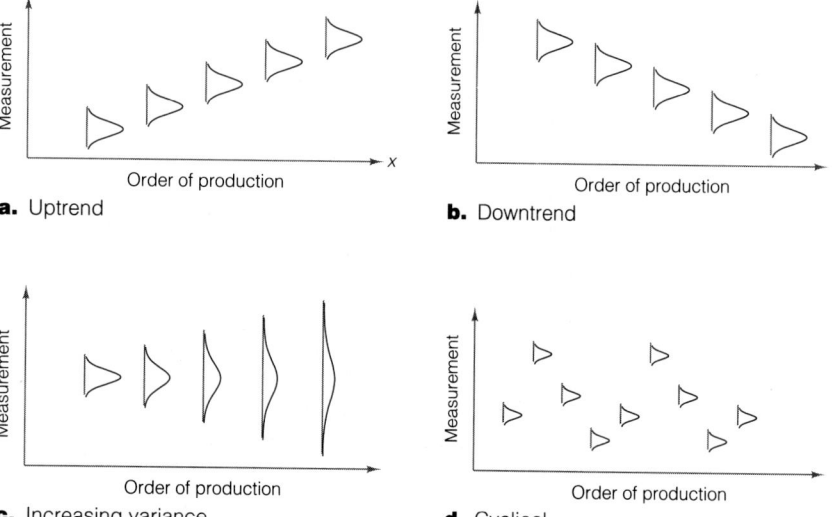

a. Uptrend

b. Downtrend

c. Increasing variance

d. Cyclical

Continued

FIGURE 11.9 ▶
Continued

e. Meandering

f. Shock/Freak/Outlier

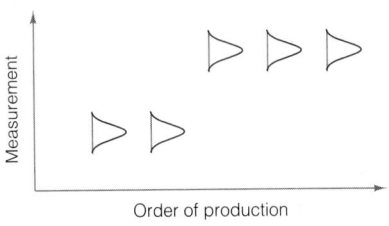

g. Level shift

result of worker fatigue. At the beginning of a shift, workers—whether they be typists, machine operators, waiters, or managers—are fresh and pay close attention to every item that they process. But as the day wears on, concentration may wane and the workers may become more and more careless or more easily distracted. As a result, some items receive more attention than other items, causing the variance of the workers' output to increase.

The sudden shift in the level of the measurements in Figure 11.6(g) can be thought of as resulting from a process whose mean suddenly increases but whose variance remains constant, as shown in Figure 11.9(g). This type of pattern may be caused by such things as a change in the quality of raw materials used in the process or bringing a new machine or new operator into the process.

One thing that all these examples have in common is that the distribution of the output variable *changes over time*. In such cases, we say the process lacks **stability**. We formalize the notion of stability in the following definition.

Definition 11.4

A process whose output distribution does *not* change over time is said to be in a state of **statistical control**, or simply **in control**. If it does change, it is said to be **out of statistical control**, or simply **out of control**.

Figure 11.10 illustrates a sequence of output distributions for both an in-control and an out-of-control process. To see what the pattern of measurements looks like on a

FIGURE 11.10 ▶

Comparison of in-control and out-of-control processes

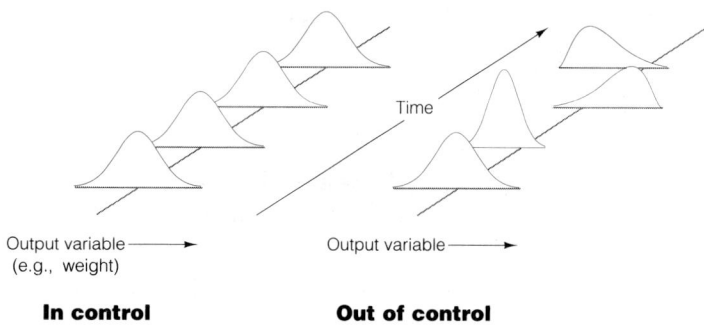

Time

Output variable ——▶
(e.g., weight)

Output variable ——▶

In control   **Out of control**

time series plot for a process that is in statistical control, consider Figure 11.11. These data are from the same paint-filling process we described earlier, but the sequence of measurements was made *after* the faulty valve was replaced. Notice that there are no discernible persistent, systematic patterns in the sequence of measurements such as those in Figures 11.5 and 11.6(a)–(g). Nor, are there level shifts or transitory shocks as in Figures 11.6(e)–(f). This "patternless" behavior is called **random behavior. The output of processes that are in statistical control exhibits random behavior. Thus, even the output of stable processes exhibits variation.**

If a process is in control and remains in control, its future will be like its past. Accordingly, the process is predictable, in the sense that its output will stay within certain limits. This cannot be said about an out-of-control process. As illustrated in Figure 11.12 (page 622), with most out-of-control processes you have no idea what the

FIGURE 11.11 ▶

Time series plot of 50 consecutive paint can fills collected after replacing faulty valve

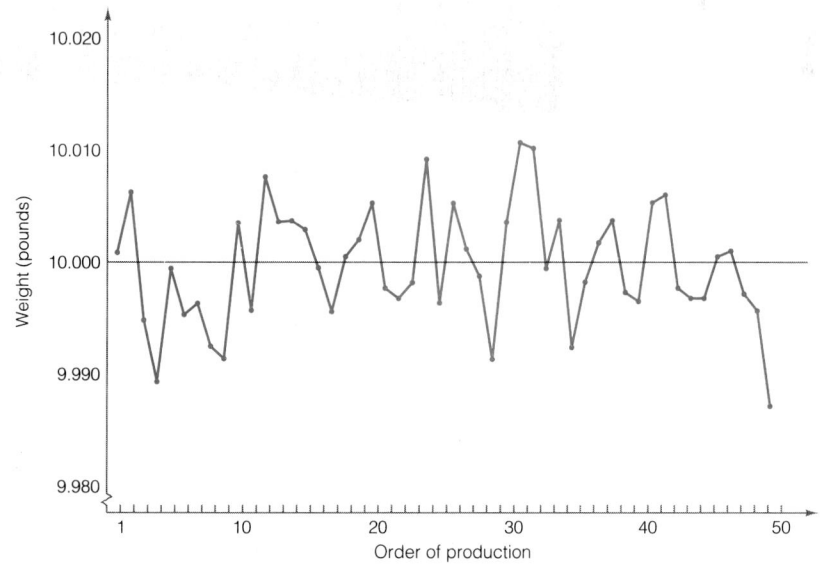

FIGURE 11.12 ▶

In-control processes are predictable; out-of-control processes are not.

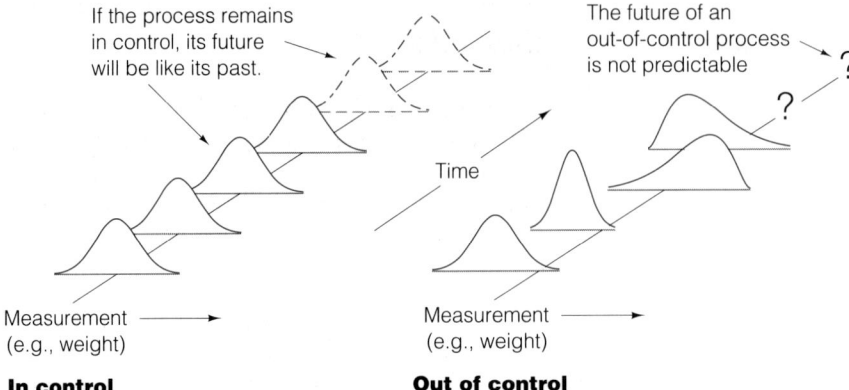

future pattern of output from the process may look like.* You simply do not know what to expect from the process. Consequently, a business that operates out-of-control processes runs the risk of (1) providing inferior quality products and services to its internal customers (people within the organization who use the outputs of the processes) and (2) selling inferior products and services to its external customers. In short, it risks losing its customers and threatens its own survival.

One of the fundamental goals of process management is to identify out-of-control processes, to take actions to bring them into statistical control, and to keep them in a state of statistical control. The series of activities used to attain this goal is referred to as **statistical process control**.

Definition 11.5

The process of monitoring and eliminating variation in order to *keep* a process in a state of statistical control or to *bring* a process into statistical control is called **statistical process control (SPC)**.

Everything discussed in this section and the remaining sections of this chapter is concerned with statistical process control. We now continue our discussion of statistical control.

The variation that is exhibited by processes that are in control is said to be due to *common causes of variation*.

---

*The output variables of in-control processes may follow approximately normal distributions, as in Figures 11.10 and 11.12, or they may not. But any in-control process will follow the *same* distribution over time. Do not misinterpret the use of normal distributions in many figures in this chapter as indicating that all in-control processes follow normal distributions.

> ## Definition 11.6
>
> **Common causes of variation** are the methods, materials, machines, personnel, and environment that make up a process and the inputs required by the process. Common causes are thus attributable to the design of the process. Common causes affect all output of the process and may affect everyone who participates in the process.

The total variation that is exhibited by an in-control process is due to many different common causes, most of which affect process output in very minor ways. In general, however, each common cause has the potential to affect every unit of output produced by the process. Examples of common causes include the lighting in a factory or office, the grade of raw materials required, and the extent of worker training. Each of these factors can influence the variability of the process output. Poor lighting can cause workers to overlook flaws and defects that they might otherwise catch. Inconsistencies in raw materials can cause inconsistencies in the quality of the finished product. The extent of the training provided to workers can affect their level of expertise and, as a result, the quality of the products and services for which they are responsible.

Since common causes are, in effect, designed into a process, the level of variation that results from common causes is viewed as being representative of the capability of the process. If that level is too great (i.e., if the quality of the output varies too much), the process must be redesigned (or modified) to eliminate one or more common causes of variation. Since process redesign is the responsibility of management, *the elimination of common causes of variation is typically the responsibility of management*, not of the workers.

Processes that are out of control exhibit variation that is the result of both common causes and **special causes of variation**.

> ## Definition 11.7
>
> **Special causes of variation** (sometimes called **assignable causes**) are events or actions that are not part of the process design. Typically, they are transient, fleeting events that affect only local areas or operations within the process (e.g., a single worker, machine, or batch of materials) for a brief period of time. Occasionally, however, such events may have a persistent or recurrent effect on the process.

Examples of special causes of variation include a worker accidentally setting the controls of a machine improperly, a worker becoming ill on the job and continuing to work, a particular machine slipping out of adjustment, and a negligent supplier shipping a batch of inferior raw materials to the process.

In the latter case, the pattern of output variation may look like Figure 11.6(f). If instead of shipping just one bad batch the supplier continued to send inferior materials, the pattern of variation might look like Figure 11.6(g). The output of a machine that is gradually slipping out of adjustment might yield a pattern like Figure 11.6(a), (b), or (c). All these patterns owe part of their variation to common causes and part to the noted special causes. In general, we treat any pattern of variation other than a random pattern as due to both common and special causes.*

Since the effects of special causes are frequently localized within a process, *special causes can often be diagnosed and eliminated by workers or their immediate supervisor.* Occasionally, they must be dealt with by management, as in the case of a negligent or deceitful supplier.

It is important to recognize that **most processes are not naturally in a state of statistical control**. As Deming (1986, p. 322) observed:

Stability [i.e., statistical control] is seldom a natural state. It is an achievement, the result of eliminating special causes one by one . . . leaving only the random variation of a stable process.

Process improvement first requires the identification, diagnosis, and removal of special causes of variation. Removing all special causes puts the process in a state of statistical control. Further improvement of the process then requires the identification, diagnosis, and removal of common causes of variation. The effects on the process of the removal of special and common causes of variation are illustrated in Figure 11.13.

FIGURE 11.13 ▶
The effects of eliminating causes of variation.

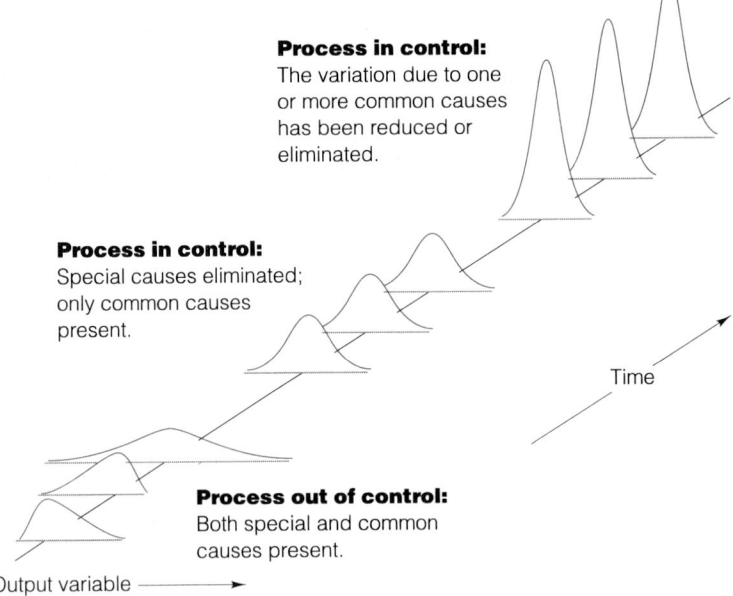

Process in control:
The variation due to one or more common causes has been reduced or eliminated.

Process in control:
Special causes eliminated; only common causes present.

Time

Process out of control:
Both special and common causes present.

Output variable ───────▶

---

*For certain processes (e.g., those affected by seasonal factors), a persistent systematic pattern—such as the cyclical pattern of Figure 11.6(d)—is an inherent characteristic. In these special cases, some analysts treat the cause of the systematic variation as a common cause. This type of analysis is beyond the scope of this text. We refer the interested reader to Alwan and Roberts (1988).

In the remainder of this chapter, we introduce you to some of the methods of statistical process control. In particular, we address how control charts help us determine whether a given process is in control.

11.3   The Logic of Control Charts

We use control charts to help us differentiate between process variation due to common causes and special causes. That is, we use them to determine whether a process is under statistical control (only common causes present) or not (both common and special causes present). Being able to differentiate means knowing when to take action to find and remove special causes and when to leave the process alone. If you take actions to remove special causes that do not exist—this is called tampering with the process—you may actually end up increasing the variation of the process and, thereby, hurting the quality of the output.

In general, control charts are useful for evaluating the past performance of a process and for monitoring its current performance. We can use them to determine whether a process was in control during, say, the past two weeks or to determine whether the process is remaining under control from hour to hour or minute to minute. In the latter case, our goal is the swiftest detection and removal of any special causes of variation that might arise. Keep in mind that **the primary goal of quality improvement activities is variance reduction**.

In this chapter we show you how to construct and use control charts for both quantitative and qualitative quality variables. Important quantitative variables include such things as weight, width, and time. An important qualitative variable is product status: defective or nondefective.

An example of a control chart is shown in Figure 11.14. It is simply a time series plot of the individual measurements of a quality variable (i.e., an output variable), to

FIGURE 11.14 ▶
A control chart

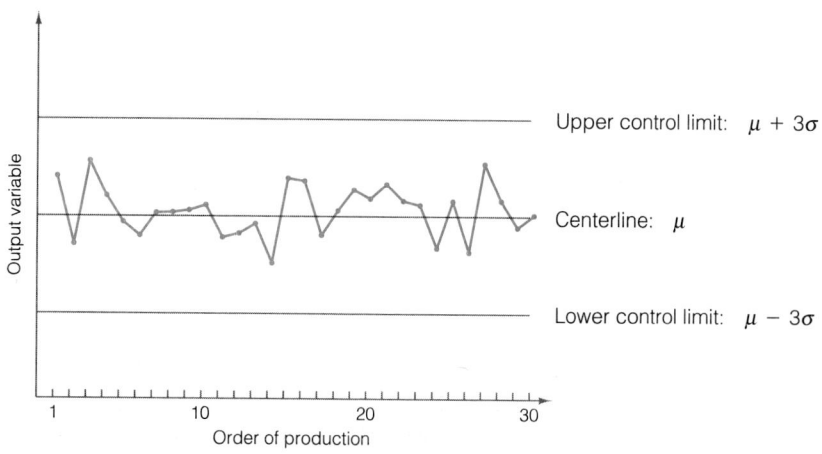

which a centerline and two other horizontal lines called **control limits** have been added. The centerline represents the mean of the process (i.e., the mean of the quality variable) *when the process is in a state of statistical control*. The **upper control limit** and the **lower control limit** are positioned so that *when the process is in control* the probability of an individual value of the output variable falling outside the control limits is very small. Most practitioners position the control limits a distance of three standard deviations from the centerline (i.e., from the process mean) and refer to them as **3-sigma limits**. If the process is in control and following a normal distribution, the probability of an individual measurement falling outside the control limits is .0027 (less than 3 chances in 1,000). This is shown in Figure 11.15.

FIGURE 11.15 ▶

The probability of observing a measurement beyond the control limits when the process is in control

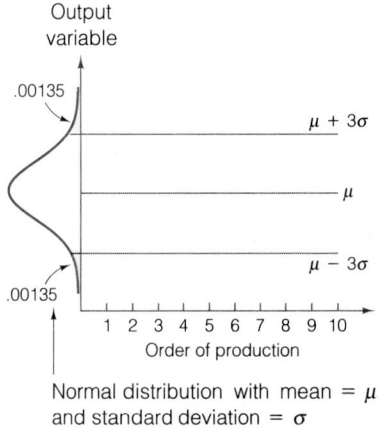

Normal distribution with mean = μ and standard deviation = σ

As long as the individual values stay between the control limits, the process is considered to be under control, meaning that no special causes of variation are influencing the output of the process. If one or more values fall outside the control limits, either a **rare event** has occurred or the process is out of control. Following the rare-event approach to inference described earlier in the text, such a result is interpreted as evidence that the process is out of control and that actions should be taken to eliminate the special causes of variation that exist.

Other evidence to indicate that the process is out of control may be present on the control chart. For example, if we observe any of the patterns of variation shown in Figure 11.6, we can conclude the process is out of control *even if all the points fall between the control limits*. In general, any persistent, systematic variation pattern (i.e., any nonrandom pattern) is interpreted as evidence that the process is out of control. We discuss this in detail in the next section.

In Chapter 8 we described how to make inferences about populations using hypothesis-testing techniques. What we do in this section should seem quite similar. Although our focus now is on making inferences about a *process* rather than a *population*, we are again testing hypotheses. In this case, we test

H_0:   Process is under control H_a: Process is out of control

Each time we plot a new point and see whether it falls inside or outside of the control limits, we are running a two-sided hypothesis test. The control limits function as the critical values for the test.

What we learned in Chapter 8 about the types of errors that we might make in running a hypothesis test holds true in using control charts as well. Any time we reject the hypothesis that the process is under control and conclude that the process is out of control, we run the risk of making a Type I error (rejecting the null hypothesis when the null is true). Anytime we conclude (or behave as if we conclude) that the process is in control, we run the risk of a Type II error (accepting the null hypothesis when the alternative is true). There is nothing magical or mystical about control charts. Just as in any hypothesis test, the conclusion suggested by a control chart may be wrong.

One of the main reasons that 3-sigma control limits are used (rather than 2-sigma or 1-sigma limits, for example) is the small Type I error probability associated with their use. The probability we noted previously of an individual measurement falling outside the control limits—.0027—is a Type I error probability. Since we interpret a sample point that falls beyond the limits as a signal that the process is out of control, the use of 3-sigma limits yields very few signals that are "false alarms."

To make these ideas more concrete, we will construct and interpret a control chart for the paint-filling process discussed in Section 11.2. Our intention is simply to help you better understand the logic of control charts. Structured, step-by-step descriptions of how to construct control charts will be given in later sections.

The sample measurements from the paint-filling process, presented in Table 11.1, were previously plotted in Figure 11.11. We use the mean and standard deviation of the sample, $\bar{x} = 9.9997$ and $s = .0053$, to estimate the mean and the standard deviation of the process. Although these are estimates, in using and interpreting control charts we treat them *as if* they were the actual mean μ and standard deviation σ of the process. This is standard practice in control charting.

TABLE 11.1 Fill Weights of 50 Consecutively Produced Cans of Paint				
1. 10.0008	11. 9.9957	21. 9.9977	31. 10.0107	41. 10.0054
2. 10.0062	12. 10.0076	22. 9.9968	32. 10.0102	42. 10.0061
3. 9.9948	13. 10.0036	23. 9.9982	33. 9.9995	43. 9.9978
4. 9.9893	14. 10.0037	24. 10.0092	34. 10.0038	44. 9.9969
5. 9.9994	15. 10.0029	25. 9.9964	35. 9.9925	45. 9.9969
6. 9.9953	16. 9.9995	26. 10.0053	36. 9.9983	46. 10.0006
7. 9.9963	17. 9.9956	27. 10.0012	37. 10.0018	47. 10.0011
8. 9.9925	18. 10.0005	28. 9.9988	38. 10.0038	48. 9.9973
9. 9.9914	19. 10.0020	29. 9.9914	39. 9.9974	49. 9.9958
10. 10.0035	20. 10.0053	30. 10.0036	40. 9.9966	50. 9.9873

The centerline of the control chart, representing the process mean, is drawn so that it intersects the vertical axis at 9.9997, as shown in Figure 11.16 on page 628. The upper control limit is drawn at a distance of $3s = 3(.0053) = .0159$ above the centerline, and the lower control limit is $3s = .0159$ below the centerline. Then the 50 sample weights are plotted on the chart in the order that they were generated by the paint-filling process.

As can be seen in Figure 11.16, all the weight measurements fall within the control limits. Further, there do not appear to be any systematic nonrandom patterns in the data such as displayed in Figures 11.5 and 11.6. Accordingly, we are unable to conclude that the process is out of control. That is, we are unable to reject the null hypothesis that the process is in control. However, instead of using this formal hypothesis-testing language in interpreting control chart results, we prefer simply to say that the data suggest or indicate that the process is in control. We do this, however, with the full understanding that the probability of a Type II error is generally unknown in control chart applications and that we might be wrong in our conclusion. What we are really saying when we conclude that the process is in control is that *the data indicate that it is better to behave as if the process were under control than to tamper with the process.*

FIGURE 11.16 ▶

Control chart of fill weights for 50 consecutive paint can fills

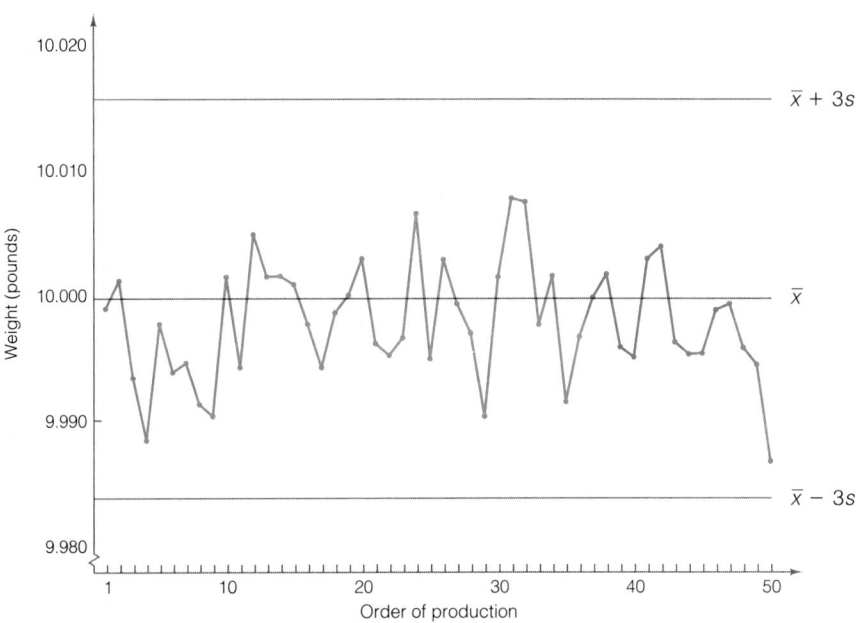

We have portrayed the control chart hypothesis test as testing "in control" versus "out of control." Another way to look at it is this: When we compare the weight of an *individual* can of paint to the control limits, we are conducting the following two-tailed hypothesis test:

$$H_0: \quad \mu = 9.9997 \qquad H_a: \quad \mu \neq 9.9997$$

where 9.9997 is the centerline of the control chart. The control limits delineate the two rejection regions for this test. Accordingly, with each weight measurement that we plot and compare to the control limits, we are testing whether the process mean (the mean fill weight) has changed. Thus, what the control chart is monitoring is the mean of the process. **The control chart leads us to accept or reject statistical control on the basis of whether the mean of the process has changed or not.** This type of process instability is illustrated in the top graph of Figure 11.8. In the paint-filling process example, the process mean apparently has remained constant over the period in which the sample weights were collected.

Other types of control charts—one of which we will describe in Section 11.6— help us determine whether the *variance* of the process has changed, as in the middle and bottom graphs of Figure 11.8.

The control chart we have just described is called an **individuals chart**, or an **x-chart**. The term *individuals* refers to the fact that the chart uses individual measurements to monitor the process—that is, measurements taken from individual units of process output. This is in contrast to plotting sample means on the control chart, for example, as we do in the next section.

Students sometimes confuse control limits with product **specification limits**. We have already explained control limits, which are a function of the natural variability of the process. Assuming we always use 3-sigma limits, the position of the control limits is a function of the size of σ, the process standard deviation.

Definition 11.8

Specification limits are boundary points that define the acceptable values for an output variable (i.e., for a quality characteristic) of a particular product or service. They are determined by customers, management, and product designers. Specification limits may be two-sided, with upper and lower limits, or one-sided, with either an upper or a lower limit.

Process output that falls inside the specification limits is said to **conform to specifications**. Otherwise it is said to be **nonconforming**.

Unlike control limits, specification limits are not dependent on the process in any way. A customer of the paint-filling process may specify that all cans contain no more than 10.005 pounds of paint and no less than 9.995 pounds. These are specification limits. The customer has reasons for these specifications but may have no idea whether the supplier's process can meet them. Both the customer's specification limits and the control limits of the supplier's paint-filling process are shown in Figure 11.17 on page 630. Do you think the customer will be satisfied with the quality of the product received? We don't. Although some cans are within the specification limits, most are not, as indicated by the shaded region on the figure.

FIGURE 11.17 ▶
Comparison of control limits and specification limits

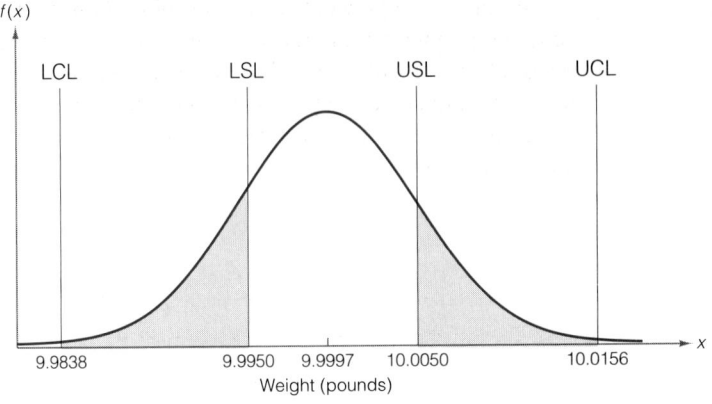

LCL = Lower control limit
UCL = Upper control limit
LSL = Lower specification limit
USL = Upper specification limit

11.4   A Control Chart for Monitoring the Mean of a Process: The $\bar{x}$-Chart

In the last section we introduced you to the logic of control charts by focusing on a chart that reflected the variation in individual measurements of process output. We used the chart to determine whether the process mean had shifted. The control chart we present in this section—the $\bar{x}$-chart—is also used to detect changes in the process mean, but it does so by monitoring the variation in the mean of samples that have been drawn from the process. That is, instead of plotting individual measurements on the control chart, in this case we plot sample means. Because of the additional information reflected in sample means (because each sample mean is calculated from n individual measurements), the $\bar{x}$-chart is more sensitive than the individuals chart for detecting changes in the process mean.

In practice, the $\bar{x}$-chart is rarely used alone. It is typically used in conjunction with a chart that monitors the variation of the process, usually a chart called an R-chart. The $\bar{x}$- and R-charts are the most widely used control charts in industry. Used in concert, these charts make it possible to determine whether a process has gone out of control because the variation has changed or because the mean has changed. We present the R-chart in the next section, at the end of which we discuss their simultaneous use. For now, we focus only on the $\bar{x}$-chart. **Consequently, we assume throughout this section that the process variation is stable.** *

To the instructor: Technically, the R-chart should be constructed and interpreted before the $\bar{x}$-chart. However, in our experience, students more quickly grasp control-chart concepts if they are familiar with the underlying theory. We begin with $\bar{x}$-charts because their underlying theory was presented in Chapters 5–7.

Figure 11.18 provides an example of an $\bar{x}$-chart. As with the individuals chart, the centerline represents the mean of the process and the upper and lower control limits are positioned a distance of three standard deviations from the mean. However, since the chart is tracking sample means rather than individual measurements, the relevant standard deviation is the standard deviation of $\bar{x}$, not σ, the standard deviation of the output variable.

FIGURE 11.18 ▶
$\bar{x}$-Chart

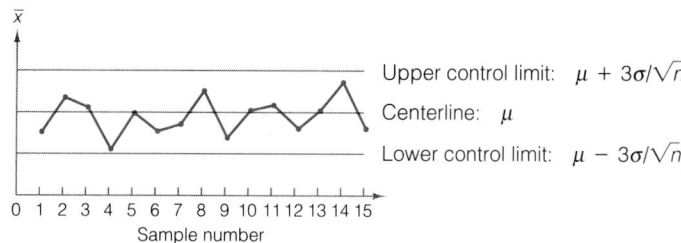

If the process were in statistical control, the sequence of $\bar{x}$'s plotted on the chart would exhibit random behavior between the control limits. Only if a rare event occurred or if the process went out of control would a sample mean fall beyond the control limits.

To better understand the justification for having control limits that involve $\sigma_{\bar{x}}$, consider the following. The $\bar{x}$-chart is concerned with the variation in $\bar{x}$ which, as we saw in Chapter 5, is described by $\bar{x}$'s sampling distribution. But what is $\bar{x}$'s sampling distribution? If the process is in control and its output variable x is characterized at each point in time by a normal distribution with mean μ and standard deviation σ, the distribution of $\bar{x}$ (i.e., $\bar{x}$'s sampling distribution) also follows a normal distribution with mean μ at each point in time. But, as we saw in Chapter 5, its standard deviation is $\sigma_{\bar{x}} = \sigma/\sqrt{n}$. The control limits of the $\bar{x}$-chart are determined from and interpreted with respect to the sampling distribution of $\bar{x}$, not the distribution of x. These points are illustrated in Figure 11.19 on page 632.*

In order to construct an $\bar{x}$-chart, you should have at least 20 samples of n items each, where $n \geq 2$. This will provide sufficient data to obtain reasonably good estimates of the mean and variance of the process. The centerline, which represents the mean of the process, is determined as follows:

$$\text{Centerline:} \quad \bar{\bar{x}} = \frac{\bar{x}_1 + \bar{x}_2 + \cdots + \bar{x}_k}{k}$$

where k is the number of samples of size n from which the chart is to be constructed and $\bar{x}_i$ is the sample mean of the ith sample. Thus $\bar{\bar{x}}$ is an estimator of μ.

---

*The sampling distribution of $\bar{x}$ can also be approximated using the central limit theorem (Chapter 5). That is, when the process is under control and $\bar{x}$ is to be computed from a large sample from the process ($n \geq 30$), the sampling distribution will be approximately normally distributed with mean μ and standard deviation $\sigma/\sqrt{n}$. Even for samples as small as 4 or 5, the sampling distribution of $\bar{x}$ will be approximately normal as long as the distribution of x is reasonably symmetric and roughly bell-shaped.

FIGURE 11.19 ▶
The sampling distribution of $\bar{x}$

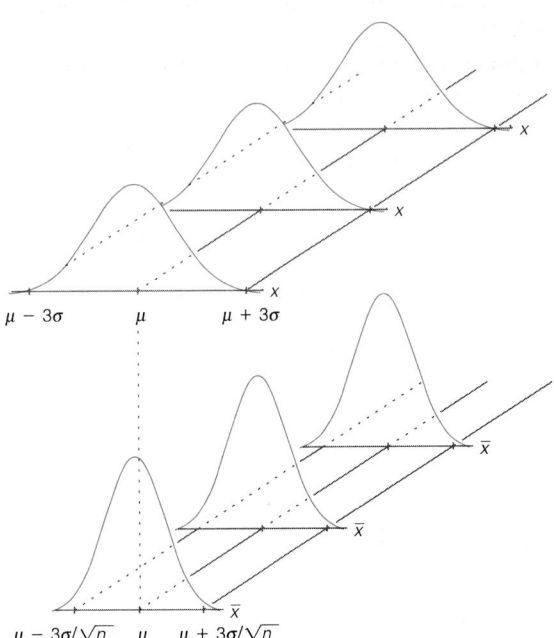

If the process is under control and follows a normal distribution with mean μ and standard deviation σ...

$\bar{x}$ also follows a normal distribution with mean μ but has standard deviation $\sigma/\sqrt{n}$.

The control limits are positioned as follows:

Upper control limit: $\bar{\bar{x}} + \dfrac{3\sigma}{\sqrt{n}}$

Lower control limit: $\bar{\bar{x}} - \dfrac{3\sigma}{\sqrt{n}}$

Since σ, the process standard deviation, is virtually always unknown, it must be estimated. This can be done in several ways. One approach involves calculating the standard deviations for each of the k samples and averaging them. Another involves using the sample standard deviation s from a large sample that was generated while the process was believed to be in control. We employ a third approach, however—the one favored by industry. It has been shown to be as effective as the other approaches for sample sizes of $n = 10$ or less, the sizes most often used in industry.

This approach utilizes the ranges of the k samples to estimate the process standard deviation, σ. Recall from Chapter 2 that the range, R, of a sample is the difference between the maximum and minimum measurements in the sample. It can be shown that dividing the mean of the k ranges, $\bar{R}$, by the constant d_2, obtains an unbiased estimator for σ. [For details, see Ryan (1989).] The estimator, denoted by $\hat{\sigma}$, is calculated as follows:

$$\hat{\sigma} = \frac{\bar{R}}{d_2} = \frac{R_1 + R_2 + \cdots + R_k}{k}\left(\frac{1}{d_2}\right)$$

where R_i is the range of the ith sample and d_2 is a constant that depends on the sample size. Values of d_2 for samples of size $n = 2$ to $n = 25$ can be found in Appendix B, Table XIV.

Substituting $\hat{\sigma}$ for σ in the formulas for the upper control limit (UCL) and the lower control limit (LCL), we get

$$\text{UCL:} \quad \bar{\bar{x}} + \frac{3\left(\dfrac{\bar{R}}{d_2}\right)}{\sqrt{n}} \qquad \text{LCL:} \quad \bar{\bar{x}} - \frac{3\left(\dfrac{\bar{R}}{d_2}\right)}{\sqrt{n}}$$

Notice that $(\bar{R}/d_2)/\sqrt{n}$ is an estimator of $\sigma_{\bar{x}}$. The calculation of these limits can be simplified by creating the constant

$$A_2 = \frac{3}{d_2\sqrt{n}}$$

Then the control limits can be expressed as

$$\text{UCL:} \quad \bar{\bar{x}} + A_2\bar{R} \qquad \text{LCL:} \quad \bar{\bar{x}} - A_2\bar{R}$$

where the values for A_2 for samples of size $n = 2$ to $n = 25$ can be found in Appendix B, Table XIV.

The degree of sensitivity of the $\bar{x}$-chart to changes in the process mean depends on two decisions that must be made in constructing the chart.

The Two Most Important Decisions in Constructing an $\bar{x}$-Chart

1. The sample size, n, must be determined.
2. The frequency with which samples are to be drawn from the process must be determined (e.g., once an hour, once each shift, or once a day).

In order to quickly detect process change, we try to choose samples in such a way that the change in the process mean occurs *between* samples, not *within* samples (i.e., not during the period when a sample is being drawn). In this way, every measurement in the sample before the change will be unaffected by the change and every measurement in the sample following the change will be affected. The result is that the $\bar{x}$ computed from the latter sample should be substantially different from that of the former sample—a signal that something has happened to the process mean.

Definition 11.9

Samples whose size and frequency have been designed to make it likely that process changes will occur between, rather than within, the samples are referred to as **rational subgroups**.

Rational Subgrouping Strategy

The samples (rational subgroups) should be chosen in a manner that:

1. Gives the maximum chance for the *measurements* in each sample to be similar (i.e., to be affected by the same sources of variation).
2. Gives the maximum chance for the *samples* to differ (i.e., be affected by at least one different source of variation).

The following example illustrates the concept of **rational subgrouping**. An operations manager suspects that the quality of the output in a manufacturing process may differ from shift to shift because of the preponderance of newly hired workers on the night shift. The manager wants to be able to detect such differences quickly, using an $\bar{x}$-chart. Following the rational subgrouping strategy, the control chart should be constructed with samples that are drawn *within* each shift. None of the samples should span shifts. That is, no sample should contain, say, the last three items produced by shift 1 and the first two items produced by shift 2. In that way, the measurements in each sample would be similar, but the $\bar{x}$'s would reflect differences between shifts.

Constructing an $\bar{x}$-Chart: A Summary

1. Using a rational subgrouping strategy, collect at least 20 samples (subgroups), each of size $n \geq 2$.
2. Calculate the mean and range for each sample.
3. Calculate the mean of the sample means, $\bar{\bar{x}}$, and the mean of the sample ranges, $\bar{R}$:

$$\bar{\bar{x}} = \frac{\bar{x}_1 + \bar{x}_2 + \cdot\cdot\cdot + \bar{x}_k}{k} \qquad \bar{R} = \frac{R_1 + R_2 + \cdot\cdot\cdot + R_k}{k}$$

where k = The number of samples (i.e., subgroups)
          $\bar{x}_i$ = The sample mean for the ith sample
          R_i = The range of the ith sample

4. Plot the centerline and control limits:

     Centerline: $\bar{\bar{x}}$
     Upper control limit: $\bar{\bar{x}} + A_2\bar{R}$ *Lower control limit:* $\bar{\bar{x}} - A_2\bar{R}$

where A_2 is a constant that depends on n. Its values are given in Appendix B, Table XIV, for samples of size $n = 2$ to $n = 25$.

5. Plot the k sample means on the control chart in the order that the samples were produced by the process.

The secret to designing an effective x̄-chart is to anticipate the *types of special causes of variation* that might affect the process mean. Then purposeful rational subgrouping can be employed to construct a chart that is sensitive to the anticipated cause or causes of variation.

The preceding discussion and example focused primarily on the timing or frequency of samples. Concerning the size of the samples, practitioners typically work with samples of size $n = 4$ to $n = 10$ consecutively produced items. Using small samples of consecutively produced items helps to ensure that the measurements in each sample will be similar (i.e., affected by the same causes of variation).

When interpreting a control chart, it is convenient to think of the chart as consisting of six zones, as shown in Figure 11.20. Each zone is one standard deviation wide. The two zones within one standard deviation of the centerline are called **C zones**; the regions between one and two standard deviations from the centerline are called **B zones**; and the regions between two and three standard deviations from the centerline are called **A zones**. The box describes how to construct the *zone boundaries* for an x̄-chart.

FIGURE 11.20 ▶

The zones of a control chart

Practitioners use six simple rules that are based on these zones to help determine when a process is out of control. The six rules are summarized in Figure 11.21 on page 637. They are referred to as **pattern-analysis rules**.

Rule 1 is the familiar point-beyond-the-control-limit rule that we have mentioned several times. The other rules all help to determine when the process is out of control *even though all the plotted points fall within the control limits*. That is, the other rules help to identify nonrandom patterns of variation that have not yet broken through the control limits (or may never break through).

All the patterns shown in Figure 11.21 are **rare events** under the assumption that the process is under control. To see this, let's assume that the process is under control and follows a normal distribution. We can then easily work out the probability that an individual point will fall in any given zone. (We dealt with this type of problem in Chapter 4.) Just focusing on one side of the centerline, you can show that the probability of a point falling beyond Zone A is .00135, in Zone A is .02135, in Zone B is .1360, and in Zone C is .3413. Of course, the same probabilities apply to both sides of the centerline.

Constructing Zone Boundaries for an $\bar{x}$-Chart

The zone boundaries can be constructed in either of the following ways:

1. Using the 3-sigma control limits:

$$\text{Upper A–B boundary:} \quad \bar{\bar{x}} + \frac{2}{3}(A_2\bar{R})$$

$$\text{Lower A–B boundary:} \quad \bar{\bar{x}} - \frac{2}{3}(A_2\bar{R})$$

$$\text{Upper B–C boundary:} \quad \bar{\bar{x}} + \frac{1}{3}(A_2\bar{R})$$

$$\text{Lower B–C boundary:} \quad \bar{\bar{x}} - \frac{1}{3}(A_2\bar{R})$$

2. Using the estimated standard deviation of $\bar{x}$, $(\bar{R}/d_2)/\sqrt{n}$:

$$\text{Upper A–B boundary:} \quad \bar{\bar{x}} + 2\left[\frac{\left(\frac{\bar{R}}{d_2}\right)}{\sqrt{n}}\right]$$

$$\text{Lower A–B boundary:} \quad \bar{\bar{x}} - 2\left[\frac{\left(\frac{\bar{R}}{d_2}\right)}{\sqrt{n}}\right]$$

$$\text{Upper B–C boundary:} \quad \bar{\bar{x}} + \left[\frac{\left(\frac{\bar{R}}{d_2}\right)}{\sqrt{n}}\right]$$

$$\text{Lower B–C boundary:} \quad \bar{\bar{x}} - \left[\frac{\left(\frac{\bar{R}}{d_2}\right)}{\sqrt{n}}\right]$$

From these probabilities we can determine the likelihood of various patterns of points. For example, let's evaluate rule 1. The probability of observing a point outside the control limits (i.e., above the upper control limit or below the lower control limit) is $.00135 + .00135 = .0027$. This is clearly a rare event.

As another example, rule 5 indicates that the observation of two out of three points in a row in Zone A or beyond is a rare event. Is it? The probability of being in Zone A or beyond is $.00135 + .02135 = .0227$. We can use the binomial distribution (Chapter 4) to find the probability of observing 2 out of 3 points in or beyond Zone A. The binomial probability $P(x = 2)$ when $n = 3$ and $p = .0227$ is $.0015$. Again, this is clearly a rare event.

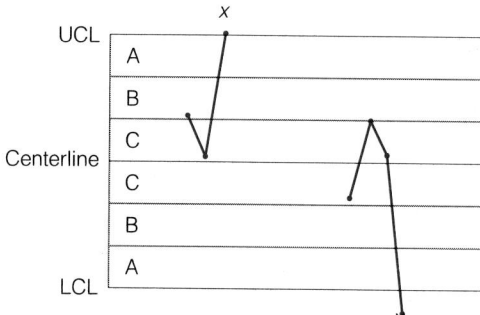

Rule1: One point beyond Zone A

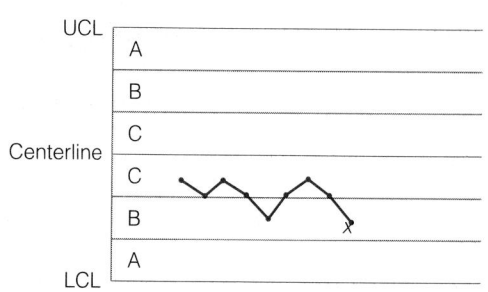

Rule 2: Nine points in a row in Zone C or beyond

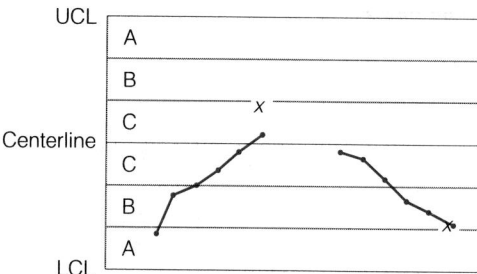

Rule 3: Six points in a row steadily increasing or decreasing

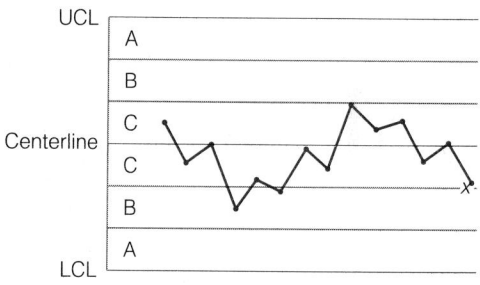

Rule 4: Fourteen points in a row alternating up and down

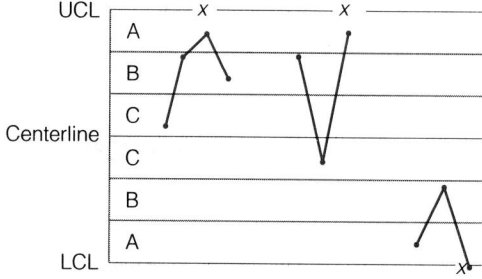

Rule 5: Two out of three points in a row in Zone A or beyond

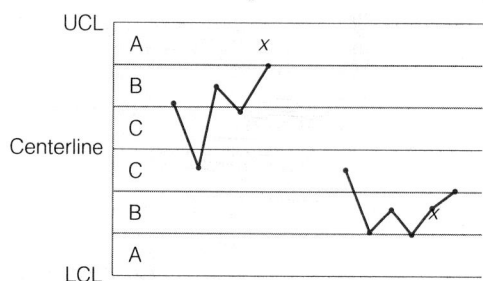

Rule 6: Four out of five points in a row in Zone B or beyond

Rules 1, 2, 5, and 6 should be applied separately to the upper and lower halves of the control chart. Rules 3 and 4 should be applied to the whole chart.

FIGURE 11.21 ▲ Pattern-analysis rules for detecting the presence of special causes of variation

In general, when the process is in control and normally distributed, the probability of any one of these rules *incorrectly* signaling the presence of special causes of variation is less than .005, or 5 chances in 1,000. If all of the first four rules are applied, the overall probability of a false signal is about .01. If all six of the rules are applied, the overall probability of a false signal rises to .02, or 2 chances in 100. These three probabilities can be thought of as Type I error probabilities. Each indicates the probability of incorrectly rejecting the null hypothesis that the process is in a state of statistical control.

Explanation of the possible causes of these nonrandom patterns is beyond the scope of this text. We refer the interested reader to AT&T's *Statistical Quality Control Handbook* (1956).

We use these rules again in the next section when we interpret the R-chart.

Interpreting an $\bar{x}$-Chart

1. The **process is out of control** if one or more sample means fall beyond the control limits or if any of the other five patterns of variation of Figure 11.21 are observed. Such signals are an indication that one or more special causes of variation are affecting the process mean. We must identify and eliminate them to bring the process into control.

2. The **process is treated as being in control** if none of the previously noted out-of-control signals are observed. Processes that are in control should not be tampered with. However, if the level of variation is unacceptably high, common causes of variation should be identified and eliminated.

Assumption: The variation of the process is stable. (If it were not, the control limits of the $\bar{x}$-chart would be meaningless, since they are a function of the process variation. The R-chart, presented in the next section, is used to investigate this assumption.)

In theory, the centerline and control limits should be developed using samples that were collected during a period in which the process was in control. Otherwise, they will not be representative of the variation of the process (or, in the present case, the variation of $\bar{x}$) when the process is in control. However, we will not know whether the process is in control until after we have contructed a control chart. Consequently, when a control chart is first constructed, the centerline and the control limits are treated as **trial values**. If the chart indicates that the process was in control during the period when the sample data were collected, then the centerline and control limits become "official" (i.e., no longer treated as trial values). It is then appropriate to extend the control limits and the centerline to the right and to use the chart to monitor future process output.

However, if in applying the pattern-analysis rules of Figure 11.21 it is determined that the process was out of control while the sample data were being collected, the trial values (i.e., the trial chart) should, in general, not be used to monitor the process. The points on the control chart that indicate that the process is out of control should be investigated to see if any special causes of variation can be identified. A graphical method that can be used to facilitate this investigation—a *cause-and-effect diagram*—is described in Section 11.7. If special causes of variation are found, (1) they should be eliminated, (2) any points on the chart determined to have been influenced by the special causes—whether inside or outside the control limits—should be discarded, and (3) *new* trial centerline and control limits should be calculated from the remaining data. However, the new trial limits may still indicate that the process is out of control. If so, repeat these three steps until all points fall within the control limits.

If special causes cannot be found and eliminated, the severity of the out-of-control indications should be evaluated and a judgment made as to whether (1) the out-of-control points should be discarded anyway and new trial limits constructed, (2) the original trial limits are good enough to be made official, or (3) new sample data should be collected to construct new trial limits.

EXAMPLE 11.1

Let's return to the paint-filling process described in Sections 11.2 and 11.3. Suppose instead of sampling 50 consecutive gallons of paint from the filling process to develop a control chart, it was decided to sample five consecutive cans once each hour for the next 25 hours. The sample data are presented in Table 11.2 on page 640. This sampling strategy (rational subgrouping) was selected because several times a month the filling head in question becomes clogged. When that happens, the head dispenses less and less paint over the course of the day. However, the pattern of decrease is so irregular that minute-to-minute or even half-hour-to-half-hour changes are difficult to detect.

a. Explain the logic behind the rational subgrouping strategy that was used.

b. Construct an x̄-chart for the process using the data in Table 11.2.

c. What does the chart suggest about the stability of the filling process (whether the process is in or out of statistical control)?

d Should the control limits be used to monitor future process output?

Solution

a. The samples are far enough apart in time to detect hour-to-hour shifts or changes in the mean amount of paint dispensed, but the individual measurements that make up each sample are close enough together in time to ensure that the process has changed little, if at all, during the time the individual measurements were made. Overall, the rational subgrouping employed affords the opportunity for process changes to occur between samples and therefore show up on the control chart as differences between the sample means.

TABLE 11.2   Twenty-five Samples of Size 5 from the Paint-Filling Process

Sample	Measurements					Mean	Range
1	10.0042	9.9981	10.0010	9.9964	10.0001	9.99995	.0078
2	9.9950	9.9986	9.9948	10.0030	9.9938	9.99704	.0092
3	10.0028	9.9998	10.0086	9.9949	9.9980	10.00082	.0137
4	9.9952	9.9923	10.0034	9.9965	10.0026	9.99800	.0111
5	9.9997	9.9883	9.9975	10.0078	9.9891	9.99649	.0195
6	9.9987	10.0027	10.0001	10.0027	10.0029	10.00141	.0042
7	10.0004	10.0023	10.0024	9.9992	10.0135	10.00358	.0143
8	10.0013	9.9938	10.0017	10.0089	10.0001	10.00116	.0151
9	10.0103	10.0009	9.9969	10.0103	9.9986	10.00339	.0134
10	9.9980	9.9954	9.9941	9.9958	9.9963	9.99594	.0039
11	10.0013	10.0033	9.9943	9.9949	9.9999	9.99874	.0090
12	9.9986	9.9990	10.0009	9.9947	10.0008	9.99882	.0062
13	10.0089	10.0056	9.9976	9.9997	9.9922	10.00080	.0167
14	9.9971	10.0015	9.9962	10.0038	10.0022	10.00016	.0076
15	9.9949	10.0011	10.0043	9.9988	9.9919	9.99822	.0124
16	9.9951	9.9957	10.0094	10.0040	9.9974	10.00033	.0137
17	10.0015	10.0026	10.0032	9.9971	10.0019	10.00127	.0061
18	9.9983	10.0019	9.9978	9.9997	10.0029	10.00130	.0051
19	9.9977	9.9963	9.9981	9.9968	10.0009	9.99798	.0127
20	10.0078	10.0004	9.9966	10.0051	10.0007	10.00212	.0112
21	9.9963	9.9990	10.0037	9.9936	9.9962	9.99764	.0101
22	9.9999	10.0022	10.0057	10.0026	10.0032	10.00272	.0058
23	9.9998	10.0002	9.9978	9.9966	10.0060	10.00009	.0094
24	10.0031	10.0078	9.9988	10.0032	9.9944	10.00146	.0134
25	9.9993	9.9978	9.9964	10.0032	10.0041	10.00015	.0077

b. Twenty-five samples ($k = 25$ subgroups), each containing $n = 5$ cans of paint, were collected from the process. The first step after collecting the data is to calculate the 25 sample means and sample ranges needed to construct the $\bar{x}$-chart. The mean and range of the first sample are

$$\bar{x} = \frac{10.0042 + 9.9981 + 10.0010 + 9.9964 + 10.0001}{5} = 9.99995$$

$$R = 10.0042 - 9.9964 = .0078$$

All 25 means and ranges are displayed in Table 11.2.

Next, we calculate the mean of the sample means and the mean of the sample ranges:

$$\bar{\bar{x}} = \frac{9.99995 + 9.99704 + \cdots + 10.00015}{25} = 9.9999$$

$$\bar{R} = \frac{.0078 + .0092 + \cdots + .0077}{25} = .01028$$

The centerline of the chart is positioned at $\bar{\bar{x}} = 9.9999$. To determine the control limits, we need the constant A_2, which can be found in Table XIV of Appendix B. For $n = 5$, $A_2 = .577$. Then

$$\text{UCL:} \quad \bar{\bar{x}} + A_2\bar{R} = 9.9999 + .577(.01028) = 10.0058$$
$$\text{LCL:} \quad \bar{\bar{x}} - A_2\bar{R} = 9.9999 - .577(.01028) = 9.9940$$

After positioning the control limits on the chart, we plot the 25 sample means in the order of sampling and connect the points with straight lines. The resulting trial $\bar{x}$-chart is shown in Figure 11.22.

FIGURE 11.22 ▶

$\bar{x}$-chart for the paint-filling process

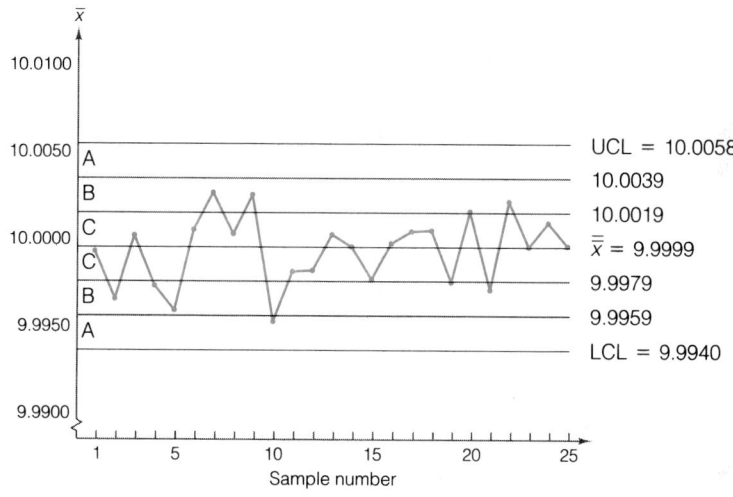

c. To check the stability of the process, we use the six pattern-analysis rules for detecting special causes of variation, which were presented in Figure 11.21. To apply most of these rules requires identifying the A, B, and C zones of the control chart. These are indicated in Figure 11.22. We describe how they were constructed below.

The boundary between the A and B zones is two standard deviations from the centerline, and the boundary between the B and C zones is one standard deviation from the centerline. Thus, using $A_2\bar{R}$ and the 3-sigma limits previously calculated, we locate the A, B, and C zones above the centerline:

$$\text{A–B boundary} = \bar{\bar{x}} + \tfrac{2}{3}(A_2\bar{R})$$
$$= 9.9999 + \tfrac{2}{3}(.577)(.01028) = 10.0039$$
$$\text{B–C boundary} = \bar{\bar{x}} + \tfrac{1}{3}(A_2\bar{R})$$
$$= 9.9999 + \tfrac{1}{3}(.577)(.01028) = 10.0019$$

Similarly, the zones below the centerline are located:

$$A\text{–}B \text{ boundary} = \bar{\bar{x}} + \tfrac{2}{3}(A_2\overline{R}) = 9.9959$$
$$B\text{–}C \text{ boundary} = \bar{\bar{x}} + \tfrac{1}{3}(A_2\overline{R}) = 9.9979$$

A careful comparison of the six pattern-analysis rules with the sequence of sample means yields no out-of-control signals. All points are inside the control limits and there appear to be no nonrandom patterns within the control limits. That is, we can find no evidence of a shift in the process mean. Accordingly, we conclude that the process is in control.

d. Since the process was found to be in control during the period in which the samples were drawn, the trial control limits constructed in part **b** can be considered official. They should be extended to the right and used to monitor future process output.

EXAMPLE 11.2

Ten new samples of size $n = 5$ were drawn from the paint-filling process of the previous example. The sample data, including sample means and ranges, are shown in Table 11.3. Investigate whether the process remained in control during the period in which the new sample data were collected.

TABLE 11.3   Ten Additional Samples of Size 5 from the Paint-Filling Process

Sample	Measurements					Mean	Range
1	10.0019	9.9981	9.9952	9.9976	9.9999	9.99841	.0067
2	10.0041	9.9982	10.0028	10.0040	9.9971	10.00125	.0070
3	9.9999	9.9974	10.0078	9.9971	9.9923	9.99890	.0155
4	9.9982	10.0002	9.9916	10.0040	9.9916	9.99713	.0124
5	9.9933	9.9963	9.9955	9.9993	9.9905	9.99498	.0088
6	9.9915	9.9984	10.0053	9.9888	9.9876	9.99433	.0177
7	9.9912	9.9970	9.9961	9.9879	9.9970	9.99382	.0091
8	9.9942	9.9960	9.9975	10.0019	9.9912	9.99614	.0107
9	9.9949	9.9967	9.9936	9.9941	10.0071	9.99726	.0135
10	9.9943	9.9969	9.9937	9.9912	10.0053	9.99626	.0141

Solution

We begin by simply extending the control limits, centerline, and zone boundaries of the control chart in Figure 11.22 to the right. Next, beginning with sample number 26, we plot the 10 new sample means on the control chart and connect them with straight lines. This extended version of the control chart is shown in Figure 11.23.

FIGURE 11.23 ▶
Extended $\bar{x}$-chart for paint-filling process

Now that the control chart has been prepared, we apply the six pattern-analysis rules for detecting special causes of variation (Figure 11.21) to the new sequence of sample means. No points fall outside the control limits, but we notice six points in a row that steadily decrease (samples 27–32). Rule 3 says that if we observe six points in a row steadily increasing or decreasing, that is an indication of the presence of special causes of variation.

Notice that if you apply the rules from left to right along the sequence of sample means, the decreasing pattern also triggers signals from Rules 5 (samples 29–31) and 6 (samples 28–32).

These signals lead us to conclude that the process has gone out of control. Apparently, the filling head began to clog about the time that either sample 26 or 27 was drawn from the process. As a result, the mean of the process (the mean fill weight dispensed by the process) began to decline.

Exercises 11.1–11.15

Learning the Mechanics

11.1 What is a control chart? Describe its use.

11.2 Explain why rational subgrouping should be used in constructing control charts.

11.3 When a control chart is first constructed, why are the centerline and control limits treated as trial values?

11.4 Which process parameter is an $\bar{x}$-chart used to monitor?

11.5   Even if all the points on an $\bar{x}$-chart fall between the control limits, the process may be out of control. Explain.

11.6   What must be true about the variation of a process before an $\bar{x}$-chart is used to monitor the mean of the process? Why?

11.7   Use the six pattern-analysis rules described in Figure 11.21 to determine whether the process being monitored with the accompanying $\bar{x}$-chart is out of statistical control.

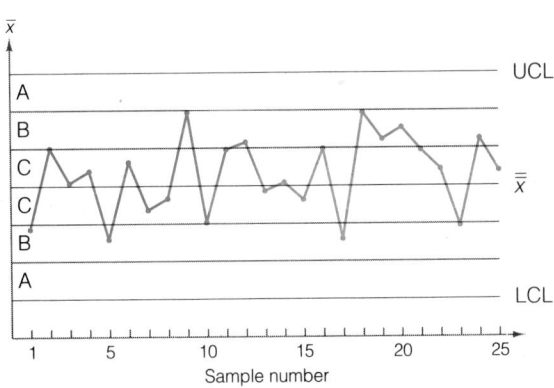

11.8   Is the process for which the accompanying $\bar{x}$-chart was constructed affected by only special causes of variation, only common causes of variation, or both? Explain.

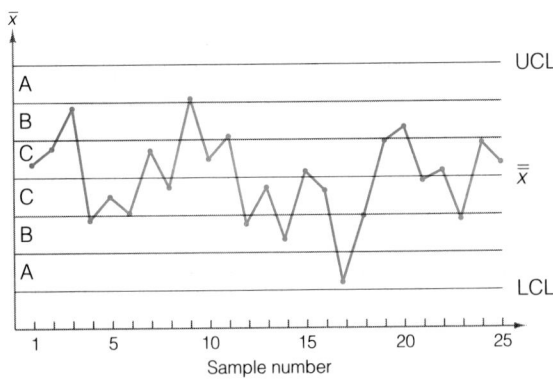

11.9   Use Table XIV in Appendix B to find the value of A_2 for each of the following sample sizes.
   a. $n = 3$ **b.** $n = 10$ **c.** $n = 22$

11.10   Twenty-five samples of size $n = 5$ were collected to construct an $\bar{x}$-chart. The accompanying sample means and ranges were calculated for these data.

Sample	x̄	R	Sample	x̄	R	Sample	x̄	R
1	80.2	7.2	10	85.3	7.1	18	75.9	9.9
2	79.1	9.0	11	77.7	9.8	19	78.1	6.0
3	83.2	4.7	12	82.3	10.7	20	81.4	7.4
4	81.0	5.6	13	79.5	9.2	21	81.7	10.4
5	77.6	10.1	14	83.1	10.2	22	80.9	9.1
6	81.7	8.6	15	79.6	7.8	23	78.4	7.3
7	80.4	4.4	16	80.0	6.1	24	79.6	8.0
8	77.5	6.2	17	83.2	8.4	25	81.6	7.6
9	79.8	7.9						

a. Calculate the mean of the sample means, x̄̄, and the mean of the sample ranges, R̄.
b. Calculate and plot the centerline and the upper and lower control limits for the x̄-chart.
c. Calculate and plot the A, B, and C zone boundaries of the x̄-chart.
d. Plot the 25 sample means on the x̄-chart and use the six pattern-analysis rules to determine whether the process is under statistical control.

11.11 The following data were collected for the purpose of constructing an x̄-chart.

Sample	Measurements				Sample	Measurements			
1	19.4	19.7	20.6	21.2	11	22.7	21.2	21.5	19.5
2	18.7	18.4	21.2	20.7	12	20.1	20.6	21.0	20.2
3	20.2	18.8	22.6	20.1	13	19.7	18.6	21.2	19.1
4	19.6	21.2	18.7	19.4	14	18.6	21.7	17.7	18.3
5	20.4	20.9	22.3	18.6	15	18.2	20.4	19.8	19.2
6	17.3	22.3	20.3	19.7	16	18.9	20.7	23.2	20.0
7	21.8	17.6	22.8	23.1	17	20.5	19.7	21.4	17.8
8	20.9	17.4	19.5	20.7	18	21.0	18.7	19.9	21.2
9	18.1	18.3	20.6	20.4	19	20.5	19.6	19.8	21.8
10	22.6	21.4	18.5	19.7	20	20.6	16.9	22.4	19.7

a. Calculate x̄ and R for each sample.
b. Calculate x̄̄ and R̄.
c. Calculate and plot the centerline and the upper and lower control limits for the x̄-chart.
d. Calculate and plot the A, B, and C zone boundaries of the x̄-chart.
e. Plot the 20 sample means on the x̄-chart. Is the process in control? Justify your answer.

Applying the Concepts

11.12 The central processing unit (CPU) of a microcomputer is a computer chip containing millions of transistors. Connecting the transistors are slender circuit paths only .5 to .85 micron wide. To understand how narrow these paths are, consider that a micron is a millionth of a meter, and a human hair is 70 microns wide (Wood, 1992). A manufacturer of CPU chips knows that if the circuit paths are not .5–.85 micron wide, a variety of problems will arise in the chips' performance. The manufacturer sampled four CPU chips six times a day (every 90 minutes from 8:00 A.M. until 4:30 P.M.) for five consecutive days and measured the circuit path widths. These data and Minitab were used to construct the x̄-chart shown on page 646.

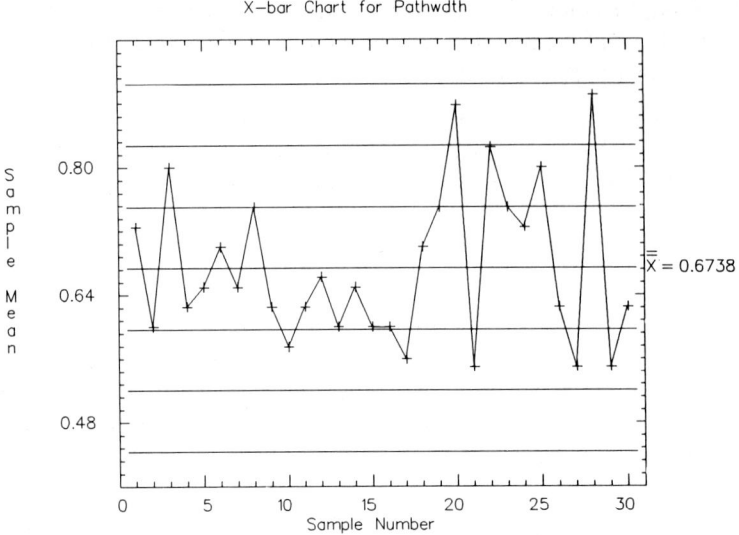

X-bar Chart for Pathwdth

a. Assuming that $\overline{R} = .3162$, calculate the chart's upper and lower control limits, the upper and lower A–B boundaries, and the upper and lower B–C boundaries.
b. What does the chart suggest about the stability of the process used to put circuit paths on the CPU chip? Justify your answer.
c. Should the control limits be used to monitor future process output? Explain.

11.13 A machine at K-Company fills boxes with bran flakes cereal. The target weight for the filled boxes is 24 ounces. The company would like to use an $\bar{x}$-chart to monitor the performance of the machine. To develop the control chart, the company decides to sample and weigh five consecutive boxes of cereal five times each day (at 8:00 and 11:00 A.M. and 2:00, 5:00, and 8:00 P.M.) for four consecutive days. The data are presented in the table.

Day	Weight of Cereal Boxes (oz.)					Day	Weight of Cereal Boxes (oz.)				
1	24.02	23.91	24.12	24.06	24.13	11	24.10	23.90	24.11	23.98	23.95
2	23.89	23.98	24.01	24.00	23.91	12	24.01	24.07	23.93	24.09	23.98
3	24.11	24.02	23.99	23.79	24.04	13	24.14	24.07	24.08	23.98	24.02
4	24.06	23.98	23.95	24.01	24.11	14	23.91	24.04	23.89	24.01	23.95
5	23.81	23.90	23.99	24.07	23.96	15	24.03	24.04	24.01	23.98	24.10
6	23.87	24.12	24.07	24.01	23.99	16	23.94	24.07	24.12	24.00	24.02
7	23.88	24.00	24.05	23.97	23.97	17	23.88	23.94	23.91	24.06	24.07
8	24.01	24.03	23.99	23.91	23.98	18	24.11	23.99	23.90	24.01	23.98
9	24.06	24.02	23.80	23.79	24.07	19	24.05	24.04	23.97	24.08	23.95
10	23.96	23.99	24.03	23.99	24.01	20	24.02	23.96	23.95	23.89	24.04

a. Construct an $\bar{x}$-chart from the given data.
b. What does the chart suggest about the stability of the filling process (whether the process is in or out of statistical control)? Justify your answer.
c. Should the control limits be used to monitor future process output? Explain.

d. Two shifts of workers run the filling operation. Each day the second shift takes over at 3:00 P.M. Will the rational subgrouping strategy used by K-Company facilitate or hinder the identification of process variation caused by differences in the two shifts? Explain.

11.14 A precision parts manufacturer produces bolts for use in military aircraft. Ideally, the bolts should be 37 centimeters in length. The company sampled four consecutively produced bolts each hour on the hour for 25 consecutive hours and measured them using a computerized precision instrument. The data are presented here.

Hour	Bolt Lengths (cm)				Hour	Bolt Lengths (cm)			
1	37.03	37.08	36.90	36.88	14	37.08	37.07	37.10	37.04
2	36.96	37.04	36.85	36.98	15	37.03	37.04	36.89	37.01
3	37.16	37.11	36.99	37.01	16	36.95	36.98	36.90	36.99
4	37.20	37.06	37.02	36.98	17	36.97	36.94	37.14	37.10
5	36.81	36.97	36.91	37.10	18	37.11	37.04	36.98	36.91
6	37.13	36.96	37.01	36.89	19	36.88	36.99	37.01	36.94
7	37.07	36.94	36.99	37.00	20	36.90	37.15	37.09	37.00
8	37.01	36.91	36.98	37.12	21	37.01	36.96	37.05	36.96
9	37.17	37.03	36.90	37.01	22	37.09	36.95	36.93	37.12
10	36.91	36.99	36.87	37.11	23	37.00	37.02	36.95	37.04
11	36.88	37.10	37.07	37.03	24	36.99	37.07	36.90	37.02
12	37.06	36.98	36.90	36.99	25	37.10	37.03	37.01	36.90
13	36.91	37.22	37.12	37.03					

a. What process is the manufacturer interested in monitoring?
b. Construct an x̄-chart from the data.
c. Does the chart suggest that special causes of variation are present? Justify your answer.
d. Provide an example of a special cause of variation that could potentially affect this process. Do the same for a common cause of variation.
e. Should the control limits be used to monitor future process output? Explain.

11.15 A walk-in freezer thermostat at a restaurant is set at 5°F. Because of the perishability of the food in the freezer, the restaurant's manager has decided to begin monitoring the temperature inside the freezer. In order to establish the centerline and control limits of an x̄-chart, the manager used a precision thermometer to take sample temperature readings at five randomly chosen times per day for 20 days. The data are presented here.

Day	Temperature Readings (°F)					Day	Temperature Readings (°F)				
1	5.22	5.29	5.11	4.95	4.78	11	5.10	5.17	4.65	5.20	4.93
2	4.40	4.41	4.63	6.03	4.83	12	4.86	4.97	5.35	4.81	4.72
3	5.11	5.43	4.90	4.55	5.23	13	5.03	3.91	5.16	4.80	4.98
4	5.65	4.24	5.09	4.82	5.50	14	5.16	4.80	5.61	5.06	4.91
5	4.68	5.92	4.71	4.67	4.75	15	4.92	4.33	5.25	4.93	4.81
6	5.01	5.26	6.10	5.20	5.25	16	5.21	5.17	4.79	4.80	5.30
7	5.20	4.99	5.15	5.96	5.35	17	3.82	5.19	5.24	4.60	4.78
8	4.30	4.91	5.03	4.97	4.80	18	4.33	4.88	5.21	5.18	5.07
9	5.45	5.62	6.11	5.13	4.90	19	5.16	5.83	5.29	4.75	4.77
10	5.06	5.13	4.95	5.59	5.80	20	5.26	4.61	5.34	5.40	4.71

   a. What process is the manager interested in monitoring?
   b. What parameter of that process can be monitored using an $\bar{x}$-chart?
   c. Construct an $\bar{x}$-chart from the data.
   d. What does the chart suggest about the stability of the temperature in the freezer unit? Explain.
   e. Should the control limits be used to monitor future temperatures? Explain.
   f. Critique the rational subgrouping strategy employed by the restaurant manager.

11.5 A Control Chart for Monitoring the Variation of a Process: The *R*-Chart

Recall from Section 11.2 that a process may be out of statistical control because its mean or variance or both are changing over time (see Figure 11.8). The $\bar{x}$-chart of the previous section is used to detect changes in the process mean. The control chart we present in this section—the R-chart—is used to detect changes in process variation.

The primary difference between the $\bar{x}$-chart and the R-chart is that instead of plotting *sample means* and monitoring their variation, we plot and monitor the variation of *sample ranges*. Changes in the behavior of the sample range signal changes in the variation of the process.

We could also monitor process variation by plotting *sample standard deviations*. That is, we could calculate s for each sample (i.e., each subgroup) and plot them on a control chart known as an **s-chart**. In this chapter, however, we focus on just the R-chart because (1) when using samples of size 9 or less, the s-chart and the R-chart reflect about the same information, and (2) the R-chart is used much more widely by practitioners than is the s-chart (primarily because the sample range is easier to calculate and interpret than the sample standard deviation). For more information about s-charts, see the references at the end of the chapter.

The underlying logic and basic form of the R-chart are similar to the $\bar{x}$-chart. In monitoring $\bar{x}$, we use the standard deviation of $\bar{x}$ to develop 3-sigma control limits. Now, since we want to be able to determine when R takes on unusually large or small values, we use the standard deviation of R, σ_R, to construct 3-sigma control limits. The centerline of the $\bar{x}$-chart represents the process mean μ or, equivalently, the mean of the sampling distribution of $\bar{x}$, $\mu_{\bar{x}}$. Similarly, the centerline of the R-chart represents μ_R, the mean of the sampling distribution of R. These points are illustrated in the R-chart of Figure 11.24.

FIGURE 11.24 ▶
R-chart

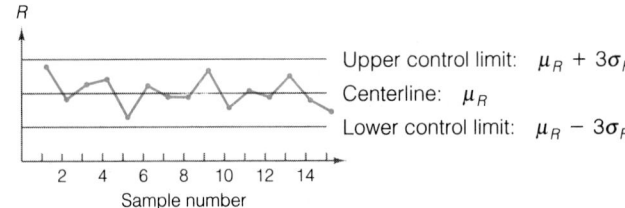

As with the $\bar{x}$-chart, you should have at least 20 samples of n items each ($n \geq 2$) to construct an R-chart. This will provide sufficient data to obtain reasonably good estimates of μ_R and σ_R. Rational subgrouping is again used for determining sample size and frequency of sampling.

The centerline of the R-chart is positioned as follows:

$$\text{Centerline:} \quad \bar{R} = \frac{R_1 + R_2 + \cdots + R_k}{k}$$

where k is the number of samples of size n and R_i is the range of the ith sample. $\bar{R}$ is an estimate of μ_R.

In order to construct the control limits, we need an estimator of σ_R. The estimator recommended by Montgomery (1991) and Ryan (1989) is

$$\hat{\sigma}_R = d_3\left(\frac{\bar{R}}{d_2}\right)$$

where d_2 and d_3 are constants whose values depend on the sample size, n. Values for d_2 and d_3 for samples of size $n = 2$ to $n = 25$ are given in Table XIV of Appendix B.

The control limits are positioned as follows:

$$\text{Upper control limit:} \quad \bar{R} + 3\hat{\sigma}_R = \bar{R} + 3d_3\left(\frac{\bar{R}}{d_2}\right)$$

$$\text{Lower control limit:} \quad \bar{R} - 3\hat{\sigma}_R = \bar{R} - 3d_3\left(\frac{\bar{R}}{d_2}\right)$$

Notice that $\bar{R}$ appears twice in each control limit. Accordingly, we can simplify the calculation of these limits by factoring out $\bar{R}$:

$$\text{UCL:} \quad \bar{R}\left(1 + \frac{3d_3}{d_2}\right) = \bar{R}D_4 \qquad \text{LCL:} \quad \bar{R}\left(1 - \frac{3d_3}{d_2}\right) = \bar{R}D_3$$

where

$$D_4 = \left(1 + \frac{3d_3}{d_2}\right) \qquad D_3 = \left(1 - \frac{3d_3}{d_2}\right)$$

The values for D_3 and D_4 have been tabulated for samples of size $n = 2$ to $n = 25$ and can be found in Appendix B, Table XIV.

For samples of size $n = 2$ through $n = 6$, D_3 is negative, and the lower control limit falls below zero. Since the sample range cannot take on negative values, such a control limit is meaningless. Thus, when $n \leq 6$ the R-chart contains only one control limit, the upper control limit.

Although D_3 is actually negative for $n \leq 6$, the values reported in Table XIV in Appendix B are all zeros. This has been done to discourage the inappropriate construction of negative lower control limits. If the lower control limit is calculated using $D_3 = 0$, you obtain $D_3\bar{R} = 0$. This should be interpreted as indicating that the R-chart has no lower 3-sigma control limit.

Constructing an *R*-Chart: A Summary

1. Using a rational subgrouping strategy, collect at least 20 samples (i.e., subgroups), each of size $n \geq 2$.
2. Calculate the range of each sample.
3. Calculate the mean of the sample ranges, $\overline{R}$:

$$\overline{R} = \frac{R_1 + R_2 + \cdots + R_k}{k}$$

   where k = The number of samples (i.e., subgroups)
   R_i = The range of the ith sample

4. Plot the centerline and control limits:

   Centerline: $\overline{R}$ *Upper control limit:* $\overline{R}D_4$ *Lower control limit:* $\overline{R}D_3$

   where D_3 and D_4 are constants that depend on n. Their values can be found in Appendix B, Table XIV. When $n \leq 6$, $D_3 = 0$, indicating that the control chart does not have a lower control limit.

5. Plot the k sample ranges on the control chart in the order that the samples were produced by the process.

Constructing Zone Boundaries for an *R*-Chart

The simplest method of construction uses the estimator of the standard deviation of R, which is $\hat{\sigma}_R = d_3(\overline{R}/d_2)$:

Upper A–B *boundary:* $\overline{R} + 2d_3\left(\dfrac{\overline{R}}{d_2}\right)$

Lower A–B *boundary:* $\overline{R} - 2d_3\left(\dfrac{\overline{R}}{d_2}\right)$

Upper B–C *boundary:* $\overline{R} + d_3\left(\dfrac{\overline{R}}{d_2}\right)$

Lower B–C *boundary:* $\overline{R} - d_3\left(\dfrac{\overline{R}}{d_2}\right)$

Note: Whenever $n \leq 6$ the R-chart has no lower 3-sigma control limit. However, the lower A–B and B–C boundaries can still be plotted if they are nonnegative.

We interpret the completed *R*-chart in basically the same way as we did the $\bar{x}$-chart. We look for indications that the process is out of control. Those indications include points that fall outside the control limits as well as any nonrandom patterns of variation that appear between the control limits. To help spot nonrandom behavior, we include the A, B, and C zones (described in the previous section) on the *R*-chart. The next box describes how to construct the zone boundaries for the *R*-chart. It requires only rules 1 through 4 of Figure 11.21, because rules 5 and 6 are based on the assumption that the statistic plotted on the control chart follows a normal (or nearly normal) distribution, whereas *R*'s distribution is skewed to the right.[*]

Interpreting an *R*-Chart

1. The **process is out of control** if one or more sample ranges fall beyond the control limits (rule 1) or if any of the three patterns of variation described by rules 2, 3, and 4 (Figure 11.21) are observed. Such signals indicate that one or more special causes of variation are influencing the *variation* of the process. These causes should be identified and eliminated to bring the process into control.

2. The **process is treated as being in control** if none of the noted out-of-control signals are observed. Processes that are in control should not be tampered with. However, if the level of variation is unacceptably high, common causes of variation should be identified and eliminated.

As with the $\bar{x}$-chart, the centerline and control limits should be developed using samples that were collected during a period in which the process was in control. Accordingly, when an *R*-chart is first constructed, the centerline and the control limits are treated as **trial values** (see Section 11.4) and are modified, if necessary, before being extended to the right and used to monitor future process output.

EXAMPLE 11.3

Refer to Example 11.1.

a. Construct an *R*-chart for the paint-filling process.

b. What does the chart indicate about the stability of the filling process during the time when the data were collected?

c. Is it appropriate to use the control limits constructed in part **a** to monitor future process output?

---

[*]Some authors (e.g., Kane, 1989) apply all six pattern-analysis rules as long as $n \geq 4$.

Solution   a. The first step after collecting the data is to calculate the range of each sample. For the first sample the range is

$$R = 10.0042 - 9.9964 = .0078$$

All 25 sample ranges appear in Table 11.2 (page 640).
    Next, calculate the mean of the ranges:

$$\bar{R} = \frac{.0078 + .0092 + \cdots + .0077}{25} = .01028$$

The centerline of the chart is positioned at $\bar{R} = .01028$. To determine the control limits, we need the constants D_3 and D_4, which can be found in Table XIV of Appendix B. For $n = 5$, $D_3 = 0$ and $D_4 = 2.115$. Since $D_3 = 0$, the lower 3-sigma control limit is negative and is not included on the chart. The upper control limit is calculated as follows:

$$\text{UCL:} \quad \bar{R}D_4 = (.01028)(2.115) = .0217$$

After positioning the upper control limit on the chart, we plot the 25 sample ranges in the order of sampling and connect the points with straight lines. The resulting trial R-chart is shown in Figure 11.25.

b. To facilitate our examination of the R-chart, we plot the four zone boundaries. Recall that in general the A–B boundaries are positioned two standard deviations from the centerline and the B–C boundaries are one standard deviation from the centerline. In the case of the R-chart, we use the estimated standard deviation of R, $\hat{\sigma}_R = d_3(\bar{R}/d_2)$, and calculate the boundaries:

$$\text{Upper A–B boundary:} \quad \bar{R} + 2d_3\left(\frac{\bar{R}}{d_2}\right) = .01792$$

$$\text{Lower A–B boundary:} \quad \bar{R} - 2d_3\left(\frac{\bar{R}}{d_2}\right) = .00264$$

$$\text{Upper B–C boundary:} \quad \bar{R} + d_3\left(\frac{\bar{R}}{d_2}\right) = .01410$$

$$\text{Lower B–C boundary:} \quad \bar{R} - d_3\left(\frac{\bar{R}}{d_2}\right) = .00646$$

where (from Table XIV of Appendix B) for $n = 5$, $d_2 = 2.326$ and $d_3 = .864$. Notice in Figure 11.25 that the lower A zone is slightly narrower than the upper A zone. This occurs because the lower 3-sigma control limit (the usual lower boundary of the lower A zone) is negative.

FIGURE 11.25 ▶

R-chart for the paint-filling process

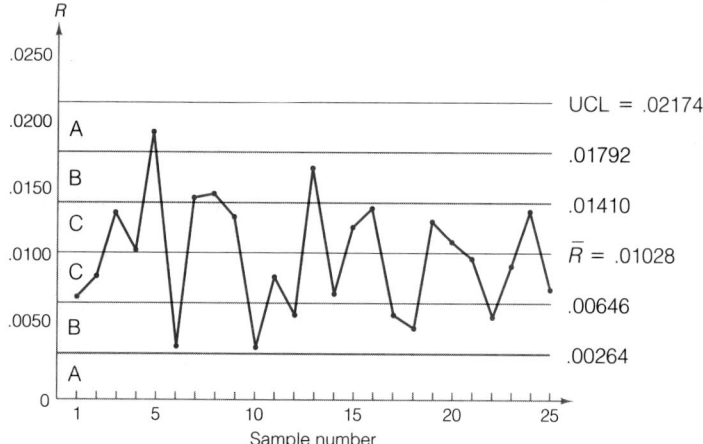

All the plotted R values fall below the upper control limit. This is one indication that the process is under control (i.e., is stable). However, we must also look for patterns of points that would be unlikely to occur if the process were in control. To assist us with this process, we use pattern-analysis rules 1–4 (Figure 11.21). None of the rules signal the presence of special causes of variation. Accordingly, we conclude that it is reasonable to treat the process—in particular, the variation of the process—as being under control during the period in question. Apparently, no significant special causes of variation are influencing the variation of the process.

c. Yes. Since the variation of the process appears to be in control during the period when the sample data were collected, the control limits appropriately characterize the variation in R that would be expected when the process is in a state of statistical control.

In practice, the $\bar{x}$-chart and the R-chart are not used in isolation, as our presentation so far might suggest. Rather, they are used together to monitor the mean (i.e., the location) of the process and the variation of the process simultaneously. In fact, many practitioners plot them on the same piece of paper.

One important reason for dealing with them as a unit is that the control limits of the $\bar{x}$-chart are a function of R. That is, the control limits depend on the variation of the process. (Recall that the control limits are $\bar{x} \pm A_2\bar{R}$.) Thus, if the process variation is out of control, the control limits of the $\bar{x}$-chart have little meaning. This is because when the process variation is changing (as in the bottom two graphs of Figure 11.8), any single estimate of the variation (such as $\bar{R}$ or s) is not representative of the process. Accordingly, **the appropriate procedure is to first construct and then interpret the R-chart. If it indicates that the process variation is in control, then it makes sense to construct and interpret the $\bar{x}$-chart.**

Figure 11.26 is reprinted from Kaoru Ishikawa's classic text on quality-improvement methods, *Guide to Quality Control* (1986). It illustrates how particular changes in a process over time may be reflected in $\bar{x}$- and R-charts. At the top of the figure, running across the page, is a series of probability distributions A, B, and C that describe the process (i.e., the output variable) at different points in time. In practice, we never have this information. For this example, however, Ishikawa worked with a known process (i.e., with its given probabilistic characterization) to illustrate how sample data from a known process might behave.

FIGURE 11.26 ▶
Combined $\bar{x}$- and R-chart
(Ishikawa, 1986)

The control limits for both charts were constructed from $k = 25$ samples of size $n = 5$. These data were generated by Distribution A. The 25 sample means and ranges were plotted on the $\bar{x}$- and R-charts, respectively. Since the distribution did not change over this period of time, it follows from the definition of statistical control that the process was under control. If you did not know this—as would be the case in practice—what would you conclude from looking at the control charts? (Remember, always interpret the R-chart before the $\bar{x}$-chart.) Both charts indicate that the process is under control. Accordingly, the control limits are made official and can be used to monitor future output, as is done next.

Toward the middle of the figure, the process changes. The mean shifts to a higher level. Now the output variable is described by Distribution B. The process is out of control. Ten new samples of size 5 are sampled from the process. Since the variation of the process has not changed, the R-chart should indicate that the variation remains stable. This is, in fact, the case. All points fall below the upper control limit. As we would hope, it is the $\bar{x}$-chart that reacts to the change in the mean of the process.

Then the process changes again (Distribution C). This time the mean shifts back to its original position, but the variation of the process increases. The process is still out of control but this time for a different reason. Checking the R-chart first, we see that it has reacted as we would hope. It has detected the increase in the variation. Given this R-chart finding, the control limits of the $\bar{x}$-chart become inappropriate (as described before) and we would not use them. Notice, however, how the sample means react to the increased variation in the process. This increased variation in $\bar{x}$ is consistent with what we know about the variance of $\bar{x}$. It is directly proportional to the variance of the process, $\sigma_{\bar{x}}^2 = \sigma^2/n$.

Keep in mind that what Ishikawa did in this example is exactly the opposite of what we do in practice. In practice we use sample data and control charts to make inferences about changes in unknown process distributions. Here, for the purpose of helping you to understand and interpret control charts, known process distributions were changed to see what would happen to the control charts.

Exercises 11.16–11.25

Learning the Mechanics

11.16 What characteristic of a process is an R-chart designed to monitor?

11.17 In practice, $\bar{x}$- and R-charts are used together to monitor a process. However, the R-chart should be interpreted before the $\bar{x}$-chart. Why?

11.18 Use Table XIV in Appendix B to find the values of D_3 and D_4 for each of the following sample sizes.
   a. $n = 4$ **b.** $n = 12$ **c.** $n = 24$

11.19 Construct and interpret an R-chart for the data in Exercise 11.10.
   a. Calculate and plot the upper control limit and, if appropriate, the lower control limit.
   b. Calculate and plot the A, B, and C zone boundaries on the R-chart.
   c. Plot the sample ranges on the R-chart and use pattern-analysis rules 1–4 of Figure 11.21 to determine whether the process is under statistical control.

11.20 Construct and interpret an R-chart for the data in Exercise 11.11.
   a. Calculate and plot the upper control limit and, if appropriate, the lower control limit.
   b. Calculate and plot the A, B, and C zone boundaries on the R-chart.
   c. Plot the sample ranges on the R-chart and determine whether the process is in control.

11.21 Construct and interpret an R-chart and an $\bar{x}$-chart from the sample data on page 656. Remember to interpret the R-chart *before* the $\bar{x}$-chart.

Sample	Measurements							$\bar{x}$	R
	1	2	3	4	5	6	7		
1	20.1	19.0	20.9	22.2	18.9	18.1	21.3	20.07	4.1
2	19.0	17.9	21.2	20.4	20.0	22.3	21.5	20.33	4.4
3	22.6	21.4	21.4	22.1	19.2	20.6	18.7	20.86	3.9
4	18.1	20.8	17.8	19.6	19.8	21.7	20.0	19.69	3.9
5	22.6	19.1	21.4	21.8	18.4	18.0	19.5	20.11	4.6
6	19.1	19.0	22.3	21.5	17.8	19.2	19.4	19.76	4.5
7	17.1	19.4	18.6	20.9	21.8	21.0	19.8	19.80	4.7
8	20.2	22.4	22.0	19.6	19.6	20.0	18.5	20.33	3.9
9	21.9	24.1	23.1	22.8	25.6	24.2	25.2	23.84	3.7
10	25.1	24.3	26.0	23.1	25.8	27.0	26.5	25.40	3.9
11	25.8	29.2	28.5	29.1	27.8	29.0	28.0	28.20	3.4
12	28.2	27.5	29.3	30.7	27.6	28.0	27.0	28.33	3.7
13	28.2	28.6	28.1	26.0	30.0	28.5	28.3	28.24	4.0
14	22.1	21.4	23.3	20.5	19.8	20.5	19.0	20.94	4.3
15	18.5	19.2	18.0	20.1	22.0	20.2	19.5	19.64	4.0
16	21.4	20.3	22.0	19.2	18.0	17.9	19.5	19.76	4.1
17	18.4	16.5	18.1	19.2	17.5	20.9	19.6	18.60	4.4
18	20.1	19.8	22.3	22.5	21.8	22.7	23.0	21.74	3.2
19	20.0	17.5	21.0	18.2	19.5	17.2	18.1	18.79	3.8
20	22.3	18.2	21.5	19.0	19.4	20.5	20.0	20.13	4.1

Applying the Concepts

11.22 Refer to Exercise 11.12, where the desired circuit path widths were .5 to .85 micron. The manufacturer sampled four CPU chips six times a day (every 90 minutes from 8:00 A.M. until 4:30 P.M.) for five consecutive days. The path widths were measured and used to construct the R-chart shown.

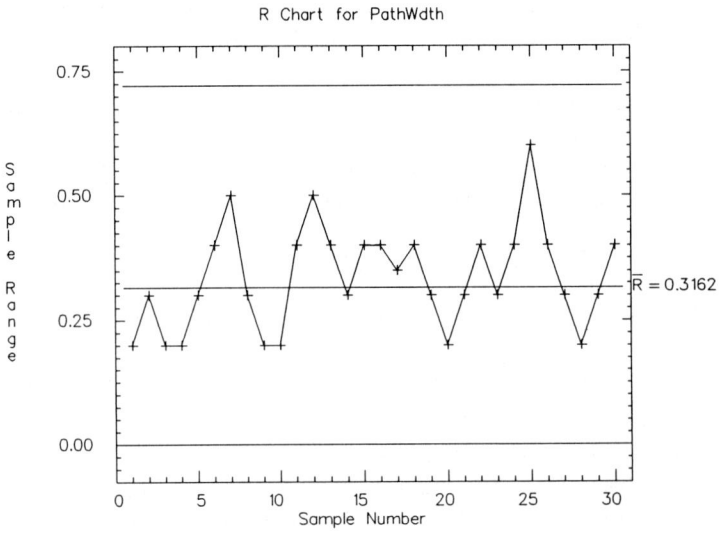

a. Calculate the chart's upper and lower control limits.
b. What does the R-chart suggest about the presence of special causes of variation during the time when the data were collected?
c. Should the control limit(s) be used to monitor future process output? Explain.
d. How many different R values are plotted on the control chart? Notice how most of the R values fall along three horizontal lines. What could cause such a pattern?

11.23 A soft-drink bottling company is interested in monitoring the amount of cola injected into 16-ounce bottles by a particular filling head. The process is entirely automated and operates 24 hours a day. At 6 A.M. and 6 P.M. each day, a new dispenser of carbon dioxide capable of producing 20,000 gallons of cola is hooked up to the filling machine. In order to monitor the process using control charts, the company decided to sample five consecutive bottles of cola each hour beginning at 6:15 A.M. (i.e., 6:15 A.M., 7:15 A.M., 8:15 A.M., etc.). The data for the first day are given here.

Sample	Measurements					Sample	Measurements				
1	16.01	16.03	15.98	16.00	16.01	13	15.96	16.00	16.01	16.00	15.98
2	16.03	16.02	15.97	15.99	15.99	14	15.98	16.01	16.02	15.99	15.99
3	15.98	16.00	16.03	16.04	15.99	15	15.99	16.03	16.00	15.98	16.01
4	16.00	16.03	16.02	15.98	15.98	16	16.02	16.02	16.01	15.97	16.00
5	15.97	15.99	16.03	16.01	16.04	17	16.01	16.05	15.99	15.99	16.03
6	16.01	16.03	16.04	15.97	15.99	18	15.98	16.03	16.04	15.98	16.01
7	16.04	16.05	15.97	15.96	16.00	19	15.97	15.96	15.99	15.99	16.01
8	16.02	16.05	16.03	15.97	15.98	20	16.03	16.01	16.04	15.96	15.99
9	15.97	15.99	16.02	16.03	15.95	21	15.99	16.03	15.97	16.05	16.03
10	16.00	16.01	15.95	16.04	16.06	22	15.98	15.95	16.07	16.01	16.04
11	15.95	16.04	16.07	15.93	16.03	23	15.99	16.06	15.95	16.03	16.07
12	15.98	16.07	15.94	16.08	16.02	24	16.00	16.01	16.08	15.94	15.93

a. Will the rational subgrouping strategy that was used enable the company to detect variation in fill caused by differences in the carbon dioxide dispensers? Explain.
b. Construct an R-chart from the data.
c. What does the R-chart indicate about the stability of the filling process during the time when the data were collected? Justify your answer.
d. Should the control limit(s) be used to monitor future process output? Explain.
e. Given your answer to part c, should an $\bar{x}$-chart be constructed from the given data? Explain.

11.24 Refer to the data in Exercise 11.13.
a. Construct an R-chart for the process.
b. What does the R-chart suggest about the presence of special causes of variation during the time when the data were collected?
c. Should the control limit(s) be used to monitor future process output? Explain.

11.25 Refer to the data in Exercise 11.14.
a. Construct an R-chart for the production process.
b. What does the R-chart indicate about the stability of the process?
c. Should the control limits be used to monitor future output? Explain.

11.6 A Control Chart for Monitoring the Proportion of Defectives Generated by a Process: The p-Chart

Among the dozens of different control charts that have been proposed by researchers and practitioners, the $\bar{x}$- and R-charts are by far the most popular for use in monitoring **quantitative** output variables such as time, length, and weight. Among the charts developed for use with **qualitative** output variables, the chart we introduce in this section is the most popular. Called the **p-chart**, it is used when the output variable is categorical (i.e., measured on a nominal scale). With the p-chart, the proportion, p, of units produced by the process that belong to a particular category (e.g., defective or nondefective; successful or unsuccessful; early, on-time, or late) can be monitored.

The p-chart is typically used to monitor the proportion of defective units produced by a process (i.e., the proportion of units that do not conform to specification). This proportion is used to characterize a process in the same sense that the mean and variance are used to characterize a process when the output variable is quantitative. Examples of process proportions that are monitored in industry include the proportion of billing errors made by credit-card companies; the proportion of nonfunctional semiconductor chips produced; and the proportion of checks that a bank's magnetic ink character-recognition system is unable to read.

As is the case for the mean and variance, the process proportion can change over time. For example, it can drift upward or downward or jump to a new level. In such cases, the process is out of control. **As long as the process proportion remains constant, the process is in a state of statistical control.**

As with the other control charts presented in this chapter, the p-chart has a centerline and control limits that are determined from sample data. After k samples of size n are drawn from the process, each unit is classified (e.g., defective or nondefective), the proportion of defective units in each sample—$\hat{p}$—is calculated, the centerline and control limits are determined using this information, and the sample proportions are plotted on the p-chart. It is the variation in the $\hat{p}$'s over time that we monitor and interpret. Changes in the behavior of the $\hat{p}$'s signal changes in the process proportion, p.

The p-chart is based on the assumption that the number of defectives observed in each sample is a binomial random variable. What we have called the process proportion is really the binomial probability, p. (We discussed binomial random variables in Chapter 4.) When the process is in a state of statistical control, p remains constant over time. Variation in $\hat{p}$—as displayed on a p-chart—is used to judge whether p is stable.

To determine the centerline and control limits for the p-chart we need to know $\hat{p}$'s sampling distribution. We described the sampling distribution of $\hat{p}$ in Section 6.4. Recall that

$$\hat{p} = \frac{\text{Number of defective items in the sample}}{\text{Number of items in the sample}} = \frac{x}{n}$$

$$\mu_{\hat{p}} = p$$

$$\sigma_{\hat{p}} = \sqrt{\frac{p(1-p)}{n}}$$

and that for large samples $\hat{p}$ is approximately normally distributed. Thus, if p were known, the centerline would be p and the 3-sigma control limits would be $p \pm 3\sqrt{p(1-p)/n}$. However, since p is unknown, it must be estimated from the sample data. The appropriate estimator is $\bar{p}$, the overall proportion of defective units in the nk units sampled:

$$\bar{p} = \frac{\text{Total number of defective units in all } k \text{ samples}}{\text{Total number of units sampled}}$$

To calculate the control limits of the p-chart, substitute $\bar{p}$ for p in the preceding expression for the control limits, as illustrated in Figure 11.27.

FIGURE 11.27 ▶
p-chart

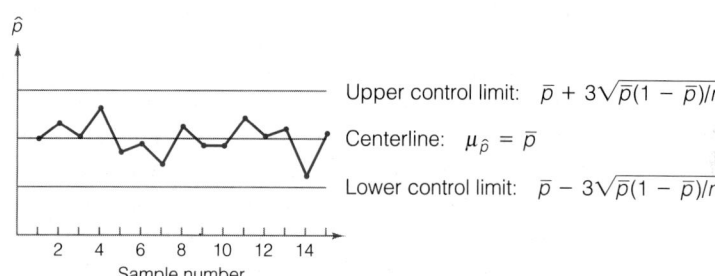

In constructing a p-chart it is advisable to use a much larger sample size than is typically used for $\bar{x}$- and R-charts. Most processes that are monitored in industry have relatively small process proportions, often less than .05 (i.e., less than 5% of output is nonconforming). In those cases, if a small sample size is used, say $n = 5$, samples drawn from the process would likely not contain any nonconforming output. As a result, most, if not all, $\hat{p}$'s would equal zero.

We present a rule of thumb that can be used to determine a sample size large enough to avoid this problem. This rule will also help protect against ending up with a negative lower control limit, a situation that frequently occurs when both p and n are small. See Montgomery (1991) or Duncan (1986) for further details.

Sample-Size Determination

Choose n such that $\quad n > \dfrac{9(1 - p_0)}{p_0}$

where

$\qquad n = $ Sample size

$\qquad p_0 = $ An estimate (perhaps judgmental) of the process proportion p

For example, if p is thought to be about .05, the rule indicates that samples of at least size 171 should be used in constructing the p-chart:

$$n > \frac{9(1 - .05)}{.05} = 171$$

In the next three boxes we summarize how to construct a p-chart and its zone boundaries and how to interpret a p-chart.

Constructing a p-Chart: A Summary

1. Using a rational subgrouping strategy, collect at least 20 samples, each of size

$$n > \frac{9(1 - p_0)}{p_0}$$

where p_0 is an estimate of p, the proportion defective (i.e., nonconforming) produced by the process. p_0 can be determined from sample data (i.e., $\hat{p}$) or may be based on expert opinion.

2. For each sample, calculate $\hat{p}$, the proportion of defective units in the sample:

$$\hat{p} = \frac{\text{Number of defective items in the sample}}{\text{Number of items in the sample}}$$

3. Plot the centerline and control limits:

$$Centerline:\quad \bar{p} = \frac{\text{Total number of defective units in all } k \text{ samples}}{\text{Total number of units in all } k \text{ samples}}$$

$$Upper\ control\ limit:\quad \bar{p} + 3\sqrt{\frac{\bar{p}(1 - \bar{p})}{n}}$$

$$Lower\ control\ limit:\quad \bar{p} - 3\sqrt{\frac{\bar{p}(1 - \bar{p})}{n}}$$

where k is the number of samples of size n and $\bar{p}$ is the overall proportion of defective units in the nk units sampled. $\bar{p}$ is an estimate of the unknown process proportion p.

4. Plot the k sample proportions on the control chart in the order that the samples were produced by the process.

As with the $\bar{x}$- and R-charts, the centerline and control limits should be developed using samples that were collected during a period in which the process was in control. Accordingly, when a p-chart is first constructed, the centerline and the control limits should be treated as *trial values* (see Section 11.4) and, if necessary, modified before being extended to the right on the control chart and used to monitor future process output.

Constructing Zone Boundaries for a *p*-Chart

Upper A–B boundary: $\bar{p} + 2\sqrt{\dfrac{\bar{p}(1 - \bar{p})}{n}}$

Lower A–B boundary: $\bar{p} - 2\sqrt{\dfrac{\bar{p}(1 - \bar{p})}{n}}$

Upper B–C boundary: $\bar{p} + \sqrt{\dfrac{\bar{p}(1 - \bar{p})}{n}}$

Lower B–C boundary: $\bar{p} - \sqrt{\dfrac{\bar{p}(1 - \bar{p})}{n}}$

Note: When the lower control limit is negative, it should not be plotted on the control chart. However, the lower zone boundaries can still be plotted if they are nonnegative.

Interpreting a *p*-Chart

1. The **process is out of control** if one or more sample proportions fall beyond the control limits (rule 1) or if any of the three patterns of variation described by rules 2, 3, and 4 (Figure 11.21) are observed. Such signals indicate that one or more special causes of variation are influencing the process proportion, *p*. These causes should be identified and eliminated in order to bring the process into control.

2. The **process is treated as being in control** if none of the above noted out-of-control signals are observed. Processes that are in control should not be tampered with. However, if the level of variation is unacceptably high, common causes of variation should be identified and eliminated.

EXAMPLE 11.4

A manufacturer of auto parts is interested in implementing statistical process control in several areas within its warehouse operation. The manufacturer wants to begin with the order-assembly process. Too frequently orders received by customers contain the wrong items or too few items.

For each order received, parts are picked from storage bins in the warehouse, labeled, and placed on a conveyor belt system. Since the bins are spread over a 3-acre area, items that are part of the same order may be placed on different spurs of the conveyor belt system. Near the end of the belt system all spurs converge and a worker sorts the items according to the order they belong to. That information is contained on the labels that were placed on the items by the pickers.

The workers have identified three errors that cause shipments to be improperly assembled: (1) pickers pick from the wrong bin, (2) pickers mislabel items, and (3) the sorter makes an error.

The firm's quality manager has implemented a sampling program in which 90 assembled orders are sampled each day and checked for accuracy. An assembled order is considered nonconforming (defective) if it differs in any way from the order placed by the customer. To date, 25 samples have been evaluated. The resulting data are shown in Table 11.4.

a. Construct a p-chart for the order-assembly operation.

b. What does the chart indicate about the stability of the process?

c. Is it appropriate to use the control limits and centerline constructed in part **a** to monitor future process output?

TABLE 11.4   Twenty-five Samples of Size 90 from the Warehouse Order-Assembly Process

Sample	Size	Defective Orders	Sample Proportion
1	90	12	.13333
2	90	6	.06666
3	90	11	.12222
4	90	8	.08888
5	90	13	.14444
6	90	14	.15555
7	90	12	.13333
8	90	6	.06666
9	90	10	.11111
10	90	13	.14444
11	90	12	.13333
12	90	24	.26666
13	90	23	.25555
14	90	22	.24444
15	90	8	.08888
16	90	3	.03333
17	90	11	.12222
18	90	14	.15555
19	90	5	.05555
20	90	12	.13333
21	90	18	.20000
22	90	12	.13333
23	90	13	.14444
24	90	4	.04444
25	90	6	.06666
Totals	2,250	292	

Solution

a. The first step in constructing the p-chart after collecting the sample data is to calculate the sample proportion for each sample. For the first sample,

$$\hat{p} = \frac{\text{Number of defective items in the sample}}{\text{Number of items in the sample}} = \frac{12}{90} = .13333$$

All the sample proportions are displayed in Table 11.4. Next, calculate the proportion of defective items in the total number of items sampled:

$$\bar{p} = \frac{\text{Total number of defective items}}{\text{Total number of items sampled}} = \frac{292}{2250} = .12978$$

The centerline is positioned at $\bar{p}$, and $\bar{p}$ is used to calculate the control limits:

$$\bar{p} \pm 3 \sqrt{\frac{\bar{p}(1 - \bar{p})}{n}} = .12978 \pm 3 \sqrt{\frac{.12978(1 - .12978)}{90}}$$

$$= .12978 \pm .10627$$

UCL: .23605

LCL: .02351

After plotting the centerline and the control limits, plot the 25 sample proportions in the order of sampling and connect the points with straight lines. The completed control chart is shown in Figure 11.28.

FIGURE 11.28 ▶

p-chart for order-assembly process

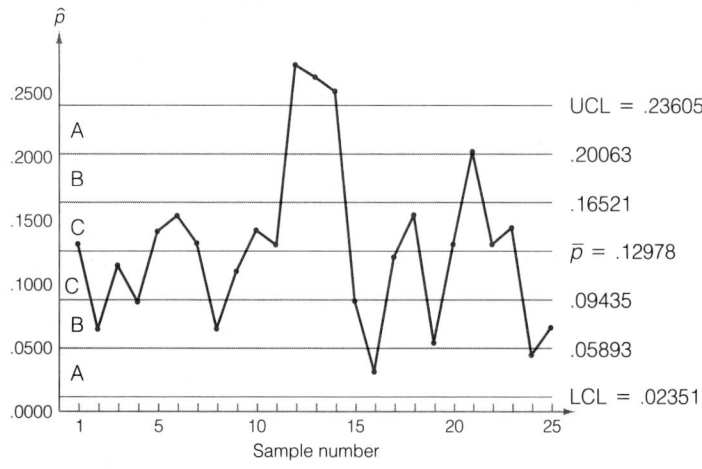

b. To assist our examination of the control chart, we add the one- and two-standard-deviation zone boundaries. The boundaries are located by substituting $\bar{p} = .12978$ into the following formulas:

$$\textit{Upper A–B boundary:} \quad \bar{p} + 2 \sqrt{\frac{\bar{p}(1 - \bar{p})}{n}} = .20063$$

$$\text{Upper B–C boundary:} \quad \bar{p} + \sqrt{\frac{\bar{p}(1 - \bar{p})}{n}} = .16521$$

$$\text{Lower A–B boundary:} \quad \bar{p} - 2\sqrt{\frac{\bar{p}(1 - \bar{p})}{n}} = .05893$$

$$\text{Lower B–C boundary:} \quad \bar{p} - \sqrt{\frac{\bar{p}(1 - \bar{p})}{n}} = .09435$$

Because three of the sample proportions fall above the upper control limit (rule 1), there is strong evidence that the process is out of control. None of the nonrandom patterns of rules 2, 3, and 4 (Figure 11.21) are evident. The process proportion appears to have increased dramatically somewhere around sample 12.

c. Because the process was apparently out of control during the period in which sample data were collected to build the control chart, it is not appropriate to continue using the chart. The control limits and centerline are not representative of the process when it is in control. The chart must be revised before it is used to monitor future output.

In this case, the three out-of-control points were investigated and it was discovered that they occurred on days when a temporary sorter was working in place of the regular sorter. Actions were taken to ensure that in the future better-trained temporary sorters would be available.

Since the special cause of the observed variation was identified and eliminated, all sample data from the three days the temporary sorter was working were dropped from the data set and the centerline and control limits were recalculated:

$$\text{Centerline:} \quad \bar{p} = \frac{223}{1980} = .11263$$

$$\text{Control limits:} \quad \bar{p} \pm 3\sqrt{\frac{\bar{p}(1 - \bar{p})}{n}} = .11263 \pm 3\sqrt{\frac{.11263(.88737)}{90}}$$

$$= .11263 \pm .09997$$

$$\text{UCL:} \quad .21259 \qquad \text{LCL:} \quad .01266$$

The revised zones are calculated by substituting $\bar{p} = .11263$ in the following formulas:

$$\text{Upper A–B boundary:} \quad \bar{p} + 2\sqrt{\frac{\bar{p}(1 - \bar{p})}{n}} = .17927$$

$$\text{Upper B–C boundary:} \quad \bar{p} + \sqrt{\frac{\bar{p}(1 - \bar{p})}{n}} = .14595$$

$$\text{Lower A–B boundary:} \quad \bar{p} - 2\sqrt{\frac{\bar{p}(1 - \bar{p})}{n}} = .04598$$

$$\text{Lower B–C boundary:} \quad \bar{p} - \sqrt{\frac{\bar{p}(1 - \bar{p})}{n}} = .07931$$

The revised control chart appears in Figure 11.29. Notice that now all sample proportions fall within the control limits. These limits can now be treated as official, extended to the right on the chart, and used to monitor future orders.

FIGURE 11.29 ▶
Revised p-chart for order-assembly process

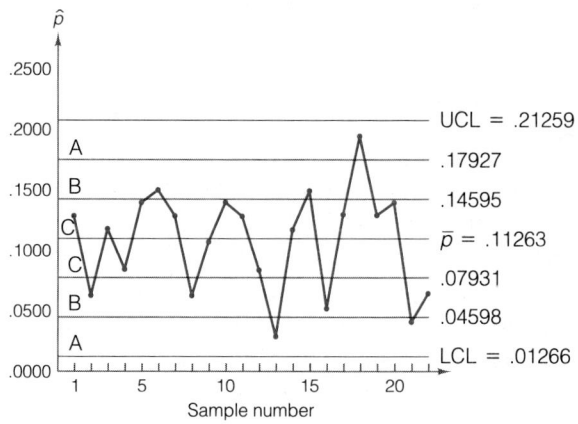

Exercises 11.26–11.34

Learning the Mechanics

11.26 What characteristic of a process is a p-chart designed to monitor?

11.27 The proportion of defective items generated by a manufacturing process is believed to be 8%. In constructing a p-chart for the process, determine how large the sample size should be to avoid ending up with a negative lower control limit.

11.28 To construct a p-chart for a manufacturing process, 25 samples of size 200 were drawn from the process. The number of defectives in each sample is listed here.

Sample	Sample Size	Defectives	Sample	Sample Size	Defectives
1	200	16	14	200	12
2	200	14	15	200	14
3	200	9	16	200	11
4	200	11	17	200	8
5	200	15	18	200	7
6	200	8	19	200	12
7	200	12	20	200	15
8	200	16	21	200	9
9	200	17	22	200	16
10	200	13	23	200	13
11	200	15	24	200	11
12	200	10	25	200	10
13	200	9			

a. Calculate the proportion defective in each sample.
b. Calculate and plot $\bar{p}$ and the upper and lower control limits for the p-chart.
c. Calculate and plot the A, B, and C zone boundaries on the p-chart.
d. Plot the sample proportions on the p-chart and connect them with straight lines.
e. Use the pattern-analysis rules 1–4 for detecting the presence of special causes of variation (Figure 11.21) to determine whether the process is out of control.

11.29   To construct a p-chart, 20 samples of size 150 were drawn from a process. The proportion of defective items found in each of the samples is listed in the accompanying table.

Sample	Proportion Defective	Sample	Proportion Defective	Sample	Proportion Defective
1	.03	8	.05	15	.07
2	.05	9	.07	16	.06
3	.10	10	.06	17	.07
4	.02	11	.07	18	.02
5	.08	12	.04	19	.05
6	.09	13	.06	20	.03
7	.08	14	.05		

a. Calculate and plot the centerline and the upper and lower control limits for the p-chart.
b. Calculate and plot the A, B, and C zone boundaries on the p-chart.
c. Plot the sample proportions on the p-chart.
d. Is the process under control? Explain.
e. Should the control limits and centerline of part a be used to monitor future process output? Explain.

11.30   In each of the following cases, use the sample-size formula on page 659 to determine a sample size large enough to avoid constructing a p-chart with a negative lower control limit.
   a. $p_0 = .01$ b. $p_0 = .05$ c. $p_0 = .10$ d. $p_0 = .20$

Applying the Concepts

11.31   A manufacturer produces disks for personal computers. From past experience the production manager believes that 1% of the disks are defective. The company collected a sample of the first 1,000 disks manufactured after 4:00 P.M. every other day for a month. The disks were analyzed for defects, then these data and Minitab were used to construct the p-chart shown on page 667.
   a. From a statistical perspective, is a sample size of 1,000 adequate for constructing the p-chart? Explain.
   b. Calculate the chart's upper and lower control limits.
   c. What does the p-chart suggest about the presence of special causes during the time when the data were collected?
   d. Critique the rational subgrouping strategy used by the disk manufacturer.

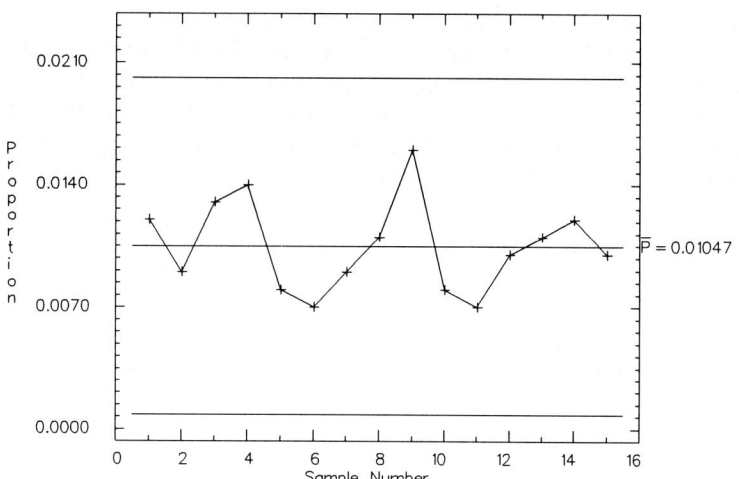

11.32 Goodstone Tire & Rubber Company is interested in monitoring the proportion of defective tires generated by the production process at its Akron, Ohio, production plant. The company's chief engineer believes that the proportion is about 7%. Because the tires are destroyed during the testing process, the company would like to keep the number of tires tested to a minimum. However, the engineer would also like to use a *p*-chart with a positive lower control limit. A positive lower control limit makes it possible to determine when the process has generated an unusually small proportion of defectives. Such an occurrence is good news and would signal the engineer to look for causes of the superior performance. That information can be used to improve the production process. Using the sample-size formula on page 659, the chief engineer recommended that the company randomly sample and test 120 tires from each day's production. To date, 20 samples have been taken. The data are presented here.

Sample	Sample Size	Defectives	Sample	Sample Size	Defectives
1	120	11	11	120	10
2	120	5	12	120	12
3	120	4	13	120	8
4	120	8	14	120	6
5	120	10	15	120	10
6	120	13	16	120	5
7	120	9	17	120	10
8	120	8	18	120	10
9	120	10	19	120	3
10	120	11	20	120	8

a. Use the sample-size formula to show how the chief engineer arrived at the recommended sample size of 120.

b. Construct a *p*-chart for the tire-production process.

c. What does the chart indicate about the stability of the process? Explain.

d. Is it appropriate to use the control limits to monitor future process output? Explain.

e. Is the *p*-chart you constructed in part **b** capable of signaling hour-to-hour changes in *p*? Explain.

11.33 With the recent increase in competition among credit-card companies, the banks issuing VistaCard are interested in improving customer service as a means of retaining current customers and attracting new ones. The banks targeted a reduction in customer billing errors as a top priority. All customer accounts are processed at a central billing center in Eureka, California. The director of the billing center believes that billing errors may run as high as 4%. A program was implemented at the center to check a random sample of 250 customer bills each day for accuracy. To date, 24 samples have been evaluated. The data are presented in the table.

Sample	Sample Size	Bills with Errors	Sample	Sample Size	Bills with Errors
1	250	11	13	250	12
2	250	9	14	250	4
3	250	8	15	250	9
4	250	14	16	250	10
5	250	16	17	250	13
6	250	12	18	250	19
7	250	7	19	250	18
8	250	17	20	250	10
9	250	14	21	250	16
10	250	3	22	250	19
11	250	11	23	250	8
12	250	6	24	250	7

a. Construct a p-chart for the customer billing operation.
b. What does the chart indicate about the stability of the process? Explain.
c. Should the control limits be used to monitor the billing process in the future? Explain.

11.34 A manufacturing company makes hemostats for hospital emergency rooms. The company is interested in implementing statistical process control procedures in its production operation. The production manager believes that the proportion of defective hemostats generated by the process is about 3%. The company collected one sample of 300 consecutively manufactured hemostats each day for 20 days. Each day sampling began at 10:00 A.M. The data are given here.

Sample	Sample Size	Defectives	Sample	Sample Size	Defectives
1	300	8	11	300	12
2	300	6	12	300	11
3	300	11	13	300	14
4	300	15	14	300	8
5	300	12	15	300	7
6	300	11	16	300	3
7	300	9	17	300	9
8	300	6	18	300	11
9	300	5	19	300	10
10	300	4	20	300	6

a. Use the sample-size formula on page 659 to show that a sample size of 300 is large enough to prevent the lower control limit of the p-chart from being negative.
b. Construct a p-chart for the manufacturing process.

   c. Does the chart indicate the presence of special causes of variation? Explain.

   d. Provide an example of a special cause of variation that could potentially affect this process. Do the same for a common cause of variation.

   e. Should the control limits and centerline be used to monitor future process output? If not, what should be done to develop a centerline and control limits that can be used to monitor future output?

11.7   Diagnosing Causes of Variation

Statistical process control (SPC) consists of three major activities or phases: (1) monitoring process variation, (2) diagnosing causes of variation, and (3) eliminating those causes. A more detailed description of SPC is shown in Figure 11.30, which depicts SPC as a quality improvement cycle. In the monitoring phase, statistical signals from the process are evaluated in order to uncover opportunities to improve the process. This is the phase we have dealt with in Sections 11.3–11.6. We turn our attention now to the diagnosis phase.

FIGURE 11.30 ▶
SPC viewed as a quality improvement cycle

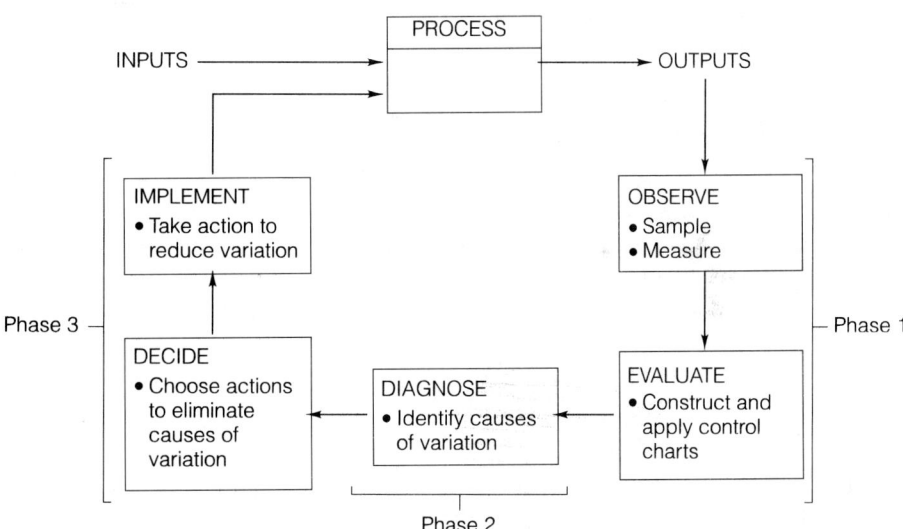

The diagnosis phase is the critical link in the SPC improvement cycle. The monitoring phase simply identifies *whether* problems exist; the diagnosis phase identifies *what* the problems are. If the monitoring phase detected the presence of special causes of variation (i.e., an out-of-control signal was observed on a control chart), the diagnosis phase is concerned with tracking down the underlying cause or causes. If no special causes were detected in the monitoring phase (i.e., the process is under statistical control) and further improvement in the process is desired, the diagnosis phase concentrates on uncovering common causes of variation.

It is important to recognize that the achievement of process improvement requires more than the application of statistical tools such as control charts. This is particularly evident in the diagnosis phase. The diagnosis of causes of variation requires expert knowledge about the process in question. Just as you would go to a physician to diagnose a pain in your back, you would turn to people who work in the process or to engineers or analysts with process expertise to help you diagnose the causes of process variation.

Several methods have been developed for assisting process experts with process diagnosis, including *flowcharting* and the simple but powerful graphical tool called *Pareto analysis* (Chapter 2). Another graphical method, the **cause-and-effect diagram**, is described in this section. A fourth methodology, *experimental design*, is beyond the scope of this text. (Consult the references for details.)

The cause-and-effect diagram was developed by Kaoru Ishikawa of the University of Tokyo in 1943. As a result, it is also known as an *Ishikawa diagram*. The cause-and-effect diagram facilitates the construction of causal chains that explain the occurrence of events, problems, or conditions. It is often constructed through brainstorming sessions involving a small group of process experts. It has been employed for decades by Japanese firms, but was not widely applied in the United States until the mid-1980s.

The basic framework of the cause-and-effect diagram is shown in Figure 11.31. In the right-hand box in the figure, we record the effect whose cause(s) we want to diagnose. For instance, Figures 11.32 and 11.33 (page 672), record two examples of effects to be diagnosed: why the wrong meals are being served to hospital patients, and the reasons for high variation in the fill weights of 20-pound bags of dry dog food.

FIGURE 11.31 ▶
The basic framework for a cause-and-effect diagram

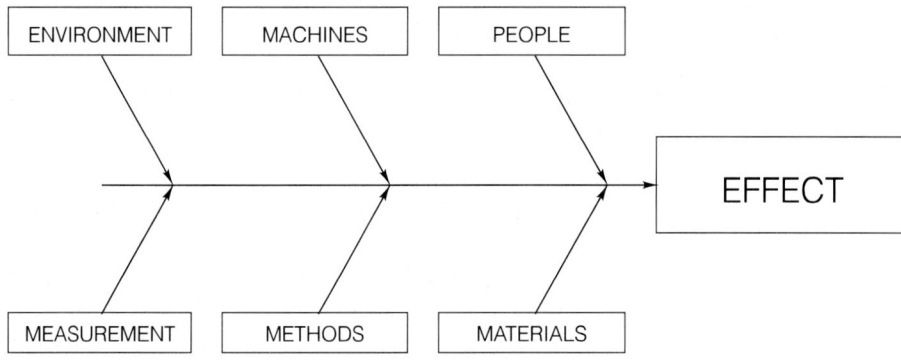

Examining Figure 11.31, we see the branches of the cause-and-effect diagram, which represent the major factors that influence the process and that could be responsible for the effect. These are often taken to be the six universal sources of process variation that we described in Section 11.1: people, machines, materials, methods, measurement, and environment. Notice that in the examples of Figures 11.32 and 11.33 these categories were tailored to fit the process in question. The set of categories must be broad enough to include virtually all possible factors that could influence the

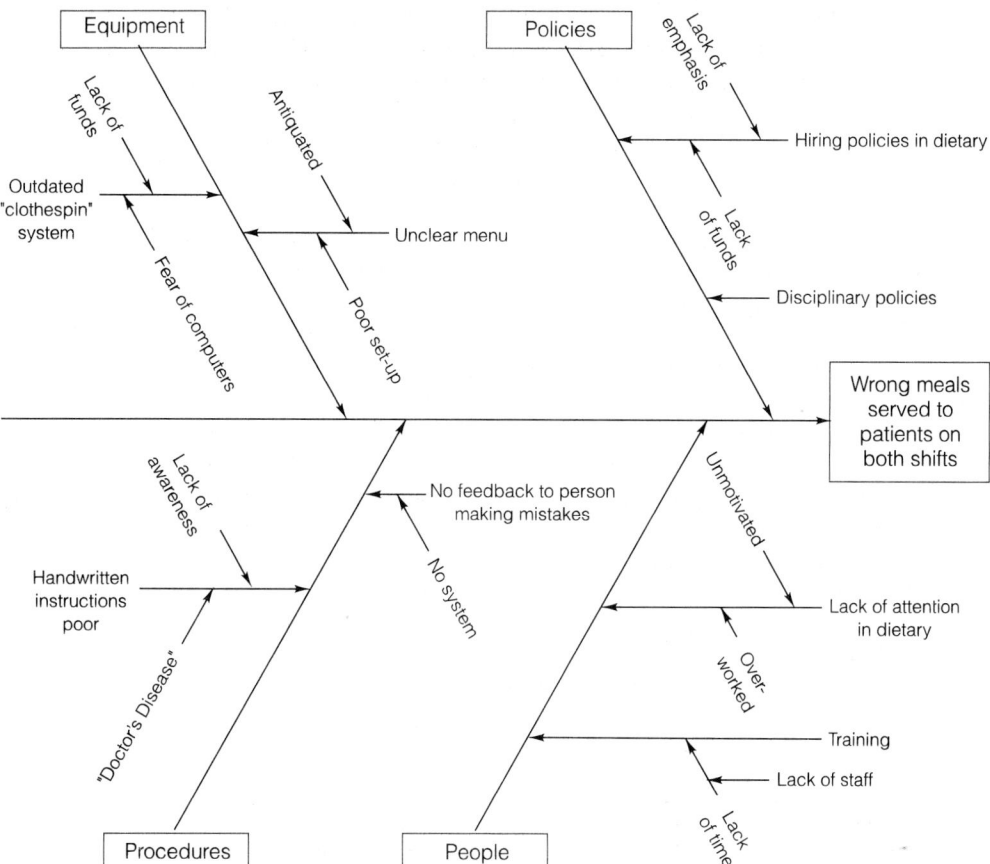

FIGURE 11.32 ▲ Cause-and-effect diagram for the meal service at a hospital [Source: *The Memory Jogger*, The Growth Opportunity Alliance of Greater Lawrence, Lawrence, Mass., 1985. p. 24.]

process. It is less important how many categories are used or how you label the categories.

The cause-and-effect diagram is constructed using effect-to-cause reasoning. That is, you begin by specifying the effect of interest and then move backward to identify *potential* causes of the effect. After a potential cause has been identified, you treat it as an effect and try to find its cause, and so forth. The result is a **causal chain.** A completed cause-and-effect diagram typically contains many causal chains. These chains help us to track down causes whose eradication will reduce, improve, or eliminate the effect in question.

After setting up the basic framework for the cause-and-effect diagram and recording the effect of interest in the box on the right, you construct the causal chains, proceeding backward from general potential causes to increasingly specific causes. Begin by choosing one of the universal cause categories—say, people—and asking, "What factors related to people could cause the effect in question?" In the hospital

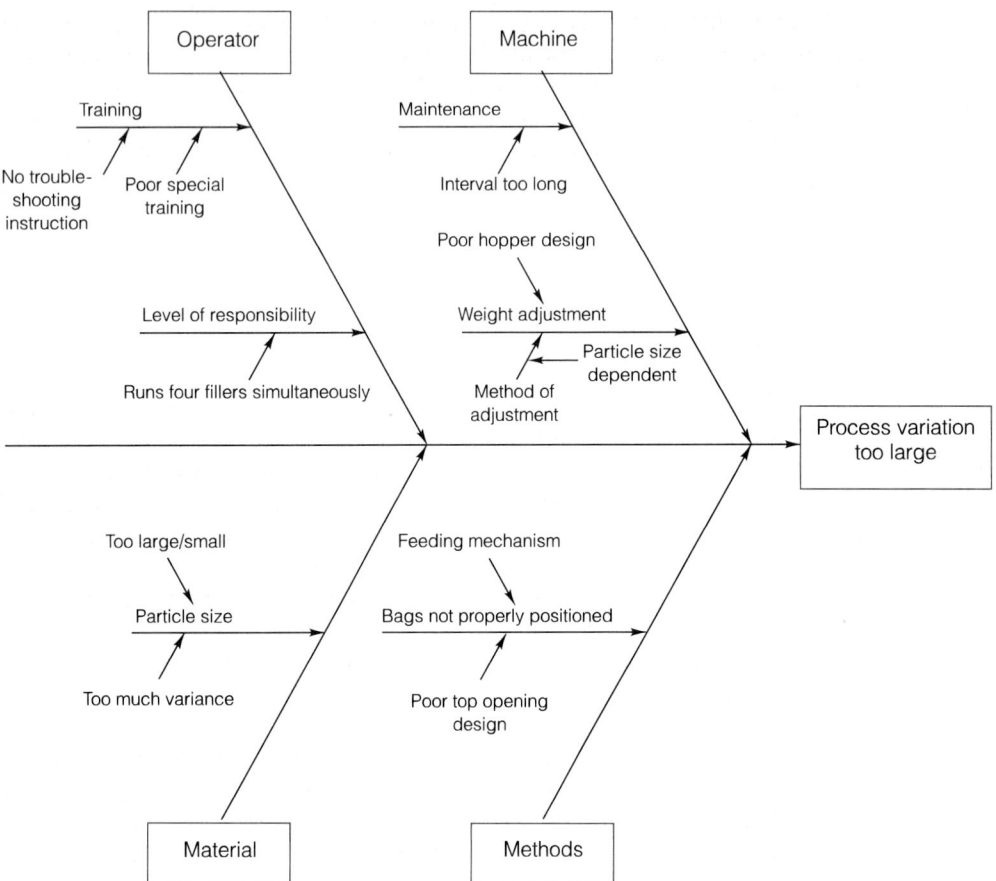

FIGURE 11.33 ▲ Cause-and-effect diagram for the filling process for 20-lb. bags of dog food; from DeVor, Chang, and Southerland (1992, p. 191)

example of Figure 11.32, two factors were identified: (1) insufficient training and (2) lack of attention to detail by workers in the dietary department. Each of these causes is written on a twig of the People branch. Next, each cause is treated as an effect and an attempt is made to identify its cause. That is, we look for subcauses. The insufficient training was blamed on a lack of available time to train the hospital staff. This in turn was blamed on a shortage of hospital personnel. Thus, the Training twig has a Lack of time twig attached to it, which in turn has a Lack of staff twig attached. Multiple causal chains like this should be constructed for each branch of the cause-and-effect diagram, as illustrated in Figures 11.32 and 11.33.

Once completed, the various causal chains of the cause-and-effect diagram must be evaluated (often subjectively) to identify one or more factors thought most likely to be causes of the effect in question. Then actions can be chosen and implemented (see Figure 11.30) to eliminate the causes and improve the process.

Besides facilitating process diagnosis, cause-and-effect diagrams serve to document the causal factors that may potentially affect a process and to communicate that information to others in the organization. The cause-and-effect diagram is a very flexible tool that can be applied in a variety of situations. It can be used as a formal part of the SPC improvement cycle, as suggested above, or simply as a means of investigating the causes of organizational problems, events, or conditions. It can also help select the appropriate process variables to monitor with control charts.

Summary

We learned that a **process** is a series of actions or operations that transform inputs to outputs. In this chapter we focused on methods for monitoring and improving processes. The methods discussed can be applied to any process, whether a personal process or an organizational process. The primary target of the methods is **variation** in process output. Variation is inherent in all processes and is caused by **people, machines, materials, methods, measurement,** and the **environment.** Consumers' perceptions of the quality of a particular product or service are strongly influenced by the amount of variation in that product or service. Variation may plague the **performance, reliability, conformance, durability,** and **serviceability** of a product. Other product dimensions that influence customers' perceptions of quality include the product's **features** and **aesthetics.**

We learned that unless a process is brought into *statistical control* its full capability will remain unknown. The set of methods and activities used to bring a process into control and keep it in control is called **statistical process control.** Processes that are in control reflect only **common causes of variation;** processes that are out of control reflect both common and **special causes of variation.**

Control charts are used to identify the presence of special causes of variation. Control charts help us decide when to take action to find and remove special causes and when to leave the process alone. The $\bar{x}$-chart monitors the mean of the process; the **R-chart** monitors the variation of the process; and the *p*-chart monitors the proportion defective produced by the process.

In constructing a control chart, we try to anticipate the special causes of variation that might affect the process and employ a **rational subgrouping strategy** that makes the chart sensitive to the anticipated variation. In interpreting a control chart, we consider the process out of control if one or more points fall beyond the **control limits** or if any of the other five sequences of points shown in the **pattern-analysis rules** of Figure 11.21 are observed between the control limits.

We learned that statistical process control can be viewed as a quality improvement cycle in which we **observe and evaluate** process data, **diagnose** causes of variation, **decide** what action to take to eliminate the cause of the variation, and **implement** the action to improve the process. Repetition of this cycle will ensure continuous improvement of the process. We saw that **cause-and-effect diagrams** are helpful in the diagnosis phase of the cycle.

Supplementary Exercises 11.35–11.61

11.35   Define *quality* and lists its important dimensions.

11.36   What is a system? Give an example of a system with which you are familiar, and describe its inputs, outputs, and transformation process.

11.37   What is a process? Give an examle of an organizational process and a personal process.

11.38   Select a personal process that you would like to better understand or to improve and construct a flowchart for it.

11.39   Describe the six major sources of process variation.

11.40   What is process management?

11.41   What is systems thinking and how does it benefit process management?

11.42   Compare and contrast the detection–reaction and preventative styles of process management.

11.43   Select an organizational process that you would like to improve.
   a. Construct a process flowchart.
   b. What are the inputs and outputs of the process?
   c. Analyze the flowchart and suggest one or more ways that the process can be simplified.
   d. Choose one operation in the process (i.e., one of the rectangles in the flowchart of part **a**) and identify the inputs and outputs of the operation. (Note that this operation is a *subprocess* of the process described in your flowchart.)
   e. Define a variable associated with the subprocess of part **d** that would be useful to monitor in managing the subprocess.
   f. Construct a cause-and-effect diagram for the variable you defined in part **e** to help explain why it takes on different values over time. Label the effect box "Variation in x," where x is your chosen variable.

11.44   Select a problem, event, or condition whose cause or causes you would like to diagnose. Construct a cause-and-effect diagram that would facilitate your diagnosis.

11.45   What are the two properties of a system that make it an "indivisible whole"?

11.46   Why is it important for managers who implement statistical process control to have a basic understanding of systems theory?

11.47   In estimating a population mean μ using a sample mean $\bar{x}$, why is it likely that $\bar{x} \neq \mu$? Construct a cause-and-effect diagram for the effect $\bar{x} \neq \mu$.

11.48   Construct a cause-and-effect diagram to help explain why customer waiting time at the drive-in window of a fast-food restaurant is a variable.

11.49   Processes that are in control are predictable; out-of-control processes are not. Explain.

11.50   Compare and contrast special and common causes of variation.

11.51   Explain the role of the control limits of a control chart.

11.52 Explain the difference between control limits and specification limits.

11.53 A process is under control and follows a normal distribution with mean 100 and standard deviation 10. In constructing a standard $\bar{x}$-chart for this process, the control limits are set three standard deviations from the mean—i.e., $100 + 3(10/\sqrt{n})$. The probability of observing an $\bar{x}$ outside the control limits is $.00135 + .00135 = .0027$. Suppose it is desired to construct a control chart that signals the presence of a potential special cause of variation for less extreme values of $\bar{x}$. How many standard deviations from the mean should the control limits be set such that the probability of the chart falsely indicating the presence of a special cause of variation is .10 rather than .0027?

11.54 Consider the following time series data.

Order of Production	Weight (grams)	Order of Production	Weight (grams)
1	6.0	9	6.5
2	5.0	10	9.0
3	7.0	11	3.0
4	5.5	12	11.0
5	7.0	13	3.0
6	6.0	14	12.0
7	8.0	15	2.0
8	5.0		

a. Construct a time series plot. Be sure to connect the points and add a centerline.
b. Which type of variation pattern in Figure 11.9 (pages 619–620) best describes the pattern revealed by your plot?

11.55 The accompanying length measurements were made on 20 consecutively produced pencils.

Order of Production	Length (inches)	Order of Production	Length (inches)
1	7.47	11	7.57
2	7.48	12	7.56
3	7.51	13	7.55
4	7.49	14	7.58
5	7.50	15	7.56
6	7.51	16	7.59
7	7.48	17	7.57
8	7.49	18	7.55
9	7.48	19	7.56
10	7.50	20	7.58

a. Construct a time series plot. Be sure to connect the plotted points and add a centerline.
b. Which type of variation pattern in Figure 11.9 best describes the pattern shown in your plot?

11.56 Use the appropriate pattern-analysis rules (page 637) to determine whether the process being monitored by the control chart on page 676 is under the influence of special causes of variation.

11.57 A company that manufactures plastic molded parts believes it is producing an unusually large number of defects. To investigate this suspicion, each shift drew seven random samples of 200 parts, visually inspected each part to determine whether it was defective, and tallied the primary type of defect present (Hart, 1992). These data are presented in the table.

| | | | | | *Type of Defect* | | |
Sample	Shift	# of Defects	Crack	Burn	Dirt	Blister	Trim
1	1	4	1	1	1	0	1
2	1	6	2	1	0	2	1
3	1	11	1	2	3	3	2
4	1	12	2	2	2	3	3
5	1	5	0	1	0	2	2
6	1	10	1	3	2	2	2
7	1	8	0	3	1	1	3
8	2	16	2	0	8	2	4
9	2	17	3	2	8	2	2
10	2	20	0	3	11	3	3
11	2	28	3	2	17	2	4
12	2	20	0	0	16	4	0
13	2	20	1	1	18	0	0
14	2	17	2	2	13	0	0
15	3	13	3	2	5	1	2
16	3	10	0	3	4	2	1
17	3	11	2	2	3	2	2
18	3	7	0	3	2	2	0
19	3	6	1	2	0	1	2
20	3	8	1	1	2	3	1
21	3	9	1	2	2	2	2

a. From a statistical perspective, are the number of samples and the sample size of 200 adequate for constructing a p-chart for these data? Explain.

b. Construct a p-chart for this manufacturing process.

c. Should the control limits be used to monitor future process output? Explain.

d. Suggest a strategy for identifying the special causes of variation that may be present.

11.58 A hospital has used control charts continuously since 1978 to monitor the quality of its nursing care. A set of 363 scoring criteria, or standards, are applied at critical points in the patients' stay to determine whether the patients are receiving beneficial nursing care. Auditors regularly visit each hospital unit, sample two patients, and evaluate their care. The auditors review patients' records; interview the patients, the nurse, and the head nurse; and observe the nursing care given (Cheng, 1992). The data in the table were collected over a 3-month period for a newly opened unit of the hospital.

Sample	Scores	Sample	Scores	Sample	Scores
1	345,341	8	344,344	15	345,329
2	331,328	9	359,334	16	358,351
3	343,355	10	346,361	17	353,352
4	351,352	11	360,355	18	334,340
5	360,348	12	325,335	19	341,335
6	342,336	13	350,348	20	358,345
7	328,331	14	336,337		

a. Construct an R-chart for the nursing care process.

b. Construct an $\bar{x}$-chart for the nursing care process.

c. Should the control charts of parts **a** and **b** be used to monitor future process output? Explain.

d. The hospital would like all scores to exceed 335 (their specification limit). Over the 3-month periods, what proportion of the sampled patients received care that did not conform to the hospital's requirements?

11.59 AirExpress, an overnight mail service, is concerned about the operating efficiency of the package-sorting department at its Toledo, Ohio, terminal. The company would like to monitor the time it takes for packages to be put in outgoing delivery bins from the time they are received. The sorting department operates 6 hours per day, from 6 P.M. to midnight. The company randomly sampled four packages during each hour of operation during four consecutive days. The time for each package to move through the system, in minutes, is given.

Sample	Transit Time (min.)				Sample	Transit Time (min.)			
1	31.9	33.4	37.8	26.2	13	24.6	29.9	31.8	37.9
2	29.1	24.3	33.2	36.7	14	30.6	36.0	40.2	30.8
3	30.3	31.1	26.3	34.1	15	29.7	33.2	34.9	27.6
4	39.6	29.4	31.4	37.7	16	24.1	26.8	32.7	29.0
5	27.4	29.7	36.5	33.3	17	29.4	31.6	35.2	27.6
6	32.7	32.9	40.1	29.7	18	31.1	33.0	29.6	35.2
7	30.7	36.9	26.8	34.0	19	27.0	29.0	35.1	25.1
8	28.4	24.1	29.6	30.9	20	36.6	32.4	28.7	27.9
9	30.5	35.5	36.1	27.4	21	33.0	27.1	26.2	35.1
10	27.8	29.6	29.0	34.1	22	33.2	41.2	30.7	31.6
11	34.0	30.1	35.9	28.8	23	26.7	35.2	39.7	31.5
12	25.5	26.3	34.8	30.0	24	30.5	36.8	27.9	28.6

a. Construct an $\bar{x}$-chart from these data. In order for this chart to be meaningful, what assumption must be made about the variation of the process? Why?

b. What does the chart suggest about the stability of the package-sorting process? Explain.
c. Should the control limits be used to monitor future process output? Explain.

11.60 Officials at Mountain Airlines are interested in monitoring the length of time customers must wait in line to check in at their airport counter in Reno, Nevada. In order to develop a control chart, five customers were sampled each day for 20 days. The data, in minutes, are presented here.

Sample	Waiting Time (min.)					Sample	Waiting Time (min.)				
1	3.2	6.7	1.3	8.4	2.2	11	3.2	2.9	4.1	5.6	.8
2	5.0	4.1	7.9	8.1	.4	12	2.4	4.3	6.7	1.9	4.8
3	7.1	3.2	2.1	6.5	3.7	13	8.8	5.3	6.6	1.0	4.5
4	4.2	1.6	2.7	7.2	1.4	14	3.7	3.6	2.0	2.7	5.9
5	1.7	7.1	1.6	.9	1.8	15	1.0	1.9	6.5	3.3	4.7
6	4.7	5.5	1.6	3.9	4.0	16	7.0	4.0	4.9	4.4	4.7
7	6.2	2.0	1.2	.9	1.4	17	5.5	7.1	2.1	.9	2.8
8	1.4	2.7	3.8	4.6	3.8	18	1.8	5.6	2.2	1.7	2.1
9	1.1	4.3	9.1	3.1	2.7	19	2.6	3.7	4.8	1.4	5.8
10	5.3	4.1	9.8	2.9	2.7	20	3.6	.8	5.1	4.7	6.3

a. Construct an R-chart from these data.
b. What does the R-chart suggest about the stability of the process? Explain.
c. Explain why the R-chart should be interpreted prior to the $\bar{x}$-chart.
d. Construct an $\bar{x}$-chart from these data.
e. What does the $\bar{x}$-chart suggest about the stability of the process? Explain.
f. Should the control limits for the R-chart and $\bar{x}$-chart be used to monitor future process output? Explain.

11.61 A company called CRW runs credit checks for a large number of banks and insurance companies. Credit history information is typed into computer files by trained administrative assistants. The company is interested in monitoring the proportion of credit histories that contain one or more data-entry errors. Based on her experience with the data-entry operation, the director of the data-processing unit believes that the proportion of histories with data-entry errors is about 6%. CRW audited 150 randomly selected credit histories each day for 20 days. The sample data are presented here.

Sample	Sample Size	Histories with Errors	Sample	Sample Size	Histories with Errors
1	150	9	11	150	7
2	150	11	12	150	6
3	150	12	13	150	12
4	150	8	14	150	10
5	150	10	15	150	11
6	150	6	16	150	7
7	150	13	17	150	6
8	150	9	18	150	12
9	150	11	19	150	14
10	150	5	20	150	10

a. Use the sample size formula on page 659 to show that a sample size of 150 is large enough to prevent the lower control limit of the p-chart they plan to construct from being negative.

b. Construct a *p*-chart for the data-entry process.

c. What does the chart indicate about the presence of special causes of variation? Explain.

d. Provide an example of a special cause of variation that could potentially affect this process. Do the same for a common cause of variation.

e. Should the control limits be used to monitor future credit histories produced by the data-entry operation? Explain.

On Your Own

Choose a process that is of interest to you and that you know something about. It can be an organizational process, such as those used in the examples of this chapter, or a personal process. Examples of personal processes include cooking, changing diapers, studying for exams, making a cup of coffee, balancing a checkbook, and so on.

a. Describe the objective or purpose of the process.

b. Identify the suppliers and customers of the process and the input(s) and output(s) of the process.

c. Identify the owner of the process. That is, identify the person closest to the process with the power to change the design of the process.

d. Identify two listening points within the process. That is, identify opportunities for monitoring the performance of various aspects of the process. Define the variables to be monitored.

e. Construct a cause-and-effect diagram that identifies the potential causes of variation in one of the variables you defined in part **d**.

f. Indicate which of the three control charts discussed in this chapter, if any, are appropriate for monitoring the variables you identified above. Justify your answer.

References

Ackoff, R. "The Second Industrial Revolution," speech transcript, undated.

Alwan, L. C., and Roberts, H. V. "Time-series modeling for statistical process control." *Journal of Business and Economic Statistics*, 1988, Vol. 6, pp. 87–95.

Banks, J. *Principles of Quality Control*. New York: Wiley, 1989.

Brassard, M. *The Memory Jogger Plus+*. Methuen, Mass.: GOAL/QPC, 1989.

Checkland, P. *Systems Thinking, Systems Practice*. New York, Wiley, 1981.

Cheng, T. C. E. "A case study of hospital quality assurance." *International Journal of Quality and Reliability Management*, 1992, Vol. 9, No. 4, p. 21.

Deming, W. E. *Out of the Crisis*. Cambridge, Mass.: M.I.T. Center for Advanced Engineering Study, 1986.

DeVor, R. E., Chang, T., and Southerland, J. W. *Statistical Quality Design and Control*. New York: Macmillan, 1992.

Duncan, A. J. *Quality Control and Industrial Statistics*. Homewood, Ill.: Irwin, 1986.

Feigenbaum, A. V. *Total Quality Control*, 3rd ed. New York: McGraw-Hill, 1983.

Fuller, T. "Eliminating complexity from work: Improving productivity by enhancing quality." *National Productivity Review*, 1985.

Garvin, D. A. *Managing Quality*. New York: Free Press/ Macmillan, 1988.

Gitlow, H., Gitlow, S., Oppenheim, A., and Oppenheim, R. *Tools and Methods for the Improvement of Quality*. Homewood, Ill.: Irwin, 1989.

Grant, E. L., and Leavenworth, R. S. *Statistical Quality Control*, 6th ed. New York: McGraw-Hill, 1988.

Hart, Marilyn K. "Quality tools for improvement." *Production and Inventory Management Journal*, First Quarter 1992, Vol. 33, No. 1, p. 59.

Ishikawa, K. *Guide to Quality Control*, 2nd ed. White Plains, N.Y.: Kraus International Publications, 1986.

Joiner, B. L., and Goudard, M. A. "Variation, management, and W. Edwards Deming." *Quality Process*, Dec. 1990, pp. 29–37.

Juran, J. M. *Planning for Quality*. New York: Free Press/Macmillan, 1988.

Juran, J. M., and Gryna, F. M., Jr. *Quality Planning and Analysis*, 2nd ed. New York: McGraw-Hill, 1980.

Kane, V. E. *Defect Prevention*. New York: Marcel Dekker, 1989.

Latzko, W. J. *Quality and Productivity for Bankers and Financial Managers*, New York: Marcel Dekker, 1986.

Melan, E. H. "Process management in service and administrative operations." *Quality Progress*, June 1985, pp. 52–59.

Moen, R. D., Nolan, T. W., and Provost, L. P. *Improving Quality Through Planned Experimentation*. New York: McGraw-Hill, 1991.

Montgomery, D. C. *Introduction to Statistical Quality Control*, 2nd ed. New York: Wiley, 1991.

Nelson, L. S. "The Shewhart control chart—Tests for special causes." *Journal of Quality Technology*, Oct. 1984, Vol. 16, No. 4, pp. 237–239.

Optner, S. L. *Systems Analysis for Business and Industrial Problem Solving*. Englewood Cliffs, N.J.: Prentice-Hall, 1965.

Roberts, H. V. *Data Analysis for Managers*, 2nd ed. Redwood City, Calif.: Scientific Press, 1991.

Rosander, A. C. *Applications of Quality Control in the Service Industries*. New York: Marcel Dekker, 1985.

Rummler, G. A., and Brache, A. P. *Improving Performance: How to Manage the White Space on the Organization Chart*. San Francisco: Jossey-Bass, 1991.

Ryan, T. P. *Statistical Methods for Quality Improvement*. New York: Wiley, 1989.

Statistical Quality Control Handbook. Indianapolis, Ind.: AT&T Technologies, Select Code 700-444 (Inquiries: 800-432-6600); originally published by Western Electric Company, 1956.

The Ernst and Young Quality Improvement Consulting Group. *Total Quality: An Executive's Guide for the 1990s*. Homewood, Ill.: Dow-Jones Irwin, 1990.

Wadsworth, H. M., Stephens, K. S., and Godfrey, A. B. *Modern Methods for Quality Control and Improvement*. New York: Wiley, 1986.

Walton, M. *The Deming Management Method*. New York: Dodd, Mead, & Company, 1986.

Wheeler, D. J., and Chambers, D. S. *Understanding Statistical Process Control*. Knoxville, Tenn.: Statistical Process Controls, Inc., 1986.

Wood, L. "MIPS, BIPS, and super-chips." *Compute*, 1992, Vol. 14, No. 9, pp. 58–66.

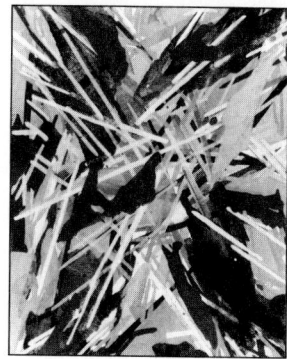

APPENDIX A

Basic Counting Rules

Simple events associated with many experiments have identical characteristics. If you can develop a counting rule to count the number of simple events, it can be used to aid in the solution of many probability problems. For example, many experiments involve sampling n elements from a population of N. Then, as explained in Section 3.1, we can use the formula

$$\binom{N}{n} = \frac{N!}{n!(N - n)!}$$

to find the number of different samples of n elements that could be selected from the total of N elements. This gives the number of simple events for the experiment.

Here, we give you a few useful counting rules. You should learn the characteristics of the situation to which each rule applies. Then, when working a probability problem, carefully examine the experiment to see whether you can use one of the rules.

Learning how to decide whether a particular counting rule applies to an experiment takes patience and practice. If you want to develop this skill, try to use the rules to solve some of the exercises in Chapter 3. You will also find large numbers of exercises in the texts listed in the references at the end of Chapter 3. Proofs of the rules below can be found in the text by W. Feller listed in the references to Chapter 3.

1. **Multiplicative rule:** You have k sets of different elements, n_1 in the first set, n_2 in the second set, . . . , and n_k in the kth set. Suppose you want to form a sample of k elements *by taking one element from each of the k sets.* The number of different samples that can be formed is the product

$$n_1 \cdot n_2 \cdot n_3 \cdot \ \cdot \ \cdot \ \cdot \ n_k$$

EXAMPLE A.1

If a product can be shipped by four different airlines and each airline can ship via three different routes, how many ways can you ship the product?

Solution

A method of shipment corresponds to a pairing of one airline and one route. There-fore, $k = 2$, the number of airlines is $n_1 = 4$, the number of routes is $n_2 = 3$, and the number of ways to ship the product is $n_1 \cdot n_2 = (4)(3) = 12$.

How the multiplicative rule works can be seen by using a **decision tree**. The airline choice is shown by three branching lines in Figure A.1.

FIGURE A.1 ▶

Decision tree for Example A.1

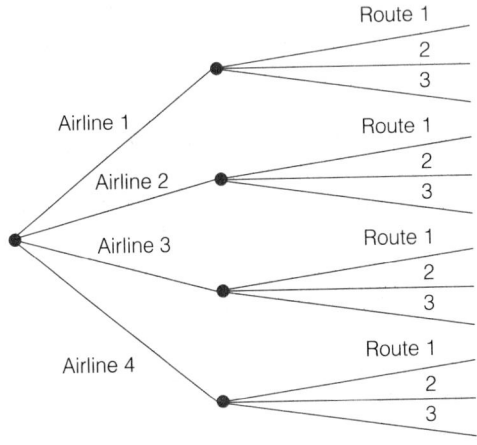

EXAMPLE A.2

You have twenty candidates for three different executive positions, E_1, E_2, and E_3. How many different ways could you fill the positions?

Solution

For this example, there are $k = 3$ sets of elements:

Set 1:   The candidates available to fill position E_1

Set 2:   The candidates remaining (after filling E_1) that are available to fill E_2

Set 3:   The candidates remaining (after filling E_1 and E_2) that are available to fill E_3

The numbers of elements in the sets are $n_1 = 20$, $n_2 = 19$, $n_3 = 18$. Thus, the number of different ways to fill the three positions is $n_1 \cdot n_2 \cdot n_3 = (20)(19)(18) = 6,840$.

2. **Partitions rule:** You have a *single set* of N distinctly different elements, and you want to partition them into k sets, the first set containing n_1 elements, the second containing n_2 elements, . . . , and kth containing n_k elements. The number of different partitions is

$$\frac{N!}{n_1! n_2! \cdot \cdot \cdot \cdot \cdot n_k!} \quad \text{where} \quad n_1 + n_2 + n_3 + \cdot \cdot \cdot + n_k = N$$

EXAMPLE A.3

You have twelve construction workers and you want to assign three to job 1, four to job 2, and five to job 3. How many different ways could you make this assignment?

Solution

For this example, $k = 3$ (corresponding to the $k = 3$ job sites), $N = 12$, and $n_1 = 3$, $n_2 = 4$, $n_3 = 5$. Then, the number of different ways to assign the workers to the job sites is

$$\frac{N!}{n_1!n_2!n_3!} = \frac{12!}{3!4!5!} = \frac{12 \cdot 11 \cdot 10 \cdot \cdots \cdot 3 \cdot 2 \cdot 1}{(3 \cdot 2 \cdot 1)(4 \cdot 3 \cdot 2 \cdot 1)(5 \cdot 4 \cdot 3 \cdot 2 \cdot 1)} = 27{,}720$$

3. **Combinations rule:**   The combinations rule given in Chapter 3 is a special case ($k = 2$) of the partitions rule. That is, sampling is equivalent to partitioning a set of N elements into $k = 2$ groups: elements that appear in the sample and those that do not. Let $n_1 = n$, the number of elements in the sample, and $n_2 = N - n$, the number of elements remaining. Then the number of different samples of n elements that can be selected from N is

$$\frac{N!}{n_1!n_2!} = \frac{N!}{n!(N - n)!} = \binom{N}{n}$$

This formula was given in Section 3.1.

EXAMPLE A.4

How many samples of four fire fighters can be selected from a group of ten?

Solution

We have $N = 10$ and $n = 4$; then,

$$\binom{N}{n} = \binom{10}{4} = \frac{10!}{4!6!} = \frac{10 \cdot 9 \cdot 8 \cdot \cdots \cdot 3 \cdot 2 \cdot 1}{(4 \cdot 3 \cdot 2 \cdot 1)(6 \cdot 5 \cdot \cdots \cdot 2 \cdot 1)} = 210$$

APPENDIX B

Tables

Contents

TABLE I Random Numbers

Row	1	2	3	4	5	6	7	8	9	10	11	12	13	14
1	10480	15011	01536	02011	81647	91646	69179	14194	62590	36207	20969	99570	91291	90700
2	22368	46573	25595	85393	30995	89198	27982	53402	93965	34095	52666	19174	39615	99505
3	24130	48360	22527	97265	76393	64809	15179	24830	49340	32081	30680	19655	63348	58629
4	42167	93093	06243	61680	07856	16376	39440	53537	71341	57004	00849	74917	97758	16379
5	37570	39975	81837	16656	06121	91782	60468	81305	49684	60672	14110	06927	01263	54613
6	77921	06907	11008	42751	27756	53498	18602	70659	90655	15053	21916	81825	44394	42880
7	99562	72905	56420	69994	98872	31016	71194	18738	44013	48840	63213	21069	10634	12952
8	96301	91977	05463	07972	18876	20922	94595	56869	69014	60045	18425	84903	42508	32307
9	89579	14342	63661	10281	17453	18103	57740	84378	25331	12566	58678	44947	05585	56941
10	85475	36857	53342	53988	53060	59533	38867	62300	08158	17983	16439	11458	18593	64952
11	28918	69578	88231	33276	70997	79936	56865	05859	90106	31595	01547	85590	91610	78188
12	63553	40961	48235	03427	49626	69445	18663	72695	52180	20847	12234	90511	33703	90322
13	09429	93969	52636	92737	88974	33488	36320	17617	30015	08272	84115	27156	30613	74952
14	10365	61129	87529	85689	48237	52267	67689	93394	01511	26358	85104	20285	29975	89868
15	07119	97336	71048	08178	77233	13916	47564	81056	97735	85977	29372	74461	28551	90707
16	51085	12765	51821	51259	77452	16308	60756	92144	49442	53900	70960	63990	75601	40719
17	02368	21382	52404	60268	89368	19885	55322	44819	01188	65255	64835	44919	05944	55157
18	01011	54092	33362	94904	31273	04146	18594	29852	71585	85030	51132	01915	92747	64951
19	52162	53916	46369	58586	23216	14513	83149	98736	23495	64350	94738	17752	35156	35749
20	07056	97628	33787	09998	42698	06691	76988	13602	51851	46104	88916	19509	25625	58104
21	48663	91245	85828	14346	09172	30168	90229	04734	59193	22178	30421	61666	99904	32812
22	54164	58492	22421	74103	47070	25306	76468	26384	58151	06646	21524	15227	96909	44592
23	32639	32363	05597	24200	13363	38005	94342	28728	35806	06912	17012	64161	18296	22851
24	29334	27001	87637	87308	58731	00256	45834	15398	46557	41135	10367	07684	36188	18510
25	02488	33062	28834	07351	19731	92420	60952	61280	50001	67658	32586	86679	50720	94953

(continued)

TABLE I Continued

Row \ Column	1	2	3	4	5	6	7	8	9	10	11	12	13	14
26	81525	72295	04839	96423	24878	82651	66566	14778	76797	14780	13300	87074	79666	95725
27	29676	20591	68086	26432	46901	20849	89768	81536	86645	12659	92259	57102	80428	25280
28	00742	57392	39064	66432	84673	40027	32832	61362	98947	96067	64760	64584	96096	98253
29	05366	04213	25669	26422	44407	44048	37937	63904	45766	66134	75470	66520	34693	90449
30	91921	26418	64117	94305	26766	25940	39972	22209	71500	64568	91402	42416	07844	69618
31	00582	04711	87917	77341	42206	35126	74087	99547	81817	42607	43808	76655	62028	76630
32	00725	69884	62797	56170	86324	88072	76222	36086	84637	93161	76038	65855	77919	88006
33	69011	65795	95876	55293	18988	27354	26575	08625	40801	59920	29841	80150	12777	48501
34	25976	57948	29888	88604	67917	48708	18912	82271	65424	69774	33611	54262	85963	03547
35	09763	83473	73577	12908	30883	18317	28290	35797	05998	41688	34952	37888	38917	88050
36	91576	42595	27958	30134	04024	86385	29880	99730	55536	84855	29080	09250	79656	73211
37	17955	56349	90999	49127	20044	59931	06115	20542	18059	02008	73708	83517	36103	42791
38	46503	18584	18845	49618	02304	51038	20655	58727	28168	15475	56942	53389	20562	87338
39	92157	89634	94824	78171	84610	82834	09922	25417	44137	48413	25555	21246	35509	20468
40	14577	62765	35605	81263	39667	47358	56873	56307	61607	49518	89656	20103	77490	18062
41	98427	07523	33362	64270	01638	92477	66969	98420	04880	45585	46565	04102	46880	45709
42	34914	63976	88720	82765	34476	17032	87589	40836	32427	70002	70663	88863	77775	69348
43	70060	28277	39475	46473	23219	53416	94970	25832	69975	94884	19661	72828	00102	66794
44	53976	54914	06990	67245	68350	82948	11398	42878	80287	88267	47363	46634	06541	97809
45	76072	29515	40980	07391	58745	25774	22987	80059	39911	96189	41151	14222	60697	59583
46	90725	52210	83974	29992	65831	38857	50490	83765	55657	14361	31720	57375	56228	41546
47	64364	67412	33339	31926	14883	24413	59744	92351	97473	89286	35931	04110	23726	51900
48	08962	00358	31662	25388	61642	34072	81249	35648	56891	69352	48373	45578	78547	81788
49	95012	68379	93526	70765	10592	04542	76463	54328	02349	17247	28865	14777	62730	92277
50	15664	10493	20492	38391	91132	21999	59516	81652	27195	48223	46751	22923	32261	85653
51	16408	81899	04153	53381	79401	21438	83035	92350	36693	31238	59649	91754	72772	02338
52	18629	81953	05520	91962	04739	13092	97662	24822	94730	06496	35090	04822	86774	98289
53	73115	35101	47498	87637	99016	71060	88824	71013	18735	20286	23153	72924	35165	43040
54	57491	16703	23167	49323	45021	33132	12544	41035	80780	45393	44812	12512	98931	91202
55	30405	83946	23792	14422	15059	45799	22716	19792	09983	74353	68668	30429	70735	25499
56	16631	35006	85900	98275	32388	52390	16815	69290	82732	38480	73817	32523	41961	44437
57	96773	20206	42559	78985	05300	22164	24369	54224	35083	19687	11052	91491	60383	19746
58	38935	64202	14349	82674	66523	44133	00697	35552	35970	19124	63318	29686	03387	59846
59	31624	76384	17403	53363	44167	64486	64758	75366	76554	31601	12614	33072	60332	92325
60	78919	19474	23632	27889	47914	02584	37680	20801	72152	39339	34806	08930	85001	87820
61	03931	33309	57047	74211	63445	17361	62825	39908	05607	91284	68833	25570	38818	46920
62	74426	33278	43972	10110	89917	15665	52872	73823	73144	88662	88970	74492	51805	99378

Row \ Column	1	2	3	4	5	6	7	8	9	10	11	12	13	14
63	09066	00903	20795	95452	92648	45454	09552	88815	16553	51125	79375	97596	16296	66092
64	42238	12426	87025	14267	20979	04508	64535	31355	86064	29472	47689	05974	52468	16834
65	16153	08002	26504	41744	81959	65642	74240	56302	00033	67107	77510	70625	28725	34191
66	21457	40742	29820	96783	29400	21840	15035	34537	33310	06116	95240	15957	16572	06004
67	21581	57802	02050	89728	17937	37621	47075	42080	97403	48626	68995	43805	33386	21597
68	55612	78095	83197	33732	05810	24813	86902	60397	16489	03264	88525	42786	05269	92532
69	44657	66999	99324	51281	84463	60563	79312	93454	68876	25471	93911	25650	12682	73572
70	91340	84979	46949	81973	37949	61023	43997	15263	80644	43942	89203	71795	99533	50501
71	91227	21199	31935	27022	84067	05462	35216	14486	29891	68607	41867	14951	91696	85065
72	50001	38140	66321	19924	72163	09538	12151	06878	91903	18749	34405	56087	82790	70925
73	65390	05224	72958	28609	81406	39147	25549	48542	42627	45233	57202	94617	23772	07896
74	27504	96131	83944	41575	10573	08619	64482	73923	36152	05184	94142	25299	84387	34925
75	37169	94851	39117	89632	00959	16487	65536	49071	39782	17095	02330	74301	00275	48280
76	11508	70225	51111	38351	19444	66499	71945	05422	13442	78675	84081	66938	93654	59894
77	37449	30362	06694	54690	04052	53115	62757	95348	78662	11163	81651	50245	34971	52924
78	46515	70331	85922	38329	57015	15765	97161	17869	45349	61796	66345	81073	49106	79860
79	30986	81223	42416	58353	21532	30502	32305	86482	05174	07901	54339	58861	74818	46942
80	63798	64995	46583	09785	44160	78128	83991	42865	92520	83531	80377	35909	81250	54238
81	82486	84846	99254	67632	43218	50076	21361	64816	51202	88124	41870	52689	51275	83556
82	21885	32906	92431	09060	64297	51674	64126	62570	26123	05155	59194	52799	28225	85762
83	60336	98782	07408	53458	13564	59089	26445	29789	85205	41001	12535	12133	14645	23541
84	43937	46891	24010	25560	86355	33941	25786	54990	71899	15475	95434	98227	21824	19585
85	97656	63175	89303	16275	07100	92063	21942	18611	47348	20203	18534	03862	78095	50136
86	03299	01221	05418	38982	55758	92237	26759	86367	21216	98442	08303	56613	91511	75928
87	79626	06486	03574	17668	07785	76020	79924	25651	83325	88428	85076	72811	22717	50585
88	85636	68335	47539	03129	65651	11977	02510	26113	99447	68645	34327	15152	55230	93448
89	18039	14367	61337	06177	12143	46609	32989	74014	64708	00533	35598	58408	13261	47908
90	08362	15656	60627	36478	65648	16764	53412	09013	07832	41574	17639	82163	60859	75567
91	79556	29068	04142	16268	15387	12856	66227	38358	22478	73373	88732	09443	82558	05250
92	92608	82674	27072	32534	17075	27698	98204	63863	11951	34648	88022	56148	34925	57031
93	23982	25835	40055	67006	12293	02753	14827	23235	35071	99704	37543	11601	35503	85171
94	09915	96306	05908	97901	28395	14186	00821	80703	70426	75647	76310	88717	37890	40129
95	59037	33300	26695	62247	69927	76123	50842	43834	86654	70959	79725	93872	28117	19233
96	42488	78077	69882	61657	34136	79180	97526	43092	04098	73571	80799	76536	71255	64239
97	46764	86273	63003	93017	31204	36692	40202	35275	57306	55543	53203	18098	47625	88684
98	03237	45430	55417	63282	90816	17349	88298	90183	36600	78406	06216	95787	42579	90730
99	86591	81482	52667	61582	14972	90053	89534	76036	49199	43716	97548	04379	46370	28672
100	38534	01715	94964	87288	65680	43772	39560	12918	86537	62738	19636	51132	25739	56947

Source: Abridged from W. H. Beyer (ed.). *CRC Standard Mathematical Tables*, 24th edition. (Cleveland: The Chemical Rubber Company), 1976. Reproduced by permission of the publisher.

TABLE II   Binomial Probabilities

Tabulated values are $\sum_{x=0}^{k} p(x)$. *(Computations are rounded at the third decimal place.)*

a. $n = 5$

k	.01	.05	.10	.20	.30	.40	.50	.60	.70	.80	.90	.95	.99
0	.951	.774	.590	.328	.168	.078	.031	.010	.002	.000	.000	.000	.000
1	.999	.977	.919	.737	.528	.337	.188	.087	.031	.007	.000	.000	.000
2	1.000	.999	.991	.942	.837	.683	.500	.317	.163	.058	.009	.001	.000
3	1.000	1.000	1.000	.993	.969	.913	.812	.663	.472	.263	.081	.023	.001
4	1.000	1.000	1.000	1.000	.998	.990	.969	.922	.832	.672	.410	.226	.049

b. $n = 6$

k	.01	.05	.10	.20	.30	.40	.50	.60	.70	.80	.90	.95	.99
0	.941	.735	.531	.262	.118	.047	.016	.004	.001	.000	.000	.000	.000
1	.999	.967	.886	.655	.420	.233	.109	.041	.011	.002	.000	.000	.000
2	1.000	.998	.984	.901	.744	.544	.344	.179	.070	.017	.001	.000	.000
3	1.000	1.000	.999	.983	.930	.821	.656	.456	.256	.099	.016	.002	.000
4	1.000	1.000	1.000	.998	.989	.959	.891	.767	.580	.345	.114	.033	.001
5	1.000	1.000	1.000	1.000	.999	.996	.984	.953	.882	.738	.469	.265	.059

c. $n = 7$

k	.01	.05	.10	.20	.30	.40	.50	.60	.70	.80	.90	.95	.99
0	.932	.698	.478	.210	.082	.028	.008	.002	.000	.000	.000	.000	.000
1	.998	.956	.850	.577	.329	.159	.063	.019	.004	.000	.000	.000	.000
2	1.000	.996	.974	.852	.647	.420	.227	.096	.029	.005	.000	.000	.000
3	1.000	1.000	.997	.967	.874	.710	.500	.290	.126	.033	.003	.000	.000
4	1.000	1.000	1.000	.995	.971	.904	.773	.580	.353	.148	.026	.004	.000
5	1.000	1.000	1.000	1.000	.996	.981	.937	.841	.671	.423	.150	.044	.002
6	1.000	1.000	1.000	1.000	1.000	.998	.992	.972	.918	.790	.522	.302	.068

TABLE II   Continued

d. $n = 8$

k \ p	.01	.05	.10	.20	.30	.40	.50	.60	.70	.80	.90	.95	.99
0	.923	.663	.430	.168	.058	.017	.004	.001	.000	.000	.000	.000	.000
1	.997	.943	.813	.503	.255	.106	.035	.009	.001	.000	.000	.000	.000
2	1.000	.994	.962	.797	.552	.315	.145	.050	.011	.001	.000	.000	.000
3	1.000	1.000	.995	.944	.806	.594	.363	.174	.058	.010	.000	.000	.000
4	1.000	1.000	1.000	.990	.942	.826	.637	.406	.194	.056	.005	.000	.000
5	1.000	1.000	1.000	.999	.989	.950	.855	.685	.448	.203	.038	.006	.000
6	1.000	1.000	1.000	1.000	.999	.991	.965	.894	.745	.497	.187	.057	.003
7	1.000	1.000	1.000	1.000	1.000	.999	.996	.983	.942	.832	.570	.337	.077

e. $n = 9$

k \ p	.01	.05	.10	.20	.30	.40	.50	.60	.70	.80	.90	.95	.99
0	.914	.630	.387	.134	.040	.010	.002	.000	.000	.000	.000	.000	.000
1	.997	.929	.775	.436	.196	.071	.020	.004	.000	.000	.000	.000	.000
2	1.000	.992	.947	.738	.463	.232	.090	.025	.004	.000	.000	.000	.000
3	1.000	.999	.992	.914	.730	.483	.254	.099	.025	.003	.000	.000	.000
4	1.000	1.000	.999	.980	.901	.733	.500	.267	.099	.020	.001	.000	.000
5	1.000	1.000	1.000	.997	.975	.901	.746	.517	.270	.086	.008	.001	.000
6	1.000	1.000	1.000	1.000	.996	.975	.910	.768	.537	.262	.053	.008	.000
7	1.000	1.000	1.000	1.000	1.000	.996	.980	.929	.804	.564	.225	.071	.003
8	1.000	1.000	1.000	1.000	1.000	1.000	.998	.990	.960	.866	.613	.370	.086

f. $n = 10$

k \ p	.01	.05	.10	.20	.30	.40	.50	.60	.70	.80	.90	.95	.99
0	.904	.599	.349	.107	.028	.006	.001	.000	.000	.000	.000	.000	.000
1	.996	.914	.736	.376	.149	.046	.011	.002	.000	.000	.000	.000	.000
2	1.000	.988	.930	.678	.383	.167	.055	.012	.002	.000	.000	.000	.000
3	1.000	.999	.987	.879	.650	.382	.172	.055	.011	.001	.000	.000	.000
4	1.000	1.000	.998	.967	.850	.633	.377	.166	.047	.006	.000	.000	.000
5	1.000	1.000	1.000	.994	.953	.834	.623	.367	.150	.033	.002	.000	.000
6	1.000	1.000	1.000	.999	.989	.945	.828	.618	.350	.121	.013	.001	.000
7	1.000	1.000	1.000	1.000	.998	.988	.945	.833	.617	.322	.070	.012	.000
8	1.000	1.000	1.000	1.000	1.000	.998	.989	.954	.851	.624	.264	.086	.004
9	1.000	1.000	1.000	1.000	1.000	1.000	.999	.994	.972	.893	.651	.401	.096

(continued)

TABLE II   Continued

g. $n = 15$

k	.01	.05	.10	.20	.30	.40	.50	.60	.70	.80	.90	.95	.99
0	.860	.463	.206	.035	.005	.000	.000	.000	.000	.000	.000	.000	.000
1	.990	.829	.549	.167	.035	.005	.000	.000	.000	.000	.000	.000	.000
2	1.000	.964	.816	.398	.127	.027	.004	.000	.000	.000	.000	.000	.000
3	1.000	.995	.944	.648	.297	.091	.018	.002	.000	.000	.000	.000	.000
4	1.000	.999	.987	.838	.515	.217	.059	.009	.001	.000	.000	.000	.000
5	1.000	1.000	.998	.939	.722	.403	.151	.034	.004	.000	.000	.000	.000
6	1.000	1.000	1.000	.982	.869	.610	.304	.095	.015	.001	.000	.000	.000
7	1.000	1.000	1.000	.996	.950	.787	.500	.213	.050	.004	.000	.000	.000
8	1.000	1.000	1.000	.999	.985	.905	.696	.390	.131	.018	.000	.000	.000
9	1.000	1.000	1.000	1.000	.996	.966	.849	.597	.278	.061	.002	.000	.000
10	1.000	1.000	1.000	1.000	.999	.991	.941	.783	.485	.164	.013	.001	.000
11	1.000	1.000	1.000	1.000	1.000	.998	.982	.909	.703	.352	.056	.005	.000
12	1.000	1.000	1.000	1.000	1.000	1.000	.996	.973	.873	.602	.184	.036	.000
13	1.000	1.000	1.000	1.000	1.000	1.000	1.000	.995	.965	.833	.451	.171	.010
14	1.000	1.000	1.000	1.000	1.000	1.000	1.000	1.000	.995	.965	.794	.537	.140

h. $n = 20$

k	.01	.05	.10	.20	.30	.40	.50	.60	.70	.80	.90	.95	.99
0	.818	.358	.122	.012	.001	.000	.000	.000	.000	.000	.000	.000	.000
1	.983	.736	.392	.069	.008	.001	.000	.000	.000	.000	.000	.000	.000
2	.999	.925	.677	.206	.035	.004	.000	.000	.000	.000	.000	.000	.000
3	1.000	.984	.867	.411	.107	.016	.001	.000	.000	.000	.000	.000	.000
4	1.000	.997	.957	.630	.238	.051	.006	.000	.000	.000	.000	.000	.000
5	1.000	1.000	.989	.804	.416	.126	.021	.002	.000	.000	.000	.000	.000
6	1.000	1.000	.998	.913	.608	.250	.058	.006	.000	.000	.000	.000	.000
7	1.000	1.000	1.000	.968	.772	.416	.132	.021	.001	.000	.000	.000	.000
8	1.000	1.000	1.000	.990	.887	.596	.252	.057	.005	.000	.000	.000	.000
9	1.000	1.000	1.000	.997	.952	.755	.412	.128	.017	.001	.000	.000	.000
10	1.000	1.000	1.000	.999	.983	.872	.588	.245	.048	.003	.000	.000	.000
11	1.000	1.000	1.000	1.000	.995	.943	.748	.404	.113	.010	.000	.000	.000
12	1.000	1.000	1.000	1.000	.999	.979	.868	.584	.228	.032	.000	.000	.000
13	1.000	1.000	1.000	1.000	1.000	.994	.942	.750	.392	.087	.002	.000	.000
14	1.000	1.000	1.000	1.000	1.000	.998	.979	.874	.584	.196	.011	.000	.000
15	1.000	1.000	1.000	1.000	1.000	1.000	.994	.949	.762	.370	.043	.003	.000
16	1.000	1.000	1.000	1.000	1.000	1.000	.999	.984	.893	.589	.133	.016	.000
17	1.000	1.000	1.000	1.000	1.000	1.000	1.000	.996	.965	.794	.323	.075	.001
18	1.000	1.000	1.000	1.000	1.000	1.000	1.000	.999	.992	.931	.608	.264	.017
19	1.000	1.000	1.000	1.000	1.000	1.000	1.000	1.000	.999	.988	.878	.642	.182

TABLE II   Continued

i. $n = 25$

k	.01	.05	.10	.20	.30	.40	.50	.60	.70	.80	.90	.95	.99
0	.778	.277	.072	.004	.000	.000	.000	.000	.000	.000	.000	.000	.000
1	.974	.642	.271	.027	.002	.000	.000	.000	.000	.000	.000	.000	.000
2	.998	.873	.537	.098	.009	.000	.000	.000	.000	.000	.000	.000	.000
3	1.000	.966	.764	.234	.033	.002	.000	.000	.000	.000	.000	.000	.000
4	1.000	.993	.902	.421	.090	.009	.000	.000	.000	.000	.000	.000	.000
5	1.000	.999	.967	.617	.193	.029	.002	.000	.000	.000	.000	.000	.000
6	1.000	1.000	.991	.780	.341	.074	.007	.000	.000	.000	.000	.000	.000
7	1.000	1.000	.998	.891	.512	.154	.022	.001	.000	.000	.000	.000	.000
8	1.000	1.000	1.000	.953	.677	.274	.054	.004	.000	.000	.000	.000	.000
9	1.000	1.000	1.000	.983	.811	.425	.115	.013	.000	.000	.000	.000	.000
10	1.000	1.000	1.000	.994	.902	.586	.212	.034	.002	.000	.000	.000	.000
11	1.000	1.000	1.000	.998	.956	.732	.345	.078	.006	.000	.000	.000	.000
12	1.000	1.000	1.000	1.000	.983	.846	.500	.154	.017	.000	.000	.000	.000
13	1.000	1.000	1.000	1.000	.994	.922	.655	.268	.044	.002	.000	.000	.000
14	1.000	1.000	1.000	1.000	.998	.966	.788	.414	.098	.006	.000	.000	.000
15	1.000	1.000	1.000	1.000	1.000	.987	.885	.575	.189	.017	.000	.000	.000
16	1.000	1.000	1.000	1.000	1.000	.996	.946	.726	.323	.047	.000	.000	.000
17	1.000	1.000	1.000	1.000	1.000	.999	.978	.846	.488	.109	.002	.000	.000
18	1.000	1.000	1.000	1.000	1.000	1.000	.993	.926	.659	.220	.009	.000	.000
19	1.000	1.000	1.000	1.000	1.000	1.000	.998	.971	.807	.383	.033	.001	.000
20	1.000	1.000	1.000	1.000	1.000	1.000	1.000	.991	.910	.579	.098	.007	.000
21	1.000	1.000	1.000	1.000	1.000	1.000	1.000	.998	.967	.766	.236	.034	.000
22	1.000	1.000	1.000	1.000	1.000	1.000	1.000	1.000	.991	.902	.463	.127	.002
23	1.000	1.000	1.000	1.000	1.000	1.000	1.000	1.000	.998	.973	.729	.358	.026
24	1.000	1.000	1.000	1.000	1.000	1.000	1.000	1.000	1.000	.996	.928	.723	.222

TABLE III   Poisson Probabilities

Tabulated values are $\sum_{x=0}^{k} p(x)$. *(Computations are rounded at the third decimal place.)*

λ \ x	0	1	2	3	4	5	6	7	8	9
.02	.980	1.000								
.04	.961	.999	1.000							
.06	.942	.998	1.000							
.08	.923	.997	1.000							
.10	.905	.995	1.000							
.15	.861	.990	.999	1.000						
.20	.819	.982	.999	1.000						
.25	.779	.974	.998	1.000						
.30	.741	.963	.996	1.000						
.35	.705	.951	.994	1.000						
.40	.670	.938	.992	.999	1.000					
.45	.638	.925	.989	.999	1.000					
.50	.607	.910	.986	.998	1.000					
.55	.577	.894	.982	.998	1.000					
.60	.549	.878	.977	.997	1.000					
.65	.522	.861	.972	.996	.999	1.000				
.70	.497	.844	.966	.994	.999	1.000				
.75	.472	.827	.959	.993	.999	1.000				
.80	.449	.809	.953	.991	.999	1.000				
.85	.427	.791	.945	.989	.998	1.000				
.90	.407	.772	.937	.987	.998	1.000				
.95	.387	.754	.929	.981	.997	1.000				
1.00	.368	.736	.920	.981	.996	.999	1.000			
1.1	.333	.699	.900	.974	.995	.999	1.000			
1.2	.301	.663	.879	.966	.992	.998	1.000			
1.3	.273	.627	.857	.957	.989	.998	1.000			
1.4	.247	.592	.833	.946	.986	.997	.999	1.000		
1.5	.223	.558	.809	.934	.981	.996	.999	1.000		

TABLE III   Continued

λ \ x	0	1	2	3	4	5	6	7	8	9
1.6	.202	.525	.783	.921	.976	.994	.999	1.000		
1.7	.183	.493	.757	.907	.970	.992	.998	1.000		
1.8	.165	.463	.731	.891	.964	.990	.997	.999	1.000	
1.9	.150	.434	.704	.875	.956	.987	.997	.999	1.000	
2.0	.135	.406	.677	.857	.947	.983	.995	.999	1.000	
2.2	.111	.355	.623	.819	.928	.975	.993	.998	1.000	
2.4	.091	.308	.570	.779	.904	.964	.988	.997	.999	1.000
2.6	.074	.267	.518	.736	.877	.951	.983	.995	.999	1.000
2.8	.061	.231	.469	.692	.848	.935	.976	.992	.998	.999
3.0	.050	.199	.423	.647	.815	.916	.966	.988	.996	.999
3.2	.041	.171	.380	.603	.781	.895	.955	.983	.994	.998
3.4	.033	.147	.340	.558	.744	.871	.942	.977	.992	.997
3.6	.027	.126	.303	.515	.706	.844	.927	.969	.988	.996
3.8	.022	.107	.269	.473	.668	.816	.909	.960	.984	.994
4.0	.018	.092	.238	.433	.629	.785	.889	.949	.979	.992
4.2	.015	.078	.210	.395	.590	.753	.867	.936	.972	.989
4.4	.012	.066	.185	.359	.551	.720	.844	.921	.964	.985
4.6	.010	.056	.163	.326	.513	.686	.818	.905	.955	.980
4.8	.008	.048	.143	.294	.476	.651	.791	.887	.944	.975
5.0	.007	.040	.125	.265	.440	.616	.762	.867	.932	.968
5.2	.006	.034	.109	.238	.406	.581	.732	.845	.918	.960
5.4	.005	.029	.095	.213	.373	.546	.702	.822	.903	.951
5.6	.004	.024	.082	.191	.342	.512	.670	.797	.886	.941
5.8	.003	.021	.072	.170	.313	.478	.638	.771	.867	.929
6.0	.002	.017	.062	.151	.285	.446	.606	.744	.847	.916

λ	10	11	12	13	14	15	16
2.8	1.000						
3.0	1.000						
3.2	1.000						
3.4	.999	1.000					
3.6	.999	1.000					
3.8	.998	.999	1.000				
4.0	.997	.999	1.000				
4.2	.996	.999	1.000				
4.4	.994	.998	.999	1.000			
4.6	.992	.997	.999	1.000			
4.8	.990	.996	.999	1.000			
5.0	.986	.995	.998	.999	1.000		
5.2	.982	.993	.997	.999	1.000		
5.4	.977	.990	.996	.999	1.000		
5.6	.972	.988	.995	.998	.999	1.000	
5.8	.965	.984	.993	.997	.999	1.000	
6.0	.957	.980	.991	.996	.999	.999	1.000

(continued)

TABLE III   Continued

λ \ x	0	1	2	3	4	5	6	7	8	9
6.2	.002	.015	.054	.134	.259	.414	.574	.716	.826	.902
6.4	.002	.012	.046	.119	.235	.384	.542	.687	.803	.886
6.6	.001	.010	.040	.105	.213	.355	.511	.658	.780	.869
6.8	.001	.009	.034	.093	.192	.327	.480	.628	.755	.850
7.0	.001	.007	.030	.082	.173	.301	.450	.599	.729	.830
7.2	.001	.006	.025	.072	.156	.276	.420	.569	.703	.810
7.4	.001	.005	.022	.063	.140	.253	.392	.539	.676	.788
7.6	.001	.004	.019	.055	.125	.231	.365	.510	.648	.765
7.8	.000	.004	.016	.048	.112	.210	.338	.481	.620	.741
8.0	.000	.003	.014	.042	.100	.191	.313	.453	.593	.717
8.5	.000	.002	.009	.030	.074	.150	.256	.386	.523	.653
9.0	.000	.001	.006	.021	.055	.116	.207	.324	.456	.587
9.5	.000	.001	.004	.015	.040	.089	.165	.269	.392	.522
10.0	.000	.000	.003	.010	.029	.067	.130	.220	.333	.458

λ	10	11	12	13	14	15	16	17	18	19
6.2	.949	.975	.989	.995	.998	.999	1.000			
6.4	.939	.969	.986	.994	.997	.999	1.000			
6.6	.927	.963	.982	.992	.997	.999	.999	1.000		
6.8	.915	.955	.978	.990	.996	.998	.999	1.000		
7.0	.901	.947	.973	.987	.994	.998	.999	1.000		
7.2	.887	.937	.967	.984	.993	.997	.999	.999	1.000	
7.4	.871	.926	.961	.980	.991	.996	.998	.999	1.000	
7.6	.854	.915	.954	.976	.989	.995	.998	.999	1.000	
7.8	.835	.902	.945	.971	.986	.993	.997	.999	1.000	
8.0	.816	.888	.936	.966	.983	.992	.996	.998	.999	1.000
8.5	.763	.849	.909	.949	.973	.986	.993	.997	.999	.999
9.0	.706	.803	.876	.926	.959	.978	.989	.995	.998	.999
9.5	.645	.752	.836	.898	.940	.967	.982	.991	.996	.998
10.0	.583	.697	.792	.864	.917	.951	.973	.986	.993	.997

λ	20	21	22
8.5	1.000		
9.0	1.000		
9.5	.999	1.000	
10.0	.998	.999	1.000

TABLE III Continued

λ \ x	0	1	2	3	4	5	6	7	8	9
10.5	.000	.000	.002	.007	.021	.050	.102	.179	.279	.397
11.0	.000	.000	.001	.005	.015	.038	.079	.143	.232	.341
11.5	.000	.000	.001	.003	.011	.028	.060	.114	.191	.289
12.0	.000	.000	.001	.002	.008	.020	.046	.090	.155	.242
12.5	.000	.000	.000	.002	.005	.015	.035	.070	.125	.201
13.0	.000	.000	.000	.001	.004	.011	.026	.054	.100	.166
13.5	.000	.000	.000	.001	.003	.008	.019	.041	.079	.135
14.0	.000	.000	.000	.000	.002	.006	.014	.032	.062	.109
14.5	.000	.000	.000	.000	.001	.004	.010	.024	.048	.088
15.0	.000	.000	.000	.000	.001	.003	.008	.018	.037	.070

λ	10	11	12	13	14	15	16	17	18	19
10.5	.521	.639	.742	.825	.888	.932	.960	.978	.988	.994
11.0	.460	.579	.689	.781	.854	.907	.944	.968	.982	.991
11.5	.402	.520	.633	.733	.815	.878	.924	.954	.974	.986
12.0	.347	.462	.576	.682	.772	.844	.899	.937	.963	.979
12.5	.297	.406	.519	.628	.725	.806	.869	.916	.948	.969
13.0	.252	.353	.463	.573	.675	.764	.835	.890	.930	.957
13.5	.211	.304	.409	.518	.623	.718	.798	.861	.908	.942
14.0	.176	.260	.358	.464	.570	.669	.756	.827	.883	.923
14.5	.145	.220	.311	.413	.518	.619	.711	.790	.853	.901
15.0	.118	.185	.268	.363	.466	.568	.664	.749	.819	.875

λ	20	21	22	23	24	25	26	27	28	29
10.5	.997	.999	.999	1.000						
11.0	.995	.998	.999	1.000						
11.5	.992	.996	.998	.999	1.000					
12.0	.988	.994	.997	.999	.999	1.000				
12.5	.983	.991	.995	.998	.999	.999	1.000			
13.0	.975	.986	.992	.996	.998	.999	1.000			
13.5	.965	.980	.989	.994	.997	.998	.999	1.000		
14.0	.952	.971	.983	.991	.995	.997	.999	.999	1.000	
14.5	.936	.960	.976	.986	.992	.996	.998	.999	.999	1.000
15.0	.917	.947	.967	.981	.989	.994	.997	.998	.999	1.000

(continued)

| TABLE III | Continued | | | | | | | | |

λ＼X	4	5	6	7	8	9	10	11	12	13
16	.000	.001	.004	.010	.022	.043	.077	.127	.193	.275
17	.000	.001	.002	.005	.013	.026	.049	.085	.135	.201
18	.000	.000	.001	.003	.007	.015	.030	.055	.092	.143
19	.000	.000	.001	.002	.004	.009	.018	.035	.061	.098
20	.000	.000	.000	.001	.002	.005	.011	.021	.039	.066
21	.000	.000	.000	.000	.001	.003	.006	.013	.025	.043
22	.000	.000	.000	.000	.001	.002	.004	.008	.015	.028
23	.000	.000	.000	.000	.000	.001	.002	.004	.009	.017
24	.000	.000	.000	.000	.000	.000	.001	.003	.005	.011
25	.000	.000	.000	.000	.000	.000	.001	.001	.003	.006

	14	15	16	17	18	19	20	21	22	23
16	.368	.467	.566	.659	.742	.812	.868	.911	.942	.963
17	.281	.371	.468	.564	.655	.736	.805	.861	.905	.937
18	.208	.287	.375	.469	.562	.651	.731	.799	.855	.899
19	.150	.215	.292	.378	.469	.561	.647	.725	.793	.849
20	.105	.157	.221	.297	.381	.470	.559	.644	.721	.787
21	.072	.111	.163	.227	.302	.384	.471	.558	.640	.716
22	.048	.077	.117	.169	.232	.306	.387	.472	.556	.637
23	.031	.052	.082	.123	.175	.238	.310	.389	.472	.555
24	.020	.034	.056	.087	.128	.180	.243	.314	.392	.473
25	.012	.022	.038	.060	.092	.134	.185	.247	.318	.394

	24	25	26	27	28	29	30	31	32	33
16	.978	.987	.993	.996	.998	.999	.999	1.000		
17	.959	.975	.985	.991	.995	.997	.999	.999	1.000	
18	.932	.955	.972	.983	.990	.994	.997	.998	.999	1.000
19	.893	.927	.951	.969	.980	.988	.993	.996	.998	.999
20	.843	.888	.922	.948	.966	.978	.987	.992	.995	.997
21	.782	.838	.883	.917	.944	.963	.976	.985	.991	.994
22	.712	.777	.832	.877	.913	.940	.959	.973	.983	.989
23	.635	.708	.772	.827	.873	.908	.936	.956	.971	.981
24	.554	.632	.704	.768	.823	.868	.904	.932	.953	.969
25	.473	.553	.629	.700	.763	.818	.863	.900	.929	.950

	34	35	36	37	38	39	40	41	42	43
19	.999	1.000								
20	.999	.999	1.000							
21	.997	.998	.999	.999	1.000					
22	.994	.996	.998	.999	.999	1.000				
23	.988	.993	.996	.997	.999	.999	1.000			
24	.979	.987	.992	.995	.997	.998	.999	.999	1.000	
25	.966	.978	.985	.991	.991	.997	.998	.999	.999	1.000

TABLE IV   Normal Curve Areas

z	.00	.01	.02	.03	.04	.05	.06	.07	.08	.09
.0	.0000	.0040	.0080	.0120	.0160	.0199	.0239	.0279	.0319	.0359
.1	.0398	.0438	.0478	.0517	.0557	.0596	.0636	.0675	.0714	.0753
.2	.0793	.0832	.0871	.0910	.0948	.0987	.1026	.1064	.1103	.1141
.3	.1179	.1217	.1255	.1293	.1331	.1368	.1406	.1443	.1480	.1517
.4	.1554	.1591	.1628	.1664	.1700	.1736	.1772	.1808	.1844	.1879
.5	.1915	.1950	.1985	.2019	.2054	.2088	.2123	.2157	.2190	.2224
.6	.2257	.2291	.2324	.2357	.2389	.2422	.2454	.2486	.2517	.2549
.7	.2580	.2611	.2642	.2673	.2704	.2734	.2764	.2794	.2823	.2852
.8	.2881	.2910	.2939	.2967	.2995	.3023	.3051	.3078	.3106	.3133
.9	.3159	.3186	.3212	.3238	.3264	.3289	.3315	.3340	.3365	.3389
1.0	.3413	.3438	.3461	.3485	.3508	.3531	.3554	.3577	.3599	.3621
1.1	.3643	.3665	.3686	.3708	.3729	.3749	.3770	.3790	.3810	.3830
1.2	.3849	.3869	.3888	.3907	.3925	.3944	.3962	.3980	.3997	.4015
1.3	.4032	.4049	.4066	.4082	.4099	.4115	.4131	.4147	.4162	.4177
1.4	.4192	.4207	.4222	.4236	.4251	.4265	.4279	.4292	.4306	.4319
1.5	.4332	.4345	.4357	.4370	.4382	.4394	.4406	.4418	.4429	.4441
1.6	.4452	.4463	.4474	.4484	.4495	.4505	.4515	.4525	.4535	.4545
1.7	.4554	.4564	.4573	.4582	.4591	.4599	.4608	.4616	.4625	.4633
1.8	.4641	.4649	.4656	.4664	.4671	.4678	.4686	.4693	.4699	.4706
1.9	.4713	.4719	.4726	.4732	.4738	.4744	.4750	.4756	.4761	.4767
2.0	.4772	.4778	.4783	.4788	.4793	.4798	.4803	.4808	.4812	.4817
2.1	.4821	.4826	.4830	.4834	.4838	.4842	.4846	.4850	.4854	.4857
2.2	.4861	.4864	.4868	.4871	.4875	.4878	.4881	.4884	.4887	.4890
2.3	.4893	.4896	.4898	.4901	.4904	.4906	.4909	.4911	.4913	.4916
2.4	.4918	.4920	.4922	.4925	.4927	.4929	.4931	.4932	.4934	.4936
2.5	.4938	.4940	.4941	.4943	.4945	.4946	.4948	.4949	.4951	.4952
2.6	.4953	.4955	.4956	.4957	.4959	.4960	.4961	.4962	.4963	.4964
2.7	.4965	.4966	.4967	.4968	.4969	.4970	.4971	.4972	.4973	.4974
2.8	.4974	.4975	.4976	.4977	.4977	.4978	.4979	.4979	.4980	.4981
2.9	.4981	.4982	.4982	.4983	.4984	.4984	.4985	.4985	.4986	.4986
3.0	.4987	.4987	.4987	.4988	.4988	.4989	.4989	.4989	.4990	.4990

Source: Abridged from Table I of A. Hald, *Statistical Tables and Formulas* (New York: Wiley), 1952. Reproduced by permission of A. Hald and the publisher, John Wiley & Sons, Inc.

TABLE V   Exponentials

λ	$e^{-\lambda}$	λ	$e^{-\lambda}$	λ	$e^{-\lambda}$	λ	$e^{-\lambda}$	λ	$e^{-\lambda}$
.00	1.000000	2.05	.128735	4.05	.017422	6.05	.002358	8.05	.000319
.05	.951229	2.10	.122456	4.10	.016573	6.10	.002243	8.10	.000304
.10	.904837	2.15	.116484	4.15	.015764	6.15	.002133	8.15	.000289
.15	.860708	2.20	.110803	4.20	.014996	6.20	.002029	8.20	.000275
.20	.818731	2.25	.105399	4.25	.014264	6.25	.001930	8.25	.000261
.25	.778801	2.30	.100259	4.30	.013569	6.30	.001836	8.30	.000249
.30	.740818	2.35	.095369	4.35	.012907	6.35	.001747	8.35	.000236
.35	.704688	2.40	.090718	4.40	.012277	6.40	.001661	8.40	.000225
.40	.670320	2.45	.086294	4.45	.011679	6.45	.001581	8.45	.000214
.45	.637628	2.50	.082085	4.50	.011109	6.50	.001503	8.50	.000204
.50	.606531	2.55	.078082	4.55	.010567	6.55	.001430	8.55	.000194
.55	.576950	2.60	.074274	4.60	.010052	6.60	.001360	8.60	.000184
.60	.548812	2.65	.070651	4.65	.009562	6.65	.001294	8.65	.000175
.65	.522046	2.70	.067206	4.70	.009095	6.70	.001231	8.70	.000167
.70	.496585	2.75	.063928	4.75	.008652	6.75	.001171	8.75	.000158
.75	.472367	2.80	.060810	4.80	.008230	6.80	.001114	8.80	.000151
.80	.449329	2.85	.057844	4.85	.007828	6.85	.001059	8.85	.000143
.85	.427415	2.90	.055023	4.90	.007447	6.90	.001008	8.90	.000136
.90	.406570	2.95	.052340	4.95	.007083	6.95	.000959	8.95	.000130
.95	.386741	3.00	.049787	5.00	.006738	7.00	.000912	9.00	.000123
1.00	.367879	3.05	.047359	5.05	.006409	7.05	.000867	9.05	.000117
1.05	.349938	3.10	.045049	5.10	.006097	7.10	.000825	9.10	.000112
1.10	.332871	3.15	.042852	5.15	.005799	7.15	.000785	9.15	.000106
1.15	.316637	3.20	.040762	5.20	.005517	7.20	.000747	9.20	.000101
1.20	.301194	3.25	.038774	5.25	.005248	7.25	.000710	9.25	.000096
1.25	.286505	3.30	.036883	5.30	.004992	7.30	.000676	9.30	.000091
1.30	.272532	3.35	.035084	5.35	.004748	7.35	.000643	9.35	.000087
1.35	.259240	3.40	.033373	5.40	.004517	7.40	.000611	9.40	.000083
1.40	.246597	3.45	.031746	5.45	.004296	7.45	.000581	9.45	.000079
1.45	.234570	3.50	.030197	5.50	.004087	7.50	.000553	9.50	.000075
1.50	.223130	3.55	.028725	5.55	.003887	7.55	.000526	9.55	.000071
1.55	.212248	3.60	.027324	5.60	.003698	7.60	.000501	9.60	.000068
1.60	.201897	3.65	.025991	5.65	.003518	7.65	.000476	9.65	.000064
1.65	.192050	3.70	.024724	5.70	.003346	7.70	.000453	9.70	.000061
1.70	.182684	3.75	.023518	5.75	.003183	7.75	.000431	9.75	.000058
1.75	.173774	3.80	.022371	5.80	.003028	7.80	.000410	9.80	.000056
1.80	.165299	3.85	.021280	5.85	.002880	7.85	.000390	9.85	.000053
1.85	.157237	3.90	.020242	5.90	.002739	7.90	.000371	9.90	.000050
1.90	.149569	3.95	.019255	5.95	.002606	7.95	.000353	9.95	.000048
1.95	.142274	4.00	.018316	6.00	.002479	8.00	.000336	10.00	.000045
2.00	.135335								

TABLE VI   Critical Values of *t*

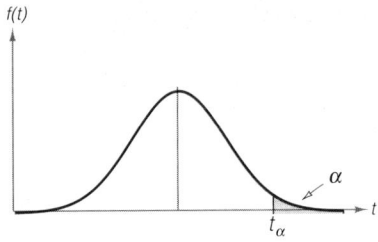

ν	$t_{.100}$	$t_{.050}$	$t_{.025}$	$t_{.010}$	$t_{.005}$	$t_{.001}$	$t_{.0005}$
1	3.078	6.314	12.706	31.821	63.657	318.31	636.62
2	1.886	2.920	4.303	6.965	9.925	22.326	31.598
3	1.638	2.353	3.182	4.541	5.841	10.213	12.924
4	1.533	2.132	2.776	3.747	4.604	7.173	8.610
5	1.476	2.015	2.571	3.365	4.032	5.893	6.869
6	1.440	1.943	2.447	3.143	3.707	5.208	5.959
7	1.415	1.895	2.365	2.998	3.499	4.785	5.408
8	1.397	1.860	2.306	2.896	3.355	4.501	5.041
9	1.383	1.833	2.262	2.821	3.250	4.297	4.781
10	1.372	1.812	2.228	2.764	3.169	4.144	4.587
11	1.363	1.796	2.201	2.718	3.106	4.025	4.437
12	1.356	1.782	2.179	2.681	3.055	3.930	4.318
13	1.350	1.771	2.160	2.650	3.012	3.852	4.221
14	1.345	1.761	2.145	2.624	2.977	3.787	4.140
15	1.341	1.753	2.131	2.602	2.947	3.733	4.073
16	1.337	1.746	2.120	2.583	2.921	3.686	4.015
17	1.333	1.740	2.110	2.567	2.898	3.646	3.965
18	1.330	1.734	2.101	2.552	2.878	3.610	3.922
19	1.328	1.729	2.093	2.539	2.861	3.579	3.883
20	1.325	1.725	2.086	2.528	2.845	3.552	3.850
21	1.323	1.721	2.080	2.518	2.831	3.527	3.819
22	1.321	1.717	2.074	2.508	2.819	3.505	3.792
23	1.319	1.714	2.069	2.500	2.807	3.485	3.767
24	1.318	1.711	2.064	2.492	2.797	3.467	3.745
25	1.316	1.708	2.060	2.485	2.787	3.450	3.725
26	1.315	1.706	2.056	2.479	2.779	3.435	3.707
27	1.314	1.703	2.052	2.473	2.771	3.421	3.690
28	1.313	1.701	2.048	2.467	2.763	3.408	3.674
29	1.311	1.699	2.045	2.462	2.756	3.396	3.659
30	1.310	1.697	2.042	2.457	2.750	3.385	3.646
40	1.303	1.684	2.021	2.423	2.704	3.307	3.551
60	1.296	1.671	2.000	2.390	2.660	3.232	3.460
120	1.289	1.658	1.980	2.358	2.617	3.160	3.373
∞	1.282	1.645	1.960	2.326	2.576	3.090	3.291

TABLE VII   Percentage Points of the F Distribution, $\alpha = .10$

| | Numerator Degrees of Freedom | | | | | | | | |
ν_2 \ ν_1	1	2	3	4	5	6	7	8	9
1	39.86	49.50	53.59	55.83	57.24	58.20	58.91	59.44	59.86
2	8.53	9.00	9.16	9.24	9.29	9.33	9.35	9.37	9.38
3	5.54	5.46	5.39	5.34	5.31	5.28	5.27	5.25	5.24
4	4.54	4.32	4.19	4.11	4.05	4.01	3.98	3.95	3.94
5	4.06	3.78	3.62	3.52	3.45	3.40	3.37	3.34	3.32
6	3.78	3.46	3.29	3.18	3.11	3.05	3.01	2.98	2.96
7	3.59	3.26	3.07	2.96	2.88	2.83	2.78	2.75	2.72
8	3.46	3.11	2.92	2.81	2.73	2.67	2.62	2.59	2.56
9	3.36	3.01	2.81	2.69	2.61	2.55	2.51	2.47	2.44
10	3.29	2.92	2.73	2.61	2.52	2.46	2.41	2.38	2.35
11	3.23	2.86	2.66	2.54	2.45	2.39	2.34	2.30	2.27
12	3.18	2.81	2.61	2.48	2.39	2.33	2.28	2.24	2.21
13	3.14	2.76	2.56	2.43	2.35	2.28	2.23	2.20	2.16
14	3.10	2.73	2.52	2.39	2.31	2.24	2.19	2.15	2.12
15	3.07	2.70	2.49	2.36	2.27	2.21	2.16	2.12	2.09
16	3.05	2.67	2.46	2.33	2.24	2.18	2.13	2.09	2.06
17	3.03	2.64	2.44	2.31	2.22	2.15	2.10	2.06	2.03
18	3.01	2.62	2.42	2.29	2.20	2.13	2.08	2.04	2.00
19	2.99	2.61	2.40	2.27	2.18	2.11	2.06	2.02	1.98
20	2.97	2.59	2.38	2.25	2.16	2.09	2.04	2.00	1.96
21	2.96	2.57	2.36	2.23	2.14	2.08	2.02	1.98	1.95
22	2.95	2.56	2.35	2.22	2.13	2.06	2.01	1.97	1.93
23	2.94	2.55	2.34	2.21	2.11	2.05	1.99	1.95	1.92
24	2.93	2.54	2.33	2.19	2.10	2.04	1.98	1.94	1.91
25	2.92	2.53	2.32	2.18	2.09	2.02	1.97	1.93	1.89
26	2.91	2.52	2.31	2.17	2.08	2.01	1.96	1.92	1.88
27	2.90	2.51	2.30	2.17	2.07	2.00	1.95	1.91	1.87
28	2.89	2.50	2.29	2.16	2.06	2.00	1.94	1.90	1.87
29	2.89	2.50	2.28	2.15	2.06	1.99	1.93	1.89	1.86
30	2.88	2.49	2.28	2.14	2.05	1.98	1.93	1.88	1.85
40	2.84	2.44	2.23	2.09	2.00	1.93	1.87	1.83	1.79
60	2.79	2.39	2.18	2.04	1.95	1.87	1.82	1.77	1.74
120	2.75	2.35	2.13	1.99	1.90	1.82	1.77	1.72	1.68
∞	2.71	2.30	2.08	1.94	1.85	1.77	1.72	1.67	1.63

Denominator Degrees of Freedom

ν_2 \ ν_1	Numerator Degrees of Freedom									
	10	12	15	20	24	30	40	60	120	∞
1	60.19	60.71	61.22	61.74	62.00	62.26	62.53	62.79	63.06	63.33
2	9.39	9.41	9.42	9.44	9.45	9.46	9.47	9.47	9.48	9.49
3	5.23	5.22	5.20	5.18	5.18	5.17	5.16	5.15	5.14	5.13
4	3.92	3.90	3.87	3.84	3.83	3.82	3.80	3.79	3.78	3.76
5	3.30	3.27	3.24	3.21	3.19	3.17	3.16	3.14	3.12	3.10
6	2.94	2.90	2.87	2.84	2.82	2.80	2.78	2.76	2.74	2.72
7	2.70	2.67	2.63	2.59	2.58	2.56	2.54	2.51	2.49	2.47
8	2.54	2.50	2.46	2.42	2.40	2.38	2.36	2.34	2.32	2.29
9	2.42	2.38	2.34	2.30	2.28	2.25	2.23	2.21	2.18	2.16
10	2.32	2.28	2.24	2.20	2.18	2.16	2.13	2.11	2.08	2.06
11	2.25	2.21	2.17	2.12	2.10	2.08	2.05	2.03	2.00	1.97
12	2.19	2.15	2.10	2.06	2.04	2.01	1.99	1.96	1.93	1.90
13	2.14	2.10	2.05	2.01	1.98	1.96	1.93	1.90	1.88	1.85
14	2.10	2.05	2.01	1.96	1.94	1.91	1.89	1.86	1.83	1.80
15	2.06	2.02	1.97	1.92	1.90	1.87	1.85	1.82	1.79	1.76
16	2.03	1.99	1.94	1.89	1.87	1.84	1.81	1.78	1.75	1.72
17	2.00	1.96	1.91	1.86	1.84	1.81	1.78	1.75	1.72	1.69
18	1.98	1.93	1.89	1.84	1.81	1.78	1.75	1.72	1.69	1.66
19	1.96	1.91	1.86	1.81	1.79	1.76	1.73	1.70	1.67	1.63
20	1.94	1.89	1.84	1.79	1.77	1.74	1.71	1.68	1.64	1.61
21	1.92	1.87	1.83	1.78	1.75	1.72	1.69	1.66	1.62	1.59
22	1.90	1.86	1.81	1.76	1.73	1.70	1.67	1.64	1.60	1.57
23	1.89	1.84	1.80	1.74	1.72	1.69	1.66	1.62	1.59	1.55
24	1.88	1.83	1.78	1.73	1.70	1.67	1.64	1.61	1.57	1.53
25	1.87	1.82	1.77	1.72	1.69	1.66	1.63	1.59	1.56	1.52
26	1.86	1.81	1.76	1.71	1.68	1.65	1.61	1.58	1.54	1.50
27	1.85	1.80	1.75	1.70	1.67	1.64	1.60	1.57	1.53	1.49
28	1.84	1.79	1.74	1.69	1.66	1.63	1.59	1.56	1.52	1.48
29	1.83	1.78	1.73	1.68	1.65	1.62	1.58	1.55	1.51	1.47
30	1.82	1.77	1.72	1.67	1.64	1.61	1.57	1.54	1.50	1.46
40	1.76	1.71	1.66	1.61	1.57	1.54	1.51	1.47	1.42	1.38
60	1.71	1.66	1.60	1.54	1.51	1.48	1.44	1.40	1.35	1.29
120	1.65	1.60	1.55	1.48	1.45	1.41	1.37	1.32	1.26	1.19
∞	1.60	1.55	1.49	1.42	1.38	1.34	1.30	1.24	1.17	1.00

Denominator Degrees of Freedom

TABLE VIII Percentage Points of the F Distribution, $\alpha = .05$

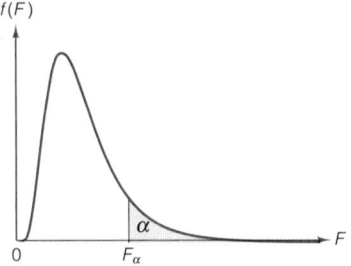

ν_1	Numerator Degrees of Freedom								
ν_2	1	2	3	4	5	6	7	8	9
1	161.4	199.5	215.7	224.6	230.2	234.0	236.8	238.9	240.5
2	18.51	19.00	19.16	19.25	19.30	19.33	19.35	19.37	19.38
3	10.13	9.55	9.28	9.12	9.01	8.94	8.89	8.85	8.81
4	7.71	6.94	6.59	6.39	6.26	6.16	6.09	6.04	6.00
5	6.61	5.79	5.41	5.19	5.05	4.95	4.88	4.82	4.77
6	5.99	5.14	4.76	4.53	4.39	4.28	4.21	4.15	4.10
7	5.59	4.74	4.35	4.12	3.97	3.87	3.79	3.73	3.68
8	5.32	4.46	4.07	3.84	3.69	3.58	3.50	3.44	3.39
9	5.12	4.26	3.86	3.63	3.48	3.37	3.29	3.23	3.18
10	4.96	4.10	3.71	3.48	3.33	3.22	3.14	3.07	3.02
11	4.84	3.98	3.59	3.36	3.20	3.09	3.01	2.95	2.90
12	4.75	3.89	3.49	3.26	3.11	3.00	2.91	2.85	2.80
13	4.67	3.81	3.41	3.18	3.03	2.92	2.83	2.77	2.71
14	4.60	3.74	3.34	3.11	2.96	2.85	2.76	2.70	2.65
15	4.54	3.68	3.29	3.06	2.90	2.79	2.71	2.64	2.59
16	4.49	3.63	3.24	3.01	2.85	2.74	2.66	2.59	2.54
17	4.45	3.59	3.20	2.96	2.81	2.70	2.61	2.55	2.49
18	4.41	3.55	3.16	2.93	2.77	2.66	2.58	2.51	2.46
19	4.38	3.52	3.13	2.90	2.74	2.63	2.54	2.48	2.42
20	4.35	3.49	3.10	2.87	2.71	2.60	2.51	2.45	2.39
21	4.32	3.47	3.07	2.84	2.68	2.57	2.49	2.42	2.37
22	4.30	3.44	3.05	2.82	2.66	2.55	2.46	2.40	2.34
23	4.28	3.42	3.03	2.80	2.64	2.53	2.44	2.37	2.32
24	4.26	3.40	3.01	2.78	2.62	2.51	2.42	2.36	2.30
25	4.24	3.39	2.99	2.76	2.60	2.49	2.40	2.34	2.28
26	4.23	3.37	2.98	2.74	2.59	2.47	2.39	2.32	2.27
27	4.21	3.35	2.96	2.73	2.57	2.46	2.37	2.31	2.25
28	4.20	3.34	2.95	2.71	2.56	2.45	2.36	2.29	2.24
29	4.18	3.33	2.93	2.70	2.55	2.43	2.35	2.28	2.22
30	4.17	3.32	2.92	2.69	2.53	2.42	2.33	2.27	2.21
40	4.08	3.23	2.84	2.61	2.45	2.34	2.25	2.18	2.12
60	4.00	3.15	2.76	2.53	2.37	2.25	2.17	2.10	2.04
120	3.92	3.07	2.68	2.45	2.29	2.17	2.09	2.02	1.96
∞	3.84	3.00	2.60	2.37	2.21	2.10	2.01	1.94	1.88

Denominator Degrees of Freedom

ν_1	Numerator Degrees of Freedom									
ν_2	10	12	15	20	24	30	40	60	120	∞
1	241.9	243.9	245.9	248.0	249.1	250.1	251.1	252.2	253.3	254.3
2	19.40	19.41	19.43	19.45	19.45	19.46	19.47	19.48	19.49	19.50
3	8.79	8.74	8.70	8.66	8.64	8.62	8.59	8.57	8.55	8.53
4	5.96	5.91	5.86	5.80	5.77	5.75	5.72	5.69	5.66	5.63
5	4.74	4.68	4.62	4.56	4.53	4.50	4.46	4.43	4.40	4.36
6	4.06	4.00	3.94	3.87	3.84	3.81	3.77	3.74	3.70	3.67
7	3.64	3.57	3.51	3.44	3.41	3.38	3.34	3.30	3.27	3.23
8	3.35	3.28	3.22	3.15	3.12	3.08	3.04	3.01	2.97	2.93
9	3.14	3.07	3.01	2.94	2.90	2.86	2.83	2.79	2.75	2.71
10	2.98	2.91	2.85	2.77	2.74	2.70	2.66	2.62	2.58	2.54
11	2.85	2.79	2.72	2.65	2.61	2.57	2.53	2.49	2.45	2.40
12	2.75	2.69	2.62	2.54	2.51	2.47	2.43	2.38	2.34	2.30
13	2.67	2.60	2.53	2.46	2.42	2.38	2.34	2.30	2.25	2.21
14	2.60	2.53	2.46	2.39	2.35	2.31	2.27	2.22	2.18	2.13
15	2.54	2.48	2.40	2.33	2.29	2.25	2.20	2.16	2.11	2.07
16	2.49	2.42	2.35	2.28	2.24	2.19	2.15	2.11	2.06	2.01
17	2.45	2.38	2.31	2.23	2.19	2.15	2.10	2.06	2.01	1.96
18	2.41	2.34	2.27	2.19	2.15	2.11	2.06	2.02	1.97	1.92
19	2.38	2.31	2.23	2.16	2.11	2.07	2.03	1.98	1.93	1.88
20	2.35	2.28	2.20	2.12	2.08	2.04	1.99	1.95	1.90	1.84
21	2.32	2.25	2.18	2.10	2.05	2.01	1.96	1.92	1.87	1.81
22	2.30	2.23	2.15	2.07	2.03	1.98	1.94	1.89	1.84	1.78
23	2.27	2.20	2.13	2.05	2.01	1.96	1.91	1.86	1.81	1.76
24	2.25	2.18	2.11	2.03	1.98	1.94	1.89	1.84	1.79	1.73
25	2.24	2.16	2.09	2.01	1.96	1.92	1.87	1.82	1.77	1.71
26	2.22	2.15	2.07	1.99	1.95	1.90	1.85	1.80	1.75	1.69
27	2.20	2.13	2.06	1.97	1.93	1.88	1.84	1.79	1.73	1.67
28	2.19	2.12	2.04	1.96	1.91	1.87	1.82	1.77	1.71	1.65
29	2.18	2.10	2.03	1.94	1.90	1.85	1.81	1.75	1.70	1.64
30	2.16	2.09	2.01	1.93	1.89	1.84	1.79	1.74	1.68	1.62
40	2.08	2.00	1.92	1.84	1.79	1.74	1.69	1.64	1.58	1.51
60	1.99	1.92	1.84	1.75	1.70	1.65	1.59	1.53	1.47	1.39
120	1.91	1.83	1.75	1.66	1.61	1.55	1.50	1.43	1.35	1.25
∞	1.83	1.75	1.67	1.57	1.52	1.46	1.39	1.32	1.22	1.00

Denominator Degrees of Freedom

TABLE IX Percentage Points of the F Distribution, $\alpha = .025$

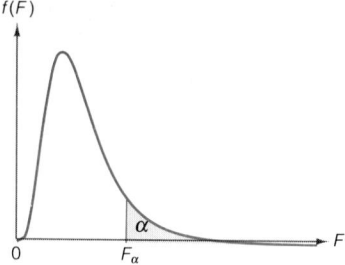

ν_2	Numerator Degrees of Freedom								
	1	2	3	4	5	6	7	8	9
1	647.8	799.5	864.2	899.6	921.8	937.1	948.2	956.7	963.3
2	38.51	39.00	39.17	39.25	39.30	39.33	39.36	39.37	39.39
3	17.44	16.04	15.44	15.10	14.88	14.73	14.62	14.54	14.47
4	12.22	10.65	9.98	9.60	9.36	9.20	9.07	8.98	8.90
5	10.01	8.43	7.76	7.39	7.15	6.98	6.85	6.76	6.68
6	8.81	7.26	6.60	6.23	5.99	5.82	5.70	5.60	5.52
7	8.07	6.54	5.89	5.52	5.29	5.12	4.99	4.90	4.82
8	7.57	6.06	5.42	5.05	4.82	4.65	4.53	4.43	4.36
9	7.21	5.71	5.08	4.72	4.48	4.32	4.20	4.10	4.03
10	6.94	5.46	4.83	4.47	4.24	4.07	3.95	3.85	3.78
11	6.72	5.26	4.63	4.28	4.04	3.88	3.76	3.66	3.59
12	6.55	5.10	4.47	4.12	3.89	3.73	3.61	3.51	3.44
13	6.41	4.97	4.35	4.00	3.77	3.60	3.48	3.39	3.31
14	6.30	4.86	4.24	3.89	3.66	3.50	3.38	3.29	3.21
15	6.20	4.77	4.15	3.80	3.58	3.41	3.29	3.20	3.12
16	6.12	4.69	4.08	3.73	3.50	3.34	3.22	3.12	3.05
17	6.04	4.62	4.01	3.66	3.44	3.28	3.16	3.06	2.98
18	5.98	4.56	3.95	3.61	3.38	3.22	3.10	3.01	2.93
19	5.92	4.51	3.90	3.56	3.33	3.17	3.05	2.96	2.88
20	5.87	4.46	3.86	3.51	3.29	3.13	3.01	2.91	2.84
21	5.83	4.42	3.82	3.48	3.25	3.09	2.97	2.87	2.80
22	5.79	4.38	3.78	3.44	3.22	3.05	2.93	2.84	2.76
23	5.75	4.35	3.75	3.41	3.18	3.02	2.90	2.81	2.73
24	5.72	4.32	3.72	3.38	3.15	2.99	2.87	2.78	2.70
25	5.69	4.29	3.69	3.35	3.13	2.97	2.85	2.75	2.68
26	5.66	4.27	3.67	3.33	3.10	2.94	2.82	2.73	2.65
27	5.63	4.24	3.65	3.31	3.08	2.92	2.80	2.71	2.63
28	5.61	4.22	3.63	3.29	3.06	2.90	2.78	2.69	2.61
29	5.59	4.20	3.61	3.27	3.04	2.88	2.76	2.67	2.59
30	5.57	4.18	3.59	3.25	3.03	2.87	2.75	2.65	2.57
40	5.42	4.05	3.46	3.13	2.90	2.74	2.62	2.53	2.45
60	5.29	3.93	3.34	3.01	2.79	2.63	2.51	2.41	2.33
120	5.15	3.80	3.23	2.89	2.67	2.52	2.39	2.30	2.22
∞	5.02	3.69	3.12	2.79	2.57	2.41	2.29	2.19	2.11

Denominator Degrees of Freedom

Source: From M. Merrington and C. M. Thompson, "Tables of Percentage Points of the Inverted Beta (F)-Distribution," *Biometrika*, 1943, 33, 73–88. Reproduced by permission of the *Biometrika* Trustees.

ν_1	Numerator Degrees of Freedom									
ν_2	10	12	15	20	24	30	40	60	120	∞
1	968.6	976.7	984.9	993.1	997.2	1,001	1,006	1,010	1,014	1,018
2	39.40	39.41	39.43	39.45	39.46	39.46	39.47	39.48	39.49	39.50
3	14.42	14.34	14.25	14.17	14.12	14.08	14.04	13.99	13.95	13.90
4	8.84	8.75	8.66	8.56	8.51	8.46	8.41	8.36	8.31	8.26
5	6.62	6.52	6.43	6.33	6.28	6.23	6.18	6.12	6.07	6.02
6	5.46	5.37	5.27	5.17	5.12	5.07	5.01	4.96	4.90	4.85
7	4.76	4.67	4.57	4.47	4.42	4.36	4.31	4.25	4.20	4.14
8	4.30	4.20	4.10	4.00	3.95	3.89	3.84	3.78	3.73	3.67
9	3.96	3.87	3.77	3.67	3.61	3.56	3.51	3.45	3.39	3.33
10	3.72	3.62	3.52	3.42	3.37	3.31	3.26	3.20	3.14	3.08
11	3.53	3.43	3.33	3.23	3.17	3.12	3.06	3.00	2.94	2.88
12	3.37	3.28	3.18	3.07	3.02	2.96	2.91	2.85	2.79	2.72
13	3.25	3.15	3.05	2.95	2.89	2.84	2.78	2.72	2.66	2.60
14	3.15	3.05	2.95	2.84	2.79	2.73	2.67	2.61	2.55	2.49
15	3.06	2.96	2.86	2.76	2.70	2.64	2.59	2.52	2.46	2.40
16	2.99	2.89	2.79	2.68	2.63	2.57	2.51	2.45	2.38	2.32
17	2.92	2.82	2.72	2.62	2.56	2.50	2.44	2.38	2.32	2.25
18	2.87	2.77	2.67	2.56	2.50	2.44	2.38	2.32	2.26	2.19
19	2.82	2.72	2.62	2.51	2.45	2.39	2.33	2.27	2.20	2.13
20	2.77	2.68	2.57	2.46	2.41	2.35	2.29	2.22	2.16	2.09
21	2.73	2.64	2.53	2.42	2.37	2.31	2.25	2.18	2.11	2.04
22	2.70	2.60	2.50	2.39	2.33	2.27	2.21	2.14	2.08	2.00
23	2.67	2.57	2.47	2.36	2.30	2.24	2.18	2.11	2.04	1.97
24	2.64	2.54	2.44	2.33	2.27	2.21	2.15	2.08	2.01	1.94
25	2.61	2.51	2.41	2.30	2.24	2.18	2.12	2.05	1.98	1.91
26	2.59	2.49	2.39	2.28	2.22	2.16	2.09	2.03	1.95	1.88
27	2.57	2.47	2.36	2.25	2.19	2.13	2.07	2.00	1.93	1.85
28	2.55	2.45	2.34	2.23	2.17	2.11	2.05	1.98	1.91	1.83
29	2.53	2.43	2.32	2.21	2.15	2.09	2.03	1.96	1.89	1.81
30	2.51	2.41	2.31	2.20	2.14	2.07	2.01	1.94	1.87	1.79
40	2.39	2.29	2.18	2.07	2.01	1.94	1.88	1.80	1.72	1.64
60	2.27	2.17	2.06	1.94	1.88	1.82	1.74	1.67	1.58	1.48
120	2.16	2.05	1.94	1.82	1.76	1.69	1.61	1.53	1.43	1.31
∞	2.05	1.94	1.83	1.71	1.64	1.57	1.48	1.39	1.27	1.00

Denominator Degrees of Freedom

TABLE X Percentage Points of the F Distribution, $\alpha = .01$

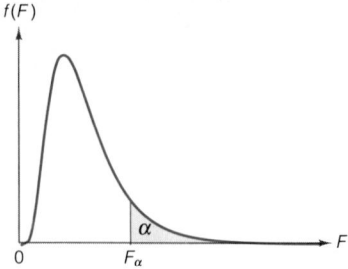

ν_2	Numerator Degrees of Freedom								
	1	2	3	4	5	6	7	8	9
1	4,052	4,999.5	5,403	5,625	5,764	5,859	5,928	5,982	6,022
2	98.50	99.00	99.17	99.25	99.30	99.33	99.36	99.37	99.39
3	34.12	30.82	29.46	28.71	28.24	27.91	27.67	27.49	27.35
4	21.20	18.00	16.69	15.98	15.52	15.21	14.98	14.80	14.66
5	16.26	13.27	12.06	11.39	10.97	10.67	10.46	10.29	10.16
6	13.75	10.92	9.78	9.15	8.75	8.47	8.26	8.10	7.98
7	12.25	9.55	8.45	7.85	7.46	7.19	6.99	6.84	6.72
8	11.26	8.65	7.59	7.01	6.63	6.37	6.18	6.03	5.91
9	10.56	8.02	6.99	6.42	6.06	5.80	5.61	5.47	5.35
10	10.04	7.56	6.55	5.99	5.64	5.39	5.20	5.06	4.94
11	9.65	7.21	6.22	5.67	5.32	5.07	4.89	4.74	4.63
12	9.33	6.93	5.95	5.41	5.06	4.82	4.64	4.50	4.39
13	9.07	6.70	5.74	5.21	4.86	4.62	4.44	4.30	4.19
14	8.86	6.51	5.56	5.04	4.69	4.46	4.28	4.14	4.03
15	8.68	6.36	5.42	4.89	4.56	4.32	4.14	4.00	3.89
16	8.53	6.23	5.29	4.77	4.44	4.20	4.03	3.89	3.78
17	8.40	6.11	5.18	4.67	4.34	4.10	3.93	3.79	3.68
18	8.29	6.01	5.09	4.58	4.25	4.01	3.84	3.71	3.60
19	8.18	5.93	5.01	4.50	4.17	3.94	3.77	3.63	3.52
20	8.10	5.85	4.94	4.43	4.10	3.87	3.70	3.56	3.46
21	8.02	5.78	4.87	4.37	4.04	3.81	3.64	3.51	3.40
22	7.95	5.72	4.82	4.31	3.99	3.76	3.59	3.45	3.35
23	7.88	5.66	4.76	4.26	3.94	3.71	3.54	3.41	3.30
24	7.82	5.61	4.72	4.22	3.90	3.67	3.50	3.36	3.26
25	7.77	5.57	4.68	4.18	3.85	3.63	3.46	3.32	3.22
26	7.72	5.53	4.64	4.14	3.82	3.59	3.42	3.29	3.18
27	7.68	5.49	4.60	4.11	3.78	3.56	3.39	3.26	3.15
28	7.64	5.45	4.57	4.07	3.75	3.53	3.36	3.23	3.12
29	7.60	5.42	4.54	4.04	3.73	3.50	3.33	3.20	3.09
30	7.56	5.39	4.51	4.02	3.70	3.47	3.30	3.17	3.07
40	7.31	5.18	4.31	3.83	3.51	3.29	3.12	2.99	2.89
60	7.08	4.98	4.13	3.65	3.34	3.12	2.95	2.82	2.72
120	6.85	4.79	3.95	3.48	3.17	2.96	2.79	2.66	2.56
∞	6.63	4.61	3.78	3.32	3.02	2.80	2.64	2.51	2.41

Denominator Degrees of Freedom (left axis label)

Source: From M. Merrington and C. M. Thompson, "Tables of Percentage Points of the Inverted Beta (F)-Distribution," *Biometrika*, 1943, 33, 73–88. Reproduced by permission of the *Biometrika* Trustees.

ν_1	Numerator Degrees of Freedom									
ν_2	10	12	15	20	24	30	40	60	120	∞
1	6,056	6,106	6,157	6,209	6,235	6,261	6,287	6,313	6,339	6,366
2	99.40	99.42	99.43	99.45	99.46	99.47	99.47	99.48	99.49	99.50
3	27.23	27.05	26.87	26.69	26.60	26.50	26.41	26.32	26.22	26.13
4	14.55	14.37	14.20	14.02	13.93	13.84	13.75	13.65	13.56	13.46
5	10.05	9.89	9.72	9.55	9.47	9.38	9.29	9.20	9.11	9.02
6	7.87	7.72	7.56	7.40	7.31	7.23	7.14	7.06	6.97	6.88
7	6.62	6.47	6.31	6.16	6.07	5.99	5.91	5.82	5.74	5.65
8	5.81	5.67	5.52	5.36	5.28	5.20	5.12	5.03	4.95	4.86
9	5.26	5.11	4.96	4.81	4.73	4.65	4.57	4.48	4.40	4.31
10	4.85	4.71	4.56	4.41	4.33	4.25	4.17	4.08	4.00	3.91
11	4.54	4.40	4.25	4.10	4.02	3.94	3.86	3.78	3.69	3.60
12	4.30	4.16	4.01	3.86	3.78	3.70	3.62	3.54	3.45	3.36
13	4.10	3.96	3.82	3.66	3.59	3.51	3.43	3.34	3.25	3.17
14	3.94	3.80	3.66	3.51	3.43	3.35	3.27	3.18	3.09	3.00
15	3.80	3.67	3.52	3.37	3.29	3.21	3.13	3.05	2.96	2.87
16	3.69	3.55	3.41	3.26	3.18	3.10	3.02	2.93	2.84	2.75
17	3.59	3.46	3.31	3.16	3.08	3.00	2.92	2.83	2.75	2.65
18	3.51	3.37	3.23	3.08	3.00	2.92	2.84	2.75	2.66	2.57
19	3.43	3.30	3.15	3.00	2.92	2.84	2.76	2.67	2.58	2.49
20	3.37	3.23	3.09	2.94	2.86	2.78	2.69	2.61	2.52	2.42
21	3.31	3.17	3.03	2.88	2.80	2.72	2.64	2.55	2.46	2.36
22	3.26	3.12	2.98	2.83	2.75	2.67	2.58	2.50	2.40	2.31
23	3.21	3.07	2.93	2.78	2.70	2.62	2.54	2.45	2.35	2.26
24	3.17	3.03	2.89	2.74	2.66	2.58	2.49	2.40	2.31	2.21
25	3.13	2.99	2.85	2.70	2.62	2.54	2.45	2.36	2.27	2.17
26	3.09	2.96	2.81	2.66	2.58	2.50	2.42	2.33	2.23	2.13
27	3.06	2.93	2.78	2.63	2.55	2.47	2.38	2.29	2.20	2.10
28	3.03	2.90	2.75	2.60	2.52	2.44	2.35	2.26	2.17	2.06
29	3.00	2.87	2.73	2.57	2.49	2.41	2.33	2.23	2.14	2.03
30	2.98	2.84	2.70	2.55	2.47	2.39	2.30	2.21	2.11	2.01
40	2.80	2.66	2.52	2.37	2.29	2.20	2.11	2.02	1.92	1.80
60	2.63	2.50	2.35	2.20	2.12	2.03	1.94	1.84	1.73	1.60
120	2.47	2.34	2.19	2.03	1.95	1.86	1.76	1.66	1.53	1.38
∞	2.32	2.18	2.04	1.88	1.79	1.70	1.59	1.47	1.32	1.00

Denominator Degrees of Freedom

TABLE XI   Critical Values of T_L and T_U for the Wilcoxon Rank Sum Test: Independent Samples

Test statistic is the rank sum associated with the smaller sample (if equal sample sizes, either rank sum can be used).

a. $\alpha = .025$ one-tailed; $\alpha = .05$ two-tailed

n_2 \ n_1	3 T_L	3 T_U	4 T_L	4 T_U	5 T_L	5 T_U	6 T_L	6 T_U	7 T_L	7 T_U	8 T_L	8 T_U	9 T_L	9 T_U	10 T_L	10 T_U
3	5	16	6	18	6	21	7	23	7	26	8	28	8	31	9	33
4	6	18	11	25	12	28	12	32	13	35	14	38	15	41	16	44
5	6	21	12	28	18	37	19	41	20	45	21	49	22	53	24	56
6	7	23	12	32	19	41	26	52	28	56	29	61	31	65	32	70
7	7	26	13	35	20	45	28	56	37	68	39	73	41	78	43	83
8	8	28	14	38	21	49	29	61	39	73	49	87	51	93	54	98
9	8	31	15	41	22	53	31	65	41	78	51	93	63	108	66	114
10	9	33	16	44	24	56	32	70	43	83	54	98	66	114	79	131

b. $\alpha = .05$ one-tailed; $\alpha = .10$ two-tailed

n_2 \ n_1	3 T_L	3 T_U	4 T_L	4 T_U	5 T_L	5 T_U	6 T_L	6 T_U	7 T_L	7 T_U	8 T_L	8 T_U	9 T_L	9 T_U	10 T_L	10 T_U
3	6	15	7	17	7	20	8	22	9	24	9	27	10	29	11	31
4	7	17	12	24	13	27	14	30	15	33	16	36	17	39	18	42
5	7	20	13	27	19	36	20	40	22	43	24	46	25	50	26	54
6	8	22	14	30	20	40	28	50	30	54	32	58	33	63	35	67
7	9	24	15	33	22	43	30	54	39	66	41	71	43	76	46	80
8	9	27	16	36	24	46	32	58	41	71	52	84	54	90	57	95
9	10	29	17	39	25	50	33	63	43	76	54	90	66	105	69	111
10	11	31	18	42	26	54	35	67	46	80	57	95	69	111	83	127

Source: From F. Wilcoxon and R. A. Wilcox, "Some Rapid Approximate Statistical Procedures," 1964, 20–23. Reproduced with the permission of American Cyanamid Company.

TABLE XII Critical Values of T_0 in the Wilcoxon Paired Difference Signed Rank Test

One-Tailed	Two-Tailed	$n = 5$	$n = 6$	$n = 7$	$n = 8$	$n = 9$	$n = 10$
$\alpha = .05$	$\alpha = .10$	1	2	4	6	8	11
$\alpha = .025$	$\alpha = .05$		1	2	4	6	8
$\alpha = .01$	$\alpha = .02$			0	2	3	5
$\alpha = .005$	$\alpha = .01$				0	2	3

One-Tailed	Two-Tailed	$n = 11$	$n = 12$	$n = 13$	$n = 14$	$n = 15$	$n = 16$
$\alpha = .05$	$\alpha = .10$	14	17	21	26	30	36
$\alpha = .025$	$\alpha = .05$	11	14	17	21	25	30
$\alpha = .01$	$\alpha = .02$	7	10	13	16	20	24
$\alpha = .005$	$\alpha = .01$	5	7	10	13	16	19

One-Tailed	Two-Tailed	$n = 17$	$n = 18$	$n = 19$	$n = 20$	$n = 21$	$n = 22$
$\alpha = .05$	$\alpha = .10$	41	47	54	60	68	75
$\alpha = .025$	$\alpha = .05$	35	40	46	52	59	66
$\alpha = .01$	$\alpha = .02$	28	33	38	43	49	56
$\alpha = .005$	$\alpha = .01$	23	28	32	37	43	49

One-Tailed	Two-Tailed	$n = 23$	$n = 24$	$n = 25$	$n = 26$	$n = 27$	$n = 28$
$\alpha = .05$	$\alpha = .10$	83	92	101	110	120	130
$\alpha = .025$	$\alpha = .05$	73	81	90	98	107	117
$\alpha = .01$	$\alpha = .02$	62	69	77	85	93	102
$\alpha = .005$	$\alpha = .01$	55	61	68	76	84	92

One-Tailed	Two-Tailed	$n = 29$	$n = 30$	$n = 31$	$n = 32$	$n = 33$	$n = 34$
$\alpha = .05$	$\alpha = .10$	141	152	163	175	188	201
$\alpha = .025$	$\alpha = .05$	127	137	148	159	171	183
$\alpha = .01$	$\alpha = .02$	111	120	130	141	151	162
$\alpha = .005$	$\alpha = .01$	100	109	118	128	138	149

One-Tailed	Two-Tailed	$n = 35$	$n = 36$	$n = 37$	$n = 38$	$n = 39$	
$\alpha = .05$	$\alpha = .10$	214	228	242	256	271	
$\alpha = .025$	$\alpha = .05$	195	208	222	235	250	
$\alpha = .01$	$\alpha = .02$	174	186	198	211	224	
$\alpha = .005$	$\alpha = .01$	160	171	183	195	208	

One-Tailed	Two-Tailed	$n = 40$	$n = 41$	$n = 42$	$n = 43$	$n = 44$	$n = 45$
$\alpha = .05$	$\alpha = .10$	287	303	319	336	353	371
$\alpha = .025$	$\alpha = .05$	264	279	295	311	327	344
$\alpha = .01$	$\alpha = .02$	238	252	267	281	297	313
$\alpha = .005$	$\alpha = .01$	221	234	248	262	277	292

One-Tailed	Two-Tailed	$n = 46$	$n = 47$	$n = 48$	$n = 49$	$n = 50$	
$\alpha = .05$	$\alpha = .10$	389	408	427	446	466	
$\alpha = .025$	$\alpha = .05$	361	379	397	415	434	
$\alpha = .01$	$\alpha = .02$	329	345	362	380	398	
$\alpha = .005$	$\alpha = .01$	307	323	339	356	373	

Source: From F. Wilcoxon and R. A. Wilcox, "Some Rapid Approximate Statistical Procedures," 1964, p. 28. Reproduced with the permission of American Cyanamid Company.

TABLE XIII   Critical Values of χ^2

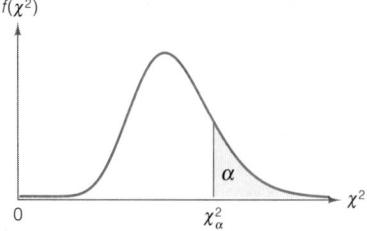

Degrees of Freedom	$\chi^2_{.995}$	$\chi^2_{.990}$	$\chi^2_{.975}$	$\chi^2_{.950}$	$\chi^2_{.900}$
1	.0000393	.0001571	.0009821	.0039321	.0157908
2	.0100251	.0201007	.0506356	.102587	.210720
3	.0717212	.114832	.215795	.351846	.584375
4	.206990	.297110	.484419	.710721	1.063623
5	.411740	.554300	.831211	1.145476	1.61031
6	.675727	.872085	1.237347	1.63539	2.20413
7	.989265	1.239043	1.68987	2.16735	2.83311
8	1.344419	1.646482	2.17973	2.73264	3.48954
9	1.734926	2.087912	2.70039	3.32511	4.16816
10	2.15585	2.55821	3.24697	3.94030	4.86518
11	2.60321	3.05347	3.81575	4.57481	5.57779
12	3.07382	3.57056	4.40379	5.22603	6.30380
13	3.56503	4.10691	5.00874	5.89186	7.04150
14	4.07468	4.66043	5.62872	6.57063	7.78953
15	4.60094	5.22935	6.26214	7.26094	8.54675
16	5.14224	5.81221	6.90766	7.96164	9.31223
17	5.69724	6.40776	7.56418	8.67176	10.0852
18	6.26481	7.01491	8.23075	9.39046	10.8649
19	6.84398	7.63273	8.90655	10.1170	11.6509
20	7.43386	8.26040	9.59083	10.8508	12.4426
21	8.03366	8.89720	10.28293	11.5913	13.2396
22	8.64272	9.54249	10.9823	12.3380	14.0415
23	9.26042	10.19567	11.6885	13.0905	14.8479
24	9.88623	10.8564	12.4011	13.8484	15.6587
25	10.5197	11.5240	13.1197	14.6114	16.4734
26	11.1603	12.1981	13.8439	15.3791	17.2919
27	11.8076	12.8786	14.5733	16.1513	18.1138
28	12.4613	13.5648	15.3079	16.9279	18.9392
29	13.1211	14.2565	16.0471	17.7083	19.7677
30	13.7867	14.9535	16.7908	18.4926	20.5992
40	20.7065	22.1643	24.4331	26.5093	29.0505
50	27.9907	29.7067	32.3574	34.7642	37.6886
60	35.5346	37.4848	40.4817	43.1879	46.4589
70	43.2752	45.4418	48.7576	51.7393	55.3290
80	51.1720	53.5400	57.1532	60.3915	64.2778
90	59.1963	61.7541	65.6466	69.1260	73.2912
100	67.3276	70.0648	74.2219	77.9295	82.3581

Source: From C. M. Thompson, "Tables of the Percentage Points of the χ^2-Distribution," *Biometrika*, 1941, 32, 188–189. Reproduced by permission of the *Biometrika* Trustees.

Degrees of Freedom	$\chi^2_{.100}$	$\chi^2_{.050}$	$\chi^2_{.025}$	$\chi^2_{.010}$	$\chi^2_{.005}$
1	2.70554	3.84146	5.02389	6.63490	7.87944
2	4.60517	5.99147	7.37776	9.21034	10.5966
3	6.25139	7.81473	9.34840	11.3449	12.8381
4	7.77944	9.48773	11.1433	13.2767	14.8602
5	9.23635	11.0705	12.8325	15.0863	16.7496
6	10.6446	12.5916	14.4494	16.8119	18.5476
7	12.0170	14.0671	16.0128	18.4753	20.2777
8	13.3616	15.5073	17.5346	20.0902	21.9550
9	14.6837	16.9190	19.0228	21.6660	23.5893
10	15.9871	18.3070	20.4831	23.2093	25.1882
11	17.2750	19.6751	21.9200	24.7250	26.7569
12	18.5494	21.0261	23.3367	26.2170	28.2995
13	19.8119	22.3621	24.7356	27.6883	29.8194
14	21.0642	23.6848	26.1190	29.1413	31.3193
15	22.3072	24.9958	27.4884	30.5779	32.8013
16	23.5418	26.2962	28.8454	31.9999	34.2672
17	24.7690	27.5871	30.1910	33.4087	35.7185
18	25.9894	28.8693	31.5264	34.8053	37.1564
19	27.2036	30.1435	32.8523	36.1908	38.5822
20	28.4120	31.4104	34.1696	37.5662	39.9968
21	29.6151	32.6705	35.4789	38.9321	41.4010
22	30.8133	33.9244	36.7807	40.2894	42.7956
23	32.0069	35.1725	38.0757	41.6384	44.1813
24	33.1963	36.4151	39.3641	42.9798	45.5585
25	34.3816	37.6525	40.6465	44.3141	46.9278
26	35.5631	38.8852	41.9232	45.6417	48.2899
27	36.7412	40.1133	43.1944	46.9630	49.6449
28	37.9159	41.3372	44.4607	48.2782	50.9933
29	39.0875	42.5569	45.7222	49.5879	52.3356
30	40.2560	43.7729	46.9792	50.8922	53.6720
40	51.8050	55.7585	59.3417	63.6907	66.7659
50	63.1671	67.5048	71.4202	76.1539	79.4900
60	74.3970	79.0819	83.2976	88.3794	91.9517
70	85.5271	90.5312	95.0231	100.425	104.215
80	96.5782	101.879	106.629	112.329	116.321
90	107.565	113.145	118.136	124.116	128.299
100	118.498	124.342	129.561	135.807	140.169

TABLE XIV   Control Chart Constants

Number of Observations in Subgroup, n	A_2	d_2	d_3	D_3	D_4
2	1.880	1.128	.853	.000	3.267
3	1.023	1.693	.888	.000	2.574
4	.729	2.059	.880	.000	2.282
5	.577	2.326	.864	.000	2.114
6	.483	2.534	.848	.000	2.004
7	.419	2.704	.833	.076	1.924
8	.373	2.847	.820	.136	1.864
9	.337	2.970	.808	.184	1.816
10	.308	3.078	.797	.223	1.777
11	.285	3.173	.787	.256	1.744
12	.266	3.258	.778	.283	1.717
13	.249	3.336	.770	.307	1.693
14	.235	3.407	.762	.328	1.672
15	.223	3.472	.755	.347	1.653
16	.212	3.532	.749	.363	1.637
17	.203	3.588	.743	.378	1.622
18	.194	3.640	.738	.391	1.608
19	.187	3.689	.733	.403	1.597
20	.180	3.735	.729	.415	1.585
21	.173	3.778	.724	.425	1.575
22	.167	3.819	.720	.434	1.566
23	.162	3.858	.716	.443	1.557
24	.157	3.895	.712	.451	1.548
25	.153	3.931	.709	.459	1.541
More than 25	$3/\sqrt{n}$				

Source: ASTM *Manual on the Presentation of Data and Control Chart Analysis*, Philadelphia, PA: American Society for Testing Materials, pp. 134–136, 1976.

APPENDIX C
Demographic Data Set

A demographic data set was assembled based on a systematic random sample of 1,000 United States zip codes. To obtain the sample, the more than 30,000 zip codes were sorted, and approximately every 30th was selected. The map in Figure C.1 shows the number of zip codes selected in each state. Note that each state is classified according to its census region: North Central, Northeast, South, and West.

Demographic data for each zip code area selected were supplied by CACI, an international demographic and market information firm, and are reproduced with its permission. CACI produces interim estimates of many of the demographic variables measured decennially by the Bureau of the Census. CACI also produces market information based on the Bureau of the Census Consumer Expenditure Survey (such

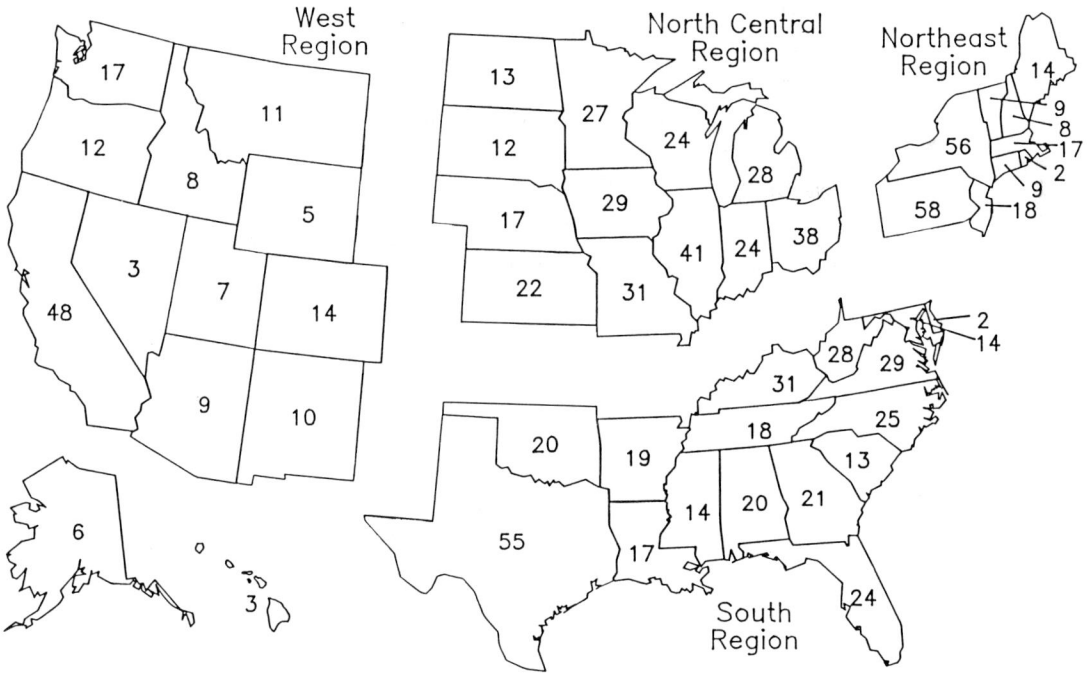

FIGURE C.1 ▲ Number of zip code areas selected by state and census region

as the four purchasing indexes given below for each zip code), which measure the relative propensity of a given market (zip code) to purchase the goods, a higher index value indicating a higher propensity to buy such goods as compared to other similar zip codes in the same census region. In general, the 1980 measurements are official U.S. Bureau of the Census estimates, while the 1986 measurements are CACI estimates.

Fifteen demographic measurements are presented for each zip code area. Portions of the data are referenced at the end of each chapter in "Using the Computer." The objectives are to enable the student to analyze real data in a relatively large sample using the computer, and to gain experience using statistical techniques and concepts on real data. Of course, neither the student nor the instructor need be bound by the suggestions in "Using the Computer"; the data are rich enough to support many more analyses than could be listed (or imagined) by the authors.

The following 15 measurements are reported for each zip code in the sample:

1. Population (1986):   Total population for the zip code, 1986.

2. Number of Households (1986):   Number of households for the zip code in 1986.

3. Age (Median, 1986):   Median age for the zip code in 1986.

4. Household Income (Median, 1986):   Median household income for the zip code in 1986.

5. Home Value (Median, 1980):   Median residential owner-occupied home value for the zip code in 1980.

6. Monthly Cost of Housing (Median, 1980):   Median monthly homeowner cost, including mortgage payments, real estate taxes, property insurance, utilities, and fuels, for the zip code in 1980.

7. Household Size (Average, 1980):   Average number of persons per household in the zip code, 1980.

8. Years of Education (Median, 1980):   Median years of education for adults (persons 25 years of age and over) in the zip code, 1980.

9. College Education (Percentage, 1980):   Percentage of adults in the zip code having a college education.

10. Women in Labor Force (Percentage, 1980):   Percentage of women age 16 and over in the zip code who are in the labor force (either having jobs or actively seeking one).

11. Unemployment (Percentage, 1980):   Percentage of the labor force in the zip code that is unemployed and actively seeking work.

12. Average Purchasing Potential (1986):   Purchasing potential index for all consumer items over the zip code area, based on the Bureau of Labor Statistics Consumer Expenditure Survey. The index compares a zip code to similar urban or rural zip codes in the same census region, with 100 set as the average value.

13. Sporting Goods Purchasing Potential (1986):   Purchasing potential index for sporting goods over the zip code area.

14. Groceries Purchasing Potential (1986):   Purchasing potential index for groceries over the zip code area.

15. Home Improvement Purchasing Potential (1986):   Purchasing potential index for home improvements over the zip code area.

Numerical codes have been assigned to each state and census region to facilitate computer utilization of these data. The codes were assigned alphabetically as shown in Tables C.1 and C.2.

TABLE C.1   Census Region Codes

Code	Census Region
1	North Central region
2	Northeast region
3	South region
4	West region

TABLE C.2   State Codes

Code	State		Code	State	
01	AK:	Alaska	26	MT:	Montana
02	AL:	Alabama	27	NC:	North Carolina
03	AR:	Arkansas	28	ND:	North Dakota
04	AZ:	Arizona	29	NE:	Nebraska
05	CA:	California	30	NH:	New Hampshire
06	CO:	Colorado	31	NJ:	New Jersey
07	CT:	Connecticut	32	NM:	New Mexico
08	DE:	Delaware	33	NV:	Nevada
09	FL:	Florida	34	NY:	New York
10	GA:	Georgia	35	OH:	Ohio
11	HI:	Hawaii	36	OK:	Oklahoma
12	IA:	Iowa	37	OR:	Oregon
13	ID:	Idaho	38	PA:	Pennsylvania
14	IL:	Illinois	39	RI:	Rhode Island
15	IN:	Indiana	40	SC:	South Carolina
16	KS:	Kansas	41	SD:	South Dakota
17	KY:	Kentucky	42	TN:	Tennessee
18	LA:	Louisiana	43	TX:	Texas
19	MA:	Massachusetts	44	UT:	Utah
20	MD:	Maryland	45	VA:	Virginia
21	ME:	Maine	46	VT:	Vermont
22	MI:	Michigan	47	WA:	Washington
23	MN:	Minnesota	48	WI:	Wisconsin
24	MO:	Missouri	49	WV:	West Virginia
25	MS:	Mississippi	50	WY:	Wyoming

The demographic data base is contained in two ASCII files, which are both sorted by census region and state within census region. The file names and corresponding layouts are given in Tables C.3 and C.4. The data files are available on magnetic tape or diskette from the publisher.

TABLE C.3   ZIPCOD01.DAT

Columns	Description
1–4	Observation number
7	Census region number
9–10	State number
12–16	Zip code
18–22	Population in '86
24–28	Number of households in '86
30–33	Median age in '86
35–39	Median household income in '86
41–46	Median home value in '80
48–50	Median monthly homeowner cost in '80
52–54	Median household size in '80
56–59	Median years of education in '80

TABLE C.4   ZIPCOD02.DAT

Columns	Description
1–4	Observation number
7	Census region number
9–10	State number
12–16	Zip code
18–21	Percent college education in '80
23–26	Percent women in work force in '80
28–31	Percent unemployed in '80
33–37	Purchasing potential index '86: Overall average
39–43	Purchasing potential index '86: Sporting goods
45–49	Purchasing potential index '86: Grocery
51–55	Purchasing potential index '86: Home improvement

APPENDIX D

ASP Tutorial

This appendix provides an overview of the ASP program. It gives the minimal hardware requirements and start-up procedures necessary to begin an ASP session on a personal computer (PC). This tutorial is not intended to replace any of the ASP documentation manuals available from the publisher or DMC Software, Inc.

Hardware Requirements

ASP must be run on an IBM-compatible PC with at least 512K of memory, two disk drives (either one hard drive and one floppy drive, or two floppy drives), and DOS 2.0 or higher. A blank formatted floppy disk is also required for data storage, unless your PC has a hard drive (i.e., fixed disk) available for storing data.

Getting Started

To use the ASP program, you must first load it into the memory of the computer. To accomplish this when starting ASP from a floppy disk:

1. Insert your copy of ASP into either of your two disk drives, drive A or drive B. (Assume drive A.)
2. Type **A:** and press **ENTER** to make drive A the current drive:

    A: ⟨ENTER⟩

3. Type **ASP** and press **ENTER** to load the ASP program into memory.

    ASP ⟨ENTER⟩

The ASP disk must remain in drive A for as long as you are using the program.

To start ASP from a fixed disk or hard drive (e.g., drive C), it is first necessary to install ASP on the fixed disk. This is accomplished by placing your copy of the ASP disk into floppy drive A and entering the following commands at the DOS prompt:

    C: ⟨ENTER⟩
    MD \ASP   ⟨ENTER⟩
    CD \ASP   ⟨ENTER⟩
    COPY A:*.*   ⟨ENTER⟩

(This sequence of DOS commands assumes the drive letter of the fixed disk is **C** and that the subdirectory in which the ASP program resides is **\ASP**.) Once ASP has been installed on the fixed disk, it need not be installed again. The ASP program can then be started at any point in the future by entering the following commands at the DOS prompt:

```
C:        ⟨ENTER⟩
CD \ASP  ⟨ENTER⟩
ASP      ⟨ENTER⟩
```

The Main Menu

The initial screen to appear as the ASP program is loaded into memory displays copyright and licensing information. After reading this information, press any key to obtain the MAIN MENU shown in Figure D.1.

The MAIN MENU is a typical ASP "bounce bar" menu. The highlighted bar can be moved from option to option by pressing the SPACE BAR, the cursor control keys ($\rightarrow \leftarrow \uparrow \downarrow$), or the TAB key. Once your selection is made, press **ENTER** to display submenus associated with the option. (You can also make a selection by pressing the letter of the desired option.)

Table D.1 gives a brief description of each of the MAIN MENU options and the corresponding chapters in the text. Several of these options contain statistical procedures that are beyond the scope of the text. Only the statistical routines covered in the text are described in the table.

FIGURE D.1 ▶
The ASP Main Menu

```
*********************   MAIN MENU   *********************
      A Statistical Package for Business, Economics, and The Social Sciences
                 Copyright 1992 by DMC Software, Inc. (Version 2.xx)
─────────────────────────────────────────────────────────────────────────

   A.  Analysis of Variance      B.  Regression Analysis     C.  Correlation Matrix

   D.  Summary Statistics        E.  Probability Dists.      F.  File Management Menu

   G.  Time Series Analysis      H.  Hypothesis Tests        I.  INSTRUCTIONS

   J.  Factor Analysis           K.  Miscellaneous Plots     L.  Crosstab/Contingency

   M.  Auxiliary Programs        N.  Enter a DOS Command     O.  Scr./Data Dir. Dflts
─────────────────────────────────────────────────────────────────────────
   F1=ALT COMMANDS MENU   F2=CALCULATOR   F3=TOGGLE PRINT (OFF)   X=EXIT
```

TABLE D.1   Options on the Main Menu

Option	Description	Chapter(s)
A. Analysis of Variance	One-way and two-way ANOVAs	—
B. Regression Analysis	Simple and multiple regression; residual analysis	11
C. Correlation Matrix	Bivariate correlations	11
D. Summary Statistics	Mean, median, standard deviation, etc.	2
E. Probability Dists.	Binomial and normal distributions	4
F. File Management Menu	Creating, saving, editing data	—
G. Time Series Analysis	(Beyond the scope of this text)	—
H. Hypothesis Tests	Confidence intervals and hypothesis tests for means, proportions, and variances; one-way table χ^2 test; nonparametric tests	6, 7, 8, 9
I. INSTRUCTIONS	A short tutorial on the use of ASP	—
J. Factor Analysis Menu	(Beyond the scope of this text)	—
K. Miscellaneous Plots	Stem-and-leaf display, box plot, normal probability plot, scatter plot	2, 10
L. Crosstab/Contingency	Two-way (contingency) table χ^2 test	9
M. Auxiliary Programs	(Beyond the scope of this text)	—
N. Enter a DOS Command	Enter and execute DOS commands within an ASP session	—
O. Scr./Data Dir. Dflts.	Set the color scheme on the monitor; set the default directory and printer port	—

Alternate Commands Menu

All of the statistical routines in ASP are accessible through the MAIN MENU. However, additional commands can be executed through the ALT COMMANDS MENU. The ALT COMMANDS MENU is called by pressing the **F1** function key from the main menu or from any menu one level below the main menu. The ALT COMMANDS MENU appears as shown in Figure D.2 on page 722.

FIGURE D.2 ▶
The Alt Commands Menu

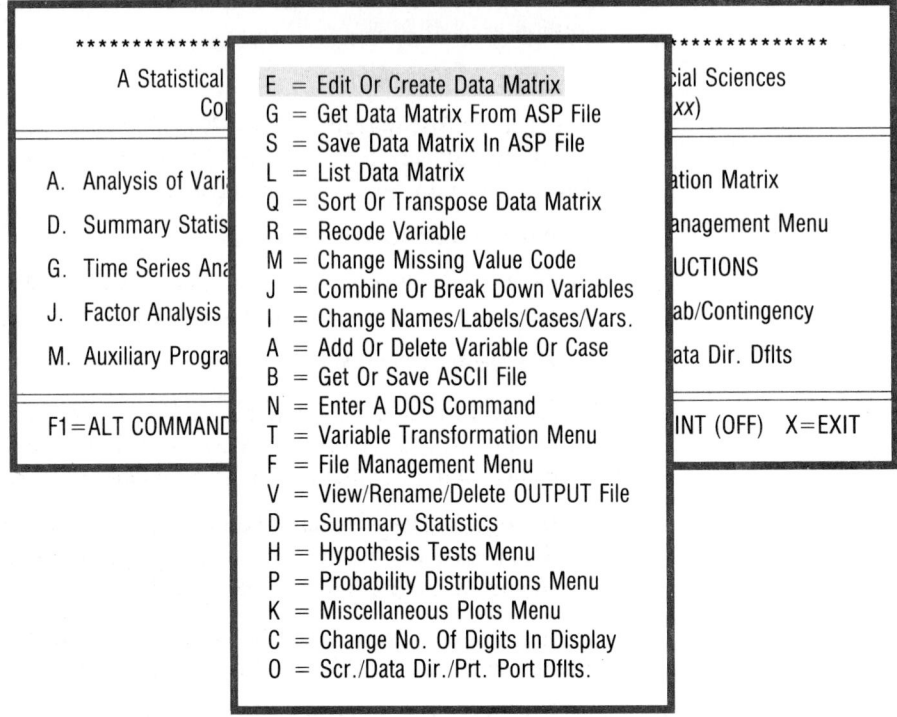

```
***********           *********
   A Statistical   E = Edit Or Create Data Matrix       cial Sciences
            Co     G = Get Data Matrix From ASP File     xx)
                   S = Save Data Matrix In ASP File
  A.  Analysis of Vari   L = List Data Matrix            ation Matrix
                         Q = Sort Or Transpose Data Matrix
  D.  Summary Statis     R = Recode Variable             anagement Menu
  G.  Time Series Ana    M = Change Missing Value Code   UCTIONS
                         J = Combine Or Break Down Variables
  J.  Factor Analysis    I = Change Names/Labels/Cases/Vars.  ab/Contingency
                         A = Add Or Delete Variable Or Case
  M.  Auxiliary Progra   B = Get Or Save ASCII File      ata Dir. Dflts
                         N = Enter A DOS Command
                         T = Variable Transformation Menu
  F1=ALT COMMAND         F = File Management Menu         INT (OFF)   X=EXIT
                         V = View/Rename/Delete OUTPUT File
                         D = Summary Statistics
                         H = Hypothesis Tests Menu
                         P = Probability Distributions Menu
                         K = Miscellaneous Plots Menu
                         C = Change No. Of Digits In Display
                         O = Scr./Data Dir./Prt. Port Dflts.
```

You can execute the commands on this menu either by moving the cursor to the desired option and pressing **ENTER** or by pressing the letter associated with the option. You will find this menu most useful for:

creating or editing data sets (option **E**)

listing data (option **L**)

getting data from an already created ASP data set (option **G**)

creating new variables for a data set (option **T**)

adding or deleting variables and/or cases (option **A**)

changing the names of variables (option **I**)

getting or saving data in an external ASCII file (option **B**)

saving an ASP data set (option **S**)

Creating a Data Matrix

Typically, you will use ASP to analyze a data set. To do this, you must first create an ASP "data matrix." Select **E = Edit or Create Data Matrix** on the ALT COM-

MANDS MENU, and ASP responds with a series of questions and prompts. The first question is:

EDIT or CREATE?   E

Note that the ASP default answer is **E** for EDIT. This is used when you want to edit an existing ASP data matrix. To create a data matrix, press the letter **C** (for CREATE). You are now prompted with the question:

Number of Variables?   1

Change the default to the correct number and press **ENTER**. ASP creates names for the variables using the convention Var1, Var2, Var3, etc., then asks:

Are Names OK?   Y

To change the name, Press **N** (for No). ASP will then ask you to enter the new name of each variable. Once this is completed, ASP will prompt you, one case (i.e., one observation) and one variable at a time, to enter the data into the data matrix.

Important: The ASP data editor will not accept letters or special characters (e.g., dollar sign, comma) as data. Only whole numbers or numbers with decimals should be entered into the data matrix.

When data entry is complete, press **X** to exit the numerical data editor. Several questions will be asked, the most important being:

Do You Wish to Save the Data Matrix?   Y

Answer "yes" by pressing **ENTER**. ASP will then ask for the drive letter (e.g., drive A) and directory of the disk where you want to save the data:

DATA DIRECTORY: A:

If the default is correct, press **ENTER**. Otherwise, enter the correct drive/path. You will be asked to name the ASP data file, provide a file label (optional), and whether you want to save all variables and all cases.

Suppose you enter the following file name:

File Name: MYDATA

ASP will save your data matrix in the ASP file named MYDATA.ASP in the directory specified earlier. In future ASP sessions, you can access this data set by first selecting the option **G = Get Data Matrix from ASP File** from the ALT COMMANDS MENU, and then selecting MYDATA from the resulting menu-list of ASP data files.

Analyzing a Data Matrix

To analyze an ASP data matrix that you have just created or accessed, return to the MAIN MENU by pressing **X** or **ESC**. From the MAIN MENU, select the desired statistical routine. Each choice will result in a series of submenus, prompts, and/or questions similar to those shown previously. After making your selections, ASP will perform the analysis and display the results immediately on the monitor screen. ASP menu selections at the bottom of the screen permit you to send the output directly to a printer or to save the output in a file for future use.

Available Documentation

ASP User's Manual (by DMC Software, Inc.)—available free to adopters of the text from the publisher of the text, Prentice Hall.

ASP Tutorial and Student Guide (by George Blackford)—can be purchased directly from DMC Software, Inc., or from your campus bookstore.

Answers to Exercises

··

Chapter 1

1.7a. Population: all the students in the class; variable: GPA of a student in the class   **b.** Census   **c.** Sample   **d.** 100% **e.** No   **1.8** Every member of the class must have an equal chance of being selected.   **1.9a.** All citizens of the United States   **b.** View of each citizen as to whether the president is doing a good or bad job   **c.** The 2,000 individuals selected for the poll   **d.** Estimate the proportion of all citizens who believe the president is doing a good job.   **1.10a.** All citizens of the United States   **b.** The rating of the presidential job performance from 0 to 100   **b.** The rating of the presidential job performance from 0 to 100   **c.** The 2,000 individuals selected for the poll   **d.** The average job performance rating of the president by all citizens   **1.11a.** The set of Fortune 500 companies   **b.** The number of new employees the company is likely to hire in the coming year   **c.** The 50 companies selected from the 500 companies   **d.** Estimate the number of new employees the Fortune 500 companies are likely to hire in the coming year.   **e.** Inferential statistics   **f.** Descriptive statistics **1.12a.** The process of filling beverage cans with soft drink at CCSB's Wakefield plant   **b.** The amount of carbon dioxide added to each can of beverage   **c.** The total number of cans selected   **d.** Estimate the mean amount of carbon dioxide added to all the cans on the process line.   **e.** Population   **1.13a.** Population: the set of all medical doctors; variable: whether the doctor was involved in one or more malpractice suits   **b.** Sample: the 500 doctors; inference: estimate the proportion of all medical doctors who have been involved in one or more malpractice suits   **c.** All medical doctors had an equal chance of being selected for the sample.   **1.14a.** The 497 corporations listed on the New York Stock Exchange who acquired control of the assets of another firm that resulted in the listing of the acquired firms' stock during the period from 1958 to 1980   **b.** The change in the value of the holdings of the bidder firm's bondholders   **c.** The 38 corporations selected   **d.** Estimate the proportion of all firms whose value of the holdings increased as a result of the merger. **1.15a.** All companies that offer job-sharing   **b.** Whether the firm's director was satisfied or not with the productivity of workers who shared jobs   **c.** The 100 firms selected   **d.** Estimate the proportion of all firms that offer job-sharing that are satisfied with the productivity of their workers with shared jobs.   **1.16a.** All department store executives   **b.** Job satisfaction of the executives and "Machiavellian" rating of each executive   **c.** The 218 department store executives selected **d.** Executives with higher job satisfaction scores are likely to have a lower "Mach" rating.   **1.17a.** Population: all RV owners in the United States; variable: preferences with respect to the features of a portable generator (e.g., size, manual or electric start, etc.); sample: the 1,052 RV owners who returned the questionnaire; inference: estimate the true proportion of RV owners who like each feature suggested on the questionnaires   **1.18a.** The distribution of pipes, valves, and fittings to the refining, chemical, and petrochemical industries by Wallace Company of Houston   **b.** Speed of the deliveries, accuracy of the invoices; quality of the packaging of the products   **c.** The total numbers of questionnaires received   **d.** Estimate the mean speed of its deliveries to all its customers; estimate the mean accuracy of its deliveries to all its customers; estimate the mean rating of the quality of its packaging to all its customers.

Chapter 2

2.2a. Interval   **b.** Nominal   **c.** Ordinal   **d.** Ratio   **2.3** Qualitative; qualitative   **2.4a.** Ratio   **b.** Nominal   **c.** Ratio **d.** Ordinal   **e.** Nominal   **f.** Ratio   **2.5a.** Nominal   **b.** Ratio   **c.** Ratio   **d.** Ratio   **e.** Interval   **2.6a.** Qualitative **b.** Quantitative   **c.** Quantitative   **d.** Qualitative   **e.** Quantitative   **2.7** I. Nominal, II. Ratio, III. Ordinal, IV. Nominal, V. Ordinal, VI. Ratio   **2.8a.** Quantitative   **b.** Quantitative   **c.** Quantitative   **d.** Qualitative   **e.** (a) Ratio (b) Ratio (c) Ratio (d) Nominal   **2.11a.** Frequency histogram   **b.** 14   **c.** 49   **2.12a.** 23   **b.** 0; 0, 1, and 2; 0, 1, and 2

2.13b. 24; .8   **c.** The area of the bottom four rectangles   **2.16** Yes   **2.17b.** Yes   **2.18b.** The number of trading days between announcement and the effective merger date is usually between 35 and 143.

2.19a.

Stem	Auto Parts Leaf		Stem	Electronics Leaf
0	7 8 8 9 9 9 9		0	8
1	0 0 0 1 2 2 3 3 3 4 4 5 5		1	0 1 2 2 2 4 4 4 5 6 9 9
			2	0 2 4 7 7
			3	9
			4	
			5	
			6	
			7	
			8	5

b. P/E ratios of firms in the electronics industry tend to be larger than the P/E ratios for the auto parts industry.
2.20a. Cigarette sales for six companies in 1985   **b.** Philip Morris; $\approx$211.8 billion   **2.22a.** 23,859   **b.** Service
2.23 Mean = 1.545; median = 15; mode = 15   **2.24** Mean = 2.717; median = 2.65   **2.28a.** 34.35   **b.** 30.6
c. Skewed to the right   **2.29a.** Mean = 180; median = 162   **b.** Skewed to the right   **2.30** 26.303   **2.31a.** Mean = 70.01; median = 68.75; 64.6 and 76.8 are both modes.   **b.** Mean = 68.83; median = 68.5; modes are 64.6 and 76.8
c. 69.0125   **2.32a.** McDonald's: $1,068,493.15; Burger King: $705,882.35   **b.** 41.67 per month; 9.62 per week; 1.37 per day   **2.33** $.35   **2.37a.** 2; 37.5; 6.124   **b.** 1.25; 1.835; 1.355   **2.38a.** 30; 200; 900   **b.** 9; 39; 81   **c.** 157; 10,069; 24,649   **d.** 9; 43; 81   **e.** 12; 102; 144   **2.39a.** 6.2; 77.2; 8.786   **b.** 28.25; 2,304.92; 48.010   **2.40a.** 5.6; 17.3; 4.1593
b. 13.75 feet; 152.25 square feet; 12.339 feet   **c.** -2.5; 4.3; 2.0736   **d.** .33 ounce; .0587 square ounce; .2422 ounce
2.41 Data set 1: 1, 1, 2, 2, 3, 3, 4, 4, 5, 5; Data set 2: 1, 1, 1, 1, 1, 5, 5, 5, 5, 5   **2.42** Data set 1: 0, 1, 2, 3, 4, 5, 6, 7, 8, 9; Data set 2: 0, 0, 1, 1, 2, 2, 3, 3, 9, 9   **2.43** No; possibly   **2.44a.** 138.2542; 139.05   **b.** 7.3; 7.4   **c.** 2.3931
2.45a. Worker A: 33.14; Worker B: 34.57   **b.** Worker A: 3.98; Worker B: .98   **d.** Worker A: .82; Worker B: 2.12
e. Choose workers similar to worker B to perform subtask 1; choose workers similar to Worker A to perform subtask 2.
2.46a. 1,325.49; 240,952.1478; 490.8688   **c.** Decrease; decrease   **2.47** Any data set; mound-shaped data   **2.48a.** Dollars; ratio   **b.** At least ¾; at least ⁸⁄₉; nothing; nothing   **2.49** At least 0%; at least 75%; at least 88.9%   **2.50a.** Miles
b. Favorably   **d.** Yes   **e.** 68%; 95%; 100%   **f.** 75%; 94.4%; 100%   **2.51** Between 104.17 and 156.25; no   **2.52a.** 61; data are skewed to the right.   **b.** No   **c.** At most 100%; at most 25%; at most 11.1%   **d.** 15%; 5%; 0%   **2.53a.** $\bar{x}$ = .1488; s^2 = .0273; s = .1652   **b.** Possibly none; at least 84%; at least 93.75%   **c.** 68%; 96%; 100%   **d.** 0%   **2.54a.** 16%
b. 2.5%   **c.** Mix A   **d.** At most 100%; at most 25%; possibly mix A   **2.55** At most 13 weeks   **2.56** .025   **2.57** At least .889   **2.58** 2.5%; 2.5%; 0%   **2.59a.** At least ⁸⁄₉   **b.** .16   **c.** Yes   **2.60** 11:30 A.M. and 4:00 P.M.   **2.61** Do not buy
2.62 Median   **2.63a.** 1   **b.** -1.5 **c.** 1.765   **d.** $-.6$ **2.64a.** $z = 2$ **b.** $z = -3$ **c.** $z = -2$ **d.** $z = 1.67$
2.65a. 3.7; 2.2; 2.95; 1.45   **b.** 1.9   **c.** Greater than 3.7; greater than 3.2; distribution is mound-shaped   **2.66** $\mu = 60$; $\sigma = 10$ **2.67a.** Brazil: -3.825; Egypt: 1.745; France: -2.787; Italy: -5.510; Japan: -56.326; Mexico: -5.689; Panama: .387; Soviet Union: 1.055; Sweden: -2.864; Turkey: .622   **b.** Japan: $z = -2.81$; Soviet Union: $z = .48$ **2.68** United States: $z = -.29$; Australia: $z = .32$; Japan: $z = -1.35$ **2.69** 1989: 69.4th percentile; 1984: 85.8th percentile   **2.70a.** .4
b. .4 above the mean   **c.** No   **2.71a.** 68%; 100%   **b.** 31   **c.** Large store: $z = 2$; rival store: $z = 3$; large store
2.72a. Greenspan: $z = -.20$; Wilson: $z = 1.93$ **b.** Average = 8.82%; standard deviation = .61%   **2.73a.** At most 25%; undetermined; at most 11.1%   **b.** 1.5   **2.74a.** $\approx$2.5%; $\approx$16%; $\approx$0%   **b.** 3.5   **c.** Over $190   **2.76** IQR = 25; lower inner fence = 22.5; upper inner fence = 122.5; lower outer fence = -15; upper outer fence = 160   **2.77a.** 39   **b.** 31.5; 45   **c.** 13.5   **d.** Skewed to the left   **e.** 50%; 75%   **2.80c.** A: 84 and 100 are outliers, 122 and 196 may be outliers; B: 40.4 and 206.4 may be outliers.   **2.81a.** Highest: 3.03; lowest: -2.68; mean: 0   **b.** 14,000, 37,200, and 40,000

2.82a. Washington Post (15.50)   **b.** 3.75   **2.83b.** 238, 268, 269, and 264   **c.** 238: 192; 268: 2.06; 269: 2.13; 264: 3.14
2.84a. Honda   **b.** Honda   **c.** Ford   **d.** Honda; 51.1   **2.85a.** Ratio   **b.** Nominal   **c.** Interval   **d.** Ordinal
e. (a) Quantitative; (b) Qualitative; (c) Quantitative; (d) Qualitative   **2.86** Median is preferred to the mean when a data set
has extreme values present.   **2.87a.** 239; 29; 841   **b.** 634; 50; 2,500   **c.** 254; 2; 4   **d.** 10,004; 102; 10,404   **2.88a.** 17.7;
4.21   **b.** 33.5; 5.79   **c.** 50.67; 7.12   **d.** 2,467.67; 49.68   **2.89b.** Add scale to vertical axis; start scale at 0.
2.92a. 3.1234   **b.** 9.0233   **c.** 9.7857   **2.93a.** 11.65   **b.** 6.6441   **c.** At least 75%; 29   **2.95a.** Skewed to the right
b. Chebyshev's theorem   **c.** At least 38 homes   **d.** $z = 3.33$; no   **2.96a.** 63   **b.** 14; 1   **2.97a.** Frequency bar chart
c. 70% of the imprints were successful.   **2.102** The amount spent by all consumers who bought new cars in 1985
2.106a. Marketing: $z = .67$; engineering: $z = .51$; accounting: $z = .77$; total: $z = .52$ **b.** Marketing: 12.51; engineering:
16.56; accounting: 22.43; total: 33.92   **c.** Marketing: 9.93; engineering: 12.72; accounting: 16.17; total: 27.10
d. 2-standard-deviation guideline   **2.108a.** Maintenance and production   **b.** Burns and back strain   **2.109a.** At least 0
b. At most 25%   **2.110a.** Approximately 68%   **b.** Approximately 2.5%   **2.112** Division B   **2.113a.** $7,500   **b.** Over
$120,000   **c.** Yes, but very unlikely since $z = 6.67$ **2.114a.** 8.0328   **b.** .70   **c.** 40; 40   **d.** No   **2.115** 0   **2.116a.** −3
b. Approximately 0   **c.** 90 or above   **2.117b.** More variability in the fill weights of operator #2 than in those of operator
#1   **c.** Yes   **2.118a.** Magazines   **b.** Magazines; newspapers   **c.** Magazines; newspapers   **e.** No   **2.119a.** United States:
$\bar{x} = 41.08\%$, $s^2 = 330.08$; Canada: $\bar{x} = 70.83\%$, $s^2 = 529.24$; United Kingdom: $\bar{x} = 60.42\%$, $s^2 = 634.27$; Sweden: $\bar{x} =$
83.42%, $s^2 = 511.17$; France: $\bar{x} = 66.33\%$, $s^2 = 1,051.88$; West Germany: $\bar{x} = 56.08\%$; $s^2 = 907.17$ **b.** Brewing: $\bar{x} =$
54.17, $s^2 = 640.97$; cigarettes: $\bar{x} = 91.00$, $s^2 = 142.00$; fabric weaving: $\bar{x} = 35.67$, $s^2 = 365.07$; paints; $\bar{x} = 40.67$, $s^2 =$
727.47; petroleum refining: $\bar{x} = 62.5$, $s^2 = 666.70$; shoes: $\bar{x} = 20.33$, $s^2 = 71.87$; glass bottles: $\bar{x} = 85.83$, $s^2 = 210.97$;
cement: $\bar{x} = 67.67$, $s^2 = 805.07$; ordinary steel: $\bar{x} = 60.67$, $s^2 = 352.67$; antifriction bearings: $\bar{x} = 80.67$, $s^2 = 390.27$;
refrigerators: $\bar{x} = 77.50$, $s^2 = 202.70$; storage batteries: $\bar{x} = 79.67$, $s^2 = 269.87$ **c.** United States; Sweden   **d.** Shoes,
fabric weaving, and paints; cigarettes, glass bottles, and antifriction bearings   **2.121c.** Brands approved by the ADA tend to
have lower costs.   **2.122c.** Yes, 18 of the 40 tires fall below the standard.

Chapter 3

3.2a. Venn diagram   **b.** $P(A) = .3$; $P(B) = .2$ **c.** $P(A) = .25$; $P(B) = .3$ **3.3a.** .3   **b.** .25   **c.** .6   **3.4a.** 126   **b.** 21
c. 1   **d.** 1   **e.** 6   **3.5a.** E_1 = loan is under $2,000; E_2 = loan is $2,000–$4,999; E_3 = loan is $5,000–$7,999; E_4 = loan
is $8,000 or over   **b.** .184   **c.** .216   **3.6** $P(A) = .31$; $P(B) = .41$; $P(C) = .81$; $P(D) = .91$ **3.7** 1/20   **3.8a.** G_1G_2, G_1P_1,
G_1P_2, G_2P_1, G_2P_2, and P_1P_2 **b.** 1/6   **c.** $P(A) = 1/6$; $P(B) = 5/6$ **3.10a.** 10/35   **b.** 20/35   **c.** 5/35   **3.11a.** Visa and
MasterCard, Diners Club, Carte Blanche, and Choice   **b.** .632, .232, .032, .105   **c.** .368   **3.12a.** 1/2   **b.** .225   **c.** .2
3.13b. 1/16   **c.** 5/16   **3.14a.** (I, S, L), (I, L, S), (S, I, L), (S, L, I), (L, I, S), (L, S, I)   **b.** 1/3; 1/3; 1/6   **3.15a.** 1 to 2   **b.** 1/2
c. 2/5   **3.16a.** .5   **b.** .19   **c.** .5   **d.** 1   **e.** .31   **f.** .69   **3.18a.** $A = \{(1, 4), (4, 1), (2, 3), (3, 2)\}$; $B = \{(2, 3), (3, 2),$
$(1, 3), (3, 1), (3, 3), (4, 3), (3, 4), (5, 3), (3, 5), (6, 3), (3, 6)\}$; $A \cap B = \{(2, 3), (3, 2)\}$; $A \cup B = \{(1, 4), (4, 1), (2, 3),$
$(3, 2), (1, 3), (3, 1), (3, 3), (4, 3), (3, 4), (5, 3), (3, 5), (6, 3), (3, 6)\}$ **b.** $P(A) = 4/36$; $P(B) = 11/36$ **c.** $P(A \cap B) = 2/36$;
$P(A \cup B) = 13/36$ **d.** 13/36   **e.** No   **3.19a.** 7/8   **b.** 3/8   **c.** 3/8   **d.** 0   **e.** Yes   **f.** 3/4   **3.20a.** 1/2   **b.** 51/160   **c.** 1/8   **d.** 3/4
e. 3/4   **f.** 5/16   **g.** A and B; A and C; B and C; D and E; D and F; E and F **3.21a.** $A \cap F$ **b.** $B \cup C$ **c.** A^c
3.22a. $B \cup C \cup D$; 7/8   **b.** E^c; 7/8   **3.23a.** $B \cap C$ **b.** A^c **c.** $C \cup B$ **d.** $A \cap C^c$ **3.24a.** Yes   **b.** $P(A) = .26$; $P(B) =$
$.35$; $P(C) = .72$; $P(D) = .28$; $P(E) = .05$ **c.** $P(A \cup B) = .56$; $P(A \cap B) = .05$; $P(A \cup C) = .77$ **d.** .74   **e.** C and D; D
and E **3.25a.** (1, R), (1, S), (1, E), (2, R), (2, S), (2, E), (3, R), (3, S), (3, E)   **b.** Sample space   **c.** .24   **d.** .10
e. .47   **f.** .62   **g.** .28   **3.26a.** 0; yes;   **b.** .45; no   **c.** .11; no   **d.** .57; yes   **e.** .68; no   **3.27a.** 20 simple events
b. .184; yes   **c.** .008   **d.** .556   **e.** .326   **3.28a.** $P \cap S \cap A$; 6 and 7   **b.** 1/5   **c.** $A \cup S$; 4/5   **d.** $P \cap S$; 3/10   **3.29a.** .81
b. .65   **c.** .41   **d.** .22   **e.** B and C; B and D; C and D **3.30b.** .25   **c.** .53   **d.** .35   **e.** .78   **3.31a.** .052   **b.** .259
c. .157   **d.** .692   **3.32a.** .85   **b.** 0   **c.** 0   **d.** .70   **e.** No   **3.33a.** $P(A) = .8$; $P(B) = .7$; $P(A \cap B) = .6$ **d.** No
3.34a. .37   **b.** .68   **c.** .15   **d.** .2206   **e.** 0   **f.** 0   **3.35a.** No   **b.** No   **c.** No   **3.36a.** 3/8   **b.** 1   **c.** 0   **d.** 7/8   **e.** 1/8
f. 0   **g.** None are independent   **3.38** $P(R \mid S) = 0$; $P(S \mid R) = 0$ **3.39** No   **3.40a.** 5/8   **b.** 1/2   **c.** 4/5   **d.** 5/8   **e.** A and
B are dependent   **f.** No   **3.41a.** .550   **b.** .450   **c.** .272   **d.** .040   **e.** .182   **f.** .857   **g.** .182   **3.42a.** .9883
b. .0117   **c.** .7917   **d.** .1183   **3.43** .005   **3.44a.** .0093   **b.** .9940   **3.45a.** .18   **b.** .82   **c.** .31   **d.** .69   **e.** .26
3.46a. .2778   **b.** .5806   **3.47a.** .3; .6   **b.** Dependent   **c.** Independent   **3.48a.** 45   **b.** 1/45   **3.51a.** (0001, 0002),

(0001, 0003), (0001, 0004), (0001, 0005), (0002, 0003), (0002, 0004), (0002, 0005), (0003, 0004), (0003, 0005), (0004, 0005) **b.** $\frac{1}{10}$ **c.** $\frac{3}{10}$ **3.54a.** .000000008; .457 **b.** .0000000014; .373 **c.** $1.284105861 \times 10^{-16}$ **3.56** Yes **3.57** .5 **3.58a.** Not mutually exclusive **b.** Mutually exclusive **c.** Mutually exclusive **3.59a.** .8145 **b.** .0135 **c.** Probability = .000475; doubt the validity of the manufacturer's claim **d.** No **3.60** 462 **3.61a.** .75 **b.** .2875 **c.** .6 **d.** .06 **3.62a.** No **b.** Employee does not plan to retire at age 68 or employee is not on the technical staff. **c.** Yes **3.63** .801 **3.64a.** $\frac{124}{153}$; $\frac{111}{153}$ **b.** $\frac{101}{153}$; $\frac{19}{153}$ **c.** $\frac{33}{153}$; $\frac{120}{153}$ **3.65b.** .95 **c.** .25 **d.** .5 **3.66a.** .26 **b.** The longer a person lives, the higher the probability of surviving until age 65. **3.68a.** $\frac{6}{30}$ **b.** $\frac{6}{29}$ **c.** .634 **3.69a.** .7127 **b.** .2873 **3.70a.** .9639 **b.** .3078 **c.** .0361 **d.** ≈ 3 **3.71** No, probability = .1 **3.72b.** .05 **3.73a.** $\frac{1}{15}$ **b.** $\frac{6}{15}$ **c.** $\frac{14}{15}$ **d.** $\frac{6}{14}$ **e.** $\frac{5}{14}$ **3.74a.** .2361 **b.** .6711 **3.75** .79 **3.76** No **3.79** False

Chapter 4

4.3a. Continuous **b.** Discrete **c.** Continuous **d.** Discrete **4.4a.** Discrete **b.** Continuous **c.** Continuous **d.** Discrete **e.** Discrete **4.11a.**

Simple Event	x		x	$p(x)$
(H, H, H)	3		0	$\frac{1}{8}$
(H, H, T)	2		1	$\frac{3}{8}$
(H, T, H)	2		2	$\frac{3}{8}$
(T, H, H)	2		3	$\frac{1}{8}$
(T, T, H)	1			
(T, H, T)	1			
(H, T, T)	1			
(T, T, T)	0			

b. x and **b. x, p(x)** columns shown above.

4.12a.

x	1	2	3	4	5	6
$p(x)$	$\frac{1}{6}$	$\frac{1}{6}$	$\frac{1}{6}$	$\frac{1}{6}$	$\frac{1}{6}$	$\frac{1}{6}$

4.13a. Not valid; $\Sigma\, p(x) \neq 1$ **b.** Valid **c.** Not valid; $p(4) = -.3$ **d.** Not valid; $\Sigma\, p(x) > 1$ **4.14a.** .3 **b.** .1 **c.** .2 **d.** .7 **e.** .9 **f.** .9 **4.15a.** 3.85 **4.16a.** .25; 3.2875; 1.813 **c.** $(-1.563, 2.063)$; .85 **d.** $(-5.189, 5.689)$; 1 **4.17b.** .56; .32

4.18a.

x	0	1	2	3
$p(x)$	.000125	.007125	.135375	.857375

c. .99275

4.19a. $E(x) = 2,450$ **b.** Firm A: $\sigma = 661.44$; Firm B: $\sigma = 701.78$; Firm B **4.20**

x	0	300,000
$p(x)$	.7	.3

4.21a. .729; .001 **b.** .243; .027 **c.** Yes **4.22a.** Bank: 173.5; finance company = 147.54 **b.** Bank: 23.37; finance company: 21.73 **4.23a.**

Disease	Hepatitis	Cirrhosis	Gallstones	Panc. Cancer
Cost	$700	$1,110	$3,320	$16,450
$p(cost)$	.4	.1	.45	.05

b. $2,707.50

c.

Disease	Hepatitis	Cirrhosis
Cost	$700	$1,110
$p(cost)$	.8	.2

d. $782 **4.24** $1,000 **4.25a.**

x	$1,000	$2,000	$3,000
$p(x)$	.25	.25	.50

b. .25 **c.** $2,250 **d.** $2,250 **4.26a.** $p(0) = .0081$; $p(1) = .0756$; $p(2) = .2646$; $p(3) = .4116$; $p(4) = .2401$ **4.27a.** .218 **b.** .025 **c.** .1296

4.28a.

x	0	1	2	3	4	5	6
$p(x)$	.000007	.000131	.001178	.006478	.024291	.065587	.131173

x	7	8	9	10	11	12	13
$p(x)$	.196760	.221355	.184462	.110677	.045277	.011319	.001306

b. $\mu = 7.8$; $\sigma^2 = 3.12$ **c.** (4,267, 11.333) **d.** .955291 **4.29a.** .097672 **b.** .998684 **c.** .228845 **4.30a.** .515 **b.** .000 **c.** .999 **d.** .012 **e.** .000 **f.** 1 **4.31a.** .5 **b.** Smaller than .5 **c.** Larger than .5 **4.32** .009 **4.33a.** .006; .014; .046 **b.** .0293; .0003 **c.** .0662; .0019 **d.** .8992 **4.34a.** .013 **b.** .783 **4.35b.** $\mu = 2.4$; $\sigma = 1.47$ **c.** $p = .90$; $q = .10$; $n = 24$; $\mu = 21.60$; $\sigma = 1.47$ **4.36** $\mu = .5$, $\sigma = .707$; no; guarantee is probably inaccurate. **4.37a.** 1 **b.** .998 **c.** .537 **d.** .009 **e.** ≈ 0 **f.** ≈ 0 **g.** ≈ 0 **h.** ≈ 0 **4.38a.** 1 **b.** 1 **c.** .764 **d.** .033 **e.** ≈ 0 **f.** ≈ 0 **g.** ≈ 0 **h.** ≈ 0 **4.39a.** $\mu = 520$; $\sigma = 13.4907$ **b.** No; -3.56 **c.** No **4.40a.** Discrete **b.** Poisson **d.** $\mu = 2$; $\sigma = 1.4142$ **e.** $\mu = 2$; $\sigma = 1.4142$ **4.41a.** .265 **b.** .647 **c.** .981 **d.** Increases **4.42a.** .397 **b.** .620 **c.** .223 **d.** .955 **e.** .781 **f.** .784 **4.43b.** $\mu = 5$; $\sigma = 2.2361$; (.5278, 9.4772) **c.** .961 **4.44a.** $E(x) = 124.5$; $\sigma = 11.158$

b. 8.65 **c.** $\dfrac{124.5^0 e^{-124.5}}{0!} + \dfrac{124.5^1 e^{-124.5}}{1!} + \cdots + \dfrac{124.5^{145} e^{-124.5}}{145!}$ **4.45a.** 2 **b.** No; probability = .003

4.46a. .0000075 **b.** $E(x) = 11.8$; $\sigma = 3.435$ **c.** ≈ 0 **4.47** .193; .660 **4.48** .090; .910 **4.49** .224; .050; .05^8 **4.50** .08; yes, probability = .019 **4.51** .632 **4.52a.** .765 **b.** .116 **4.53a.** $f(x) = .04$ ($20 \le x \le 45$) **b.** $\mu = 32.5$; $\sigma^2 = 52.0833$ **c.** (18.0662, 46.9338); 1 **4.54a.** .4 **b.** .4 **c.** .6 **d.** 0 **e.** .8 **f.** .8 **g.** .6 **h.** .4 **4.55a.** $f(x) = \frac{1}{4}$ ($3 \le x \le 7$) **b.** $\mu = 5$; $\sigma^2 = 1.333$ **c.** (3.845, 6.155); .5775 **4.56a.** 4.6 **b.** 4 **c.** 7 **d.** 6 **e.** 6.2 **4.57a.** 0 **b.** 1 **c.** 1 **4.58** $d = 11.732$; $c = 8.268$; $f(x) = .289$ **4.60** .333; 15 minutes **4.61b.** .5; .2; .2 **4.62b.** $\mu = .5$; $\sigma^2 = .083$ **c.** .05; .95 **d.** $f(p) = 20$ ($.90 \le p \le .95$) **4.63** .4444 **4.64a.** .4772 **b.** .4987 **c.** .4332 **d.** .2881 **4.65a.** .2789 **b.** .9544 **c.** .0819 **d.** .9974 **e.** .4878 **f.** .4878 **4.66a.** .1587 **b.** .0102 **c.** .0049 **d.** .0228 **e.** 0 **f.** .05 **4.67a.** .6826 **b.** .95 **c.** .90 **d.** .9544 **4.68a.** 1.645 **b.** 1.96 **c.** -1.96 **d.** 1.28 **e.** 1.28 **4.69a.** $-.81$ **b.** .55 **c.** 1.43 **d.** .21 **e.** -2.05 **f.** .50 **4.70a.** -2.5 **b.** 0 **c.** $-.625$ **d.** -3.75 **e.** 1.25 **f.** -1.25 **4.71a.** 1.25 below **b.** 1.875 above **c.** 0 **d.** 1.5 above **4.72a.** .9544 **b.** .0918 **c.** .0228 **d.** .8607 **e.** .0927 **f.** .7049 **4.73a.** .0456; .0026 **b.** .6826; .9544 **c.** 1,008.4; 987.2 **4.74a.** 53 **b.** 55.88 **c.** 45.065 **d.** 53.3 **4.75** 182 **4.76** .0351; .0080 **4.77a.** .2843 **b.** .0228 **c.** 71.64 **4.78a.** 25.14% **b.** 90.375 **4.79a.** .1151 **b.** .6554 **c.** 10.50 **4.80a.** 456 **b.** 3,174 **c.** 3,174 **4.81a.** XYZ **b.** ABC: \$105; XYZ: \$107 **c.** ABC **4.82a.** .0307 **b.** .0893 **4.83** 5.068 **4.85a.** .367879 **b.** .082085 **c.** .000553 **d.** .223130 **4.86a.** .002479 **b.** .011109 **c.** .000123 **d.** .259240 **4.87a.** .999447 **b.** .999955 **c.** .981684 **d.** .632121 **4.88** $\mu = .5$; $\sigma = .5$; .950213 **4.89a.** .018316 **b.** .950213 **c.** .383401 **4.90a.** 20 minutes **b.** .22313 **c.** .049787; .950213 **4.91** .223130 **4.92** .657481; .510458; .300327 **4.93a.** .367879; .212248 **b.** .049787 **c.** Less than 58 **d.** 40.6 **4.94a.** $\mu = 23.81$; $\sigma = 23.81$; (0, 47.62) **b.** 23.81 days **c.** .716346 **d.** .864665 **e.** .950213 **4.95a.** $e^{-.5x}$ **b.** .135335 **c.** .367879 **d.** .367879 **e.** 820.85; 3,934.69 **f.** 37 days **4.96** b, c, d, and f **4.97a.** Yes **b.** $\mu = 17.5$; $\sigma^2 = 5.25$ **c.** .902 **d.** .9049 **4.98a.** .5398 **b.** .7330 **c.** .9345 **4.99a.** .488 **b.** .2334 **c.** 0 **4.100** .5160 **4.101a.** .0559 **c.** No **4.102a.** No **b.** .6026 **c.** No; yes; yes **d.** .7190 **4.103b.** 0 **c.** No **d.** Yes **4.104** .2676; no **4.105a.** .2734 **b.** .4096 **c.** .3432 **4.106a.** No **b.** No **c.** Yes **4.107a.** $f(x) = \frac{1}{80}$, $10 \le x \le 90$ **b.** $\mu = 50$; $\sigma = 23.094011$ **c.** (3.812, 96.188) **d.** .625 **e.** 0 **f.** .875 **g.** .577 **h.** .1875 **4.108a.** .6915 **b.** .1587 **c.** .1915 **d.** .3085 **e.** 0 **f.** 1.0 **4.109a.** .084 **b.** .073 **c.** .028 **4.110a.** 47.68 **b.** 47.68 **c.** 30.13 **d.** 30.13 **e.** 41.5 **f.** 38.5 **4.111a.** .451188 **b.** .406570 **c.** 0 **d.** .877544 **e.** .27387 **4.112a.** .9441 **b.** .9429 **c.** .9988 **d.** .0031 **4.113a.** Discrete **b.** Continuous **c.** Continuous **d.** Continuous **4.114a.** True **b.** .017 **4.115a.** 497,000 **b.** 6.6055975×10^{11} **4.116a.** 288 **b.** .2483 **c.** No **4.117** \$9.6582 **4.118a.** .20 **b.** .003 **4.119a.** .0918 **b.** 0 **c.** 4.87 decibels **4.120a.** .001 **d.** Yes; probability = .012 **4.121** .036 **4.122** .632121 **4.123a.** .0548 **b.** .6006 **c.** .3446 **d.** \$6,503.80 **4.124** .051 **4.125a.** 13.33 weeks **b.** .860708; .637628 **c.** .59343 **4.126** Probability of observing 400 or more who favor the product is ≈ 0. **4.127a.** $\mu = 5$; $\sigma^2 = 4$ **b.** .617 **c.** .006 **4.128** .265; .176 **4.129a.** .8264 **b.** 17 **c.** .6217 **d.** 0; -157 **4.130a.** Company A: 4.60; company B: 3.70 **b.** Company A: \$46,000; company B: \$55,500 **c.** Company A: $\sigma^2 = 1.34$, $\sigma = 1.16$; company B: $\sigma^2 = 1.21$, $\sigma = 1.10$ **d.** Company A: .95; company B: .95 **4.131** .303

Chapter 5

5.2a. Decrease **c.** $\bar{x}$ **d.** $\sigma_{\bar{x}} = 1.25$; $\sigma_A = 2.5$ **5.3a.** 8; .75 **b.** 200; 3.873 **c.** 50; .4 **d.** -10; 1.621 **5.4a.** 10; 2 **b.** Normal **c.** 1.7 **d.** $-.85$ **5.5a.** .3085 **b.** .6915 **c.** .0606 **d.** .3830 **e.** .0495 **5.6a.** .5 **b.** .5 **c.** .8413 **d.** .9772 **e.** .2090 **f.** .8975 **g.** .2005 **h.** .3115 **5.7a.** 2.5; .1904 **b.** Approximately normal **5.10a.** 6; .3536 **b.** .5222 **c.** .0793 **d.** Standard deviation would decrease. **5.11a.** 6: (chip 1, chip 2), (chip 2, chip 3), (chip 1, chip 3), (chip 2, chip 4), (chip 1, chip 4), (chip 3, chip 4)   **b.** $1/6$ **c.** $\bar{x}_{(1,2)} = 1.5$; $\bar{x}_{(1,2)} = 1.5$; $\bar{x}_{(1,3)} = 2$; $\bar{x}_{(2,2)} = 2$; $\bar{x}_{(2,3)} = 2.5$; $\bar{x}_{(2,3)} = 2.5$ **d.**

$\bar{x}$	$p(\bar{x})$
1.5	$2/6 = 1/3$
2	$2/6 = 1/3$
2.5	$2/6 = 1/3$

5.12a. (3 ones); (3 zeros); (2 ones, 1 zero); (2 zeros, 1 one)   **b.** $\bar{x}_{3 \text{ ones}} = 1$; $\bar{x}_{3 \text{ zeros}} = 0$; $\bar{x}_{2o,1z} = 2/3$; $\bar{x}_{1o,2z} = 1/3$

c.

$\bar{x}$	$p(\bar{x})$
1	$1/8$
$2/3$	$3/8$
$1/3$	$3/8$
0	$1/8$

5.13

n	1	5	10	20	30	40	50
$\sigma/\sqrt{n}$	10	4.472	3.162	2.236	1.826	1.581	1.414

5.14 No   **5.15a.** 36.515   **b.** 120   **c.** 54   **5.16a.** .0031; doubt the claim   **b.** More likely; less likely   **c.** Less likely; more likely   **5.17a.** Approximately normal with $\mu_{\bar{x}} = 10$ and $\sigma_{\bar{x}} = 2.0486$ **b.** .0446; not very likely   **c.** Forecasts very accurate   **5.18a.** Increase   **b.** Risk = 1.6   **5.19a.** 95.25%   **b.** 100%   **5.20** .0456   **5.21a.** Approximately normal, $\mu_{\bar{x}} = 840$, $\sigma_{\bar{x}} = 2.1213$ **b.** 0   **c.** $\mu < 840$ **d.** Approximately normal, $\mu_{\bar{x}} = 840$, $\sigma_{\bar{x}} = 6.3640$; .0582   **5.22a.** 16.274   **b.** 16.548   **c.** 16.411   **d.** No   **5.23** .4514   **5.24** .0082   **5.25a.** Approximately normal with $\mu_{\bar{x}}$ unknown and $\sigma_{\bar{x}} = .0717$ **b.** Approximately normal with $\mu_{\bar{y}}$ unknown and $\sigma_{\bar{y}} = .0536$ **c.** 502   **5.26a.** Market values of all single-family homes in a particular county in 1994   **b.** .5   **c.** .8904   **5.27a.** 1.5%   **b.** .0026   **c.** .1587   **5.28a.** 1.1775% and 2.8225%   **b.** .9131   **5.29a.** .05   **b.** 1   **c.** .000625   **5.30a.** Approximately normal with $\mu_{\bar{x}} = 75.11$ and $\sigma_{\bar{x}} = .025$ **b.** 0   **c.** Yes   **5.31** .9332   **5.32a.** Approximately normal with mean 7,500 and standard deviation 246.475   **b.** .9576   **c.** .0075

Chapter 6

6.1a. 1.645   **b.** 2.575   **c.** 1.96   **d.** 1.28   **6.2a.** 95%   **b.** 90%   **c.** 99%   **d.** 80%   **e.** 67.78%   **6.3a.** 17 ± 2.720 **b.** 95% confident that μ lies between 14.28 and 19.72   **6.4a.** $26.2 \pm .96$ **b.** 26.2 ± 1.26 **c.** Increases   **d.** Yes   **6.5a.** 26.2 ± 1.271 **b.** Wider, narrower   **6.6** 95% of intervals generated by repeated sampling contain μ.   **6.10a.** Changes in rent for two-bedroom apartments in metropolitan Minneapolis between May 1989 and May 1990   **b.** $1.5 \pm .587$ **c.** No   **6.11a.** Set of amounts credit card customers spent on their first visit to the chain store's new store   **b.** μ **c.** 62.56 ± 4.65 **6.12a.** 35.442 ± 7.447 **6.13a.** Set of differences between the actual amounts owed the company and the amounts indicated on the invoices   **b.** Difference between the actual amount owed the company and the amount indicated on the invoice   **c.** 1 ± 48.84 **d.** 98% confident that the mean difference between the actual amount owed the company and the amount indicated on the invoice is between $-\$47.84$ and $\$49.84$ **e.** Not very accurate   **6.14** 480 ± 3.016 **6.15a.** 23.43 ± 1.817 **b.** 90% confident the true mean number of years of service lies between 21.613 years and 25.247 years   **c.** n is large   **d.** Yes   **6.16** ≈ 308 **6.17** $\approx 1,230$ **6.18a.** 1.7167; .8583; .5722; .2575   **6.19a.** 68   **b.** 31   **6.20a.** Yes   **b.** No   **6.21a.** 656   **b.** Wider   **c.** 38.3%   **6.22** 43; 171; 385   **6.23** 55   **6.24** 27   **6.25** 271   **6.27a.** $z_{.10} = 1.28$; $t_{.10} = 1.533$ **b.** $z_{.05} = 1.645$; $t_{.05} = 2.132$ **c.** $z_{.025} = 1.96$; $t_{.025} = 2.776$ **d.** $z_{.01} = 2.33$; $t_{.01} = 3.747$ **e.** $z_{.005} = 2.575$; $t_{.005} = 4.604$ **6.28a.** 2.201   **b.** 2.821   **c.** -3.707 **d.** -1.734 **6.29a.** 2.228   **b.** 2.228   **c.** -1.812 **d.** 2.086   **e.** 4.032   **6.30a.** 5 ± 2.132 **b.** 5 ± 2.776 **c.** 5 ± 4.604 **d.** (a) $5 \pm .865$ (b) 5 ± 1.047 (c) 5 ± 1.431 **6.31a.** 100 ± 3.72 **b.** 100 ± 5.83 **6.32a.** $3.8 \pm .464$ **b.** 90% confident that mean LOS in 1990 is between 3.336 and 4.264 days   **c.** 90% of all intervals constructed will contain the population mean.   **6.33a.** 78.364 ± 4.408 **b.** 95% confident that mean participation rate for Fortune 500 companies is between 73.956% and 82.772%   **c.** Population of Fortune 500 participation rates is normal.   **d.** Center: same; width: narrower   **6.34a.** Balance of all home mortgages foreclosed by the bank due to default by the borrower during the last 3 years; normally distributed   **b.** $67,648.58 \pm 9,939.55$ **c.** 90% confident that the true mean outstanding principal lies between $\$57,709.03$ and $\$77,588.13$ **6.35a.** All the costs of hiring secretaries in the corporation for the last 2 years   **b.** $1,901.875 \pm 213.743$ **c.** 427.486; wider   **6.36** 180.975 ± 119.605 **6.37a.** 135 ± 13.839 **b.** Population of all health insurance costs per worker per month is normally distributed.   **c.** 95% of all similarly constructed intervals will contain the true value of μ.   **6.38** Approximately normal with $\mu_{\hat{p}} = p$ and $\sigma_{\hat{p}} = \sqrt{pq/n}$ **6.40a.** Yes   **b.** $.46 \pm .065$ **c.** 95% confident the true value of p will fall

between .395 and .525 **6.41a.** Yes **b.** .88 ± .049 **c.** Sample is random. **6.42a.** Yes **b.** No **c.** Yes **d.** No
6.43a. .3 ± .083 **6.44a.** .623 ± .086 **d.** Probably not **6.45** .565 ± .120 **6.46a.** .4 ± .047 **b.** .094; narrower
6.47a. All owners and managers of small U.S. businesses **b.** Yes **c.** .4 ± .06 **d.** Narrower **6.48** .08 ± .024
6.49a. 482 **b.** 752 **6.50a.** 385 **b.** 601 **6.51** 34 **6.52** 425 **6.53** 980 **6.54** 788 **6.55** 322 **6.56** No; $n = 457$
6.57a. t **b.** z **c.** z **d.** z **e.** Neither **6.58a.** -1.725 **b.** 3.250 **c.** 1.860 **d.** 2.898 **6.60a.** 12.2 ± 1.645
b. 166 **6.62a.** 985.6 ± 25.610 **b.** Not out of control **c.** 985.6 ± 14.198; out of control **d.** 99% confidence interval
e. Breaking strengths are normally distributed. **6.63a.** 12,522 ± 784 **6.64** μ: $n = 43$; p: $n = 260$; choose $n = 260$
6.65 .613 ± .051 **6.66a.** 42,250 **b.** 42,250 ± 1,683.713 **c.** Interval estimation **6.67a.** 42,250 **b.** 42,250 ±
506.570 **c.** Interval estimation **6.68a.** .094 **b.** Yes **c.** .094 ± .037 **6.69** 818 **6.70a.** 34.76 ± 6.344
b. Population of all claims is normally distributed. **6.71a.** 853 **b.** Random sample

Chapter 7

7.1 Null; alternative **7.2** Test statistic, rejection region **7.3** $\alpha = P(\text{Reject } H_0 \text{ when } H_0 \text{ is true})$ **7.4** $\alpha = P(\text{Type I error})$;
$\beta = P(\text{Type II error})$ **7.5** Rejecting the null hypothesis when it is true; accepting the null hypothesis when it is true;
rejecting the null hypothesis when it is false; accepting the null hypothesis when it is false **7.7** No **7.8a.** Type I error: say
a person is a liar when he is telling the truth; Type II error: believe a person is telling the truth when he is not **b.** .370;
.240 **7.9a.** Unsafe; safe **b.** Type I error: concluding the drug is safe when it is not; Type II error: concluding the drug is
not safe when it is **c.** α **7.10a.** Type I error: concluding the new product is better when the current product is better;
Type II error: concluding the current product is better when the new product is better **b.** $1,200,000; $30,000 **c.** .01
7.11a. $z > 1.96$ **b.** $z > 1.645$ **c.** $z > 2.575$ **d.** $z < -1.29$ **e.** $|z| > 1.645$ **f.** $|z| > 2.575$ **g.** .025; .05;
.005; .0985; .10; .01 **7.12a.** $z = -1.47$; reject H_0. **b.** $z = 1.47$; do not reject H_0. **7.13a.** Reject H_0 if $z > 2.14$.
b. .0162 **7.14a.** $z = 1.85$; reject H_0. **b.** $z = 1.85$; do not reject H_0. **7.15a.** .1056 **b.** .0384 **c.** Yes; $z = 3.88$
7.16a. Yes; $z = 7.02$ **7.17a.** H_0: $\mu = 35$; H_a: $\mu > 35$ **b.** Yes; $z = 2.16$ **7.18a.** H_0: $\mu = 10$; H_a: $\mu < 10$ **b.** Type I
error: decide that the equipment can inspect less than 10 joints per second on the average when it can inspect at least 10
joints per second; Type II error: decide that the equipment can inspect at least 10 joints per second on the average when it
really cannot **c.** $z = -2.33$; reject H_0. **7.19a.** H_0: $\mu = 1,502.5$; H_a: $\mu > 1,502.5$ **b.** Yes; $z = 3.74$ **7.20a.** Do not
reject H_0. **b.** Do not reject H_0. **c.** Reject H_0. **d.** Reject H_0. **e.** Do not reject H_0. **f.** Reject H_0. **7.21a.** Do not
reject H_0. **b.** Reject H_0. **c.** Reject H_0. **d.** Do not reject H_0. **e.** Do not reject H_0. **7.24** .0336 **7.25** .0768
7.26 .0166 **7.27** .0119; reject H_0 for $\alpha > .0119$ **7.28** .1442; no evidence to reject H_0 for $\alpha \leq .10$ **7.29a.** No; $z =$
-1.29 **b.** .0985 **c.** Small p-values **7.30** ≈ 0 **7.31a.** H_0: $\mu = \$9,083$; H_a: $\mu > \$9,083$ **7.32a.** H_0: $\mu = \$101,335$;
H_a: $\mu > \$101,335$ **b.** .0174; reject H_0 for $\alpha \geq .0174$. **7.33a.** Do not reject H_0 for $\alpha = .05$; reject H_0 for $\alpha = .10$.
b. .1706; do not reject H_0 for $\alpha \leq .10$. **7.35** Population is approximately normal and σ is unknown. **7.37a.** .10
b. .05 **c.** .05 **7.38a.** $t = -1.76$; do not reject H_0. **b.** $t = -1.76$; do not reject H_0. **7.39a.** .05 < p-value < .10
b. .10 < p-value < .20 **7.40a.** 10.178 ± 1.202 **b.** 2.015 **7.41a.** Random sample from a normal population
b. Reject H_0 for $\alpha > .0382$. **c.** .0764; reject H_0 for $\alpha = .10$. **7.42a.** Yes; $t = -3$ **b.** .01 < p-value < .02
c. Population of content weights that is approximately normal **d.** 19.7 ± .186 **7.43** Yes; $t = -4.193$ **7.44a.** H_0: $\mu =$
1,047.34; H_a: $\mu > 1,047.34$ **b.** $t = 2.36$; reject H_0. **7.45a.** No, $t = 1.113$ **b.** Population of differences is normal.
7.46a. H_0: $\mu = .004$; H_a: $\mu > .004$ **c.** Plant 1: no evidence to reject H_0 for $\alpha \leq .10$; Plant 2: no evidence to reject H_0 for
$\alpha = .05$ **7.47** When the population is not normal **7.48a.** .5 **b.** .5 **c.** Cannot be determined **d.** .5
7.49a. .035 **b.** .363 **c.** .004 **d.** .1515 **e.** .2119 **7.50a.** $S = 6$, p-value = .377; do not reject H_0. **b.** $S = 6$,
p-value = .754; do not reject H_0. **c.** $S = 9$, p-value = .011; reject H_0. **d.** $S = 9$, p-value = .022; reject H_0.
e. (a) p-value $\approx .3745$; (b) p-value $\approx .7490$; (c) p-value $\approx .0136$; (d) p-value $\approx .0272$ **7.51** $S = 17$, p-value = .054; reject
H_0. **7.52a.** 43 **b.** H_0: $M = 37$; H_a: $M > 37$ **c.** $S = 11$, p-value = .059; do not reject H_0 at $\alpha = .05$; reject H_0 for
$\alpha > .059$. **d.** Yes **7.53a.** Sign test **b.** H_0: $M = 30$; H_a: $M < 30$ **c.** $S = 5$; reject H_0 if p-value < .01. **d.** p-value =
.109; do not reject H_0. **7.54a.** $S = 17$, p-value = .0329; reject H_0. **b.** .0329 **7.55a.** Yes **b.** No **c.** Yes **d.** No
e. No **7.56b.** $z = -1.53$; do not reject H_0. **c.** .0630 **7.57a.** -2.33 **c.** Reject H_0. **d.** .0099 **7.58a.** No
b. p-value would double. **7.59a.** $z = 1.13$; do not reject H_0. **b.** .1292 **7.60a.** Yes; $z = 2.31$ **b.** Yes **c.** .0104
7.61a. $z = -4.83$; reject H_0. **b.** Yes **c.** No; $z = -.48$ **7.62** 0; .3156 **7.63a.** Yes; $z = 2.66$ **b.** .0039 **7.64a.** H_0:

$p = .52$; H_a: $p < .52$ **c.** Do not reject H_0 for $\alpha \leq .10$.   **d.** p-value would double.   **7.65** Yes; $z = 2.80$ **7.66** Power = $1 - \beta$ **7.68a.** Approximately normal with $\mu_{\bar{x}} = 500$ and $\sigma_{\bar{x}} = 20$ **b.** 532.9   **d.** .1949   **e.** .8051   **7.69a.** .0174
b. .9826   **7.70a.** Approximately normal with $\mu_{\bar{x}} = 75$ and $\sigma_{\bar{x}} = 2.143$ **b.** Approximately normal with $\mu_{\bar{x}} = 70$ and $\sigma_{\bar{x}} = 2.143$ **c.** .1469   **d.** .8531   **7.71** .3632   **7.72a.** .7910; .4522; .1469; .0233; .0018   **c.** .62   **d.** .2090; .5478; .8531; .9767; .9982   **7.73a.** Approximately normal with $\mu_{\bar{x}} = 30$ and $\sigma_{\bar{x}} = .109$.   **b.** Approximately normal with $\mu_{\bar{x}} = 29.8$ and $\sigma_{\bar{x}} = .109$ **c.** .5359   **d.** .0409   **7.74a.** .1949; Type II error   **b.** .05; Type I error   **c.** .8051   **7.75** .1075
7.76a. .1251; .2578; .4404; .6406; .8051   **c.** .5438   **d.** 1; 0   **7.77** .2090; .5080; .8051; .9545; .9941   **7.78** Null hypothesis, alternative hypothesis, and rejection region based on α **7.79** Alternative   **7.81a.** H_0: Individual does not have the disease; H_a: Individual does have the disease   **b.** Type I error: false positive; Type II error: false negative   **c.** Minimize β **7.82** Small   **7.83** As α decreases, β increases for a fixed value of the parameter and a fixed sample size.   **7.84a.** No; $z = 1.41$ **b.** Small   **c.** .0793   **7.85a.** Decide not to halt production when mean amount of PCB exceeds 3 parts per million   **b.** .8212   **c.** .1788   **d.** $\beta = .3121$; power = .6879   **7.86a.** No   **b.** $\beta = .5910$; power = .4090   **c.** Increases   **7.87a.** No; $t = .93$ **c.** $S = 4$, p-value = .344; do not reject H_0.   **7.88** No; $t = -1.28$ **7.89** p-value $> .10$
7.90a. Yes; $z = -3.03$ **7.91** .0012   **7.92** .7422; .2578   **7.93** $z = 3.79$; reject H_0 **7.94a.** H_0: $\mu = 1$; H_a: $\mu > 1$
b. Rejection region: $t > 1.345$ **c.** Population of beta coefficients of technology stocks is normally distributed.   **d.** $t = 2.41$; reject H_0.   **e.** $.01 < p$-value $< .025$ **7.95a.** Reject H_0 at $\alpha = .10$.   **b.** .0152   **7.96** $z = 1.41$; do not reject H_0.
7.97 .0793   **7.98a.** Concluding the newsletter does not significantly increase the odds of winning when in fact it does
b. .8264   **c.** .7389   **7.99a.** H_0: $p = .5$; H_a: $p > .5$ **b.** Reject H_0 for $\alpha > .0329$.

Chapter 8

8.1a. 150 ± 6 **b.** 150 ± 8 **c.** $\mu_{\bar{x}_1 - \bar{x}_2} = 0$; $\sigma_{\bar{x}_1 - \bar{x}_2} = 5$ **d.** 0 ± 10 **e.** Variability of the difference between independent sample means is larger than the variability of individual sample means.   **8.2a.** $\mu_{\bar{x}_1} = 12$; $\sigma_{\bar{x}_1} = .5$ **b.** $\mu_{\bar{x}_2} = 10$; $\sigma_{\bar{x}_2} = .375$ **c.** $\mu_{\bar{x}_1 - \bar{x}_2} = 2$; $\sigma_{\bar{x}_1 - \bar{x}_2} = .625$ **d.** Yes   **8.3a.** $z = .4$ **b.** .3446   **c.** .6554   **d.** .9726   **8.4a.** .5
c. Yes   **d.** $|z| > 1.96$ **e.** $z = -42.2$; reject H_0.   **f.** $-11.1 \pm .98$ **g.** Confidence interval   **8.5a.** Reject H_0 for $\alpha \leq .10$.   **b.** p-value = $.1150/2 = .0575$; do not reject H_0 for $\alpha = .05$.   **8.6a.** Yes; $z = -2.76$ **b.** .0029   **c.** Samples are independent and randomly selected.   **d.** No   **8.7a.** Yes; $z = -2.78$ **b.** .0027   **8.8** -1.9 ± 1.123 **8.9a.** Yes; $z = 12.71$, p-value = 0   **b.** Type I error: decide there is a significant decline in the average number of defects when there is not; Type II error: decide there is not a significant decline in the average number of defects when there is a significant decline   **8.10** $z = 1.96$; reject H_0.   **8.11b.** Yes; $z = 4.27$ **c.** 0   **8.12** $1.9 \pm .87$; wider   **8.13a.** Asking prices for all houses in both Edina and St. Louis Park   **b.** Mean asking prices for all houses in both Edina and St. Louis Park   **c.** Yes; $z = 2.30$ **d.** $108,842 \pm 41,654.21$ **8.14** Normal distributions and equal variances; randomly and independently selected
8.15a. No   **b.** No   **c.** No   **d.** Yes   **e.** No   **8.17a.** 110   **b.** 14.5714   **c.** .1821   **d.** 2,741.9355   **e.** Near the variance with the larger sample size   **8.18a.** .4263   **b.** Yes; $t = -2.27$ **c.** $.01 < p$-value $< .025$ **d.** $-.897 \pm .725$
e. Confidence interval   **8.19a.** 15.3612   **b.** Yes; $t = -5.35$ **c.** p-value $< .01$ **d.** -8 ± 3.077 **8.20a.** No; $t = .013$
b. 10.025 ± 4.817 **8.21a.** H_0: $\mu_1 - \mu_2 = 0$; H_a: $\mu_1 - \mu_2 > 0$ **b.** $t = 2.616$, $.01 < p$-value $< .025$; reject H_0.
8.22a. Yes, $t = 3.19$ **b.** 5 ± 2.676 **8.23a.** Yes; $t = -1.96$ **c.** $.05 < p$-value $< .10$ **d.** -7.4 ± 6.382 **8.24a.** No; $t = -.81$ **b.** $-.0184 \pm .0446$ **8.25a.** Yes; $t = 4.46$ **b.** $.001 < p$-value $< .005$ **8.26a.** H_0: $\mu_1 - \mu_2 = 0$; H_a: $\mu_1 - \mu_2 \neq 0$ **b.** Do not reject H_0 for $\alpha \leq .10$.   **8.27a.** $t > 1.796$ **b.** $t > 1.319$ **c.** $t > 3.182$ **d.** $t > 2.998$
8.28a. $\bar{x}_D = -8.2$; $s_D = 3.8987$ **c.** Yes; $t = -4.70$ **d.** $.002 < p$-value $< .01$ **e.** Population of differences is normal.   **8.29** -8.2 ± 4.84 **8.30a.** $t < -1.333$ **b.** $t = -3.24$; reject H_0.   **d.** -3.5 ± 1.88 **e.** Confidence interval   **8.32a.** $t = -1.14$; do not reject H_0.   **b.** p-value $> .20$ **8.33a.** Each pair came from the same house.   **b.** Houses
c. $t = 1.866$; reject H_0.   **8.34a.** Yes; $t = -1.92$ **8.35a.** No; $t = .078$ **b.** 3.3 ± 1.874 **8.36a.** Yes; $t = 7.68$ **b.** .01
d. $.4167 \pm .1395$ **8.37a.** No; $t = .40$ **b.** $.4167 \pm 2.2963$ **d.** No   **8.38a.** H_0: $\mu_D = 0$; H_a: $\mu_D \neq 0$ **b.** Reject H_0; no   **d.** Yes   **8.39** $n_1 = n_2 = 34$ **8.40** 41   **8.41** 40   **8.42** $n_1 = n_2 = 1,729$ **8.43** 293   **8.44** 42   **8.45** 38   **8.46** 55
8.47a. T_B; $T_B \leq 35$ or $T_B \geq 67$ **b.** T_A; $T_A \geq 43$ **c.** T_B; $T_B \geq 93$ **d.** z; $|z| > 1.96$ **8.48a.** H_0: Two sampled populations have identical distributions; H_a: The probability distribution for population A is shifted to the left of that for B
b. $T_B = 42.5$; reject H_0.   **8.50a.** $z = -4.23$; reject H_0.   **b.** 0   **8.51a.** $T_B = 53$; reject H_0.   **8.52** Yes; $T_A = 39$
8.53 $T_{After} = 86$; reject H_0.   **8.54a.** No; $T_A = 82$ **b.** No; paired-difference design   **8.55a.** $t = -1.26$; do not reject H_0.
b. $T_A = 37.5$; do not reject H_0.   **8.56a.** $z = 1.77$; reject H_0.   **8.57a.** The smaller of T_- or T_+; $T \leq 152$ **b.** T_-;

$T_- \leq 60$ **c.** $T_+; T_+ \leq 0$ **8.58a.** H_0: The two sampled populations have identical probability distributions; H_a: The probability distribution for population A is shifted to the right of that for population B   **b.** $T_- = 5.5$; reject H_0. **8.61a.** H_0: The two sampled populations have identical probability distributions; H_a: The probability distribution for population A is shifted to the right of that for population B   **b.** $z = 2.499$; reject H_0.   **c.** .0062   **8.62a.** Paired difference **b.** H_0: The two sampled populations have identical probability distributions; H_a: The probability distribution for the teleconferencing groups is shifted to the right of that for the face-to-face group   **c.** $T_+ = 3.5$; reject H_0.   **8.63** $T_+ = 2$; reject H_0.   **8.64** Yes; $T_+ = 3$ **8.65** No; $T_+ = 6$ **8.66** No; $T- = 8$ **8.67a.** $t = .802$; do not reject H_0.   **b.** $T_- = 8$; do not reject H_0.   **8.68a.** No; $t = .13$ **b.** Type I error: decide the R&D expenditures have increased when they have not; Type II error: decide the R&D expenditures have not increased when they have increased   **c.** Population of differences is normal.   **8.69** $.3 \pm 5.381$ **8.71a.** H_0: $\mu_D = 0$; H_a: $\mu_D > 0$ **b.** Paired experiment   **c.** A*ad*: reject H_0 for $\alpha = .05$; A*b*: reject H_0 for $\alpha = .05$; *Intention*: reject H_0 for $\alpha = .05$.   **8.72a.** Yes; $T_B = 19$ **b.** Doubtful that the number of accidents is normally distributed   **8.73a.** Yes; $T_- = 22$ **b.** $.025 < p$-value $< .05$ **8.74a.** Yes; $t = -4.02$ **b.** $.001 < p$-value $< .005$ **8.75a.** H_0:$\mu_1 - \mu_2 = 0$; H_a: $\mu_1 - \mu_2 \neq 0$ **b.** Reject H_0 for $\alpha > .0072$.   **8.76** Yes; $z = -4.00$ **8.77a.** Reject H_0. **b.** Do not reject H_0.   **c.** Reject H_0.   **d.** Reject H_0.   **e.** Do not reject H_0.   **f.** Do not reject H_0.   **8.78a.** H_0: $\mu_D - \mu_N$ $= 0$; H_a: $\mu_D - \mu_N \neq 0$ **b.** Hours of work: do not reject H_0 for $\alpha \leq .10$; Free time: reject H_0 for $\alpha > .047$; Breaks: reject H_0 for $\alpha > .0073$.   **8.79a.** H_0: $\mu_J - \mu_A = 180$; H_A: $\mu_J - \mu_A \neq 180$ **b.** Yes; $z = -2.07$, p-value $= .0384$ **d.** 164 ± 15.144 **8.80a.** $t = -2.96$; reject H_0.   **b.** $T_+ = 1$; reject H_0.   **8.81** Yes; $T_{Before} = 132.5$

Chapter 9

9.3a. No   **b.** No   **c.** Yes   **d.** No   **e.** Yes   **9.4a.** $z < -2.33$ **b.** $z < -1.96$ **c.** $z < -1.645$ **d.** $z < -1.28$ **9.5a.** $\hat{p}_1 = .235$; $\hat{p}_2 = .327$ **b.** $|z| > 1.645$ **c.** $z = -2.09$; reject H_0.   **d.** .0366   **f.** $-.092 \pm .1015$ **9.6a.** $z <$ -1.96 **b.** $z = -2.55$; reject H_0.   **c.** .0054   **e.** $-.053 \pm .0266$ **9.7** $z = 1.14$; do not reject H_0.   **9.8a.** H_0: $p_1 - p_2 =$ 0; H_a: $p_1 - p_2 \neq 0$ **b.** Yes   **c.** $z = -4.30$; reject H_0.   **9.9** $.41 \pm .070$ **9.10a.** Age: yes; education: yes; employment: yes   **b.** Yes, $z = 5.03$ **9.11** $-.535 \pm .086$ **9.12a.** $z = -5.22$; reject H_0.   **b.** $-.215 \pm .109$ **c.** Confidence interval **9.13a.** Yes; $z = 4.48$ **b.** ≈ 0 **9.14a.** $.1732 \pm .0076$ **b.** $.0756 \pm .0064$ **c.** $.0976 \pm .0099$ **9.15** Yes; $z = 17.87$ **9.16** Less likely   **9.17a.** $n_1 = n_2 = 30$ **b.** $n_1 = n_2 = 542$ **c.** $n_1 = n_2 = 271$ **9.18** $n_1 = n_2 = 3383$ **9.19** $n_1 = n_2$ $= 812$ **9.20** Yes; $n_1 = n_2 = 136$ **9.21a.** $n_1 = n_2 = 911$ **b.** Yes   **9.22** $n_1 = n_2 = 542$ **9.23** $n_1 = n_2 = 4,802$ **9.24** 347   **9.25a.** 27.5871   **b.** 70.0648   **c.** 22.3072   **d.** 12.8381   **9.26a.** .010   **b.** .010   **c.** .900   **d.** .005 **9.27a.** $X^2 > 6.25139$ **b.** $X^2 > 15.0863$ **c.** $X^2 > 14.0671$ **9.29** Expected cell count ≥ 5 **9.30a.** No; $X^2 = 3.941$ **b.** p-value $> .10$ **9.31a.** No; $X^2 = 2.145$ **b.** Type I error: conclude the multinomial probabilities differ when they do not; Type II error: conclude the multinomial probabilities do not differ when they do   **9.32** $.286 \pm .060$ **9.33a.** Yes; X^2 $= 26.66$ **b.** No; $X^2 = 1$ **9.34** $.55 \pm .082$ **9.35a.** $X^2 = 12.374$; do not reject H_0.   **b.** $.05 < p$-value $< .10$ **9.36a.** Yes; $X^2 = 1,037.83$ **b.** p-value $< .005$ **9.37** Yes; $X^2 = 10.3$ **9.38a.** H_0: $p_1 = p_2 = p_3 = p_4 = .25$; H_a: At least one $p_i \neq .25$, $i = 1, 2, 3, 4$ **b.** Yes; $X^2 = 68.62$ **c.** $.3443 \pm .0352$ **d.** Yes   **9.39a.** $X^2 > 21.0261$ **b.** $X^2 > 22.3072$ **c.** $X^2 > 13.2767$ **9.40a.** H_0: The row and column variables are independent; H_a: The row and column variables are dependent   **b.** Rejection region: $X^2 > 9.21034$ **c.** $E(n_{11}) = 15.67$; $E(n_{12}) = 34.14$; $E(n_{13}) = 39.18$; $E(n_{21}) = 12.33$; $E(n_{22}) = 26.86$; $E(n_{23}) = 30.82$ **d.** $X^2 = 4.22$; do not reject H_0. **9.41a.**

		Column			
		1	*2*	*3*	
Row	1	42.9%	52.5%	64.3%	56.0%
	2	57.1%	47.5%	35.7%	44.0%

c. Row percentages in each column would be close to the row total percentages; no   **9.42** $X^2 = 14.457$; reject H_0.
9.43

	B₁	*B₂*	*B₃*	
A_1	28.7%	44.0%	30.4%	34.9%
A_2	49.3%	32.1%	50.7%	43.4%
A_3	22.1%	23.9%	18.8%	21.7%

9.44 $X^2 = 37.111$; reject H_0.   **9.47a.** Yes; $X^2 = 20.78$ **b.** Sprain; older employees; younger employees
d.

	Kind of Accident			
	Sprain	Burn	Cut	Total
Under 25	12.9%	56.7%	29.4%	26.50%

9.48a. Union: $X^2 = 13.36$, reject H_0; nonunion: $X^2 = 9.64$, do not reject H_0.   **b.** Union: $.025 < p\text{-value} < .05$; nonunion, $.1 < p\text{-value} < .9$.   **9.49a.** H_0: Viewing and buying are independent; H_a: Viewing and buying are dependent
b. $X^2 = 89.09$; reject H_0.   **9.50a.** Yes; $X^2 = 4.975$, reject H_0.   **b.** Type I error: conclude a relationship exists between a board's level of participation and its composition when it does not; Type II error: conclude no relationship exists between a board's level of participation and its composition when it really does   **c.** $.05 < p\text{-value} < .10$ **9.51** Yes; $X^2 = 40.70$
9.52a. No; $X^2 = 1.35$ **b.** $.10 < p\text{-value} < .90$ **9.53a.** Contra: $.17 \pm .063$; Santa Clara: $-.004 \pm .006$; San Bernardino: $.102 \pm .070$ **9.54** $n_1 = n_4 = 1,905$ **9.55a.** H_0: $p_1 - p_2 = 0$; H_a: $p_1 - p_2 > 0$ **b.** $z = .66$; do not reject H_0.   **c.** H_0: $p_1 - p_3 = 0$; H_a: $p_1 - p_3 > 0$ **d.** Yes   **9.56a.** $n_1 = n_3 = 546$ **b.** $z = 2.30$, $p\text{-value} = .0107$; reject H_0 for $\alpha > .0107$.
9.57 Yes; $X^2 = 6.58$ **9.58a.** Yes; $z = 2.60$ **b.** $.0047$ **9.59a.** No   **c.** H_0: The January change and the next 11-month change are independent; H_0: The January change and the next 11-month change are dependent   **d.** $X^2 = 2.373$; do not reject H_0.   **e.** Yes   **9.60** $n_1 = n_2 = 542$
9.61a.

		Committee		
		Acceptable	Rejected	Totals
Inspector	Acceptable	101	23	124
	Rejected	10	19	29
	Totals	111	42	153

b. Yes   **c.** $X^2 = 26.034$; reject H_0.   **9.62a.** $.52 \pm .113$ **9.63a.** $.69 \pm .039$ **b.** $-.01 \pm .058$ **9.64a.** Yes; $X^2 = 87.38$
b. Yes: 65.8%; uncertain: 25.7%; no: 8.4%   **9.65a.** $X^2 = 6.66$; reject H_0.   **b.** $.025 < p\text{-value} < .05$ **d.** $.5625 \pm .1215$
9.66a. Yes; $X^2 = 8.125$ **b.** $.01 \le p\text{-value} \le .025$
9.67a.

	1	2	3	4	Quit or Fired A	Totals
Job-matched	178	792	634	277	99	1980
Not job-matched	79	673	990	1228	991	3961
	257	1465	1624	1505	1090	5941

b. Yes; $X^2 = 895.79$ **c.** Yes; $z = 12.53$ **9.68** $.0308 \pm .0341$ **9.69** $-.0467 \pm .0839$ **9.70** No; $X^2 = 3.13$
9.71a. Yes; $X^2 = 47.98$ **b.** $.125 \pm .046$ **9.72a.** Yes; $X^2 = 46.25$ **b.** $p\text{-value} < .005$

Chapter 10

10.2 $\beta_1 = .625$; $\beta_0 = 2.25$; $y = 2.25 + .625x$ **10.3a.** $y = \dfrac{-10}{3} + \dfrac{5}{3}x$ **b.** $y = \dfrac{3}{4}x$ **c.** $y = -2 + \dfrac{8}{7}x$ **d.** $y = \dfrac{-8}{5} + \dfrac{7}{5}x$ **10.5a.** $\beta_1 = 1$; $\beta_0 = 4$ **b.** $\beta_1 = 1$; $\beta_0 = -4$ **c.** $\beta_1 = 2$; $\beta_0 = 4$ **d.** $\beta_0 = 0$; $\beta_1 = -2$ **e.** $\beta_0 = 0$; $\beta_1 = 1$
f. $\beta_1 = .75$; $\beta_0 = .5$ **10.8** No   **10.9a.** $\Sigma x_i = 24$, $\Sigma y_i = 31$, $\Sigma x_i^2 = 116$, $\Sigma x_i y_i = 80$ **b.** -26.2857143 **c.** 33.71428571
d. $-.7797$ **e.** $\bar{x} = 3.4286$; $\bar{y} = 4.4286$ **f.** 7.1017 **g.** $\hat{y} = 7.1017 - .7797x$ **10.10c.** $SSE_a = 1.2205$; $SSE_b = 108$
10.11b. $y = 1 + x$ **d.** $SSE_1 = 1.5$; $SSE_2 = 3.5$ **e.** $\hat{y} = 1 + x$ **10.12b.** Negative linear relationship   **c.** $\hat{\beta}_1 = -.994$; $\hat{\beta}_0 = 8.543$ **d.** $\hat{y} = 8.543 - .994x$ **10.13a.** $y = \beta_0 + \beta_1 x + \epsilon$ **b.** $\hat{\beta}_0 = -30,000$, $\hat{\beta}_1 = 70$ **c.** Not meaningful
d. For each additional square foot of living space, the mean selling price of a house is estimated to increase by $70.

e. $180,000; yes **f.** $320,000; no **10.14a.** Decreases **b.** $\hat{y} = 575.0287 - .00219x$ **d.** Not meaningful **e.** When salary increases by $1, the mean retaliation index decreases by .00219. **10.15a.** $\hat{y} = 36.3511 + 2.8442x$ **c.** 79.0141 cents per gallon **10.16b.** $\hat{\beta}_1 = 3.125$; $\hat{\beta}_0 = -.125$ **c.** $\hat{y} = -.125 + 3.125x$ **d.** Not meaningful; for every additional salesperson on duty, mean number of cars sold will increase by 3.125. **e.** 15.5 **10.17a.** Positive **b.** Yes **c.** $\hat{y} = -37.435 + 455.271x$ **d.** Yes **10.18a.** $\hat{y} = 141.347 - .208x$ **10.19** .3475 **10.20a.** SSE = 442.1429; $s^2 = 34.01099$ **b.** SSE = 5,022.232207; $s^2 = 59.08508$ **c.** SSE = 18,370.9217; $s^2 = 2,624.4174$ **10.21** Exercise 10.9: $s^2 = .2441$, $s = .4940$; Exercise 10.12: $s^2 = 1.14269$; $s = 1.0690$ **10.22** c **10.23a.** $\hat{y} = 7.381 + .373x$ **b.** $604.181 billion **c.** SSE = 2,225.6298; $s^2 = 741.8766$ **d.** Expect almost all of the observed values of y to fall within 1,483.7532 of their predicted values **10.24b.** Brand A: $\hat{y} = 6.62 - .0727x$; Brand B: $\hat{y} = 9.31 - .0177x$ **c.** Brand A: SSE = 19.056, $s^2 = 1.4658$, $s = 1.211$; Brand B: SSE = 4.8329889, $s^2 = .3717$, $s = .610$ **d.** Brand A: 1.531 + 2.422; Brand B: 1.771 ± 1.22 **e.** Brand B **10.25a.** Yes; $\hat{y} = 74.713 - 1.288x$ **c.** SSE = 6,341.088676, $s^2 = 352.2827$, $s = 18.769$; ± 37.538 **10.26a.** $\hat{y} = 3.068 - .015x$ **c.** 2.918; 2.828 **d.** SSE = .019263335, $s^2 = .0064211$, $s = .0801$ **e.** .1602 **10.27a.** 31 ± 1.17; 31 ± .94 **b.** 64 ± 5.08; 64 ± 4.16 **c.** $-8.4 \pm .75$; $-8.4 \pm .62$ **10.28b.** $\hat{y} = .536 + .821x$ **d.** $H_0: \beta_1 = 0$; $H_a: \beta_1 \neq 0$ **e.** $t = 3.646$; df = 5 **f.** Reject H_0. **10.29** .8214 ± .3325; .8214 ± .7581 **10.30** No; $t = -.33$ **10.31a.** .0010; reject H_0. **b.** For each additional square foot of living space, the price of the house is estimated to increase from $49.1 to $90.9; decrease the level of confidence. **10.32b.** $\hat{y} = 44.13 + .2366x$ **c.** SSE = 6,400.594072, $s^2 = 376.505536$, $s = 19.4038$; approximately 95% of the manager success indexes lie within 38.8 of the least squares line. **e.** $t = 1.27$; do not reject H_0. **f.** .2366 ± .3935 **10.33a.** $\hat{y} = 12.71 + 1.50x$ **b.** Yes; $t = 18.25$ **c.** Independence of error terms **10.34a.** Conoco: reject H_0; DuPont: reject H_0; Mobil: reject H_0; Mobil: reject H_0; Seagram: reject H_0. **b.** Increase by .14; increase by .076 **c.** Conoco **10.35** Yes; $t = -.96$ **10.36** Yes; $t = 2.56$ **10.37** Yes; $t = -4.43$ **10.39a.** Perfect positive linear relationship **b.** Perfect negative linear relationship **c.** No linear relationship **d.** Strong positive linear relationship **e.** Weak positive linear relationship **f.** Strong negative linear relationship **10.40a.** Positive **b.** Negative **c.** 0 slope **d.** Positive or negative **10.41a.** $r = .985$; $r^2 = .971$ **b.** $r = -.9934$; $r^2 = .987$ **c.** $r = 0$; $r^2 = 0$ **d.** $r = 0$; $r^2 = 0$ **10.42a.** .9438 **b.** .802 **c.** .727 **10.43** $r = .9046$; $r^2 = .8183$; no **10.44** $r = -.0166$; $r^2 = .0003$ **10.45** Price **10.46** $r^2 = .456$; $r = -.675$ **10.47c.** y_1: $r = .965$; y_2: $r = .996$ **d.** Yes **10.48a.** $\hat{y} = 44.17 - .0255x$ **c.** $t = -.03$; do not reject H_0. **d.** No **e.** .0003 **10.49b.** $\hat{y} = 1.5 + .946x$ **c.** 2.22143 **d.** 4.338 ± 1.170 **e.** 4.338 ± 3.223 **f.** Prediction interval **10.50c.** 4.644 ± 1.118 **d.** $-.414 \pm 1.172$ **10.51a.** 2.2 ± 1.382 **c.** Yes **d.** $t = 6.10$; reject H_0. **10.52a.** $\hat{y} = 1.375 + .875x$ **c.** 1.5 **d.** .1875 **e.** 3.5625 ± .3279 **f.** 4.875 ± 1.062 **10.53b.** $\hat{y} = 5,761.227 - 246.81x$ **c.** Yes; $t = -8.63$ **d.** $r = -.9502$; $r^2 = .9029$ **e.** 3,293.127 ± 102.001 **f.** 3,293.127 ± 318.358 **10.54b.** $\hat{y} = 4.861 - .3466x$ **c.** Yes, $t = -5.91$; negative relationship **d.** 1.74 ± 1.09 **e.** 2.61 ± .38 **10.55** 93.2351 ± 4.5558 **10.56a.** $\hat{y} = 5.325 + .5861x$ **b.** No **c.** $t = 15.35$; reject H_0 **d.** 28.183 ± 1.273; 28.183 ± 4.629 **10.57a.** Brand A: 3.3485 ± .5873; Brand B: 4.4635 ± .2529 **b.** Brand A: 3.3485 ± 2.2237; Brand B: 4.4635 ± 1.201 **c.** $-.65 \pm 3.606$; assume that the relationship observed between x and y extends to $x = 100$. **10.59a.** $\hat{\beta}_0 \approx 575.03$; $\hat{\beta}_1 = -.002186$ **b.** SSE = 293,208.461; $s^2 = 22,554.497$, $s = 150.18155$ **c.** .0664 **d.** $t = -.962$; p-value = .3538; do not reject H_0. **e.** (414.7, 582.3) **10.60a.** $\hat{y} = 44.13 + .2366x$ **b.** 19.40375 **c.** .0865 **d.** No; $t = 1.269$; .2216 **10.61a.** $\hat{\beta}_0 = 506.346$, $\hat{\beta}_1 = -941.9$, $\hat{\beta}_2 = -429.06$ **b.** $\hat{y} = 506.34 - 941.9x_1 - 429.06x_2$ **c.** SSE = 151,015.72376, MSE = 8,883.27787, $s = 94.25114$; about 95% of the observations will fall within ±188.50228 of the fitted regression surface. **d.** $t = -3.424$, p-value = .0032; reject H_0. **e.** -429.06 ± 801.432 **10.62a.** $t = 1.45$; do not reject H_0. **b.** $t = 3.21$; reject H_0. **c.** $s_{\hat{\beta}_3} < s_{\hat{\beta}_2}$ **10.63a.** .8911 **b.** $F = 65.462$; reject H_0. **c.** .0001; strong evidence to reject H_0. **d.** $t = -6.803$, reject H_0; p-value $\leq .0001$ **10.64a.** Yes **b.** Yes; $F = 32.12$ **10.65a.** $\hat{y} = 1.4326 + .01x_1 + .379x_2$ **b.** Yes; $t = 3.15$ **c.** Yes **10.66a.** 55.6214 **b.** Yes; $t = -2.8$ **c.** $.005 < p$-value $< .01$ **10.67a.** $\hat{y} = 20.09 - .6705x + .0095x^2$ **b.** No **c.** No; $t = 1.51$ **d.** $\hat{y} = 19.2791 - .4449x$ **e.** $-.4449 \pm .0727$ **10.68a.** Yes; $t = -3.33$ **10.69a.** $\hat{y} = 93,074 + 4,152x_1 - 855x_2 + .92x_3 + 2,692x_4 + 15.5x_5$ **b.** 33,225.9; expect 95% of the observations to be ±66,451.8 dollars from the mean selling price. **c.** $t = 2.784$, p-value = .0059; reject H_0. **d.** Mean sale price will increase by $4,152 for each additional unit, all other variables held constant. **f.** $t = -2.865$, reject H_0. **g.** .00495 **10.70a.** $E(y) = \beta_0 + \beta_1x_1 + \beta_2x_2 + \beta_3x_3 + \beta_4x_4 + \beta_5x_5$ **b.** $\hat{y} = 15.491 + 12.774x_1 + .713x_2 + 1.519x_3 + .32x_4 + .205x_5$ **c.** $R^2 = .240$; yes, $F = 11.68$ **d.** p-value $< .025$, reject H_0. **f.** Relationship between salary and tenure may depend on gender. **10.71a.** y_1: $F = 1.616$, do not reject H_0; y_2: $F = 2.148$, do not reject H_0. **b.** Greater than .10 **10.72** $F = 1.06$; do not reject H_0. **10.73a.** $\hat{y} = 295.327 - 480.838x_1 - 829.465x_2 + .0079x_3 + 2.3608x_4$

b. 46.76747; expect 95% of the observations to be ±93.5294 beds from the mean survival size.   **c.** $F = 28.180$, p-value = .0001; reject H_0.   **d.** Yes; $t = -3.197$, p-value = .003   **10.74a.** $\hat{y} = 2.41 + 1.43x_1 - .366x_2$ **b.** $F = 54.807$, p-value ≤ .0001; reject H_0.   **c.** .9400   **d.** $\hat{y} = -.349 + 2.065x_1 + .0215x_2 - .0919x_1x_2$ **e.** .9865   **g.** $t = -4.544$, p-value = .0039; reject H_0.   **h.** No   **10.75** Yes; yes   **10.76** x_1: no; x_2: possibly   **10.77a.** $\hat{y}_1 = 1.43 + .00999x_1 + .379x_2$; $\hat{y}_2 = 1.16 + .0187x_1 + .406x_2$ **b.** $s_1 = .2769$; $s_2 = .5581$ **c.** $F_1 = 100.80$, reject H_0; $F_2 = 33.88$, reject H_0.   **d.** .379 ± .0575; .406 ± .1149   **10.78a.** Yes; 26th household   **10.79** $n = 25$: normal; $n = 26$: nonnormal   **10.80a.** Decreasing   **b.** $\hat{y} = 148.055 - 7.57x$; $F = 196.615$, reject H_0; $s = 18.74$ **c.** Second-order model may be more appropriate; constant variance assumption may be violated.   **10.81a.** $F = 799.634$, reject H_0.   **b.** Assumption appears to be satisfied.   **c.** $t = -28.278$, reject H_0.   **10.82a.** Yes   **b.** .7825   **c.** $\hat{y} = -29.497 + 8.865x$ **d.** .6123   **e.** $t = 6.03$; reject H_0.   **f.** Yes   **g.** 679.703 ± 370.191   **h.** 679.703 ± 80.054   **10.83b.** $\hat{y} = 12.594 + .10936x$ **c.** Yes; $t = 3.50$ **d.** 29.988 ± 12.500   **10.84a.** 57.143 ± 34.818   **b.** Extrapolation   **c.** 44   **10.85a.** $r = -.443$; $r^2 = .1963$ **b.** No, $t = -1.85$ **10.86a.** Positive   **b.** $\hat{y} = 12,024 + 3.582x$ **c.** .7972   **d.** Yes; $t = 8.641$, p-value ≤ .0001   **e.** (12,862.6, 16,915.3)   **10.87b.** $\hat{y} = -15,124 + 76.1745x$ **c.** .9185   **d.** Yes; $t = 15.743$ **e.** 76.1745 ± 10.0350; yes   **f.** .0001   **g.** (146,713, 158,206)   **10.88** Step 1: $y = \beta_0 + \beta_1 x + \epsilon$; Step 2: $\hat{y} = 2,407.663 + 136.746x$; Step 3: assume (1) mean of ϵ is 0, (2) variance of ϵ is constant, (3) distribution of ϵ is normal, (4) errors are independent; Step 4: $t = 2.79$, reject H_0: $\beta_1 = 0$; $r = .5498$; $r^2 = .3023$; Step 5: 9,244.963 ± 17,797.970   **10.89a.** $R^2 = .45$; yes, $F = 6.38$ **c.** Yes, p-value = .002   **10.90a.** $\hat{y} = -13.062 + .742x_1 + 18.603x_2 + 13.419x_3$ **b.** $R^2 = .9098$; $F = 188.33$, reject H_0.   **10.91a.** $\hat{y} = .601 + .595x_1 - 3.725x_2 - 16.232x_3 + .235x_1x_2 + .308x_1x_3$ **b.** $R^2 = .928$; $F = 139.42$, reject H_0.   **10.92a.** Test H_0: $\beta_2 = \beta_3 = 0$ **b.** City slope = 40; suburb–city slope = 50   **c.** Yes; $t = -3.33$ **10.93** $t = -1.10$; do not reject H_0.   **10.94a.** $\hat{\beta}_1$: mean GPA increases by .02573 for each 1-point increase in verbal score, mathematics score held constant; $\hat{\beta}_2$: mean GPA increases by .03361 for each 1-point increase in mathematics score, verbal score held constant   **b.** 95% of the observations to fall with ±.80456 of the predicted value; 68% of the sample variability in GPA's is explained by the model containing verbal and mathematics scores.   **c.** Yes; $F = 39.505$, p-value = .0000   **10.95** x_1: yes; x_2: yes   **10.96a.** First-order model: ±.8046; second-order model: ±.3742   **b.** $F = 100.409$, p-value = .0000; reject H_0.   **c.** $t = 1.675$, p-value = .1032; do not reject H_0.   **10.97** Second-order model

Chapter 11

11.4 Process mean   **11.6** Stable   **11.7** Out of control   **11.8** Both   **11.9a.** 1.023   **b.** .308   **c.** .167   **11.10a.** $\bar{\bar{x}} = 80.352$; $\bar{R} = 7.948$ **b.** Centerline = 80.352; UCL = 84.938; LCL = 75.766   **c.** Upper A–B: 83.409, Lower A–B: 77.295; Upper B–C: 81.881, Lower B–C: 78.823   **d.** Out of control

Sample	$\bar{x}$	R	Sample	$\bar{x}$	R
1	20.225	1.8	11	21.225	3.2
2	19.750	2.8	12	20.475	0.9
3	20.425	3.8	13	19.650	2.6
4	19.725	2.5	14	19.075	4.0
5	20.550	3.7	15	19.400	2.2
6	19.900	5.0	16	20.700	4.3
7	21.325	5.5	17	19.850	3.6
8	19.625	3.5	18	20.200	2.5
9	19.350	2.5	19	20.425	2.2
10	20.550	4.1	20	19.900	5.5

11.11a. (table above)   **b.** $\bar{\bar{x}} = 20.11625$; $\bar{R} = 3.31$ **c.** Centerline = 20.116; UCL = 22.529; LCL = 17.703   **d.** Upper A–B: 21.725, Lower A–B: 18.507; Upper B–C: 20.920, Lower B–C: 19.312   **e.** No   **11.12a.** UCL = .9043; LCL = .4433; Upper A–B: .8275, Lower A–B: .5201; Upper B–C: .7506, Lower B–C: .5970   **b.** Out of control   **c.** No   **11.13a.** Centerline = 23.9971; UCL = 24.102; LCL = 23.892; Upper A–B: 24.067, Lower A–B: 23.927; Upper B–C: 24.032, Lower B–C: 23.962   **b.** In control   **c.** Yes   **d.** Facilitate

11.14a. Production of bolts used in military aircraft   **b.** Centerline = 37.007; UCL = 37.143, LCL = 36.871; Upper A–B: 37.098, Lower A–B: 39.916; Upper B–C: 37.052, Lower B–C: 36.962   **c.** In control   **e.** Yes   **11.15a.** Mechanical process that produces and monitors the freezer temperature   **b.** Mean temperature   **c.** Centerline = 5.042; UCL = 5.601, LCL = 4.483; Upper A–B: 5.415, Lower A–B: 4.669; Upper B–C: 5.228, Lower B–C: 4.856   **d.** Out of control   **e.** No

11.16 Process variation   **11.18a.** $D_3 = .000$, $D_4 = 2.282$ **b.** $D_3 = .283$, $D_4 = 1.717$ **c.** $D_3 = .451$, $D_4 = 1.548$
11.19a. UCL $= 16.802$ **b.** Upper A–B: 13.853, Lower A–B: 2.043; Upper B–C: 10.900, Lower B–C: 4.996   **c.** In control   **11.20a.** UCL $= 7.553$ **b.** Upper A–B: 6.139, Lower A–B: .481; Upper B–C: 4.725, Lower B–C: 1.895   **c.** In control   **11.21** R-chart: UCL $= 7.754$, LCL $= 0.306$; Upper A–B: 6.513, Lower A–B: 1.547; Upper B–C: 5.271, Lower B–C: 2.789; in control; $\bar{x}$-chart: Centerline $= 21.728$; UCL $= 23.417$, LCL $= 20.039$; Upper A–B: 22.854; Lower A–B: 20.602; Upper B–C: 22.291; Lower B–C: 21,165; out of control   **11.22a.** UCL $= .7216$ **b.** In control   **c.** Yes   **d.** 6
11.23a. Yes   **b.** Centerline $= .0796$, UCL $= .168$; Upper A–B: .139, Lower A–B: .020; Upper B–C: .109, Lower B–C: .050   **c.** Out of control   **d.** No   **e.** No   **11.24a.** Centerline $= .1815$, UCL $= .3837$; Upper A–B: .3163, Lower A–B: .0467; Upper B–C: .2489, Lower B–C: .1141   **b.** In control   **c.** Yes   **11.25a.** Centerline $= .1868$, UCL $= .426$; Upper A–B: .346, Lower A–B: .027; Upper B–C: .267, Lower B–C: .107   **b.** In control   **c.** Yes   **11.26** Proportion of defective units   **11.27** 104

11.28a.

Sample	$\hat{p}$	Sample	$\hat{p}$
1	.080	14	.060
2	.070	15	.070
3	.045	16	.055
4	.055	17	.040
5	.075	18	.035
6	.040	19	.060
7	.060	20	.075
8	.080	21	.045
9	.085	22	.080
10	.065	23	.065
11	.075	24	.055
12	.050	25	.050
13	.045		

b. $\bar{p} = .0606$, UCL $= .1112$, LCL $= .0100$ **c.** Upper A–B: .0943, Lower A–B: .0269; Upper B–C: .0775, Lower B–C: .0437   **e.** In control   **11.29a.** Centerline $= .0575$; UCL $= .1145$, LCL $= .0005$ **b.** Upper A–B: .0955, Lower A–B: .0195; Upper B–C: .0765, Lower B–C: .0385   **d.** Out of control   **e.** No   **11.30a.** 892   **b.** 172   **c.** 82   **d.** 37   **11.31a.** Yes   **b.** UCL $= .02013$, LCL $= .00081$ **c.** Upper A–B: .01691, Lower A–B: .00403; Upper B–C: .01369, Lower B–C: .00725; in control   **11.32b.** Centerline $= .071$, UCL $= .141$, LCL $= .001$; Upper A–B: .118, Lower A–B: .024; Upper B–C: .094, Lower B–C: .048   **c.** In control   **d.** Yes   **e.** No   **11.33a.** Centerline $= .0455$, UCL $= .085$, LCL $= .006$; Upper A–B: .072, Lower A–B: .019; Upper B–C: .059, Lower B–C: .032   **b.** Out of control   **c.** No   **11.34b.** $\bar{p} = .0297$, UCL $= .0591$, LCL $= .0003$; Upper A–B: .0493, Lower A–B: .0101; Upper B–C: .0395, Lower B–C: .0199   **c.** Out of control   **e.** No   **11.53** 1.645   **11.54b.** Increasing variance   **11.55b.** Level shift   **11.56** Out of control

11.57a. Yes   **b.** Centerline $= .0614$, UCL $= .1123$, LCL $= .0105$; Upper A–B: .0953, Lower A–B: .0275; Upper B–C: .0784, Lower B–C: .0444   **c.** No; out of control   **11.58a.** $\bar{R} = 7.4$, UCL $= 24.1758$; Upper A–B: 18.5918, Lower A–B: -3.7918; Upper B–C: 12.9959, Lower B–C: 1.8041; out of control   **b.** $\bar{\bar{x}} = 344.15$, UCL $= 358.062$, LCL $= 330.238$; Upper A–B: 353.425, Lower A–B: 334.875; Upper B–C: 348.787, Lower B–C: 339.513; out of control   **c.** No   **d.** .25
11.59a. $\bar{\bar{x}} = 31.468$, UCL $= 38.205$, LCL $= 24.731$; Upper A–B: 35.960, Lower A–B: 26.976; Upper B–C: 33.714, Lower B–C: 29.222   **b.** In control   **c.** Yes   **11.60a.** $\bar{R} = 5.455$, UCL $= 11.532$; Upper A–B: 9.508, Lower A–B: 1.402; Upper B–C: 7.481, Lower B–C: 3.429   **b.** In control   **d.** $\bar{\bar{x}} = 3.867$, UCL $= 7.015$, LCL $= .719$; Upper A–B: 5.965, Lower A–B: 1.769; Upper B–C: 4.916, Lower B–C: 2.818   **e.** In control   **f.** Yes   **11.61a.** Yes   **b.** Centerline $= p = .063$, UCL $= .123$, LCL $= .003$; Upper A–B: .103, Lower A–B: .023; Upper B–C: .083, Lower B–C: .043   **c.** Out of control   **e.** No

Index

Symbol	Description
A^c	Complement of event A 145
A, B	Events 129
$A \cup B$	Union of events A and B 140
$A \cap B$	Intersection of events A and B 140
α (alpha)	Probability of rejecting H_0 if in fact H_0 is true (Type I error) 329
β (beta)	Probability of accepting H_0 if in fact H_0 is false (Type II error) 331
β_0	y-intercept in regression models 496
$\hat{\beta}_0$	Least squares estimator of β_0 501
β_1	Slope of straight-line regression model 496
$\hat{\beta}_1$	Least squares estimator of β_1 501
c_j	Total count in column j of a contingency table 473
df	Degrees of freedom for the t and F distributions 306
$E(x)$	Expected value of the random variable x 186
ϵ (epsilon)	Random error component in regression models 496
f_i	Frequency for category i in a data set 30
$f(x)$	Probability density function for a continuous random variable x 214
F	Test statistic used to test global usefulness of multiple regression model 554
F_α	Value of F distribution with area α to its right 554
H_a	Alternative (or research) hypothesis 328
H_0	Null hypothesis 328
IQR	Interquartile range 92
λ (lambda)	(1) Mean of the Poisson distribution 209 (2) Reciprocal of mean for exponential distribution 235
M	Population median 355
μ (mu)	Population mean 53
μ_D	Population mean of differences in a paired difference experiment 406
$\mu_{\bar{x}}$	Mean of the sampling distribution of $\bar{x}$ 268
n	(1) Sample size, total number of measurements in a sample 51 (2) Number of trials in a binomial experiment 198
n_D	Number of differences (or pairs) in a paired difference experiment 408
n_{ij}	Observed count in cell (i, j) in a contingency table 473
$n!$	n factorial; product of first n integers ($0! = 1$) 135

Continued inside back cover

Symbol	Description
$\dbinom{N}{n}$	Number of possible combinations when n elements are drawn without replacement from N elements 135
ν_1 (nu)	Numerator degrees of freedom for an F statistic 554
ν_2	Denominator degrees of freedom for an F statistic 554
p	(1) Observed significance level for a hypothesis test 344 (2) Probability of success for the binomial distribution 198
$p(x)$	Probability distribution for a discrete random variable x 183
p_{ij}	Probability associated with the (i, j) cell in a contingency table 468
$p_1 - p_2$	Difference between true probabilities of success in two independent binomial experiments 449
$\bar{p}$	Overall proportion of defective units, used to construct p-chart 660
$\hat{p}$	(1) Estimator of binomial probability p; sample proportion of successes 313 (2) Pooled estimator of $p_1 = p_2 = p$ in test of equality of two population proportions 450
$\hat{p}_1 - \hat{p}_2$	Difference between sample proportions of success in two independent binomial samples 449
$P(A)$	Probability of event A 130
$P(A \mid B)$	Probability of event A given that event B occurs 152
q	Probability of failure for the binomial distribution 198
Q_L	Lower quartile 91
Q_U	Upper quartile 91
r	Pearson product moment coefficient of correlation between two samples 520
r^2	Coefficient of determination in simple regression 525
r_i	Total count in row i of a contingency table 473
$\bar{R}$	Mean of sample ranges for $\bar{x}$-chart, R-chart 634
ρ (rho)	Pearson product moment coefficient of correlation between two populations 523
s	Sample standard deviation 67
s^2	Sample variance 67
s_D	Sample standard deviation of differences in a paired difference experiment 407
s_p^2	Pooled sample variance in two-sample t test 396
S	(1) Sample space 128 (2) Statistic used in sign test for population median 356

· ·

Library of Congress Cataloging-in-Publication Data

McClave, James T.
   A first course in business statistics / James T. McClave, P.
George Benson/Terry Sincich.—6th ed.
   Includes bibliographical references and indexes.
   ISBN 0-02-379175-6
   1. Commercial statistics.   2. Statistics—Data processing.
3. Commercial statistics—Case studies.   I. Benson, P. George,
1946–   .   II. Sincich, Terry.   III. Title.
HF1017.M358   1995
519.5—dc20

94-40678
CIP

On the cover: "Untitled" was executed by Los Angeles artist Charles Arnoldi. The work is watercolor on paper. Arnoldi's work may be seen at the Stremmel Gallery in Reno, Nevada, the Hampton Gallery in Venice, California, and the Charles Cowles Gallery in New York City. His work is included in the permanent collection of the Albright-Knox Museum in Buffalo, New York, the Chicago Art Institute, the Museum of Modern Art in New York City, the Metropolitan Museum, the Los Angeles County Museum, and the San Francisco Museum of Modern Art.

 © 1995 by Prentice-Hall, Inc.
A Simon & Schuster Company
Englewood Cliffs, New Jersey 07632

Printed in the United States of America

10 9 8 7 6 5 4 3 2 1

ISBN 0-02-379175-6

Prentice-Hall International (UK) Limited, *London*
Prentice-Hall of Australia Pty. Limited, *Sydney*
Prentice-Hall Canada Inc., *Toronto*
Prentice-Hall Hispanoamericana, S.A., *Mexico*
Prentice-Hall of India Private Limited, *New Delhi*
Prentice-Hall of Japan, Inc., *Tokyo*
Simon & Schuster Asia Pte. Ltd., *Singapore*
Editora Prentice-Hall do Brasil, Ltda., *Rio de Janeiro*

A First Course in

BUSINESS
STATISTICS

....

SIXTH EDITION

James T. McClave
Info Tech, Inc.
University of Florida

P. George Benson
Graduate School of Management
Rutgers University

Terry Sincich
University of South Florida

 PRENTICE HALL
Englewood Cliffs, New Jersey 07632